Professional ASP.NET 3.5 Security, Membership, and Role Management with C# and VB

GE P

12/10/2008

Professional

ASP.NET 3.5 Security, Membership, and Role Management with C# and VB

Professional
ASP.NET 3.5 Security, Membership, and Role Management with C# and VB

Bilal Haidar

Stefan Schackow

WILEY

Wiley Publishing, Inc.

Professional ASP.NET 3.5 Security, Membership, and Role Management with C# and VB

Published by
Wiley Publishing, Inc.
10475 Crosspoint Boulevard
Indianapolis, IN 46256
www.wiley.com

Portions based on the previous work *Professional ASP.NET 2.0 Security, Membership, and Role Management*, by Stefan Schackow, copyright © 2006 Stefan Schackow, published by Wiley Publishing, Inc.

Published simultaneously in Canada

ISBN: 978-0-470-37930-1

Manufactured in the United States of America

10 9 8 7 6 5 4 3 2 1

Library of Congress Cataloging-in-Publication Data

Haidar, Bilal.
  Professional ASP.NET 3.5 security, membership, and role management with C# and VB / Bilal Haidar,
  Stefan Schackow.
     p. cm.
  Includes index.
  ISBN 978-0-470-37930-1 (paper/website)

  1. Active server pages. 2. Microsoft .NET. 3. Computer security. 4. Web site development.
  I. Schackow, Stefan, 1970- II. Title.
  QA76.9.A25H344 2008
  005.8—dc22
                      2008036129

About the Author

Bilal Haidar has a BE in Computer Engineering and a BS in Computer Science with a minor in Mathematics from the Lebanese American University (LAU). He has authored several online articles for www.aspalliance.com, www.code-magazine.com, and www.aspnetpro.com, and is one of the top posters at the ASP.NET forums. Bilal has been a Microsoft MVP in ASP.NET since 2004, as well as a Microsoft Certified Trainer, and currently works as a senior developer for Consolidated Contractors Company (CCC), a multinational company whose headquarters are based in Athens, Greece (www.ccc.gr). Bilal runs his own blog, where he shares his technical experience and can be reached at http://www.bhaidar.net.

About the Previous Author

Stefan Schackow is a Program Manager on the Web Platform and Tools Team at Microsoft. During the Visual Studio 2005 cycle, he worked on the new application services stack in Visual Studio 2005 and owned the Membership, Role Manager, Profile, Personalization and Site Navigation features in ASP.NET 2.0. He also worked on features for Microsoft's ASP.NET hosting solution. Currently, Stefan is working and speaking on Silverlight for Microsoft. He is a frequent speaker at Microsoft developer conferences. Prior to joining the ASP.NET team, Stefan worked as an application development consultant in Microsoft Consulting Services (MCS) with enterprise customers.

Credits

Acquisitions Director
Jim Minatel

Development Editors
John Sleeva
Gus Miklos

Technical Editor
Alexei Gorkov

Production Editor
Kathleen Wisor

Copy Editor
Christopher M. Jones

Editorial Manager
Mary Beth Wakefield

Production Manager
Tim Tate

Vice President and Executive Group Publisher
Richard Swadley

Vice President and Executive Publisher
Joseph B. Wikert

Project Coordinator, Cover
Lynsey Stanford

Compositor
James D. Kramer, Happenstance Type-O-Rama

Proofreader
Publication Services, Inc.

Indexer
Jack Lewis

Acknowledgments

The idea of working on this book started when Jim Minatel, Acquisitions Director at Wrox, emailed me about updating the previous version of this book. Despite the fact that I have been publishing articles for magazines and online websites for the past few years, I felt the experience of working on such a book would be really interesting and unique. Only the days later proved me right and made me proud that I accepted Jim's offer.

I spent many hours researching new features and upgrades, writing down everything I learned so that I could share it with you. Many people supported me and provided me with valuable information, including Scott Guthrie, Billy Hoffman, Mike Volodarsky, Steve Scofield, and Anil Ruia. (I apologize if I forgot anyone!)

I want to thank the Wiley publishing family, including Jim Minatel, John Sleeva, Gus Miklos, Carol Kessel, Katie Wisor, and Ashley Zurcher, as well as technical editor Alexei Gorkov.

I cannot forget the support and flexibility that my company, CCC, represented by my managers and colleagues, showed me during all the stages of writing this book. Your support and understanding gave me enough strength to carry on and finish this book.

Finally, a special thanks to my parents and brother and sister, who followed up with me from the beginning of this work and were even more excited about this book than I myself was.

Contents

Contents

Contents

Contents

Contents

Introduction

This book covers security topics on a wide range of areas in ASP.NET 2.0 and ASP.NET 3.5. It starts with an introduction to Internet Information Services 7.0 (IIS 7.0) and then explains in detail the new IIS 7.0 Integrated mode of execution. Next is detailed coverage of how security is applied when an ASP.NET application starts up and when a request is processed in the newly introduced integrated request-processing pipeline. The book then branches out to cover security information for features such as trust levels, forms authentication, session state, page security, and configuration system security. You will also see how you can benefit from the IIS 7.0 Integrated mode to make use of ASP.NET features to handle non-managed or native requests such as classic ASP due to the fact that ASP.NET and IIS 7.0 join efforts to form an integrated request-processing pipeline to handle requests. Over the course of these topics, you will gain a solid understanding of many of the less publicized security features in ASP.NET 2.0 and ASP.NET 3.5.

The book switches gears in Chapter 10 to address two security services in ASP.NET 2.0 and ASP.NET 3.5: Membership and Role Manager. You start out learning about the provider model that underlies both of these features. Then you get a detailed look at the internals of both features, as well as the SQL- and Active Directory-based providers included with them. After reading through these topics, you will have a thorough background on how you can work with those providers and how you can extend them in your applications. The discussion about the ASP.NET features continues, with Chapter 17 dedicated to the ASP.NET AJAX 3.5 security integration with ASP.NET 3.5, showing how to authenticate/authorize users with JavaScript code written on the client-side.

Finally, the book closes with a chapter on the best practices ASP.NET developers should follow to protect their ASP.NET applications from malicious attacks.

Who This Book Is For

This book is intended for developers who already have a solid understanding of ASP.NET 1.1 and ASP.NET 2.0 security concepts in the area of forms authentication, page security, and website authorization. Where the book addresses functionality such as Membership and Role Manager, it assumes that you have already used these features and have a good understanding of the general functionality provided by both of them. It is also assumed that you have already worked with ASP.NET AJAX 3.5. This book does not rehash widely available public information on various features or API reference documentation.

Instead, you will find that the book has been written to "peel back the covers" of various ASP.NET security features so that you can gain a much deeper understanding of the security options available to you. The book focuses on explaining the new IIS 7.0 and its Integrated mode of execution, showing the importance of this new mode and how ASP.NET applications benefit from it. The book also addresses lesser known security functionality such as ASP.NET trust levels so that you can take advantage of these approaches in your own applications.

If you are looking for an overview on IIS 7.0 and its unified/integrated request-processing pipeline, you will find Chapters 1 and 2 useful. If you are seeking a deep dive on general ASP.NET 2.0 and ASP.NET 3.5

security, you will find Chapters 2-9 useful. If your initial focus is on the Membership and Role Manager features, Chapters 10-15 will be immediately useful to you. Chapter 17 focuses on explaining the authentication/authorization features in ASP.NET AJAX 3.5 to show you how to benefit from some of ASP.NET security features from the client-side JavaScript code, thereby developing more responsive but more secure applications without reinventing the wheel. Finally, Chapter 18 covers a number of threats and attacks that ASP.NET applications might face and provides solutions and on how to handle such threats.

After you have read through these topics, you will have a thorough understanding of why ASP.NET security works the way it does, and you will have insights into just how far you can "stretch" ASP.NET 2.0 and ASP.NET 3.5 to match your application's security requirements.

What This Book Covers

The subject of ASP.NET security can refer to a lot of different concepts: security features, best coding practices, lockdown procedures, and so on. This book addresses ASP.NET security features from the developer's point of view. It gives you detailed information on every major area of ASP.NET security you will encounter while developing web applications. And it shows you how you can extend or modify these features.

❑   Chapter 1, "Introducing IIS 7.0," starts by refreshing the ideas on application pools and worker processes before diving into explaining the major components that constitute IIS 7.0. The new modular architecture in IIS 7.0 is explained and a list of both native and managed modules is provided. At the end of the chapter you will learn about the two modes of processing inside IIS 7.0: Integrated and Classic.

❑   Chapter 2, "IIS 7.0 and ASP.NET Integrated Mode," starts by introducing the advantages of using the IIS 7.0 and ASP.NET integrated mode. The discussion expands into exploring the internals and architecture of the new integrated mode of execution. In addition, the chapter highlights the migration problems that a developer or administrator faces when upgrading an application to run inside IIS 7.0 under the integrated mode. The chapter ends with a section on extending the IIS 7.0 infrastructure by developing managed `HttpHandlers` and `HttpModules` and installing these features from inside the application's `web.config` configuration file without the need to have access to the IIS 7.0 Manager tool.

❑   Chapter 3, "HTTP Request Processing in IIS 7.0 Integrate Model," starts by introducing the new built-in IUSR account and IIS_IUSRS group inside IIS 7.0. It then gives you a detailed walkthrough of the security processing that both IIS 7.0 and ASP.NET perform in the integrated/unified request-processing pipeline. The unified processing pipeline and all its events and stages are introduced with a detailed focus on some of the important stages. You will also see how the default authentication and authorization modules work, as well as the new techniques at the IIS 7.0 level to block access to content based on new IIS 7.0 configuration settings. A section is dedicated to the new native `UrlAuthorizationModule` that ships as part of the native modules in IIS 7.0. This chapter also describes subtleties in how request identity works with ASP.NET 2.0's and ASP.NET 3.5's asynchronous pipeline events and asynchronous page model.

❑   Chapter 4, "A Matter of Trust," describes what an ASP.NET trust level is, and how ASP.NET trust levels work to provide more secure environments for running web applications. The chapter goes into detail on how you can customize trust levels and how to write privileged code that works in partial trust applications.

❑ Chapter 5, "Configuration System Security," covers the security features in the 2.0 and 3.5 Frameworks' configuration systems. It discusses the configuration options for locking down configuration sections as well as protecting configuration sections from prying eyes. The chapter discusses managing the IIS 7.0 configuration system versus the ASP.NET configuration system, and introduces IIS 7.0 feature delegation, which enables administrators to specify which IIS 7.0 configuration sections ASP.NET applications can change and modify. It also discusses how ASP.NET trust levels and configuration system security work together.

❑ Chapter 6, "Forms Authentication," explains ASP.NET 2.0 and ASP.NET 3.5 features for forms authentication. You will learn about the integrated cookieless support and the support forms authentication has for passing authentication tickets across web applications. The chapter also presents an extensive example of implementing a lightweight single sign on solution using forms authentication, as well as how to enforce a single login using a combination of forms authentication and Membership.

❑ Chapter 7, "Integrating ASP.NET Security with Classic ASP," demonstrates using IIS 7.0 wild-card mappings and ASP.NET 2.0's and ASP.NET 3.5's support for wildcard mappings to share authentication and authorization information with Classic ASP applications when an ASP.NET application is operating in the IIS 7.0 Classic mode. The chapter shows how easy it is to inte-grate ASP.NET security with Classic ASP or any other non-managed content through the Inte-grated mode of processing introduced with IIS 7.0. The chapter ends with a detailed discussion on authenticating and authorizing classic ASP Content through ASP.NET Membership and Role Manager in an application operating under the IIS 7.0 Integrated mode.

❑ Chapter 8, "Session State," covers security features and guidance for session state. Session state security features in ASP.NET 2.0 and ASP.NET 3.5 are covered, as well as security options for out-of-process state and the effect ASP.NET trust levels have on the session state feature. In addition is a detailed discussion on how to enable session state for non-managed content when ASP.NET applications are operating under the IIS 7.0 Integrated mode.

❑ Chapter 9, "Security for Pages and Compilation," describes some lesser known page security features from ASP.NET 1.1. It also describes ASP.NET 2.0 and ASP.NET 3.5 options for securing viewstate and postback events. Chapter 9 also covers how the dynamic compilation model in ASP.NET 3.5, originally introduced with ASP.NET 2.0, can be used with code access security.

❑ Chapter 10, "The Provider Model," gives you an architectural overview of the provider model in both ASP.NET 2.0 and ASP.NET 3.5. The chapter covers the various Framework classes that are "the provider model," along with sample code showing you how to write your own custom provider-based features.

❑ Chapter 11, "Membership," talks about the Membership feature in ASP.NET 2.0 and ASP.NET 3.5. The chapter goes into detail about the core classes of the Membership feature as well as how you can extend the feature with custom hash algorithms.

❑ Chapter 12, "SqlMembershipProvider," delves into both the SqlMembershipProvider as well as general database design assumptions that are baked into all of ASP.NET 2.0's and ASP.NET 3.5's SQL-based features. You will learn how you can extend the provider to support automatically unlocking user accounts. The sample code also covers custom password encryption, storing password histories, and extending the provider to work in portal environments.

❑ Chapter 13, "ActiveDirectoryMembershipProvider," covers the other membership provider that ships in ASP.NET 2.0 and ASP.NET 3.5 — ActiveDirectoryMembershipProvider. You will learn about how this provider maps its functionality onto Active Directory, and you will see how to set up both Active Directory and Active Directory Lightweight Directory Service (introduced with Windows Server 2008) servers to work with the provider.

❑ Chapter 14, "Role Manager," describes the Role Manager feature that provides built-in authorization support for ASP.NET 2.0 and ASP.NET 3.5. You will learn about the core classes in Role Manager. The chapter also details how the `RoleManagerModule` is able to automatically set up a principal for downstream authorization and how the module and Role Manager's caching work hand in hand. Chapter 14 also covers the `WindowsTokenRoleProvider`, one of the providers that ships with Role Manager.

❑ Chapter 15, "SqlRoleProvider," discusses the `SqlRoleProvider` and its underlying SQL schema. You will learn about using the provider in conjunction with Windows authentication, extending the provider to support custom authorization logic, and how you can use its database schema for data layer authorization logic. Although not specific to just `SqlRoleProvider`, the chapter covers how to get the provider working in a partial trust non-ASP.NET environment.

❑ Chapter 16, "AuthorizationStoreRoleProvider," covers the `AuthorizationStoreRoleProvider`, a provider that maps Role Manager functionality to the Authorization Manager feature that first shipped in Windows Server 2003 and is now part of Windows Server 2008. You will learn how to set up and use both file-based and directory-based policy stores with the provider. The chapter covers special Authorization Manager functionality that is supported by the provider, as well as how to use both the `ActiveDirectoryMembershipProvider` and `Authorization StoreRoleProvider` to provide Active Directory-based authentication and authorization in your web applications.

❑ Chapter 17, "Membership and Role Management in ASP.NET AJAX 3.5," discusses how ASP.NET AJAX 3.5 integrates with ASP.NET 3.5 Membership and Role management features through newly introduced web services that act as an interface to the ASP.NET application services. The chapter starts by recapping the Membership and Role Management features in ASP.NET 2.0 and ASP.NET 3.5. The discussion then moves to the steps required to enable existing ASP.NET applications with ASP.NET AJAX 3.5 and then how to enable client-side authentication and role services in the application. Chapter 17 ends by dissecting the authentication and role services in ASP.NET AJAX by detailing all the server-side and client-side classes that make the ASP.NET AJAX 3.5 integration with the ASP.NET application services possible.

❑ Chapter 18, "Best Practices for Securing ASP.NET Web Applications," covers the best practices that can be followed to secure ASP.NET applications. The discussion takes the form of a list of best practices that you can follow and apply in your web application. Each recommended best practice is explained in detail, with a sample code included when possible. The chapter ends by introducing you to the vulnerabilities exposed by introducing AJAX techniques into your applications, and the possible best practices in securing such applications.

What You Need to Use This Book

This book was written using the .NET 3.5 Framework together with .NET 3.5 Framework SP1 on both Windows Server 2008 and Windows Vista. The sample code in the book has been verified to work with .NET 3.5 Framework and .NET 3.5 Framework SP1 on Windows Vista. To run all of the samples in the book, you will need the following:

❑ Windows Server 2008 or Windows Vista

❑ Internet Information Services 7.0 (IIS 7.0)

- ❑ Visual Studio 2008 RTM

- ❑ Either SQL Server 2000 or SQL Server 2005

- ❑ A Windows Server 2008 domain running at Windows Server 2008 functional level

Most of the samples should also work when using Windows Server 2008, as Windows Server 2008 and Windows Vista both share the same IIS 7.0. Note that the information in most of the book refers to security credential configuration using IIS 7.0 application pools.

Note that all of the book's chapters require you to have IIS 7.0 installed.

Chapters 12 and 15 use the SQL-based providers. You should have either SQL Server 2000 or SQL Server 2005 setup to use these samples. Scattered throughout the book are other samples that rely on the Membership feature. These samples also require either SQL Server 2000 or SQL Server 2005.

To run the samples in Chapter 13, you will need either a Windows Server 2008 domain controller or a machine running Active Directory Lightweight Directory Service (ADLDS) or Application Mode (ADAM). Chapter 13 addresses using the `ActiveDirectoryMembershipProvider` in both Active Directory and ADLDS environments.

The sample code in Chapter 16 uses the Authorization Manager functionality in Windows Server 2008 (both setting up policies and consuming them). As a result, to run most of the samples, you will need a Windows Server 2008 domain controller that has been set up to work with Authorization Manager. For file-based policy stores, you do not need your own domain controller if you just want to try out file-based policy stores with the `AuthorizationStoreRoleProvider`. In addition, Windows Server 2008 enriches the Authorization Manager with the ability to store the authorization information in a Microsoft SQL Server. Therefore, either SQL Server 2000 or SQL Server 2005 is required to show how this new feature works on Windows Server 2008.

Conventions

To help you get the most from the text and keep track of what's happening, we've used a number of conventions throughout the book.

> Boxes like this one hold important, not-to-be forgotten information that is directly relevant to the surrounding text.

Notes, tips, hints, tricks, and asides to the current discussion are offset and placed in italics like this.

As for styles in the text:

- ❑ We *highlight* new terms and important words when we introduce them.

- ❑ We show keyboard strokes like this: Ctrl+A.

❏   We show file names, URLs, and code within the text like so: `persistence.properties`.

❏   We present code in two different ways:

```
We use a monofont type with no highlighting for most code examples.
```

```
We use gray highlighting to emphasize code that's particularly important
in the present context.
```

Source Code

As you work through the examples in this book, you may choose either to type in all the code manually or to use the source code files that accompany the book. All of the source code used in this book is available for download at `http://www.wrox.com`. Once at the site, simply locate the book's title (either by using the Search box or by using one of the title lists) and click the Download Code link on the book's detail page to obtain all the source code for the book.

Because many books have similar titles, you may find it easiest to search by ISBN; this book's ISBN is 978-0-470-37930-1.

Once you download the code, just decompress it with your favorite compression tool. Alternately, you can go to the main Wrox code download page at `http://www.wrox.com/dynamic/books/download.aspx` to see the code available for this book and all other Wrox books.

Errata

We make every effort to ensure that there are no errors in the text or in the code. However, no one is perfect, and mistakes do occur. If you find an error in one of our books, like a spelling mistake or faulty piece of code, we would be very grateful for your feedback. By sending in errata you may save another reader hours of frustration and at the same time you will be helping us provide even higher quality information.

To find the errata page for this book, go to `http://www.wrox.com` and locate the title using the Search box or one of the title lists. Then, on the book details page, click the Book Errata link. On this page you can view all errata that has been submitted for this book and posted by Wrox editors. A complete book list including links to each book's errata is also available at `www.wrox.com/misc-pages/booklist.shtml`.

If you don't spot "your" error on the Book Errata page, go to `www.wrox.com/contact/techsupport.shtml` and complete the form there to send us the error you have found. We'll check the information and, if appropriate, post a message to the book's errata page and fix the problem in subsequent editions of the book.

p2p.wrox.com

For author and peer discussion, join the P2P forums at p2p.wrox.com. The forums are a Web-based system for you to post messages relating to Wrox books and related technologies and interact with other readers and technology users. The forums offer a subscription feature to e-mail you topics of interest of your choosing when new posts are made to the forums. Wrox authors, editors, other industry experts, and your fellow readers are present on these forums.

At http://p2p.wrox.com you will find a number of different forums that will help you not only as you read this book, but also as you develop your own applications. To join the forums, just follow these steps:

1. Go to p2p.wrox.com and click the Register link.

2. Read the terms of use and click Agree.

3. Complete the required information to join as well as any optional information you wish to provide and click Submit.

4. You will receive an e-mail with information describing how to verify your account and complete the joining process.

You can read messages in the forums without joining P2P but in order to post your own messages, you must join.

Once you join, you can post new messages and respond to messages other users post. You can read messages at any time on the Web. If you would like to have new messages from a particular forum e-mailed to you, click the Subscribe to this Forum icon by the forum name in the forum listing.

For more information about how to use the Wrox P2P, be sure to read the P2P FAQs for answers to questions about how the forum software works as well as many common questions specific to P2P and Wrox books. To read the FAQs, click the FAQ link on any P2P page.

1

Introducing IIS 7.0

Microsoft Internet Information Services (IIS) version 7.0 was introduced with the Windows Vista operating system as the main Windows web server. The same web server is going to be utilized by Windows Server 2008 with the same features, which means developing with Windows Vista IIS 7.0 will cost nothing when it is time to deploy on Windows Server 2008 IIS 7.0.

IIS 7.0 is a revolution in terms of web application processing and handling. It has been re-architected to provide a more robust, extensible, componentized web server that gives developers a better opportunity to integrate more into its features.

This chapter starts with an overview of new IIS 7.0 features. Application pools and worker processes are reviewed before diving into more advanced topics. The discussion goes deeper to cover the major components inside IIS 7.0. IIS 7.0 introduces the concept of modules as a new architectural design. Both native and managed modules are covered, with a brief description of each. The chapter ends by giving an overview on the request processing in IIS 7.0 and the new application pool modes: Integrated and Classic.

By the end of this chapter, you will have a good knowledge of the following:

- ❏ IIS 7.0 features overview
- ❏ Application pool and worker processes
- ❏ IIS 7.0 components
- ❏ Managed and native modules inside IIS 7.0
- ❏ IIS 7.0 request processing pipeline
- ❏ Integrated and Classic mode application pools

Overview of IIS 7.0

IIS 7.0 is the new web server that ships with Windows Vista and Windows Server 2008. Similar to the previous versions of IIS, this new version will continue to handle and process web requests that arrive at the Windows machine. The most mature version of IIS before the current one is IIS 6.0 which ships with Windows Server 2003. IIS 6.0 is very robust in terms of security, speed, process management, and reliability. IIS 7.0 builds its core engine on its predecessor and improves several areas. In addition, many new features have been added, making it extensible and manageable, thus leveraging IIS 7.0 to be a web server platform powerful enough to handle the challenges of present and future web applications.

The new IIS 7.0 features and characteristics are briefly summarized and presented in the next few sections to give a high-level overview of what has been done to improve the web server.

Modular Architecture

As mentioned above, IIS 7.0 bases its core engine on the best features of IIS 6.0 and adds to them the extensibility and accessibility for developers through its modular core engine. IIS 7.0 is based on a plug-in architecture that allows developers to have a hand in the processing of web requests. IIS 7.0 provides extensibility through its runtime pipeline, configuration management, and operational features to have a customizable web server for varying needs and requirements.

Making IIS 7.0 modular gives you the chance to customize it according to personal preferences and needs. Contrary to how the IIS 6.0 was configured, IIS 7.0 has most of its modules available but not installed. An administrator or developer can choose what modules or features to install and activate and what modules to deactivate. This provides both administrators and developers with a robust and reliable capability to configure the web server as needed. Figure 1-1 shows the new IIS 7.0 Manager listing the 40 available managed and native modules or features that ship with a full installation.

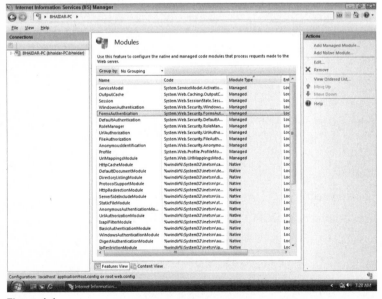

Figure 1-1

All modules are not installed by default, unless specified. Any module can be uninstalled and removed from the runtime pipeline processing, giving a flexible and dynamic experience in terms of choosing what to configure from built-in modules or even adding new modules and features. From the security point of view, an administrator or developer can choose what modules to include in the processing, hence affecting the overall performance of loading the configured modules to handle requests. This modular architecture helps reduce surface attacks by having the freedom to choose the modules to include and provides better performance by having the administrator or developer install only the required set of modules or features. IIS 7.0 managed and unmanaged modules are covered in detail later in this chapter.

Web server features or modules are configured through XML configuration files. The configuration files (discussed in a later section) are built into a hierarchy where at every level modules or features are configurable.

A Microsoft TechNet resource is available online that lists all the modules and features contained in IIS 7.0 and shows which modules are installed by default and which can be added later:
http://technet2.microsoft.com/WindowsServer2008/en/library/
0d35e92b-ddb7-4423-b1e5-df550e25713b1033.mspx

Developing Modules and Features

The modular architecture introduced above discusses the ability to customize the modules installed on the web server whether by adding new ones or uninstalling existing ones. Adding new modules is easier with the new extensibility API for developing modules to integrate into IIS.

All of the native modules installed or shipped with IIS are developed on top of this extensibility API and this API is public, which means any developer can take that API and either redevelop an existing module or develop a new module as required.

The new extensibility API is built with C++ and it fully represents the new web server object model. The set of classes allows the developer to develop modules that can participate in request processing on IIS. This model is a replacement of the ISAPI extensibility model and is much easier to develop with since the new model includes a type-safe and well-encapsulated object model. Every needed web server object has a corresponding specialized object interface in the new API. For example, the IHttpRequest interface allows custom modules developed on top of the new extensibility API to access all the information related to the request under processing. The IHttpResponse interface allows custom modules to interact with the response generated for a request processed by IIS 7.0.

The new extensibility API even excels in terms of memory allocation and state management over ISAPI. In the days of ISAPI extensions, the developer had to take care of allocating and unallocating memory as required. The new extensibility API and most of the new IIS 7.0 APIs allocate server-managed memory for the data processed, which is different from the days of ISAPI extensions where developers had to take care of all the mess.

Finally, the new extensibility API allows modules to access features that were impossible to access before, such as request buffering and other IIS request processing tasks.

What about ASP.NET developers who are not ready to learn C++ to develop new modules for IIS? IIS 7.0 allows ASP.NET developers to utilize their existing ASP.NET module or create new ones using both the .NET 2.0 and 3.5 Frameworks and plug them automatically into the IIS request pipeline. In a later section, the ASP.NET integration process is explained in more depth.

Deployment and Configuration Management

IIS 7.0 uses a new configuration system that is conceptually much different from the IIS 6.0 centralized metabase configuration system. The new configuration system borrows many ideas from the current .NET 2.0 and 3.5 Frameworks configuration system, which is based on section groups and sections.

IIS 7.0 configuration system is based on XML configuration files mainly the `ApplicationHost.config` and `Administration.config` configuration files. Both of these files get deployed on the machine when IIS 7.0 is installed The configuration file of concern for most of the tasks related to IIS 7.0 is the `ApplicationHost.config` configuration file that contains all the new web server meta-data.

This configuration file contains global- and application-specific configuration sections. It resembles the .NET Frameworks configuration files: `machine.config` and the root `web.config` configuration files. The web server configuration file can be reached by browsing to the `%WINDIR%/System32/inetsrv/config` folder. Figure 1-2 shows the two main sections of the `ApplicationHost.config` configuration file.

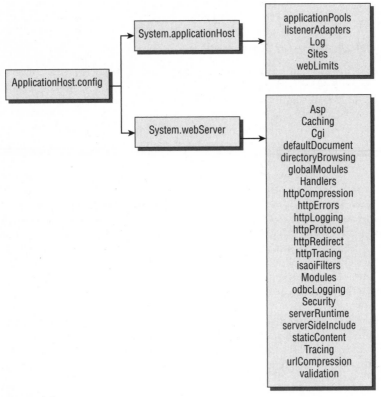

Figure 1-2

The two main section groups are the `<system.applicationHost>` and the `<system.webServer>` section groups. The `<system.applicationHost>` section group contains all the global settings for the web server, including the sites, applicationPools, listenerAdapaters, and so forth. This section is locked down and cannot be extended by any application hosted insideIIS.

```
<sites>
    <site name="Default Web Site" id="1" serverAutoStart="true">
        <application path="/">
            <virtualDirectory path="/" physicalPath="%SystemDrive%\inetpub\
wwwroot" />
        </application>
        <application path="/MyApp">
            <virtualDirectory path="/" physicalPath="%SystemDrive%\inetpub\
wwwroot\MyApp" />
        </application>
        <bindings>
            <binding protocol="http" bindingInformation="*:80:" />
        </bindings>
    </site>
```

The <sites> section defines all the configuration information on all sites hosted by the web server. At the root node there is the Default Web Site that points to the site located at %SystemDrive%\ inetpub\wwwroot. To add a new website to IIS 7.0, simply add a new application node specifying the virtual path attributes together with a virtualDirectory sub-node setting the path and physicalPath attributes. With the above configuration, a new website has been added to IIS and can be accessed by http://localhost/MyApp.

The other section group, <system.webServer>, holds all the configurable sections for an application. For instance, this section contains configuration information about all the modules installed on the web server, a configuration section for directory browsing, and all the rest of the sections shown in Figure 1-2.

Note that with the new configuration system introduced by IIS 7.0, an administrator can configure the <system.applicationHost> and then select which section groups and sections from the <system .webServer> can be changed and edited by the application's web.config configuration file. This eliminates the need for a site owner to contact the administrator to change any settings in IIS, which was always happening before the release of IIS 7.0. This makes deployment with IIS 7.0 much easier. A developer can configure the <system.webServer> configuration section group during the development stage and then once the application is deployed, all the settings that were applied locally on IIS 7.0 would have the same effect on the hosting server given the fact that the administrator on the hosting server has already unlocked most of the configurable sections within the <system.webServer>. For instance, a developer can override the default web server settings for the default document for an application and set it to a customized page name.

```
<system.webServer>
    <defaultDocument>
        <files>
            <clear />
            <add value="MyPage.aspx" />
        </files>
    </defaultDocument>
</system.webServer>
```

The <system.webServer> configuration section group is the only section group in the Application Host.config configuration file that can be extended and configured in the web.config configuration file of an application. The default documents configured on the web server are cleared out and a new customized default document for the current application is set to point to MyPage.aspx.

In regard to security, administrators are allowed to select which sections of the `<system.webServer>` to allow for editing and which are locked. For instance, an administrator can unlock many sections that do not pose any threat to the security of the web server as a whole and leave open all the sections that site owners usually require to change per application.

When a request reaches IIS for a resource, the different configuration files are joined together in a hierarchy to form single, unified configuration settings that apply to the current request. Figure 1-3 shows the process of how the different configuration files are grouped together to form a final `web.config` configuration file.

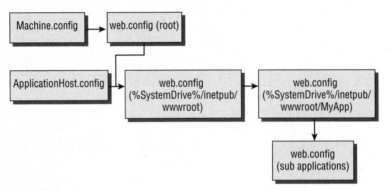

Figure 1-3

The `machine.config` file is merged with the `web.config` configuration file located in the root folder of the .NET 2.0 Framework, which is a shared folder used by both ASP.NET 2.0 and ASP.NET 3.5. The `ApplicationHost.config` configuration file is added to the result of the above grouping, and then the combined configuration settings are grouped with the `web.config` configuration file in the root website of the web server. The final result is added to the grouped configuration settings of the `web.config` configuration file of the executing application with its sub-applications' `web.config` configuration files.

An IIS resource is available online that gives a detailed overview of the `ApplicationHost.config` configuration file: `http://learn.iis.net/page.aspx/124/introduction-to-applicationhostconfig/`

Improved Administration

The IIS 7.0 Manager has been developed from scratch to replace the previous version. The difference is evident through the new UI experience and quick availability for any section to check and configure.

The IIS 7.0 Manager provides the UI interface experience for administrators and developers to configure the `ApplicationHost.config` configuration file without touching any physical resources. For instance, Figure 1-4 lists the available application pools in the `ApplicationHost.config` configuration file.

The Manager is just a UI representation to whatever is stored in the `ApplicationHost.config` configuration file. Using the manager to configure IIS 7.0 helps to prevent imposing possible wrong XML tag placement.

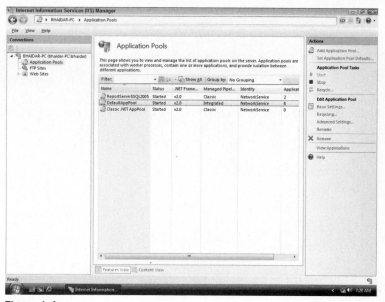

Figure 1-4

```
<applicationPools>
    <add name="DefaultAppPool" />
    <add name="Classic .NET AppPool" managedPipelineMode="Classic" />
    <applicationPoolDefaults>
        <processModel identityType="NetworkService" />
    </applicationPoolDefaults>
</applicationPools>
```

Application pools can be removed and edited, and new ones can be added. The result is stored in the `ApplicationPool` configuration section group inside the `ApplicationHost.config` configuration file.

The IIS 7.0 Manager inherits the idea of extensibility from IIS 7.0 and provides an extensible API that can be used to extend its UI features, hence extending the UI experience with much more features as required. In addition, the Manager allows management delegation that helps in administrating remote websites. For example, administrators in hosting companies can configure IIS 7.0 with the major and most secure configurations and allow the sites' owners to configure their sites remotely through their version of IIS 7.0 Manager. This does away with the need for special control panels for site owners to log into and configure their websites.

Moreover, the IIS 7.0 team thought of providing developers with a managed API to allow them to configure the IIS 7.0 configuration settings programmatically. The new API is called the `Microsoft.Web.Administration` API. Before this API can be used in Visual Studio, a reference has to be added to the `Microsoft.Web.Administration.dll` found at `%SystemDrive%:\Windows\System32\inetsrv`. The main class in this new API is the `ServerManager` .NET class. This class contains properties for the sites, applications, virtual directories, application pools, and worker processes.

C#

```
using System;
using System.Collections.Generic;
using System.Linq;
using System.Text;
using Microsoft.Web.Administration;

namespace Microsoft.Web.Administration
{
    public class Program
    {
        static void Main(string[] args)
        {
            // Get a reference to the factory object
            // ServerManager
            var manager = new ServerManager();

            // Define a new website
            manager.Sites.Add(
                "ProgrammaticSite",
                @"D:\ProgrammaticSite\",
                8080);

            // Commit changes to the ApplicationHost.config
            manager.CommitChanges();
        }
    }
}
```

VB.NET

```
Imports System
Imports System.Collections.Generic
Imports System.Linq
Imports System.Text
Imports Microsoft.Web.Administration

Namespace Microsoft.Web.Administration
    Public Class Program
        Shared Sub Main(ByVal args() As String)
            ' Get a reference to the factory object
            ' ServerManager
            Dim manager = New ServerManager()

            ' Define a new website
            manager.Sites.Add("ProgrammaticSite", "D:\ProgrammaticSite\",_
            8080)

            ' Commit changes to the ApplicationHost.config
            manager.CommitChanges()
        End Sub
    End Class
End Namespace
```

The preceding code creates a new instance of the `ServerManager` factory object. Then it adds a new site by accessing the `Sites` property and specifying the site name, physical path, and the port, and finally, a call to the `CommitChanges` method to reflect the changes in the `ApplicationHost.config` configuration file. The result of executing the preceding code can be checked in the `<sites>` configuration section:

```
<site name="ProgrammaticSite" id="20">
    <application path="/">
        <virtualDirectory path="/" physicalPath="D:\ProgrammaticSite\" />
    </application>
    <bindings>
        <binding protocol="http" bindingInformation="*:8080:" />
    </bindings>
</site>
```

A new `site` entry is created within the `<sites>` configuration section group. The new site specifies the application's physical `path`, `virtualDirectory`'s *physicalPath*, and the `protocol` binding.

Moreover, IIS 7.0 provides an additional tool called `appcmd.exe` that allows administrators and developers to configure the web server from the command prompt to create and configure sites, applications, virtual directories, start and stop application pools, recycle application pools, and much more. The utility is very rich in options and even presents a deeper configuration interface than that of IIS 7.0 Manager.

The book titled *Professional IIS 7 and ASP.NET Integrated Programming* (Wrox) explains in detail the IIS 7.0 Manager and the new Administration API. In addition, it includes informative chapters on the new IIS 7.0 configuration system and many more topics. An IIS resource is available online that gives a detailed overview of the Microsoft.Web.Administration API: `http://learn.iis.net/page.aspx/165/how-to-use-microsoftwebadministration/`

ASP.NET Integration

ASP.NET, since its release, has been used for several years to provide high level and powerful web applications developed purely within the context of the .NET Framework. A revolutionary stage has been introduced with the release of ASP.NET 2.0 that introduced new concepts and services to web development in ASP.NET. ASP.NET 3.5 continues to use the ASP.NET 2.0 at its core and adds to it additional new features and improvements to help developers build better and robust Web solutions.

So far, ASP.NET has been used only as a framework for developing dynamic web applications. IIS 7.0 leverages ASP.NET 2.0 and ASP.NET 3.5 to extensibility frameworks to extend the new web server.

IIS 6.0 handles requests for ASP.NET pages through ISAPI filters and extensions. Request handling is delegated to the ASP.NET ISAPI extension, the ASP.NET pipeline is triggered to handle the new request, and a response is generated and finally handed back to the IIS to deliver it to the requesting client. APS.NET has no control over what is being sent to its engine, since it is solely controlled by the IIS core engine. Only requests defined by the ASP.NET engine can be passed and processed, but what about other content? For instance, what if an ASP.NET application wants to secure access to some old Classic ASP pages using the same `FormsAuthenticationModule` used to protect ASP.NET resources? Before IIS 7.0, that was hard to do, if not impossible. If you are in a hurry to learn how to control and process non-ASP.NET content and resources through the ASP.NET pipeline, you can jump directly to

Chapter 7 for a detailed discussion on how to integrate ASP.NET security with Classic ASP pages. Note that whatever applies to Classic ASP applies also to any other non-ASP.NET resource including .php, .jpg, .htm, and so on.

In IIS 7.0, ASP.NET 2.0 and 3.5 can run in two different modes: Classic and Integrated. The Classic mode resembles the same model as that of IIS 6.0 and ASP.NET. ASP.NET 1.1 applications running inside IIS 7.0 can only be run using the Classic mode. When an ASP.NET 2.0 or 3.5 application is running in the Integrated mode, however, the ASP.NET engine gets unified with the IIS 7.0 engine, hence they share the same request pipeline. IIS's native C++ modules and ASP.NET HttpModules work together on processing a request. A request is processed by the configured native modules and any module registered with ASP.NET. One of the clear and shining results of this unified integration is that ASP.NET can now have a say when processing any content resource (and not only ASP.NET resources), a feature not present before the days of IIS 7.0. Figure 1-5 shows the unified request pipeline in processing a request in IIS 7.0.

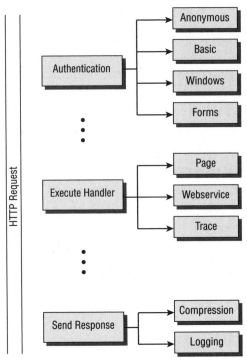

Figure 1-5

When it is time for IIS to authenticate a request, it executes all the configured native and managed authentication modules at the same time. The same applies for any stage inside IIS 7.0. This signifies again the power of having both ASP.NET modules and native modules execute side by side in handling a request.

More on ASP.NET integration with IIS 7.0 is covered in detail in Chapter 2.

Security Improvements

IIS 7.0 security is based on the robustness of IIS 6.0's security. By default, when IIS 6.0 is installed, it is installed in a locked-down mode, meaning that only handling of static files and the World Wide Web Publishing Service (WWW Service) are installed and enabled. The rest of services that operate on top of IIS 6.0 (including ASP, ASP.NET, and so forth) are disabled and can be added and enabled at any time by the administrator.

IIS 7.0 takes the locked-down strategy of IIS 6.0 one step further and follows the same locked-down pattern by installing fewer services at installation time. Having fewer features installed and enabled minimizes the risk of attack on the web server and minimizes the work done by the administrator to keep updating with patches and service packs on the different services installed, whether enabled or not. By making use of the modular architecture, an administrator can easily, at any time, install a new module or feature required by applications hosted by the web server.

Enabling the unified request pipeline in IIS 7 by configuring applications with the Integrated mode, the web server gains a more secure environment through the use of ASP.NET security modules. These modules include the `FormsAuthenticationModule` and the Membership and Role management services introduced early in ASP.NET 2.0 that still constitute a major feature in ASP.NET 3.5. Not only can ASP.NET benefit from these modules, but IIS 7.0 also gets better protection by utilizing these modules to protect the resources hosted in its environment.

In addition, IIS 7.0 introduces URL Authorization, which is inspired (more or less) by the architecture of the ASP.NET URL Authorization. The new authorization system allows administrators to add declarative access control rules for the hosted applications to protect their resources. This new feature integrates well with the ASP.NET Membership and Role management services. A more detailed discussion on URL Authorization is given in Chapter 3 of this book.

Moreover, the IIS 7.0 team replaced the old URL Scan security tool with a new `RequestFilteringModule` that gives administrators finer control on what to allow and disallow in a request targeting the web server. The `RequestFilteringModule`, as shown in the following code, can be configured through the `<system.webServer>` configuration section group either in the `ApplicationHost.config` configuration file or through the application's `web.config` configuration file.

```
<configuration>
 <system.webServer>
  <security>
   <requestFiltering>
    <fileExtensions allowUnlisted="false" >
    <add fileExtension=".aspx" allowed="true"/>
    </fileExtensions>
   </requestFiltering>
  </security>
 </system.webServer>
</configuration>
```

For instance, to configure IIS 7.0 to process ASP.NET web pages only, the `RequestFilteringModule` is configured to allow only ASP.NET web pages and prevent all other file extensions from being served and processed.

For further details, an IIS resource is available online that gives a wider overview of the new `Request FilteringModule`: http://learn.iis.net/page.aspx/143/how-to-use-request-filtering/

Another security feature in which IIS 7.0 excels is the IIS Manager. As mentioned above, when applications are hosted locally, the site owner can configure IIS 7.0 settings by either direct access to the `ApplicationHost.config` configuration file, or through the `appcmd.exe` command-line utility, or programmatically by utilizing the `Microsoft.Web.Adminsitration` API. When configuring remote applications, IIS Manager provides remote connections to site owners through their local instance of the manager through firewall-friendly HTTPs connections. Based on the restrictions set by the remote administrator, a site owner connects to the remote web server through the local instance of the manager. The user gets authenticated on the remote server either by Windows authentication, if the user has a Windows account on the remote server, or by custom authentication of the ASP.NET Membership services. Once authenticated, the site owner can now configure the web server's settings under the limitations set by the remote administrator.

Not only does IIS Manager allow remote connections; it also allows administrators to configure the IIS Manager UI to select the features to show for remote connections. This is yet another security protection on the hosting web server.

Finally, IIS 7.0 introduces a new IIS anonymous account, the `IIS_USR`. This built-in account has no expiration date, nor does it need any password synchronization among different machines. Also, a new group is `IIS_IUSRS` that replaces the old `IIS_WPG` group. This group injects itself into the identity of the Worker process automatically at runtime. This makes the process of specifying another custom account for the Worker process identity easier without having to worry about adding this custom account to the `IIS_IUSRS` group. Since the `IIS_IUSR` and `IIS_IUSRS` are built-in, any Windows access control lists (ACLs) that an administrator or developer assigns on one machine can be copied to another machine, for instance, from the development machine to the testing and deployment machine, without any further worries, making the deployment process easier and more flexible.

Troubleshooting Improvements

IIS modular architecture not only introduces flexibility and robustness in configuring the web server, but it also adds more complexities when it comes to debugging or tracing requests when a problem occurs while a resource is being executed by the web server. Therefore, several new troubleshooting improvements have been added to allow administrators and developers to better detect what is going wrong with their applications.

A new, improved tracing system is added to the IIS infrastructure that is capable of capturing all related information for a request being processed by the web server. This way, an administrator can refer back at any time to check the status of requests being served by IIS. The trace information generated by the web server can be monitored and listened to by a new feature, the Failed Request Tracing feature. This new feature is basically configured to listen only to *failure* requests and logs them to the hard-disk. Before using this feature, it must be enabled in the IIS Manager tool. Figure 1-6 shows how to open up the Failure Request Tracing form to enable/disable the feature and to specify the path where to log the trace data.

By default, the Failure Request Tracing feature passes all successful requests and logs only the failed ones, as mentioned above. In addition, an administrator can define Failure Request Tracing Rules to specify what trace information to listen to in the web server tracing system. To define these rules, the Failing Request Tracing Rules feature can be configured inside the IIS Manager tool reached by selecting Server Name ⇨ Web Sites ⇨ Default Web Site ⇨ Failed Request Tracing Rules under the IIS section.

Figure 1-6

In addition, IIS provides new error information pages when errors are detected in the resources being processed. These error pages are similar in concept to the error pages generated by ASP.NET when an exception or error occurs in the application while a request is being made to any of its resources. The IIS error information pages give details about the problem that occurred, what module caused the problem, if any, where to find more tracing information about the specific failure of the request, and even more information that helps the administrator or developer to locate the problem quickly. The detailed error pages are configured for local access only by default and can be localized for any culture of preference.

To better benefit from the unified integration model between IIS and ASP.NET, the new web server's tracing system exposes its functionality to the modules created by the managed code in ASP.NET. The new tracing system is extensible enough to allow the managed modules registered in IIS to make use of the tracing information and to emit tracing data to the IIS tracing system. ASP.NET 2.0 and ASP.NET 3.5 contain the `System.Diagnostics.TraceSource` class that makes the developer's life easier in handling tracing events, data, and information (shown in the following code). The tracing system present in IIS 7.0 integrates with the tracing system in ASP.NET 2.0 and 3.5, thus allowing tracing information generated by ASP.NET to flow to the IIS 7.0 tracing system.

C#

```csharp
using System;
using System.Diagnostics;
using System.Web;

public class CustomTracing : IHttpModule
{
    // Private member to hold a reference to the
    // TraceSource class
    private TraceSource tsTracing;
```

```
/// <summary>
/// Initialize event in the HttpModule
/// </summary>
/// <param name="application"></param>
public void Init(HttpApplication application)
{
    // Attach to the EndRequest event
    application.EndRequest += new EventHandler(application_EndRequest);

    // Define the trace source
    tsTracing = new TraceSource("tsTracing");
}

/// <summary>
/// Handles the end request event
/// </summary>
/// <param name="sender"></param>
/// <param name="e"></param>
void application_EndRequest(object sender, EventArgs e)
{
    // Write a message to the configured trace listeners mentioning the start of
    // a logical operation  or event, which is in this case beginning of the
    // EndRequest method.
    this.tsTracing.TraceEvent(
        TraceEventType.Start,
        0,
        "[CustomTracing MODULE] START EndRequest");

    // Get a reference to the HttpContext
    var app = (HttpApplication)sender;
    var context = app.Context;

    // Write some text to the response stream
    context.Response.Write(
        "Testing Tracing from ASP.NET and integrating into IIS 7.0");

    this.tsTracing.TraceEvent(
        TraceEventType.Verbose,
        0,
        "A debugging trace message to the trace listener!");
    this.tsTracing.TraceEvent(
        TraceEventType.Critical,
        0,
        "A fatal error or crash message to the trace listener!");
    this.tsTracing.TraceEvent(
        TraceEventType.Error,
        0,
        "A recoverable error message to the trace listener!");
    this.tsTracing.TraceEvent(
        TraceEventType.Information,
        0,
        "An informational message to the trace listener!");

    // Write a message to the configured trace listeners mentioning the end of a
    // logical operation or event, which is in this case end of the EndRequest
    // method
```

```
            this.tsTracing.TraceEvent(
                TraceEventType.Stop,
                0,
                "[CustomTracing MODULE] STOP EndRequest");
        }


    #region IHttpModule Members

    public void Dispose()
    {
        throw new NotImplementedException();
    }
    #endregion
}
```

VB.NET

```
Imports System
Imports System.Diagnostics
Imports System.Web

Namespace CustomTracingModule
    Public Class CustomTracing
        Implements IHttpModule
        ' Private member to hold a reference to the
        ' TraceSource class
        Private tsTracing As TraceSource

        ''' <summary>
        ''' Initialize event in the HttpModule
        ''' </summary>
        ''' <param name="application"></param>
        Public Sub Init(ByVal application As HttpApplication) Implements_
        IHttpModule.Init
            ' Attach to the EndRequest event
            AddHandler application.EndRequest, AddressOf application_EndRequest

            ' Define the trace source
            tsTracing = New TraceSource("tsTracing")
        End Sub

        ''' <summary>
        ''' Handles the end request event
        ''' </summary>
        ''' <param name="sender"></param>
        ''' <param name="e"></param>
        Private Sub application_EndRequest(ByVal sender As Object,_
        ByVal e As EventArgs)
            ' Write a message to the configured trace listeners
            ' mentioning the start of a logical operation
            ' or event, which is in this case beginning of the EndRequest method.
            Me.tsTracing.TraceEvent(TraceEventType.Start,_
                    0,_
                    "[CustomTracing MODULE] START EndRequest")
```

```
                    ' Get a reference to the HttpContext
                    Dim app = CType(sender, HttpApplication)
                    Dim context = app.Context

                    ' Write some text to the response stream
        context.Response.Write("Testing Tracing from ASP.NET and integrating into IIS 7.0")

            Me.tsTracing.TraceEvent(TraceEventType.Verbose,_
                        0,_
                        "A debugging trace message to the trace listener!")
            Me.tsTracing.TraceEvent(TraceEventType.Critical,_
                        0,_
                        "A fatal error or crash message to the trace listener!")
            Me.tsTracing.TraceEvent(TraceEventType.Error,_
                        0,_
                        "A recoverable error message to the trace listener!")
            Me.tsTracing.TraceEvent(TraceEventType.Information,_
                        0,_
                        "An informational message to the trace listener!")

            ' Write a message to the configured trace listeners
            ' mentioning the end of a logical operation
            ' or event, which is in this case end of the EndRequest method
            Me.tsTracing.TraceEvent(TraceEventType.Stop,_
                        0,
                        "[CustomTracing MODULE] STOP EndRequest")
        End Sub


#Region "IHttpModule Members"

        Public Sub Dispose() Implements IHttpModule.Dispose
            Throw New NotImplementedException()
        End Sub
#End Region
    End Class
End Namespace
```

The preceding code defines a local instance of the `TraceSource` class to hold all the tracing information by the managed ASP.NET module. The name of the `TraceSource` is important, as it will be referenced later as a source for the IIS trace listener. The `HttpModule` subscribes to the `EndRequest` event of the module and writes some dummy text into the response stream. Several trace messages have been written to the ASP.NET tracing system using the `TraceSource` object. Several methods are available in the aforementioned object, one of which is the `TraceEvent` method that takes as one of the inputs a value from the `TraceEventType` enumeration that defines the purpose of the trace message and another input, the trace message to be sent to the trace listener. There are several values in the `TraceEventType` enumeration that defines the different contexts in which a trace message might be present.

.NET 3.5 Framework ships with the `System.Web.IisTraceListner` class, which is used to route tracing information from ASP.NET tracing system to the IIS tracing infrastructure. To define the trace listener and attach it as a listener to the `TraceSource`, the `<system.diagnostics>` configuration section in the `web.config` configuration file is used.

```
<system.diagnostics>
    <sharedListeners>
       <add name="IisTraceListener" type="System.Web.IisTraceListener, System.Web,
Version=2.0.0.0, Culture=neutral, PublicKeyToken=b03f5f7f11d50a3a" />
    </sharedListeners>
     <switches>
     <add name="DefaultSwitch" value="All" />
    </switches>
    <sources>
      <source name="tsTracing" switchName="DefaultSwitch">
        <listeners>
          <add name="IisTraceListener" type="System.Web.IisTraceListener, System.
Web, Version=2.0.0.0, Culture=neutral, PublicKeyToken=b03f5f7f11d50a3a" />
        </listeners>
      </source>
    </sources>
  </system.diagnostics>
```

The preceding configuration section defines the new IIS trace listener with a switch to capture all tracing information. In addition, the tracing source, which is in this case the `TraceSource` instance defined previously in the custom tracing managed module, is added and configured with the `IISTraceListener`. The preceding configuration section makes sure all the tracing information from ASP.NET is routed correctly to the IIS tracing system. The Failed Request Tracing feature can then be used, either through the default behavior to capture only failure trace information for failing requests or by adding custom rules to capture specific tracing information descending from the ASP.NET tracing system.

Finally, native developers can now troubleshoot the state of the IIS web server through the new Runtime Status and Control (RSCA) API known as "reeska." This new API allows native developers, mainly C++ developers, to examine the real-time status of the server by checking the active states of the sites and application pools, the running worker processes, and even to check current requests that are being processed. Developers can check the normal flow of page execution on the server and identify bottlenecks, while the different modules take their part in the request processing in the IIS pipeline. In addition, RSCA provides a means to control the state of the web server by stopping and starting the service, recycling application pools, starting and stopping sites, etc. These features are similar to the `appcmd.exe` command-line tool mentioned previously in this chapter.

An IIS resource is available online that gives an overview on developing managed tracing modules and routing the ASP.NET trace information to the IIS 7.0 tracing system: `http://learn.iis.net/page .aspx/171/how-to-add-tracing-to-iis-7-managed-modules/`

Application Pools

IIS 6.0 introduced the concept of application pools when operating in the worker process isolation-mode compared to working in the IIS 5 mode. An application pool by definition is a unit of separation, at the web server level, that is used to logically group applications into different boundaries, hence providing an isolation of execution from one application to another. If an application in one of the application pools on the web server crashes, not all the applications on the web server will be crashed too. This is because if each application is assigned to a separate application pool, then only this specific application pool will recycle and all applications assigned to the same application pool will also crash. Other applications assigned to other application pools continue to function properly as if nothing happened on the web server. Therefore, application pools provide isolation of execution under the boundaries of the server resources allocated to every application pool, which are allocated differently from one application pool to another.

In the previous release of IIS, the web server was configured to either run in the worker process isolation mode or in the IIS 5.0 mode. However, in IIS 7.0, an application pool is created and its managed pipeline mode property is either set to *Integrated mode* or *Classic mode*. This means that the managed pipeline mode is not configured on the web server as a whole. On the contrary, several application pools can be created on IIS 7.0 with different managed pipeline modes, and applications can be assigned to any of those application pools, hence it is possible to run applications on the same web server with different modes of execution. Figure 1-7 shows the basic settings window for any application created inside IIS 7.0.

Figure 1-7

By opening the IIS manager tool, on the Actions tab on the right of the manager, there is a link to view application pools. All of the application pools created on the web server are listed. Right-clicking any of the application pools and selecting basic settings yields the screen shown in Figure 1-7. There is nothing special about it, but the managed pipeline mode combo box that allows you to choose either the Integrated or Classic mode.

Integrated Mode

When an ASP.NET 2.0 or 3.5 application is assigned to an application pool running in the Integrated mode, the application will benefit from the IIS and ASP.NET unified request processing pipeline. This means the request is processed by both the native and managed installed modules and ASP.NET will have the ability to process all types of content within that specific application. This mode is recommended when there is a need to execute an application in the Integrated mode, and it is the preferred mode to configure the application pools. Several additional and advanced settings can be set by right-clicking on the specific application pool and selecting Advanced Settings.

Classic Mode

The Classic mode resembles an IIS 6.0 application pool when the web server is running in a worker process isolation-mode. In IIS 7.0, applications are still given the opportunity to function as if they are being served by IIS 6.0. When an application is assigned to an application pool configured to run in the Classic mode, IIS 7.0 handles the execution of the application in the same way as IIS 6.0. For instance, if an ASP.NET application is assigned to function under an application pool configured with Classic mode, the default and only available option for ASP.NET 1.1 application, when a request reaches IIS for that application, only the native modules will be executed on the request, then IIS 7.0 hands the request to the `aspnet_isapi.dll` extension to be processed by the ASP.NET runtime. Hence, IIS is able to process the request with all the installed native modules and ASP.NET will have another round in executing its managed modules; the same old-fashioned way of executing applications under IIS 6.0 when configured to run in the worker process isolation mode. If any ASP.NET application for some reason cannot run inside the application pool Integrated mode, it is recommended to keep it configured with the Classic mode under IIS 7.0. It will be executed and processed as if it is hosted in an IIS 6.0 environment.

IIS 7.0 Components

IIS 7.0 is made up of several components that form the web server internal core engine. These components include protocol listeners, services such as the w3svc service and the WAS service, protocol adapters, and many more core components. This section will present an overview of some of the protocols and services that handle request processing inside IIS 7.0.

Protocol Listeners

Protocol listeners are services in which each service is configured to listen and process a specific protocol request coming from the network on which the machine hosting the web server resides. For instance, one of the listeners installed on a Windows machine keeps on waiting and listening for any web request arriving on the machine. There are additional listeners also present to listen to other, different protocols. When a request is received by a listener, it forwards it to IIS 7.0 to be processed. Once a request is processed by IIS 7.0, the response generated is sent back to the protocol listener that originally sent the request. Finally, the response is handed back to the requestor.

An example of a protocol listener is the HTTP listener called Hyper Text Protocol Stack. This is the main protocol listener for all HTTP requests arriving on a Windows machine. When an HTTP request is first received by Windows Vista or Windows Server 2008, the initial handling is actually performed by the kernel-mode HTTP driver: `http.sys`.

World Wide Web Publishing Service

In IIS 6.0 the WWW service was responsible for several tasks at once. These tasks included HTTP administration and configuration, process management, and performance monitoring. In IIS 7.0, this has changed and the WWW Service now acts as a listener adapter for `http.sys`. A listener adapter is responsible for configuring the `http.sys` protocol listener with the IIS 7.0 configuration information stored in the `ApplicationHost.config` configuration file. It then waits for changes in the configuration information to reflect them into the `http.sys`, and finally notifies the Windows Process Activation Service (WAS) when a new HTTP request enters the local queue.

WWW Service functionality has been split into other services. It has preserved its role as a listener adapter, however, the rest of its responsibilities have been passed into another service called the Windows Process Activation Service.

Windows Process Activation Service

In IIS 7.0, the WAS is the second half of the WWW service that was present in the IIS 6.0 days. The WAS is a new service that has three main parts. Figure 1-8 shows the architecture and main components of the WAS.

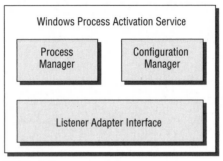

Figure 1-8

The configuration manager is responsible for reading the configuration information from the ApplicationHost.config configuration file. This manager reads global configuration information and protocol configuration information for both HTTP and non-HTTP protocols in order to be able to configure all protocol listeners installed on the web sever machine. It also reads application pool configuration information to know what application pools are present when processing requests on the server. It reads site configuration information, including the different applications included in each site together with the bindings defined on each application, and finally, reads the application pool each application belongs to. Such information helps the WAS when processing a request to know which site and application the request belongs to so that it gets handled by the right application pool.

In addition, the configuration manager gets a notification when the ApplicationHost.config configuration file changes so that it updates its data with the new ones and reflects this on the available protocol listeners.

The process manager is responsible for managing the application pools and worker processes for both HTTP and non-HTTP requests. It manages the state of the application pool by stopping, starting, and recycling it. In addition, when WAS receives a new request from one of the configured protocol listeners, it determines to which application the request belongs. It then checks with the configuration manager for the application pool of the application that the current request belongs to. Once the application pool is determined, it checks to see if there is any worker process currently active. If it finds one, it sends the request to the application pool to be processed by the worker process. If there is no worker process active inside the application pool, WAS instantiates a new one to process the current and upcoming requests.

The last component of the WAS is the unmanaged listener adapter interface. This layer inside the WAS defines how the external listeners communicate the requests they receive into the WAS in order to process them by the web server.

On startup of IIS 7.0, WAS gets initiated and performs several tasks. Figure 1-9 shows the flow of inter-action when WAS first configures the protocol listener adapters.

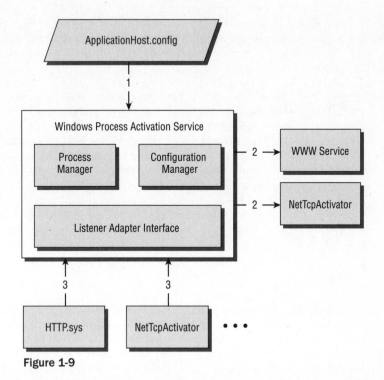

Figure 1-9

When WAS is instantiated, it first reads the configuration data from the `ApplicationHost.config` con-figuration file. Once the configuration information is read, it interacts with the configured protocol listener adapters to pass to them the needed configuration information. Protocol listener adapters function as the glue between the WAS and the protocol listeners. For instance, the WAS passes the configuration informa-tion into the WWW Service, the `http.sys` protocol listener adapter, which in turn configures `http.sys` to start listening for HTTP requests.

Once a new request comes in, the specific protocol listener communicates the request to the WAS through the listener adapter interface, so that the request gets processed. Once a response is ready for the request, WAS passes the response back to the protocol listener responsible for delivering the response back to the client. Again, WAS uses the listener adapter interface for the incoming and outgoing communication with the protocol listeners.

As shown in Figure 1-9, `NetTcpActivator` is the protocol listener and adapter for handling WCF requests. This indicates that WAS can process HTTP and non-HTTP requests; that means WAS can function properly without the need for the WWW Service by serving only non-HTTP requests. A good MSDN resource on the WCF listener adapters and hosting WCF applications inside IIS 7.0 is available online at `http://msdn2.microsoft.com/en-us/library/ms730158.aspx`

IIS 7.0 Modules

The modular architecture of IIS 7.0 has been discussed thoroughly at the beginning of this chapter. It is the new architecture that characterizes the web server core engine. Modules or features can be thought of as classes or objects embedding certain functionality that get executed whenever a new request is being processed by the IIS pipeline. Every installed module gets its turn in processing every request entering the IIS 7.0 pipeline.

This modular architecture has several goals, but above all it protects the web server from security attacks. When a small number of modules are installed on the web server, this means there is a lower probability for a security attack on the server, hence lowering the surface attack to hackers. In addition, when a small number of modules are installed, this means less security patches and updates are required for the administrator to maintain. Moreover, being able to customize the web server to this extent gives the administrator the chance of deciding on the role of the web server by installing and uninstalling modules in the way best suited for the role intended for the web server.

IIS 7.0 ships with a set of unmanaged or native modules that are all installed in case of a full installation of the web server. In addition, IIS 7.0 allows you to extend its functionality with managed modules. Each of these modules is discussed in detail.

Unmanaged Modules

The native modules are grouped by functionality. There are HTTP-related modules that perform tasks specific to HTTP; another set of modules perform tasks related to security; and anther set of modules perform tasks related to content (static files, directory browsing, and so on). There are a set of modules responsible for compression, modules concerned with caching, modules responsible for logging and diagnostics, and modules that help in integrating managed modules. All of these modules are fired and executed during the request-processing pipeline. The available native modules at the time of this writing together with a description are listed in the following table.

Module Name	Description
HTTP Modules	
CustomErrorModule	Sends default and configured HTTP error messages when an error status code is set on a response.
HttpRedirectionModule	Supports configurable redirection for HTTP requests.
OptionsVerbModule	Provides information about allowed verbs in response to OPTIONS verb requests.
ProtocolSupportModule	Performs protocol-related actions, such as setting response headers and redirecting headers based on configuration.
RequestForwarderModule	Forwards requests to external HTTP servers and captures responses.

Module Name	Description
TraceVerbModule	Returns request headers in response to TRACE verb requests
Security Modules	
AnonymousAuthModule	Performs Anonymous authentication when no other authentication method succeeds.
BasicAuthModule	Performs Basic authentication.
CertificateMappingAuthenticationModule	Performs Certificate Mapping authentication using Active Directory.
DigestAuthModule	Performs Digest authentication.
IISCertificateMappingAuthenticationModule	Performs Certificate Mapping authentication using IIS certificate configuration.
RequestFilteringModule	Performs URLScan tasks, such as configuring allowed verbs and file extensions, setting limits, and scanning for bad character sequences.
UrlAuthorizationModule	Performs URL authorization.
WindowsAuthModule	Performs NTLM integrated authentication.
Content Modules	
CgiModule	Executes CGI processes to build response output.
DavFSModule	Sets the handler for Distributed Authoring and Versioning (DAV) requests to the DAV handler.
DefaultDocumentModule	Attempts to return the default document for requests made to the parent directory.
DirectoryListingModule	Lists the contents of a directory.
IsapiModule	Hosts ISAPI extension DLLs.
IsapiFilterModule	Supports ISAPI filter DLLs.
ServerSideIncludeModule	Processes server-side includes code.
StaticFileModule	Serves static files.
FastCgiModule	Supports FastCGI, which provides a high-performance alternative to CGI.

Continued

23

Module Name	Description
Compression Modules	
DynamicCompressionModule	Compresses responses, and applies Gzip compression transfer coding to responses.
StaticCompressionModule	Performs precompression of static content.
Caching Modules	
FileCacheModule	Provides user-mode caching for files and file handles.
HTTPCacheModule	Provides kernel-mode and user-mode caching in http.sys.
SiteCacheModule	Provides user-mode caching of site information.
TokenCacheModule	Provides user-mode caching of user name and token pairs for modules that produce Windows user principals.
UriCacheModule	Provides user mode caching of URL information.
Logging and Diagnostics Modules	
CustomLoggingModule	Loads custom logging modules.
FailedRequestsTracingModule	Supports the Failed Request Tracing feature.
HttpLoggingModule	Passes information and processing status to http.sys for logging.
RequestMonitorModule	Tracks requests currently executing in worker processes, and reports information with Runtime Status and Control Application (RSCA) Programming Interface.
TracingModule	Reports events to Microsoft Event Tracing for Windows (ETW).
Managed Support Modules	
ManagedEngine	Provides integration of managed code modules in the IIS request-processing pipeline.
ConfigurationValidationModule	Validates configuration issues, such as when an application is running in Integrated mode but has handlers or modules declared in the system.web section.

The preceding modules are all installed with a full installation of IIS 7.0. However, if IIS 7.0 is installed with the default configuration and modules, a subset of those modules are installed. The modules installed by default are listed as follows.

- ❑ HTTP modules
    - ❑ `CustomErrorModule`
    - ❑ `ProtoclSupportModule`
- ❑ Security modules
    - ❑ `RequestFilteringModule`
    - ❑ `AnonymousAuthenticationModule`
- ❑ Content modules
    - ❑ `DefaultDocumentModule`
    - ❑ `DirectoryListingModule`
    - ❑ `StaticFileModule`
- ❑ Content modules
    - ❑ `StaticCompressionModule`
- ❑ Logging and diagnostics modules
    - ❑ `HTTPLoggingModule`
    - ❑ `RequestMonitorModule`
- ❑ Caching modules
    - ❑ `HttpCacheModule`

Managed Modules

IIS 7.0 infrastructure allows the installation of .NET managed modules to participate in the request-processing pipeline. Allowing managed modules to function properly depends mostly on the `Managed EngineModule` mentioned above. Managed modules are ASP.NET 2.0 and 3.5 `HttpModules` that a .NET developer has always been used to writing, however with IIS 7.0, these modules will get the chance to work upon requests during the request-processing pipeline managed by the web server itself.

The existing managed modules that can be configured with IIS 7.0 are listed in the following table.

Module Name	Description
`AnonymousIdentification`	Manages anonymous identifiers, which are used by features that support anonymous identification such as ASP.NET profile engine.
`DefaultAuthentication`	Ensures that an authentication object is present in the context.
`FileAuthorization`	Verifies that a user has permission to access the requested file.

Continued

Module Name	Description
FormsAuthentication	Supports authentication by using Forms authentication.
OutputCache	Supports output caching
Profile	Manages user profiles by using ASP.NET profile, which stores and retrieves user settings in a data source such as a database.
RoleManager	Manages a RolePrincipal instance for the current user.
Session	Supports maintaining session state, which enables storage of data specific to a single client within an application on the server.
UrlAuthorization	Determines whether the current user is permitted access to the requested URL, based on the user name or the list of roles that a user is member of.
UrlMappingsModule	Supports mapping a real URL to a more user-friendly URL.
WindowsAuthentication	Sets the identity of the user for an ASP.NET application when Windows authentication is enabled.

This managed modules' information has been gathered from the official ASP.NET 2.0/3.5 documentation on MSDN.

Summary

In this chapter you were introduced to the new web server engine by Microsoft, IIS 7.0. IIS 7.0 ships with a new architecture that is more modular and allows administrators and developers to configure it the way they want.

The main point to keep in mind about the new web server is its modular architecture. IIS 7.0 is installed with minimal modules or features. Additional modules can be installed whenever they are needed. In addition, IIS 7.0 allows developing both native and managed modules using C++ and .NET, respectively.

A lot of improvements have been introduced to IIS 7.0, including security, administration and configuration, and troubleshooting improvements. New APIs are now ready for use by native and managed developers to extend the functionality of the web server.

IIS 7.0 now integrates well with ASP.NET infrastructure for request processing; hence, applications now can run either in the Integrated mode or in the Classic mode application pool.

❑ **Integrated mode:** When running under the Integrated mode, the ASP.NET 2.0 or 3.5 application can take benefit from the integration between IIS 7.0 and ASP.NET so that a single unified pipeline is present where both IIS native modules and configured ASP.NET modules have a say while processing a specific request.

❑ **Classic mode:** With the Classic mode, an application will have the same environment as it had once under IIS 6.0, where the IIS 7.0 request-processing pipeline happens separately from the ASP.NET request-processing pipeline.

In addition, IIS 7.0 components have been enhanced and a new major component that has been added is the Windows Process Activation Service (WAS). This service is the brain of the web server that interacts with the web server configuration system and configures protocol listener adapters that in turn configure their corresponding protocol listeners. This new service handles both HTTP and non-HTTP requests, and this gives IIS a broader field to handle so many requests from different sources. Also, this service is responsible for the process management including application pool states, stopping, starting, recycling them, and creating new worker process instances.

The next chapter continues this discussion with a look at the new IIS 7.0 and ASP.NET Integrated mode. The discussion includes a thorough examination of the Integrated mode architecture as well as developing new modules and handlers in ASP.NET and integrating them with IIS 7.0 infrastructure. In addition, a study on handling migration errors is given to help in migrating an existing ASP.NET application to run under the IIS 7.0 and ASP.NET Integrated mode.

2

IIS 7.0 and ASP.NET Integrated Mode

Internet Information Services (IIS) version 7.0 introduces two modes of processing: Classic and Integrated mode. The Classic mode resembles the same mode of execution as that of IIS 6.0. What is new is the Integrated mode, which unifies the request-processing pipeline between the IIS infrastructure and the ASP.NET runtime.

One of the striking advantages of this new mode of execution is that ASP.NET runtime is now capable of processing all types of content files including ASP.NET, HTML, ASP, PHP, and many other web resources. This is by far an improvement that makes all ASP.NET services including forms authentication, membership, role management, and many others available to different kinds of content file types in an application.

This chapter starts by introducing the advantages of using the IIS 7.0 and ASP.NET Integrated mode. The discussion expands into exploring the internals and architecture of the new Integrated mode of execution. In addition, the chapter highlights the migration problems that a developer or administrator faces when upgrading an application to run inside IIS 7.0 under the Integrated mode. The chapter ends with a section on extending the IIS 7.0 infrastructure by developing managed `HttpHandlers` and `HttpModules` and installing these features from inside the application's `web.config` configuration file without the need to have access to the IIS 7.0 Manager tool.

When you finish reading this chapter, you will be armed with a good knowledge in:

❑   Advantages of using IIS 7.0 and ASP.NET Integrated mode.

❑   IIS 7.0 and ASP.NET Integrated mode architecture.

❑   Handling migration errors for applications to run under IIS 7.0 Integrated mode.

❑   Extending IIS 7.0 with managed `HttpModules` and `HttpHandlers`.

Advantages of IIS 7.0 and ASP.NET Integrated Mode

IIS 7.0 introduces a new era of web development with a solid integration with ASP.NET 3.5. Web development witnessed a huge change and improvement with the release of ASP.NET 1.x, and with ASP.NET 2.0. In ASP.NET 3.5 many services were added. There is more control over the ASP.NET request-processing pipeline, new APIs were developed to make development tasks easier, in addition to many other improvements. IIS 7.0 goes far beyond and leverages ASP.NET 3.5 from being just a technology or framework to develop dynamic web applications to a framework to extend its core engine.

IIS 7.0 gives the developer the choice to either continue working with the Classic mode, i.e., the IIS 6.0 mode, or enhance the development and move to the Integrated mode. Integrated mode means the integration between IIS 7.0 and ASP.NET working together, joining their efforts for a better web development experience. The benefits of such an Integrated mode can be summarized as follows:

❑ **ASP.NET 3.5 services can now be used for all content types:** In previous releases of IIS, ASP.NET did not have a say when it comes to content file types that are not registered with ASP.NET runtime. For example, when processing an ASP classic page, ASP.NET runtime could not perform any processing on that specific file type. This is due to the fact that IIS used to map several file types, including .aspx, .ascx, etc., to the ASP.NET ISAPI extension, while other file types, including .ASP, and so on, were mapped to another ISAPI extension different from that of the ASP.NET. However, with the new Integrated mode offered by IIS 7.0, ASP.NET can operate on any file type regardless of its extension and this is because when an ASP.NET application is executing under the new IIS 7.0 Integrated mode, it gets the chance to process any request, that IIS 7.0 accepts, regardless of its type. As an example, ASP.NET FormsAuthenticationModule can now be used to authenticate non-ASP.NET pages similar to the way used to authenticate ASP.NET resources. In addition, all the ASP.NET 3.5 services, including Membership, Role, and Profile management services, can be used not only with ASP.NET resources, but also with any other resource.

❑ **Extend IIS 7.0 with ASP.NET:** Previously, to extend IIS, developers had to develop native modules using both the ISAPI API and C++. Such a task was not easy at all and this forced developers who are developing in .NET, the managed code, to learn other languages like C++ to be able to develop and extend the web server core engine. In the Integrated mode, ASP.NET developers can extend the web server core engine by developing ASP.NET HttpModules. Once a module is developed, it can be registered inside IIS 7.0 modules so that it can operate during the IIS request-processing pipeline. Later in the chapter, a section is dedicated to developing a new ASP.NET module and registering it with IIS 7.0.

❑ **Unified processing pipeline:** IIS 7.0 integrates its own request-processing pipeline with ASP.NET. For instance, you can disable all native authentication modules and enable the FormsAuthenticationModule through IIS. When the authentication event fires, IIS 7.0 runs all configured authentication modules registered in an application. When it detects that forms authentication is enabled, it hands off the request to the ASP.NET module to process the request. What happens, in fact, is that the IIS 7.0 engine uses the native ManagedEngineModule to instantiate a new AppDomain instance. Inside the new AppDomain, the Common Language Runtime (CLR) is first instantiated, and after that the needed module is loaded, hence giving it the chance to operate on the request instead of a native module inside IIS. It can be seen how the native and managed modules can be used interchangeably as though they are both of the same type of modules, which they are not, but the Integrated mode gives that impression.

This was a brief summary on the advantages of the new Integrated mode. In the coming sections, the IIS 7.0 Integrated mode architecture and an example of developing an ASP.NET module and integrating it with IIS is shown in detail.

IIS 7.0 Integrated Mode Architecture

The initial processing of an HTTP request on IIS 7.0 running in the Classic mode, resembling the same IIS 6.0 functionality, occurs within IIS and a supporting protocol driver. As a result, depending on the configuration for IIS, a request may never make it far enough to be processed by ASP.NET. Figure 2-1 shows the salient portions of IIS 7.0 running in the Classic mode and Windows Server 2008 or Windows Vista/2003 that participate in request processing.

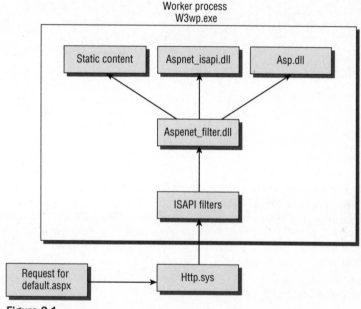

Figure 2-1

A request must first pass the restrictions enforced by the kernel mode HTTP driver: http.sys. The request is handed off to a worker process, where it then flows through a combination of the internal request processing provided by IIS and several ISAPI filters and extensions. Ultimately, the request is routed to the appropriate content handler, which for ASP.NET pages is the ASP.NET runtime's ISAPI extension.

The ASP.NET ISAPI extension contains the ASP.NET runtime request-processing pipeline. It can be easily concluded how the request first passes through the IIS request-processing pipeline for authentication, authorization, and all other modules. When it is time to determine the handler for the request based on the request's file extension, in case of an ASP.NET page, IIS passes the request to the ASP.NET ISAPI extension. Once the extension is activated, the ASP.NET request-processing pipeline is fired. Figure 2-2 shows a basic sketch of what goes on inside the ASP.NET request-processing pipeline.

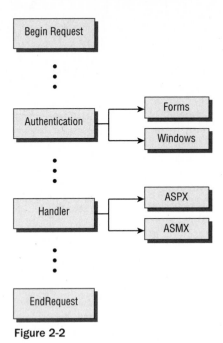

Figure 2-2

Once the request enters the ASP.NET request-processing pipeline, the different registered events start to execute. The first event is the BeginRequest event. Following is a set of events each linked to execute a specific feature until the authentication stage is reached. Based on which authentication type the application is configured with, the corresponding module executes: FormsAuthenticationModule or WindowsAuthenticationModule. Later on, the stage is reached where a handler should be selected to handle the execution of the current request according to the file extension of the request resource. Finally, the EndRequest event is fired and the response of executing the request is handed off to the IIS request-processing pipeline so that a response is generated for the client that issued the request.

In IIS 7.0, the story is different. The unified request-processing pipeline that was explained earlier takes control over the execution inside IIS 7.0 when running in the Integrated mode. Unified pipeline means that both the IIS 7.0 and ASP.NET request-processing pipeline unite and execute as though they were the same pipeline of execution. This means that ASP.NET is given the privilege to have access to any IIS 7.0 intrinsic object and being able to have a hand at every stage of execution. For instance, an ASP.NET authentication module can be used to substitute any authentication native module used by IIS 7.0.

With the Integrated mode enabled, ASP.NET modules become first-class citizens. They can operate on the request before any IIS module operates on it, which means ASP.NET can, for example, change the request headers before any other native module gets access to it. In addition, ASP.NET modules can operate on requests even after IIS modules finish processing the request and even sometimes, ASP.NET modules can replace existing IIS modules. Figure 2-3 shows the unified request-processing pipeline inside IIS 7.0 when operating in the Integrated mode.

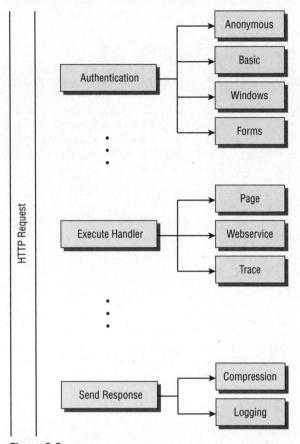

Figure 2-3

When a request reaches IIS 7.0 to be processed, the different stages inside the request-processing pipe-line start to execute. For instance, once the `AuthenticateRequest` event fires, IIS 7.0 checks to see what authentication modules are configured inside the `<system.webServer />` configuration section group and accordingly it executes the right module(s) in the order specified in the `<modules>` configuration section. At this stage, an ASP.NET module that attaches to the authentication event and provides the logic to authenticate users can be added in the application's `web.config` configuration file, thus remov-ing all other native modules registered by IIS for the authentication stage. There is one exception in that, at minimum, the native `AnonymousAuthenticationModule` should be enabled when no other native authentication module is enabled.

This unified Integrated mode allows ASP.NET modules to execute as though they were part of the IIS 7.0 infrastructure. The question that arises now is how an application interacts with the IIS engine to decide what module to run; is it the native one or the managed one? Going back to Chapter 1 when the `ApplicationHost.config` configuration file was introduced, it was clear that IIS infrastructure and every ASP.NET application can share the same `<system.webServer />` configuration sec-tion group. The `ApplicationHost.config` configuration file fills the aforementioned section with global configurations and leaves it to each specific application to decide whether to use the defaults set globally by the web server or to update the section with specific information targeting the specific application. An important discussion to have at this stage is how IIS installs and registers the native and managed modules and who decides on which module to use.

system.webServer Configuration Section Group

The `<system.webServer />` configuration section group located inside the `ApplicationHost.config` configuration file contains dedicated sections to list the native and managed modules installed on the web server. The native modules usually require not only installation but also registration, while the managed modules need only to be registered. The first section inside the `<system.webServer />` that is discussed is the `<globalModules />` configuration section.

The globalModules Configuration Section

The `<globalModules />` configuration section installs all the native modules listed. In the `Application Host.config` configuration file the `<globalModules />` configuration section usually contains the following native modules.

```
<globalModules>
    <add name="UriCacheModule"
        image="%windir%\System32\inetsrv\cachuri.dll" />
    <add name="FileCacheModule"
        image="%windir%\System32\inetsrv\cachfile.dll" />
    <add name="TokenCacheModule"
        image="%windir%\System32\inetsrv\cachtokn.dll" />
    <add name="HttpCacheModule"
        image="%windir%\System32\inetsrv\cachhttp.dll" />
    <add name="StaticCompressionModule"
        image="%windir%\System32\inetsrv\compstat.dll" />
    <add name="DefaultDocumentModule"
        image="%windir%\System32\inetsrv\defdoc.dll" />
    <add name="DirectoryListingModule"
        image="%windir%\System32\inetsrv\dirlist.dll" />
    <add name="ProtocolSupportModule"
        image="%windir%\System32\inetsrv\protsup.dll" />
    <add name="StaticFileModule"
        image="%windir%\System32\inetsrv\static.dll" />
    <add name="AnonymousAuthenticationModule"
        image="%windir%\System32\inetsrv\authanon.dll" />
    <add name="RequestFilteringModule"
        image="%windir%\System32\inetsrv\modrqflt.dll" />
    <add name="CustomErrorModule"
        image="%windir%\System32\inetsrv\custerr.dll" />
    <add name="HttpLoggingModule"
        image="%windir%\System32\inetsrv\loghttp.dll" />
    <add name="RequestMonitorModule"
        image="%windir%\System32\inetsrv\iisreqs.dll" />
    <add name="IsapiModule"
        image="%windir%\System32\inetsrv\isapi.dll" />
    <add name="IsapiFilterModule"
        image="%windir%\System32\inetsrv\filter.dll" />
```

```
        <add name="ConfigurationValidationModule"
             image="%windir%\System32\inetsrv\validcfg.dll" />
        <add name="ManagedEngine"
             image="%windir%\Microsoft.NET\Framework\v2.0.50727\webengine.dll"
             preCondition="integratedMode,runtimeVersionv2.0,bitness32" />
        <add name="BasicAuthenticationModule"
             image="%windir%\System32\inetsrv\authbas.dll" />
    </globalModules>
```

Depending on which native modules have been installed on the web server, they will be shown in the <globalModules /> configuration section. Before being able to use any native module it should be installed and this is exactly what the <globalModules /> configuration section does. It installs every module listed inside so that it can be used later by any IIS feature. Every module is listed by specifying the (friendly) name of the module name and the image where the module is located. All the above native modules are C++ modules and each module is located within its own assembly.

Now that the modules are installed, they need to be registered so that they attach to the request-processing pipeline. The <modules /> configuration section is the one that registers both native and managed modules.

The modules Configuration Section

The <modules /> configuration section is the place where both native and managed modules get registered by the web server so that they can participate in the processing of requests inside the unified request-processing pipeline. Native modules registered in this section should have already been installed as mentioned in the previous section.

```
    <location path="" overrideMode="Allow">
        <system.webServer>
            <modules>
                <add name="HttpCacheModule" />
                <add name="StaticCompressionModule" />
                <add name="DefaultDocumentModule" />
                <add name="DirectoryListingModule" />
                <add name="ProtocolSupportModule" />
                <add name="StaticFileModule" />
                <add name="AnonymousAuthenticationModule" />
                <add name="RequestFilteringModule" />
                <add name="CustomErrorModule" />
                <add name="IsapiModule" />
                <add name="BasicAuthenticationModule" />
                <add name="HttpLoggingModule" />
                <add name="RequestMonitorModule" />
                <add name="IsapiFilterModule" />
                <add name="ConfigurationValidationModule" />
                <add name="OutputCache"
                     type="System.Web.Caching.OutputCacheModule"
                     preCondition="managedHandler" />
                <add name="Session"
                     type="System.Web.SessionState.SessionStateModule"
                     preCondition="managedHandler" />
```

```
                    <add name="WindowsAuthentication"
                        type="System.Web.Security.WindowsAuthenticationModule"
                        preCondition="managedHandler" />
                    <add name="FormsAuthentication"
                        type="System.Web.Security.FormsAuthenticationModule"
                        preCondition="managedHandler" />
                    <add name="DefaultAuthentication"
                        type="System.Web.Security.DefaultAuthenticationModule"
                        preCondition="managedHandler" />
                    <add name="RoleManager"
                        type="System.Web.Security.RoleManagerModule"
                        preCondition="managedHandler" />
                    <add name="UrlAuthorization"
                        type="System.Web.Security.UrlAuthorizationModule"
                        preCondition="managedHandler" />
                    <add name="FileAuthorization"
                        type="System.Web.Security.FileAuthorizationModule"
                        preCondition="managedHandler" />
                    <add name="AnonymousIdentification"
                        type="System.Web.Security.AnonymousIdentificationModule"
                        preCondition="managedHandler" />
                    <add name="Profile"
                        type="System.Web.Profile.ProfileModule"
                        preCondition="managedHandler" />
                    <add name="UrlMappingsModule"
                        type="System.Web.UrlMappingsModule"
                        preCondition="managedHandler" />
                </modules>
            </system.webServer>
        </location>
```

Every module, whether it is a native or managed one, is added to the <modules> configuration section by the add element.

❑ name: The name attribute specifies a friendly and human readable name of the registered module. If the module registered is a native one, the name should match the same name used when the module was installed in the <globalModules /> configuration section. In case of a managed module, any friendly and expressive name can be used.

❑ type: This attribute contains the value of the fully qualified namespace of the managed module registered. It applies only to managed modules.

❑ precondition: This attribute specifies whether the module should be loaded for all requests or only managed requests, that is, request for ASP.NET resources. If you want to enable a module to run for every request, whether it is an ASP.NET or not, simply clear this attribute in the ApplicationHost.config configuration file. In most cases, when hosting a website on a remote server you will not get the chance to play around with this file. A better solution is to configure the module through the web.config configuration file as will be shown soon.

The modules defined at this level are defined globally at the web server's level, which means all the lower-level sites, applications, and virtual directories inherit all these modules. This means all the registered modules will process any request that is part of your site, application, or virtual directory.

To prevent this from happening, you can add a web.config configuration file into the application and remove any module that you do not want to take part in the processing of requests that belong to the application.

```
<configuration>
  <system.webServer>
    <modules>
      <remove name="BasicAuthenticationModule"/>
    </modules>
  </system.webServer>
</configuration>
```

The preceding configuration can be placed inside the application's web.config configuration file. What the above configuration settings do is remove the installed and registered BasicAuthenticationModule. Now, regardless whether the BasicAuthenticationModule is enabled or not for the application, requests belonging to the application will not be processed by the native BasicAuthenticationModule.

```
<configuration>
  <system.webServer>
    <modules>
      <remove name="BasicAuthenticationModule"/>
      <add name="MyBasicAuthenticationModule"/>
    </modules>
  </system.webServer>
</configuration>
```

If, on the other hand, you want to replace an existing module with a custom module, you can simply remove the module in question and then add your own module by specifying its name. It goes without saying that the new module should be listed in the <globalModules /> configuration section of the ApplicationHost.config configuration file. In other words, the module must be installed inside IIS 7.0 before being able to use it in your applications.

It is important to know the order in which the above registered modules get executed by the IIS runtime. As previously mentioned, the <modules> configuration section registers both the native and managed modules. Every module registers itself to a specific event in the request-processing pipeline. When an event fires in the pipeline, IIS 7.0 looks at the registered modules and decides on which modules should be run (remember again, modules can be both native and managed modules). Once the selection is made, IIS then looks to see the order they are registered with in the <modules /> configuration section. The order decides which module would run before another module. So it is very possible that a managed module might be placed before a native module, both registered for the same event. Therefore, the managed module will be executed first by ASP.NET runtime and then followed by the native module that will be executed within the context of IIS runtime.

It is important to remember that native and managed modules are executed according to their order of appearance in the <modules /> configuration section. In addition, the order can be set programmatically. However, this is available only for native modules, as you will see later on with the native AnonymousAuthenticationModule.

The security Configuration Section Group

The <security /> configuration section group is the place where you specify security options for your application. It contains two major sections, as described next.

The authentication Configuration Section

In the <globalModules /> configuration section, several authentication modules were installed and then later on were registered in the <modules> configuration section. Which of these modules does IIS 7.0 use for authentication? The answer lies in the <authentication> configuration section that enables/disables modules as required. Looking at the <authentication> configuration section in the ApplicationHost.config configuration file yields the configuration section shown here.

```
<authentication>

    <anonymousAuthentication enabled="true" userName="IUSR" />

    <basicAuthentication enabled="false" />

    <clientCertificateMappingAuthentication />

    <digestAuthentication />

    <iisClientCertificateMappingAuthentication>
    </iisClientCertificateMappingAuthentication>

    <windowsAuthentication>
    </windowsAuthentication>

</authentication>
```

The installed and registered modules in the <globalModules /> and <modules /> configuration sections are shown in the <authentication /> configuration section above with configuration attributes.

For instance, the BasicAuthenticationModule shown above with an attribute of enabled="false" was already installed and registered in the <globalModules /> and <modules /> configuration sections. The other modules without any configurable attributes were neither installed nor registered, hence the fact that only registered and installed native modules show up in the authentication section with configurable attributes. In other words, the IIS 7.0 <modules /> configuration section determines whether or not a module (authentication or any other module) will even run. The <authentication /> configuration section configures the behavior of each authentication type. However, the settings in the <authentication /> configuration section will not take effect unless the associated module has already been configured to run in the first place.

The AnonymousAuthenticationModule shown previously has a set of important attributes that are worth discussing, especially from the security context. This module is usually installed as part of the default installation of IIS 7.0. For a list of the modules installed with a default installation of IIS, refer back to Chapter 1.

This module is enabled by default and hence it applies to all requests that belong to all sites configured under the IIS 7.0 web server. The <anonymousAuthentication /> element defines userName and password attributes that are used together to specify the identity or Windows account that IIS uses when an anonymous user accesses an application when no other authentication module is enabled. By default, IIS 7.0 sets the userName attribute to the built-in account IUSR that replaces the old IUSR_MachineName account in IIS 6.0 and has minimum and limited privileges. The new IUSR built-in user account and the IIS_IUSRS built-in group are discussed in detail in Chapter 3.

Moreover, you can configure IIS 7.0 to use the application pool or worker process identity as the username and password for the AnonymousAuthenticationModule. This can be configured by setting an empty string for the value of userName attribute. An empty string can be represented by double quotes as follows:

```
<anonymousAuthentication enabled="true" userName=""/>
```

In case you want to disable any of the registered native modules, you can do so from inside the application's web.config configuration file using the enabled attribute as shown here.

```
<system.webServer>
  <security>
    <authentication>
      <anonymousAuthentication enabled="true"/>
      <basicAuthentication enabled="false"/>
      <clientCertificateMappingAuthentication enabled="false"/>
      <digestAuthentication enabled="false"/>
      <iisClientCertificateMappingAuthentication enabled="false"/>
      <windowsAuthentication enabled="false"/>
    </authentication>
  </security>
</system.webServer>
```

By specifying enabled="false" you simply disabled the module from having any role in processing a request that belongs to the current application.

Another important trick to mention here is: What if you want to enable, for example, Forms AuthenticationModule to handle all content file types and not only ASP.NET resource files? In other words, what if you want to remove the preCondition attribute set for each managed module in the <modules /> configuration section in the ApplicationHost.config configuration file? This can be easily done by removing the module element then adding it again without specifying a value for the preCondition attribute.

```
<system.webServer>
  <modules>
    <!-- Allow the FormsAuthentication module to run for all requests -->
    <remove name="FormsAuthentication"/>
    <add name="FormsAuthentication" type="System.Web.Security.
FormsAuthenticationModule"/>
  </modules>
</system.webServer>
```

As the preceding listing shows, the `FormsAuthenticationModule` element has been removed and another element has been added, setting the `name` attribute to `FormsAuthentication`. It is very important to use the same friendly name used by IIS in the `ApplicationHost.config` configuration file and set the `type` attribute to the full namespace of the `FormsAuthenticationModule` defined in the .NET Framework base class library.

To enable all managed modules to run for all request types, you set the value of the `runAllManagedModulesForAllRequests` attribute to `true`.

```
<system.webServer>
        <modules runAllManagedModulesForAllRequests="true"></modules>
</system.webServer>
```

The attribute is added to the `<modules />` configuration section in the `<system.webServer />` configuration section group inside the application's `web.config` configuration file.

Note, though, that when IIS 7.0 finds out that a managed module has to be run and executed, a switch happens from a native mode to the managed mode for the managed module to be run within the ASP .NET runtime in the CLR. In general, it is recommended not to automatically run all managed modules for all requests. This incurs an overhead and low performance in throughput because of the switch of context. What you can do is selectively choose the managed modules that make sense for non-ASP.NET content and enable only those modules for all requests, managed and native.

To decide on what authentication type to use in an application, the same old way of specifying the authentication in an ASP.NET application still works. To configure what authentication type the application should use, add an `<authentication />` configuration section inside the `<system.web />` configuration section group of the application's `web.config` configuration file.

```
<system.web>
  <authentication mode="Forms" />
</system.web>
```

The preceding listing configures an application to use forms authentication. However, if you want an application to be configured with Windows authentication, change the `mode` attribute value from `Forms` to a value of `Windows` and make sure the managed `WindowsAuthenticationModule` is registered correctly with IIS 7.0.

Authorization Configuration Section

When installing IIS 7.0, you get the chance to install a new native `UrlAuthorizationModule` that has been introduced to the IIS 7.0 runtime. Once this native module is installed, it shows up in both the `<globalModules />` and `<modules>` configuration sections of the `<system.webServer />` configuration section group.

```
<globalModules>
    <add name="ManagedEngine"
        image="%windir%\Microsoft.NET\Framework\v2.0.50727\webengine.dll"
        preCondition="integratedMode,runtimeVersionv2.0,bitness32" />
    <add name="BasicAuthenticationModule"
        image="%windir%\System32\inetsrv\authbas.dll" />
```

```
        <add name="UrlAuthorizationModule"
              image="%windir%\System32\inetsrv\urlauthz.dll" />
    </globalModules>
```

Once the native `UrlAuthorization` feature is installed, IIS 7.0 configures the `ApplicationHost.config` configuration file and adds an entry inside the `<globalModules />` configuration section.

```
        <modules>
            <add name="UrlMappingsModule"
                 type="System.Web.UrlMappingsModule"
                 preCondition="managedHandler" />
            <add name="UrlAuthorizationModule" />
        </modules>
```

In addition, the module gets registered by having a new entry in the `<modules />` configuration section. If you would like to disable this module for your application, you can easily do so by removing it from the `<modules />` configuration section of the `<system.webServer />` configuration section group inside the application's `web.config` configuration file.

```
    <system.webServer>
      <modules>
        <remove name="UrlAuthorizationModule"/>
      </modules>
    </system.webServer>
```

The native `UrlAuthorizationModule` uses authorization rules that determine whether the user accessing the application is authorized to access specific parts of the application or specific page URLs. These authorization rules are configured by adding some declarative rules into the `<authorization />` configuration section inside the `<security />` section group of the application's `web.config` configuration file.

```
    <system.webServer>
      <security>
        <authorization>
          <add accessType="Deny" users="?"/>
          <add accessType="Allow" users="bhaidar"/>
        </authorization>
      </security>
    </system.webServer>
```

This can be achieved by adding sub-elements inside the `<authorization />` configuration section specifying the `accessType`, whether to allow or deny, the `users` to whom you want to grant access and finally, the `verbs` attribute.

Moreover, when ASP.NET is installed on IIS 7.0, it registers with the `ApplicationHost.config` configuration file a managed `UrlAuthorizationModule` that is configured to run for ASP.NET resources processed by the application.

```
        <modules>
            <add name="AnonymousIdentification"
                 type="System.Web.Security.AnonymousIdentificationModule"
```

```
                              preCondition="managedHandler" />
              <add name="Profile"
                    type="System.Web.Profile.ProfileModule"
                    preCondition="managedHandler" />
              <add name="UrlAuthorization"
                    type="System.Web.Security. UrlAuthorizationModule"
                    preCondition="managedHandler" />
              <add name="UrlAuthorizationModule" />
          </modules>
```

Once again notice the `preCondition` attribute set to `managedHandler`, which means that this module will be invoked only for managed resources. To activate this module for all types of requests, simply use the `web.config` configuration file in your application to remove the module and add it again without specifying a value for the `preCondition` attribute.

```
<system.webServer>
  <modules>
    <remove name="UrlAuthorization"/>
    <add name="UrlAuthorization" type="System.Web.Security.
UrlAuthorizationModule"/>
  </modules>
</system.webServer>
```

The code in the listing above removes the managed `UrlAuthorizationModule` element and then adds it again so that it functions against all requests processed by the IIS runtime.

The managed `UrlAuthorizationModule` uses authorization rules that determine whether the user accessing the application is authorized to access specific parts of the application or not. These authorization rules are defined in the `<authorization>` configuration section inside the `<system.web />` configuration section group of the application's `web.config` configuration file. There is nothing different here from what has always been used to configure ASP.NET authorization before the days of IIS 7.0.

```
<system.web>
  <authorization>
    <deny users="?"/>
  </authorization>
</system.web>
```

The preceding configuration settings prevent anonymous users from accessing the website.

Migrating ASP.NET Applications to Integrated Mode

When a new ASP.NET application is created using Visual Studio 2008 under IIS 7.0, it is by default configured to run under the Integrated mode application pool. However, having ASP.NET running for several years, there is a huge number of applications that need to be migrated in order to function properly under IIS 7.0 Integrated mode. If, however, you decide to keep your applications the same without introducing any changes to them, then simply add the application to IIS and assign it to the Classic mode application pool. With this configuration, you are sure the application will run properly the same as it did under IIS 6.0.

When you consider migrating old applications into the Integrated mode, you should be looking at three important sections within the web.config configuration file: <httpModules />, <httpHandlers />, and the <identity /> configuration sections.

httpModules Configuration Section

When an ASP.NET application wants to register an HttpModule it usually adds an entry inside the <httpModules /> configuration section inside the <system.web> configuration section group of the application's web.config configuration file. Now to make the application run properly under IIS 7.0 Integrated mode, simply copy all the registered modules inside the <httpModules /> configuration section into the <modules> configuration section inside the <system.webServer /> configuration section group. Not all modules registered within the <httpModules /> configuration section will take effect when the application is running in the Integrated mode. Only those registered within the <modules /> configuration section of the <system.webServer /> configuration section group will run and execute. If any new module is to be registered in an application, it is best to place it inside the <modules /> configuration section of the <system.webServer /> configuration section group.

C#

```csharp
public class BasicHttpModule : IHttpModule
{
    public BasicHttpModule()
    {
    }

    public void Dispose()
    {
        // Leave it blank since we will not add any code
    }

    /// <summary>
    /// This method is used to register for events in the
    /// request-processing pipeline stages
    /// </summary>
    /// <param name="context"></param>
    public void Init(HttpApplication context)
    {
        // Register for the BeginRequest event
        context.BeginRequest += new EventHandler(BeginRequest);
    }

    static void BeginRequest(object sender, EventArgs e)
    {
        HttpContext context=
        HttpContext.Current;
        context.Write("<h3 align='center'>
            Welcome message from the Basic Http Module !</h3>");
    }

}
```

VB.NET

```vbnet
Imports System
Imports System.Web

''' <summary>
''' Summary description for BasicHttpModule
''' </summary>
Public Class BasicHttpModule
    Implements IHttpModule
    Public Sub New()
        '
        ' TODO: Add constructor logic here
        '
    End Sub

#Region "IHttpModule Members"

    Public Sub Dispose() Implements IHttpModule.Dispose
        ' Leave it blank since we will not add any code
    End Sub

    ''' <summary>
    ''' This method is used to register for events in the
    ''' request-processing pipeline stages
    ''' </summary>
    ''' <param name="context"></param>
    Public Sub Init(ByVal context As HttpApplication) Implements IHttpModule.Init
        ' Register for the BeginRequest event
        AddHandler context.BeginRequest, AddressOf BeginRequest
    End Sub

    Private Shared Sub BeginRequest(ByVal sender As Object, ByVal e As EventArgs)
        HttpContext context=
        HttpContext.Current;
        context.Write("<h3 align='center'>
            Welcome message from the Basic Http Module !</h3>");
    End Sub

#End Region
End Class
```

The preceding listing shows a simple HttpModule that registers the BeginRequest event of the unified request-processing pipeline to display a message on the user's screen.

To register this module in the application's web.config configuration file, simply add the following:

```xml
<system.webServer>
        <modules>
    <!-- Register the BasicHttpModule  -->
    <add name="BasicHttpModule" type="BasicHttpModule" />
        </modules>
</system.webServer>
```

When registering an `HttpModule` located in the `App_Code` system folder of an ASP.NET application, simply add the module by specifying a friendly `name` for the module and by setting the module name as a value for the `type` attribute.

When any ASP.NET page is requested by the application, the following message is attached as the first thing to display on the page:

```
Welcome message from the Basic Http Module!
```

The module gets executed during the `BeginRequest` event during the unified request-processing pipeline.

Moreover, if you move the registered module into the `<modules />` configuration section and keep the `<httpModules />` section inside the application's `web.config` configuration file, you should turn off validation done by IIS, to ensure that the `web.config` configuration is valid, so that IIS does not generated migration error messages. Turning off validation simply suppresses the error messages generated. This also applies for the `<httpHandlers />` configuration section and enabling impersonation as you will see in the next two sections.

httpHandlers Configuration Section

When an ASP.NET application wants to register an `HttpHandler` to process a specific content file type, usually a custom one, it adds an entry into the `<httpHandlers />` configuration section inside the `<system.web />` configuration section group in the application's `web.config` configuration file. Now to make the application run properly under IIS 7.0 Integrated mode, simply copy all the registered handlers from inside the `<httpHandlers />` configuration section into the `<handlers />` configuration section inside the `<system.webServer />` configuration section group. The `<handlers />` configuration section is originally defined inside the `ApplicationHost.config` configuration file. It lists all the mappings between content file extensions and their corresponding handlers.

```xml
<location path="" overrideMode="Allow">
    <system.webServer>
        <handlers accessPolicy="Script, Read">
            <add name="TraceHandler-Integrated"
                path="trace.axd"
                verb="GET,HEAD,POST,DEBUG"
                type="System.Web.Handlers.TraceHandler"
                preCondition="integratedMode" />
            <add name="WebAdminHandler-Integrated"
                path="WebAdmin.axd"
                verb="GET,DEBUG"
                type="System.Web.Handlers.WebAdminHandler"
                preCondition="integratedMode" />
            <add name="PageHandlerFactory-Integrated"
                path="*.aspx"
                verb="GET,HEAD,POST,DEBUG"
                type="System.Web.UI.PageHandlerFactory"
                preCondition="integratedMode" />
            <add name="SimpleHandlerFactory-Integrated"
                path="*.ashx"
                verb="GET,HEAD,POST,DEBUG"
```

```
                        type="System.Web.UI.SimpleHandlerFactory"
                        preCondition="integratedMode" />
            <add name="WebServiceHandlerFactory-Integrated"
                        path="*.asmx"
                        verb="GET,HEAD,POST,DEBUG"
                        type="System.Web.Services.Protocols.WebServiceHandlerFactory,
                            System.Web.Services, Version=2.0.0.0, Culture=neutral,
                            PublicKeyToken=b03f5f7f11d50a3a"
                        preCondition="integratedMode" />
            <add name="PageHandlerFactory-ISAPI-2.0"
                        path="*.aspx"
                        verb="GET,HEAD,POST,DEBUG"
                        modules="IsapiModule" scriptProcessor="%windir%\Microsoft.NET\
                            Framework\v2.0.50727\aspnet_isapi.dll"
                        preCondition="classicMode,runtimeVersionv2.0,bitness32"
                            responseBufferLimit="0" />
            <add name="StaticFile" path="*"
                        verb="*"
                        modules="StaticFileModule,DefaultDocumentModule,
                            DirectoryListingModule" resourceType="Either"
                            requireAccess="Read" />
        </handlers>
      </system.webServer>
    </location>
```

The preceding listing shows a subset of the handlers defined in the `ApplicationHost.config` configuration file. For instance, the `PageHandlerFactory-Integrated` handler maps all `.aspx` pages into the `System.Web.UI.PageHandlerFactory` class. This handler is used when an application is running in the Integrated mode. There is also a counterpart handler that runs when the application is configured in the Classic mode application pool; the handler name is `PageHandlerFactory-ISAPI-2.0`.

Adding a custom `HttpHandler` for new content file types was not an easy task in IIS 6.0, and sometimes it was impossible when the IIS 6.0 server was running remotely in a hosting company. Making use of the IIS 7.0 Integrated mode processing, it is now considered a piece of cake to add a new handler for any content file type you want by simply adding a new entry into the `<handlers />` configuration section of the `<system.webServer />` configuration section group located in the application's `web.config` configuration file.

```
    <system.webServer>
            <handlers>
        <add name="BasicHttpHandler"
            preCondition="integratedMode"
            path="*.info"
            type="BasicHttpHandler"
            verb="GET, POST" " />
        </handlers>
    </system.webServer>
```

The preceding configuration settings add a registration entry into the `<handlers />` configuration section. The handler entry should specify at a minimum the `name` of the `HttpHandler`; in this case, it is `BasicHttpHandler`. Also specified is the `path` attribute for which the handler will be triggered; in this case, all requests to content files with an extension of .info. And finally, the verb attribute is specified; in this case, the handler will accept requests with GET and POST verbs.

C#

```csharp
using System;
using System.Web;
using System.Web.Security;
using System.Web.UI;

public class BasicHttpHandler : IHttpHandler
{
    public BasicHttpHandler()
    {
    }

    #region IHttpHandler Members

    public bool IsReusable
    {
        get { return true;}
    }

    public void ProcessRequest(HttpContext context)
    {
        HttpResponse objResponse = context.Response;
objResponse.Write("<html><body><h1>Thank you for visiting our <b>info<b> page!!");
        objResponse.Write("</body></html>");
    }

    #endregion
}
```

VB.NET

```vbnet
Imports System
Imports System.Data
Imports System.Configuration
Imports System.Linq
Imports System.Web
Imports System.Web.Security
Imports System.Web.UI
Imports System.Web.UI.HtmlControls
Imports System.Web.UI.WebControls
Imports System.Web.UI.WebControls.WebParts
Imports System.Xml.Linq


''' <summary>
''' Summary description for BasicHttpHandler
''' </summary>
Public Class BasicHttpHandler
    Implements IHttpHandler
```

```
        Public Sub New()
            '
            ' TODO: Add constructor logic here
            '
        End Sub

    #Region "IHttpHandler Members"

        Public ReadOnly Property IsReusable() As Boolean Implements _
            IHttpHandler.IsReusable
            Get
                Return True
            End Get
        End Property

        Public Sub ProcessRequest(ByVal context As HttpContext) Implements _
            IHttpHandler.ProcessRequest()
            Dim objResponse As HttpResponse = context.Response
objResponse.Write("<html><body><h1>Thank you for visiting our <b>info<b> page!!")
            objResponse.Write("</body></html>")
        End Sub

    #End Region
    End Class
```

The preceding `BasicHttpHandler` code defines the HTML markup to show when a request for a page with an extension of `.info` is request by the client.

Identity Configuration Section

If the application you are migrating to work under IIS 7.0 is configured with client impersonation in the `<identity />` configuration section, it is recommended to disable impersonation, since the application might not behave correctly. This is especially true in that client impersonation is not available in early ASP.NET request processing stages. Alternatively, you can assign the application configured with client impersonation to an application pool with Classic mode.

Figure 2-4 shows the error page when you try to run an application that enables client impersonation that is configured with an application pool set to run in the Integrated mode.

When you create a new application to run under IIS 7.0, you will notice the following inside the `<system.webServer />` configuration section group:

```
<system.webServer>
        <validation validateIntegratedModeConfiguration="false"/>
</system.webServer>
```

The `validation` configuration section determines whether the IIS 7.0 runtime shall display error messages to help in upgrading the application to fit the IIS 7.0 Integrated mode. As mentioned above, if you keep the `<httpModules />` and `<httpHandlers />` configuration sections' entries outside the `<system.webServer />` configuration section group, they will not take effect in the unified request processing. In addition, keeping the aforementioned configuration sections inside the `<system.web />` configuration section group does not show any error message by IIS 7.0 notifying you that there are errors with running the application in the Integrated mode due to the presence of undesirable sections in the application's `web.config` configuration file. This is because the `validateIntegratedMode Configuration` attribute of the `<validation />` configuration section is set to a value of `false`. Changing this attribute to `true` will cause IIS 7.0 to show detailed error messages about the migration problems of the running application and what is recommended to fix the upgrading problems. The screen shown in Figure 2-4 would not have been displayed unless the aforementioned attribute was set to `true`. In other words, you can keep the `<httpModules />`, `<httpHandlers />`, and `<identity />` configuration sections in their place, while setting the `validateIntegratedModeConfiguration` attribute to `false`, or simply remove the three sections from inside the `<system.web />` configuration section group and leave the validation attribute either `true` or `false`.

Figure 2-4

This section covered the migration configuration errors that you may receive when you migrate an application to run under IIS 7.0 Integrated mode. For a more detailed discussion on the different errors you may face when migrating your application, see: `http://mvolo.com/blogs/serverside/archive/2007/12/08/IIS-7.0-Breaking-Changes-ASP.NET-2.0-applications-Integrated-mode.aspx`

Extending IIS 7.0 with Managed Handlers and Modules

Throughout this book, it has been mentioned several times that the new IIS 7.0 architecture is extensible. It allows developers to extend its core functionality by developing modules or features in two flavors:

❏ Native code modules

❏ Managed code modules

Developing native modules requires working with the C++ API. On the other hand, managed modules take advantage of the .NET framework and allow developers to use their existing ASP.NET `HttpModules` or develop new ones to integrate with the IIS 7.0 infrastructure and benefit from the IIS 7.0 and ASP.NET Integrated mode of execution.

Managed Handlers

A managed handler is an ASP.NET object that is responsible for the processing handling of an ASP.NET resource that has a specific file extension. In other words, a managed handler is linked to a particular file extension that is configured inside the `<httpHandlers />` configuration section of the application's `web.config` configuration file. `HttpHandlers` do not require operating on physically available content files. The resources might be virtual ones that do not exist physically in the application.

C#

```csharp
public class SampleHttpHandler : IHttpHandler
{
    public SampleHttpHandler()
    {
    }

    public bool IsReusable
    {
        get { throw new NotImplementedException(); }
    }

    public void ProcessRequest(HttpContext context)
    {
        throw new NotImplementedException();
    }
}
```

VB.NET

```vbnet
Imports System
Imports System.Data
Imports System.Configuration
Imports System.Linq
Imports System.Web
Imports System.Web.Security
Imports System.Web.UI
Imports System.Web.UI.HtmlControls
Imports System.Web.UI.WebControls
Imports System.Web.UI.WebControls.WebParts
Imports System.Xml.Linq

''' <summary>
''' Summary description for SampleHttpHandler
''' </summary>
Public Class SampleHttpHandler
    Implements IHttpHandler
    Public Sub New()
```

```
            '
            ' TODO: Add constructor logic here
            '
        End Sub

    #Region "IHttpHandler Members"

        Public ReadOnly Property IsReusable() As Boolean Implements _
            IHttpHandler.IsReusable
            Get
                Throw New NotImplementedException()
            End Get
        End Property

        Public Sub ProcessRequest(ByVal context As HttpContext) Implements _
            IHttpHandler.ProcessRequest
            Throw New NotImplementedException()
        End Sub

    #End Region
    End Class
```

The code in the preceding listing shows the skeleton of an HttpHandler. You create a new handler by implementing the IHttpHandler interface. This interface has two main methods to implement:

❑ **ProcessRequest:** This method is the brain of an HttpHandler. It is the method that gets executed when the handler is activated. It is responsible for handling the specific request execution and generation of the correct markup text that will be sent back to the requestor as a response. The nature of the markup text generated depends on the type of the request. For example, if the request is for an ASP.NET page, then the ProcessRequest method generates HTML markup text to be sent back to the requestor. If on the other hand the handler is configured to process and handle .xml content file extensions, then the response shall be XML markup text. This method accepts as an input parameter an instance of type HttpContext. This parameter contains the context in which the request is being processed and handled. Usually when a new request comes in, ASP.NET runtime creates a new HttpContext object. This object can store request-specific information and is disposed when the request is sent back to the requestor.

❑ **IsReusable:** This is a read-only property that returns a value of type Boolean and specifies whether the current handler can be used to process different requests for the configured resource. If the handler has some state that is expensive to initialize, and that is invariant from request to request, it should return a value of true so that ASP.NET has the opportunity to cache it. Otherwise, if the handler has nothing in common for different requests, then it is recommended to return a value of false.

Developing a Managed Handler

In this section, a custom managed handler is to be developed to handle displaying employees' profile pages in an application that manages employees' information in a department, company, you name it! The name of the handler is EmployeeHandler and will process requests for resources that have a .info extension.

Displaying employees' profile information can be easily done by developing an ASP.NET UserControl that serves as a template to show information about an employee. However, using a page to hold this template is a waste of resources and more processing is done with no extra benefit. For instance, when an employee's profile page is requested, the ASP.NET runtime handles the request and fires all the events during the page's life cycle. None of the events are of interest in this specific case and hence more processing is done with no extra benefit. In that case, to get rid of all the extra non-useful steps, an HttpHandler is recommended.

The EmployeeHandler handles requests targeting specific employee as follows:

```
http://localhost/Employees/1234.info
```

What the handler does is extract the employee number from the URL, access the Employees data table inside the database, and if the employee is present in the database, an employee profile page is displayed with all the details from the database.

The Employees data table used in this example is a simple data table used to collect information about an employee. Figure 2-5 shows the Employees data table structure.

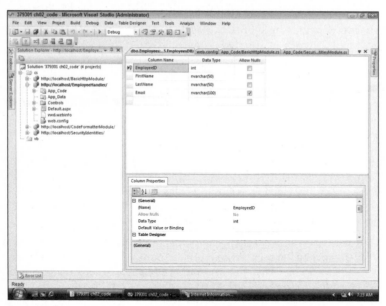

Figure 2-5

The Employees data table contains the EmployeeID, FirstName, LastName, and Email data columns. This is just an example of simple collected information. In a production environment, this would be much more serious and according to the context of the application.

For the sake of this example, a new LINQ DataContext class is added to the application to represent the Employees data table in an object-like fashion, which makes querying the database an easy task. Figure 2-6 shows the new .dbml LINQ object in the solution.

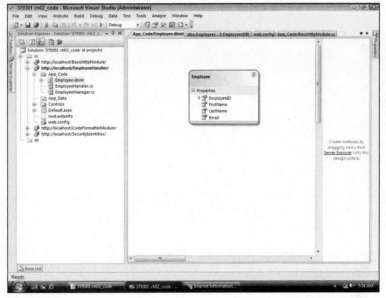

Figure 2-6

C#

```csharp
[Table(Name="dbo.Employees")]
public partial class Employee : INotifyPropertyChanging, INotifyPropertyChanged
{
  private int _EmployeeID;

  private string _FirstName;

  private string _LastName;

  private string _Email;


  public Employee()
    {
    }

[Column(Storage="_EmployeeID", DbType="Int NOT NULL", IsPrimaryKey=true)]
public int EmployeeID
    {
        get
        {
            return this._EmployeeID;
        }
        set
        {
            if ((this._EmployeeID != value))
            {
```

```
                                    this._EmployeeID = value;
                    }
            }
    }

[Column(Storage="_FirstName", DbType="NVarChar(50) NOT NULL", CanBeNull=false)]
public string FirstName
    {
        get
        {
                return this._FirstName;
        }
        set
        {
                if ((this._FirstName != value))
                {
                        this._FirstName = value;
                }
        }
    }

[Column(Storage="_LastName", DbType="NVarChar(50) NOT NULL", CanBeNull=false)]
public string LastName
    {
        get
        {
                return this._LastName;
        }
        set
        {
                if ((this._LastName != value))
                {
                        this._LastName = value;
                }
        }
    }

[Column(Storage="_Email", DbType="NVarChar(100)")]
public string Email
    {
        get
        {
                return this._Email;
        }
        set
        {
                if ((this._Email != value))
                {
                        this._Email = value;
                }
        }
    }
}
```

VB.NET

```vbnet
<Table(Name:="dbo.Employees")> _
Partial Public Class Employee Implements INotifyPropertyChanging, _
        INotifyPropertyChanged

    Private Shared emptyChangingEventArgs As _
        PropertyChangingEventArgs = New PropertyChangingEventArgs(String.Empty)

    Private _EmployeeID As Integer

    Private _FirstName As String

    Private _LastName As String

    Private _Email As String

    Public Sub New()
        MyBase.New
        OnCreated
    End Sub

    <Column(Storage:="_EmployeeID", DbType:="Int NOT NULL", IsPrimaryKey:=true)> _
    Public Property EmployeeID() As Integer
        Get
            Return Me._EmployeeID
        End Get
        Set
            If ((Me._EmployeeID = value) _
                    = false) Then
                Me.OnEmployeeIDChanging(value)
                Me.SendPropertyChanging
                Me._EmployeeID = value
                Me.SendPropertyChanged("EmployeeID")
                Me.OnEmployeeIDChanged
            End If
        End Set
    End Property

    <Column(Storage:="_FirstName", _
        DbType:="NVarChar(50) NOT NULL", _
        CanBeNull:=false)> _
    Public Property FirstName() As String
        Get
            Return Me._FirstName
        End Get
        Set
            If (String.Equals(Me._FirstName, value) = false) Then
                Me.OnFirstNameChanging(value)
                Me.SendPropertyChanging
                Me._FirstName = value
                Me.SendPropertyChanged("FirstName")
                Me.OnFirstNameChanged
            End If
        End Set
```

```
            End Property

            <Column(Storage:="_LastName", _
                DbType:="NVarChar(50) NOT NULL", _
                CanBeNull:=false)>  _
            Public Property LastName() As String
                Get
                    Return Me._LastName
                End Get
                Set
                    If (String.Equals(Me._LastName, value) = false) Then
                        Me.OnLastNameChanging(value)
                        Me.SendPropertyChanging
                        Me._LastName = value
                        Me.SendPropertyChanged("LastName")
                        Me.OnLastNameChanged
                    End If
                End Set
            End Property

            <Column(Storage:="_Email", DbType:="NVarChar(100)")>  _
            Public Property Email() As String
                Get
                    Return Me._Email
                End Get
                Set
                    If (String.Equals(Me._Email, value) = false) Then
                        Me.OnEmailChanging(value)
                        Me.SendPropertyChanging
                        Me._Email = value
                        Me.SendPropertyChanged("Email")
                        Me.OnEmailChanged
                    End If
                End Set
            End Property

    End Class
```

This code shows the Employee object automatically generated by the LINQ DataContext object once the Employees data table is added to it. Additional generated events and properties are removed because they are not of concern when it is all about using the object to hold single employee information. This object will be used in the application to represent a single employee.

The EmployeeHandler developed for this example is shown in the following code.

C#

```
public class EmployeeHandler : IHttpHandler
{
    public EmployeeHandler()
    {
    }

    #region IHttpHandler Members
```

```csharp
    public bool IsReusable
    {
        get { return false; }
    }

    public void ProcessRequest(HttpContext context)
    {
        // Determine the employee's ID
        string empID = Path.GetFileNameWithoutExtension(
            context.Request.PhysicalPath);

        // Try to parse the employee's ID
        int id = -1;
        if (!int.TryParse(empID, out id))
        {
context.Response.Write("Employee ID is invalid or doesn't exist in the database!!");
            return;
        }

        // Get the employee from the database
        var employee = EmployeeManager.GetEmployeeByID(id);

        // Make sure there is an employee in
        // the database with the requested number
        if (employee == null)
        {
            // Write out an error message
context.Response.Write("Employee ID is invalid or doesn't exist in the database!!");
            return;
        }

        // Add the employee information to the Items
        // collection of the context
        context.Items["Employee"] = employee;

        // Display the employee info
        DisplayEmployee(context, employee);
    }

    #endregion

    #region Utils
    private void DisplayEmployee(HttpContext context, Employee employee)
    {
        // Create a new page instance
        Page page = new Page();

        // Load the employee profile usercontrol dynamically
        UserControl employeeCtrl =
            (UserControl)page.LoadControl("~/Controls/EmployeeProfile.ascx");

        // Add the control to the page instance
        page.Controls.Add(employeeCtrl);

        // Execute the page containing the usercontrol
```

```
            StringWriter writer = new StringWriter();

            // Add the HTML header to the page
            writer.WriteLine(
            string.Format("<html><head><title>Employee {0} Profile</title></head>",
            employee.EmployeeID));
            writer.WriteLine("<body>");

            HttpContext.Current.Server.Execute(page, writer, false);

            // Add the HTML footer
            writer.WriteLine("</body>");
            writer.WriteLine("</html>");

            // Write the response out to the screen
            context.Response.Write(writer.ToString());
        }    #endregion
}
```

VB.NET

```
Imports System
Imports System.Data
Imports System.Configuration
Imports System.IO
Imports System.Web
Imports System.Web.Security
Imports System.Web.UI
Imports System.Web.UI.HtmlControls
Imports System.Web.UI.WebControls
Imports System.Web.UI.WebControls.WebParts


''' <summary>
''' Summary description for EmployeeHandler
''' </summary>
Public Class EmployeeHandler
    Implements IHttpHandler
    Public Sub New()
        '
        ' TODO: Add constructor logic here
        '
    End Sub

#Region "IHttpHandler Members"

    Public ReadOnly Property IsReusable() As Boolean Implements _
    IHttpHandler.IsReusable
        Get
            Return False
        End Get
    End Property


    ''' <summary>
    ''' This method handles the processing of .info requests
```

```vb
    ''' Gets the specific employee from the database based on the
    ''' employee id specified before the .info extension and
    ''' fills in an employee record inside the context's
    ''' items collection
    ''' </summary>
    ''' <param name="context"></param>
    Public Sub ProcessRequest(ByVal context As HttpContext) _
        Implements IHttpHandler.ProcessRequest
        ' Determine the employee's ID
        Dim empID As String = _
        Path.GetFileNameWithoutExtension(context.Request.PhysicalPath)

        ' Try to parse the employee's ID
        Dim id As Integer = -1
        If (Not Integer.TryParse(empID, id)) Then
            context.Response.Write("Employee ID is invalid" & _
            "or doesn't exist in the database!!")
            Return
        End If

        ' Get the employee from the database
        Dim employee = EmployeeManager.GetEmployeeByID(id)

        ' Make sure there is an employee in
        ' the database with the requested number
        If employee Is Nothing Then
            ' Write out an error message
            context.Response.Write("Employee ID is invalid" & _
            "or doesn't exist in the database!!")
            Return
        End If

        ' Add the employee information to the Items
        ' collection of the context
        context.Items("Employee") = employee

        ' Display the employee info
        DisplayEmployee(context, employee)
    End Sub

#End Region

#Region "Utils"
    Private Sub DisplayEmployee(ByVal context As HttpContext, _
        ByVal employee As Employee)
        ' Create a new page instance
        Dim page As Page = New Page()

        ' Load the employee profile usercontrol dynamically
        Dim employeeCtrl As UserControl = _
            CType(page.LoadControl("~/Controls/EmployeeProfile.ascx"), UserControl)

        ' Add the control to the page instance
        page.Controls.Add(employeeCtrl)
```

```
                    ' Execute the page containing the usercontrol
                    Dim writer As StringWriter = New StringWriter()

                    ' Add the HTML header to the page
                    writer.WriteLine(
                    String.Format("<html><head><title>Employee {0} Profile</title></head>", _
                    employee.EmployeeID))
                    writer.WriteLine("<body>")

                    HttpContext.Current.Server.Execute(page, writer, False)

                    ' Add the HTML footer
                    writer.WriteLine("</body>")
                    writer.WriteLine("</html>")

                    ' Write the response out to the screen
                    context.Response.Write(writer.ToString())
            End Sub
    #End Region
    End Class
```

This code shows the implementation of the `EmployeeHandler`. Each of the methods used inside the handler is explained in detail in the next few sections.

IsReusable

This method is inherited from the `IHttpHandler` interface and has been explained in detail above.

C#

```csharp
public bool IsReusable
{
    get { return false; }
}
```

VB.NET

```vb
Public ReadOnly Property IsReusable() As Boolean Implements _
IHttpHandler.IsReusable
    Get
        Return False
    End Get
End Property
```

In the preceding code, it returns a value of `false`, which means the handler instance will not process several requests of the same extension. Every request will generate a new instance of the handler.

ProcessRequest

The `ProcessRequest` method is the bulk of the `EmployeeHandler` and every developed handler. This method is responsible for processing a request. For instance, when the `ProcessRequest` method of the `.aspx` handler executes, it processes the page by starting the page life cycle events. Every event will add some bits into the response and the end response is ready to be sent back to the requestor. The same is followed in the `ProcessRequest` method of the `EmployeeHandler`.

C#

```
        // Determine the employee's ID
        string empID = Path.GetFileNameWithoutExtension(
            context.Request.PhysicalPath);

        // try to parse the employee id
        int id = -1;
        if (!int.TryParse(empID, out id))
        {
context.Response.Write("Employee ID is invalid or doesn't exist in the database!!");
            return;
        }
```

VB.NET

```
        ' Determine the employee's ID
        Dim empID As String = Path.GetFileNameWithoutExtension(
            context.Request.PhysicalPath)

        ' try to parse the employee id
        Dim id As Integer = -1
        If (Not Integer.TryParse(empID, id)) Then
context.Response.Write("Employee ID is invalid or doesn't exist in the database!!")
            Return
        End If
```

The method starts by extracting the page requested without an extension. The usual URL requested to display an employee's profile is as follows:

```
http://localhost/Employees/1234.info
```

What the preceding code will do is extract the `EmployeeID`, which is in this case "1234". Once the EmployeeID is extracted, it is validated to make sure the client did not request a non-integer EmployeeID.

C#

```
        // Get the employee from the database
        var employee = EmployeeManager.GetEmployeeByID(id);

        // Make sure there is an employee in
        // the database with the requested number
        if (employee == null)
        {
            // Write out an error message
context.Response.Write("Employee ID is invalid or doesn't exist in the database!!");
            return;
        }
```

VB.NET

```
            ' Get the employee from the database
            Dim employee = EmployeeManager.GetEmployeeByID(id)

            ' Make sure there is an employee in
            ' the database with the requested number
            If employee Is Nothing Then
                ' Write out an error message
context.Response.Write("Employee ID is invalid or doesn't exist in the database!!")
                Return
            End If
```

After the `EmployeeID` is extracted and validated, a call to the `EmployeeManager.GetEmployeeByID` is issued.

C#

```csharp
    public static Employee GetEmployeeByID(int empID)
    {
        // Get a new instance of the DataContext
        EmployeeDataContext context = new EmployeeDataContext();

        // Query the database to get the employee
        var query = (from e in context.Employees
                        where e.EmployeeID == empID
                        select e).Single();

        return query;
    }
```

VB.NET

```vbnet
    Public Shared Function GetEmployeeByID(ByVal empID As Integer) As Employee
        ' Get a new instance of the DataContext
        Dim context As EmployeeDataContext = New EmployeeDataContext()

        ' Query the database to get the employee
        Dim query = (From e In context.Employees Where _
            e.EmployeeID = empID Select e).SingleOrDefault()

        Return query
    End Function
```

The `GetEmployeeByID` method instantiates a new LINQ `DataContext`; in this case it is the `Employee DataContext` that was added before. Then a LINQ query is defined to select the employee record that has an `EmployeeID` matching that present in the requested URL. Finally, the employee record represented as `Employee` object is returned out of the method.

Once the `GetEmployeeByID` method is called inside the `ProcessRequest` method, the returned `Employee` object is validated to make sure there is an employee with the requested `EmployeeID` in the database. If there is one, then the employee's record is added to the `Items` collection of the `HttpContext` object. As previously explained, the `HttpContext` object is created at the beginning of the request processing and it stays valid until the response is returned back to the requestor. In this sense, the code is making use of the Items collection to store the employee's record so that it is retrieved later on to display the details of the employee. Once the employee record is stored in the context of the request, the employee's profile is displayed on the screen by calling the DisplayEmployee method.

DisplayEmployee

This method is responsible for generating the HTML markup text and sending it back to the client that initiated the request. Before diving into the details of the implementation of this method, however, let's review the EmployeeProfile user control.

C#

```
<%@ Control Language="C#" AutoEventWireup="true"
    CodeFile="EmployeeProfile.ascx.cs" Inherits="Controls_EmployeeProfile" %>
<h1 align="center">Employee Profile</h1>
<asp:Label ID="Label1" runat="server" Font-Bold="True" Text="Employee ID">
</asp:Label>
<br />
<asp:Label ID="lblEmployeeID" runat="server"></asp:Label>
<p></p>
<asp:Label ID="Label3" runat="server" Font-Bold="True" Text="First Name">
</asp:Label>
<br />
<asp:Label ID="lblFirstName" runat="server"></asp:Label>
<p></p>
<asp:Label ID="Label4" runat="server" Text="Last Name" Font-Bold="True">
</asp:Label>
<br />
<asp:Label ID="lblLastName" runat="server"></asp:Label>
<p></p>
<asp:Label ID="Label5" runat="server" Font-Bold="True" Text="Email"></asp:Label>
<br />
<asp:Label ID="lblEmail" runat="server"></asp:Label>
```

VB.NET

```
<%@ Control Language="VB" AutoEventWireup="false"
    CodeFile="EmployeeProfile.ascx.vb" Inherits="Controls_EmployeeProfile" %>
<h1 align="center">Employee Profile</h1>
<asp:Label ID="Label1" runat="server" Font-Bold="True" Text="Employee ID">
</asp:Label>
<br />
<asp:Label ID="lblEmployeeID" runat="server"></asp:Label>
<p></p> ·
<asp:Label ID="Label3" runat="server" Font-Bold="True" Text="First Name">
</asp:Label>
<br />
<asp:Label ID="lblFirstName" runat="server"></asp:Label>
<p></p>
<asp:Label ID="Label4" runat="server" Text="Last Name" Font-Bold="True">
</asp:Label>
<br />
<asp:Label ID="lblLastName" runat="server"></asp:Label>
```

```
<p></p>
<asp:Label ID="Label5" runat="server" Font-Bold="True" Text="Email"></asp:Label>
<br />
<asp:Label ID="lblEmail" runat="server"></asp:Label>
```

The HTML part of the user control is very simple. It displays a few labels that display the details of the employee such as the EmployeeID, FirstName, LastName, and Email properties.

C#

```csharp
public partial class Controls_EmployeeProfile : System.Web.UI.UserControl
{
    protected void Page_Load(object sender, EventArgs e)
    {
        // Get the Employee info from the HttpContext
        Employee emp =
            (Employee)HttpContext.Current.Items["Employee"];

        // Bind the values on the screen
        if (emp == null) return;

        this.lblEmployeeID.Text = emp.EmployeeID.ToString();
        this.lblFirstName.Text = emp.FirstName;
        this.lblLastName.Text = emp.LastName;
        this.lblEmail.Text = emp.Email;
    }
}
```

VB.NET

```vbnet
Partial Public Class Controls_EmployeeProfile
    Inherits System.Web.UI.UserControl


    Protected Sub Page_Load(ByVal sender As Object, ByVal e As System.EventArgs) _
    Handles Me.Load
        ' Get the Employee info from the HttpContext
        Dim emp As Employee = CType(HttpContext.Current.Items("Employee"), _
        Employee)

        ' Bind the values on the screen
        If emp Is Nothing Then
            Return
        End If

        Me.lblEmployeeID.Text = emp.EmployeeID.ToString()
        Me.lblFirstName.Text = emp.FirstName
        Me.lblLastName.Text = emp.LastName
        Me.lblEmail.Text = emp.Email
    End Sub
End Class
```

The code underlying usercontrol extracts the employee's record from the same HttpContext object instance that had its Items collection filled during the ProcessRequest method, casts the data into a strongly typed `Employee` object, and finally binds each label on the usercontrol to the data retrieved from the request's context.

C#

```csharp
private void DisplayEmployee(HttpContext context, Employee employee)
{
    // Create a new page instance
    Page page = new Page();

    // Load the employee profile usercontrol dynamically        UserControl
      employeeCtrl =
      (UserControl)page.LoadControl("~/Controls/EmployeeProfile.ascx");

    // Add the control to the page instance
    page.Controls.Add(employeeCtrl);

    // Execute the page containing the usercontrol
    StringWriter writer = new StringWriter();

    // Add the HTML header to the page
    writer.WriteLine(
    string.Format("<html><head><title>Employee {0} Profile</title></head>",
    employee.EmployeeID));
    writer.WriteLine("<body>");

    HttpContext.Current.Server.Execute(page, writer, false);

    // Add the HTML footer
    writer.WriteLine("</body>");
    writer.WriteLine("</html>");

    // Write the response out to the screen
    context.Response.Write(writer.ToString());
}    #endregion
}
```

VB.NET

```vbnet
Private Sub DisplayEmployee(ByVal context As HttpContext, _
        ByVal employee As Employee)
    ' Create a new page instance
    Dim page As Page = New Page()

    ' Load the employee profile usercontrol dynamically
    Dim employeeCtrl As UserControl = _
    CType(page.LoadControl("~/Controls/EmployeeProfile.ascx"), UserControl)

    ' Add the control to the page instance
    page.Controls.Add(employeeCtrl)

    ' Execute the page containing the usercontrol
    Dim writer As StringWriter = New StringWriter()
```

```
        ' Add the HTML header to the page
        writer.WriteLine(
        String.Format("<html><head><title>Employee {0} Profile</title></head>", _
        employee.EmployeeID))
        writer.WriteLine("<body>")

        HttpContext.Current.Server.Execute(page, writer, False)

        ' Add the HTML footer
        writer.WriteLine("</body>")
        writer.WriteLine("</html>")

        ' Write the response out to the screen
        context.Response.Write(writer.ToString())
    End Sub
```

Going back to the `DisplayEmployee` method, it starts by creating a new instance of the `Page` class. This page object will be used as a place holder to load the `EmployeeProfile` usercontrol inside it. After that, the `EmployeeProfile` usercontrol is dynamically loaded and then added as the first and only control inside the page object. Once the usercontrol is initialized and added to the page, a new instance of the `StringWriter` is created to hold the HTML markup text generated by executing the page object. The page is executed by issuing a call to the `HttpContext.Current.Server.Execute` method. Finally, the generated HTML markup text is added to the context's response to be sent back to the requestor.

Figure 2-7 shows the employee's profile when employee data is requested.

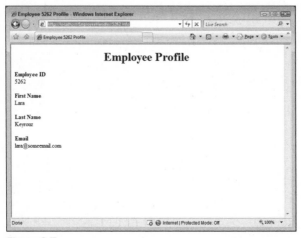

Figure 2-7

If you notice the URL, the requested page is `5262.info`, which does not exist physically inside the application. However, the `EmployeeHandler` intercepts the request and processes it as though it were a real page. The result shows the employee's profile displayed on the screen without having the request go through all the page life cycle events that add nothing to the task of showing an employee's profile from the database.

Installing a Managed Handler

Now that the handler is developed, there are two ways of installing it. One way is for the administrator or developer to use the IIS 7.0 Manager tool and add a handler mapping similar to the way it was done in the days of IIS 6.0. However, the power of developing managed handlers and deploying them in IIS 7.0 eliminates the need to access the IIS 7.0 Manager tool! This is done by simply adding the following to the application's `web.config` configuration file.

```
<system.webServer>
        <handlers>
                <!-- Add the EmployeeHandler here -->
                <add name="EmployeeHandler" type="EmployeeHandler" verb="*"
path="*.info" />
        </handlers>
</system.webServer>
```

The new managed handler is configured by adding an entry into the handler section of the `<system.webServer>` section group located in the application's `web.config` configuration file.

However, if the handler is to be used among several applications, then it should be installed at the IIS 7.0 web server level. The details of installing it on the web server level is out of the scope of this chapter because it is more related to IIS 7.0 administration and configuration, but you can find good walk-throughs on this topic in the book *Professional IIS 7.0 and ASP.NET Integrated Programming* (Wrox). The book is a complete reference on all the details about the IIS 7.0 and ASP.NET Integrated model.

Managed Modules

A managed module is an ASP.NET object that inherits from the `IHttpModule` interface. A module is used to handle the pre-processing and post-processing of a request. This means a module can register itself to process a request before it is being handed off to the managed handler for execution, and then once the request is processed by the handler, the module can again register itself to handle the request after it has been processed by the handler. The one thing to notice here is that a module does not process the request; it just registers itself to operate on the request before and after it has been operated on by the managed handler.

C#

```
public class SampleHttpModule : IHttpModule
{
  public SampleHttpModule()
    {
    }

    #region IHttpModule Members

    public void Dispose()
    {
        throw new NotImplementedException();
    }

    public void Init(HttpApplication context)
```

```
        {
            context.AuthenticateRequest +=
                new EventHandler(context_AuthenticateRequest);
        }

        void context_AuthenticateRequest(object sender, EventArgs e)
        {
            throw new NotImplementedException();
        }

        #endregion
}
```

VB.NET

```
Public Class SampleHttpModule
    Implements IHttpModule
    Public Sub New()
    End Sub

#Region "IHttpModule Members"

    Public Sub Dispose() Implements IHttpModule.Dispose
        Throw New NotImplementedException()
    End Sub

    Public Sub Init(ByVal context As HttpApplication) Implements IHttpModule.Init
        AddHandler context.AuthenticateRequest, AddressOf context _
        AuthenticateRequest
    End Sub

    Private Sub context_AuthenticateRequest(ByVal sender As Object, _
            ByVal e As EventArgs)
        Throw New NotImplementedException()
    End Sub

#End Region
End Class
```

This code shows the skeleton of an HttpModule. You create a new module by implementing the IHttpModule interface. This interface has one main method, Init, to implement.

When the ASP.NET runtime is processing a request, several events are fired throughout the request-processing pipeline. Every event handles a specific task within the life cycle of the request processing. For example, there is an event to handle the authentication of the request. Based on what the application specifies for the authentication type, a specific .NET module will subscribe to the authentication event and execute its codes to authenticate the request. Because of the extensible nature of the .NET runtime, developers are allowed to build their own modules that attach to the list of events fired by the pipeline. To register any of those events, you need to create a new module and utilize the Init method to subscribe to the specific event.

When an ASP.NET request is to be processed by the ASP.NET runtime, it is usually handled inside an instance of the HttpApplication object. When the runtime starts processing an ASP.NET request, it checks to see if there is a live instance of the HttpApplication object inside a pool that it maintains for all

`HttpApplication` instances that the request belongs to. If there is no instance, a new `HttpApplication` instance is created, used by the runtime to process the request, and finally added to the pool. On the other hand, if an instance was found, it is used by the runtime to process the request.

During the processing of the request, the `HttpApplication` instance fires a set of events such as `BeginRequest`, `AuthenticateRequest`, and so forth. Each of these events plays a role in the request-processing pipeline. This explains why the `Init` method accepts as input a parameter of type `Http Application`. The custom module can use this parameter to subscribe to the events that are exposed by the `HttpApplication` object. As is the case in the previous code listing, the `Init` method subscribes to the `AuthenticateRequest` event to execute some custom code. More on the `HttpApplication` events and request-processing pipeline is discussed in later sections.

What has been said above is an old story about `HttpModules`. In the IIS 7.0 infrastructure, the managed `HttpModule` does not fire only for managed resources. On the contrary, when an application is running inside an application pool configured with the Integrated mode, all the `HttpApplication` events fire while processing any request, whether the request is a managed request or a native request. This has been mentioned several times and once again shows how powerful the new integration architecture is between IIS 7.0 and ASP.NET.

Developing a Managed Module

In this section, a custom managed module is to be developed to handle displaying formatted code, whether it is VB or C# code. Usually IIS 7.0 is configured to disable accessing a code file through a browser for security and safety reasons. However, there are times when you want to present the code files online for an article that you have posted on your blog or for some other reason. The name of the module is `CodeFormatterModule` and it will process requests that include the `Code/CodeFileName` segment in the URL.

The `CodeFormatterModule` handles requests targeting specific code file names as follows:

```
http://localhost/Code/Default.aspx.cs/
```

Notice the / at the end of the URL. Without it the `RequestFilteringModule` will show a `404.7 Not Found Error` since accessing code files by a browser is disabled for security concerns.

What the module does is extract the code file name from the URL for all requests that include the `Code/` segment, and then the code file is read as a normal text file and sent back as a response to the requestor embedded in a `pre` tag. The formatting can be done in a better way with colorful code lines. However, for the sake of this sample, the `pre` tag is more than enough to clarify the idea of developing a managed module and running it under IIS 7.0.

The `CodeFormatterModule` developed for this example is shown in the following code listing.

C#

```csharp
public class CodeFormatterModule : IHttpModule
{
    public CodeFormatterModule()
    {
    }
    #region IHttpModule Members
```

```csharp
public void Dispose()
{
}

public void Init(HttpApplication context)
{
    context.BeginRequest +=
        new EventHandler(context_BeginRequest);
}

void context_BeginRequest(object sender, EventArgs e)
{
    // Get an instance of the HttpApplication
    HttpApplication application = (HttpApplication)sender;

    // Get an instance of the HttpContext
    HttpContext context = application.Context;

    // Find if the current request ends with
    // Code/ClassName so that to show the class's code
    // formatted on the screen.
    // The url to access the formatter should be something
    // as: http://localhost/Code/Default.aspx.cs/
    // The "/" at the end is very important because without
    // it the RequestFiltering module installed on IIS will prevent the
    // the access to a .cs or .vb file.
    Regex regEx = new Regex(@"Code/(.*)", RegexOptions.IgnoreCase);
    Match match = regEx.Match(context.Request.Path);

    // there is a match, this means
    // the request is for code formatting
    if (match.Success)
    {
        // Code file holds the code file name
        string codeFile = "";

        // Split the path based on the /
        string[] tokens = context.Request.Path.Split(new char[] {'/'});
        if (tokens.Length <= 0)
            return;

        // Grab the code file name which should be
        // the item before the last one
        codeFile = tokens[tokens.Length-2];

        // Get the physical path to the code file
        string pathtoCodeFile =
            context.Request.PhysicalPath.Replace(@"Code\", "");

        // Remove the \ from the end of the file name
        pathtoCodeFile =
            pathtoCodeFile.Substring(0, pathtoCodeFile.Length - 1);
```

```
                // If the file exists, read it and display it
                if (!File.Exists(pathtoCodeFile))
                {
                    // inform the user that the file doesn't exist
                    context.Response.Write("File doesn't exist!");

                    // End the request
                    context.Response.End();
                }

                // read the contents of the file
                string fileContent = File.ReadAllText(pathtoCodeFile);

                // Set the response to
                context.Response.ContentType = "text/html";

                // Write the formatted code
                context.Response.Write("<pre>");
                context.Response.Write(fileContent);
                context.Response.Write("</pre>");

                // End the request
                context.Response.End();
            }
        }

        #endregion
    }
```

VB.NET

```
Imports System
Imports System.Data
Imports System.Configuration
Imports System.Linq
Imports System.IO
Imports System.Text
Imports System.Text.RegularExpressions
Imports System.Web
Imports System.Web.Security
Imports System.Web.UI
Imports System.Web.UI.HtmlControls
Imports System.Web.UI.WebControls
Imports System.Web.UI.WebControls.WebParts
Imports System.Xml.Linq

''' <summary>
''' Summary description for CodeFormatterModule
''' </summary>
Public Class CodeFormatterModule
    Implements IHttpModule
    Public Sub New()
        '
```

```vb
            ' TODO: Add constructor logic here
            '
        End Sub

#Region "IHttpModule Members"

        Public Sub Dispose() Implements IHttpModule.Dispose
        End Sub

        ' Subscribe to the BeginRequest to process
        ' a request to the code formatter so that
        ' if the request was to show formatted code,
        ' the rest of the HttpApplication events get
        ' ignored, hence improving performance.
        Public Sub Init(ByVal context As HttpApplication) Implements IHttpModule.Init
            AddHandler context.BeginRequest, AddressOf context_BeginRequest
        End Sub

        Private Sub context_EndRequest(ByVal sender As Object, ByVal e As EventArgs)

        End Sub

        Private Sub context_BeginRequest(ByVal sender As Object, ByVal e As EventArgs)
            ' Get an instance of the HttpApplication
            Dim application As HttpApplication = CType(sender, HttpApplication)

            ' Get an instance of the HttpContext
            Dim context As HttpContext = application.Context

            ' Find if the current request ends with
            ' Code/ClassName so that to show the class's code
            ' formatted on the screen.
            ' The url to access the formatter should be something
            ' as: http://localhost/Code/Default.aspx.cs/
            ' The "/" at the end is very important because without
            ' it the RequestFiltering module installed on IIS will prevent the
            ' the access to a .cs or .vb file.
            Dim regEx As Regex = New Regex("Code/(.*)", RegexOptions.IgnoreCase)
            Dim match As Match = regEx.Match(context.Request.Path)

            ' There is a match, which means
            ' the request is for code formatting
            If match.Success Then
                ' Code file holds the code file name
                Dim codeFile As String = ""

                ' Split the path based on the /
                Dim tokens As String() = context.Request.Path.Split(New Char() {"/"c})
                If tokens.Length <= 0 Then
                    Return
                End If

                ' Grab the code file name which should be
                ' the item before the last one
```

```
        codeFile = tokens(tokens.Length - 2)

        ' Get the physical path to the code file
        Dim pathtoCodeFile As String = _
        context.Request.PhysicalPath.Replace("Code\", "")

        ' Remove the \ from the end of the file name
        pathtoCodeFile = pathtoCodeFile.Substring(0, pathtoCodeFile.Length - 1)

        ' If the file exists, read it and display it
        If (Not File.Exists(pathtoCodeFile)) Then
            ' Inform the user that the file doesn't exist
            context.Response.Write("File doesn't exist!")

            ' End the request
            context.Response.End()
        End If

        ' Read the contents of the file
        Dim fileContent As String = File.ReadAllText(pathtoCodeFile)

        ' Set the response to
        context.Response.ContentType = "text/html"

        ' Write the formatted code
        context.Response.Write("<pre>")
        context.Response.Write(fileContent)
        context.Response.Write("</pre>")

        ' End the request
        context.Response.End()
    End If
End Sub

#End Region
End Class
```

This code shows the implementation of the `CodeFormatterModule`. Each of the methods used inside the module is explained in detail in the next few sections.

Init

The `Init` method is the core of the `HttpModule`. It is the best place inside the `HttpModule` to subscribe to the `HttpApplication`'s events. The module above subscribes to the `BeginRequest` event.

C#

```
public void Init(HttpApplication context)
{
    context.BeginRequest +=
        new EventHandler(context_BeginRequest);
}
```

VB.NET

```
Public Sub Init(ByVal context As HttpApplication) Implements IHttpModule.Init
    AddHandler context.BeginRequest, AddressOf context_BeginRequest
End Sub
```

Subscribing to an event is done the usual way in the .NET framework. The `context_BeginRequest` method is the method to be called when the `HttpApplication`'s `BeginRequest` event fires.

Context_BeginRequest

The `context_BeginRequest` method does the bulk of the processing by extracting the code file name and displaying the code inside it as formatted code.

C#

```
// Get an instance of the HttpApplication
HttpApplication application = (HttpApplication)sender;

// Get an instance of the HttpContext
HttpContext context = application.Context;
```

VB.NET

```
' Get an instance of the HttpApplication
Dim application As HttpApplication = CType(sender, HttpApplication)

' Get an instance of the HttpContext
Dim context As HttpContext = application.Context
```

The method starts by getting a reference to the `HttpApplication` and the `HttpContext` objects.

C#

```
Regex regEx = new Regex(@"Code/(.*)", RegexOptions.IgnoreCase);
Match match = regEx.Match(context.Request.Path);

// There is a match, which means
// the request is for code formatting
if (match.Success)
{
```

VB.NET

```
Dim regEx As Regex = New Regex("Code/(.*)", RegexOptions.IgnoreCase)
Dim match As Match = regEx.Match(context.Request.Path)

' There is a match, which means
' the request is for code formatting
If match.Success Then
```

Then the URL of the current request is matched against a pattern that contains the `Code/` segment. If the URL has such a token, this means that the requestor is trying to access a code file.

C#

```csharp
// Code file holds the code file name
string codeFile = "";

// Split the path based on the /
string[] tokens = context.Request.Path.Split(new char[] {'/'});
if (tokens.Length <= 0)
    return;

// Grab the code file name which should be
// the item before the last one
codeFile = tokens[tokens.Length-2];

// Get the physical path to the code file
string pathtoCodeFile =
context.Request.PhysicalPath.Replace(@"Code\", "");

// Remove the \ from the end of the file name
pathtoCodeFile =
pathtoCodeFile.Substring(0, pathtoCodeFile.Length - 1);
```

VB.NET

```vbnet
' Code file holds the code file name
Dim codeFile As String = ""

' Split the path based on the /
Dim tokens As String() = context.Request.Path.Split(New Char() {"/"c})
If tokens.Length <= 0 Then
    Return
End If

' Grab the code file name which should be
' the item before the last one
codeFile = tokens(tokens.Length - 2)

' Get the physical path to the code file
Dim pathtoCodeFile As String = _
context.Request.PhysicalPath.Replace("Code\", "")

' Remove the \ from the end of the file name
pathtoCodeFile = pathtoCodeFile.Substring(0, pathtoCodeFile.Length - 1)
```

The code file name is extracted from the URL, and the `Code/` segment is removed from the URL, since this is a virtual token and does not exist in the application. It is only used to distinguish requests for normal resources and requests for code files. After that, the physical path of the code file is retrieved.

C#

```csharp
// If the file exists, read it and display it
if (!File.Exists(pathtoCodeFile))
{
    // Inform the user that the file doesn't exist
```

```
            context.Response.Write("File doesn't exist!");

            // End the request
            context.Response.End();
    }

    // Read the contents of the file
    string fileContent = File.ReadAllText(pathtoCodeFile);

    // Set the response to
    context.Response.ContentType = "text/html";

    // Write the formatted code
    context.Response.Write("<pre>");
    context.Response.Write(fileContent);
    context.Response.Write("</pre>");

    // End the request
    context.Response.End();
```

VB.NET

```
    ' If the file exists, read it and display it
    If (Not File.Exists(pathtoCodeFile)) Then
        ' Inform the user that the file doesn't exist
        context.Response.Write("File doesn't exist!")

        ' End the request
        context.Response.End()
    End If

    ' Read the contents of the file
    Dim fileContent As String = File.ReadAllText(pathtoCodeFile)

    ' Set the response to
    context.Response.ContentType = "text/html"

    ' Wite the formatted code
    context.Response.Write("<pre>")
    context.Response.Write(fileContent)
    context.Response.Write("</pre>")

    ' End the request
    context.Response.End()
```

If the file exists, the content of the file is read into a string, the response's content type is set to text/html, and then a pre tag is inserted into the response stream, followed by the content of the code file, and finally a closing pre tag.

Figure 2-8 shows the result of accessing a code file in an application.

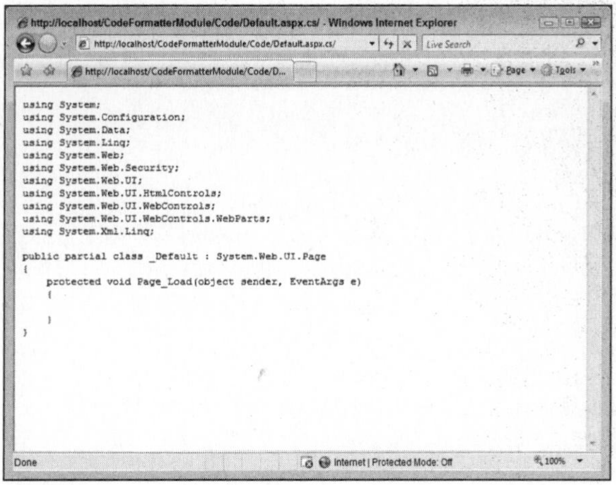

Figure 2-8

Figure 2-8 shows the content of the `Default.aspx.cs` code file displayed as normal text.

Installing a Managed Module

Now that the module is developed, there are two ways of installing it. One of the ways is to go to the IIS 7.0 Manager tool and install the module as a managed one that can be applied to any application hosted on the web server. The other way is to just add an entry to the `<modules>` section of the `<system .webServer>` configuration section group inside the application's `web.config` configuration file.

```
<system.webServer>
<modules>
        <!-- Add the CodeFormatterModule -->
        <add name="CodeFormatterModule" type="CodeFormatterModule"/>
</modules>
</system.webServer>
```

As mentioned previously, if the module is to be executed for any application hosted on the IIS 7.0 web server, it is recommended to install it at the web server level. The details of installing it at the web server level are out of the scope of this chapter. (See the reference to the book mentioned earlier for details about IIS 7.0 and ASP.NET Integrated mode.)

Summary

In this chapter you were introduced to the new IIS 7.0 Integrated mode of execution. The new mode unifies the request-processing pipeline between IIS 7.0 infrastructure and ASP.NET runtime, thus leveraging ASP.NET from a framework to develop web applications to a framework to extend IIS 7.0 runtime.

While upgrading an ASP.NET application from previous versions of IIS to host it under IIS 7.0 Integrated mode, it is essential to consider several sections within the application's `web.config` configuration file to get rid of the inconsistencies and abide by the new rules. Some of the new rules are as follows:

- ❑ `httpModules` section: It is recommended to remove this section from the `<system.web />` configuration section group file of the application's `web.config` configuration file and place its entries inside the `<modules />` configuration section of the `<system.webServer />` configuration section group. Only modules defined inside the `<modules>` section will take effect and execute. Every managed module defined can be configured to run for either all resources or just ASP.NET resources.

- ❑ `httpHandlers` section: The `httpHandlers` section should also be removed from the `<system.web />` configuration section group of the application's `web.config` configuration file, with its entries placed inside the `<modules />` configuration section inside the `<system.webServer />` configuration section group. What is important about configuring a handler is that there is no need to use the IIS 7.0 Manager tool to map a content file extension to a specific handler in an application; only a single configuration entry is required and that's it!

- ❑ `identity` section: Impersonation is not allowed during the early stages of a request processing and that is why an application should either turn off impersonation or upgrade the application and make it run under the Classic mode. Impersonation could be kept on and at the same time set the value of the `validateIntegratedModeConfiguration` attribute on the validation section to `false` that is located inside the `<modules />` configuration section inside the `<system.webServer />` configuration section group.

The main point to keep in mind about the new Integrated mode is the extensibility IIS 7.0 offers for ASP.NET developers. IIS 7.0 HTTP request processing integrates itself with ASP.NET to form a unified request-processing pipeline. Both IIS 7.0 and ASP.NET respond to the same events at the same time and IIS decides on the native and managed modules to run and execute.

The unified request-processing pipeline gives ASP.NET services and modules the ability to handle and process any resource and not just ASP.NET resources. You can now enable `FormsAuthentication` module to protect images, `.php`, `.html`, `.asp` resources, etc. in an application without having to do any workaround to make this happen. Moreover, you can now develop ASP.NET `HttpModules` and `HttpHandlers`, configure them through the application's `web.config` configuration file, and let them take part of the request processing without having to do any configuration settings using the IIS 7.0 Manager tool.

The next chapter continues this discussion to explore the security context of a request when it is processed inside the unified IIS 7.0 Integrated mode. The discussion is focused on the authentication and authorization events that get fired through the life cycle of the unified request-processing pipeline. In addition, the new `IUSR` built-in user and `IIS_IUSRS` built-in group will be explained in detail, showing their advantages and portability when deploying applications.

3

HTTP Request Processing in IIS 7.0 Integrated Model

The previous chapter discussed the architecture of the new IIS 7.0 integrated mode in detail. This chapter starts by introducing the advantages, the new `IUSR` built-in account and `IIS_IUSRS` built-in group, replacing the old `IUSR_MACHINENAME` user account and `IIS_WPG` group. The chapter continues to describe security-related processing that occurs each time the unified request-processing pipeline processes a request. A combination of the application's configuration in IIS and the ASP.NET configuration for the application determines the security context that is initialized for each request.

Once a request enters IIS 7.0, the first defense gate takes control to validate the request before starting the unified request-processing pipeline. Once accepted, the unified pipeline starts processing and handling the request. The added value of the new IIS 7.0 integrated mode is that IIS and ASP.NET both subscribe to the same events fired during the processing of the request.

After a request is running through the unified pipeline, the authentication and authorization options that have been configured for the application take affect. If a request passes authentication and authorization checks, there is still one last hurdle to clear; the `HttpHandler` that is assigned to process the request, in case the request is an ASP.NET resource.

In this chapter, you will learn about:

- ❑ The new `IUSR` built-in account and `IIS_IUSRS` built-in group.
- ❑ How the security identity of a request is constructed during the unified processing.
- ❑ Security issues around the ASP.NET asynchronous programming model.
- ❑ Authentication steps that occur in the HTTP pipeline.
- ❑ Authorization processing in the HTTP pipeline.
- ❑ How the new IIS native filtering module controls access to files.

Built-in IUSR Account and IIS_IUSRS Group

Before going on to start analyzing the security context of requests while they take the journey through the IIS 7.0 and ASP.NET unified request-processing pipeline, it is important to give an overview on the new IUSR account and IIS_USRS group.

IIS 7.0 introduces a new built-in account IUSR and a built-in group IIS_IUSRS. The IUSR account replaces the old IUSR_*MachineName* account that was used previously by the IIS 6.0 web server. The new account is a built-in account, which means its password never expires and hence this improves deployment by not having to worry about password differences between the local IIS_IUSR *MachineName* account and the remote user account.

Another benefit of the new IUSR account is when you set access control lists (ACLs) for the IUSR account folders inside your application, there is no need to worry about copying these ACLs from your local machine to the remote web server machine. The reason lies behind the fact that the operating system creates unique security identifiers (SIDs) for every account created in Windows, and ACLs are applied on the SID of the account and not anything else. This means when you apply ACLs locally on the IUSR for a folder in your application, those ACLs will be copied with the folder when moved from the local server to the remote web server and the same ACLs will take effect, since all Windows machines that have IIS 7.0, whether the client IIS 7.0 or server IIS 7.0, share the same SID for the IUSR account.

An important feature to mention about the new IUSR account is that it acts anonymously on the network. This means when you try to access resources located somewhere on the network from inside your application, you need to impersonate some other account that the network recognizes as a machine user account that can authenticate against it. One could use the NT AUTHORITY\NETWORK SERVICE account that acts as a machine account and can be authenticated. This limitation on the IUSR account has been done as a security precaution so as not to elevate the privileges of the IUSR account.

On the other hand, the IIS_IUSRS group replaces the old IIS_WPG group. This group has been granted the necessary permissions on all necessary files and resources so that when an account is attached to this group, it can act as a normal application pool worker process identity without the need for any additional action.

Whatever applies on the IUSR account regarding setting of the ACL applies also to the IIS_IUSRS group. If you apply ACLs to this group on your files and folders and then move your application from your local web server to the remote one, the same ACLs are also copied. This is due to the fact that Windows operating system applies ACLs based on the SID of the group or user account.

Moreover, when IIS 7.0 starts a new worker process, it usually passes a token that is going to be used as the identity of the worker process.

```
<applicationPools>
    <applicationPoolDefaults>
        <processModel identityType="NetworkService" />
    </applicationPoolDefaults>
</applicationPools>
```

In IIS 7.0, the default identity that the application pool uses is the NT AUTHORITY\NETWORK SERVICE and this has been configured in the <applicationPools /> section group inside the ApplicationHost .config configuration file.

The good news is that if you configure the application pool to run with a custom user account, no matter what the account is, IIS 7.0 infrastructure automatically adds at run time the worker process token or identity, no matter what the account is, to the IIS_IUSRS group and hence there is no need to worry about giving the worker process identity account the necessary privileges to function properly.

Integrated Mode Per-Request Security

It has been previously mentioned how the request-processing pipeline gets unified when an ASP.NET application is running in the IIS 7.0 integrated mode. It is clear how the duplication of effort has been eliminated since both ASP.NET and IIS 7.0 now share the same request-processing pipeline.

The unified pipeline indicates that at every stage in the pipeline, IIS and ASP.NET modules subscribe to the same event and hence they run side by side. IIS runtime will check the configured modules and executes them according to their order of listing inside the <modules /> configuration section with some exceptions. The native modules have the capability to change the order programmatically, which is the case with the native AnonymousAuthenticationModule. This module always runs at the end of the authentication event fired by the pipeline no matter what other authentication modules are enabled. As you will see later, this proves why the managed WindowsAuthenticationModule does not fire its Authenticate event since AnonymousAuthenticationModule, when enabled, fires after the managed WindowsAuthenticationModule.

The configured modules for a specific pipeline event could include both native and managed modules. For instance, the FormsAuthenticationModule has been integrated into the authentication modules in IIS. This allows you now to enable this module for your application from inside the IIS Manager tool. When the managed FormsAuthenticationModule is enabled, no other native authentication module can be enabled at the same time except that of the AnonymousAuthenticationModule. Therefore, while an application is running in the integrated mode, IIS can execute only a single authentication module at once with the exception of the AnonymousAuthenticationModule that gets executed after all configured authentication modules have been executed.

This is quite different from what has been happening in the pre-releases of IIS 7.0. In IIS 6.0, for example, the request has to pass first through the IIS request-processing pipeline. After it has been handed off to the ASP.NET ISAPI extension, another processing pipeline starts, this time in the boundaries of the .NET Framework.

From an ASP.NET perspective, the security choices in IIS boil down to the following:

❑   Does the ASP.NET application require a WindowsPrincipal for each user that authenticates with the website?

❑   Will ASP.NET handle authentication using forms-based authentication, or some other custom authentication strategy?

❑   Will the ASP.NET site run from a remote file share, that is, a share defined with a Universal Naming Convention (UNC) name? This question is related to the previous two considerations because using a UNC share is primarily a deployment decision, but one that does have ramifications for security.

From a technical perspective, when IIS 7.0 starts a new worker process to initiate the execution of the request, it passes a token to the worker process. Usually, it is the `NT AUTHORITY\NETWORK SERVICE` token that is configured in the `ApplicationHost.config` configuration file as mentioned previously. Once the worker process is initiated, if the application is an ASP.NET application, a list of Application Domains called the application domain pool is checked to see if the application targeted has an active application domain to load. If there is no active application domain for the current application, a new application domain is created and then the CLR is loaded inside the new application domain. After that the unified request-processing pipeline starts execution, the different events start firing, and the different modules start executing according to the events they have already been registered for. Both IIS 7.0 and ASP.NET subscribe to the same events and hence IIS 7.0 and ASP.NET processing for the same event happens at the same time.

In IIS 7.0, the following directory security options are available:

❑ Authenticated access using Windows Security (either NTLM- or Kerberos-based), Basic Authentication, Digest Authentication

❑ Authenticated access using certificate mapping

❑ Anonymous access

The first two security configurations result in a security token that represents a specific user from either the local machine's security database or a domain. The token returned varies from request to request, depending on which user is currently making a request to IIS. The last option also results in a security token representing a specific user; however, on every request made to IIS, the same security token is returned because IIS uses a fixed identity to represent an anonymous user, which is the IUSR account by default. However, it can be any other user account or even the account configured on the worker process.

When a new request enters the unified request-processing pipeline and the stage where authentication should take place is reached, a check is done on both the authentication type the application is configured to run with (Forms, Windows, and None) and the authentication modules enabled on IIS.

In determining the authenticated identity of a request, IIS takes the following considerations:

❑ **If a username/password is configured at the application or virtual directory level, it is used as the identity of the current request, which is the impersonation token.** To configure a fixed account on an application or virtual directory, do the following:

    1. Open the IIS 7.0 Manager tool.

    2. Select the specific application or virtual directory.

    3. Click on Advanced Settings.

    4. Edit the Physical Path Credentials field.

❑ Figure 3-1 shows the window used to configure a fixed user for the anonymous identity on an application or virtual directory.

❑ The figure shows the window that is used to configure a specific user account on the application or virtual directory. On the other hand, you can select not to impersonate the access to the application or virtual directory to any user account, instead using the impersonation token generated later on by the IIS runtime.

Figure 3-1

❑ **If the application or virtual directory is not configured with fixed user credentials, IIS checks the type of authentication enabled on the application, whether it is Windows, Basic, Digest, or anonymous authentication.** If the AnonymousAuthenticationModule is enabled, it will automatically rule over all the other enabled native authentication modules and no negotiation happens between IIS and the user. The issue is different when authorization rules are set on the application. At this time, IIS postpones the execution of the AnonymousAuthenticationModule to the end of the authentication stage of the unified request-processing pipeline. However, if the AnonymousAuthenticationModule is disabled and any other native authentication module is enabled, IIS would request a username/password to authenticate the request. If the request is authenticated successfully, an impersonation token is generated and stored by IIS to be accessed later by the managed WindowsAuthenticationModule, in the case that the ASP.NET application is running in the IIS 7.0 classic mode. However, if the application is running in IIS 7.0 integrated mode and a user has been authenticated, the native authentication module sets the value of the native User principal, and then the integrated request processing pipeline proxies that native User principal to managed code automatically. In other words, if a native authentication module sets the value of the native User principal, it gets brought over to ASP.NET as the HttpContext.Current.User. In addition, IIS sets the value of the server variable LOGON_USER to the username that was used in the authentication process. This is done for both modes of processing in IIS 7.0: Classic and Integrated.

❑ However, if IIS finds out that all the native authentication modules are disabled, not mentioning the AnonymousAuthenticationModule, the impersonation token generated is that of the default identity assigned for the native AnonymousAuthenticationModule or any custom identity, and there will be no value set for the managed HttpContext.Current.User property when the application is running in the IIS 7.0 Integrated mode. This implies that the managed `Windows` `AuthenticationModule` will not fire its `Authenticate` event. You will see why in much more detail when you reach the section on the managed `WindowsAuthenticationModule` later in the chapter.

❑ On the other hand, if an impersonation token is generated by IIS runtime and the ASP.NET application is configured to run under IIS 7.0 classic mode, the managed `WindowsAuthentication` `Module` grabs the impersonation token from IIS and generates the `WindowsPrincipal` object and sets the value of the `User` property on the `HttpContext` class, all based on the received impersonation token. Finally it triggers its `Authenticate` event. In the case of an application running in IIS 7.0 Integrated mode, the managed `WindowsAuthenticationModule` ignores the impersonation token set by IIS 7.0 and simply extracts a `WindowsPrincipal` instance from the `Http` `Context.Current.User` and creates a new instance of the `WindowsIdentity` class based on the `Identity` property located at the `WindowsPrincipal` class extracted from the `HttpContext` `.Current.User` property. The module then decides if there is a valid `WindowsIdentity` instance (i.e. the request is not anonymous and authentication took place inside a native module), and triggers its `Authenticate` event; otherwise, the `Authenticate` event will not get a chance to be fired. As mentioned above, when IIS 7.0 detects that the ASP.NET application is running in IIS 7.0 Integrated mode, the integrated request-processing pipeline automatically maps the authenticated user represented by a native `User` principal, if any, to the `HttpContext.Current` `.User` property to be accessible by the managed `WindowsAuthenticationModule`. Thus, you can conclude that you can simply remove the managed `WindowsAuthenticationModule` and the `HttpContext.Current.User` will always be set in case authentication took place inside IIS 7.0's native authentication modules.

❑ At this stage, if the `AnonymousAuthenticationModule` is enabled, it executes. After its execution, the impersonation token is generated based on the identity set on the `Anonymous` `AuthenticationModule`. In addition, if the application is running inside IIS 7.0 Integrated mode, the `HttpContext.Current.User`'s value is set to a dummy instance of the `Windows` `Principal` class with its `Identity.Name` property set to an empty string.

❑ At the end of the authentication stage, IIS gets the value of the impersonation token generated by either a native authentication module, in case the `AnonymousAuthenticationModule` is disabled, or by the `AnonymousAuthenticationModule` in case it is enabled. The value of the impersonation token is stored by IIS so that it can be accessed later. Moreover, if the application is running under the IIS 7.0 Integrated mode, at the end of the authentication stage, the `Http` `Context.Current.User`'s value would also have been set to a complete `WindowsPrincipal` instance if the native `AnonymousAuthenticationModule` was disabled, and it gets set to a dummy instance of the `WindowsPrincipal` class with its `Identity.Name` property set to an empty string if the native `AnonymousAuthenticationModule` was enabled and got executed.

❑ **If there is no authenticated user, this is the case when the native AnonymousAuthentication-Module is enabled with or without the managed FormsAuthenticationModule.** ASP.NET automatically handles the authentication of the request with the managed `FormsAuthentication` `Module` if enabled. Regardless of the user account configured for the `AnonymousAuthentication` `Module`, IIS will use the identity of the worker process as the impersonation token, which is by default the `NT AUTHORITY\NETWORK SERVICE`. If the request is successfully authenticated, IIS stores the `username` used in the authentication process into the server variable `LOGON_USER`.

Usually, the enabled configured native module executes within the boundaries of the web server core engine, and any enabled managed authentication module is handed off to ASP.NET runtime to process. Just because an impersonation token might be generated by IIS 7.0 or the `HttpContext.Current.User`'s value might be set by the integrated-request processing pipeline and is available to ASP.NET does not mean that the same security credentials will be used by ASP.NET. Instead, the security context for each request is dependent on the following settings and information:

❑ The identity of the operating system thread

❑ The request authenticated identity from IIS

❑ The value of the impersonate attribute in the `<identity />` configuration element

❑ The value of the username and password attributes in the `<identity />` configuration element

❑ Whether the mode attribute of the `<authentication />` configuration element has been set to `Windows`

Before diving into how these settings interact with each other, an understanding of the `AnonymousAuthenticationModule` is required, as well as a review of where security information can be stored.

❑ *Native AnonymousAuthentication Module*

This module is configured with the new built-in `IUSR` account. This can be configured in both the `ApplicationHost.config` configuration file and the `<system.webServer />` configuration section group of the application's `web.config` configuration file.

```
<anonymousAuthentication enabled="true" userName="IUSR" />
```

You are given the choice to set the anonymous user account to the same identity used by the worker process inside an application pool that is the `NT AUTHORITY\NETWORK SERVICE` account. To change the default user, right-click the Anonymous Authentication method listed in the Authentication section. Figure 3-2 shows the window that you can use to edit the identity assigned to the module.

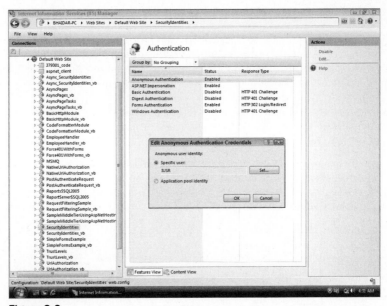

Figure 3-2

You can assign the Application Pool Identity as the identity of the anonymous user. In addition, you can click the Set… button and a small window pops up allowing you to specify a Windows account of your choice to use as the anonymous user identity.

When the Application Pool Identity account is selected, you will notice the following change in the application's `web.config` configuration file:

```
<anonymousAuthentication enabled="true" userName="" />
```

However, if you have chosen to set the anonymous user identity to another Windows account of choice, the following would appear in the application's `web.config` configuration file:

```
<anonymousAuthentication enabled="true" userName="test" password="test" />
```

As you can see, both the `userName` and `password` attributes have been set to the custom user account that you have specified.

It is important to mention that the native `AnonymousAuthenticationModule` runs during the authentication stage of the unified request-processing pipeline, and it is the last module to run in this stage. This is the programmatic reordering that was mentioned before when it comes to running different modules, managed and native, at the same stage of the pipeline. It is true that IIS runs the modules according to the order of appearance in the `<modules />` section with the exception of programmatic ordering that only native modules have the right to make use of. In addition, if the `AnonymousAuthenticationModule` is enabled, regardless of the other native authentication modules, the request will be considered anonymous and none of the native authentication modules would run.

> Remember that the `AnonymousAuthenticationModule` is executed by the IIS core engine at the end of the authentication stage after all other authentication modules, native or managed, have executed.

Here are some scenarios on how the native `AnonymousAuthenticationModule` works:

❑ When the native `AnonymousAuthenticationModule` is enabled, it rules over all other native authentication modules. For this scenario, assume the managed `FormsAuthenticationModule` is disabled, the ASP.NET application is configured with Windows authentication, and all other native authentication modules are disabled. Hence, an impersonation token is generated based on the user identity assigned for the `AnonymousAuthenticationModule`, which is by default the `IUSR` account. In addition, if IIS 7.0 detects that the application is running under the Integrated mode, the `HttpContext.Current.User` property is set to a dummy instance of the `WindowsPrincipal` class.

❑ If the native `AnonymousAuthenticationModule` is enabled and any other native authentication is also enabled, such as the Basic or Windows authentication modules, nothing changed to what has been mentioned above. IIS 7.0 knows that the native `AnonymousAuthenticationModule` is enabled and does not request any username/password from the user.

❑ In this last case, if the native `AnonymousAuthenticationModule` is enabled and the managed `FormsAuthenticationModule` is also enabled, the `FormsAuthenticationModule` will check if there is a valid user on the `HttpContext.Current.User` property. If not, it creates a new `GenericPrincipal` instance and assigns it to the `HttpContext.Current.User` property, along with other tasks you will learn more about in Chapter 6, "Forms Authentication." The native `AnonymousAuthenticationModule` would still generate the impersonation token based on the default identity assigned for the module itself or any other custom identity.

Where Is the Security Identity for a Request?

In reality, no single location in ASP.NET defines the identity for a request. This is a case where the differences between the older Win32-oriented programming model and the managed world sort of collide.

Before the .NET Framework was implemented, the question of security identity always rested with the currently executing operating system thread. An operating system thread always has a security token associated with it representing either a local (potentially a built-in identity) or a domain account. Win32 programmers have always had the ability to create new security tokens and use these to change the security context of an operating system thread. This behavior includes reverting the identity of a thread and explicitly impersonating a security identity.

With the introduction of the .NET Framework, a managed representation of a thread is available from the `System.Threading.Thread` class. The `Thread` class has a `CurrentPrincipal` property that represents the security identity of the managed thread. It is entirely possible for the security identity of the operating system thread (obtainable by calling `System.Security.Principal.WindowsIdentity` `.GetCurrent()`) to differ in type and in value from the managed `IPrincipal` reference available from an instance of `Thread.CurrentPrincipal`.

As if that was not complicated enough, ASP.NET introduced the concept of an `HttpContext` associated with each request flowing through ASP.NET. The `HttpContext` instance for a request has a `User` property that also contains a reference to an `IPrincipal` implementation. This additional reference to a security identity opened up the possibility of having a third set of security credentials available to a developer that differed from the information associated with the operating system thread and the managed thread.

To demonstrate, the following example is a simple application that displays three different identities. The sample code stores the operating system's security identity and the managed thread identity as they exist during the `Application_BeginRequest` event, and when a page is running. The value for the `User` property on the `HttpContext` is also stored.

The initial identity information is collected in a managed `SecurityIdentitiesModule` developed for the sake of this demonstration:

C#

```
void context_BeginRequest(object sender, EventArgs e)
{
    HttpContext current = HttpContext.Current;

    current.Items["OperatingSystem_ThreadIdentity_BeginRequest"] =
        WindowsIdentity.GetCurrent().Name;
```

```
        if (String.IsNullOrEmpty(Thread.CurrentPrincipal.Identity.Name))
        {
            current.Items["ManagedThread_ThreadIdentity_BeginRequest"] =
                "[null or empty]";
            current.Items["ManagedThread_IsGenericPrincipal"] =
                (Thread.CurrentPrincipal is GenericPrincipal);
        }
        else
            current.Items["ManagedThread_ThreadIdentity_BeginRequest"] =
                Thread.CurrentPrincipal.Identity.Name;

        if (current.User == null)
            current.Items["HttpContext_User_BeginRequest"] = "[null]";
        else
            current.Items["HttpContext_User_BeginRequest"] =
                current.User.Identity.Name;
    }
```

VB.NET

```
Private Sub context_BeginRequest(ByVal sender As Object, ByVal e As EventArgs)
    Dim current As HttpContext = HttpContext.Current
    current.Items("OperatingSystem_ThreadIdentity_BeginRequest") _
        = WindowsIdentity.GetCurrent().Name()

    If String.IsNullOrEmpty(Thread.CurrentPrincipal.Identity.Name) Then
        current.Items("ManagedThread_ThreadIdentity_BeginRequest") _
            = "[null or empty]"

        current.Items("ManagedThread_IsGenericPrincipal") = _
            (TypeOf Thread.CurrentPrincipal Is GenericPrincipal)
    Else
        current.Items("ManagedThread_ThreadIdentity_BeginRequest") = _
            Thread.CurrentPrincipal.Identity.Name()
    End If

    If current.User Is Nothing Then
        current.Items("HttpContext_User_BeginRequest") = "[null]"
    Else
        current.Items("HttpContext_User_BeginRequest") = _
            current.User.Identity.Name()
    End If
End Sub
```

This code contains checks for null or empty strings because `Application_BeginRequest` occurs as the first event in the integrated unified request-processing pipeline. As a result, neither IIS nor ASP. NET has configured any security context for the current request. From the ASP.NET point of view, it has not attempted to associate an `IPrincipal` with the current `HttpContext`. Additionally, ASP.NET has not synchronized user information on the `HttpContext` to the current managed thread. The managed thread principal is instead associated with an instance of a `System.Security.Principal.Generic Principal` with a username set to the empty string. The value of the `User` property on the `HttpContext` though is not even initialized, and returns a null value instead.

The values for this information are displayed in a page load event using the following code:

C#

```
using System;
using System.Security.Principal;
using System.Threading;

public partial class _Default : System.Web.UI.Page
{
    protected void Page_Load(object sender, EventArgs e)
    {
        Response.Write("The OS thread identity during BeginRequest is: " +
            Context.Items["OperatingSystem_ThreadIdentity_BeginRequest"] + "<br />");

        Response.Write("The managed thread identity during BeginRequest is: " +
            Context.Items["ManagedThread_ThreadIdentity_BeginRequest"] + "<br />");

        Response.Write("The managed thread identity during BeginRequest is " +
            "a GenericPrincipal: " +
            Context.Items["ManagedThread_IsGenericPrincipal"] + "<br />");

        Response.Write("The user on the HttpContext during BeginRequest is: " +
            Context.Items["HttpContext_User_BeginRequest"] + "<br />");

        Response.Write("<hr />");

        Response.Write("The OS thread identity when the page executes is: " +
            WindowsIdentity.GetCurrent().Name + "<br />");

        if (String.IsNullOrEmpty(Thread.CurrentPrincipal.Identity.Name))
    Response.Write("The managed thread identity when" +
        "the page executes is: " + "[null or empty]" + "<br />");
else
    Response.Write("The managed thread identity when the " +
        "page executes is: " +
        Thread.CurrentPrincipal.Identity.Name + "<br />");
    Response.Write("The managed thread identity is of type: " +
            Thread.CurrentPrincipal.ToString() + "<br />");

        if (String.IsNullOrEmpty(User.Identity.Name))
    Response.Write("The user on the HttpContext when " +
        "the page executes is: " + "[null or empty]" + "<br />");
else
    Response.Write("The user on the HttpContext when the " +
        "page executes is:" + User.Identity.Name + "<br />");

        Response.Write("The user on the HttpContext is of type: " +
            User.ToString() + "<br />");

        Response.Write("The user on the HttpContext and the " +
            "thread principal point at the same object: " +
```

```
                    (Thread.CurrentPrincipal == User) + "<br />");

        Response.Write("The impersonation token set by IIS is: " +
            Request.LogonUserIdentity.Name + "<br />");
    }
}
```

VB.NET

```
Imports System
Imports System.Security.Principal
Imports System.Threading

Partial Public Class _Default
    Inherits System.Web.UI.Page
    Protected Sub Page_Load(ByVal sender As Object, _
                            ByVal e As System.EventArgs) _
                            Handles Me.Load
        Response.Write("The OS thread identity during BeginRequest is: " & _
            Context.Items("OperatingSystem_ThreadIdentity_BeginRequest") & _
            "<br />")

        Response.Write("The managed thread identity during BeginRequest is: " & _
            Context.Items("ManagedThread_ThreadIdentity_BeginRequest") & _
            "<br />")

        Response.Write("The managed thread identity during BeginRequest is " & _
            "a GenericPrincipal: " & _
            Context.Items("ManagedThread_IsGenericPrincipal") & _
            "<br />")

        Response.Write("The user on the HttpContext during BeginRequest is: " & _
            Context.Items("HttpContext_User_BeginRequest") & _
            "<br />")
        Response.Write("<hr />")

        Response.Write("The OS thread identity when the page executes is: " & _
            WindowsIdentity.GetCurrent().Name & _
            "<br />")

        If String.IsNullOrEmpty(Thread.CurrentPrincipal.Identity.Name) Then
            Response.Write("The managed thread identity when the " & _
                        "page executes is:" & "[null or empty]" & _
                        "<br />")
        Else
            Response.Write("The managed thread identity when " & _
                "the page executes is:" & _
                Thread.CurrentPrincipal.Identity.Name & "<br />")
        End If
        Response.Write("The managed thread identity is of type: " & _
                    Thread.CurrentPrincipal.ToString() & "<br />")

        If String.IsNullOrEmpty(User.Identity.Name) Then
            Response.Write("The user on the HttpContext when " & _
```

```
                              "the page executes is:" & "[null or empty]" & "<br />")
        Else
    Response.Write("The user on the HttpContext when the " & _
            "page executes is: " & User.Identity.Name & "<br />")
    End If

    Response.Write("The user on the HttpContext is of type: " & _
        CType(User,Object).ToString() & "<br />")

    Response.Write("The user on the HttpContext and the " & _
        "thread principalpoint at the same object: " & _
        (Thread.CurrentPrincipal Is User) & "<br />")

    Response.Write("The impersonation token set by IIS is: " & _
         Request.LogonUserIdentity.Name & "<br />")
    End Sub
    End Class
```

The information is displayed running on an ASP.NET 3.5 application with the following characteristics:

- ❏ The site is running locally on the web server (that is, not on a UNC share).

- ❏ IIS has Anonymous Authentication and Windows Authentication modules enabled.

- ❏ ASP.NET is using the default mode of Windows for authentication.

- ❏ The <identity /> element's impersonate attribute is set to false.

The page output is shown here:

```
The OS thread identity during BeginRequest is: NT AUTHORITY\NETWORK SERVICE
The managed thread identity during BeginRequest is: [null or empty]
The managed thread identity during BeginRequest is a GenericPrincipal: True
The user on the HttpContext during BeginRequest is: [null]
-------------------------------------------------------------------------------
The OS thread identity when the page executes is: NT AUTHORITY\NETWORK SERVICE
The managed thread identity when the page executes is: [null or empty]
The managed thread identity is of type: System.Security.Principal.WindowsPrincipal
The user on the HttpContext when the page executes is: [null or empty]
The user on the HttpContext is of type: System.Security.Principal.WindowsPrincipal
The user on the HttpContext and the thread principal point at the same object: True
```

The operating system thread identity makes sense because this is the identity of the underlying IIS 7.0 worker process. The ASP.NET runtime is not impersonating any identity, so the security context of the thread is not reset by ASP.NET. As mentioned earlier, during BeginRequest neither the HttpContext nor the Thread object have had any security information explicitly set by ASP.NET.

The security information during page execution is a bit more interesting. The operating system thread identity has not changed. However, the IPrincipal associated with the current thread, and the IPrincipal associated with HttpContext is a reference to a WindowsPrincipal. Furthermore, the managed thread and HttpContext are referencing the same object instance. Clearly something occurred after Application_BeginRequest that caused a WindowsPrincipal to come into the picture. "Going back to the conditions under which the above code is running, it explains clearly what have been mentioned before that in the case of an application running under the IIS 7.0 Integrated mode, the native

AnonymousAuthenticationModule is enabled, WindowsAuthenticationModule is enabled, and the ASP.NET application is configured to run with Windows authentication, the HttpContext.Current .User's value will be set to a dummy instance of a WindowsPrincipal class having its Identity.Name property set to an empty string."

At this point, the important thing to keep in mind is that before the AuthenticateRequest event in the integrated request-processing pipeline occurs, neither the thread principal nor the User property of HttpContext should be relied on for identifying the security identity for the current request. The operating system identity, though, has been established. However, this identity can be affected by a number of factors, as you will see in the next section.

Establishing the Operating System Thread Identity

Both ASP.NET and IIS have a say in the identity of the underlying operating system thread that is used for request processing. By default, the identity is set to that of the IIS 7.0 worker process: NT AUTHORITY\ NETWORK SERVICE. However, developers and administrators have the option to change the default identity of the application pool by several ways, two of which follow:

- ❑ The default identity of the application pool is set in the ApplicationHost.config configuration file of the web server.

  ```
  <applicationPools>
      <applicationPoolDefaults>
          <processModel identityType="NetworkService" />
      </applicationPoolDefaults>
  </applicationPools>
  ```

- ❑ A developer or administrator can open the ApplicationHost.config configuration file, find the <applicationPoolDefaults /> configuration section located inside the <application Pools /> configuration section group and then change the identityType attribute of the <processModel /> element.

- ❑ Another way of changing the default identity associated with the application pool is by visiting the IIS 7.0 Manager tool, clicking on the View Application Pools on the Actions menu on the right, selecting the application pool you want to change its identity, and finally clicking on the Advanced Settings. Figure 3-3 shows the Advanced Settings window used to configure advanced options for an application pool.

In earlier versions of ASP.NET, determining the actual impersonation token set by the IIS core engine was difficult because the technique involved some rather esoteric code. However, it is easy to get a reference to it in ASP.NET 2.0 and 3.5. The following line of code gets a reference to the identity determined by IIS for the current request by its core engine:

```
WindowsIdentity wi = Request.LogonUserIdentity;
```

With this information, it is much simpler to see the IIS impersonation without the sometimes confusing effects of other authentication and configuration settings. For example, with the sample application used in the previous section (anonymous access allowed in IIS, Windows authentication enabled in ASP.NET, no impersonation), some of the security information for a page request is:

```
The OS thread identity during BeginRequest is: NT AUTHORITY\NETWORK SERVICE
The OS thread identity when the page executes is: NT AUTHORITY\NETWORK SERVICE
The impersonation token set by IIS is: NT AUTHORITY\IUSR
```

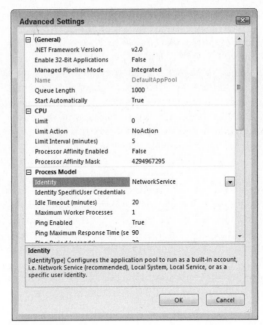

Figure 3-3

As you can see, the authenticated identity determined by IIS for the current request is the default identity of the anonymous authentication module. Recall that this application is running with the Anonymous AuthenticationModule enabled, the default identity of the aforementioned module was not changed and left with its default value. In addition, the application was not configured with a username or password hence the identity of the anonymous authentication module was used as the authenticated identity of the current request. Also notice that, even though the native WindowsAuthenticationModule was enabled, the AnonymousAuthenticationModule takes control over any other enabled native authentication module.

The following table shows the various IIS security options and the resulting request authenticated identity set by IIS that can be accessed by ASP.NET:

IIS Authentication Type	Impersonation Token Generated
Windows, Basic, Digest, or Certificate Mapping	Token corresponding to the authenticated (or mapped) browser user.
Anonymous	The default identity configured in IIS for anonymous authentication module. If not changed, it is by default IUSR built-in.
Running on a UNC share with explicit credentials	The configured UNC identity. This identity is used regardless of the IIS authentication type.

During the early stages of the request, enabling impersonation in an application running in the integrated mode has no real effect up until the request is authenticated by both IIS and ASP.NET. The setting of the impersonate attribute on the <identity /> element will affect the operating system thread

93

identity. Once the authentication stage is over and the page starts execution, ASP.NET will initialize the identity of the operating system thread based on a combination of the settings in the `<identity />` attribute and the request authenticated identity set by IIS core engine.

When an ASP.NET application is configured to impersonate the authenticated user for the current request, the impersonation usually has an effect through all the stages of the request-processing pipeline, starting from the `BeginRequest` stage. However, with the IIS 7.0 Integrated mode, ASP.NET modules can now execute at early stages of the integrated request-processing pipeline. Therefore, impersonation is not available for ASP.NET applications running in the Integrated mode, only after the `Authenticate Request` stage. If your ASP.NET application makes use of impersonation in early stages of the request-processing pipeline, the IIS team at Microsoft recommends moving the application into the IIS 7.0 Classic mode. On the other hand, if you are not concerned with enabling impersonation for your application in the early stages of the request-processing pipeline, then the application operates according to the rules set by the IIS 7.0 Integrated mode. If the impersonate attribute of the `<identity />` element is set to `true`, then ASP.NET will change the operating system thread's identity using the request authenticated identity set by IIS. However, if ASP.NET does not explicitly set the thread token, the operating system thread will run with the credentials configured for the worker process in IIS.

Continuing with previous sample, if the following configuration change is made to the application, ASP.NET explicitly impersonates using the IIS impersonation token:

```
<identity impersonate="true" />
```

The security information for the request changes to reflect the identity value of the impersonation token set by IIS. (At this point the sample application is not requiring IIS to authenticate the browser user):

```
The OS thread identity during BeginRequest is: NT AUTHORITY\NETWORK SERVICE
The OS thread identity when the page executes is: NT AUTHORITY\IUSR
The impersonation token set by IIS is: NT AUTHORITY\IUSR
```

An mentioned above, ASP.NET impersonation does not have a real effect on the identity of the operating system in the early stages of the integrated request processing pipeline; this is clear from the operating system thread identity inside the `BeginRequest` event. However, once the authentication stage is over, the impersonation effect is clear. ASP.NET sets the identity of the operating system thread to the impersonation token set by IIS core engine.

Changing the settings in IIS to instead allow only native `BasicAuthenticationModule` causes IIS to set the impersonation token to the identity of the authenticated user. Again, if you look back at the section that talks about how IIS 7.0 determines the identity of the request, you will notice that the exact same thing is happening. Because ASP.NET impersonates this identity, the thread identity will reflect the impersonation token:

```
The OS thread identity during BeginRequest is: NT AUTHORITY\NETWORK SERVICE
The OS thread identity when the page executes is: bhaidar-PC\test
The impersonation token set by IIS is: bhaidar-PC\test
```

If the configuration for `<identity />` includes an explicit value for the username and password attributes then ASP.NET ignores the impersonation token set by IIS native modules, and ASP.NET instead explicitly sets the operating system's thread token based on the credentials in the `<identity />` element. For example, if the sample application is switched back to allow Anonymous access in IIS and the configuration is changed to use the following:

```
<identity impersonate="true" userName="test" password="test"/>
```

Then the security information reflects the application impersonation identity:

```
The OS thread identity during BeginRequest is: NT AUTHORITY\NETWORK SERVICE
The OS thread identity when the page executes is: bhaidar-PC\test
The impersonation token set by IIS is: bhaidar-PC\bhaidar
```

Notice that since `Basic Authentication` module is still the only native module configured in IIS, the user gets authenticated with basic authentication and IIS generates the impersonation token based on the username and password supplied by the user for the basic authentication. But since, ASP.NET application impersonates to a Windows account, it is clear that the operating system thread's identity is set to the same username configured for the `<identity />` configuration section, inside the application's `web.config` configuration file, when the impersonation is enabled.

Prior to IIS 7.0, configuring application impersonation required that you manually edit the `<identity />` section in the application's `web.config` configuration file. However, with IIS 7.0 you have a visual interface that allows you to edit the application impersonation, which is now known as *ASP.NET impersonation*, from inside the IIS 7.0 Manager tool. To use IIS 7.0 Manager to configure ASP.NET impersonation, locate the ASP.NET application in the list of hosted sites inside IIS 7.0. Figure 3-4 shows the IIS 7.0 Manager tool with an ASP.NET application selected.

Figure 3-4

Double-click the selected Authentication icon and you will get a list of all authentication modules registered and installed by IIS 7.0. Figure 3-5 shows the available authentication modules for the ASP.NET application under study:

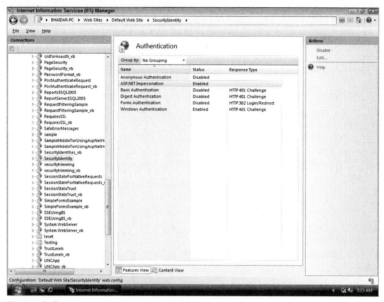

Figure 3-5

In Figure 3-5 the ASP.NET Impersonation icon is selected. This icon has been added to allow developers and administrators to configure the `<identity />` configuration section through the IIS 7.0 Manager tool and is located explicitly within the authentication applet in IIS 7.0 Manager. Keep the ASP.NET Impersonation icon selected and click the Edit link from the Actions pane on the right-hand side. Figure 3-6 shows the dialog box that pops up when you click this link.

Figure 3-6

This small dialog box is all you need to use to configure the ASP.NET impersonation, whether you want to configure client impersonation or application impersonation. As you can see, there are two main radio buttons: Specific user and Authenticated user.

The Specific user option resembles what you already know as application impersonation. It is here that you can explicitly specify a username and password to impersonate the authentication identity of the request. Simply click on the Set button. Another dialog box appears that lets you enter a username, password, and confirmation password.

On the other hand, the Authenticated user option simply impersonates the authentication identity of the request to the impersonation token set by IIS 7.0. This option resembles client impersonation.

Throughout the previous samples, the sample application was running locally on the web server. If instead the sample application is placed on a UNC share configured with explicit UNC credentials, the only security identities used for the operating system thread are either the UNC credentials or the application impersonation credentials. This is due in part because IIS always set the impersonation token to the explicit UNC identity, regardless of whether or not the application in IIS is configured to require some type of authentication with the browser.

When running the sample application on a UNC share without impersonation enabled, the security information looks like:

```
The OS thread identity during BeginRequest is: bhaidar-PC\uncidentity
The OS thread identity when the page executes is: bhaidar-PC\uncidentity
The impersonation token set by IIS is: bhaidar-PC\uncidentity
```

This highlights an important piece of ASP.NET security behavior. ASP.NET always ignores the `true`/`false` state of the impersonate attribute when running on a UNC share. Instead, ASP.NET will impersonate the UNC identity. Running on a UNC share with client impersonation enabled (`<identity impersonate="true" />`), the security information is exactly the same because of this behavior:

```
The OS thread identity during BeginRequest is: bhaidar-PC\uncidentity
The OS thread identity when the page executes is: bhaidar-PC\uncidentity
The impersonation token set by IIS is: bhaidar-PC\uncidentity
```

However, if application impersonation is configured for an application (that is, the username and password attributes of the `<identity />` element are set), then ASP.NET will ignore the impersonation token set by IIS and will instead set the operating system thread identity to the values specified in the `<identity />` element. Notice in the following output that the UNC identity is only available from the impersonation token set by IIS:

```
The OS thread identity during BeginRequest is: bhaidar-PC\test
The OS thread identity when the page executes is: bhaidar-PC\test
The impersonation token set by IIS is: bhaidar-PC\uncidentity
```

To summarize all this information, the following table lists the combinations of the impersonation token from IIS and operating system thread identities based on various configuration settings when running on IIS 7.0 integrated mode. Remember that client impersonation means `<identity impersonate="true"/>`, whereas application impersonation means an explicit username and password were configured in the `<identity />` element. In the following table, when running on a UNC share is yes, this means that the application in IIS has an explicit set of UNC credentials configured for accessing the share. As noted earlier, "officially" ASP.NET 3.5 is not supported running on a UNC share that uses pass-through authentication.

On UNC Share	IIS Authentication	ASP.NET Impersonation	OS Thread Identity	IIS Impersonation Token
No	Anonymous allowed	None	NETWORK SERVICE	IUSR
No	Anonymous allowed	Client	IUSR	IUSR
No	Anonymous allowed	Application	The application impersonation credentials	IUSR
No	Authenticated access required	None	NETWORK SERVICE	The credentials of the browser user
No	Authenticated access required	Client	The credentials of the browser user	The credentials of the browser user
No	Authenticated access required	Application	The application impersonation credentials	The credentials of the browser user
Yes	Anonymous allowed	None	The configured UNC identity	The configured UNC identity
Yes	Anonymous allowed	Client	The configured UNC identity	The configured UNC identity
Yes	Anonymous allowed	Application	The application impersonation credentials	The configured UNC identity
Yes	Authenticated access required	None	The configured UNC identity	The configured UNC identity
Yes	Authenticated access required	Client	The configured UNC identity	The configured UNC identity
Yes	Authenticated access required	Application	The application impersonation credentials	The configured UNC identity

The Unified Processing Pipeline

In the new unified integrated mode of execution, both native and managed modules get the chance to subscribe to the same events during the request-processing pipeline. The different stages of execution are exposed to all the managed modules and hence, the new integrated mode can make heavy use of the modules developed by ASP.NET.

A request in IIS 7.0 integrated mode passes through the same set of events as that of the ASP.NET pipeline events. As you know, the new integrated mode leverages ASP.NET to a framework to extend IIS 7.0 and hence, the ASP.NET pipeline will play a very important role from now on. Requests would pass through the same old ASP.NET pipeline events, both native and managed modules would subscribe to these events and hence, the expanded use of ASP.NET powers.

And now for a brief interlude to review the processing pipeline in ASP.NET 3.5: A basic understanding of the pipeline is useful for knowing when authentication and authorization occur within the lifecycle of the integrated request-processing pipeline.

Developers who have worked with the ASP.NET pipeline are usually familiar with the synchronous events that can be hooked. ASP.NET 3.5 expands on the original pipeline provided by ASP.NET 2.0 by adding three new events, which will be discussed shortly.

The current ASP.NET 3.5 synchronous pipeline events are listed in the order that they occur as follows:

1. `BeginRequest`
2. `AuthenticateRequest`
3. `PostAuthenticateRequest`
4. `AuthorizeRequest`
5. `PostAuthorizeRequest`
6. `ResolveRequestCache`
7. `PostResolveRequestCache`
8. `MapRequestHandler`
9. `PostMapRequestHandler`
10. `AcquireRequestState`
11. `PostAcquireRequestState`
12. `PreRequestHandlerExecute`

    At this stage, the selected handler executes the current request. The most familiar handler is the Page handler.

13. `PostRequestHandlerExecute`
14. `ReleaseRequestState`
15. `PostReleaseRequestState`
16. `UpdateRequestCache`
17. `PostUpdateRequestCache`
18. `LogRequest`
19. `PostLogRequest`
20. `EndRequest`

ASP.NET 3.5 adds three new stages to the unified integrated request-processing pipeline. These events are only used when the integrated mode is configured:

1. `MapRequestHandler` : At this stage a handler is selected based on the content file type extension that is requested. Either a native module such as the `StaticFileModule` handler or a managed module such as `PageHandlerFactory` can be selected

2. `LogRequest`: Fires just after the `PostUpdateRequestCache` event. Even if an error occurs in the request processing, this even still fires. Both native and managed modules can subscribe to this event.

3. `PostLogRequest`: This event fires just after `LogRequest` event fires.

The discussion will drill down to explain what happens during `AuthenticateRequest`, `PostAuthenticateRequest`, and `AuthorizeRequest` in more detail shortly. Suffice it to say that prior to the completion of `AuthenticateRequest` and `PostAuthenticateRequest`, only the operating system thread identity should be used. Other identities have not been completely initialized until these two events complete.

For most developers, the operating system thread identity that is established prior to `BeginRequest` remains stable for the duration of the entire pipeline. Similarly, after authentication has occurred during `AuthenticateRequest` and `PostAuthenticateRequest`, the values of `HttpContext.Current.User` as well as `Thread.CurrentPrincipal` remain constant for the remainder of the pipeline.

ASP.NET continues to support the ASP.NET 2.0's asynchronous processing in the pipeline as well. After all, the core runtime of ASP.NET 3.5 is no different from ASP.NET 2.0, with some additional integrated features such as ASP.NET AJAX. For example, each of the synchronous events in the previous list also has a corresponding asynchronous event that developers can hook. Asynchronous pipeline processing makes it possible for developers to author long-running tasks without tying up ASP.NET worker threads. Instead, in ASP.NET 3.5 developers can start long running tasks in a way that quickly returns control to the current ASP.NET 3.5 worker thread. Then at a later point the ASP.NET runtime will be notified of the completion of the asynchronous work, and a worker thread is scheduled to continue running the pipeline again.

Thread Identity and Asynchronous Pipeline Events

Because of the support for asynchronous processing in ASP.NET 3.5, developers need to be cognizant of the security values available at different phases of asynchronous processing. In general, asynchronous pipeline events are handled in the following manner:

1. The developer subscribes to an asynchronous pipeline event in `global.asax` or with an `HttpModule`. Subscribing involves supplying a `Begin` and an `End` event handler for the asynchronous pipeline event.

2. ASP.NET runs the `Begin` event handler. The developer's code within the `Begin` event handler kicks off an asynchronous task and returns the `IAsyncResult` handle to ASP.NET.

3. The asynchronous work actually occurs on a *framework thread pool* thread. This is a critical distinction, because when the actual work occurs, ASP.NET is not involved. No security information from the ASP.NET world will be auto-magically initialized. As a result, it is the responsibility of the developer to ensure that any required security identity information is explicitly passed to the asynchronous task. Furthermore, if the asynchronous task expects to be running

under a specific identity, the task is responsible for impersonating prior to performing any work as well as reverting impersonation when the work is completed.

4. Once the asynchronous work is done, the thread pool thread will call back to ASP.NET to notify it that the work has completed.

5. As part of the callback processing, ASP.NET will call the developer's End event handler. Normally in the End event handler, the developer uses the IAsyncResult handle from step 2 to call EndInvoke and process the results.

6. ASP.NET starts up processing the page request again using a different ASP.NET worker thread. Before ASP.NET resumes running the request, it reinitializes the ASP.NET worker thread to ensure that the correct security context and security identities are being used.

To make this a bit clearer, let's walk through a variation of the identity sample used earlier. The asynchronous sample hooks the asynchronous version of PostAuthenticateRequest with an HttpModule. The reason behind subscribing to the PostAuthenticateRequest event is due to the breaking changes introduced by IIS 7.0 regarding impersonation. If you had to subscribe to the BeginRequest event, you would not have been able to see the effect of impersonation on the asynchronous pipeline events.

The module is registered as follows:

```
<modules>
        <add name="AsyncEventModule" type="AsyncEventsModule" />
</modules>
```

The module's Init method is where the asynchronous event registration actually occurs. Notice that both a Begin and an End event handler are registered.

C#

```csharp
using System;
using System.Collections;
using System.Data;
using System.Configuration;
using System.Security.Principal;
using System.Threading;
using System.Web;
using System.Web.Security;

public class AsyncEventsModule : IHttpModule
{
  public AsyncEventsModule()
  {
  }

    #region IHttpModule Members

public void Dispose()
{
    throw new Exception("The method or operation is not implemented.");
}

public void Init(HttpApplication context)
{
```

```
            context.AddOnPostAuthenticateRequestAsync(
                new BeginEventHandler(this.PostAuthenticateRequest_BeginEventHandler),
                new EndEventHandler(this. PostAuthenticateRequest_EndEventHandler)
                );
        }

        #endregion

    //Implementations of being and end event handlers shown later
}
```

VB.NET

```
Imports System
Imports System.Collections
Imports System.Data
Imports System.Configuration
Imports System.Security.Principal
Imports System.Threading
Imports System.Web
Imports System.Web.Security
Imports System.Web.UI
Imports System.Web.UI.WebControls
Imports System.Web.UI.WebControls.WebParts
Imports System.Web.UI.HtmlControls

Public Class AsyncEventsModule
    Implements IHttpModule
    Public Sub New()
    End Sub

#Region "IHttpModule Members"

    Public Sub Dispose() Implements IHttpModule.Dispose
    End Sub

    Public Sub Init(ByVal context As HttpApplication) Implements IHttpModule.Init
        context.AddOnPostAuthenticateRequestAsync( _
            New BeginEventHandler( _
                AddressOf Me.PostAuthenticateRequest_BeginEventHandler), _
            New EndEventHandler( _
                AddressOf Me.PostAuthenticateRequest_EndEventHandler))
    End Sub

#End Region

    'Implementations of being and end event handlers shown later

End Class
```

Within the same ASP.NET application, there is a class called Sleep that will sleep for one second when one of its methods is called. The Sleep class simulates a class that would perform some type of lengthy work that is best executed in the background. The constructor for the Sleep class accepts a reference to an IDictionary. This will be used to initialize the Sleep class with a reference to the HttpContext's Items collection. Using the Items collection, an instance of the Sleep class can log the operating system thread identity, both during asynchronous execution and after completion of asynchronous processing.

C#

```csharp
using System.Collections;
using System.Security.Principal;
using System.Threading;
...
public class Sleep
{
    private IDictionary state;

    public Sleep(IDictionary appState)
    {
        state = appState;
    }

    public void DoWork()
    {
        state["AsyncWorkerClass_OperatingSystemThreadIdentity"] =
            WindowsIdentity.GetCurrent().Name;
        Thread.Sleep(1000);
    }

    public void StoreAsyncEndID()
    {
        state["AsyncWorkerClass_EndEvent_OperatingSystemThreadIdentity"] =
            WindowsIdentity.GetCurrent().Name;
    }
}
```

VB.NET

```vbnet
Imports System
Imports System.Collections
Imports System.Security.Principal
Imports System.Threading
...
Public Class Sleep
    Private state As IDictionary
    Private aspnetThreadToken As IntPtr

    Public Sub New(ByVal appState As IDictionary, ByVal token As IntPtr)
        state = appState
    End Sub
    Public Sub DoWork()
state("AsyncWorkerClass_OperatingSystemThreadIdentity") = _
   WindowsIdentity.GetCurrent().Name
        Thread.Sleep(1000)
    End Sub

    Public Sub StoreAsyncEndID()
state("AsyncWorkerClass_EndEvent_OperatingSystemThreadIdentity") _
   = WindowsIdentity.GetCurrent().Name
    End Sub
End Class
```

The `Begin` event handler for `PostAuthenticateRequest` will use a `delegate` to trigger an asynchronous call to the `DoWork` method. The module defines a `delegate` that is used to wrap the `DoWork` method on the `Sleep` class as follows:

C#

```
public delegate void AsyncSleepDelegate();
```

VB.NET

```
Public Delegate Sub AsyncSleepDelegate()
```

For simplicity, the `Begin` and `End` pipeline event handlers are also implemented as part of the same `HttpModule`. The `Begin` event handler (which follows), first obtains a reference to the `HttpContext` associated with the current request by casting the sender parameter to an instance of `HttpApplication`. Using the context, the module stores the operating system thread identity. Then the module creates an instance of the class that will perform the actual asynchronous work. After wrapping the `DoWork` method with an `AsyncSleepDelegate`, the module calls `BeginInvoke`. The code passes the `AsyncCallback` reference supplied by ASP.NET as one of the parameters to `BeginInvoke`. This is necessary because it is the ASP.NET runtime that is called back by the .NET Framework thread pool thread carrying out the asynchronous work. Without hooking up the callback, there would be no way for the flow of execution to return back to ASP.NET after an asynchronous piece of work was completed. The second parameter passed to `BeginInvoke` is a reference to the very `AsyncSleepDelegate` being called. As a result, the delegate reference will be available when asynchronous processing is completed and `EndInvoke` is called on the delegate.

The return value from any call made to a `BeginInvoke` method is a reference to an `IAsyncResult`. The `BeginInvoke` method is auto-generated by the .NET Framework to support asynchronous method calls without developers needing to explicitly author asynchronous class definitions. Returning an `IAsyncResult` allows ASP.NET to pass the reference back to the developer's `End` event later on when asynchronous processing is complete.

C#

```
private IAsyncResult PostAuthenticateRequest_BeginEventHandler(
    object sender, EventArgs e, AsyncCallback cb, object extraData)
{
    HttpApplication a = (HttpApplication)sender;
    a.Context.Items["PostAuthenticateRequestAsync_OperatingSystemThreadID"] =
        WindowsIdentity.GetCurrent().Name;

    Sleep s = new Sleep(a.Context.Items);
    AsyncSleepDelegate asd = new AsyncSleepDelegate(s.DoWork);
    IAsyncResult ar = asd.BeginInvoke(cb, asd);

    return ar;
}
```

VB.NET

```
Private Function PostAuthenticateRequest_BeginEventHandler( _
    ByVal sender As Object, _
    ByVal e As EventArgs, _
    ByVal cb As AsyncCallback, _
```

```
           ByVal extraData As Object) As IAsyncResult

        Dim a As HttpApplication = CType(sender, HttpApplication)
    a.Context.Items("PostAuthenticateRequestAsync_OperatingSystemThreadID") _
      = WindowsIdentity.GetCurrent().Name

        'the Sleep class is now constructed with:
        Dim s As New Sleep(a.Context.Items, WindowsIdentity.GetCurrent().Token)

        Dim asd As New AsyncSleepDelegate(AddressOf s.DoWork)
        Dim ar As IAsyncResult = asd.BeginInvoke(cb, asd)

        Return ar
    End Function
```

When asynchronous work has completed, the .NET Framework calls back to ASP.NET using the call-back reference that was supplied earlier to the BeginInvoke call. As part of the callback processing, ASP.NET calls the End event (which follows) that was registered, passing it the IAsyncResult that was returned from the BeginInvoke call. This allows the End event to cast the AsyncState property available from IAsyncResult back to a reference to the AsyncSleepDelegate. The End event can now call EndInvoke against the AsyncSleepDelegate to gather the results of the asynchronous processing. In the sample application, there is no return value, but in practice any asynchronous processing would probably return a reference to a query or some other set of results.

Because the End event now has a reference to the AsyncSleepDelegate, it can use the Target property of the delegate to get back to the original instance of Sleep that was used. The End event then logs the current operating system thread identity as it exists during the End event using the StoreAsyncEndID method on the Sleep instance. At this point, having the Sleep instance log the thread identity is acceptable because this method call is synchronous and thus executes on the same thread running the End event handler.

C#

```csharp
private void PostAuthenticateRequest_EndEventHandler(IAsyncResult ar)
{
    AsyncSleepDelegate asd = (AsyncSleepDelegate)ar.AsyncState;
    asd.EndInvoke(ar);

    Sleep s = (Sleep)asd.Target;
    s.StoreAsyncEndID();

}
```

VB.NET

```vbnet
Private Sub PostAuthenticateRequest_EndEventHandler(ByVal ar As IAsyncResult)
    Dim asd As AsyncSleepDelegate = CType(ar.AsyncState, AsyncSleepDelegate)
    asd.EndInvoke(ar)

    Dim s As Sleep = CType(asd.Target, Sleep)
    s.StoreAsyncEndID()

End Sub
```

You can run the sample with a variety of different settings for `<identity />` in the web.config configuration file, as well as the directory security settings in IIS. Using the sample code earlier, the following extra lines of code show the asynchronous identity information.

C#

```
Response.Write("The OS thread identity during " +
        "PostAuthenticateRequest_BeginEventHandler is: " +
        Context.Items["PostAuthenticateRequestAsync_OperatingSystemThreadID"] +
            "<br/>");

Response.Write("The OS thread identity during " +
        "the actual async work is: " +
        Context.Items["AsyncWorkerClass_OperatingSystemThreadIdentity"] +
            "<br />");

Response.Write("The OS thread identity during " +
        "PostAuthenticateRequest_EndEventHandler is: " +
        Context.Items["AsyncWorkerClass_EndEvent_OperatingSystemThreadIdentity"] +
            "<br />");
```

VB.NET

```
Response.Write("The OS thread identity during " & _
        "PostAuthenticateRequest_BeginEventHandler is: " & _
        Context.Items("PostAuthenticateAsync_OperatingSystemThreadID") & _
        "<br />")

Response.Write("The OS thread identity during " & _
        "the actual async work is: " & _
        Context.Items("AsyncWorkerClass_OperatingSystemThreadIdentity") & _
        "<br />")

Response.Write("The OS thread identity during " & _
        "PostAuthenticateRequest_EndEventHandler is: " & _
        Context.Items("AsyncWorkerClass_EndEvent_OperatingSystemThreadIdentity") & _
        "<br />")
```

The following results show the identity information with Anonymous access allowed in IIS and the `<identity />` configured for application impersonation:

```
The OS thread identity during BeginRequest is: NT AUTHORITY\NETWORK SERVICE
The OS thread identity during PostAuthenticateRequest_BeginEventHandler is:
bhaidar-PC\test
The OS thread identity during the actual async work is: NT AUTHORITY\NETWORK
SERVICE
The OS thread identity during PostAuthenticateRequest_EndEventHandler is: NT
AUTHORITY\NETWORK SERVICE


The OS thread identity when the page executes is: bhaidar-PC\test
The impersonation token from IIS is: NT AUTHORITY\IUSR
```

As you can see, the `Begin` event handler uses the default application pool identity NT AUTHORITY\ NETWORK SERVICE instead of the application impersonation account. As previously mentioned above, when an ASP.NET application is running inside the IIS 7.0 Integrated mode, the application imperson-ation has no effect before the `AuthenticateRequest` stage, where the request would have been authen-ticated by both IIS 7.0 and ASP.NET. However, remember from above that the code subscribed to the `PostAuthenticateRequest`. At this stage the ASP.NET application impersonation has an effect on the operating system thread, which is clear from the output above where the operating system thread in the `PostAuthenticateRequest` represents that of the ASP.NET application impersonation.

However, during the asynchronous work in the `Sleep` instance, a thread from the .NET Framework thread pool was used. Because the application is running in an IIS 7.0 worker process, the default identity for any operating system threads is the identity of the worker process. In this case, the worker process is using the default identity of `NT AUTHORITY\NETWORK SERVICE`. You can clearly see that the application impersonation has no effect at all here and is regardless of the fact that the request is operating in the `PostAuthenticateRequest` stage (where application impersonation takes effect).

The `End` event handler also executes on a thread pool thread. As a result, the operating system thread identity is also `NT AUTHORITY\NETWORK SERVICE`. Do not be mixed up with the fact that the `Begin` and `End` events were registered during the `PostAuthenticateRequest` stage. The asynchronous work is done on a separate thread that the .NET Framework has chosen from the thread pool, and hence the application authentication has no effect on those threads located in the thread pool.

Because the work that occurs in the `End` event handler is usually limited to just retrieving the results from the asynchronous call, the identity of the thread at this point should not be an issue. Note that just from an architectural perspective, you should not be performing any "heavy" processing at this point. The general assumption is that the `End` event handler is used for any last pieces of work after asynchro-nous processing is completed.

This highlights the fact that if a developer depends on the thread identity during asynchronous work (for example, a call is made to SQL Server using integrated security), the developer is responsible for impersonating and reverting identities during the asynchronous call, regardless of whether the asyn-chronous work is performed before or after `PostAuthenticateRequest` event and whether application impersonation is enabled or not. Because you own the work of safely manipulating the thread identity at this point, you may need to carefully wrap all work in a `try/finally` block to ensure that the thread pool's thread identity is always reset to its original state. Although some tricks can be used to marshal an appropriate security token over to an asynchronous worker class, performing work that requires specific credentials will always be a bit complicated.

For example, the sample intentionally used application impersonation to show that the application impersonation identity is not available during asynchronous processing. If an application required this identity to perform a piece of asynchronous work, you would need to first get a copy of the operating system thread token in the `Begin` event (there is a `Token` property on `WindowsIdentity`), and then pass the token to the asynchronous worker class. If the `Sleep` class is modified to accept a token in its constructor, it can impersonate the necessary identity in the `DoWork` method when asynchronous work is performed:

C#

```
//the Sleep class is now constructed with:
Sleep s = new Sleep(a.Context.Items,WindowsIdentity.GetCurrent().Token);

public class Sleep
{
    private IDictionary state;
```

```csharp
    private IntPtr aspnetThreadToken;

    public Sleep(IDictionary appState, IntPtr token)
    {
        state = appState;
        aspnetThreadToken = token;
    }

    public void DoWork()
    {

        WindowsIdentity wi = new WindowsIdentity(aspnetThreadToken);
        WindowsImpersonationContext wic = null;
        try
        {
            wic = wi.Impersonate();

            state["AsyncWorkerClass_OperatingSystemThreadIdentity"] =
                WindowsIdentity.GetCurrent().Name;
            Thread.Sleep(1000);
        }
        finally
        {
            if (wic != null)
                wic.Undo();
        }
    }

    //StoreAsyncEndID snipped for brevity

}
```

VB.NET

```vbnet
'the Sleep class is now constructed with:
Dim s As New Sleep(a.Context.Items, WindowsIdentity.GetCurrent().Token)

Public Class Sleep
    Private state As IDictionary
    Private aspnetThreadToken As IntPtr

    Public Sub New(ByVal appState As IDictionary, ByVal token As IntPtr)
        state = appState
        aspnetThreadToken = token
    End Sub

    Public Sub DoWork()
        Dim wi As WindowsIdentity = Nothing
        If aspnetThreadToken <> IntPtr.Zero Then
            wi = New WindowsIdentity(aspnetThreadToken)
        End If

        Dim wic As WindowsImpersonationContext = Nothing
        Try
```

```
                    If aspnetThreadToken <> IntPtr.Zero Then
                        wic = wi.Impersonate()
                    End If

    state("AsyncWorkerClass_OperatingSystemThreadIdentity") _
        = WindowsIdentity.GetCurrent().Name

                    Thread.Sleep(1000)
            Finally
                    If wic IsNot Nothing Then
                        wic.Undo()
                    End If
            End Try
        End Sub

    'StoreAsyncEndID snipped for brevity

End Class
```

The result of impersonating the identity during the asynchronous work shows that now the application impersonation identity is available:

```
The OS thread identity during BeginRequest_BeginEventHandler is: NT AUTHORITY\IUSR
The OS thread identity during the actual async work is: bhaidar-PC\testThe OS
thread identity during BeginRequest_EndEventHandler is: NT AUTHORITY\NETWORK
SERVICE
```

Once again it is important to mention that the AsyncEventsModule has been updated to register for the AddOnPostAuthenticateRequestAsync since only at this event can you see the effect of impersonating an ASP.NET application. Before the AuthenticateReqesut event occurs, the impersonation will have no effect on the operating system thread. Moreover, if you plan to see the effect of the ASP.NET application impersonation during the processing and execution of asynchronous work, you should also impersonate to retrieve the operating system thread identity, which in this case is also an impersonated identity due to application impersonation and the location where the asynchronous work is registered (the PostAuthenticateRequest stage).

Overall, the moral of the story here is that when planning for asynchronous pipeline events, the question of the identity needed to carry out the background work needs to be considered early on. If using the worker process identity is not an option, for simplicity using a fixed set of identity information that can be loaded from configuration or encapsulated in a worker class may be a better choice than trying to "hop" the ASP.NET thread's security identity over the wall to the asynchronous worker class. Although the modifications shown earlier were pretty simple, the actual identity that is used will vary depending on IIS and ASP.NET security settings. Trying to debug why a background task is failing will be much more difficult if the task depends on an identity that can be easily changed with a few misconfigurations.

Although it is not shown here, if the security information required by your asynchronous task is instead just the IPrincipal from either HttpContext.Current.User or Thread.CurrentPrincipal, you can pass the IPrincipal reference to your asynchronous worker class. In the case of HttpContext.Current.User, it is even easier because you can just pass an HttpContext reference to your worker class (the sample passed the Items collection from the current HttpContext). You may need the IPrincipal, for example, if you pass user information to your middle tier for authorization or auditing purposes.

Also, note that in some cases the value of `Thread.CurrentPrincipal` may appear to be retained across the main ASP.NET request, and your asynchronous task. However, this behavior should not be relied on, because it is entirely dependent on which managed thread is selected from the framework's thread pool to execute asynchronous tasks.

One last piece of information about managing security for asynchronous tasks is in order. The sample you looked at used a separate class to carry out the asynchronous work. However, a number of .NET Framework classes provide methods that return an `IAsyncResult` reference. For example, both the `System.IO.FileStream` and the `System.Data.SqlClient.SqlCommand` classes support asynchronous reads. As another example, the `System.Net.HttpWebRequest` class also supports making asynchronous requests to HTTP endpoints. In cases like these, you need to look at the class signatures and determine if they have any built-in support for passing a security identity along to their asynchronous processing. In the case of `System.Net.HttpWebRequest`, there is a `Credentials` property that you can explicitly set. When the `HttpWebRequest` class asynchronously makes a request, it will use the security information that you set in the `Credentials` property. A similar ability to automatically pass along the correct credentials exists when using the `SqlCommand` and `SqlConnection` classes.

AuthenticateRequest

The `AuthenticateRequest` event is the point in the unified HTTP pipeline where both IIS and ASP.NET participate in authenticating the request. It is at this stage the IIS 7.0 core engine detects the configured authentication modules and executes them.

The process that IIS follows to authenticate a request has been discussed in details above. Therefore the focus here will be on the managed authentication side of the authentication process done by ASP.NET. It is this one that gives developers the opportunity to write code to examine the current security information for a request and based upon it, create an `IPrincipal` implementation and attach it to the current ASP.NET request. The end result of `AuthenticateRequest` is that both the managed thread's identity (available from `Thread.CurrentPrincipal`) and the `User` property of the current `HttpContext` will be initialized to an `IPrincipal` that can be used by downstream code.

Be default, ASP.NET ships with a number of `HttpModules` that hook the `AuthenticateRequest` event. You can see this list (and modify it) in the root `web.config` configuration file that is available in the following location:

```
%windir%\Microsoft.NET\Framework\v2.0.50727\CONFIG
```

The `web.config` configuration file in the framework's `CONFIG` directory is a concept that was introduced with ASP.NET 2.0. The development teams at Microsoft decided to separate web-specific configuration out of the `machine.config` configuration file to speed up load times for non-web applications. As a result, non-ASP.NET applications do not have to chug through configuration sections for features unsupported outside of a web environment.

Looking at the `<httpModules />` configuration element in the root `web.config` configuration file, the following entries are for modules that hook `AuthenticateRequest`:

```
<add name="WindowsAuthentication"
     type="System.Web.Security.WindowsAuthenticationModule" />
<add name="FormsAuthentication"
```

```
        type="System.Web.Security.FormsAuthenticationModule" />
    <add name="PassportAuthentication"
        type="System.Web.Security.PassportAuthenticationModule" />
```

Of the three default modules, we will only take a closer look at the `WindowsAuthenticationModule` and `FormsAuthenticationModule`. The `PassportAuthentication` is not supported anymore on Windows Vista and Windows Server 2008.

WindowsAuthenticationModule

When the ASP.NET application is running under IIS 7.0 classic mode, the managed `Windows AuthenticationModule` is the only authentication module that depends on impersonation token set by IIS. Its purpose is to construct a `WindowsPrincipal` based on the authenticated identity set by IIS when a `web.config` configuration file contains the setting `<authentication mode="Windows"/>`. The resultant `WindowsPrincipal` is set as the value of the `User` property for the current `HttpContext`. If a different authentication mode has been configured, the `WindowsAuthenticationModule` imme- diately returns whenever it is called during the `AuthenticateRequest` event. Note that the module does not look at or use the security identity of the underlying operating system thread when creating a `WindowsPrincipal`. As a result, the settings in the `<identity />` element have no effect on the output from the `WindowsAuthenticationModule`.

On the other hand, when the ASP.NET application is running under IIS 7.0 integrated mode, the managed `WindowsAuthenticationModule` behaves differently. It simply disregards the impersonation token set by IIS 7.0 and focuses on the `HttpContext.Current.User` property. In case a native authentication mod- ule was executed and successful, this means there is a valid and authenticated user. As mentioned above, there is an integrated request processing pipeline mechanism that sets the `HttpContext.Current.User` property to the value of the native `User` principal. The managed `WindowsAuthenticationModule` simply casts the value in the `HttpContext.Current.User` property into a valid `WindowsPrincipal` instance. However, if the native `AnonymousAuthenticationModule` is enabled, the `HttpContext.Current.User` property will be null and not set by the integrated request processing pipeline, since the native `Anonymous AuthenticationModule` runs after all the authentication modules configured in IIS 7.0. Therefore, if the native `AnonymousAuthenticationModule` is enabled and the application is running under the IIS 7.0 integrated mode, the managed `WindowsAuthenticationModule` has no use and can be easily removed without causing any problem to the application.

The name of the module `WindowsAuthenticationModule` is a little misleading because in reality this module does not actually authenticate a user. Authentication usually implies some kind of challenge (username and password), a response and a resultant representation of the success or failure of the challenge/response. However, this module is not involved in any challenge/response sequence.

Instead, all this occurs up front in IIS. If IIS is configured to require some type of authenticated access to an application (Windows using NTLM or Kerberos, Basic, Digest, or Certificate Mapping), then it is IIS that challenges the browser for credentials according to the enabled authentication types. If the response succeeds (and in some cases the response involves multiple network round trips to complete all of the security negotiations), then it is IIS that creates the data that represents a successfully authen- ticated user by doing all of the following:

❑   Generating the impersonation token that represents the authenticated user and making this identity available to ASP.NET.

❑ Setting the values of the LOGON_USER and AUTH_TYPE server variables to reflect the authenticated user and the authentication type that was used.

❑ If the ASP.NET application is running under the IIS 7.0 integrated mode and a native authentication module like Basic or Windows authentication is enabled, the integrated request processing pipeline uses a mechanism to set the HttpContext.Current.User property to the value of the native User principal.

In IIS 7.0 classic mode, WindowsAuthenticationModule just consumes the results of the security negotiations with IIS and makes the results of these negotiations available as a WindowsPrincipal. When the LOGON_USER and AUTH_TYPE server variables are empty (that is, no authentication challenge took place at the IIS 7.0 native authentication modules (the managed WindowsAuthenticationModule initializes the HttpContext.Current.User property to an anonymous identity that is the value of WindowsIdentity.GetAnonymous().

This anonymous identity has the following characteristics:

❑ The value of Name is the empty string.

❑ The value of AuthenticationType is the empty string.

❑ IsAnonymous is set to true.

❑ IsAuthenticated is set to false.

In other words, the managed WindowsAuthenticationModule inspects the LOGON_USER and AUTH_TYPE server variables for the current request. If those variables are empty, no authentication challenge took place at the IIS 7.0 level. Consequently, it constructs a WindowsPrincipal containing an anonymous WindowsIdentity, which determines that no browser user was authenticated for the current request and simply ignores the impersonation token set by IIS. If the server variables were not empty, the managed WindowsAuthenticationModule constructs a new WindowsPrincipal instance and assigns it to the HttpContext.Current.User property based on the server variables mentioned at the beginning of this paragraph. In addition, the Identity property on the User property is initialized to a new instance of the WindowsIdentity class.

On the other hand, when an application is running in the IIS 7.0 integrated mode, the managed Windows AuthenticationModule has a minimal job to do. It simply does some internal initialization based on the HttpContext.Current.User property's value that was originally passed a WindowsPrincipal instance by an integrated request processing pipeline mechanism based on the native User principal.

It was mentioned above that when the native AnonymousAuthenticationModule is enabled and the application is configured for Windows authentication and running under the integrated mode, the managed WindowsAuthenticationModule will not fire its Authenticate event and will perform only internal tasks. The reason behind this is that when the native AnonymousAuthenticationModule is enabled, regardless of the native authentication module configured, no authentication process takes place and hence regardless what native authentication modules have been configured, the HttpContext.Current .User property is empty. Internally the managed WindowsAuthenticationModule checks if the Identity property on the HttpContext.Current.User is null in C# or Nothing in VB.NET the Authenticate event never fires.

To illustrate how the `HttpContext.Current.User` property is determined when the native `AnonymousAuthenticationModule` is enabled, let's go back and check the output log that was generated by the previous sample code shown above:

```
The managed thread identity when the page executes is: [null or empty]
The managed thread identity is of type: System.Security.Principal.WindowsPrincipal
The user on the HttpContext when the page executes is: [null or empty]
The user on the HttpContext is of type: System.Security.Principal.WindowsPrincipal
The user on the HttpContext and the thread principal point at the same object: True
```

Now you know why the `IPrincipal` attached to both the context and the thread is a `WindowsPrincipal` with a `username` of empty string. The native `AnonymousAuthenticationModule` is enabled, meaning that no authentication challenge takes place and hence the integrated request processing pipeline does not set any value to the `HttpContext.Curent.User` property. The application is configured by default with Windows authentication and since the native `AnonymousAuthenticationModule` runs as the last authentication module at the AuthenticateRequest stage, it finds out that the `User` property is still invalid, and it informs the integrated request processing pipeline to instantiate the `HttpContext.Current.User` property to an anonymous `WindowsPrincipal` instance that has an anonymous `Identity` property of type `WindowsIdentity`.

On the other hand, if an authenticated browser user is detected (i.e., LOGON_USER and AUTH_TYPE are not empty strings) and the application runs under the IIS 7.0 classic mode, `WindowsAuthenticationModule` looks at the impersonation token set by IIS and creates a `WindowsIdentity` with the token.

Regardless of whether the application is running in either the integrated or classic mode, after the module creates a `WindowsIdentity` (either an authenticated identity in both classic and integrated mode or an anonymous identity in the classic mode), it raises the `Authenticate` event. If the event is fired, a developer can choose to hook the `Authenticate` event from `WindowsAuthenticationModule`. The `WindowsIdentity` that the module created is passed as part of the event argument of type `Windows AuthenticationEventArgs`. A developer can choose to create a custom principal in their event handler by setting the `User` property on the `WindowsAuthenticationEventArgs` event argument. The thing that is a little weird about this event is that a developer can actually do some pretty strange things with it. For example:

❑ A developer could technically ignore the `WindowsIdentity` supplied by the module and create a custom `IIdentity` wrapped in a custom `IPrincipal` implementation and then set this custom `IPrincipal` on the `WindowsAuthenticationEventArgs` User property.

❑ Alternatively, a developer could obtain a completely different `WindowsIdentity` (in essence ignoring the request authenticated identity set by IIS) and then wrap it in a `WindowsPrincipal` and set it on the event argument's `User` property.

In general, though, there is not a compelling usage of the `Authenticate` event for most applications. The `Authenticate` event was originally placed on this module (and others) to make it easier for developers to figure out how to attach custom `IPrincipal` implementations to an `HttpContext` without needing to create an `HttpModule` or hook events in `global.asax`. Architecturally, though, it makes more sense to just let `WindowsAuthenticationModule` carry out its work, and not hook the `Authenticate` event. If a web application needs to implement a custom authentication mechanism, it should use a custom `HttpModule` that itself hooks the `AuthenticateRequest` pipeline event. Both ASP.NET 2.0 and

ASP.NET 3.5 make this approach even easier because you can author the module with a class file inside of the App_Code directory and just reference the type (without all of the other assembly identification information) inside of the <httpModules /> configuration section of the web.config configuration file when the application is running under IIS 7.0 Classic mode, or inside of the <modules /> configuration section of the web.config configuration file when the application is running under IIS 7.0 Integrated mode.

Once the Authenticate event returns, WindowsAuthenticationModule looks at the User property on the WindowsAuthenticationEventArgs that was passed to the event. If an IPrincipal was set, the module sets the value of HttpContext.Current.User to the IPrincipal reference. If the User property on the event argument is null, though (the normal case), the module wraps the WindowsIdentity it determined earlier (either an anonymous WindowsIdentity, or a WindowsIdentity corresponding to the IIS impersonation token) in a WindowsPrincipal, and sets this principal on HttpContext.Current.User.

Using the sample application shown earlier in the chapter, look at a few variations of IIS security settings and UNC locations while using Windows authentication. Earlier, you saw the results of running with AnonymousAuthenticationModule enabled in IIS for a local web application. If instead, some type of authenticated access is required in IIS (Windows, Digest, Basic, or Certificate Mapping), the output changes to reflect the authenticated browser user.

```
The OS thread identity when the page executes is: bhaidar-PC\test
The managed thread identity when the page executes is: bhaidar-PC\bhaidar
The managed thread identity is of type: System.Security.Principal.WindowsPrincipal
The user on the HttpContext when the page executes is: bhaidar-PC\bhaidar
The user on the HttpContext is of type: System.Security.Principal.WindowsPrincipal
```

Regardless of whether impersonation is in effect (in this case, I enabled application impersonation), the value of Thread.CurrentPrincipal and HttpContext.Current.User will always reflect the authenticated browser user (and hence the request authenticated identity set by IIS) when some type of browser authentication is required.

If the application is running on a UNC share using explicit UNC credentials, continues to function properly with an exception, which is that when authentication is enabled for an application, it will ignore the impersonation token generated by IIS that is based on the UNC share credentials and simply uses the credentials of the authenticated user. Remember that in earlier UNC examples you saw that the impersonation token from IIS always reflected the explicit UNC credentials. Because WindowsAuthentication Module creates a WindowsPrincipal that is either an anonymous identity, or an identity matching the impersonation token from IIS, this means that even in the UNC case there will only ever be one of two possible WindowsPrincipal objects attached to the thread and the context: an anonymous Windows Identity, or an identity matching the authenticated credentials negotiated by the IIS when authentication was performed.

The following output is for the same application using application impersonation and running on a UNC share with anonymous access allowed:

```
The OS thread identity when the page executes is: bhaidar-PC\test
The managed thread identity when the page executes is: [null or empty]
The managed thread identity is of type: System.Security.Principal.WindowsPrincipal
The user on the HttpContext when the page executes is: [null or empty]
The user on the HttpContext is of type: System.Security.Principal.WindowsPrincipal
```

When authenticated access to the application is required, the UNC identity will not have any effect on the thread and the context identities. Instead, the application impersonation identity will take control. The account bhaidar-PC\test was used as the application impersonation account throughout this chapter.

```
The OS thread identity when the page executes is: bhaidar-PC\test
The managed thread identity when the page executes is: bhaidar-PC\bhaidar
The managed thread identity is of type: System.Security.Principal.WindowsPrincipal
The user on the HttpContext when the page executes is: bhaidar-PC\bhaidar
The user on the HttpContext is of type: System.Security.Principal.WindowsPrincipal
```

The following table summarizes the type of WindowsIdentity that is set on the HttpContext for various settings:

Running on a UNC Share?	Authenticated Access Required in IIS?	WindowsIdentity Set on the HttpContext
No	No	A WindowsIdentity corresponding to an anonymous user. WindowsIdentity.GetAnonymous()
No	Yes	A WindowsIdentity corresponding to the authenticated browser user
Yes	No	The value of WindowsIdentity.GetAnonymous()
Yes	Yes	A WindowsIdentity corresponding to the authenticated browser user

FormsAuthenticationModule

To start with, FormsAuthenticationModule is now registered on IIS 7.0 once the ASP.NET feature is enabled on the web server. Hence, this module can now be enabled for an application from the IIS 7.0 Manager tool and of course from inside the <system.webServer /> configuration section group of the application's web.config configuration file. In addition, taking advantage of the IIS 7.0 and ASP.NET integrated mode of execution, FormsAuthenticationModule can be used to authenticate requests for non-ASP.NET resources. This is because when it is time to authenticate a request, IIS 7.0 and ASP.NET would be executing the enabled native and managed authentication modules at the same authentication stage in the unified request-processing pipeline.

FormsAuthenticationModule inspects the cookies and the URL of the incoming request, looking for a forms authentication ticket (an encrypted representation of a FormsAuthenticationTicket instance). If the authentication mode is set to forms <authentication mode="Forms" />, the module will use a valid ticket to create a GenericPrincipal containing a FormsIdentity, and set the principal on HttpContext.Current.User. If a different authentication mode has been configured, then the module immediately exits during the AuthenticateRequest event.

Before the module attempts to extract a forms authentication ticket, it raises an Authenticate event. This event is similar in behavior to the Authenticate event raised by WindowsAuthenticationModule. Developers can choose to hook the Authenticate event on the FormsAuthenticationModule and supply a custom IPrincipal implementation by setting the User property on the FormsAuthentication EventArgs parameter that is passed to the event. After the event fires, if an IPrincipal was set on the event argument, FormsAuthenticationModule sets the value of HttpContext.Current.User to the same value, and then exits.

In forms authentication, the Authenticate event is a bit more useful, because conceptually "forms" authentication implies some type of logon form that gathers credentials from a user. Hooking the Authenticate event can be useful if developers programmatically create a FormsAuthentication Ticket, but then need to manage how the ticket is issued and processed on each subsequent request. As with the WindowsAuthenticationModule, the Authenticate event can be used as just a convenient way to author a completely custom authentication scheme without needing to author and then register an HttpModule.

If you do not hook the event, the normal processing of FormsAuthenticationModule occurs. In Chapter 6, on forms authentication, you learn more about the options available for handling forms authentication tickets. Briefly though, the sequence of steps the module goes through to arrive at a FormsIdentity are:

1. The module first gets the encrypted ticket that may have been sent as part of the request. The ticket could be in a cookie, in a custom HTTP header, in a query-string variable, or in a posted form variable.

2. After the module has the ticket, it attempts to decrypt it. If decryption succeeds, the module now has a reference to an instance of FormAuthenticationTicket. Some other validations occur, including confirming that the ticket has not expired, and that if SSL is required for cookie-based tickets that the current request is running under SSL.

3. If decryption or any of the subsequent validations fail, then the ticket is invalid and the Forms AuthenticationModule explicitly clears the ticket by either issuing an outdated cookie or clearing the cookieless representation from the HTTP_ASPFILTERSESSIONID header. At this point the module exits, which means no IPrincipal is created or attached to the context.

4. If a valid ticket was found but the ticket was in a query-string variable or was part of a posted form variable, the module will transfer the ticket into either a cookie or the cookieless representation of a forms authentication ticket. A side effect of this is that the module will trigger a redirect if transferring the ticket to a cookieless representation.

5. The module then creates an instance of a GenericPrincipal. Because forms authentication has no concept of roles and requires no custom properties or methods on the principal, it uses a GenericPrincipal. The custom representation for forms authentication is the FormsIdentity class. By this point, the module has a reference to a FormsAuthenticationTicket instance as a side effect of the earlier decryption step. It constructs a FormsIdentity, passing in the Forms AuthenticationTicket reference to the constructor. The FormsIdentity instance is then used to construct a GenericPrincipal.

6. GenericPrincipal is set as the value of the User property on the current HttpContext.

7. The module may update the expiration date for the ticket if sliding expirations have been enabled for forms authentication. As with step 4, when working with cookieless tickets, automatically updating the expiration date will trigger a redirect.

8. FormsAuthenticationModule sets the public SkipAuthorization property on the current HttpContext. Note that even though the module sets this property, it does not actually use it. Instead downstream managed authorization modules can inspect this property when authorizing a request. The module will set the property to true if either the configured forms authentication login page is being requested (it would not make any sense to deny access to

the application's login page), or if the current request is for the ASP.NET assembly resource handler (AssemblyResourceLoader-Integrated), which is configured in the <handlers /> configuration section of the ApplicationHost.config configuration file. The reason for the extra check for webresource.axd is that it is possible to remove the handler definition from configuration, in which case ASP.NET no longer considers webresource.axd to be a special request that should skip authorization.

Unlike WindowsAuthenticationModule, FormsAuthenticationModule sets up security information that is divorced from any information about the operating system thread identity. In some ways, forms authentication is a much easier authentication model to use because developers do not have to wrestle with the intricacies of IIS native authentication modules, UNC shares and ASP.NET's impersonation settings.

Tweaking some of the earlier samples to require forms authentication, the following output shows the results of running an application with the native AnonymousAuthenticationModule enabled in IIS and application impersonation enabled in ASP.NET.

```
The OS thread identity when the page executes is: bhaidar-PC\test
The managed thread identity when the page executes is: testuser
The managed thread identity is of type: System.Security.Principal.GenericPrincipal
The user on the HttpContext when the page executes is: testuser
The user on the HttpContext is of type: System.Security.Principal.GenericPrincipal
The request authenticated identity set by IIS is: NT AUTHORITY\NETWORK SERVICE
```

As you can see, HttpContext and the current thread reflect the GenericPrincipal that is created by FormsAuthenticationModule. The fact that application impersonation is being used is ignored, as is the value of the impersonation token set by IIS. Also notice here that, since there is no native authentication module enabled on IIS 7.0 other than the AnonymousAuthenticationModule and the managed FormsAuthenticationModule, the impersonation token generated by IIS defaults to the identity currently configured for the worker process, in this case it is the NT AUTHORITY\NETWORK SERVICE identity.

When developing with forms authentication, you probably should still be aware of the operating system thread identity because it is this identity that will be used when using some type of integrated security with back-end resources such as SQL Server. However, from a downstream authorization perspective, using forms authentication means that only the GenericPrincipal (and the contained FormsIdentity) are relevant when making authorization decisions.

DefaultAuthentication and Thread.CurrentPrincipal

Most of the sample output has included information about the identity of Thread.CurrentPrincipal and the identity on HttpContext.Current.User. However, in the previous discussions on Windows AuthenticationModule and FormsAuthenticationModule, you saw that these modules only set the value of the User property for the current context.

How then did the same IPrincipal reference make it onto the CurrentPrincipal property of the current thread? The answer lies within the ASP.NET runtime. Since ASP.NET 1.0, there has been a "hidden" pipeline event called DefaultAuthentication. This event is not publicly exposed, so as a module author you cannot directly hook the event. However, there is an ASP.NET authentication module that runs during the `DefaultAuthentication` event called `DefaultAuthentication` module. As a developer, you never explicitly configure this module. Instead when the ASP.NET runtime is initializing an application and is hooking up all of the `HttpModules` it also automatically registers the `DefaultAuthenticationModule`. As a result, this module is always running in every ASP.NET application. There is no way to "turn off" or unregister the `DefaultAuthenticationModule`.

This module provides a number of services for an ASP.NET application:

1. It exposes a public `Authenticate` event (like the other authentication modules) that a developer can hook. When running an application in the IIS integrated mode, this event is not fired. It is required to register for the `AuthenticateRequest` event instead. Subscribing to the `Authenticate` event would throw a `PlatformNotSupportedException`.

2. It provides a default behavior for failed authentication attempts.

3. The module ensures that if the `User` property has not been set yet, a `GenericPrincipal` is created and set on the current context's `User` property.

4. The module explicitly sets the `CurrentPrincipal` property of the current thread to the same value as the current context's `User` property.

Initially, `DefaultAuthenticationModule` looks at the value of `Response.StatusCode`, and if the status code is set to a value greater than 200, then the module routes the current request directly to the `End Request` pipeline event. Normally, unless a piece of code explicitly changes the value of `Response.StatusCode`, it defaults to 200 when the `Response` object is initially created. As a side effect of `Default AuthenticationModule` checking the `StatusCode`, if `DefaultAuthenticationModule` detects that `Response.StatusCode` was set to 401 (indicating an Access Denied error has occurred), the module writes out a custom 401 error message to `Response` prior to handing off the request to the `EndRequest` event.

Note that neither `WindowsAuthenticationModule` nor `FormsAuthenticationModule` sets the `StatusCode` property. So, the behavior in `DefaultAuthenticationModule` around status codes is only useful for developers who write custom authentication mechanisms that explicitly set the `StatusCode` for failed authentication attempts.

To see this behavior, look at a simple application with an `HttpModule` that hooks the `Authenticate Request` event. The module just sets the `StatusCode` property on the response to 401. The application has *only* the native `AnonymousAuthenticationModule` enabled in IIS (this prevents an IIS credentials prompt from occurring in the sample). In ASP.NET, the application has its authentication mode set to None, because the normal scenario for depending on the 401 behavior of `DefaultAuthentication Module` makes sense only when you write a custom authentication mechanism:

```
<!-- registering the HttpModule in web.config -->
<modules>
<add name="Fake401" type="ModuleThatForces401"/>
</modules>

<!-- Authentication mode in web.config is set to None --->
<authentication mode="None"/>
```

C#

```
public class ModuleThatForces401 : IHttpModule
{
  //Default implementation details left out…

    private void FakeA401(Object source, EventArgs e)
    {
        HttpContext.Current.Response.StatusCode = 401;
    }

    public void Init(HttpApplication context)
    {
        context.AuthenticateRequest += new EventHandler(this.FakeA401);
    }
}
```

VB.NET

```
Public Class ModuleThatForces401
    Implements IHttpModule
    ' Default implementation details left out…

    Private Sub FakeA401(ByVal source As Object, ByVal e As EventArgs)
        HttpContext.Current.Response.StatusCode = 401
    End Sub

#Region "IHttpModule Members"

    Public Sub Dispose() Implements IHttpModule.Dispose
        Throw New Exception("The method or operation is not implemented.")
    End Sub

    Public Sub Init(ByVal context As HttpApplication) Implements IHttpModule.Init
        AddHandler context.AuthenticateRequest, AddressOf FakeA401
    End Sub

#End Region
End Class
```

Running a website with this module results in a custom error page containing an "Access is denied" error message generated by DefaultAuthenticationModule.

The DefaultAuthenticationModule does not fire the Authenticate event when an application is running in the new IIS integrated mode. Therefore, if you want to provide custom authentication, you should develop an HttpModule and hook into the AuthenticateRequest event. Custom authentication code running in this event should create an IPrincipal and set it on the current context's User property if the custom authentication succeeds. Optionally, you can set StatusCode to 401 (or some other error code depending on the type of failure). After the managed authentication module finishes executing, DefaultAuthenticationModule runs and looks at the StatusCode of the current authenticated request and will output custom error information if a 401 is in the StatusCode. Also, any StatusCode greater than 200 will cause the module to short-circuit the request and reroute it to the EndRequest pipeline event.

If `StatusCode` is still set to 200 or lower and any custom authentication in the `AuthenticateRequest` event succeeds, the `DefaultAuthenticationModule` checks the current context's `User` property. If the `User` property is still `null` (remember that the property defaults to null back when `BeginRequest` occurs), the module constructs a `GenericPrincipal` containing a `GenericIdentity` with the following characteristics:

❑ The username is set to the empty string.

❑ The authentication type is set to the empty string.

❑ A zero-length string array is assigned as the set of roles associated with the principal.

❑ The `IsAuthenticated` property in the identity returns `false`.

The reason the module creates the `GenericPrincipal` is that most downstream authorization code expects some kind of `IPrincipal` to exist on the current `HttpContext`. If the module did not place at least a default `IPrincipal` implementation on the `User` property, developers would probably be plagued with null reference exceptions when various pieces of authorization code attempted to perform `IsInRole` checks.

After ensuring that default principal exists, the module sets `Thread.CurrentPrincipal` to the same value as `HttpContext.Current.User`. It is this behavior that automatically ensures the thread principal and the context's principal are properly synchronized. The fact that ASP.NET has an `Http Context` with a property for holding an `IPrincipal` creates the potential for an identity mismatch with the .NET Framework's convention of storing an `IPrincipal` on the current thread. Having the `DefaultAuthenticationModule` synchronize the two values ensures that developers can use either the ASP.NET coding convention (`HttpContext.Current.User`) or the .NET Framework's coding convention (`Thread.CurrentPrinicpal`) for referencing the current `IPrincipal`, and both coding styles will reference the same identity and result in the same security decisions. Another nice side effect of this synchronization is that developers using the declarative syntax for making access checks (`[PrincipalPermission(SecurityAction.Demand, Role="Administrators"]`) will also get the same behavior because `PrincipalPermission` internally performs an access check against `Thread.CurrentPrincipal` (not `HttpContext.Current.User`).

However, when an application is running in integrated mode, things are much different. Given the native `AnonymousAuthenticationModule` is enabled, native `WindowsAuthenticationModule` is enabled, ASP.NET application is configured with Windows authentication, this means `Anonymous AuthenticationModule` takes control all over the authentication. It has been mentioned above that the native `AnonymousAuthenticationModule` when it finds that there is no native User principal set yet, it creates a new Windows anonymous principal and through an integrated request processing pipeline mechanism, the value is passed to the `HttpContext.Current.User` property. Therefore, when the `DefaultAuthenticationModule` runs, it will find out that the `HttpContext.Current .User` property already assigned a value (either an authenticated or anonymous `WindowsPrincipal` instance) and hence it does nothing and exits.

PostAuthenticateRequest

This event has already been added in ASP.NET 2.0, along with most of the other Post* events in the pipeline. The two ASP.NET modules that hook this event are the managed `AnonymousIdentifica- tionModule` and `RoleManagerModule`. Of the two, only `RoleManagerModule` is actually involved in security-related work. The `AnonymousIdentificationModule` hooks `PostAuthenticateRequest` because it is early enough in the pipeline for it to issue an anonymous identifier for use with the Profile feature, but it is late enough in the pipeline that it can determine if the current user is authenticated, and thus an anonymous identifier would not be needed in that case.

Because `RoleManagerModule`, and the Role Manager feature, is covered in much more detail later in the book, I will simply say at this point that the purpose of the `RoleManagerModule` is to create a `RolePrincipal` class and set it as the value for both `HttpContext.Current.User` and `Thread.CurrentPrincipal`. The `RolePrincipal` class fulfills `IsInRole` access checks with user-to-role mappings stored using the Role Manager feature.

It is important for developers to understand that because the `PostAuthenticateRequest` event occurs *after* the `DefaultAuthenticationModule` has run, any changes made to either `HttpContext.Current.User` or `Thread.CurrentPrincipal` *will not* be automatically synchronized. For example, this is why `RoleManagerModule` has to set both the context and the thread's principals. If the module did not perform this extra work, developers would be left with two different principals and two different sets of results from calling `IPrincipal.IsInRole`.

A simple application that hooks `PostAuthenticateRequest` illustrates this subtle problem. The application uses forms authentication, which initially results in same `GenericPrincipal` on both the context's `User` property and the current principal of the thread. However, the sample application changes the principal on `HttpContext.Current.User` to a completely different value during the `PostAuthenticateRequest` event.

C#

```
//Hook PostAuthenticateRequest inside of global.asax
    void Application_PostAuthenticateRequest(Object sender, EventArgs e)
    {
        IPrincipal p = HttpContext.Current.User;

        //Only reset the principal after having logged in with
        //forms authentication.
        if (p.Identity.IsAuthenticated)
        {
            GenericIdentity gi =
                new GenericIdentity("CompletelyDifferentUser", "");
            string[] roles = new string[0];

            HttpContext.Current.User =
                new GenericPrincipal(gi, roles);

            //Ooops - forgot to sync up with Thread.CurrentPrincipal!!
        }
    }
```

VB.NET

```
    Private Sub Application_PostAuthenticateRequest(ByVal sender As Object, _
                                        ByVal e As EventArgs)

        Dim p As IPrincipal = HttpContext.Current.User

        'Only reset the principal after having logged in with
        'forms authentication.
```

```
        If p.Identity.IsAuthenticated Then
            Dim gi As New GenericIdentity("CompletelyDifferentUser", "")
            Dim roles(-1) As String

            HttpContext.Current.User = New GenericPrincipal(gi, roles)

            'Ooops - forgot to sync up with Thread.CurrentPrincipal!!
        End If

    End Sub
```

The resulting output shows the mismatch between the thread principal and the context's principal. The testuser account is the identity that was logged in with forms authentication.

```
The managed thread identity when the page executes is: testuser
The managed thread identity is of type: System.Security.Principal.GenericPrincipal
The user on the HttpContext when the page executes is: CompletelyDifferentUser
The user on the HttpContext is of type: System.Security.Principal.GenericPrincipal
The user on the HttpContext and the thread principal point at the same object:
False
```

Now in practice you would not create a new identity during PostAuthenticateRequest. However, you may have a custom mechanism for populating roles, much like the Role Manager feature, whereby the roles for a user are established after an IIdentity implementation has been created for a user. Hooking PostAuthenticateRequest is a logical choice because by this point you are guaranteed to have some type of IIdentity implementation available off of the context. But as shown previously, if you reset the principal during PostAuthenticateRequest, it is your responsibility to also set the value on Thread.CurrentPrincipal to prevent mismatches later on in the pipeline.

AuthorizeRequest

Now you will turn your attention to the portion of the pipeline that authorizes users to content and pages. As the name of the pipeline event implies, decisions on whether the current user is allowed to continue are made during this pipeline event.

ASP.NET ships with two HttpModules configured in the <httpModules /> or <modules /> section that enforce authorization:

❑   FileAuthorizationModule

❑   UrlAuthorizationModule

If you have configured the application to run in the unified integrated mode, the <modules /> section entries will take effect, else if the application is operating in the classic mode, then the old usual <httpModules /> section takes effect.

In addition, IIS adds a new native URLAuthorizationModule that you can enable to run for all content file types. Configuring this module is similar to the way you configure URLAuthorizationModule in ASP.NET. The module will be discussed shortly.

Developers can hook this event and provide their own custom authorization implementations as well, whether it is through native or managed code. By the time the AuthorizeRequest event occurs, the

`IPrincipal` references for the current context and the current thread have been set and should be stable for the remainder of the request. Although it is technically possible to change either of these identities during this event (or any other event later in the pipeline), this is not a practice you want to adopt!

FileAuthorizationModule

`FileAuthorizationModule` authorizes access to content by checking the ACLs on the underlying requested file and confirming that the current user has either read or read/write access (more on what defines the "current user" in a bit). For HEAD, GET, and POST requests, the module checks for read access. For all other verbs, the module checks for both read and write access.

Because ACL checks only make sense when working with a `WindowsIdentity`, `FileAuthorization Module` is really only useful if both of the following are true:

❑ The ASP.NET application uses Windows authentication.

❑ The ASP.NET application is not running on a UNC share.

If an ASP.NET application is running on a UNC share, `FileAuthorizationModule` does not attempt any file ACL checks. Instead it just immediately exits. The module has this behavior because UNC based ASP.NET applications run with the explicit UNC credentials. If these credentials did not have access to all of the files on the UNC share, the application would fail in IIS anyway. As a result, performing a file ACL check is redundant (the app made it far enough to start running in ASP.NET; therefore, the UNC identity has access to the share). Although configuring `FileAuthorizationModule` in `web.config` configuration file for these types of applications is innocuous, developers should probably remove `File AuthorizationModule` from their configuration files because it serves no purpose in the UNC case.

Because `FileAuthorizationModule` performs file ACL checks, it requires that a `WindowsIdentity` be available on `HttpContext.Current.User`. If some other type of `IIdentity` implementation is on the `User` property, the module automatically grants access and immediately exits. This means file ACLs are not checked when the authentication mode is set to `Forms` or `None`.

Assuming that you are using Windows authentication in ASP.NET, the question arises on how to use file ACL checks when the `AnonymousAuthenticationModule` is enabled in IIS. If your site has a mixture of public and private content, you can set more restrictive ACLs on the private content. If an unauthenticated browser user attempts to access the private content, then `FileAuthorizationModule` will force the browser to authenticate itself (more on this later). If an authenticated user is allowed access to the file, then he or she will be able to access the private content.

The user token that the `FileAuthorizationModule` uses for making the access check is the request authenticated identity set by IIS. From earlier topics, you know that in non-UNC scenarios, the request authenticated identity is either IUSR or the token associated with an authenticated browser user. This means that if you want to grant access to anonymous users, what you really need to do is set the NTFS ACLs on the filesystem to allow read (or read/write access depending the HTTP verbs being used) access to the IUSR account. If you happened to change the default anonymous user account in the IIS 7.0 Manager tool or through the `<anonymousAuthentication />` section in the `web.config` configuration file, you would grant access to whatever anonymous user account is currently configured for the application in IIS.

You can see this behavior pretty easily by explicitly denying access for IUSR when you set up the ACLs for a file. In IIS, set the application to *only* allow Anonymous access, i.e., enabling the native Anonymous

`AuthenticationModule`; this prevents IIS from attempting to negotiate an authenticated identity with the browser. Now when you try to browse to the file, `FileAuthorizationModule` will return a 401 status code and write out some custom error information stating that access is denied. If you then grant access on the file to `IUSR` again, you will be able to successfully browse to the file.

Because it is the request authenticated identity set by IIS that is used for file ACL checks by the module, other security identities are ignored by `FileAuthorizationModule`. For example, if you are using application impersonation, the operating system thread identity will be running as the application impersonation identity. Although technically nothing prevents you from using application impersonation with file authorization, application impersonation does not affect the request authenticated identity set by IIS. Because `FileAuthorizationModule` does not use the operating system thread identity for its access checks, it ignores the effects of application impersonation and instead the access checks will always be made against the anonymous or authenticated user account from IIS.

The concept to always remember when using `FileAuthorizationModule` is that only the anonymous user account from IIS or the authenticated browser user will be used for the access checks. This also means that an application needs to run with client impersonation (that is, `<identity impersonate ="true" />` for file authorization checks to really make any sense.

When `FileAuthorizationModule` determines that the identity represented by the IIS request authenticated identity does not have read (or read/write access depending on the HTTP verb used), it sets `Response.StatusCode` to 401, writes custom error information indicating that access is denied, and reroutes the request to the `EndRequest` event in the pipeline.

If the application is configured in IIS to allow authenticated access as part of the security options, when the 401 result is detected by IIS, it will attempt to negotiate an authenticated connection with the browser after the 401 occurs. If this negotiation succeeds, the next request to ASP.NET will be made as an authenticated browser identity. Of course, if the authenticated browser identity also lacks the appropriate file access, the subsequent 401 error results in the custom error information from the ASP.NET module, and no additional authentication negotiation with the browser occurs.

Managed UrlAuthorizationModule

Because an authorization strategy tightly tied to Windows security identities is not always useful for Internet-facing applications, a more generic authorization mechanism is implemented in `Url AuthorizationModule`. Based on the URL authorization rules defined in configuration, the module uses the `IPrincipal` on the `User` property of the current context to compare against the users and roles that are defined in the authorization rules. Because URL authorization works only against the `User` property and the configuration-based authorization rules, it can be used with any type of authentication that sets an `IPrincipal` on the current context's `User` property. For example, if you use Windows authentication with `UrlAuthorizationModule`, the module uses the `WindowsIdentity` in the context's `User` property in a generic fashion. The module does not "know" the extra security semantics available from Windows authenticated users. Instead, the module performs its access checks based solely off of the value of the `Name` property on the associated `IIdentity` and the results of calling `IPrincipal.IsInRole`.

As with file authorization, URL authorization also does not depend on the operating system thread identity. However, URL authorization can be used in conjunction with file authorization. Remember from previous topics though that the security identity represented by the IIS impersonation token will not necessarily match the `IPrincipal` in the `User` property on the current context. In the case of unauthenticated browser users and Windows authentication, the User property will contain a dummy principal (username set to empty string) while the request authenticated identity represents the anonymous access account configured in IIS. Because of this, be careful when mixing file and URL authorization, and keep in mind the different identities that each authorization module depends on.

Before attempting any type of authorization, UrlAuthorizationModule first checks to see if the value of HttpContext.Current.SkipAuthorization is set to true. Authentication modules have the option of setting this property to true as a hint to UrlAuthorizationModule. As mentioned earlier, one example of this is FormsAuthenticationModule, which indicates that authorization should be skipped when a user requests the forms authentication login page. If SkipAuthorization is set to true, UrlAuthorizationModule immediately exits, and no further work is performed.

The module delegates the actual work of authorizing the current User to the AuthorizationSection configuration class. This class is the root of the portion of the configuration hierarchy that defines the <authorization /> configuration element and all of the nested authorization rules. Because <authorization /> definitions can be made at the level of the machine, website, application or an individual subdirectory, the AuthorizationSection class merges the rules from the hierarchy of applicable configuration files to determine the set of rules that apply for the given page. Note that because of the merge behavior, the authorization rules defined in configuration files at the most granular configuration level take precedence. For example, this means authorization rules defined in a subdirectory are evaluated before authorization rules defined at the application level.

The default authorization rules that ship with ASP.NET are defined in the root web.config configuration file located at:

```
%windir%\Microsoft.NET\Framework\v2.0.50727\CONFIG\web.config
```

The default rules just grant access to everyone:

```
<authorization>
    <allow users="*" />
</authorization>
```

However, rules can either allow or deny access and can do so based on a combination of username, roles, and HTTP verbs. For example:

```
<allow verbs="GET" users="John Doe", role="Browser Users" />
<deny verbs="POST" />
```

After the merged set of rules have been determined, each authorization rule (defined with <allow /> or <deny /> elements) is iterated over sequentially. The result from the first authorization rule that matches either the name (User.Identity.Name) or one of the roles (User.IsInRole) is used as the authorization decision. The sequential nature of the authorization processing has two implications:

1. It is up to you to order the authorization rules in configuration so that they are evaluated in the correct order. For example, having a rule that allows access to a user based on a role precede a rule that denies access to the same user based on name results in the user always being granted access. ASP.NET does not perform any automatic rule reordering.

2. A URL authorization check is a linear walk of all authorization rules. From a performance perspective, for a specific resource or directory you should place the most commonly applicable

rules at the top of the `<authorization />` section. For example, if you need to deny access on a resource for most users, but you allow access to only a small subset of these users, it makes sense to put the `<deny />` element first because that is the most common case.

Using a simple application with a few pages, subdirectories, and authorization rules, we can get a better idea of the merge behavior and rule ordering behavior for URL authorization. The directory structure for the sample application is shown in Figure 3-7.

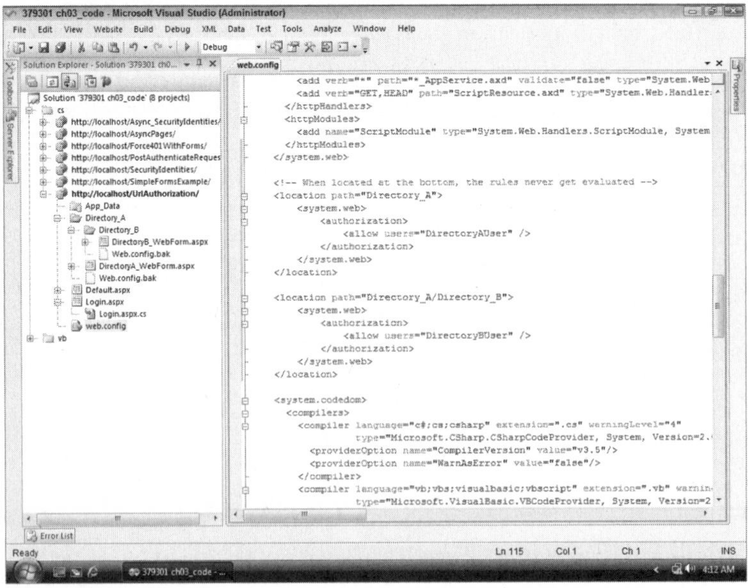

Figure 3-7

There is an `.aspx` page located in the application root, as well as in each of the two subdirectories. The application uses forms authentication, with three fixed users defined in the configuration:

```
<authentication mode="Forms" >
    <forms>
        <credentials passwordFormat="Clear">
            <user name="Admin" password="password"/>
            <user name="DirectoryAUser" password="password"/>
            <user name="DirectoryBUser" password="password"/>
        </credentials>
    </forms>
</authentication>
```

The `web.config` configuration file located in the root of the application initially defines authorization rules as:

```
<authorization>
    <allow users="Admin"/>
    <deny users="*" />
</authorization>
```

When attempting to browse to any page in the application, you must log in as the `Admin` user to successfully reach the page. However, you can add a `web.config` configuration file into Directory A with the following authorization rule:

```
<authorization>
    <allow users="DirectoryAUser" />
</authorization>
```

Now both the `Admin` user and the `DirectoryAUser` can access the web page located in Directory A. The reason for this is that, as mentioned earlier, `AuthorizationSection` merges authorization rules from the bottom up. The result of defining rules in a `web.config` configuration file located in a subdirectory as well as in the application's `web.config` configuration file is the following evaluation order:

1. First, rules from Directory A are evaluated.

2. If no match is found based on the combination of verbs, users and roles, then the rules from the application's `web.config` configuration file are evaluated.

3. If no match was found using the application's `web.config` configuration file, then the root `web.config` configuration file located in the framework `CONFIG` directory is evaluated. Remember that the default authorization configuration grants access to all users.

With this evaluation order, `DirectoryAUser` matches the rule defined in the `web.config` configuration file located in Directory A. However, for the `Admin` user, no rules matched, so instead the rules in the application's `web.config` configuration file are consulted.

Now add a third `web.config` configuration file, this time dropping it into Directory B. This configuration file defines the following authorization rule:

```
<authorization>
    <allow users="DirectoryBUser" />
</authorization>
```

Because the evaluation order for accessing pages in Directory B will first reference the `web.config` configuration file from Directory B, the `DirectoryBUser` has access to files in the directory. If you log in though with `DirectoryAUser`, you will find that you can still access the files in Directory B. The reason is that when there is a rule evaluation miss from the `web.config` configuration file in Directory B, ASP.NET moves up the configuration hierarchy to next available `web.config` configuration file—in this case, the one located in Directory A. Because that `web.config` configuration file grants access to `DirectoryAUser`, that user can also access all resources in Directory B. The same effect of hierarchal configuration evaluation allows the `Admin` user access to the all resources in Directory B because the application's `web.config` configuration file grants access to `Admin`.

You can also get the same effect, and still centralize authorization rules in a single configuration file, by using `<location />` configuration elements. Using `<location />` tags, the authorization rules for the subdirectories are instead defined in the application's main `web.config` configuration file:

```
<system.web>
  <authorization>
    <allow users="Admin"/>
    <deny users="*" />
  </authorization>
</system.web>
```

```
<location path="Directory_A">
  <system.web>
    <authorization>
        <allow users="DirectoryAUser" />
    </authorization>
  </system.web>
</location>

<location path="Directory_A/Directory_B">
  <system.web>
    <authorization>
        <allow users="DirectoryBUser" />
    </authorization>
  </system.web>
</location>
```

You will have the exact the same login behavior as described earlier when using separate web.config configuration files. The configuration system treats each <location /> tag as a logically separate "configuration" file. The end result is that even though the authorization rules are defined in the same physical web.config configuration file, the <location /> tags preserve the hierarchal nature of the configuration definitions.

Developers sometimes want to control configuration in a central configuration file for an entire web server but are unsure of the value to use for the path attribute when referencing individual web applications. For example, if you want to centrally define configuration for an application called "Test" located in the Default Web Site in IIS, you can use the following <location /> definition:

```
<location path="Default Web Site/Test" />
```

So far, the sample application has demonstrated the hierarchal merge behavior of different configuration files and different <location /> elements. If the authorization rule for the Admin user is reversed with the deny rule:

```
<authorization>
    <deny users="*" />
    <allow users="Admin"/>
</authorization>
```

the Admin user can no longer access any of the pages. The behavior for DirectoryBUser and DirectoryA User remains the same because the other <location /> elements grant these users access. But when the last set of authorization rules are evaluated, the blanket <deny /> is evaluated first. As a result, any authorization evaluation that reaches this <authorization /> element always results in access being denied.

Note that even though the previous samples relied on authorizing based on the user's name; the same logic applies when authorizing based on verb or based on a set of one or more roles.

Of course, what cannot be shown here (but you will see the behavior if you download and try out the sample) is the behavior when UrlAuthorizationModule denies access to a user. When the module denies access, it sets Response.StatusCode to 401, writes out some custom error text in the response, and then short circuits the request by rerouting it to the EndRequest event (basically, the same behavior as the FileAuthorizationModule). However, for those of you that have used URL authorization before, you know that typically you do not see an access denied error page. Instead, in the case of forms authentication, the browser user is redirected to the login page configured for forms authentication. If an application is using Windows authentication and configured to run in the Classic mode, the 401 is a signal to IIS to attempt to negotiate credentials with the browser based on the application's security settings in IIS. If, however, the application is configured to run in the new Intgrated mode and Windows authentication is enabled, the user will get the chance to see the error text on the screen. Again this is because the application is running in the unified processing pipeline. When the AuthorizeReqesut event fires IIS runtime checks the configured authorization modules. If a native authorization module is enabled, IIS core engine starts executing it and if there is a managed authorization module enabled, ASP.NET will take care of processing the authorization process, let it be file or URL authorization

How Character Sets Affect URL Authorization

The character set used to populate the IPrincipal on the context's User property plays an important role when authorizing access with UrlAuthorizationModule. When performing an access check based on the users attribute defined for an authorization rule, UrlAuthorizationModule performs a case-insensitive string comparison with the value from HttpContext.Current.User.Name. Furthermore, the comparison is made using the casing rules for the invariant culture and ordering rules based on ordinal sort ordering.

Because of this, there may be subtle mismatches in character comparisons due to a different character set being used for the value of a username. For example, the Membership feature in ASP.NET 3.5 stores usernames in a SQL Server database by default. If a website selects a different collation order than the default Latin collation, the character comparison rules that are applied at user creation time will not be the same as the comparison rules UrlAuthorizationModule applies when comparing usernames.

Overall though, there are two simple approaches to avoid any problems caused by using different character sets for user creation and user authorization:

- ❑ Do not authorize based on usernames. Instead, only authorize based on roles because the likelihood of any organization creating two role names that differ only in characters with culture-specific semantics is extremely low.

- ❑ Use a character set/collation order in your back-end user store that is a close match with the invariant culture. For SQL Server, the default Latin collation is a pretty close approximation of the invariant culture. If you are authorizing against WindowsIdentity instances, then you won't encounter a problem because usernames in Active Directory are just plain Unicode strings without culture-specific character handling.

Native UrlAuthorizationModule

IIS 7.0 introduces a new native URLAuthorizationModule that allows administrators or developers to configure URL authorization for an entire application or for a single page within the application. It is a much advanced and improved module over the previous authorization modules that used to ship with previous releases of IIS. Before the days of IIS 7.0, authorization was based on ACLs and Windows accounts only. This means that when you want to set authorization rules for Windows users or groups on resources in an application, you would configure ACLs for specific files or folders located in an application. Depending on ACLs only, limits the authorization to files and folder only, without being able to use this feature for real URLs. In addition, in previous releases of IIS, only Windows accounts or groups can be used for file or folder authorization.

The new native `URLAuthorizationModule` introduced by IIS 7.0 has many features:

❑ It can be used to enable authorization for all content types served by IIS. This means, you can enable the new module to authorize access for an entire application regardless of the content file types included inside it.

❑ It enables authorization rules for both Windows and non-Windows user accounts. Non-Windows user accounts can be users configured with the application's ASP.NET Membership and Role management services.

❑ It can be used to enable authorization for an entire application or for a specific page URL within an application.

❑ It has the ability to function properly when the managed `FormsAuthenticationModule` is enabled. The native `URLAuthorizationModule` can detect and parse `FormsAuthenticion Tickets`, hence being able to retrieve the authenticated `username` of the current request and execute the authorization rules to authorize the currently authenticated user.

IIS 7.0 supports the new native module by shipping a new authorization rules UI interface. Selecting an application in the Features View of IIS, you will notice a new icon called Authorization Rules. Figure 3-8 shows the new UI displayed when the Authorization Rules icon is double-clicked.

Figure 3-8

On the Actions menu you see two links to configure the authorization rules for an application. The Add Allow Rule… is used to add a new `Allow` authorization rule to *allow* a user or group to access the application. On the other hand, the Add Deny Rule… is used to provide a `Deny` rule to prevent a user or group from accessing the application.

Both links have a similar UI window. The only difference is that one will add an `Allow` rule and the other will add a `Deny` rule.

Figure 3-9 shows the UI window that ships with IIS 7.0 to configure URL authorization rules.

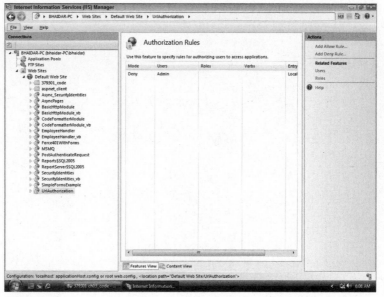

Figure 3-9

You can add URL authorization rules based on the following criteria:

❑   To allow all users to access the application

❑   To allow only anonymous users to access the application

❑   To allow specific role(s) or group(s) to access the application. You can specify multiple roles or users separated by a comma (,) and can be mixed between Windows groups and ASP.NET roles.

❑   To allow specific users to access the application. You can specify multiple users separated by a comma (,) and can be mixed between Windows users and ASP.NET Membership users.

You can also apply the rule you add to a specific verb by setting the value of the last textbox on the UI window.

If you look back at Figure 3-9, you will notice two handy links to add ASP.NET users and roles. If you have already enabled membership and role management services in an application, you will be able to view the list of all users and roles that are stored in the database of the application. Figure 3-10 shows a listing of users that are configured in the application.

These steps show you how to configure URL authorization for an entire application. What if you want to configure URL authorization for a single page? This task has been made easy with the new native authorization module. Click the application name on the tree of applications in the IIS 7.0 Manager tool, and then click the Content View tab. A list of all the resources inside the application is listed. Right-click the specific resource and choose Switch to Features View. You will see a new node with the resource name selected underneath the application on the tree of applications. Clicking this new node enables you to configure different features per resource in IIS 7.0. You can now follow the same steps taken above to add authorization rules for the specific resource in the application.

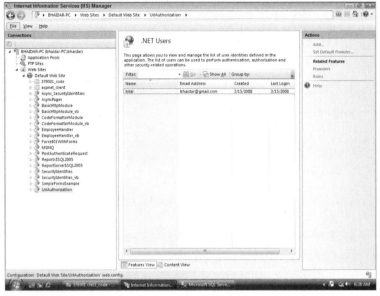

Figure 3-10

Figure 3-11 shows the Features view for a specific selected resource.

Figure 3-11

The new native `URLAuthorization` module can also be configured using the `web.config` configuration file of an application. The `<authorization />` section located inside the `<security />` section group in the `<system.webServer />` section group is used to configure URL authorization for an application or a single page inside the `web.config` configuration file.

Figure 3-12 shows the hierarchy of a sample application that is used to demonstrate configuring native URL authorization through configuration settings.

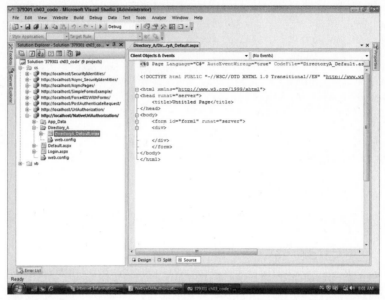

Figure 3-12

The application assumes the following settings:

❑ `AnonymousAuthenticationModule` is enabled on IIS.

❑ `BasicAuthenticationModule` is enabled on IIS.

In addition, two new Windows accounts have been created: `bhaidar` and `test`. These accounts will be used with the basic authentication. The plan is to allow `bhaidar` to access the entire application and deny access to the `test` account. In addition, the `DirectoryA_Default.aspx` page should allow access to the `test` user account *only*.

To add the configuration settings, you can either use the IIS Manager tool or add the configuration settings yourself into the `web.config` configuration file. We will select the second option for demonstration purposes.

First of all make sure the native `URLAuthorizationModule` is installed. Go to the application's `web.config` configuration file and locate the `<system.webServer />` section group. You will need to add a sub-section group called the `<security />` section group. To enable URL authorization, you will need to add the rules inside the `<authorization />` section.

```
<system.webServer>
        <security>
               <authorization>
               <remove users="*" roles="" verbs="" />
                        <add accessType="Allow" users="bhaidar" />
               <add accessType="Deny" users="test" />
               </authorization>
        </security>
</system.webServer>
```

First of all, the default URL authorization rule added by IIS 7.0 is removed. To remove the default rule completely, make sure to empty the `roles` and `verbs` attributes, and set * as the value for the `users` attribute. Removing the authorization rule allows all users to access the application.

A new authorization rule is added to allow access to the Windows user account `bhaidar`. The `access Type` attribute is an enumeration that can take as a value either `Allow` or `Deny`. Another authorization rule is added that denies the user `test`.

Inside the `Directory_A`, add a new `web.config` configuration file to configure the authorization rules for the only .aspx page included inside it.

```
<location path="DirectoryA_Default.aspx">
    <system.webServer>
        <security>
            <authorization>
                <remove users="bhaidar" roles="" verbs="" />
                <remove users="test" roles="" verbs="" />
                <add accessType="Allow" users="test" />
            </authorization>
        </security>
    </system.webServer>
</location>
```

A new location element is created to configure the authorization settings for a single .aspx page. Going back to the requirements, *only* the `test` user account should be allowed access to this .aspx page. Therefore, two new authorization rules are added to remove the propagating effect of the authorization rule that was set at the application level and that grants access to the `bhaidar` user account. In addition, you should also remove the propagation effect of the authorization rule that denies access to the `test` account set on the application level. Finally, add a new authorization rule that allows access to the `test` user account on the .aspx page.

A major difference between the managed URL authorization and the native URL authorization can be summarized in the following:

❑ **Managed URL authorization is configured by default to serve only managed resources, whereas the native URL authorization is enabled to serve all content types.** This can be solved by removing the managed `URLAuthorizationModule` entry and adding it once again by skipping out the `preCondition` attribute or setting its value to an empty string (double quotes).

❑ **Managed URL authorization starts calculating the authorization rules following the *Bottom-up* strategy that has been previously explained.** On the other hand, the native URL authorization calculates the authorization rules following the *top-down* strategy meaning that authorization rules at the parent will be evaluated first. In addition, the native URLAuthorizationModule evaluates Deny rules before evaluating the Allow rules.

IIS will execute the enabled modules according to their order of appearance when they were registered in the <module /> configuration section with the exception of programmatic ordering that only native modules can do. The same rule applies on the managed and native URLAuthorizationModules. Depending on the order of appearance, those modules would execute. The important thing to remember here is that no matter who runs and executes first, any of the aforementioned modules, if the authorization process fails, the SkipAuthorization property on the HttpContext class will be set to true. For instance, if the native module runs first and the authorization process fails, when it is time for the managed module to run, it will check the SkipAuthorization property. If the value is true, then the managed module will not run, else it will run and authorize the request.

PostAuthorizeRequest Through PreRequestHandlerExecute

After the AuthorizeRequest event, developers can hook the PostAuthorizeRequest event if there is custom authorization work that needs to be performed. ASP.NET does not ship with any HttpModules that hook this event. After PostAuthorizeRequest, there are no other pipeline events intended for authentication- or authorization-related processing. Although many of the subsequent pipeline events may use the identity of the current user, the pipeline events up through PreRequestHandlerExecute are intended for setting up and initializing other information, such as session state data or cached information used by output and fragment caching.

Technically, you could manipulate the operating system thread identity, the current thread principal, or the current context's User property during any subsequent pipeline event. However, there is an implicit assumption that after PostAuthenticateRequest the security information for the request is stable, and that after PostAuthorizeRequest no additional authorization is necessary. Because the pipeline events after PostAuthorizeRequest are involved in retrieving data tied to a user identity (state and cached data), it is important that any custom authentication or authorization mechanism honors these assumptions.

Blocking Requests at the IIS Level

IIS 7.0 replaces the old URLScan security add-on with a new native module, RequestFiltering module. The new module is configurable through the configuration settings just like any other native module configured in the ApplicationHost.config configuration file. The module includes all the core features of the URLScan add-on and adds a new feature called Hidden Segments.

If you open the ApplicationHost.config configuration file, you will notice the <requestFiltering /> configuration section group:

```
<security>
    <requestFiltering>
        <fileExtensions allowUnlisted="true">
```

```
                    <add fileExtension=".asax" allowed="false" />
                    <add fileExtension=".ascx" allowed="false" />
                    <add fileExtension=".master" allowed="false" />
                    . . . . .
                    <add fileExtension=".cs" allowed="false" />
                    <add fileExtension=".vsdisco" allowed="false" />
                </fileExtensions>
                <verbs allowUnlisted="true" />
                <hiddenSegments>
                    <add segment="web.config" />
                    <add segment="bin" />
                    <add segment="App_code" />
                    <add segment="App_GlobalResources" />
                    <add segment="App_LocalResources" />
                    <add segment="App_WebReferences" />
                    <add segment="App_Data" />
                    <add segment="App_Browsers" />
                </hiddenSegments>
            </requestFiltering>
        </security>
```

The `<fileExtensions />` configuration section lists all the file extensions that are not allowed to be accessed directly by users. For instance, you may notice an entry for the `.ascx` extension, which represents the extension for ASP.NET `UserControls`.

In addition, the `allowUnlisted` attribute is a `Boolean` value, which takes either `false` or `true`. By default, it has the value of `true`. This means the `<fileExtensions />` configuration section allows requests to all the file types except those listed inside it.

The `RequestFiltering` module runs before any request-processing pipeline happens inside the IIS engine. That is why ASP.NET now delegates preventing access to sensitive file type extensions to this native module. This is done by listing all the file type extensions for which ASP.NET has configured `HttpHandlers` to prevent access.

As with other configuration sections, you can configure the file extensions from inside the application's `web.config` configuration file. For instance, to prevent access to content file types with an extension of `.asp`, you add the following to the configuration file:

```
<system.webServer>
        <security>
                <requestFiltering>
                        <fileExtensions allowUnlisted="true">
                                <add allowed="false" fileExtension=".asp"/>
                        </fileExtensions>
                </requestFiltering>
        </security>
</system.webServer>
```

When a resource with an extension of `.asp` is requested through the browser, an error page prepared by the IIS engine is displayed to the user, as shown in Figure 3-13.

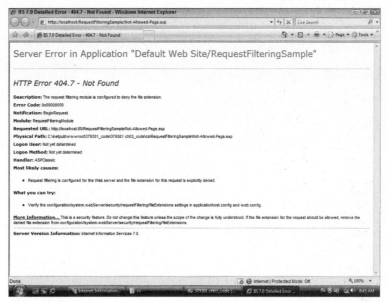

Figure 3-13

You have full control over the allowed and prevented extensions in an application. But remember that the `<requestFilering />` configuration section group is locked down by default and to be able to edit its sections in the application's `web.config` configuration file, the module's `overrideModeDefault` attribute should be set to `Allow` in the `ApplicationHost.config` configuration file.

```
<section name="requestFiltering" overrideModeDefault="Allow" />
```

Another important configuration section inside the `<requestFiltering />` configuration section group is the `<hiddenSegments />` section. You can use this section to reject URLs that contain certain segments. For instance, if you try to access a URL such as `http://localhost/Request FilteringSample/bin/`, you will get an error page prepared by IIS that mentions the existence of a `hiddenSegment` that denies access to URLs containing the `bin` segment. In addition, all ASP.NET system folders are added to this section and considered to be sensitive segments that no URL should have direct access to. You can also add any segment you want to the default list found in the `ApplicationHost.config` configuration file. IIS makes sure to reject any direct access to the hidden segments specified.

The `RequestFiltering` module has several important security features that are worth looking at. You can read more on this new native module by checking the online resource at `http://learn.iis.net/page.aspx/143/how-to-use-request-filtering/`.

Identity during Asynchronous Page Execution

Earlier in the chapter, I discussed issues with flowing security identities through asynchronous pipeline event handlers. The `Page` handler in ASP.NET 3.5 also supports the concept of asynchronous execution, and as a result, developers using this functionality should be aware of the security identities for this case.

Things can be a little confusing with asynchronous pages because the `Page` class supports two different patterns for carrying out asynchronous tasks. Both approaches, along with the flow of security information, are discussed in the next two sections.

Asynchronous PreRender Processing

A developer can request asynchronous support in a page by including the `Async` attribute in the page directive:

C#

```
<%@ Page Language="C#" Async="true" %>
```

VB.NET

```
<%@ Page Language="VB" Async="true" %>
```

To leverage this asynchronous page model, you need to register `begin` and `end` event handlers for your asynchronous task. This approach is exactly the same model as discussed earlier for asynchronous pipeline events. You typically hook up the async `begin` and `end` event handlers inside of a page or control event where a long-running task would normally occur. For example, instead of making a call to a high-latency Web Service from inside of a button click event handler, you would instead register your asynchronous event handlers in the click event handler. Furthermore, you can hook up multiple `begin` and `end` event handlers, and ASP.NET will call each pair of asynchronous event handlers in sequence.

ASP.NET calls into your async `begin` event handler after the `PreRender` phase of the page life cycle. The idea is that high-latency work can be safely deferred until the `PreRender` phase because the results of any processing are not needed until the subsequent `Render` phase of a `Page`. Inside of your async `begin` event handler, you collect whatever data you need to pass to your asynchronous task (page variables, context data, and so on), and then you invoke the asynchronous task. As with asynchronous pipeline events, the asynchronous task that is called during asynchronous page processing runs on a .NET thread-pool thread. This means it is your responsibility to gather any necessary security information and "throw it over the wall" to the asynchronous task.

After some indeterminate amount of time has passed, the asynchronous task completes and the ASP.NET runtime is signaled via a callback. Just as you saw with asynchronous pipeline events, the async `end` event for pages executes on a thread-pool thread. The operating system thread identity at this point will not reflect the security settings you have set in IIS and ASP.NET. Note though that if you implement your async `begin` and `end` event handlers as part of the page's code-behind class, you can always get back to the `HttpContext` associated with the page (that is, `this.Context` is available). This at least gives you access to the `IPrincipal` associated with the request from inside of both the async `begin` and `end` event handlers.

After the `end` event handler runs, ASP.NET reschedules the page for execution, at which point ASP.NET reinitializes the operating system thread identity, managed thread identity, and the `HttpContext` (including its associated `IPrincipal`) for the current managed thread.

To demonstrate the security identity handling during asynchronous page execution, you can create an application with a single asynchronous page that registers for asynchronous `PreRender` handling. The page has a single button on it, and the application registers the async `begin` and `end` event handlers in its click event.

C#

```
protected void Button1_Click(object sender, EventArgs e)
{
    //Hook up the async begin and end events
    BeginEventHandler bh = new BeginEventHandler(this.BeginAsyncPageProcessing);
    EndEventHandler eh = new EndEventHandler(this.EndAsyncPageProcessing);

    AddOnPreRenderCompleteAsync(bh, eh);
}
```

VB.NET

```
Protected Sub Button1_Click(ByVal sender As Object, ByVal e As EventArgs)
    'Hook up the async begin and end events
    Dim bh As New BeginEventHandler(AddressOf Me.BeginAsyncPageProcessing)
    Dim eh As New EndEventHandler(AddressOf Me.EndAsyncPageProcessing)

    AddOnPreRenderCompleteAsync(bh, eh)
End Sub
```

Notice that the event handler delegates are of the exact same type used with asynchronous pipeline events. The async `begin` handler is responsible for triggering the asynchronous work and returns the `IAsyncResult` reference to ASP.NET.

C#

```
// Defined as part of the page class
public delegate void AsyncSleepDelegate();

private IAsyncResult BeginAsyncPageProcessing(
    object sender, EventArgs e, AsyncCallback cb, object extraData)
{
    //Output the security information
    //.. code snipped out for brevity …

    //Do the actual asynchronous work
    Sleep s = new Sleep(this.Context.Items);
    AsyncSleepDelegate asd = new AsyncSleepDelegate(s.DoWork);
    return asd.BeginInvoke(cb, asd);
}
```

VB.NET

```
' Defined as part of the page class
Public Delegate Sub AsyncSleepDelegate()

Private Function BeginAsyncPageProcessing(ByVal sender As Object, _
            ByVal e As EventArgs, _
            ByVal cb As AsyncCallback, _
            ByVal extraData As Object) _
            As IAsyncResult


    'Output the security information
```

```
'.. code snipped out for brevity …

'Do the actual asynchronous work
Dim s As New Sleep(Me.Context.Items)
Dim asd As New AsyncSleepDelegate(AddressOf s.DoWork)
Return asd.BeginInvoke(cb, asd)
End Function
```

The async end event handler in the sample application just outputs more security identity information. In a real application, you would gather the results of the asynchronous work and probably set the values of various controls on the page or perhaps data-bind the results to one of the data controls.

C#

```csharp
private void EndAsyncPageProcessing(IAsyncResult ar)
{
    //Normally you would harvest the results of async processing here
    AsyncSleepDelegate asd = (AsyncSleepDelegate)ar.AsyncState;
    asd.EndInvoke(ar);

    //Output security information
    //.. code snipped out for brevity …
}
```

VB.NET

```vbnet
Private Sub EndAsyncPageProcessing(ByVal ar As IAsyncResult)
    'Normally you would harvest the results of async processing here
    Dim asd As AsyncSleepDelegate = CType(ar.AsyncState, AsyncSleepDelegate)
    asd.EndInvoke(ar)

    'Output the security information
    '.. code snipped out for brevity …

End Sub
```

As with the asynchronous pipeline event sample, the asynchronous page uses a simple class that sleeps for one second to simulate a long-running task. A reference to the current `HttpContext` is passed in the constructor so that the class can log the operating system thread identity.

C#

```csharp
public class Sleep
{
    private IDictionary state;

    public Sleep(IDictionary appState)
    {
        state = appState;
    }

    public void DoWork()
    {
        state["AsyncWorkerClass_OperatingSystemThreadIdentity"] =
```

```
                       WindowsIdentity.GetCurrent().Name;
           Thread.Sleep(1000);
       }
   }
```

VB.NET

```
Public Class Sleep
    Private state As IDictionary


    Public Sub New(ByVal appState As IDictionary)
        state = appState
    End Sub

    Public Sub DoWork()
        state("AsyncWorkerClass_OperatingSystemThreadIdentity") = _
            WindowsIdentity.GetCurrent().Name()
        Thread.Sleep(1000)
    End Sub

End Class
```

I ran the sample application with the following IIS and ASP.NET configuration settings:

1. The application ran locally on the web server.

2. Authenticated access was required in IIS.

3. An explicit application impersonation identity was used for ASP.NET.

The results of running the application with this configuration are shown here:

```
The OS thread identity during the beginning of page async processing is:
bhaidar-PC\test
The OS thread identity in the async worker class is: NT AUTHORITY\NETWORK SERVICE
The OS thread identity during the end of page async processing is: NT AUTHORITY\
NETWORK SERVICE
The OS thread identity in Render is: bhaidar-PC\test
```

You can see that the background worker and the end event run with the default credentials of the process, despite the fact that the ASP.NET application is configured with application impersonation. Once the page starts running again in the Render event, though, ASP.NET has reinitialized all of the security information, and the application impersonation identity is once again used for the operating system thread identity. The exact same approaches for flowing credentials discussed earlier in the section "Thread Identity and Asynchronous Pipeline Events" also apply to the asynchronous PreRender processing.

Asynchronous Page Using PageAsyncTask

An alternative approach to attributing a page as being is the concept of asynchronous page tasks. This second approach has many similarities to the previous discussion. As a developer, you still need to delegate your high-latency work as a piece of asynchronous processing. Additionally, you hook into the PageAsyncTask-based processing with a pair of begin and end event handlers.

However, there are some important differences in the `PageAsyncTask` approach. You can create one or more asynchronous units of work, wrap each piece of work with individual `PageAsyncTask` instances, and then hand all of the work off as a single "package" to the page. With the `PreRender`-based approach, handling multiple asynchronous tasks is a little more awkward because you either have to coalesce all of the work yourself inside of a custom class, or you have to carefully hook up a chain of `begin` and `end` event handlers.

Also, when you are wrapping your asynchronous work, you can pass a timeout handler to the `PageAsyncTask` that will execute if your asynchronous work takes too long. The actual timeout that is honored for each piece of asynchronous work defaults to 45 seconds, though this can be changed by setting the `AsyncTimeout` property on the page, or by setting an application-wide default in the `<pages />` configuration section. There is also an option to allow all or some of the asynchronous work to execute in parallel. For example, if a web page required three lengthy web service calls to fetch data, you could indicate to ASP.NET that all three asynchronous tasks should be kicked off in parallel on separate worker threads.

Once you have wrapped your asynchronous task with one or more instances of `PageAsyncTask`, you register the instances with the `Page` using the `RegisterAsyncTask` method. At this point, you have one of two options: you can do nothing else, in which case ASP.NET will call your asynchronous work immediately after the `PreRender` event. You can also take control of exactly when you want the page to stop normal processing by explicitly calling the `ExecuteRegisteredAsyncTasks` method. Personally, I think it is more intuitive to explicitly trigger asynchronous processing in a click event handler, as opposed to waiting for the default `PreRender` processing.

Up to this point, the differences between `PageAsycTask`-based processing and the default `PreRender` processing have all been in the area of programmability and flexibility. The interesting security behavior around `PageAsyncTask`-based processing is that ASP.NET will actually reinitialize the operating system thread identity, managed thread identity, and `HttpContext` for the *end event handler*. Note that you are still responsible for flowing security information to your asynchronous work, but now ASP.NET at least ensures a balanced set of security information in both the `begin` and `end` event handlers.

To highlight this behavior, modify the `PreRender` example to instead use a `PageAsyncTask`. The only difference is that the button click handler has been modified:

C#

```csharp
protected void Button1_Click(object sender, EventArgs e)
{
    //Hook up the async begin and end events
    //using the PageAsyncTask pattern
    BeginEventHandler bh =
        new BeginEventHandler(this.BeginAsyncPageProcessing);
    EndEventHandler eh =
        new EndEventHandler(this.EndAsyncPageProcessing);

    Object someState = new Object();
    PageAsyncTask pt = new PageAsyncTask(bh, eh, null, someState);

    this.RegisterAsyncTask(pt);

    //Explicitly trigger the async page task at this point
```

```
        //rather than waiting for PreRender to occur
        this.ExecuteRegisteredAsyncTasks();
    }
```

VB.NET

```vbnet
    Protected Sub Button1_Click(ByVal sender As Object, ByVal e As EventArgs)
        'Hook up the async begin and end events
        'using the PageAsyncTask pattern
        Dim bh As New BeginEventHandler(AddressOf Me.BeginAsyncPageProcessing)
        Dim eh As New EndEventHandler(AddressOf Me.EndAsyncPageProcessing)

        Dim someState As New Object()
        Dim pt As New PageAsyncTask(bh, eh, Nothing, someState)

        Me.RegisterAsyncTask(pt)

        'Explicitly trigger the async page task at this point
        'rather than waiting for PreRender to occur
        Me.ExecuteRegisteredAsyncTasks()
    End Sub
```

Notice that the begin and end event handlers use the same definitions. However, instead of calling AddOnPreRenderCompleteAsync, the page wraps the event handlers in an instance of PageAsyncTask (in this case, no timeout event handler is registered) and registers the asynchronous task with the page. Last, the button click event handler explicitly triggers the execution of the asynchronous work.

Everything else in the sample application remains the same. Running with the same IIS and ASP.NET configuration as before (local application, application impersonation enabled, authenticated access required in IIS), the output looks like this:

```
The OS thread identity during the beginning of page async processing is:
bhaidar-PC\test
The OS thread identity in the async worker class is: NT AUTHORITY\NETWORK SERVICE
The OS thread identity during the end of page async processing is: bhaidar-PC\test
The OS thread identity in Render is: bhaidar-PC\test
```

As you can see, the third line of output with the operating system thread identity shows that ASP.NET has restored the application impersonation identity on the thread. Although it is not shown in the output, the IPrincipal available from both Thread.CurrentPrincipal and the context's User property correctly reflect the authenticated user in both the begin and end event handlers. Remember, though, that you cannot rely on the value of Thread.CurrentPrincipal in the asynchronous work itself for the reasons discussed earlier in the asynchronous pipeline section.

EndRequest

The EndRequest event is the last event in the unified request-processing pipeline. Once a request starts running in the pipeline, situations can occur that result in termination of the request. As a result, EndRequest is the only pipeline event that is guaranteed to occur after BeginRequest. Terminating a request usually results in bypassing all remaining pipeline events and going directly to EndRequest, with the exception introduced in ASP.NET 3.5, which is the LogRequest event that will also get fired even if an error occurred in the processing of the current request.

If you remember the discussion of the `AuthenticateRequest` and `AuthorizeRequest` events, `DefaultAuthenticationModule`, `FileAuthorizationModule`, and `UrlAuthorizationModule` all have the capability to forward a request directly to the `EndRequest` event.

Because `EndRequest` is guaranteed to always run, it is a convenient place in the pipeline to perform cleanup tasks or final processing that absolutely must run at the completion of a request. Aside from security-related processing, `EndRequest` is also used by other ASP.NET code such as the `Session StateModule` to ensure that session teardown and persistence always occur.

For security purposes, the event is used by `FormsAuthenticationModule` to carry out custom actions when an unauthenticated user attempts to access a protected resource. The `FormsAuthentication Module` relies on the value of `Response.StatusCode` to determine whether any special end request processing is necessary. Because forms authentication is the most common authentication mode used for Internet-facing ASP.NET sites, we will concentrate on what the `FormsAuthenticationModule` does during this event.

During `AuthenticateRequest`, the `FormsAuthenticationModule` is only concerned with verifying the forms authentication ticket and attaching a `FormsIdentity` to the current `HttpContext`. However, you know that the forms authentication feature supports the ability to automatically redirect unauthenticated users to a login page. `FormsAuthenticationModule` supports this functionality by checking the `Response.StatusCode` property for each request during `EndRequest`. If it sees that `StatusCode` is set to 401 (and, of course, if the authentication mode is set to forms), then the module fetches the currently configured redirect URL for logins and appends to it a query-string variable called `ReturnUrl`. This query-string variable is assigned the value of the currently requested path plus any query string variables associated with the current request. Then `FormsAuthenticationModule` issues a redirect to the browser telling it to navigate to the redirect URL.

Although `FormsAuthenticationModule` itself never sets a 401 status code, you saw earlier that both `FileAuthorizationModule` and `UrlAuthorizationModule` will set a 401 status code if either module determines that the user for the current request does not have access to the requested resource.

As an extremely simple example, if you author a page on a site that is configured with forms authentication and put the following code in the Load event:

```
Response.StatusCode = 401;
```

After the page completes, the browser is redirected to the forms authentication login page because of the 401. In a production application though you would use a custom HTTP module or hook one of the `Authenticate` events and set the `StatusCode` there instead.

Summary

On each ASP.NET request, there are four different security identities to be aware of:

- ❑ The operating system thread identity.
- ❑ The request authenticated identity set by IIS.
- ❑ The `IPrincipal` available on `Thread.CurrentPrincipal`.
- ❑ The `IPrincipal` available from `HttpContext.Current.User`

If you are using Windows authentication in your ASP.NET application, then the impersonation token from IIS is used to create a `WindowsIdentity` for both the current thread and the current context. If the current request is an anonymous user, then the `WindowsIdentity` is just the value of `WindowsIdentity` `.GetAnonymous`. For authenticated users, the `WindowsIdentity` represents the authenticated user credentials from the IIS impersonation token. For applications running on a UNC share, the `Windows Identity` that is created represents either the anonymous user account configured in IIS or the credentials that were used to authenticate the user.

If you are using forms authentication, though, the impersonation token set by IIS has no bearing on the security information set on the thread and the context. Instead, for authenticated users, the `FormsAuthenticationModule` will create a `GenericPrincipal` containing a `FormsIdentity` and set this value on the current context's `User` property.

If no authentication module sets an `IPrincipal` on the current context's user property, the hidden `DefaultAuthenticationModule` will create a `GenericPrincipal` with a username set to the empty string and set this value on the current context's `User` property. This module is also responsible for synchronizing the value of the `User` property with `Thread.CurrentPrincipal`.

The operating system thread identity starts out as the identity of the IIS6 worker process. However, if the ASP.NET application is running locally and is using client impersonation, then ASP.NET uses the IIS impersonation token to switch the operating system thread identity. If the application is running on a UNC share though, then the operating system thread identity is that of the explicit UNC credentials configured in IIS. If application impersonation is used (regardless of running on a UNC share), ASP.NET switches the operating system thread identity to match the credentials of the application impersonation account.

After all of the security identity information is established, developers still need to be careful when dealing with asynchronous pipeline events and asynchronous page handling. The main thing to remember is that you need to pass any required security information over to the asynchronous tasks. Neither ASP.NET nor the .NET Framework will automatically propagate security identities to asynchronous tasks, though there are some .NET Framework classes that make it pretty easy to accomplish this.

Furthermore, a new native module has been introduced in IIS 7.0 named `RequestFiltering` module that allows administrators and developers, at the IIS level, to block access to requests based on the file type extensions. The extensions can be existing ones like `.asp`, `.aspx`, `.xml`, and so forth, or new customized file extensions. It can be configured through the application's `web.config` configuration file. In addition, this module gives a variety of handy features to manage the security of a request including a special section to define hidden segments, in such a way that if any of the listed hidden segments is found in the URL of a request, the request is automatically rejected by IIS runtime.

4

A Matter of Trust

The topics discussed so far have centered on various pieces of security information: encryption key material, security identities, authentication and authorization, and so on. They dealt with security decisions that were tied to some concept of identity. The security identity may have been that of the browser user, or it may have been the identity of the running process.

A different aspect of ASP.NET security uses the .NET Framework code access security (CAS) functionality to secure the code that runs in an ASP.NET site. Although the concept of code having its own set of rights has been around since the first version of the .NET Framework, more often than not the actual use of CAS by developers has been limited. In large part, this has been due to the complexities of understanding just what CAS is as well as how to effectively use CAS with your code.

ASP.NET 1.1 substantially reduced the learning curve with CAS by introducing the concept of ASP.NET trust levels. In essence, an ASP.NET trust level defines the set of rights that you are willing to grant to an application's code. This chapter thoroughly reviews the concept of ASP.NET trust levels, as well as new features in ASP.NET 3.5 around enforcement of trust levels that have not changed since ASP.NET 2.0

You will learn about the following areas of ASP.NET trust levels:

❑   Configuring and working with ASP.NET trust levels.

❑   What an ASP.NET trust level looks like.

❑   How a trust level definition actually works.

❑   Creating your own custom trust levels.

❑   Details on frequently asked questions for trust level customizations.

❑   A review of all the permissions defined in ASP.NET trust policy files.

❑   Advanced topics on writing code for partial trust environments.

What Is an ASP.NET Trust Level?

ASP.NET 1.1, ASP.NET 2.0, and ASP.NET 3.5 have the concept of trust levels. In a nutshell, a *trust level* is a declarative representation of security rules that defines the set of .NET Framework classes your ASP.NET code can call as well as a set of .NET Framework features that your ASP.NET code can use. The declarative representation of this information is called a trust policy file. Because a trust level is a declarative representation, you can view the definitions of trust levels by looking at the trust policy files on disk, and you can edit these files to suit your needs. When you configure an ASP.NET site with a specific trust level, the application is said to be running in XYZ trust (where XYZ is specific trust level). Much of the code that runs in an ASP.NET application and certainly all of the code you write in code-behind files is restricted by the rules defined for the current trust level. Note that ASP.NET trust levels apply to only ASP.NET applications. Console applications, NT services, Winforms, and other applications still rely on a developer understanding the .NET Framework CAS features. Currently, no other execution environments provide a developer-friendly CAS abstraction like ASP.NET trust levels do.

The specific trust levels that ship with ASP.NET 1.1, ASP.NET 2.0, and ASP.NET 3.5 (no new trust levels were added in ASP.NET 3.5) are listed here from the most permissive to the most restrictive trust level:

- ❑ Full trust
- ❑ High trust
- ❑ Medium trust
- ❑ Low trust
- ❑ Minimal trust

When trust levels were introduced in ASP.NET 1.1, the decision was made to default all ASP.NET applications to Full trust. Because many ASP.NET sites were already written with the 1.0 version of the framework, it was considered too much of a breaking change to default ASP.NET applications to a more restrictive trust level. In ASP.NET 3.5 this is also the case, with all ASP.NET 3.5 applications also defaulting to Full trust.

As the name implies, Full trust code can use any class in the .NET Framework and perform any privileged operation available to managed code. However, I admit that this is a pretty theoretical description of Full trust. A much simpler way to think of Full trust is that your code can call any arbitrary Win32 API. For most IT developer shops this may not be a particularly big deal, especially because you could already call any Win32 API back in ASP days. However, the .NET Framework was supposed to bring a security sandbox to managed code developers, and arguably being able to call interesting Win32 APIs that do things like reformat disk drives does not seem like much of a security sandbox. The .NET Framework did introduce a very robust code access security framework that allowed developers to prevent managed code from doing things like reformatting hard drives; there was just the "minor" problem that you needed to get a PhD in what is definitely one of the more esoteric (though incredibly powerful) areas of the framework. As a result, ASP.NET 1.0 development left CAS usage up to the individual developer, with the result being that future versions of ASP.NET allow Full trust by default.

Running an ASP.NET application in anything other than Full trust means that the application is running in *partial trust*, which simply means any piece of managed code (not just ASP.NET code) that has one or more CAS restrictions being enforced on it. In the case of ASP.NET, because all trust levels below Full trust enforce varying degrees of CAS restrictions, running applications in less than Full trust means these applications are partially trusted by the .NET Framework. As you will see throughout this chapter, partial trust applications are blocked from certain features of the .NET Framework.

Moving an application from Full trust to High trust is actually a pretty big security move, because running High trust restricts an ASP.NET application to only the set of rights defined in the High trust policy file. The specifics of what is allowed for each trust level will be reviewed in detail in the next few sections, but for now an easy way to think of High trust is that it prevents your ASP.NET code from calling unmanaged Win32 APIs. If you are unable to apply any of the other information covered in this chapter, at least try to switch your Internet-facing ASP.NET applications from running in Full trust to running in High trust. Turning off access to unmanaged Win32 APIs reduces the potential for mischief and unexpected consequences in your applications.

The next restrictive trust level is Medium trust. Think of Medium trust as the trust level that a shared hosting company would want to use. The ASP.NET team attempted to model the set of permissions in Medium trust to match the set of restrictions that an Internet hosting company would probably want enforced for each of their customers. In addition to the previous restriction on calling Win32 APIs, the Medium trust level restricts file I/O access for an ASP.NET application to only the files and folders that are located within the application's directory structure. In a shared hosting environment with many customers, each of whom does not trust any of the other customers, the restrictions in Medium trust prevent a malicious user from attempting to surf around the host machine's local hard drive.

Low trust is appropriate for a read-only web server and for web servers running specialized no-code or low-code applications. The default set of permissions in Low trust allow only read access to the application's directory structure. In addition, Low trust does not allow ASP.NET code to reach out across the network. For example, in Low trust an ASP.NET application cannot call a SQL Server or use the `System.Net.HttpWebRequest` class to make HTTP calls to other web servers. Overall, Low trust is appropriate for web servers with applications that can effectively run in a standalone mode without relying on any other external servers. It is also the recommended trust level for developers that implement no-code or low-code execution environments. For example, SharePoint is an example of an application environment that requires no `.aspx` pages or very few `.aspx` pages on the web server's file system. Developers usually work within the SharePoint environment (which is effectively its own sandbox) and typically do not need to place many `.aspx` files directly onto the file system. SharePoint developers also work within the coding guidelines and restrictions enforced by the SharePoint runtime, which in turn sits on top of the ASP.NET runtime.

> *SharePoint v3 (the current version) actually uses a modified variation of ASP.NET's Minimal trust level known as WSS_Minimal. The WSS_Minimal is an ASP.NET custom trust level.*

The last ASP.NET trust level is Minimal trust. As its name implies, this trust level allows only the most minimal capabilities for an ASP.NET application. Other than running innocuous code (for example, a web-based calculator or basic `.aspx` pages), ASP.NET code running in Minimal trust cannot call into classes or attempt operations that could cause any type of security risk. This trust level is suitable for highly secure applications where 99 percent of any complex logic lives within compiled binaries that are deployed in the Global Assembly Cache (GAC). Because deploying a binary in the GAC requires administrative privileges, locking an ASP.NET web server down to Minimal trust effectively requires administrator intervention to deploy any code of consequence onto a web server.

To summarize at a high level, the following table shows the ASP.NET trust levels and the general concept behind each trust level:

Trust Level	Used For
Full	Any and all code is allowed to run. Mainly intended for backwards compatibility with ASP.NET 1.0 and 1.1 applications that were not aware of how to use CAS or how to work with ASP.NET trust levels.
High	Among other restrictions, ASP.NET code cannot call into unmanaged Win32 APIs. A good first step for securing Internet-facing ASP.NET applications.
Medium	Intended as the default trust level for shared hosting environments where multiple untrusted customers use the same machine. Also recommended for any Internet-facing production applications.
Low	A set of permissions suitable for applications such as SharePoint that provide their own sandboxed execution environment. Also useful for read-only applications that don't require network access to other backend servers.
Minimal	Locked down web servers that allow only the barebones minimum in your ASP.NET code. You will be able to add two numbers together and write out the results to a web page, but not much else.

Configuring Trust Levels

Now that you have a general idea of the target audience for each trust level, you need to know how to configure a trust level for your ASP.NET applications. The default of Full trust is defined in the root web.config file located in the CONFIG subdirectory of the framework installation directory:

```
%windir%\Microsoft.NET\Framework\v2.0.50727\CONFIG\web.config
```

At the top of the root web.config file is a location tag with a trust level definition that looks as follows:

```
<location allowOverride="true" >
    <system.web>
        <!--  security policies snipped for brevity -->

        <trust level="Full" originUrl="" />

    </system.web>
</location>
```

Changing the <trust /> configuration element in the root web.config file affects all ASP.NET applications running on the machine. The <trust /> element is conveniently located inside of a <location /> element to make it even easier for you to set the trust level for an entire machine, and then prevent anyone from changing the trust level on other web.config files. For example, if you make the following change to the location tag:

```
<location allowOverride="false">
```

then the individual applications that attempt to redefine the `<trust />` configuration element in their `web.config` files will end up with an exception. Because all configuration files located in the `CONFIG` directory are ACL'd to only allow the local Adminstrators group and SYSTEM write access, a malicious developer cannot use an ASP.NET application to make changes to `machine.config` or the root `web.config` file. Chapter 5 goes into more detail about how the configuration system in ASP.NET 3.5 can be used to prevent websites and web applications from changing machine wide settings.

Although making changes to the root `web.config` file gives a machine administrator a great deal of leverage over the trust level setting for all applications on the machine, it is also likely that on some machines you will not be able to enforce a single trust level for all applications.

The `<trust />` configuration element can also be defined in the `web.config` file for individual applications. This gives you the flexibility to pick and choose the appropriate trust level for different applications. However, allowing individual applications to change the trust level in their `web.config` files may not be something you want to allow for security reasons. As an alternative, you can define multiple `<location />` tags in the root `web.config` using the syntax shown earlier, but with the addition of a path attribute that indicates which application the settings apply to. For example, the following configuration element defines the Medium trust level, but the setting applies only to a specific application, as opposed to all applications on the web server:

```
<location path="Default Web Site/sampleapp" allowOverride="false" >
    <system.web>

        <trust level="Medium" originUrl="" />

    </system.web>
</location>
```

Working with Different Trust Levels

To give you a better idea of how trust levels affect an application, let's use a sample application that attempts the following operations:

❑   Create an ADO (not ADO.NET) recordset using the primary interop assembly (PIA) that ships for ADO.

❑   Open `Notepad.exe` for read access. This file is located in the Windows directory.

❑   Connect to the Pubs database running on a local SQL Server.

❑   Open the application's local `web.config` file for reading.

❑   Add two numbers together and output the results using a label control.

The first operation is interesting because it uses the ADODB primary interop assembly (PIA) that provides a managed type wrapper around the older COM ADO objects. Calling into a PIA (or any managed code wrapper for a COM object) involves calling unmanaged code. As a result, running the following code will only work in Full trust.

C#

```
…
    using ADODB;
…
    private void CreateRecordset()
    {
        RecordsetClass rc = new RecordsetClass();
        int fieldCount = rc.Fields.Count;
    }

    protected void btnFull_Click(object sender, EventArgs e)
    {
        try
        {
            //Need to call a separate method so that the exception
            //occurs there, and can then be trapped from the click event.
            this.CreateRecordset();

            lblResults.Text =
                "Successfully created an ADO recordset using the ADO PIA.";
        }
        catch (Exception ex)
        {
            lblResults.Text = ex.Message + "<br />" +
                Server.HtmlEncode(ex.StackTrace);
        }
    }
```

VB.NET

```
…
    Imports ADODB
…
    Private Sub CreateRecordset()
        Dim rc As New RecordsetClass()
        Dim fieldCount As Integer = rc.Fields.Count
    End Sub

    Protected Sub btnFull_Click( _
    ByVal sender As Object, _
    ByVal e As System.EventArgs) Handles btnFull.Click
        Try
            'Need to call a separate method so that the exception
            'occurs there, and can then be trapped from the click event.
            Me.CreateRecordset()

lblResults.Text = "Successfully created an ADO recordset using the ADO PIA."
        Catch ex As Exception
            lblResults.Text = ex.Message & "<br />" & _
            Server.HtmlEncode(ex.StackTrace)
        End Try
    End Sub
```

This sample code also requires that the website reference the ADO PIA from `web.config`, as follows:

```
<compilation debug="false">
    <assemblies>
        <add assembly="ADODB, Version=7.0.3300.0,
                        Culture=neutral, PublicKeyToken=B03F5F7F11D50A3A"/>
    </assemblies>
</compilation>
```

If you attempt to create an ADO object in less then Full trust, you receive an error message saying, "assembly does not allow partially trusted callers." This is .NET Framework shorthand for saying that the application is running in something other than Full trust, and thus does not have rights to make calls into the ADO PIA.

You should keep this scenario in mind if you migrate an ASP application to ASP.NET and then attempt to run the migrated ASP.NET application in anything other than Full trust. Older ASP applications usually depend on all sorts of COM objects, with ADO just being one of the most prevalent COM objects. Because calling COM objects from managed code always requires a managed-to-unmanaged code transition, migrated ASP applications can be a bit problematic to get running in partial trust. Although I discuss strategies that allow partially trusted applications to call into unmanaged code, migrated ASP applications are typically so dependent on COM objects that it can be expensive for developers to go through a converted application and implement workarounds just so the COM interop wrappers can be used in partial trust.

The second piece of code attempts to open `Notepad.exe` for read access. Because `Notepad.exe` is located in the Windows directory, it clearly lies outside of the file and directory structure of the ASP.NET application.

C#

```
string filePath = "c:\\windows\\notepad.exe";
FileStream fs = File.OpenRead(filePath);
fs.Close();
```

VB.NET

```
Dim filePath As String = "c:\windows\notepad.exe"
Dim fs As FileStream = File.OpenRead(filePath)
fs.Close()
```

This code will successfully run in Full and High trust, but at any other trust level it will result in a `SecurityException`, indicating that the request for a `FileIOPermission` failed. If you have applications that read and write data files located outside the directory structure of an ASP.NET application, High trust is realistically as low as you can go in terms of tightening trust levels without using the sandboxing approach described later in the chapter. You would need to move this type of code to a separate assembly and assert the necessary permissions in order to be able to read and write files outside the application's directory structure in Medium or lower trust levels.

The next piece of code uses `System.Data.SqlClient` to connect to a local database.

C#

```
string connString =
    @"server=.\SQL2005;database=pubs;Integrated Security=True;";
sqlConn =
    new SqlConnection(connString);
sqlConn.Open();
```

VB.NET

```
Dim connString As String = _
    "server=.\SQL2005;database=pubs;Integrated Security=True;"
sqlConn = New SqlConnection(connString)
sqlConn.Open()
```

At Medium trust or above, the code runs without a problem. However, Low and Minimal trust do not grant the necessary permissions to application code. As a result, Low or Minimal trust will result in a `SecurityException`, indicating that the request for a `SqlClientPermission` failed. The ability to connect to SQL Server is allowed in Medium trust because it is the trust level recommended for shared hosting machines. Because customers at Internet hosters usually want some type of database access, `SqlClientPermission` made sense to add to the Medium trust policy file.

Opening files located within an application's directory structure in read-only mode is allowed at Low trust or above.

C#

```
string filePath = Server.MapPath("~") + "\\web.config";
FileStream fs = File.OpenRead(filePath);
fs.Close();
```

VB.NET

```
Dim filePath As String = Server.MapPath("~") & "\web.config"
Dim fs As FileStream = File.OpenRead(filePath)
fs.Close()
```

However, if you lower the trust level to Minimal trust, this code fails with a `SecurityException` indicating that the request for a `FileIOPermission` failed. Although these types of exceptions seem a bit unclear, it is intentional that the exception information and messages do not expose additional information. It can be a bit of a pain as a developer to track down what is happening, but the tradeoff is that additional information, such as specific file paths, or requested access modes, is not accidentally exposed in an error message that my be rendered in the browser.

I will not show the last piece of sample code, because it is not terribly interesting to add two numbers together and output the results on a page. The point of the last sample code, though, is to prove that in Minimal trust you still have the ability to write some code in your ASP.NET pages. Basically, Minimal trust allows you to write code that depends only on the object instances available on the page and .NET Framework classes that operate entirely against data located in the application's memory. However, any attempt to use .NET Framework classes that read and write files, communicate with databases and directory stores, reach out across the network, and so on results in some type of `SecurityException`.

Anatomy of a Trust Level

You have seen the general idea of how a trust level works. In the following sections, you get a better idea of how a trust level is defined, as well as the meaning of various security restrictions. The intent of the next few sections is to give you the information you need to be able to interpret the trust level policy files that ship with ASP.NET 3.5. Note, though, that the discussion intentionally tries to avoid diving too deep into the esoteric nature of how .NET Framework CAS works. Thankfully, the information you need to effectively use trust levels is much smaller than the knowledge required to become a CAS guru!

Finding the Trust Policy File

Medium trust is the default level recommended for hosters supporting untrusted customers. If you configure your server or application to run in Medium trust, ASP.NET must first determine just where the rules for Medium trust are located. Earlier you saw the configuration example for selecting a trust level, but some other configuration information was removed. The configuration that follows is what actually ships with the .Net Framework:

```
<location allowOverride="true">
    <system.web>
        <securityPolicy>
            <trustLevel name="Full" policyFile="internal" />
            <trustLevel name="High" policyFile="web_hightrust.config" />
            <trustLevel name="Medium" policyFile="web_mediumtrust.config" />
            <trustLevel name="Low" policyFile="web_lowtrust.config" />
            <trustLevel name="Minimal" policyFile="web_minimaltrust.config" />

          <!-- the following is not in the default web.config
            <trustLevel name="CustomLevel" policyFile="mycustomlevel.config" />
            -->

        </securityPolicy>
        <trust level="Full" originUrl="" />
    </system.web>
</location>
```

The `<securityPolicy />` element contains the information ASP.NET needs to map a trust level name to a specific policy file location on disk. Furthermore, you have the option to define additional trust level names (in essence, additional trust levels) by adding your own `<trustLevel />` configuration elements within the `<securityPolicy />` section. Any trust level defined in this section can be used as a value for the "level" attribute in the `<trust />` element.

All locations defined in the preceding `policyFile` attributes are assumed to be relative to the following location:

```
%windir%\Microsoft.NET\Framework\v2.0.50727\CONFIG
```

If you create a custom trust level, the associated policy file must be placed in the CONFIG directory for ASP.NET to be able to use it. When you look in the CONFIG directory, you will actually see two copies of every policy file. For example, the medium trust policy file is defined in `web_mediumtrust.config`; a backup copy of the original medium trust policy file is defined in `web_mediumtrust.config.default`. Because you can edit the `.config` files to customize an individual trust policy, and because most of us will probably also do something wrong the first few times, the `.default` files are a handy way to get back to the original policy definitions. Needless to say, don't edit the .default files, or at the very least, make a copy of them in a safe place!

String Replacements in Policy Files

After ASP.NET locates the appropriate policy file, it loads it into memory and performs some basic string replacements inside of it. If you open the medium trust policy file (`web_mediumtrust.config`) in a text editor, you will see the following string replacement tokens:

- ❑　　$AppDir$
- ❑　　$AppDirUrl$
- ❑　　$CodeGen$
- ❑　　$OriginHost$

These replacement tokens exist primarily because the dynamic nature of ASP.NET applications makes it difficult to statically define all of the security information required to effectively use CAS.

As you can probably infer from the first two string replacement tokens, because ASP.NET applications can be located anywhere on disk, ASP.NET needs a way to define permissions such that physical file paths can be flexibly defined. Both $AppDir$ and $AppDirUrl$ are representations of the physical file path for the application root. For example, if you create an application called `MyApplication` located within your `wwwroot` directory, and you are running off of the C drive, the string replacement tokens will have values of:

- ❑　　$AppDir$ = c:\inetpub\wwwroot\MyApplication
- ❑　　$AppDirUrl$ = file:///c:/inetpub/wwwroot/MyApplication

Because different permission classes require different path representations, ASP.NET supports these two representations.

The next replacement token, $CodeGen$, is used to represent the physical location on disk where all compiled code used by ASP.NET is located. As a side note, the term *codegen* is also shorthand in the ASP.NET world for any kind of auto-generated code artifacts that ASP.NET emits while running your application. Using the `MyApplication` example again, ASP.NET will create a directory structure that looks something like the following:

```
%windir%\Microsoft.NET\Framework\v2.0.50727\Temporary ASP.NET Files\MyApplication \
e63333b8
```

This entire path, including the random hash value at the end (and there may actually be a few levels of these strange looking hash values) is used to create the value for $CodeGen$. The actual $CodeGen$ value is a `file:///` URL-style representation of this physical path (just like the $AppDirUrl$ used previously).

This location is important from a .NET Framework perspective because most of the executable assemblies for an ASP.NET application (both the assemblies you drop into the /bin directory and the ones ASP.NET auto-generates for pages, controls, and so on) are located somewhere within the directory tree represented by $CodeGen$. This set of code represents user code—the code that you, as a developer, have written. When running with any trust level other than Full trust, it is primarily user code that is restricted based on the security settings in the policy file. $CodeGen$ is the way ASP.NET can tell the .NET Framework where this user code exists.

The last string replacement token, $OriginHost$, does not deal with file locations, but instead is used to allow developers to define either a specific URL or a URL pattern to be used with classes such as System.Net.HttpWebRequest. Some of the System.Net classes support CAS restrictions that allow you to define the set of URL endpoints that can be connected to using these classes. You can supply the value for $OriginHost$ by putting a value in the originUrl attribute of the <trust /> element, as shown here:

```
<trust level="Medium" originUrl="http://www.internalwebserviceendpoint.contoso
.com/" />
```

Defining Sets of Permissions

A central concept to .NET Framework CAS is the idea of a permission set. Because code access security is all about applying a set of restrictions to one or more pieces of code, a permission set is a convenient way of grouping multiple restrictions into one logical definition—for example, a permission set. Because effective CAS usage typically requires varying levels of software restrictions within a single application, the .NET Framework supports the idea of naming individual permission sets so that developers can keep track of the intended use of the permission sets.

Inside of the Medium trust policy file, ASP.NET defines the following named permission sets.

❑ FullTrust

❑ Nothing

❑ ASP.Net

As the first named permission set implies, it defines a CAS policy that allows any kind of code or behavior in the .NET Framework. The definition for FullTrust in the policy file looks like:

```
<PermissionSet
class="NamedPermissionSet"
        version="1"
        Unrestricted="true"
        Name="FullTrust"
        Description="Allows full access to all resources"
    />
```

<PermissionSet /> elements can contain child elements defining specific permissions. However, the FullTrust permission set clearly has no child elements. The reason this permission set allows managed code to pretty much do anything is because of the attribute definition: Unrestricted="true". This syntax indicates that any code that is granted the FullTrust permission set has unrestricted access to all functionality (including calling Win32 APIs and native code) in the .NET Framework.

The next permission set, called Nothing, defines absolutely zero permissions, which, given the name, is what you would expect. The definition for Nothing in the policy file looks like this:

```
<PermissionSet
class="NamedPermissionSet"
        version="1"
        Name="Nothing"
        Description="Denies all resources, including the right to execute"
 />
```

Because the Nothing named permission set has no child elements, and no other attribute values of note, the permission set effectively defines an empty set of permissions.

The last permission set is the most interesting one, because it is the ASP.NET named permission set that differs across the various policy files. The FullTrust and Nothing permission set definitions are the same in all of the policy files. However, it is the varying definitions of the ASP.NET permission set that gives each trust level its unique behavior. The partial definition for the ASP.NET named permission set is shown here:

```
<PermissionSet
class="NamedPermissionSet"
        version="1"
        Name="ASP.Net">

        <!-- multiple child permissions that will be discussed shortly -->

</PermissionSet>
```

Because the ASP.NET permission set would be pretty useless without a set of defined permissions, it is the only named permission set with child elements defining a number of specific security rights for code.

Defining Individual Permissions

An individual permission in a policy file is defined with an `<IPermission />` element. The in-memory representation of many interesting .NET Framework CAS permissions are classes that derive from a class called `CodeAccessPermission`. Because the `CodeAccessPermission` class happens to implement the `IPermission` interface, the declarative representation of a `CodeAccessPermission` is an `<IPermission />` element.

For example, the Medium trust policy file allows user code to make use of the `System.Data.SqlClient` classes. The definition of this permission looks like this:

```
<IPermission
class="SqlClientPermission"
        version="1"
        Unrestricted="true"
 />
```

Because the `System.Data.SqlClient` classes do not support more granular permission definitions, the `System.Data.SqlClient.SqlClientPermission` is used to allow all access to the main functionality in the namespace, or deny access to this functionality. The previous definition sets the `Unrestricted` attribute to `true`, which indicates that user code in the ASP.NET application can use any functionality in `System.Data.SqlClient` that may demand this permission.

Some permissions, though, have more complex representations. Usually, the permissions you will find in the ASP.NET policy files will support multiple attributes on an <IPermission /> element, with the attributes corresponding to specific aspects of a customizable permission. For example, remember the earlier section describing string replacement tokens in policy files. The System.Security.Permissions .FileIOPermission is defined in the Medium trust policy file as follows:

```
<IPermission
class="FileIOPermission"
          version="1"
          Read="$AppDir$"
          Write="$AppDir$"
          Append="$AppDir$"
          PathDiscovery="$AppDir$"
/>
```

This permission supports a more extensive set of attributes for customizing security behavior. In this definition, the policy file is stating that user code in an ASP.NET application has rights to read and write files located within the application's directory structure. Furthermore, user code in an ASP.NET application has rights to modify files (the Append attribute) and retrieve path information within the application's directory structure. When ASP.NET first parses the policy file, it replaces $AppDir$ with the correct rooted path for the application. That way when the <IPermission /> is deserialized by the .NET Framework into an actual instance of a FileIOPermission, the correct path information is used to initialize the permission class.

Later in this chapter in the section titled "The Default Security Permissions Defined by ASP.NET," you walk through the individual permissions that are used throughout the various policy files so that you get a better idea of the default CAS permissions.

How Permission Sets Are Matched to Code

At this point, you have a general understanding of permission sets and the individual permissions that make up a permission set. The next part of a policy file defines the rules that the .NET Framework uses to determine which permission sets apply to specific pieces of code. Clearly, CAS wouldn't be very useful if, for example, all of the assemblies in the GAC were accidentally assigned the named permission set Nothing. So, there must be some way that the framework can associate the correct code with the correct set of permissions.

The first piece of the puzzle involves the concept of code *evidence*, information about a piece of running code that meets the following criteria:

❑   The .NET Framework can discover, either by inferring it or by having the evidence explicitly associated with the code. Evidence includes things such as where an assembly is located and the digital signature (if any) of the assembly.

❑   The .NET Framework can interpret evidence and use it when making decisions about assigning a set of CAS restrictions to a piece of code. This type of logic is called a *membership condition* and is represented declaratively with the <IMembershipCondition /> element.

The unit of work that the .NET Framework initially uses as the basis for identifying code is the current stack frame. Essentially, each method that you write has a stack frame when the code actually runs (ignore compiler optimizations and such). At runtime, when a security demand occurs and the framework needs to determine the correct set of permissions to check against, the framework looks at the current stack frame. Based on the stack frame, the framework can backtrack and determine which assembly actually contains the code for that stack frame. And then backtracking farther, the framework can look at that assembly and start inferring various pieces of evidence about that assembly.

Looking through the policy file, you will see a number of <CodeGroup /> elements that make use of evidence. The <CodeGroup /> elements are declarative representations of evidence-based comparisons used to associate security restrictions to code. I won't delve into the inner workings of specific code group classes, because that is a topic suitable to an entire book devoted only to code access security. Generally speaking, though, a code group is associated with two concepts:

- ❑ A code group is always associated with a named permission set. Thus, the code group definitions in the ASP.NET policy files are each associated with one of the following named permission sets discussed earlier: ASP.Net, FullTrust, or Nothing.

- ❑ A code group defines a set of one or more conditions that must be met for the framework to consider a piece of code as being restricted to the named permission set associated with the code group. This is why <IMembershipCondition /> elements are nested within <CodeGroup /> elements. The definitions of membership conditions rely on the evidence that the framework determines about an assembly.

The ASP.NET policy files define several <CodeGroup /> elements, with some code groups nested inside of others. If you scan down the elements, though, a few specific definitions stand out. The very first definition is shown here:

```
<CodeGroup
class="FirstMatchCodeGroup"
        version="1"
        PermissionSetName="Nothing">
          <IMembershipCondition
              class="AllMembershipCondition"
              version="1"
          />
```

This definition effectively states the following: if no other code group definitions in the policy file happen to match the currently running code, then associate the code with the named permission set called "Nothing." In other words, if some piece of unrecognized code attempts to run, it will fail because the "Nothing" permission set is empty.

Continuing down the policy file, the next two code group definitions are very important.

```
<CodeGroup
class="UnionCodeGroup"
        version="1"
        PermissionSetName="ASP.Net">
          <IMembershipCondition
              class="UrlMembershipCondition"
              version="1"
              Url="$AppDirUrl$/*"
            />
</CodeGroup>
<CodeGroup
class="UnionCodeGroup"
```

```
                version="1"
                PermissionSetName="ASP.Net">
                    <IMembershipCondition
                        class="UrlMembershipCondition"
                        version="1"
                        Url="$CodeGen$/*"
                />
    </CodeGroup>
```

These two definitions are where the proverbial rubber hits the road when it comes to the ASP.NET trust feature. The $AppDirUrl$ token in the first membership condition indicates that any code loaded from the file directory structure of the current ASP.NET application should be restricted to the permissions defined in the ASP.NET named permission set. Also notice that the "Url" attribute ends with a /*, which ensures that any code loaded at or below the root of the ASP.NET application will be restricted by the ASP.NET permission set.

Similarly, the second code group definition restricts any code loaded from the code generation directory for the ASP.NET application to the permissions defined in the ASP.NET named permission set. As with the first code group, the membership condition also ends in a /* to ensure that all assemblies loaded from anywhere within the temporary directory structure used for the application's codegen will be restricted to the ASP.NET permission set.

It is this pair of <CodeGroup /> definitions that associates the ASP.NET named permission set to all the code that you author in your ASP.NET applications. The pair of definitions also restricts any of the code you drop into the /bin directory because of course that lies within the directory structure of an ASP.NET application. These two definitions are also why trust-level customizations (discussed a little later in this chapter) can be easily made to the ASP.NET named permission set without you needing to worry about any of the other esoteric details necessary to define and enforce CAS.

The remaining <CodeGroup /> elements in the policy files define a number of default rules, with the most important one being the following definition:

```
    <CodeGroup
    class="UnionCodeGroup"
            version="1"
            PermissionSetName="FullTrust">
                <IMembershipCondition
                    class="GacMembershipCondition"
                    version="1"
                />
    </CodeGroup>
```

This definition states that any code that is deployed in the GAC is assigned the FullTrust named permission set. This permission set allows managed code to make use of all the features available in the .NET Framework. Because you can author code and deploy assemblies in the GAC, you have the ability to create an ASP.NET application with two different levels of security restrictions. User code that lives within the directory structure of the ASP.NET application will be subjected to the ASP.NET permission set, but any code that you deploy in the GAC will have the freedom to do whatever it needs to. This concept of full trust GAC assemblies will come up again in the section "Advanced Topics on Partial Trust" where there is a discussion of strategies for sandboxing privileged code.

Other Places that Define Code Access Security

Although the previous topics focused on how ASP.NET defines the permission set associations using a trust policy file, the .NET Framework defines a more extensive hierarchy of code access security settings. Using the .NET Framework 2.0 Configuration MMC, you can create security policies for any of the following:

❑ Enterprise

❑ Machine

❑ User

This means that you can create declarative representations of permissions, permission sets, and code groups beyond those defined in the ASP.NET trust policy file.

If your organization defines security policies at any of these levels, it is possible that the permissions defined in the ASP.NET trust policy file may not exactly match the behavior exhibited by your application. This occurs because each successive level of security policy (with the lowest level being the ASP.NET trust policy) acts sort of like a filter. Only security rights allowed across all of the levels will ultimately be granted to your code.

With that said, though, in practice many organizations are either unaware of the security configuration levels, or have considered them too complicated to deal with. That is why ASP.NET trust policies with their relatively easy-to-understand representations are ideally suited for quickly and easily enforcing CAS restrictions on all of your web applications.

By default, the .NET Framework defines only restrictive CAS policies for the Machine level. The framework defines a number of different code groups that divvy up code based on where the code was loaded from. These code group definitions depend on the concept of security zones that you are probably familiar with from Internet Explorer. You might wonder why ASP.NET needs to define its own concept of CAS with trust levels when zone-based CAS restrictions are already defined and used by the Framework.

ASP.NET cannot really depend on the default Machine level CAS definitions because, for all practical purposes, ASP.NET code always runs locally. The ASP.NET pages exist on the local hard drive of the web server, as does the Temporary ASP.NET Files directory. Even in when running from a UNC share, most of the actual compiled code in an application is either auto-generated by ASP.NET or shadow copied into the local Temporary ASP.NET Files directory.

As a result, if ASP.NET didn't use trust levels, all ASP.NET code that you write would fall into the code group called `My_Computer_Zone`. The membership condition for this code group is the My Computer zone, which includes all code installed locally. Because the code group grants full trust to any assemblies that are installed locally, this means in the absence of ASP.NET trust levels, all ASP.NET code runs at full trust. This is precisely the outcome in ASP.NET 1.0, which predated the introduction of ASP.NET trust levels.

A Second Look at a Trust Level in Action

Earlier you saw an example of using various pieces of code in different trust levels and the failures that occurred. Now that you have a more complete picture of what exists inside of a trust policy file, reviewing how trust levels and CAS all hang together is helpful. Figure 4-1 outlines a number of important steps.

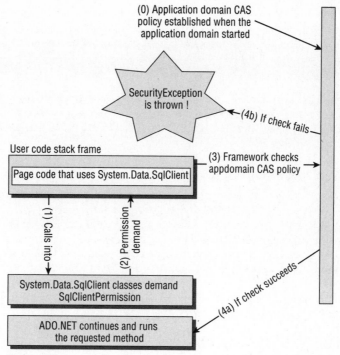

Figure 4-1

Step 0: Application Domain Policy

As part of ASP.NET's application domain initialization process, ASP.NET reads configuration to determine the appropriate trust policy that should be loaded from the CONFIG directory. When the file is loaded, and the string replacement tokens are processed, ASP.NET calls System.AppDomain.SetAppDomainPolicy to indicate that permissions defined in the trust level's policy file are the CAS rules for the application domain. If your organization also defines CAS rules for the Enterprise, Machine, or User levels, then the application domain policy is intersected with all of the other predefined CAS rules.

Step 1: User Code Calls into a Protected Framework Class

One of the pieces of code from the sample application shown in the beginning of the chapter attempted to call into ADO.NET:

C#

```
string connString =
    @"server=.\SQL2005;database=pubs;Integrated Security=True;";
sqlConn =
    new SqlConnection(connString);
sqlConn.Open();
```

VB.NET

```
Dim connString As String = _
    "server=.\SQL2005;database=pubs;Integrated Security=True;"
sqlConn = New SqlConnection(connString)
sqlConn.Open()
```

Attempting to open a connection or run a command using the `System.Data.SqlClient`'s classes results in a demand being made in ADO.NET for the `SqlClientPermission`. ADO.NET makes the demand by having the framework construct an instance of the `SqlClientPermission` class and then calling the `Demand` method on it.

Step 2: The Demand Flows up the Stack

The technical details of precisely how the Framework checks for a demanded permission are not something you need to delve into. Conceptually, though, demanding a permission causes the Framework to look up the call stack at all of the code that was running up to the point that the permission demand occurred. Underneath the hood, the Framework has a whole set of performance optimizations so that in reality the code that enforces permission demands doesn't have to riffle through every last byte in what could potentially be a very lengthy call stack.

Ultimately, though, the Framework recognizes the user code from the sample page, and it decides to check the set of permissions associated with the page.

Step 3: Checking the Current CAS Policy

This is where the effects of the ASP.NET trust policy come into play. Because ASP.NET earlier initialized a set of permissions (code groups and membership conditions for the application domain) the Framework now has a set of rules that it can reference. If the user code sits on an ASP.NET page, the Framework uses the `UrlMembershipCondition` definitions defined earlier in the trust policy file to determine the permissions associated with the page code. The page code at this point has actually been compiled into a page assembly (either automatically or from an earlier precompilation), and this assembly is sitting somewhere in the Temporary ASP.NET Files directory structure for the current application. Because the permissions for files located in the codegen directory are the ones from the ASP.NET named permission set, the Framework looks for the existence of `SqlClientPermission` in that permission set.

Step 4: The Results of the Check

If the ASP.NET application is running at Medium trust or above, the Framework will find the `SqlClientPermission` in the permission set associated with user code. In this case, the Framework determines that the user code passes the security check, and as a result the original ADO.NET call is allowed to proceed. What isn't shown in Figure 4-1 is the extended call stack that sits on top of the code sitting in the `.aspx` page. When the Framework determines that the user code has the necessary permissions, it continues up the call stack, checking every assembly that is participating on the current thread. In the case of ASP.NET, though, all code prior to the button click event handler calling ADO.NET is code that exists in `System.Web.dll` or some other .NET Framework assembly. Because all these assemblies exists in the GAC, and GAC'd assemblies have full trust, all of the other code on the class stack is considered to implicitly have all possible permissions.

On the other hand, if the ASP.NET application is running in Low or Minimal trust, the .NET Framework will not find a `SqlClientPermission` for the page's code, and the permission demand fails with a stack that looks roughly like:

```
Request for the permission of type 'System.Data.SqlClient.SqlClientPermission,
System.Data, Version=2.0.0.0, Culture=neutral, PublicKeyToken=b77a5c561934e089'
failed.
at System.Security.CodeAccessSecurityEngine.Check(Object demand, StackCrawlMark&
stackMark, Boolean isPermSet) at System.Security.PermissionSet.Demand() at
```

The downside of CAS is that when a security exception occurs, it usually results in semi-intelligible results like those shown previously.

However, when you encounter a security exception (and it is usually an instance of System.Security.SecurityException that is thrown), with a little probing you can usually pick apart the call stack to get some idea of what happened. For the previous example, you can see that the bottom of the call stack is the button click handler; that immediately tells you the user code triggered the call that eventually failed. Moving up the call stack a bit, System.Data.SqlClient.SqlConnection.PermissionDemand() gives you an idea of which System.Data.SqlClient class your code is calling.

Moving up the stack a bit more, you see various calls into System.Security.CodeAccessSecurity Engine. This class is part of the internal guts of the CAS enforcement capability in the .NET Framework. Finally, at the top of the stack trace is the information pertaining to the specific permission request that failed, which in this case is SqlClientPermission. In this example, the SqlClientPermission is a very simple permission class that represents a binary condition: either code has rights to call into System.Data.SqlClient, or it doesn't. As a result, you don't need additional information to investigate the problem.

So, troubleshooting this problem boils down to figuring out why the code in the button click event doesn't have rights to call into various ADO.NET classes. With an understanding of ASP.NET trust levels in mind, the first thing you would do is determine the current trust level. In this case, I set the application to run in Minimal trust. In the policy file for Minimal trust, SqlClientPermission has not been granted to ASP.NET code.

Troubleshooting More Complex Permissions

Although troubleshooting SqlClientPermission is pretty simple, other more complex permission types are not so easy. For example, the System.Security.Permissions.FileIOPermission class supports much more granular permission definitions. As you saw earlier in some snippets from the ASP.NET trust policy files, you can selectively grant access to read files, create files, modify existing files, and so on. Using the sample application from the beginning of the chapter again, you can attempt to read a file running in Minimal trust:

C#

```csharp
string filePath = Server.MapPath("~") + "\\web.config";
FileStream fs = File.OpenRead(filePath);
fs.Close();
```

VB.NET

```vbnet
Dim filePath As String = Server.MapPath("~") & "\web.config"
Dim fs As FileStream = File.OpenRead(filePath)
fs.Close()
```

This code results in the following stack trace:

```
Request for the permission of type 'System.Security.Permissions.FileIOPermission,
mscorlib, Version=2.0.0.0, Culture=neutral, PublicKeyToken=b77a5c561934e089'
failed.

at System.Security.CodeAccessSecurityEngine.Check(Object demand, StackCrawlMark&
stackMark, Boolean isPermSet) at
System.Security.CodeAccessPermission.Demand() at
System.Web.HttpRequest.MapPath(VirtualPath virtualPath, VirtualPath baseVirtualDir,
Boolean allowCrossAppMapping) at
System.Web.HttpServerUtility.MapPath(String path) at _Default.btnLow_Click(Object
sender, EventArgs e)
```

Unfortunately, from this stack trace, you can glean only that some piece of user code (the click event handler at the bottom of the trace) triggered a call to System.Web.HttpRequest.MapPath and that this call eventually resulted in a SecurityException because the check for FileIOPermission failed. The information about the FileIOPermission failure, though, says absolutely nothing about why it failed. At this point, about the only thing you can do is sleuth around the rest of the stack trace and attempt to infer what kind of FileIOPermission check failed. Was it read access, write access, or what?

In this case, the call to MapPath gives you a clue because ASP.NET has a MapPath method on the HttpServerUtility class. Because the purpose of MapPath is to return the physical file path representation for a given virtual path, you have a clue that suggests something went wrong when attempting to discover the physical file path.

Because the application is running at Minimal trust, you know that there are no FileIOPermission definitions inside of the Minimal trust policy file. With the information about MapPath, you can make a reasonable guess that if you wanted the code in the click event handler to succeed, you would at least need to create a declarative <IPermission /> for a FileIOPermission that granted PathDiscovery to the application's physical directory structure.

One of the other samples attempts to open a file outside of the directory structure of the application while running in Medium trust. Doing so still fails with a SecurityException complaining about the lack of a FileIOPermission. However, this time the stack trace includes the following snippet:

```
Snip...
at System.Security.CodeAccessPermission.Demand()
at System.IO.FileStream.Init(String path, FileMode mode, FileAccess access, Int32
rights, Boolean useRights, FileShare share, Int32 bufferSize, FileOptions options,
SECURITY_ATTRIBUTES secAttrs, String msgPath, Boolean bFromProxy)
at System.IO.FileStream..ctor(String path, FileMode mode, FileAccess access,
FileShare share)
Snip...
```

Now the stack trace looks a bit more interesting. The snippet shows that one type of file I/O operation was attempted and during initialization of the FileStream, a demand occurred. Because the failure involved FileIOPermission, you have enough information in the stack trace to realize that you need to look at the code that opened the file stream. Depending on the location of the requested file, as well as the type of access requested, you can look in the trust policy file (Medium trust in this case) and see which file permissions are granted by default. In this case, because only file I/O permissions within the scope of the application's directory structure are granted, and the code is attempting to open a file in the %windir% directory, you need to grant extra permissions.

Adding the following permission element allows the application to open notepad.exe even though the application is running in Medium trust:

```
<IPermission
class="FileIOPermission"
        version="1"
        Read="c:\\windows\\notepad.exe"
        PathDiscovery="c:\\windows\\notepad.exe"
    />
```

Troubleshooting permission failures and the need to edit policy files to fix the failures leads us to the next topic.

Creating a Custom Trust Level

At some point, you may need to edit the permissions in a trust policy file and create a custom trust level. Creating a custom trust level involves the following tasks:

1. Creating a policy file containing your updated permission definitions
2. Determining the declarative representation of the new permissions
3. Applying the new trust level to your application

Creating a Policy File

Although you can edit the existing policy files located in the CONFIG directory, unless you are making minor edits for an existing trust level, you should create a separate policy file that represents the new custom set of permissions you are defining. Start with the policy file that has the closest set of permissions to those you want to define. This discussion starts with the Medium trust policy file. I made a copy of the Medium trust policy file and called it web_mediumtrust_custom.config.

After you have a separate copy of the policy file, you need to edit some configuration settings so that a trust level is associated with the policy file. Hooking up the policy file up so that it is available for use requires editing the root web.config file located in the framework's CONFIG subdirectory. Remember earlier that you looked at the <securityPolicy /> configuration element. Creating the following entry inside of the <securityPolicy /> element makes the custom policy file available for use as a custom trust level:

```
<securityPolicy>

        <!--  default trust levels -->
            <trustLevel name="Medium_Custom"
    policyFile="web_mediumtrust_custom.config" />

        </securityPolicy>
```

Now ASP.NET applications that need the set of permissions defined inside of web_mediumtrust_custom .config can simply reference the Medium_Custom trust level.

Determining Declarative Permission Representations

So far you have been looking at preexisting permission definitions. However, these declarative representations must have come from somewhere and must follow some type of expected schema; otherwise, it would be a free-for-all when class implementers tried to determine the correct <IPermission /> definitions for a permission.

Two pieces of information are necessary for enabling new permissions in a policy file:

❑ The class information for the security permission class

❑ The declarative XML representation of the permission

Determining the class information for a new permission is pretty simple. Usually you know what piece of code you are attempting to enable in a partial trust application, so you know the calls that are being made and that are failing.

The first example of creating a new custom permission attempts to enable OleDb for use in Medium trust. You can determine the permission that is necessary to enable usage of the classes in System .Data.OleDb by first attempting to run a page that uses OleDb in Medium trust and looking at the failure information. The following code initially does not work in Medium trust because the policy file for Medium trust only grants the SqlClientPermission:

C#

```
            OleDbConnection oc =
                new OleDbConnection("Provider=SQLOLEDB;" +
                    @"Data Source=.\SQL2005;Initial Catalog=pubs;" +
                    "Integrated Security=True;Connect Timeout=30");
            oc.Open();

            OleDbCommand ocmd = new OleDbCommand("select * from authors", oc);
            OleDbDataReader or = ocmd.ExecuteReader();
```

VB.NET

```
            Dim oc As New OleDbConnection("Provider=SQLOLEDB;" & _
                ControlChars.CrLf & _
                "Data Source=.\SQL2005;Initial Catalog=Pubs;" _
                & ControlChars.CrLf & "Integrated Security=SSPI;")
            oc.Open()
            Dim ocmd As New OleDbCommand("select * from authors", oc)
            Dim orr As OleDbDataReader = ocmd.ExecuteReader()
```

Running the code results in the following exception information:

```
[SecurityException: Request for the permission of type 'System.Data.OleDb.
OleDbPermission, System.Data, Version=2.0.0.0, Culture=neutral, PublicKeyToken=b77a
5c561934e089' failed.]
```

How convenient! The first piece of information is right there in the exception information. Using <IPermission /> elements in a trust policy file requires that you first register the type of the permission class that you are defining. This is necessary because the IPermission interface is a generic representation of a code-access permission, but you are attempting to define very specific permissions, sometimes with additional attributes or nested permissions that are unique to the specific class of permission you are working with.

You can register the `OleDbPermission` type in your custom policy file by copying the information out of the exception dump, and into a `<SecurityClass />` element, as shown here:

```
<SecurityClasses>
  <!-- pre-defined security classes snipped for brevity -->

  <SecurityClass
      Name="OleDbPermission"
      Description="System.Data.OleDb.OleDbPermission, System.Data,
                  Version=2.0.0.0, Culture=neutral,
                  PublicKeyToken=b77a5c561934e089"/>

</SecurityClasses>
```

The `Name` attribute can actually be set to any string value because it is used by individual `<IPermission />` elements to reference the correct permission type. However, you would normally use the class name without other type or namespace information as the value for the `Name` attribute. The `Description` attribute is set to a type string that the .NET Framework uses to resolve the correct permission type at runtime. In the previous example, the `Descrption` attribute has been set to the strong type definition that is conveniently available from the exception text.

Now that the permission class information has been entered into the policy file, the next step is to determine the declarative representation of an `OleDbPermission`. The easiest way to do this in the absence of any documentation for a XML representation as follows:

C#

```csharp
using System.Data.OleDb;
using System.Security;
using System.Security.Permissions;
...
    protected void Page_Load(object sender, EventArgs e)
    {
        OleDbPermission odp =
            new OleDbPermission(PermissionState.Unrestricted);

        SecurityElement se = odp.ToXml();

        Response.Write(Server.HtmlEncode(se.ToString()));
    }
```

VB.NET

```vbnet
Imports System.Data.OleDb
Imports System.Configuration
Imports System.Collections
Imports System.Security
Imports System.Security.Permissions
...
    Protected Sub Page_Load(ByVal sender As Object, ByVal e As System.EventArgs) _
        Handles Me.Load
```

```
            Dim odp As New OleDbPermission(PermissionState.Unrestricted)

            Dim se As SecurityElement = odp.ToXml()

            Response.Write(Server.HtmlEncode(se.ToString()))
      End Sub
```

The sample code constructs an instance of the permission class, passing it a value from the `System`
`.Security.Permissions.PermissionState` enumeration. The sample code essentially creates a
permission that grants unrestricted permission to the full functionality of the `System.Data.OleDb`
namespace. The XML representation of the permission is created by calling `ToXML()` on the permission, which results in an instance of a `System.Security.SecurityElement`. A `SecurityElement` is
the programmatic representation of the XML for a permission. You can get the string representation of
the XML by calling `ToString()` on the `SecurityElement`. The end result of running this code is the
declarative representation of an `OleDbPermission` instance:

```
<IPermission
      class="System.Data.OleDb.OleDbPermission, System.Data, Version=2.0.0.0,
Culture=neutral, PublicKeyToken=b77a5c561934e089"
      version="1"
      Unrestricted="true"
/>
```

This representation is almost exactly what you need to drop into your custom policy file, with one
minor change. Because you already defined a `<SecurityClass />` earlier for the `OleDbPermission`
type, the lengthy type definition isn't required. Instead, you want to enter the following XML into your
custom policy file:

```
<IPermission
      class="OleDbPermission"
      version="1"
      Unrestricted="true"
/>
```

The `class` attribute will be interpreted as a reference to a permission class that is keyed by the name
`OleDbPermission`. Because you created a `<SecurityClass />` earlier named `OleDbPermission`,
at runtime the Framework will correctly infer that the `<IPermission />` definition here is for an
instance of the type defined by the `OleDbPermission` security class.

You can place the `<IPermission />` declaration anywhere within the list of `<IPermission />` elements that are nested underneath the `<PermissionSet />` element for the ASP.NET named permission set. The following XML shows where to place the `OleDbPermission` declaration:

```
<PermissionSet
      class="NamedPermissionSet"
      version="1"
      Name="ASP.Net">

<!-- other default IPermission definitions -->
<IPermission
      class="OleDbPermission"
      version="1"
      Unrestricted="true"
```

```
    />

    </PermissionSet>
```

At this point, the edits to the policy file are complete, and the only task left is to associate the sample application with the custom trust level defined by this policy file.

Applying the New Trust Level

Earlier, you defined a new trust level called Medium_Custom for the modified policy file. The sample ASP.NET application can use this trust level by redefining the trust level in its web.config:

```
    <trust level="Medium_Custom" />
```

With the creation of the custom trust policy file and the use of the custom trust level, when you run the sample code shown earlier, the application is able to open an OleDb connection and make a query against the pubs database.

Additional Trust Level Customizations

You have seen how to enable unrestricted OleDb permissions for an ASP.NET application. However, permission classes sometimes allow for more extensive customizations. In this section, you will take a look at a few of the more common (or more confusing!) permissions classes you may encounter

Customizing OleDbPermission

The OleDbPermission class allows more than just a simple binary decision on class usage. For example, hosters frequently want to enable Access (aka Jet) databases for their customers, but at the same time they don't want to throw the doors wide open to any kind of OleDb drivers being used.

For example, let's say you wanted to allow use of only the System.Data.OleDb classes with the following restrictions:

❑   Only Access could be used through OleDb. Any other data provider, including OleDb-based SQL Server access, is disallowed.

❑   To prevent any type of extended information from being passed on the connection string, you allow only customers to set the database location, username, and password.

You can model this set of restrictions in code using the OleDbPermission class, as shown here:

C#

```csharp
OleDbPermission odp =
new OleDbPermission(PermissionState.None);

odp.Add("Provider=Microsoft.Jet.OLEDB.4.0",
        "data source=;user id=;password=;",
        KeyRestrictionBehavior.AllowOnly);

SecurityElement se = odp.ToXml();
Response.Write(Server.HtmlEncode(se.ToString()));
```

VB.NET

```
Dim odp As New OleDbPermission(PermissionState.Unrestricted)

odp.Add("Provider=Microsoft.Jet.OLEDB.4.0", _
    "data source=;user id=;password=;", _
    KeyRestrictionBehavior.AllowOnly)

Dim se As SecurityElement = odp.ToXml()
Response.Write(Server.HtmlEncode(se.ToString()))
```

Unlike the first example of using OleDbPermission, this code uses the Add method to selectively add the set of allowed connection strings that can be used with System.Data.OleDb. The Add method in the previous code says that connection strings that reference the Jet provider are allowed. Allowable connection strings can be further modified with the data source, user id, and password attributes. Attempts to create an OleDbConnection with a connection string that does not follow these constraints will result in a SecurityException.

Writing out the XML representation of the permission, and modifying the class attribute as mentioned earlier results in the following declarative syntax that can be placed in a custom policy file:

```
<IPermission class="OleDbPermission" version="1" >

<add ConnectionString="Provider=Microsoft.Jet.OLEDB.4.0"
    KeyRestrictions="data source=;user id=;password=;"
    KeyRestrictionBehavior="AllowOnly"
/>
</IPermission>
```

Notice how you now have a <IPermission /> element that itself contains nested security information. Permission classes are free to define whatever XML representation they require and this additional information can be nested within <IPermission />. This allows permission classes to manage collections of security information, rather than being restricted to a single static definition of one security rule. In the case of OleDbPermission, this enables you to define as many connection string constraints as you need, although this example defines only the single constraint.

If you run the sample code shown earlier that connects to SQL Server, a security exception is thrown. However, if instead you attempt to connect to an MDB database, as the following example shows, everything works:

C#

```
//Using a Sql connection string at this point will result in a SecurityException
        OleDbConnection oc = new OleDbConnection(
            "Provider=Microsoft.Jet.OLEDB.4.0;" +
            @"data source=C:\inetpub\wwwroot\379301_code\379301 +
            @ch04_code\cs\TrustLevels\\ASPNetdb_Template.mdb;");
        oc.Open();

    OleDbCommand ocmd = new OleDbCommand("select * from aspnet_Applications", oc);
        OleDbDataReader or = ocmd.ExecuteReader();
```

VB.NET

```
Dim oc As New OleDbConnection( _
"Provider=Microsoft.Jet.OLEDB.4.0;" & _
"data source=C:\inetpub\wwwroot\379301_code\379301 ch04_code\" & _
"cs\TrustLevels\\ASPNetdb_Template.mdb;")
oc.Open()

Dim ocmd As New OleDbCommand("select * from aspnet_Applications", oc)
Dim orr As OleDbDataReader = ocmd.ExecuteReader()
```

If a hoster provisioned only a specific database name (or names), you could even go one step further and define the <IPermission /> in the custom policy file to restrict access to a predefined name:

```
<IPermission class="OleDbPermission" version="1" >

<add ConnectionString="Provider=Microsoft.Jet.OLEDB.4.0;datasource=$AppDir$\
ASPNetdb_Template.mdb"
    KeyRestrictions="user id=;password=;"
    KeyRestrictionBehavior="AllowOnly"
/>

</IPermission>
```

Notice how the ConnectionString attribute in the <add /> element now also includes the data source definition. Furthermore, KeyRestrictions no longer allows you to specify a custom value for data source. Because ASP.NET performs a string search-and-replace for all tokens in a trust policy file, you can use the replacement token $AppDir$ inside of the ConnectionString attribute. The previous definition has the net effect of restricting an ASP.NET application to using only an Access database called ASPNetdb_Template.mdb located in the root of the application's physical directory structure. Attempting to use any other Access MDB will result in a SecurityException.

Customizing OdbcPermission

Another data access technology that many folks use in ASP.NET is ODBC. Even though it probably seems a bit old-fashioned to still be using ODBC (as I like to half-joke: every few years Microsoft needs to release an entirely new data access technology due to our predilection for reorgs), it is still widely used due to the prevalence of ODBC drivers that have been around for years. In many cases, database back ends that are no longer actively supported are accessible only through proprietary APIs or custom ODBC drivers. Another reason ODBC can be found on ASP.NET servers is that customers using the open-source MySQL database used to need the MySQL ODBC driver, although recently a .NET driver for MySQL was released.

If you want to enable ODBC for your ASP.NET applications, you can follow the same process shown earlier for OleDb. A <SecurityClass /> element needs to be added to the custom policy file that registers the OdbcPermission class:

```
<SecurityClass Name="OdbcPermission"
    Description="System.Data.Odbc.OdbcPermission, System.Data, Version=2.0.0.0,
Culture=neutral, PublicKeyToken=b77a5c561934e089"/>
```

Next, you need to determine what the declarative representation of an `OdbcPermission` looks like. Modifying the OleDb sample code used earlier, the following snippet outputs the XML representation of a permission that allows only the use of the Access provider via the `System.Data.Odbc` classes:

C#

```
OdbcPermission odp =
        new OdbcPermission(PermissionState.None);

odp.Add("Driver={Microsoft Access Driver (*.mdb)};",
                "Dbq=;uid=;pwd=;",
                KeyRestrictionBehavior.AllowOnly);

SecurityElement se = odp.ToXml();
Response.Write(Server.HtmlEncode(se.ToString()));
```

VB.NET

```
Dim odp As New OdbcPermission(PermissionState.None)

odp.Add("Driver={Microsoft Access Driver (*.mdb)};", _
    "Dbq=;uid=;pwd=;", KeyRestrictionBehavior.AllowOnly)

Dim se As SecurityElement = odp.ToXml()

Response.Write(Server.HtmlEncode(se.ToString()))
```

The `OdbcPermission` class actually has a programming model that is very similar to the `OleDb Permission` class. You can add multiple connection string related permissions into a single instance of `OdbcPermission`. Running the previous code, and then tweaking the output to use the shorter reference in the `class` attribute, results in the following `<IPermission />` declaration:

```
<IPermission class="OdbcPermission" version="1" >
 <add ConnectionString="Driver={Microsoft Access Driver (*.mdb)};"
     KeyRestrictions="Dbq=;uid=;pwd=;"
     KeyRestrictionBehavior="AllowOnly"/>
</IPermission>
```

Although the syntax of the connection string text is a bit different to reflect the ODBC syntax, you can see that the permission declaration mirrors what was shown earlier for OleDb.

With this permission added to the custom trust policy file, the code that uses Access will run without triggering any security exceptions.

C#

```
//The following won't work when only Access connection strings are allowed in the
//trust policy file.
//OdbcConnection oc =
//    new OdbcConnection("Driver={SQL Server};" +
//                       "Server=foo;Database=pubs;Uid=sa;Pwd=blank;");
```

```
        OdbcConnection oc = new OdbcConnection(
            "Driver={Microsoft Access Driver (*.mdb)};" +
            @"Dbq=C:\inetpub\wwwroot\379301_code\379301 ch04_code\cs\" +
            @TrustLevels\\ASPNetdb_Template.mdb;");
        oc.Open();


    OdbcCommand ocmd = new OdbcCommand("select * from aspnet_Applications", oc);
        OdbcDataReader or = ocmd.ExecuteReader();
```

VB.NET

```
        'The following won't work when only Access
        'conn strings are allowed for ODBC
        'OdbcConnection oc =
        '    new OdbcConnection("Driver={SQL Server};Server=foo;
            Database=pubs;Uid=sa;Pwd=blank;");
        Dim oc As New OdbcConnection( _
            "Driver={Microsoft Access Driver (*.mdb)};" & _
            "Dbq=C:\inetpub\wwwroot\379301_code\379301 ch04_code\cs" & _
            "\TrustLevels\\ASPNetdb_Template.mdb;")
        oc.Open()

        Dim ocmd As New OdbcCommand("select * from aspnet_Applications", oc)
        Dim orr As OdbcDataReader = ocmd.ExecuteReader()
```

However, attempting to create an `OdbcConnection` with a SQL Server-style connection string results in a `SecurityException` because it is disallowed by the permission definition in the trust policy file.

Allowing ODBC and OLEDB in ASP.NET

Now that you have seen how to enable ODBC and OleDb inside of partial trust ASP. NET applications, you should be aware that running either of these technologies reduces the security for your web applications. Many drivers written for ODBC and OleDb predate ASP.NET and for that matter predated widespread use of the Internet in some cases. The designs for these drivers didn't take into account scenarios such as shared hosters selling server space to customers on the Internet.

For example, the Jet provider for Access can be used to open Excel files and other Office data formats in addition to regular MDB files. Because many Office files, including Access databases, support scripting languages like VBScript, it is entirely possible for someone to use an Access database as a tunnel of sorts to the unmanaged code world. If you lockdown an ASP.NET application to partial trust but still grant selective access with the `OleDbPermission`, developers can write code to open an arbitrary Access database. After that happens, a developer can issue commands against the database that in turn trigger calls into VBScript or to operating system commands and of course when that happens, you are basically running the equivalent of an ASP page with the capability to call arbitrary COM objects.

Continued

> Because the .NET Framework CAS system does not extend into the code that runs inside of an Access database, after the `OleDbPermission` demand occurs, the Framework is no longer in the picture. In the case of Access, the Jet engine supports Registry settings that enable a sandboxed mode of operation. The sandbox prevents arbitrary code from being executed as the side effect from running a query. There may be additional avenues, though, for running scripts in Access databases. (I admit to having little experience in Access, which is probably a good thing!) Overall, the general advice is to thoroughly research the vagaries of whatever ODBC or OleDb drivers you are supporting and as much as possible, implement the mitigations suggested by the various vendors.

Using the WebPermision

One of the permissions defined in the Medium and High trust files is for the `System.Net.Web Permission`. This is probably one of the most confusing permissions for developers to use due to the interaction between the `<trust />` element and the settings for this permission. The default declaration looks like this:

```
<IPermission
      class="WebPermission"
      version="1">
   <ConnectAccess>
      <URI uri="$OriginHost$"/>
   </ConnectAccess>
</IPermission>
```

As with some of the other permissions you have looked at, the `WebPermission` supports multiple sets of nested information. Although a `WebPermission` can be used to define both outbound and inbound connection permissions, normally, you use `WebPermission` to define one or more network endpoints that your code can connect to. The default declaration shown previously defines a single connection permission that allows partially trusted code the right to make a connection to the network address defined by the `<URI />` element.

However, the definition for this element has the string replacement token: `$OriginHost$`. This definition is used conjunction with the `<trust />` element, which includes an attribute called `originHost` and its value is used as the replacement value for `$OriginHost$`. For example, if you define the following `<trust />` element:

```
<trust level="Medium_Custom" originUrl="http://www.microsoft.com/"/>
```

. . . when ASP.NET processes the trust policy file, it will result in a permission that grants connect access to `http://www.microsoft.com/`. Although the attribute is called `originUrl`, the reality is that the value you put in this attribute does not have to be your web server's domain name or host name. You can set a value that corresponds to your web farm's domain name if, for example, you make web service calls to other machines in your environment. However, you can just as easily use a value that points at any arbitrary network endpoint as was just shown. One subtle and extremely frustrating behavior to note here is that you need to have a trailing / at the end of the network address defined in the `originUrl` attribute. Also, when you write code that actually uses `System.Net` classes to connect to this endpoint, you also need to remember to use a trailing / character.

With the `<trust />` level setting shown previously, the following code allows you to make an HTTP request to the Microsoft home page and process the response:

C#

```
HttpWebRequest wr = (HttpWebRequest)WebRequest.Create("http://www.microsoft.com/");
HttpWebResponse resp = (HttpWebResponse)wr.GetResponse();

Response.Write(resp.Headers.ToString());
```

VB.NET

```
Dim wr As HttpWebRequest = CType( _
WebRequest.Create("http://www.microsoft.com/"), _
HttpWebRequest)
Dim resp As HttpWebResponse = CType(wr.GetResponse(), HttpWebResponse)

Response.Write(resp.Headers.ToString())
```

Because the `WebPermission` class also supports regular expression based definitions of network endpoints, you can define `originUrl` using a regular expression. The reason regular expression-based URLs are useful is that the `WebPermission` class is very precise in terms of what it allows. Defining a permission that allows access to only `www.microsoft.com` means that your code can access only that specific URL. If you happened to be curious about new games coming out, and created an `HttpWebRequest` for `www.microsoft.com/games/default.aspx`, then a `SecurityException` occurs.

You can rectify this by instead defining `originUrl` to allow requests to any arbitrary page located underneath `www.microsoft.com`.

```
<trust level="Medium_Custom" originUrl="http://www\.microsoft\.com/.*"/>
```

Notice the trailing .* at the end of the `originUrl` attribute. Now the `System.Net.WebPermission` class will interpret the URL as a regular expression; the trailing .* allows any characters to occur after the trailing slash. With that change, the following code will work without throwing any security exceptions:

C#

```
HttpWebRequest wr =
  (HttpWebRequest)WebRequest.Create("http://www.microsoft.com/games/default.aspx");
```

VB.NET

```
Dim wr As HttpWebRequest = CType( _
WebRequest.Create("http://www.microsoft.com/games/default.aspx"), _
HttpWebRequest)
```

Although the examples shown all exercise the `HttpWebRequest` class directly, the most likely use you will find for a custom `WebPermission` is in partial trust ASP.NET applications that call into web services. Without defining one or more `WebPermissions`, your web service calls will fail with less than enlightening security errors.

Because your web application may need to connect to multiple web service endpoints, potentially located under different DNS namespaces, you need to define a <IPermission /> element in your custom policy file with multiple nested <URI /> entries. As an example, the following code gives you the correct XML representation for a set of two different endpoints:

C#

```
WebPermission wp = new WebPermission();

Regex r = new Regex(@"http://www\.microsoft\.com/.*");
wp.AddPermission(NetworkAccess.Connect,r);

r = new Regex(@"http://www\.google\.com/.*");
wp.AddPermission(NetworkAccess.Connect, r);

SecurityElement se = wp.ToXml();
Response.Write(Server.HtmlEncode(se.ToString()));
```

VB.NET

```
Dim wp As New WebPermission()

Dim r As New Regex("http://www\.microsoft\.com/.*")
wp.AddPermission(NetworkAccess.Connect, r)

r = New Regex("http://www\.google\.com/.*")
wp.AddPermission(NetworkAccess.Connect, r)

Dim se As SecurityElement = wp.ToXml()
Response.Write(Server.HtmlEncode(se.ToString()))
```

The resulting XML, adjusted again for the class attribute, looks like this:

```
<IPermission class="WebPermission" version="1">
   <ConnectAccess>
      <URI uri="http://www\.microsoft\.com/.*"/>
      <URI uri="http://www\.google\.com/.*"/>
   </ConnectAccess>
</IPermission>
```

The $OriginHost$ replacement token is no longer being used. Realistically, after you understand how to define a WebPermission in your policy file, the originUrl attribute isn't really needed anymore. Instead, you can just build up multiple <URI /> elements as needed inside of your policy file. With the previous changes, you can now write code that connects to any page located underneath www.microsoft.com or www.google.com.

C#

```
HttpWebRequest wr =
(HttpWebRequest)WebRequest.Create("http://www.microsoft.com/games/default.aspx");
HttpWebResponse resp = (HttpWebResponse)wr.GetResponse();

...
```

```
resp.Close();

wr = (HttpWebRequest)WebRequest.Create("http://www.google.com/microsoft");
resp = (HttpWebResponse)wr.GetResponse();
```

VB.NET

```
        Dim wr As HttpWebRequest = CType( _
        WebRequest.Create("http://www.microsoft.com/games/default.aspx"), _
        HttpWebRequest)
        Dim resp As HttpWebResponse = CType(wr.GetResponse(), HttpWebResponse)
        ...
        resp.Close()
        wr = CType( _
        WebRequest.Create("http://www.google.com/microsoft"), _
        HttpWebRequest)
        resp = CType(wr.GetResponse(), HttpWebResponse)
```

Although I won't cover it here, the companion classes to HttpWebRequest/HttpWebResponse are the various System.Net.Socket* classes. As with the Http classes, the socket classes have their own permission: SocketPermission. Just like WebPermission, SocketPermission allows the definition of network endpoints for both socket connect and socket receive operations.

LINQ in Medium/Partial Trust ASP.NET Applications

Language Integrated Query (LINQ), introduced in the .NET Framework 3.5, is a standard way of accessing data, whether the data is stored in databases, XML files, objects, or other data sources. The purpose behind LINQ is to provide a standard set of query operators that the developer can make use of to query against different data sources by utilizing the same queries with some or minor changes between a data source and another.

By default, LINQ features, prior to the .NET Framework 3.5 final release mainly in .NET Framework 3.5 Beta 2, cannot run in an ASP.NET application that is configured with medium or partial trust. As you have learned above, the set of permissions granted to an ASP.NET web application running in the medium or partial trust is determined by a Code Access Security (CAS) policy file located on the web server. When the .NET Framework 3.5 Beta 2 is installed on the machine, the existing or new ASP.NET web applications or websites continue to use the same CAS policy files that were defined with the .NET Framework 2.0. However, this has been resolved with the final release of the .NET Framework 3.5 in such a way that when you install the .NET Framework 3.5 on the machine, the CAS policy files get updated and modified to reflect the permission changes required to make LINQ function properly in ASP.NET applications running under the medium or partial trust levels. The following paragraphs describe a step-by-step process to show you the permissions required by LINQ to function properly in web applications running in the medium or partial trust, and how to configure them manually. Remember, the following configurations are already done for you when you install the .NET Framework 3.5 final release on your machine.

LINQ features require the application running inside it to be granted the RestrictedMemberAccess permission, which is not granted by default for ASP.NET 2.0 running in medium or partial trust. The RestrictedMemberAccess permission indicates whether the restricted invocation of non-public types and members is allowed or not for partially trusted code. The restricted invocation means that for a partially trusted code to access non-public types and members, the set of permissions granted to it must contain all the permissions granted to the assembly that has the non-public types and members.

Before getting into how to enable an ASP.NET application running in the medium or partial trust level to function properly with LINQ, let's look at a sample code that makes use of a LINQ to SQL query:

C#

```
PubsDataContext context = new PubsDataContext();
var query = from emp in context.employees
            select emp;
foreach (employee empl in query)
{
    Response.Write("Employee Name: " + empl.fname + "<br/>");
}
```

VB.NET

```
Dim context As New PubsDataContext()
Dim query = From emp In context.employees _
            Select emp

For Each empl As employee In query
    Response.Write("Employee Name: " & empl.fname & "<br/>")
Next empl
```

The preceding code assumes that there is a `PubsDataContext` created in the application that points to the famous Pubs database on Microsoft SQL Server 2000 or 2005. Without going into much detail on the `DataContext` class, consider it as the gateway to access the data tables that were loaded from the database and converted into .NET objects. The same above shows a simple query that retrieves all the employees' records from the Employees data table. Once the data is retrieved, a `foreach`-loop goes through every item returned and displays onscreen the first name of every employee in the result set of the query.

When you run the preceding code in an ASP.NET application configured with a Medium trust level in such a way the machine running the application is still using the unmodified .NET Framework 2.0 CAS policy files, you will receive the following exception:

```
[SecurityException: Request for the permission of type 'System.Security.
Permissions.ReflectionPermission, mscorlib, Version=2.0.0.0, Culture=neutral, Publi
cKeyToken=b77a5c561934e089' failed.]
```

As you can see, a request for the permission of type `ReflectionPermission` is done to allow the code to browse the members on the `employee` class above. Hence, the need for granting access for the `ReflectionPermission` for the LINQ features to work properly in an ASP.NET web application running under the medium or partial trust level.

To allow ASP.NET web applications running under the .NET Framework 3.5 to use the new LINQ features, you need to modify the CAS policy file that corresponds to the trust level that is configured for the applications, which is a task that has been already done for you when the .NET Framework 3.5 final release was installed on your machine.

Assuming that you have installed .NET Framework 3.5 Beta 2 and your application is configured with the medium trust level, the changes should target the web_mediumtrust.config configuration file. To start, open the aforementioned configuration file, which located in the following directory on your machine:

```
%windir%\Microsoft.NET\Framework\v2.0.50727\CONFIG
```

Make sure to back up the CAS policy file you want to modify. This is recommended so that no harm is generated on your existing ASP.NET web applications in the event something wrong went on while modifying the policy file.

Locate the <SecurityClasses> configuration section inside the web_mediumtrust.config file and check if an entry is found for the ReflectionPermission class. If not, make sure to add the following entry:

```
<SecurityClass Name="ReflectionPermission"     Description="System.Security.
Permissions.ReflectionPermission, mscorlib,Version=2.0.0.0, Culture=neutral, Public
KeyToken=b77a5c561934e089"/>
```

The ReflectionPersmission class controls access to non-public types and members through the System.Reflection classes with the help of the appropriate ReflectionPermissionFlag enumeration. Once the preceding entry is added, you also need to add the following <IPermission> entry to the <NamedPermissionSets>, as follows:

```
<IPermission
     class="ReflectionPermission"
     version="1"
     Flags="RestrictedMemberAccess"/>
</PermissionSet>
```

For the LINQ features to function properly, the ReflectionPermission should be granted on the CAS policy file with the ReflectionPermissionFlag set to RestrictedMemberAccess. That is everything you need to do to make the LINQ features function properly in an application configured to run with the medium trust level.

If you are using another trust level that already contains an entry for the ReflectionPersmission, make sure that ReflectionPermissionFlag contains a value of RestrictedMemberAccess, as follows:

```
<IPermission
     class="ReflectionPermission"
     version="1"
     Flags="ReflectionEmit, RestrictedMemberAccess"/>
```

Save the file and make sure to restart the IIS 7.0 web server. Now running the sample code above should work smoothly without any exceptions.

Remember that the preceding changes and demonstration is required only on a machine that has .NET Framework 3.5 Beta 2 installed and not the final release of the framework; as you know by now, .NET Framework 3.5 final release modifies the CAS policy files on your behalf. However, the demonstration was to show you in depth what LINQ features require to function properly in applications running under .NET Framework 3.5 and configured with medium or partial trust levels.

The Default Security Permissions Defined by ASP.NET

ASP.NET ships with default trust policy files for High, Medium, Low, and Minimal trust. You have already read about several different permissions that are configured in these files. This section covers all the permissions that appear in the files in the ASP.NET named permission set, along with information on the different rights that are granted depending on the trust level.

AspNetHostingPermission

To support the trust level model, ASP.NET created a new permission class: `System.Web.AspNet HostingPermission`. The permission class is used as the runtime representation of the application's configured trust level. Although you could programmatically determine the trust level of an application by looking at the `level` attribute of the `<trust />` element, that programming approach isn't consistent with how you would normally use CAS permissions. Because `AspNetHostingPermission` inherits `CodeAccessPermission`, code can instead demand an `AspNetHostingPermission` just like any other permissions class. The Framework will perform its stack walk, ensuring that all code in the current call stack has the demanded trust level. ASP.NET uses this capability extensively within its runtime to protect access to pieces of functionality that are not intended for use at lower trust levels.

The permission class has a public property `Level` that indicates the trust level represented by the permission instance. In the various trust policy files, there is always a definition of `AspNetHostingPermission`.

```
<IPermission
class="AspNetHostingPermission"
         version="1"
         Level="High"
/>
```

The usual convention is to set the `Level` attribute in the `<IPermission />` element to the effective trust level represented by the policy file.

There is nothing to prevent you from setting the `Level` attribute to a value that is inconsistent with the overall intent of the trust policy file. For example, you could declare an `AspNetHostingPermission` with a `Level` of High inside of the minimal trust policy file. However, you should normally not do this, because the value of the `Level` property is used by ASP.NET to protect access to certain pieces of functionality. Artificially increasing the trust level can result in ASP.NET successfully checking for a specific trust level and then failing with `SecurityException` when the runtime attempts a privileged operation that isn't allowed based on the other permissions defined in the trust policy file.

The problem also exists with the reverse condition; you could define a lower trust level than what the permissions in the trust policy file would normally imply. For example, you could copy the policy file for High trust, and then change the `AspNetHostingPermission` definition's `Level` attribute to `Medium`. Even though ASP.NET internally won't run into unexpected exceptions, you now have the problem that ASP.NET "thinks" it is running at Medium trust, but the permissions granted to the application are actually more appropriate for a High trust application.

All this brings us to a very important point about the `AspNetHostingPermission`. The intent of the `Level` property is to be a broad indicator of the level of trust that you are willing to associate with the application. Although the `<IPermission />` definitions in the rest of the policy file are a concrete representation of the trust level, the `Level` property is used as a surrogate for making other trust-related decisions in code. Whenever possible you should set the `Level` attribute appropriately based on the level of trust you are willing to grant to the application. Internally ASP.NET needs to make a number of security decisions based on an application's trust level. Rather than creating concrete permissions for each and every security decision (this would result in dozens of new permission classes at a bare minimum), ASP.NET instead looks at the `AspNetHostingPermission` for an application and makes security judgments based on it. This is the main reason why you should ensure that the "Level" attribute is set appropriately for your application.

Trust Level Intent

So, what specifically are the implications behind each trust level? Full trust is easy to understand because it dispenses with the need for a trust policy file and a definition of `AspNetHostingPermission`. The following table lists the conceptual intent behind the other trust levels.

Trust Level	Intent
Full	The ASP.NET application can call anything it wants.
High	The ASP.NET application should be allowed to call most classes within the .NET Framework without any restrictions. Although the High trust policy file does not contain an exhaustive list of all possible Framework permissions (the file would be huge if you attempted this), High trust implies that aside from calling into unmanaged code (this is disallowed), it is acceptable to use most of the remainder of the Framework's functionality. Although sandboxing privileged operations in GAC'd classes is preferred, adding new permissions directly to the High trust policy file instead would not be considered "breaking the contract" of High trust.
Medium	The ASP.NET application is intended to be constrained in terms of the classes and Framework functionality it is allowed to use. A Medium trust application isn't expected to be able to directly call dangerous or privileged pieces of code. However, a Medium trust application is expected to be able to read and write information; it is just that the reading and writing may be constrained, or require special permissions before it is allowed. If problems arise because of a lack of permissions, you try to avoid adding the requisite permission classes to the Medium trust policy file. Instead, if privileged operations require special permissions, the code should be placed in a separate assembly and installed in the GAC. Furthermore, if at all possible, this type of assembly should demand some kind of permission that you would expect the Medium trust application to possess. For example you could demand the `AspNetHostingPermission` at the Medium level to ensure that even less trusted ASP.NET applications cannot call into your GAC'd assembly.
Low	The ASP.NET application is running in an environment where user code should not be trusted with any kind of potentially dangerous operations. Low trust applications are frequently considered to be read-only applications; this would cover things like a reporting application. Because this is such a "low" level of trust, you should question any application running in this trust level that is allowed to reach out and modify data. For example, in the physical world someone that you had a low level of trust for is probably not an individual you would trust to make changes to your bank account balance. As with Medium trust, you should use GAC'd assemblies to solve permission problems, although you should look at the operations allowed in your assemblies to see if they are really appropriate for a Low trust application. Note that Low trust is also appropriate for web applications like SharePoint that provide their own hosted environment and thus their own security model on top of ASP.NET. Applications like SharePoint lock down the rights of pages that are just dropped on the web server's file system. Developers instead make use of privileged functionality through the SharePoint APIs or by following SharePoint's security model.

Continued

Trust Level	Intent
Minimal	A Minimal trust application means that you don't trust the code in the application to do much of anything. If permission problems arise, you should not work around the issue with GAC'd assemblies. Instead, you should question why a minimally trusted application needs to carry out a protected operation. Realistically, this means that a Minimal trust application is almost akin to serving out static HTML files, with the additional capability to use the ASP.NET page model for richer page development.

ASP.NET Functionality Restricted by Trust Level

ASP.NET makes a number of decisions internally based on the trust level defined by the AspNetHosting Permission. Because High and Full trust applications imply the ability to use most Framework functionality, the allowed ASP.NET functionality at these levels isn't something you need to worry about.

However, the Medium trust level is the lowest level at which the following pieces of ASP.NET functionality are allowed. Below Medium trust, the following features and APIs are not allowed:

❑ Accessing asynchronous pages (the Async page attribute)

❑ Accessing transacted pages (the Transaction page attribute)

❑ Using the Culture page attribute

❑ Setting debug=true for a page or the entire application

❑ Sending mail with System.Web.Mail.SmtpMail

❑ Calling Request.LogonUserIdentity

❑ Calling Response.AppendToLog

❑ Explicitly calling HttpRuntime.ProcessRequest

❑ Retrieving the MachineName property from HttpServerUtility

❑ Setting the ScriptTimeout property on HttpServerUtility

❑ Using the System.Web.Compilation.BuildManager class

❑ Displaying a source error and source file for a failing pages

At Low trust, there are a still a few pieces of ASP.NET functionality available that are not allowed when running at Minimal trust:

❑ Retrieving Request.Params.

❑ Retrieving Request.ServerVariables.

❑ Retrieving HttpRuntime.IsOnUNCShare.

❑ Calling into the provider-based features: Membership, Role Manager, Profile, Web Parts Personalization, and Site Navigation. Note, though, that most of the providers for these features will not work in Low trust because their underlying permissions are not in the Low trust policy file.

Implications of AspNetHostingPermission Outside of ASP.NET

As you may have inferred from the name of the permission, it is primarily intended for use with ASP.NET-specific code. Most of the time, this means Framework code that has the `AspNetHostingPermission` attribute or that internally demands this permission to be called from inside of ASP.NET. In fully trusted code-execution environments outside of ASP.NET you may not realize this is happening. For example, the following code runs without a problem in a console application.

C#

```
Console.WriteLine(HttpUtility.HtmlEncode("<br />"));
```

VB.NET

```
Console.WriteLine(HttpUtility.HtmlEncode("<br />"))
```

Notice that this code is using the `System.Web.HttpUtility` class. Running the console application from the local hard drive works, even though the `HttpUtility` class has the following declarative `LinkDemand`:

C#

```
[AspNetHostingPermission(SecurityAction.LinkDemand,
            Level=AspNetHostingPermissionLevel.Minimal]
```

VB.NET

```
<AspNetHostingPermission(SecurityAction.LinkDemand, _
        Level:=AspNetHostingPermissionLevel.Minimal)>
```

This works by default because applications running from the local hard drive are considered by the .NET Framework to be running in the My Computer security zone. Any code running from this zone is fully trusted. As a result, when it evaluates the `LinkDemand`, the Framework the application is running in full trust, and thus ignores any permission checks.

However, if you move the compiled executable to a universal naming convention (UNC) share and then run it, you end up with a `SecurityException` and the following stack dump information:

```
System.Security.SecurityException: Request for the permission of type 'System.Web.
AspNetHostingPermission, System, Version=2.0.0.0, Culture=neutral, PublicKeyToken=b
77a5c561934e089' failed.
....
The assembly or AppDomain that failed was:
UsingAspNetCodeOutsideofAspNet, Version=1.0.0.0, Culture=neutral,
PublicKeyToken=null
The Zone of the assembly that failed was: Internet
The Url of the assembly that failed was: file://remoteserver/c$/
UsingAspNetCodeOutsideofAspNet.exe
```

Now the Framework considers the application to be running in partial trust. Because the executable was moved to a UNC share, the Framework applied the security restrictions from the Internet zone. When `LinkDemand` occurred for `AspNetHostingPermission`, the Framework looked for that permission in the named permission set that the Framework associates with the Internet zone. Of course, it couldn't find it because the `AspNetHostingPermission` is typically found only inside of the ASP.NET trust policy files.

I won't cover how to fix this security problem in this chapter, because most of the ASP.NET classes are not intended for use outside of a web application anyway. However, in Chapter 15, "SqlRoleProvider," I walk through an example of using a provider-based feature from inside of a partial trust non-ASP.NET application. Both Membership and Role Manager are examples of ASP.NET classes that were explicitly tweaked to make them useable outside of a web application. However, the classes for these features make extensive use of AspNetHostingPermission, so it is necessary to understand how to grant the AspNetHostingPermission to partial trust non-ASP.NET applications that use these two features.

Using AspNetHostingPermission in Your Code

Because AspNetHostingPermission models the conceptual trust that you grant to an application, you can make use of this permission as a surrogate for creating a permission class from scratch. In fact, one of the reasons ASP.NET uses AspNetHostingPermission to protect certain features is to reduce the class explosion that would occur if every protected feature had its own permission class. So, rather than creating TransactedPagePermission, AsyncPagePermission, SetCultureAttributePermission, and so on, ASP.NET groups functionality according to the trust level that is appropriate for the feature.

You can follow a similar approach with standalone assemblies that you author. This applies to custom control assemblies as well as to assemblies that contain middle-tier code or other logic. For example, you can create a standalone assembly that uses the permission with the following code:

C#

```
public class SampleBusinessObject
{
    public SampleBusinessObject() { }

    public string DoSomeWork()
    {
        AspNetHostingPermission perm =
            new AspNetHostingPermission(AspNetHostingPermissionLevel.Medium);

        perm.Demand();

        //At this point it is safe to perform privileged work
        return "Successfully passed the permission check.";
    }
}
```

VB.NET

```
Public Class SampleBusinessObject
    Public Sub New()
    End Sub

    Public Function DoSomeWork() As String
        Dim perm As New AspNetHostingPermission( _
        AspNetHostingPermissionLevel.Medium)

        perm.Demand()

        'At this point it is safe to perform privileged work
```

```
            Return "Successfully passed the permission check."
        End Function
End Class
```

Drop the compiled assembly into the /bin folder of an ASP.NET application. Because the assembly demands Medium trust, the following simple page code in an ASP.NET application works at Medium trust or above.

C#

```
        SampleBusinessObject obj = new SampleBusinessObject();
        Response.Write(obj.DoSomeWork());
```

VB.NET

```
        Dim obj As New SampleBusinessObject()
        Response.Write(obj.DoSomeWork())
```

However, if you configure the ASP.NET application to run at Low or Minimal trust, the previous code will fail with a SecurityException stating that the request for the AspNetHostingPermission failed. Unfortunately, though, the exception information will not be specific enough to indicate additional any extra information; in this case, it would be helpful to know the level that was requested but failed.

In cases like this where you probably control or have access to the code in the standalone assemblies, you can determine which security permissions are required by using the permcalc tool located in the .NET Framework's SDK directory. (This directory is available underneath the Visual Studio install directory if you chose to install the SDK as part the Visual Studio setup process.) I ran permcalc against the sample assembly with the following command line:

```
"C:\Program Files\Microsoft Visual Studio 8\SDK\v2.0\Bin\permcalc"
SampleBusinessTier.dll
```

The tool outputs an XML file containing all declarative and code-based permission demands. Although declarative permission requirements are the easiest to infer (remember there is also an AspNetHosting Permission attribute that you can use to adorn a class or a method), the tool does a pretty good job of inspecting the actual code and pulling out the code-based permission demands. In the case of the sample assembly, it returned the following snippet of permission information:

```
<Method Sig="instance string DoSomeWork()">
- <Demand>
- <PermissionSet version="1" class="System.Security.PermissionSet">
    <IPermission
        Level="Medium"
        version="1"
        class="System.Web.AspNetHostingPermission, System,
        Version=2.0.0.0, Culture=neutral,  PublicKeyToken=b77a5c561934e089"
    />
  </PermissionSet>
  </Demand>
```

The <Demand /> element in the permcalc output shows that the tool determined that the DoSomeWork method is demanding AspNetHostingPermission with the Level at Medium.

DnsPermission

As the name implies, the `System.Net.DnsPermission` class defines the ability of your code to perform forward and reverse address lookups with the `System.Net.Dns` class. The permission is a binary permission in that it either grants code the right call into the `Dns` class or it denies the ability to use the `Dns` class. An interesting side note is that if you do not add `DnsPermission` to a trust policy file, but you have added `WebPermission`, you can still make use of the `HttpWebRequest` and related classes. Internally, `System.Net` assumes that if you have the necessary `WebPermission`, it can perform any required DNS lookups internally on your behalf.

The rights for `DnsPermission` at the various trust levels are shown in the following table:

Trust Level	Granted Permission
Full	Unrestricted
High	Unrestricted
Medium	Unrestricted
Low	No rights to use the `Dns` class
Minimal	No rights to use the `Dns` class

EnvironmentPermission

The `System.Security.Permissions.EnvironmentPermission` class defines the ability of user code to access environment variables via the `System.Environment` class. If you drop to a command line and run the `SET` command, all sorts of interesting information is available from the environment variables. Because this could be used as a backdoor for gathering information about the web server, the ASP.NET trust policy files restrict access to only a few environment variables in the lower trust levels.

The `EnvironmentPermission` supports defining access levels on a more granular basis, even down to the level of protecting individual environment variables. As a result, you can control the ability to read and write individual environment variables. Each security attribute (All, Read, and Write) in the declarative representation of an `EnironmentPermission` can contain a semicolon delimited list of environment variables.

The rights for `EnvironmentPermission` at the various trust levels are shown in the following table:

Trust Level	Granted Permission
Full	Unrestricted
High	Unrestricted
Medium	Can only read the following environment variables: TEMP, TMP, USERNAME, OS, COMPUTERNAME. No ability to set environment variables.
Low	No rights to read or write any environment variables
Minimal	No rights to read or write any environment variables

FileIOPermission

I have already covered most of the functionality for the `System.Security.Permissions.File`
`IOPermission` class in other sections. This permission also supports defining different permissions
for different directory and file paths. The thing that is a little odd about this permission class is that it
takes a somewhat nonoptimal approach to declaring multiple permissions. Unlike `WebPermission` or
`SocketPermission`, `FileIOPermission` does not output nested elements within a `<IPermission />`
element. Instead, it has a fixed set of attributes, but each path-related attribute can contain a semicolon-
delimited list of multiple paths. For example, the declarative syntax of a `FileIOPermission` with different permissions for two different directory paths is shown here:

```
<IPermission
    class="FileIOPermission"
    version="1"
    Read="d:\temp;d:\somedummylocation"
    Write="d:\somedummylocation"
    Append="d:\temp;d:\somedummylocation"
/>
```

This permission defines only allowable file I/O operations at the Framework level. This means the
permission class is only able to define the ability of user code to perform logical operations (read, write,
and so on based on a set of defined file paths. However, the `FileIOPermission` does not protect access
to files and directories based on NT file system (NTFS) file ACLs. As a result, it is completely possible
that from a CAS perspective the Framework will allow your code to issue a file I/O operation, but from
an NTFS perspective, your code may not have the necessary security permissions. When performing
any type of file I/O, you also need to ensure that the identity of the operating system thread has been
granted the necessary rights on the file system.

The following table lists the default permissions for the different trust levels.

Trust Level	Granted Permission
Full	Unrestricted.
High	Unrestricted: Remember, this means the ability to read and write files anywhere in the file system.
Medium	Read, write, append, and path discovery are all allowed for directories and paths located within the directory structure of the web application. Operations outside of the application's directory structure are not allowed.
Low	Only read and path discovery are all allowed for directories and paths located within the directory structure of the web application. Write operations are not allowed within the application's directory structure. Also, operations outside of the application's directory structure are not allowed.
Minimal	No file I/O rights.

IsolatedStorageFilePermission

The `System.Security.Permissions.IsolatedStorageFilePermission` class controls the allowable
file operations when using the `System.IO.IsolatedStorage.IsolatedStorageFile` class. I honestly

have never encountered any customers using isolated file storage in an ASP.NET application. Although you could technically use isolated storage as a way to store information locally on the web server for each website user, there are probably not any web applications that work this way: A database would be better choice, especially in web farm environments. However, because IsolatedStoragePermission is also defined by the Framework in the machine CAS policy, the permission is included in the ASP.NET trust policy files to ensure that ASP.NET has the final say on what is allowed when using isolated storage.

The following table lists the default permissions for the different trust levels.

Trust Level	Granted Permission
Full	Unrestricted.
High	Unrestricted.
Medium	Isolated storage is allowed, but the only storage mode that can be used isolates data by user identity. The disk quota for each user is effectively set to infinite.
Low	Isolated storage is allowed, but the only storage mode that can be used isolates data by user identity. The disk quota for each user is set to 1MB.
Minimal	Not allowed.

PrintingPermission

Before you double over laughing at why this permission exists in an ASP.NET trust policy file, I'll state that the reason is the same as mentioned earlier for the IsolatedStorageFilePermission. The default machine CAS policy grants System.Drawing.Printing.PrintingPermission to code running in the various predefined security zones. So, ASP.NET also defines the PrintingPermission in its trust files to ensure that it has a final say in the level of access granted to user code that works with printers.

The following table lists the default permissions for the different trust levels.

Trust Level	Granted Permission
Full	Unrestricted.
High	User code can issue commands to print to the default printer attached to the web server.
Medium	User code can issue commands to print to the default printer attached to the web server.
Low	Not allowed.
Minimal	Not allowed.

ReflectionPermission

The System.Security.Permissions.ReflectionPermission class defines the types of reflection operations you can perform with classes in the System.Reflection namespaces. This is a very important permission for ensuring the safety of partial trust applications because reflecting against code introduces the potential for calling private/internal methods, and inspecting private/internal variables. As a result, in the default ASP.NET policy files only High trust code has rights to use some of the reflection APIs. In practice, you should not grant reflection permission to partially trusted user code due to the potential for malicious code to deconstruct the code that is running on your server.

The following table lists the default permissions for the different trust levels.

Trust Level	Granted Permission
Full	Unrestricted.
High	User code can use only classes in the `System.Reflection.Emit` namespace. These classes can be used to generate code programmatically as well as a compiled representation of the generated code. This functionality can be useful for an application that dynamically generates assemblies to disk and then references these classes from page code.
Medium	Not allowed.
Low	Not allowed.
Minimal	Not allowed.

RegistryPermission

The `System.Security.Permissions.RegistryPermission` defines permissions for creating, reading, and writing Registry keys and values. Much as with `FileIOPermission`, you can use this permission class to define a set of permission rules that vary depending on the Registry path. The various security attributes on the `<IPermission />` element contain a semicolon delimited list of Registry keys to protect. This permission is enforced whenever you use the `Microsoft.Win32.RegistryKey` class to manipulate the registry. Because there usually isn't a need to directly read and write Registry data in web applications, ASP.NET by default only defines a `RegistryPermission` for High trust. If you need access to Registry information at lower trust levels, you should put Registry access code into a separate GAC'd assembly that has the necessary permissions. Normally, though, the restrictions on Registry access are not too onerous because in web applications you use configuration files as opposed to Registry keys for storing application configuration data.

The following table lists the default permissions for the different trust levels.

Trust Level	Granted Permission
Full	Unrestricted
High	Unrestricted
Medium	Not allowed
Low	Not allowed
Minimal	Not allowed

SecurityPermission

The System.Security.Permissions.SecurityPermission class is a proverbial jack-of-all-trades permissions class. Instead of defining a narrow set of permissions used by a specific set of classes in the framework, a SecurityPermission class can define around fifteen permissions that apply to different privileged operations in the framework. For example, these permissions define the ability to call unmanaged code and the ability for code to execute. The list of possible permissions that can be granted with a SecurityPermission can be found in the SecurityPermissionFlag enumeration.

In partial trust applications, ASP.NET allows a subset of the available permissions by defining progressively more restrictive security permissions for the lower trust levels. The specific permissions that ASP.NET may grant are listed here:

❑ **Assertion:** This permission allows code to assert that it has the right to call into other code that may demand certain permissions. The advanced topics sections of this chapter cover how to write GAC'd assemblies that use this permission. In partially trusted applications, assertion is usually not granted because code doesn't have sufficient rights to assert other arbitrary permission defined in the Framework.

❑ **ControlPrincipal:** Allows code to change the IPrincipal reference available from Thread .CurrentPrincipal. ASP.NET also demands this right if you attempt to set the User property on an HttpContext. Keep this permission in mind if you write custom authentication or custom authorization modules. If your modules need to set the thread principal when running in Low trust or below, you need to deploy your modules in the GAC and assert a Security Permission with the ControlPrincipal right.

❑ **ControlThread:** Grants code the right to perform privileged operations on an instance of System .Threading.Thread. For example, with this permission code is allowed to call Thread.Abort, Thread.Suspend, and Thread.Resume.

❑ **Execution:** Allows .NET Framework code to run. If ASP.NET did not define this permission in the various trust policy files, none of your code would ever be allowed to run. Removing this permission from any of the ASP.NET trust policy files effectively disables the ability to run .aspx pages.

❑ **RemotingConfiguration:** Allows an application to configure and start up a remoting infrastructure. Many ASP.NET applications don't need to expose or call into remotable objects. However, if you want to run a partial trust ASP.NET application that consumes objects using .NET Remoting, make sure this permission is defined in the trust policy file. Note that RemotingConfiguration isn't needed if your application calls Web Services.

The following table lists the security permissions granted at the different trust levels.

Trust Level	Granted Permission
Full	Unrestricted
High	Assertion, Execution, ControlThread, ControlPrincipal, RemotingConfiguration
Medium	Assertion, Execution, ControlThread, ControlPrincipal, RemotingConfiguration
Low	Execution
Minimal	Execution

As you can see from this list, at Low and Minimal trust user code has only the ability execute. Because ASP.NET restricts the `SecurityPermission` at Low and Minimal trust, you need to deploy all sensitive business or security logic in GAC'd assemblies.

Due to the sensitive nature of the Assertion and ControlPrincipal rights, you should look into removing these if you create a custom trust level. The Assertion right is really intended for trusted code that can successfully assert some kind of underlying permission. However, partially trusted code by its very nature lacks many permissions, and thus it is unlikely that user code in a code-behind page could successfully assert a permission (if the code already had the necessary permission, it wouldn't need to assert anything in the first place).

The ControlPrincipal right is a security-sensitive right appropriate only for code that manipulates identity information for a request. Although it is a little bit more difficult to write a standalone HTTP authentication/authorization module and deploy it in the GAC, it is much more secure to do so and then remove the ControlPrincipal right in a trust policy file. Doing so ensures that some random piece of application code can't arbitrarily change the security information for a request, something especially trivial to accomplish when using forms authentication.

SmtpPermission

In ASP.NET 1.0 and 1.1, the closest thing to a managed mail class was found in `System.Web.Mail` `.SmtpMail`. Internally, `SmtpMail` is just a wrapper around CDONTS, which itself is unmanaged code. Because it would be excessive to grant unmanaged code permission to a partially trusted ASP.NET application, ASP.NET instead protects access to this mail class by using the `AspNetHostingPermission` as surrogate permission. At Medium trust or above, you can use `SmtpMail`, whereas at lower trust levels you cannot send mail.

Starting with the v2.0 of the Framework, though, the `System.Web.Mail.SmtpMail` class has been deprecated and is replaced by the classes in the `System.Net.Mail` namespace. These classes protect access to mail operations using the `System.Net.Mail.SmtpPermission` class. To maintain parity with the mail behavior of earlier ASP.NET release, the trust policy files are defined to allow all mail operations at Medium trust and above as shown in the following table.

Trust Level	Granted Permission
Full	Unrestricted
High	Unrestricted
Medium	Unrestricted
Low	Not allowed
Minimal	Not allowed

SocketPermission

`System.Net.SocketPermission` is the companion permission class to the `System.Net.WebPermission` class discussed earlier. It supports defining connect and receive access in a granular fashion segmented by different network endpoints. Because of the potential for mischief when using the socket classes, ASP.NET grants access to only High trust applications. If you have web applications that need to make outbound socket connections (receiving socket connections is unlikely in a web application), you can use the same approach described earlier for the WebPermission class to determine the exact XML syntax necessary to restrict socket connections to specific endpoints.

The following table lists the security permissions granted at the different trust levels.

Trust Level	Granted Permission
Full	Unrestricted
High	Unrestricted
Medium	Not allowed
Low	Not allowed
Minimal	Not allowed

SqlClientPermission

The System.Data.SqlClient.SqlClientPermission class is used to allow or disallow use of the classes in the System.Data.SqlClient namespace. There is no support for granular permissions along the lines of the SocketPermission or WebPermission classes. Because Medium trust is the recommended default trust level for shared hosters, the permission is available at Medium trust and above.

The following table lists the security permissions granted at the different trust levels.

Trust Level	Granted Permission
Full	Unrestricted
High	Unrestricted
Medium	Unrestricted
Low	Not allowed
Minimal	Not allowed

WebPermission

System.Net.WebPermission is used to define a granular set of connection rules for making HTTP requests to various network endpoints. Because it is a potentially complex permission with multiple nested permission elements, you can use the techniques described in the section "Using the WebPermission" to determine the correct XML.

The following table lists the security permissions granted at the different trust levels.

Trust Level	Granted Permission
Full	Unrestricted.
High	Unrestricted.

Trust Level	Granted Permission
Medium	Only connect access is granted to a single network endpoint. This endpoint is defined by the `originUrl` attribute in the `<trust />` configuration element.
Low	Not allowed.
Minimal	Not allowed.

Advanced Topics on Partial Trust

There are a few advanced issues on partial trusts that you may encounter while developing your application:

❑   Exception behavior when dealing with Link demands

❑   Requirements for using the "allow partially trusted callers attribute" (APTCA) when writing trusted types for use by ASP.NET

❑   Sandboxing access to security sensitive code with GAC'd assemblies

❑   The `processRequestInApplicationTrust` attribute in the `<trust />` element

LinkDemand Exception Behavior

All the sample code used so far to highlight exception behavior has involved full permission demands made by different classes in the Framework. However, this type of permission demand can be expensive because the Framework has to crawl up the current call stack each and every time a full permission demand occurs. Even if the exact same code is executing on subsequent page requests, the Framework still has to perform a fair amount of work to reevaluate the results of a demand.

To mitigate the performance hit of full demands, the Framework also includes the concept of a link demand, also referred to as a `LinkDemand`. The idea behind a `LinkDemand` is that the Framework needs to make a permission check only the first time code from one assembly attempts to call a piece of protected code in another assembly. After that check is made, the Framework does not perform any additional security evaluations on subsequent calls.

The issue you may run into when developing partial trust applications is that `LinkDemands` are evaluated before your code even starts running. The reason for this is that a `LinkDemand` occurs when the Framework is attempting to link the code that you wrote with the compiled code that exists in another assembly. Establishing this link occurs before the first line of code in your method executes. As a result, even though you may have try/catch blocks set up to explicitly catch `SecurityExceptions`, you still end up with an unhandled exception. To highlight this behavior, let's use one of the sample pieces of code from the beginning of the chapter to make a call into the ADO PIA.

C#

```
try
{
    //An unhandled exception due to LinkDemands will occur before this code runs
    RecordsetClass rc = new RecordsetClass();
```

```
        int fieldCount = rc.Fields.Count;

    Response.Write("Successfully created an ADO recordset using the ADO PIA.");
}
catch (Exception ex)
{
    Response.Write(ex.Message + "<br />" +
        Server.HtmlEncode(ex.StackTrace));
}
```

VB.NET

```
    Try
        'The next two lines of code result '
        'in an unhandled exception from the
        LinkDemand()
        Dim rc As New RecordsetClass()
        Dim fieldCount As Integer = rc.Fields.Count

        Response.Write( _
            "Successfully created an ADO " & _
            "recordset using the ADO PIA.")
    Catch ex As Exception
        Response.Write(ex.Message & "<br />" & _
            Server.HtmlEncode(ex.StackTrace))
    End Try
```

Even though this code is catching almost every exception, when you attempt to run this code in a partial trust ASP.NET application (I used Medium trust for the test), the page fails with an unhandled exception. Some of the abbreviated exception information is shown here:

```
[SecurityException: That assembly does not allow partially trusted callers.]

System.Security.CodeAccessSecurityEngine.ThrowSecurityException(Assembly
asm, PermissionSet granted, PermissionSet refused, RuntimeMethodHandle rmh,
SecurityAction action, Object demand, IPermission permThatFailed) at LinkDemand.
CreateRecordset() at LinkDemand.Button1_Click(Object sender, EventArgs e) in c:\
inetpub\wwwroot\379301_code\379301 ch04_code\cs\WorkingWithTrustLevels\LinkDemand.
aspx.cs:line 36
```

The call stack shows the code appears to have transitioned from the button click handler immediately into the internals of the .NET Framework security system. The reason is that the ADO primary interop assembly (PIA) is installed in the GAC, and thus the Framework requires that any calling code itself be fully trusted. The security check immediately failed when it detected that the calling code was partially trusted. In fact, one of the most common symptoms of a failed LinkDemand is the exception text stating that some assembly doesn't allow partially trusted callers.

The way around the unhandled exception problem is to place code that may encounter LinkDemand failures inside of a separate method or function. Then have your main code path call the helper method, wrapping the call in an exception handler. For example, you can change the sample code to use a private method for calling ADO:

C#

```csharp
private void CreateRecordset()
{
    //This code will never run due to a LinkDemand failure
    RecordsetClass rc = new RecordsetClass();
    int fieldCount = rc.Fields.Count;
}

protected void Button1_Click(object sender, EventArgs e)
{
    try
    {
        //The LinkDemand failure from the private method will bubble up as a
        //catch-able exception
        this.CreateRecordset();

        Response.Write("Successfully created an ADO recordset using the ADO PIA.");
    }
    catch (Exception ex)
    {
        Response.Write(ex.Message + "<br />" +
            Server.HtmlEncode(ex.StackTrace));
    }
}
```

VB.NET

```vbnet
Private Sub CreateRecordset()
    Dim rc As New RecordsetClass()
    Dim fieldCount As Integer = rc.Fields.Count
End Sub

Protected Sub Button1_Click( _
ByVal sender As Object, _
ByVal e As System.EventArgs) Handles Button1.Click
    Try
        ' The LinkDemand failure from the private method will bubble up as a
        ' catch-able exception

        Me.CreateRecordset()

        Response.Write( _
        "Successfully created an ADO " & _
        "recordset using the ADO PIA.")
    Catch ex As Exception
        Response.Write(ex.Message & "<br />" & _
        Server.HtmlEncode(ex.StackTrace))
    End Try
End Sub
```

Now the LinkDemand failure occurs when the Framework attempts to link the code in CreateRecordset to the code inside of the ADO PIA. The resulting SecurityException is successfully caught inside of the button click handler, and you can react appropriately to the error.

Although this example demonstrates the problem with a LinkDemand requiring a full trust caller, any LinkDemand-induced failure will exhibit this behavior. As a developer, you should be aware of this and code defensively when you know you are using classes that implement LinkDemands.

LinkDemand Handling When Using Reflection

Because LinkDemands are intended to protect an assembly when another assembly links to it, there is a potential problem when using reflection to call into a protected assembly. With reflection, the immediate caller into a protected assembly is the .NET Framework code for the System.Reflection namespace. Because Framework code all lives in the GAC, any LinkDemand would appear to immediately pass the security checks. However, if this were really the case, any partial trust application with the appropriate ReflectionPermission could subvert the intent of a LinkDemand.

To prevent this kind of "end run" around security, the Framework first checks the security of the *true* caller rather than the code running System.Reflection. Additionally, the Framework converts the LinkDemand into a full demand. If the previous example used a GAC'd assembly to call the ADO PIA via reflection on behalf of the ASP.NET page, the following would occur:

1. The reflection code sees the LinkDemand for full trust.

2. The Framework enforces the LinkDemand against the assembly in the GAC because it is the GAC'd assembly that is really making the method call.

3. The Framework converts the LinkDemand into a full demand because reflection is being used.

4. The Framework walks up the call stack, inspecting each assembly involved in the current call stack to see if it is fully trusted.

5. When the stack crawl reaches the partial trust page code the security check fails and a SecurityException is thrown.

Keep this behavior in mind if you write a GAC'd wrapper assembly that calls a protected assembly on behalf of a partial trust ASP.NET application. The section on sandboxing titled "Sandboxing with Strongly Named Assemblies" will cover how a GAC'd assembly can ensure that it always has the necessary rights to call protected code, regardless of whether the call is made directly or via reflection.

Working with the AllowPartiallyTrustedCallers Attribute

You would be in a real quandary if there was no way to call protected code from a partial trust ASP.NET application. If you think about it, though, ASP.NET code is calling into what would technically be considered "protected code" all the time. Whenever you write a line of code that uses the Request or Response objects, you are accessing classes that live inside of SystemWeb.dll, which itself is installed in the GAC. However, in all the previous examples where sample code was writing information out using Response, there weren't any unexpected security exceptions.

The reason for this behavior is the AllowPartiallyTrustedCallersAttribute class located in the System.Security namespace. If an assembly author includes this attribute as part of the assembly's metadata, when the .NET Framework sees a call being made from partially trusted code to the assembly, it does not trigger a LinkDemand for full trust. The System.Web.dll assembly uses AllowPartiallyTrustedCallersAttribute to allow partial trust code to call into its classes. You can see this if you run the `ildasm` utility (available in the SDK subdirectory inside of the Visual Studio install directory if you chose to install the SDK) against the `System.Web.dll` file located in the framework's installation directory. You will see a line of metadata like the following if you look at the assembly's manifest inside of `ildasm`.

```
[mscorlib]System.Security.AllowPartiallyTrustedCallersAttribute::.ctor()
```

If you are using assemblies that you don't directly control or own, and you are wondering whether the assemblies can even be used in a partially trusted web application, you should `ildasm` them and look for the `AllowPartiallyTrustedCallersAttribute`. If the assemblies lack the attribute, then without additional work on your part (sandboxing the assemblies which is discussed later), you will not be able to install the code in the GAC and consume it directly from a partially trusted ASP.NET application.

A few technical details about using `AllowPartiallyTrustedCallersAttribute` are listed here:

❑   Although you can add this attribute to any assembly, it makes sense to use it only with an assembly that is strongly named.

❑   Strongly named assemblies require a signing key and an extra step in the assembly's build process to create the digital signature for the assembly's code. You can set this all up in Visual Studio 2008 so that the work is done automatically for you.

❑   In ASP.NET 3.5 you can deploy strongly named assemblies either in the GAC or in the `/bin` directory of your application. Deploying a strongly named assembly in the `/bin` directory has some extra implications in partial trust ASP.NET applications.

In the interest of brevity, folks frequently refer to the `AllowPartiallyTrustedCallersAttribute` *as APTCA, or "app-ka" when talking about it. Trust me; it's a lot faster to talk about APTCA rather than the full name of the attribute!*

To demonstrate using the attribute, create a really basic standalone assembly that is strongly named. The assembly exposes a dummy worker method just so there is something that you can call.

C#

```csharp
public class SampleClass
{
    public string DoSomething()
    {
        return "I did something";
    }
}
```

VB.NET

```vbnet
Public Class SampleClass
    Public Function DoSomething() As String
        Return "I did something"
    End Function
End Class
```

Initially, the assembly will be strongly named, but won't have APTCA in its metadata. If you are wondering how to get Visual Studio to strongly name the assembly, just use the following steps:

1. Right-click the Project node in the Solution Explorer.

2. Select the Signing tab in the Property page that is displayed.

3. Check the Sign the assembly check box on the Signing property page.

4. If you are just creating a key file for a sample application like I am, choose New from the Choose a strong name key file drop-down list. In a secure development environment, though, you should delay sign the assembly and manage the private key information separately.

5. Type the key file name in the dialog box that pops up, and optionally choose to protect the file with a username and password.

The end result is that when you build the standalone assembly, Visual Studio signs it for you. You can confirm this by running `ildasm` against the assembly. You will see the public key token, albeit with a different value, when you look at the assembly's manifest:

```
.publickey = (00 24 00 00 04 80 00 00 94 00 00 00 06 02 00 00
            ...
            )
```

Now you have a strongly named assembly and can start working with it from a partial trust ASP.NET application. First, install the assembly into the GAC using the `gacutil` tool: This tool is also available from the SDK directory. Run the following command to install the assembly into the GAC:

```
"C:\..path..to..VS\SDK\v2.0\Bin\gacutil" -i SampleAPTCAAssembly.dll
```

Next, you can try instantiating and calling the assembly from ASP.NET. Because I keep the standalone assembly in a separate project, I can't use the project reference feature in Visual Studio. In a case like this, you can manually hook up a reference to any assembly located in the GAC by doing the following:

1. Navigate to `%windir%\assembly` to view the GAC.

2. Find your registered assembly in the list, and note the version number, culture, and public key token information.

3. Using that information, manually register the GAC'd assembly using the `<assemblies />` element in `web.config`.

For the sample application, I added the following GAC reference into `web.config`:

```
<compilation debug="true">
  <assemblies>
    <add assembly="SampleAPTCAAssembly, Version=1.0.0.0, Culture=neutral,
    PublicKeyToken=ffd374f46df42d28"/>
  </assemblies>
</compilation>
```

With this reference in the configuration, the sample application can reference the namespace from the assembly and use the sample class.

C#

```
using SampleAPTCAAssembly;
…


protected void Page_Load(object sender, EventArgs e)
{
    SampleClass sc = new SampleClass();
    Response.Write(sc.DoSomething());
}
```

VB.NET

```
Imports SampleAPTCAAssembly_vb.SampleAPTCAAssembly_vb
…

    Protected Sub Page_Load( _
    ByVal sender As Object, _
    ByVal e As System.EventArgs) Handles Me.Load
        Dim sc As New SampleClass()
        Response.Write(sc.DoSomething())
    End Sub
```

Because the sample web application is set to run at Medium trust, running the sample page results in the following now familiar SecurityException:

```
System.Security.SecurityException: That assembly does not allow partially trusted
callers.
```

However, armed with the information that the standalone assembly requires APTCA to be success-fully called, this problem can quickly be rectified. Going back to the standalone assembly project, the APTCA attribute is added to the assembly by placing the attribute definition inside of the project's AssemblyInfo.cs file. This file can be found by expanding the Properties node for the project inside of Solution Explorer.

C#

```
using System.Security;
…
//Allow partially trusted callers
[assembly: AllowPartiallyTrustedCallers()]
```

VB.NET

```
Imports System.Security
…
'Allow partially trusted callers
<Assembly: AllowPartiallyTrustedCallers()>
```

Recompiling the application and reinstalling the new assembly into the GAC gives you an assembly that will now allow a partial trust web application to call into it. Running the sample's ASP.NET page in Medium trust succeeds, and the text from the standalone assembly is written out without triggering any exceptions.

Sometimes changing GAC'd assemblies doesn't seem to always take immediate effect. If you are sure that you have updated a GAC'd assembly with APTCA, and it still isn't working, try closing down Visual Studio and running `iisreset`.

Strong Named Assemblies, APTCA, and the Bin Directory

One variation on the issue with APTCA and partial trust callers deals with the issue of deploying strongly named assemblies in `/bin` and then attempting to use them. You might think that you could create a strong named assembly for versioning purposes but then deploy it into the `/bin` directory of a web application for convenience. However, if you attempt to do this, the .NET Framework still enforces a `LinkDemand` when a partially trusted caller attempts to use a strong named assembly.

You can see this if you take the standalone assembly used earlier and recompile it without APTCA. Drop it into the `/bin` directory of the web application (make sure to remove the old assembly from the GAC) and remove the GAC reference from `web.config`. Now when you run the sample web page it once again fails with a `SecurityException`.

This behavior may take you by surprise if you have ASP.NET applications that formerly ran in full trust and that you are now attempting to tweak to get running in High trust or lower. If you have strongly named assemblies sitting in `/bin` (which admittedly in ASP.NET 1.1 you might have avoided because there were problems with loading strong named assemblies from `bin`), and if those assemblies never had APTCA applied to them, then your ASP.NET application will suddenly start throwing the familiar `SecurityException` complaining about partially trusted callers.

This boils down to a simple rule: If you are creating strongly named assemblies, you should make the decision up front on whether the assemblies are intended to support partial trust environments like ASP.NET. If so, you should review the code to ensure that partially trusted applications are not allowed to call dangerous code (for example, a strong named assembly shouldn't be just a proxy for directly calling random Win32 APIs), and then add the APTCA attribute to the assembly. For some developers who have large numbers of middle tier assemblies, quite a few assemblies may require this type of security review and the application of APTCA prior to being useable in a partial trust application.

Another area where APTCA is enforced is for any type that ASP.NET dynamically loads on your behalf. Because you can create custom configuration section handlers, custom `HttpModules`, custom providers, and so on, ASP.NET is responsible for dynamically loading the assemblies that contain these custom extensions.

Consider the following scenario:

1. An ASP.NET application runs in Medium trust.
2. You write a custom Membership provider in a strongly named standalone assembly.
3. The assembly isn't attributed with APTCA.
4. For ease of deployment, you place the assembly in `/bin`.

What happens? From a .NET Framework perspective, it triggers a `LinkDemand` for full trust when ASP.NET attempts to load the custom provider. Because it is ASP.NET that is loading the provider, the initial `LinkDemand` check succeeds. The provider loader code is buried somewhere in `System.Web.dll`, which itself sits in the GAC. So, from a .NET Framework perspective, everything is just fine with the immediate caller. Because ASP.NET dynamically loads providers with the `System.Activator` type, though, the Framework will continue to demand Full trust from all other code sitting in the calls stack. Because it is probably user code in a page that is making use of Membership in this scenario, the full stack walk to check for Full trust will end up failing.

To give an example of this, you can use the standalone assembly from the earlier APTCA discussion, and add a simple Membership provider to it.

C#

```csharp
public class DummyMembershipProvider : SqlMembershipProvider {}
```

VB.NET

```vbnet
Public Class DummyMembershipProvider Inherits SqlMembershipProvider
End Class
```

The assembly is again deployed into the /bin directory of the ASP.NET application. Because this is a Membership provider, the Membership feature must be configured to use the custom provider. A full strong type definition isn't necessary, because the containing assembly is in /bin:

```xml
<membership>
  <providers>
   <add name="DummyProvider"
        type="SampleAPTCAAssembly.DummyMembershipProvider, SampleAPTCAAssembly" />
  </providers>
</membership>
```

A sample page that forces the Membership feature to initialize, and thus load all configured providers, is shown here:

C#

```csharp
protected void Page_Load(object sender, EventArgs e)
{
    Response.Write(Membership.ApplicationName);
}
```

VB.NET

```vbnet
Protected Sub Page_Load( _
    ByVal sender As Object, _
    ByVal e As System.EventArgs) Handles Me.Load
    Response.Write(Membership.ApplicationName)
End Sub
```

Running this page at Medium trust results in a page failure:

```
Description: An error occurred during the processing of a configuration file
required to service this request. Please review the specific error details below
and modify your configuration file appropriately.

Parser Error Message: That assembly does not allow partially trusted callers.
```

Depending on which piece of ASP.NET code is actually responsible for loading custom types, you will get different error messages. In this case, because loading custom Membership providers is considered part of the configuration for Membership, the error information is returned as an instance of System.Configuration.ConfigurationErrorsException. Again, this kind of failure can be solved by attributing the assembly with APTCA. After the assembly is updated with APTCA and redeployed to the /bin directory, the Medium trust application is able to load the custom provider.

Now say that you instead make use of the GAC for a custom provider. The scenario looks like:

1. An ASP.NET application runs in Medium trust.

2. You write a custom Membership provider in a strongly named standalone assembly.

3. The assembly is not attributed with APTCA.

4. You deploy the provider in the GAC.

In this case, ASP.NET adds an extra layer of enforcement. Before even attempting to spin up the provider with System.Activator, ASP.NET first checks to see of the provider's assembly is attributed with APTCA. If ASP.NET cannot find the APTCA attribute, it immediately fails with a ConfigurationErrors Exception (though in this case the text of the error will be a bit different because it is ASP.NET's APTCA check that is failing as opposed to the Framework's APTCA enforcement). Although the provider case would still fail even if ASP.NET did not make this check (the page code in a partial trust web application would still be on the stack), there are other cases where ASP.NET dynamically loads code (for example, custom handlers and modules), and thus no user code exists on the stack. This is the main reason why ASP.NET adds its own additional APTCA check for dynamically loaded types that exist in GAC'd assemblies. All of this should serve to reinforce the fundamental tenet of strongly named assemblies: determine whether the strongly named assembly is intended for use in any type of partial trust scenario, and if so perform a security review and attribute with APTCA. Do not assume that you can "fake out" ASP.NET or the .NET Framework by using some level of indirection to get a reference to a strongly named type. Reflection will not help, because the Framework converts LinkDemands into full demands. In the case of ASP.NET, code that loads types from the GAC based on information in configuration explicitly looks for APTCA on an assembly before loading it on behalf of a partially trusted ASP.NET application.

Sandboxing with Strongly Named Assemblies

With an understanding of APTCA, the GAC, and partial trust callers under your belt, you can put the pieces together for wrapping code in a sandbox of sorts such that partially trusted callers can use more privileged code. The idea behind the sandbox is that a partial trust web application doesn't require access to every possible API in the .NET Framework.

For example, if you are developing a Medium trust web application that communicates with a database, chances are that the web application doesn't really need to use every class in System.Data.SqlClient. Furthermore, it is likely that the web application does not require the ability to issue any arbitrary query. Instead, your web application probably has a very specific set of requirements—a specific set of tables and stored procedures that it should interact with. As a result, you could encapsulate this restricted functionality inside of an assembly (or assemblies) that exposes methods performing only the required query operations. With such an approach you have effectively created a sandbox within which your partial trust application can issue a limited set of SQL queries.

Creating a sandbox assembly for use by a partial trust application requires the following:

1. A clear understanding of the specific functionality that needs to be publicly available to the partial trust application

2. Knowledge of the security expectations that the sandbox assembly can realistically demand from the partial trust code

3. Knowledge of the security requirements of lower-level code that the sandboxed assembly itself relies on

Of the these three items, you can pretty easily scope out the requirements for point 1 because you would normally do this anyway in the course of designing and developing your web application. However, point 2 is something that you may not have given consideration to before.

If you work on a development team where everyone knows who writes specific pieces of code, then you may not need to give too much though to the security expectations the sandbox assembly demands. You could instead author a sandbox assembly, install it on one or more web servers, and be done with it. However, if you write a sandboxed assembly for use by anonymous or unknown customers, then you should definitely enforce point 2.

If you think about it, System.Web.dll could be considered a really, really big sandbox assembly. On behalf of millions of developers not personally known by the ASP.NET development team, the ASP.NET runtime is allowing partial trust web applications to do all sorts of interesting things. AspNetHostingPermission, which was covered earlier, is the programmatic representation of a security requirement that ASP.NET demands from all partial trust applications. In the absence of a "personal trust" relationship, ASP.NET instead uses the custom permission to establish an understanding of the level of trust granted to a web application. As you saw, based upon that level of trust, ASP.NET will turn on and off various features.

If you are planning on authoring a strongly named assembly, regardless of whether it goes in the GAC, you need to consider what types of permissions you expect (.demand) from calling code. Of course, another reason for doing this is that some code that calls into your assembly may be malicious code that is attempting to use your sandboxed assembly to subvert other security restrictions on the web server.

In Figure 4-2, the general pattern of a sandboxed assembly requesting some type of permission from its caller is shown.

For example, say that your strongly named assembly internally makes a request for a bank account balance lookup from some mainframe. The assembly exposes a public method for making this request that hides all of the internals necessary for setting up a call to a mainframe, parsing the response, authenticating the web server to the mainframe, and so on. In normal circumstances, your assembly is deployed on a web server, probably in the GAC, and the following call flow occurs:

1. The partially trusted web application calls a public method on your assembly, requesting the bank account balance lookup.

2. Rather than just blindly trusting the caller, your assembly requires that the web application has a custom permission defined by your company. It makes this check by constructing an instance of the custom permission and then programmatically demanding it.

3. Assuming that the web application has the required permission, your assembly makes the necessary calls into other privileged code to retrieve the bank account balance.

Because of step 2, your sandboxed assembly is safer for use in partial trust applications and by any random and anonymous set of developers. Because your assembly requires a custom permission, the logical place to assign the permission to an ASP.NET application is in a custom trust policy file. Remember from earlier all of the permission classes that were registered with <SecurityClass /> elements in a trust policy file? You could author your own permission that derives from System.Security.CodeAccess Permission and then configure it in the trust policy file and grant it in with <IPermission /> element.

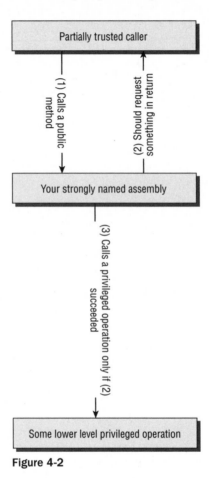

Figure 4-2

Now a malicious user who obtains your sandboxed assembly and attempts to call it would need to overcome the following hurdles:

❑   They would need to obtain the assembly with the definition of the custom permission you are demanding.

❑   The custom permission would need to be installed in the GAC, but this requires machine administrator privileges.

❑   The trust policy file for the web application would need to be changed. Again, though, creating or editing trust policy files requires machine administrator privileges.

Because the likelihood of compromising someone with machine administrator privileges is pretty low (if someone with machine admin privileges on your Internet-facing web farms has malicious intent, it's all over!), any attempt by a partial trust web application to use your sandboxed assembly immediately fails when your assembly demands a custom permission.

> *Always demand some kind of permission in your sandbox assemblies when you don't know who is writing the partially trusted code that calls into your assembly.*

The last point mentioned earlier (step 3) noted that you also have to have an understanding of the security requirements of the code that your sandboxed assembly will call. This is necessary because it is likely that some of the classes you call also have their own demands. For example, if you were wrapping calls to `System.Data.SqlClient`, you know that the various classes in that namespace will demand `SqlClientPermission`. Even though your assembly is strongly named, and may be in the GAC, it doesn't change the fact that the demand for `SqliClientPermission` will flow right up the call stack, and when the demand hits a partially trusted web application, the demand will fail.

So, the third thing a sandboxed assembly may need to do is assert one or more permissions. When calling `System.Data.SqlClient`, your sandboxed assembly needs to assert `SqliClientPermission`. Doing so has the effect of stopping the stack walk for `SqliClientPermission` when your assembly is reached. Figure 4-3 shows this.

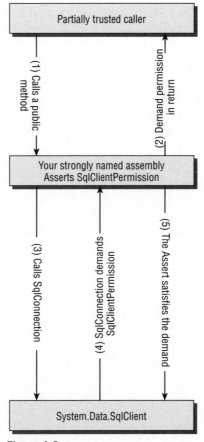

Figure 4-3

Walking through the steps that occur:

1. The partial trust web application calls into the sandboxed assembly.

2. The sandboxed assembly demands permission from the partial trust web application rather than just immediately executing code on its behalf.

3. Assuming that the permission demand succeeds, the sandboxed assembly makes a call into ADO.NET.

4. ADO.NET demands `SqlClientPermission`, which starts a stack walk to check that all assemblies in the current call stack have this permission.

5. When the stack walk "sees" that the sandboxed assembly asserted `SqlClientPermission`, the stack walk stops.

6. Control returns back to ADO.NET, and the appropriate method is allowed to execute.

The need to demand some type of permission from the calling code is, hopefully, a little clearer now. Because sandbox assemblies may very well assert one or more permissions, it makes good sense to require some type of permission in return from the calling code. Think of this as the equivalent of giving your car keys to your teenager on the weekend (you are effectively asserting that you trust he or she will not do anything wrong with the car, but in return you expect your teenager to drive responsibly).

There is one thing to keep in mind with the concept of asserting permissions. Even though any code can `new()` up a permission class and call the `Assert` method, this doesn't necessarily mean that `Assert` will succeed. The reason a sandboxed assembly in the GAC can successfully call `Assert` for any permission class lies in the way the .NET Framework evaluates the `Assert`. When a piece of code calls `Assert`, the Framework looks at the assembly that contains the code making the assertion. Based on the evidence for that assembly (where is the assembly physically located, what is its digital signature, and so on), the Framework matches the assembly to the appropriate portion of the security policy currently in effect for that application domain. The Framework then looks for the asserted permission in the security policy; if the permission is found, the assertion succeeds. If the assertion fails, a `SecurityException` occurs.

When assemblies are deployed in the GAC, code always has full trust, which means that GAC'd code can call any other code and use any of the functionality in the Framework. As a result, GAC'd code that calls `Assert` always succeeds. I won't go into it here, but it is possible to structure the membership conditions for the .NET Framework's security to allow code in other locations to also be assigned full trust. For most folks, though, installation in the GAC is the most straightforward way of obtaining full trust and, thus, being able to assert permissions.

Sandboxed Access to ADODB

Earlier in the section "Working with Different Trust Levels" a few samples attempted to use the old ADO data access technology from a partial trust web application. In this scenario, you can move the ADO data access code into its own sandbox assembly and then enable the assembly for use in partial trust.

The sandbox assembly contains code that attempts to create a new recordset:

C#

```
public int CreateRecordset()
{
    AspNetHostingPermission asp =
            new AspNetHostingPermission(AspNetHostingPermissionLevel.Medium);
    asp.Demand();

    RecordsetClass rc = new RecordsetClass();
    int fieldCount = rc.Fields.Count;
    return fieldCount;
}
```

VB.NET

```
        Public Function CreateRecordset() As Integer
            Dim asp As New AspNetHostingPermission( _
                AspNetHostingPermissionLevel.Medium)
            asp.Demand()

            Dim rc As New RecordsetClass()
            Dim fieldCount As Integer = rc.Fields.Count
            Return fieldCount
        End Function
```

The assembly is attributed with APTCA to allow partially trusted callers. The class also demands Medium trust from its callers. Because this method is working with ADO, which is effectively the precursor to ADO.NET, and ASP.NET grants `SqlClientPermission` at Medium trust, the `CreateRecordset` method works with ADO on behalf of any partially trusted caller running at Medium trust or higher.

After installing the assembly into the GAC, the web application is updated so that it has a reference to the GAC'd assembly.

```
<add assembly="SampleAPTCAAssembly, Version=1.0.0.0, Culture=neutral, PublicKeyToke
n=ffd374f46df42d28"/>
```

The web page that uses the GAC'd assembly is shown here:

C#

```
using SampleAPTCAAssembly;
...
protected void Page_Load(object sender, EventArgs e)
{
    ADODBWrapper wrapper = new ADODBWrapper();
    Response.Write(wrapper.CreateRecordset().ToString());
}
```

VB.NET

```
Imports SampleAPTCAAssembly_vb.SampleAPTCAAssembly_vb
...
Protected Sub Page_Load( _
    ByVal sender as Object, _
    ByVal e As System.EventArgs) Handles Me.Load
        Dim wrapper As New ADODBWrapper()
        Response.Write(wrapper.CreateRecordset().ToString())
    End Sub
```

At this point the page still won't work, because the COM interop layer for ADO is demanding `File-IOPermission`. However, because calling into a PIA means that you are calling into unmanaged code, the sandbox assembly also needs `SecurityPermission` to grant unmanaged code assert permission. It isn't uncommon for sandbox assemblies to need to assert permissions to prevent demands in the underlying code from flowing up the call stack. To rectify the problem when calling the ADO PIA, the assembly asserts file IO permission and unmanaged code permission as shown here:

C#

```
//If we get this far, we trust the caller and are willing to assert
//permissions on its behalf.
PermissionSet ps = new PermissionSet(null);
try
{

    FileIOPermission fp = new FileIOPermission(PermissionState.Unrestricted);
    SecurityPermission sp =
        new SecurityPermission(SecurityPermissionFlag.UnmanagedCode);

    ps.AddPermission(fp);
    ps.AddPermission(sp);

    ps.Assert();

    RecordsetClass rc = new RecordsetClass();
    int fieldCount = rc.Fields.Count;
    return fieldCount;
}
finally
{
    CodeAccessPermission.RevertAssert();
}
```

VB.NET

```
                'If we get this far, we trust the caller and are willing to assert
                'permissions on its behalf.
                Dim ps As New PermissionSet(PermissionState.Unrestricted)
                Try

                    Dim fp As New FileIOPermission( _
                        PermissionState.Unrestricted)
                    Dim sp As New SecurityPermission( _
                        SecurityPermissionFlag.UnmanagedCode)
```

```
                    ps.AddPermission(fp)
                    ps.AddPermission(sp)

                    ps.Assert()

                    Dim rc As New RecordsetClass()
                    Dim fieldCount As Integer = rc.Fields.Count
                    Return fieldCount
            Finally
                    CodeAccessPermission.RevertAssert()
            End Try
```

In this example, two permissions were asserted: `FileIOPermission` and a `SecurityPermission`. However, you cannot create individual permission classes and then call `Assert` on each instance. When you call `Assert`, the Framework temporarily changes the security information associated with the current stack frame. At that point, you cannot `Assert` a second permission unless you tear down the first `Assert`. To get around this, use the class `System.Security.PermissionSet` to add one or more permissions to a permission set. You can then call `Assert` on the `PermissionSet`, and all the individual permissions that were added to the set are associated with the current stack frame. In the sample code, the `PermissionSet` allows the code to assert the file IO permission and the unmanaged code permission.

When you need to assert permissions, you should try to assert only the specific permissions your code needs. The sample asserts unrestricted `FileIOPermission`, which technically states that the wrapper code may attempt any file IO operation anywhere on the file system. In this case, I don't know specifically what file path (or paths) the COM interop layer is looking at, so I used `PermissionState.Unrestricted`. However, if the wrapper assembly is calling another piece of code that works with only a specific file or directory, it would be a better to assert `FileIOPermission` for only the required file or directory.

All the example code is wrapped in a try/finally exception block. I did this to demonstrate how to call the static method `CodeAccessPermission.RevertAssert`. This isn't strictly necessary when your code exits a method shortly after asserting permissions and doing some work (which is the case in the sample). However, if you have methods that need to briefly assert one or more permissions to call some other code, but your method then continues with other work, you should call `RevertAssert` to remove the extra security rights from the current stack frame. This call ensures that the remainder of the code in your method doesn't inadvertently run with an elevated set of CAS permissions.

At this point, if you run the sample ASP.NET page, everything finally works. To summarize, the following work is necessary to enable calling ADO from a Medium trust application:

1. Create a strongly named wrapper assembly.

2. Assign the APTCA attribute to the assembly to allow partial trust code like the web application to call into it.

3. Install the assembly in the GAC, thus allowing the assembly to assert any permission that it needs because GAC code is always fully trusted.

4. In the assembly, assert `FileIOPermission` and a `SecurityPermission` for unmanaged code to prevent the underlying COM interop demands from flowing up the call stack.

Sandboxed Access to System.Data.SqlClient

Access to some type of relational database is a common requirement for web applications, so this section describes what is involved in running queries against SQL Server for an application running in Low trust. Remember that the default trust policy file for Low trust doesn't include the SqlClientPermission.

Here, I reuse the assembly from the ADODB example because it already gets installed in the GAC and has the APTCA attribute applied to it. Because the new class in this assembly needs to prevent the demand for SqlClientPermission from making it to the user code running in the page, the new class needs to assert SqlClientPermission. As a basic protection though, the wrapper class requires at least Low trust from its callers. The code to do all this is:

C#

```
public class PubsDatabaseHelper
{
    public DataSet RetrieveAuthorsTable()
    {
        //This class is only intended for use at Low trust or above
(new AspNetHostingPermission(AspNetHostingPermissionLevel.Low)).Demand();

        try
        {
            //Prevent SqlClientPermission demand from flowing up the call stack.
            SqlClientPermission scp =
                new SqlClientPermission(PermissionState.Unrestricted);
            scp.Assert();

            string connectionString =
                @"server=.\SQL2005;integrated security=true;database=pubs";

            using (SqlConnection conn =
                    new SqlConnection(connectionString))
            {
                SqlCommand cmd
                    = new SqlCommand("select * from authors", conn);
                SqlDataAdapter da = new SqlDataAdapter(cmd);

                DataSet ds = new DataSet("authors");
                da.Fill(ds);

                return ds;
            }
        }
        finally
        {
            CodeAccessPermission.RevertAssert();
        }
    }
}
```

VB.NET

```
    Public Class PubsDatabaseHelper
        Public Function RetrieveAuthorsTable() As DataSet
            'This class is only intended for use at Low trust or above
CType(New AspNetHostingPermission(AspNetHostingPermissionLevel.Low),
AspNetHostingPermission).Demand()

            Try
                'Prevent SqlClientPermission demand from flowing up the call stack.
                Dim scp As New SqlClientPermission(PermissionState.Unrestricted)
                scp.Assert()

Dim connectionString As String = "server=.\SQL2005;integrated
security=true;database=pubs"

                Using conn As New SqlConnection(connectionString)
                    Dim cmd As New SqlCommand("select * from authors", conn)
                    Dim da As New SqlDataAdapter(cmd)

                    Dim ds As New DataSet("authors")
                    da.Fill(ds)

                    Return ds
                End Using
            Finally
                CodeAccessPermission.RevertAssert()
            End Try
        End Function
    End Class
```

In the sample ASP.NET application, the trust level is reduced to Low. The page that uses the PubsDatabaseHelper has a GridView control on it, and some code in the page load event to programmatically data-bind the dataset returned from the PubsDatabaseHelper.

C#

```
using SampleAPTCAAssembly;
...
    protected void Page_Load(object sender, EventArgs e)
    {
        PubsDatabaseHelper ph = new PubsDatabaseHelper();

        grdView.DataSource = ph.RetrieveAuthorsTable();
        grdView.DataBind();
    }
```

VB.NET

```
Imports SampleAPTCAAssembly_vb.SampleAPTCAAssembly_vb
...
    Public Sub Page_Load( _
```

```
        ByVal sender As Object, _
        ByVal e As System.EventArgs) Handles Me.Load
        Dim ph As New PubsDatabaseHelper()

        grdView.DataSource = ph.RetrieveAuthorsTable()
        grdView.DataBind()
    End Sub
End Class
```

When you run the sample page, it successfully calls the GAC'd sandbox assembly and populates the GridView control with the returned DataSet.

This basic example of sandboxing ADO.NET access shows how the same techniques can be used for any arbitrary middle tier. Sandboxed assemblies are yet another reason why an architecturally sound middle tier is so important to web applications. Even if you are running all of your ASP.NET applications today in full trust, if you have a well-designed middle tier you've already taken the most important step toward enabling your web application for partial trust. The extra steps of security review, adding the APTCA attribute, and selectively asserting permissions are comparatively easy when there is already a clean separation of presentation layer and business layer code.

ProcessRequestInApplicationTrust

The last advanced topic that I want to cover is a security feature that was introduced in ASP.NET 2.0 and still exists in ASP.NET 3.5. There is a new attribute on the <trust /> element called processRequest InApplicationTrust. By default, this attribute is set to true in the default trust level configuration:

```
<location allowOverride="true">
    <system.web>
        <!-- security policy definition snipped for brevity -->

        <trust level="Medium" processRequestInApplicationTrust="true"
                originUrl="" />
    </system.web>
</location>
```

If you look at the root web.config file, you will not see the new attribute because the trust level configuration class internally defaults the attribute's value to true. Because this attribute deals with trust-related security in ASP.NET, the attribute was added to the <trust /> element. So, along with the ability to globally define the trust level for all applications on the machine, you can also globally control the value of the new attribute. However, unlike trust levels where there are valid reasons why you would want different trust levels for different applications, the setting for processRequestInApplicationTrust should be left alone at its default value of true.

The attribute was introduced primarily to handle backwards compatibility issues when moving from ASP.NET 1.1 to 2.0. Because ASP.NET 2.0 tightens its enforcement of trust levels, some earlier applications and controls may fail with security exceptions when they run on ASP.NET 2.0 or ASP.NET 3.5. As a result, set the new attribute to false only when you encounter this kind of problem and even then after the applications or controls are tweaked to work in ASP.NET 2.0 and ASP.NET 3.5, you should revert to the default value of true for the attribute.

The Interaction between Trust and ASP.NET Internal Code

To get a better understanding of what the processRequestInApplicationTrust attribute really addresses, you need to understand a potential security issue for partial trust web applications. In several scenarios in ASP.NET, only trusted code is running on the stack. Probably the easiest example to explain is the no-compile page that was introduced in ASP.NET 2.0.

A no-compile page has no user code in a code-behind file. Instead, the only code is the declarative markup in an .aspx. For example, the following page definition is an example of a no-compile page.

C#

```
<%@ Page Language="C#" CompilationMode="Never" %>

<!DOCTYPE html PUBLIC "-//W3C//DTD XHTML 1.1//EN" "http://www.w3.org/TR/xhtml11/
DTD/xhtml11.dtd">


<html xmlns="http://www.w3.org/1999/xhtml" >
<head id="Head1" runat="server">
    <title>Untitled Page</title>
</head>
<body>
    <form id="form1" runat="server">
    <div>
        <asp:SqlDataSource ID="SqlDataSource1" runat="server"
          ConnectionString="<%$ ConnectionStrings: pubsConnectionString %>"
          ProviderName="<%$ ConnectionStrings: pubsConnectionString.ProviderName %>"
    SelectCommand="SELECT [au_id], [au_lname], [au_fname], [phone] FROM [authors]">
        </asp:SqlDataSource>

    </div>
        <asp:GridView ID="GridView1" runat="server"
            AutoGenerateColumns="False" DataKeyNames="au_id"
          DataSourceID="SqlDataSource1">
          <Columns>
              <asp:BoundField DataField="au_id" HeaderText="au_id"
                ReadOnly="True" SortExpression="au_id" />
              <asp:BoundField DataField="au_lname" HeaderText="au_lname"
                SortExpression="au_lname" />
              <asp:BoundField DataField="au_fname" HeaderText="au_fname"
                SortExpression="au_fname" />
              <asp:BoundField DataField="phone" HeaderText="phone"
                SortExpression="phone" />
          </Columns>
        </asp:GridView>
    </form>
</body>
</html>
```

VB.NET

```
<%@ Page Language="VB" CompilationMode="Never" %>

<!DOCTYPE html PUBLIC "-//W3C//DTD XHTML 1.0 Transitional//EN" "http://www.w3.org/
TR/xhtml1/DTD/xhtml1-transitional.dtd">

<html xmlns="http://www.w3.org/1999/xhtml">
<head runat="server">
    <title>Untitled Page</title>
</head>
<body>
    <form id="form1" runat="server">
    <div>
        <asp:SqlDataSource ID="SqlDataSource1" runat="server" ConnectionString="<%$
ConnectionStrings:pubsConnectionString %>" SelectCommand="SELECT [au_id], [au_
lname], [au_fname], [phone] FROM [authors]">
        </asp:SqlDataSource>

    </div>
        <asp:GridView ID="GridView1" runat="server" AutoGenerateColumns="False"
DataKeyNames="au_id"
            DataSourceID="SqlDataSource1">
            <Columns>
                <asp:BoundField DataField="au_id" HeaderText="au_id"
ReadOnly="True" SortExpression="au_id" />
                <asp:BoundField DataField="au_lname" HeaderText="au_lname"
SortExpression="au_lname" />
                <asp:BoundField DataField="au_fname" HeaderText="au_fname"
SortExpression="au_fname" />
                <asp:BoundField DataField="phone" HeaderText="phone"
SortExpression="phone" />
            </Columns>
        </asp:GridView>
    </form>
</body>
</html>
```

The page contains only a declarative representation of a `GridView` control bound to a `SqlDataSource` control. Furthermore, the page directive explicitly disallows compilation by specifying `Compilation Mode='Never'`. If you run this page and then look in the Temporary ASP.NET Files directory, you will see that there is no auto-generated page assembly. When the page runs, ASP.NET effectively acts like a parsing engine, using the control declarations to decide which ASP.NET control classes to instantiate and then calling various methods on the instantiated controls.

There is a potential security issue here because the call stack at the time the `GridView` is data-bound contains only ASP.NET code, and because all the ASP.NET code exists in the GAC, technically all of the code is running in full trust. The rough call stack at the time `DataBind` is called is listed as follows. Notice that every class involved in the call is fully trusted:

❑ **SqlDataSource:** Located in `System.Web.dll`.

❑ **GridView:** Located in `System.Web.dll`.

❑ **Page:** Located in `System.Web.dll`.

- ❏ **HttpRuntime:** Located in System.Web.dll.
- ❏ **HostingEnvironment:** Located in `System.Web.dll`.
- ❏ **ISAPIRuntime:** Located in `System.Web.dll`.
- ❏ **Unmanaged code:** Located in `aspnet_isapi.dll`.

Clearly, if the only security check for no-compile pages was the demand for `SqlClientPermission` that comes from `SqlDataSource` calling into ADO.NET, a no-compile page would always succeed in calling into SQL Server. However, if you run the sample page in a Low trust application (because Low trust doesn't have `SqlClientPermission`), you get a security-related exception.

You can't take advantage of no-compile pages to call privileged code, because ASP.NET restricts the page by forcing it to execute with the restrictions of the application's current trust level. This is where the phrase "process request in application trust" comes from. Internally, when ASP.NET runs a no-compile page, it temporarily restricts the executing thread to the application's trust level by calling `PermitOnly` on the `NamedPermissionSet` that was declared for the ASP.NET permission set in the trust policy file. So, not only does the trust policy file result in an application domain security policy, it also results in a reference to a `NamedPermissionSet` that ASP.NET can use. Calling `PermitOnly` tells the Framework that all subsequent method calls made on that thread should have CAS demands evaluated against only the permissions defined by the named permission set. As a result, on no-compile pages ASP.NET is effectively telling the Framework that ASP.NET's GAC'd code should be treated as if it were regular user code that you wrote in a code-behind file.

This behavior is all well and good for no-compile pages, and in fact there is no way for you to turn this behavior off for no-compile pages. Because no-compile pages are present since ASP.NET 2.0, there can't be any backward-compatibility issues around trust level enforcement. However, in ASP.NET 1.1 you can write your own custom web controls, and if you choose you can sign them and deploy them in the GAC. Even though an ASP.NET 1.1 page auto-generates an assembly that is restricted by the application's trust level, a GAC'd web control still has the freedom to run in full trust. That means in ASP.NET 1.1 it is possible to author a web control that asserts permissions and then calls into other protected assemblies despite the web control being placed on a page in a partially trusted web application. The reason for this loophole is that there are places when a `Page` is running where only ASP.NET code is on the stack, even for pages with code-behind and auto-generated page assemblies. The various internal lifecycle events (Init, Load, and so on) execute as part of the `Page` class, which is a GAC'd class. If the `Page` class constructs or initializes a control that in turn exists in the GAC, you have the problem where only fully trusted code sitting on the stack.

ASP.NET 2.0, and consequently ASP.NET 3.5, tightens enforcement of trust levels by calling `PermitOnly` on the trust level's `PermissionSet` just prior to starting the page lifecycle. The net result is that all activities that occur as a consequence of running a page, including management of each individual control's lifecycle, are constrained to only those CAS permissions explicitly granted in the trust policy file. This enforcement occurs because the `processRequestInApplicationTrust` attribute on the `<trust />` configuration element is set to `true` by default. Hopefully, you now have a better understanding of why this setting should normally not be changed.

However, if `processRequestInApplicationTrust` is set to `false`, then for compiled pages ASP.NET 2.0 and ASP.NET 3.5 will not call `PermitOnly`, and the loophole whereby GAC'd controls can avoid the application trust level still exists. Figure 4-4 shows two different call paths involving a GAC'd web control: one call path is the normal one; the other call path shows what occurs if "processRequestInApplication Trust" is set to false.

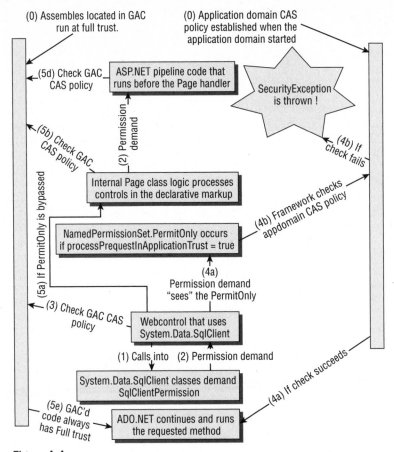

Figure 4-4

0. When the application domain is initialized, the permissions in the trust policy file are applied as the application domain CAS policy.

1. A request for a page that contains a GAC'd web control occurs. When the web control's Render method is called, it internally calls into System.Data.SqlClient classes.

2. This triggers a demand for SqlClientPermission.

3. The Framework first checks to see that the GAC'd web control has the necessary permission. Because the control is in the GAC, and thus running in full trust, the check succeeds.

4a. If processRequestInApplicationTrust is true, then when the permission demand flows up the call stack, it encounters the security restriction put in place by the Page class's call to PermitOnly.

4b. The Framework now checks the set of permissions that were defined in the trust policy file, looking for SqlClientPermission.

4c. If the application is running in Medium or higher trust, the check succeeds, and the ADO.NET call eventually continues.

4d. If the application is running in Low or Minimal trust, the check fails, and a `SecurityException` is thrown.

5a. If `processRequestInApplicationTrust` is `false`, the permission demand continues to flow up the call stack.

5b. The demand passes through various internal `Page` methods involved in instantiating the web control. Because the `Page` class is in the GAC, it runs at full trust and the demand succeeds.

5c. The demand eventually makes it to the top of the managed call stack. All code at this level is GAC'd ASP.NET code that was initially responsible for receiving the call from the ISAPI extension and starting up the HTTP pipeline. So again, the demand succeeds.

5d. Because only fully trusted code is in the current call stack, the demand succeeds, and the ADO. NET call eventually continues.

To demonstrate how this actually works in code, you can create a simple web control that retrieves data from the pubs database in SQL Server and renders it on the page.

C#

```csharp
public class MyCustomControl : WebControl
{
    protected override void  Render(System.Web.UI.HtmlTextWriter writer)
    {
string connectionString = @"server=.\SQL2005;database=pubs;integrated security=true";
        SqlConnection conn = new SqlConnection(connectionString);

        SqlCommand cmd = new SqlCommand("select * from authors", conn);
        DataSet ds = new DataSet("foo");

        SqlDataAdapter da = new SqlDataAdapter(cmd);

        da.Fill(ds);
    }
}
```

VB.NET

```vbnet
Public Class MyCustomControl
    Inherits WebControl
    Protected Overrides Sub Render( _
        ByVal writer As System.Web.UI.HtmlTextWriter)
        Dim connectionString As String = "server=.\SQL2005;database=pubs;" & _
        "integrated security=true"
        Dim conn As New SqlConnection(connectionString)
        Dim cmd As New SqlCommand("select * from authors", conn)
        Dim ds As New DataSet("foo")
        Dim da As New SqlDataAdapter(cmd)
        da.Fill(ds)
    End Sub
End Class
```

The assembly is attributed with APTCA, signed with a signing key, and then installed in the GAC. In the web application, a reference is established to the GAC'd assembly.

```
<add assembly="GacdWebControl, Version=1.0.0.0, Culture=neutral,
PublicKeyToken=8d9c3421c2f25fff" />
```

Notice that this GAC'd class does *not* assert SqlClientPermission. A page is created that uses the web control in the declarative markup of the page.

C#

```
<%@ Register
  TagPrefix="GCW" Namespace="GacdWebControl" Assembly="GacdWebControl"  %>

.. other HTML snipped …

    <form id="form1" runat="server">
    <div>
        <GCW:MyCustomControl runat="server" ID="customControl" />
    </div>
    </form>
```

VB.NET

```
<%@ Register Assembly="GacdWebControl_vb, Version=1.0.0.0, Culture=neutral, PublicK
eyToken=b2748bd5f288dfd2"
    Namespace="GacdWebControl_vb.GacdWebControl_vb" TagPrefix="cc1" %>
.. other HTML snipped …
    <form id="form1" runat="server">
    <div>
        <GCW:MyCustomControl runat="server" ID="customControl" />
    </div>
    </form>
```

If you first run the page in Low trust, you receive a SecurityException due to the failed SqlClient Permission demand. The call stack that follows shows only trusted code on the stack because the code in the GAC'd web control is called as part of the Render processing for a Page.

```
[SecurityException: Request failed.]
..snip..
System.Data.Common.DbConnectionOptions.DemandPermission()
...
System.Data.Common.DbDataAdapter.Fill(DataSet dataSet)
GacdWebControl.MyCustomControl.Render(HtmlTextWriter writer)
...
System.Web.UI.Control.RenderControl(HtmlTextWriter writer)
System.Web.UI.Page.ProcessRequestMain(Boolean includeStagesBeforeAsyncPoint,
Boolean includeStagesAfterAsyncPoint)
...
System.Web.UI.Page.ProcessRequest(HttpContext context)
...
```

Because `PermitOnly` occurs inside of the initial call to `Page.ProcessRequest`, when the `SqlCli-entPermission` demand reaches that point in the call stack, it fails and the GAC'd web control is not allowed to issue a command against SQL Server.

Now change the `<trust />` level element, either in the root `web.config` or by overriding it in the application's `web.config`, to the following:

```
<trust level="Low" processRequestInApplicationTrust="false"/>
```

When you rerun the page, there is no longer a `PermitOnly` call restricting the permissions on the `Page`. Instead the `SqlClientPermission` demand flows up a call stack that consists of nothing but trusted code, and so the permission demand succeeds and the page successfully renders the dataset XML generated by the GAC'd web control.

The best advice for the `processRequestInApplicationTrust` attribute on `<trust />` is to leave it at its default setting of `true`, and if at all possible also set the `allowOverride` attribute on the enclosing `<location />` tag to `false`. This prevents enterprising developers from attempting an end run around the application trust level by way of a GAC'd control. However, if you do encounter applications being moved from ASP.NET 1.1 that run into problems with the new trust level enforcement in the `Page` class, you can temporarily set `processRequestInApplicationTrust` to `false`, but only for the specific application that requires the workaround. You should never disable the `Page`'s trust level enforcement for all applications on a machine, even though it is a little bit of a hassle, use application-specific `<location />` elements or the application's `web.config` instead to tweak the behavior for the offending applications. After you track down the problematic code and fix it (usually there are a few asserts necessary and a quick security review to make sure the asserts are appropriate), you can remove the `<trust />` level workaround for the application and revert to the intended ASP.NET 2.0 or ASP.NET 3.5 behavior.

Summary

In this chapter, you took a comprehensive look at the concept of code access security (CAS) in ASP.NET. Although the .NET Framework has a rich set of classes and configuration information for enforcing code access security, ASP.NET simplifies CAS by introducing the concept of a trust level. A trust level is represented as a piece of XML in a trust policy file that defines the set of .NET Framework permissions granted to an ASP.NET application. You can choose permissions for your application by using the `<trust />` configuration element and setting it to one of the following trust levels:

❑   **Full:** The web application can call any code in the Framework as well as Win32 APIs.

❑   **High:** The web application cannot call into Win32 APIs. Also, a default set of restricted permissions is defined by ASP.NET that gives your web application access to a reasonably large set of the Framework.

❑   **Medium:** The recommended trust level for hosting machines. Also recommended for any Internet-facing web server.

❏ **Low:** This trust level has a very limited set of CAS permissions. It is appropriate for applications that perform only local read-only operations. It is also used for applications that provide their own sandboxed execution model on top of ASP.NET such as SharePoint.

❏ **Minimal:** The lowest trust level available. It allows you to write only code that deals with in-memory data. Your web application can't touch the file system or the network.

Make your web applications more secure by at least moving from Full to High trust. Although doing so will likely require a few tweaks in your web applications and your business tiers, changing your applications so that they are only partially trusted is a major step in restricting the capabilities of malicious code. You can choose to customize the default trust levels by editing the policy files that ship with ASP.NET 3.5, or creating new custom trust levels and registering them inside a `<securityPolicy />` element.

If you are writing an application in which you want to strictly limit the kind of code that can be called from the presentation layer, use a trust level (such as Low or Minimal) that grants very few permissions to application code. You can instead deploy your business logic inside of sandboxed assemblies that are deployed in the GAC and that expose only public APIs for a limited functionality set. Internally, your sandboxed assemblies need to assert various CAS permissions when calling other protected assemblies. Ideally, sandboxed assemblies should also demand some kind of permission from partially trusted applications prior to calling privileged code on behalf of the web application.

5

Configuration System Security

Many .NET Framework features depend on initialization information stored in various configuration files. ASP.NET especially is heavily dependent on configuration sections for defining the behavior of many aspects of the ASP.NET runtime. As a result the configuration information frequently contains sensitive information (usernames, passwords, connections strings, and so on). Configuration information can also directly affect the security settings enforced by certain features. As a result, configuration security is an important aspect of ensuring that a web application works as expected.

This chapter covers the following aspects of securing configuration information:

❑ Using the `<location />` element.

❑ Implementing granular inheritance control using the new "lock" attributes.

❑ Setting access rights to read and modify configuration.

❑ Managing IIS 7.0 configuration versus ASP.NET configuration.

❑ IIS 7.0 Feature Delegation.

❑ Implementing partial trust restrictions when using configuration.

❑ Using the new protected configuration feature.

Using the `<location />` Element

The `<location />` element has existed since ASP.NET 1.0 as a convenient way to define configuration inheritance without the need to create and deploy multiple separate configuration files. Because web applications always have some type of hierarchy, and thus the concept of configuration inheritance, you commonly need to define configuration settings at different levels of the ASP.NET inheritance hierarchy. The following list shows the ASP.NET 3.5 inheritance chain:

1. **Settings defined in** `machine.config`: In ASP.NET 2.0 many of the default ASP.NET settings have been moved out of `machine.config` to minimize startup time of non-web applications.

2. **Settings defined in the root** `web.config`: This new configuration file exists in `%windir%\ Microsoft.NET\Framework\v2.0.50727\CONFIG`. Most of the ASP.NET-specific default settings are now defined in the root `web.config` file.

3. **Settings defined in the** `web.config` **file located in the root folder of a website:** For the default web site, this would be a folder resembling `c:\inetpub\wwwroot`.

4. **Settings defined in the root directory of the application:** This is the `web.config` file that you normally work with in your applications. If the application is the website (meaning the application exists at "/"), the website configuration file and the application's configuration file are one and the same.

5. **Settings defined in a configuration file located in a subdirectory of a web application:** Settings that can be changed on a per-directory basis can be placed in a `web.config` file in a directory. For example, you can define `<authorization />` elements in `web.config` files that apply only to a specific virtual directory.

Usually, you set some global defaults once in the `machine.config` and root `web.config` files, and spend most of your time editing the application's `web.config` file.

The contents of the `<location />` element are the same configuration sections that you would normally set up inside of the various configuration files. Using the URL authorization section as an example, you could place the following into the `web.config` located at the root of a website (for example, at `c:\inetpub\wwwroot\yourwebsite\web.config`) as follows:

```
<location path="Virtual Path A">
  <system.web>
    <authorization>
        <allow roles="Secured, Administrators" />
        <deny  users="*" />
    </authorization>
  </system.web>
</location>
```

The `<location />` element is interpreted as the beginning of a new virtual configuration file, meaning the element (or elements) nested immediately beneath the `<location />` element must be top-level elements allowed in a normal configuration file. Thus, in the example just shown, the `<system.web>` declaration is needed. You cannot place the `<authorization />` element inside a `<location />` element because it wouldn't be allowed as a top-level element in a `web.config` file.

The thing that becomes awkward with configuration inheritance is that you can quickly end up with a proliferation of `.config` files. For example, the URL authorization section (`<authorization />`) often requires many configuration files because the `<authorization />` section can be applied down to the level of a specific web page. Developers who need to lock individual folders can drop a `web.config` file into each separate folder containing the folder-specific authorization rules. You saw an example of this back in Chapter 3 when URL authorization was covered.

You can determine how far down the inheritance chain a configuration section can be defined by looking at the section definitions. Most section definitions can be found within `<section />` elements up in `machine.config`. (Configuration section definitions are typically global to a machine so it makes sense to define them up in `machine.config`.) In a section definition like the following one:

```
<section name="healthMonitoring"
         type="..."
         allowDefinition="MachineToApplication" />
```

...the `allowDefinition` attribute indicates that the health-monitoring configuration section can be defined all the way down to the `web.config` file for an application. So, you are not going to run into a problem with needing health-monitoring definitions for each your application's subfolders.

As a counterpoint, the URL authorization configuration section definition is:

```
<section name="authorization" type="..." />
```

The lack of the `allowDefinition` attribute for this configuration section is an indication that the authorization configuration can be redefined to any level of folder nesting. As a result, this configuration section is a good candidate for centralizing in an application's `web.config` to prevent the number of folder-specific `web.config` files from growing out of control.

Just looking at the section definition in `machine.config` is not always going to tell you whether the configuration makes sense at nested configuration levels. For example, the browser capabilities section can also be redefined at any level of the configuration hierarchy. Most likely, though, you would not redefine this section beneath the level of the application's `web.config`.

The Path Attribute

The `<location />` element is a way to control the number of `.config` files deployed for an application. The `path` attribute within the `<location />` element tells the configuration system where in the configuration inheritance chain the information contained within the `<location />` element should be applied. You can place a `<location />` element inside of any configuration file within the inheritance chain, from `machine.config` all the way down to a configuration file in a subfolder of a web application, and then use the `path` attribute to indicate where the enclosed configuration information applies.

Probably the most confusing aspect, though, of the `<location />` element is the potential values for the `path` attribute. You can place the following values inside of the `path` attribute:

❑   A specific page (that is, `default.aspx`)

❑   A specific folder (that is, `"subfolder"`)

❑   A combined path (that is, `"subfolder/default.aspx"` or `"subfolderA/subfolderB"`*.
The name of a website as defined in IIS (that is, `"Default Web Site"`)

❑   The combination of a website name and nested path information (that is, `"Default Web Site/subfolderA"`)

With the `path` attribute, you can centralize configuration settings into a single physical configuration while still having the flexibility to define configuration settings for different applications, folders, pages, and so on.

Your decision about how to centralize configuration settings should be based on the relationship between the desired configuration information and the location of the configuration file. The root web.config file is an appropriate location for defining configuration information applicable to all web applications on a server. For example, this is the reason that the trust level configuration exists within a <location /> element in the root web.config file.

The web.config file that can be placed at the root of an IIS website is probably used as an application configuration file by most developers. When you have no applications running at /, the website's configuration file is an appropriate location for defining configuration information applicable to all applications running beneath the website's root.

Each application's web.config file can be used for centralizing configuration information applicable to the application's subfolders. Although you can spread out configuration information into configuration files in subfolders (as was shown in the URL authorization discussion in Chapter 3), it can be confusing to debug application problems. Unless someone who knows the application intimately realizes that configuration files are located in subfolders, you may end up scratching your head wondering why an application is behaving in a specific manner. Centralizing configuration information using <location /> tags in the application's web.config file makes it easier for you to know exactly which configuration settings are in effect in different parts of the application.

The allowOverride Attribute

An additional level of security is available with the <location /> element through the allowOverride attribute. Commonly, a web server administrator defines some ASP.NET settings in machine.config. However, this wouldn't be very useful if in each web application the developer simply redefined the configuration sections. The solution is to set the allowOverride attribute to false. After this is done, any attempt to redefine the configuration information contained within the <location /> element results in a configuration exception.

If you globally define the trust level in machine.config as follows:

```
<location allowOverride="false">
    <system.web>
        <trust level="Medium" />
    </system.web>
</location>
```

...attempting to redefine this in your application's web.config file results in an error page telling you that the parser encountered an error because the section has been locked down in a higher-level configuration file (in this case, machine.config). The amount of leverage the <location /> element plus the allowOverride attribute gives you is the reason security-sensitive configuration sections should be defined in either machine.config or the new root web.config file. Both of these files are also ACL'd on the file system to allow only write access by machine administrators so individual application developers can't subvert the settings. Setting allowOverride to false guarantees the person who can change a locked configuration section is a member of the machine's Administrator group.

Using the lockAttributes

Around the time that Beta 1 of ASP.NET 2.0 was worked on, the development team came up with the idea of allowing the session state feature to lock portions of its configuration. The idea was to allow developers using session state to configure application-specific behavior such as the session timeout, while allowing machine administrators to define more global settings such as the session state mode and connection string. As part of this work, the team realized that the existing 1.0/1.1 <location /> -based lockdown approach was too restrictive.

For instance, if an administrator wanted to enforce just the connection string used by all applications with SQL Server session state, an administrator would also have to drag in enforced settings for session timeout, cookieless support, and so on. On some web servers, this constraint might be reasonable, but in corporate hosting environments the likelihood is rather high that different internal corporate customers want different application-specific behavior.

Rather than taking the early work for session state and limiting it to that feature, the concept of locking down individual configuration attributes as well as nested configuration elements was expanded and made available to any arbitrary configuration section. The following list describes the set of common attributes:

❑ **lockAttributes:** You can specify specific attributes on a configuration element that cannot be redefined lower down in the configuration hierarchy.

❑ **lockElements:** You can specify nested elements for a given configuration element that should not be redefined in child configuration files. This attribute is applicable only to complex configuration sections that contain nested elements.

❑ **lockAllAttributesExcept:** This is the companion attribute to lockAttributes. Depending on how many attributes you are locking down, it may be faster to lock all attributes except for a select few, rather than listing specific locked attributes with lockAttributes.

❑ **lockAllElementsExcept:** The companion attribute to lockElements. For complex configuration sections, it may be easier to define the nested elements that can be redefined, rather than list the locked elements with lockElements.

Locking Attributes

You can define the configuration for a feature in a higher-level configuration file and then selectively choose which attributes are allowed to be redefined in child configuration files. The lockAttributes and lockAllAttributesExcept attributes can be placed inside of any configuration element to limit the attributes that can be redefined in child configuration files.

Take the Membership feature as an example of how you can lock individual attributes of a configuration element. The <membership /> element has three attributes: defaultProvider, userIsOnline TimeWindow, and hashAlgorithmType. Of the three attributes, perhaps as an administrator you would like to ensure that any providers configured to use hashing should always use a stronger hashing variant, specifically SHA256.

To test the effect of locking the hashAlgorithmType attribute, you can write a sample application that defines the <membership /> element in its web.config:

```
<membership
            hashAlgorithmType="SHA1"
            userIsOnlineTimeWindow="15" >
```

The membership feature comes preconfigured in machine.config with just an empty <membership /> element. However, for testing the attribute-based configuration lockdown, machine.config can be modified to look as follows:

```
<membership hashAlgorithmType="SHA256"> …
```

You can see the hash algorithm that has been configured for the Membership feature by just outputting the setting on a web page in the sample application:

```
Response.Write(Membership.HashAlgorithmType);
```

The first time you run the sample application the redefined configuration in the application takes effect, and thus the output on the web page is "SHA1." Now lock the settings in machine.config to prevent redefinition of the hashAlgorithmType attribute:

```
<membership hashAlgorithmType="SHA256" lockAttributes="hashAlgorithmType">
```

Now when you attempt to run the sample application you get a configuration error stating that the hashAlgorithmType attribute has been locked in a higher-level configuration file. If you remove the hashAlgorithmType attribute from the application's web.config file, the application runs successfully and the new hash algorithm is SHA256. Just for the heck of it, you can extend the attribute lock in machine.config to include the userIsOnlineTimeWindow and defaultProvider attributes as well:

```
<membership hashAlgorithmType="SHA256"
            lockAttributes="hashAlgorithmType;userIsOnlineTimeWindow;defaultProvider">
```

Use a comma or a semicolon to delimit the individual attributes defined in lockAttributes and lockAllAttributesExcept.

This basic example with the <membership /> element shows that lockAttributes gets pretty verbose. Locking something like the <sessionState /> element with its 14 different attributes results in a lengthy definition for lockAttributes. Taking the <membership /> section again as an example, allowing the userIsOnlineTimeWindow attribute to be changed in child configuration files, you could use the following more succinct machine.config definition:

```
<membership hashAlgorithmType="SHA256"
            lockAllAttributesExcept="userIsOnlineTimeWindow" >
```

This construct allows you to redefine just a subset of the <membership /> element in the application's web.config file:

```
<membership userIsOnlineTimeWindow="15" >
```

As with the lockAttributes element, you can specify multiple attributes within lockAllAttributes Except. The comma and semicolon characters are also used as delimiters.

A shorthand for locking all attributes on a configuration element is to use an asterisk for the value of `lockAttributes`. The following example shows how to prevent the redefinition of any attribute on the `<membership />` element:

```
<membership … lockAttributes="*" />
```

Finding Out Which Elements Are Available for Lockdown

To find out which elements are available for lockdown for a specific configuration element, you can create a bogus `lockAttributes` value. For example, with the following configuration definition (this is in `machine.config`, but the technique works in any configuration file):

```
<membership hashAlgorithmType="SHA256"
            lockAllAttributesExcept="this doesn't exist" >
```

The error returned from ASP.NET is:

```
The attribute 'this doesn't exist' is not valid in the locked
list for this section. The following attributes can be locked:
'defaultProvider', 'userIsOnlineTimeWindow', 'hashAlgorithmType'.
Multiple attributes may be listed separated by commas.
```

Self-documenting errors are a good thing in this case!

Although locking specific attribute configuration is a powerful feature of the configuration system, bear in mind that just because a lockdown is technically possible it may not always make much sense in practice. For example, the previous examples showing how to lock down the hash algorithm for the `<membership />` feature wouldn't be useful if all membership providers used by an application were configured with reversible encryption instead. In this case, the configuration system happily enforces the attribute lockdown, but the end result would have no effect at runtime. This means attribute lockdowns (and element lockdowns discussed in the next section) still require you to look at the final runtime effect to determine whether the locked down configuration really makes sense.

Locking Elements

Because many configuration sections have nested elements, the configuration system provides the ability to lock elements within a configuration section. The `lockElements` and `lockAllElementsExcept` attributes control this behavior for any configuration section.

For example, the `<membership />` section enables you to define providers using the `<providers />` element and `<add />`, `<remove />`, and `<clear />` elements nested with the `<providers />` element. You could allow application developers to change attributes on the `<membership />` element but disallow them from changing any of the providers with the following configuration in `machine.config`:

```
<membership lockElements="providers">
```

Attempting to make any changes to the `<providers />` element for `<membership />` in a child `web.config` file results in an error because the `providers` element has been locked in higher-level configuration file.

To allow an individual application to add new providers but disallow individual applications from removing or clearing providers defined in parent configuration files, your configuration in `machine.config` could look like the following:

```
<membership>
    <providers lockAllElementsExcept="add">
        <!-- provider definitions here -->
    </providers>
</membership>
```

In this example, the `lockAllElementsExcept` attribute is used as a shortcut for allowing only child `web.config` files to use the `<add />` element within the membership provider definition.

A shorthand for locking all elements nested within a configuration element is to use an asterisk for the value of `lockElements`. The following example shows how to prevent the redefinition of any providers for the membership feature:

```
<membership>
    <providers lockElements="*">
        <!-- provider definitions here -->
    </providers>
</membership>
```

The utility of element-based lockdown in Add-Remove-Clear (ARC) collections such as the membership provider collection is somewhat open to question. Locking `<membership />` by preventing changes to the `<providers />` element is for all practical purposes locking the configuration of the entire Membership feature. Because providers are central to the feature, using a `<location />`-based lock would achieve about the same result. About the only benefit you gain from using `lockElements` with a feature like `<membership />` is that you could still allow individual applications to customize the online time window setting. A `machine.config` definition that allowed this would look as follows:

```
<membership lockElements="providers"
            lockAttributes="defaultProvider,hashAlgorithmType">
```

However, some provider-based features like the health-monitoring benefit from the use of the element-based lock. For example, as an administrator you could prevent removal or clearing of health-monitoring providers with the following configuration definition:

```
<healthMonitoring>
    <providers lockElements="remove,clear">
        <add name="admin configured provider goes here" … />
    </provider>
</healthMonitoring>
```

With this definition, you can add providers to individual web applications. However, you cannot remove any providers defined in `machine.config`. This approach allows a box administrator to ensure that specific providers are always configured and in use on the machine for centralized web event collection, regardless of whatever other providers may be added by individual applications.

The following list describes the combinations of element-based locks that make sense for any Add-Remove-Clear collection (provider definitions, the Profile properties definition, and so on):

❑ Lock all ARC elements to prevent child modifications by locking the parent collection element. This means putting a `lockElements='*'` definition in the parent element as was shown earlier (for example the `<providers />` element, the `<properties />` element for a feature like Profile, and so on).

❑ Allow individual applications to add elements to an ARC collection, but disallow changing any inherited collection elements. This means using a lock definition such as "`lockAllElementsExcept='add'` in the parent collection element.

❑ Allow individual applications to remove elements from an ARC collection, but disallow additions. This can be accomplished with a definition such as `lockElements='add'` in the parent collection element. This approach can be useful if you configure multiple providers on a machine, but leave it up to the individual applications to choose the specific ones to use. Individual applications can then remove the providers they don't want to use.

Although you can technically do other things, such as disallow `<remove />` but not `<clear />`, or vice versa, these types of locks are ineffective. The `<clear />` and `<remove />` elements are basically interchangeable. You can simulate a `<clear />` with a series of `<remove />` elements, so preventing a child configuration file from using `<clear />` but not `<remove />` is pointless. Similarly, preventing the use of `<remove />` but not `<clear />` is questionable because `<clear />` is just a fast way of removing all previously defined items in a configuration collection.

Locking Provider Definitions

Because a good chunk of this book is about Membership and Role Manager, you may be wondering how the attribute lock feature works with provider-based features. You may be thinking that with the attribute-based lock feature, you can customize portions of your provider definitions and restrict the redefinition of many of the provider attributes.

To see which attributes in a provider `<add />` element are lockable by default you can use the trick mentioned earlier. Take the sample application and create the following membership provider `<add />` element:

```
<add lockAttributes="foo"
     name="AspNetSqlMembershipProvider"
     type="…"
     connectionStringName="LocalSqlServer"
     enablePasswordRetrieval="false"
     enablePasswordReset="false"
     requiresQuestionAndAnswer="false"
     applicationName="ConfigurationSample"
     requiresUniqueEmail="true"
     passwordFormat="Hashed"
     description="some description here" />
```

The following error statement returns:

```
The following attributes can be locked: 'name', 'type', 'connectionStringName',
'enablePasswordRetrieval', 'enablePasswordReset', 'requiresQuestionAndAnswer',
'applicationName', 'requiresUniqueEmail', 'passwordFormat', 'description'.
```

All provider definitions use the same underlying strongly typed configuration class (this is covered extensively in Chapter 10 on the Provider Model). The strongly typed provider configuration class defines only "name" and "type" as common provider attributes. Clearly, though, each provider-based feature has a rich set of feature-specific provider attributes, and the error message shown previously lists much more than the "name" and "type" attributes as available for lock.

This behavior occurs because the strongly typed configuration class for the <add /> element includes a collection used to contain feature-specific provider attributes. When you place a lockAttributes or lockAllAttributesExcept attribute on a provider <add /> element, the configuration system considers the feature-specific provider attributes lockable along with the "name" and "type" attributes. (These two attributes are required on a provider <add /> definition, so they are always lockable).

This still leaves the question as to how you actually lock a specific provider definition. Provider configuration always uses Add-Remove-Clear (ARC) collections, meaning that the provider definitions are built up through a series of <add /> elements, with optional <remove /> and <clear /> elements in child configuration sections. However, there is no such thing as a <modify /> element. Without a modification element, what use are the locking attributes?

If you define a provider with an <add /> element and then subsequently use <remove > and then add the provider in another configuration file, the configuration system remembers the original set of locked attributes from the first <add /> definition. It enforces the attribute lock when the provider is redefined. To see an example of this, you can define a membership provider in machine.config as follows:

```
<membership>
    <providers>
        <add lockAttributes="passwordFormat"
            name="AspNetSqlMembershipProvider"
            .../>
    </providers>
</membership>
```

Then in the web.config for an application, you can redefine the provider as follows:

```
<membership>
    <providers>
        <remove name="AspNetSqlMembershipProvider" />
        <add name="AspNetSqlMembershipProvider"
            passwordFormat="Encrypted"
            .../>
    </providers>
</membership>
```

If you attempt to run any pages in the sample application at this point, you end up with an error saying that the passwordFormat attribute was already defined and locked in a parent configuration file. Unfortunately, you can easily "fake out" the configuration system by using a <clear /> element instead. If you substitute a <clear /> element for the <remove /> element, the web application will run without a problem. Basically in ASP.NET 3.5 the configuration system lacks the "smarts" to retain attribute lock information when a `<clear />` element is used.

Hopefully, in a future release of ASP.NET, this problem will be resolved. For ASP.NET 3.5, though, this means that you can only lockdown provider definitions with the following approaches:

❏ Use a `<location />` tag to lock the entire provider-based feature. For example, configure the `<membership />` section in a parent configuration file and disallow any type of redefinition in child configuration files.

❏ Use the `lockElements` and `lockAllElementsExcept` attributes to control whether child configuration files are allowed to use the `<add />`, `<remove />`, and `<clear />` elements. You might allow for child configuration files to add new provider definitions or you might allow child configuration files to remove previously defined providers.

❏ Use the `lockElements='providers'` attribute to prevent any kind of changes to the `<providers />` element, while still allowing child configuration files the leeway to change attributes on the feature's configuration element (for example, allow edits to the attribute contained in `<membership />` or `<roles />`).

Managing IIS 7.0 Configuration versus ASP.NET Configuration

Chapter 1 provided an overview of the new IIS 7.0 configuration system. There was a big step moving away from the old IIS 6.0 metabase configuration system into the new .NET-like configuration system. The structure and concept of the IIS 7.0 configuration system is based on the .NET Framework configuration system. They both make use of XML configuration files, proving the tight integration when it comes to mixing both configuration systems in a single file (for instance, the application's `web.config` file, as you will see later in this section).

The IIS 7.0 configuration system constitutes a hierarchy of XML configuration files that are distributed among the .NET Framework and IIS 7.0. This hierarchy includes

❏ The `machine.config` file that contains all the global settings and configurations for the .NET Framework.

❏ The root `web.config` configuration file that contains the .NET configurations in the `web.config` configuration file that was introduced since ASP.NET 2.0 as a way to delegate some of the configuration settings from the `machine.config` configuration file.

❏ The site's `web.config` configuration file that contains specific configuration for a specific site.

❏ The application's `web.config` configuration file that holds specific configuration for a specific application in the site.

❏ Finally, the site directory's `web.config` configuration file that contains the most specific configuration settings for a directory within an application.

In addition to the .NET Framework configuration files, there is the famous `applicationHost.config` file, which represents the overall configuration settings specific to IIS 7.0.

Figure 5-1 shows a graphical representation of the different configuration files that constitute the new IIS 7.0 configuration system. The components of the IIS 7.0 configuration system include the .NET Framework configuration files in addition to the IIS 7.0-specific configuration file.

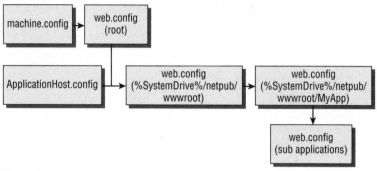

Figure 5-1

As you already know by now, the `applicationHost.config` file is composed of two main section groups: `<system.applicationHost />` and `<system.webServer />`. The `<system.applicationHost />` configuration section group holds global configuration settings used by the Windows Process Activation Service that apply to all Web sites hosted inside of IIS 7.0. Among the different global configuration sections are the `<applicationPools />` configuration section group, which holds information about the different application pools created inside the IIS 7.0 engine, and the `<sites />` configuration section group, which holds information for every site and its inner applications installed on the IIS 7.0 web server. Such configuration settings are not allowed to be edited or modified on the site or application level; only web server administrators are allowed to modify these settings to apply to all sites and applications running on the machine.

The other important configuration section group in the `applicationHost.config` file is the `<system .webServer />` section group. This section contains all the configuration settings for the IIS 7.0 Web server engine, including `<modules />`, `<handlers />`, `<asp />`, and `<security />`. The major difference between this configuration section group and the `<applicationHost />` configuration section group is that IIS 7.0 allows application developers to play around with this section and modify entries inside it that best suits the application they are developing, taking into consideration the ability of the web server administrator to lock down certain sections inside the `<system.webServer />` that he or she finds important for the functionality of the web server and that application developers should keep intact.

Now that the preceding two major sections of the `applicationHost.config` configuration file have been introduced, you have a better understanding that the aforementioned IIS 7.0 configuration file contains global settings that only web server administrators have access to, and global/specific settings that can be defined globally on the IIS 7.0 web server level and can also be overridden by application developers.

As mentioned previously, the new IIS 7.0 configuration system is a mixture of the .NET Framework configuration files and the IIS 7.0 `applicationHost.config` configuration file. Now the question arises: how does IIS 7.0 handle the distributed hierarchy of configuration files when an application is running and executing inside IIS? What happens is that the IIS 7.0 configuration system has access to all the .NET Framework configuration files. At runtime the .NET Framework combines the different configuration sections from the different configuration files starting with the `machine.config` configuration file, adding to it any changes or editions made in the root `web.config` file, adding to it any changes or editions in the site `web.config` configuration file, and finally arriving at the application `web.config` file. In the case a subdirectory is accessed in an application, and then the `web.config` configuration file of that specific directory is also added to the combination of configuration sections. The .NET Framework piles up all the configuration settings into a single configuration file. At this time, the IIS 7.0 reads the .NET Framework joined configuration settings and more specifically the `<system.webServer />` configuration section group. It ignores the rest of the ASP.NET configuration settings and reads the IIS 7.0-specific configuration section. This way, IIS 7.0 would have access to the ASP.NET configuration settings, just as ASP.NET itself has access to them, with one major difference: ASP.NET will be reading the ASP.NET-specific settings and ignoring the `<system.webServer />` configuration section, and IIS 7.0 would ignore all ASP.NET related configuration sections and process the `<system.webServer />` configuration section. Referring to the idea of delegation, IIS 7.0 *should* access and read the `<system.webServer />` configuration section defined inside the ASP.NET piled-up configuration settings because, as you have read above, ASP.NET developers are given the privilege to configure IIS 7.0-specific settings from inside the different .NET Framework configuration files and, hence, if some IIS 7.0-specific settings were changed for a specific web application, the IIS 7.0 configuration system has to know about the changes so that it configures the application at the IIS 7.0 level with the changes or modifications required.

From an architectural point of view, the IIS 7.0 configuration system inherits the structure of the .NET Framework configuration system. This led the IIS team at Microsoft to decide on grouping both configuration settings in the same configuration file. This improves portability and deployment, of course, since the developer has to move only the application's `web.config` configuration file with the application when it is time to deploy it on a server. The IIS 7.0 installed on the production server will read all the specific IIS 7.0 configuration settings and customize the application's specific configurations inside it. The only concern with such a design is the overlap between configuration settings in the sense that IIS 7.0 might be accessing and reading ASP.NET configuration sections and ASP.NET would be accessing the `<system.webServer />` configuration sections, and hence problems and exceptions might occur. For this reason, the IIS 7.0 configuration system was designed to ignore the ASP.NET-specific configuration sections. In fact, the 2.0 .NET Framework's `machine.config` configuration file, which is shared between ASP.NET 2.0 and ASP.NET 3.5, now has a new section called `system.webServer` that maps the `<system.webServer />` configuration section to a handler that simply ignores that section as follows:

```
<section name="system.webServer" type="System.Configuration.IgnoreSection, System
.Configuration, Version=2.0.0.0, Culture=neutral, PublicKeyToken=b03f5f7f11d50a3a"
/>
```

As you can see, the `<system.webServer />` configuration section is mapped to the `System.Configuration.IgnoreSection` class, which simply ignores the IIS 7.0-specific configuration section when ASP.NET is reading the application's compiled `web.config` configuration file. However, if you are running an application in ASP.NET 1.1 that is hosted inside an IIS 7.0 web server, you need to add the above section manually (since ASP.NET 1.1 existed a long time before IIS 7.0 came into the picture) so that no errors are generated when the application is running and executing.

Extending IIS 7.0 with Managed Modules and Handlers

Now that you understand the IIS 7.0 configuration system and its general architectural design, it is important to discuss some the changes that were made on some configuration sections, especially the `<httpHandlers />` and `<httpModules />` configuration sections that were originally located in the `<system.web />` configuration section group of the .NET Framework configuration files. As you already know, IIS 7.0 introduced the Integrated mode of execution (explained in Chapter 2). With the new Integrated mode, ASP.NET developers can now build their custom handlers and modules in .NET and make them participate in the processing of HTTP requests that go into the unified HTTP request pipeline. At every stage in the unified HTTP request pipeline, the IIS 7.0 core engine checks to see if there are any native and managed modules to initialize using an internal native module that takes care of querying the managed modules to see whether there are managed modules registered to run in the Integrated mode.

Because IIS 7.0 has no clue about any configuration sections defined inside the ASP.NET specific configuration sections, it has no way of knowing which managed modules and handlers are registered inside the ASP.NET `<system.web />` configuration section group that need to run and execute when the web application is executing in the IIS 7.0 Integrated mode.

The only way for the IIS 7.0 configuration system to know which managed modules and handlers the application developer has attached to the running application is to query the `<system.webServer />` configuration section that the application developer used to register the managed modules and handlers to run in the Web application that is configured in the Integrated mode. In other words, the `<system.webServer />` configuration section is the only interface ASP.NET developers have inside the application's `web.config` configuration file to interact with the IIS 7.0 configuration system. Of course, administrators and developers can use the IIS 7.0 Manager tool to do all the configuration settings for the application, but this privilege is not always available for developers hosting their application in remote servers, so `<system.webServer />` configuration section is their only way out.

Therefore, the `<httpModules />` and `<httpHandlers />` configuration sections located inside the `<system.web />` configuration section group have no effect when the application is running in the IIS 7.0 Integrated mode—thus, the need was to move the aforementioned configuration sections inside the `<system.webServer />` configuration section so that IIS 7.0 can understand which managed modules and handlers can be used to extend its functionality. Currently, the `<system.webServer />` configuration section includes the `<modules />` and `<handlers />` configuration section groups that you can use to configure your managed modules and handlers that are to be run inside the unified HTTP request pipeline.

Managing the Native versus Managed Configuration Systems

Reading about the IIS 7.0 configuration system might bring fears and worries to you on how to manage both configuration systems and what to count on. In this context there is no magical solution that you can follow when it comes to managing both configuration systems. At the same time, having flexibility and richness with both configuration systems should be a source of power for you as a developer, giving you more control in configuring both the IIS 7.0 and ASP.NET specific features.

For instance, IIS 7.0 contains the CustomErrorModule, a native module running in the IIS 7.0 Web server core engine that maps to the <httpErrors /> configuration section that allows you to define custom HTML/ASPX pages to handle specific errors that might occur during the processing of HTTP requests inside IIS 7.0. The <httpErrors /> configuration section, for example, looks something similar to the following:

```
<httpErrors>
          <error statusCode="401"
                 prefixLanguageFilePath="%SystemDrive%\inetpub\custerr"
                 path="401.htm" />
          <error statusCode="403"
                 prefixLanguageFilePath="%SystemDrive%\inetpub\custerr"
                 path="403.htm" />
</httpErrors>
```

The preceding configuration section configures a possible error through its statusCode attribute and maps its handler to an .htm static page. In your application, you can map to a custom .aspx page that is part of the theme and layout of the application you are developing.

Another flexibility is given to you through the native UrlAuthorizationModule that ships as part of the IIS 7.0 and is configured inside the <system.webServer /> configuration section. Now developers have the option of either using the ASP.NET UrlAuthorizationModule or the IIS 7.0 UrlAuthorization Module by simply editing the application's web.config configuration file for either the ASP.NET or IIS 7.0-specific configuration sections. By default, the native module works automatically with both native and managed requests; however, the managed module has to be removed from the <modules /> section inside the application's web.config configuration file and then added again with the precondition attribute set to an empty string, a trick you have learned about before. Nevertheless, the richness of the authorization feature and its ease of configuration inside either the <system.web /> or <system.webServer /> give you a powerful way of authorizing your users.

In addition to the previous features introduced with IIS 7.0 is the output caching module. The caching module is defined in the applicationHost.config as follows:

```
<add name="HttpCacheModule" image="%windir%\System32\inetsrv\cachhttp.dll" />
```

And it is configured through the following configuration section:

```
<caching enabled="true" enableKernelCache="true"></caching>
```

This native module caches an application's output in the kernel mode cache, thereby reducing the application's response time. Once again you are given the option of configuring output caching either with the native IIS 7.0 module or through the managed output caching module in ASP.NET, the OutputCacheModule represented by the <OutputCache /> configuration section.

You have witnessed above the new native and configurable modules that are introduced by IIS 7.0. All of the above modules are easily configured through the flexible IIS 7.0 configuration system. However, you can clearly see the overlapping in functionalities between the features that have already existed in ASP.NET and the ones introduced with IIS 7.0.

A general recommendation for the above overlapping configurable native and managed modules is to continue using ASP.NET custom errors for ASP.NET content because the custom errors feature in ASP.NET is tied directly into ASP.NET's logic for dealing with unhandled exceptions. Regarding authorization, once again the recommendation is to use the native `UrlAuthorizationModule` with any new project you start developing for the main reason that this native module works fine with both native and managed requests without any modifications. However, for current applications that are already configured with the managed `UrlAuthorizationModule`, keep using the managed module when the application gets upgraded to run under IIS 7.0. Finally, regarding the output caching feature that is present in both ASP.NET and IIS 7.0, originally output caching in IIS 7 is intended for classic ASP applications as opposed to ASP.NET content. As a result, for anything but the most trivial ASP.NET caching scenarios, you are better off sticking with ASP.NET's output caching.

IIS 7.0 Feature Delegation

IIS 7.0 provides a new feature that gives administrators a visual tool to decide which configuration sections in the `ApplicationHost.config` file can be configured on the application level. By default most of the configuration sections in the `ApplicationHost.config` file are locked down, meaning that applications hosted on the IIS web server cannot re-configure those locked-down configuration sections in the application's `web.config` file. The main two configuration section groups in the `ApplicationHost.config` configuration file are the `<system.applicationHost>` and the `<system.webServer>` configuration section groups:

```
<configSections>
    <sectionGroup name="system.applicationHost">
        <section name="applicationPools"
                allowDefinition="AppHostOnly"
                overrideModeDefault="Deny" />
        <section name="sites"
                allowDefinition="AppHostOnly"
                overrideModeDefault="Deny" />
    </sectionGroup>

    <sectionGroup name="system.webServer">
        <section name="defaultDocument"
                overrideModeDefault="Allow" />
        <section name="directoryBrowse"
                overrideModeDefault="Allow" />
        <section name="globalModules"
                allowDefinition="AppHostOnly"
                overrideModeDefault="Deny" />
        <section name="handlers"
                overrideModeDefault="Deny" />
        <section name="httpRedirect"
                overrideModeDefault="Allow" />
        <section name="modules"
                allowDefinition="MachineToApplication"
                overrideModeDefault="Deny" />
        <sectionGroup name="security">
            <section name="access"
                    overrideModeDefault="Deny" />
```

```
            <section name="applicationDependencies"
                     overrideModeDefault="Deny" />
        <sectionGroup name="authentication">
            <section name="anonymousAuthentication"
                     overrideModeDefault="Allow" />
            <section name="basicAuthentication"
                     overrideModeDefault="Deny" />
            <section name="windowsAuthentication"
                     overrideModeDefault="Deny" />
        </sectionGroup>
        <section name="authorization"
                 overrideModeDefault="Deny" />
        <section name="requestFiltering"
                 overrideModeDefault="Allow" />
        </sectionGroup>
        <section name="serverRuntime"
                 overrideModeDefault="Deny" />
        <section name="staticContent"
                 overrideModeDefault="Deny" />
        </sectionGroup>
    </configSections>
```

The `<system.applicationHost>` configuration section group is a global section that is usually configured by administrators and cannot be edited by specific applications or virtual directories. However, the `<system.webServer>` configuration section group is the section that developers can override through the application's `web.config` configuration file.

Figure 5-2 shows the Feature Delegation applet when opened in IIS 7.0 Manager.

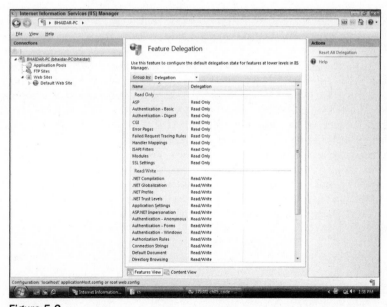

Figure 5-2

You can see that some of the managed and native modules are listed with either Read Only or Read/Write. Read-Only delegation for a feature means that applications can only read the configuration settings set for that specific feature in the `ApplicationHost.config` configuration file and cannot change any settings. For example, the Error Pages module has a Read-Only delegation that means no application can change or configure the error pages' global settings. On the other hand, when a feature has a Read/Write delegation, it means that an application's `web.config` file can read and change the default or global configuration settings. An example is the Authentication – Anonymous feature configured with Read/Write delegation. Having a Read/Write delegation allows an application's `web.config` file to configure the `AnonymousAuthenticationModule`. For instance, you can now disable the `AnonymousAuthentication` native module by adding the following configuration section in the application's `web.config` file:

```
<system.webServer>
    <security>
        <authentication>
            <anonymousAuthentication enabled="false" />
        </authentication>
    </security>
</system.webServer>
```

If you try to configure a locked-down module inside the application's `web.config` file, you receive the following exception:

```
This configuration section cannot be used at this path. This happens when
the section is locked at a parent level. Locking is either by default
(overrideModeDefault="Deny"), or set explicitly by a location tag with
overrideMode="Deny" or the legacy allowOverride="false".
```

The exception message is clear enough to inform you that you are trying to configure a locked-down configuration section at the `ApplicationHost.config` file.

When you set the delegation for a feature to Read Only, a new `<location />` section is added at the end of the `ApplicationHost.config` configuration file. This section has a `Path` attribute that is used to specify the path to a specific application or if left as empty string meaning that the `<location />` section applies to the entire applications hosted on the web server. The other attribute this section has is the `overrideMode` attribute that is set to `Deny`. Setting this attribute to `Deny` means that the configuration sections listed inside the `<location />` configuration section are locked down and applications hosted on the web server can neither configure the listed configuration sections nor change any of them. If, on the other hand, the value of the `overrideMode` is `Allow`, the subconfiguration sections listed are allowed to be changed and modified by the hosted application's `web.config` files.

It is recommended to unlock configuration sections by using a `<location />` configuration section whether you are unlocking manually or by using the Feature Delegation in IIS 7.0. For instance, consider that the `<defaultDocument />` configuration section is locked down in the `ApplicationHost.config` file as follows:

```
<section name="defaultDocument" overrideModeDefault="Deny" />
```

To unlock the above native module configuration section so that an application's `web.config` file can change the default documents assigned to an application, you could either use the Feature Delegation to unlock it or do it manually. Unlocking sections manually or through Feature Delegation results in the same `<location />` section being added to the `ApplicationHost.config` file, as follows:

```
<location path="" overrideMode="Allow">
    <system.webServer>
        <defaultDocument enabled="true">
            <files>
                <add value="Default.htm" />
                <add value="Default.asp" />
                <add value="index.htm" />
                <add value="index.html" />
                <add value="iisstart.htm" />
                <add value="default.aspx" />
            </files>
        </defaultDocument>
    </system.webServer>
</location>
```

The new `<location />` section applies to all the applications hosted on the IIS web server since the `Path` attribute has the value of an empty string. The `Allow` value of the `overrideMode` attribute means that any subconfiguration section is automatically unlocked so that applications can re-configure it using the `<system.webServer>` configuration section group in the `web.config` file. You can notice the presence of the `<system.webServer>` configuration section group in the `<location />` section above. To unlock any configuration section, you should place it inside the `<system.webServer>` configuration section group since an application's `web.config` file uses the `<system.webServer>` configuration section group to configure IIS features. Hence, placing the features' sections you want to unlock inside this configuration section group means that those features are unlocked and can be re-configured inside the same configuration section of the application's `web.config` file.

The `<system.webServer>` configuration section has been newly added into the IIS 7.0 `application Host.config` file. Having this configuration section as part of the `applicationHost.config` configuration file gives the web server administrator a way to define IIS features globally. In addition, developers can add this section into the application's `web.config` file to customize the IIS features per the current web application.

Once you have unlocked the `<defaultDocument>` configuration section using the Feature Delegation, you will configure the default documents for a hosted application. Figure 5-3 shows the Default Document applet in IIS 7.0 that can be used to edit the default documents in an application.

Any changes you make here are reflected into the application's `web.config` file. For example, only the `default.aspx` page has been added to the list of default documents; therefore, you would expect the `<system.webServer>` configuration section group to look like the following:

```
<system.webServer>
    <defaultDocument>
        <files>
            <clear />
            <add value="default.aspx" />
        </files>
    </defaultDocument>
</system.webServer>
```

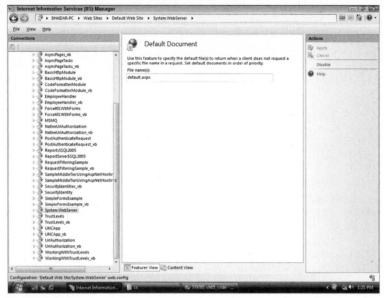

Figure 5-3

As you can see in the preceding configuration settings, all the preset default documents have been cleared out and only one web page has been added: the default.aspx. Without having an administrator add a new <location /> configuration section to allow modifying of the above <defaultDocument> native module, you would not have been able to change or configure this section. This applies to all the sections located inside the <system.webServer> configuration section group located in the ApplicationHost.config configuration file.

Using IIS 7.0 Feature Delegation provides administrators with an easy way to control which configuration sections are allowed to be re-configured and overridden by an application's web.config files and which sections are not allowed. It is through this feature that IIS 7.0 protects the configuration sections inside the ApplicationHost.config from being edited or changed by applications as a way to protect the global settings set by administrators on web servers.

Moreover, this feature gives developers an easier way of configuring the web server from their application's web.config file without the need to contact the web server administrator or connect to the web server. However, this depends on how much configuration sections are unlocked by administrators taking into consideration security attacks and other safety measures.

In addition to using the <location /> configuration section to lock and unlock features, you can lock specific elements and attributes the same way as you have read about at the beginning of this chapter. For instance, if you want to enable the native WindowsAuthenticationModule at the ApplicationHost.config file level and prevent the application from editing the value of the enabled attribute, you would add something such as:

```
<location path="" overrideMode="Allow">
    <system.webServer>
        <security>
```

```
          <authentication>
            <windowsAuthentication
                enabled="true"
                lockAttributes="enabled">
                  <providers>
                      <add value="Negotiate" />
                      <add value="NTLM" />
                  </providers>
            </windowsAuthentication>
          </authentication>
        </security>
      </system.webServer>
  </location>
```

As you can see, the configuration settings use the same `lockAttributes` attribute to lock down specific attributes. To lock all the attributes of a feature, simply set the value of the `lockAttributes` to the list of attributes, separated by a comma (,).

You can also lock elements for any feature. For instance, suppose you want to enable the native `WindowsAuthenticationModule` to all hosted applications on the web server but lock the `Providers` element from being edited by specific applications. The following configuration settings make sure that the `Providers` element will not be touched by any hosted application:

```
<location path="" overrideMode="Allow">
    <system.webServer>
        <security>
          <authentication>
              <windowsAuthentication enabled="true" lockElements="providers">
                  <providers>
                      <add value="Negotiate" />
                      <add value="NTLM" />
                  </providers>
              </windowsAuthentication>
          </authentication>
        </security>
      </system.webServer>
  </location>
```

In addition to being able to lock down specific elements, you can also lock down multiple elements by simply setting the value of the `lockElements` to a comma-separated list of all the elements to be locked down.

If you want to lock down all elements or attributes except a single element or attribute, you can make use of the `lockAllElementsExcept` or `lockAllAttributesExcept` to list the only unlocked element or attribute for a feature while locking down the rest of elements or attributes that belong to a feature.

As you can see, the same locking sections and attributes that were used and explained above for ASP.NET apply to the configuration sections of IIS 7.0. In fact, the IIS team imported the concepts and ideas from the ASP.NET configuration system and applied them on the IIS 7.0 configuration system, which is why you see so many similarities between the ASP.NET and IIS 7.0 configuration systems. The locking by elements and attributes will not be explained further since the same concepts that apply to ASP.NET and that were explained above apply to IIS 7.0 configuration system locking features.

Reading and Writing Configuration

Before diving into specifics on ACL requirements for reading and writing configuration, a quick primer on using the strongly typed configuration API is useful. Even though a detailed discussion of the new strongly typed configuration API is out of the scope of this book, it is helpful for you to understand the basic coding approaches for manipulating configuration before you see the various security requirements that are enforced when using these APIs.

You may never end up using the strongly typed configuration API. For example, if you use the Membership feature, almost all of the configuration information about the feature itself (the <membership /> configuration element) and the individual providers (the various <add /> elements) are available from the Membership and various MembershipProvider-derived classes. Other features like Forms Authentication follow a similar approach.

However, some features, such as session state, don't mirror every configuration setting via a property from a well-known feature class. Also for administrative-style applications, it makes sense to deal with configuration information using the configuration APIs as opposed to using different feature classes that are potentially scattered through different namespaces.

Reading configuration for a web application can be accomplished in two different ways. If you want to use the configuration APIs available to all Framework applications, you use the ConfigurationManager class, as shown here:

C#

```
...
using System.Web.Configuration;
using System.Configuration;
...
protected void Page_Load(object sender, EventArgs e)
{
  SessionStateSection sts =
              (SessionStateSection)
                    ConfigurationManager.GetSection("system.web/sessionState");
  Response.Write("The session state mode is: " + sts.Mode.ToString() + "<br/>");
}
```

VB.NET

```
...
Imports System.Configuration
Imports System.Web.Configuration
...

    Protected Sub Page_Load(ByVal sender As Object, ByVal e As EventArgs) Handles _
    Me.Load

        Dim sts As SessionStateSection = _
        CType(ConfigurationManager.GetSection("system.web/sessionState"), _
        SessionStateSection)
        Response.Write("The session state mode is: " & _
        sts.Mode.ToString() & "<br/>")

    End Sub
```

The ConfigurationManager class has a static GetSection method that you can use to obtain a reference to a strongly typed configuration class representing a configuration section. You tell the ConfigurationManager which section you want by specifying an XPath-like syntax to the configuration section you want. Because in this case the sample is showing how to access the configuration information for the session state configuration information, and this configuration section is nested within the <system.web> configuration section, the path that you pass is system.web/sessionState. The path information is case-sensitive because configuration files are XML files.

After ConfigurationManager finds the section, you cast the returned object to the correct type. ASP.NET includes several strongly typed configuration section classes within the System.Web.Configuration namespace. In the sample code you cast to an instance of SessionStateSection, which is the strongly typed configuration class used for the Session State feature. With the reference to SessionStateSection in hand, you can access any properties exposed by the class; the sample uses the Mode property to write the session state mode for the current application.

The ConfigurationManager class is scoped only to the current application, though, so it is not flexible enough for applications that need to edit arbitrary configuration files for different web applications. As a result, there is a companion configuration class called WebConfigurationManager, which includes additional overloads for its methods to allow loading of arbitrary web application configuration files.

C#

```
...
using System.Web.Configuration;
using System.Configuration;
...
protected void Page_Load(object sender, EventArgs e)
{
    MembershipSection ms =
      (MembershipSection)
       WebConfigurationManager.GetSection("system.web/membership", "~/web.config");

    Response.Write("The default provider as set in config is: " +
                   ms.DefaultProvider + "<br/>");
}
```

VB.NET

```
...
Imports System.Configuration
Imports System.Web.Configuration
...

    Protected Sub Page_Load(ByVal sender As Object, ByVal e As EventArgs) _
    Handles Me.Load()

        Dim ms As MembershipSection = _
        CType(WebConfigurationManager.GetSection("system.web/membership", _
                   "~/web.config"), MembershipSection)
        Response.Write("The default provider as set in config is: " _
        & ms.DefaultProvider & "<br/>")
```

In this sample, the GetSection method includes a second parameter specifying the virtual path to the current application's web.config file. You can change the value of this parameter to point at other web application configuration files, or at configuration files located in subdirectories within a web application. Various overloads let you use physical file paths as well as virtual file paths when referencing configuration files.

Writing to configuration requires that you actually open the entire configuration file, as opposed to just getting a reference to an individual configuration section. This returns a reference to an instance of the System.Configuration.Configuration class. (It's not a typo; the class that represents a configuration file is really called Configuration within the System.Configuration namespace.) As with read operations, you can use the ConfigurationManager or the WebConfigurationManager to accomplish this. However, the available methods on the ConfigurationManager are not intuitive from the perspective of a web application developer because the various overloads refer to variations of configuration files for client executables. As a result, you will probably find the WebConfigurationManager makes more sense when you edit web.config for your web applications.

After you programmatically open a configuration file, you get a reference to the specific configuration section you want to edit from the Configuration instance. You can set various properties on the strongly typed configuration section as well as manipulate any writable collections exposed on the configuration class. After all the edits are made, you call the Save method on the Configuration instance to commit the changes to disk. The following code demonstrates using the WebConfigurationManager to load and update a <membership /> configuration section.

C#

```
...
using System.Web.Configuration;
...
protected void Page_Load(object sender, EventArgs e)
{
    Configuration config = WebConfigurationManager.OpenWebConfiguration("~");

    MembershipSection ms =
      (MembershipSection)config.GetSection("system.web/membership");

    ms.DefaultProvider = "someOtherProvider";

    config.Save();
}
```

VB.NET

```
...
Imports System.Web.Configuration

    Protected Sub Page_Load(ByVal sender As Object, ByVal e As EventArgs) _
    Handles Me.Load
        Dim config As Configuration = WebConfigurationManager.OpenWebConfiguration("~")

        Dim ms As MembershipSection = _
        CType(config.GetSection("system.web/membership"), _
        MembershipSection)
```

```
                ms.DefaultProvider = "someOtherProvider"

            config.Save()
    End Sub
```

Several overloads to the `OpenWebConfiguration` method allow you to specify the exact configuration file you want to open for editing. As shown in the sample, the `"~"` shorthand can be used for loading the current application's `web.config` file.

The configuration system does not enforce any kind of concurrency or locking if multiple threads attempt to update the same configuration file. For this reason, you should ensure that any code that edits configuration files serializes access to the configuration file, or is written to handle the exception that is returned from the configuration system if it detects that changes occurred to the underlying configuration file. If you write console applications for editing configuration files, you probably won't run into this issue. However, an administrative website that allows editing of any `web.config` file located on a web server should be written with concurrency in mind.

Permissions Required for Reading Local Configuration

The most common scenario is reading configuration information for a web application located on the same server as the code that performing the read operation. For example, each time a web application starts up, ASP.NET is reading configuration information down the entire inheritance chain of configuration files. Furthermore, as you use various features, such as Membership, Role Manager, Session State, and so on, your code triggers additional reads to occur from the various configuration files.

As mentioned in Chapter 2, when an application domain first starts up, the identity that is used is either the process identity or the application impersonation identity. So under normal conditions, the Read ACL on web directories that is granted to IIS_USRS allows the default process identity to read configuration information.

Looking up the configuration inheritance chain, the default ACLs on the various configuration files are:

❑　The web application's directory grants Read access to IIS_USRS, so IIS_USRS has Read access to the application's `web.config` file.

❑　The root `web.config` file located at `%windir%\Microsoft.NET\Framework\v2.0.XYZ\CONFIG\web.config` grants Read access to IIS_USRS.

❑　The `machine.config` located in the same `CONFIG` subdirectory also grants Read access to IIS_USRS.

This set of ACLs allows the configuration system to merge configuration sections up the inheritance chain. If you remove these Read ACLs from any one of these configuration files, ASP.NET would be unable to Read configuration during application startup and your web application will fail to start.

Either the process identity or the application impersonation identity is also used when reading configuration information during normal runtime processing, specifically when using the `GetSection` method on `WebConfigurationManager` or `ConfigurationManager`. For example, if you use Windows authentication in a web application and enable client impersonation, even if the impersonated account does not have access to read the application's `web.config` file, the web application still runs and configuration information is still successfully read.

If you think about it, this behavior makes sense. It would be a pretty onerous security requirement if every possible Windows user of an application with client impersonation turned on was required to have Read access up the configuration inheritance chain. Although the default ACLs on the CONFIG subdirectory do grant Read access to the local Users group (and hence any authenticated user on the machine has Read access), it is not uncommon to remove this ACL on hardened servers.

The GetSection call succeeds because GetSection is considered to be a "runtime" configuration API. When you call GetSection the configuration system accesses cached configuration information that was previously loaded while running as either the process identity or the application impersonation identity. From a runtime perspective, loading configuration information is a service that the configuration system provides to running code.

This behavior becomes clearer when you compare the difference between the runtime configuration API and the design-time configuration API. Earlier you saw that an alternative approach for getting a configuration section was to use a method such as WebConfigurationManager.OpenWebConfiguration or ConfigurationManager.OpenExeConfiguration. These Open* methods are considered "design-time" configuration APIs. As a result, they have different security semantics when accessing configuration information.

When you call an Open* method the configuration system attempts to open one or more physical configuration files on disk. For example, if you attempt to open a web application's configuration, a file open attempt will occur up the entire inheritance chain of configuration files. These file open operations are like any other call to the File.Open method. The security token on the operating system thread must have Read access to one or more configuration files.

If you have a web application using Windows authentication with client impersonation enabled, and you write the following line of code:

```
Configuration config = WebConfigurationManager.OpenWebConfiguration("~");
```

… the open attempt will fail unless the impersonated client identity has Read access to the application's web.config as well as the root web.config and machine.config files located in the Framework's CONFIG subdirectory. You can see this behavior if you add an explicit Deny ACE to the application's web.config that disallows Read access to the application's web.config. The call to Open WebConfiguration will fail with an Access Denied error. You will have the same failure if you add a Deny ACE on the root web.config or on machine.config. However, if you change your code to call WebConfigurationManager.GetSection, your code will run without a problem.

The following list summarizes the security requirements for the runtime and design-time configuration APIs:

❑   GetSection: Regardless of whether this is called from WebConfigurationManager or ConfigurationManager, the process identity or the application impersonation identity (if application impersonation is being used) requires Read access to the application's web.config file, the root web.config file and the machine.config file. If you are attempting to read configuration at a path below the level of the root of a web application, Read access is also required on the lower-level configuration files. This level of access will normally exist because without it the web application would fail to start up.

❑   GetWebApplicationSection: This is just another variation of GetSection available on WebConfigurationManager. It has the same security requirements as GetSection.

❑ `OpenWebConfiguration`: This method is available only on `WebConfigurationManager`. The operating system thread identity at the time the call is made requires Read access to the application's `web.config` file, the root `web.config` file and the `machine.config` file. If you are attempting to read configuration at a path below the level of the root of a web application, the operating system thread identity also requires Read access to the lower-level configuration files.

❑ Other `Open*` methods: Both `WebConfigurationManager` and `ConfigurationManager` have a variety of methods starting with `Open` that provide different overloads for opening configuration files at different levels of the inheritance chain (that is, open just `machine.config`) as well as different ways for referencing virtual directories in a web application. No matter which `Open*` method you use, the operating system thread identity requires Read access to all configuration files that contribute to the configuration for the desired application or virtual path. When only `machine.config` is being opened, Read access is required only on `machine.config` because the lower-level configuration files will not be opened (for example, root `web.config` and application-specific configuration files have no effect on determining machine-level configuration information).

Permissions Required for Writing Local Configuration

Writing configuration is not something that a web application would normally attempt. Hence, the default ACLs up the configuration hierarchy don't grant any Write access to commonly used ASP.NET accounts. Looking up the configuration inheritance chain, the Write ACLs on the various configuration files are as follows:

❑ Only the local Administrators group and SYSTEM have write access to files (including `web.config` files) located beneath `inetpub\wwwroot`.

❑ The root `web.config` file located at `%windir%\Microsoft.NET\Framework\v2.0.XYZ\CONFIG\web.config` grants Write access only to the local Administrators group as well as SYSTEM.

❑ The `machine.config` located in the same `CONFIG` subdirectory also grants Write access only to the local Administrators group as well as SYSTEM.

This set of ACLs shows that the default privileges pretty much expect only interactive editing of configuration files by a machine administrator using Notepad.

Write access alone, however, is not sufficient for editing configuration files using the configuration API. Updating configuration information results in the following file operations:

1. A temporary file is created in the appropriate directory where the updated configuration file will be written. For example, if you are updating a configuration section in a web application's configuration file, the configuration system will create a temporary file with a random file name in the web application's root directory.

2. The original configuration file is deleted.

3. The temporary file is renamed to either `web.config` or `machine.config`, depending on which type of configuration file is being edited.

From this list it is pretty obvious that editing and updating configuration files requires very powerful privileges.

Because of the creation and deletion of configuration files, the operating system thread identity that is updating configuration effectively requires Full Control to the directory containing the configuration file that will ultimately be rewritten (technically, you can get away with just Write and Modify access on the directory, but realistically there isn't much difference between Full Control and Write+Modify). Although you could go out of your way and attempt to grant Full Control on a directory but restrict the rights on all files except the configuration file located within a directory, such a security lockdown doesn't buy you much. Full Control on a directory gives an account wide latitude to make changes in it, and arguably the ability to change the configuration file means an account also has broad privileges to change the behavior of an application.

An important side note here is that because local administrators do have Full Control to directories, a website with Windows authentication and client impersonation enabled could "accidentally" write to any of these configuration files. If a user account that was a member of the local Administrators group happened to surf to a web application that included malicious code that attempted to rewrite configuration, the malicious code would succeed. This type of subtle attack vector is another reason users with elevated privileges in a domain should never perform routine day-to-day work logged in with "super" privileges; its far too easy for someone to slip a piece of interesting code into an unsuspecting web application that maliciously makes use of such elevated privileges.

Unlike the Read-oriented methods in configuration that are split between a set of runtime and design-time APIs, Write operations are considered design-time APIs. There is no equivalent to GetSection for writing configuration. In fact, if you obtain a configuration section via GetSection, although you can call the property setters on the strongly typed configuration section that is returned, no methods are available to commit the changes to the underlying configuration file.

Instead, you commit changes to disk with a call to the Save or SaveAs method available on System .Configuration.Configuration. The Configuration instance can be obtained via a call to one of the Open* methods available on ConfigurationManager or WebConfigurationManager. Remember that the operating system thread identity requires Read access to successfully load a configuration file (or files) from disk; loading these files is always the first step whenever you want to edit configuration. After a call to WebConfigurationManager.OpenWebConfiguration, you have a Configuration object that is a reference to an in-memory representation of the loaded configuration file.

Subsequently calling Configuration.Save or Configuration.SaveAs results in the file creation and deletion operations listed earlier. The following code snippet loads a web application's configuration, modifies the configuration information in memory, and then writes the results to disk:

C#

```
Configuration config =
    WebConfigurationManager.OpenWebConfiguration("~");

MembershipSection ms =
    (MembershipSection)config.GetSection("system.web/membership");

ms.DefaultProvider = "someOtherProvider";

config.Save();
```

VB.NET

```
Dim config As Configuration = WebConfigurationManager.OpenWebConfiguration("~")

Dim ms As MembershipSection = _
CType(config.GetSection("system.web/membership"), _
MembershipSection)

ms.DefaultProvider = "someOtherProvider"

config.Save()
```

In the sample code, the configuration information being edited is the web.config file for a web application; thus, Full Control is required only on the root of the web application's directory. The configuration information represented by the Configuration instance is loaded by reading all the configuration files up the configuration inheritance chain. In an application using Windows authentication and client impersonation, the resulting operating system thread identity needs Read access on each of these configuration files. However, because the web application's configuration was loaded (as opposed to the root web.config or the machine.config), Full Control is needed only on the web application's root directory when the call to Save is made.

The requirements for Full Control raise the question of exactly when it makes sense to use the design-time APIs. The safest approach would be to never deploy code to a production web server that calls Configuration.Save. The design-time aspect of configuration makes a lot of sense to use in a development environment or in an automated build process. However, after you have programmatically generated the desired configuration file, you would copy it to a production server.

If the need to edit the configuration files used in production arises, it still makes sense to have the code that performs the configuration updates run on some type of staging or test server. After you verify that the updated configuration works, the updated configuration file can be staged and copied to production. I think having code that writes to configuration sitting on a production server, along with a set of file permissions granting Full Control, is simply a hacker attack waiting to happen.

There is no escaping the fact that you need Full Control to save configuration changes to disk. The idea of having Full Control ACLs for anything other than local administrators placed on the directories of various application folders is pretty scary. Although there will surely be many elegant and powerful configuration-editing UIs created for ASP.NET 3.5 (IIS 7.0 allows editing web server configuration settings remotely using IIS 7.0 Manager), such tools should be tightly controlled. Setting up a website or a Web Service that allows for remote editing of configuration files on a production server is just a security incident waiting to happen.

Permissions Required for Remote Editing

The configuration system for ASP.NET includes the ability to have code on one machine remotely bind to ASP.NET configuration data on a remote server and read or write that configuration information. For security reasons, this capability is not enabled by default. A DCOM object can be enabled on your web server to allow remote machines to connect to the web server and carry out configuration operations.

To enable remote reading and writing of a web server's configuration information, you use the `aspnet_regiis` tool:

```
%windir%\Microsoft.NET\Framework\v2.0.5727\aspnet_regiis -config+
```

The `config+` switch causes the Framework to register a DCOM endpoint with the following PROGID:

```
System.Web.Configuration.RemoteWebConfigurationHostServer_32
```

If you use the DCOMCNFG tool (which is now an MMC console showing both COM+ and standard DCOM information) after running `aspnet_regiis -config+`, you can open the DCOM configuration node to see the newly registered DCOM endpoint, as shown in Figure 5-4.

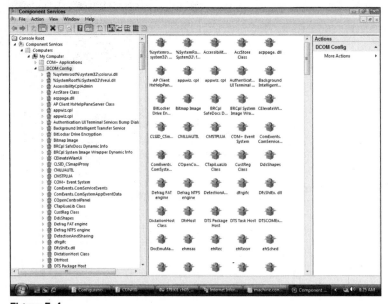

Figure 5-4

You can subsequently disable remote editing of configuration by using `aspnet_regiis -config-`.

You run the `aspnet_regiis` tool on the web servers that you want to manage. However, it isn't necessary to run the tool on the machine that will be running the configuration code. Within the web configuration code, whenever you attempt to open configuration information on a remote server, the configuration code attempts to create an instance of the DCOM object on the remote server. This requires that DCOM calls are able to flow across the network between the machine running the configuration editing code, and the remote server.

Due the sensitive nature of allowing code to remotely manipulate a server's configuration information, the DCOM object on the remote web server has its launch permissions restricted to only members of the remote server's local Administrators group. Remember that this is the same security requirement needed by default for editing local configuration information. This means that even if you call one of the `Open`* methods with the intent of only reading configuration information from a remote server, the operating system thread identity making the calls still needs to be a member of the remote server's Administrators group. The more stringent security requirement is necessary because you don't want random machines on your network trolling through your servers attempting to remotely read configuration information.

The utility of allowing remote editing of configuration is suspect due to the security risks involved. With the additional requirement of configuring DCOM to work through firewalls if you are attempting to manage web servers in a DMZ, remote configuration editing in ASP.NET is most useful for web servers running inside of a corporate network. Even then you should use additional security such as IPSEC restrictions to prevent random machines on your network from attempting to launch the DCOM server on your web machines.

For additional security, you should change the access permissions on the DCOM object. Although the launch permissions are locked to the local Administrators group, after the DCOM server is launched the default DCOM access permissions control which identities can invoke methods on the DCOM server. Creating a custom set of access permissions for the configuration DCOM object ensures that only selected users or groups can invoke methods on the DCOM server after it is already started.

Using Configuration in Partial Trust

The configuration examples you have seen so far all depended implicitly on one additional security setting in order to work: the trust level for the sample application. The sample applications have all been running in Full trust when calling into the configuration system. If you attempt to use the strongly typed configuration API, you can only do so by default when running in either Full or High trust. At lower trust levels, the strongly typed configuration API will fail.

For example, say you attempt to read the Membership configuration with code like the following:

C#

```
MembershipSection ms =
    (MembershipSection)ConfigurationManager.GetSection("system.web/membership");
```

VB.NET

```
Dim ms As MembershipSection = _
  CType(config.GetSection("system.web/membership"), _
  MembershipSection)
```

If your application is running in Medium trust or below, you get an exception with the following information:

```
Request for the permission of type 'System.Security.Permissions.FileIOPermission,
mscorlib, Version=2.0.0.0, Culture=neutral, PublicKeyToken=b77a5c561934e089'
failed. (machine.config)
Stack Trace:
...
    at System.Web.UI.Page.ProcessRequestMain(Boolean includeStagesBeforeAsyncPoint,
Boolean includeStagesAfterAsyncPoint)
```

Chapter 4 explained that when you encounter permission-related exceptions, the exception information and stack trace can sometimes give you a clue as to what happened. In this case, it looks like the configuration system made a check for a permission, specifically the System.Configuration.Configuration Permission. The configuration system always demands the ConfigurationPermission whenever an attempt is made to retrieve a configuration object with a call to GetSection.

If you look in the policy file for High trust, you can see that the ConfigurationPermission is explicitly granted:

```
<SecurityClasses>
    <!--other classes snipped for brevity -->
    <SecurityClass
      Name="ConfigurationPermission"
      Description="System.Configuration.ConfigurationPermission,
                   System.Configuration, Version=2.0.0.0, Culture=neutral,
                   PublicKeyToken=b03f5f7f11d50a3a"/>
</SecurityClasses>

<NamedPermissionSets>
  <PermissionSet class="NamedPermissionSet"
                 version="1" Name="ASP.Net">
  <!-- other permissions snipped for brevity -->

  <IPermission
    class="ConfigurationPermission" version="1"
    Unrestricted="true" />
  </PermissionSet>

</NamedPermissionSets>
```

The High trust policy file defines the necessary security class for ConfigurationPermission and then grants unrestricted permission on ConfigurationPermission to any ASP.NET application running in High trust. When running at Full trust (the default for all ASP.NET applications), the demand for ConfigurationPermission always succeeds. If you look in the trust policy files for Medium, Low, and Minimal trust, you will see that these policy files do not define a <SecurityClass /> for ConfigurationPermission and thus do not grant this permission in the ASP.NET NamedPermissionSet.

With this behavior, you might be wondering how any of the ASP.NET 3.5 features that depend on configuration even work in lower trust levels. For example, the Membership feature clearly depends heavily on a variety of configuration information. You can definitely use the Membership feature in Medium trust without any SecurityExceptions being thrown, so what is going on to make this work? ASP.NET 3.5 features that retrieve their configuration sections use an internal helper class that asserts unrestricted ConfigurationPermission. Because the core of ASP.NET 3.5 lives in the GAC'd System.Web.dll assembly, the assertion is allowed. At runtime when various ASP.NET features retrieve their configuration information, the ConfigurationPermission demand from the configuration system succeeds when the demand encounters the assertion during the stack crawl.

The combination of the configuration system's demand and the assertion within ASP.NET is why in many places in this book I note that strongly typed configuration information is not something that can be depended on when running in partial trust (Medium trust or lower to be specific). This is also why most of the ASP.NET features mirror their configuration information through some portion of their API.

For example almost all of the configuration attributes found on the <membership /> configuration element and its provider <add /> elements can be found on Read-Only properties, either Read-Only properties on the static Membership class or exposed as Read-Only properties from MembershipProvider.

The design approach of echoing back configuration properties on a feature class is one you should keep in mind when designing configuration-driven features. If you design a feature intending that aspects of its configuration be available to developers, then you can do the following:

1. Author the feature to live in the GAC. Follow the design guidelines in Chapter 4 for writing a sandboxed GAC-resident assembly.

2. Within your feature code, assert the ConfigurationPermission when your feature reads its configuration information.

3. Create one or more Read-Only properties on your feature classes that echo back the appropriate portions of your configuration information.

Of course, there is one flaw with this approach: You may not be allowed to deploy your feature into the GAC. Especially if you write code for use by customers running on shared hosting servers, it is likely that your customers will be unable to deploy your feature's assembly into the GAC. There is a workaround for this scenario, though.

The requirePermission Attribute

The <section /> configuration element introduced in 2.0 Framework a new attribute, require Permission. By default, this attribute is set to true, which triggers the configuration system to demand the ConfigurationPermission. However, if you set it to false, the configuration system bypasses the permission demand. For example if you tweak the definition of the <membership /> configuration section to look like the following:

```
<section name="membership"
        type="System.Web.Configuration.MembershipSection, System.Web, …"
        allowDefinition="MachineToApplication"
        requirePermission="false" />
```

… the sample shown earlier using GetSection will work when running Medium trust or below. However, even though you can add the requirePermission attribute, it is not a recommended approach for the built-in ASP.NET features.

The ConfigurationPermission is intended to close the following loophole. Because the configuration system is fully trusted (it lives in the various GAC'd assemblies), and the configuration system is usually invoked initially without any user code on the stack, the configuration system ends up loading configuration data that is potentially sensitive. The theory is that the configuration data should be treated in such a way that only fully trusted code is allowed Read and Write access to it. If the configuration system allowed partially trusted code (that is, partial trust ASP.NET pages) to read and write configuration data, then the configuration system theoretically opens itself to a luring attack. Partially trusted code would be able to gain access to some configuration data that it normally would not be able to read.

Of course, one quirk with this theory is that even in Medium and Low trust you can write code in your pages that opens up the application's web.config as a raw text file, at which point you can parse through it and find the configuration information. However, configuration information is hierarchical, so it is likely that some of your application's configuration information lives in the parent configuration files. Using simple file I/O, you will not be able to discover the settings stored in either the root web.config or in machine.config when running in Medium trust or below.

The use of the ConfigurationPermission is a code access security (CAS)-based approach to ensuring that partial trust code cannot use the configuration system to gain access to these parent configuration files when a simple file I/O based approach would fail. The ConfiguartionPermission is granted to High trust because High trust applications also have the necessary FileIOPermission to read the root web.config and machine.config files. So, the default High trust policy file ensures that the configuration system and the permissions for performing raw file I/O are in sync. Of course, as with all security policies defined using trust policy files, you can create a trust policy file that breaks this; you could, for example, grant ConfigurationPermission in the Medium trust policy file, although this is not something you should do.

So, when should you use the requirePermission attribute to override the default demand for ConfigurationPermission? If you author a configuration-driven feature that will not live in the GAC, it makes sense to include the requirePermission attribute in the <section /> definition for your custom configuration section. A feature that does not live in the GAC is basically a partially trusted feature itself; conceptually, it would not be considered any more sensitive than the partially trusted code that calls it. Hence, it is reasonable to allow partially trusted code access to the strongly typed configuration class for such a feature. Of course, if partially trusted code attempts to write changes for the feature back to the underlying configuration files, it still needs the appropriate FileIOPermission and the appropriate NTFS permissions. With these additional security requirements required for updating configuration, setting the requirePermission attribute in your custom configuration sections for non-GAC'd features doesn't open any security holes.

The behavior of the requirePermission attribute suggests that you should ensure that all GAC'd features have <section /> definitions in machine.config or web.config because after a <section /> is defined in a configuration file, child configuration files cannot override the definition. Even if a child configuration file like an application web.config attempts to add the requirePermission='false' attribute, the configuration system disallows this redefinition of the configuration section.

When setting up the configuration section for a feature, you should do one of the following:

❑ For GAC, based features, define <section /> in machine.config or the root web.config file.

❑ For non-GAC'd features running in shared hosting environments, define the <section /> in the application's web.config file, and set requirePermission to false. This also means that you will only be able to include the feature's configuration section in the application's web.config file. If you place the feature's configuration in a higher level configuration file you get an exception because the <section /> has not been defined yet.

❑ For non-GAC'd features running in some type of trusted environment (such as an internal corporate web server), you can define the <section /> wherever it makes sense for manageability. You may define your <section /> in machine.config or root web.config to allow multiple web applications to take advantage of the feature. This is one case where it is reasonable for a non-GAC'd feature to have its <section /> definition in a parent configuration file while still setting requirePermission to false.

There are two configurations sections defined in machine.config that set requirePermission to false: <connectionStrings /> and <appSettings />. Because these configuration sections are typically used directly by application code, locking them down for partial trust applications does not make sense. As a result, these two configuration sections are the exception to the rule that GAC'd configuration sections disallow strongly typed configuration access to partial trust applications.

Demanding Permissions from a Configuration Class

There is little-known capability in the configuration system that you can use for supporting partial trust applications. You can use a custom configuration class as a kind of gatekeeper to a feature and prevent the feature from being used in a partial trust application. If you remember back to the Chapter 4 on trust levels, and the discussion on the "processRequestInApplicationTrust" attribute, there is a subtle issue with features and code being called when only trusted code is on the stack.

Custom configuration classes are part of this issue because when configuration is being loaded, it is not guaranteed that there will be any user code on the stack. More important, the feature that carries out work and that consumes the configuration information may itself always be called with trusted code on the stack. Scenarios like GAC'd classes that are HttpModules have this problem. An HttpModule only has the ASP.NET pipeline code sitting above it, so any demands a custom HttpModule located in the GAC makes always succeed.

A feature can indirectly work around this problem by taking advantage of the fact that the configuration system calls PermitOnly on the named permission set for the current trust level. This behavior is the same approach that the page handler takes when it calls PermitOnly prior to running a page. The configuration system makes this call just before attempting to deserialize a configuration section. As a result, a custom configuration class that overrides ConfigurationSection.PostDeserialize can demand an appropriate permission in an override of this method.

C#

```
using System;
using System.Data.SqlClient;
using System.Security.Permissions;
using System.Configuration;

public class SkeletalConfigClass: ConfigurationSection
{
 public SkeletalConfigClass() {}

    protected override void PostDeserialize()
    {
        SqlClientPermission scp =
            new SqlClientPermission(PermissionState.Unrestricted);
        scp.Demand();
    }

    //the rest of the configuration class…
}
```

VB.NET

```
Imports System
Imports System.Configuration
Imports System.Security.Permissions
Imports System.Data.SqlClient
```

```
Public Class SkeletalConfigClass
    Inherits ConfigurationSection

    Public Sub New()
    End Sub

    Protected Overrides Sub PostDeserialize()
        Dim scp As New SqlClientPermission(PermissionState.Unrestricted)
        scp.Demand()
    End Sub

    'the rest of the configuration class…
End Class
```

The previous configuration class demands the `SqlClientPermission`. Because the configuration system restricts the set of allowed permissions to whatever is defined for the application's current trust level prior to the deserialization process, the sample configuration class is usable only if the current trust level grants the `SqlClientPermission`. If a feature living in the GAC attempts to read its configuration information and the current trust level doesn't grant this permission, the feature initialization fails because any attempt to read its configuration always fails with a `SecurityException`.

Given this capability, when would you actually use it? Should you always demand something from your custom configuration class? If you know your GAC'd code is going to be called in scenarios where only trusted code exists on the stack, you should make use of the `PostDeserialize` method. It is the only point when you will have a chance to enforce a CAS restriction. Identifying these scenarios can be difficult, though. If your feature includes a GAC'd `HttpModule`, this is one obvious case. A custom handler that is deployed in the GAC would be another example where using `PostDeserialize` as a surrogate trust enforcement mechanism makes sense.

However, it may impossible to make an intelligent demand in `PostDeserialize` if you depend on the code that consumes your feature to supply dynamic information. For example, if your feature reads and writes to the file system, you may not know which path to demand permission against until after some consumer code sets some properties on your feature. As a result, the `PostDeserialize` method is appropriate only for demanding permissions that always need to be statically configured in a trust policy file.

FileIOPermission and the Design-Time API

Unlike the runtime portion of the configuration API (for example, `GetSection`), the design-time API always results in physical file I/O operations occurring up the chain of parent configuration files. Because in Medium trust an ASP.NET application only has rights to read and write files within the application's directory structure, partial trust code doesn't have rights to open files outside the application. For this reason, the design-time API is basically useless when running in Medium trust or below. Although you could theoretically tweak the lower trust levels' policy files to get the design-time API working, it is better to consider the design-time API suitable only for Full trust or High trust applications.

If you attempt to use one of the design-time APIs such as `WebConfigurationManager.OpenWeb Configuration` in partial trust, you will run into an exception like the following:

```
SecurityException: Request for the permission of type 'System.Security.Permissions.
FileIOPermission, …' failed.]
…snip…
System.Security.CodeAccessPermission.Demand()
```

```
System.IO.FileStream.Init(String path, FileMode mode, FileAccess access, Int32
rights, Boolean useRights, FileShare share, Int32 bufferSize, FileOptions options,
SECURITY_ATTRIBUTES secAttrs, String msgPath, Boolean bFromProxy)
System.IO.FileStream..ctor(String path, FileMode mode, FileAccess access, FileShare
share)
...snip...
System.Configuration.UpdateConfigHost.OpenStreamForRead(String streamName)
System.Configuration.BaseConfigurationRecord.InitConfigFromFile()
```

This stack trace shows that the open attempt eventually results in the use of the `FileStream` object. Attempting to open a `FileStream` on top of a file always results in a demand for a `FileIOPermission`. So, long before the configuration system ever gets around to demanding `ConfigurationPermission`, the file I/O that occurs during a call to `OpenWebConfiguration` in a partial trust application will fail. This behavior is another reason the design-time APIs are useful only in High and Full trust web applications.

Protected Configuration

Since ASP.NET 1.0, a common request has been for a way to safely store sensitive configuration information and shield it from prying eyes. The most common information that developers want to protect is connection strings because these frequently contain username-password pairs. But sorts of interesting information beyond connection strings is contained within ASP.NET configuration files. If you use the `<identity />` section, you again have credentials stored in configuration. If you use classes in the `System.Net` namespace, you may have configuration elements listing out SMTP servers or other network endpoints and so on.

Since the 2.0 Framework, there has been a feature to deal with this problem called *protected configuration*. Protected configuration is a way to take selected pieces of any configuration file and store the configuration information instead in a secure and encrypted format. The great thing about the protected configuration feature is that it can be used with just about any configuration section—both ASP.NET and non-ASP.NET configuration sections. As with other features in ASP.NET, protected configuration is provider-based, so you can buy or write alternative protected configuration providers instead of using the built-in providers.

Out of the box, the .NET Framework ships with two protected configuration providers:

❑   `System.Configuration.DPAPIProtectedConfigurationProvider`

❑   `System.Configuration.RsaProtectedConfigurationProvider`

As the class names suggest, the first provider uses the data protection API (DPAPI) functionality in Windows to encrypt and decrypt configuration sections. The second provider uses the public-key RSA algorithm for performing the same functionality.

The basic idea behind protected configuration is that you use the `aspnet_regiis` command-line tool, or the configuration API (the `SectionInformation.ProtectSection` and `SectionInformation.UnprotectSection` methods, to be precise) to encrypt selected pieces of your configuration information prior to putting an application into production. Then at runtime the configuration system decrypts the protected configuration information just prior to handing the configuration information back to the requesting code. The important thing is that protecting a configuration section is transparent to the features that rely on the configuration section. No feature code has to change just because an underlying configuration section has been encrypted.

When you use protected configuration you start with configuration section that might look like the following:

```
<machineKey
    validationKey="12345678901234567890123456789012345678901234567890"
    decryptionKey="12345678901234567890123456789012345678901234567890" />
```

This is a perfect example of the type of section you probably would like to protect. You would rather not have any random person with Read access to your web.config walking away with the signing and validation keys for your application.

You can encrypt this configuration section from the command line using the aspnet_regiis tool:

```
aspnet_regiis -pe system.web/machineKey -app / ConfigurationSample
              -prov DataProtectionConfigurationProvider
```

After you use the protected configuration feature, the <machineKey /> section looks something like the following:

```
<machineKey configProtectionProvider="DataProtectionConfigurationProvider">
    <EncryptedData>
        <CipherData>
            <CipherValue>encrypted data here</CipherValue>
        </CipherData>
    </EncryptedData>
</machineKey>
```

Of course, instead of the text "encrypted data here," the actual result has about five lines of text containing the base-64 encoded representation of the encrypted blob for the <machineKey /> section. When you run the application, everything still works normally, though, because internally the configuration system transparently decrypts the section using the extra information added to the <machineKey /> element.

Depending on whether you use the RSA- or the DPAPI-based provider, different information will show up within the <machineKey /> element. In the previous example, the configuration, system added the configProtectionProvider attribute to the <machineKey/> element. This is a pointer to one of the protected configuration providers defined in machine.config. At runtime, the configuration system instantiates the specified provider and asks it to decrypt the contents of the <EncryptedData /> element. This means that custom protected configuration providers can place additional information within the <EncryptedData /> element containing any extra information required by the provider to successfully decrypt the section. In the case of the DPAPI provider, no additional information behind the encrypted blob is necessary.

What Can't You Protect?

Protected configuration sounds like the final answer to the age-old problem of encrypting connection strings. However, due to the interaction between app-domain startup and configuration, you cannot blindly encrypt every single configuration section in your configuration files. In some cases, you have a "chicken-and-egg" effect where ASP.NET or the Framework needs to read configuration information to bootstrap itself, but it has to do this prior to having read the configuration information that defines the protected configuration providers.

The following list names some configuration sections (this is not an exhaustive list) that you may have in your various configuration files that *can't* be encrypted with protected configuration:

❑ `processModel`: ASP.NET needs to be able to read this just as it is starting up. Furthermore, for IIS 5 and IIS 5.1 it controls the identity of the worker process, so you would be in a Catch-22 situation if you needed the correct worker process identity in order to read protected configuration.

❑ **startup and runtime:** These configuration sections are used by the Framework to determine things such as which version of the Framework to load as well as information on assembly redirection.

❑ `cryptographySettings`: This configuration section defines the actual cryptography classes used by the framework. Because protected configuration depends on some of these classes, you can't encrypt the configuration section that contains information about the algorithms used by the protected configuration feature.

❑ `configProtectedData`: This is the configuration section that contains the definition of the protected configuration providers on the machine. This would also be a Catch-22 if the section were encrypted because the configuration system needs to be able to read this section to get the appropriate provider for decrypting other configuration sections.

Selecting a Protected Configuration Provider

Now that you know you have at least two different options for encrypting configuration information, you need to make a decision about which one to use. Additionally, you need to determine how you want to use each provider. The criteria for selecting and then configuring a provider revolve around two questions:

❑ Do you need to share configuration files across machines?

❑ Do you need to isolate encrypted configuration data between applications?

The first question is relevant for those of you that need to deploy an application across multiple machines in a web farm. Obviously in a load-balanced web farm, you want an application that is deployed on multiple machines to use the same set of configuration data. You can use either the DPAPI provider or the RSA provider for this scenario.

Both providers require some degree of setup to work properly in a web farm. Of the two providers, the RSA provider is definitely the more natural fit. With the DPAPI provider, you would need to do the following to deploy a `web.config` file across multiple machines:

1. Deploy the unencrypted configuration file to each web server.

2. On each web server, run `aspnet_regiis` to encrypt the desired configuration sections.

The reason for this is that the DPAPI provider relies on machine-specific information, and this information it not portable across machines. Although you can make the DPAPI provider work in a web farm, you will probably get tired of constantly re-encrypting configuration sections each time you push a new configuration file to a web farm.

The RSA provider depends on key containers that contain the actual key material for encrypting and decrypting configuration sections. For a web farm, you would perform a one-time setup to synchronize a key container across all the machines in a web farm. After you create a common key container across all machines in the farm, you can encrypt a configuration file once on one of the machines, perhaps even using a utility machine that is not part of the web farm itself but that still has the common key container. When you push the encrypted configuration file to all machines in the web farm, each web server is able to decrypt the protected configuration information because each machine has access to a common set of keys.

The second question around isolation of encryption information deals with how the encryption keys are protected from other web applications. Both the DPAPI and the RSA providers can use keys that are accessible machine-wide, or use keys that are accessible to only a specific user identity. RSA has the additional functionality of using machine-wide keys that only grant access to specific user accounts.

Currently, the recommendation is that if you want to isolate key material by user account, you should separate your web applications into different application pools in IIS 7.0, and you should use the RSA provider. This allows you to specify a different user account for each worker process. Then when you configure the RSA-protected configuration providers, you take some extra steps to ensure that encryption succeeds only while running as a specific user account. At runtime, this means that even if one application can somehow gain access to another application's configuration data, the application will not be able to decrypt it because the required key material is associated with a different identity.

Both the DPAPI and RSA have per-user modes of operation that can store encryption material directly associated with a specific user account. However, both of these technologies have the limitation that the Windows user profile for the process identity needs to be loaded into memory before it can access the necessary keys. Loading of the Windows user profile does not happen on IIS 6 and 7.0 (it will occur, though, for other reasons in IIS 5/5.1). As a result, the per-user modes for the DPAPI and RSA providers really aren't useful for web applications.

There is another aspect to isolating encryption data for the DPAPI provider because the provider supports specifying an optional entropy value to use during encryption and decryption. The entropy value is essentially like a second piece of key material. Two different applications using different entropy values with DPAPI will be unable to read each other's data. However, using entropy is probably more suitable when you want the convenience of using the machine-wide store in DPAPI, but you still want some isolation between applications.

The following table summarizes the provider options that you should consider before setting up protected configuration for use in ASP.NET:

	Need to Support Multiple Machines	Only Deploy on a Single Machine
Sharing key material is acceptable	RSA provider. Use the default machine-wide key container, and grant Read access to all accounts.	Either the RSA or the DPAPI provider will work. Use the machine-wide options for either provider. Can optionally use key entropy with DPAPI provider. Can optionally use RSA key containers with different ACLs.

	Need to Support Multiple Machines	**Only Deploy on a Single Machine**
Key material should be isolated	RSA provider. Use machine-wide RSA key containers, but ACL different key containers to different user identities.	RSA provider. Use machine-wide RSA key containers, but ACL different key containers to different identities. DPAPI per-user key containers require a loaded user profile and thus should not be used. RSA per-user key containers also require a loaded user profile and thus should not be used.

Caveat When Using Stores That Depend on User Identity

If you choose to use either provider with their per-user mode of operation or if you use machine-wide RSA key containers that are ACL'd to specific users, you need to be aware of an issue with using protected configuration. The sequence in which ASP.NET reads and then deserializes configuration sections is not fixed. Although ASP.NET internally obtains configuration sections in a certain sequence during app-domain startup, this sequence may very well change in the future.

One very important configuration section that is read early on during app-domain startup is the <identity /> section. You can use <identity /> to configure application impersonation for ASP.NET. However, if you use RSA key containers, for example, that depend on specific user identities, you can end up in a situation where ASP.NET starts initially running as a specific process identity (NETWORK SERVICE by default on IIS 6 and 7.0), and then after reading the <identity /> section it switches to running as the defined application impersonation identity.

This can lead to a situation where you have granted permission on an RSA key container to an IIS 6 or 7.0 worker process account, and suddenly other configuration sections are no longer decrypting properly because they are being decrypted after ASP.NET switches over to the application impersonation account. As a result, you should always configure and ACL key stores on the basis of a known process identity.

For IIS 6 or 7.0 this means setting up protected configuration based on the identity that will be used for an individual worker process. If your applications need to run as different identities, instead of using application impersonation on IIS 7.0, you should separate the applications into different application pools (aka worker processes). This guarantees that at runtime ASP.NET will always be running with a stable identity, and thus regardless of the order in which ASP.NET reads configuration sections during app-domain startup, protected configuration sections will always be capable of being decrypted using the same identity.

For older versions like IIS 5 and IIS 5.1, you can choose a different process identity using the <processModel /> element. However, application impersonation is really the only way to isolate applications by identity on these older versions of IIS. Although you could play around with different configuration sections to determine which ones are being read with the identity defined in <processModel /> and which ones are

Continued

> read using the application impersonation identity in <identity />, you could very well end up with a future service pack subtly changing the order in which configuration sections are deserialized.
>
> As a result, the recommendation for IIS 5/5.1 is to upgrade to IIS 6 or IIS 7.0 if you want to use a feature like RSA key containers with user-specific ACLs. Granted that this may sound a bit arbitrary, but using key storage that depends on specific identities with protected configuration gets somewhat complicated as you will see in a bit. Attempting to keep track of the order of configuration section deserialization adds to this complexity and if depended on would result in a rather brittle approach to securing configuration sections. Separating applications with IIS 6 or 7.0 worker processes is simply a much cleaner and more maintainable approach over the long term.

Defining Protected Configuration Providers

The default protected configuration providers are defined in machine.config:

```
<configProtectedData defaultProvider="RsaProtectedConfigurationProvider">
        <providers>
            <add name="RsaProtectedConfigurationProvider"
                type="System.Configuration.RsaProtectedConfigurationProvider, … "
                description="Uses RsaCryptoServiceProvider to encrypt and decrypt"
                keyContainerName="NetFrameworkConfigurationKey"
                cspProviderName=""
                useMachineContainer="true"
                useOAEP="false" />

            <add name="DataProtectionConfigurationProvider"
                type="System.Configuration.DpapiProtectedConfigurationProvider,…"
                description="Uses CryptProtectData and CryptUnProtectData… "
                useMachineProtection="true"
                keyEntropy="" />
        </providers>
</configProtectedData>
```

If you author or purchase a custom provider, you would configure it in the <configProtectedData /> section and assign it a name so that tools like aspnet_regiis can make use of it. Other than the "name" and "type" attributes, all of the information you see on the provider <add /> elements is unique to each specific provider. Custom providers can support their own set of configuration properties that you can then define when you configure them with the <add /> element.

As with most other provider-based features, you can define as many protected configuration providers as you want. Then when using a tool like aspnet_regiis, writing code with the ProtectSetion method, or creating web.config files, you can reference one of the protected configuration providers from <configProtectedData /> by name. For example, the -prov command-line switch you saw earlier on aspnet_regiis refers to a named provider within <configProtectedData/>. In these scenarios, if you do not explicitly select a provider, then the value of defaultProvider on the <configProtectedData /> element is used. This means that by default the RSA provider is used for protected configuration.

DpapiProtectedConfigurationProvider

This protected configuration provider uses the data protection API (DPAPI) that is part of Windows. This functionality will probably be familiar to those of you who used the aspnet_setreg tool back in ASP.NET 1.1 or who wrote a managed DPAPI wrapper for use in applications. The nice thing about the DPAPI provider is that it is very easy to use. Configuring the provider is quite simple because you need to consider only two provider-specific options:

❑   keyEntropy: This is a string value containing some random information that will be used during the encryption process. If you use a different keyEntropy value for each application, applications that share the same set of DPAPI encryption keys still cannot read each other's protected configuration data.

❑   useMachineProtection: Because DPAPI has the concept of a machine store and a per-user store, this configuration attribute indicates which one to use. If you set this attribute to true (the default), all applications can decrypt each other's protected configuration data. If you set this attribute to false, then only applications running under the same credentials will be able to decrypt each other's protected configuration data.

The DPAPI provider should really be used only for single-machine applications. Although you can go through a manual step whereby you always re-encrypt your configuration files after they have been deployed to a machine, this is inconvenient. Furthermore, it opens up the possibility of someone forgetting to encrypt a configuration file (and remember that you may need to encrypt multiple configuration files up the configuration inheritance hierarchy).

keyEntropy

The keyEntropy option is only useful for giving a modicum of protection against two different applications reading each other's configuration data when useMachineProtection is set to true. With the machine-wide DPAPI key store, technically anyone who can get code onto the machine will be able to decrypt your protected configuration data. Specifying an entropy value gives you a lightweight approach to protecting the encrypted data. You can use keyEntropy with the per-user mode of operation for DPAPI as an additional layer of protection, although the per-user mode for the DPAPI provider is not suitable for use with web applications.

If each web application uses a different keyEntropy parameter in its configuration, only code with knowledge of that value will be able to read the configuration data. Of course, the management problem with using keyEntropy is that you need a separate provider definition for each different keyEntropy value. If you have a fair number of applications to protect on a server, and you want to isolate the encrypted data between each application, you can easily end up with dozens of provider definitions just so that you can use a different keyEntropy value for each application.

There is also the related issue that you need to ACL the appropriate configuration files so that random users cannot open them and read the configuration. Placing the different provider definitions in machine.config or the root web.config prevents applications running at Medium trust or lower from being able to use the strongly typed configuration classes to read the raw provider definitions (note that the actual provider class DpapiProtectedConfigurationProvider doesn't expose the keyEntropy value as a property).

However High and Full trust applications have the ability to open any file on the file system (ACLs permitting). For these types of applications, you need to run each application in a separate application pool with each application pool being assigned a different user identity. With this approach, you can then place each application's provider definition within the application's web.config file, and the ACLs prevent one worker process from reading the configuration file from another application. If you were to leave the application-specific provider definition in machine.config or web.config, Full and High trust applications would be able to open these files and read the keyEntropy attribute.

Using keyEntropy is pretty basic: You just define another instance of the DPAPI provider and put any value you want as a value for this attribute:

```
<configProtectedData>
  <providers>
    <add name="AppSpecificDPAPIProvider"
         type="System.Configuration.DpapiProtectedConfigurationProvider…"
         useMachineProtection="true"
         keyEntropy="AD50GC20FKQ43%dj!@4F" />
  </providers>
</configProtectedData>
```

You should set the keyEntropy value to something that cannot be easily guessed. In this case, I just used a random string of characters. Any long string of random values will work; there are no restrictions on the length of the keyEntropy configuration attribute. If another application attempts to decrypt a protected configuration section and uses a different entropy value, it receives an error message stating that the data in the configuration section is invalid.

useMachineProtection

The default DPAPI configuration uses the machine-wide DPAPI key store; if you configure the DPAPI provider and fail to set the useMachineProtection attribute, internally the provider will also default to using the machine-wide store. If you are running in a trusted environment and it doesn't really matter if applications can read each other's configuration data, this setting is reasonable.

However, if you are on a machine that hosts applications from development groups that don't trust each other, or if you have a business requirement that different applications should not be able to read each other's configuration data, setting useMachineProtection to false is an option. If you set this attribute to false, the identity of the application needs to be switched to a different user account (see the earlier section on using per-user key stores). Of course, after you change your application to run as a different identity, you already have the option of using file ACLs as a protection mechanism for preventing other applications from reading your configuration data. In a sense, using the per-user mode of the DPAPI provider is an additional layer of protection above and beyond what you gain just by changing applications to run as different user identities.

As mentioned earlier, though, there is a pretty severe limitation if you set useMachineProtection to false. Due to the way DPAPI works, it needs access to the user profile for the process identity to access the key material. On IIS 7 the user profile for a worker process account (specifically machine or domain accounts other than LOCAL SERVICE or NETWORK SERVICE) is never loaded by IIS. If you follow the steps outlined in this section everything will work until you reboot the machine and the side effects of the runas command window are lost. If you really, really want to get per-user DPAPI working, you need a hack such as launching runas from a scheduled task or having an NT service that forcibly loads the profile for a user identity. Realistically, though, I would never depend on such workarounds for a production application, and hence the machine store for the DPAPI protected configuration provider is the only really viable option for web applications. Non-ASP.NET applications do not have the limitation with the Windows user profile, though, so you may be interested in using DPAPI user stores for securing configuration information used by a fat client application.

To set up the provider for per-user DPAPI, just change the useMachineProtection attribute to false:

```
<configProtectedData>
  <providers>
    <add name="AppSpecificDPAPIProvider"
         type="System.Configuration.DpapiProtectedConfigurationProvider…"
         useMachineProtection="false"
  </providers>
</configProtectedData>
```

If you use DPAPI with per-user keys you must run interactive tools like aspnet_regiis with the process credentials that will be used at runtime. The simplest way to do this is with the runas command to spawn a separate command window. Of course, this also implies that you should choose a local or domain user account for your process identity because you aren't going to know the password for the built-in NETWORK SERVICE account.

After you spawn a command window running as the proper credentials, you can use the aspnet_regiis command to encrypt the desired configuration section. Because encrypting a configuration file requires writing a temporary file, replacing the original configuration file, and then cleaning up afterward, the identity you are running as will temporarily need Read, Write, and Modify access to the application's directory. After the encryption operation is done, you can remove the Write and Modify privileges from the directory.

After the configuration file has been encrypted, try moving the web application into an IIS 7 application pool running with the same credentials that were used to run aspnet_regiis in the spawned command window. Now when you run your web application, the encrypted sections will be transparently decrypted using the DPAPI key associated with the worker process identity. If you assign your application to a different application pool, for example the default application pool running as NETWORK SERVICE, you will see the effect of the per-user DPAPI key. Running as NETWORK SERVICE instead returns an error message that the key is not valid for the specified state, meaning that you are attempting to decrypt the data with an invalid key.

However, if you reboot your machine after the previous steps, your web application will stop working, even with everything set up properly, due to the dependence DPAPI has on the Windows user profile. As a result I would not recommend trying to get the per-user mode working for IIS 7. Also be aware that if you are running IIS 5 on a production machine, you can get the per-user mode of DPAPI to work because ASP.NET loads the user profile of the account specified in the <processModel /> element. However, if you move the application to an IIS 7 machine, it will fail because of the lack of a loaded Windows user profile for IIS 7.

RsaProtectedConfigurationProvider

As the name suggests this protected configuration provider uses the RSA public-key encryption algorithm for encrypting configuration sections. To be precise, the provider encrypts configuration sections using 3DES, but it then encrypts the symmetric 3DES key using the asymmetric RSA algorithm.

Of the two providers included in the Framework, this is definitely the preferred provider for a variety of reasons:

❑ It works well in multi-machine environments.

❑ It supports per-user key container ACLing without any awkward dependence on user profiles.

❑ As a result of its use of RSA, you can use other Windows cryptographic service providers for the RSA algorithm.

Because the provider internally uses the RSA classes in the framework, it is able to support exporting and importing key material. This means there is a viable approach for synchronizing key material across multiple machines in a web farm.

The concept of securing key containers to specific users does not depend on a Windows user profile; instead, it relies on having ACLs set up that grant access to specific user accounts that need to open and read key containers. As a result, using machine-wide containers with specific user ACLs is the preferred approach for isolating the encrypted configuration information for multiple applications.

Because the provider uses RSA, and internally the Framework RSA classes rely on the Windows cryptographic API (CAPI), you get the added benefit of being able to use RSA key containers other than the default software-based Microsoft implementation. Although this last point is probably relevant for a small percentage of developers, if you happen to work in a bank or in the defense industry you are probably familiar with hardware cryptographic service providers (CSPs) for CAPI. If your organization uses Active Directory as a certificate store, you also may be using hardware-based CSPs. With the RsaProtectedConfigurationProvider, you have the option of configuring the protected configuration provider to use a custom CSP instead of the default software-based CSP.

The configuration options of the RSA provider are a bit more extensive than those of the DAPI provider. Aside from the standard name, type, and description attributes, you can configure the following:

❑ useMachineContainer: As with the DPAPI provider you can use per-user key containers instead of machine-wide key containers. Like DPAPI, per-user key containers require a loaded Windows profile. Unlike DPAPI, machine-wide RSA key containers can be ACL'd to specific users.

❑ keyContainerName: The RSA provider always accesses keys from a software abstraction called a key container. From a manageability and security perspective, it makes it easier to separate different applications through the use of different key containers that are locked down to specific users.

❑ useOAEP: This option tells the providers to use Optional Asymmetric Encryption and Padding (OAEP) when encrypting and decrypting. Windows 2000 does not support this, so the default for this setting in configuration and inside of the provider is false. If you are running on Windows Server 2003, Server 2008, XP, or Vista, you can use this option because these operating systems support OAEP with RSA.

❑ cspProviderName: Assuming that you have registered a custom CSP for use with CAPI, you can tell the RSA configuration provider to use it by specifying the CSP's name with this parameter.

Of the various parameters listed here, I will only drill into the useMachineContainer and key ContainerName attributes because these settings are the ones you will most commonly worry about. For IIS 7 on Windows Server 2008 or Windows Vista, you can optionally set useOAEP to true. For the cspProviderName attribute, if you already have a custom CSP configured on your web servers, you will already know the string name for using it with your applications. Beyond that, there is not anything else special that you need to do from the perspective of protected configuration.

keyContainerName

Regardless of whether you use a machine key container or a user-specific key container, the RSA-protected configuration provider needs to be pointed at the appropriate container. Unlike the DPAPI provider, the RSA provider does not have some central pool where keys are held. Instead, key material is always segmented into specific containers. The following default RSA provider configuration uses a default container name of NetFrameworkConfigurationKey:

```
<add name="RsaProtectedConfigurationProvider"
     type="System.Configuration.RsaProtectedConfigurationProvider,…"
     keyContainerName="NetFrameworkConfigurationKey"
     cspProviderName=""
     useMachineContainer="true"
     useOAEP="false"  />
```

Encrypting a configuration section with aspnet_regiis using the RSA provider looks like the following:

```
aspnet_regiis -pe system.web/machineKey -app /ConfigurationSample
```

In this case, the -prov option was not used, meaning the default provider for protected configuration will be used, which is the RSA-based provider. Contrasted with the output from the DPAPI provider, the output from the RSA provider is substantially more verbose:

```
<machineKey configProtectionProvider=" RsaProtectedConfigurationProvider ">
  <EncryptedData Type="http://www.w3.org/2001/04/xmlenc#Element"
                 xmlns="http://www.w3.org/2001/04/xmlenc#">
    <EncryptionMethod Algorithm="http://www.w3.org/2001/04/xmlenc#tripledes-cbc" />
    <KeyInfo xmlns="http://www.w3.org/2000/09/xmldsig#">
      <EncryptedKey xmlns="http://www.w3.org/2001/04/xmlenc#">
        <EncryptionMethod Algorithm="http://www.w3.org/2001/04/xmlenc#rsa-1_5" />
        <KeyInfo xmlns="http://www.w3.org/2000/09/xmldsig#">
          <KeyName>Rsa Key</KeyName>
        </KeyInfo>
        <CipherData>
          <CipherValue>encrypted 3DES key goes here</CipherValue>
        </CipherData>
      </EncryptedKey>
    </KeyInfo>
    <CipherData>
      <CipherValue>encrypted machine key section here</CipherValue>
    </CipherData>
  </EncryptedData>
</machineKey>
```

The format for the RSA and DPAPI providers is based on the W3C XML Encryption Recommendation. However, the RSA provider output really needs the expressiveness of this format due to all of the information it needs to output.

There are actually two separate `<CipherValue />` elements. The first `<CipherValue />` element contains an encrypted version of a 3DES key. The idea behind the RSA provider is that for each configuration section that is encrypted, the provider creates a new random symmetric key for 3DES. However, you don't want to communicate that signing key in the clear. So, the symmetric key is encrypted using an asymmetric RSA public-private key pair.

The end result of the asymmetric RSA encryption is placed within the first occurrence of the `<CipherValue />` element. The only way that someone can actually decrypt the 3DES encryption key is to have the same public-private key pair in the appropriate RSA container on their system. The `<EncryptionMethod />` element that ends in `rsa-1_5` tells the configuration system (or more precisely the XML Encryption support in the Framework) to use the RSA algorithm to decrypt the 3DES encryption key. Internally, the protected configuration provider will hand the Framework an instance of a `System.Security.Cryptography.RSACryptoServiceProvider` that has already been initialized with the appropriate RSA key container based on the configuration provider's settings.

The second `<CipherValue />` element contains the actual results of encrypting the configuration section using 3DES. At runtime, the protected configuration provider will use the results of the RSA decryption for the 3DES key to in turn decrypt the second `<CipherValue />` section into the cleartext version of a configuration section.

Although a bit counterintuitive, if you rush out and use `aspnet_regiis` to encrypt a configuration section with the RSA provider, when you then run your ASP.NET application, it will fail with an error stating that the RSA key container cannot be opened. This is because although the Framework ensures that an RSA container called `NetFrameworkConfigurationKey` is created on the machine, by default the process account for your web application does not have rights to retrieve key material from the key container.

You have to first grant read access on the key container using `aspnet_regiis`. For ASP.NET, you need to grant read access on the container to only the appropriate process account. Although `aspnet_regiis` supports granting Full access to a key container, you don't want the identity of a web application to have rights to write to or delete containers. As a result, for the default provider configuration, the process account for your web application needs only Read access. The following `aspnet_regiis` command grants Read access to the default RSA key container used by protected configuration:

```
aspnet_regiis -pa "NetFrameworkConfigurationKey" "NT AUTHORITY\NETWORK SERVICE"
```

After you do this, your web applications will be able to decrypt configuration sections using the default machine-wide container.

Now that you understand the basics of using the default key container, the next question is when would you use alternate key containers? The combination of using machine-wide containers (for example, the `useMachineContainer` attribute is set to `true`) with key containers is compelling. You can log on to a web server as local machine administrator and create a machine-wide RSA key pair in a new container using the `aspnet_regiis` tool. You can then selectively grant Read access on the container to certain accounts.

This means you can segment your applications into different worker processes running with different user accounts, and grant each user account Read access to a specific key container. Unlike DPAPI, just because an RSA key container is available machine-wide, it does not mean that any arbitrary account can access it. The required step of granting Read access makes this approach secure and effective. It is reasonably simple to set up, and it allows you to isolate configuration data between applications. As you will see in the next section on useMachineContainer, RSA key containers that are usable machine-wide are really the only viable mechanism for providing configuration isolation to ASP.NET applications.

Creating a RSA key container can be accomplished with the following command line:

```
aspnet_regiis -pc "Application_A_Container"
```

This command creates a new RSA key container called Application_A_Container that is accessible machine-wide assuming the appropriate access control lists (ACLs) are granted. As an aside, the -pc option supports an additional -size option that allows you to specify how large you want the RSA key to be. By default, the tool will create 1024-bit keys, but the RSA standard supports keys as large as 16,384 bits if necessary.

You grant access to the newly created container using the -pa switch, as shown a little bit earlier. For this to make sense, though, you must separate your applications into separate worker processes running as something other than NETWORK SERVICE. Obviously, granting key container access to NETWORK SERVICE is pointless if your intent is to isolate access by worker process identity. Assuming that you use a different identity for each of your worker processes, you can use the -pa switch to grant access in such a way that each new key container is accessible by only a specific worker process account.

This approach does have a similar manageability issue to using keyEntropy with the DPAPI provider. Using a different key container per process identity means that you have to create a different RSA provider definition for each separate key container. However, you do not have to worry about where you place the different RSA provider definitions. Even if applications are able to physically read protected configuration definitions for other applications, the key container ACLs will prevent applications running with different identities from successfully decrypting other application's configuration sections.

useMachineContainer

As with the DPAPI provider, the RSA provider allows you to use a per-user mode of operation. The previous discussions on the RSA provider have been using key containers that are visible machine-wide. For an additional level of security, you might think that you could create key containers that are only "visible" to specific user accounts. This approach is dependent on Windows user profiles as you will see in a bit.

The first step is to define a protected configuration provider to use a user-specific key container. Something like the following:

```
<add name="AppSpecificRSAProvider"
     type="System.Configuration.RsaProtectedConfigurationProvider,…"
     keyContainerName="UserSpecificContainer"
     useMachineContainer="false"  />
```

After you have a provider defined, the general sequence of steps enables you to use user-specific containers:

1. Open a command window running as the user account that will "own" the key container. You can log in interactively as the account or use the `runas` command.

2. Use the `aspnet_regiis -pc` command to create a key container.

3. Use `aspnet_regiis -pe` to encrypt the desired configuration sections. You need to perform the encryption while running as the specific user account; otherwise, the configuration system is not going to be using the correct user-specific key container. Make sure to use the `-prov` option so that the tool knows to use the appropriate provider definition.

4. Log off or close the spawned command window.

5. Change the identity of your web application's application pool to the same identity that was used to create the key container and encrypt the configuration sections.

When you run your web application, it will be able to decrypt the encrypted configuration sections using the key pair located in the user-specific key container.

Unfortunately, this entire process suffers from the same dependency on Windows user profiles as DPAPI. If you reboot the machine, causing the user profile that was loaded in step 1 to go away, your web application can no longer decrypt the configuration section. As with DPAPI the per-user key containers are not really usable in ASP.NET applications; you need to stick with machine-wide containers and selectively ACL the RSA key containers to get configuration isolation across applications.

Synchronizing Key Containers across Machines

The biggest advantage of the RSA provider over the DPAPI provider is that RSA provides a viable approach for synchronizing the contents of a key container across a web farm. Unlike DPAPI, RSA key pairs are exportable. The most important thing you need to do to ensure that you can synchronize keys is create your key containers so that they are exportable. The following command uses the `-exp` option to create a machine-wide key container with exportable keys. If you forget the `-exp` option the resultant key container will not be exportable. Note that for this discussion, only machine-wide key containers are used because per-user key containers aren't really suitable for ASP.NET.

```
aspnet_regiis -pc ExportableContainer -size 2048 -exp
```

The next step is to export the key material so that it can be physically transported. The `aspnet_regiis` command line for export is shown here:

```
aspnet_regiis -pri -px ExportableContainer  c:\exportedkey.xml
```

The `-px` option tells the tools that the key information in the container should be exported to the file name shown on the command line. The bold `-pri` option is important because it also tells the tool to ensure that the private half of the RSA key pair is exported as well. If you forget to export the private key, when you import the result on another server it will be useless because you need the private half of the key pair to be able to decrypt the 3DES encryption key from the XML in the protected configuration section.

With the export file in hand, you can go to each machine that needs to share the key material and import the key container with the following command:

```
aspnet_regiis -pi ExportableContainer c:\exportedkey.xml
```

The -pi command tells the tool to import the contents of the XML file into the specified RSA key container. After you import the file on any given machine, you should immediately delete it and wipe the directory that contained it. It would be a major security breach if the XML export file is left lying around for someone to copy and walk away with. The same holds true for the machine where the original export occurred; you should also ensure that the original export file is not lying around on disk waiting for someone to snoop.

As a last step, because this approach creates a new key container upon import, you need to use aspnet_regiis with the -pa switch on each web server to grant Read access on the key container to the appropriate worker process accounts.

At this point you have a key container called ExportableContainer on one or more machines. In a really secure web environment, you can perform the encryption of your configuration sections using a system that is not directly connected to the internet. After you create a config file with all of the appropriate encrypted configuration sections, you copy the result to all of the machines in your web farm. The previous steps of importing containers and ACLing the containers are one-time setup tasks. After they have been accomplished, you only need to copy encrypted configuration files to all of your web servers.

This is a much cleaner approach than using DPAPI, where you would need to perform in-place encryption on each of your production web servers. In-place encryption is not only error-prone, but it also means the web server administrator always gets to see the before image of the configuration data. With the RSA provider, you can go so far as having a security group responsible for encrypting your production configuration files; the security group members could be the only ones that know sensitive information such as connection string passwords. Then when the security group is done with the encryption process they could hand the results back to your development team for deployment onto a production farm. In this way, only a small set of individuals actually knows the sensitive pieces of cleartext configuration information.

aspnet_regiis Options

Several different command-line options have been thrown around for aspnet_regiis. The following table briefly summarizes the main options that have been used for the various samples. Each of these options usually has additional suboptions for things like per-user RSA containers, more specific virtual path information, and so on. However, the table shows only the most common options that you are likely to need:

Command-Line Option	Description
-pc Container_Name -exp -size 4096	Creates a new RSA key container that is available to any account, assuming Read access is granted.
	If you plan to export the key container, you need to include the -exp option.
	The -size option lets you specify the size of the RSA key that will be created in the container.

Continued

Command-Line Option	Description
`-pa Container_Name "DOMAIN\user"`	Grants Read access on an RSA key container to the specified user account.
`-pri -px Container_ Name file name`	Exports an RSA key container to the specified file. The export file includes the private RSA key information as well.
`-pi Container_Name file name`	Imports an RSA key container.
`-pe config_section_ path -app /app_path -prov provider_name`	Encrypts the configuration section identified by the configuration section path. This path looks something like `system.web/membership`. The application path specified by `-app` denotes a virtual path within the default web site, unless you specify a site with the `-site` option. The encryption uses the provider specified by `-prov`. This provider must have been defined in the `<configProtectedData />` section. If you want to use the default protected configuration provider, then `-prov` is not necessary.
`-pd config_section_ path -app /app_path`	Decrypts the configuration section identified by the configuration section path. This path looks something like `system.web/membership`. The application path specified by `-app` denotes a virtual path within the default web site, unless you specify a site with the `-site` option.

The `aspnet_regiis` tool really has only two modes of operation when working with protected configuration providers:

❑ The tool has rich support for the RSA-based provider that ships in the framework. `aspnet_regiis` includes many configuration switches to carry out various operations that are specific to the RSA-based provider.

❑ The tool can invoke any arbitrary provider, but it cannot support any special behavior that may be required by the provider. You can see that the command line (the `-pe` and `-pd` options) does not include any special switches beyond the basics that are required to identify a specific configuration section to protect.

This means that if you use a different protected configuration provider, and if you need to support special operations related to that provider (for example, the key container setup required when using RSA), you will need to write your own code to carry out these types of provider-specific tasks.

Using Protected Configuration Providers in Partial Trust

You have seen how protected configuration works transparently with the features that depend on the underlying configuration data. However, because protected configuration relies on providers, and these providers are public, there is not anything preventing you from just creating an instance of either the

RSA or the DPAPI provider and calling the methods on these providers directly. The `Decrypt` method on a `ProtectedConfigurationProvider` accepts a `System.Xml.XmlNode` as an input parameter and returns the decrypted version as another `XmlNode` instance.

Combining the simplicity of this method with the fact that most ASP.NET trust levels allow some Read access to the file system means that malicious developers could potentially attempt the following steps:

1. Open the application's `web.config` file as a text file or through a class like `System.Xml.XmlTextReader`.

2. Get a reference to the appropriate DPAPI or RSA provider based on the provider name in the `configProtectionProvider` attribute that is on the configuration element being protected.

3. Pass the contents of the `<EncryptedData />` element for a protected configuration section to the `Decrypt` method of the protected configuration provider obtained in the previous step.

In some scenarios, you do not want any piece of code to be able to accomplish this. Even in High trust where your code has access to read the `machine.config` and root `web.config` files, you probably do not want this loophole to exist.

If a feature is written to mirror configuration properties in a public API, then that is where developers should access the values. In some cases, if you author a feature so that certain pieces of configuration information are read, but are never exposed from a feature API, then you do not want random code that outflanks your feature and decrypts sensitive data directly from configuration.

To prevent this, the DPAPI and the RSA providers include the following class-level demand on their class signatures:

```
[PermissionSet(SecurityAction.Demand, Name="FullTrust")]
```

This declarative demand requires that all callers up the call stack must be running in Full trust. The `FullTrust` value for the `Name` property is actually a reference to one of the built-in .NET Framework permission sets that you can see if you use a tool like the .NET Framework Configuration MMC. As a result, all code in the call stack needs to be running in the GAC or the entire ASP.NET application needs to be running in the ASP.NET Full trust level. For a partial trust application, any attempt to directly call the providers will fail with a `SecurityException`.

You can see how this works by writing some sample code to load an application's `web.config` file, extract an encrypted section out of it, and then pass it to the correct provider.

C#

```csharp
using System.Configuration;
using System.Xml;
...
protected void Page_Load(object sender, EventArgs e)
{
    XmlDocument xd = new XmlDocument();
    xd.Load(Server.MapPath("~/web.config"));
```

```
    XmlNamespaceManager ns = new XmlNamespaceManager(xd.NameTable);
    ns.AddNamespace("u", "http://schemas.microsoft.com/.NetConfiguration/v2.0");
    XmlNode ec =
        xd.SelectSingleNode("//u:configuration/u:system.web/u:machineKey",ns);

    RsaProtectedConfigurationProvider rp =
        (RsaProtectedConfigurationProvider)
            ProtectedConfiguration.Providers["AppSpecificRSAProvider"];
    XmlNode dc = rp.Decrypt(ec);
}
```

VB.NET

```
Imports System.Configuration
Imports System.Xml
...

    Protected Sub Page_Load(ByVal sender As Object, ByVal e As EventArgs) _
    Handles Me.Load
        Dim xd As New XmlDocument()
        xd.Load(Server.MapPath("~/web.config"))

        Dim ns As New XmlNamespaceManager(xd.NameTable)
        ns.AddNamespace("u", "http://schemas.microsoft.com/.NetConfiguration/v2.0")
        Dim ec As XmlNode = _
        xd.SelectSingleNode("//u:configuration/u:system.web/u:machineKey", _
                ns)

        Dim rp As RsaProtectedConfigurationProvider = _
            CType(ProtectedConfiguration.Providers("AppSpecificRSAProvider"), _
        RsaProtectedConfigurationProvider)
        Dim dc As XmlNode = rp.Decrypt(ec)
    End Sub
```

The sample code uses an XPath query to extract an XmlNode reference to the encrypted <machineKey /> section. It then uses the ProtectedConfiguration class to get a reference to the correct provider for decryption. If you run this code in a Full trust ASP.NET application it will work. However, if you drop the trust level to High or lower, a SecurityException occurs when the call to Decrypt occurs.

Even though the protected configuration providers demand Full trust, you can still protect your own custom configuration sections in partial trust applications when using either the DPAPI or the RSA providers. At runtime when a call is made to GetSection from ConfigurationManager or WebConfiguration Manager, internally the configuration system asserts Full trust on your behalf prior to decrypting the contents of your custom configuration section. This behavior makes sense because the assumption is that if a piece of code can successfully call GetSection (for example, if ConfigurationPermission has been granted to the partial trust application, or requirePermission has been set to false, or your code is running in the GAC and asserts ConfigurationPermission), there is no reason why access to configuration via a strongly typed configuration class should fail even if the underlying data requires decryption.

If you have a sample application running in High trust (High trust is necessary for this sample because the "runtime" configuration APIs fail by default when called below High trust), you can attempt to open the protected <machineKey /> section with the following code:

C#

```
MachineKeySection mk =
    (MachineKeySection)WebConfigurationManager.GetSection("system.web/machineKey");
```

VB.NET

```
Dim mk As MachineKeySection = _
    CType(config.GetSection("system.web/machineKey"), _
    MachineKeySection)
```

The preceding code will work in both High and Full trust. In High trust, the code succeeds because it makes it over the hurdle of the two following security checks:

❑   The application is running in High trust, so the configuration system demand for Configuration Permission succeeds.

❑   The configuration system internally asserts Full trust when deserializing the configuration section, so the declarative security demand from the protected configuration provider passes as well.

However, if you use the *design-time* configuration API as follows in High trust, the same logical operation fails:

C#

```
//This will fail in High trust or below with a protected config section
Configuration config = WebConfigurationManager.OpenWebConfiguration("~");
MachineKeySection mk =
    (MachineKeySection)config.GetSection("system.web/machineKey");
```

VB.NET

```
'These two pieces of code fail in partial trust when using protected config
'because Open is a "design time" API
Dim config As Configuration = WebConfigurationManager.OpenWebConfiguration("~")
Dim mk As MachineKeySection = _
    CType(config.GetSection("system.web/machineKey"), _
    MachineKeySection)
```

In this scenario, three security checks occur, and the last one fails:

❑   The configuration system opens the file using file I/O, which generates a FileIOPermission demand. The demand passes because High trust has rights to read all configuration files in the inheritance chain.

❑   The NTFS ACLs on machine.config, root web.config, and the application's web.config also allow Read access.

❑ The protected configuration provider demands Full trust. The demand fails because the sample code is running in the `Page_Load` method of a partial trust ASP.NET application. Internally, the configuration does not assert Full trust on your behalf when calling the `Open*` methods.

The interaction of trust levels with protected configuration can be a bit mind-numbing to decipher. Excluding intervention on your part with configuration files or sandboxed GAC assemblies, the following list summarizes the behavior of the RSA and DPAPI protected configuration providers:

❑ Protected configuration providers *work in partial trust* applications that load configuration using the `GetSection` method. This method is the normal way a custom feature that you author would load configuration.

❑ Protected configuration providers *fail in partial trust* when using the design-time configuration APIs (that is, the various `Open*` methods). Normally, you will not call these methods from anything other than administrative applications or command-line configuration tools.

Redirecting Configuration with a Custom Provider

So far, all of the discussion on protected configuration has revolved around the idea of encrypting and decrypting configuration sections. Given the feature's heritage with the old `aspnet_setreg.exe` tool, this is understandable. Traditionally, when customers asked for a way to secure sensitive pieces of configuration data, they were looking for a way to encrypt the information. However, there is no reason that the concept of "protection" can't be interpreted differently.

A common problem some of you probably have with your web applications is with promoting an application through various environments. Aside from development environments you may have test servers, staging servers, live production servers, and potentially warm backup servers. Encrypting your configuration data does make it safer, but it also increases your management overhead in attempting to synchronize configuration data properly in each of these environments. This overhead is even more onerous if you work in a security-sensitive environment where only a limited number of personnel are allowed to encrypt the final configuration information prior to pushing it into production.

Protected configuration is probably manageable with manual intervention for a few servers and is tolerable with the help of automated scripts in environments that deal with dozens if not hundreds of servers. However, you can kill two birds with one stone if you think about "protected" actually being a problem of getting important configuration data physically off your web servers. If you store selected configuration sections in a central location (such as a central file share or a central configuration database), you have a more manageable solution and, depending on how you implement this, a more secure solution as well.

You can write a custom protected configuration provider that determines information about the current server and the currently running application. Because a protected configuration provider controls the format of the data that is written into a protected configuration section, you can store any additional information you need in this format. For example, you could have a custom XML format that includes hints to your provider so that it knows if a configuration section for `machine.config`, the root `web.config`, or an application `web.config` is requested. Even though the DPAPI and RSA providers use the W3C XML Encryption Recommendation, this is not a strict requirement for the format of encrypted data that is used by a custom provider.

A custom provider can then reach out to a central repository of configuration information and return the appropriate information. Depending on how stringent your security needs are you can layer extra protection in the form of transport layer security (such as an SSL connection to a SQL Server machine as well as IPSEC connection rules) and encrypt the configuration data prior to storing it in a central location. When you have a select group of individuals who manage the configuration data for live production servers, it is probably much easier to have such a group manage updates to a single database as opposed to encrypting a file and then having to worry about getting the synchronization of said file correct across multiple machines.

Implementing a custom protected configuration provider requires you to derive from the `System` `.Configuration.ProtectedConfigurationProvider` class. As you can see, the class signature is very basic:

C#

```csharp
public abstract class ProtectedConfigurationProvider : ProviderBase
{
    public abstract XmlNode Encrypt(XmlNode node);
    public abstract XmlNode Decrypt(XmlNode encryptedNode);
}
```

VB.NET

```vbnet
Public MustInherit Class ProtectedConfigurationProvider
    Inherits ProviderBase
    Public MustOverride Function Decrypt(ByVal encryptedNode As XmlNode) As XmlNode
    Public MustOverride Function Encrypt(ByVal node As XmlNode) As XmlNode
End Class
```

For a sample provider that demonstrates redirecting configuration to a database, you implement only the `Decrypt` method because this is the method used at runtime to return configuration data to the caller. If you store more complex data inside your protected configuration format, implementing the `Encrypt` method will make life easier when storing configuration sections in a custom data store.

First look at what a "protected" configuration section in a `web.config` file will look like using the custom provider:

```xml
<membership configProtectionProvider="CustomDatabaseProvider">
    <EncryptedData>
        <sectionInfo name="membership" />
    </EncryptedData>
</membership>
```

As with previous snippets of protected configuration, the `<membership />` section references a protected configuration provider. Instead of the actual definition of the `<membership />` section though, the `<EncryptedData />` element is common to all protected configuration sections. However, what is enclosed within this element is determined by each provider. In this case, to keep the sample provider very simple, the protected data consists of only a single element: a `<sectionInfo />` element.

Unlike protected configuration providers that blindly encrypt and decrypt data, this provider needs to know the actual configuration section that is being requested. The RSA and DPAPI providers actually have no idea what they are operating against. Both providers work against a fixed schema and consider the encrypted blob data to be opaque from a functionality standpoint. The custom provider, however, needs to know what section is really being requested because its purpose is to store configuration data in a database for any arbitrary configuration section. The name attribute within the <sectionInfo /> element gives the custom provider the necessary information. Although this is just a basic example of what you can place with <EncryptedData />, you can encapsulate any kind of complex data your provider may need within the XML.

The custom provider will store configuration sections in a database, keying off of a combination of the application's virtual path and the configuration section. The database schema that follows shows the table structure for storing this:

```
create table ConfigurationData (
ApplicationName nvarchar(256) NOT NULL,
SectionName nvarchar(150) NOT NULL,
SectionData ntext
)
go

alter table ConfigurationData
   add constraint PKConfigurationData
   PRIMARY KEY (ApplicationName,SectionName)
go
```

Retrieving this information will similarly be very basic with just a single stored procedure pulling back the SectionData column that contains the raw text of the requested configuration section:

```
create procedure RetrieveConfigurationSection
   @pApplicationName nvarchar(256),
   @pSectionName nvarchar(256)
as

select SectionData
from   ConfigurationData
where  ApplicationName  = @pApplicationName
and    SectionName      = @pSectionName
go
```

Because the custom protected configuration provider needs to connect to a database, a connection string must be included within the definition of the provider. Writing and configuring custom providers is the subject of Chapter 10; the important point for this sample is that ASP.NET allows you to add arbitrary information to the configuration element for providers.

```
<configProtectedData>
  <providers>
    <add name="CustomDatabaseProvider"
         type="CustomProviders.DatabaseProtectedConfigProvider,CustomProviders"
         connectionStringName="ConfigurationDatabase"
    />
  </providers>
</configProtectedData>
```

The provider configuration looks similar to the configurations for the RSA and DPAPI providers. In this case, however, the custom provider requires a connectionStringName element so that it knows which database and database server to connect to. The value of this attribute is simply a reference to a named connection string in the <connectionStrings /> section, as shown here:

```
<connectionStrings>
    <add name="ConfigurationDatabase"
        connectionString="server=.;Integrated _
            Security=true;database=CustomProtectedConfiguration"/>
</connectionStrings>
```

When creating your own custom providers, you have the freedom to place any provider-specific information you deem necessary in the <add /> element.

Now that you have seen the data structure and configuration related information, take a look at the code for the custom provider. Because a protected configuration provider ultimately derives from System.Configuration.Provider.ProviderBase, the custom provider can override portions of ProviderBase as well as ProtectedConfigurationProvider. Chapter 10 goes into more detail on ProviderBase; for now, though, the custom provider will override ProviderBase.Initialize so that the provider can retrieve the connection string from configuration:

C#

```
using System;
using System.Data;
using System.Data.SqlClient;
using System.Configuration;
using System.Configuration.Provider;
using System.Web;
using System.Web.Hosting;
using System.Web.Configuration;
using System.Xml;

namespace CustomProviders
{
    public class DatabaseProtectedConfigProvider : ProtectedConfigurationProvider
    {
        private string connectionString;

        public DatabaseProtectedConfigProvider() { }

        public override void Initialize(string name,
            System.Collections.Specialized.NameValueCollection config)
        {
            string connectionStringName = config["connectionStringName"];
            if (String.IsNullOrEmpty(connectionStringName))
                throw new ProviderException("You must specify " +
                    "connectionStringName in the provider configuration");

            connectionString =
                WebConfigurationManager.ConnectionStrings[connectionStringName] _
                                    .ConnectionString;
            if (String.IsNullOrEmpty(connectionString))
                throw new ProviderException("The connection string " +
```

```
                                    "could not be found in <connectionString />.");
            config.Remove("connectionStringName");

            base.Initialize(name, config);
        }

    //Remainder of provider implementation
    }
}
```

VB.NET

```vb
Imports System
Imports System.Data
Imports System.Data.SqlClient
Imports System.Configuration
Imports System.Configuration.Provider
Imports System.Web
Imports System.Web.Hosting
Imports System.Web.Configuration
Imports System.Xml

Namespace CustomProviders
    Public Class DatabaseProtectedConfigProvider
        Inherits ProtectedConfigurationProvider
        Private connectionString As String

        Public Sub New()
        End Sub

        Public Overrides Sub Initialize( _
        ByVal name As String, _
        ByVal config As System.Collections.Specialized.NameValueCollection)
            Dim connectionStringName As String = config("connectionStringName")
            If String.IsNullOrEmpty(connectionStringName) Then
            Throw New ProviderException( _
                "You must specify connectionStringName in the provider configuration")
            End If

            connectionString = _
    WebConfigurationManager.ConnectionStrings(connectionStringName).ConnectionString
            If String.IsNullOrEmpty(connectionString) Then
            Throw New ProviderException( _
                "The connection string could not be found in <connectionString />.")
            End If
            config.Remove("connectionStringName")

            MyBase.Initialize(name, config)
        End Sub

    'Remainder of provider implementation

    End Class
End Namespace
```

The processing inside of the `Initialize` method performs a few sanity checks to ensure that the `connectionStringName` attribute was specified in the provider's `<add />` element, and that furthermore the name actually points at a valid connection string. After the connection string is obtained from the `ConnectionStrings` collection, it is cached internally in a private variable.

Of course, the interesting part of the provider is its implementation of the `Decrypt` method:

C#

```csharp
public override XmlNode Decrypt(XmlNode encryptedNode)
{
    //Application name
    string applicationName = HostingEnvironment.ApplicationVirtualPath;
    XmlNode xn = encryptedNode.SelectSingleNode("/EncryptedData/sectionInfo");
    //Configuration section to retrieve from the database
    string sectionName = xn.Attributes["name"].Value;

    using (SqlConnection conn = new SqlConnection(connectionString))
    {
        SqlCommand cmd =
            new SqlCommand("RetrieveConfigurationSection", conn);
        cmd.CommandType = CommandType.StoredProcedure;
        SqlParameter p1 = new SqlParameter("@pApplicationName", applicationName);
        SqlParameter p2 = new SqlParameter("@pSectionName", sectionName);

        cmd.Parameters.AddRange(new SqlParameter[] { p1, p2 });

        conn.Open();
        string rawConfigText = (string)cmd.ExecuteScalar();
        conn.Close();

        //Convert string from the database into an XmlNode
        XmlDocument xd = new XmlDocument();
        xd.LoadXml(rawConfigText);

        return xd.DocumentElement;
    }
}
```

VB.NET

```vbnet
Public Overrides Function Decrypt( _
ByVal encryptedNode As XmlNode) As XmlNode()
    Dim applicationName As String = _
        HostingEnvironment.ApplicationVirtualPath
    Dim xn As XmlNode = _
        encryptedNode.SelectSingleNode("/EncryptedData/sectionInfo")
    Dim sectionName As String = xn.Attributes("name").Value

    Using conn As New SqlConnection(connectionString)
        Dim cmd As New SqlCommand("RetrieveConfigurationSection", conn)
        cmd.CommandType = CommandType.StoredProcedure
        Dim p1 As New SqlParameter("@pApplicationName", applicationName)
        Dim p2 As New SqlParameter("@pSectionName", sectionName)
```

```
                cmd.Parameters.AddRange(New SqlParameter() {p1, p2})

            conn.Open()
            Dim rawConfigText As String = CStr(cmd.ExecuteScalar())
            conn.Close()

            'Convert string from the database into an XmlNode
            Dim xd As New XmlDocument()
            xd.LoadXml(rawConfigText)

            Return xd.DocumentElement
        End Using
    End Function
```

The Decrypt method's purpose is take information about the current application and information available from the <sectionInfo /> element and use it to retrieve the correct configuration data from the database.

The provider determines the correct application name by using the System.Web.Hosting.Hosting Environment class to determine the current application's virtual path. The name of the configuration section to retrieve is determined by parsing the <EncryptedData /> section to get to the name attribute of the custom <sectionInfo /> element. With these pieces of data the provider connects to the database using the connection string supplied by the provider's configuration section.

The configuration data stored in the database is just the raw XML fragment for a given configuration section. For this example, which stores a <membership /> section in the database, the database table just contains the text of the section's definition taken from machine.config stored in an ntext field in SQL Server. Because protected configuration providers work in terms of XmlNode instances, and not raw strings, the provider converts the raw text in the database back into an XmlDocument, which can then be subsequently returned as an XmlNode instance. Because the data in the database is well-formed XML, the provider can just return the DocumentElement for the XmlDocument.

The provider's implementation of the Encrypt method is just stubbed out. For your own custom providers, you could implement the inverse of the logic shown in the Decrypt method that would scoop the configuration section out of the config file and stored in the database.

C#

```csharp
public override XmlNode Encrypt(XmlNode node)
{
    throw new NotImplementedException("This method is not implemented.");
}
```

VB.NET

```vbnet
        Public Overrides Function Encrypt(ByVal node As XmlNode) As XmlNode
            Throw New NotImplementedException("This method is not implemented.")
        End Function
```

What is really powerful about custom protected configuration providers is that you can go back to some of the sample configuration code used earlier in the chapter and run it, with the one change being that you use the "protected" configuration section for <membership />.

C#

```
MembershipSection ms =
        (MembershipSection)ConfigurationManager.GetSection("system.web/membership");
```

VB.NET

```
Dim ms As MembershipSection = _
    CType(config.GetSection("system.web/membership"), _
    MembershipSection)
```

This code works unchanged after you swap in the new <membership /> section using the custom protected configuration provider. This is exactly what you would want from protected configuration. Nothing in the application code needs to change despite the fact that now the configuration section is stored
remotely in a database as opposed to locally on the file system.

Clearly, the sample provider is pretty basic in terms of what it supports. However, with a modicum of
work you could extend this provider to support features like the following:

❑ Machine-specific configuration

❑ Environment-specific configuration, separating data by terms like TEST, DEV, PROD, and so on

❑ Encrypting the actual data inside of the database so that database administrators can't see what
is stored in the tables

Nothing requires you to store configuration data in a traditional data store like a database or on the file
system. You could author a custom provider that uses a Web Service call or socket call to a configuration system as opposed to looking up data in a database.

One caveat to keep in mind with custom protected configuration providers is that after the data is physically stored outside of a configuration file, ASP.NET is no longer able to automatically trigger an app-domain
restart whenever the configuration data changes. With the built-in RSA and DPAPI providers, this is not an
issue because the encrypted text is still stored in web.config and machine.config files. ASP.NET listens
for change notifications and triggers an app-domain restart in the event any of these files change.

However, ASP.NET does not have a facility to trigger changes based on protected configuration data
stored in other locations. For this reason, if you do write a custom provider along the lines of the sample
provider, you need to incorporate operational procedures that force app-domains to recycle whenever
you update configuration data stored in locations other than the standard file-based configuration files.

Summary

Configuration security in ASP.NET 2.0 included quite a number of improvements that ASP.NET 3.5
builds on top of them. While the original <location />-based locking approach is still supported (and
is definitely still useful), ASP.NET 3.5's configuration system now gives you the ability to enforce more
granular control over individual sections. The lockAttributes attribute restricts the ability of child
configuration files to override selected attributes defined on the parent. The lockElements attribute
prevents entire configuration elements from being redefined in child configuration files. Both of these
attributes support an alternate syntax to make it easier to configure fine-grained security when many
attributes or many nested configuration elements need to be controlled.

In addition, IIS 7.0 ships with the Feature Delegation feature that allows administrators to decide which configuration sections of the `<system.webServer>` configuration section group located in the `ApplicationHost.config` configuration file can be edited by developers through the application's `web.config` file. It is the IIS 7.0 way of protecting configuration settings in the `ApplicationHost.config` file.

Because configuration data exists within physical files, NTFS permissions come into play when reading or writing configuration data. Under normal conditions, configuration data only needs to be read; although it has to be read up the entire inheritance chain from the most derived `web.config` file all the way up to the root `web.config` and `web.config` files. Because ASP.NET reads runtime configuration data using the process account or application impersonation identity, reading configuration usually succeeds assuming the file ACLs have been set up properly. Physically writing configuration data is something that should be reserved only for administrative-style applications or command-line tools due to the need for Full Control on these files. ASP.NET also supports remote editing of configuration files, although for security reasons this functionality is turned off by default.

Because ASP.NET supports running in partial trust, the configuration system makes use of the Framework's CAS support to limit what can be done in partial trust. Access to strongly typed configuration sections is allowed only in High and Full trust. If you need to access the configuration classes directly in Medium trust or lower, you will need to use the `requirePermission` attribute. For the built-in configuration sections, you should avoid doing so because most ASP.NET features expose public APIs that already give access to most of the configuration data you need.

Customers have long asked for the ability to secure configuration data so that prying eyes cannot see sensitive information such as database connection strings. The protected configuration feature that was introduced in .NET Framework 2.0 allows you to encrypt configuration sections using either DPAPI or RSA. Because the protected configuration feature is based on the provider model, you also have the option to write or purchase custom protected configuration providers. This gives you the freedom to implement different encryption strategies or, as seen with the sample provider, different storage locations for your configuration data.

6

Forms Authentication

Forms authentication is the most widely used authentication mechanism for Internet-facing ASP.NET sites. The appeal of forms authentication is that sites with only a few pages and simple authentication requirements can make use of forms authentication, and complex sites can still rely on forms authentication for the basic handling of authenticating users. ASP.NET 3.5 continues to use the same forms authentication that was improved in ASP.NET 2.0, with some enhancements that allow the integration of forms authentication on IIS 7.0 so that not only ASP.NET resources can be authenticated, but also other types of content. Moreover, the ASP.NET 3.5 runtime resembles that of ASP.NET 2.0, with additional features.

This chapter covers the following topics on ASP.NET 3.5 forms authentication:

- ❑ Reviewing how forms authentication works in the HTTP pipeline (most of this was covered in Chapter 3).
- ❑ Making changes to the behavior of persistent forms authentication tickets.
- ❑ Securing the forms authentication payload.
- ❑ Securing forms authentication cookies with `HttpOnly` and `requireSSL`.
- ❑ Using cookieless support in forms authentication.
- ❑ Using forms authentication across ASP.NET 1.1 and ASP.NET 3.5.
- ❑ Using forms authentication across different content types.
- ❑ Leveraging the `UserData` property of `FormsAuthenticationTicket`.
- ❑ Passing forms authentication tickets between applications.
- ❑ Enforcing a single login and preventing replayed tickets after logout.

A Quick Recap of Forms Authentication

In Chapter 3, the sections on `AuthenticateRequest`, `AuthorizeRequest` and `EndRequest` described how forms authentication works throughout the HTTP pipeline. In summary, forms authentication performs the following tasks:

1. During `AuthenticateRequest`, the `FormsAuthenticationModule` checks the validity of the forms authentication ticket (carried in a cookie or in a cookieless format on the URL) if one exists. If a valid ticket is found, this results in a `GenericPrincipal` referencing a `FormsIdentity` as the value for `HttpContext.Current.User`. The actual information in the ticket is available as an instance of a `FormsAuthenticationTicket` off of the `FormsIdentity`.

2. During `AuthorizeRequest`, other modules and logic such as the `UrlAuthorizationModule` attempt to authorize access to the currently requested URL. If an authenticated user was not created earlier by the `FormAuthenticationModule`, any URL that requires some type of authenticated user will fail authorization. However, even if forms authentication created a user, authorization rules that require roles can still fail unless you have written custom logic to associate a `FormsIdentity` with a set of roles or used a feature like Role Manager that performs this association automatically.

3. If authorization fails during `AuthorizeRequest`, the current request is short-circuited and immediately forwarded to the `EndRequest` phase of the pipeline. The `FormsAuthentication Module` runs during `EndRequest` and if it detects that `Response.StatusCode` is set to 401, the module automatically redirects the current request to the login page that is configured for forms authentication (`login.aspx` by default).

This basic summary of forms authentication demonstrates that the forms authentication ticket is the piece of persistent authentication information around which the forms authentication feature revolves. The next few sections delve into more details about how the forms authentication ticket is protected, persisted, and passed around applications. For all practical purposes, developers use the terms "forms authentication ticket" and "forms authentication cookie" interchangeably.

Understanding Persistent Tickets

Since ASP.NET 1.0, the forms authentication feature has supported persistent and nonpersistent tickets. In ASP.NET 1.0 and 1.1 the forms authentication ticket was always stored in a cookie (again excluding the Mobile Internet Toolkit which most developers probably have not used). So, the decision between using a persistent versus nonpersistent ticket is a choice between using persistent or session-based cookies. The lifetime of a session-based cookie is the duration of the interactive browser session; when you shut down the browser, any session-based cookies held in memory are gone. The forms authentication feature included the option for persistent cookies to enable lower-security applications (message boards, personal websites with minimal security requirements, and so on) to store a representation of the authenticated user without constantly requiring users to log in again.

Clearly, for some sites where users infrequently access the application (and hence are always forgetting their credentials), persistent cookies are a great usability enhancement. The one "small" problem is that on ASP.NET 1.0 and ASP.NET 1.1 sites, persistent cookies are given a 50-year lifetime. Now, I am all for making certain types of websites easier to use (like everybody else I have an idiotic number of username-password combinations to deal with), but I think 50 years is pushing it a bit! You can see this for older ASP.NET sites that issue cookies if you take a look at the expiration date for their forms authentication tickets. For example, the following code issues a persistent ticket:

C#

```
FormsAuthentication.RedirectFromLoginPage("testuser", true);
```

VB.NET

```
FormsAuthentication.RedirectFromLoginPage("testuser", True)
```

The resulting expiration date on the cookie when I was writing this was "4/5/2058 11:18:25 AM." The net result is that a digitally encrypted and digitally signed forms authentication ticket is left lying around a user's computer until by happenstance the cookie is deleted. On one hand, if you regularly delete cookies, then 50-year lifetimes are probably not a big deal. On the other hand, as a website developer you definitely can bet that some percentage of your user population is accruing cookies ad infinitum. From a security perspective the 50-year lifetime is really, really bad. Although the default security for forms authentication cookies encrypts and signs the cookies, it is likely that sometime in the next 50 years computing power will have reached a point that the present-day forms authentication ticket can be cracked in a reasonably short time. It's unlikely that anybody will ever have their original computer from 50 years ago (where would you put that old UNIVAC today?). But some website users will still be on the same machine 5 to 7 years later, and if they regularly visit the same site, the forms authentication ticket issued years earlier will still be lying around waiting to be hijacked and cracked.

As a result of this type of security concern with excessively long-lived forms authentication tickets, in ASP.NET 3.5, as in ASP.NET 2.0, persistent cookies set their expiration based upon the value of the cookie timeout set in configuration. Taking the same code shown earlier and running it on ASP.NET 3.5 with the default cookie timeout of 30 minutes results in a persistent cookie that expires 30 minutes later (you can see this if you view the files in your browser cache and look for the cookie file). This change may take a number of developers by surprise, and their first inkling of the new behavior may be complaints from website users suddenly being forced to login.

However, even though the ASP.NET 2.0 and ASP.NET 3.5 behavior changes the cookie expiration for *new* cookies issued using forms authentication, the new behavior has no effect on preexisting cookies. If you upgrade an ASP.NET 1.1 application to ASP.NET 3.5, any users with 50-year cookies floating around will continue to retain these cookies. Even if you use sliding expiration for your forms authentication tickets, because ASP.NET has not been around for 25 years, none of the preexisting persistent cookies will be reissued due to time passing for sliding expirations (forms authentication attempts to reissue a cookie when 50 percent or more of the configured cookie timeout has elapsed).

This raises the question of whether developers should take explicit steps to reissue their persistent cookies with more reasonable timeouts. I believe that a little more security is better than 50-year cookie lifetimes, and recommend that developers using persistent forms authentication cookies add some logic to their applications after upgrade. First, developers should determine a reasonable persistent cookie timeout. This may be a few weeks or months, although I wouldn't recommend going beyond one year. Even for sites that do not care too much about security, it does not seem unreasonable to ask people to reauthenticate themselves once a year.

ASP.NET 2.0 and ASP.NET 3.5 have only one cookie timeout setting (the `timeout` attribute in the `<forms />` configuration element). If your site needs to issue a mixture of persistent and session-based cookies, both types of cookies will use the timeout set in configuration; however, expiration enforcement happens through different mechanisms. In these situations it makes sense to ask why a website (or perhaps a set of websites) mixes the comparatively insecure persistent cookie option with session-based forms authentication tickets. Cookie-based websites should use one type of cookie persistence for all website users, and stick with a single persistence model.

After you have determined a new value for timeout, the next step is to add some code to your site that automatically swaps out the old persistent cookie for a new one with an updated expiration. `Post AuthenticateRequest` is a convenient point to perform this work. The following code for `global .asax` shows how this can be accomplished.

C#

```csharp
void Application_PostAuthenticateRequest(Object sender, EventArgs e)
{
    if (User.Identity is FormsIdentity)
    {
        if (((FormsIdentity)User.Identity).Ticket.Expiration >
                (DateTime.Now.Add(new TimeSpan(0,40320,0))))
        {
            FormsAuthentication.RedirectFromLoginPage(User.Identity.Name, true);
        }
    }
}
```

VB.NET

```vbnet
Private Sub Application_PostAuthenticateRequest( _
ByVal sender As Object, _
ByVal e As EventArgs)
   If TypeOf User.Identity Is FormsIdentity Then
            If (CType(User.Identity, FormsIdentity)).Ticket.Expiration > _
            (DateTime.Now.Add(New TimeSpan(0,40320,0))) Then
                FormsAuthentication.RedirectFromLoginPage(User.Identity.Name, True)
            End If
    End If
End Sub
```

The code first checks to see whether an authenticated `FormsIdentity` exists on the current context. If one exists, the `Identity` that is available from the `User` property on the context is cast to a `FormsIdentity` so that you can get access to the `FormsAuthenticationTicket` available off of the `Ticket` property. The `FormsAuthenticationTicket` conveniently exposes its expiration with the `Expiration` property. In the sample code, if the ticket expires more than 40320 minutes (roughly one month) from now, the credentials are reissued as a persistent ticket.

Running this code on ASP.NET 3.5 results in a forms authentication cookie being reissued with the updated behavior for computing cookie expiration based on the timeout attribute in configuration. One thing to note is that the forms authentication API does not expose the value of the timeout attribute in a convenient manner. Although you could technically use the strongly typed configuration classes in ASP.NET 3.5 to get the correct value, you cannot really depend on that approach if you plan to run in partial trust (more on issues with strongly typed configuration classes and partial trust in Chapter 5).

As a result, the somewhat simplistic workaround is to duplicate the expiration value either by hard-coding it as in the sample code or, for better maintenance, by storing it as a value in a place like the `<appSettings />` section in configuration.

How Forms Authentication Enforces Expiration

The `timeout` attribute on the `<forms />` configuration element controls the expiration of the forms authentication ticket. However, in the case of session based cookies the `Expires` property of the cookie created by forms authentication is never set. Furthermore, with the cookieless support in ASP.NET 2.0 and ASP.NET 3.5, there may not even be a cookie created for the forms authentication ticket.

Forms authentication computes the expiration time for a forms authentication ticket by adding the value of the `timeout` attribute to `DateTime.Now`. This value is passed as one of the parameters to the `FormsAuthenticationTicket` constructor. After a `FormsAuthenticationTicket` is created, it is converted to a hex-string representation using some custom internal serialization logic. This means the expiration date is packaged within the custom serialized representation of the ticket, regardless of whether the ticket is subsequently issued as a cookie or is instead placed on the URL for the cookieless case.

Each time a forms authentication ticket arrives back at the web server, `FormsAuthenticationModule` opens either the cookie or the cookieless value on the URL, and converts the enclosed hex-string to an instance of `FormsAuthenticationTicket`. With a fully inflated ticket, the module checks the `Expiration` property to determine whether the ticket is still valid. This means that when a ticket is carried inside a cookie, `FormsAuthenticationModule` ignores any implied statement about expiration. Technically, if a cookie is sent to the web server, the browser agent that sent the cookie must consider the cookie still to be valid, meaning that the cookie has not expired yet.

However, from a security perspective, it is trivial for a malicious user to generate a cookie and send it to the web server. As a result, forms authentication never depends on the expiration mechanism supported by HTTP cookies. It always consults the expiration date contained within the serialized ticket when determining whether the ticket is valid. If a cookie arrives at the web server, but the expiration date contained within the serialized ticket indicates that the ticket has expired, `FormsAuthenticationModule` recognizes this and doesn't create a `FormsIdentity` based on the ticket. Furthermore, it removes the expired cookie from the `Request.Cookies` collection to prevent any downstream logic from making incorrect decisions based on the presence of the expired ticket.

This approach also has the side benefit of forms authentication performing date comparisons based on the web server's time. Although clock-skew probably exists between the current time on the web server and the current time on a client's machine, as long as the cookie gets sent to the web server, the expiration date comparison is made using the server's time.

One question that arises from time to time is whether the expiration date of the ticket is maintained in Universal Coordinate Time (UTC). Unfortunately, when forms authentication was first implemented, it used the local date-time representation for the expiration date. Back in ASP.NET 2.0, the team considered changing this behavior through a configuration setting, but ultimately decided against it due to the following problems:

❏   Changing to a UTC-based expiration would break authentication in mixed ASP.NET 1.1 and ASP.NET 2.0 and ASP.NET 3.5 environments. The ASP.NET 1.1 servers would think the expiration date was in local time, when in reality the time was offset by many hours from the local time (assuming that your web server wasn't sitting in the GMT time zone, of course!).

❑ Although a configuration switch for ASP.NET 2.0 and ASP.NET 3.5 was a possibility, this would introduce a fair amount of confusion around when to turn it on or off. If the UTC time handling was turned on, and then later an ASP.NET 1.1 application was introduced into your web farm, ASP.NET 2.0 and ASP.NET 3.5 would have to be switched back to the original behavior.

In two scenarios, local times potentially introduce problems for computing expiration times.

❑ In the United States, twice during the year, clocks are reset forward or backward by one hour. When a forms authentication ticket that was issued before the clock reset is sent back to the web server, the forms authentication feature incorrectly interprets the local time in that ticket. This means that one of two things happens: an extra hour is added to the ticket's expiration, or one hour is subtracted from the ticket's expiration. However, because this occurs at 1 AM local time (for the United States time adjustments), there probably is not a lot of traffic on your website that will encounter this oddity.

❑ If a website user browses across servers located in different physical time zones, and if the servers in each time zone are not set to use the same time zone internally, servers will incorrectly interpret the expiration date. For example, if a website load balances some of its users across servers on the West Coast and the East Coast of the United States, there is a three-hour time difference between the two coasts. If a forms authentication ticket is initially issued on the West coast at 10 AM local time, when the ticket is sent to a server on the East Coast, that server is going to compare the 10AM issuance against the fact that it is now 1 PM. This kind of discrepancy can lead to a user being forced to log in again.

Because of these potential discrepancies, developers should be aware of the limitations of the local date time value stored in the forms authentication ticket. In the case of the clocks being reset twice a year, the current behavior is likely limited only to a few night owls.

However, if your websites use geographic load balancing, keep in mind the forms authentication behavior. You could ensure that when a user has accessed a server in one geographic region, the user is routed back to the same geographic region on all subsequent requests. Alternatively, you could have a standard time zone that all servers use regardless of the time zone for the physical region that the servers are deployed in. On the other hand, if all of your geographically dispersed servers lie in the same time zone (maybe you have servers in New York City and others in Miami), you will not run into the forms authentication expiration issue.

Working with the DateTime Issue with Clock Resets

You do not need to read this section unless you are really, really curious about what happens when the server clock is reset! After struggling with this problem during the ASP.NET 2.0 design cycle, I figured I would share the code snippets and results.

The following code is for a simple console application that simulates the problem with date time comparisons when the clock resets.

C#

```
static void Main(string[] args)
{
    DateTime dtNow = DateTime.Now;
```

```
        Console.WriteLine("Use a 30 minute timeout just like forms authentication.");

        Console.WriteLine("The date value for now is: " +
            dtNow.ToShortTimeString());
        Console.WriteLine("Has the time expired: " +
            (dtNow.Add(new TimeSpan(0, 30, 0)) < DateTime.Now));

        string breakHere = "Manually reset the clock ";

        DateTime dtNow2 = DateTime.Now;
        Console.WriteLine("The date value for now after the clock reset is: " +
            dtNow2.ToShortTimeString());
        Console.WriteLine("Has the time expired: " +
            (dtNow.Add(new TimeSpan(0, 30, 0)) < DateTime.Now));

        Console.ReadLine();

    }
```

VB.NET

```
Shared Sub Main(ByVal args() As String)
    Dim dtNow As DateTime = DateTime.Now
    Console.WriteLine("Use a 30 minute timeout just like forms authentication.")
    Console.WriteLine("The date value for now is: " & dtNow.ToShortTimeString())
    Console.WriteLine("Has the time expired: " & _
    (dtNow.Add(New TimeSpan(0, 30, 0)) < DateTime.Now))

    Dim breakHere As String = "Manually reset the clock "
    Dim dtNow2 As DateTime = DateTime.Now
    Console.WriteLine("The date value for now after the clock reset is: " & _
    dtNow2.ToShortTimeString())
    Console.WriteLine("Has the time expired: " & _
    (dtNow.Add(New TimeSpan(0, 30, 0)) < DateTime.Now))
    Console.ReadLine()
End Sub
```

Running this inside of the debugger with a breakpoint in the dummy string assignment in the middle allows you to set the clock forward or backward prior to the next date comparison. The comparison against DateTime.Now is the same as the comparison that FormsAuthenticationTicket makes when you check the Expired property. Running the sample code and setting the clock back one hour during the breakpoint results in the following output:

```
Use a 30 minute timeout just like forms authentication.
The date value for now is: 10:27 AM
Has the time expired: False
The date value for now after the clock reset is: 9:27 AM
Has the time expired: False
```

The net result is that after the clock was set back one hour (just as is done during the last Sunday of October in most of the United States), an expiration time based on a 30-minute timeout will be valid until 10:57 AM. However, with the clock reset back to 9:27 AM, the lifetime of a ticket with this expiration is accidentally extended to 90 minutes.

Running the same code, but this time setting the clock forward one hour results in the following output:

```
Use a 30 minute timeout just like forms authentication.
The date value for now is: 10:33 AM
Has the time expired: False
The date value for now after the clock reset is: 11:33 AM
Has the time expired: True
```

Now the original expiration of 11:03 AM (10:33 AM issuance plus a 30-minute lifetime) is considered expired after the clock was set forward one hour (just as is done during the first Sunday in April). This occurs because after the clock is reset, the original expiration time of 11:03 AM (which is considered a local time) is compared against the newly updated local time of 11:33 AM and is considered to have immediately expired.

The underlying technical reason for this similar behavior with forms authentication tickets is twofold:

❑ The serialization of the forms authentication ticket's DateTime expiration uses a local time conversion (DateTime.ToFileTime and DateTime.FromFileTime). As a result, whenever a forms authentication ticket is deserialized on a web server, the .NET Framework hands back a DateTime instance that contains a local time value.

❑ The Expired property on FormsAuthenticationTicket is always compared against Date Time.Now. For the ticket to be UTC capable, you really need the ticket to be compared against DateTime.UtcNow.

There is not an easy workaround to this whole issue. Aside from physical deployment steps, you can take to prevent part of the problem, the only ironclad way to ensure handling for all of these scenarios is for you to take over much of the management and verification of the forms authentication ticket, including the following:

❑ Manually construct the ticket and store the UTC expiration date inside of the UserData property of the FormsAuthenticationTicket.

❑ Manually issue the ticket.

❑ Hook a pipeline event prior to AuthenticateRequest (for example, BeginRequest), or hook the Authenticate event on the FormsAuthenticationModule directly. Then manually crack open and verify the ticket based on the UTC date previously stored in the UserData property of the FormsAuthenticationTicket. If you detect a discrepancy between the UTC-based comparison and the value of FormsAuthenticationTicket.Expired, you could force a redirect to reissue an updated cookie that contains an adjusted local time for the Expiration property.

Whether this effort is worth it depends on the specific kind of application you are trying to secure. I suspect that for all but the most sensitive sites (for example, financial sites), the extra effort to deal with time mismatches that occur twice a year will probably not warrant the investment in time and effort.

Securing the Ticket on the Wire

By default, the forms authentication ticket is digitally encrypted and signed using a keyed hash. This security has been available since ASP.NET 1.0, and ASP.NET 3.5 uses the same security for the ticket. However, there have been some new questions over hash security and support for new encryption options in ASP.NET 2.0 and ASP.NET 3.5.

How Secure Are Signed Tickets?

Since ASP.NET 1.0, forms authentication tickets have been digitally signed using a keyed hash that uses the SHA1 algorithm. When SHA1 was originally chosen years ago, it was considered a very secure hashing algorithm with no likelihood of being cryptographically weakened. In 2005, there were reports that SHA1 had been "broken"; in the cryptographic community, someone reported a theoretical collision-based attack on SHA1 hashes.

In summary, some researchers proposed a way to reduce the chance of inducing a hash collision in SHA1 to only 2^{69} attempts. Normally, you would expect to take around 2^{80} attempts to create a collision in SHA1 (SHA1 hashes are 160 bits in length, so you can figure that on average you only need to flip half as many possible bits to eventually find a piece of text that results in a matching SHA1 hash.)

So, this new attack against SHA1 theoretically reduces the number of attempts by a pretty hefty 1208335523804270469054464 iterations (after notepad, I think `calc.exe` is the most frequently entered command from the Run option in Windows). Suffice it say that that the current estimate of 2^{69} attempts to find a SHA1 collision would still entail enormous computing resources. Depending on who you believe, it takes a few million years with commodity hardware or a few years with specialized cracking computers backed by the resources of the NSA. Regardless, it all boils down to the fact that "breaking" SHA1 is still incredibly difficult and time-consuming and realistically isn't feasible with 2005-class hardware.

However, in the cryptography community, weaknesses with hashing or encryption algorithms are like snowballs rolling down a steep hill. Weaknesses start out small, but as time passes and attacks are better understood, the combination of increased mathematical focus on these algorithms combined with ever-increasing computing power eventually leads to present-day algorithms being susceptible to viable attacks.

Given the news about the SHA1 attack, there has been concern in the cryptography community around the long-term viability of SHA1 as a hashing algorithm. Some companies will probably start moving to SHA256 as a preemptive measure. There had been discussion on the ASP.NET team about whether one of the stronger SHA variants should have been added to <machineKey /> (remember that <machineKey /> defines the encryption and signing options for forms authentication, among other things). However, the team decided to stick with SHA1 because, technically speaking, forms authentication really uses HMACSHA1 (frequently referred to as a "keyed hash"), not just plain SHA1. In the case of <machineKey />, and thus forms authentication tickets, sticking with HMACSHA1 is a reasonable choice for the current ASP.NET 2.0 and ASP.NET 3.5 products.

The transient nature of nonpersistent forms authentication tickets means that in future framework releases, support for stronger SHA variants like SHA256 and SHA512 can be easily added. Such a change would impact applications that persistently store forms authentication tickets. Any application that truly needs security, though, should not be using persistent forms authentication tickets. The most likely future impact for developers would be around edge cases dependent on the total length of the characters in a forms authentication cookie. The stronger SHA variants contain more bits, and thus require more hex characters when converted to a string representation. This is normally more of a concern for cookieless tickets where ticket lengths are constrained. I cover issues with cookieless forms authentication tickets, including effective length restrictions, later in this chapter.

Another reason for sticking with SHA1 as the hashing algorithm for forms authentication is that, as mentioned earlier, ASP.NET really uses HMACSHA1 (specifically the `System.Security.Cryptography.HMACSHA1` class). This means that the value of the `validationKey` attribute in `<machineKey />` is used as part of the input to generate a SHA1 hash. As a result, for any attacker to force a hashing collision, not only does an attacker have to force a collision with the SHA1 result, an attacker also has to guess the key that was used with HMACSHA1. Just brute forcing SHA1 is not sufficient, because an attacker needs to know the `validationKey` that was provided as input to the HMACSHA1 algorithm.

You can set the `validationKey` attribute of `<machineKey />` to a maximum length of 128 characters, which represents a 64-byte key value. The minimum allowable length for `validationKey` is 40 characters, which represents a 20-byte value. That means if you take advantage of the maximum allowable length, you have a 512 bit random value being used as the key, and an attacker has to somehow guess this value to create a viable hashing collision. I admit that I am definitely not a crypto-guru, so I can't state how much stronger keying with HMACSHA1 is versus the plain SHA1 algorithm. However, with the added requirement of dealing with an unknown 512-bit key, the number of iterations necessary to force a collision with HMACSHA1 far exceeds either 2^{69} or 2^{80} iterations.

One final note: developers may use a little-known method in the forms authentication API: `FormsAuthentication.HashPasswordForStoringInConfigFile`. In ASP.NET 1.1, this was a convenient way to obtain a hex-string representation of a hashed password using MD5 or SHA1. Although originally intended for making it easier to securely populate the `<credentials />` section contained within `<forms />` (since superseded by the more powerful and secure Membership feature in ASP.NET 2.0 and ASP.NET 3.5), customers have found this method handy as an easy-to-use interface to the hash algorithms. The problem today, though, is that with MD5's strength in question, and now SHA1 potentially declining in strength, developers should really think about moving to SHA256 or SHA512 instead. However, the `HashPasswordForStoringInConfigFile` was not updated in ASP.NET 2.0 and ASP.NET 3.5 to support any of the other hash algorithms in the framework.

Instead, you will need to write code to accomplish what this method used to do (and I strongly encourage moving to other hashing algorithms over time even though it will take a little more work). To make the transition a bit easier, the following console sample below shows how to perform the equivalent functionality but with the extra option of specifying the desired hashing algorithm.

C#

```
using System;
using System.Security.Cryptography;
using System.Collections.Generic;
using System.Text;

namespace HashPassword
```

```
{
    class Program
    {
        static void Main(string[] args)
        {
            if ((args.Length < 2) || (args.Length > 2))
            {
                Console.WriteLine("Usage:  hashpassword password hashalgorithm");
                return;
            }

            string password = args[0];
            HashAlgorithm hashAlg = HashAlgorithm.Create(args[1]);

            //Make sure the hash algorithm actually exists
            if (hashAlg == null)
            {
                Console.WriteLine("Invalid hash algorithm.");
                return;
            }

            string result = HashThePassword(password, hashAlg);
            Console.WriteLine("The hashed password is: " + result);
        }

        private static string HashThePassword(string password,
                                    HashAlgorithm hashFunction)
        {
            if (password == null)
                throw new ArgumentNullException("The password cannot be null.");

            byte[] bpassword = Encoding.UTF8.GetBytes(password);
            byte[] hashedPassword = hashFunction.ComputeHash(bpassword);

            //Transform the byte array back into hex characters
            StringBuilder s = new StringBuilder(hashedPassword.Length * 2);
            foreach (byte b in hashedPassword)
                s.Append(b.ToString("X2"));

            return s.ToString();
        }
    }
}
```

VB.NET

```
Imports Microsoft.VisualBasic
Imports System
Imports System.Collections.Generic
Imports System.Linq
Imports System.Text
Imports System.Web
Imports System.Security.Cryptography
Imports System.Security.Authentication
```

```vb
Namespace HashPassword
  Friend Class Program
        Shared Sub Main(ByVal args() As String)
            If (args.Length < 2) OrElse (args.Length > 2) Then
            Console.WriteLine("Usage:  hashpassword password hashalgorithm")
                Return
            End If

            Dim password As String = args(0)
            Dim hashAlg As HashAlgorithm = HashAlgorithm.Create(args(1))

            'Make sure the hash algorithm actually exists
            If hashAlg Is Nothing Then
                Console.WriteLine("Invalid hash algorithm.")
                Return
            End If

            Dim result As String = HashThePassword(password, hashAlg)
            Console.WriteLine("The hashed password is: " & result)
        End Sub

        Private Shared Function HashThePassword( _
        ByVal password As String, _
        ByVal hashFunction As HashAlgorithm) As String
            If password Is Nothing Then
                Throw New ArgumentNullException("The password cannot be null.")
            End If

            Dim bpassword() As Byte = Encoding.UTF8.GetBytes(password)
            Dim hashedPassword() As Byte = hashFunction.ComputeHash(bpassword)

            'Transform the byte array back into hex characters
            Dim s As New StringBuilder(hashedPassword.Length * 2)
            For Each b As Byte In hashedPassword
                s.Append(b.ToString("X2"))
            Next b
            Return s.ToString()
        End Function
      End Class
End Namespace
```

The main entry point performs a few validations, the important one being the confirmation of the hash algorithm. You can indicate the hash algorithm using any of the string representations defined in the documentation for the HashAlgorithm.Create method. As you would expect, you can use strings such as SHA1, SHA256, and SHA512. After the hash algorithm has been validated and created using the HashAlgorithm.Create method, the actual work is performed by the private HashThePassword method.

The password is converted to a byte representation because the hash algorithms operate off of byte arrays rather than strings. Calling ComputeHash on the hash object results in the new hashed value. Because you are probably hashing these values with the intent of storing them somewhere and retrieving the values later, the hashed value is converted back into a string where two hex characters are used to represent each byte value.

I have included a few sample results from running this utility:

```
C:\inetpub\wwwroot\379301_code\379301 ch06_code\cs\HashPassword\bin\Debug>Has
hPassword pass!word MD5
The hashed password is: 0033A636A8B61F9EE199AE8FA8185F2C

C:\inetpub\wwwroot\379301_code\379301 ch06_code\cs\HashPassword\bin\Debug>Has
hPassword pass!word SHA1
The hashed password is: 24151F57F8F9C408380A00CC4427EADD4DDEBFC6

C:\inetpub\wwwroot\379301_code\379301 ch06_code\cs\HashPassword\bin\Debug>Has
hPassword pass!word SHA256
The hashed password is: DE98DD461F166808461A3CA721C41200A7982B7EB12F32C57C62572C
6F2E5509

C:\inetpub\wwwroot\379301_code\379301 ch06_code\cs\HashPassword\bin\Debug>Has
hPassword pass!word SHA512
The hashed password is: E84C057E3B6271ACC5EF6A8A81C55F2AB8506B7F464929417387BDC6
03E49BC0278DFAF063066A98EE074B15A956624B840DADBA65EDCF896521167C5DDE61CE
```

As you would expect, the strong SHA variants result in substantially longer hash values. The simplicity of the sample code shows how easy it is to start using stronger hash algorithms in your code. Because the utility generates hashed values, you can validate user-entered passwords later with similar code; just convert a user-entered password into either the hex string representation or byte representation of the hash value, and compare it against the hash value that was previously generated with the sample code. Also note that the sample code uses *unkeyed* hash algorithms. As a result, you will get the same hash values for a given piece of input text regardless of the machine you use the utility on. This is because unkeyed hash algorithms apply the hash algorithm against the values you provide and do not inject any additional key material, as is done with an algorithm like HMACSHA1.

Encryption Options in ASP.NET 2.0 and 3.5

In ASP.NET 1.0 and 1.1, you could encrypt the forms authentication ticket with either DES or 3DES. Normally, most developers use 3DES because DES has already been cracked. 3DES, however, is considered to be an old encryption algorithm as of 2005. In 2001, the National Institute of Standards and Technology (NIST) published the details for a new common encryption standard called the Advanced Encryption Standard (AES). AES is the replacement for 3DES, and over time most application developers and companies will shift away from 3DES and start using AES.

ASP.NET 2.0 and ASP.NET 3.5 have support for AES so that developers can easily take advantage of the new encryption standard. AES has the benefit of supporting much longer keys than 3DES does. 3DES uses a 168-bit key (essentially three 56-bit keys), whereas AES supports key lengths of 128, 192, and 256 bits. To support the new encryption algorithm, ASP.NET 2.0 and ASP.NET 3.5 have a new configuration attribute in the <machineKey /> section:

```
<machineKey  …  decryption=[Auto|DES|3DES|AES] />
```

By default, the decryption attribute of <machineKey /> is set to Auto. In this case, ASP.NET 2.0 and ASP.NET 3.5 will look at the value in the decryptionKey attribute of <machineKey /> to determine the appropriate encryption algorithm. If a 16-character value is used for decryptionKey, ASP.NET 2.0

and ASP.NET 3.5 choose DES as the encryption algorithm (16 hex characters equate to an 8-byte value, which is the number of bytes needed for a DES key). If a longer string of characters is set in decryption Key, ASP.NET 2.0 and ASP.NET 3.5 choose AES.

> *In the .NET Framework, if you look for a class called "AES" or "Advanced Encryption Standard" you will not find one. Instead, there is a class in the* System.Security.Cryptography *namespace called* RijndaelManaged. *Because the AES encryption standard uses the Rijndael encryption algorithm, ASP.NET used the* RijndealManaged *class when you choose AES.*

If an application's decryptionKey attribute is at the default setting of Autogenerate, IsolateApps, ASP.NET will automatically use the randomly generated 24-byte (192-bit) value that was created for the current process or application identity. This also results in ASP.NET automatically selecting AES as the encryption option.

You can see from this the symmetry in byte sizes for keys between 3DES and AES. In 3DES, the three 56-bit keys need to be packaged into three 64-bit values (8 bits in each value are unused as key material by 3DES), which works out to a 192-bit value. The same auto-generated key can be used with AES because AES supports 192-bit key lengths as well.

If you choose to explicitly specify a value for decryptionKey (and I would highly recommend this because explicit keys are consistent values that you can depend on), you should ensure that the text value you enter in the <machineKey /> section is one of those shown in the following table.

Desired AES Key Length in Bits	Number of Hex Characters Required for decryptionKey
128	32
192	48
256	64

If you are working on anything other than a hobby or personal website, always do the following with <machineKey />:

1. Explicitly set the decryptionKey and validationKey attributes. Avoid using the auto-generated options.

2. Explicitly set the new decryption attribute to the desired encryption algorithm. Choose either 3DES for backward compatibility (more on this later) or AES.

3. Explicitly set the validation attribute. Choose SHA1, 3DES, or AES (remember that this setting is overloaded for viewstate encryption handling, hence the oddity of 3DES or AES specified for a validation algorithm). MD5 is not recommended because it isn't as strong as SHA1. And of course, just to add to the confusion, choosing SHA1 here really means that forms authentication uses the keyed version: HMACSHA1.

Depending on the auto-generated keys is fraught with peril. For a personal site or a hobbyist site that lives on a single machine, the auto-generated keys are convenient and easy to use. However, any website that needs to run on more than two machines has to use explicit keys because auto-generated keys, by definition, vary from machine to machine.

There is another subtle reason why you should avoid auto-generated keys. Each time you run `aspnet_regiis` with the `ga` option for different user accounts, the next time ASP.NET starts up in a worker process that uses these new credentials, a new set of auto-generated keys is generated! This means if you persistently store any encrypted information (maybe persisted forms authentication tickets, for example) that depends on stable values for the key material, you are only one command-line invocation of `aspnet_regiis` away from accidentally changing the key material. Also, when you upgrade an ASP.NET 1.1 site to ASP.NET 3.5, the auto-generated keys have all been regenerated with new values. I cover the implications of this in the section about upgrade implications from ASP.NET 1.1 to 3.5.

Generating Keys Programmatically

Encouraging developers to use explicit keys is not very useful if there is not a way to generate the necessary keys in the first place. Following is a simple console application that outputs the hex representation of a cryptographically strong random key given the number of desired hex characters. If you create similar code on your machine, make sure that the project includes `System.Security` in the project references.

C#

```
using System;
using System.Security.Cryptography;
using System.Collections.Generic;
using System.Text;

namespace GenKeys
{
 class Program
 {
    static void Main(string[] args)
    {
        if ((args.Length == 0) || (args.Length > 1))
        {
            Console.WriteLine("Usage:  genkeys numcharacters");
            return;
        }

        int numHexCharacters;
        if (!Int32.TryParse(args[0], out numHexCharacters))
        {
            Console.WriteLine("Usage:  genkeys numcharacters");
            return;
        }

        if ((numHexCharacters % 2) != 0)
        {
            Console.WriteLine("The number of characters must be a multiple of 2.");
            return;
        }
        //Two hex characters are needed to represent one byte
        byte[] keyValue = new byte[numHexCharacters / 2];

        //Use the crypto support in the framework to generate the random value
        RNGCryptoServiceProvider r = new RNGCryptoServiceProvider();
        r.GetNonZeroBytes(keyValue);
```

```
        //Transform the random byte values back into hex characters
        StringBuilder s = new StringBuilder(numHexCharacters);
        foreach (byte b in keyValue)
            s.Append(b.ToString("X2"));
        Console.WriteLine("Key value: " + s.ToString());
    }
  }
}
```

VB.NET

```
Imports Microsoft.VisualBasic
Imports System
Imports System.Collections.Generic
Imports System.Linq
Imports System.Text
Imports System.Web
Imports System.Security.Authentication
Imports System.Security.Cryptography

Namespace GenKeys
  Friend Class Program
        Shared Sub Main(ByVal args() As String)
            If (args.Length = 0) OrElse (args.Length > 1) Then
                Console.WriteLine("Usage:  genkeys numcharacters")
                Return
            End If

            Dim numHexCharacters As Integer
            If (Not Int32.TryParse(args(0), numHexCharacters)) Then
                Console.WriteLine("Usage:  genkeys numcharacters")
                Return
            End If

            If (numHexCharacters Mod 2) <> 0 Then
        Console.WriteLine("The number of characters must be a multiple of 2.")
                Return
            End If
            'Two hex characters are needed to represent one byte
            Dim keyValue(numHexCharacters \ 2 - 1) As Byte

        'Use the crypto support in the framework to generate the random value
            Dim r As New RNGCryptoServiceProvider()
            r.GetNonZeroBytes(keyValue)

            'Transform the random byte values back into hex characters
            Dim s As New StringBuilder(numHexCharacters)
            For Each b As Byte In keyValue
                s.Append(b.ToString("X2"))
            Next b
            Console.WriteLine("Key value: " & s.ToString())
        End Sub
  End Class
End Namespace
```

After some basic validations, the program determines the number of bytes needed based on the requested number of hexadecimal characters: because it takes two hex characters to represent a single byte value, you simply divide the command line parameter by two. To create the actual random value, call the `RNGCryptoServiceProvider` class in the `System.Security.Cryptography` namespace. In this example, I requested that the result not include any byte values of zero.

Converting the byte array back into a hex string is also pretty trivial. The code simply iterates through the byte array of random values, converting each byte into its string equivalent. The "X2" string format indicates that each byte value should be converted to hexadecimal format, and that an extra "0" charac- ter should be included where necessary to ensure that each byte is represented by exactly two charac- ters. If you do not do this, byte values from zero to fifteen require only a single hex character.

The following example of using the tool is generating a 64-character (256-bit) value suitable for use with the AES encryption option.

```
C:\inetpub\wwwroot\379301_code\379301 ch06_code\cs\\GenKeys\bin\Debug>genkeys
64
Key value: C5D08A900770821F2AC4CFA3727B28F68C8A8A1BC7A857BE6E588210051C0968
```

Setting Cookie-Specific Security Options

Most developers probably use forms authentication in cookie mode. In fact, unless you happened to use the Microsoft Mobile Internet Toolkit (MMIT) in ASP.NET 1.1, ASP.NET could not automatically issue and manage tickets in a cookieless format.

In ASP.NET 1.1 the `requireSSL` attribute on the `<forms />` element enabled developers to require SSL when handling forms authentication tickets carried in a cookie. The `slidingExpiration` attribute on `<forms />` allowed you to enforce whether forms authentication tickets would be automatically renewed as long as a website user stayed active on the site. In addition to these options, ASP.NET 2.0 and ASP.NET 3.5 include a security feature for the forms authentication ticket by always setting the `HttpOnly` property on the cookie to `true`.

requireSSL

The `HttpCookie` class has a property called `Secure`. When this property is set to `true`, it includes the string `secure` in the `Set-Cookie` command that is sent back to the browser. Browsers that recognize and honor this cookie setting send the cookie back to the web server only if the connection is secured with SSL. For any high-security site, the `requireSSL` attrbitue should always be set to `true` to maxi- mize the likelihood that the cookie is only communicated over a secure connection.

However, depending on client-side behavior is always problematic. The browser may not support secure cookies (unlikely but still possible with older browsers). Additionally, not every user on a web- site is a person sitting in a chair using a browser. You may have users that are really programs making HTTP calls to your site, in which case it is highly likely that such programs do not bother looking at or honoring any of the extended cookie settings like the `secure` attribute. In these cases, it becomes pos- sible for the forms authentication cookie to be sent back to the web server over an insecure connection.

The forms authentication feature protects against this by explicitly checking the state of the connection before it starts processing a forms authentication cookie. If the FormsAuthenticationModule receives a valid cookie (meaning, the cookie decrypts successfully, the signature is valid, and the cookie has not expired yet), the module ignores it and clears the cookie from the Request collection if the requireSSL attribute in the <forms /> configuration section was set to true and ASP.NET detects that the connection is not secure. From a user perspective, the cookie will not be used to create a FormsIdentity, and as a result no authenticated identity is set on the context's User property. As a result, the user will be redirected to the login page. Programmatically, the check is easy to do and looks similar to the following:

C#

```
if (FormsAuthentication.RequireSSL && (!Request.IsSecureConnection))
```

VB.NET

```
If FormsAuthentication.RequireSSL AndAlso ((Not Request.IsSecureConnection)) Then
```

Both the requireSSL setting and the secured state of the current HTTP connection are available from public APIs.

As a quick example, you can configure an application to use forms authentication but not require an SSL connection, as shown here:

```
<authentication mode="Forms">
    <forms requireSSL="false" />
</authentication>
```

Run the application and login so that a valid forms authentication ticket is issued. Then change the configuration for <forms /> to require SSL:

```
<forms requireSSL="true" />
```

Now when you refresh the page in your browser, you are redirected to the login page. If you attempt to log in again, the FormsAuthentication class will throw an HttpException when the code attempts to issue a ticket. For example, with code like the following:

C#

```
FormsAuthentication.RedirectFromLoginPage("testuser", false);
```

VB.NET

```
FormsAuthentication.RedirectFromLoginPage("testuser", False)
```

You encounter the HttpException if you attempt this when the connection is insecure. Although you would probably think this is unlikely to occur (if you set requireSSL to true in configuration, you probably have SSL on your site), it is possible to run into this behavior when testing or developing an application in an environment that does not have SSL. Because returning unhandled exceptions to the browser is a bad thing, you should defensively code for this scenario with something like the following:

C#

```
protected void  Button1_Click(object sender, EventArgs e)
{
    if (FormsAuthentication.RequireSSL && (!Request.IsSecureConnection))
    {
        lblErrorText.Text = "You can only login over an SSL connection.";
        txtPassword.Text = String.Empty;
        txtUsername.Text = String.Empty;
        return;
    }
    else
    {
        //Authenticate the credentials here and then …
        FormsAuthentication.RedirectFromLoginPage(txtUsername.Text, false);
    }
}
```

VB.NET

```
Protected Sub Button1_Click( _
    ByVal sender As Object, _
    ByVal e As EventArgs) Handles Button1.Click
        If FormsAuthentication.RequireSSL AndAlso _
        ((Not Request.IsSecureConnection)) Then
        lblErrorText.Text = "You can only login over an SSL connection."
        txtPassword.Text = String.Empty
        txtUsername.Text = String.Empty
        Return
    Else
        'Authenticate the credentials here
        FormsAuthentication.RedirectFromLoginPage(txtUsername.Text, False)
    End If
```

The check for the security setting and the current connection security duplicate the similar check that is made internally in a number of places in forms authentication. However, by explicitly checking for this, you avoid the problem of the forms authentication feature throwing any unexpected exceptions. It also gives you the chance to tell the browsers users to use an HTTPS connection to log in. This type of check should be used when calling any forms authentication APIs that may issue cookies such as RedirectFromLoginPage, and SetAuthCookie.

The requireSSL *attribute applies mainly to forms authentication tickets issued in cookies. If an application uses cookieless tickets, or if it has the potential to issue a mixture of cookie-based and cookie-less tickets, it is possible to send cookieless tickets over a non-SSL connection. Although ASP.NET still disallows you from issuing cookieless tickets over insecure connections, ASP.NET accepts and processes cookieless tickets received over non-SSL connections. Keep this behavior in mind if you set* requireSSL *to* true *and still support cookieless tickets.*

HttpOnly Cookies

HttpOnly cookies are a Microsoft-specific security extension for reducing the likelihood of obtaining cookies through client script. In ASP.NET, the System.Web.HttpCookie class adds the HttpOnly property. If you create a cookie and set this property to true, ASP.NET includes the HttpOnly string in the Set-Cookie header returned to the browser. This is a Microsoft-specific extension to the cookie header. I am only aware of it being supported on IE6 SP1 or higher, although there are discussions on the Internet about building in support for it on other browsers, and most recently Firefox 2.0.0.5 has added the HttpOnly checking. Most other browsers just ignore the HttpOnly option in the cookie header, so setting HttpOnly for a cookie is usually innocuous. In some cases, however, browsers will drop a cookie with the HttpOnly option (for example, Internet Explorer 5). ASP.NET's cookie writing logic will not emit the HttpOnly option for these cases.

Technically, the way HttpOnly cookies work is that if a piece of client-side script attempts to retrieve the cookie, Internet Explorer honors the HttpOnly setting and will not return a cookie object. ASP.NET 3.5 enforces HttpOnly cookies all the time for forms authentication, as was the case in ASP.NET 2.0. This means that all forms authentication tickets contained in cookies issued by the FormsAuthentication API (for example, RedirectFromLoginPage and SetAuthCookie) will *always* have the HttpOnly setting appended to them.

There was a fair amount of discussion about this internally because the change has the potential to be a pain for some customers. However, given the fact that many developers are not aware of the HttpOnly option (its original introduction was buried somewhere in IE6 SP1) having a configuration option to change this behavior did not seem like a great idea. If few people know about a certain capability, adding a configuration option to turn the capability on doesn't really do anything to get the word out about it.

Of course, ASP.NET 2.0 and ASP.NET 3.5 could still have added support for HttpOnly cookies by defaulting to turning the behavior on and then exposing a configuration setting to turn it back off again. The counterpoint to this option is that doing so gives developers a really easy way to open themselves up to cross-site scripting attacks that harvest and hijack client-side cookies. The reality is that if developers need a way to grab the forms authentication cookie client-side, the forms authentication APIs can still be pretty easily used to manually create the necessary cookie, but without the HttpOnly option turned on.

Lest folks think that the pain around the decision to enforce HttpOnly for forms authentication tickets is limited to the developer community at large, the ASP.NET team has actually pushed back a number of times when internal groups asked for HttpOnly to be turned off. Repeatedly, the ASP.NET team has seen that architectures that depend on retrieving the forms authentication ticket client-side are flawed from a security perspective. If you really need the forms authentication ticket to be available from a client application, using the browser's cookie cache as a surrogate storage mechanism is a bad idea. In fact, scenarios that require passing a forms authentication ticket around on the client-side frequently also depend on the need for persistent tickets (if the ticket were session-based, there would be no guarantee that the cookie would still be around for some other client application). So, now you start going down the road of persistent cookies that are retrievable with a few lines of basic JavaScript, which is not a big deal for low-security sites, but definitely something to avoid in any site that cares about security.

To see how the behavior affects forms authentication in ASP.NET 3.5, you can write client-side JavaScript like the sample shown here.

```
<html>
 <head><title>You were logged in!</title></head>
<body>
<script language=javascript>
function ShowAllCookies()
{
    var c = document.cookie;
    alert(c);
}
</script>

  <form id="form1" >
    <input type=button onclick="ShowAllCookies();" value="Click to see cookies." />
  </form>
</body>
</html>
```

If you run this code on an ASP.NET 1.1 site that requires forms authentication, you get a dialog box that conveniently displays your credentials such as the one shown in Figure 6-1:

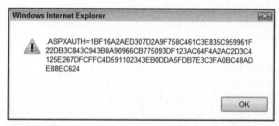

Figure 6-1

If you run, same client-side script in an ASP.NET 3.5 application after logging in, you will not get anything back. Figure 6-2 shows the results on ASP.NET 3.5, which resembles that of ASP.NET 2.0.

Figure 6-2

As mentioned earlier, if you really need client-side access to the forms authentication cookie, you need to manually issue the cookie and to manage reissuance of the authentication cookie in case you want to support sliding expirations. (With sliding expirations, FormsAuthenticationModule may reissue the cookie on your behalf.)

Although `HttpOnly` cookies make it much harder to obtain cookies through a client-side attack, it is still possible to trick a web server into sending back a page (including cookies) in a way that bypasses the protections within Internet Explorer. There are a number of discussions on the Internet about using the `TRACE/TRACK` command to carry out what is called a cross-site tracing attack. In essence, these commands tell a web server to send a dump of a web request back to the browser, and with sufficient client-side code, you can parse this information and extract the forms authentication cookie. Luckily, this loophole can be closed by explicitly disabling the `TRACE/TRACK` command on your web servers and/or firewalls.

slidingExpiration

You may not think of the sliding expiration feature as much of a security feature, but this setting does have a large effect on the length of time that a forms authentication cookie is considered valid. By default, in ASP.NET 2.0 and ASP.NET 3.5 sliding expiration is enabled (the `slidingExpiration` attribute is set to `true` in `<forms />`). As long a website user sends a valid forms authentication cookie back to the web server before the ticket expires (30-minute expiration by default), the `FormsAuthenticationModule` periodically refreshes the expiration date of the cookie. The `FormsAuthentication.RenewTicket IfOld` method is used to create an updated ticket if more than 50 percent of the ticket's lifetime has elapsed.

The security issue is that with sliding expirations a website user could potentially remain logged on to a site forever. Even with the 30 minute default, as long as something or someone sends a valid ticket back to the server every 29 minutes and 59 seconds, the ticket will continue to be valid. On private computers or computers that are not in public areas, this really is not an issue. However, for computers in public areas like kiosks or public libraries, if a user logs into a site and does not logout, the potential exists for anyone to come along and reuse the original login session.

You can't control the behavior of your customers. (Even with a logout button on a website, only a small percentage of users actually use it.) You do, however, have the option to disable sliding expirations. When `slidingExpiration` is set to `false`, regardless of how active a user is on the website, when the expiration interval passes, the forms authentication ticket is considered invalid and the website user is forced to log in again. Of course, this leads to the problem of determining an appropriate value for the `timeout` attribute. Setting this to an excessively low interval annoys users, whereas setting it to a long interval leaves a larger window of opportunity for someone's forms authentication ticket to be reused.

Using Cookieless Forms Authentication

ASP.NET 2.0 and ASP.NET 3.5 automatically support issuing and managing forms authentication tickets in a cookieless manner. The process starts by ASP.NET inspecting the request URL, looking for any cookieless tickets. In ASP.NET 2.0 and 3.5, cookieless tickets are supported for session state (this was also available in 1.1), forms authentication (previously available as part of the mobile support in ASP.NET), and anonymous identification (introduced since ASP.NET 2.0). A sample URL with a cookieless session state ticket is shown here:

```
http://localhost/inproc/(S(tuucni55xfzj2qxlmnqdg55))/Default.aspx
```

ASP.NET reserves the path segment immediately after the application's virtual root as the location on the URL where cookieless tickets are stored. In this example, the application was called `inproc`, so the next path segment is where ASP.NET stored the cookieless tickets. All cookieless tickets are stored within an outer pair of parentheses. Within these, there can be a number of cookieless tickets, each starting with a single letter indicating the feature that consumes the ticket, followed by a pair of parentheses that contain the cookieless ticket. Currently, the following three identifiers are used:

❑ **S:** Cookieless ticket for session state

❑ **A:** Cookieless ticket for anonymous identification

❑ **F:** Cookieless ticket for forms authentication

At some stage during the request life cycle, ASP.NET removes the cookieless tickets from the URL and inserts a new custom HTTP header to the current HTTP request called `ASPFILTERSESSIONID` that contains all the cookieless tickets that were already found in the current HTTP request. ASP.NET 2.0 and ASP.NET 3.5 base themselves on the above mechanism to support cookieless representations of forms authentication tickets, as well as anonymous identifiers (this second piece of information is only used with the Profile feature). You can enable cookieless forms authentication simply by setting the new `cookieless` attribute to in the `<forms />` configuration section:

```
- AG<forms … cookieless="UseUri" />
```

The following table lists the options for the `cookieless` attribute.

Cookieless Attribute Value	Descrption
UseUri	Always issues the forms authentication ticket so that it shows up as part of the URL. Cookies are never issued.
UseCookies	Always issues the forms authentication ticket in a cookie.
AutoDetect	Detects whether the browser supports cookies through various heuristics. If the browser does not appear to support cookies, issues the ticket on the URL instead.
UseDeviceProfile	Finds a device profile for the current browser agent, and based upon the information in the profile, uses cookies if the profile indicates they are supported. This is the default setting in ASP.NET 2.0 and ASP.NET 3.5. Information for the device profiles is stored in the Browsers subdirectory of the framework's CONFIG directory. ASP.NET ships with a set of browser information, including cookie support, for widely used browsers. You can edit the files in this directory, or add additional setting files, and then make the changes take effect with the aspnet_regbrowsers.exe tool.

The default setting for the `cookieless` attribute is `UseDeviceProfile`. This means that your site will issue a mixture of cookie-based and URL-based forms authentication tickets, depending on the type of browser agent accessing your website. If you do not want to deal with some of the edge cases that occur when using cookieless tickets, you should set the `cookieless` attribute to `UseCookies`.

The nice thing about cookieless support in ASP.NET 2.0 and ASP.NET 3.5 is that other than changing a single configuration attribute, forms authentication continues to work. As a very basic example, issuing a cookieless forms authentication ticket on a login page with the familiar `FormsAuthentication` `.RedirectFromLoginPage` method results in a URL that looks something like the following (the URL is wrapped because the cookieless representation bloats the URL size):

```
http://localhost/cookieless/(F(DJflxUBV0oD-JNW_FmuLwsvIEzBTYRk19QYcPG7gT9-
5lkplFeRFwI-KxSdBIjDpzvSYGi5VQ8GY1PA2h9m6l4LwPa60gQ91nYGly9Bo79c1))/Default.aspx
```

The bold portion of the URL is, of course, the forms authentication ticket. As mentioned above, ASP.NET takes care of removing the cookieless tickets from the URL and stores them into a custom HTTP header so that the ASP.NET engine can later on make use of the these tickets. Internally, cookieless features such as forms authentication rely on internal helper classes to move data from the custom HTTP header into feature specific classes, such as `FormsAuthenticationTicket`. If you dump the HTTP headers for the page in the previous URL, you will see the end result of the work performed by the ASP.NET runtime:

```
HTTP_ASPFILTERSESSIONID=F(DJflxUBV0oD-JNW_FmuLwsvIEzBTYRk19QYcPG7gT9-5lkplFeRFwI-Kx
SdBIjDpzvSYGi5VQ8GY1PA2h9m6l4LwPa60gQ91nYGly9Bo79c1)
```

Unfortunately, in ASP.NET 2.0 and ASP.NET 3.5, the general-purpose class used internally for parsing the cookieless headers is not available as a public API. So, unlike the `HttpCookie` class, which gives developers the flexibility to create their own custom cookie-based mechanisms, cookieless data in ASP.NET 2.0 and ASP.NET 3.5 is supported only for the few features like forms authentication that have baked the support into their APIs.

Cookieless Options

You have seen the various cookie options that you can set on the `cookieless` attributes. Of the four options, `UseCookies` and `UseUri` are self-explanatory. However, I want to drill in a bit more on the other two options: `AutoDetect` and `UseDeviceProfile`.

AutoDetect

The `AutoDetect` option comes into play when forms authentication needs to determine whether a forms authentication ticket should be placed on the URL. ASP.NET 2.0 and ASP.NET 3.5 will go through several checks to see whether the browser supports cookies. Although going through this evaluation means that the initial ticket issuance takes a little longer, it does mean that for each and every new user on your website, you have a very high likelihood of being able to issue the forms authentication ticket in a way that can be received by the user's browser. If new browsers are introduced, and the device profile information is not available yet on your server (an extremely common case in the mobile world where there seems to be a new device/browser/etc. every day), the `AutoDetect` option is very handy.

When a browser first accesses a site, it is requesting one of three possible types of pages:

❑   Pages that allow anonymous users and, thus, do not require authentication.

❑   The forms authentication login page for the site.

❑   A secured page that requires some type of authenticated user. In this case, authorization will eventually fail and force a redirect back to the login page.

Phase 1 of Auto-Detection

In the first case, forms authentication lies dormant and the auto-detect setting has no effect. After a browser accesses the types of pages indicated by the second and third bullet points, the `Forms AuthenticationModule` starts the process to detect whether or not the browser supports cookies. Depending on whether the browser is accessing the login page or a secured page, the internal path leading to auto-detection is a bit different. However, from a functionality perspective, the browser experiences the same behavior.

The detection process goes through the following steps in sequence:

1. A check is made using the browser capabilities object available from `Request.Browser`. The information returned by this object is based on an extensive set of browser profiles stored on disk in the Browsers directory. If the browser capabilities definitively indicate that cookies are not supported, there is no additional detection needed. Short-circuiting the auto-detection process at this point saves time and unnecessary redirects. For classes of devices that simply do not support cookies, there isn't any point in probing further in an attempt to send cookies.

2. If the browser capabilities for the current request indicate that cookies are supported, then a check is made to see if auto-detection occurred previously. If a previous browse path through the site already occurred, and if the results of that browsing indicated that cookies weren't supported, the URL will already contain extra information indicating that this check occurred. Normally though, a user browses to the login page or a secured page for the first time, and thus auto-detection will not already have occurred.

3. A check is made to see if cookies have been sent with the request. For example, your site may have already issued some other kind of cookies previously when the user was browsing around. In this case, the mere presence of cookies sent back to the server is an indication that cookies are supported.

4. If all of the previous checks fail, ASP.NET adds some information to the current response. It adds a cookie to `Response.Cookies` called "AspxAutoDetectCookieSupport." It also appends a query-string name-value pair to the current request path; the query-string variable is also called "AspxAutoDetectCookieSupport." Because it is the only way to get this query-string variable onto the path in a way that the browser can replay it, a redirect to the currently requested page is then issued.

The net result of this initial detection process is that for the nominal case of a browser first accessing the login page, or a secured page, a redirect to the login page always occurs. In the case that the user was attempting to directly access a secured page, the extra query-string and cookie information is just piggybacked onto the redirect that normally occurs anyway. On the other hand, if the user navigated to the login page directly, then ASP.NET forces a redirect back to the login page in order to set the query-string variable. In the browser's address bar, the result looks something like the following:

```
http://bhaidar-pc/cookieless/login.aspx?AspxAutoDetectCookieSupport=1
```

At this point if the browser supports cookies, there is also a session cookie held in the browser's cookie cache called "AspxAutoDetectCookieSupport." So, there is potentially both a query-string variable and a cookie value client-side in the browser waiting to be sent back to the web server. Of course, on browsers that don't support cookies, only they query-string variable will exist.

Phase 2 of Auto-Detection

After the user types in credentials and submits that login page back to the server, the auto-detect steps listed earlier are evaluated again because the FormsAuthenticationModule always triggers these steps for the login page. However, because the auto-detection process already started, one of two decisions is made:

❑ If the browsers supports cookies, the auto-detect cookie will exist and the forms authentication feature will determine that cookies are supported.

❑ If the auto-detect cookie was not sent back by the browser, a check is made for the auto-detect query-string variable. Because this query-string variable now exists, ASP.NET will add a cookieless value to the URL that indicates the browser does not support cookies. A value of "X(1)" is inserted into the URL and will exist in all subsequent requests that the browser makes to the site for the duration of the browser session.

Phase 3 of Auto Detection

The code in the login page needs to process the credentials that were posted back to it at this point. If the credentials are invalid, then the browser remains on the login page, and Phase 2 will repeat itself when the user attempts another login. If the credentials are valid, though, then usually either Forms Authentication.RedirectFromLoginPage or FormsAuthentication.SetAuthCookie is called to create the forms authentication ticket and package it up to send back to the client.

In the case that the browser supports cookies, the ticket is simply packaged into a cookie and added to the Response.Cookies collection. However, if the auto-detect process determined that cookies are not supported then both of these methods will package the hex string representation of the forms authentication ticket into the URL. The general form of the cookieless ticket in the URL is F(ticket value here).

The sample address bar below shows the results of a successful login on a site that uses auto-detection. Note how both the "X" and the "F" identifiers exist in the URL: one indicating the cookies are not supported and the other containing the cookieless ticket. To make it bit easier to see everything, the X and F identifiers are bolded.

```
http://bhaidar-pc/cookieless/(X(1)F(eKZT5gWUi7Le_4tXEei9Lgu2l1crhX23Kq-zdV6P8D8ActC
VtgVWOsLMlvGiwEynmTbYLCzVWnj0n5MJtidRjf9kij0gkv-DL-1MxzqnlRU1))/Default.aspx
```

Subsequent Authenticated Access

After logging in, there really aren't additional phases to the initial auto-detection process. Auto-detection has occurred, and the results of the process are now indelibly stamped into the URL and maintained on each and every request. ASP.NET automatically takes care of hoisting the embedded URL values into the custom header using ASP.NET runtime, and various downstream components like forms authentication contain the necessary logic to check for cookieless artifacts (such as the X identifier and the F ticket in the URL).

How to Simulate This in Internet Explorer

It can be a bit of a pain to actually get auto-detection to slip into cookieless mode using a browser like Internet Explorer. By default, IE of course supports cookies, so setting "AutoDetect" in config will only show you the parts of the first two phases of auto-detection before defaulting to using cookies.

However, with a bit of rooting around inside of IE, you can force it to reject or prompt for cookies—at which point you have a way to simulate a cookieless browser.

First, go to Tools ➪ Internet Options and click the Privacy tab. Clicking the Advanced button pops up another dialog box, as shown in Figure 6-3. In my case, I set the options for cookies to Prompt, though if you don't want the hassle of always rejecting cookies you can just set the options to Block.

Figure 6-3

Now you can navigate to your website to test it in cookieless mode. However, you must request your pages using the machine name of your web server. Looking at the last few URL samples, notice how the URL starts with a machine name (http://bhaidar-PC) as opposed to the usual http://localhost. If you use http://localhost, the cookie options you set on the Privacy tab are ignored.

UseDeviceProfile

Device profiles are another mechanism for determining browser cookie support. Although an exhaustive description of devices profiles is outside the scope of this book (the current browser profiles include reams of information that mobile developers care about but that aren't terribly relevant to security or forms authentication), it is still important to understand where the profiles are located and, in general, how profile information affects detection of cookie support.

UseDeviceProfile is the default setting of the cookieless attribute in forms authentication. This means that whenever the forms authentication feature needs to determine whether a browser supports cookies, it looks only at the values of Request.Browser.Cookies and Request.Browser.Supports RedirectWithCookie. If both those values return true, then forms authentication issues tickets in a cookie; otherwise, it uses the F() identifier in the URL.

The information in the Browser property, which is an instance of System.Web.HttpBrowser Capabilities, comes from browser information files located at:

```
%windir%\Microsoft.NET\Framework\v2.0.50727\CONFIG\Browsers
```

ASP.NET 3.5 Uses the .NET Framework 2.0 Installation Folder

You should have noticed the Windows path that points to the Browsers folder inside the .NET Framework 2.0 installation folder. In fact, ASP.NET 3.5, in its core, depends on ASP.NET 2.0 and adds only a few new features.

This is also shown when you configure a web application in IIS 7.0 and notice that its application pool points to the .NET 2.0 Framework and not .NET 3.5 Framework; hence, ASP.NET 3.5 uses the same engine as ASP.NET 2.0 and adds some new features.

Note that the actual version number for the framework may be slightly different at release. This directory contains two dozen different files, all ending in .browser. ASP.NET internally parses the information in the .browser files, and based on the regular expression-based matching rules defined in these files, determines which .browser file applies based on the user agent string for a specific request.

For example, when running Internet Explorer on my machine, the user agent string that IE sends down to the web server looks like this:

```
Mozilla/4.0 (compatible; MSIE 7.0; Windows NT 6.0; SLCC1; .NET CLR 2.0.50727; Media
Center PC 5.0; .NET CLR 3.0.04506; .NET CLR 3.5.21022) HTTP_UA_CPU:x86
```

If you look in the Browsers subdirectory, and open up the file ie.browser, you will see that the browser capabilities files define a regular expression matching rule like the following:

```
<userAgent match="^Mozilla[^(]*\([C|c]ompatible;\s*MSIE (?'version'(?'major'\d+)
(?'minor'\.\d+)(?'letters'\w*))(?'extra'[^)]*)" />
```

Just from glancing at the regular expression syntax you can see how a match occurs, anchored around the Mozilla and MSIE identifiers in the user agent string. When ASP.NET evaluates this regular expression at runtime, and finds a match, it consults the other information in the ie.browser file and uses it for the information returned in Request.Browser. For example, if you were to query Request .Browser.TagWriter, you would get back the string System.Web.UI.HtmlTextWriter. I use the TagWriter property as an example because without the browser capabilities files, there is no way ASP.NET could possibly come up with a .NET Framework class name just from the information sent in the HTTP request headers.

If you open up ie.browser in Notepad, and scroll down a bit to the <capabilities> section, you see a number of individual <capability> elements. The one of interest to forms authentication is:

```
<capability name="cookies" value="true" />
```

Because this capability is set to true, in the default out-of-box ASP.NET configuration, forms authentication will always assume that IE browsers support cookies. You can verify this behavior by doing the following:

1. Change the value in the capability to false and save the .browser file.
2. Recompile the browser capabilities assembly. You can do this by running the command aspnet_regbrowsers -I from the framework install directory. This has the effect of reparsing all of the .browser files and then encapsulating their settings inside of a GAC'd assembly. Note that if you fail to do this the changes made in step 1 will not have any effect.

3. Within Internet Explorer, make sure you carried out the steps described earlier in the "How To Simulate This" section.

4. Set the cookieless attribute in web.config to UseDeviceProfile.

Now if you request an authenticated page in the browser, forms authentication will use the device profile information, and thus automatically assume that the browser doesn't support cookies. No auto-detection mechanism is necessary. When you log in, forms authentication will place the forms authentication ticket in the URL inside of the `F()` characters. Unlike the auto-detect case, though, there will be no `X(1)` in the URL, because the device profile deterministically indicates that the browser does not support cookies.

Although editing the IE device profile is a bit contrived, device profiles provide a fixed way for determining cookie support in a browser. The downside of `UseDeviceProfile` is that it can't accommodate new browser types that have totally new user agent strings (for example, if I created a new browser that sent back a user agent string `My New Browser`, this isn't going to match any of the predefined regular expressions defined in the various browser capabilities files). In this case, ASP.NET will simply fall back to the settings in the `Default.browser` file, which may or may not contain correct information.

As a side note, `Default.browser` indicates that cookies are supported, so any user agent that is not recognized by the myriad `.browser` files shipping in ASP.NET 2.0, which are also shared with ASP.NET 3.5, will automatically be considered to support cookies.

Another limitation of `UseDeviceProfile` is that device profiles don't honor the intent of the browser user. A website user may intentionally disable cookies in any of the major desktop browsers. However, with `UseDeviceProfile` the user can never log in to your site because ASP.NET will always assume that cookies are supported. Each time the user attempts to log in, ASP.NET will send the forms authentication cookie back, and of course the browser will promptly reject it. Then when the browser redirects to a secured page, the lack of the cookie will simply dump the browser right back to the login page.

Although you definitely have the option of telling website customers up front that cookies are required to log in, you also have the option of switching to AutoDetect instead. If you have a sizable percentage of customers that do not want to use cookies (or perhaps you have regulations that mandate support for cookieless clients), then the AutoDetect option may be a better choice than `UseDeviceProfile`. However, make sure to read the topic about security implications of cookieless tickets below so that you understand the ramifications of placing the authentication ticket in the URL.

Replay Attacks with Cookieless Tickets

Although both cookie-based and cookieless forms authentication tickets are susceptible to replay attacks, the ease with which a cookieless ticket can be disseminated makes it especially vulnerable. As an example of how easy it is to reuse a cookieless ticket, try the following sequence of steps on an ASP.NET site that is configured to run in cookieless mode.

1. Log in with valid credentials and confirm that the cookieless ticket shows up in the address bar of the browser.

2. Copy and paste the contents of the address bar into some other location like notepad.

3. Shut down the browser.

At this point, you have your very own forms authentication ticket sitting around and available for replay for as long as the expiration date inside of the authentication ticket remains valid. If you paste the URL back into a new instance of your browser, you will successfully navigate to the page indicated in the URL. If you know the names of other pages in the site, you can edit the pasted URL; the important and interesting piece of the URL is the forms authentication ticket embedded within it.

Probably the most likely potential for security mischief with cookieless tickets in this case is not a malicious user or hacker. Rather, website users that don't understand the ramifications of having the forms authentication ticket in the URL are the most likely candidates for accidentally inflicting a replay attack on themselves. Imagine the following scenario:

1. A website customer visits an e-commerce site that issues cookieless authentication tickets. The customer adds some items to a shopping cart and then logs in to start the checkout process.

2. At some part into the checkout process, the customer has a question—maybe about price. So, the customer copies the URL into an email message. Or for a nontechnical user, just selects File ⇨ Send ⇨ Link by Email. Now the customer has a URL with a valid forms authentication ticket sitting in an email message.

3. When the recipient receives the message, the recipient clicks the URL in the email (or the URL may be packaged as a clickable URL attachment), and surprise! The recipient just "logged in" to the e-commerce site as the original user.

Given the default of sliding expirations in ASP.NET 2.0 and ASP.NET 3.5 forms authentication, after a cookieless ticket makes it outside of the boundaries of the browser session where the ticket was originally issued, it can be reused as long someone uses the ticket before the expiration period is exhausted.

This scenario gives rise to a very specific piece of security guidance when using cookieless forms authentication:

> *Never use sliding expirations when there is any chance of issuing cookieless tickets!*

I understand many of the arguments that can be made against this advice—chiefly that authentication tickets with absolute timeouts lead to a poor customer experience. However, I guarantee that if website customers accidentally email their forms authentication ticket, their ire over exposing their personal account will vastly exceed the pain of customers having to periodically log back in again. And don't forget that after someone accidentally leaks his or her forms authentication ticket in an email, every server and network route along the delivery path has the potential of sniffing and stealing a perfectly valid cookieless ticket.

Although the scenario I described earlier involves a customer sending a link to a secured page in a site, the reality is that after the forms authentication ticket is embedded on the URL, it remains there for the duration of the browser session. This means that if a customer logs in to start a checkout process but then clicks back to a publicly available page (maybe the customer clicks back out to an items detail page in a web catalog), the forms authentication ticket is still in the URL. I will grant you that sending an email link from deep inside a checkout process is probably unlikely. However, accidentally emailing the forms authentication credentials from a catalog page in an e-commerce site strikes me as a very likely occurrence.

This leads to a few additional pieces of advice about cookieless tickets:

1. Do not use cookieless tickets for any type of high-security site. For example, do not use cookieless tickets for an online banking or investment site. The risk of someone accidentally compromising themselves far outweighs the convenience factor.

2. If you set the requireSSL attribute on your site to true, ask yourself why you are allowing cookieless tickets. The requireSSL attribute doesn't protect cookieless tickets; it works only for cookie-based tickets. Although it is reasonable to set requireSSL to true on sites that support mixed clients (the theory being that at least the browsers that do support cookies will have a more secure experience), be aware that for cookieless users the forms authentication ticket can be issued and received over non-SSL connections.

3. Try to set the timeout attribute on sites that support cookieless clients to as small a value as possible. I would not recommend setting a timeout greater than 60 minutes, although it is understandable if you can't get much shorter than 45 minutes given the usage trends on e-commerce sites.

4. If you think your cookieless customer base will accept it, you should reauthenticate the customers prior to carrying out any sensitive transaction. This would mean requiring cookieless customers to reenter their username and password when they attempted to finalize a purchase or when they attempt to retrieve or update credit card information.

The Cookieless Ticket and Other URLs in Pages

Throughout the discussion, it has been stated that ASP.NET automatically handles maintaining the cookieless ticket in the URL. Although this is true for server-side code, the placement of the cookieless ticket in the URL also depends on browser behavior with relative URLs. If you look carefully at the sample URLs shown earlier, you can see that the URL consists of a few pieces. For a page like default.aspx, the browser considers the current path to the application to be:

```
http://bhaidar-pc/cookieless/(X(1)F(eKZT5gWUi7Le_4tXEei9Lgu2l1crhX23Kq-zdV6P8D8ActC
VtgVWOsLMlvGiwEynmTbYLCzVWnj0n5MJtidRjf9kij0gkv-DL-1MxzqnlRU1))
```

This means that the browser sees the cookieless information as part of the directory structure for the site. If you embed relative URLs into your page such as:

```
<a href=SomeOtherPage.aspx>Click me. I'm a regular A tag.</a>
```

Then whenever you click these types of links, the browser will prepend it with the current path information from the current page. So, this <a /> tag is interpreted by the browser as:

```
http://bhaidar-pc/cookieless/(X(1)F(eKZT5gWUi7Le_4tXEei9Lgu2l1crhX23Kq-zdV6P8D8ActC
VtgVWOsLMlvGiwEynmTbYLCzVWnj0n5MJtidRjf9kij0gkv-DL-1MxzqnlRU1))/SomeOtherPage.aspx
```

On the other hand, if you embed absolute hrefs in your pages, you will lose the forms authentication ticket when someone clicks on the link. For example, if you accidentally created the <a/> tag as:

```
<a href="/SomeOtherPage.aspx">Click me. I'm a regular A tag.</a>
```

The address that your browser will navigate to is:

```
http://bhaidar-pc/SomeOtherPage.aspx
```

With this style of URL, you can see that the forms authentication ticket is lost. Now, for a simple application, you may not need to use absolute URLs. However, if you have a more complex navigation structure, perhaps with a common menu or navigation bar on your pages, you may very well have a set of fixed URLs that users can click. Unfortunately, cookieless forms authentication and absolute URLs do not mix, so you will need to write extra code to account for this behavior. Although a bit kludgy, an easy way to maintain a common set of URL endpoints like this is with a redirection page.

Instead of the browser "knowing" the correct endpoint URL it should navigate to, you can convert these types of links into GET requests against a common redirection page. For example, you can use the LinkButton control to postback to ASP.NET:

```
<asp:LinkButton ID="linkRedirectMe" runat="server"
            OnClick="linkRedirectMe_Click">
        SomeOtherPage
</asp:LinkButton>
```

In the code-behind, the click event looks like:

```
Response.Redirect("/cookieless/SomeOtherPage.aspx");
```

Now when you click the link the browser, the page posts back to ASP.NET, and a server-side redirect is issued that retains in the all cookieless ticket information in the URL. The reason server-side redirects work is that Response.Redirect includes extra logic that ensures all of the information in the custom HTTP_ASPFILTERSESSIONID HTTP header is added back into the URL that is sent back to the browser. When the redirect reaches the browser, it has the full URL including the cookieless tickets.

One last area where URL format matters is in any postback event references in the page. In fact, the LinkButton example depended on the correct behavior when posting the page back to itself. Because just about every ASP.NET control depends on postbacks, it would be pretty painful if postbacks did not correctly retain all cookieless tickets. ASP.NET is able to retain the cookieless tickets by explicitly embedding them in the "action" tag of the page's <form /> element. Taking the previous LinkButton example, if you view the source of the page in the browser, the form element looks like:

```
<form method="post" action="/cookieless/(X(1)F(eKZT5gWUi7Le_4tXEei9Lgu2l1crhX23Kq-z
dV6P8D8ActCVtgVWOsLM1vGiwEynmTbYLCzVWnj0n5MJtidRjf9kij0gkv-DL-1MxzqnlRU1))/default.
aspx" id="form1">
```

Because much of the postback infrastructure depends on calling the JavaScript submit() method of a form, and the action attribute on the form includes the cookieless information, any attempt to programmatically submit a form (whether this is ASP.NET code or JavaScript code that you write) will include the cookieless information.

Overall, ASP.NET will, for the most part, correctly retain the cookieless tickets in a transparent manner. Only if you embed absolute URLs in your pages, or if you use absolute URLs in your code-behind, will you lose the cookieless tickets. You should try to use relative URLs in page markup, and application-relative URLs in code-behind and for attributes of ASP.NET server controls. Although there are cases in server-side code where you can write code with URLs that are absolute virtual paths (that is,

/myapproot/somepage.aspx), depending on whether you use this style of URL with Response .Redirect versus in a control property, you will get different behavior. Coding with application-relative URLs (that is, ~/somepage.aspx) gives you consistent behavior with cookieless tickets regardless of where you use the application-relative URL. The following table shows various pieces of code and whether or not cookieless tickets are preserved.

Code That Uses URLs	Are Tickets Retained?
Response.Redirect("~/SomeOtherPage.aspx");	Yes
Response.Redirect("SomeOtherPage.aspx");	Yes
Response.Redirect("/cookieless/SomeOtherPage.aspx");	Yes
Response.Redirect("http://bhaidar-PC/ cookieless/SomeOtherPage. aspx");	No
<asp:HyperLink ID="HyperLink1" runat="server" NavigateUrl="~/SomeOtherPage.aspx">	Yes
<asp:HyperLink ID="HyperLink2" runat="server" NavigateUrl="/ cookieless/SomeOtherPage.aspx">	No
<a href=SomeOtherPage.aspx>	Yes
<a href="/SomeOtherPage.aspx">	No

Payload Size with Cookieless Tickets

When you support cookieless tickets with forms authentication, you need to be careful of the size of the forms authentication ticket in the URL. Although forms authentication in cookie mode technically also has issues with the size of the ticket, you have roughly 4K of data that you can work with in cookie mode.

However, in cookieless mode, two factors work against you and limit the overall amount of data that you can place in a FormsAuthenticationTicket:

❑ There are other cookieless features in ASP.NET that also may place cookieless identifiers on the URL. Both session state and anonymous identification can take up space in the URL.

❑ On IIS 7, you cannot have more than 260 characters in any individual path segment (assuming you do not edit the <requestFiltering> configuration section in either the Application Host.config file or in the application's web.config file).

If you think about it, the 260-character constraint is actually pretty limiting and basically means that little more than username and expiration date can be effectively shipped around in a cookieless ticket. The previous sections on cookieless tickets regularly resulted in 100 or more characters being used on the URL for the ticket.

You can turn on anonymous identification and session state in `web.config`, and force them to run in cookieless mode with the following configuration settings, respectively (they use the same values for the `cookieless` attribute as forms authentication):

```
<anonymousIdentification enabled="true" cookieless="UseUri"/>
<sessionState cookieless="UseUri" />
```

Without even logging in to a sample application with these settings, the URL includes the following cookieless tickets (assume auto-detection is used for forms authentication for the absolute worst-case scenario).

```
(
   X(1)
A(ABa15sfNyAEkAAAAOTVkYmQ4MjYtZjM0Zi00NmYxLWE4MTMtYjNkOGMzMDA2N2ZiDvoszMRsIAPx3LnxE
4OL-yxa0Bg1)
S(vufwu245awzb32v21oyir245)
)
```

Adding this all up, and ignoring the line breaks because those exist just for formatting in the book, there are:

❏ 2 characters for the beginning and closing parentheses

❏ 4 characters for the auto-detection marker "X"

❏ 95 characters for the anonymous identification ticket "A"

❏ 27 characters for the session state identifier "S"

Without forms authentication even being involved, ASP.NET has already consumed 128 characters on the URL, which leaves a paltry 132 characters for forms authentication.

The most obvious piece of information that drives variability in the size of the forms authentication ticket is the username. You may not realize it, but the value of the `path` configuration attribute could also contribute to the variable size of the ticket. By default, the path is set to `/`, so this only adds one additional character to the ticket prior to its encryption. In cookieless mode though, because the ticket is embedded in the URL, there isn't really a concept of path information. As a result, in cookieless mode the path is *always* set to `/` by forms authentication, and hence there is always the same overhead in cookieless tickets for the path value.

Other information such as a ticket version number and the issue and expiration date information are fixed size and don't vary from one website to another. Logging in to a sample application with a comparatively short username (`testuser`) adds the following forms authentication ticket to the URL:

```
F(hZ-dwIinilHGQZ76f7fHcvJqG3iJngm1M-wnx3w6DSmV8FZcQSF6p6GpBXSK85G4YHXRUOlfdzmtV7cUv
doDGZu3mGiwmOMYBtcdB8RPVao1)
```

This adds another whopping 111 characters to the URL. Now with all cookieless features enabled there are 239 characters consumed for the various cookieless representations. Playing around a bit with different usernames on the sample application, the longest username that worked was `testuser 123456789012` (that is, a 20-character username). This results in an F ticket that is 132 characters long—resulting in a path segment that is 260 characters long. That is right on the 260 character path segment limit enforced by the `<requestFiltering>` configuration section in the `ApplicationHost.config` configuration file and the limitations set by the `http.sys` file that was introduced in Chapter 1.

After the username increases to 21 characters, a 400 Bad Request error is returned.

```
HTTP Error 404.14 - URL_TOO_LONG
```

Going back to the path configuration attribute, you can explicitly set it to match the application's root:

```
<forms cookieless="AutoDetect" path="/cookieless" />
```

Logging, with just `testuser` for the username results in a 111-character length for the forms authentication cookieless ticket (the same as before). And as before, the upper limit on the username is 20 characters. If you are curious what happened to the path information from configuration, the value of `FormsAuthenticationTicket.CookiePath` is hard-coded to /, regardless of the value in configuration. At one point earlier in the ASP.NET 2.0 development cycle, the full path value from configuration was included in cookieless tickets. Because this consumed far too much space on the URL (you could come up with a long enough path that even a zero-length username was too much to fit in the URL), the decision was made to always use the hard-coded / value. Keep this quirk in mind if for any reason you were depending on the `FormsAuthenticationTicket.CookiePath` property anywhere in your code; it should not be relied upon if your application ever issues cookieless forms authentication tickets.

Of course, the size constraints on the URL are a bit more relaxed if you do not use other cookieless features. Turning off anonymous identification (because that is gobbling up 95 characters), a 40-character username results in around a 230-character URL. Because 40-character usernames are pretty unlikely, you have breathing room on the URL after anonymous identification is disabled.

If you use cookieless forms authentication tickets, keep the following points in mind:

❑   With all cookieless features turned on, you are limited to a maximum length of around 20 characters for usernames with forms authentication.

❑   With anonymous identification turned off, you will probably not run into any real-world constraints on username length, unless of course you allow email addresses for usernames. Because email addresses can be upwards of 256 characters long, you will need to limit username length for such applications.

One final point on how cookieless tickets are embedded in the URL: Even though ASP.NET 2.0 and ASP.NET 3.5 embed them all into a single path segment, future releases may choose to split out the cookieless tickets for various features into separate path segments. If this approach is ever taken, it would free up quite a bit more space for forms authentication, enough space that even `UserData` could store limited amounts of information. For this reason, I would recommend that developers avoid writing code that explicitly parses the URL format used by ASP.NET 2.0 and ASP.NET 3.5 or that depends on the specific layout of cookieless tickets. Continue to manipulate URLs with the built-in ASP.NET APIs and the application-relative path syntax. Writing code that has an explicit dependency on the ASP.NET 2.0 and ASP.NET 3.5 cookieless format may lead to the need to rework such code in future releases.

Unexpected Redirect Behavior

Cookieless forms authentication introduces another subtle gotcha due to the reliance on redirects. The initial set of redirects that occur during autodetection does't complicate matters because this logic runs as part of the normal redirection to a login page. In existing ASP.NET 1.1 applications, developers already have to deal with the possibility of a website user posting data back to a secured page, only to get redirected to the login page instead—along with the subsequent loss of any posted data.

However, a bit of an edge case arises when using cookieless tickets, regardless of the selected cookieless mode. If you allow sliding expirations with cookieless tickets (and for security reasons this is not advised), then it is possible that at some point `FormsAuthenticationModule` may detect that more than 50% of a ticket's lifetime has elapsed. The module always calls `FormsAuthentication.RenewTicketIfOld` on each request, for both cookied and cookieless modes. In the case of cookieless modes, though, if the module detects that a new forms authentication ticket was issued with an updated expiration time due to the renewal call, the module needs to ensure that the new ticket value is embedded on the URL.

The module accomplishes this by repackaging the new `FormsAuthenticationTicket` into the custom `HTTP_ASPFILTERSESSIONID` header and then calling `Response.Redirect`, specifically the overload of `Response.Redirect` that accepts only the redirect path. This means the current request is immediately short-circuited to the `EndRequest` phase of the pipeline, and the redirect with the updated URL is sent back to the browser.

From the user's perspective, this means that anytime the user is working in the website (and this can be on a secured page or a publicly accessible page), enough of the ticket expiration may have elapsed to trigger a redirect. If by happenstance this redirect occurs when posting back user-entered data, the user is going to be one unhappy camper. Imagine entering a form full of registration data, hitting submit, and the net result is that you end up back on the same page with all of the fields showing as empty!

You can simulate this behavior with a simple page that has a few text boxes for entering data. Add a button that posts the page back to the server. Set the `timeout` attribute in the `<forms />` configuration element to 2 minutes. Log in to the site, and navigate to the page with the text boxes. Type in some data, and then wait around 1.5 minutes, long enough for the ticket to need renewal. Now when you post back, you can see that all of the data you entered has been lost. This behavior is another reason why sliding expirations should be avoided when using cookieless tickets.

About the only workaround (and an admittedly crude one at that) is for developers to identify pages in their site where user-entered information is not posted back in a form variable. For example, maybe viewing a catalog page in a website relies on query-string variables and a GET request, which allows the query-string variables to be preserved across redirects. You can write some code that runs in the pipeline (after `FormsAuthenticationModule` runs) and pro-actively checks the expiration date of the ticket. Rather than waiting for the ASP.NET default of 50% or more of the ticket lifetime to elapse, you could be more aggressive and force a ticket to be reissued at shorter intervals. This at least gives you some control over when the ticket is reissued, and it increases the likelihood that the ticket is reissued at well-defined points in the website where you can be assured that user-entered data is not lost.

Of course, there are myriad side effects with this workaround:

❏ Redirection behavior is still hard to test. You have to laboriously test each page in the site where you may inject a proactive renewal of the forms authentication ticket.

❑   The extra, and potentially unnecessary, redirects make the website seem slower.

❑   The workaround still doesn't solve the problem of a user entering a checkout process, getting up from the computer, and coming back a little later after more than 50 percent of the lifetime for his or her current ticket has elapsed. This specific scenario is one where dumping the user back to the page they were just on, with empty fields, is likely to cause the user to bail out of the checkout process.

Unfortunately, there isn't an elegant solution to the unintended redirect problem with cookieless tickets. The best advice is to turn off sliding expirations, and set the forms authentication ticket lifetime to a "reasonable" value (say somewhere around 30 to 60 minutes).

Configuring Forms Authentication Inside IIS 7.0

The <forms /> configuration section is usually edited inside the application's web.config. If you want to change the default predefined values, you configure a <forms /> section by specifying the name, path, login page, cookieless mode, authentication cookie time-out, sliding expiration, whether forms authentication requires SSL, and whether the authentication cookie is enabled for cross-application redirects. Although the application's web.config configuration file provides a very good IntelliSense to manipulate the different configuration sections, IIS 7.0, among the many new integration features with ASP.NET, provides a graphical user interface to edit the application's <forms /> authentication configuration section and some other configuration sections, too (SessionState is an example). To edit the <forms> authentication section, right-click on the FormsAuthenticationModule inside the Authentication applet window. Figure 6-4 shows the IIS 7.0 Windows Form used to edit the <forms /> section for an application.

As you can see, the entire <forms /> authentication configuration section is now editable through the IIS 7.0 Manager tool.

Figure 6-4

Sharing Tickets between 1.1 and 2.0/3.5

It is likely that most organizations will need to run ASP.NET 1.1, 2.0, and 3.5 applications side by side for a few years. In many cases, if corporate developers integrate custom internal ASP.NET sites with web-based applications from third-party vendors, they may need to wait for the next upgrade from their vendors before moving a web application over to ASP.NET 2.0 or ASP.NET 3.5. It is worth mentioning that ASP.NET 3.5 uses the same runtime as that of ASP.NET 2.0. Upgrading an application from ASP.NET 2.0 to ASP.NET 3.5 requires no major changes at all, contrary to the case of upgrading an ASP.NET 1.1 to either ASP.NET 2.0 or ASP.NET 3.5. An application configured with .NET Framework 3.5 inside Visual Studio 2008 functions the same as an application running with .NET Framework 2.0 in Visual Studio 2008. However, the difference is in the added features that are part of ASP.NET 3.5 only (AJAX, LINQ, and so on).

> *The bottom line here is that ASP.NET 3.5 and ASP.NET 2.0 applications share the same application pool on IIS 7.0 since the runtime is the same and, hence, whatever applies on ASP.NET 2.0 applies also on ASP.NET 3.5.*

You can accomplish both of the following scenarios when running in mixed environments:

❑   You can issue forms authentication tickets from ASP.NET 2.0 and ASP.NET 3.5 applications and the tickets will work properly when they are sent to an ASP.NET 1.1 application.

❑   You can issue forms authentication tickets from ASP.NET 1.1 applications and the tickets will work properly when they are sent to ASP.NET 2.0 and ASP.NET 3.5 applications.

To interoperate tickets between the two versions, you must ensure the following:

1.   ASP.NET 2.0 and ASP.NET 3.5 must be configured to use 3DES for encryption. Remember that by default ASP.NET 2.0 and ASP.NET 3.5 use AES for their encryption algorithm.

2.   Both ASP.NET 1.1 and ASP.NET 2.0 or ASP.NET 3.5 must share common decryption and validation keys.

The first point was discussed earlier in the section on ticket security. However, the second point may not be immediately obvious for some types of applications. By default, both the `validationKey` and `decryptionKey` attributes are set to `AutoGenerate,IsolateApps`. This holds true for ASP.NET 1.1, ASP.NET 2.0 and ASP.NET 3.5. If a developer changes the settings to instead be `AutoGenerate`, that temporarily solves the problem of sharing the auto-generated key material across multiple ASP.NET applications on the same machine.

However, when ASP.NET 2.0 is installed on a machine running ASP.NET 1.1 (that is, `aspnet_regiis -I` is run), the auto-generated key material is regenerated for ASP.NET 2.0. This means on a single web server that has both ASP.NET 1.1 and ASP.NET 2.0 running, setting any of the key attributes in `<machineKey />` to `AutoGenerate` is not sufficient. If you need to share forms authentication tickets between ASP.NET 1.1 and ASP.NET 2.0 or ASP.NET 3.5, you *must* use explicitly generated keys, and you must set the key values in the `encryptionKey` and `decryptionKey` attributes of `<machineKey />`. The section earlier on generating keys programmatically has sample code that makes it easy to generate the necessary values.

To demonstrate these concepts, use two simple applications. Both applications are initially configured as follows:

```
<authentication mode="Forms" />

<authorization>
    <deny users="?"/>
</authorization>
```

Each application has a login page that simply issues a session-based forms authentication cookie after clicking a button on the page (interoperating 1.1 and 2.0 or 3.5 only works with cookies because there was no URL-based forms authentication in the base ASP.NET 1.1 product). With this basic web.config, forms authentication tickets will not work between the two applications because the defaults in <machineKey /> are being used. If you try logging in against the 1.1 application and then change the address in the URL to reference a secure page in the 2.0 or 3.5 application, the ASP.NET 2.0 or ASP.NET 3.5 application returns you to the login page for the ASP.NET 2.0 or ASP.NET 3.5 page.

The reason for this is twofold: The keys are different between the two applications, and ASP.NET 2.0 or ASP.NET 3.5 is using AES by default. To rectify this, place a <machineKey /> section into both applications with explicit decryption and validation keys. In the case of ASP.NET 2.0 or ASP.Net 3.5, the <machineKey /> section must also specify the correct encryption algorithm:

```
<machineKey
   decryptionKey="A225194E99BCCB0F6B92BC9D82F12C2907BD07CF069BC8B4"
   validationKey="6FA5B7DB89076816248243B8FD7336CCA360DAF8"
   decryption="3DES"
/>
```

decryptionKey is 48 characters long, which is the recommended length when using 3DES (48 characters = 24 bytes = three 8 byte keys of which only 56-bits are used for each of the three keys used in 3DES), validationKey is 40-characters long, which is the minimum length supported by this attribute.

With the updated <machineKey /> sections, you can now log in to the ASP.NET 1.1 application, and then change the URL to reference a 2.0 or 3.5 page without being forced to log in again. The reverse scenario also works properly: you can log in to the 2.0 or 3.5 application and then reference a 1.1 page without being forced to log in again.

The only slight difference between tickets issued by ASP.NET 1.1 and ASP.NET 2.0 or ASP.NET 3.5 is the version property. If the forms authentication ticket is generated by ASP.NET 1.1, the FormsAuthentication Ticket.Version is set to 1. If the forms authentication ticket is generated by ASP.NET 2.0 or ASP.NET 3.5, then the property returns 2. Because neither ASP.NET 1.1 nor 2.0 or 3.5 do anything internally with the Version property (aside from packing and unpacking the value), the different values are innocuous. If for some reason you have business logic that depends on the value of the Version property, be aware that in a mixed ASP.NET environment there is no guarantee of a stable value.

Using Forms Authentication Across Different Content Types

It has been mentioned several times throughout the book that one of the major advantages of running applications in the new IIS 7.0 integrated mode is the ability of ASP.NET runtime to process requests for non-ASP.NET resources. Added to this, the managed `FormsAuthenticationModule` is now integrated into IIS 7.0, which means that in addition to having the native authentication modules listed and registered inside IIS, you now have the managed `FormsAuthenticationModule` listed so that administrators or developers can enable/disable it the same way they enable/disable any other native authentication module.

Figure 6-5 shows the list of authentication modules listed inside the IIS 7.0 Manager tool.

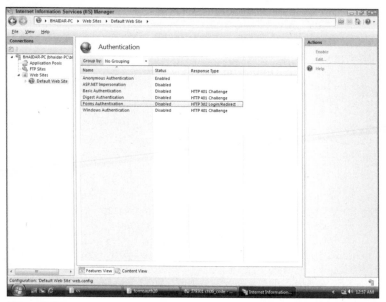

Figure 6-5

There are some limitations on using the managed module. If the managed `FormsAuthentication Module` is enabled, you cannot enable any other native authentication module. There is a workaround to this limitation to enable both the native `WindowsAuthenticationModule` and the managed `Forms AuthenticationModule`, which you can read more about at `http://mvolo.com/blogs/serverside/archive/2008/02/11/IIS-7.0-Two_2D00_Level-Authentication-with-Forms-Authentication-and-Windows-Authentication.aspx`. But as a rule. and without any workarounds, you cannot enable the manage `FormsAuthenticationModule` while enabling any other native authentication module.

The second limitation comes from the fact that IIS 7.0 cannot process any request if no native authentication module is enabled. The end result will be `Access Denied!` That is why when you want to enable ASP.NET `FormsAuthenticationModule` to authenticate requests to IIS 7.0, you should also enable the native `AnonymousAuthenticationModule`. This is an exception to the previously listed limitation, but this is a requirement by IIS 7.0.

IIS 7.0 can now make use of the powers of ASP.NET features when authenticating requests other than ASP.NET resources. For instance, if you have an ASP.NET application that contains .html, .asp, etc. file content types, you can easily protect them as if they were normal ASP.NET resources. The story starts with the new IIS 7.0 integrated mode where ASP.NET runtime can have access to all requests processed by IIS. Now enabling the managed `FormsAuthenticationModule` gives a chance for ASP.NET to handle the authentication and protection for all the content file types placed inside an application.

To enable an application to use the managed `FormsAuthenticationModule` for non-ASP.NET resources, perform the following steps:

1. Configure the application to run under the `DefaultAppPool`. In other words, make sure the application is running in the integrated mode.

2. Configure the `FormsAuthenticationModule` to execute for all content types, not only ASP.NET resources. This is a trick that has been mentioned before. All you need to do is add the following into the application's `web.config` file:

```
<system.webServer>
    <validation validateIntegratedModeConfiguration="false" />
    <modules>
       <remove name="FormsAuthentication" />
          <add
             name="FormsAuthentication"
              type="System.Web.Security.FormsAuthenticationModule" />
    </modules>
    <security>
       <authentication>
          <anonymousAuthentication enabled="true" />
       </authentication>
    </security>
</system.webServer>
```

If you do not want to add the above configuration elements manually, removing the `Forms AuthenticationModule` entry and re-adding it with the precondition attribute removed, you can make use of the rich IIS 7.0 Manager tool to configure a managed module to function properly on both managed and non-managed resources. Locate the Modules applet icon on the home page of the Web application you are configuring, and then double-click the Modules icon. A list of all the native and managed modules enabled for the application appears. Right-click the `FormsAuthentication` entry and choose Edit.

Notice the checkbox displayed at the bottom of the dialog box that says "Invoke only for requests to ASP.NET applications or managed handlers." This checkbox is selected by default, which means the `FormsAuthenticationModule` is enabled only for managed and ASP.NET resources, nothing else. To enable this module to function properly on non-managed and non-ASP.NET resources, simply unselect the checkbox and notice the changes that were reflected back on the application's `web.config` configuration file:

```
<system.webServer>
    <validation validateIntegratedModeConfiguration="false" />
    <modules>
       <remove name="FormsAuthentication" />
          <add
             name="FormsAuthentication"
```

```
                type="System.Web.Security.FormsAuthenticationModule"
                preCondition=""
                />
    </modules>
    <security>
       <authentication>
          <anonymousAuthentication enabled="true" />
       </authentication>
    </security>
</system.webServer>
```

Instead of removing the precondition attribute, the preceding configuration keeps the attribute as it is but replaces its value with an empty string, signaling that the managed module is now enabled for all content types, not only for managed resources.

3.   In addition to enabling FormsAuthenticationModule to protect non-ASP.NET content, you also need to configure the UrlAuthorizationModule to execute and authorize non-ASP.NET content. What you need to do is add the following into the application's web.config file.

```
<system.webServer>
     <validation validateIntegratedModeConfiguration="false" />
     <modules>
        <remove name="UrlAuthorization" />
          <add
             name="UrlAuthorization"
             type="System.Web.Security.UrlAuthorizationModule"/>
     </modules>
</system.webServer>
```

Again you can make use of the same alternative trick that was mentioned above to configure the managed UrlAuthorizationModule to function properly with managed and non-managed resources.

When configuring the managed UrlAuthorizationModule to handle both native and managed resources, you might consider utilizing the native UrlAuthorizationModule introduced as part of the IIS 7.0 core engine. One of the major advantages of the native authorization module is its capability to handle all content types, whether managed or non-managed, and above all, its ability to understand the FormsAuthenticationTicket (hence its tight and seamless integration with the managed authentication module, FormsAuthenticationModule).

The existence of this new native UrlAuthorizationModule gives you the opportunity either to keep on using the existing managed UrlAuthorizationModule for managed resources and enabling it for non-managed ones with some configuration settings, or to directly make use of the new native module that gives you a seamless integration with the managed Forms AuthenticationModule and protects your managed and non-managed resources with zero effort from your side.

For a more in-depth explanation on the new native UrlAuthorizationModule, visit Chapter 3 and read the full explanation about the new native module introduced by IIS 7.0.

4.   Finally, configure the application for forms authentication, and configure any needed attributes on the authentication configuration section in the application's web.config file.

To the test the above configuration, I have included the `aspnetForAllContent` web application, which contains a mix of ASP.NET resources and non-ASP.NET resources. The application has been configured with forms authentication, and a "deny all anonymous users" authorization rule has been added under the `<authorization>` configuration section to protect all the content included. Now if you try to access a protected .asp, .htm, or any other non-ASP.NET content types, you will notice that you are always redirected into the ASP.NET login page to provide your credentials before accessing any of the resources included in an application, whether the resources are ASP.NET or belong to any other type.

Leveraging the UserData Property

I will start out by saying up front that you can only leverage the `UserData` property for applications that run in cookie mode. Although the constructor for creating a `FormsAuthenticationTicket` with user data is public, there is no publicly available API for setting an instance of a `FormsAuthentication Ticket` onto a URL. As a result, the only way that the `UserData` can be used is if authentication tickets are sent in cookies.

The nice aspect of the `UserData` property is that after you get custom data into the forms authentication ticket, the information is always there and available on all subsequent page requests. The problem in ASP.NET 1.1, ASP.NET 2.0 and ASP.NET 3.5 is that there is no single method that you can call wherein you supply both custom data for the `UserData` property and the username of the authenticated user. This oversight in ASP.NET 2.0 and ASP.NET 3.5 is somewhat unfortunate because I run across internal and external customers over and over again that need to store a few extra pieces of identification or personalization information after a user logs in. Storing this information in the forms authentication ticket is logical, and it can eliminate the need to cobble together custom caching mechanisms just to solve basic performance problems such as displaying a friendly first name and last name of a customer on every single web page.

So, how do you store extra information in a forms authentication ticket and then issue the ticket in a way that all of the other settings (mainly the issue date and expiration date) are set to the correct values? More importantly, how do you do this without the need to hard-code assumptions into your code around cookie timeouts? In the `FormsAuthentication` class in ASP.NET 2.0, which is the same in ASP.NET 3.5, there is one glaring omission: you cannot retrieve the `timeout` attribute that is set in the `<forms />` element in configuration. Although you can technically retrieve this information with the strongly typed configuration classes in ASP.NET 2.0 and ASP.NET 3.5 (there is a `FormsAuthenticationConfiguration` class that provides strongly typed access to the values set in configuration), as was discussed in Chapter 5, you cannot use the strongly typed configuration classes when running in partial trust.

The following solution uses a simple workaround to ensure that all of the forms authentication settings are still used when manually issuing a forms authentication ticket, and it does it in a way that will still work in partial trust applications.

C#

```
protected void Button1_Click(object sender, EventArgs e)
{
    HttpCookie cookie =
            FormsAuthentication.GetAuthCookie(txtUsername.Text, false);
```

```csharp
    FormsAuthenticationTicket ft =
        FormsAuthentication.Decrypt(cookie.Value);

    //Cutom user data
    string userData = "John Doe";

    FormsAuthenticationTicket newFt =
        new FormsAuthenticationTicket(
            ft.Version,       //version
            ft.Name,          //username
            ft.IssueDate,     //Issue date
            ft.Expiration,    //Expiration date
            ft.IsPersistent,
            userData,
            ft.CookiePath);

    //re-encrypt the new forms auth ticket that includes the user data
    string encryptedValue = FormsAuthentication.Encrypt(newFt);

    //reset the encrypted value of the cookie
    cookie.Value = encryptedValue;

    //set the authentication cookie and redirect
    Response.Cookies.Add(cookie);
    Response.Redirect(
        FormsAuthentication.GetRedirectUrl(txtUsername.Text, false),false);
}
```

VB.NET

```vbnet
Protected Sub Button1_Click( _
ByVal sender As Object, _
ByVal e As EventArgs) Handles Button1.Click
    Dim cookie As HttpCookie = _
    FormsAuthentication.GetAuthCookie(txtUsername.Text, False)

    Dim ft As FormsAuthenticationTicket = _
    FormsAuthentication.Decrypt(cookie.Value)

    'Cutom user data
    Dim userData As String = "John Doe"

    Dim newFt As New FormsAuthenticationTicket(ft.Version, _
    ft.Name, ft.IssueDate, ft.Expiration, ft.IsPersistent, _
    userData, ft.CookiePath)

    're-encrypt the new forms auth ticket that includes the user data
    Dim encryptedValue As String = FormsAuthentication.Encrypt(newFt)

    'reset the encrypted value of the cookie
    cookie.Value = encryptedValue
```

```
        'set the authentication cookie and redirect
        Response.Cookies.Add(cookie)
        Response.Redirect( _
    FormsAuthentication.GetRedirectUrl(txtUsername.Text, False), _
    False)
    End Sub
```

Because you need to ultimately issue a forms authentication cookie, the first step is to call Forms Authentication.GetAuthCookie, passing it the values that you would normally pass directly to FormsAuthentiction.RedirectFromLoginPage. This results in a cookie that has the correct settings for items such as cookie domain and cookie path. It also results in an encrypted cookie payload containing a forms authentication ticket. You can easily extract the FormsAuthenticationTicket by passing the cookie's Value to the Decrypt method.

At this point, you have a fully inflated FormsAuthenticationTicket with the correct values of Issue Date and ExpirationDate already computed for you. You can create a new FormsAuthentication Ticket instance based on the values of the FormsAuthenticationTicket that was just extracted from the cookie. The only difference is that for the userData parameter in the constructor, you supply the custom data that you want to be carried along in the ticket. In the case of the sample, I just stored a first name and last name as an example. Because the user data needs to fit within the limits of a single forms authentication ticket, there are some constraints on just how much information can be stuffed into this parameter.

Internally, when you call FormsAuthentication.Encrypt, a 4K buffer is allocated to hold some of the interim results of encrypting the data. The net result is that that you cannot exceed roughly 2000 characters in the userData parameter if you need to call the Encrypt method. However, because the ultimate result needs to be stored in a cookie, you really only have 4096 bytes available for storing the entire ticket in the cookie. By the time the encryption bloat and hex string conversions occur, the realistic upper boundary on userData is around 900–950 characters. This still leaves a pretty hefty amount of space for placing information into the forms authentication ticket. And it is certainly enough space for common uses such as storing first name and last name, or storing a few IDs that are needed elsewhere in the application.

In the sample code shown previously, the new FormsAuthentication instance is encrypted with a call to FormsAuthentication.Encrypt, and the result is placed in the Value property of the cookie that we started with. At this point, you now have a valid forms authentication cookie, with an encrypted representation of a FormsAuthenticationTicket that includes custom data. Notice that nowhere does the sample code need to rely on hard-coded values for determining date-time information. Also, the sample does not call in to any configuration APIs to look up any of the configuration values for the forms authentication feature.

The last step in the sample is to add the forms authentication cookie into the response and then issue the necessary redirect. The Response.Redirect call shown in the sample roughly mirrors what occurs inside of that last portion of FormsAuthentication.RedirectFromLoginPage. Note that the Redirect overload that is used issues a "soft" redirect. The second parameter to the method is passed a false value, which means the remainder of the page will continue to run. Only when the page is done executing, and the remainder of the HTTP pipeline completes, will ASP.NET send back the redirect to the browser.

The call to `GetRedirectUrl` causes the forms authentication feature to find the appropriate value for the redirect URL based on information in the query-string (the familiar `RedirectURL` query-string variable you see in the address bar when you are redirected to a login page), or in the form post variables. Calling `GetRedirectUrl` eliminates the need for you to write any parsing code for determining the correct redirect target.

You can run the sample application by attempting to access a simple home page that displays the `UserData` property on the ticket.

C#

```
//Display some user data
FormsAuthenticationTicket ft =
    ((FormsIdentity)User.Identity).Ticket;

Response.Write("Hello " + ft.UserData);
```

VB.NET

```
'Display some user data
Dim ft As FormsAuthenticationTicket = (_
CType(User.Identity, FormsIdentity)).Ticket

Response.Write("Hello " & ft.UserData)
```

As you can see, after you jump through the hoops necessary to set the `UserData` in the ticket, it is very handy and easy to get access to it elsewhere in an application. Hopefully in future releases, ASP.NET will make it a bit easier to issue tickets with custom data as well as extending this functionality over to the cookieless case.

Passing Tickets Across Applications

Another title for this section could be "how to roll a poor man's single sign-on (SSO) solution." In ASP.NET 2.0 and ASP.NET 3.5, forms authentication includes the ability to pass forms authentication tickets across applications. Although prior to 2.0 you could create a custom solution that passed the forms authentication ticket around as a string, you had to write extra code to handle hopping the ticket across applications.

ASP.NET 2.0 and ASP.NET 3.5 support setting the domain value of the forms authentication cookie from inside of configuration. ASP.NET 2.0 and ASP.NET 3.5 also add explicit support built into the APIs and the `FormsAuthenticationModule` for handling tickets that are passed using either query-strings or form posts. As long as you follow the basic conventions expected by forms authentication, the work of converting information sent in these alternative locations into a viable forms authentication ticket is automatically done by ASP.NET.

Cookie Domain

The ASP.NET 2.0 and ASP.NET 3.5 forms authentication configuration section includes a domain attribute. By default, this attribute is set to the empty string, which means that cookies issued by forms authentication APIs will use the default value of the `Domain` property for a `System.Web.HttpCookie`. As a result, the `Domain` property of the cookie will be set to the full DNS address for the issuing web-site. For example, if a page is located at `http://bhaidar-PC/login.aspx`, the resulting cookie has a domain of `bhaidar-PC`. On the other hand, if the full DNS address for the server is used in the URL (`http://bhaidar-PC.somedomain.com/login.aspx`). Then the resulting cookie has its domain set to `bhaidar-PC.somedomain.com`.

In ASP.NET 1.1, this was the only behavior supported by forms authentication, which made it problem-atic when attempting to share cookies across websites that only shared a portion of the domain name. For instance, you might need to authenticate users to `bhaidar-PC.somedomain.com` as well as `someotherapp.somedomain.com`, but the set of users is the same for both applications.

With ASP.NET 2.0 and ASP.NET 3.5 this is easy to accomplish. Add the domain attribute to the `<forms />` element and set its value to the portion of the domain name that is shared across all of your applications.

```
<forms … path="/" domain="somedomain.com" />
```

With this setting, each time a cookie is issued by forms authentication, the cookie's domain value will be set to `somedomain.com`. As a result, the browser will automatically send the cookie anytime you request a URL where the network address ends with `somedomain.com`. Another nice side effect of this support for the domain attribute in ASP.NET 2.0 and ASP.Net 3.5 is that renewed forms authentication cookies (remem-ber that with sliding expirations enabled, cookies can be renewed as they age) will also pick up the same value for the domain. In ASP.NET 1.1, if you enabled sliding expirations but you manually issued the forms authentication cookie with a different domain than the default, it was possible that the cookie would be automatically renewed by the `FormsAuthenticationModule`. When that happened in ASP.NET 1.1, it reis-sued the cookie and never set the domain attribute on the new cookie.

Cross-Application Sharing of Ticket

The ability to customize the domain of the forms authentication cookie is useful when all of your appli-cations live under a common DNS namespace. What happens, though, if your applications are located in completely different domains? Companies that support multiple web properties, potentially with dif-ferent branding, have to deal with this. The URLs of public websites are frequently chosen so as to be easy for customers to remember and, thus, are not necessarily chosen for purposes of DNS naming consistency. ASP.NET 2.0 and ASP.NET 3.5 have the ability to share forms authentication tickets across arbitrary sites by passing the forms authentication ticket around in the query-string or in a form post variable. This capability allows developers to intelligently flow authentication credentials across dis-parate ASP.NET sites without forcing a website user to repeatedly log in.

Prior to ASP.NET 2.0, your only options were to manually create some type of workaround for this or to purchase a third-party vendor's single sign on (SSO) product. A number of developers, though, really don't need all the complexities and costs of full-blown SSO products. If the problem that you need to solve is primarily centered on sharing forms authentication tickets across multiple ASP.NET websites with different DNS namespaces, the support for passing forms authentication tickets across ASP.NET 2.0 and ASP.NET 3.5 applications will be a good fit.

That leads to the question of when wouldn't you use the cross-application capabilities in ASP.NET 2.0 and ASP.NET 3.5? There are still valid reasons for using true SSO products, some of which are listed below:

1. You need to share authenticated users across heterogeneous platforms. For example you need to support logging users in across UNIX-based websites and ASP.NET sites. Clearly forms authentication won't help here because there is no native support for the forms authentication stack on web platforms other than ASP.NET.

2   You need to share authenticated users across different untrusted organizations. This is a scenario where loose "federations" of different organizations need some way for website customers to seamlessly interact with different websites, but need to do so in a way that does not force the customer to constantly log in. For example, maybe a company wants the ability for a website customer to seamlessly navigate over to a parcel-tracking site to retrieve shipment information, and then over to a payment site to see the status of purchases and payments. Because each site is run by a different company, it is very hard to solve this problem today. There are a number of companies, including Microsoft, working on SSO solutions that can interoperate in a way allowing for a seamless authentication experience for this type of problem.

3. You may need to map the credentials of a logged-in user to credentials for other back-end data stores. For example, after logging in to a website the user may also have credentials in a mainframe system or a back-end resource planning system. Some SSO products support the ability to map authentication credentials so that a website user logs in once and then is seamlessly reauthenticated against these types of systems.

As you can see from this partial list, most of the SSO scenarios involve more complexity in the form of other companies or other systems that are external to the website. Many extranet and internet sites don't need to solve these problems, or can live with comparatively simple solutions for reaching into back-end data stores. For these types of sites, the cross-application support in forms authentication is a lower-cost and easier solution to the single sign on problem.

How Cross-Application Redirects Work

By default, the "SSO-lite" functionality in ASP.NET 2.0 and ASP.NET 3.5 is not enabled. To turn it on, you need to set the `enableCrossAppRedirects` attribute to `true`:

```
<forms … enableCrossAppRedirects="true" />
```

Doing so turns on a few pieces of logic within forms authentication. First, the `FormsAuthentication` `.RedirectFromLoginPage` method has extra logic to automatically place a forms authentication ticket into a query-string variable when it detects that it will be redirecting outside of the current application. Second, the `FormsAuthenticationModule` will look on the query-string and in the form post variables for a forms authentication ticket if it could not find a valid ticket in the other standard locations (that is, in a cookie or embedded in the URL, for the cookieless case).

Because cookie-based tickets automatically flow across applications that share at least a portion of a DNS namespace, you really only need to set `enableCrossAppRedirects` to `true` for the following cases:

❑   You need to send a forms authentication ticket between applications that do not share any portion of a DNS namespace. In this case, the "domain" attribute isn't sufficient to solve the problem.

❑   You need to send a cookieless ticket between different applications, regardless of whether or not the applications share the same DNS namespace. Cookieless tickets, by their very nature, are limited to only URLs in the current application.

Cookieless Cross-Application Behavior

Examine the cookieless case first. You can create two sample applications and in configuration set up forms authentication and the authorization rules as follows:

```
<authentication mode="Forms">
    <forms cookieless="UseUri" />
</authentication>

<authorization>
    <deny users="?"/>
</authorization>
<machineKey
  decryptionKey="A225194E99BCCB0F6B92BC9D82F12C2907BD07CF069BC8B4"
  validationKey="6FA5B7DB89076816248243B8FD7336CCA360DAF8"
/>
```

With this configuration, both applications are forced to use cookieless tickets. Additionally, both applications share common key information which ensures that a ticket from one application is consumable by the other application.

To focus on the cross-application redirect issue, we will keep the rest of the application very simple. Both applications will have a default.aspx page, and a login page. Both login pages (for now) will simply issue a forms authentication ticket for a fixed username and then pass the user back to the original requesting URL:

C#

```
FormsAuthentication.RedirectFromLoginPage("testuser", false);
```

VB.NET

```
FormsAuthentication.RedirectFromLoginPage("testuser", False)
```

After you end up on default.aspx, there is a button you can click to redirect yourself over to the other application:

C#

```
Response.Redirect("/cookielessAppB/default.aspx");
```

VB.NET

```
Response.Redirect("/cookielessAppB/default.aspx")
```

The preceding code is in the sample application called cookielessAppA, so default.aspx redirects over to the other sample application: cookielessAppB. If you were to run both sample applications, and try to seamlessly ping-pong between the two applications, you would find yourself constantly logging in. The culprit of course is that Response.Redirect that punts you to the other application; when that redirect is issued, the cookieless credentials embedded in the current URL are lost.

Unfortunately, you can't just call one API or use some new parameter on the Redirect method to solve this problem when running in cookieless mode. Although FormsAuthentication.Redirect FromLoginPage has logic to store a ticket on the query-string, the scenario above is one where you click on a link inside of one application, and it takes you over to a second application. For this case, you need a wrapper around Response.Redirect that includes the logic to pass the forms authentication ticket along with the redirection.

I created a simple query-string wrapper:

C#

```
public static class RedirectWrapper
{
    public static string FormatRedirectUrl(string redirectUrl)
    {
        HttpContext c = HttpContext.Current;
        if (c == null)
throw new InvalidOperationException("You must have an active context to
perform a redirect");

        //Don't append the forms auth ticket for unauthenticated users or
        //for users authenticated with a different mechanism
        if (!c.User.Identity.IsAuthenticated ||
            !(c.User.Identity.AuthenticationType == "Forms"))
            return redirectUrl;

        //Determine if we need to append to an existing query-string or not
        string qsSpacer;
        if (redirectUrl.IndexOf("?") > 0)
            qsSpacer = "&";
        else
            qsSpacer = "?";

        //Build the new redirect URL
        string newRedirectUrl;
        FormsIdentity fi = (FormsIdentity)c.User.Identity;
        newRedirectUrl = redirectUrl + qsSpacer +
                FormsAuthentication.FormsCookieName + "=" +
                FormsAuthentication.Encrypt(fi.Ticket);

        return newRedirectUrl;
    }
}
```

VB.NET

```
Public NotInheritable Class RedirectWrapper
  Private Sub New()
  End Sub
  Public Shared Function FormatRedirectUrl(ByVal redirectUrl As String) As String
        Dim c As HttpContext = HttpContext.Current
        If c Is Nothing Then
Throw New InvalidOperationException("You must have an active context to
perform a redirect")
        End If

        'Don't append the forms auth ticket for unauthenticated users or
        'for users authenticated with a different mechanism
        If (Not c.User.Identity.IsAuthenticated) OrElse _
        Not(c.User.Identity.AuthenticationType = "Forms") Then
            Return redirectUrl
        End If

        'Determine if we need to append to an existing query string or not
        Dim qsSpacer As String
        If redirectUrl.IndexOf("?") > 0 Then
            qsSpacer = "&"
        Else
            qsSpacer = "?"
        End If

        'Build the new redirect URL
        Dim newRedirectUrl As String
        Dim fi As FormsIdentity = CType(c.User.Identity, FormsIdentity)
        newRedirectUrl = redirectUrl & _
        qsSpacer & _
        FormsAuthentication.FormsCookieName & _
        "=" & _
        FormsAuthentication.Encrypt(fi.Ticket)

        Return newRedirectUrl
  End Function
End Class
```

Given a query-string, the static method FormatRedirectUrl makes a few validation checks and then appends a query-string variable with the forms authentication ticket to the URL. If the current request doesn't have an authenticated user, or if it's not using forms authentication, calling the method is a no-op. Assuming that there is a forms-authenticated user, the method determines whether or not it needs to add a query-string to the current URL, or if instead it just needs to append a query-string variable (there may already be one or more query-strings on the URL, hence the need to check for this condition).

Last, the method reencrypts the current user's forms authentication ticket back into a string, and it places it on the query-string. Notice how the value of FormsAuthentication.FormsCookieName is used as the name of the query-string variable. Even though the code isn't really sending a cookie, the FormsCookieName is the identifier used for a forms authentication ticket regardless of whether the ticket is in the query-string, in a form post variable or contained in a cookie.

To use the new helper method, we can rework the previous redirect logic to look like this:

C#

```
Response.Redirect(
    RedirectWrapper.FormatRedirectUrl("/cookielessAppB/default.aspx"));
```

VB.NET

```
Response.Redirect(
    RedirectWrapper.FormatRedirectUrl("/cookielessAppB/default.aspx"))
```

You can update both sample applications to include the new helper class in their App_Code directories. Also, update the forms authentication configuration to enable cross-application redirects. This is necessary for the forms authentication module to recognize the incoming ticket on the query-string properly.

```
<forms cookieless="UseUri" enableCrossAppRedirects="true" />
```

Now when you use both applications, you can seamlessly ping-pong between both applications without being challenged to log in again. Each hop from application A to application B results in a redirect underneath the hood that includes the ticket on the query-string:

```
http://localhost/cookielessAppB/default.aspx?.ASPXAUTH=F2CB90DA66DE1044FEEE4FE676
AB6C1226EF04F5FDE104002CEA29448E2CC0CD3AF7BA33E4022C5E786BAD23F98163F708AB21A52893
9502ADBCAB5031C918F47AD1A317AC183883
```

The FormsAuthenticationModule detects this and properly converts the query-string variable back into a cookieless ticket embedded on a URL. Due to the reliance on redirect behavior, you can't post any data from one application to the other. Instead, you have to pass information between applications with query-string variables. Even if you attempt to use a form post as a mechanism for transferring from one application to another, you can't avoid at least one redirect. When the FormsAuthenticationModule in the second application issues a forms authentication ticket based on the ticket that was carried in the query-string, the module issues a redirect to embed the new ticket onto the URL. The only way to avoid a redirect in this case is if you run in cookie mode, which we shall see shortly.

As an aside, there is one slight quirk in how this all works. Remember earlier in the discussion on cookieless tickets where it was mentioned that the requireSSL attribute in the <forms /> element is ignored when using cookieless tickets? If you enable cross application redirects, the requireSSL attribute still affects the FormsAuthenticationModule. Under the following conditions, the Forms AuthenticationModule will ignore any query-string or forms variable containing a ticket:

❑   The requireSSL attribute is set to true.

❑   The module could not find a ticket either in a cookie or embedded in a URL, and hence reverted to looking in the query-string and forms variable collection.

❑   The current connection is not secured with SSL.

If you think you have cross-application redirects setup properly, and you are still being challenged with a login prompt, double-check and make sure that you have not set requireSSL to true and then attempted to send the ticket to another application over a non-SSL connection.

Cookied Cross-Application Behavior

You can use a similar application to the cookieless sample to also show cross-application redirects in the cookied case. Again using two sample applications, both applications need to share a common configuration:

```
<forms cookieless="UseCookies" enableCrossAppRedirects="true"
 path="/cookiedAppA"/>

<machineKey
   decryptionKey="A225194E99BCCB0F6B92BC9D82F12C2907BD07CF069BC8B4"
   validationKey="6FA5B7DB89076816248243B8FD7336CCA360DAF8"
 />
```

To simulate isolation of the forms authentication cookies, each application explicitly sets the path attribute as shown above. Because this sample uses cookies, the path attribute prevents the browser from sending the forms authentication cookie for one application over to the second application. Remember that setting the path attribute only takes effect when using cookied modes (for example, setting the path attribute would have no effect on the previous cookieless example). For starters, we will use the same redirection helper as we did earlier, and pages in both applications will issue a Response.Redirect to get to the second application.

When you run the sample applications, you get almost the same result as the cookieless applications. You can bounce around between applications without the need to log in again. However, one noticeable difference is the lack of a second redirect each time you transition from one application to another. When the FormsAuthenticationModule converts the query-string variable into a forms authentication ticket encapsulated inside of a cookie, it does not need to issue a redirect. Instead, it just sets a new cookie in the response, and the remainder of the request is allowed to execute. As a result, when you transition from application A to application B, the URL in the browser address bar still retains the query-string variable used during the redirect:

```
http://localhost/cookiedAppB/default.aspx?.ASPXAUTH=23CB12E603239A53830866D67D38DE6
E8AAAA3647A05220FB278A5B6A3A0C0927FC498D3E6ED46AEBD7EF770AC3359CABE08EDC63385D8C058
B58D0C63782A27F948A8A8BFF5DFE9CE2C78463C68E1C0EB390B6C89CB594D21564EF94B2866CA112AF
E132F904FF87FF728B6DD3A48E6
```

Although it looks a bit strange, this is actually innocuous. After you start navigating around in the second application, the query-string variable will go away:

1. When the current page posts back to itself, the query-string variable will flow down to the application.

2. The FormsAuthenticationModule first looks for valid tickets in cookies and embedded in the URL. Because it finds a valid ticket in a cookie, it never makes it far enough to look at the query-string variable.

3. The current page runs.

4. Eventually you click on a link or trigger a redirect to some other page in the application. When this occurs the query-string is not sent along with the request, and as a result other pages in the application won't have the ticket sitting in the address bar.

Because the point at which step 4 occurs is probably not deterministic (a website user may be able to enter into the application from any number of different pages), the query-string variable can end up in the address bar for any of your entry pages.

As with cookieless cross application redirection, if you happen to set `requireSSL` to `true` in your applications, the hop from one application to another will cause the `FormsAuthenticationModule` to check the secured state of the connection. If the module detects that the cross-application redirect occurred on a non-SSL connection, it will throw an `HttpException`, just as it would for the cookieless scenario.

Unlike the cookieless case, though, you do have another option for hopping credentials from one application over to another. You can choose to post the forms authentication ticket from one application to another because you don't need to worry about the extra redirect the `FormsAuthenticationModule` performs when embedding the ticket into the URL. To show this, create another page in the first application:

```
<html xmlns="http://www.w3.org/1999/xhtml" >
<head runat="server">
    <title>Untitled Page</title>
</head>
<body>
 <form id="form1" runat="server" >
  <div>
  <asp:TextBox ID="txtSomeInfo" runat="server"></asp:TextBox><br />
  <br />
  <asp:Button ID="Button1" runat="server"
      PostBackUrl="/cookiedAppB/ReceivePostFromAnotherApplication.aspx"
      Text="Button" />
  </div>
  <input id="Hidden1" type="hidden" runat="server" />
 </form>
</body>
</html>
```

This page markup takes advantage of a feature that was originally introduced in ASP.NET 2.0 called *cross-page postings*. Although this sample application is not showing the primary purpose of cross-page posting (which is posting between two different pages within the *same* application), it turns out that you can use cross-page posting just as well to make it easier to post form data across applications. The markup above has set the `PostBackUrl` property on a standard `Button` control to a URL located in the second sample application. By doing so, ASP.NET injects some extra information into the page that causes the page to post back to the second application.

In addition to using cross-page posting, the code-behind for the page sets some values for the hidden control that is on the page:

C#

```
protected void Page_Load(object sender, EventArgs e)
{
    this.Hidden1.ID = FormsAuthentication.FormsCookieName;
    this.Hidden1.Value =
```

```
FormsAuthentication.Encrypt(((FormsIdentity)User.Identity).Ticket);

}
```

VB.NET

```
Protected Sub Page_Load( _
ByVal sender As Object, _
ByVal e As EventArgs) Handles Me.Load()
    Me.Hidden1.ID = FormsAuthentication.FormsCookieName
    Me.Hidden1.Value = _
    FormsAuthentication.Encrypt((CType(User.Identity, FormsIdentity)).Ticket)
End Sub
```

The hidden control has its ID set to the same value as the forms authentication cookie. This is necessary because when the request flows to the second application, one of the places the FormsAuthentication Module will look for a forms authentication ticket is in Request.Form["name of the forms authentication cookie"]. The value of the hidden control is set to the encrypted value of the FormsAuthenticationTicket for the current user. This is the same operation we saw earlier for the redirection scenarios, with the difference being that in this sample the forms authentication ticket is being packaged and stored inside of a hidden form variable rather than a query-string variable.

When you request this page from the first application in the browser, viewing the source shows how everything has been lined up for a successful cross-page post. An abbreviated version of the <form /> element is shown here:

```
<form method="post" action="PostToAnotherApplication.aspx" id="form1">

<input type="hidden" name="__VIEWSTATE" id="__VIEWSTATE" value="/
wEPDwUKMTUyMjMyNTkyOWRk/xqxNcEwAvNgbY4ERISdsKcovBo=" />

<input name="txtSomeInfo" type="text" id="txtSomeInfo" /><br />

<input id="Button1" type="submit" name="Button1" value="Button"
        onclick="javascript:WebForm_DoPostBackWithOptions(new WebForm_PostBackO
ptions('Button1','',false,'', '/cookiedAppB/ReceivePostFromAnotherApplication.
aspx',false,false))" />

<input name=".ASPXAUTH" type="hidden" id=".ASPXAUTH"
value="8CA4D2EB5407E67A6E9950337562ABDEDDBA305644DB3E4B51490F715B4D313A275CE9FB6912
7BE6780462B6570DF8347F282E8FA25E28B1958B13FD710EDF956BD315E40F64B4D44FE3534BA857BA2
F99225E63EA4E65FD40357D995DA1E3F8E4C4D7BAA6E8A4CFC828D357EECEDC27" />

</form>
```

The forms authentication ticket is packaged up in the hidden form variable. You can also see that the form's action is set to PostToAnotherApplication.aspx, which at first glance doesn't look like a page in another application. The form will actually post to another application because the button on the form has a click handler that calls WebForm_DoPostBackWithOptions. This method is one of the many ASP.NET client-side JavaScript methods returned from webresource.axd (webresource.axd is the replacement for the JavaScript files that you used to deploy underneath the aspnet_client subdirectory back in ASP.NET 1.1 and 1.0).

When you press the button on this page, two things occurs:

1. The `WebForm_DoPostBackWithOptions` client-side method sets the `action` attribute on the client-side form to the value `/cookiedAppB/ReceivePostFromAnotherApplication.aspx`.

2. The client-side method returns, at which point because the button is of type "submit," the client-side form is submitted by the browser, using the "action" that was just set.

As a result of this, you have a form-submit from a page in Application A flowing over to application B. When the request hits application B, it starts running through the HTTP pipeline. The `Forms AuthenticationModule` sees the request, and attempts to find a forms authentication ticket. Eventually, the module looks in `Request.Form[".ASPXAUTH"]` for a forms authentication ticket. Because there is a hidden field on the form called `.ASPXAUTH`, the module is able to find the string value stored there. The module then converts the string value into a forms authentication ticket and sets a cookie on the response that contains this ticket.

At this point the request continues to run, which in the case of the sample application results in a call on the page to:

C#

```
Response.Write("The posted value was: " + Request.Form["txtSomeInfo"]);
```

VB.NET

```
Response.Write("The posted value was: " & Request.Form("txtSomeInfo"))
```

If you run the sample application, you will see that the preceding line of code will successfully play back to you whatever value you typed into the text box back in application A. The other nice thing about this approach is that not only are posted variables retained across the two applications, when you end up on the page in the second application there isn't the somewhat odd (maybe unsettling?) behavior of the authentication ticket showing up in the address bar of the browser. Additionally, if you view the source of the second page in the browser, there isn't any authentication ticket there either. For both of these reasons, when running sites with cookie-based forms authentication, POST-based transfers of control between applications are preferred to the approach that relies on calling `Response.Redirect`.

One last comment on the cross-page posting case: remember that you always need to explicitly set the keys in the `<machineKey />` element for all participating applications. Without this, the forms authentication ticket in the hidden field will not be decryptable in the second application.

Cookie-based "SSO-Lite"

Now that you have seen the various permutations of passing forms authentication tickets between applications, let's tie the concepts together with some sample applications that use a central login form. This approach is conceptually similar to how Passport works with all tickets being issued from central login application. Note that this design only works with cookie-based forms authentication because it relies on issuing forms authentication cookies that can authenticate the browser back to the original application. Websites that use cookieless forms authentication need more explicit code inside of each application due to the need to manually create some approach for hopping authentication tickets from one application to another.

The general design of our "hand-rolled" single sign-on solution is shown in Figure 6-6.

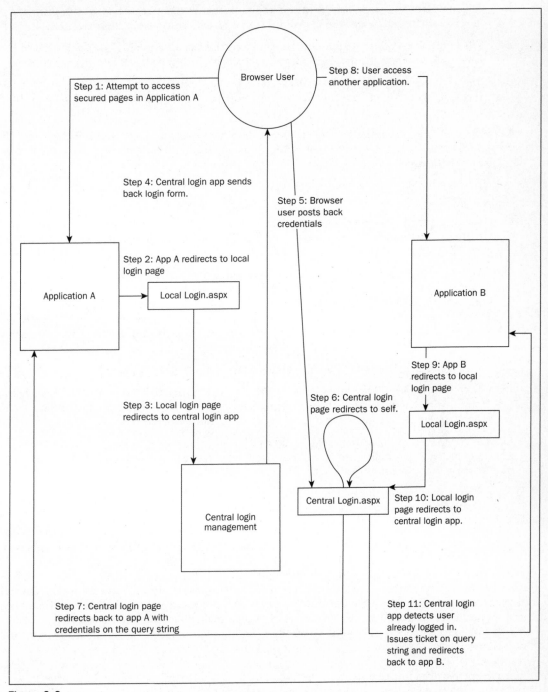

Figure 6-6

The desired behavior of the solution is described in the following list:

1. A user attempts to access a secured application, in this case Application A. At this point, the user has not logged in anywhere and thus has no forms authentication tickets available.

2. When the request reaches application A, it detects that the application allows authenticated users only. As a result, it redirects the browser to a login page that is local to the application.

3. The local login page does not actually send back a login form to the user at this point. Instead, the local login form places some information onto the query-string and then redirects to a central login application.

4. The central login application detects that the user has never logged in against it, and so it redirects the user to a login page in the central login application. This is the only point at which the browser user ever sees a login UI.

5. At this point the browser user enters credentials into a form and submits the form back to the central login application.

6. Assuming that the credentials are valid, the login page in the central login application redirects back to itself. This is because the login page handles both interactive logins and noninteractive logins.

7. When the login page redirects to itself, it detects that the user already has a valid forms authentication ticket for the central login application. So instead, the login page clones the forms authentication ticket and sends this new ticket by way of a redirect back to application A. In Application A, the `FormsAuthenticationModule` will see the ticket on the query-string, convert it into a cookie, and then start running the original page that the user was attempting to access back in step 1.

8. Some time later, the user attempts to access a secured page in application B.

9. Because there is no forms authentication ticket for application B, it redirects to the local login page. As with application A though, the local login page just exists to place information on the query-string and redirect to the central login application.

10. When the redirect reaches the login page in the central login application, the forms authentication ticket issued back in step 6 will flow along with the request. As a result, the login page detects that the user already logged in.

11. Rather than sending back a login form, the login page creates another clone of the forms authentication ticket and places it on a query-string. It then redirects back to application B.

12. The `FormsAuthenticationModule` in application B converts the forms authentication ticket on the query-string into a forms authentication cookie. The original page that the user requested back in step 8 then runs.

You can see that the primary underpinning of the SSO-lite solution in forms authentication is the ability to pass forms authentication tickets across disparate applications. A website user logs in against a central application, which results in a forms authentication cookie being sent to the user's browser. That forms authentication ticket becomes the master authentication ticket for all subsequent attempts to access other sites.

Whenever a participating website redirects back into the central login application, the master forms authentication cookie is sent by the user's browser to the login page in the central application. The central login page can then crack open this ticket and extract most of the values in it, and create a new forms authentication ticket. The new ticket is what is packaged on the query-string and sent back to the original application by way of a redirect.

The benefit of generating application-specific forms authentication tickets off of the central application's forms authentication ticket is that all participating applications receive a forms authentication ticket with a common set of issue and expiration dates. It is the central login application that defines for how long the master ticket is valid (if sliding expirations are even allowed). The cloned tickets for all of the participating applications simply reflect these settings as established in the central login application.

Now that you have reviewed the conceptual design, it's time to drill into the actual implementation. There are two important pieces of information that all participating applications need to send over to the central application:

❏ The URL of the page that was originally requested in the application

❏ The desired cookie path that should be used when creating a forms authentication ticket in the participating application

The first piece of information is pretty intuitive. Because you want your SSO-lite solution to roughly mirror the standard forms authentication behavior, we need the website user to eventually end up on the page that was originally requested. However, the second piece of information is very important to get right because the solution will be issuing forms authentication tickets in one place (the central login application), but the ticket needs to be converted into a valid cookie in a completely different place (the `FormsAuthenticationModule` of the participating application).

It turns out that the login in forms authentication for handling cross-application redirects is dependent on the `CookiePath` property of `FormsAuthenticationTicket`. When a `FormsAuthenticationModule` receives a ticket on the query-string, it does *not* look at the `path` attribute set in the `<forms />` element for the application. Instead, when the module cracks open the ticket that was sent on the query-string, it uses the `CookiePath` that it finds there as the value for the Path property on the resulting forms authentication `HttpCookie`.

In our SSO-lite solution, the two necessary pieces of information are passed from participating applications to the central login application with two query-string variables:

❏ `CustomCookiePath`: Each participating application sets this value to `FormsAuthentication` `.CookiePath`. That has the effect of ensuring the forms authentication ticket issued inside of each application actually uses the path as set in each application's configuration.

❏ `CustomReturnUrl`: Each participating application sets this value to the original URL that the website user was attempting to access. The central login application eventually issues a redirect back to this URL.

For those of you that poke around a bit in the internal workings of forms authentication, you may be wondering why the solution needs a custom definition of a return URL. Whenever forms authentication performs its automatic redirect-to-login-page logic, there is a query-string variable called `ReturnUrl`. You cannot overload this query-string variable for the purposes of cross-application redirects because forms authentication only places a server-relative virtual path into this variable. Forms authentication does not have the ability in ASP.NET 2.0 and ASP.NET 3.5 to add the DNS or server name into the `ReturnUrl` variable (that is, forms authentication never prepends `http://some.server.address.here/` to this variable).

An SSO-lite solution would not be very useful, though, if the only return URLs sent to the central login application were to other applications deployed on the same IIS server. In fact, if that were the only problem you were trying to solve, chances are all you would need to do is set the domain attribute in configuration. As a result, the SSO-lite solution uses the CustomReturnUrl variable to hold the fully qualified address of the original page the website user was attempting to access. This ensures that the central login application can exist in a completely different DNS namespace from any of the participating applications.

Sample Participating Application

The web.config for a participating application is defined as shown here:

```
<configuration xmlns="http://schemas.microsoft.com/.NetConfiguration/v2.0">
  <appSettings>
    <add key="centralLoginUrl"
        value="http://bhaidar-PC/CentralLogin/Login.aspx"/>
  </appSettings>
  <system.web>

  <machineKey
    decryptionKey="A225194E99BCCB0F6B92BC9D82F12C2907BD07CF069BC8B4"
    validationKey="6FA5B7DB89076816248243B8FD7336CCA360DAF8"
  />

  <authentication mode="Forms">
      <forms loginUrl="Login.aspx"
            cookieless="UseCookies" enableCrossAppRedirects="true"
            path="/AppAUsingCentralLogin" slidingExpiration="False"
      />
  </authentication>

  <authorization>
    <deny users="?"/>
  </authorization>

  </system.web>
</configuration>
```

The bolded portions of the configuration require some explanation. First, the <appSettings /> variable defines the full URL needed to reach the login page in the central login application. You would need to set this in the configuration of every participating application so that applications know where to send the authentication redirect. The enableCrossAppRedirects setting is necessary so that the FormsAuthenticationModule inside the application will look in the query-string or form post variables for a ticket. With this setting turned on, the participating application can successfully convert tickets send from the central application back into an application-specific forms authentication ticket.

Last, note that slidingExpiration is set to false. Because the central login application issues the master forms authentication ticket, it is the timeout and slidingExpiration settings of the central login application that take precedence. You don't want participating applications to be renewing forms authentication tickets; rather, you want the central login application to do this for you.

Because the configuration above denies access to all anonymous users, any attempt to access a page in the application results in a redirect to the *local* login page. The local version of Login.aspx is shown here:

C#

```csharp
    protected void Page_Load(object sender, EventArgs e)
    {
        Redirector.PerformCentralLogin(this);
    }
```

VB.NET

```vbnet
    Protected Sub Page_Load(ByVal sender As Object, ByVal e As EventArgs) _
    Handles Me.Load
        Redirector.PerformCentralLogin(Me)
    End Sub
```

It is intentionally kept simple because you don't want to duplicate the redirection login in every single application. In this case, there is a static helper class called Redirector that has a single helper method called PerformCentralLogin.

C#

```csharp
public static class Redirector
{
    //snip….
    private static string centralLoginUrl;

    static Redirector()
    {
        centralLoginUrl = ConfigurationSettings.AppSettings["centralLoginUrl"];

        //snip…
    }

    public static void PerformCentralLogin(Page p)
    {
        string redirectUrl =
            FormsAuthentication.GetRedirectUrl(string.Empty, false);

        //snip…
        string baseServer = p.Request.Url.DnsSafeHost;

        string customRedirectUrl = "http://" + baseServer + redirectUrl;

        p.Response.Redirect(
            centralLoginUrl + "?CustomReturnUrl=" +
            p.Server.UrlEncode(customRedirectUrl) +
            "&CustomCookiePath=" +
            p.Server.UrlEncode(FormsAuthentication.FormsCookiePath));
    }
}
```

VB.NET

```
Public NotInheritable Class Redirector
    //snip…
    Private Shared centralLoginUrl As String

    Shared Sub New()
            centralLoginUrl = ConfigurationSettings.AppSettings("centralLoginUrl")

            //snip…
    End Sub

    Public Shared Sub PerformCentralLogin(ByVal p As Page)
            Dim redirectUrl As String = _
            FormsAuthentication.GetRedirectUrl(String.Empty, False)
            //snip…
            Dim baseServer As String = p.Request.Url.DnsSafeHost

            Dim customRedirectUrl As String = "http://" & baseServer & redirectUrl

            p.Response.Redirect(centralLoginUrl & _
                    "?CustomReturnUrl=" & _
                    p.Server.UrlEncode(customRedirectUrl) & _
                    "&CustomCookiePath=" & _
                    p.Server.UrlEncode(FormsAuthentication.FormsCookiePath))
    End Sub
End Class
```

For simplicity, I placed the static class definition into the App_Code directory of each participating application. In a production application, you would take this one step further and at least compile the code into a bin-deployable assembly, if not the GAC.

When the Redirector class is first used, the static constructor runs. For now, the code snippet shows only part of the work in the static constructor where it fetches the central login URL once for future use. The single parameter to the PerformCentralLogin method is a reference to the current page. This ensures the helper method has access to any request-specific objects necessary to build up the redirect information. The PerformCentralLogin method fetches the redirect URL using FormsAuthentication .GetRedirectUrl. At this point, calling GetRedirectUrl works because it returns the virtual path to the originally requested page. However, as noted earlier, the path lacks the server information necessary to allow redirects to work against any arbitrary set of servers and DNS namespaces.

Ignoring some other functionality for a second, the method fetches the server portion of the current URL. With both the server's address, and the virtual path in hand, the method constructs the fully qualified redirect path. The method can now redirect to the central login application's login page, including the fully qualified return URL in the CustomReturnUrl query-string variable and the correct cookie path information for the forms authentication ticket in the CustomCookiePath query-string variable.

So, the net result of the original call in the Load event of Login.aspx is that the participating application silently constructs and issues a redirect into the central login application. No user interface for login is ever returned by a participating application.

Let's return the code that was snipped out earlier. The following includes bolded code that shows some additional logic:

C#

```csharp
public static class Redirector
{
    private static Dictionary<string, string> pages;
    private static string centralLoginUrl;

    static Redirector()
    {
        centralLoginUrl = ConfigurationSettings.AppSettings["centralLoginUrl"];

        //Register page mappings to force correct casing for the cookie
        //that will eventually be issued.
        pages =
         new Dictionary<string, string>(StringComparer.InvariantCultureIgnoreCase);

        pages.Add("/AppAUsingCentralLogin/Default.aspx",
                "/AppAUsingCentralLogin/Default.aspx");

        pages.Add("/AppAUsingCentralLogin/AnotherPage.aspx",
                "/AppAUsingCentralLogin/AnotherPage.aspx");

    }

    public static void PerformCentralLogin(Page p)
    {
        string redirectUrl =
            FormsAuthentication.GetRedirectUrl(string.Empty, false);

        //Fix the casing of the redirect URL to prevent problems with new cookies
        //being issued for a request with incorrect casing on the URL.
        redirectUrl = pages[redirectUrl];
        string baseServer = p.Request.Url.DnsSafeHost;

        string customRedirectUrl = "http://" + baseServer + redirectUrl;

        p.Response.Redirect(
                centralLoginUrl + "?CustomReturnUrl=" +
                p.Server.UrlEncode(customRedirectUrl) +
                "&CustomCookiePath=" +
                p.Server.UrlEncode(FormsAuthentication.FormsCookiePath));
    }
}
```

VB.NET

```vbnet
Public NotInheritable Class Redirector
    Private Shared pages As Dictionary(Of String, String)
    Private Shared centralLoginUrl As String

    Shared Sub New()
        centralLoginUrl = ConfigurationSettings.AppSettings("centralLoginUrl")

        'Register page mappings to force correct casing for the cookie
        'that will eventually be issued.
```

```
            pages = _
    New Dictionary(Of String, String)(StringComparer.InvariantCultureIgnoreCase)

        pages.Add("/AppAUsingCentralLogin_vb/Default.aspx", _
            "/AppAUsingCentralLogin_vb/Default.aspx")

        pages.Add("/AppAUsingCentralLogin_vb/AnotherPage.aspx", _
            "/AppAUsingCentralLogin_vb/AnotherPage.aspx")

    End Sub

    Public Shared Sub PerformCentralLogin(ByVal p As Page)
        Dim redirectUrl As String =
        FormsAuthentication.GetRedirectUrl(String.Empty, False)
        'Fixup the casing of the redirect URL to prevent problems
        'with new cookies being issued for a request with
        'incorrect casing on the URL.
        redirectUrl = pages(redirectUrl)
        Dim baseServer As String = p.Request.Url.DnsSafeHost

        Dim customRedirectUrl As String = "http://" & baseServer & redirectUrl

        p.Response.Redirect(centralLoginUrl & _
            "?CustomReturnUrl=" & _
            p.Server.UrlEncode(customRedirectUrl) & _
            "&CustomCookiePath=" & _
            p.Server.UrlEncode(FormsAuthentication.FormsCookiePath))
    End Sub

    End Class
```

The bolded code in the preceding code deals with a quirk in cookie handling. If you depend on setting the Path property of an HttpCookie, the path information is case-sensitive. For many developers, using forms authentication this isn't an issue because forms authentication defaults to a path of /. However, when putting together this sample, there were some frustrating moments before realizing that some of the test URLs I was using had incorrect casing compared to the path of the forms authentication cookie.

If you plan to create your own SSO-lite solution, and if you intend to segment forms authentication tickets between applications through the use of a cookie's path property, you need to be very careful about how URLs are handled in your code. In the case of the sample SSO-lite solution, the bolded code is a simple workaround for ensuring proper casing. The helper class holds a dictionary containing every URL in the application. The trick here is that the dictionary uses a case-insensitive string comparer, and it uses the invariant culture. This means whenever a lookup is made into the dictionary, the key comparison ignores case, and treats culture-sensitive characters in a neutral manner.

When the PerformCentralLogin method runs, it always takes the redirect URL as returned from forms authentication and converts it into the correct casing. The theory here is that if this method is called, it is very likely that it is being called due to an end user (like myself) accidentally typing in the wrong casing for a URL in the IE address bar. By performing a lookup into the static dictionary, the method can convert any arbitrary casing on the redirect URL into a URL with correct casing. Because the SSO-lite solution does partition forms authentication tickets with paths other than / (from the configuration a few pages back, the current application we are looking at uses a cookie path of /AppAUsingCentralLogin), it is important to perform this conversion prior to sending the redirect URL to the central login application.

Central Login Application

The configuration for the central login application pretty much mirrors that of the participating applications.

```
<configuration xmlns="http://schemas.microsoft.com/.NetConfiguration/v2.0">
 <system.web>

  <machineKey
    decryptionKey="A225194E99BCCB0F6B92BC9D82F12C2907BD07CF069BC8B4"
    validationKey="6FA5B7DB89076816248243B8FD7336CCA360DAF8"
  />

  <authentication mode="Forms">
    <forms cookieless="UseCookies" enableCrossAppRedirects="true"
           path="/CentralLogin" slidingExpiration="true"
           timeout="30"/>
  </authentication>

  <authorization>
    <deny users="?"/>
  </authorization>

 </system.web>
</configuration>
```

Unlike the participating applications, the central login application does not register any URL in the <appSettings /> section. In fact, the SSO-lite solution shown here has zero knowledge of any of the other participating applications.

The bolded attributes in the <forms /> element are of interest because these settings not only define behavior for the master forms authentication ticket issued by the central login application, the settings also influence the ticket behavior for the participating application. Of course, enableCrossApp Redirects is set to true because without that, there is no way to hop tickets between applications. The path attribute ensures that the forms authentication ticket for the central login application stays in the central login application. This is why I refer to the forms authentication ticket from the central login application as the "master" forms authentication ticket. After it is issued, the cookie never flows to any other application.

The slidingExpiration and timeout attributes define the expiration behavior for the master forms authentication ticket. Because the master ticket is also cloned and used as the source for tickets sent to other participating applications, this means these attributes also define the expiration behavior for all other applications. In the case above, the central login application is using the standard timeout of 30 minutes, and it is allowing sliding expirations. Remember, though, that slidingExpiration is always set to false in all of the participating applications. This point will be expanded on below when I cover the login page.

The login page in the central login application normally would have the user interface for collecting credentials and validating them. However, because this is just a sample that focuses on the mechanics of passing tickets around, the actual "login" on the page is pretty basic and uses a fixed credential:

C#

```csharp
protected void Button1_Click(object sender, EventArgs e)
{
    FormsAuthentication.SetAuthCookie("testuser", false);

    string redirectUrl = Request.QueryString["CustomReturnUrl"];
    string cookiePath = Request.QueryString["CustomCookiePath"];

    Response.Redirect("Login.aspx?CustomReturnUrl=" + redirectUrl +
                  "&CustomCookiePath=" + cookiePath, true);
}
```

VB.NET

```vbnet
Protected Sub Button1_Click( _
ByVal sender As Object, _
ByVal e As EventArgs) Handles Button1.Click
    FormsAuthentication.SetAuthCookie("testuser", False)

    Dim redirectUrl As String = Request.QueryString("CustomReturnUrl")
    Dim cookiePath As String = Request.QueryString("CustomCookiePath")

    Response.Redirect("Login.aspx?CustomReturnUrl=" & redirectUrl &
    "&CustomCookiePath=" & cookiePath, True)
End Sub
```

Rather than calling `FormsAuthentication.RedirectFromLoginPage`, the button click handler for login calls `SetAuthCookie`. Calling `SetAuthCookie` ensures that the master forms authentication cookie is set in the `Response`, but it also allows the login page to do other work and then programmatically issue a redirect.

Because the `CustomReturnUrl` and `CustomCookiePath` attributes are still needed, the click event handler simply moves the values from the inbound Request query-string to the query-string variables on the redirect. The important thing to note about the click event handler is that it will only be called when an interactive login is required. The very first time website users enter any participating site, they will end up with the interactive login and their response will flow to the click event handler. However, as the following code shows, the login page also supports noninteractive login:

C#

```csharp
protected void Page_Load(object sender, EventArgs e)
{
    //If the user is already authenticated, then punt them back
    //to the original application, but place a new forms authentication
    //ticket on the query string.
    if (User.Identity.IsAuthenticated == true)
    {
        //This information comes from the forms authentication cookie for the
```

```
                    //central login site.
                    FormsIdentity fi = (FormsIdentity)User.Identity;
                    FormsAuthenticationTicket originalTicket = fi.Ticket;

                    //For sliding expirations, ensure the ticket is periodically refreshed.
                    DateTime expirationDate;
                    if (FormsAuthentication.SlidingExpiration == true)
                    {
                        TimeSpan timeout =
                         originalTicket.Expiration.Subtract(originalTicket.IssueDate);
                        expirationDate =
                         originalTicket.IssueDate.Add(new TimeSpan(timeout.Ticks / 2));
                        expirationDate.AddMinutes(1);
                    }
                    else
                        expirationDate = originalTicket.Expiration;

                    FormsAuthenticationTicket ft =
                        new FormsAuthenticationTicket
                            (originalTicket.Version,
                             originalTicket.Name,
                             originalTicket.IssueDate,
                             expirationDate,
                             originalTicket.IsPersistent,
                             originalTicket.UserData,
                             Request.QueryString["CustomCookiePath"]
                            );

                    string redirectUrl = Request.QueryString["CustomReturnUrl"];

                    Response.Redirect(
                        redirectUrl + "?" +
                        FormsAuthentication.FormsCookieName + "=" +
                        FormsAuthentication.Encrypt(ft));
                }
            }
```

VB.NET

```
Protected Sub Page_Load(ByVal sender As Object, ByVal e As EventArgs) _
Handles Me.Load
    'If the user is already authenticated, then punt them back
    'to the original application, but place a new forms authentication
    'ticket on the query string.
    If User.Identity.IsAuthenticated = True Then
        'This information comes from the forms authentication cookie for the
        'central login site.
        Dim fi As FormsIdentity = CType(User.Identity, FormsIdentity)
        Dim originalTicket As FormsAuthenticationTicket = fi.Ticket

        'For sliding expirations, ensure the ticket is periodically refreshed.
        Dim expirationDate As DateTime
        If FormsAuthentication.SlidingExpiration = True Then
            Dim timeout As TimeSpan = _
            originalTicket.Expiration.Subtract(originalTicket.IssueDate)
```

```
                    expirationDate = _
                    originalTicket.IssueDate.Add(New TimeSpan(timeout.Ticks / 2))
                    expirationDate.AddMinutes(1)
                Else
                    expirationDate = originalTicket.Expiration
                End If


                Dim ft As New FormsAuthenticationTicket( _
                originalTicket.Version, originalTicket.Name, _
                originalTicket.IssueDate, expirationDate, originalTicket.IsPersistent, _
                originalTicket.UserData, Request.QueryString("CustomCookiePath"))

                Dim redirectUrl As String = Request.QueryString("CustomReturnUrl")

                Response.Redirect(redirectUrl & "?" & FormsAuthentication.FormsCookieName
                & "=" & FormsAuthentication.Encrypt(ft))
            End If
        End Sub
```

Actually, what happens when a website used first needs to login against the central login application is that the Load event handler runs. However, because this event handler falls through for unauthenticated users, the very first time a user needs to log in he or she instead ends up with the login page being rendered and can perform an interactive login.

The noninteractive login occurs on most subsequent requests. For example, the button click handler for the login page redirects back to the same page. When the redirect comes back to the login page, there is now a master forms authentication ticket sent along with the request (from the SetAuthCookie call in the button click handler). As a result, when the Load event runs again, it sees that the user is authenticated, and so no interactive UI is even rendered.

The Load event first gets a reference to the master forms authentication ticket because it needs most of the information in that ticket to create a forms authentication ticket for the participating site. The Load event creates a new forms authentication ticket and carries over almost all of the settings from the master forms authentication ticket. For example, this means a participating site gets the exact same issue date and expiration date as the master forms authentication ticket. If you build a similar solution, you could choose to actually store DateTime.Now for the IssueDate of the new ticket. The main point, though, is that the expiration date for tickets sent to participating sites is based on the expiration date for the login against the central login application.

If you use absolute ticket expiration in the central login application, the behavior when tickets timeout in participating applications is pretty clear. When a forms authentication ticket times out in a participating application, the request is redirected through the local login page, which ends up requesting the central login page. However, because all tickets use the same timeout values, the master forms authentication ticket has also timed out. As a result, the redirect to the central login application falls through the Load event (the user is no longer considered authenticated), and instead the interactive login is shown. When the interactive login completes, a new master forms authentication ticket is issued, and the second execution of the login page results in a redirect with a new ticket and a new expiration date back to the participating application.

On the other hand, if you use sliding expirations in the central login application, the reauthentication should be transparent to the website user. The ticket for the participating application is issued with a modified expiration date. Instead of using the same expiration date as the master forms authentication ticket, the time to live for the ticket is set to half the TTL for the master forms authentication ticket, plus one extra minute. Because you know that forms authentication automatically reissues tickets when 50 percent or more of the remaining time to live has passed for a ticket, the idea is to create a ticket for the participating applications that will timeout in a similar manner. The extra one minute is added to account for clock-skew between the central login application and participating applications.

What happens now is that in the participating applications with absolute expirations, the forms authentication ticket eventually times out at (IssueDate + 50 percent of the central login application's timeout + 1 minute). This results in a redirect back to the central login page. However, because (Expiration Date – 50 percent of the central login application's timeout – 1 minute) of time remains on the master forms authentication ticket, the master ticket is still considered valid. On the other hand, though, because the master forms authentication ticket has less than 50 pertcent of its remaining lifetime left, the FormsAuthenticationModule in the central login application will automatically renew the master forms authentication ticket, which results in a new IssueDate and a new ExpirationDate.

Because the renewal occurs in the HTTP pipeline before the login page ever runs, by the time the Load event executes, a new master forms authentication ticket is available. As a result, the ticket that is created for the participating application contains a new IssueDate and an ExpirationDate roughly equal to (DateTime.Now + 50 percent of the central login application's timeout + 1 minute). When this ticket is sent back to the participating application, it results in a valid forms authentication ticket, and the website user is returned to the originally requested page. Although a few redirects occurred underneath the hood, there was no interactive login required to renew the cookie.

Another property in the new forms authentication ticket that differs is the CookiePath. Rather than cloning over the cookie path from the forms authentication ticket, the value from the CustomCookiePath query-string variable is used instead. This is how the central login application ensures that the ticket sent back to the participating application has the correct path information. The FormsAuthentication Module in the participating application will use the CookiePath value from this ticket when it constructs and issues the forms authentication cookie.

The CustomReturnUrl query-string variable is used to build the redirect URL. Because this value includes the full qualified path back to a page in the participating application, the redirect issued by the central login page can cross servers and domains. You can see the chain that leads up to this point as well:

1. Participating application creates the fully qualified return URL.

2. Central login application replays fully qualified return URL when it redirects to itself.

3. Central login application uses replayed fully qualified return URL when it redirects back to the participating application.

The actual redirect includes the query-string variable and value with the forms authentication ticket. It uses the exact same code as you saw earlier when cross-application redirects were first introduced.

The Final Leg of the SSO Login

At this point, a redirect has been issued back to the participating application, to the specific page that the website user was originally trying to access. The user is able to navigate around the participating application because now there is a valid forms authentication cookie. If the cookie eventually times out, the behavior described earlier around ExpirationDate takes effect, and a new ticket is issued.

If the website user surfs over to another participating application, there is of course no forms authentication cookie for this third application. However, the exact same logic applies. In the third application:

1. A redirect to the local login page occurs.

2. The local login page redirects to the central login application.

3. Because the master forms authentication ticket exists, the central login application transparently creates a new ticket and sends it back to the participating application.

4. The participating application converts the ticket in the query-string into a valid forms authentication cookie, and the originally requested page runs.

Examples of Using the SSO-Lite Solution

Using a sample participating application called AppAUsingCentralLogin, the initial attempt to fetch default.aspx results in a redirect to the interactive login page in the central login application. The URL at this point looks like (bolded areas inserted for clarity):

```
http://bhaidar-pc/CentralLogin/Login.aspx?CustomReturnUrl=http%3a%2f%2flocalhost%2f
AppAUsingCentralLogin%2fDefault.aspx&CustomCookiePath=%2fAppAUsingCentralLogin
```

You can see that the URL is pointed at the central login page. The CustomReturnUrl query-string variable contains the URL-encoded representation of a test server as well as the full path to default.aspx. The CustomCookiePath query-string variable contains the path information that was set in the <forms /> configuration element of the participating application /AppAUsingCentralLogin.

After successfully logging in, you are redirected back to the originally requested URL. The URL in the address bar at this point looks like:

```
http://localhost/AppAUsingCentralLogin/Default.aspx?.ASPXAUTH=090AC8BAD650B5186DD7B
A78D7A5A88F310F2C69CCD6C640C2541AC1CF2559F6D8283EC9339A957B8005CEB6C8306715471654A8
53E33BD57859C0BFED309DBDC08C582A0FDBBB3C7E0B5993A23E8BBD2BD8ACBC6ABC04607A423067273
F4A83112C5F52679FA71AB36D5F8144BB20586832623F6BB17EC1
```

Because the SSO-lite solution relies on cross-application redirects, the very first page accessed after the redirect from the central login application includes the forms authentication ticket sitting in the query-string. If you navigate around into the site though, this query-string variable goes away:

```
http://localhost/AppAUsingCentralLogin/AnotherPage.aspx
```

If you now navigate over to a second participating application:

```
http://bhaidar-PC/AppBUsingCentralLogin/Default.aspx
```

There is a slight pause while the redirects occur, but you end up on default.aspx, with the address bar showing the following:

```
http://localhost/AppBUsingCentralLogin/Default.aspx?.ASPXAUTH=079B144714F15D4934761
64AC79DBE45D91DD19A1DB728F591CFB9B08307E4B0ECCE05E4A4DE5F62E997F4521477F1B3C9FD7A31
A8F25387BE18A64E1B50954C126353791741AC698165140E4C71A12D31A9E22F0AC8BD425D026F6A800
5B5028D039253F66A23AB97DED3F1DB3D9009B691C615B77BAE20
```

No prompt for login occurs, though, because the master forms authentication cookie has already been issued. As with the first participating application, the initial redirect from the central login application back to application B (in this case), results in the forms authentication ticket showing on the URL. When you navigate deeper into the site, this will go away.

Although I can't show it here in a book, if you take the code for the central login application in Visual Studio and attach to w3wp.exe with the debugger, you can see how tickets are renewed in the sliding expiration case with the following steps:

1.   Set the timeout attribute in the central login application to three minutes or more.

2.   Access one of the participating applications and go through the login process.

3.   Attach the central login application with the debugger and set breakpoints in the Load event of the login page.

4.   Wait for 2.5 minutes (50 percent of the central application's timeout plus one minute). This is the timeout on the ticket sent to the participating application.

5.   Access another page in the participating application. At this point, you will see that the breakpoints in the central login page are hit and a new forms authentication ticket is issued for the participating application. If you inspect the new IssueDate and ExpirationDate, you will see that they have all been updated with new values. Because the master forms authentication ticket was 2.5 minutes old when the redirect back to the central login application occurred, the FormsAuthenticationModule in the central login application automatically renewed the master ticket as well.

Final Notes on the SSO-Lite Solution

You have seen that with cross-application redirects in ASP.NET 2.0 and ASP.NET 3.5's forms authentication, it is possible to sort of cobble together an SSO-like solution. However, now that I have shown how to accomplish it, there are a number of technical points that you still need to keep in mind.

❑   The solution depends entirely on redirects between different servers and different domains. There may be the possibility of getting browser security warnings when running under SSL and a redirect occurs to a completely different application and DNS domain.

❑   Because of the dependency on redirects, you need to be careful in how participating applications are structured as well as in the ticket timeouts. It is entirely possible that a user working on a form in an application posts data back to the server and then loses all of the information when a silent reauthentication with the central login site occurs.

❑   In the case of sliding expirations, the sample depends on very specific behavior around the renewal of forms authentication tickets. Although this renewal behavior is documented, the trick with adding a one minute offset is fragile, both due to the potential for changes in the underlying forms authentication behavior as well as the variability around clock skew between participating applications and the central login server. A more robust solution could involve a custom HttpModule installed on each participating site that would optionally renew the ticket based on information carried in the UserData property of the ticket.

❑   You may want more control over how ticket timeouts are handled in general, both for the master forms authentication ticket and for the participating sites. For example, you may want configurable ticket timeouts that vary depending on which participating application is requesting a ticket.

❑ There was no concept of federation or trust shown in the sample SSO solution. For an in-house IT shop, this probably would not be an issue because developers at least know of other development organizations sharing server farms and there is an implicit level of trust. However, in the case of disparate Internet facing sites run by different companies, trust is an incredibly important aspect of any SSO solution. Attempting to create an SSO solution on top of forms authentication for such a scenario probably isn't realistic.

❑ Last, the sample application allows any participating application to make use of it. With the prevalence of phishing attacks on the Internet these days, you would want to add some additional security in an SSO-lite solution. At a minimum, you would want the central login application to only accept login attempts from URLs that are "trusted" by the central login application. This would prevent attacks where a malicious website poses as the login page to a legitimate site, and then through social engineering attacks (that is, an unwary user clicking through a spam email) harvests a valid forms authentication ticket issued by the central login application. This specific scenario is why, for more complex SSO scenarios, you would want to use a commercial SSO product that incorporates the concept of trust, both trust between participating sites as well as trust between applications and the website that issues credentials.

Overall, I think these points highlight the fact that cross-application redirects can definitely be used for solving some of the simpler problems companies run into around single sign-on. However, if you find that your websites require more than just a basic capability to share tickets across servers and applications, you will probably need to either write more code to handle your requirements or go with a third-party SSO solution.

Enforcing Single Logons and Logouts

A question that comes up from time to time is the desire to ensure the following behavior when users login with forms authentication:

❑ Users should be allowed to login once, and only once. If they attempt to log in a second time in an application, the login should be rejected.

❑ If users explicitly log out, the fact that they logged out should in some way be remembered to prevent replaying previous authentication tickets.

Both of these design questions highlight the fact that forms authentication is a lightweight mechanism for enforcing authentication. Forms authentication as a feature does not have any back-end data store. As a result there isn't an out-of-box solution that automatically keeps track of login sessions and subsequent logouts. However, with a little bit of coding, it is possible to deal with both scenarios in ASP.NET 2.0 and ASP.NET 3.5.

The solution outlined in this section relies on the Membership feature of ASP.NET 2.0 and ASP.NET 3.5. There is an extensive discussion of extending Membership in Chapters 11, 12, and 13. However, because this chapter deals with forms authentication, it makes more sense to show the Membership-based solution at this point rather than deferring it. Because Membership is designed to work hand-in-hand with forms authentication, it is a logical place to store "interesting" information about the logged-in or logged-out state of a user account. Of course, you could write your own database solution for the same purposes, or possibly even use the Profile feature in ASP.NET 2.0 and ASP.NET 3.5 for similar purposes, but given that Membership is readily available and is part of the authentication stack in ASP.NET 2.0 and ASP.NET 3.5, it makes sense to leverage it.

Enforcing a Single Logon

For the first scenario of preventing duplicate login attempts, the fact that Membership stores its information in a database (or in AD and ADAM, if you so choose) makes it very useful in web farms. Any information stored into the `MembershipUser` instance for a logged-on user will be available from any other web server in the farm. In the same vein, because Membership providers can be configured in multiple applications to point at the same database, it is also possible to use information in a `MembershipUser` instance across multiple applications.

The `MembershipUser` object doesn't have many places for storing additional information. However, the `Comment` property on `MembershipUser` is not used by ASP.NET, so it is a convenient place to store information without needing to write derived versions of `MembershipUser` as well as derived versions of `MembershipProvider`(s).

Enforcing the concept of a single logon requires tracking two pieces of information associated with a successful logon:

❑ The expiration time for the successful logon

❑ Some type of identifier associated with the logon

Knowing when a successful logon expires is important because most website users probably never use explicit logout mechanisms. Instead, most users navigate through a site, perform whatever required work there is and then close the browser. In this case, if a user comes back to the site at a later point after the original logon session has expired, you do not want to nag the user about preexisting logon sessions that have since expired. Instead, you want an authentication solution that recognizes the previous logon has expired and silently cleans up after the fact.

The second piece of information is important to keep track of because you need some concrete representation of the fact that a user logged in to the website. Just storing an expiration date is not sufficient. An expiration date indicates when an active logon session expires, but the date alone does not give you enough information to correlate to the fact that someone logged in to a website. By tracking some type of session identifier, you can check on each inbound request whether the authentication data is for the active logon session or for some other logon session.

A logon session identifier also gives the website user the ability to forcibly logout another active session. This scenario is important if, for example, a user logs in to your website on one machine and forgets about it. Then the user walks down the hallway to another machine and attempts to log in again. With the logon session identifier, you have a way to allow the user to log on using other machines while ensuring that the previous logon session (or sessions) that are sitting idle on some other machine cannot be reused when the individual gets back to his or her desk.

So, just from this brief overview of the main problems involved with enforcing a single login, you can see that there is a fair amount of tracking and enforcement necessary to get all this working. The good thing, though, is that it is possible to build this type of enforcement using the existing forms authentication and Membership features.

You will start out building the solution by looking at a sample login page. Since ASP.NET 2.0 and ASP.NET 3.5 conveniently include the UI login controls, building the basic UI with logical events during the login process is a snap. Drop a login control onto a page, and then convert it into a template. Converting it into a template allows you to add UI customizations as needed. In this case, you need to add a check box that allows an end user to forcibly logout other active logon sessions.

```
<!-- snip -->
<tr>
 <td colspan="2">
    <asp:CheckBox ID="ForceLogout" runat="server"
                   Text="Check here to invalidate other logon sessions." />
 </td>
</tr>
<!-- snip -->
```

So much for the UI aspect of the login control. Switching to the code-behind for the page, there are two events that you want to handle:

❑   LoggingIn: This event gives you the opportunity to perform some checks before the Login control attempts to validate credentials using the Membership feature. It is a good place to check and see whether or not another active logon session is in progress.

❑   LoggedIn: This event occurs after the Login control has successfully validated credentials. Because enforcing a single login requires some extra work on your part, this is the logical point to create a FormsAuthenticationTicket with extra information and issue it.

The LoggedIn event is where you store information inside of Membership that indicates the logon session ID as well as the session expiration inside of the forms authentication ticket.

C#

```
//snip...
protected MembershipUser loginUser;

protected void Login1_LoggedIn(object sender, EventArgs e)
    {
        if (loginUser == null)
            loginUser = Membership.GetUser(Login1.UserName);

        //represents the active login "session"
        Guid g = System.Guid.NewGuid();

        HttpCookie c = Response.Cookies[FormsAuthentication.FormsCookieName];
        FormsAuthenticationTicket ft = FormsAuthentication.Decrypt(c.Value);

        //Generate a new ticket that includes the login session ID
        FormsAuthenticationTicket ftNew =
            new FormsAuthenticationTicket(
                ft.Version,
                ft.Name,
                ft.IssueDate,
                ft.Expiration,
                ft.IsPersistent,
```

```
                g.ToString(),
                ft.CookiePath);

        //Store the expiration date and login session ID in Membership
        loginUser.Comment =
            "LoginExpiration;" + ft.Expiration.ToString() +
            "|LoginSessionID;" + g.ToString();
        Membership.UpdateUser(loginUser);

        //Re-issue the updated forms authentication ticket
        Response.Cookies.Remove(FormsAuthentication.FormsCookieName);

        //Basically clone the original cookie except for the payload
        HttpCookie newAuthCookie =
            new HttpCookie(
                FormsAuthentication.FormsCookieName,
                FormsAuthentication.Encrypt(ftNew));
        //Re-use the cookie settings from forms authentication
        newAuthCookie.HttpOnly = c.HttpOnly;
        newAuthCookie.Path = c.Path;
        newAuthCookie.Secure = c.Secure;
        newAuthCookie.Domain = c.Domain;
        newAuthCookie.Expires = c.Expires;

        //And set it back in the response
        Response.Cookies.Add(newAuthCookie);

    }
```

VB.NET

```
...
Protected loginUser As MembershipUser
    Protected Sub Login1_LoggedIn( _
    ByVal sender As Object, _
    ByVal e As EventArgs) Handles Login1.LoggedIn
        If loginUser Is Nothing Then
            loginUser = Membership.GetUser(Login1.UserName)
        End If

        'DetermineExpirationForNewLogin();

        'represents the active login "session"
        Dim g As Guid = System.Guid.NewGuid()

        Dim c As HttpCookie = Response.Cookies(FormsAuthentication.FormsCookieName)
        Dim ft As FormsAuthenticationTicket = _
        FormsAuthentication.Decrypt(c.Value.ToString)

        'Generate a new ticket that includes the login session ID
        Dim ftNew As New FormsAuthenticationTicket( _
        ft.Version, ft.Name, ft.IssueDate, ft.Expiration, _
        ft.IsPersistent, g.ToString(), ft.CookiePath)
```

```
                  'Store the expiration date and login session ID in Membership
                  loginUser.Comment = "LoginExpiration;" & ft.Expiration.ToString() &
                  "|LoginSessionID;" & g.ToString()
                  Membership.UpdateUser(loginUser)

                  'Re-issue the updated forms authentication ticket
                  Response.Cookies.Remove(FormsAuthentication.FormsCookieName)

                  'Basically clone the original cookie except for the payload
                  Dim newAuthCookie As New HttpCookie(FormsAuthentication.FormsCookieName,
                  FormsAuthentication.Encrypt(ftNew))
                  newAuthCookie.HttpOnly = c.HttpOnly
                  newAuthCookie.Path = c.Path
                  newAuthCookie.Secure = c.Secure
                  newAuthCookie.Domain = c.Domain
                  newAuthCookie.Expires = c.Expires

                  'And set it back in the response
                  Response.Cookies.Add(newAuthCookie)

          End Sub
```

After a successful login, the page first ensures there is a MembershipUser reference available for the user that is logging in. The GetUser(…) overload that accepts a username must be used because even though the user's credentials have been successfully verified at this point, from a forms authentication viewpoint, the page is still running with an anonymous user on the current HttpContext. It won't be until the next page request that the FormsAuthenticationModule has a cookie on the request that it can convert into a FormsIdentity.

Because the LoggedIn event won't run unless other preliminary checks ensure that it is alright for the user to login, there aren't any other validation checks in this event handler. To reach this event, the credentials will already have been verified as matching, and the other checks in the LoggingIn event (shown a little bit later) will also have been passed.

For this sample, a Guid was chosen as the representation of a login session—so the event handler creates a new Guid to represent a new instance of a login session. As you have seen in other sections, because the forms authentication APIs do not expose timeout information, you need to get to it through a workaround. In this case, because the Login control has already called SetAuthCookie internally, there is a valid forms authentication cookie sitting in the Response. With this cookie, you can get the FormsAuthenticationTicket for the user that is logging in.

A new FormsAuthenticationTicket is created that is a clone of the already issued ticket, with one difference. The UserData information in the ticket is where the Guid login session identifier is stored. Note that because this sample application relies on the UserData property, enforcing a single logon in this manner will only work with clients that support cookies. The Expiration and the Guid for the ticket are also packaged up and stored in the MembershipUser instance for the user logging in. In more complex applications, you could create a custom class that represented this type of information, run the class through the XmlSerializer, and store the output in the Comment property. For simplicity though, the sample application stores the information with the following format:

```
LoginExpiration;expiration_date|LoginSessionID;the_Guid
```

Each piece of information is a name-value pair, with different name-value pairs delimited with the pipe character. Within a name-value pair, the two pieces of information are delimited by a semicolon. Once the Comment field has the new information, Membership.UpdateUser is called to store the changes back to the database.

The last piece of work during login is to replace the forms authentication cookie issued by the Login control with the FormsAuthenticationTicket that has the UserData in it. Again, rather than attempting to hard-code pieces of forms authentication configuration information into the application, the sample code simply reuses all of the settings from the Login control's cookie to create a new cookie with all of the correct settings. The Login control's original cookie is then removed from the Response, and the new cookie is added in its place.

At this point, when the login page completes, the user is successfully logged in with the session identifier flowing back and forth between the browser and the web server inside of the forms authentication ticket. There is also a persistent representation of the expiration time for the login as well as the session identifier stored in the Membership system. These pieces of information form the basis for checking the validity of a login on each and every request.

Because the FormsAuthenticationModule runs during the AuthenticateRequest event in the pipeline, it makes sense to perform additional validations after forms authentication has performed the basic work of determining whether or not there is a valid forms-authenticated user for the request. A custom HttpModule is used to enforce that the current request is associated with the current login session.

C#

```csharp
public class FormsAuthSessionEnforcement : IHttpModule
{
    public FormsAuthSessionEnforcement(){}
    public void Dispose() {}

    public void Init(HttpApplication context)
    {
        context.PostAuthenticateRequest += new EventHandler(OnPostAuthenticate);
    }

    private void OnPostAuthenticate(Object sender, EventArgs e)
    {
        HttpApplication a = (HttpApplication)sender;
        HttpContext c = a.Context;

        //If the user was authenticated with Forms Authentication
        //Then check the session ID.
        if (c.User.Identity.IsAuthenticated == true)
        {
            FormsAuthenticationTicket ft =
                ((FormsIdentity)c.User.Identity).Ticket;

            Guid g = new Guid(ft.UserData);

            MembershipUser loginUser = Membership.GetUser(ft.Name);
            string currentSessionString =
```

```
                    loginUser.Comment.Split("|".ToCharArray())[1];
                Guid currentSession =
                    new Guid(currentSessionString.Split(";".ToCharArray())[1]);

                //If the session in the cookie does not match the current session as
                // stored in the Membership database, then terminate this request
                if (g != currentSession)
                {
                    FormsAuthentication.SignOut();
                    FormsAuthentication.RedirectToLoginPage();
                }
            }
        }
    }
}
```

VB.NET

```
Public Class FormsAuthSessionEnforcement
  Implements IHttpModule
  Public Sub New()
  End Sub

  Public Sub Init(ByVal context As HttpApplication) Implements IHttpModule.Init
      AddHandler context.PostAuthenticateRequest, AddressOf OnPostAuthenticate
  End Sub

    Private Sub OnPostAuthenticate(ByVal sender As Object, ByVal e As EventArgs)
        Dim a As HttpApplication = CType(sender, HttpApplication)
        Dim c As HttpContext = a.Context

        If c.User Is Nothing Then
            Return
        End If

        'If the user was authenticated with Forms Authentication
        'Then check the session ID.
        If c.User.Identity.IsAuthenticated = True Then
            Dim ft As FormsAuthenticationTicket = _
            (CType(c.User.Identity, FormsIdentity)).Ticket

            Dim g As New Guid(ft.UserData)

            Dim loginUser As MembershipUser = Membership.GetUser(ft.Name)
            Dim currentSession As Guid
            'If there isn't any session information in Membership at this point
            'then it is likely the user logged out, and an old cookie is
            'being replayed.
            If (Not String.IsNullOrEmpty(loginUser.Comment)) Then
                Dim currentSessionString As String = _
                loginUser.Comment.Split("|".ToCharArray())(1)
                currentSession = _
                New Guid(currentSessionString.Split(";".ToCharArray())(1))
            Else
                currentSession = Guid.Empty
            End If
```

```
                    'If the session in the cookie does not match the current session as
                    'stored in the Membership database, then terminate this request
                    If g <> currentSession Then
                        FormsAuthentication.SignOut()
                        FormsAuthentication.RedirectToLoginPage()
                    End If

            End If
        End Sub

        Public Sub Dispose() Implements IHttpModule.Dispose
        End Sub

End Class
```

The custom module hooks the PostAuthenticateRequest event so that it can inspect the authenticated credentials after the FormsAuthenticationModule has run. If the current request doesn't have an authenticated user, the module exits. On the other hand, if there is an authenticated user, the module gets a reference to the FormsAuthenticationTicket and extracts the Guid login session identifier. The login information for the authenticated user is also retrieved from the Membership database.

The module is only concerned with checking the validity of the session identifier so that it doesn't bother retrieving the expiration date from the MembershipUser instance because the FormsAuthentication Module will already have made this check. The module does check the session identifier in the ticket against the session identifier stored in the database. If they match, the request is allowed to proceed. However, if the two identifiers do not match, this is an indication that the current request is not associated with an active and valid login session. In this case, the module calls FormsAuthentication.SignOut, which has the effect of issuing a cookie that will clear the forms authentication cookie in the browser. Then the module redirects the current request to the login page for the application.

Because all this logic is encapsulated in an HttpModule, the module needs to be registered in each application that wants to make use of its services. In terms of code deployment, for the sample application the code is in the App_Code directory; although again you can instead choose to author it in a separate assembly deployed in the bin or the GAC. Depending on how the module is deployed, you will need to add more information to the type attribute.

```
<system.webServer>
    <modules>
        <add
            name="FormsAuthSessionEnforcement"
            type="FormsAuthSessionEnforcement"/>
    </modules>
</system.webServer>
```

Note that the sample code shown here only includes checks that make sense in the case of absolute ticket expirations. The custom module and login page do not handle the case where sliding expirations are enabled. You would need extra logic to periodically update the expiration data in the Membership database whenever the FormsAuthenticationModule renewed the ticket. As a result, the configuration for the sample application only allows absolute expirations.

```
<forms slidingExpiration="false" />
```

When the module exits, one of two outcomes has occurred: either the login session is valid and the request continues, or the session is invalid and the user is prompted to log in again. Assuming that the user is prompted for a login, this brings us full circle back to the login page. As shown earlier, there is a check box on the login page that allows a user to clear active login sessions. The setting of this check box, as well as the logic to prevent duplicate logins, is in the LoggingIn event of the Login control.

C#

```csharp
protected void Login1_LoggingIn(object sender, LoginCancelEventArgs e)
    {
        if (loginUser == null)
            loginUser = Membership.GetUser(Login1.UserName);

        //See if the user indicates that they want an existing login session
        //to be forcibly terminated
        CheckBox cb = (CheckBox)Login1.FindControl("ForceLogout");
        if (cb.Checked)
        {
            loginUser.Comment = String.Empty;
            Membership.UpdateUser(loginUser);
            return;
        }

        //Only need to check if the user instance already has login information
        //stored in the Comment field.
        if ((!String.IsNullOrEmpty(loginUser.Comment)) &&
             loginUser.Comment.Contains("LoginExpiration"))
        {
            string currentExpirationString =
                loginUser.Comment.Split("|".ToCharArray())[0];
            DateTime currentExpiration =
             DateTime.Parse((currentExpirationString.Split(";".ToCharArray()))[1]);

            //The user was logged in at some point previously and the login is
            //still valid
            if (DateTime.Now <= currentExpiration)
            {
                e.Cancel = true;
                Literal tx = (Literal)Login1.FindControl("FailureText");
                tx.Text = "You are already logged in.";
            }
        }
    }
```

VB.NET

```vbnet
Protected Sub Login1_LoggingIn( _
    ByVal sender As Object, _
    ByVal e As LoginCancelEventArgs) _
    Handles Login1.LoggingIn

    If loginUser Is Nothing Then
        loginUser = Membership.GetUser(Login1.UserName)
    End If
```

```
                    'See if the user indicates that they want an existing login session
                    'to be forcibly terminated
                    Dim cb As CheckBox = CType(Login1.FindControl("ForceLogout"), CheckBox)
                    If cb.Checked Then
                        loginUser.Comment = String.Empty
                        Membership.UpdateUser(loginUser)
                        Return
                    End If

                    'Only need to check if the user instance already has login information
                    'stored in the Comment field.
                    If ((Not String.IsNullOrEmpty(loginUser.Comment))) AndAlso _
                    loginUser.Comment.Contains("LoginExpiration") Then
                        Dim currentExpirationString As String = _
                        loginUser.Comment.Split("|".ToCharArray())(0)
                        Dim currentExpiration As DateTime = _
                        DateTime.Parse((currentExpirationString.Split(";".ToCharArray()))(1))

                        'The user was logged in at some point previously and the login is still
                        'valid
                        If DateTime.Now <= currentExpiration Then
                            e.Cancel = True
                            Dim tx As Literal = _
                            CType(Login1.FindControl("FailureText"), Literal)
                            tx.Text = "You are already logged in."
                        End If
                    End If
                End Sub
```

Duplicate login checks always require a MembershipUser to be handy, so the event first ensures that an instance is available. Because the LoggingIn event is always fired by the Login control before the LoggedIn event, the check that is made in the LoggedIn event will always find a MembershipUser instance already available for use.

If the check box is selected (that is, the website user indicated that they want any active login session to be invalidated), the session information inside of the MembershipUser instance is cleared and the information is saved back to the Membership database. In essence, a setting of String.Empty in the MembershipUser.Comment field is an indication that the user is not logged in. One side note: Placing the check box on the Login control required converting the control into a template. Template editing mode for the control allows you to add arbitrary controls to the layout. However, there is not a convenient strongly typed reference to any controls that you add (hence the need for calling FindControl to get a reference to the check box).

If there is login information contained in the Comment property, then the expiration date is extracted. From this, you can see that there are two different points in the application where expiration date and session identifiers are checked. The login session identifier is checked *after* the user is logged in. The expiration date is checked *before* the user is logged in. If the expiration date from the MembershipUser instance indicates that there is still a valid login session (that is, there is a session that will expire sometime in the future), the remainder of the processing of the Login control is halted by setting the Cancel property on the event arguments to true. A reference to the Literal control that displays error text is found, and appropriate error information is displayed to the user.

Each time a user logs in there are a few possible decision trees that will occur on the `Login` page:

1. The user is logging in for the very first time to the application. As a result, all the checks in the `LoggingIn` event are bypassed, and a login occurs.

2. The user is logging in after a previous login session already expired. In this case, the expiration date check in the `LoggingIn` event detects this, and the user is allowed to log in.

3. The user is logging in, but there is already a valid login session as indicated by the expiration date information within the `Comment` field. In this case, the login is not allowed to proceed and an error is returned.

4. The user is logging in and explicitly states that any previous session should be invalidated. This is similar to the first point, with some extra work performed to clear the `Comment` field prior to allowing the login to proceed.

You can try all this out by stepping through the process of logging in multiple times:

1. If you don't already have a user, you can quickly create one by using the ASP.NET Configuration tool inside of Visual Studio (Website ⇨ ASP.NET Configuration Tool).

2. Log in with a user to the sample site. If you look in the database, you will see login information inside of the Comment column of the aspnet_Membership database table. The data looks like:
    ```
    LoginExpiration;5/22/2005 12:52:51 PM|LoginSessionID;71fa38d5-97f8-4c62-
    8bbb-bac4ab2f352b.
    ```

3. Open up a second browser window and type the address of a secured page in the application. This will require you to log in again.

4. Note that when you attempt to log in in the second browser instance, the login fails because of the checks being made in the `LoggingIn` event on the login page.

5. Now attempt to log in but make sure to click the check box to invalidate other login sessions. You will be able to log in at this point successfully. If you check the Comment column in the database, you will see updated information there.

6. Flip back to the first browser window and attempt to continue navigating around the site. You will instead get redirected back to the login page because of the login session ID check being made by the custom `HttpModule`. The module detects the login session in the first browser is no longer the active login session.

Enforcing a Logout

An issue related to the single login scenario is the potential for a user to reenter the site as a logged-in user after he or she has already logged out. If this sounds a bit strange, the following sequence of events can lead to this:

1. The user logs in and gets back a valid forms authentication ticket.

2. At some point in the future, the authentication ticket is hijacked or exposed.

3. The user logs out, thus clearing the forms authentication cookie from his or her browser.

4. The malicious individual from step 2 replays the ticket back to the site. Assuming that the expiration date in the ticket is still valid, the malicious user can now run as an authenticated user.

In reality, the possibility of step 2 is open to quite a bit of debate. If you run your entire site under SSL (or at the very least set requireSSL to true in configuration), hijacking a forms authentication from a network trace is not possible. Prior to ASP.NET 2.0, though, it was still possible to use some type of cross-site scripting attack to hijack a cookie using client-side browser code. However, in ASP.Net 2.0 and ASP.NET 3.5 the HttpOnly property of forms authentication cookies is set to true, so this attack vector is quite a bit harder to accomplish (though, as noted earlier, it may be possible to use the TRACE/TRACK command which, if supported on the web server, still allows access to the cookie).

Furthermore, there isn't anything in the steps listed earlier that would prevent this type of replay attack from occurring with a technically savvy user that sits down at a coworker's machine and attempts to physically copy a cookie and email it back to himself (though even this attack would be partially mitigated by using only session based cookies). Anyway, the point here is that for high-security sites, you don't want to allow theoretical vulnerabilities, especially if there are reasonable steps that you can take to prevent the problem in the first place.

Because you have already seen the solution for preventing multiple logins, it is pretty easy to extend it one step further. A value of String.Empty in the MembershipUser.Comment field is already treated as an indicator that there is no active login session. If you add a LoginStatus control to the pages in your site, you can hook the LoggingOut event and perform some extra cleanup.

C#

```
protected void LoginStatus1_LoggingOut(object sender, LoginCancelEventArgs e)
{
    //Clear the information in Membership that tracks the
    //the current login session.
    MembershipUser mu = Membership.GetUser();
    mu.Comment = String.Empty;
    Membership.UpdateUser(mu);
}
```

VB.NET

```
Protected Sub LoginStatus1_LoggingOut( _
ByVal sender As Object, _
ByVal e As LoginCancelEventArgs) _
Handles LoginStatus1.LoggedOut
    'Clear the information in Membership that tracks the
    'the current login session.
    Dim mu As MembershipUser = Membership.GetUser()
    mu.Comment = String.Empty
    Membership.UpdateUser(mu)
End Sub
```

Now whenever a website user explicitly logs out of a site, the login information for that user is deleted from the user record in the Membership database. With this change, there is one extra modification needed in the custom `HttpModule` as well.

C#

```
private void OnPostAuthenticate(Object sender, EventArgs e)
    {
        HttpApplication a = (HttpApplication)sender;
        HttpContext c = a.Context;

        //If the user was authenticated with Forms Authentication
        //Then check the session ID.
        if (c.User.Identity.IsAuthenticated == true)
        {
            FormsAuthenticationTicket ft =
                ((FormsIdentity)c.User.Identity).Ticket;

            Guid g = new Guid(ft.UserData);
            MembershipUser loginUser = Membership.GetUser(ft.Name);

            Guid currentSession;
            //If there isn't any session information in Membership at this point
            //then it is likely the user logged out, and an old cookie is
            //being replayed.
            if (!String.IsNullOrEmpty(loginUser.Comment))
            {
                string currentSessionString =
                    loginUser.Comment.Split("|".ToCharArray())[1];
                currentSession =
                    new Guid(currentSessionString.Split(";".ToCharArray())[1]);
            }
            else
                currentSession = Guid.Empty;

            //If the session in the cookie does not match the current session as
            // stored in the Membership database, then terminate this request
            if (g != currentSession)
            {
                FormsAuthentication.SignOut();
                FormsAuthentication.RedirectToLoginPage();
            }
        }

    }
```

VB.NET

```
Private Sub OnPostAuthenticate(ByVal sender As Object, ByVal e As EventArgs)
    Dim a As HttpApplication = CType(sender, HttpApplication)
    Dim c As HttpContext = a.Context

    If c.User Is Nothing Then
        Return
    End If
```

```
                    'If the user was authenticated with Forms Authentication
                    'Then check the session ID.
                If c.User.Identity.IsAuthenticated = True Then
                    Dim ft As FormsAuthenticationTicket = _
                    (CType(c.User.Identity, FormsIdentity)).Ticket

                    Dim g As New Guid(ft.UserData)
                    Dim loginUser As MembershipUser = Membership.GetUser(ft.Name)

                    Dim currentSession As Guid
                    'If there isn't any session information in Membership at this point
                    'then it is likely the user logged out, and an old cookie is
                    'being replayed.
                    If (Not String.IsNullOrEmpty(loginUser.Comment)) Then
                        Dim currentSessionString As String = _
                        loginUser.Comment.Split("|".ToCharArray())(1)
                        currentSession = _
                        New Guid(currentSessionString.Split(";".ToCharArray())(1))
                    Else
                        currentSession = Guid.Empty
                    End If

                    'If the session in the cookie does not match the current session as
                    'stored in the Membership database, then terminate this request
                    If g <> currentSession Then
                        FormsAuthentication.SignOut()
                        FormsAuthentication.RedirectToLoginPage()
                    End If

                End If
            End Sub
```

The bolded section shows the changes to the module. Instead of just assuming that there will always be a value in the Comment property for the authenticated user, the module instead checks to see if the Comment property has any valid information in it. If there is no information in the Comment property, then the comparison between the session identifier in the forms authentication ticket and the value Guid.Empty always fails. If a malicious user attempts to replay an otherwise valid forms authentication cookie, and the true user logged out of the application, the replayed ticket will never be accepted.

Looking at this code, you can see why for very secure sites, sliding expirations should never be used. Although you now have sample code that keeps track of the logged-in versus logged-out status of a user, there really isn't much you can do to force a user to actually log out. How many of us just close down the browser when we are done with a site? In cases like this, the only remaining protection is for the forms authentication ticket to eventually expire. At least with absolute expirations the window of opportunity for a successful replay attack can be substantially narrowed. With sliding expirations, as long as a valid ticket is replayed to the site, the ticket will continue to work and will be periodically updated as well.

Summary

Out of the box, forms authentication in ASP.NET 2.0 and ASP.NET 3.5 adds new protections by including the HttpOnly attribute on all forms authentication cookies. Used in conjunction with encryption and signing of the forms authentication ticket, the requireSSL attribute and absolute ticket expirations, you can quickly restrict the ability of malicious users to gain access to a forms authentication cookie.

When running an application in the new IIS 7.0 integrated mode, you can enable the managed Forms-AuthenticationModule to authenticate ASP.NET and non-ASP.NET resources. This comes as a result of having ASP.NET access to all request types when running under the integrated mode in IIS 7.0.

ASP.NET 2.0 and ASP.NET 3.5 also include a cookieless mode of operation, whereby the forms authentication ticket is embedded in the URL. This makes it much easier for developers to author sites that work with mobile browsers as well as standard desktop browsers. In the interest of security, though, developers should avoid cookieless forms authentication tickets for sites that require high degrees of security. It is simply too easy to "leak" or expose a cookieless forms authentication ticket to someone other than the original user.

Although forms authentication seems pretty simple, with a bit of custom code, you can actually solve some rather complex authentication problems. The ability in ASP.NET 2.0 and ASP.NET 3.5 to pass forms authentication tickets across applications makes it possible to solve some single sign-on issues that previously required complex third-party SSO applications. Of course, there is also a limit to how far you can stretch the new cross-application capabilities of forms authentication. For many developers, commercial SSO solutions will still make sense.

The combination of forms authentication and Membership finally gives developers the basic plumbing needed to solve the single-logon problem. Although neither feature includes support for enforcing single-logons, both features are sufficiently extensible that with a reasonable amount of custom code you can prevent users from performing multiple logons. You can also provide protection so that when a user explicitly signs out, cookie replay attacks with a forms authentication cookie are not allowed.

7
Integrating ASP.NET Security with Classic ASP

All the great security features in ASP.NET do not really help you when you look at your older classic ASP applications. Although forms authentication and URL authorization have been around since the ASP.NET 1.0 days, these features have not been of any use in the ASP world. With the introduction of the Membership and Role Manager features in ASP.NET 2.0, you had even more authentication and authorization functionality built into ASP.NET, which ASP.NET 3.5 continues to support. But again, it seems like that functionality is orphaned in the ASP.NET world and never made it over to the world of classic ASP.

Why attempt to bring the ASP.NET and classic ASP worlds together? In terms of sheer volume of code written, the majority of web applications out there are still running on classic ASP. Even if you surf around Microsoft's own sites, such as the MSDN online library and various links and subsites of www.microsoft.com, you still encounter a lot of classic ASP pages.

In ASP.NET 2.0 a number of small changes were made in some admittedly esoteric aspects of the runtime to make it possible to more tightly integrate ASP.NET and classic ASP. These changes also rely on modifications made earlier to IIS 6 around handling for ISAPI extensions. Both of these changes taken together make it possible to wrap classic ASP sites inside of ASP.NET.

With the release of ASP.NET 3.5 and IIS 7.0, the integration between ASP.NET and classic ASP is made even easier, especially with IIS 7.0's new integrated mode. As you know, IIS 7.0 provides two main modes of executing: the classic mode, which resembles that of IIS 6, and, integrated mode, which is new and unites the ASP.NET and IIS request pipeline into a single, integrated request pipeline.

This chapter covers the following topics:

- ISAPI extension mapping behavior in IIS 5.
- Wildcard mappings in IIS 7.0 and how they work.
- The `DefaultHttpHandler` in ASP.NET 3.5.
- Using the `DefaultHttpHandler` with ASP.NET and classic ASP.
- Authenticating classic ASP using ASP.NET in IIS 7.0 classic and integrated modes.
- Authorizing classic ASP using ASP.NET in IIS 7.0 classic and integrated modes.
- Adding roles from Role Manager for use in classic ASP.
- Passing data from classic ASP pages to ASP.NET pages.

IIS 5 ISAPI Extension Behavior

Before ASP.NET there was IIS 5, and it was good. You could write classic ASP applications that incorporated their own authentication and authorization behavior. And you could add other external resources like images, stylesheets, and so on and reference them from your classic ASP applications. However, sometimes you wanted to perform some preliminary work prior to passing a request on to ASP. Probably the most frequently asked-for capability was URL rewriting, for which the new IIS 7.0 Integration mode offers an easy solution.

However, in IIS 5 the only way to accomplish something like this was by writing an ISAPI filter, a rather daunting prospect for most us. The underlying reason for this restriction is that in IIS5 the core runtime is only extensible through ISAPI filters and extensions; that was the extensibility mechanism at the time.

Of course, one nice side effect in IIS 5 was that the authentication model for classic ASP was the IIS authentication model. There was no artificial bifurcation between IIS authentication modes and some other ASP-like authentication mode. This meant that after you had things configured in IIS, your ASP security just worked with IIS's implementation of integrated security. Furthermore, when an ASP application relied on just plain HTML pages, image files, CSS files, and the like, there was no need for special security configuration work to get these to work. ASP, IIS, and static files lived together peacefully.

Then along came ASP.NET 1.0 and 1.1 running on top of IIS 5, and the security story became a little weird. ASP.NET security was in its own world and hence one scenario that was definitely lost was that ASP.NET pages and classic ASP pages were oblivious of one another.

In ASP.NET, you finally had a way to modify parameters of an incoming request prior to having a page run. But if you were thinking you could shoehorn classic ASP into ASP.NET to take advantage of the `HttpModule` extensibility in ASP.NET, you were sorely disappointed. The core technical reason for this is that in IIS 5, when a request is mapped to an ISAPI extension that is the end of the road for that request. After the request is handed off to a specific ISAPI extension, the mapped extension owns the request for the rest of its lifetime.

There was no concept in IIS 5 of being able to route a request to one extension (`aspnet_isapi.dll`, for instance) and then somehow reroute the request to another extension, for example, `asp.dll`, which is responsible for .asp and .asa files. Of course, you could get a little enterprising and implement some redirection-based mechanisms that hopped information back and forth between classic ASP and ASP.NET, but those solutions always end up being a bit awkward. Any customer on a slow Internet link is also aware of the overhead involved with all these redirects, which usually makes any such solution chancy at best for those still living in a 56K world.

There was another problem with the ISAPI extension handling in IIS 5 when using ASP.NET and that was in the area of static file handling. As you saw in Chapter 3 in the section on blocking access to non-ASP.NET file types, most common static file extensions are already mapped to ISAPI extensions or to the core IIS runtime itself. As a result, if you wrote an ASP.NET application that needed to protect access to XML or .htm files, you had to explicitly map each of these file extensions to the ASP.NET ISAPI extension. If you did not carry out this step, IIS 5 would happily serve the files directly without any authentication or authorization by ASP.NET. Of course, if your HTML or XML files happened to include sensitive data, this was not exactly the desired outcome.

What was especially aggravating with IIS 5 was that if you had more than one or two static file extensions to be protected by ASP.NET, you had to go through a fair amount of manual configuration on each of your web servers to ensure the correct association of static file types to ASP.NET. And of course if you wanted a mixture of authentication and authorization policies for these files (for example, maybe some images were viewable by everyone, but others need to be secured) you had two choices:

❑   Have all requests for the static files flow through ASP.NET, in which case you would encounter slower performance when serving the static files for anonymous users.

❑   Separate the files that were accessible to anonymous users into one directory structure outside of ASP.NET, so they could take advantage of the faster file-serving performance afforded by IIS 5.

Both of these options had their shortcomings: You could trade off performance for centralized management of authentication, or you could get optimal performance but with the overhead of keeping two different directory structures for anonymous and authenticated users.

IIS 7.0 Wildcard Mappings

IIS 6 introduced the concept of wildcard mappings. Wildcard mappings are a way to tell IIS 6 that every incoming request, regardless of file type, should be routed to one or more ISAPI extensions. Since these extensions are configured in IIS 6 to handle any incoming request, the term "wildcard" is used to indicate that request handling is independent of a specific file type. Not only can you configure a single ISAPI extension with wildcard mappings, but you can also configure multiple ISAPI extensions to act as a chain of wildcard mappings. IIS 6 will walk through the list of configured mappings in sequence, passing control of the request to each extension in turn.

After the wildcard mapped extensions have completed their processing, IIS 6 passes control of the request to the extension or internal runtime handling appropriate for the file type. The IIS 6 ISAPI API also included additional functionality for extension authors that know their extensions will be used as part of a wildcard mapping. In the case of ASP.NET 3.5, the DefaultHttpHandler class (covered in the "DefaultHttpHanlder" section this chapter) includes extra logic that allows ASP.NET to gain control of a request for non-ASP.NET resources both before and after the default processing for that request occurs. This enables you to integrate ASP.NET 3.5 so that it can perform both preprocessing and post-processing of a classic ASP request.

When an application is hosted in IIS 7.0 and configured to run under the classic application pool, it resembles an application running under IIS 6.0. For the coming sections the demonstration will handle applications hosted inside IIS 7.0 and configured to run under the classic application pool. When an application is running in the new IIS 7.0 Integration mode, the process of ASP.NET handling non-ASP.NET resources differs, as you have seen throughout the previous chapters in the book. However, a review on the how ASP.NET can handle non-ASP.NET resources when the application is running under the default application pool is worth repeating.

Configuring a Wildcard Mapping

To keep things simple initially, let's take a simple ASP page and a simple ASP.NET application and configure the two to work together using an IIS 7.0 wildcard mapping for an application running under the classic application pool. After creating the basic folder structure, and marking the folder as an application in IIS 7.0 running under the classic application pool, the next step is to add a wildcard mapping so that all requests for resources will first flow through ASP.NET.

After you click on the web application hosted in IIS 7.0, the Handler Mappings applet shows under the IIS features, as you can see in Figure 7-1.

Figure 7-1

Double-click the Handler Mappings applet icon to check the list of all extension mappings inherited by your application from the Default Web Site. Figure 7-2 shows the list of handlers defined on the application running under the classic application pool in IIS 7.0.

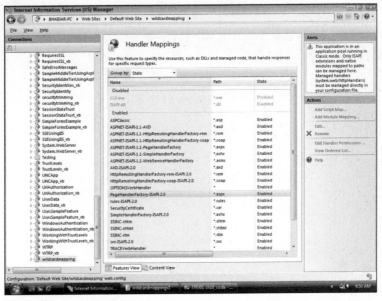

Figure 7-2

Unless you have a photographic memory, you probably do not remember the full path to the ASP.NET ISAPI extension. So, before configuring wildcard mappings, it is helpful to select one of the preexisting mappings (for example, the `.aspx` mapping) and click the Edit link on the action pane on the right side of the IIS Manager tool. The Edit Script Map dialog box, shown in Figure 7-3, conveniently holds the full path to the ASP.NET ISAPI extension in the Executable text box.

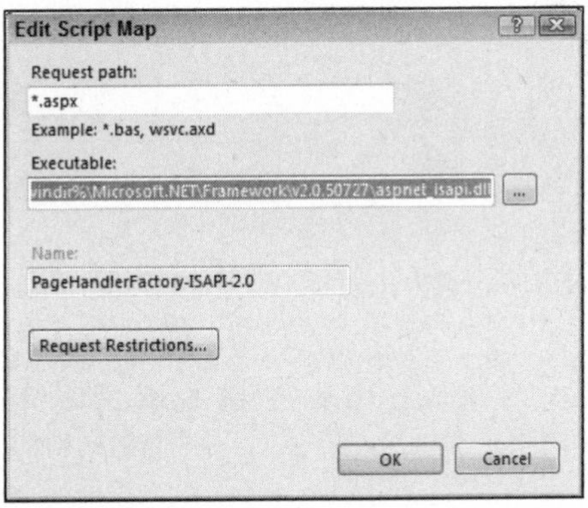

Figure 7-3

Copy the path and then cancel out of the dialog box. Now you can click the Add Script Map link on the action pane to open the dialog box for configuring wildcard extension mappings (see Figure 7-4.) Paste in the full path to the ASP.NET ISAPI extension into the Executable text box. In addition, enter * as the request path to capture all types of requests. Finally, give the new mapping a name of your own choice.

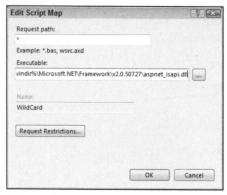

Figure 7-4

Now click the Request Restrictions button located at the bottom of the dialog box. Figure 7-5 shows the resulting dialog box that enables you to edit additional configuration settings for the new wild-card mapping.

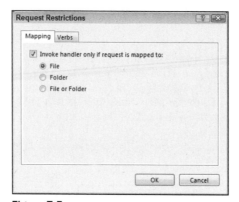

Figure 7-5

The tab of concern for now is the Mapping tab. The "Invoke handler only if request is mapped to" checkbox helps you to decide when to allow the mapping to run and execute. You have several options either when a physically existing file in the filesystem is requested, when a physically existing directory in the filesystem is requested, and finally an option for both a file and directory at the same time. However, if you unselect the check box, you are telling the current extension mapping not to verify if the file or directory physically exists in the filesystem prior to passing the request to ASP.NET. This has the same functionality as the "Verify that File Exists" option in IIS 6.0 when adding a new extension mapping. By default this checkbox is selected and the File option is chosen. This means that the wildcard mapping you are creating will check if the resource requested physically exists in the filesystem prior to sending it to the ASP.NET engine.

Close out of all of the dialog boxes by clicking OK. You have now configured an application hosted inside of IIS 7.0 and running under the classic application pool that will forward all requests initially to the ASP.NET 2.0 ISAPI extension, which is still the same ISAPI for ASP.NET 3.5. Due to the functionality of the DefaultHttpHandler inside of ASP.NET 3.5, these requests will hand off to IIS 7.0 for execution by the appropriate extension or internal runtime logic. After the appropriate extension or IIS 7 has completed its processing, ASP.NET 3.5 will have the chance to perform some postprocessing, after which the request will complete.

If you look at the application's web.config configuration file, you will notice the following entry that was added to the <handlers> configuration section inside the <system.webServer> configuration section group.

```
<add
    name="WildCard"
    path="*"
    verb="*"
    modules="IsapiModule"
    scriptProcessor="%windir%\Microsoft.NET\Framework\v2.0.50727\aspnet_isapi.dll"
    resourceType="File"
    requireAccess="None"
/>
```

The preceding configuration element simply resembles the wildcard mapping configuration that you have just added inside the IIS 7.0 Manager tool.

For now just a simple ASP page is used:

```
<%
Response.Write("This is text from the classic ASP application" + "<br/>")
%>
```

When you access this page (in the sample application this is default.asp), the classic ASP ISAPI extension (ASP.dll) will eventually get the chance to parse and run the page, resulting in a string being output to the browser.

Now it's time to get a little frisky and see if ASP.NET can output some text in addition to the text coming from the classic ASP application. Try adding the following code to global.asax:

C#

```
void Application_BeginRequest(Object sender, EventArgs e)
{
    HttpContext context = HttpContext.Current;
    context.Response.Write("This came from the ASP.NET global.asax eventhander");
}
```

VB.NET

```
Sub Application_BeginRequest(ByVal sender As Object, ByVal e As EventArgs)
    Dim context As HttpContext = HttpContext.Current
    context.Response.Write("This came from the ASP.NET global.asaxevent hander")
End Sub
```

When you run `default.asp`, instead of getting back two pieces of text (one from ASP.NET and one from classic ASP), you instead get an error saying, "This type of page is not served." Hmmm—what happened? First everything was working with the wildcard mapping, and now that you add one simple line of code to ASP.NET, everything breaks!

The reason for this behavior is quite simple. When ASP.NET detects that a response has been modified, prior to handing the request back to IIS 7.0 it checks to see if the request was either a POST request, or a request for a classic ASP page. If the request is a POST request or a classic ASP request, ASP.NET will throw an exception rather than hand control back to IIS 7.0. ASP.NET considers a response to have been modified if any of the following occur:

- ❏ One or more HTTP headers in the response have been set or modified (for example setting a cookie).

- ❏ Text has been written to the response, regardless of whether this text has been buffered or already sent to the client.

- ❏ Code in the ASP.NET application modified the `HttpCachePolicy` associated with the response.

- ❏ A `Stream` was assigned to the `Response.Filter` property. This is an advanced operation and is normally used by developers who need to modify the raw contents of the response prior to sending it back to the browser.

The last two restrictions probably are not particularly onerous for developers. However, the first two restrictions effectively mean that you need to be careful about what an ASP.NET application is doing when you use it as a wildcard mapping. If you think about it, though, these restrictions do make sense; ASP.NET and classic ASP still live in separate worlds and know nothing about the internal processing logic of the other's ISAPI extension.

Without some major surgery to the guts of IIS, ASP, and ASP.NET, it is basically impossible for two ISAPI extensions to manipulate the data that is sent back in a response. For example, how would you integrate ASP.NET's fragment caching with the response written from a classic ASP page? Or how would the response buffering behavior in classic ASP (the Enable Buffering check box for ASP) coexist with response buffering in ASP.NET? The simple answer is that both ISAPI extensions have many internal assumptions about a request lifecycle and ownership of the actual response data. There is no easy way to reconcile these assumptions in ASP.NET 3.5 or IIS 7.0 when an application is running under the classic application pool.

Now that you understand that ASP.NET cannot touch anything in the response when interacting with classic ASP, what are some of the things you can safely do in ASP.NET? Any ASP.NET APIs that do not touch the response are safe to use. So, for example, you can call any of the following:

- ❏ Forms authentication APIs that create tickets as well as encrypting and decrypting string representations of the tickets. However you cannot call methods like `SetAuthCookie` or `RedirectFromLoginPage`.

- ❏ Application services that do not directly interact with the `Response` object are safe to call. You could call most of the Membership, Role Manager, and Profile APIs without any problems.

- ❏ You can freely use the `Request` object to inspect information; you could look at the forms authentication cookie (if one was sent) or query-string and forms variables.

- ❏ You can access other application services such as session state or the Cache API.

As a simple example, you can take the sample ASP.NET application used earlier, and instead of touching the Response, log information about the incoming request to a text file:

C#

```csharp
void Application_BeginRequest(Object sender, EventArgs e)
{
    StreamWriter sw = File.CreateText(Server.MapPath("~/App_Data/logfile.txt"));
    sw.WriteLine("A request was made to: " + Request.Path);
    sw.Flush();
    sw.Close();
}
```

VB.NET

```vbnet
Sub Application_BeginRequest(ByVal sender As Object, ByVal e As EventArgs)
    Dim sw As StreamWriter = _
    File.CreateText(Server.MapPath("~/App_Data/logfile.txt"))
    sw.WriteLine("A request was made to: " & Request.Path)
    sw.Flush()
    sw.Close()
End Sub
```

If you access `default.asp`, everything still works, and the ASP.NET applications `App_Data` directory contains the text log file containing information about the request. So, you can safely carry out complex operations from inside of the ASP.NET application. From a design standpoint, this means you can think of a wild-carded ASP.NET application as something of a bridge to the managed world for a classic ASP application.

At this point, you might be thinking there is a sneaky way to start doing interesting "stuff" inside of ASP.NET and then pass the results off to classic ASP. Obviously, from the previous sample you could hack up an approach whereby ASP.NET writes information to a file in a common location, and classic ASP reads from it. But that approach is going to fall apart quickly. How about just stuffing information onto the query string inside of ASP.NET and then picking these values up over in the classic ASP code?

C#

```csharp
Request.QueryString.Add("foo", "It would be nice if this worked.");
```

VB.NET

```vbnet
Request.QueryString.Add("foo", "It would be nice if this worked.")
```

This code is a nice idea, but it is not going to work, because inside of ASP.NET, information such as `Request.QueryString` and `Request.Form` are contained in read-only collections. You could write code inside of the classic ASP application that would place values on the query-string, and then when a redirect occurred the ASP.NET application could read these values and do some work, but the problem that is being addressed in this chapter involves authentication and authorization. In these cases, the flow of data is in the other direction; you need ASP.NET to communicate the results of an authentication or authorization decision to the classic ASP application (or at least store the results in a way that protects the classic ASP application).

Of course, the issue with using all of the ASP.NET capabilities is that the results are still "locked up" as it were inside of the ASP.NET application. How do you actually throw any of the data over the wall to the classic ASP application? Prior to ASP.NET 2.0, you would probably pursue options such as:

❑　Write a web service that wraps managed code, and then access it using SOAP tools from your classic ASP applications

❑　Wrap the managed code into a COM component, thus making the logic available to the classic ASP world as well

Both of these approaches are still valid in the world of ASP.NET 2.0 and ASP.NET 3.5. However, they also tend to be a bit heavyweight. Writing a web service or a COM-callable wrapper to an inventory control API might make sense; sometimes all you want to accomplish is basic authentication and authorization. Even for these two aspects of a website, writing a web service and making something like forms authentication globally available as a service can be appealing.

However, considering that forms authentication and URL authorization are already built into ASP.NET, it seems like overkill to wrap these features just to make them useful in classic ASP. And there is also the extra overhead of having to write and maintain the wrappers as well as figure out how to configure them in production. A much easier approach would be to use these types of ASP.NET features from inside an ASP.NET code-base and make the results available as necessary to the classic ASP application.

The Resource Type Setting

You might have noticed that the dialog box for editing additional configuration settings for the wild-card mapping had a check box, "Invoke handler only if request is mapped to", that was checked by default, having the File option selected. Such a configuration setting tells IIS 7.0 that it should first verify that the requested resource actually exists on the filesystem prior to passing the request on to ASP.NET. If you use wildcard mappings for only basic ASP.NET processing, this may be an acceptable setting.

The configuration setting is reflected in the <handlers> configuration section by adding the resourceType attribute. The resourceType attribute, already shown above, takes several input values, including File, Directory, Either, or Unspecified. All the values' meanings are clear and direct, except perhaps the Unspecified value. This value is set when the "Invoke handler only if request is mapped to" check box is unchecked and hence this tells IIS not to verify that the resource physically exists prior to sending it to ASP.NET or any other extension configured.

However, if you look at the default file associations that are mapped to ASP.NET, you will see quite a few mappings that have this setting turned off. As a result, if you plan to run application running in IIS 7.0 that contains a mixture of ASP.NET and ASP content, you should leave this setting unchecked. The reason is that a number of "resources" that are requested from an ASP.NET site do not physically exist on the filesystem.

The easiest way to demonstrate this is by dropping a TreeView control onto a form and hooking it up to a sitemap file:

```
<asp:TreeView ID="TreeView1" runat="server" DataSourceID="SiteMapDataSource1">
</asp:TreeView>
<br />
<asp:SiteMapDataSource ID="SiteMapDataSource1" runat="server" />
```

If you add a `web.sitemap` file to a project and the ASP.NET application is configured with a wildcard mapping, when the `TreeView` renders all collapse icons will be missing. Furthermore, the page will load with a JavaScript error because the HTML source for the page contains references like:

```
<img
    src="/wildcardmapping/WebResource.axd?d=OXSMoGK15Uw3RgQR7RCe_WMrxaink7zs4hqaurgE
2G81&amp;t=633408398072242656"
    alt="Collapse foo1"
    style="border-width:0;"
/>
```

These types of references point back at `webresource.axd`, the central content handler in ASP.NET 3.5 for serving up JavaScript and images. If the "Invoke handler only if request is mapped to" check box is checked, then IIS 7.0 will fail requests like these because it cannot locate any file called `webresource.axd` on the filesystem.

Because `webresource.axd` serves the JavaScript used by validator controls, and it is likely that you will need the validator controls for any ASP.NET login page that front-ends a classic ASP site, remember that you must uncheck this setting when setting up a wildcard mapping.

DefaultHttpHandler

All of the previous discussions have lead up to the need for some kind of "glue" that ASP.NET can use to pass data to classic ASP. The solution to this need is the `DefaultHttpHandler` class. In the previous examples, it was the `DefaultHttpHandler` that was responsible for passing the request back to IIS 7.0 whenever an ASP page was requested. Also, it was the `DefaultHttpHandler` that performed the various checks to ensure that the response had not been modified prior to either processing a POST request or passing control to classic ASP.

The `DefaultHttpHandler` runs during the handler execution phase of the ASP.NET HTTP pipeline. In other words, `DefaultHttpHandler` runs at the same point in time as the `.aspx` page handler; although instead of running an `.aspx` page, the `DefaultHttpHandler` deals with handing control to IIS 7.0. This means that the earlier events in the HTTP pipeline are available, and any of the logic associated with those events will run (for example, the `FormsAuthenticationModule` will run during `Authenticate Request` and so on).

The `DefaultHttpHandler` is configured in the root `web.config` file as shown here:

```
<add path="*" verb="GET,HEAD,POST"
  type="System.Web.DefaultHttpHandler" validate="True" />
```

Because this handler mapping is the second to last mapping, it means that any GET, HEAD, or POST request made to an ASP.NET application for a file type other than ones that are explicitly recognized by ASP.NET, will be routed to the `DefaultHttpHandler`. Prior to the configuration for `DefaultHttpHandler`, the default root `web.config` contains a number of obvious mappings (for example, `.aspx` requests are mapped to the `PageHandlerFactor`) and some other less obvious mappings (for example, SQL Server `.mdf` and `.ldf` files are mapped to the `ForbiddenHandler`).

If a request is made for an unrecognized file type, but the HTTP verb for the request is not GET, HEAD, or POST, then the request will bypass the `DefaultHttpHandler` and fall through to the final handler mapping, which points at the `HttpMethodNotAllowedHandler`.

It is important to remember here that when an application is running under the classic application pool hosted inside IIS 7.0, the HttpHandlers that take effect are those defined within the root web.config or the application's web.config configuration files inside the <httphandlers> configuration section. So, to detect the above handler mapping, you now know where exactly you should be looking. This is different from the case when the application is running under the default application pool hosted inside IIS 7.0, where only the handlers defined within the <handlers> configuration section, located inside the <system.webServer> configuration section group, in either the applicationHost.config or the application's web.config configuration files take effect at runtime.

Internally, the DefaultHttpHandler has two code paths: one that eventually hands control back to IIS, and a separate path that handles the case where the response has already been modified in some manner. On one hand, when an ASP.NET application modifies the response, if the DefaultHttpHandler determines that the request is really for a static file, then the DefaultHttpHandler passes the request to another internal handler called the StaticFileHandler. On the other hand, if the DefaultHttpHandler determines that the conditions for passing control back to IIS 7.0 have not been violated, the handler passes control back to IIS 7.0 using the HSE_REQ_EXEC_UNICODE_URL server support function in the ISAPI API.

Normally, this means that requests for any kind of non-ASP.NET resource will be automatically routed to IIS 7.0, at which point IIS 7.0 will either serve the file itself (in the case of static files), or pass the request on to the appropriate ISAPI extension (in the case of ASP pages). There is a boundary scenario with static files in that you can programmatically configure an HttpCachePolicy for the Response when a request is made for a static file (remember, this is one of the conditions the DefaultHttpHandler checks for). Doing so allows you to use some aspects of ASP.NET output caching to explicitly configure the way you want to cache static file content. Because the cache policy is modified, the DefaultHttpHandler will never pass the request back out to IIS 7.0; there is no logic in IIS 7.0 that would know what to do with an ASP.NET HttpCachePolicy. So, instead the internal StaticFileHandler is used to serve the static content, taking into account the output cache settings set on the Response.Cache property. Because the StaticFileHandler defaults a number of output cache settings, programmatically modifying the response's cache policy in such a way that it plays well with the StaticFileHandler is tricky; it is also an extensibility scenario that really hasn't been tested extensively.

Using the DefaultHttpHandler

The DefaultHttpHandler is a public class with a number of virtual methods that you can override. As a first step towards integrating ASP.NET authentication and authorization with classic ASP, you can create a custom HttpHandler that derives from DefaultHttpHandler:

C#

```
public class CustomHandler : DefaultHttpHandler
{
    public CustomHandler() {}

    public override string OverrideExecuteUrlPath()
    {
        //gets called just before control is handed back to IIS 6
        return null;
    }
}
```

```
        public override void EndProcessRequest(IAsyncResult result)
        {
            //gets called when the original ISAPI extension is done processing
            //This step is useful for post-processing
            base.EndProcessRequest(result);
        }
}
```

VB.NET

```
Public Class CustomHandler
    Inherits DefaultHttpHandler

    Public Sub New()
    End Sub

    Public Overrides Function OverrideExecuteUrlPath() As String
            'gets called just before control is handed back to IIS 7.0
            Return Nothing
    End Function

    Public Overrides Sub EndProcessRequest(ByVal result As IAsyncResult)
            'gets called when the original ISAPI extension is done processing
            'This step is useful for post-processing
            MyBase.EndProcessRequest(result)
    End Sub
End Class
```

This code represents the basic skeleton of a custom HttpHandler. It overrides the two core methods available on DefaultHttpHandler: OverrideExecuteUrlPath and EndProcessRequest. You want to override the method OverrideExecuteUrlPath rather than the virtual BeginProcessRequest method for the following reasons:

❑ Although you could override BeginProcessRequest (it is virtual), this method contains the internal logic used by DefaultHttpHandler to determine whether the request can be forwarded to IIS 7.0, or whether the request needs to be passed to the static file handler (or failed in the case of a classic ASP request). The logic for making this determination is internal and, thus, is not accessible to developers.

❑ The OverrideExecuteUrlPath and the OnExecuteUrlPreconditionFailure virtual methods are intended as the two integration points for custom handlers when the request is being processed. Although this chapter deals only with OverrideExecuteUrlPath, you also have the option to override OnExecuteUrlPreconditionFailure. This second method is called when the DefaultHttpHandler determines that the current request cannot be passed to IIS 7.0; if you know that you do not want the static file handler attempting to process your requests, then you can override OnExecuteUrlPreconditionFailure and throw some other kind of error instead.

❑ The DefaultHttpHandler will have already populated the protected Context property for you before calling into OverrideExecuteUrlPath. Without access to a valid HttpContext, there would not be much point in writing a custom handler in the first place.

Unlike `BeginProcessRequest`, you can override `EndProcessRequest` if needed. For purposes of this chapter, nothing needs to be cleaned up or postprocessed in an override of `EndProcessRequest`. However, if you were attempting to integrate session state between ASP.NET and classic ASP, overriding `EndProcessRequest` would be the correct place to write session data modified in classic ASP back into the ASP.NET session state store. (Of course, the whole issue with integrating ASP.NET and classic ASP session state would warrant at least part of another book.)

The current sample code does not actually do anything inside of the overrides. `EndProcessRequest` simply delegates control to the base class. `OverrideExecuteUrlPath` returns a null value, which in the case of an ASP.NET application applying authentication and authorization logic to a classic ASP application is the correct thing to do. If you return a null value, the currently requested path is the one that IIS 6 will continue executing when it regains control of the request.

The secondary idea behind `OverrideExecuteUrlPath`, and the reason that it returns a string value, is that developers can choose to modify the actual path that is returned back to IIS 7.0. As a quick side note, if you were to change the logic inside of `OverrideExecuteUrlPath` to look as follows:

C#

```
public override string OverrideExecuteUrlPath()
{
    //gets called just before control is handed back to IIS 7.0
    return "/wildcardmapping/default2.asp";
}
```

VB.NET

```
Public Overrides Function OverrideExecuteUrlPath() As String
    'gets called just before control is handed back to IIS 7.0
    Return "/wildcardmapping_vb/default.asp"
End Function
```

When you ran the sample application and request `default.asp`, the actual classic ASP page that would run would be `default2.asp`. This is a pretty powerful extensibility point but again not something that you need for front-ending a classic ASP application. Some Microsoft development teams, such as Share-Point, use this ability to modify the path prior to passing control to the SharePoint ISAPI extension.

Having written a custom `HttpHandler`, you still need to register the handler with ASP.NET so that it recognizes it.

```
<httpHandlers>
  <add path="*.asp" verb="GET,HEAD,POST" type="CustomHandler" validate="true" />
</httpHandlers>
```

You register HTTP handlers inside of the `<httpHandlers />` configuration element. In this case, because the custom handler is intended to work with only classic ASP pages, the `path` attribute is set to `*.asp`. You want the custom handler to work with any of the likely HTTP verbs, so `GET`, `HEAD`, and `POST` are all specified. The type registration is simply a .NET Framework type string. In the sample application the `CustomHandler` class is located inside the `App_Code` directory, so only the classname is needed. Because I did not add an explicit namespace definition in the file located in `App_Code`, the class ends up in the default namespace and hence does not include a namespace in the type definition. Chances are that in a real production scenario you would implement the custom handler in a stand-alone assembly, in which case the `type` attribute requires the namespace qualified class name and at least an assembly reference—something like `MyNamespace.CustomHandler, TheHandlerAssembly`.

Although the default HTTP handler definitions in the root `web.config` include a mapping of `*` to the `DefaultHttpHandler`, the previous registration is still sufficient. When ASP.NET processes the set of defined `<httpHandlers />`, it will see the handlers defined in the application's `web.config` file after the handlers defined in the root `web.config` file. Because the last matching handler definition takes precedence, the mapping to `*.asp` inside of the application's `web.config` will always win out over the more generic mapping defined in the root `web.config` file.

To see if everything is working at this point, you can set some breakpoints inside of `CustomHandler`, and then run the application requesting the `default.asp` page. The breakpoint in `OverrideExecute UrlPath` is hit first (as expected, this also shows that the `DefaultHttpHandler` is ready to forward the request to IIS 7.0). Later, the breakpoint in `EndProcessRequest` is reached as well. And finally the output from the classic ASP page appears in your browser. So at this point, you have a functioning custom handler and both ASP.NET and classic ASP are working properly.

Serving Classic ASP in IIS 7.0 Integration Mode

The preceding sections emphasized how to define a wildcard mapping for an application that is hosted inside IIS 7.0 and running under the classic .NET application pool that resembles that of the IIS 6.0 functioning mode. As you can see, it was obvious that the process of serving classic ASP pages in an ASP.NET application has not changed at all. You still need to define a wildcard mapping so that the `.asp` pages are processed by the ASP.NET ISAPI extension before IIS 7.0 takes back control on those resources.

Chapter 2 explained in depth the details of the new IIS 7.0 Integration mode. The discussion will not be repeated here; however, refreshing your memory with the major concepts behind the new integration mode should be helpful.

With the new IIS 7.0 Integration mode, ASP.NET unites with the IIS request pipeline and hence the name integration! Prior to IIS 7.0, a request used to pass through the IIS request pipeline where a set of events would be fired and handled by core native modules inside IIS only. Once IIS finishes its processing on the request, it is handed off to the correct ISAPI extension configured at the level of IIS. Assuming an .aspx page was requested, the ASP.NET engine starts its own managed request pipeline to serve the request and generate a response to be sent back to IIS in order to be sent back to the client making the request.

Now things have changed drastically! The IIS and ASP.NET request pipelines unite and integrate into a single request pipeline, getting rid of the overhead that we had before because of the presence of two different request pipelines. Integrating both pipelines has so many advantages and improvements, among which is that managed and native modules will be executing side by side in the same request pipeline. Throughout the request pipeline, the IIS core engine fires events during the life cycle of the request. Modules, whether native or managed, subscribe to these events and fire accordingly. IIS 7.0 core web server makes use of the Managed Engine in making the integration successful. The Managed Engine works as a wrapper over all the managed modules and hence when an event is fired by the IIS core engine, the native modules that subscribe to the current event are retrieved and executed on the spot, whereas the managed modules are accessed through the Managed Engine that checks which managed modules subscribe to the event fired by the IIS core engine and requests executing the modules, as necessary.

The presence of the unified and integrated mode gives the ASP.NET engine a chance to have a say in every request that hits the IIS web server. Why? The reasoning is simple and comes from the fact that inside the integration mode, both managed and native modules can subscribe to the same events that are fired by the IIS core engine when a new request comes in. This means that there is no additional work required by the administrator or developer to give the ASP.NET engine a chance to process a request for a non-ASP.NET resource. ASP.NET in the integration mode has full access to every request that passes through the integrated mode and hence the ASP.NET engine treats a request for an ASP.NET page the same as it treats a classic ASP page.

Another important advantage that ASP.NET developers gain is that all the ASP.NET features can now be applied on the non-ASP.NET resources. For instance, FormsAuthenticationModule, Membership, and Role management can all be used now with resources that are not ASP.NET. Hence, a developer working on a classic ASP application can now make use of those features instead of having to re-write them from scratch. You will see in the coming sections of this chapter how you can authenticate and authorize classic ASP pages using ASP.NET core features.

By default, when you open the IIS 7.0 Manager tool and create a new website, application, or virtual directory, the application is automatically set to run under the default application pool. The default application pool puts the application running into the new IIS 7.0 integrated mode and hence you can notice the difference between the classic .NET application pool that puts the application to run as if it were running inside IIS 6.0. There is nothing special to configure an application to run in the integrated mode, except to assign the default application pool as the application's application pool, which again is set by default on any new application that is created inside IIS 7.0.

To test the power of the new IIS 7.0 integrated mode, create a new application and add a simple .asp page that contains the following code:

```
<%
Response.Write("A classic ASP page running inside the IIS 7.0 Integrated mode!")
%>
```

The code is simple but it serves the purpose of showing how you can easily run and execute a non-ASP.NET application inside an ASP.NET application without having to do any configurations or workarounds on the IIS web server level.

Later in this chapter, you will learn how to authenticate and authorize classic ASP requests using the ASP.NET features.

Finally, it is important to mention that when an application is running under the integrated mode, you cannot use the `DefaultHttpHandler` or any other custom class derived from that handler. While running under the integration mode, the `DefaultHttpHandler` will not be able to return back the request to IIS 7.0 and hence it will treat a non-ASP.NET resource as a static resource and executes accordingly. This is not bad news at all, because by now you know that when an application is running under the integration mode, the ASP.NET engine has access to all requests, whether those requests are ASP.NET or non-ASP.NET resources.

Authenticating Classic ASP with ASP.NET

The next step is to build the functionality inside of the ASP.NET application to support forms authentication for classic ASP users. The general idea is that with both ASP pages and ASP.NET pages located in same virtual directory (and, thus, the same application in IIS 7.0), you want unauthenticated users to be forced to authenticate using ASP.NET's forms authentication mechanism.

After a user successfully logs in with forms authentication, the user should be redirected to the original requested page. This should occur regardless of whether the originally requested resource was an ASP.NET page or a classic ASP page. On subsequent requests, again regardless of the type of requested resource, you want ASP.NET to transparently verify the validity of the forms authentication cookie and then pass the request along.

For starters, you need to configure the ASP.NET application with the basics necessary to enable forms authentication and enforce authenticated access:

```
<authentication mode="Forms"/>

<authorization>
<deny users="?"/>
</authorization>
```

With these settings, anonymous users will be redirected to the forms authentication login page. For now, just add a basic login page called `Login.aspx` to the sample application, and place a `Login` control onto the web page.

You can't directly access `default.asp` at this point. Instead, because the wildcard mapping first routes the request to ASP.NET, and the ASP.NET configuration denies access to all anonymous users, you are redirected to the login page. In fact, anonymous requests never even make it to the logic inside of the `CustomHandler` class. The `UrlAuthorizationModule` running during the `AuthorizeRequest` event in the HTTP pipeline detects that the user is anonymous and immediately forwards the call to `EndRequest`—in effect short-circuiting the request processing and bypassing the custom handler. The information about the original request to `default.asp` is still retained:

```
http://localhost/wildcardmapping/login.aspx?ReturnUrl=%2fwildcardmapping%2fDefault.asp
```

The next step is to add in a basic user store and authenticate credentials against that user store. I cover the new Membership feature in detail in Chapter 10, but for now the sample just uses the Membership feature with only a minor change to its default configuration. Because I happen to be running a local instance of SQL Server 2005, the connection string for all of the SQL-based providers (including Membership) needs to be changed:

```
<connectionStrings>
  <remove name="LocalSqlServer"/>
  <add
  name="LocalSqlServer"
  connectionString="server=.\SQL2005;Integrated Security=true;database=aspnetdb"
  />
</connectionStrings>
```

All of the provider-based features that have SQL providers use the same connection string, `LocalSqlServer`. For the sample application the default definition of `LocalSqlServer` is removed and is redefined to point at a local SQL Server instance running the `aspnetdb` database.

The login page for the application is `Login.aspx`, and again no special behavior is needed here. Just dropping a `Login` control onto the page is sufficient because the `Login` control automatically works with the Membership feature.

C#

```
<%@ Page Language="C#" AutoEventWireup="true"
CodeFile="Login.aspx.cs" Inherits="Login" %>

<html xmlns="http://www.w3.org/1999/xhtml" >
<head runat="server">
    <title>Login Page</title>
</head>
<body>
    <form id="form1" runat="server">
    <div>
        <asp:Login ID="Login1" runat="server">
        </asp:Login>
    </div>
    </form>
</body>
</html>
```

VB.NET

```
<%@ Page Language="vb" AutoEventWireup="true" _
CodeFile="Login.aspx.vb" Inherits="Login" %>

<!DOCTYPE html PUBLIC "-//W3C//DTD XHTML 1.0 Transitional//EN" _
"http://www.w3.org/TR/xhtml1/DTD/xhtml1-transitional.dtd">

<html xmlns="http://www.w3.org/1999/xhtml">
<head runat="server">
    <title>Untitled Page</title>
</head>
<body>
    <form id="form1" runat="server">
    <div>
        <asp:Login ID="Login1" runat="server">
        </asp:Login>
    </div>
    </form>
</body>
</html>
```

Now if you attempt to navigate to `default.asp`, you will be redirected to `Login.aspx`. Type in some valid credentials (if you need to create some credentials first just use the ASP.NET Configuration tool from inside of Visual Studio), and log in. Assuming that the credentials are valid, you will be redirected back to `default.asp`, and you will have a valid forms authentication cookie for subsequent pages.

At this point in the sample, the custom handler is not really adding anything, though you will rectify this shortly. The main thing to keep in mind is that with nothing more than a wildcard mapping, a slight tweak to a connection string, the forms authentication feature, and one login page, you now have an ASP.NET application authenticating and logging users in prior to handing the users to classic ASP. Now that you know the steps involved, you can whip up all this up in about five minutes flat! In fact, for many smaller ASP.NET-to-classic ASP integration problems, this may actually be all you need.

Will Cookieless Forms Authentication Work?

Cookieless forms authentication may not work as an authentication mechanism for classic ASP. For the heck of it, try adding the following to `web.config`.

```
<authentication mode="Forms">
    <forms cookieless="UseUri" />
</authentication>
```

Initially, things will look like they are working, and you will successfully get redirected to `default.asp`. The resultant URL looks something like:

```
http://localhost/wildcardmapping/(F(kc9ofAIFfj1TpnvRRoC9_me0TPhW4m9_x8n0od-
KUmjaLB__BWQplUyZ7lWW4ORKjkGJZcYMAIH662Evl4CRiA0sXEfOp1mHhH6WpzBoJkI1))/Default.asp
```

The problem with this URL is not the fact that the cookieless forms authentication ticket is embedded in the URL. That actually will not impact classic ASP because the ASP.NET ISAPI filter removes the ticket from the URL long before the request is forwarded to `ASP.dll`. Problems arise if your classic ASP code starts constructing redirects from inside of its code-base.

Chapter 6 explained that there were some restrictions on the way in which ASP.NET code could construct URLs and still retain the forms authentication ticket. ASP.NET provides the handy syntax to indicate an application-relative reference. However no such shorthand exists in classic ASP. You might have code in your classic ASP application that issues redirects with code like the following:

C#
```
Response.Redirect("/wildcardmappings/SomeOtherPage.aspx");
```

VB.NET
```
Response.Redirect("/wildcardmappings/SomeOtherPage.aspx")
```

This style of redirect will lose the forms authentication ticket that was embedded on the URL. Given the limited programming model available in classic ASP, there is not an easy way to grab the ticket out of the URL and preserve it when you redirect. If your classic ASP application uses only relative redirects like the following then you will most likely be able to use cookieless forms authentication with a classic ASP application.

```
'This type of redirect preserves the cookie-less ticket
Response.Redirect("default2.asp")
```

The same approach will work if you have any <a /> tags or other relative URL references in your classic ASP pages. From the browser's standpoint, relative URL references are always considered relative to the last path in the URL, which in the case of cookieless forms authentication means relative to the full URL including the cookieless ticket.

Passing Data to ASP from ASP.NET

Up to this point, you have seen the mechanics of getting forms authentication working with classic ASP. The next step is to come up with a way to pass the authenticated username over to the classic ASP application. There probably are not many ASP sites out there that require authentication but then throw away the authenticated username. The problem of getting the authenticated username over to the ASP application, however, is just a specific example of the more general problem of passing data from ASP. NET over to a classic ASP application.

This is where the custom `HttpHandler` comes in handy. Rather than having to cobble together some kind of redirection-based mechanism, you can use the HTTP headers for the request as a way to pass information along from ASP.NET into a classic ASP application. In fact, for quite a few years, a variety of third-party authentication products have relied on manipulating HTTP headers as a platform-neutral way to pass information between different web applications.

In the case of a custom `HttpHandler`, you can change the HTTP headers for a request by using the protected `ExecuteUrlHeaders` property. You might think that you could just use the `Context` property to get to the `Request.Headers` property and then manipulate the resulting `NameValueCollection`. This will not work because `Request.Headers` is a read-only collection; its intended use in earlier versions of ASP.NET never included modifying the headers of a request. `DefaultHttpHandler` gets around this by storing a copy if the incoming HTTP headers in a separate `NameValueCollection` and making this collection available to developers via the `ExecuteUrlHeaders` property.

As an example, you can try adding an arbitrary header to the incoming request from inside of the custom handler.

C#

```
public override string OverrideExecuteUrlPath()
{
        this.ExecuteUrlHeaders.Add("Some Custom Header", "Some Custom Value");
        return null;
}
```

VB.NET

```
Public Overrides Function OverrideExecuteUrlPath() As String
        Me.ExecuteUrlHeaders.Add("Some Custom Header", "Some Custom Value")
        Return Nothing
End Function
```

Now, the custom `HttpHandler` inserts a new header value for the request. To verify that this custom HTTP header made it to the classic ASP page, you can add code to `default.asp` that dumps out the request headers.

```
<%
For Each value In Request.ServerVariables
    if (value <> "ALL_HTTP") AND (value <> "ALL_RAW") then
%>
<b><%= value %></b> = <%= Request.ServerVariables(value) %> <br/><%
    End if
Next
%>
```

The ASP code intentionally skips over the ALL_HTTP and ALL_RAW variables because these contain a concatenated dump of all of the headers in a rather unreadable form. If you open a browser and log in to default.asp, you get nicely formatted output showing all the request headers. At the end of the list, you will see the following:

```
HTTP_SOME CUSTOM HEADER = Some Custom Value
```

You can easily access custom HTTP header values from inside of classic ASP by just indexing into Request.ServerVariables. With this basic technique, you can pass information from ASP.NET 3.5 to classic ASP. As long as the information you need to pass can be serialized into a string in ASP.NET, and your classic ASP code can do something useful with that string value, you have a very easy way to pass information between the two environments. No need for kludgy redirects or expensive web service calls!

Although the samples in this chapter do not need to move very much information around from ASP.NET to classic ASP, you might be wondering just how much data you can actually stuff into an HTTP header. As an experiment, you can try adding large strings into the header. The following code uses a 32KB string as the value for a custom HTTP header:

C#

```
public override string OverrideExecuteUrlPath()
{
    //gets called just before control is handed back to IIS 7.0
    this.ExecuteUrlHeaders.Add("Some Custom Header", "Some Custom Value");

    StringBuilder largeString = new StringBuilder();
    largeString.Append(new String(char.Parse("a"), 32768));
    this.ExecuteUrlHeaders.Add("A Very Large Header", largeString.ToString());

    return null;
}
```

VB.NET

```
Public Overrides Function OverrideExecuteUrlPath() As String
    'gets called just before control is handed back to IIS 7.0
    Me.ExecuteUrlHeaders.Add("Some Custom Header", "Some Custom Value")

    Dim largeString As New StringBuilder()
    largeString.Append(New String(Char.Parse("a"), 33870))
    Me.ExecuteUrlHeaders.Add("A Very Large Header", largeString.ToString())

    Return Nothing
End Function
```

The custom header value "A Very Large Header" was passed to classic ASP without a problem, and the entire 32KB string showed up on default.asp. Part of the reason such enormous headers are allowed is that by the time ASP.NET is handing a request back to IIS 7.0, the normal URL length and header size restrictions enforced by http.sys and ASP.NET have already occurred. Playing around with this a bit more, it turns out you can send as much as 65,535 bytes in an additional custom header (that is, 1 byte less than 64KB). Realistically, though, for purposes of authentication and authorization, you aren't going to need much more than a few kilobytes of space for username and role information.

Passing Username to ASP

Now that you have seen most of the work necessary to move information from ASP.NET over to classic ASP, the sample application should be extended to pass the authenticated username from ASP.NET forms authentication over to classic ASP. However, there is one very convenient piece of work that ASP.NET already performs on your behalf! A side effect of running the request through ASP.NET first is that the authenticated user information is automatically placed in the appropriate HTTP headers. For example, if you log in with the account classicASP from ASP.NET, the header information that ASP.NET sets up for classic ASP already includes the following:

```
AUTH_USER = classicASP
LOGON_USER = classicASP
```

For classic ASP code that was already using either of these server variables to identify the user, integrating forms authentication and ASP couldn't be easier.

Authenticating Classic ASP with IIS 7.0 Integrated Mode

Authenticating a classic ASP page that is part of an ASP.NET application running under the classic .NET application pool inside IIS 7.0 does not require any extra efforts except the trick of defining a wildcard mapping inside IIS 7.0 so that ASP.NET gets the chance to process the classic ASP page. Defining and enforcing authentication on classic ASP pages, as you have seen in the above section, is no different from what you do for ASP.NET resources. First, you define the <authentication> configuration section inside the web.config configuration file of the application. Once the web.config configuration file is configured properly to handle authentication, you add an .aspx login page to allow users to enter their credentials to be authenticated by the application.

The preceding section shows how to authenticate classic ASP pages inside an ASP.NET application that is running under the classic .NET application pool. The same configurations and additions are needed when you want to authenticate classic ASP pages when running inside an ASP.NET application that is configured with the default application pool or in other words the integrated mode. You still need to define the <authentication> configuration section inside the web.config configuration file and add an .aspx Login page to gather credentials and authenticate users.

Until now there has been nothing mentioned about wildcard mapping when it is time to authenticate classic ASP pages with IIS 7.0 integration mode. With the new IIS 7.0 integrated mode there is no need for any extension mapping, since the ASP.NET engine has full control and access to any request that hits the IIS web server; hence, no additional configuration is needed by IIS 7.0 except putting the application to run under the default application pool. However, there is one step required to authenticate a request for non-ASP.NET resources, in this case classic ASP pages, which is to configure any ASP.NET authentication type you choose to authenticate non-ASP.NET resources.

As mentioned previously in this book, when an application runs in the integrated mode, IIS 7.0 makes full use of all the configuration sections defined within the `<system.webServer>` configuration section group to load any custom `HttpHandler`, `HttpModule` or any other custom configuration setting while the application is running. ASP.NET existed before the days of IIS 7.0 and hence all the ASP.NET modules and features target only ASP.NET resources. For instance, the managed `FormsAuthentication Module`, if installed on IIS 7.0, for applications running under the default application pool, is defined inside the `<modules>` configuration section within the `<system.webServer>` configuration section group located inside the `applicationHost.config` IIS 7.0 configuration file, as follows:

```
<add name="FormsAuthentication" type="System.Web.Security.
FormsAuthenticationModule" preCondition="managedHandler" />
```

The preceding shows how the managed `FormsAuthenticationModule` is added into the list of managed modules on IIS 7.0. For an in-depth discussion on the new IIS 7.0 integrated mode and the `applicationHost.config` IIS 7.0 configuration file, please refer back to Chapter 2.

The important attribute to watch for now is the `preCondition` attribute. In the above configuration section, it is set to the `managedHandler` value. This means that the added module will serve and run only for managed resources (i.e. ASP.NET resources). To be able to use the same module to authenticate non-ASP.NET resources (in this case, classic ASP pages), you need to add the following configuration sections into the `<modules>` configuration section inside the `<system.webServer>` configuration section group located in the application's `web.config` configuration file:

```
<system.webServer>
  <modules>
    <remove name="FormsAuthentication"/>
    <add
     name="FormsAuthentication"
     type="System.Web.Security.FormsAuthenticationModule"
     preCondition=""
    />
  </modules>
</system.webServer>
```

As you know by now, the `FormsAuthenticationModule` is already added inside the `applicationHost.config` IIS 7.0 configuration file. What you need to do first is remove the module's entry by specifying the module's name, as specified in the `<add />` element above.

After removing the module, you need to add it again, but this time setting the value of the `preCondition` attribute to an empty string represented by empty double quotes. This instructs the IIS 7.0 web server core engine to list the `FormsAuthenticationModule` as a managed authentication module that can be applied to all resources that are processed by ASP.NET engine. That is all you need to ensure that non-ASP.NET resources, in this case classic ASP pages, get authenticated using ASP.NET features and modules.

Once the above has been added to the application's `web.config` configuration file, you still need to configure the `<authentication />` configuration section group to work with Forms authentication. The same steps that were mentioned in the above section can be used here without any changes except for adding/removing the authentication module of choice, whether Forms or Windows authentication.

A closing note here is that the above configuration change works not only for classic ASP pages but also for any non-ASP.NET resource, including images, cascading style sheets, PHP pages, etc. You can now benefit from pre-existing ASP.NET features to manage other non-ASP.NET resources and even pages from other technologies.

Authorizing Classic ASP with ASP.NET

You have seen that forms authentication is already working with classic ASP application, in part because there is a URL authorization rule that denies access to anonymous users. In effect, you already have the basics of authorization working. The sample application, though, can be modified a bit more to include more extensive authorization rules.

For example, let's say there is an administrative folder for the ASP application that should only grant access to users that are in the "Administrators" role. You can create a URL authorization rule that protects the ASP subdirectory.

```
<location path="ASPAdminPages">
    <system.web>
        <authorization>
            <allow roles="Administrators"/>
            <deny users="*"/>
        </authorization>
    </system.web>
</location>
```

Now, whenever an attempt is made to access a classic ASP page in the ASPAdminPages subdirectory, ASP.NET's URL authorization will enforce this rule. Using the ASP.NET Configuration tool available from inside of Visual Studio, you can enable the Role Manager feature, create a new role called "Administrators" and add a user to the new role. The only change that occurs in configuration is the addition of the <roleManager /> element (by default Role Manager is not enabled, hence the need to turn it on):

```
<roleManager enabled="true" />
```

As with the Membership feature, the default Role Manager provider uses the LocalSqlServer connection string. Because this was changed earlier, Role Manager will automatically associate role information in the aspnetdb database with the user account information located in the same database.

At this point, if you try logging into a classic ASP page located within the ASPAdminPages directory, you get redirected to the login page for the application. If you log in with an account that you added to the "Administrators" role, you can access pages in this subdirectory.

Once again you can see that once wildcard mappings are setup in IIS 7.0, you just go about building authentication and authorization inside of ASP.NET as you normally would. The only difference is that the authorization rules also automatically protect access to the classic ASP pages. As with the authentication setup discussed earlier, even though there is a custom HTTP handler in the ASP.NET application, it still is not needed at this point. You could pull the custom HTTP handler, and everything shown so far with forms authentication and URL authorization would still function properly.

Passing User Roles to Classic ASP

By this point, you are probably wondering why there even is a custom HTTP handler in the ASP.NET application. Forms authentication and URL authorization seem to be working just fine; why is this handler sitting around in the application? Well, you finally made it to the point where the built-in magic of wildcard mappings runs out of steam. Even though authorizing classic ASP pages is useful, chances are that some of your ASP applications need the full role information for an authenticated user. Just protecting individual pages or entire subdirectories is not sufficient.

Solving this problem does require passing data from ASP.NET to classic ASP, and as a result you will need a custom HTTP handler to hand the role information to your classic ASP pages. Because the sample application uses Role Manager, you can modify the custom handler in the application to pack the user's roles into a custom header.

C#

```csharp
public override string OverrideExecuteUrlPath()
{
    //gets called just before control is handed back to IIS 6
    HttpContext c = this.Context;

    StringBuilder userRoles = new StringBuilder();
    RolePrincipal rp = (RolePrincipal)c.User;

    //Move the user roles into a semi-colon delimited string
    string rolesHeader;
    if ( (rp != null) && (rp.GetRoles().Length > 0) )
    {
        foreach (string role in rp.GetRoles())
            userRoles.Append(role + ";");
        rolesHeader = userRoles.ToString(0, userRoles.Length - 1);
    }
    else
        rolesHeader = String.Empty;

    this.ExecuteUrlHeaders.Add("Roles", rolesHeader);
    return null;
}
```

VB.NET

```vbnet
Public Overrides Function OverrideExecuteUrlPath() As String
    'gets called just before control is handed back to IIS 7.0
    Dim c As HttpContext = Me.Context

    Dim userRoles As New StringBuilder()
    Dim rp As RolePrincipal = CType(c.User, RolePrincipal)

    Dim rolesHeader As String
    If (rp IsNot Nothing) AndAlso (rp.GetRoles().Length > 0) Then
        For Each role As String In rp.GetRoles()
            userRoles.Append(role & ";")
        Next role
```

```
            rolesHeader = userRoles.ToString(0, userRoles.Length - 1)
        Else
            rolesHeader = String.Empty
        End If

        Me.ExecuteUrlHeaders.Add("Roles", rolesHeader)

        Return Nothing
    End Function
```

First the custom HTTP handler gets a reference to the authenticated user on the context. Because the sample application enabled the Role Manager feature, the RolePrincipal is the object representation of an authenticated user that is attached to the current context automatically by the RoleManagerModule. You can then retrieve all the roles that a user belongs to from the RolePrincipal.GetRoles method.

When you run the sample application again, the role information can be seen in the "Roles" custom header. The original header name is prepended with HTTP_ by ASP, which is why the following sample output has a header called HTTP_ROLES rather than just ROLES.

HTTP_ROLES = Administrators;Regular User;Valued Customer

The classic ASP pages can retrieve this role information in a more useful form by just cracking the header apart into an array.

```
<%
Dim arrRoles
arrRoles = split(Request.ServerVariables("HTTP_ROLES"),";")

For Each role In arrRoles
    Response.Write(role) + "<br/>"
Next
%>
```

This ASP page simply converts the string into an array, and then dumps the array out on the page. Assuming your classic ASP applications have some type of wrapper or common include function for retrieving roles and checking role access, you simply need to tweak that type of code to fetch the role information from the custom HTTP header instead.

Safely Passing Sensitive Data to Classic ASP

At this point, it almost looks like the authentication and authorization scenario is solved. Everything works, and you have a simple but very effective way for passing role information over to classic ASP. There is however one security problem with the previous code. Because the custom handler is manipulating a custom HTTP header, there are no special protections enforced for the header's value. As a result, there is nothing that would prevent a malicious user from logging in and attempting to send a forged HTTP header called Roles that contained some roles that the user really didn't belong to. This type of attack will not work with HTTP headers such as LOGON_USER, because the value of these headers is automatically set in IIS and by ASP.NET. There is no way that a malicious user could forge their username by sending fake headers to ASP.NET. However, with the theory that it is better to be safe than sorry, you can add extra protections into the custom HTTP handler that will make it impossible to create a forged header—regardless of how ASP.NET handles header merging. Just as forms authentication and other cookie-based features support digitally signing their payloads, you can also add a hash-based signature to your sensitive custom HTTP headers.

The sample defines a helper class that encapsulates the work involved in hashing string values as well as verifying hash values. The creation of a hash value for a custom HTTP header is performed from inside of the custom HTTP handler, while verification of the hashed header occurs inside of the classic ASP code. The need to access the same logic in both places means that the hash helper class also needs to be exposed via COM so that classic ASP can call into it.

Start by just defining the hash helper class and its static constructor:

C#

```csharp
namespace HashLibrary
{
 public class Helper
 {
     private static string hashKey =
       "a 128 character random key goes here";

     private static byte[] bKey;

     static Helper()
     {
         //Cache the byte representation of the signing key
         bKey = ConvertStringKeyToByteArray(hashKey);
     }

     //snip...
 }
}
```

VB.NET

```vbnet
Namespace HashLibrary
Public Class Helper

 Private Shared hashKey As String = "a 128 character random key goes here"

   Private Shared bKey() As Byte

   Shared Sub New()
         'Cache the byte representation of the signing key
       bKey = ConvertStringKeyToByteArray(hashKey)
   End Sub

  'snip...

End Class
```

Because the intent of this helper class is for it to create and verify hashes, some common key material must be shared across all applications that perform these operations. For a production application, you would use configurable keys, along the lines of <machineKey />, because this allows for flexible definition of keys and makes it easier to rotate keys. For simplicity, though, the sample application hard-codes a 128-character (that is, a 64-byte) key. You can easily generate one using the GenKeys sample code that was covered in Chapter 6. Needless to say, in a secure application you should never store key material inside code. For our purposes, though, building a custom configuration section or dragging protected configuration into the mix at this point will simply clutter up the sample.

The hash functions inside the .NET Framework use byte arrays, so the string hash key needs to be converted. Because the private static variable holds the hash key as a string, it performs a one-time conversion of the key into a byte array inside of the static constructor. This one-time conversion eliminates the parsing overhead of having to convert the string hash key into a byte array every time the key is needed. The ConvertStringKeyToByteArray method is covered later in this chapter, although the purpose of the method is pretty clear from its name.

The helper class exposes a public static method that hashes a string value and returns the resulting hash as a string.

C#

```csharp
public static string HashStringValue(string valueToHash)
{
    using (HMACSHA1 hms = new HMACSHA1(bKey))
    {
        return ConvertByteArrayToString(
                hms.ComputeHash(Encoding.Unicode.GetBytes(valueToHash))
            );
    }
}
```

VB.NET

```vbnet
Public Shared Function HashStringValue(ByVal valueToHash As String) As String
    Using hms As New HMACSHA1(bKey)
        Return ConvertByteArrayToString( _
        hms.ComputeHash(Encoding.Unicode.GetBytes(valueToHash)))
    End Using
End Function
```

Because you do not want an external user to be able to forge any of the custom HTTP header values, you need to use a hash algorithm that cannot be spoofed by other users. As with forms authentication, the sample code uses the HMACSHA1 algorithm because it relies on a secret key that will only be known by your application. Given a string value to hash, the HashStringValue method does the following:

1. Creates an instance of the HMACSHA1 algorithm, initializing it with the secret key.

2. Converts the string into a byte array because hash functions operate on byte arrays—not strings.

3. Hashes the resulting byte array.

4. Converts the result back into a string using another helper method that will be covered a little later.

Now that you have a convenient way to securely sign a string, you need a way to verify the signature.

C#

```csharp
    public static bool ValidateHash(string value, string hash)
    {
        using (HMACSHA1 hms = new HMACSHA1(bKey))
        {
            if (HashStringValue(value) != hash)
                return false;
            else
                return true;
        }
    }
```

VB.NET

```vbnet
    Public Shared Function ValidateHash(ByVal value As String, ByVal hash As String) _
    As Boolean
        Using hms As New HMACSHA1(bKey)
            If HashStringValue(value) <> hash Then
                Return False
            Else
                Return True
            End If
        End Using
    End Function
```

The ValidateHash method is the companion to the HashStringValue method. In ValidateHash, given a piece of string data (the value parameter), and the digital signature for the data (the hash parameter), the method uses HMACSHA1 to generate a hash of the string data. Assuming that the piece of code that initially signed the string data, and thus generated the hash parameter, shares the same signing key, then hashing the value parameter should yield a hash value that matches the hash parameter.

Because the intent is for classic ASP pages to verify the hash values for custom HTTP headers, the logic inside of the ValidateHash method must also be made available through a COM interop.

C#

```csharp
#region COM support
    public Helper() { }

    public bool ValidateHashCOM(string value, string hash)
    {
        return Helper.ValidateHash(value, hash);
    }
#endregion
```

VB.NET

```vbnet
#Region "COM support"
 Public Sub New()
 End Sub
```

```
Public Function ValidateHashCOM(ByVal value As String, ByVal hash As String) _
As Boolean
    Return Helper.ValidateHash(value, hash)
End Function
```

There are a few requirements to make a .NET Framework class visible via a COM wrapper. The class needs a default constructor because there is no concept of parameterized class construction in COM. Additionally, any methods exposed to COM must have signatures that are compatible with COM types. Because there is no concept of static methods in COM, it was just easier to add a default constructor to the Helper class as well as a public instance method that simply wraps the public static ValidateHash method. From ASP.NET, you would use the static methods on the Helper class. From classic ASP and COM, you first instantiate an instance of the Helper class and then call ValidateHashCOM on the instance.

The Helper class also has two methods for converting hex strings to and from byte arrays.

C#

```csharp
public static byte[] ConvertStringKeyToByteArray(string stringizedKeyValue)
{
    byte[] keyBuffer = new byte[64];

    if (stringizedKeyValue.Length > 128)
        throw new ArgumentException(
            "This method is hardcoded to accept only a 128 character string");

    for (int i = 0; i < stringizedKeyValue.Length; i = i + 2)
    {
     //Convert the string key - every 2 characters represents 1 byte
     keyBuffer[i / 2] =
       Byte.Parse(
         stringizedKeyValue.Substring(i, 2),
                   System.Globalization.NumberStyles.HexNumber
       );
    }

    return keyBuffer;
}
```

VB.NET

```vbnet
Public Shared Function ConvertStringKeyToByteArray( _
ByVal stringizedKeyValue AsString) As Byte()
        Dim keyBuffer(63) As Byte
        If stringizedKeyValue.Length > 128 Then
            Throw New ArgumentException("This method is " & _
                      "hardcoded to accept only a 128 character string")
        End If
        For i As Integer = 0 To stringizedKeyValue.Length - 1 Step 2
            'Convert the string key - every 2 characters represents 1 byte
            keyBuffer(i \ 2) = Byte.Parse( _
            stringizedKeyValue.Substring(i, 2), _
            System.Globalization.NumberStyles.HexNumber)
```

```
            Next i
            Return keyBuffer
    End Function
```

The `ConvertStringKeyToByteArray` method is currently hard-coded to work only with 64-byte keys. Given a 128 character string (which is the hex string representation of a 64-byte value), the method iterates through the string extracting each set of two hex characters (0-9 and A-F). Each pair of hex characters is then converted into a byte value with a call to `Byte.Parse`. The net result is that a 128 character string is converted into a `byte[64]`.

The reverse operation of converting a byte array into a string is shown here:

C#

```csharp
public static string ConvertByteArrayToString(byte[] value)
{
    StringBuilder sb = new StringBuilder(128);

    if (value.Length > 64)
        throw new ArgumentException(
            "This method is hardcoded to accept only a byte[64].");

    foreach (byte b in value)
    {
        sb.Append(b.ToString("X2"));
    }
    return sb.ToString();
}
```

VB.NET

```vbnet
Public Shared Function ConvertByteArrayToString(ByVal value() As Byte) As String
    Dim sb As New StringBuilder(128)
    If value.Length > 64 Then
            Throw New ArgumentException("This method is " & _
                    "hardcoded to accept only a byte[64].")
    End If
    For Each b As Byte In value
        sb.Append(b.ToString("X2"))
    Next b

    Return sb.ToString()
End Function
```

As with `ConvertStringKeyToByteArray`, the `ConvertByteArrayToString` method assumes 128-character strings. Converting a byte array to a string is much easier because you can convert each byte value to a hex-string equivalent by using the string format of X2.

The only other work needed in the hash helper is to attribute the assembly so that the public `Helper` class is visible to COM. The assembly is also strongly named and will be deployed in the GAC.

C#

```
//from assemblyinfo.cs
[assembly: ComVisible(true)]

// The GUID is for the ID of the typelib if this project is exposed to COM
[assembly: Guid("5252f41f-a404-43eb-8d55-8fbdeb2011df")]

[assembly: AssemblyVersion("1.0.0.0")]
[assembly: AssemblyFileVersion("1.0.0.0")]

[assembly: AllowPartiallyTrustedCallers()]
```

VB.NET

```
'from assemblyinfo.vb
<Assembly: ComVisible(True)>

' The following GUID is for the ID of the typelib if this project is exposed to COM
<Assembly: Guid("42de7270-c824-4ed1-9c24-59caaaaf24d3")>

<Assembly: AssemblyVersion("1.0.0.0")>
<Assembly: AssemblyFileVersion("1.0.0.0")>
<Assembly: System.Security.AllowPartiallyTrustedCallers()>
```

At this point, you can integrate the Helper class into the custom HTTP handler. Rather than passing the role information for the user in the clear as a simple string, the custom handler will instead calculate the signed hash for all of the roles.

C#

```
public override string OverrideExecuteUrlPath()
{
    //gets called just before control is handed back to IIS 6
    HTTPContext c = this.Context;

    StringBuilder userRoles = new StringBuilder();
    RolePrincipal rp = (RolePrincipal)c.User;

    string rolesHeader;
    if ( (rp != null) && (rp.GetRoles().Length > 0) )
    {
        foreach (string role in rp.GetRoles())
            userRoles.Append(role + ";");
        rolesHeader = userRoles.ToString(0, userRoles.Length - 1);
        rolesHeader = rolesHeader + "," +
                        Helper.HashStringValue(rolesHeader);
    }
    else
        rolesHeader = String.Empty;

    this.ExecuteUrlHeaders.Add("Roles", rolesHeader);
    return null;
}
```

VB.NET

```
Public Overrides Function OverrideExecuteUrlPath() As String
    'gets called just before control is handed back to IIS 7.0
    Dim c As HttpContext = Me.Context

    Dim userRoles As New StringBuilder()
    Dim rp As RolePrincipal = CType(c.User, RolePrincipal)

    Dim rolesHeader As String
    If (rp IsNot Nothing) AndAlso (rp.GetRoles().Length > 0) Then
        For Each role As String In rp.GetRoles()
            userRoles.Append(role & ";")
        Next role
        rolesHeader = userRoles.ToString(0, userRoles.Length - 1)
        rolesHeader = rolesHeader & "," & Helper.HashStringValue(rolesHeader)
    Else
        rolesHeader = String.Empty
    End If

    Me.ExecuteUrlHeaders.Add("Roles", rolesHeader)
    Return Nothing
End Function
```

The extra code appends the HMACSHA1 hash of the role string to the end of the custom header. Now when you log in to the ASP application, the header looks like:

HTTP_ROLES = Administrators;Regular User;Valued Customer,
5F9AFD42A9ABCE50FE651A39A1F5EB63E5142D21

To use the hash helper from inside of the ASP.NET application, you also need to add an assembly reference because the helper is deployed in the GAC:

```
<compilation debug="true">
  <assemblies>
  <add assembly="HashLibrary, Version=1.0.0.0, Culture=neutral,
      PublicKeyToken=729492b6d2638318" />
  </assemblies>
</compilation>
```

The only work left to do at this point is make the hash helper available to the classic ASP application. Because the helper assembly was already compiled with the necessary attributes to make it visible in COM, you just need to register the assembly with the regasm.exe utility:

```
%windir%\Microsoft.NET\Framework\v2.0.50727\regasm HashLibrary.dll
```

The result of running `regasm` is that the `Helper` class is registered as a COM type in the Windows Registry and is associated with the type library GUID that was defined in the helper project's `AssemblyInfo.cs` file. Because the intent for now is to just call the `Helper` class from ASP, there wasn't any additional information specified in the `Helper` project to give the `Helper` class a fixed COM CLSID. Classic ASP uses late-bound COM calls anyway so the extra work to `configure` the Helper class with a fixed class ID is not necessary.

You can use the hash helper from ASP as shown here:

```
<%
Dim objHelper, signedRoles, strRoles, strRolesHash, arrRoles

if (Request.ServerVariables("HTTP_ROLES") <> "") then
    signedRoles = split(Request.ServerVariables("HTTP_ROLES"),",")

    strRoles    = signedRoles(0)
    strRolesHash  = signedRoles(1)

    Set objHelper = Server.CreateObject("HashLibrary.Helper")
    result = objHelper.ValidateHashCOM(strRoles, strRolesHash)
    if (result = true) then
        arrRoles = split(strRoles,";")
        For Each role In arrRoles
            Response.Write(role) + "<br/>"
        Next
    else
        Response.Write("No valid roles were found for the user.")
    end if
else
    Response.Write("No roles were found for the user.")
end if
%>
```

Assuming that a custom "Roles" header was sent, this ASP code splits the value into two parts: the string containing the actual role information and the string containing the digital signature of the role string. With these two values, the ASP code creates an instance of the `Helper` class using COM, and then calls the `ValidateHashCOM` method to verify the digital signature that was sent in the header. Because the custom HTTP handler is using the same key material, the `Helper` class successfully validates that the signature in the custom header is valid.

You can try testing the negative case by tweaking the custom handler to include bogus data in the signature:

C#

```
this.ExecuteUrlHeaders.Add("Roles", rolesHeader + "1");
```

VB.NET

```
Me.ExecuteUrlHeaders.Add("Roles", rolesHeader + "1")
```

Because the digital signature is the last part of the custom HTTP header, appending an extra character creates an invalid hash value. Now when you try to run the sample ASP code, the hash verification will fail.

You have seen how the hash verification is handled, with the signature being created in the handler and then validated in classic ASP. You can integrate this kind of logic into whatever ASP code you currently use for authorization. The logic for splitting the custom header and verifying it can easily be wrapped in a custom include file or function without necessarily affecting any other code in your ASP application that depends on retrieving and checking role information.

Full Code Listing of the Hash Helper

Since the hash Helper class was shown piecemeal earlier, the Helper class is shown in its entirety here:

C#

```
using System;
using System.Collections.Generic;
using System.Text;
using System.Security.Cryptography;

namespace HashLibrary
{
 public class Helper
 {
    private static string hashKey =       "179C4AB2765118F23CCB273EF2BB31016154F0103
3F237F1BC0B04662232D51BE7416119B88D52B5C346CA9E03A4EA34875C4D15A976A353155532464947
81D5";

    private static byte[] bKey;

    static Helper()
    {
        //Cache the byte representation of the signing key
        bKey = ConvertStringKeyToByteArray(hashKey);
    }

    public static byte[] ConvertStringKeyToByteArray(string stringizedKeyValue)
    {
        byte[] keyBuffer = new byte[64];

if (stringizedKeyValue.Length > 128)
    throw new ArgumentException(
        "This method is hardcoded to accept only a 128 character string");

        for (int i = 0; i < stringizedKeyValue.Length; i = i + 2)
        {
            //Convert the string key - every 2 characters represents 1 byte
            keyBuffer[i / 2] =
                Byte.Parse(
                  stringizedKeyValue.Substring(i, 2),
                  System.Globalization.NumberStyles.HexNumber
                  );
        }

        return keyBuffer;
    }

    public static string ConvertByteArrayToString(byte[] value)
    {
        StringBuilder sb = new StringBuilder(128);

        if (value.Length > 64)
          throw new ArgumentException(
```

```csharp
                    "This method is hardcoded to accept only a byte[64].");

            foreach (byte b in value)
            {
                sb.Append(b.ToString("X2"));
            }
            return sb.ToString();
        }

        public static string HashStringValue(string valueToHash)
        {
            using (HMACSHA1 hms = new HMACSHA1(bKey))
            {
                return ConvertByteArrayToString(
                        hms.ComputeHash(Encoding.Unicode.GetBytes(valueToHash)));
            }
        }

        public static bool ValidateHash(string value, string hash)
        {
            using (HMACSHA1 hms = new HMACSHA1(bKey))
            {
                if (HashStringValue(value) != hash)
                    return false;
                else
                    return true;
            }
        }

#region COM support
        public Helper() { }

        public bool ValidateHashCOM(string value, string hash)
        {
            return Helper.ValidateHash(value, hash);
        }
#endregion

    }
}
```

VB.NET

```vbnet
Imports Microsoft.VisualBasic
Imports System
Imports System.Collections.Generic
Imports System.Text
Imports System.Security.Cryptography

Namespace HashLibrary
Public Class Helper
    Private Shared hashKey As String = "179C4AB2765118F23CCB273EF2BB31016154F01033F2
37F1BC0B04662232D51BE7416119B88D52B5C346CA9E03A4EA34875C4D15A976A35315553246494781D
5"
```

```vb
    Private Shared bKey() As Byte

    Shared Sub New()
        'Cache the byte representation of the signing key
        bKey = ConvertStringKeyToByteArray(hashKey)
    End Sub

     Public Shared Function ConvertStringKeyToByteArray( _
     ByVal stringizedKeyValue As String) As Byte()
         Dim keyBuffer(63) As Byte
         If stringizedKeyValue.Length > 128 Then
             Throw New ArgumentException("This method is hardcoded " & _
                     "to accept only a 128 character string")
         End If
         For i As Integer = 0 To stringizedKeyValue.Length - 1 Step 2
             'Convert the string key - every 2 characters represents 1 byte
             keyBuffer(i \ 2) = Byte.Parse( _
             stringizedKeyValue.Substring(i, 2), _
             System.Globalization.NumberStyles.HexNumber)
         Next i
         Return keyBuffer
     End Function


Public Shared Function ConvertByteArrayToString(ByVal value() As Byte) As String
    Dim sb As New StringBuilder(128)
    If value.Length > 64 Then
        Throw New ArgumentException("This method is hardcoded _
        to accept only a byte[64].")
    End If
    For Each b As Byte In value
        sb.Append(b.ToString("X2"))
    Next b

    Return sb.ToString()
End Function

Public Shared Function HashStringValue(ByVal valueToHash As String) As String
        Using hms As New HMACSHA1(bKey)
            Return ConvertByteArrayToString( _
            hms.ComputeHash(Encoding.Unicode.GetBytes(valueToHash)))
        End Using
    End Function

    Public Shared Function ValidateHash( _
    ByVal value As String, ByVal hash As String) As Boolean
        Using hms As New HMACSHA1(bKey)
            If HashStringValue(value) <> hash Then
                Return False
            Else
                Return True
            End If
        End Using
```

```
        End Function

#Region "COM support"
    Public Sub New()
    End Sub
    Public Function ValidateHashCOM( _
    ByVal value As String, ByVal hash As String) As Boolean
        Return Helper.ValidateHash(value, hash)
    End Function
#End Region
End Class
End Namespace
```

Authorizing Classic ASP with IIS 7.0 Integrated Mode

This section is not going to repeat what has already been mentioned in the section on authenticating classic ASP with the IIS 7.0 integrated mode. As you have seen in the above section, authorizing classic ASP pages residing inside an ASP.NET application that runs under the classic .NET application pool inside IIS 7.0 requires no additional steps compared to authorizing ASP.NET resources in terms of configuration settings. The only required configuration is the wildcard mapping so that the ASP.NET engine gets the chance to receive classic ASP page requests for several sorts of processing needed.

The authorization for non-ASP.NET resources is no different from the authentication of non-ASP.NET resources in an application that is running in the integrated mode. No extension mappings are needed because the ASP.NET engine automatically has access to every request that comes into the IIS web server; hence, the mapping is done automatically for you by the IIS 7.0 web server core engine.

What is left for you as a developer to enable and make use of ASP.NET authorization modules on non-ASP.NET resources is to change some configuration settings inside the application's web.config configuration file.

For the sake of showing how to authorize non-ASP.NET resources, I will show you how the managed UrlAuthorizationModule is defined inside the <modules> configuration section under the <system .webServer> configuration section group located in the IIS 7.0 applicationHost.config configuration file:

```
<add name="UrlAuthorization" type="System.Web.Security.UrlAuthorizationModule"
preCondition="managedHandler" />
```

The preceding module entry registers the managed UrlAuthorizationModule with IIS 7.0 and makes it available to be used by applications that are configured with the new IIS 7.0 integrated mode. Again, notice the preCondition attribute that is used to specify that this module works and runs only when managed resources are accessed.

To enable the above module for resources other than ASP.NET ones, the same trick that was explained above can be used.

```
<add
 name="UrlAuthorization"
 type="System.Web.Security.UrlAuthorizationModule"
 preCondition=""
/>
```

Notice the bolded `preCondition` attribute whose value is set to an empty string, signaling to IIS 7.0 that this managed module is to be used to authorize non-ASP.NET resources.

After the above configuration has been added into the application's `web.config` configuration file, you can follow the same steps as above for authorizing classic ASP pages in an ASP.NET application—the same steps that you have always used to authorize ASP.NET resource, but now those same settings are used to authorize non-ASP.NET resources.

Passing Data from ASP.NET to Classic ASP in IIS 7.0 Integrated Mode

You have seen how to implement a custom `DefaultHttpHandler` and override the `OverrideExecute UrlPath()` method to add any custom headers you want to pass from ASP.NET to classic ASP when the request is back to IIS 7.0, by adding custom headers' entries into the protected `ExecuteUrlHeaders` property defined on the `DefaultHttpHandler` class.

When an application is running in the new IIS 7.0 integrated mode, any request that comes into the IIS web server goes through the integrated request pipeline, where ASP.NET has access to the request throughout the entire pipeline. When it is time to select a handler for the request, the IIS 7.0 Web server core engine selects the ISAPI extension mapped in IIS to run and execute classic ASP pages. At this time, the classic ASP page gets executed and then after the execution stage in the integrated request pipeline, the request continues through the rest of events that are usually fired for a request in the integrated request pipeline. In other words, and contrary to how things happen in the classic mode (IIS 6.0 mode), there is no concept of a request sent back from ASP.NET to IIS 7.0. The ASP.NET engine would have access to the request at all the stages of the integrated request pipeline and it is only that IIS 7.0 selects the correct handler to execute the page requested when it is time to actually run the page and generate its output HTML to be sent back to the server. Hence, the `DefaultHttpHandler` has no role when the application is running in the integrated mode, same pipeline, same execution path, and, therefore, the same request and response.

Given the fact that the `DefaultHttpHandler` is not used anymore in the integrated mode, this means we cannot use the same method that was explained above to pass custom headers or data from ASP.NET to classic ASP.

A way around this limitation is to define a new IIS 7.0 managed module and register it with the `<modules>` configuration section inside the `<system.webServer>` configuration section group. The new module is called `PassingDataToClassicASP` and is defined in the App_Code folder of the "managedmapping" application accompanying this chapter as part of the source code. To define the module, add the following configuration element:

```
<!-- When an application is running under IIS 7.0 Integrated Mode you should
     register the HttpModule here. -->
<add
```

```
        name="PassingDataToClassicASP"
        type="PassingDataToClassicASP"
   />
```

Because the above module is defined in the App_Code folder, you only need to specify the full name of the module without any assembly name. In this case, the full name of the module is just the name of the class since no namespace was defined in the code.

The module developed subscribes to the `BeginRequest` event to add a custom header to the collection of headers on the current request.

C#

```csharp
using System;
using System.Data;
using System.Configuration;
using System.Collections;
using System.Collections.Specialized;
using System.Web;
using System.Web.Security;
using System.Xml.Linq;

public class PassingDataToClassicASP : IHttpModule
{
    public PassingDataToClassicASP()
    {
    }
    #region IHttpModule Members

    public void Dispose()
    {
        throw new NotImplementedException();
    }

    public void Init(HttpApplication context)
    {
        // Subscribe to the BeginRequest Event
        context.BeginRequest += new EventHandler(context_BeginRequest);
    }

    void context_BeginRequest(object sender, EventArgs e)
    {
        // Add custom header
        HttpContext.Current.Request.Headers.Add("My Custom Key", "Custom Data");
    }

    #endregion
}
```

VB.NET

```vbnet
Imports Microsoft.VisualBasic
Imports System
Imports System.Data
Imports System.Configuration
```

```
Imports System.Collections
Imports System.Collections.Specialized
Imports System.Linq
Imports System.Reflection
Imports System.Web
Imports System.Web.Security
Imports System.Web.UI
Imports System.Web.UI.HtmlControls
Imports System.Web.UI.WebControls
Imports System.Web.UI.WebControls.WebParts
Imports System.Xml.Linq

Public Class PassingDataToClassicASP Implements IHttpModule
  Public Sub New()
  End Sub

    #Region "IHttpModule Members"

    Public Sub Dispose() Implements IHttpModule.Dispose
          Throw New NotImplementedException()
    End Sub

    Public Sub Init(ByVal context As HttpApplication) Implements IHttpModule.Init
          ' Subsribe to the BeginRequest Event
          AddHandler context.BeginRequest, AddressOf context_BeginRequest
    End Sub

      ''' <summary>
      ''' </summary>
      ''' <param name="sender"></param>
      ''' <param name="e"></param>
    Private Sub context_BeginRequest(ByVal sender As Object, ByVal e As EventArgs)
          HttpContext.Current.Request.Headers.Add("My Custom Key", "Custom Data")
    End Sub

    #End Region
End Class
```

This is a very simple module, code-wise. When an application is running under the new IIS 7.0 integrated mode, the `HttpRequest.Headers` collection is Read/Write, contrary to how the headers' collection behaves when the application is running in the classic .NET application pool, which is Read Only. This means that you can add as many custom headers as you want to the current request using the `Add()` method on the `HttpRequest.Headers` collection.

Inside the classic ASP page, you can retrieve the custom header as follows:

```
<% = Request.ServerVariables("HTTP_My Custom Key") %>
```

Nothing in the classic ASP page code has changed from the above sections. What is different is that the ASP.NET code is no longer making use of the `DefaultHttpHandler`'s `ExecuteUrlHeaders` property to add the custom headers. A new managed IIS 7.0 module is developed and it subscribes to the `BeginRequest` event to add the custom headers. In addition, the `HttpRequest.Headers` collection is configured as Read/Write when the application is running under the new IIS 7.0 integrated mode;

therefore, you can add new entries directly to it. The integrated mode has made the process of passing data from ASP.NET to classic ASP a matter of defining a simple managed module, subscribing to events as needed, and adding custom headers to the Read/Write `HttpRequest.Headers` collection.

What if you want to pass the username that ASP.NET used for authentication to the classic ASP page? The answer is simple: subscribe to the `PostAuthenticateRequest` event and add the currently authenticated username as a custom header to the `HttpRequest.Headers` collection.

If you have enabled role management for your application and you want to pass the set of roles that the currently authenticated user belongs to, you would subscribe to the `PostAuthorizeRequest` event and add the set of roles that the current user belongs to (the same way as was explained in the above section using the `DefaultHttpHandler`).

The most important advantage in this solution is that now you can control at what stage in the integrated request pipeline you fill in custom data to pass to the classic ASP page. With the help of the read/write `HttpRequest.Headers` collection and by developing a new managed IIS 7.0 module, you can send whatever data you want from ASP.NET to the classic ASP page before the classic ASP page gets handled by the specific page hander that is selected by the IIS 7.0 Web server core engine to execute the classic ASP page. For a full discussion on the sequence of events that fire inside the integrated request pipeline, refer to Chapter 3.

Summary

Prior to ASP.NET 2.0 and IIS 6, your options for integrating authentication and authorization rules between ASP.NET and classic ASP were limited. You could write awkward redirection-based logic that moved data around on query-strings, or you could invest a fair amount of effort attempting to wrap ASP.NET functionality inside of a web service.

With IIS 6 and ASP.NET 2.0, extra logic was added to the runtimes of both products that finally made it easier to integrate the ASP and ASP.NET environments. IIS 6 added a new feature called wildcard mappings that allow arbitrary ISAPI extensions to participate in the request lifecycle of any resource. This allows you to route all `.asp` requests to ASP.NET. ASP.NET 2.0 includes the necessary logic to recognize when wildcard mappings are being used. Unlike earlier versions of ASP.NET, ASP.NET 2.0 will route a request to IIS 6 for further processing.

The combination of IIS 6 wildcard mappings and ASP.NET 2.0's `DefaultHandler` means that you can now use ASP.NET authentication and authorization in conjunction with a classic ASP site. The basic steps necessary to enable this integration are:

1. Use wildcard mappings to route all `.asp` requests to the ASP.NET ISAPI extension.

2. Add some `.aspx` pages to your classic ASP application. The basic ASP.NET page that you will need is some kind of login page.

3. Although the ASP and ASP.NET pages all live in the same directory structure, you can still add a `web.config` file into this structure for the ASP.NET pages. This `web.config` file includes settings to turn on forms authentication, define URL authorization rules, and enable the Membership and Role Manager features for automatic authentication and authorization support.

4. Optionally, you can author a custom HTTP handler that derives from `DefaultHandler`. This is only necessary if you plan to pass information from ASP.NET over to classic ASP. For example, as was demonstrated in this chapter, a custom handler can pass the role information from Role Manager over to ASP using a custom HTTP header.

After steps 1–3 have been accomplished (and optionally step 4), access to your ASP pages is controlled by the authentication and authorization mechanisms of ASP.NET. This allows you to migrate the authentication and authorization rules for your mixed application environments exclusively into ASP.NET.

ASP.NET 2.0 and IIS 6.0 did a great job facilitating the communication between ASP.NET and classic ASP. However, there were still steps you needed to configure from the IIS 6 side, where you had to add a new wildcard mapping so that `.asp` requests get redirected to the ASP.NET engine. In addition, you had to develop a custom `DefaultHttpHandler` to be able to perform any ASP.NET processing before the `.asp` request is handed back to IIS 6 for execution by the ISAPI extension that is configured to handle such request types.

The above steps are still valid and required with ASP.NET 3.5 and IIS 7.0 when an application is running under the classic .NET application pool inside IIS 7.0. However, ASP.NET 3.5 and IIS 7.0 provide a more mature model to integrate the communication between ASP.NET and classic ASP. This model is represented by the introduction of the new integration mode in IIS 7.0, where ASP.NET and IIS 7.0 share the same request pipeline and therefore the ASP.NET engine will implicitly have access to any request that passes through the pipeline, whether the request is for an ASP.NET resource, a classic ASP resource, or any other non-ASP.NET resource.

The above improvement implies that the developer has now zero effort to make ASP.NET get control over non-ASP.NET resources. Even better, you do not need to implement any custom `DefaultHttpHandler` to pass data from ASP.NET to classic ASP. On the contrary, all you have to do is develop a new managed IIS 7.0 module, subscribe to the suitable events inside the unified request pipeline (`BeginRequest`, `PostAuthenticateRequest`, etc.), and fill in the data you want to pass to the classic ASP pages inside custom headers of the `HttpRequest.Headers` collection that has been modified to allow additions of new custom headers.

Once the application has been configured to run under the new integrated mode inside IIS 7.0, classic ASP pages can benefit from the ASP.NET 3.5 features without any cost or effort from the developer side. Data can be passed easily from ASP.NET to classic ASP by developing a new managed IIS 7.0 module. Then you can configure ASP.NET authentication and authorization in the application's `web.config` configuration file and all resources, classic ASP or any other type of resource, inside the ASP.NET application, running under the integrated mode, are forced to abide by the ASP.NET rules set in the aforementioned configuration file, whether for authentication or authorization.

8

Session State

Session state probably does not strike most people as having much of anything to do with security. However, some security-related design points are worth touching on when thinking about how session state is used in an application. ASP.NET 3.5 plays an important role in securing cookieless sessions as well as locking down behavior in lower trust levels.

This chapter covers the following topics on ASP.NET 3.5 session state:

- ❑ Session state and the concept of a logon session.
- ❑ How session data is partitioned across applications.
- ❑ Cookie-based session IDs.
- ❑ Cookieless sessions and session ID regeneration.
- ❑ Configuring session state inside IIS 7.0.
- ❑ Protecting against session state denial-of-service attacks.
- ❑ Trust-level restrictions when using session state.
- ❑ Database security when using storing session state in SQL Server.
- ❑ Securing the out-of-process state server.

Does Session State Equal Logon Session?

An architectural question that comes up time and time again with session state is whether session state can be considered equivalent to a logon session. Hopefully after reading this section, you will agree that the answer to this question is unequivocally no! When developers ask about having the concept of a logon session object in ASP.NET, not only are they looking for a convenient storage location associated with a user, but they are also usually looking for a mechanism that prevents problems such as duplicate logins. (A workaround using forms authentication for this was shown earlier in Chapter 6.)

However, in ASP.NET session state is a service that is *always* available on each and every page in an application. There is no concept of having to authenticate to obtain a valid session object. More important, no mechanism inside of ASP.NET enforces validity of a session identifier (that is, is the identifier a value that was originally generated by ASP.NET?). As long as a browser is able to send a well-formed session identifier to ASP.NET, and the session identifier meets some basic syntax checks, the corresponding session data is available to the application.

Contrast this with something like forms authentication, where, in the default configuration, it is next to impossible to create a forged forms authentication ticket. (You would need to guess an encryption key as well as the key used for the HMACSHA1 signature.) The problem with depending on session state as an indicator of a logon session is that unlike forms authentication, it is trivial to create a valid session identifier.

Because a session identifier is nothing more than a 120-bit random number encoded using letters and numbers (this works out to a 24-character cookie value due to the way session state encodes the random number), you or I can easily create a perfectly valid session identifier. Of course, if you send such an identifier to ASP.NET, there probably isn't going to be any session data associated with it. (You have 2^120 possible combinations to guess if you were actually trying to grab someone else's session.) Instead ASP.NET spins up a new session object for you based on the ID.

If your application's code stored data inside of the Session object that indicated logon information, potentially even information indicating the logon status, you can quickly see how with a trivial client-side "attack," a user already logged on can quickly get into a logged-off state. There is another more subtle problem with using session state as a kind of logon session service: session identifiers cannot flow across domains.

The configuration options for session state, unlike forms authentication, don't include options for setting a cookie domain or a cookie path. Furthermore, when using the cookieless mode of operation, there is no facility equivalent to the cross-application redirection capability in forms authentication. For both of these reasons, attempting to keep track of a logon session across a set of applications running under different DNS addresses (although at least sharing a common domain suffix, for example, mycompany.com) is simply not possible with cookieless session state. The cookieless identifier that associates a user to session information will be different across various applications and no functionality is available to synchronize session state data from multiple applications.

A second flaw with attempting to use session state as a surrogate logon session service is that even if multiple applications share the same DNS namespace (meaning that all the applications run as virtual directories underneath www.mycompany.com), the very nature of session state is to segment data by application. You take a closer look at this in the next section, but in a nutshell the session state from application A is never available to the session state in application B. It does not matter whether you use out-of-process (OOP) session state in an attempt to make session data available across a web farm; even the OOP modes of operation segment data from different applications.

A final shortcoming of using session state for tracking logon status is the inability to set the Secure property of the session state cookie (assuming that you are using cookied mode, of course). Unlike forms authentication, the session state cookie always flows across the network regardless of the state of any SSL security on the connection. If you think about it, this makes sense for a feature like session state because many applications would break if the data in session randomly became unavailable when a user surfed between secure and insecure pages.

This means that session state as implemented in the default providers that ship with ASP.NET 3.5 is not explicitly associated to a user. Although ASP.NET 3.5 exposes extensibility hooks that allow you or a third party to write such functionality, out-of-the-box session state is basically an anonymous data storage mechanism. As long you have a valid identifier, you can get and set session data. However, this is exactly the functionality you want to avoid with a logon session; the whole point of a logon session is that it requires authentication to obtain a session, and once established there is a persistent association between an authenticated user and the actual session data.

About the only situation where session state could be used is in a single-application scenario. If you are writing a single application and you never need to flow authentication information to any other application, you could potentially turn session state into a surrogate logon session service. Technically, you could create a login form, and when a user sent valid credentials, instead of issuing a forms authentication ticket, you could write some information into session state. When the user returned to the site, and the session state was still active, you could check the session data to determine the logged on status.

Even for this limited scenario, there is another argument against using session state as an indication of the logged-in status for a user. Session state can potentially live forever; there is no concept of an absolute expiry for session state data. Instead, as long as a request is periodically made with the session state expiration time window, the time to live of the session data will be renewed. Unlike forms authentication, there is no way to lock down the lifetime of session data with an absolute expiration. For secure sites, the last thing you want is for an authenticated user to "live forever" on the website.

The following table compares the important security features of forms authentication against session state and shows why session state should be used solely as a convenient data storage service, not as a login mechanism.

Security Feature	Forms Authentication	SessionState
Control DNS domain of cookie	Yes	No
Control path of cookie	Yes	No
Require SSL for cookie	Yes	No
Information is shareable across applications	Yes	No
Supports absolute expirations	Yes	No
A valid Identifier can be easily forged	No	Yes

Of course, from this discussion you might be wondering if you should use session state at all! The best way to think about session data is to treat session state as if it were data stored in forms variables on a page. The one major difference being that you do not need to move data back and forth in an HTML form when you use session state. Instead, session state acts as a server-side store for this type of information. From the point of view of data security, you should treat session state data as if it were being sent back and forth in a web page.

For example, if you were filling out an online insurance application, you might choose to store each page's entries in session state to make the application process run faster. From a security and privacy standpoint, though, this data could just as easily have ended up in hidden fields or in form elements located on different web pages. As a result, you would want to ensure that any session state data entered during the application process came from pages that were submitted over an SSL connection. Similarly, you would want to process or display this information to the user only over an SSL connection. From a developer standpoint, you would need to be diligent enough to ensure that this type of information was not accessed from an insecure page such as a non-SSL home page.

Session Data Partitioning

Another question that frequently arises is around data partitioning of session data between applications. From time to time, someone will have a panic attack because, at first glance, session state looks as if it would leak data from one application into another. Especially in the case of out-of-process session state, where all servers and all applications share a central database (or session server), it is understandable why some developers are a bit leery about accidental data sharing.

The example here starts with the simpler case of in-process session state. When using the in-process mode of operation (ASP.NET 3.5 is really an in-process session state provider, because session state is a provider-based feature as well), the data storage mechanism that is used is the ASP.NET Cache object. Because the Cache object manages a chunk of memory inside an application domain, you automatically gain the benefit of partitioning. There is no remoting capability built into either the Cache object or the in-process session state provider.

As a result, short of attaching a debugger or using Win32 APIs to poke around in memory, there isn't any way that application A's session state can accidentally show up inside of application B. Each ASP. NET application on the web server lives in its own application domain, and there is no mechanism to reach out and access session data across application domains. Of course, nothing prevents you from writing some cross-appdomain remoting objects that would give you this capability, but realistically if you want to go down that road, you would probably want to write a custom ASP.NET session state provider that runs against a central application domain used for storing common session state data.

Now for the potentially more worrisome scenarios: What happens when you run with one of the out-of-process session state providers? Is there some way that application A could reach into application B's session state data when using the SQL Server-based provider? Clearly this is not the case, because if that were actually happening, ASP.NET's out-of-process session state would have been broken all the way back in ASP.NET 1.0.

In the case of both the OOP session server, and the OOP provider that uses SQL Server, ASP.NET includes an application identifier with the session state data. For example, if you take two sample applications using the same session state configuration:

```
<sessionState mode="SQLServer" sqlConnectionString="server=.;Integrated
Security=true" />
```

and both applications manipulate session data with the following code (the application name is different in the other application, of course):

```
Session["somevariable"] = "Application A: somedata" + DateTime.Now.ToString();
```

you end up with two different sets of data in the session state SQL database. In the case of the SQL database, two tables are used: ASPStateTempApplications and ASPStateTempSessions. The temporary applications table shows information for the two different ASP.NET applications:

```
AppId        AppName
----------   ------------------------------------------
489834269    /lm/w3svc/1/root/ sessionstateappa
896781384    /lm/w3svc/1/root/ sessionstateappb
```

ASP.NET uses the IIS metabase path of each application as an identifier when partitioning session state data. Looking in the table that stores the actual session state data, along with a number of other columns containing data and lock status, there is a SessionID column:

```
SessionId
-------------------------------
2mhd20eb0op3v3eb5j05yq4504500497
2mhd20eb0op3v3eb5j05yq4504500498
```

At first glance, the IDs from the two applications look almost exactly the same. Take a look at the bolded portion of the session identifier, though. This portion of the identifier differs between the two rows of data because the extra eight characters (padded so there are two hex characters per byte of application ID) are actually the application identifiers from the ASPStateTempSessions table. The first 24 characters in the SessionId column are the same because these 24 characters represent that actual session identifier that is sent back to the browser in the cookie. You will also see this value if you retrieve the Session.SessionID property.

So, things become quite a bit clearer around data partitioning for the OOP modes of operation. ASP.NET keeps track of the different applications that have been registered in the OOP session state stores. Whenever a request comes through to get or set data, the primary key (or the cache lookup key in the case of the session state server) for the data includes the client's session identifier and some extra information identifying the specific web application that originated the request.

One interesting point is obvious from looking at how the applications are stored in the database. For applications deployed on a web farm, you must ensure that each application installation is made to the same virtual web server on each web server. If you accidentally mix up the virtual web servers during installation, one of two things will happen:

❑   One of your application installations will end up with a totally different metabase path, and it will store session data separately from all of the other application installs.

❑   If you have applications spread out across your web servers, the potential exists that you accidentally install application A in application B's virtual web server, and vice versa. If that happens, you probably will end up with exceptions inside of your web applications when you attempt to cast session data retrieved from the wrong row of session data back to an incompatible data type.

Cookie-Based Sessions

Storing the session identifier in a cookie is the most common mode of operation for developers; it is also the default mode of operation for ASP.NET 3.5. Because it follows the programming model as session state in Classic ASP, many developers never need to deal with the cookieless mode of operation.

You saw earlier that session state providers ensure that data in the back-end data store is properly partitioned by application. This is important because if you look at the session identifier in use across multiple applications on the same web server, you see that it is the exact same identifier. The application ID-based partitioning is hidden inside of the session state providers.

Sharing Cookies Across Applications

If you write other application code that depends on Session.SessionID, the same value is going to show up in different applications. If your intent is to hook other application logic and data storage off of SessionID, you may want to use a different identifier, such as a combination of authenticated user-name and application name. The one thing you definitely do *not* want to do is to come up with a solution that forces creation of a new session identifier in each unique application.

Think about a scenario in which you have multiple applications sitting on the same server. The HttpCookie that the session state feature issues will have the following characteristics:

- ❏ The Domain property is never set on the HttpCookie, so it will default to the domain of the server.
- ❏ The Path property will be hardcoded to /.
- ❏ No explicit expiration date will be set on the cookie.
- ❏ The value of the cookie is set to the 24-character identifier that you can get from Session.SessionID.

With this combination of values, anytime the browser user surfs between applications on the same server (or applications living under the same DNS name in the case of a load-balanced web farm), the session cookie will be sent to each and every application. This means that, over time, the session state feature will be accumulating session data for each application. If you were suddenly to send back a fake cookie that reset the session state cookie from one of your responses, the net result would be that all of the session state data in all of the other applications would be lost.

Let me state that a different way, because this is central to the way the ASP.NET session state feature works. For each full DNS hostname, a browser gets one, and only one, session state cookie. That cookie is shared across all applications, and if the cookie is ever lost or reset, all session data in all applications that received that cookie will be lost. I want to drive home that point because sometimes developers wonder whether they should include custom logic in their logout process for session state.

There is a method on the Session object called Abandon. Calling Session.Abandon invalidates the session state data in the back-end data store (cache entry invalidation for in-process and session state server and deleting the row of data for SQL-based session data) for the specific application that called the method. However, calling Session.Abandon doesn't clear the session cookie. If you called Session.Abandon from application A, and if ASP.NET then cleared the session cookie, any session data in other applications would be lost. The fact that the session identifier can be shared between many applications is the reason ASP.NET invalidates only session data, not the cookie, during a call to Abandon.

If you do want to enforce that session data for a user is eliminated when that user logs out of an application, calling `Abandon` is sufficient. Extending the previous sample applications a bit more, you can add a page that explicitly calls the `Abandon` method and see the effect inside of SQL Server. When you first access the sample site, you get a row of session data as expected:

```
SessionId                            Created
-------------------------------      ----------------------------------
2mhd20eb0op3v3eb5j05yq4504500497     4/8/2008 11:10:35 AM
```

When `Abandon` is called, in the case of the SQL Server-based provider, an immediate delete command is issued and the session data is removed from the database. If you then access another page in the application, thus recreating the session data, the same session ID is retained (shown in bold), but a new row in the database is created with new values for the creation and expiration date.

```
SessionId                            Created
-------------------------------      ----------------------------------
2mhd20eb0op3v3eb5j05yq4504500497     4/8/2008 11:12:30 AM
```

If you happen to be developing a standalone application, and thus you don't need the session identifier to remain stable across different applications, you can issue a clear cookie from your logout logic. However, this is the only scenario where explicitly clearing the session cookie can be done, because there aren't any other ASP.NET applications relying on the value.

Protecting Session Cookies

As with forms authentication in ASP.NET 3.5, the session state feature explicitly sets the `HttpOnly` property on the cookie to `true`. Because applications store interesting information inside of session state, ASP.NET protects the session identifier from client-side cross-site scripting (XSS) attacks (for more details on XSS attacks and other security features of `HttpOnly` cookies, see the discussion in Chapter 6 on forms authentication cookies). The likelihood of an attacker ever guessing a live session cookie is astronomically low. (With 120 bits in the session identifier, that works out to an average of 2^{60} guesses required. Come back in the next millennium when you finally get a match.)

That pretty much leaves cookie hijacking as the most viable option for getting to someone else's session data, hence the addition of `HttpOnly` protection in ASP.NET 3.5. The theory is that few (if any) applications should harvest the session identifier client-side for other uses. Typically, developers slipstream off the value of `Session.SessionID` in their server-side logic and do not need to pass it around client-side. As a result of risks of accidentally exposing a session identifier across multiple client-side applications, I definitely recommend changing that type of logic prior to upgrading to ASP.NET 3.5.

Some developers may wonder why session state doesn't include at least the encryption and signing protections found in other cookie-based features, such as forms authentication and Role Manager. There was a fair amount of debate around adding encryption and signing to the session state cookie since ASP.NET 2.0. However, because the default session state cookie is a cryptographically strong 120-bit random number, there didn't seem to be much point in layering the overhead of encryption and signing on top of it. Furthermore, not only is the session state identifier a strong random number, because the session state identifier is stored in a session-based cookie, the session ID changes from browser session to browser session.

Unlike forms authentication, which relies on a fixed encryption key and a fixed validation key, with session state the only time you can really attack someone else's session state is while that user's session is still alive. There is no such thing as an offline brute force decryption attack or hash collision attack with session state. With session state, an attacker must successfully guess (incredibly unlikely) or hijack (possible but difficult to accomplish) a session identifier while that session is still alive somewhere in an application. Although an attacker could theoretically stumble across a session identifier associated with an expired session, this is not of any use because an expired session means that the data associated with that session is no longer available.

Session ID Reuse

This leads to another point around the behavior of cookie-based sessions after the session has expired. If a browser user accesses an application and sends a session cookie along with the request, but the session has expired since the last time the application was accessed, the old session data is no longer accessible. However, when running in cookied mode, the session identifier will be reused to create a new session for the application.

Because a session identifier may be shared across multiple web applications, the session state feature will not invalidate the session identifier just because the session has expired. Instead, the session state feature sets up a new session state object that is associated with the preexisting identifier. By doing so, session state prevents the problem of one application invalidating a session identifier when there is still live session data associated with that identifier in other applications.

You can see this pretty easily by using two applications, both with session state enabled. Set the timeout for session state in one application to one minute, and leave the other application's timeout at its default. After accessing both applications at least once, wait for a bit more than one minute. This gives the application with the short timeout the opportunity for the session state to expire.

When you access the applications again (using the same browser session), the application with the short timeout has indeed expired its session data. However, the second application, with the default timeout, still has an active session, and the data in that session is still retrievable because expiration of cookie-based sessions doesn't cause the session identifier to be regenerated.

Put a different way, cookie-based session state always supports `Session ID` reuse. As long as the browser sends a well-formed session identifier to the server, that identifier will be reused. Sometimes developers assume that session state will create a new session identifier when a session expires, and as a result, developers create application functionality that depends on a new session identifier being created after a session expires. This assumption is incorrect, though, and developers cannot rely on new session identifier being generated when running in cookied mode.

Cookieless Sessions

ASP.NET 1.1 added support for a cookieless session state. As mentioned in earlier chapters, the cookieless mechanism that was added in ASP.NET 1.1 for session state has been expanded to encompass cookieless support for forms authentication as well anonymous identification. You can easily enable cookieless operations with the following configuration:

```
<sessionState cookieless="UseUri" />
```

You can also issue cookieless session identifiers based on the capabilities of a user's browser with one of the following options: `AutoDetect` or `UseDeviceProfile`. These options use different detection mechanisms to determine whether the user's browser should be sent a cookieless session identifier. Accessing an application that uses cookieless session state results in the session identifier showing up on the URL

```
http://localhost/CookielessSessionState/(S(kgtn5145tznbsymgj0xsm445))/Default.aspx
```

The value in the URL is the same value that is returned from `Session.SessionID`. If you use the following line of code on the `default.aspx` page shown earlier:

```
Response.Write(Session.SessionID + "<br />");
```

the identifier output on the page matches the value shown in the URL:

```
kgtn5145tznbsymgj0xsm445
```

This behavior should start a few security antennae wiggling! Now anybody who looks at the address bar in the browser knows his or her session identifier. A user who understands how ASP.NET works will recognize this value and a malicious user that understands ASP.NET session state may start thinking about what can be done with this information.

Especially in cookieless mode, don't use the session identifier as an indication of an authentication session. If you have logic that works this way, all a user has to do is come up with a 24-character string, and suddenly that user would be authenticated.

Of course, the real security issue with cookieless session state is the common weakness that was discussed earlier with cookieless forms authentication. It is very, very easy for a user to unwittingly leak the session identifier to other people (email it, save it to disk as an Internet Explorer shortcut, and so on). On shared machines such as kiosks, the cookieless identifier has a very real likelihood of sticking around across the browser session of completely different users.

Given the comparative weakness of cookieless session identifiers, when is cookieless session state appropriate?

❑ **For an internal corporate application that needs to be available from a mobile device that doesn't support cookies:** The likelihood of leaking the identifier is much lower in this scenario.

❑ **For Internet facing applications that need to support mobile users:** For such an application you should not store anything sensitive inside of session state: this means no personally identifiable information and definitely nothing like credit card numbers, Social Security identifiers, and so on. Furthermore, the session identifier should not be used within the application's logic as a key that can lead to any kind of sensitive or personally identifiable information.

I intentionally left out a potential third scenario of an e-commerce site that wants to support cookieless users. If you need to support these types of customers and you are thinking of using cookieless session state, exercise caution. A customer using a desktop browser with cookieless session state is at risk for leaking the session identifier outside of the browser due to the ease with which you can get to an email application from inside of all popular browsers (for example, Hi Mom; here's that item I was talking about on the Web!). If you do choose to support cookieless session state on an e-commerce site, only use it to hold anonymous information such as shopping cart items. Do not use session state in a way that a session identifier could ever be used to get back to information about a specific person. Although running the entire e-commerce site under SSL is also a way to mitigate the security problem of cookieless identifiers, for performance reasons most e-commerce sites would probably be unwilling to do this.

The following list contains many of the security limitations of cookieless session identifiers:

❑　The identifier is immediately visible inside the address bar of the browser.

❑　The only way to prevent man-in-the-middle attacks is to run the entire site under SSL, although this is also a limitation of the session state feature as a whole.

❑　The identifier can be easily pasted into an email and shared with other users.

❑　Because the identifier is in the URL, cached URLs with the session identifier can end up in the browser's URL history.

❑　Proxy servers and caching servers can end up with URLs in their caches that contain the cookieless session identifier.

Configuring Session State Inside IIS 7.0

The `<sessionState>` configuration section is usually edited inside the application's `web.config`. If you want to change the default predefined values, you can configure a `<sessionState>` section by specifying the session state mode and cookie settings. Although the application's `web.config` file provides very good IntelliSense to do this, IIS 7.0 provides a graphical user interface to edit the application's `<sessionState>` configuration section. To edit the `<sessionState>` section, double-click the Session State applet inside IIS 7.0 Manager, as shown in Figure 8-1.

Figure 8-1

Figure 8-2 shows the IIS 7.0 Windows form used to edit the `<sessionState>` section for an application.

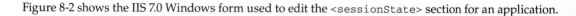

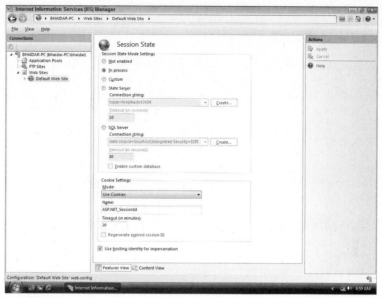

Figure 8-2

All the different session state mode options are listed so that you can select a single mode setting. If a setting requires additional information (for instance, the SQL Server session state), a UI section is enabled so that you can edit the needed information. Moreover, you can specify the session cookie mode, name, and timeout of the cookie in case Use Cookies was selected. The last checkbox on the screen, Use Hosting Identity for Impersonation, allows you to use Windows authentication and the host process identity (either ASP.NET or Windows service identity) for connections to the database.

Session State for Applications Running in IIS 7.0 Integrated Mode

When an ASP.NET application is running under the default application pool inside IIS 7.0 (i.e., integrated mode), the HTTP request processing pipelines get unified and integrated into a single pipeline, enabling the application to access any request that reaches IIS 7.0's gate. This means that both native and managed requests will pass through the unified HTTP request pipeline. If the current request is for a native or non-managed resource, the managed handler is null and the native request will be processed and executed by the IIS 7.0 core engine.

As you learned in Chapter 3, the session state of an ASP.NET web application is accessible after the `AcquireRequestState` event of the HTTP request pipeline is fired. At this stage, the `SessionState Module` that has already subscribed to the `AcquireRequestState` in the HTTP request pipeline would fire its `AcquireRequestState`'s event handler and get the session state initialized for the current request. Several conditions are checked, of course, to ensure the session state can be initialized, among which the handler for the current request implements the `IRequestSessionState` interface, which is a marker interface with no methods or properties inside to be implemented by the implementer. If the handler for the current request is a managed handler (that is, a handler for `.aspx` files, `.asmx` files, and so on), then the process of initializing the session state for the current continues successfully, else there will be no session state attached to the current request.

The preceding discussion applies to all managed resources. However, what happens when an ASP.NET web application is executing in the integrated mode and accepting not only managed requested but also non-managed or native requests? As mentioned previously, the ASP.NET runtime does not create any managed handler for the non-managed requests; therefore, when the managed `SessionStateModule` checks to see if the current handler created implements the managed `IRequiresSessionState` marker interface, the checking would fail.

What if the developer wants some sort of session management when an ASP.Net web application is executing within the new IIS 7.0 integrated mode even for non-managed resources? Such a concern has been raised on the online forums and the IIS team at Microsoft recommends the following technique.

The HTTP request pipeline contains two main events that deal with the process of mapping a managed handler for the current request being processed. Those events are the `MapRequestHandler` and `PostMapRequestHandler`. Inside the former event, the handler is decided on for the current HTTP request. If the request corresponds to a managed request, a managed handler is created; otherwise, the handler for current request will be null. The `PostMapRequestHandler` is the best place to check to determine whether a handler has been created for the current request. For now, this gives you a hint on where you can detect whether the HTTP request processed inside the integrated HTTP request pipeline is for a managed resource or a native resource.

Directly after the `PostMapRequestHandler`, the `AcquireRequestState` is fired and the managed `SessionStateModule`'s event handler for the aforementioned event gets executed only at this time. This means that if the current request corresponds to a managed resource, the managed handler for the current request would have been already created, as the `AcquireRequestState` event fires after the `MapRequestHandler` event has been fired. Therefore, if the current request is a native one, the handler for it will be null and no session state will be initialized. On the other hand, if the current request is for a managed resource, the handler will be checked to see if it requires session state, and if so, the session state will be initialized for the current request.

The trick now lies in the fact that if the managed `SessionStateModule` finds out that the current request has a managed handler created and that handler implements the `IRequiresSessionState` marker interface, the session state for the current request gets initialized regardless of whether the request was originally for a native request. What you can do is create a new C# or VB.NET class and let this class implement the `IHttpHandler` and `IRequiresSesionState`. Then, when the `PostMapRequestHandler` is fired, you check to see if the current request has a null handler (that is, that this is a native request), create a new instance of the custom dummy handler, and pass to it an instance of the current handler. Then you can make the current managed handler point to the instance you have already created for your custom handler. When the `AcquireRequestState` executes, the managed `SessionStateModule` will notice that there is a managed handler accompanying the current request and that implements the `IRequiresSessionState` marker interface. Thus, it proceeds in initializing the session state for the current native request, and you now have access to the session state at later events inside the integrated HTTP request pipeline.

However, the solution is not over yet. You want to make sure that after the `AcquireRequestState` event is fired and executed, the current request points to an instance of the custom dummy handler. This means the request is originally for a native resource and that you should reset the current managed handler to the same instance of the managed handler that was created for the current request while the request was about to enter the `PostMapRequestHandler` event. Remember that you have already passed an instance of original handler that was originally created for the current request by the ASP.NET run-time. All you need to do now is to subscribe to the `PostAcquireRequestState` event and perform the switch of the handler back to the original one in case the current handler was of the type of the custom dummy handler.

This is a workaround solution and works fine for the purpose of making sure the session state gets initialized even for non-managed requests.

To demonstrate this solution, you first need to create a new custom HTTP module to be able to subscribe to the previously mentioned events.

C#

```csharp
using System;
using System.Data;
using System.Configuration;
using System.Linq;
using System.Web;
using System.Web.Security;
using System.Web.UI;
using System.Web.UI.HtmlControls;
using System.Web.UI.WebControls;
using System.Web.UI.WebControls.WebParts;
using System.Xml.Linq;

public class SessionStateForNativeRequestsModule : IHttpModule
{
    #region IHttpModule Members

    public void Dispose()
    {
        throw new NotImplementedException();
    }

    public void Init(HttpApplication context)
    {
        // Subscribe to the PostMapRequestHandler
        context.PostMapRequestHandler +=
            new EventHandler(context_PostMapRequestHandler);

        // Subscribe to the PostAcquireRequestState
        context.PostAcquireRequestState +=
            new EventHandler(context_PostAcquireRequestState);
    }

    void context_PostAcquireRequestState(object sender, EventArgs e)
    {
```

```
        }

        void context_PostMapRequestHandler(object sender, EventArgs e)
        {
        }

    #endregion
}
```

VB.NET

```vbnet
Imports Microsoft.VisualBasic
Imports System
Imports System.Data
Imports System.Configuration
Imports System.Web
Imports System.Web.Security

Public Class SessionStateForNativeRequestsModule
    Implements IHttpModule
    #Region "IHttpModule Members"

    Public Sub Dispose() Implements IHttpModule.Dispose
        Throw New NotImplementedException()
    End Sub

    Public Sub Init(ByVal context As HttpApplication) Implements IHttpModule.Init
        ' Subscribe to the PostMapRequestHandler
        AddHandler context.PostMapRequestHandler, _
        AddressOf context_PostMapRequestHandler

        ' Subscribe to the PostAcquireRequestState
        AddHandler context.PostAcquireRequestState, _
        AddressOf context_PostAcquireRequestState
    End Sub

    Private Sub context_PostAcquireRequestState( _
    ByVal sender As Object, ByVal e As EventArgs)

    End Sub

    Private Sub context_PostMapRequestHandler( _
    ByVal sender As Object, ByVal e As EventArgs)

    End Sub

    #End Region
End Class
```

Before going into the details of the implementation of the preceding HTTP module, let's create the custom dummy handler that will implement the IRequireSessionState and that will be used as a temporary managed handler to fake the managed SessionStateModule to initialize the session state for native or non-managed resources. Create a new C# or VB.NET class that implements the IHttpHandler interface and IRequiresSessionState marker interface.

C#

```csharp
using System;
using System.Data;
using System.Configuration;
using System.Web;
using System.Web.SessionState;
using System.Web.Security;
using System.Web.UI;

public class CustomNativeHandler : IHttpHandler, IRequiresSessionState
{

    #region IHttpHandler Members

    public bool IsReusable
    {
        get { return false; }
    }

    public void ProcessRequest(HttpContext context)
    {
        // This method won't be called, but to be on the safe
        // side, through an exception.
        throw new NotImplementedException();
    }

    #endregion

    #region Fields
    internal readonly IHttpHandler ManagedHandler;
    #endregion

    #region Constructors
    public CustomNativeHandler(IHttpHandler managedHandler)
    {
        ManagedHandler = managedHandler;
    }
    #endregion
}
```

VB.NET

```vbnet
Imports Microsoft.VisualBasic
Imports System
Imports System.Data
Imports System.Configuration
Imports System.Web
Imports System.Web.SessionState
Imports System.Web.Security
```

```vb
Public Class CustomNativeHandler
   Implements IHttpHandler, IRequiresSessionState
   #Region "IHttpHandler Members"

   Public ReadOnly Property IsReusable() As Boolean Implements _
   IHttpHandler.IsReusable
         Get
                  Return False
         End Get
   End Property

   Public Sub ProcessRequest(ByVal context As HttpContext) Implements _
   IHttpHandler.ProcessRequest
         ' This method won't be called, but to be on the safe
         ' side, through an exception.
         Throw New NotImplementedException()
   End Sub

   #End Region

   #Region "Fields"
   Friend ReadOnly ManagedHandler As IHttpHandler
   #End Region

   #Region "Constructors"
   Public Sub New(ByVal managedHandler As IHttpHandler)
         Me.ManagedHandler = managedHandler
   End Sub
   #End Region
End Class
```

The preceding handler is quite basic and simple. The `ProcessRequest` method would never be called and executed; however, throwing an exception inside makes it safer and reminds you to remove this dummy handler after you are finished with it.

In addition, the handler contains an internal read-only field called `ManagedHandler` that holds the managed handler (if any) that was originally created by the .NET Framework. This handler might be null or it might be a valid managed handler.

To be able to initialize the `ManagedHandler` field, you must add a constructor passes in as input parameter a pointer to the managed handler that was created as part of the current `HttpContext` of the request.

To complete the discussion on the above handler, the `IsReusable` property has to return a value of `false`. This property decides whether to use the same instance of the handler to process more than one request. However, in this case, because each instance of the handler contains data representing the handler created originally by the .NET Framework, the `IsReusable` property should return a value of `false`, meaning that every instance should only be used once.

Now that the dummy handler is developed, let's go back to the HTTP module and fill in the blanks to the event handler for the `PostMapRequestHandler` and `PostAcquireRequestState` events.

C#

```
void context_PostMapRequestHandler(object sender, EventArgs e)
{
    // Get an instance of the current Context
    HttpContext context = ((HttpApplication)sender).Context;

    // If the current HttpHandler is null, then this must be
    // a native request being processed.
    if (context.Handler == null)
        context.Handler = new CustomNativeHandler(context.Handler);
}
```

VB.NET

```
Private Sub context_PostMapRequestHandler( _
ByVal sender As Object, ByVal e As EventArgs)
        ' Get an instance of the current Context
        Dim context As HttpContext = (CType(sender, HttpApplication)).Context

        ' If the current HttpHandler is null, then this must be
        ' a native request being processed.
        If context.Handler Is Nothing Then
                context.Handler = New CustomNativeHandler(context.Handler)
        End If
End Sub
```

Inside the `PostMapRequestHandler` event handler, a checking is done to make sure the current request is a native one by simply checking whether an instance of a managed handler has been created. If the current `HttpContext`'s handler is null, this tells you that the current request is for a native resource, and so the code creates a new instance of the `CustomNativeHandler` and assigns it to the handler's property of the current `HttpContext`; otherwise, nothing should be done.

C#

```
void context_PostAcquireRequestState(object sender, EventArgs e)
{
    // Get an instance of the current Context
    HttpContext context = ((HttpApplication)sender).Context;

    // Use "as" so that if the current handler
    // is not a CustomNativeHandler, then no exception
    // will be thrown, like in the case of casting.
    CustomNativeHandler customHandler =
        context.Handler as CustomNativeHandler;

    // If the current handler is our custom dummy handler
    // then revert back to the managed handler that was
    // originally created by the .NET Framework for the
    // current request
    if (customHandler != null)
        context.Handler = customHandler.ManagedHandler;
}
```

VB.NET

```
Private Sub context_PostAcquireRequestHandler( _
ByVal sender As Object, ByVal e As EventArgs)
            ' Get an instance of the current Context
            Dim context As HttpContext = (CType(sender, HttpApplication)).Context

            ' Use "as" so that if the current handler
            ' is not a CustomNativeHandler, then no exception
            ' will be thrown, like in the case of casting.
            Dim customHandler As CustomNativeHandler = _
            TryCast(context.Handler, CustomNativeHandler)

            ' If the current handler is our custom dummy handler
            ' then revert back to the managed handler that was
            ' originally created by the .NET Framework for the
            ' current request
            If customHandler IsNot Nothing Then
                    context.Handler = customHandler.ManagedHandler
            End If
End Sub
```

The `PostAcquireRequestState` event handler starts by getting an instance of the current `HttpContext`. Then a casting is done using the as keyword in C# instead of the normal casting. This ensures that if the current context's handler is not an instance of the `CustomNativeHandler`, no exception will be thrown. This is followed by a check for the casted handler against the value of null. If the current handler is not null, the current handler holds an instance of the `CustomNativeHandler`, and the current context's handler should be reverted back to the original handler that the .NET Framework created and that was stored as an internal instance field inside the `CustomNativeHandler`.

Now that the development of the HTTP module and handler is done, it's time to configure the application's `web.config` file and register the `SessionStateForNativeRequestModule`:

```
<system.webServer>
  <modules>
        <add
            name="SessionStateForNativeRequests"
            type="SessionStateForNativeRequests"
        />
  </modules>
</system.webServer>
```

Run the application and set some breakpoints inside the `PostAcquireRequestState` event handler. Try to access a .jpg file residing in the root of your web application. You will notice that the session state is not getting initialized for the native HTTP request. Why? Well, while I was running this sample, I was always getting an empty session state for native requests. I checked the code several times to make sure the logic was implemented successfully. It ended up that I wasn't mapping the managed `SessionStateModule` for all requests. By default, the `SessionStateModule` is defined inside the `<modules />` configuration section in the `applicationHost.config` file as follows:

```
<add
    name="Session"
    type="System.Web.SessionState.SessionStateModule"
```

```
        preCondition="managedHandler"
    />
```

Notice the text in bold, which maps the managed SessionStateModule to managed requests only by specifying a value of managedHandler for the preCondition attribute.

For the preceding solution to work, you need to map the SessionStateModule to all managed and non-managed requests so that at the AcquireRequestState event the managed SessionStateModule is queried to check if session state can be created for the current request (that is, the handler created for the current request implements the IRequiresSessionState marker interface). Without the preceding mapping, the managed SessionStateModule would never run and do the check and validation for non-managed requests.

To map the SessionStateModule for all requests, simply add the following to the <module /> configuration section inside the <system.webServer /> configuration section group located in the application's web.config configuration file:

```
<remove name="Session" />
<add
    name="Session"
    type="System.Web.SessionState.SessionStateModule"
    preCondition=""
/>
```

Notice that this time the preCondition attribute is reset to an empty string, signaling to the integrated HTTP request pipeline to allow the managed SessionStateModule to check if it can be initialized for the requests entering the pipeline.

Now you run the application included with the code included this chapter. The application name is SessionStateForNativeRequests. You will notice that the session state is getting initialized even for native requests using the trick proposed by the IIS team.

Session ID Reuse and Expired Sessions

Many of these weaknesses revolve around the ability for a URL with a session identifier to be reused by someone other than the original intended recipient of the identifier. Because the session state feature doesn't have the concept of an absolute expiration, as long as someone (or some user agent) continues to access a site with a valid session identifier, the underlying data will be kept alive. This behavior is more of a problem with cookieless session state, though.

Any browser, caching server, proxy server, and so on that keeps URLs lying around in a cache results in potentially long-term storage of URLs with embedded session identifiers. This is a much less likely problem in the cookied case because most user agents and caching software ignore session-based cookies. (The browser isn't going to keep a history of your session-based session cookie for the next 30 days.)

On the other hand, it is almost guaranteed that between the possibility of accidentally leaking session identifiers and the long-lived storage of URLs through various caching mechanisms, someone will eventually return to a site and replay a cookieless session identifier. The most likely scenario is one where the user that was originally issued the identifier comes back to the site through some kind of shortcut. You only need to use the Internet Explorer history feature to see what I mean. Or a site with cookieless sessions all URLs with the embedded session identifier in it are sitting there in the browser history waiting for you to click them.

Unlike cookied mode, though, cookieless session state automatically reissues a session identifier under the following conditions:

❑ A valid (that is, well-formed) session identifier is contained on the request URL.

❑ The session data associated with that identifier has expired.

If both of these conditions are true, then the session state feature will automatically create a new session identifier when it initializes a new session state object. Note that if you call Session.Abandon from an application using cookieless sessions, the session ID will also be regenerated the next time you access a page in the application. In this case, calling Abandon is just another way of ending up in the situation where you have a valid but expired identifier.

To see the behavior when a session expires, you can take the cookieless URL that was shown earlier:

```
http://localhost/CookielessSessionState/(S(kgtn5145tznbsymgj0xsm445))/Default.aspx
```

Paste this URL into the browser (assuming, of course, that 20 minutes have passed, which is the default session timeout). The page still runs successfully, but the URL that comes back in the browser reflects a new session identifier:

```
http://localhost/CookielessSessionState/(S(4lakxf45asdoz045slsdnb45))/Default.aspx
```

The reason for this behavior is that in ASP.NET 3.5, the session state configuration supports a new attribute: regenerateExpiredSessionId. By default this attribute is set to true, which is why when expired session identifiers are sent in the URL, ASP.NET automatically issues a new identifier. This behavior is enabled by default for a few reasons:

❑ It is the best choice from a security standpoint. Given the ease with which cookieless identifiers can live far beyond their intended life, it makes sense to invalidate the identifiers by default.

❑ Unlike cookied sessions, cookieless session identifiers are not shared across multiple applications. You can see that cookieless session identifiers do not flow across applications by setting up two applications on the same server and configuring both to use cookieless session state. When you access each application in turn, you end up with two different identifiers. This intuitively makes sense because URLs are by their very nature unique to an application; hence values embedded in the URL would also be application-local.

If for some reason you don't want session identifiers to be regenerated, you can set regenerate ExpiredSessionId to false. However, if your application depends on retaining stable session identifiers across browser sessions (this is one possible reason why you wouldn't want to issue a new identifier), you should look at why your application is depending on stable session identifiers. If at all possible, move to some other mechanism (perhaps requiring a login at which point you have a user identifier) that is more secure for tracking specific users across different browser sessions.

Session ID Denial-of-Service Attacks

The idea behind a session ID denial-of-service (DOS) attack is that a malicious user "poisons" session state by sending it numerous bogus session identifiers or by forcing the creation of sessions that will never be used after being initialized. Unlike other poisonings (for example, DNS cache poisoning) that involve placing incorrect or malicious data into a cache, session ID poisoning is very basic. A malicious user can spam the web server with session identifiers that are well formed but not associated with any active session. Hence, the term *poisoning* because the ASP.NET server ends up with an internal cache polluted with spurious session identifiers.

In a similar manner, a malicious user can access a page in an application that results in the issuance of a session identifier, but then throw away the cookie that is sent back by the application. In this manner, a malicious user can force an application to spin up a new session each time the page is accessed, again resulting in a session state store that is polluted with unused session state data.

A session identifier does take up a little bit of space and processing overhead on the web server each time a new session is started up. However, because ASP.NET has a number of internal optimizations around new and uninitialized sessions, sending a spurious identifier in and of itself is harmless. The real danger of session ID poisoning occurs if the session state object is accessed after the spurious identifier is sent. This can be code running in the Session_Start event in global.asax, or there can just be code running on a regular .aspx page that manipulates session state.

After the Session object is accessed, storage is allocated for the session data. This means that memory is consumed on the web server for the in-process session state case, and rows are allocated in the database for the SQL OOP scenario. For the session state server, memory is allocated on the OOP session state server.

For the OOP SQL session state, spurious sessions shouldn't have a big impact because each spurious session and subsequent use of that session results in a row in the database. An attacker that attempted a DOS attack against SQL-based session state causes some extra CPU and disk overhead on the SQL Server but not much more, because the lifetime of a spurious session looks roughly as follows:

1. The attacker sends a fake session ID to the server as part of the request or accesses a page that makes use of session state but then intentionally throws away the a session state identifier.

2. The ASP.NET page accesses the Session object in some manner, which results in a new row being written to the ASPStateTempSessions table.

3. The attack continues to send other fake session IDs, or continues to request the same page but with no session state cookie, thus resulting in the creation of a new session identifier for each request.

4. At some point the session associated with the identifier from step 2 times out.

5. Every minute (by default) the ASP.NET SQL Server session state cleanup job runs and deletes expired rows of session data from the database.

As a result of the automatic session cleanup in step 5, a spurious session is only going to take up space in the SQL Server for an amount of time equal to the timeout setting in configuration (20 minutes by default). If an attacker uses a standard desktop machine to send 10 spurious session identifiers per second (in other words, the attacker adds 10 requests per second (RPS) overall to your site's load), an attack can accumulate 600 spurious sessions in a minute, and 12,000 spurious sessions in the default 20 minute timeout period.

If you have 12,000 spurious sessions in the database, and each session is associated with 5KB of data, you are looking at roughly 58–59MB of extra data sitting in the session state database. Furthermore, the SQL Server machine has to chug through and delete 600 rows of bogus session data each time the cleanup job wakes up on its 60-second interval. Overall, it is not good that this type of extra overhead is being incurred, but on the other hand, short of a concentrated attack against a web farm using OOP SQL Session state, an attacker is going to have a hard time being anything more than a nuisance.

One of the reasons I picked such a low request per second value for describing the issue is that many websites have a variety of real-time security monitors in place: one of them checks on the requests per second value. If your security monitoring apparatus suddenly sees a spike in traffic (for example, the current RPS compared to the average RPS during the last 30 minutes) it probably will set off several alarms. However, slipping in an extra 10 requests per second is trivial for today's web server hardware; probably only paranoid security measures would detect such a small increase in the overall traffic of a site.

Although SQL Server-based session state is pretty hard to overrun with a session ID DOS attack, the story is a bit different when using in-process session state or the OOP session state server. In both of these cases, an attacker is causing memory consumption to occur with each and every spurious session. Unlike SQL Server session state where disk space is relatively cheap (imagine an attacker attempting to overflow a terabyte of storage on the session state server; good luck!), memory is a scarce resource on the web server.

Taking the previous scenario with 10 spurious requests per second, and 5KB of spurious data, you end up permanently losing 58–59MB of memory from your web server due to space wasted storing spurious session data. Furthermore, you incur the additional overhead of the in-memory items aging out (session state items are held in the ASP.NET Cache object) and the subsequent overhead of garbage collection attempting to recompact and reclaim memory caused by session data constantly aging out and being replaced by other spurious session data.

Although 58–59MB does not seem like a lot of memory, the real risk of a session ID DOS attack comes when you have an application that depends on storing larger amounts of data in session state. For example, if an application stores 50KB of data in session state instead of 5KB of data, you have a very real problem. An attacker could consume around 570MB of memory over a 20-minute period. On servers running multiple ASP.NET applications, that is enough memory consumption to probably force the appdomain of the problematic ASP.NET application to recycle. If you are running on Windows Server 2008 or Windows Vista and IIS 7.0, and if you have set memory-based process recycling limits, it is possible that the IIS 7.0 worker process will also be forced into periodic recycling.

The general guidance here is that if you depend on in-process session state or the OOP session state server, and if your website is Internet-facing and hence reachable by an attacker, you should do the following to detect and mitigate session ID DOS attacks:

❑　Monitor the application specific ASP.NET performance counter for Sessions Active as shown in Figure 8-3.

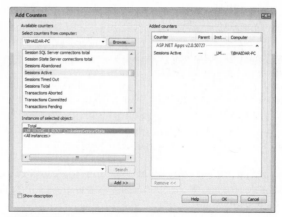

Figure 8-3

❑ Inside of the performance monitor MMC, you can get to this counter by selecting ASP.NET Apps v2.0.x.y for the performance object, and then choosing to monitor all ASP.NET instances, or just specific ones. After you choose the desired instances, the Sessions Active option is available in the Select Counters from List list box. You need to profile the usage of your application to determine an appropriate upper limit. Chances are that most applications could probably get by with a limit of somewhere between 100 and 500 sessions for an application. Because the performance monitor supports configuring alerts, you can set up an alert that sends emails or runs some other program if the number of active sessions exceeds an appropriate limit.

❑ Monitor the overall requests per second on your site. If the RPS at any point in time shows an abnormal spike relative to the last few minutes (or perhaps hours) of activity, send out an alert so that someone can investigate and determine what is happening.

❑ Set appropriate memory limits on applications that use session state. This is very easy to accomplish in IIS 7.0 because you can set a memory-based process recycling limit on the Recycling section of an application pool. Again, you will need to determine appropriate upper limits for your applications. Once set, though, the side effect of a sustained DOS is that the problematic application will periodically recycle as memory is consumed. Other applications in other application pools will be unaffected, though.

❑ The simplest way to mitigate the entire session ID DOS scenario is to use session state only on pages that require an authenticated user. As mentioned earlier, just sending a session identifier to ASP.NET does not do much of anything. ASP.NET will delay initialization of the session state object until it is actually needed. As a result, if you access the Session object only on pages that require an authenticated user, the only way an attacker could perform a DOS is to log in first. Typically, attackers want to remain anonymous and aren't going to set up a user account on your site just to launch a DOS.

Trust Levels and Session State

As with just about every other aspect of ASP.NET, the session state feature is affected by the trust-level settings for your machine and your application. For in-process session state, the effect of the trust level is limited to restrictions around serialization and deserialization, which were originally introduced with ASP.NET 2.0 (a bit more on that later in this section). However, both SQL Server and the OOP session state server require applications to run in Medium trust or higher for these features to be used.

You can take any of the previous sample applications that used SQL Server-based session state and add a <trust /> level element as follows:

```
<trust level="Low"/>
```

You get back an error page to the effect that you can't use session state at that trust level. If you tweak the trust level to Medium, the application will start working again.

Things get a bit interesting, though, if you take an additional step and edit the actual trust policy file (for all the details on trust level and their relationship to trust policy files, see Chapter 4). Change the trust level to use a custom trust level:

```
<trust level="Medium_Custom"/>
```

This custom trust level sets the AspNetHostingPermission.Level to Medium, so effectively the application is running a modified version of the Medium trust level. Then in the trust policy file associated with this trust level, remove the following permission element:

```
<IPermission
          class="SqlClientPermission"
          version="1"
          Unrestricted="true"
    />
```

When you rerun the application, session state still works! There are a few reasons for this behavior. Session state is a heavily used feature by customers, so ASP.NET should not impose excessive security requirements just to get session state working. However, in the case of SQL Server-based session state there is obviously a perfectly good permission class supplied by the framework that models access rights for using SQL Server. The problem is that if ASP.NET relied on the presence of SqlClientPermission in the trust policy, it would effectively be allowing any page in the application to use SQL Server.

However, if a developer wants to enable SQL Server session state and does not want random pieces of page code using ADO.NET and attempting to access SQL Server, having session state condition its behavior on SqlClientPermission is excessively permissive. The compromise approach for all of this is why SQL Server session state works in the absence of SqlClientPermission. Instead, ASP.NET requires that the application be running at Medium trust or above. As long as this condition is met, the session state feature will call into SQL Server on behalf of the application.

Technically, SQL Server session state works in Medium trust because the entire code stack for session state is trusted code. For example, if you think about the process by which session data is stored, the call stack from top to bottom is roughly:

1. The EndRequest event is run by the HTTP pipeline.
2. The SessionStateModule that hooks EndRequest is called.

3. As part of the processing in SessionStateModule, it calls into the internal class that implements the SQL Server session state provider.

4. That provider calls into ADO.NET.

All of this code, though, is trusted code that lives in the global assembly cache (GAC). As a result, when ADO.NET in step 4 triggers a demand for SqlClientPermission, the call stack above that demand consists entirely of ASP.NET code sitting somewhere inside of System.Web.dll which exists in the GAC. From the Framework's standpoint, only trusted code is on the stack, and as a result the call to SQL Server succeeds. In the case of the out-of-process session state server, a similar situation exists though the OOP state server uses Win32 sockets instead.

You can see from all of this that whenever significant work is performed by the session state feature, only trusted ASP.NET code is on the stack. As a result, the session state feature has to be a bit more careful in terms of what it allows because permission checks and demands will always succeed. The trust-level requirements for the various modes of session state are shown in the following table.

Session State Mode	Required CAS Permissions	Required Trust Level
In process	None	Minimal
Sql Server	None	Medium
State Server	None	Medium
Custom	Depends on custom provider implementation	Minimal. Custom providers can be more restrictive if desired.

Serialization and Deserialization Requirements

Session state is a lot like no-compile pages ASP.NET 3.5; both features involve only trusted ASP.NET code running on the stack, which means that without extra protections, a savvy and malicious developer could trick ASP.NET into running privileged code. If you think back to the discussion on processRequestInApplicationTrust in Chapter 4, the solution for no-compile pages (and for that matter, any type of .aspx page) was for ASP.NET to call PermitOnly on the PermissionSet representing the permissions granted in the application's trust policy.

Session state also internally checks the value of processRequestInApplicationTrust. If this setting is true (by default it is true, and unless there is a specific reason for it, you should not change this setting), session state calls PermitOnly prior to either serializing or deserializing session state data. This means that any types deployed in the GAC that also implement custom serialization logic are still restricted to the permission set defined by the application's trust policy when the types are serialized or deserialized by the Session state feature. Because session state uses binary serialization, this means any GAC'd types with custom implementations of ISerializable cannot be lured into performing a privileged operation through the use of session state in a partial trust application.

This protection closes a potential loophole with storing an instance of a GAC'd type in session state. If enough was understood about the internals of the GAC'd type, then when either of the out-of-process session state providers serialized the GAC'd type prior to saving it, session state would inadvertently trigger privileged code inside of the GAC'd type's serialization logic. With the PermitOnly in effect, though, a developer can no longer use session state to make an end-run around the application's trust policy.

To highlight this, you can create a simple class that attempts to connect to SQL Server:

C#

```csharp
[Serializable()]
public class SomeObject : ISerializable
{
    public SomeObject() { }

    protected SomeObject(SerializationInfo info, StreamingContext context)
    {
      SqlConnection conn =
      new SqlConnection("server=.\SQL2005;database=pubs;Integrated Security=true");
        SqlCommand cmd = new SqlCommand("select * from authors", conn);

        conn.Open();
        SqlDataReader dr = cmd.ExecuteReader();

        conn.Close();
    }

    public void GetObjectData(SerializationInfo info, StreamingContext context)
    {
        info.AddValue("foo", "bar");

      SqlConnection conn =
      new SqlConnection("server=.\SQL2005;database=pubs;Integrated Security=true");
        SqlCommand cmd = new SqlCommand("select * from authors", conn);

        conn.Open();
        SqlDataReader dr = cmd.ExecuteReader();

        conn.Close();
    }
}
```

VB.NET

```vbnet
    <Serializable()> _
    Public Class SomeObject
        Implements ISerializable
        Public Sub New()
        End Sub

        Protected Sub New(ByVal info As SerializationInfo, _
            ByVal context As StreamingContext)
         Dim conn As New _
         SqlConnection("server=.\SQL2005;database=pubs;Integrated Security=true")
            Dim cmd As New SqlCommand("select * from authors", conn)

            conn.Open()
            Dim dr As SqlDataReader = cmd.ExecuteReader()

            conn.Close()
```

```
          End Sub

          Public Sub GetObjectData(ByVal info _
                  As SerializationInfo, ByVal context _
                  As StreamingContext) Implements ISerializable.GetObjectData
              info.AddValue("foo", "bar")

           Dim conn As New _
           SqlConnection("server=.\SQL2005;database=pubs;Integrated Security=true")
              Dim cmd As New SqlCommand("select * from authors", conn)

              conn.Open()
              Dim dr As SqlDataReader = cmd.ExecuteReader()

              conn.Close()
          End Sub
      End Class
```

The sample class is marked with the Serializable attribute, indicating that it supports being binary serialized. Inside the ISerializable method associated with serialization, and in the special ISerializable constructor, the class attempts to execute a command against SQL Server. This operation results in a demand for SqlClientPermission, which you can use to show the effects of enforcing the application trust policy.

After marking the class's assembly with the APTCA attribute, signing it with a strong name, and adding it to the GAC, you can create a sample web application that makes use of this class. The web application will be configured to run in partial trust and use SQL Server session state.

```
<trust level="Medium_Custom"/>

<sessionState mode="SQLServer" sqlConnectionString="server=.\SQL2005;Integrated
Security=true" timeout="30"/>
<compilation debug="true">
 <assemblies>
  <add assembly="BusinessObjects, Version=1.0.0.0, Culture=neutral,
       PublicKeyToken=9cd23ad80158bbfe"/>
 </assemblies>
</compilation>
```

Using SQL Server-based session state means that the session state feature will use binary serialization to load and store any objects placed inside of session state. A simple page that makes use of the GAC'd type is shown here.

C#

```
protected void Page_Load(object sender, EventArgs e)
{
    if (Session["ObjectReference"] != null)
    {
        object o2 = Session["ObjectReference"];
    }
```

```
                SomeObject obj = new SomeObject();
                Session["ObjectReference"] = obj;
        }
```

VB.NET

```
        Protected Sub Page_Load(ByVal sender As Object, ByVal e As EventArgs) _
        Handles Me.Load
            If Session("ObjectReference") IsNot Nothing Then
                Dim o2 As Object = Session("ObjectReference")
            End If

            Dim obj As New SomeObject()
            Session("ObjectReference") = obj
        End Sub
```

The page stores a reference to the GAC'd type inside of Session["ObjectReference"]. Because the page attempts to get a value first, this triggers deserialization of the object instance within the session state feature. Prior to ASP.NET 3.5 and mainly in ASP.NET 2.0, there was a slight optimization added to the out-of-process session state providers. These providers load only the raw blob data when the AcquireRequestState event occurs in the HTTP pipeline. However, the session state providers will not attempt to deserialize the blob into an actual object instance until a piece of code runs and explicitly accesses the session state variable.

Attempting to get an instance of the GAC'd type from session state triggers this lazy deserialization. The page also creates an instance of the GAC'd type and stores it in session state so that later during either the ReleaseRequestState or EndRequest phase the session state provider will have to serialize the object instance.

If you run the page code while the custom trust policy still includes SqlClientPermission, the page runs without a problem. However, if you remove the SqlClientPermission from the trust policy file, the next time you run the page it will fail. Depending on whether you run the page for a brand new session or run the page after session data already exists in the database, the attempt to retrieve an instance of SomeObject fails, or the request fails after the page has run when an attempt is made to serialize the instance of SomeObject.

Overall, the sample highlights the fact that you should not use GAC'd types with out-of-process session state in partially trusted applications if the trusted type carries out any kind of privileged operation using custom serialization. Realistically, this scenario probably will not affect most developers because normally serializable types do not access external resources from inside of custom serialization logic. However, you may encounter custom types written by a development organization or third-party vendor that have this behavior.

If you have an application that was working with OOP session state under full trust, but the application stops working after you drop to High trust or lower, the application trust policy enforcement in ASP.NET 3.5 session state may be the problem. Also note that although the sample shown earlier used custom serialization with ISerializable, the same issue arises if you implement custom serialization using the version tolerant serialization (VTS) mechanism in the 2.0 version of the Framework. Essentially different methods are involved, but you still have the same effect with ASP.NET 2.0 or ASP.NET 3.5 enforcing a PermitOnly prior to any VTS-related methods being called.

Database Security for SQL Session State

SQL Server session state is the most common out-of-process session state mode used by developers. As a result of its popularity, a few quick notes around the database store are in order. The thing to keep in mind when using SQL Server session state is that the information sitting in the session state database is effectively a snapshot of various pieces of application data associated with individual users. If you have sensitive information or privacy related information stored in session, the potential exists for other malicious code to reach into the SQL Server session state store and retrieve it.

Prior to ASP.NET 2.0, you could store session state inside of `tempdb` or inside of a specific database called `ASPState`. Both of these deployment options open up the potential for session data in one application being accessible from another application. The specific risk is that each ASP.NET application that is pointed either `tempdb` or `ASPState` has to be configured with `dbo`-level credentials. The entire schema created by the SQL Server-based session state feature is owned by the `dbo` user. Furthermore, the code inside of the SQL Server session state provider prepends all of the stored procedure names with `dbo`.

As a result, if multiple ASP.NET applications are configured to point at one of the common session state databases, page code inside of these ASP.NET applications can easily issue a select statement directly against the session state database. Take the following simple command:

```
Select * from ASPStateTempSessions
```

If a page in an application issues this command using ADO.NET, it now has a `DataSet` or `SqlDataReader` that contains the raw object data. In ASP.NET 3.5, the `SessionItemShort` and `SessionItemLong` columns contain the serialized representations of session state objects. The blob values in these columns are not directly usable with the binary formatter; however, with a little snooping around and reverse engineering, you can pretty easily tease out the basic structure of the data in these fields.

After a malicious user has done this, that user can read selected byte sequences from these columns and feed them to the `BinaryFormatter`. For a single application using one of the default session state databases, this isn't a security problem because the single application is supposed to be able to manipulate its own session data. Jumping through hoops to do this through ADO.NET and the `BinaryFormatter` doesn't expose any data. However, chances are that if multiple applications are using SQL Server session state, development team A did not intend to allow its data to be snooped by the application written by development team B.

And taking paranoia one step further, in scenarios where multiple applications share the same session state data store, it is also possible for one application to synthesize the byte representation for serialized data and inject it into one of the session state rows containing data for another application. For example, maybe a marketing oriented application uses the same session state database as a web-based loan application does. The marketing application could be crafted so that a malicious developer could write code to edit a row of session data associated with the loan application, maybe to do something along the lines of editing credit information that is temporarily being stored in the session state database for use by an online approver.

So, what does this really boil down to for developers using ASP.NET 2.0 or ASP.NET 3.5? Fortunately, ASP.NET 2.0 and ASP.NET 3.5 have the ability to deploy session state into any arbitrary database (not just `tempdb` and `ASPState`). As a result, it is very easy for ASP.NET 2.0 and ASP.NET 3.5 applications to segment session state stores and prevent different applications from peeking into another application's session data. Locking down session state data in ASP.NET 2.0 and ASP.NET 3.5 should include the following steps:

1. Install the session state schema in separate databases when applications handling sensitive data may be storing some of this information temporarily into session state. You can use the Framework's `aspnet_regsql.exe` tool, located in the install directory, to do this using the `-sstype c` and `-d <database>` options.

2. In the configuration for your web applications, add the new attribute `allowCustomSqlDatabase` to the `<sessionState />` configuration element. Doing so allows you to enter the extra database information into the `sqlConnectionString` attribute of the `<sessionState />` element. If you don't set `allowCustomSqlDatabase` to `true` though and you attempt to use a custom database (something other than `tempdb` or `ASPState`), an exception is thrown at runtime.

3. Configure the connection credentials for the custom session state database so that other ASP.NET applications cannot access it. You can accomplish this by running the ASP.NET application in its own worker process with a unique identity, by setting a unique application impersonation identity for the application, or by using a unique set of standard SQL Server credentials in the connection string.

A sample configuration that would allow you to isolate a session state database to a single ASP.NET application is shown here:

```
<sessionState mode="SQLServer" allowCustomSqlDatabase="True"
    sqlConnectionString="server=.\SQL2005;Integrated Security=true;database=mycusto
mdb" />

<identity impersonate="true" userName="user" password="password"/>
```

This configuration tells the session state feature that is allowable to have a `database` attribute in the connection string that points at something other than `aspnetdb` or `ASPState`. Because application impersonation is also configured, the SQL session state provider will connect to the database using the configured application impersonation credentials. As long as no other ASP.NET applications use the same set of application impersonation credentials, the session state data is limited to only one application.

As a side note, in ASP.NET 2.0 and ASP.NET 3.5, the impersonation behavior of the SQL provider was tweaked a bit. The SQL provider by default always suspends client impersonation prior to communicating with SQL Server. This means if you have client impersonation configured in your application (for example, you are using Windows authentication and `<identity impersonate="true" />`), the SQL server provider reverts to the process identity (or application impersonation identity if application impersonation is in effect) prior to communicating with SQL Server. If you want to retain the old ASP.NET 1.1 impersonation behavior, you can use the `useHostingIdentity` attribute on the `<sessionState />` element and set it to `false`.

So, as long as the underlying process identity of the ASP.NET application or the application impersonation identity has `dbo` privileges in the SQL Server session state database, you can safely use integrated security with the session state connection string. This eliminates the need to add all your Active Directory user accounts to the session state database if you choose to use integrated security with your session state database (though there were also other bugs in ASP.NET 1.1 that made it difficult to use integrated security with session state).

Security Options for the OOP State Server

The out-of-process session state server runs as an NT service using the `aspnet_state.exe` executable. Because the state service itself simply listens on a socket, it doesn't have any built-in security protections that prevent arbitrary hosts on the network from connecting to the state server. Unlike SQL Server, the OOP state server has no concept of integrated security. As a result, server administrators should use other network security mechanisms such as IP security (IPSEC) rules to prevent random machines from attempting to connect to the state server.

Beyond network layer security mechanisms, there are two other security options you should be aware of when using the OOP state server. The first thing you should do is change the default network port that the state server listens on. By default, the state server listens on port 42424. Because this is a well-known port for the state server, you can make the state server listen on a different port by finding the following registry key:

```
HKEY_LOCAL_MACHINE\SYSTEM\CurrentControlSet\Services\aspnet_state\Parameters
```

Underneath this key, you can add a new DWORD registry value named `Port`. Set the actual value to a different port number that you want the state service to listen on. With this change a malicious network user now has to perform a port scan in order to find the state service as opposed to just connecting to port 42424.

Because the OOP state server is usually deployed to support multiple remote web servers, you will quickly find out that your remote OOP state server doesn't work out of the box. The reason for this is that the ASP.NET state service by default only allows connections from localhost. This prevents server administrators from installing ASP.NET on machines and then unknowingly having state servers sitting around listening for remote connections on the network. To allow an instance of the ASP.NET state service to accept remote connections, you can add another DWORD registry value under the `Parameters` key called `AllowRemoteConection`. Setting `AllowRemoteConnection` to "1" enables the state service to accept remote network connections.

Summary

Although session state is usually considered just a handy item in the developer's arsenal of ASP.NET tools, there are a number of subtle security issues to keep in mind. ASP.NET 2.0 and ASP.NET 3.5 include cookieless support for the session state feature. However, as with other features that support cookieless behavior, the potential to accidentally leak cookieless tickets is a risk. As a result, if you choose cookieless sessions, do not store any private or privileged information inside session state; this minimizes the impact of other users accidentally reusing a cookieless session ticket.

Session state has the concept of session ID reuse. In cookied modes, session IDs are shared across *all* applications running under a common DNS host name. This means that even if you call `Session .Abandon` in one application, the session identifier remains in the cookie and the identifier continues to be used by all applications. However, in the application where `Abandon` was called, the session data is deleted, so you end up with fresh session data the next time the user returns to that specific application.

For applications that use cookieless session identifiers, ASP.NET session state doesn't reuse session identifiers by default. Instead, if you call `Abandon` or access an application with an expired session identifier, session state detects this and issues a new session identifier. This behavior is intended to minimize the potential for a user to accidentally or intentionally use a cookieless session identifier that was originally issued to a different user.

If you use in-process session state or the out-of-process session state server, be aware of the potential for DOS attacks. DOS attacks can be launched against these types of session states in an attempt to force an excessive amount of memory consumption on your servers. A simple mitigation is to start using session state only after a user has logged in; prior to that point, if you never access session state, ASP.NET does not allocate any space in memory for session state data. Also, attackers usually want to remain anonymous and thus tend to avoid launching any of type of attack that requires an identifiable account on the website.

Last, be aware of the potential for exposing session state data in SQL Server to other applications that share the same back-end session state database. With the support in ASP.NET 2.0 and ASP.NET 3.5 for custom databases, it is easy to give each application its own session state database, thus preventing one application from snooping around in the session data of another application.

9

Security for Pages and Compilation

A good deal of writing a secure page depends on often-discussed topics such as input validation, handling malicious input, preventing SQL injection attacks, and so on. However, ASP.NET provides some lesser known configurable security features that add a degree of extra security to your pages. This chapter will review some security features for pages and compilation that have been around since ASP.NET 1.1, as well as security features in ASP.NET 2.0 and ASP.NET 3.5.

The topics that will be covered include:

- ❑ Request validation and viewstate protection.
- ❑ Options for securing page compilation.
- ❑ Protecting against fraudulent postbacks.
- ❑ Site navigation security.

Request Validation and Viewstate Protection

Two well-known protection mechanisms for ASP.NET pages are request validation and viewstate protection. Request validation has always been a bit of a mystery to developers, so in this section you will see exactly how it works in ASP.NET 2.0 and ASP.NET 3.5. Viewstate protections have been around since ASP.NET 1.0, but there have been some features added for viewstate protection in ASP.NET 2.0, which are now also part of ASP.NET 3.5.

Request Validation

Request validation is meant to detect strings posted to a web server that may contain suspicious character sequences. In general, request validation attempts to detect string information, which if subsequently rendered on a page, could result in a successful cross-site scripting attack. Request validation is not a general-purpose input validation mechanism. Constraining input to a valid set of values and preventing data from containing SQL injection attacks are still tasks the developer must implement.

By default, request validation is turned on. You can change the request validation settings with either the `validateRequest` attribute of the `<pages />` element or the `ValidateRequest` attribute of the `@Page` directive. In general, you should keep request validation turned on, and turn it off on selected pages where you are encountering problems. The request validation feature checks the following `Request` collections for suspicious strings:

❑ Form variables

❑ Query string variables

❑ The Cookie collection

The actual string checks are pretty straightforward. Request validation looks for character sequences such as:

❑ **< followed by an exclamation point:** For example, `<!` is not allowed.

❑ **< followed by the letters a through z:** The theory is that a character sequence that starts out looking like `<s` could potentially be the beginning of a `<script>` element for example. So in general, the request validation feature pessimistically rejects these types of character sequences.

❑ **& followed by a pound sign:** So, the sequence `"&#123"` would be rejected. This prevents encoding based attacks, where a person attempts to submit script code as a sequence of HTML-encoded characters in the hope that it will subsequently be accidentally decoded prematurely.

Back in the ASP.NET 2.0 development cycle, there were many more stringent checks added to request validation. However, these checks were backed out because for every case that ASP.NET was protecting against, you could come up with an innocuous reason for submitting the string in a form. For example, at one point with ASP.NET 2.0 or ASP.NET 3.5 if you submitted text in a form that said "The onclick event looks like 'onclick=alert('hello world')'", the server would reject it. Unfortunately, that level of parameter checking ended up causing early developers to turn off request validation entirely in an attempt to get their forms working. So instead, request validation was reverted to a simpler set of validation checks, the idea being that it was better to have everyone benefit from some level of request validation rather than forcing many developers to turn off the feature.

Even with the basic set of request validations, you can still run into problems if you are writing a control like a rich text box. Many of the rich text editors allow users to type in basic HTML tags such as `<b>`. Of course if you try this with request validation turned on, the page request will promptly fail because ASP.NET detects the < characters followed by a letter. If you implement rigorous input validation in your application though, you could safely turn off request validation for this case.

However, a more secure approach to this problem is to pre-encode strings on the client using your own custom mapping. For example, if you write a rich text editor that supports bold and italic characters, just before the form is submitted you could convert all instances of <b> to [html bold] and all instances of <i> to [html italic]. Then on the server side you would search for that string token and convert it the correct HTML markup. Doing this is a bit laborious because you have to preprocess and postprocess all the strings that you care about. But it does have the benefit of allowing request validation to stay in place. Also, this type of development work will make it very clear to you the specific subset of strings that you want to allow in your application.

Securing viewstate

The ability to protect viewstate with a hash signature and encryption has been available since ASP.NET 1.0. You are probably very familiar with how it works by now, so rather than rehashing the basics, I will cover what has been added in ASP.NET 2.0 that still applies to ASP.NET 3.5 as well as one dusty corner of viewstate security that some developers do not know about.

By default, all pages have their EnableViewStateMac property set to true. Combined with the default <machineKey /> setting of SHA1 for the validation attribute, this means that .aspx pages include a hash value along with their viewstate data. The only new thing in this regard was the addition of ASP.NET 2.0 to the AES algorithm to the <machineKey /> section. Although it looks a bit strange, you can set the validation attribute in ASP.NET 2.0 and ASP.NET 3.5 to SHA1, MD, 3DES, or AES. Because older versions of ASP.NET overloaded the validation attribute for viewstate protection *and* forms authentication protection, you end up with options for specifying symmetric encryption algorithms in an attribute that theoretically references one-way hashing algorithms.

Forms authentication ignores the nonhashing options for the validation attribute, but the Page class does make use of the encryption options. If you set either 3DES or AES in the validation attribute, then assuming your .aspx pages have EnableViewStateMac set to true, ASP.NET will first hash the page's viewstate data using SHA1 (HMACSHA1 to be precise), and then it will encrypt both the viewstate and the hash value using either 3DES or AES. Unlike the companion decryption attribute in <machineKey />, for the validation attribute you have to explicitly choose the type of encryption algorithm you want to use. There is no capability for ASP.NET to auto-select a viewstate encryption algorithm on your behalf.

There is an extra option that developers can use in their code to make viewstate more secure: the ViewStateUserKey property. Although this property is not new in ASP.NET 2.0 or ASP.NET 3.5, many developers are unaware of its existence. When viewstate is being hashed you can add a per-user identifier to the information that is used when hashing viewstate. By default, when ASP.NET hashes the viewstate for the page, it includes extra information derived from the .aspx page as part of the stream of data that is being hashed. This mechanism ensures that the viewstate from one page cannot be posted to a different page (excepting the cross-page posting feature in ASP.NET 2.0 and ASP.NET 3.5).

This default protection, though, won't prevent a malicious user from hijacking the viewstate data shown in one user's browser and then attempting to submit it in a separate browser. For example if a web application automatically trusts all its postback data and doesn't perform any additional security checks, it becomes possible for someone to steal the viewstate form variable and then replay it to trigger actions on the server that a user may not normally have rights to. You have the option of injecting your own user-specific information into the data stream being hashed by setting a value on the ViewStateUserKey property. Because the intent of the property is to prevent user A from posting user B's viewstate back to the server, the logical choice for a ViewStateUserKey value is the value from User.Identity.Name.

C#

```
protected void Page_Init(object sender, EventArgs e)
{
    this.ViewStateUserKey = User.Identity.Name;
}
```

VB.NET

```
Protected Sub Page_Init( ByVal sender As Object, _
    ByVal e As EventArgs) Handles Me.Init()
    Me.ViewStateUserKey = User.Identity.Name
End Sub
```

With this code, even if a malicious user attempts to submit hijacked viewstate information, the postback will fail because the viewstate hash is now derived in part from the user's name.

You have to set the ViewStateUserKey property early on in the page lifecycle during the Init event. Because the property value affects the deserialization and validation of viewstate, ASP.NET has to have the correct ViewStateUserKey value before it attempts to process the viewstate. Setting ViewStateUserKey during a page's Load event is far too late because by that point ASP.NET has already deserialized viewstate.

ASP.NET 2.0 and ASP.NET 3.5 include an option for determining when viewstate *encryption* occurs: a property on the Page class called ViewStateEncryptionMode. The possible values for this property are Auto, Never, and Always, with the default being Auto. You can set this value globally in configuration using the viewStateEncryptionMode attribute of the <pages /> configuration section. You can also customize the value on a per-page basis using the ViewStateEncryptionMode attribute of the @Page directive. Although you can set the property at runtime, either the configuration setting or the page directive are the normal approaches for setting this value. If you attempt to programmatically set ViewStateEncryptionMode, you will need to do so in an override of the FrameworkInitialize method on the page class. This is a new "ultra-early" initialization method where you can set various page properties that really can't be set during the normal page initialization phase.

During viewstate serialization, the Page class and the ObjectStateFormatter class look at the ViewStateEncryptionMode property before looking at the setting for EnableViewStateMac. Clearly, if the property setting is Never, nothing else happens and the ObjectStateFormatter follows the ASP.NET 1.1 behavior for hashing and encrypting viewstate. However, if ViewStateEncryptionMode is set to Always, regardless of the page's current setting for EnableViewStateMac, ASP.NET will *always* encrypt viewstate. Furthermore, this encryption will use the encryption algorithm determined by the decryption attribute on <machineKey />. So by default, this means with a setting of Always, your page's viewstate will be encrypted using AES. Two things to keep in mind if you set ViewStateEncryptionMode to Always:

❑ The encryption options in the validation attribute are ignored. Forcing viewstate encryption means that the selection of the encryption algorithm follows the rules for forms authentication.

❑ The other validation options in the validation attribute are also ignored. When ViewStateEncryptionMode forces viewstate encryption, *only* encryption occurs. No hashing of the viewstate data stream occurs. However, if you set a value for ViewStateUserKey, it will be added to the encrypted data stream, so you still gain the extra viewstate protection of this property.

The last (and the default) option for `ViewStateEncryptionMode` is Auto. The Auto setting is intended for use by controls in conjunction with the new `Page` method `RegisterRequiresViewStateEncryption`. Because the default page setting is Auto, various controls in the framework, or third-party controls, can proactively turn on viewstate encryption if the controls "know" that they deal with sensitive data. The idea behind the Auto setting is that individual control developers know the guts of their code much better than the developers using them do. Rather than forcing developers to slog through lengthy API documents to determine whether sensitive data is being processed by a control, a control developer can just make that determination up front.

If a control calls `Page.RegisterRequiresViewStateEncryption` and the current `ViewStateEncryptionMode` is `Auto`, regardless of the `EnableViewStateMac` setting, the page's viewstate will end up being encrypted. Because the default setting of `EnableViewStateMac` is true, but the `validation` attribute in `<machineKey />` defaults to SHA1, under normal conditions all of your page's viewstate is for all practical purposes being transmitted in the clear. Even though the hidden __VIEWSTATE is base64 encoded, with the default behavior there is nothing preventing a user from un-encoding the field and looking at the raw data. The `ViewStateEncryptionMode` behavior allows a control to increase the security of the page's viewstate by forcing this data to be encrypted, even when the page developer may not realize that sensitive information is being stored in viewstate.

Within ASP.NET, the following controls (all of them are data controls) may call `RegisterRequiresViewStateEncryption`:

- ❑   `FormView`: If there are any key values in the `DataKeyNames` property, `FormView` forces viewstate encryption.

- ❑   `DetailsView`: If there are any key values in the `DataKeyNames` property, the `DetailsView` forces viewstate encryption.

- ❑   `GridView`: If there are any key values in the `DataKeyNames` property, and the control is *not* auto-generating the columns used in the `GridView` control, then `GridView` forces viewstate encryption.

- ❑   `DataList`: If there is a key value stored in the `DataKeyField` property then the `DataList` forces viewstate encryption.

- ❑   `ListView`: If there are any key values in the `DataKeyNames` property, `ListView` forces viewstate encryption.

As you can see, the preceding are data controls that are part of ASP.NET 2.0 and ASP.NET 3.5, except for the `ListView`, which is newly introduced to ASP.NET 3.5. You should keep this behavior in mind if you port your old ASP.NET 1.1 data control logic over to use the ASP.NET 3.5 data controls.

If you choose to store the primary key values in these controls (and for some control scenarios you need to do this), you will end up triggering viewstate encryption. This isn't a "bad" thing, because chances are that you don't want the outside world looking at your database primary keys through reverse engineering client-side viewstate. However, if your application works perfectly in development, but fails when you push it out to your web farm, the `ViewStateEncryptionMode` behavior might be causing the problem. Because viewstate encryption uses the encryption key material from `<machineKey />`, the `<machineKey />` by default sets the decryption key to `AutoGenerate`, `IsolateApps`, your data pages can fail in a multiserver web farm. As with forms authentication there is a simple solution: if you use any of these four controls and you run in a web farm, explicitly set the `decryptionKey` attribute in `<machineKey />` and synchronize the value across all your web servers.

One thing to keep in mind with ViewStateEncryptionMode is that you are not always guaranteed that encryption will occur. If the page has explicitly turned off ViewStateEncryptionMode by setting it to Never, regardless of whether a control requests viewstate encryption, the page is not going to force encryption. In this case, only the protections specified in the validation attribute of <machineKey /> will apply. The interaction between ViewStateEncryptionMode and a control results in a more secure page only if the mode is set to Auto *and* if no other steps have been taken to turn off viewstate encryption for the page.

The compatabilityMode Attribute in ASP.NET 3.5 SP 1

ASP.NET 3.5 SP1 introduced a new attribute in the <machineKey /> configuration element called compatibilityMode. The new attribute can have one of the two possible values: Framework20SP1 or Framework20SP2. The attribute defaults to Framework20SP1, which maintains compatibility with the 2.0 and 3.5 ASP.NET releases. However, switching the compatibilityMode attribute to Framework20SP2 introduces a slight change to how viewstate and other page variables get encrypted/ encoded when viewstate encryption is turned on. The result is that running in the latter mode results in viewstate that cannot be decoded on web servers running older versions of ASP.NET. Therefore, to make use of the new compatibilityMode attribute to benefit from the slight changes that it introduced into the framework, you have to have ASP.NET 3.5 SP1 installed on the web server running the application(s) that is utilizing the new attribute.

Page Compilation

The dynamic page compilation model that was introduced since ASP.NET 2.0 does away with the monolithic code-behind assembly from ASP.NET 1.1. Instead, developers can just author their page markup and code-behind pages, and then deploy all the content to a web server. Although this model of XCOPY everything works well inside of a corporate firewall, for Internet-facing applications administrators understandably may not want the .vb or .cs code-behind files existing on their production servers. To address this issue, ASP.NET 2.0 and ASP.NET 3.5 have the concept of precompilation. A precompiled website is one where ASP.NET has already converted the page code and markup into multiple assemblies. The output from precompilation are just a series of .aspx/.ascx files along with compiled code in multiple assemblies sitting in the /bin directory.

With a precompiled site, the page and user control files that are left in an application's folder structure can optionally include the original markup because there are two modes of precompilation: updatable and non-updatable. If you use updatable precompilation the markup is preserved in the .aspx and .ascx files. Non-updatable precompilation still generates .aspx files, but these files are just empty stubs. In either case, you can use precompiled sites to ensure that your assemblies are deployed to a production server without the need to push any page code.

You can invoke precompilation in two ways. The easiest is to just select Publish Website from the Build menu option in Visual Studio 2005 or Visual Studio 2008. (Note: this option does not exist in the

Express editions of Visual Studio 2005 and Visual Studio 2008.) You can also invoke precompilation using the `aspnet_compiler.exe` program that is located in the framework installation directory. The command-line tool is useful if you have an automated build process that you are currently using for building websites. When you move to ASP.NET 2.0 or ASP.NET 3.5, you can update your build process to invoke the `aspnet_compiler` tool instead. A command-line invocation looks something like this:

```
aspnet_compiler -m /LM/W3SVC/1/ROOT/PageSecurity d:\inetpub\wwwroot\somedir
```

You can also reference your application code using a physical path or a virtual path. The preceding example uses an IIS metabase path to reference the specific application that should be compiled.

Some developers in ASP.NET 1.1 took advantage of the code-behind assembly by signing it. Then on their web servers, they had Framework CAS policies that only allowed signed assemblies with a specific public key to run, or that restricted permissions based on specific public keys. If you want to accomplish the same thing in ASP.NET 2.0 or ASP.NET 3.5, you must use precompilation. Both the Visual Studio 2008 (and 2005) UIs and the command-line compiler give you the option to sign your precompiled assemblies. You will need to generate a `.snk` file with the key material ahead of time. After you have generated the public/private key-pair you can then use either Visual Studio 2008 (or 2005) or the command-line compiler to generate and sign the precompiled assemblies. In Figure 9-1, you can see an example of precompiling a website and signing the precompiled assemblies.

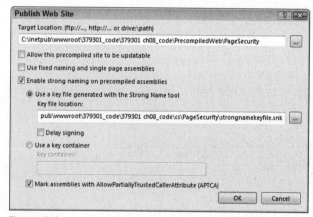

Figure 9-1

Notice that updatable precompilation wasn't selected. This ensures that all the code in the site is compiled ahead of time and that no dynamic generation of page classes will occur at runtime. This also means that all your application code, including any inline code on an `.aspx` page or `.ascx` control, will be stripped out and compiled into precompiled assemblies. Also note that the Mark assemblies with APTCA option is checked. This is necessary if you want to run a signed precompiled site in anything less than Full trust.

In Figure 9-2, you can see the result of signing precompiled output in ildasm.

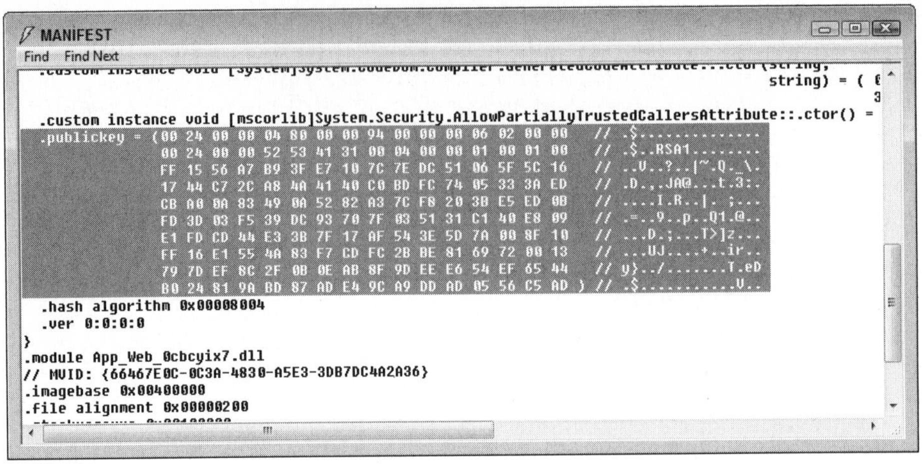

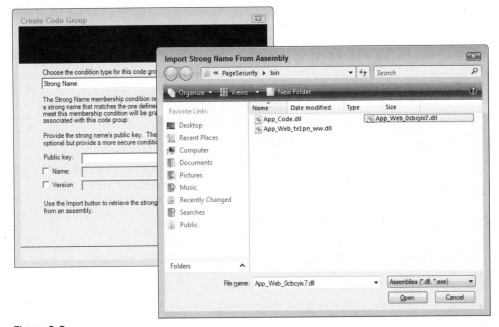

Figure 9-2

The precompiled assembly called App_Web_0cbcyix7.dll now has a public key embedded in its manifest.

With the signed assembly, you can use the .NET Framework Configuration MMC. (Look for mscorcfg.msc in the directory where you installed the Framework SDK.) The tool is no longer installed as part of the Framework itself to set up a code group with a public key based membership condition. If precompilation outputs multiple assemblies (which will normally be the case), you can just choose one of the assemblies for purposes of setting up the public key based membership condition. Figure 9-3 shows the step in the wizard that walks you through creating a new code group with a strong-name membership condition.

Figure 9-3

In this wizard step, the Strong Name condition has been chosen. In the File dialog box, the precompiled assembly has been selected so that the wizard will extract the public key token from it. Once the token is extracted, the wizard enables you to choose a permission set to associate with assemblies that match the membership condition. Although ASP.NET trust policy files are really the *de rigueur* approach for granting permissions to web applications, you may be in an environment where permissions are also locked down using the Framework's CAS policies. After you set up a new code group, you can use the .NET Framework Configuration MMC to associate a custom permission set for your precompiled ASP.NET sites.

Although it is not new to ASP.NET 2.0 and ASP.NET 3.5, you can change the location of the temporary files used by ASP.NET at runtime. Normally, any type of temporary per-application file storage for ASP.NET is placed somewhere in the following directory:

```
%windir%\Microsoft.NET\Framework\v2.0.50727\Temporary ASP.NET Files\
```

One reason you might want to change the location is that you installed the framework onto your system drive, but you want the auto-generated compiler output, spooled data from large requests, and so on to be located on a separate drive. If you host a large number of applications, it is possible to have a very large file structure within the Temporary ASP.NET Files location, in which case the system drive may not be the right place for them.

From a security perspective, the fact that many different applications are sharing the same general directory structure can also be troublesome. Even though there is no way for code in a partially trusted web application to reach out into this directory structure, many ASP.NET sites still run in Full trust. A malicious developer could take advantage of a fully trusted application and write code to open and read the temporary files in this directory structure from other applications. As a side note, this is another reason why running in Medium trust for untrusted hosting environments is so important; this attack vector simply isn't available in Medium trust.

If you want you can change the location used by ASP.NET for storing its temporary files with the `tempDirectory` attribute of the `<compilation />` configuration section. For example, the following configuration section remaps the temporary file location to a location on the D drive.

```
<compilation tempDirectory="D:\Chapter 9\NewTempDirectory" />
```

Of course, just changing the location of the temporary directory is not sufficient. You also need to ensure that the process account, or the application impersonation account if you are using application impersonation, has the following directory rights:

❏ Read/Read & Execute/List Folder Contents

❏ Write

❏ Modify

❏ Special Permission: Delete Subfolders and Files

❏ Special Permission: Change Permissions

These are the same set of rights granted to accounts on the Temporary ASP.NET Files directory if you use the `aspnet_regiis -ga` option in ASP.NET 2.0 and ASP.NET 3.5 to configure nondefault process accounts. After you configure the NTFS ACLs appropriately, you will see that your web application uses the new `tempDirectory` location for all temporary ASP.NET files.

Fraudulent Postbacks

ASP.NET relies heavily upon postbacks and on the client-side postback logic that the runtime emits. With ASP.NET 1.1, there is a potential security issue with postbacks because the client-side JavaScript that triggers postbacks is easy to modify. This security issue is referred to as the fraudulent postback problem. To illustrate the problem, you can construct a simple page with some ASP.NET controls that use the client-side postback logic.

```
<form id="form1" runat="server">
<div>
    <asp:LinkButton
         ID="btnSensitive" runat="server" Visible=false
         OnClick="btnSensitive_Click">Click Me!</asp:LinkButton> 
    <br />
    <a href="javascript:fraudulentPostback()">Trigger fraudulent postback</a>
    <br />
    <asp:LinkButton ID="LinkButton1" runat="server">
             Ignore Me!</asp:LinkButton></div>

<script type="text/javascript">
function fraudulentPostback()
{
    var theForm = document.forms['form1'];
    theForm.__EVENTTARGET.value = 'btnSensitive';
    theForm.__EVENTARGUMENT.value = '';
    theForm.submit();
}
</script>

</form>
```

This ASP.NET page has two LinkButton controls: I chose that control type because LinkButton(s) emit the __doPostBack function and the supporting form variables used by ASP.NET for submitting postbacks. Note that the same issue can also be triggered with less complex server-side controls, such as the Button control, that don't rely on the _doPostBack method. In the sample page, the first Link-Button has its Visible property set to false. Many developers use control visibility or the enabled/disabled state of a control as a kind of surrogate client-side security mechanism. For instance, you might intentionally hide a set of update controls on a page if you know the current user has only view rights to a piece of data.

The reason for the second LinkButton on the page is simply to force the rendering of the hidden __EVENTTARGET and __EVENTARGUMENT fields for this example. Most moderately complex ASP.NET pages will have multiple controls on them that can trigger postbacks, so even if one set of controls is disabled or hidden, the other controls will still trigger the rendering of these hidden fields. The sample page has an <a> tag that points at a JavaScript function called fraudulentPostback. The code in the function contains a copy of the JavaScript from the __doPostBack function, the one modification being that fraudulentPostback hardcodes the event target as the btnSensitive control. In other words, the fraudulentPostback function is faking the postback process that would occur if btnSensitive were visible on the page, and the browser user clicked it.

The server code for this page is very basic: The click event for the hidden link button simply writes some text:

C#

```
protected void btnSensitive_Click(object sender, EventArgs e)
{
    Response.Write("Sensitive operation has been carried out.");
}
```

VB.NET

```
Protected Sub btnSensitive_Click(ByVal sender As Object, _
    ByVal e As EventArgs) Handles btnSensitive.Click
    Response.Write("Sensitive operation has been carried out.")
End Sub
```

The problem in a real application, of course, occurs when the click event for a hidden or disabled control actually carries out a sensitive operation based solely on the assumption that the postback data can be trusted.

When you run the page in the browser, the HTML for the form includes only the following control tags:

```
<form name="form1" method="post" action="FraudulentPostback.aspx" id="form1">
...
<input type="hidden" name="__EVENTTARGET" id="__EVENTTARGET" value="" />
<input type="hidden" name="__EVENTARGUMENT" id="__EVENTARGUMENT" value="" />
...
<a href="javascript:fraudulentPostback()">Trigger fraudulent postback</a>
    <br />
<a id="LinkButton1" href="javascript:__doPostBack('LinkButton1','')">
Ignore Me!</a>
...
```

Notice that the rendered HTML does not have an <a> tag for the btnSensitive LinkButton control. At this point though, you can still click on the LinkButton1 link button. ASP.NET is fooled into thinking that the browser user actually clicked the nonexistent btnSensitive link button, and as a result the code in btnSensitive_Click runs. In a nutshell, this entire process is the crux of the fraudulent postback problem. As long as someone can load a page in a browser and have it run JavaScript, it is possible to run JavaScript code that sends postback data to ASP.NET for controls and actions that don't actually exist on the rendered HTML page.

The first line of defense against this problem is simply to use defense-in-depth coding techniques in your web application. A security-conscious developer would not trust the postback data in a server-side event. Instead of assuming that just because a server-side event has been fired that the business logic within it is safe to run, you would perform server-side authorization checks. For example, you could perform a role-based authorization check in the click event that confirms the current user is in the appropriate role before it carries out the requested sensitive work. Alternatively, you could perform the same type of security check farther down in your middle tier.

Unfortunately, not all developers are diligent about building this level of security into their applications. If an application relies solely on the presentation tier doing the right thing, then it is rather easy to forge postbacks as you just saw. ASP.NET 2.0 and ASP.NET 3.5 have an additional layer of protection, called *event validation*, that specifically addresses the problem of fraudulent postbacks.

By default, event validation is turned on in ASP.NET 2.0 and ASP.NET 3.5. So, if you were to take the code shown earlier and run it on ASP.NET 2.0 or ASP.NET 3.5, instead of the btnSensitive_Click event running, you get an exception and stack trace like the following:

```
[ArgumentException: Invalid postback or callback argument. …]
System.Web.UI.ClientScriptManager.ValidateEvent(String uniqueId, String argument)
System.Web.UI.Control.ValidateEvent(String uniqueID, String eventArgument)
System.Web.UI.WebControls.LinkButton.RaisePostBackEvent(String eventArgument)
…
```

Here, the LinkButton control makes use of the event validation feature in ASP.NET 2.0 and ASP.NET 3.5. When the postback event is passed to the LinkButton, it in turn uses the ClientScriptManager object to validate that the current event is actually valid. Because the LinkButton control is actually not visible on the page, clearly the postback event could not have been triggered by it, and as a result the exception occurs.

Event validation can be controlled globally in an application with the enableEventValidation attribute in the <pages /> configuration section. You can also turn validation on or off on a per-page basis with the EnableEventValidation attribute on the @Page directive. There is a property on the Page class of the same name that you can set as well, although you can only set the EnableEventValidation property during FrameworkInitialize. By default, event validation is turned on for all pages in ASP.NET 2.0 and ASP.NET 3.5.

When event validation is enabled, and a control that makes use of event validation is on the page, the following general steps occur when the page runs:

1. When the control is creating postback event references for a page, it also calls the Register-ForEventValidation method on the ClientScriptManager object associated with the page. Internally the ClientScriptManager creates and stores a hash value of the data that is passed to the RegisterForEventValidation method. A control can choose to hash just a string that uniquely identifies the control, a combination of both the control's identifier and the event arguments, or a hash can be generated from an instance of PostBackOptions. For example, the Button control generates a validation hash using its PostBackOptions, while the GridView hashes its UniqueID and the event arguments for the postback reference being created.

2. The ClientScriptManager then takes all of the hash values that it created, and it serializes them into a hidden input field called __EVENTVALIDATION. The hidden input field is protected in the same way that the hidden __VIEWSTATE field is protected. By default the serialized representation of the event validation hash codes is itself hashed using the <machineKey /> information, and this value is included in the __EVENTVALIDATION field. If encryption has been enabled (or was forced on due to the new ViewStateEncryptionMode settings), the information will be encrypted.

3. When a postback subsequently occurs, the postback is raised to a specific control on the page. For example, if a control implements IPostBackEventHandler, then if an event reference for that control triggered the event, ASP.NET will call the control's RaisePostBackEvent

implementation. At that point, it is the control's responsibility to call `ClientScriptManager`
`.ValidateEvent`, passing the same set of parameters to `ValidateEvent` that were originally
passed into the `RegisterEventForValidation` method. If you are authoring a control that registers for event validation with `PostBackOptions`, you will need to pass the `PostBackOptions`
`.TargetControl.UniqueID` and `PostBackOptions.Argument` properties to `ValidateEvent`
because there is no `ValidateEvent` overload that accepts an instance of `PostBackOptions`.

4. The `ClientScriptManager` delay loads the data in the __EVENTVALIDATION field. If no
   controls on the page ever call `ValidateEvent`, then the `ClientScriptManager` does not need
   to deserialize the event validation information, thus saving processing overhead. Only when
   `ValidateEvent` is called for the first time during a postback will the `ClientScriptManager`
   derserialize the event validation information.

5. Inside the `ValidateEvent` method, the `ClientScriptManager` looks at the string identifier and optional arguments that were passed to it. It hashes these values and then checks in
   the deserialized event validation information to see if the same hash values exist. If a match
   is found, then the postback event and its associated arguments are valid (that is, the postback
   event and its arguments were originally rendered on the page). If the hash of the information
   that the control passed to `ValidateEvent` cannot be found, this is an indication that a forged
   postback has occurred. In this case, the `ClientScriptManager` throws the exception that you
   saw earlier.

On one hand, the net result of all of this work is that if a control registers for event validation, and the
set of event information that was registered arrives at the server during a subsequent postback, then
the postback will be considered valid. On the other hand, if event data posted back to ASP.NET comes
from an event reference that was never rendered, or a control that was never rendered, when the
`ClientScriptManager` attempts to find a previous registration for the event or control it fails and
throws an exception.

One thing to note about event validation is that it is not an ironclad guarantee that a postback is valid.
Event validation is only as strong as its weakest link, specifically the hidden __EVENTVALIDATION
field. Just as viewstate from one user can potentially be hijacked and submitted by a second user, the
same attack vector exists for the event validation field. However, because the event validation field is
protected in the same way as viewstate, you can set a `ViewStateUserKey` that will make the event validation field unique to each user.

Many of the controls in ASP.NET 3.5 make use of event validation. A partial list of the ASP.NET controls
that make use of event validation is:

- ❑   Button
- ❑   CatalogZoneBase
- ❑   Checkbox
- ❑   DetailsView
- ❑   FormView
- ❑   GridView
- ❑   HiddenField
- ❑   ImageButton

- ❑ LinkButton
- ❑ ListBox
- ❑ Menu
- ❑ RadioButton
- ❑ TextBox
- ❑ TreeView
- ❑ WebPartZoneBase

Because the ClientScriptManager APIs for event validation are all public, if you author custom controls (both web controls and user controls), you can also make use of event validation. Just follow the general registration flow describer earlier. Register your control's event data for validation when your control is setting up postback event references. In the methods where your control processes postback events, first call ValidateEvent to ensure that the postback is valid prior to carrying out the rest of your control's event processing.

Also note that even though this discussion has been about event validation for postbacks, the event validation mechanism in ASP.NET 2.0 and ASP.NET 3.5 also works for callbacks. In fact, ASP.NET controls that support callbacks like the TreeView control make use of event validation for both postbacks and callbacks.

Site Navigation Security

ASP.NET 2.0 and ASP.NET 3.5 include a set of navigation controls such as Menu and TreeView that work with navigation data. One source of this navigation data is the Site Navigation feature, which makes use of SiteMapProvider(s). There is one concrete implementation of a SiteMapProvider included in ASP.NET called the XmlSiteMapProvider. Its purpose is to parse Xml in a .sitemap file and return this information as a linked set of SiteMapNode instances that controls like the Menu control can then render. The interesting aspect of the Site Navigation feature from a security perspective is that you will likely define navigation data in a .sitemap file that closely mirrors the navigation hierarchy of your site. A potential security mismatch can occur if your navigation UI renders links to pages that normally would be inaccessible to a user. Even though an unauthorized user won't be able to actually run such pages, you may not want to even display inaccessible links in the first place.

The base SiteMapProvider class has support for a feature called security trimming. If security trimming is turned on for a SiteMapProvider, prior to returning a SiteMapNode from a provider method, the SiteMapProvider first checks to see if the URL represented by the SiteMapNode is actually accessible to the current user. You enable security trimming with the securityTrimmingEnabled attribute as shown in the following sample provider definition:

```
<siteMap>
  <providers>
    <clear />
    <add name="AspNetXmlSiteMapProvider"
        type="System.Web.XmlSiteMapProvider, …"
```

```
            siteMapFile="web.sitemap"
            securityTrimmingEnabled="true"
      />
    </providers>
  </siteMap>
```

When security trimming is enabled, the XmlSiteMapProvider, its immediate base class
(StaticSiteMapProvider) and the base SiteMapProvider class all call into SiteMapProvider
.IsAccessibleToUser to determine whether a node is considered accessible. If the URL is not accessible by the current user, then the corresponding SiteMapNode is skipped and is not returned to the
user. In some cases, this means a null value is returned to the calling code; in other cases, it means
that the node is not included in a SiteMapNodeCollection returned to the user, and in some other
cases, it means that node traversal of site map data is halted when an inaccessible node is reached. If
you author a custom SiteMapProvider, you can make use of IsAccessibleToUser as well to perform authorization checks for your own node instances.

By default, security trimming is not turned on for the default XmlSiteMapProvider configured in
the <sitemap /> configuration element. This means that even if you have authorization rules set up
in web.config for your site, your navigation controls will render links to all of the URLs defined in a
sitemap even if the current user cannot access them. Even though it would technically be more secure
to have turned security trimming on, developers would probably see nodes appearing and disappear-
ing randomly each time they edited the authorization rules in web.config. Without understanding
that Site Navigation performs security trimming, this would lead folks to think the navigation feature
was broken.

The logic inside of the IsAccessibleToUser method uses the authorization logic contained in both
UrlAuthorizationModule and FileAuthorizationModule. It also works with optional role information defined using the roles attribute of a sitemap node in a .sitemap file. Because the authorization
rules in the <authorization /> configuration element can apply to only pages inside of a web application, SiteMapNode class allows you to define additional role information about a specific URL. For
example, if your .sitemap file had a node definition that pointed at www.microsoft.com, there is no
way for URL authorization to decide whether a user is authorized to this URL because it lies outside the
scope of your web application. To deal with these types of URLs, or to just define additional role information for an application's URLs, you can put a semicolon or comma delimited set of roles in the roles
attribute of a <siteMapNode /> element in a .sitemap file.

```
<siteMapNode url="http://www.microsoft.com" title="External Link"
         roles="Regular Users, Power Users" />
```

Another reason that the Site Navigation feature allows for defining roles on a <siteMapNode /> is
that not all nodes represent navigable content. For example, if your navigation structure includes menu
headers, these headers are only intended for organizing the display of navigation UI.

```
<siteMapNode title="Administrative Pages" roles="Adminstrator" >
    <siteMapNode url="ManageUsers.aspx" title="Manage Users"
             roles="Adminstrator"/>
    <siteMapNode url="ManageRoles.aspx" title="Manage Roles"
             roles="Adminstrator"/>
</siteMapNode>
```

In this example, the first node is just being used to create a menu entry that a user can hover over. However, the entry is itself not navigable; instead, you would select either Manage Users or Manage Roles in a pop-up menu to navigate to a specific page. Because no URL is associated with the first node, the only way to have SiteMapProvider determine if a user should even see the node in navigation UI is by attributing it with the roles attribute. If you write a custom provider that loads its navigation data from somewhere else, you can also supply role information for this type of node by supplying a collection of role strings in the SiteMapNode constructor.

Also note that the role information is repeated in the two child nodes for managing users and roles. The Site Navigation feature does not have the concept of role inheritance. So, even though a role definition was added to the Administrative Pages node, you still need to mirror the role information in all of the child nodes. If you don't do this, a piece of code that accesses one of the child nodes directly with a call to FindSiteMapNode would succeed, while node traversal starting at the parent node would fail. As a result, if you don't copy the role definitions to the children, you end up with inconsistent results returned from the provider, depending on what methods you are calling.

This behavior means that the IsAccessibleToUser method potentially has three different sets of authorization information that it can reference when deciding whether a SiteMapNode's URL is accessible to the current user. IsAccessibleToUser goes through the following evaluation sequence to determine whether a user is authorized to the URL of a SiteMapNode:

1. If the roles attribute was defined in the .sitemap file for a <siteMapNode /> element, then the provider calls HttpContext.Current.User.IsInRole for each and every role in the roles attribute. If the current user is in at least one of the defined roles, the provider will return the SiteMapNode. This means that the roles attribute of a <siteMapNode /> *expands access* beyond the authorization rules defined in an <authorization /> tag. As long as there is at least one match between the current user's roles and the roles in the roles attribute, SiteMapProvider considers a SiteMapNode to be visible to the user.

2. If the roles attribute is set to * (that is, roles="*"), this means all users are allowed to see the node, and thus the provider returns the node.

3. If the site map node has no URL, and no match was found in the roles attribute for the current's user's roles, then the current user is considered to not have rights to the node. Depending on the provider method that was called, this means either a null value is returned or the provider skips the node and does not include it in the results. This behavior is important to keep in mind if your sitemap contains spacer or header nodes such as the Administrative Pages node shown earlier. Without a roles attribute defining at least one piece of role information on these types of nodes, all users will not have rights to view the node when security trimming is enabled.

4. If no match is found in the roles attribute or the roles attribute does not exist, and the node has a URL, the provider will call into FileAuthorizationModule if Windows authentication is enabled for the website. With Windows authentication enabled, there will be a WindowsIdentity on the context, and as a result the provider can call an internal method on the FileAuthorizationModule that performs authorization checks against the physical file associated with the SiteMapNode. If the authorization check succeeds, then the SiteMapNode is returned to the caller.

5. If the file authorization check fails, or if Windows authentication is not enabled on the site, the provider calls an internal method on the UrlAuthorizationModule, passing it the URL

from the `SiteMapNode`. This authorization check mirrors the behavior you get from the `<authorization />` section in your `web.config`. If the check succeeds, then the `SiteMap-Node` is returned to the caller.

6. If all of the previous checks fail, the user is considered to not have the rights to view the `SiteMapNode`, and either a null value will be returned by the provider or the provider will stop walking through `SiteMapNode(s)`. On one hand, for example, if `FindSiteMapNode` was called, a `null` would be returned. On the other hand, if `GetChildNodes` was called and the current user did not have access to some of the children of the specified node, then those child nodes would not be included in the returned `SiteMapNodeCollection`.

One point of confusion about the security trimming behavior that some developers run into is that they expect the `roles` attribute to be the exclusive definition of authorization information for their nodes. You can end up being surprised when you see nodes still being rendered in your UI even though your `roles` attributes would seem to indicate that a user should not be seeing a node. What is happening in this case is that the provider falls through the `roles` attribute check and continues to the file and URL authorization checks. And then one of these two authorization checks succeed.

One side effect of all of this processing is that the performance of iterating through a sitemap with security trimming turned on is substantially less than when it is turned off. Because file authorization and URL authorization were really intended for authorization checks for single page, they tend to be rather inefficient when a feature like Site Navigation comes along and starts asking for hundreds of authorization checks on a single page request. You can run a sitemap with 150-300 nodes in it with security trimming turned on, and other than increased CPU utilization you shouldn't see any effect on your application performance. However, if you plan to create a sitemap with thousands of nodes in it, the default security trimming behavior will probably be too expensive for your application.

Another issue you might run into when you turn on security trimming is that all of your navigation UI may suddenly disappear, depending on the kind of navigation structure you have in your `.sitemap`. If your structure has a root node that you don't ever intend to display (that is, you set up your `SiteMapDataSource` to skip this node), you still need to put a `roles="*"` attribute in the root node as shown here:

```xml
<?xml version="1.0" encoding="utf-8" ?>
<siteMap xmlns="http://schemas.microsoft.com/AspNet/SiteMap-File-1.0" >
    <siteMapNode title="hidden root" roles="*">
      <siteMapNode title="Administrator Pages" roles="Administrator">
        <siteMapNode url="ManageUsers.aspx" title="Manage Users"
                 roles="Administrator" />
        <siteMapNode url="ManageRoles.aspx" title="Manage Roles"
                 roles="Administrator" />
      </siteMapNode>
      <siteMapNode title="Regular Pages" roles="*">
        <siteMapNode url="http://www.microsoft.com" title="External link"
                 roles="*" />
        <siteMapNode url="Default.aspx" title="Home Page" roles="*" />
      </siteMapNode>
    </siteMapNode>
</siteMap>
```

Without the bolded "roles" definition, any attempt to render the full sitemap will result in no nodes being returned. Because the root node has no URL, the provider only has the roles attribute to go against for authorization information. As a result, if you leave out the roles attribute, the provider will think that no one is authorized to that node, and node traversal through the rest of the sitemap will stop.

If you want the XmlSiteMapProvider that ships with ASP.NET 2.0 and ASP.Net 3.5 to rely only on the information contained in the roles attribute, you can derive from the provider and implement custom logic in an override of the IsAccessibleToUser method.

C#

```
public class CustomAuthorization : XmlSiteMapProvider
{
    public override bool IsAccessibleToUser(HttpContext context, SiteMapNode node)
    {
        if (node == null)
        {
            throw new ArgumentNullException("You must specify a node.");
        }

        if (context == null)
        {
            throw new ArgumentNullException("The supplied context cannot be null");
        }

        if (!SecurityTrimmingEnabled)
        {
            return true;
        }

        if (node.Roles != null && node.Roles.Count > 0)
        {
            foreach (string role in node.Roles)
            {
                // Grant access if one of the roles is a "*".
                if (String.Equals(role, "*",
                    StringComparison.InvariantCultureIgnoreCase))
                {
                    return true;
                }
                else if (context.User != null && context.User.IsInRole(role))
                {
                    return true;
                }
            }
        }
        //If you make it this far, the user is not authorized
        return false;
    }
}
```

VB.NET

```
Public Class CustomAuthorization Inherits XmlSiteMapProvider
   Public Overrides Function IsAccessibleToUser( _
       ByVal context As HttpContext, _
       ByVal ByVal node As SiteMapNode) As Boolean
         If node Is Nothing Then
             Throw New ArgumentNullException("node")
         End If
         If context Is Nothing Then
             Throw New ArgumentNullException("context")
         End If
         If (Not SecurityTrimmingEnabled) Then
             Return True
         End If
         If node.Roles IsNot Nothing AndAlso node.Roles.Count > 0 Then
             For Each role As String In node.Roles
                 ' Grant access if one of the roles is a "*".
                 If String.Equals( role, "*", _
                 StringComparison.InvariantCultureIgnoreCase) Then
                     Return True
                 ElseIf context.User IsNot Nothing AndAlso_
                 context.User.IsInRole(role) Then
                     Return True
                 End If
             Next role
         End If

         'If you make it this far, the user is not authorized
         Return False
   End Function
End Class
```

This code mirrors the logic inside of `SiteMapProvider.IsAccessibleToUser`, but instead of attempting other checks at the end of the method, this custom provider looks only at the information in the `roles` attribute. If you use this custom provider in your site, you will see that now the `roles` attribute is the only thing controlling whether a `SiteMapNode` is returned to calling code. A nice performance benefit of this approach is that bypassing the file and URL authorization checks substantially increases the performance of security trimming. With the preceding code you could realistically accommodate a 1000 node sitemap.

This custom code brings up a very important security point though. Don't be fooled into thinking that security trimming with the previous custom code makes your site secure. The only thing the custom code does is to give you the ability to precisely control authorization of your sitemap information *independently* of the authorization rules you have defined either in `web.config` or through NTFS ACLs. Just because Site Navigation now hides nodes based exclusively on the sitemap's role information doesn't mean that your pages are secure. A user who knows the correct URL for a page can always attempt to access it by typing it into a browser. As a result, if you use an approach like the custom provider you must always ensure that you have still correctly secured your pages and directories with URL authorization and file authorization.

Summary

Since ASP.NET 1.0, page developers have benefited from the ability to hash and encrypt viewstate. You could also make viewstate information unique to a specific user with the `ViewStateUserKey` property. With the introduction of the viewstate encryption mode feature back in ASP.NET 2.0, control developers had the option of automatically turning on viewstate encryption when they know their controls store potentially sensitive data in viewstate.

When data is submitted to an ASP.NET page, all input should initially be considered untrusted. Although the majority of the work involved in scrubbing input data lies with the developer, ASP.NET does have some protections that work on your behalf. Since ASP.NET 1.1, the runtime validates form data, query-string values and cookie values for suspicious string sequences. Although this type of check is not exhaustive, it does cover the most likely forms of malicious input. Both ASP.NET 2.0 and ASP.NET include logic to protect against fraudulent postbacks. Because postbacks can be easily triggered with a few lines of JavaScript, it is possible to forge postback data to controls and events that were not rendered on the page. By default, ASP.NET 2.0 and ASP.NET 3.5 check for this situation and will not trigger server-side events for nonvisible or disabled controls and events that were never rendered on the client.

10

The Provider Model

Many of the features in both ASP.NET 2.0 and ASP.NET 3.5, including the Membership and Role Manager features, are built using the provider model. The provider model is not just an architectural model limited to ASP.NET 2.0 or ASP.NET 3.5 features; the base classes are available for you to build your own provider-based features.

This chapter covers the theory and intent behind the provider model so that you have a good idea of the patterns used by provider-based features. You will be introduced to the base provider classes, the services they provide, and the general assumptions around the ASP.NET provider model. Last, you will see some examples of how you can create your own custom feature using the provider model.

This chapter will cover the following topics:

- ❑ Why have providers?
- ❑ Patterns found in the Provider model.
- ❑ Core provider classes.
- ❑ Building a provider-based feature.

Why Have Providers?

Traditionally, when a software vendor creates a programming framework or a software platform, a good deal of the framework logic is baked into the actual binaries. If extensibility is required, then a product like an operating system incorporates a device driver model that allows third parties to extend it. For something like the .NET Framework, extensibility is usually accomplished by deriving from certain base classes and implementing the expected functionality.

The device driver model and the derivation model are two ends of the extensibility spectrum. With device drivers, higher-level functionality such as a word processor is insulated from the specifics of how abstract commands are actually carried out. Clearly, modern-day word processors are oblivious to the technical details of how any specific graphics card displays pixels or how any vendor's printer renders fonts.

Writing software that derives from base classes defined in a framework or software development kit (SDK) usually implies another piece of code that knows about the custom classes you're writing. For example, if you implement a custom collection class, somewhere else you have code that references the assembly containing your custom collection class and that code also contains explicit references to the custom collection class.

What happens though if you want to have the best of both worlds? How do you get the separation of functionality afforded by the device driver model, while still retaining the ability to write custom code that extends or replaces core functionality in the .NET Framework? The answer in both the 2.0 and 3.5 Frameworks is the provider model that both ASP.NET 2.0 and ASP.NET 3.5 rely heavily upon. The provider model allows you to swap custom logic into your application in much the same way you would install device drivers for a new graphics card. And you can swap in this custom logic in such a way that none of your existing code needs to be touched or recompiled.

Simultaneously, though, there are well-defined provider APIs that you can code against to create your own custom business logic and business rules. If you choose, you can write applications to take a direct dependency on your custom code but this is definitely not a requirement. Well-written providers can literally be transparently "snapped into" an application.

To accomplish this, both the 2.0 and 3.5 Framework include the same base classes and helper methods that provide the basic programming structure for the provider model. Specific features within the Frameworks extend these base classes and build feature-specific providers. To make this all a bit more concrete, you can use the Membership feature as a sort of canonical example of a provider-based feature.

The Membership feature, of course, deals with the problem of creating user credentials, managing these credentials, and verifying credentials provided by applications. When the Membership feature was first designed, a number of different design options were available:

❑   Write a set of Membership-related classes that contained all the business logic and data storage functionality as designed by the ASP.NET team. This option is the "black-box" option; you would end up with functional APIs, and zero extensibility.

❑   Keep the same set of classes from option 1, but add protected virtual methods and/or event-based extensibility hooks. This model would be more akin to the control development model in ASP.NET. With this model you start out with either an ASP.NET control or a third-party control, and through event hookups or derivations you modify the behavior of a control to better suit your needs.

❑   Separate the intent of the Membership feature from the actual business logic and data storage functionality necessary to get a functional Membership feature. This approach involves defining one set of classes that all developers can use, but having concrete implementations of other classes (the provider base classes) that contain very specific functionality. Along with this separation, the design requires the ability to swap out concrete provider implementations without impacting the common set of classes that all developers rely upon.

Now, of course, because this book isn't a mystery story, you know the outcome of these various design decisions. Both ASP.NET 2.0 and ASP.NET 3.5 went with the third option: providing a common set of

Membership classes for everyone to use, while compartmentalizing most of the business logic and data storage rules inside of various Membership providers.

It is pretty clear why you wouldn't want the first option. Creating useful APIs and great functionality inside of black boxes is nice until about 60 seconds after the first developer lays eyes on it and determines that for their needs they require some different logic. The second design option is actually not all that unreasonable. Clearly, ASP.NET developers are comfortable with the event-based extensibility that has been around since ASP.NET 1.0 (and for that matter all the way back to earlier versions of Visual Basic).

However, event-driven extensibility and protected virtual methods have the shortcoming that if an application wants different behavior than what is built into the Framework, then some other piece of code needs to be explicitly linked or referenced. For example, using the second design approach, what happens if you want to create users somewhere other than the default SQL Server schema that ships in both ASP.NET 2.0 and ASP.NET 3.5? If creating users raised some kind of event where you could create the actual `MembershipUser` in a back-end data store, you could hook this event and then return the new object, probably as a property on an event argument.

The shortcoming here is that now in every application where you want to use your custom data store you also need to include code that explicitly wires up the event hookups. If the extensibility mechanism used a protected virtual method instead, then each of your applications would need code that explicitly created the custom implementations of the various Membership classes. For both cases, you effectively have a compile-time dependency on your custom code. If you ever want to choose a different custom implementation of Membership, you have the hassle of recompiling each of your applications to reference the new code.

The third option, the provider-based design approach, breaks the compilation dependency. With the 2.0 and 3.5 Frameworks, you can write code against a common set of classes (that is, `Membership`, `MembershipUser`, and `MembershipUserCollection`). Nowhere in your code-base do you need a compile-time reference to your custom implementation of a `MembershipProvider`. If you wake up tomorrow and decide to throw out your custom `MembershipProvider`, there is no problem; you drop a different assembly onto your desktops or servers, tweak a configuration setting, and the rest of your applications continue to work. Sounds a lot like swapping out graphics cards and device drivers without the "excitement" that such upgrades usually entail.

Of course, the ability to tweak some settings in configuration requires that the Membership feature use some kind of dynamic type loading mechanism. Underneath the hood, this mechanism allows a feature to convert a configuration setting into a reference to a concrete provider class. And, of course, a dynamic type loading mechanism also requires at least a basic programming contract that defines the type signature that the Membership feature expects to dynamically load.

So, a provider-based feature, in short, has the following characteristics:

❑   A well-defined set of public APIs that most application code is expected to code against.

❑   A well-defined set of one or more interfaces or class definitions that define the extensible set of classes for the feature. In both the 2.0 and 3.5 Frameworks, these are the provider base classes.

❑   A configuration mechanism that can generically associate concrete provider implementations with each feature.

❑   A type-loading mechanism that can read configuration and create concrete instances of the providers to hand back to the feature APIs.

Matching up these characteristics, you can see that the Membership feature and the Framework have the following:

1. Public classes like `Membership` and `MembershipUser` that you write most of your code against.

2. A `MembershipProvider` class that defines the programming contract for all implementations of business logic and data storage for use with the Membership feature.

3. A provider configuration class that encapsulates the configuration information for any provider. This configuration class (`System.Configuration.ProviderSettings`), and the accompanying XML configuration syntax, is used by `MembershipProvider`(s) to declaratively define type information (among other things).

4. A `System.Web.Configuration.ProvidersHelper` class that acts as a class factory mechanism for returning instances of configured providers to any feature, including Membership.

Patterns Found in the Provider Model

If you have architected a fair number of applications, you invariably have come across design patterns, both theoretical ones that you considered when writing an application and the actual design patterns that you adopted in your application. The provider model in the .NET Framework is no different, with various pieces of the provider development stack mapping to well-known design patterns.

> For the classic guide to design patterns, pick up a copy of "Design Patterns: Elements of Reusable Object-Oriented Software" by the Gang of Four: Eric Gamma, Richard Helm, Ralph Johnson, and John Vlissides. Addison-Wesley ISBN: 0-201-63361-2.

The provider-based features in both ASP.NET 2.0 and ASP.NET 3.5 are implementations of the following well-known design patterns:

❑ Strategy
❑ Factory Method
❑ Singleton
❑ Façade

Of the four common design patterns, the Strategy pattern is the core design concept that really makes the provider model so powerful.

The Strategy Pattern

In a nutshell, the Strategy design pattern is a design approach that encapsulates important pieces of a feature's functionality in a manner that allows the functionality to be swapped out with different implementations. A Strategy design approach allows a feature to define a public-facing definition of common functionality, while abstracting away the nitty-gritty of the implementation details that underlie the common functionality.

If you were to design your own feature using the Strategy pattern, you would probably find that the dividing line between a public API and a specific implementation to be somewhat fuzzy. Strategy-based approaches work best when there is a common set of well-defined functionality that you expect most developers will need. However, you also need to be able to implement that functionality in a way that can be reasonably separated from the public API; otherwise you can't engineer the ability to swap out the lower layers of the feature.

For example, say that you wanted to implement a class that could be used to balance your checkbook. The general operations you perform against a checkbook are well understood: debit, credit, reconcile balances, and so on. However, the way in which you store the checkbook information is all over the map: You could store your checkbook in Excel, in a commercially available financial package, and so forth. So, the checkbook design is one where you could define a public checkbook API for developers to consume, while still allowing developers the freedom to swap in different storage mechanisms for different data stores. With this approach you would have a Strategy-based design for storing checkbook data.

However, if you take the checkbook example a bit further, what happens to the non-storage-related operations for the checkbook? The debit and credit operations involve a few steps: loading/storing data using a configurable data store and carrying out accounting computations against that data. Does it make sense for the accounting operations to be swapped out? Are there really multiple ways to add and subtract values in a checkbook ledger?

It is this kind of design decision where the Strategy approach gets a bit murky. Realistically, you could argue this decision either way. On one hand, for a consumer application that has a checkbook, it would probably be overkill to abstract the computations via the Strategy pattern. On the other hand, if you were authoring an enterprise resource planning (ERP) package, and you needed to accommodate different accounting rules for various businesses and even different countries, then creating a configurable accounting engine would make sense.

If you take a closer look at how some of the provider-based features in both the 2.0 and 3.5 Frameworks approached these decisions, you will see different degrees of business logic configurability with the Strategy pattern:

- ❑ **Membership:** Both the data storage and the business logic are abstracted into the provider layer. Provider authors are responsible for data storage related tasks and the core business logic that makes the Membership feature work. For example, if you choose to implement self-service password resets, your provider not only has to deal with the data storage necessary to support this feature; it is up to you to write the logic that handles things like a customer entering too many wrong password answers. Although the class definitions in Membership *suggest* how you should go about implementing this kind of logic, as a provider author you have a large amount of leeway in terms of implementing business logic in your providers.

- ❑ **Role Manager:** As with Membership, both data storage and business logic are the responsibility of the providers. However, the Role Manager API is simple enough that for all practical purposes Role Manager providers are primarily data storage engines.

- ❑ **Profile:** The providers for the Profile feature deal only with data storage and serialization. However, because the Profile feature is essentially a programming abstraction for exposing data in a consistent manner without forcing the page developer to wrestle with different back-end data stores, the data-centric nature of Profile providers is expected. The only real "logic" that a provider implementer would normally deal with is around caching and mapping from a property on a customer's profile to a specific piece of data in some back-end system.

- ❑ **Web Parts Personalization:** Personalization providers can actually come in two flavors: providers that only implement data storage against a different back-end, and providers that fundamentally change the way in which web parts personalization works (that is, changing the "business logic" of web parts). However, writing a personalization provider that changes the core logic of web parts is a nontrivial undertaking to say the least, so the most likely personalization providers will be ones that work against data stores other than SQL Server. If you take a look at the nonabstract virtual methods on the `PersonalizationProvider` base class, you will see methods that deal with web parts security as well as the logic of how web parts work as opposed to just the data storage aspect of web parts.

❏   **Site Navigation:** Along the same lines as web parts, the providers in Site Navigation can either be data-centric, or they can also alter the core logic of the Site Navigation feature. On one hand, if you author a provider that derives from `StaticSiteMapProvider`, then most of the logic around traversing navigation data is already handled for you. You are left to implement one abstract method that is responsible for loading navigation data and converting it into a structure that can be consumed by the `StaticSiteMapProvider`. On the other hand, if you derive directly from `SiteMapProvider`, then you not only handle data-storage-related tasks, you can also be very creative in terms of how you handle the logic for traversing site navigation data (that is, use XPath queries, use a custom in-memory graph structure, and so on) as well as the security of individual `SiteMapNode` instances.

❏   **Health Monitoring:** Because the nature of the Health Monitoring feature (also referred to as Web Events) is to store diagnostic data, providers written for this feature only deal with data storage. Although storing data when a high volume of diagnostic events are being generated can require some very creative approaches, at the end of the day a Health Monitoring provider is just a pipe for storing or forwarding diagnostic information.

❏   **Session:** Session state is a bit of a hybrid when it comes to the provider layer. Session state providers of course have to deal with loading and storing data. However, the providers are also responsible for handling some of the logic in session state around concurrent access to session data. Additionally, you may write a custom session state provider to work in conjunction with custom session ID generators and custom partition information, in which case a bit more of the logic for session state is also in your hands. However, even in this case, 90 percent of the purpose of a session state provider revolves around data storage as opposed to session state logic. Most of the real logic around session state is bound up inside of the `SessionStateModule`.

From the previous brief overview of various provider-based features in both ASP.NET 2.0 and ASP.NET 3.5, you can see that all the providers' abstract away data storage details from developers who use a feature. To varying degrees, some of the providers also abstract away the core logic of the feature.

Factory Method

The Strategy pattern would not be very useful in the 2.0 and 3.5 Frameworks if you did not have a way to easily swap out different providers when using different features. Because the Strategy pattern is inherently about making it easy to choose different implementations of a feature, the Factory Method pattern is a logical adjunct to it. The idea behind the Factory Method is to separate the creation of certain classes from the feature that consumes those classes. As long as classes implement a common interface, or derive from a common class, a feature can encapsulate class creation using a generic mechanism that does not require any hard compile-time dependencies.

In other words, a feature that makes use of the Factory Method pattern does not hard-code references to concrete types. Instead a feature references classes via interfaces or base class references, and defers the actual creation of concrete implementations to some other piece of code. Of course, the magic of the

Factory Method lies within this "other code," and that leads to the question of how can you actually write something that generically creates types without hard-coding the type definition at compile time?

Luckily for us, both the 2.0 and 3.5 Frameworks include excellent support for reflection, which in turn makes it trivial to take a string definition of a type and convert it into an actual class. Hence, there is no need for a compile-time dependency on a concrete type. Following along this design approach, both the 2.0 and 3.5 Frameworks also have an extensive configuration system that makes it a pretty convenient place to store information such as string-ized type references. So, the combination of (configuration + reflection) is what enables both the 2.0 and 3.5 Frameworks to make use of the Factory Method pattern for its provider-based features.

If you use any of the existing provider-based features, the Factory Method implementation is transparent to you. For example, if you use the Membership feature, you just configure one or more providers as follows:

```
<membership defaultProvider="AccessMembershipProvider">
  <providers>
        <add name="AccessMembershipProvider"
             type="Samples.AccessMembershipProvider, SampleAccessProviders"
             … />
        <add name="AnotherProvider"
             type="SomeOtherNamespace.SomeOtherProvider, AnotherAssembly"
             … />
  </providers>
</membership>
```

Then at runtime, all the configured providers are automatically available for you to use with the Membership feature. Underneath the hood, the Membership feature uses a helper class (that is, a generic class factory) to instantiate each provider and hook it up to the feature.

The 2.0 and 3.5 Frameworks class that contains the logic for creating arbitrary providers is System.Web .Configuration.ProvidersHelper. It exposes two static helper methods (InstantiateProvider and InstantiateProviders) that you can use when creating your own provider based features. As you would expect, InstantiateProviders is just a helpful wrapper method for creating one or more providers; internally, it just iterates over the information passed to it and calls InstantiateProvider multiple times.

The method signature for InstantiateProviders is:

C#

```
public static void InstantiateProviders(
    ProviderSettingsCollection configProviders,
    ProviderCollection providers,
    Type providerType)
```

VB.NET

```
Public Shared Sub InstantiateProviders( _
    ByVal configProviders As providerSettingsCollection, _
    ByVal providers As ProviderCollection, _
    ByVal providerType As Type)
```

Let's take a closer look at what each of these parameters represents and how each parameter maps to a provider configuration section such as the one used for the Membership feature. The first parameter accepts a collection containing one or more instances of `System.Configuration.ProviderSettings`. A `ProviderSettings` instance is a strongly typed representation of the configuration for a single provider, although because any feature can define and use an arbitrary set of providers, the actual "strong" representation is only relevant to the common configuration information you would expect to find for any provider regardless of its associated feature.

The public properties that are available from a `ProviderSettings` instance are `Name` and `Type` (both `Strings`) as well as the `Parameters` property, which is a `NameValueCollection`. If you use the abbreviated Membership provider with the following definition:

```
<providers>
  <add name="AccessMembershipProvider"
       type="Samples.AccessMembershipProvider, SampleAccessProviders"
       connectionStringName = "some connection string"
       enablePasswordRetrieval = "false"
    … />
</providers>
```

You can see that the `name` and `type` configuration attributes on a provider's `<add/>` element are what map to the `Name` and `Type` properties on an instance of `ProviderSettings`. All the other configuration attributes are lumped into the `Parameters NameValueCollection` containing key-value pairs. It is up to the individual 2.0 and 3.5 Frameworks features to perform further processing on these key-value pairs. This is the underlying reason why most of the validation of a provider's configuration needs to be baked into each individual provider as opposed to having the smarts in the configuration class (more on this design aspect a bit later in the chapter). If you take a look at the various provider-based features in both ASP.NET 2.0 and ASP.NET 3.5, you will see that each feature's configuration classes deal with providers using the rather generic `ProviderSettings` class. For example there is no such thing currently as a "MembershipProviderSettings" versus a "RoleManagerProviderSettings" class.

The second parameter to `ProvidersHelper.InstantiateProviders` is a `ProviderCollection`. The caller to this method is responsible for creating an empty instance of a `ProviderCollection`. The `ProvidersHelper` class will populate the collection with one or more providers. Because every provider in both ASP.NET 2.0 and ASP.NET 3.5 ultimately derives from a common base class (`System.Configuration.ProviderBase`), the `ProvidersHelper` class is able to deal with any arbitrary provider type in a generic manner.

The last parameter to the `InstantiateProviders` method is a `Type` object. A provider-based feature passes in a `Type` object that represents the base provider type required by that feature. For example, when the Membership feature needs to create all its configured providers, it will pass "typeof(MembershipProvider)" as the value for this parameter. The resulting `Type` reference is used by the `ProvidersHelper` class to verify that the provider type being instantiated (remember this is defined by the `Type` property on a `ProviderSettings` instance) actually derives from the type passed in the third parameter. This allows some basic validation to occur at provider instantiation time and prevents problems such as accidentally instantiating a `RoleProvider`-derived class for the Membership feature.

As noted a little earlier, `ProvidersHelper.InstantiateProviders` is just a convenient way to convert a set of provider configuration information into multiple provider instances. If for some reason you had a provider-based feature that only supported a single provider, you could instead call `ProvidersHelper.InstantiateProvider` directly. The method signature is:

C#

```
public static ProviderBase InstantiateProvider(
    ProviderSettings providerSettings,
    Type providerType)
```

VB.NET

```
Public Shared Function InstantiateProvider( _
    ByVal providerSettings As ProviderSettings, _
    ByVal providerType As Type) As ProviderBase
```

As you can see, the parameters closely mirror the parameters for `InstantiateProviders`, but just for a single provider. Internally, this method performs a few basic tasks to create a concrete provider type:

1. A `Type` object representing the provider type as defined in the "type" configuration attribute is obtained.

2. The helper validates that the `Type` from step 1 is actually compatible with the `providerType` information that was passed to `InstantiateProvider`. This ensures that the loose type definition obtained from configuration (represented by `ProviderSettings.Type`) has been successfully translated to a type definition that is compatible with the feature that is calling `ProvidersHelper`.

3. Using the `System.Activator` class, the helper creates a concrete instance of the desired provider.

4. With the concrete instance in hand, the helper passes the configuration attributes on `ProviderSettings.Parameters` to the provider's `Initialize` method. This is covered in the "Core Provider Classes" section later in this chapter, but the `ProviderBase` class defines a common `Initialize` method that must be called for a concrete provider to bootstrap itself. Without the call to `Initialize`, an instance of any given provider is sort of in a zombie-like state: It exists but doesn't have any of the information necessary for it to function.

5. After the provider successfully initializes itself, the helper method returns the provider instance as a reference to the base type: `ProviderBase`. It is up to the calling code or feature to then cast the `ProviderBase` reference back to the base type used by the feature. However, because the helper method already validated that the `ProviderSettings.Type` was compatible with a feature's expected type, by this point the feature has the assurance that its type-cast will succeed.

To see all this working, the following sample code shows a simple example of manually creating a `ProviderSettings` instance and then using it to create an instance of the `SqlMembershipProvider`.

C#

```
using System;
using System.Configuration;
using System.Configuration.Provider;
using System.Web.Security;
using System.Web.Configuration;
namespace CreateMembershipProvider1
{
  class Program
  {
    static void Main(string[] args)
    {
```

```
     ProviderSettings ps = new ProviderSettings(
       "ManuallyCreated",
       "System.Web.Security.SqlMembershipProvider, System.Web,
       Version=2.0.0.0, Culture=neutral, PublicKeyToken=b03f5f7f11d50a3a");

     //Can add one or more provider-specific configuration attributes here
     ps.Parameters.Add("connectionStringName", "LocalSqlServer");

     //This is the expected base type of the provider instance
     Type t = typeof(MembershipProvider);

     //Use the helper class to instantiate the provider
     ProviderBase pb = ProvidersHelper.InstantiateProvider(ps, t);

     //At this point you can safely cast to either the explicit provider
     //type, or to MembershipProvider
     SqlMembershipProvider smp = (SqlMembershipProvider)pb;

     //Do something with the provider - though for other reasons this
     //won't work!
     MembershipCreateStatus status;
     smp.CreateUser("delete_this_user", "pass^word", "some@where.org",
       "question", "answer", false, null, out status);
   }
  }
}
```

VB.NET

```
Imports System
Imports System.Configuration
Imports System.Configuration.Provider
Imports System.Web.Security
Imports System.Web.Configuration

Namespace CreateMembershipProvider1
    Friend Class Program
        Shared Sub Main(ByVal args() As String)
            Dim ps As New ProviderSettings("ManuallyCreated", _
            "System.Web.Security.SqlMembershipProvider, System.Web, Version=2.0.0.0, _
            Culture=neutral, PublicKeyToken=b03f5f7f11d50a3a")

            'Can add one or more provider-specific configuration attributes here
            ps.Parameters.Add("connectionStringName", "LocalSqlServer")

            'This is the expected base type of the provider instance
            Dim t As Type = GetType(MembershipProvider)

            'Use the helper class to instantiate the provider
            Dim pb As ProviderBase = ProvidersHelper.InstantiateProvider(ps, t)

            'At this point you can safely cast to either the explicit provider
            'type, or to MembershipProvider
            Dim smp As SqlMembershipProvider = CType(pb, SqlMembershipProvider)
```

```
            'Do something with the provider - though for other reasons this
            'won't work!
            Dim status As MembershipCreateStatus
            smp.CreateUser("delete_this_user", _
            "pass^word", _
            "some@where.org", _
            "question", _
            "answer", _
            False, _
            Nothing, _
            status)
        End Sub
    End Class
End Namespace
```

This sample console application shows you roughly the same steps that the Membership feature follows when it creates the membership providers that you define in configuration. The `ProviderSettings` class that is created contains the "name" and "type" values that you use when configuring Membership providers. The sample code then adds a provider-specific configuration attribute—in this case, the `connectionStringName` attribute that references a connection string defined somewhere in the `<connectionStrings />` configuration section. Although that is the only attribute defined in this sample, you could add as many provider-specific configuration attributes as needed at this point.

`ProvidersHelper.InstantiateProvider` is called, passing in the `Type` object for `MembershipProvider` because the expectation is that the string value for the type parameter used earlier in the sample will actually resolve to a provider that derives from `MembershipProvider`. If you run this code in a debugger, you can successfully cast the return value from `InstantiateProvider` to a `SqlMembershipProvider`. However, as a result of the way many provider-based features work in both ASP.NET 2.0 and ASP.NET 3.5, attempting to subsequently call `CreateUser` on the returned provider instance will fail.

This happens because most provider-based features expect to operate in the larger context of their associated feature. As part of this assumption, there is the expectation that any individual provider can reference the `ProvidersCollection` associated with a feature. Because this sample code is creating a provider in a vacuum, when the `CreateUser` method eventually leads to some internal Membership validation, you will get an error to the effect that the provider you just created does not actually exist. When you use any of the provider-based features in both ASP.NET 2.0 and ASP.NET 3.5, though, you will not run into this issue because the various features are responsible for instantiating providers and, thus, will maintain a `ProvidersCollection` with references to all the feature providers defined in configuration.

As a second example, you can extend the sample code to instantiate multiple providers by using `ProvidersHelper.InstantiateProviders`. Instantiating multiple providers, and storing the resultant collection is the process that most ASP.NET 2.0 and ASP.NET 3.5 provider-based features follow:

C#

```
static void Main(string[] args)
{
    ProviderSettings ps = new ProviderSettings("ManuallyCreated_1",
        "System.Web.Security.SqlMembershipProvider, System.Web,
        Version=2.0.0.0, Culture=neutral, PublicKeyToken=b03f5f7f11d50a3a");
```

```
    //Add multiple provider-specific configuration attributes here
    ps.Parameters.Add("connectionStringName", "LocalSqlServer");
    ps.Parameters.Add("requiresQuestionAndAnswer", "false");

    //Create another ProviderSettings instance for a second provider
    ProviderSettings ps2 = new ProviderSettings("ManuallyCreated_2",
      "System.Web.Security.SqlMembershipProvider, System.Web,
      Version=2.0.0.0, Culture=neutral, PublicKeyToken=b03f5f7f11d50a3a");
    ps2.Parameters.Add("connectionStringName", "LocalSqlServer");
    ps2.Parameters.Add("requiresQuestionAndAnswer", "true");

    Type t = typeof(MembershipProvider);

    //Need a collection since in this case you are getting multiple
    //providers back from the helper class
    ProviderSettingsCollection psc = new ProviderSettingsCollection();
    psc.Add(ps);
    psc.Add(ps2);

    //Call the helper class to spin up each provider
    MembershipProviderCollection mp = new MembershipProviderCollection();
    ProvidersHelper.InstantiateProviders(psc, mp, t);

    //Get a reference to one of the multiple providers that was instantiated
    SqlMembershipProvider smp2 = (SqlMembershipProvider)mp["ManuallyCreated_2"];
}
```

VB.NET

```
Shared Sub Main(ByVal args() As String)
  Dim ps As New ProviderSettings("ManuallyCreated_1", "System.Web.Security.
  SqlMembershipProvider, System.Web, Version=2.0.0.0, _
  Culture=neutral, PublicKeyToken=b03f5f7f11d50a3a")

  'Add multiple provider-specific configuration attributes here
  ps.Parameters.Add("connectionStringName", "LocalSqlServer")
  ps.Parameters.Add("requiresQuestionAndAnswer", "false")

  'Create another ProviderSettings instance for a second provider
  Dim ps2 As New ProviderSettings("ManuallyCreated_2", "System.Web.Security.
  SqlMembershipProvider, System.Web, Version=2.0.0.0, _
  Culture=neutral, PublicKeyToken=b03f5f7f11d50a3a")
  ps2.Parameters.Add("connectionStringName", "LocalSqlServer")
  ps2.Parameters.Add("requiresQuestionAndAnswer", "true")

  Dim t As Type = GetType(MembershipProvider)

  'Need a collection since in this case you are getting multiple
  'providers back from the helper class
  Dim psc As New ProviderSettingsCollection()
  psc.Add(ps)
  psc.Add(ps2)
```

```
    'Call the helper class to spin up each provider
    Dim mp As New MembershipProviderCollection()
    ProvidersHelper.InstantiateProviders(psc, mp, t)

    'Get a reference to one of the multiple providers that was instantiated
    Dim smp2 As SqlMembershipProvider = CType(mp("ManuallyCreated_2"), _
    SqlMembershipProvider)
End Sub
```

In the second sample, the call to `InstantiateProviders` requires an empty `ProviderCollection`. The helper class creates and initializes each provider in turn and then places a reference to each provider inside of the supplied `ProviderCollection` object.

If you were to look inside of the code for a static feature class like `Membership`, you would see that it actually uses a derived version of `ProviderCollection` called `MembershipProviderCollection`. Additionally, if you look at a static feature class like `Membership`, you now understand where the value for the `Providers` property comes from. Once `Membership` completes its call to `ProvidersHelper` factory method, the `MembershipProviderCollection` instance becomes the return value for the `Membership.Providers` property.

The Singleton Pattern

The Singleton Pattern is used when a developer wants a single instance of class to exist within an application. Rather than the standard object-oriented approach of creating objects and destroying them after use, the Singleton Pattern results in a single object instance being used for the duration of an application's lifetime. Frequently, the Singleton Pattern is used when object instantiation and destruction of a class is very expensive, and hence you may only want one instance of the class to ever incur the overhead of object construction. The Singleton Pattern is also used when you want to mediate access to a specific resource with a single object instance gating access to the resource, it is possible to implement synchronization logic within the object instance so that only a single active thread can access the resource at a time.

ASP.NET 2.0 and ASP.NET 3.5 use the Singleton Pattern for all the providers that are instantiated by its provider-based features. However, both ASP.NET 2.0 and ASP.NET 3.5 do not require that individual providers be instantiated via a Singleton Pattern. In reality, nothing prevents you from using the `ProvidersHelper` (as shown in the previous section) or from manually creating and initializing a provider yourself. As you saw in the Membership provider example, if you step outside the boundaries of the feature's initialization behavior you will probably run into exceptions down the road.

A more precise statement would be that the provider-based features in ASP.NET implicitly use the Singleton Pattern as long as you interact with providers by way of the various feature classes (that is, `Membership`, `ProfileCommon`, `Roles`, and so on). Features will use the `ProvidersHelper` class to create and initialize one, and only one, instance of each configured provider. For the duration of the application's lifetime the providers stay in memory and are used whenever you write code that makes use of the feature. The ASP.NET 2.0 and ASP.NET 3.5 features do not `new()` up providers on each and every page request.

From your perspective as a provider implementer, this means your providers need to be structured to allow multiple concurrent callers in any of the public methods. If your providers internally have any shared state, and if you intend to modify that state inside of a method, it is up to you to synchronize access to that state. The use of the Singleton Pattern suggests the following best practices on your custom providers:

❑ If at all possible, common provider states should be initialized in the provider's `Initialize` method. For provider instances being initialized by a feature, you are guaranteed that one and only one thread of execution will ever call into the `Initialize` method. The feature classes internally serialize access during feature initialization. This means that you can safely create and set internal state in a provider's `Initialize` method without having to synchronize access to it at this point.

❑ You should not call back into a feature from inside of the `Initialize` method. For example, in a custom `Membership` provider, you should not create instances of `MembershipUser` or call into the static `Membership` class. These types of operations will usually cause a feature to attempt to initialize itself a second time, which in turn triggers initialization of your custom provider a second time. At which point you have a second instance of your provider that attempts to call back into the feature, and you end up in an infinite loop of initialization.

❑ If your provider needs to initialize some type of shared state, and if this initialization requires calling other methods in the feature, you need to separate this logic into internal methods that are "lazily" called. This means sometime after the provider is initialized, when any of its public methods are called, you need to check to see whether this secondary initialization has occurred; if it hasn't, you need to take some kind of lock and then perform the secondary initialization. This is the approach used by the `XmlSiteMapProvider` when it loads its navigation data from an XML file. The actual parsing of the XML file occurs after the provider has been initialized when a public method is first called. Internally the `XmlSiteMapProvider` serializes the initialization process to ensure that if multiple threads are calling into the provider, the secondary initialization occurs once and only once.

❑ Public instance methods on the provider should be as stateless as possible. If your custom provider needs only to read some shared state (for example, a connection string loaded earlier during Initialize), you won't need to worry about thread-safety issues. You can just write the code in each instance method without introducing any synchronization code. Writing to shared state should be avoided if at all possible, because providers must expect to have multiple concurrent requests flowing through their methods at any point in time. If for some reason a provider needs to write to shared state, it will be less performant because of the need to use some type of locking to ensure thread-safe operations. As an aside, most of the ASP.NET 2.0 and ASP.NET 3.5 providers do *not* have any type of synchronization logic in their methods. For example, the public instance methods on `SqlMembershipProvider` never need to lock anything because the only shared state used by the `SqlMembershipProvider` is read-only configuration data that was passed during the call to `Initialize`.

Façade

A Façade is a design approach for wrapping complex details from multiple subsystems with an easy-to-use class or programming interface. Another way to look at the Façade Pattern is as a "good enough" API that exposes the most common functionality needed by a developer without requiring developers to wade through complex implementations of underlying classes. You could argue that any layered API is effectively a Façade with each layer of a programming API providing an easier interface to the next level down.

In both ASP.NET 2.0 and ASP.NET 3.5, the Façade pattern is evidenced by various entry-point classes that are closely associated with the related feature. The use of these entry points eliminates the need for many developers to ever interact directly with individual providers. In other cases, the entry-point classes hide the complexities involved when mediating the flow of data between providers and other classes that manipulate data. The general application of the Façade pattern is listed here for a number of the ASP.NET 2.0 and ASP.NET 3.5 features:

❏ **Membership:** The static `Membership` class is the main entry point into the feature. Developing against this class allows you to use the feature without using a `MembershipProvider` directly. Internally, the class automatically handles initialization of the feature on your behalf. It also exposes many static methods that provide multiple options for creating and modifying data; internally the `Membership` class maps these methods to the appropriate provider methods. For example, there is only one `CreateUser` method defined on `MembershipProvider`, but the static `Membership` class provides four different `CreateUser` methods that cover the common ways to create users. Internally, the static `Membership` class "fills in the blanks" when it calls the provider.

❏ **Role Manager:** The static `Roles` class is the main feature entry point. As with the Membership feature, the `Roles` class automatically initializes the configured providers for you. It also exposes a number of overloads for adding and deleting users to and from roles that are a bit easier to use than the more generic method definitions on `RoleProvider`.

❏ **Profile:** The Profile feature actually has two main entry points. For administrative functionality, the static `ProfileManager` class is used; it performs the same functionality as described for Membership and Role Manager. However, the more common entry point for most developers is the `ProfileCommon` class that is auto-generated by the ASP.NET compiler at runtime (available from `Page.Profile`). This class derives from `ProfileBase`. The net result of these two classes is that as a developer you have an easy-to-use strongly typed object available from the `Profile` property on a `Page` class. However, underneath the hood, this object hides all the complexities of hooking up providers to properties, serializing and deserializing data, as well as the intricacies of triggering the loads and saves of individual property data. More than any other provider-based feature, the Profile feature is a great example of the Façade pattern. The more you delve into what actually makes the Profile feature tick, the more you realize the large amount of functionality that is all tucked away behind the `Profile` property on the `Page` class.

❏ **Web Parts Personalization:** Like Membership and Role Manager, Personalization has a static management class called `PersonalizationAdministration` that acts as a façade for the more generic methods defined on `PersonalizationProvider`. The `WebPartsPersonalization` class acts as a runtime façade for the `WebPartManager`. While a `WebPartManager` drives the page lifecycle for web parts, it uses the API defined on `WebPartsPersonalization` for data-related tasks including loading and storing data as well as extracting and applying personalization data. You can swap out different pieces of personalization functionality both in `WebPartsPersonalization` and lower down in the provider layer, yet the `WebPartManager` is unaware of such changes because it interacts only with a `WebPartPersonalization` instance.

❏ **Site Navigation:** The static `SiteMap` class acts as the main entry point for this feature. It will automatically initialize configured providers on your behalf. In this sense, it is a weak façade implementation because you typically call `SiteMap.CurrentNode`, after which you start working with `SiteMapNode` and `SiteMapProvider` instances directly.

❏ **Session:** You interact with the Session feature through an instance of `HttpSessionState`, usually through the `Session` property on the current context or on a page. From your point of view the Session State feature is basically a dictionary where you can add and remove objects. However, the `HttpSessionState` object and the associated `SessionStateModule` hide the large amount of complexity involved in managing session. Tasks such as serialization/deserialization, managing session concurrency, and managing session setup and expiration all happen automatically with the complexities hidden from view.

Core Provider Classes

You have seen a number of the different support classes that are common to providers. In this section, you walk through each of the core classes so that you can see in one place the different provider-related classes.

System.Configuration.Provider Classes

The core provider classes that define the base functionality for a provider are found in the `System.Configuration.Provider` namespace. These classes are available for use both in ASP.NET and non-ASP.NET applications.

ProviderBase

Of course, the most important provider class is the base class from which most providers derive: `System.Configuration.Provider.ProviderBase`. The class signature is:

C#

```
public abstract class ProviderBase {

        public virtual string Name { get };
        public virtual string Description {get };

        public virtual void Initialize(string name, NameValueCollection config);
    }
```

VB.NET

```
Public MustInherit Class ProviderBase

    Public Overridable ReadOnly Property Description As String
    Public Overridable ReadOnly Property Name As String

    Public Overridable Sub Initialize( _
    ByVal name As String, _
    ByVal config As NameValueCollection)

End Class
```

Feature-specific provider definitions derive from `ProviderBase`, and as a developer you write custom providers that in turn derive from a feature's provider base class definition. It is unlikely that you would ever author a provider that directly derives from `ProviderBase` because `ProviderBase` exposes very little functionality.

`ProviderBase` is abstract because that forces you to derive from it and it also would make little sense to `new()` up `ProviderBase`. However, the functionality that is available on `ProviderBase` is all virtual because `ProviderBase` does supply basic functionality common to all providers. If you have looked at the configuration sections for both ASP.NET 2.0 and ASP.NET 3.5 provider-based features you notice that "name" and "type" are always present. Although it is not immediately obvious, all ASP.NET providers also have a configurable "description" attribute as well.

The type attribute is not exposed by ProviderBase, because by the time you have a concrete provider in hand, you know its type. However, the "name" and "description" attributes are available on ProviderBase. The read-only Name property is important because this is how you index into provider collections for various features that support defining multiple providers. The read-only Description property is mainly intended for administrative applications where you may want to see a list of the providers currently configured for an application.

By default, the ASP.NET providers contain localized resource strings for the descriptions. This means that if you query the Description property in a French application, you get back French text for each provider description; while in an English application you get back an English description. However, if you explicitly configure the "description" attribute in your web.config, providers always return the configuration value from the Description property, regardless of locale. The default implementation of ProviderBase.Description returns the Name property if for some reason a provider implementer forgot to explicitly initialize the description.

The most important method on ProviderBase is Initialize. Normally, this method is called during a feature's initialization. As described earlier in the section on the Factory Method pattern, static feature classes use the ProvidersHelper class to call Initialize on each configured provider. The name parameter is the value of the name attribute from configuration, while the config parameter is the Parameters property from the ProviderSettings configuration class: the list of name-value pairs from the <add /> provider element without "name" and "type."

The default implementation of Initialize performs the following work on your behalf:

1. The method checks to see whether the provider has been initialized before. If the provider has already been initialized, it throws an exception. This means that provider implementers should always call base.Initialize to gain protection against double-initialization.

2. The name parameter is stored internally and is thus available from the Name property.

3. If a key called "description" is available in the NameValueCollection passed via the config parameter, the value is stored internally and thus is available from the Description property. Note that if the "description" key is found, it is removed from the NameValueCollection and is no longer available from the collection when control passes back to the provider.

The general approach provider implementers should take when using ProviderBase.Initialize is:

1. If a "description" attribute is not available from configuration, add a key called "description" to the NameValueCollection that is passed to Initialize. For the value you can follow ASP.NET's approach and insert a localized value, or for simplicity you can add a hard-coded description of the provider.

2. Immediately after any logic for "description," make a call to base.Initialize. This protects against double-initialization before your provider does anything substantial.

3. After the call to base.Initialize, your provider should carry out feature-specific initialization tasks.

ProviderException

Sometimes when an error occurs within a provider, the built-in 2.0 and 3.5 Frameworks' exception classes don't have anything that maps nicely to the problem. Furthermore, you may not want to create a plethora of custom exception classes for comparatively rare or obscure error conditions. The

`System.Configuration.Provider.ProviderException` class is intended as a convenient exception class for these cases. For example, the Membership providers throw a `ProviderException` if the password format is incorrect. Rather than creating a "PasswordFormatException" that would rarely occur, a `ProviderException` was used.

Realistically, whether you use `ProviderException` is more of a philosophical decision. The ASP.NET team didn't want to spam the `System.Web` namespace with dozens of exception classes for one-off or rare error conditions. However, there is nothing wrong if you disagree with that approach and instead create a rich and detailed set of exceptions for your applications.

The class signature for `ProviderException` is very simple. It just derives from `System.Exception`:

C#

```
[Serializable]
public class ProviderException : Exception
{
        public ProviderException();

        public ProviderException( string message );

        public ProviderException( string message, Exception innerException );

        protected ProviderException( SerializationInfo info,
                                     StreamingContext context );
}
```

VB.NET

```
<Serializable> _
Public Class ProviderException
    Inherits Exception

    Public Sub New()

    Public Sub New(ByVal message As String)

    Protected Sub New(ByVal info As SerializationInfo, _
                    ByVal context As StreamingContext)

    Public Sub New(ByVal message As String, ByVal innerException As Exception)

End Class
```

There is no custom logic inside of `ProviderException`. Each of the nondefault constructor overloads simply calls the base constructor implementations in `Exception`.

ProviderCollection

As you saw in the Factory Method section, provider-based features usually deal with multiple providers. The approach used by various features is to have a feature-specific provider collection that in turn derives from `System.Configuration.Provider.ProviderCollection`. The `ProvidersHelper` class can then work with the common `ProviderCollection` class, while individual features can expose strongly typed collection classes. From a configuration standpoint, all the `<add />` provider elements in your web.config eventually end up as concrete providers that can be referenced from a ProviderCollection-derived class.

For example, in the Membership feature the Membership.Providers property returns a reference to a MembershipProviderCollection containing a reference to every provider defined within the <membership /> configuration section. The advantage to working with MembershipProvider Collection as opposed to ProviderCollection is that you know any provider returned from the collection indexer derives from MembershipProvider. The collection also validates that any providers added to it derives from MembershipProvider.

The definition for ProviderCollection is simple, and it exposes the common collection-based functionality you would expect:

C#

```csharp
public class ProviderCollection : IEnumerable, ICollection
{
        public ProviderCollection();

        public virtual void Add(ProviderBase provider);
        public void Remove(string name);

        public ProviderBase this[string name] { get };

        public IEnumerator GetEnumerator();

        public void SetReadOnly();
        public void Clear();

        public int       Count          { get };
        public bool      IsSynchronized { get };
        public object    SyncRoot       { get };

        public void      CopyTo(ProviderBase[] array, int index);
        void ICollection.CopyTo(Array array, int index);

}
```

VB.NET

```vbnet
<DefaultMember("Item")> _
Public Class ProviderCollection
    Implements ICollection, IEnumerable

    Public Sub New()

    Public Overridable Sub Add(ByVal provider As ProviderBase)
    Public Sub Remove(ByVal name As String)

    Public ReadOnly Default Property Item(ByVal name As String) As ProviderBase

    Public Function GetEnumerator() As IEnumerator

    Public Sub SetReadOnly()
```

```
        Public Sub Clear()

        Public ReadOnly Property Count As Integer
        Public ReadOnly Property IsSynchronized As Boolean
        Public ReadOnly Property SyncRoot As Object

        Public Sub CopyTo(ByVal array As ProviderBase(), ByVal index As Integer)
        Private Sub System.Collections.ICollection.CopyTo( _
        ByVal array As Array, _
        ByVal index As Integer) Implements ICollection.CopyTo

    End Class
```

I won't cover every method and property, because you are probably already familiar with quite a number of collection classes. The two pieces of important functionality that `ProviderCollection` delivers are validation for read-only collections and a common type for `ProvidersHelper` to use when it creates multiple providers inside of the `ProvidersHelper.InstantiateProviders` method.

Usually after a feature has completed initialization, the feature will call `SetReadOnly` on its `ProviderCollection`. This ensures that the set of providers available through the feature exactly mirrors the set of providers defined in configuration. After a call to `SetReadOnly` the `ProvidersCollection` class enforces the read-only nature of the collection. Attempts to call `Add` or `Remove` will fail with an exception.

The usual implementation model is for a feature-specific provider collection to derive from `ProviderCollection` and at least override the `Add` method. For ease of use, features also commonly implement a feature-specific indexer that supplements the default indexer on `ProviderCollection` as well as a feature-specific implementation of `CopyTo`. In other words, any portion of the `ProviderCollection` type signature that deals with a parameter of type `ProviderBase` is either overridden or supplemented by feature-specific provider collections.

You can actually see that `ProviderBase` itself follows a similar approach because its implementation of `ICollection.CopyTo` requires an explicit interface cast. If instead you call `CopyTo` directly on `ProviderBase`, you will be using the method that accepts an array of `ProviderBase` instances, as opposed to just an array of `object`. The general idea is to specialize the portion of the collection that deals with common types by adding methods or overriding methods so that you can deal with a more specific type.

A feature-specific provider collection performs type-specific validation in an override of the `Add` method (that is, are you adding the correct provider type to the collection?). A feature-specific provider also performs the necessary type casts inside of its additional `CopyTo` and default indexer implementations. For example, if you work with a `MembershipProviderCollection` and if you use the default indexer, you know that the return value from its default indexer is already a `MembershipProvider`. If, instead, you worked with a `MembershipProviderCollection` instance as a `ProviderCollection` reference, you would have to perform a cast on the return value from the default indexer on `ProviderCollection`.

You may be wondering why the provider-based features didn't simply use the generic functionality that was introduced in the 2.0 Framework. Certainly, from an elegance standpoint, you would not have to muck around with collection hierarchies and the minutia of which methods to override or reimplement if `ProviderCollection` was instead defined as a generic type. The simple answer is that the provider model was already developed very early on in the lifecycle of the 2.0 Framework. A substantial number of provider-based features were pretty well fleshed out by the time that Framework generics had stabilized. (Remember that building one piece of the framework that is in turn dependent on another core piece of the framework gets pretty "interesting" at times!)

Once generics had stabilized though, there had not been a decision yet on whether generics would be considered CLS-compliant, that is, would a public API that exposed generics be reusable across many different compilers that targeted the .NET Framework? Eventually, the decision was made in late 2004 to define generics as being CLS-compliant. By that point though, the development teams were pretty much in ship mode for .NET 2.0 Beta 2, which was way too late for folks to rummage through all the provider-based features and swap out old-style 1.1 collections for 2.0 generics (sometimes making what would appear to be a common-sense design change in a large product like the .NET Framework turns out to be akin to standing a 747 on its wing and pulling a 9G turn, it would be nice if it worked, but it is more likely that various pieces will come flying off). The 3.5 Framework and especially ASP.NET 3.5 did not change the implementation of the providers that were already introduced by ASP.NET 2.0 and hence ASP.NET 3.5 uses the same providers as those in ASP.NET 2.0.

System.Web.Configuration Classes

Because most of the concrete provider implementations in both the 2.0 and 3.5 Frameworks exist within ASP.NET 2.0 and ASP.NET 3.5, the helper class for creating providers ended up in the `System.Web.Configuration` namespace. If you implement a provider-based feature or if you plan to use an existing provider-based feature outside of both ASP.NET 2.0 and ASP.NET 3.5, you can still reference this namespace though and make use of the helper class.

The `System.Web.Configuration.ProvidersHelper` class provides two convenient helper methods for instantiating providers. The class is typically used by features during feature initialization as mentioned earlier. Although you can certainly instantiate providers manually using the helper class, there are usually other feature-specific dependencies that end up breaking when you use such an approach.

I won't cover the helper class again here, because the previous section on the Factory Method went into detail on how to use the class as well how it acts as a provider factory for the Framework. The class signature is:

C#

```csharp
public static class ProvidersHelper {

   public static ProviderBase InstantiateProvider(
            ProviderSettings providerSettings, Type providerType)

   public static void InstantiateProviders(
         ProviderSettingsCollection configProviders,
         ProviderCollection providers, Type providerType)
}
```

VB.NET

```vbnet
Public Class ProvidersHelper

    Public Shared Function InstantiateProvider(ByVal providerSettings As
        ProviderSettings, ByVal providerType As Type) As ProviderBase
```

```
        Public Shared Sub InstantiateProviders(ByVal configProviders As
            ProviderSettingsCollection, ByVal providers As ProviderCollection,
            ByVal providerType As Type)

    End Class
```

System.Configuration Classes

One of the important points for provider-based features is that you can swap out providers through configuration. The configuration-driven nature of provider-based features means that you can write code that uses a feature without hard-coding any compile-time dependencies on a specific provider implementation.

To support this functionality two configuration classes represent provider configuration data.

ProviderSettings

The `System.Configuration.ProviderSettings` class is the programmatic representation of a provider `<add />` element in configuration. The `ProviderSettings` class exposes properties for some of the common configuration attributes found in a provider `<add />` element, while still retaining the flexibility for feature providers to define their own custom set of configuration (and this runtime) attributes.

The class signature for `ProviderSettings` (less configuration class-specific internals) is shown here:

C#

```csharp
public sealed class ProviderSettings : ConfigurationElement
{

    public ProviderSettings();
    public ProviderSettings(String name, String type);

    //ConfigurationElement specific methods snipped out for brevity

    [ConfigurationProperty("name", RequiredValue = true, IsCollectionKey=true)]
    public String Name { get; set; }

    [ConfigurationProperty("type", RequiredValue = true)]
    public String Type {get; set;}

    public NameValueCollection Parameters { get; }

}
```

VB.NET

```vbnet
Public NotInheritable Class ProviderSettings
    Inherits ConfigurationElement

    Public Sub New()
    Public Sub New(ByVal name As String, ByVal type As String)
```

```
'ConfigurationElement specific methods snipped out for brevity

<ConfigurationProperty("name", IsRequired:=True, IsKey:=True)> _
Public Property Name As String

Public ReadOnly Property Parameters As NameValueCollection

Protected Friend Overrides ReadOnly Property Properties As
        ConfigurationPropertyCollection

<ConfigurationProperty("type", IsRequired:=True)> _
Public Property Type As String

End Class
```

As you can see from the type signature, the only configuration attributes that are common across all providers are the "name" and "type" configuration attributes, which map respectively to the Name and Type properties. All other provider properties that you see when looking in machine.config or web.config are considered to be feature-specific provider attributes. The declarative ConfigurationProperty attributes on the Name and Type properties are interpreted by the configuration system at runtime. These attributes are what "tell" the configuration system how to translate an Xml attribute to a property on the ProviderSettings class.

Feature-specific provider attributes are parsed by the configuration system and added as name-value pairs to the NameValueCollection available from the Parameters property. As a result, the process by which configuration settings in web.config eventually end up in a provider is:

1. At runtime a feature class, such as the static Membership class, makes a call into the configuration system asking for its configuration section to be parsed and loaded.

2. After the configuration file has been parsed, the values are returned back to the feature class as one or more configuration objects. In the case of the provider <add /> elements, each configured provider results in an instance of ProviderSettings. All attributes other than "name" and "type" end up in the ProviderSettings.Parameters property.

3. The feature class calls ProvidersHelper.InstantiateProviders and passes the ProviderSettings to the helper class (to be precise an instance of ProviderSettingsCollection containing one or more ProviderSettings is passed to the helper class).

4. The ProvidersHelper class uses ProviderSettings.Type to determine the correct type that needs to be instantiated.

5. Once the provider has been instantiated, the ProviderBase.Initialize method is called. The name parameter for this method comes from ProviderSettings.Name, whereas the config parameter comes from ProviderSettings.Parameters.

6. The provider internally calls base.Initialize to set the Name of the provider and optionally the Description. Feature-specific providers then use the remainder of the name-value pairs from ProviderSettings.Parameters for feature-specific initialization logic.

If you look in both the 2.0 and 3.5 Frameworks, you won't find any feature-specific configuration classes that derive from ProviderSetting; in fact, ProviderSettings is sealed, so in both the 2.0 and 3.5 Frameworks you cannot write feature-specific ProviderSettings classes even if you wanted to.

As a result, when you are working with configuration files at design time, the IntelliSense in the design environment is only able to validate the "name" and "type" attributes. If you are configuring a `MembershipProvider`, for example, you will not get any IntelliSense for the SQL or the Active Directory/Active Directory Application Mode (AD/ADAM or ADLDS) provider properties. Instead, you are left to the documentation to determine which additional key-value pairs are allowed in the provider `<add />` element within the `<membership />` configuration element.

Early in the 2.0 Framework and currently in 3.5 Framework, this behavior was chosen to avoid having to engineer feature-specific settings classes along with an accompanying XSD schema for IntelliSense validation. The design problem with having feature-specific `ProviderSettings` classes is that for many features you cannot completely define the feature-specific attributes with a single configuration class. For example, within Membership the allowable attributes on the SQL provider only partially overlap with the allowable attributes on the AD/ADAM or ADLDS provider. Both the SQL and the AD/ADAM or ADLDS providers have implementation-specific attributes in addition to common Membership attributes.

This problem is common to all providers because the whole point of providers is to allow you to write your own custom implementations, which usually results in custom provider attributes. If each feature had a more strongly typed definition of `ProviderSettings`, you would still need a property like the `ProviderSettings.Parameters` property to allow for extensibility.

There is also an issue with XSD-based IntelliSense validation. It becomes problematic because `<add />` was chosen as the common way for configuring a provider. However, because `<add />` elements vary by their attributes, you can't define an XSD validation rule that says "allow `<add />` with the attribute set A or allow `<add />` with the attribute set B, but don't allow an `<add />` element with a mixture of attribute sets A and B." Furthermore, the existing `<add />` element has a common XSD definition that is used in every feature-specific configuration section. The same `<add />` element is used within `<membership />`, `<profile />`, `<sitemap />`, and so on. To really support strongly typed provider configuration sections and classes, you would need:

- ❏ A different configuration approach that was element-driven as opposed attribute driven. Something like a `<membershipProvider />` configuration element, a `<roleManagerProvider />` configuration element, and so on. This would allow for feature-specific XSD schemas.

- ❏ Feature-specific configuration classes that derive from `ProviderSettings`. This work would at least be pretty easy to accomplish.

- ❏ Some type of extensibility mechanism that would allow you to tell both the 2.0 and 3.5 Frameworks about new provider types and to supply provider-specific XSD extensions. This would enable IntelliSense to validate both the core set of feature-specific configuration information as well as your custom provider configuration information. Again, though, this extensibility mechanism would probably need to be element-based as opposed to attribute-based.

The nice thing about the current design though is that when you author a custom provider, you do not have to author a custom configuration section and a related custom configuration class. The existing `ProviderSettings` class and the `<add />` configuration element are flexible enough that you don't need to write any special configuration code to plug in your own custom providers.

ProviderSettingsCollection

Because most provider-based features support configuring multiple providers, the System
.Configuration.ProviderSettingsCollection class is used to hold all the ProviderSettings
that resulted from parsing a configuration file.

The class definition, less configuration class-specific methods, is shown here:

C#

```
[ConfigurationCollection(typeof(ProviderSettings))]
public sealed class ProviderSettingsCollection : ConfigurationElementCollection
{
  public ProviderSettingsCollection();

  public ProviderSettingsCollection Providers { get; }

  public void Add(ProviderSettings provider);
  public void Remove(String name);
  public void Clear();

  public ProviderSettings this[object key] { get; }
  public ProviderSettings this[int index] { get; set; }

  //Other configuration class specific methods removed for brevity
}
```

VB.NET

```
<ConfigurationCollection(GetType(ProviderSettings)), DefaultMember("Item")> _
Public NotInheritable Class ProviderSettingsCollection
    Inherits ConfigurationElementCollection

    Public Sub New()
    Public Sub Add(ByVal provider As ProviderSettings)
    Public Sub Clear()
    Public Sub Remove(ByVal name As String)

    Public Default Property Item(ByVal index As Integer) As ProviderSettings
    Public ReadOnly Default Property Item(ByVal key As String) As ProviderSettings
    Protected Friend Overrides ReadOnly Property _
    Properties As ConfigurationPropertyCollection

    'Other configuration class specific methods removed for brevity
End Class
```

The second code sample in the earlier section on the Factory Method showed how you could manually
construct a ProviderSettingsCollection, populate it with multiple ProviderSettings instances,
and then pass the collection to ProvidersHelper.InstantiateProviders. From an application development perspective though, you probably will not ever deal with a ProviderSettingsCollection.
Instead, you may use a ProviderSettingsCollection class for administrative purposes to programmatically read and modify a configuration file.

If you do author a provider-based feature, and you create a configuration section class for that feature, the configuration system will automatically convert the provider <add /> elements into an instance of ProviderSettingsCollection on your configuration section class. You do not need to manually call Add, Remove, and similar methods from inside your custom configuration class. Instead, you would simply add a property on your configuration class of type ProviderSettingsCollection and attribute it appropriately.

Using the MembershipSection class as an example, it has a public property for its <provider /> section as shown here:

C#

```
[ConfigurationProperty("providers")]
public ProviderSettingsCollection Providers { get; }
```

VB.NET

```
<ConfigurationProperty("providers")> _
Public ReadOnly Property Providers As ProviderSettingsCollection
```

So, when the configuration system is parsing a configuration file, and it is processing a <providers /> element like:

```
<providers>
    <add name="foo"  type="bar"  ... />
</providers>
```

The configuration system knows that the results of parsing everything underneath <providers /> results in a collection of information represented by ProviderSettingsCollection. Because a ProviderSettingsCollection is as an Add-Remove-Clear ( )collection, the configuration system also knows to expect the Xml elements <add />, <remove /> and <clear /> underneath the <providers /> configuration element.

As the configuration system encounters each of these elements, it converts them into a method call to the Add, Remove and Clear methods on the ProviderSettingsCollection class. Because ProviderSettingsCollection is attributed with the ConfigurationCollection attribute, and this attribute indicates that the collection contains instances of ProviderSettings, the configuration system will look at the declarative attributes on the ProviderSettings class when it processes the contents of the <providers /> section.

Because ProviderSettings has two properties adorned with the ConfigurationProperty attribute, the configuration system knows that when it parses a name or type attribute it needs to assign these to the Name and Type properties respectively on the ProviderSettings instance. Because the ConfigurationProperty attribute on ProviderSettings.Name also includes IsCollectionKey = true, the configuration system will treat the name attribute as the key value when calling various methods on ProviderSettingsCollection. For example, a <remove name="foo" /> configuration element is interpreted as a call to ProviderSettingsCollection.Remove with the value foo being used as a parameter to the method.

As mentioned earlier, from your perspective all this complexity is transparent to you. As long as you have a property of type ProviderSettingsCollection with the requisite ConfigurationProperty attribute, the configuration system will automatically parse your provider definitions for you.

Building a Provider-Based Feature

Now that you have seen the rationale and architecture behind provider-based features, walking through the basic steps of writing a simple provider-based feature along with a custom provider will help you tie together the previous concepts to the provider support classes in both the 2.0 and 3.5 Frameworks. In this section, you will walk through the steps of building a provider-based feature, as shown in Figure 10-1.

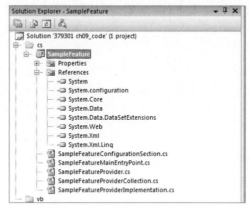

Figure 10-1

Because the intent of this section is to concentrate on creating a provider-based feature, the feature used for the sample will define and implement only one method that simply requests a string from its default provider. The sample provider base class definition is:

C#

```csharp
using System;
using System.Configuration.Provider;

namespace SampleFeature
{
    public abstract class SampleFeatureProvider : ProviderBase
    {
        //Properties
        public abstract string Color { get; }
        public abstract string Food { get; }

        //Methods
        public abstract string GetMeAString(string andPutThisOnTheEndOfIt);
    }
}
```

VB.NET

```vbnet
Imports Microsoft.VisualBasic
Imports System
Imports System.Configuration.Provider
```

```
Namespace SampleFeature
    Public MustInherit Class SampleFeatureProvider
        Inherits ProviderBase
        'Properties
        Public MustOverride ReadOnly Property Color() As String
        Public MustOverride ReadOnly Property Food() As String

        'Methods
        Public MustOverride Function GetMeAString( _
        ByVal andPutThisOnTheEndOfIt As String) As String

    End Class
End Namespace
```

A provider implementation for the sample feature is required to implement the `GetMeAString` method as well as the two abstract properties. The general convention for handling feature-specific configuration settings in a provider-based feature is to define abstract property getters on the provider base class. With this abstract class definition, the configuration settings for a "color" attribute and a "food" attribute will be available through their corresponding properties on the feature's providers. This approach allows developers to access configuration settings at runtime without having to use any of the configuration classes.

Because the sample feature will allow you to configure multiple instances of a provider, a corresponding provider collection class is also defined.

C#

```csharp
using System;
using System.Configuration.Provider;

namespace SampleFeature
{
    public class SampleFeatureProviderCollection : ProviderCollection
    {
        public override void Add(ProviderBase provider)
        {
            if (provider == null)
                throw new ArgumentNullException(
                        "You must supply a provider reference");

            if (!(provider is SampleFeatureProvider))
                throw new ArgumentException(
                 "The supplied provider type must derive from SampleFeatureProvider");

            base.Add(provider);
        }

        new public SampleFeatureProvider this[string name]
        {
            get { return (SampleFeatureProvider)base[name]; }
        }
```

```csharp
        public void CopyTo(SampleFeatureProvider[] array, int index)
        {
            base.CopyTo(array, index);
        }
    }
}
```

VB.NET

```vbnet
Imports Microsoft.VisualBasic
Imports System
Imports System.Configuration.Provider

Namespace SampleFeature
  Public Class SampleFeatureProviderCollection
        Inherits ProviderCollection
        Public Overrides Sub Add(ByVal provider As ProviderBase)
            If provider Is Nothing Then
                Throw New ArgumentNullException( _
                "You must supply a provider reference")
            End If

            If Not(TypeOf provider Is SampleFeatureProvider) Then
                Throw New ArgumentException( _
                "The supplied provider type must derive from " & _
                "SampleFeatureProvider")
            End If

            MyBase.Add(provider)
        End Sub

        Default Public Shadows ReadOnly Property Item( _
        ByVal name As String) As SampleFeatureProvider
            Get
                Return CType(MyBase.Item(name), SampleFeatureProvider)
            End Get
        End Property
            Get
                Return CType(MyBase.Item(name), SampleFeatureProvider)
            End Get
        End Property

        Public Overloads Sub CopyTo( _
        ByVal array() As SampleFeatureProvider, _
        ByVal index As Integer)
                MyBase.CopyTo(Array, index)
            End Sub
            MyBase.CopyTo(array, index)
        End Sub

  End Class
End Namespace
```

As you can see, a provider collection class is pretty much boilerplate code. The override for the Add method has some extra validation logic to ensure that only instances of SampleFeatureProvider are added to the collection. The default indexer and the CopyTo implementations simply cast the provider reference returned by the underlying ProviderCollection to a SampleFeatureProvider reference.

The public portion of the sample feature is accessible through a static entry class called SampleFeature MainEntryPoint. This design mirrors the approach used by many of the ASP.NET 2.0 and ASP.NET 3.5 provider-based features. The class definition below shows the relevant portions used for the public API.

C#

```csharp
using System;
using System.Configuration;
using System.Configuration.Provider;
using System.Web.Configuration;

namespace SampleFeature
{
    public static class SampleFeatureMainEntryPoint
    {
        //Initialization related variables and logic
        //snip…

        //Public feature API
        private static SampleFeatureProvider defaultProvider;
        private static SampleFeatureProviderCollection providerCollection;

        public static SampleFeatureProvider Provider
        {
            get
            {
                return defaultProvider;
            }
        }

        public static SampleFeatureProviderCollection Providers
        {
            get
            {
                return providerCollection;
            }
        }

        public static string GetMeAString(string someString)
        {
            return Provider.GetMeAString(someString);
        }
    }
}
```

VB.NET

```vbnet
Imports Microsoft.VisualBasic
Imports System
Imports System.Configuration
Imports System.Configuration.Provider
Imports System.Web.Configuration

Namespace SampleFeature
    Public NotInheritable Class SampleFeatureMainEntryPoint
        'Initialization related variables and logic
        'snip…

            'Public feature API
            Private Shared defaultProvider As SampleFeatureProvider
            Private Shared providerCollection As SampleFeatureProviderCollection

            Public Shared ReadOnly Property Provider() As SampleFeatureProvider
                Get
                    'Initialize();
                    Return defaultProvider
                End Get
            End Property

            Public Shared ReadOnly Property Providers() _
            As SampleFeatureProviderCollection
                Get
                    'Initialize();
                    Return providerCollection
                End Get
            End Property
                Get
                    'Initialize();
                    Return providerCollection
                End Get
            End Property

            Public Shared Function GetMeAString(ByVal someString As String) As String
                Return Provider.GetMeAString(someString)
            End Function

    End Class
End Namespace
```

The static feature class allows you to access its default provider via the `Provider` property. If you configure multiple providers with the feature, you can choose a specific provider with the corresponding `Providers` property. Last, the static feature class exposes the functionality that is implemented by way of a provider. This sample intentionally has a simplistic piece of logic; you can ask the feature for a string, and it will return a string from the default provider. Complex provider-based features like Membership have a hefty number of static feature methods providing a variety of overloads that map to methods in the underlying providers.

A provider-based feature can be considered to go through a lifecycle of sorts:

1. First the feature is in an uninitialized state. Any call to a method on the static feature class should result in initialization.

2. If initialization succeeds, the feature is considered initialized.

3. If initialization failed, the feature can still be considered initialized, but in a failed state. The fact that initialization failed needs to be stored somewhere.

So, a side effect of the feature's initialization should either be a functioning static class, or some persistent representation of the initialization failure. The sample feature's private `Initialize` method is written to throw an exception if initialization failed. As a result, any attempt to call a public property or method on the `SampleFeatureMainEntryPoint` class results in an exception if initialization failed. More specifically, any attempt to call a public static method or property will fail with an exception stating that the type initializer failed. If you then drill into the `InnerException`, you will see the specific details of what caused the failure.

Because the initialization process for the feature is the place where configuration and providers come together, let's take a look at the initialization related code for the static feature class.

C#

```csharp
public static class SampleFeatureMainEntryPoint
{
    //Initialization related variables and logic
    private static bool isInitialized = false;
    private static Exception initializationException;

    private static object initializationLock = new object();

    static SampleFeatureMainEntryPoint()
    {
        Initialize();
    }

    private static void Initialize()
    {
        //implementation
    }
}
```

VB.NET

```vbnet
Public NotInheritable Class SampleFeatureMainEntryPoint
        'Initialization related variables and logic
        Private Shared isInitialized As Boolean = False
        Private Shared initializationException As Exception

        Private Shared initializationLock As Object = New Object()

        Private Sub New()
        End Sub
        Shared Sub New()
```

```
            Initialize()
        End Sub

        Private Shared Sub Initialize()
            'implementation
        End Sub

    End Class
```

The feature class holds its initialization state inside two private variables. If the initialization process has occurred, regardless of its success, then isInitialized will be set to true. If the initialization process failed, an exception has occurred, and this exception will be cached for the lifetime of the application, using the initializationException variable. Both variables are static because the initialization process itself is triggered by the feature class's static constructor.

Because both the 2.0 and 3.5 Frameworks calls the type's static constructor before running any public properties and methods call, the very first call to any portion of the public API will cause the Initialize method to carry out the necessary initialization work. This is the one point where a call to Initialize will actually result in feature initialization. The actual logic within the Initialize method is shown here:

C#

```csharp
private static void Initialize()
{
    //If for some reason the feature has already initialized
    //then exit, or optionally throw if init failed
    if (isInitialized)
    {
        if (initializationException != null)
            throw initializationException;
        else
            return;
    }

    //Start the initialization
    lock (initializationLock)
    {
     //Need to double-check after the lock was taken
     if (isInitialized)
     {
         if (initializationException != null)
             throw initializationException;
         else
             return;
     }
     try
     {
         //Get the feature's configuration info
         SampleFeatureConfigurationSection sc =
           (SampleFeatureConfigurationSection)
           ConfigurationManager.GetSection("sampleFeature");

         if (sc.DefaultProvider == null ||
             sc.Providers == null || sc.Providers.Count < 1)
```

```csharp
                throw new ProviderException("The feature requires that you " +
                        " specify a default " +
                        "feature provider as well as at least one " +
                        "provider definition.");

            //Instantiate the feature's providers
            providerCollection = new SampleFeatureProviderCollection();
            ProvidersHelper.InstantiateProviders(
                sc.Providers,
                providerCollection,
                typeof(SampleFeatureProvider));

            providerCollection.SetReadOnly();

            defaultProvider = providerCollection[sc.DefaultProvider];
            if (defaultProvider == null)
            {
                throw new ConfigurationErrorsException(
                    "The default feature provider was not specified.",
                    sc.ElementInformation.Properties["defaultProvider"].Source,
                    sc.ElementInformation.Properties["defaultProvider"].LineNumber);
            }
        }
        catch (Exception ex)
        {
            initializationException = ex;
            isInitialized = true;
            throw ex;
        }

        isInitialized = true; //error-free initialization

    }//end of lock block
}//end of Initialize method

//Public feature API
//snip…
    }
}
```

VB.NET

```vbnet
        Private Shared Sub Initialize()
            ' If for some reason the feature has already initialized
            ' then exit, or optionally throw if init failed
            If isInitialized Then
                If initializationException IsNot Nothing Then
                    Throw initializationException
                Else
                    Return
                End If
            End If

            ' Start the initialization
```

```vbnet
        SyncLock initializationLock
            ' Need to double-check after the lock was taken
            If isInitialized Then
                If initializationException IsNot Nothing Then
                    Throw initializationException
                Else
                    Return
                End If
            End If
            Try
                'Get the feature's configuration info
                Dim sc As SampleFeatureConfigurationSection = CType( _
                ConfigurationManager.GetSection("sampleFeature"), _
                SampleFeatureConfigurationSection)

                If sc.DefaultProvider Is Nothing _
                OrElse sc.Providers Is Nothing OrElse sc.Providers.Count < 1 Then
                    Throw New ProviderException( _
                    "The feature requires that you specify a default " & _
                    "feature provider as well as at least one " & _
                    "provider definition.")
                End If

                'Instantiate the feature's providers
                providerCollection = New SampleFeatureProviderCollection()
                ProvidersHelper.InstantiateProviders( _
                        sc.Providers, _
                        providerCollection, _
                        GetType(SampleFeatureProvider))
                providerCollection.SetReadOnly()
                defaultProvider = providerCollection(sc.DefaultProvider)
                If defaultProvider Is Nothing Then
                Throw New ConfigurationErrorsException( _
                "The default feature provider was not specified.", _
                sc.ElementInformation.Properties("defaultProvider").Source, _
                sc.ElementInformation.Properties("defaultProvider").LineNumber)
                End If
            Catch ex As Exception
                initializationException = ex
                isInitialized = True
                Throw ex
            End Try

            isInitialized = True 'error-free initialization
        End SyncLock
    End Sub
```

The method first attempts to quickly return whether the feature was already initialized; if the initialization caused an error, the exception that caused the failure is thrown instead. Because this sample feature depends on a static constructor though, this type of check is not actually needed. I show it here so that you can see how the ASP.NET provider-based features carry out their initialization logic. In the case of the ASP.NET 2.0 and ASP.NET 3.5 static feature classes, the first if block is what runs 99.9 percent of the time this type of method is called, so the overhead of calling into `Initialize` from the public API is normally just the overhead of an extra method call.

However, if the `Initialize` method detects that the feature has not been initialized, the method enters a synchronization block using the C# lock syntax in the C# code block and VB.NET SyncLock syntax in the VB.NET code block shown above. Immediately after entering the lock section (now a maximum of one and only one thread can ever be running inside of the lock block), the method double-checks the initialization results. This is the classic lock-and-double-check approach to performing common synchronization for a class. Because, theoretically, two threads of execution may have simultaneously entered the static method, the code makes a second check against the initialization flag to cover the case where a second thread completed initialization after the first thread checked the Boolean `isInitialized` variable.

Again this static feature class is written a little bit differently from how ASP.NET provider-based features are written. For historical reasons, the ASP.NET provider-based features did not use static classes until later in the development cycle. As a result, their initialization processes depended on having a call to a private initialization method inside of every public method and property. This would be equivalent to having the sample class above calling `Initialize` from inside of the `Provider` and `Providers` properties as well as the `GetMeAString` method. Because the ASP.NET approach did not use a static constructor, the feature class needed to provide its own synchronization (like that shown previously) during initialization because it was very likely that there would be multiple threads running inside of the initialization method. The sample feature class, though, calls `Initialize` from its static constructor, so it is not really necessary to use the first `if`-check or the `lock` block or SyncLock block with the second `if`-check. Instead, both the 2.0 and 3.5 Frameworks will ensure thread safety when the `Initialize` method is called from the static constructor; because the method is called from the static constructor, it never needs to be called again from the public properties or methods on the sample feature class.

The `try-catch` block is where the meat of the feature initialization occurs. Using the `Configuration-Manager` class in `System.Configuration`, the `Initialize` method gets a strongly typed reference to the configuration section class for the feature (discussed later in this chapter). The feature's configuration section class exposes two important properties: `DefaultProvider` and `Providers`. These properties define the default provider that the static feature class should use as well as the set of all configured providers for the feature. If the configuration section in the application's configuration file is wrong, and it lacks definitions of a default provider and at least one feature provider, the initialization process throws a `ProviderException` indicating the problem.

With the configuration information now available, the `Initialize` method creates an empty `Sample FeatureProviderCollection` class that will eventually hold a reference to each provider that was configured for the feature. This collection is also accessible from the static feature class's `Providers` property. The `ProvidersHelper` class is called to populate this provider collection based on the providers defined in the application's configuration file. Assuming that the helper successfully ran to completion, the provider collection is then marked as read-only. You don't want application developers to be able to modify the feature's provider collection after initialization has occurred.

The `Initialize` method then attempts to get a reference to the default provider and make it available from the static feature class's `DefaultProvider` property. If there is no provider in the provider collection with a `Name` that matches the value of the feature's "defaultProvider" configuration attribute, then a `ConfigurationErrorsException` is thrown. Assuming that the application is running in a high enough trust level, the error message that is returned from the exception will include the file path to the configuration file as well as the line number on which the problematic "defaultProvider" attribute for the feature was defined.

By this point, the `Initialize` method is able to complete without error, or it catches whatever exception occurred. In either case, the feature marks itself as being initialized. In the error case, it also stores a reference to the exception that caused initialization to fail. This is another point where the ASP.NET provider-based features are a little different from the sample feature. The ASP.NET provider-based features need to store the exception and rethrow it whenever their private initialization methods are called from their public properties and methods. However, the sample feature class shown previously instead relies on the 2.0 or 3.5 Framework to do the heavy lifting.

Because `Initialize` was called from the static constructor, the 2.0 or 3.5 Framework will remember that the static constructor failed. This means if the `Initialize` method fails, subsequent attempts to call public properties or methods on the static feature class result in a `System.TypeInitialization-Exception` being thrown. The `InnerException` property on this exception instance will represent the true exception that was thrown from inside of the `Initialize` method. From a programming standpoint either the ASP.NET approach or the approach shown previously that relies on a static constructor is valid. The decision is up to you.

Using the static constructor eliminates the need for funky lock logic, but you do need to drill into the `TypeInitializationException` to find the root cause of a failure. The ASP.NET approach means that you will always have the problematic exception being thrown from public APIs and properties. But you will need to use locking inside of your feature's initialization logic and have each public property and method on your feature class call back to your initialization method to cause the initialization exception to be rethrown.

At this point, let's take a look at the feature's configuration section class. You want a configuration class that provides strongly typed access for a configuration that looks like:

```
<sampleFeature defaultProvider="DefaultSampleFeatureProvider">
  <providers>
    <add name="DefaultSampleFeatureProvider"
         type="SampleFeature.SampleFeatureProviderImplementation, SampleFeature"
         connectionStringName="SomeConnectionString"
         color="red"
         food="burgers"
         description="this came from config" />
  </providers>
</sampleFeature>
```

The feature itself has its own configuration section as indicated by the `<sampleFeature />` configuration element. The one allowable attribute on this element is the "defaultProvider" attribute. Nested within a `<sampleFeature />` is a `<providers />` section allowing for one or more provider definitions. Aside from the "name" and "type" attributes, all the other attributes are feature-specific.

The configuration section class that models this configuration section is shown here:

C#

```
using System;
using System.Configuration;

namespace SampleFeature
{
    public class SampleFeatureConfigurationSection : ConfigurationSection
    {
```

```csharp
        public SampleFeatureConfigurationSection(){}

        [ConfigurationProperty("providers")]
        public ProviderSettingsCollection Providers
        {
            get
            {
                return (ProviderSettingsCollection)base["providers"];
            }
        }

        [ConfigurationProperty("defaultProvider",
          DefaultValue = "DefaultSampleFeatureProvider")]
        [StringValidator(MinLength = 1)]
        public string DefaultProvider {
            get
            {
                return (string)base["defaultProvider"];
            }
            set
            {
                base["defaultProvider"] = value;
            }
        }
    }
}
```

VB.NET

```vbnet
Imports Microsoft.VisualBasic
Imports System
Imports System.Configuration

Namespace SampleFeature
  Public Class SampleFeatureConfigurationSection
        Inherits ConfigurationSection
      Public Sub New()
      End Sub

        <ConfigurationProperty("providers")> _
        Public ReadOnly Property Providers() As ProviderSettingsCollection
            Get
                Return CType(MyBase.Item("providers", _
                ProviderSettingsCollection
            End Get
        End Property

        DefaultValue:="DefaultSampleFeatureProvider"), _
                        StringValidator(MinLength:=1)> _
        Public Property DefaultProvider() As String
                Get
                    Return CStr(MyBase.Item("defaultProvider"))
                End Get
                Set(ByVal value As String)
```

```
                        MyBase.Item("defaultProvider") = value
                End Set
        End Property
    End Class
End Namespace
```

Inheriting from `ConfigurationSection` means that this class represents a configuration section in an application configuration file. The default constructor is used by the configuration system when it `new()`'s up configuration section classes while parsing configuration. The only custom code that you need to write in the configuration class are the custom properties that represent configuration attributes and nested configuration sections.

The `Providers` property represents the nested `<providers />` configuration section. The declarative attribute on the property causes the configuration system to parse the `<providers />` section and its nested elements into an instance of a `ProviderSettingsCollection`. By using the `ProviderSettingsCollection` class, you automatically leverage the built-in behavior of the `<providers />` configuration section without the need to write any additional code.

The `DefaultProvider` property has two declarative attributes on it. The `ConfigurationProperty` attribute indicates that if a "defaultProvider" attribute is found within the `<sampleFeature />` element that its value will be available via the `DefaultProvider` property. The `ConfigurationProperty` also has a default value indicating that the property should be set to "DefaultSampleFeatureProvider" if the attribute is not found in the configuration file. Last, the `StringValidator` attribute tells the configuration system that if the attribute exists in configuration, the attribute must be a non-empty string. This type of declarative validation rule is automatically enforced when the configuration system attempts to parse the configuration.

In the `SampleFeatureMainEntryPoint.Initialize` method, the following code is what triggers the parsing and loading of the configuration section:

C#

```
SampleFeatureConfigurationSection sc =
    (SampleFeatureConfigurationSection)ConfigurationManager.GetSection(
                                            "sampleFeature");
```

VB.NET

```
Dim sc As SampleFeatureConfigurationSection = _
        CType(ConfigurationManager.GetSection("sampleFeature"), _
        SampleFeatureConfigurationSection)
```

The configuration runtime knows to associate the `<sampleFeature />` configuration section with the `SampleFeatureConfigurationSection` class once you add the following section definition to your application's configuration file:

```
<configSections>
    <section name="sampleFeature"
            type="SampleFeature.SampleFeatureConfigurationSection, SampleFeature"
            allowDefinition="MachineToApplication" />
</configSections>
```

A <section /> element is used to associate an XML element called sampleFeature to the custom configuration class you just saw. The type attribute tells the configuration system where to find the class; in this case, the class is located in an unsigned assembly called SampleFeature.dll. Depending on whether you are defining the custom section for a web application, you can also use the "allowDefinition" attribute to control the inheritance behavior of the configuration section. Because provider-based features usually do not allow redefinition in the level of individual subdirectories, the "allowDefinition" attribute is set to limit the "sampleFeature" element to only machine.config, the root web.config or an application's web.config file.

At this point, the only piece left to implement for the sample feature is a concrete provider. The basic implementation of a concrete provider (less the initialization step) is:

C#

```csharp
using System;
using System.Configuration;
using System.Configuration.Provider;

namespace SampleFeature
{
    public class SampleFeatureProviderImplementation : SampleFeatureProvider
    {
        private string color;
        private string food;
        private String connectionString;

        public override string Color
        {
            get { return color; }
        }

        public override string Food
        {
            get { return food; }
        }

        public override string GetMeAString(string andPutThisOnTheEndOfIt)
        {
            return "This string came from the " +
                    " SampleFeatureProviderImplementation.\r\n" +
                    "The provider description is: " + Description + "\r\n" +
                    "The provider color is: " + Color + "\r\n" +
                    "The provider food is: " + Food + "\r\n" +
                    andPutThisOnTheEndOfIt;
        }

        //Initialize method snipped out for now...
    }
}
```

VB.NET

```vbnet
Imports Microsoft.VisualBasic
Imports System
Imports System.Configuration
Imports System.Configuration.Provider

Namespace SampleFeature
  Public Class SampleFeatureProviderImplementation
        Inherits SampleFeatureProvider
        Private color_Renamed As String
        Private food_Renamed As String
        Private connectionString As String

        Public Overrides ReadOnly Property Color() As String
            Get
                Return color_Renamed
            End Get
        End Property

        Public Overrides ReadOnly Property Food() As String
            Get
                Return food_Renamed
            End Get
        End Property

        Public Overrides Function GetMeAString( _
    ByVal andPutThisOnTheEndOfIt As String) As String
        Return _
        "This string came from the SampleFeatureProviderImplementation." & _
        Constants.vbCrLf & "The provider description is: " & _
        Description & _
        Constants.vbCrLf & _
        "The provider color is: " & _
        Color & Constants.vbCrLf & _
        "The provider food is: " & _
        Food & Constants.vbCrLf & _
        andPutThisOnTheEndOfIt()
    End Function

        'Initialize method snipped out for now…

  End Class
End Namespace
```

The concrete provider implementation inherits from SampleFeatureProvider and overrides the two abstract properties as well as the single abstract method defined on the provider base class. The value of the public properties is established when the provider is initialized, while the public method simply plays back the property values as well as some extra strings. Assuming that you configure an instance of SampleFeatureProviderImplementation as the default provider in configuration, a call to `SampleFeatureMainEntryPoint.GetMeAString` is simply forwarded to the method implementation shown previously. Remember that the forwarding code in the static feature class references the static `Provider` property, which contains a reference to the default provider defined in configuration:

C#

```
public static string GetMeAString(string someString) {
            return Provider.GetMeAString(someString); }
```

VB.NET

```
Public Shared Function GetMeAString(ByVal someString As String) As String
            Return Provider.GetMeAString(someString)
End Function
```

This is the same approach used by most of the ASP.NET 2.0 and ASP.NET 3.5 provider-based features and explains why you can use static classes like `Membership` and these classes just work because their static methods internally forward their calls to the default feature provider.

Of course, the concrete provider really can't accomplish anything unless it is initialized first:

C#

```
public override void Initialize(string name,
        System.Collections.Specialized.NameValueCollection config)
{
    if ( (config == null) || (config.Count == 0) )
        throw new ArgumentNullException(
                "You must supply a non-null, non-empty value for config.");

    if (string.IsNullOrEmpty(config["description"]))
    {
        config.Remove("description");
        config.Add("description",
          "This would be where you put a localized description for the provider.");
    }

    //Let ProviderBase perform the basic initialization
    base.Initialize(name, config);

    //Perform feature-specific provider initialization here

    //Color
    if (string.IsNullOrEmpty(config["color"]))
    {
        color = "The default color for the provider";
    }
    else
    {
        color = config["color"];
    }
```

```
            config.Remove("color");

            //Food
            if (string.IsNullOrEmpty(config["food"]))
            {
                food = "The default food for the provider";
            }
            else
            {
                food = config["food"];
            }
            config.Remove("food");

            //Get the connection string
            string connectionStringName = config["connectionStringName"];
            if (String.IsNullOrEmpty(connectionStringName))
                throw new ProviderException(
                    "You must specify a connectionStringName attribute for the provider");

            ConnectionStringsSection cs =
                (ConnectionStringsSection)ConfigurationManager.GetSection(
                                                    "connectionStrings");
            if (cs == null)
                throw new ProviderException(
                  "The <connectionStrings/> configuration section was not defined.");

            if (cs.ConnectionStrings[connectionStringName] == null)
                throw new ProviderException(
                    "The connectionStringName could not be found " +
                    "in the <connectionStrings /> configuration section.");
            else
                connectionString =
                    cs.ConnectionStrings[connectionStringName].ConnectionString;

            if (String.IsNullOrEmpty(connectionString))
                throw new ProviderException(
                    "The specified connection string has an invalid value.");
            config.Remove("connectionStringName");

            //Check to see if unexpected attributes were set in configuration
            if (config.Count > 0)
            {
                string extraAttribute = config.GetKey(0);
                if (!String.IsNullOrEmpty(extraAttribute))
                 throw new ProviderException("The following unrecognized attribute was " +
                                        "found in the " + Name + "'s configuration: '" +
                                        extraAttribute + "'");
                else
                    throw new ProviderException("An unrecognized attribute was " +
                                            "found in the provider's configuration.");
            }
        }
```

VB.NET

```vbnet
Public Overrides Sub Initialize( _
    ByVal name As String, _
    ByVal config As System.Collections.Specialized.NameValueCollection)
    If (config Is Nothing) OrElse (config.Count = 0) Then
        Throw New ArgumentNullException( _
        "You must supply a non-null, non-empty value for config.")
    End If

    If String.IsNullOrEmpty(config("description")) Then
        config.Remove("description")
        config.Add("description", _
        "This would be where you put a localized description " & _
        "for the provider.")
    End If

    'Let ProviderBase perform the basic initialization
    MyBase.Initialize(name, config)

    'Perform feature-specific provider initialization here

    'Color
    If String.IsNullOrEmpty(config("color")) Then
        color_Renamed = "The default color for the provider"
    Else
        color_Renamed = config("color")
    End If
    config.Remove("color")

    'Food
    If String.IsNullOrEmpty(config("food")) Then
        food_Renamed = "The default food for the provider"
    Else
        food_Renamed = config("food")
    End If
    config.Remove("food")

    'Get the connection string
    Dim connectionStringName As String = config("connectionStringName")
    If String.IsNullOrEmpty(connectionStringName) Then
        Throw New ProviderException( _
        "You must specify a connectionStringName " & _
        "attribute for the provider")
    End If

    Dim cs As ConnectionStringsSection = CType _
    (ConfigurationManager.GetSection("connectionStrings"), _
ConnectionStringsSection)
    If cs Is Nothing Then
        Throw New ProviderException( _
        "The connectionStringName could not be found " & _
        "in the <connectionStrings /> configuration section.")
    End If

    If cs.ConnectionStrings(connectionStringName) Is Nothing Then
```

```vbnet
            Throw New ProviderException( _
            "The connectionStringName could not be found " & _
            "in the <connectionStrings /> configuration section.")
    Else
            connectionString = cs.ConnectionStrings _
            (connectionStringName).ConnectionString
    End If

    If String.IsNullOrEmpty(connectionString) Then
            Throw New ProviderException( _
            "The specified connection string has an invalid value.")
    End If
    config.Remove("connectionStringName")

    'Check to see if unexpected attributes were set in configuration
    If config.Count > 0 Then
            Dim extraAttribute As String = config.GetKey(0)
            If (Not String.IsNullOrEmpty(extraAttribute)) Then
                    Throw New ProviderException( _
                    "The following unrecognized attribute was " & _
                    "found in the " & _
                    Name & _
                    "'s configuration: '" & _
                    extraAttribute & "'")
            Else
                    Throw New ProviderException( _
                    "An unrecognized attribute was " & _
                    "found in the provider's configuration.")
            End If
    End If
End Sub
```

The name parameter contains the "name" attribute from the provider's <add /> configuration element, while the config parameter contains all the other attributes that the configuration runtime found on the <add /> provider element. The provider first makes a sanity check to ensure that it was passed a valid collection of configuration attributes. When a provider is initialized via a static feature provider that in turn uses a configuration class, this sanity check is redundant. However, as mentioned earlier, there isn't anything that prevents a developer from attempting to new() up a provider and manually initialize it (hence, the sanity check).

If a "description" attribute was not supplied in the provider's <add /> element, or if it was the empty string, then the provider supplies a default description instead. Although the sample does not show it here, this is the point at which both ASP.NET 2.0 and ASP.NET 3.5 providers will fall back and return a localized description for a provider if you did not supply a "description" in configuration. With the "name" and "description" attributes squared away, the provider calls the Initialize implementation on ProviderBase. ProviderBase will automatically hook up these two attributes to the Name and Description properties defined on ProviderBase.

After the base class performs its initialization tasks, the next pieces of code transfer the "color" and "food" attributes from configuration and hook them up to the provider's Color and Food properties. Notice that the provider treats these attributes as optional and automatically supplies default values if they were not specified in configuration. Because the configuration class for providers treats all attributes other than "name" and "type" as optional, you need to implement code in your custom providers to either enforce additional required attributes or supply reasonable defaults, as shown in the sample provider. Also notice how after each configuration attribute is used, the attribute is removed from the configuration collection with a call to the `Remove` method.

The next block of logic deals with handling a connection string attribute. The sample feature obviously does not use any type of connection string, but I included the code for handling connection strings because it is pretty likely that many of you writing custom providers will need to deal with connection strings at some point. The sample provider requires a "`connectionStringName`" attribute on each provider `<add />` element. If it does not find the attribute in the attribute collection passed to `Initialize`, the provider throws an exception.

Assuming that the attribute was defined, the provider goes through the following series of steps to get the actual connection string:

1. The provider gets a reference to the strongly typed configuration class for the `<connectionStrings />` configuration section. Remember that this was a new section in the 2.0 Framework and currently supported in the 3.5 Framework and is intended to be the place for storing database connection strings (as opposed to `<appSettings />`).

2. The provider looks for the connection string defined by "`connectionStringName`" in the `<connectionStrings />` section. If there is no such connection string with that name, the provider throws an exception.

3. The provider gets the value of the specified connection string and performs a basic verification to ensure it was not set to the empty string. If the connection string's value was set to the empty string, the provider throws an exception.

4. The provider stores the connection string internally and then removes the "`connectionStringName`" attribute from the configuration attribute collection.

By this point, the provider and `ProviderBase` have processed all the configuration attributes that are known to the two classes. As a final verification, the provider checks to see if there are any remaining attributes in the configuration attribute collection. If there are remaining attributes, the provider throws an exception because it does not know what to do with them. This is an important design point because all the ASP.NET 2.0 and ASP.NET 3.5 providers perform similar processing with their configuration attributes. For example, if you were to supply additional attributes when configuring a `SqlMembershipProvider`, the provider would fail with a similar exception.

One subtle point with the way the `Initialize` method is coded is that it is possible for the provider to fail initialization and end up in a sort of "zombie" state; the provider exists in memory, but it has not completed enough of its initialization to be of any use. Theoretically, if you could get a reference to a zombie provider, you could call properties and methods on it, and depending on when the provider initialization failed, you would get different results. It turns out that the ASP.NET 2.0 and ASP.NET 3.5 providers also have the same small loophole. The ASP.NET providers do not have extra protections that throw exceptions from public properties or methods because these protections already exist in the static feature classes. Assuming that you aren't trying to create and initialize providers manually, the static feature classes will fail initialization when one of the configured providers throws an exception from an `Initialize` call. This, in turn, means that if you attempt to get a reference to a configured provider via a call to either the `Provider` or `Providers` properties on the static feature class, you will also get an exception.

This behavior holds true for the sample feature as well. If a provider fails initialization, attempting to call `SampleFeatureMainEntryPoint.Provider` (or `Providers`) will return a `TypeInitialization Exception`, and you won't actually be able to get a reference to a "zombie" provider. Of course, you could still attempt to manually create and initialize a provider, but this approach is outside the intended usage boundaries of provider-based features. You can certainly implement additional protections in your providers to cover this case, but because a developer cannot "accidentally" misuse a provider when going through a static feature class, this design loophole was not addressed in both the 2.0 and 3.5 Frameworks.

Now that you have the end-to-end sample feature coded up (finally!), let's actually try it out in a few scenarios. You can compile all the previous code into a standalone assembly. Then reference the assembly from a console application that has the following configuration:

```
<configuration>
 <configSections>
   <section name="sampleFeature"
           type="SampleFeature.SampleFeatureConfigurationSection, SampleFeature"
           allowDefinition="MachineToApplication" />
 </configSections>

 <sampleFeature >
  <providers>
    <add name="DefaultSampleFeatureProvider"
         type="SampleFeature.SampleFeatureProviderImplementation, SampleFeature"
         connectionStringName="SomeConnectionString"
         color="red"
         food="burgers"
         description="this came from config" />

    <add name="SecondSampleFeatureProvider"
         type="SampleFeature.SampleFeatureProviderImplementation, SampleFeature"
         connectionStringName="SomeConnectionString"
         color="green"
         food="milk-shake" />

    <add name="ThirdSampleFeatureProvider"
         type="SampleFeature.SampleFeatureProviderImplementation, SampleFeature"
         connectionStringName="SomeConnectionString" />

  </providers>
 </sampleFeature>

 <connectionStrings>
    <add name="SomeConnectionString"
         connectionString="the connection string value" />
 </connectionStrings>

</configuration>
```

The test application's configuration includes the `<section />` that tells the configuration system how to parse the `<sampleFeature />` configuration element. There are three providers defined for the sample feature. Notice how the "`defaultProvider`" is not defined on the `<sampleFeature />` element while there is a provider `<add />` element using the default value for this attribute of

"DefaultSampleFeatureProvider." The second and third provider definitions do not include a "description," whereas the third provider definition defines the bare minimum number of required attributes (that is, "name," "type," and "connectionStringName"). Last, there is a section that all the provider definitions reference.

You can use the feature with the following sample test console application:

C#

```
using System;
using SampleFeature;

namespace SampleFeatureConsoleTest
{
 class Program
 {
    static void Main(string[] args)
    {
        try
        {
            Console.WriteLine(
              SampleFeatureMainEntryPoint.GetMeAString("console app"));
        }
        catch(Exception ex) { }

        SampleFeatureProvider sp =
            SampleFeatureMainEntryPoint.Providers["SecondSampleFeatureProvider"];
        string anotherString = sp.GetMeAString("Using the second provider.");
        Console.WriteLine(anotherString);

        SampleFeatureProvider sp2 =
            SampleFeatureMainEntryPoint.Providers["ThirdSampleFeatureProvider"];
        string anotherString2 = sp2.GetMeAString(
                "This provider had no config attributes defined.");
        Console.WriteLine(anotherString2);
    }
 }
}
```

VB.NET

```
Imports Microsoft.VisualBasic
Imports System
Imports System.Collections.Generic
Imports System.Linq
Imports System.Text
Imports SampleFeature

Namespace SampleFeatureConsole
  Friend Class Program
        Shared Sub Main(ByVal args() As String)
            Try
                Console.WriteLine(SampleFeatureMainEntryPoint. _
                GetMeAString("console app"))
```

```
                      Catch ex As Exception
                      End Try

                      Dim sp As SampleFeatureProvider =
                      SampleFeatureMainEntryPoint.Providers("SecondSampleFeatureProvider")
                      Dim anotherString As String = sp.GetMeAString _
                      ("Using the second provider.")
                      Console.WriteLine(anotherString)

                      Dim sp2 As SampleFeatureProvider =
                      SampleFeatureMainEntryPoint.Providers("ThirdSampleFeatureProvider")
                      Dim anotherString2 As String = sp2.GetMeAString _
                      ("This provider had no config attributes defined.")
                      Console.WriteLine(anotherString2)

                      Console.Read()
                End Sub

        End Class
End Namespace
```

The sample application works just as you would expect any other provider-based feature to work. With just the provider definition in configuration, it calls the static feature class to output a string. Internally, this results in a call to the default provider. The other two code blocks demonstrate accessing the two nondefault providers and then calling methods directly on them. The sample output is:

```
This string came from the SampleFeatureProviderImplementation.
The provider description is: this came from config
The provider color is: red
The provider food is: burgers
console app

This string came from the SampleFeatureProviderImplementation.
The provider description is: This would be where you put a localized description
for the provider.
The provider color is: green
The provider food is: milk-shake
Using the second provider.

This string came from the SampleFeatureProviderImplementation.
The provider description is: This would be where you put a localized description
for the provider.
The provider color is: The default color for the provider
The provider food is: The default food for the provider
This provider had no config attributes defined.
```

You can see how the description varies between the providers, with the second and third providers relying on the default description defined inside of the provider's Initialize method. The output from the third provider also demonstrates how the provider can fall back to reasonable defaults when option feature-specific attributes are not defined in the provider's configuration.

If you run the sample console application along with the sample provider code in a debugger, you can play around with intentionally creating bad configurations. Then you can see how the exception behavior inside of the static feature class's `Initialize` method causes the second and third attempts to call into the feature to fail (this is why the test app eats all exceptions from the first attempt to use the feature).

Just for grins, you can take the sample feature and drop it into the "/bin" directory of a web application. Take the configuration section shown for the sample console application and drop it into the `web.config` for a sample web application. Then create a test page with roughly the same code as shown above for the console application and have it write out the results to a web page. You will get the exact same feature behavior as was demonstrated for the console application.

Summary

The 2.0 Framework introduced a new design concept with provider-based features, which .NET 3.5 continues to support and make good use of. Rather than creating features and services where the internal implementations are "black boxes," the new provider-based features allow you to author custom implementations of business logic and data access logic. You can then swap these custom implementations into place with a few simple configuration settings.

The core design pattern used by provider-based features is the Strategy pattern. The Strategy pattern is a design approach that allows you to plug in different implementations for the core logic of a feature. In the case of both the 2.0 or 3.5 Frameworks and both ASP.NET 2.0 and ASP.NET 3.5, the providers are the implementation of the Strategy design pattern.

A number of support classes exist in `System.Configuration`, `System.Configuration.Providers` and `System.Web.Configuration` to make it easier to write provider-based features yourself. You can use the existing provider base class in conjunction with provider-specific configuration classes to build the basic underpinnings of a provider-based feature.

Overall the sample provider-based feature that was shown had roughly 200 lines for code (and that includes the braces!). Approximately half of the code is boilerplate implementation of things like the provider collection and the configuration class. However, with around only 100 lines of actual initialization code (and again the basics of initialization are the same regardless of feature), you can create a custom provider-based feature that you can use across the spectrum of fat client and web-based applications.

11

Membership

One of the unique aspects of ASP.NET 2.0 and ASP.NET 3.5 is that they introduce a number of powerful application services that are built using the provider model. Membership is one of the services addressing the common need that websites have for creating and managing users and their credentials. Although the Membership feature ships with a great deal of functionality right out of the box, it is also flexible enough for you to customize or extend many of the core aspects of the feature.

This chapter discusses the core classes of the Membership feature: the public static `Membership` class, the base `MembershipProvider` class, and the `MembershipUser` class all include functionality that is common regardless of the kind of providers used with the feature. You will see the various coding assumptions baked into the Membership feature for each of these classes. `MembershipProvider` is covered in detail so that you get a better idea about what needs to be implemented as well as the general behavior that ASP.NET expects from custom providers.

Last, you gain some insight into miscellaneous design concepts and areas of the Membership feature. The idea of user uniqueness is covered along with guidance about how to create a custom hash algorithm for use by providers. You also see how you can use the Membership feature in applications other than ASP.NET websites.

This chapter will cover the following topics:

- ❑ The `Membership` class
- ❑ The `MembershipUser` class
- ❑ The `MembershipProvider` base class
- ❑ The "primary key" for membership
- ❑ Supported environments
- ❑ Using custom Hash algorithms

The Membership Class

Probably the first exposure many of you had to the Membership feature was through the similarly named `Membership` class. This class is defined as a public static class, and the style of programming you use with it is meant to parallel other common ASP.NET classes such as `Request`, `Response`, and so on. Rather than having to muddle around trying to figure out how to get up and running with the feature, the idea is that after developers know of the `Membership` class, they can quickly access the functionality of the feature.

As with many provider-based features, the most important task the `Membership` class provides has already completed before any of your code does anything substantial with the feature. The previous chapter, on the provider model, showed how a static feature class is responsible for initializing a feature, including the instantiation and initialization of all providers associated with the feature. Because the `Membership` class is static, it performs initialization only once during the lifetime of an application. Furthermore, it instantiates only one instance of each configured `MembershipProvider`. So, if you plan on writing custom `MembershipProviders`, you need to follow the guidelines from Chapter 10 to ensure that your custom providers are thread-safe in all public properties and methods.

Although the `Membership` class is static, for historical reasons (the Membership feature was implemented very early on in the development cycle of ASP.NET 2.0) the class doesn't take advantage of the 2.0 Framework's support for static constructors. Instead, if you were to disassemble the class you would see that it has an internal initialization method that implements locking semantics to ensure that it initializes the feature only once. Furthermore, scattered (or perhaps more accurately, liberally spammed) through all the properties and methods are internal calls to the initialization method to ensure that the feature has parsed configuration and instantiated providers before attempting to do anything substantial with the feature.

If you look at the public signature of the `Membership` class, the properties and methods are broken down into three general areas:

- ❑ Public properties that mirror data loaded from configuration
- ❑ Public methods that are just façades on top of the underlying default provider
- ❑ Utility methods that can be used by providers

Before delving into each of these areas though, you need to be familiar with the difference between the feature's providers, and the feature's default provider. By now, you have probably seen many examples of the Membership feature's configuration. The default configuration can always be found up in `machine.config` (more on why this is the case a little bit later).

Because you can configure multiple providers for the Membership feature, much of the public API on the `Membership` static class may seem a bit redundant. Furthermore, you might wonder how a method like `Membership.CreateUser` maps to all the providers you have configured. This is where the concept of the default provider comes in. The `<membership />` configuration element has a `defaultProvider` attribute that defines the specific provider that the static `Membership` class "talks" to for much of its API.

```
<membership defaultProvider="SomeProviderDefinition">
  <providers>
    <add name="SomeProviderDefinition" … />
```

```
      <add name="A_Different_Provider_Definition" … />
    </providers>
  </membership>
```

If you have only one provider defined in configuration, using the static `Membership` class and getting a reference to the single default provider are pretty much the same thing. The only difference between the two approaches is that the static `Membership` class provides several convenient overloads that map to the method signatures found on a `MembershipProvider`. For example, several `CreateUser` overloads on the static `Membership` class internally map to the single `CreateUser` method that is defined on `MembershipProvider`.

However, if you have multiple provider references in configuration, it is almost guaranteed that the static `Membership` class will be of limited use to you. In fact, I would go so far as to say that other than using the `Membership` class for reading global Membership configuration settings, you probably won't use the `Membership` class at all in this scenario. By way of example, even the login controls that rely heavily on the Membership feature don't make much use of the static `Membership` class. Instead, the login controls get a reference to individual providers via the `Membership.Providers` property and then invoke various pieces of functionality directly on the providers with a `MembershipProvider` reference.

Of all the properties available on the Membership class, only the following ones are global to the feature:

❑   `HashAlgorithmType`: This is a string property that echoes back the value of the `hashAlgorithmType` attribute from configuration. It is mainly of use to custom provider implementers that need to know which hash algorithm an application expects from its providers.

❑   `Provider`: Returns a `MembershipProvider` reference to the provider defined by the `defaultProvider` attribute on the `<membership />` configuration element. If you have only one provider, you probably won't use this property.

❑   `Providers`: Returns a `MembershipProviderCollection` containing one reference to each provider defined within the `<providers />` element contained within a `<membership />` element. If your application needs to use multiple providers, you will become very familiar this property.

❑   `UserIsOnlineTimeWindow`: Defines the number of minutes that should be used to determine whether a user has been considered active on the site.

Several other static public properties are available on the `Membership` class, but I won't list them here. These properties are just part of the `Membership` façade that maps to the same set of properties on the default provider. So, if you access the `Membership.PasswordStrengthRegularExpression` property for example, you are really retrieving the value of the `PasswordStrengthRegularExpression` property from the default Membership provider. There is also a public event definition: the `Validating Password` event. If you register an event handler with this property, in reality you are registering your event handler with the default provider.

Most of the public methods on the `Membership` class are also façades that just forward their calls internally to the default provider. The purpose of these façade methods is to make the underlying `MembershipProvider` API a little less intimidating. As such, the façade methods "fill in the blanks" for method overloads that have fewer parameters than their counterparts on the `MembershipProvider` class. On one hand, for example, administrative methods like `Membership.FindUsersByName` don't require you to supply more advanced parameters such as page index or page size; you can just call the narrower overloads on the `Membership` class without having to juggle the extra information. On the other hand, if you take advantage of this functionality with a 100,000 user data store, you will quickly regret not using the wider overloads that support paging.

This leads to a bit of a philosophical question: to use or not to use the façade methods on the static `Membership` class. If you are just writing a small site for yourself and you want to get up and running with a minimum of hassle, all the façade methods are reasonable. However, if you plan on having more than a few hundred users on your site, and definitely if you are working on production-grade line-of-business or Internet-facing applications, you should look more carefully at the façade methods that you use. At a minimum, I would recommend using the widest overloads possible because they give you full access to all the parameters from the underlying `MembershipProvider`.

To be absolutely flexible, though, and to ensure your applications are maintainable over the long haul, you should use the `Membership.Providers` property to get a reference to the desired provider, and then use the resulting `MembershipProvider` reference to carry out your tasks. This programming style will give you the flexibility in the future to use multiple providers in your application, something that will be somewhat monotonous to retrofit into an application that relied exclusively on the static `Membership` class:

C#

```
//This is OK for simpler applications
MembershipUser mu = Membership.CreateUser("I_am_new","123password@#");

//This is better to use for larger applications
MembershipProvider mp = Membership.Providers["Provider_Number_2"];

MembershipCreateStatus status;
MembershipUser mu;
mu = mp.CreateUser("username", "12password@#", "email",
            "passwordquestion", "passwordanswer",
            true /*isApproved*/, null /*providerUserKey*/, out status);
```

VB.NET

```
'This is OK for simpler applications
Dim mu As MembershipUser = Membership.CreateUser("I_am_new", "123password#")
'This is better to use for larger applications
Dim mp As MembershipProvider = Membership.Providers("Provider_Number_2")
Dim status As MembershipCreateStatus
Dim mu As MembershipUser
mu = mp.CreateUser("username", _
                "12password@#", _
                "email", _
                "passwordquestion", _
                "passwordanswer", _
                True, _
                Nothing, _
                status)
```

Obviously, it is a bit more of a hassle to use the provider directly in this case because the `CreateUser` overload supports quite a few more parameters. But after you code it this way, it is much easier to swap out providers later, potentially even adding logic that chooses a different provider on the fly based on information supplied by the user. It also makes it easier to adjust the code if you choose to turn on or off features like unique email addresses and self-service password resets.

The third set of methods on the `Membership` class are utility methods. Currently, there is only one: `GeneratePassword`. If you write custom providers that support self-service password reset with auto-generated passwords, this method comes in handy. The method signature is shown here:

C#

```
Public Shared Function GeneratePassword(ByVal length As Integer, _
        ByVal numberOfNonAlphanumericCharacters As Integer) _
        As String
```

VB.NET

```
Public Shared Function GeneratePassword(ByVal length As Integer, _
        ByVal numberOfNonAlphanumericCharacters As Integer) _
        As String
```

One mode of self-service password reset automatically generates a random password when a user has forgotten his or her password. Because generating a string random password is a pain to get correct, it is actually a handy utility to have around.

The method generates a random string of characters based on the length parameter. Furthermore, it will ensure that at least a number of these characters are considered to be nonalphanumeric characters (for example, `Char.IsLetterOrDigit` returns `false` for a certain number of random characters) based on the second parameter. Note that the method may generate a password with more nonalphanumeric characters than specified by the `numberOfNonAlphanumericCharacters` parameter; you are only guaranteed that the auto-generated password has at least this many nonalphanumeric characters. Last, the method ensures that each randomly generated character won't trigger a false positive from ASP.NET's request validation functionality. It would be frustrating to say the least if the system auto-generated a new password only for the poor website user to always be rejected on the login page because ASP.NET detected a potentially suspicious character in the submitted password when request validation was turned on.

The MembershipUser Class

Regardless of whether you code against the static `Membership` class or directly against `Membership Providers`, you will invariable deal with the `MembershipUser` class. The `MembershipUser` class is intended to be a lightweight representation of a user (though in retrospect it is just a tad bit too light-weight—hopefully, basic information such as first name, last name, and/or friendly name will be tacked on in a future release). The class is not intended to be an exhaustive or comprehensive representation of everything you would ever want to store about a user.

For ASP.NET 2.0 and ASP.NET 3.5, if you need to store more extensive information about a user, the usual approach is to leverage the Profile feature by defining the additional properties you need within the `<profile />` configuration section. Alternatively, you can author a custom provider (perhaps deriving from an existing provider type) that works with a derived version of `MembershipUser`. Using the Profile feature is definitely the simpler of the two approaches. However, writing a custom provider and custom `MembershipUser` class is appropriate if you do not want to use the Profile feature in your website. For more about the different approaches used to extend the Membership provider model in ASP.NET 2.0 and ASP.NET 3.5, see the article at `http://www.code-magazine.com/Article .aspx?quickid=0703071`). It will give you a detailed explanation on how to set up a custom Membership provider that attaches additional data into the `MembershipUser` without using the Profile feature.

The main purpose of the `MembershipUser` class is to contain the basic pieces of information relevant to authenticating a user. Some of the properties are self-explanatory, but I have listed them here with an explanation for each:

❑ `Comment`: Intended as the one generic property on `MembershipUser` that you can use to store any information you deem appropriate. No part of the Membership feature makes use of this property, and it is safe to say that future releases of the Membership feature will also leave this property alone. Although you can go overboard and implement entire universes of functionality with this property, it comes in handy when you need to store just a few extra pieces of information and need a convenient place to put them, perhaps those pesky first name and last name properties!

❑ `Username`: This is the username that your website users type when logging in. It is also one component of the primary key for users in the Membership feature and other related ASP.NET application services.

❑ `CreationDate`: The date and time when the user was first created in the back-end data store. The property returns its value as a local date time, but the expectation is that providers store it in universal coordinate date time (UTC).

❑ `ProviderUserKey`: An alternate representation of the primary key for a `MembershipUser`. Where `Username` is considered to be part of the primary key for identifying a user across all ASP.NET features, the `ProviderUserKey` is a data-store specific primary key for the user. This can be useful when retrofitting a custom `MembershipProvider` onto an existing data store and you want to integrate it with other features you have written that already rely on a data-store-specific primary key. Note that because this property is typed as object, it is up to you to make the correct type casts within your code.

❑ `ProviderName`: The string name of the provider that manages the `MembershipUser` instance. Because the `MembershipUser` class supports a number of methods that deal with the user object, each user object needs to know the provider that should be called. In other words, a `MembershipUser`'s methods act as a mini-façade on top of the provider that initially was responsible for creating the `MembershipUser`. As a side note, the reason that this property is a string (it was a `MembershipProvider` reference early on in ASP.NET 2.0 and is kept the same in ASP.NET 3.5) is to make it possible to serialize a `MembershipUser` instance. If this property had been left as a reference type, this would have required all `MembershipProvider` instances to also be serializable.

❑ `Email`: An optional email address for the user. This property is very important if you want to support self-service password resets because without an email address there is no way to communicate to the users the newly generated password or their old password.

❑ `IsApproved`: A Boolean property that provides a basic mechanism for indicating whether a user is actually allowed to log into a site. If you set `IsApproved` to `false` for a user, even if the user supplies the correct username-password credentials at login, the login attempt (that is, the call to ValidateUser) will fail. With the IsApproved property, you can implement a basic two-step user creation process where external customers request an account and internal personnel approve each account. The Web Administration Tool that is accessible inside of the Visual Studio environment provides a UI for this type of basic two-step creation process.

❑ IsOnline: A Boolean property indicating whether the user has been active on the site within the last Membership.UserIsOnlineTimeWindow minutes. The actual computation of whether a user is considered online is made inside of this property by comparing the LastActivity-Date property for the user to the current UTC time on the web server. If you rely on this property, make sure that your web servers regularly synchronize their time with a common time source. Note that the IsOnline property is not virtual in this release, so if you want to implement alternate logic for IsOnline, you have to add your own custom property to a derived implementation of MembershipUser.

❑ IsLockedOut: A Boolean property indicating whether the user account has been locked out due to a security violation. This property has a distinctly different connotation from the IsApproved property. While IsApproved simply indicates whether a user should be allowed to log into a site, IsLockedOut indicates whether an excessive number of bad login attempts have occurred. If you support self-service password reset or password retrieval using a password question-and-answer challenge, this property also indicates whether an excessive number of failed attempts were made to answer the user's password question.

❑ PasswordQuestion: You can choose to support self-service password resets or self-service password retrieval on your site. For added protection, you can require that the user answer a password question before resetting the password or retrieving the current password. This property contains the password question that was set for the user. It is up to you whether to allow each user to type in a unique question, or if you provide a canned list of password questions. Note that even though you can retrieve the password question for a user, the password answer is not exposed as a property because it should only be managed internally by providers.

❑ LastActivityDate: The last date and time that the user was considered to be active. Certain methods defined on MembershipProvider are expected to update this value in the back-end data store when called. Other companion features, such as Profile and Web Parts Personalization, update this value assuming that you use the ASP.NET SQL providers for all these features. The property is returned as a local date time, but providers should internally store the value in UTC time.

❑ LastLoginDate: The last date and time a successful call to ValidateUser occurred. Providers are expected to update this value after each successful password validation. The property is returned as a local date time, but providers should internally store the value in UTC time.

❑ LastPasswordChangedDate: The last date and time that the password was changed, either by the user explicitly updating their password or by having the system create a new auto-generated password. The property is returned as a local date time, but providers should internally store the value in UTC time.

❑ LastLockoutDate: The last date and time that the user account was locked out, either due to an excessive number of bad passwords or because too many bad password answers were supplied. This value is only expected to be reliable when the account is in a locked out state (that is, this.IsLockedOut is true). For accounts that are not locked out, this property may instead return a default value. The property is returned as a local date time, but providers should internally store the value in UTC time.

Extending MembershipUser

The MembershipUser class is public but it is not sealed, so you can write derived versions of this class. Most of its public properties are defined virtual for this reason. In fact, the ActiveDirectory MembershipProvider takes advantage of this and uses a derived version of MembershipUser to help optimize the interaction of the provider with an Active Directory or Active Directory Application Mode data store.

The class definition for MembershipUser is:

C#

```
public class MembershipUser
{
  //Virtual properties
  public virtual string UserName{ get; }
  public virtual object ProviderUserKey{ get; }
  public virtual string Email{ get; set; }
  public virtual string PasswordQuestion{ get; }
  public virtual string Comment{ get; set; }
  public virtual bool IsApproved{ get; set; }
  public virtual bool IsLockedOut{ get; }
  public virtual DateTime LastLockoutDate{ get; }
  public virtual DateTime CreationDate { get; }
  public virtual DateTime LastLoginDate { get; set; }
  public virtual DateTime LastActivityDate { get; set; }
  public virtual DateTime LastPasswordChangedDate { get; }
  public virtual string ProviderName { get; }

  //Non-virtual properties
  public bool IsOnline { get; }

  //Constructors
  public MembershipUser(
          string        providerName,
          string        name,
          object        providerUserKey,
          string        email,
          string        passwordQuestion,
          string        comment,
          bool          isApproved,
          bool          isLockedOut,
          DateTime      creationDate,
          DateTime      lastLoginDate,
          DateTime      lastActivityDate,
          DateTime      lastPasswordChangedDate,
          DateTime      lastLockoutDate )
  protected MembershipUser() { }

  //Methods - all are virtual
  public virtual string GetPassword()
  public virtual string GetPassword(string passwordAnswer)
  public virtual bool ChangePassword(string oldPassword, string newPassword)
  public virtual bool ChangePasswordQuestionAndAnswer(
          string password, string newPasswordQuestion, string newPasswordAnswer)
```

```
    public virtual string ResetPassword(string passwordAnswer)
    public virtual string ResetPassword()
    public virtual bool UnlockUser()
}
```

VB.NET

```
Public Class MembershipUser
    ' Overridable Properties
    Public Overridable Property Comment() As String
    Public Overridable ReadOnly Property CreationDate As DateTime
    Public Overridable Property Email As String
    Public Overridable Property IsApproved As Boolean
    Public Overridable ReadOnly Property IsLockedOut As Boolean
    Public Overridable Property LastActivityDate As DateTime
    Public Overridable ReadOnly Property LastLockoutDate As DateTime
    Public Overridable Property LastLoginDate As DateTime
    Public Overridable ReadOnly Property LastPasswordChangedDate As DateTime
    Public Overridable ReadOnly Property PasswordQuestion As String
    Public Overridable ReadOnly Property ProviderName As String
    Public Overridable ReadOnly Property ProviderUserKey As Object
    Public Overridable ReadOnly Property UserName As String

        ' Non-Overridable Properties
    Public ReadOnly Property IsOnline As Boolean
        ' Constructors
    Protected Sub New()

    Public Sub New(ByVal providerName As String, ByVal name As String, _
    ByVal providerUserKey As Object, ByVal email As String, _
    ByVal passwordQuestion As String, ByVal comment As String, _
    ByVal isApproved As Boolean, ByVal isLockedOut As Boolean, _
    ByVal creationDate As DateTime, ByVal lastLoginDate As DateTime, _
    ByVal lastActivityDate As DateTime, ByVal lastPasswordChangedDate As DateTime, _
    ByVal lastLockoutDate As DateTime)

        ' Methods - all are overridable
    Public Overridable Function ChangePassword(ByVal oldPassword As String, _
    ByVal newPassword As String) As Boolean

    Friend Function ChangePassword(ByVal oldPassword As String, _
    ByVal newPassword As String, ByVal throwOnError As Boolean) As Boolean

    Public Overridable Function ChangePasswordQuestionAndAnswer _
    (ByVal password As String, _
    ByVal newPasswordQuestion As String, ByVal newPasswordAnswer _
    As String) As Boolean

    Public Overridable Function GetPassword() As String
    Friend Function GetPassword(ByVal throwOnError As Boolean) As String
    Public Overridable Function GetPassword(ByVal passwordAnswer As String) As String

    Friend Function GetPassword(ByVal answer As String, _
    ByVal throwOnError As Boolean) As String
```

```
          Private Function GetPassword(ByVal answer As String, _
          ByVal useAnswer As Boolean, ByVal throwOnError As Boolean) As String

          Public Overridable Function ResetPassword() As String
          Friend Function ResetPassword(ByVal throwOnError As Boolean) As String
          Public Overridable Function ResetPassword(ByVal _
          passwordAnswer As String) As String

          Friend Function ResetPassword(ByVal passwordAnswer As String, _
          ByVal throwOnError As Boolean) As String

          Private Function ResetPassword(ByVal passwordAnswer As String, _
          ByVal useAnswer As Boolean, ByVal throwOnError As Boolean) As String

          Public Overrides Function ToString() As String
          Public Overridable Function UnlockUser() As Boolean
          Friend Overridable Sub Update()
          Private Sub UpdateSelf()
     End Class
```

As mentioned earlier, the IsOnline property cannot be overridden, so you are left with the default implementation. All the other properties, though, can be overridden. The default implementation for these properties simply returns the property values that were set when the object was first constructed. As you can see from the lengthy constructor parameter list, the usage model for MembershipUser is:

1. Either a provider or your code new()'s up an instance, passing in all the relevant data.

2. You subsequently access the properties set in the constructor via the public properties.

3. If you want to then update the MembershipUser object, you pass the modified instance back to the UpdateUser method implemented either on the static Membership class or on a specific MembershipProvider.

Note that with this approach, updating the user is a little awkward because there is no update method on the user object itself. Instead, the user object is passed as a piece of state to the UpdateUser method on a provider.

The capability to override individual properties is somewhat limited, though, because you don't have access to the private variables that back each of these properties. The most likely purpose of an override would be to throw an exception (for example, NotSupportedException) for properties that may not be supported by custom providers. For example, if you authored a custom provider that did not support the concept of account lockouts, you could throw a NotSupportedException from a LastLockoutDate override.

All the public methods currently defined on MembershipUser can be overridden. The default implementations of these methods are just façades that do two things:

❑ Get a reference to the MembershipProvider based on the providerName parameter supplied in the constructor.

❑ Call the method on the MembershipProvider reference that corresponds to the public method on the MembershipUser object (for example, the ResetPassword overloads on MembershipUser call the ResetPassword method on the appropriate provider).

The `providerName` parameter on the constructor is actually a very important piece of information that effectively limits any kind of "tricks" involving manual creation of providers. Remember from Chapter 10 that the provider initialization sequence is something that you can accomplish with a few lines of your own custom code.

However, if you attempt to instantiate `MembershipProviders` with your own code, and if you need to manipulate `MembershipUser` instances, your code will fail. Inside of the `MembershipUser` constructor, a validation check ensures `providerName` actually exists in the `Membership.Providers` collection. If the provider cannot be found, an exception is thrown. If you wanted to try something like spinning up dozens or hundreds of provider instances on the fly without first defining the providers in configuration, the basic approach or just instantiating providers manually won't work.

MembershipUser State after Updates

If you call any of the public methods on `MembershipUser` that affect the state of the user object (that is, all methods except for the `GetPassword` overloads), then the `MembershipUser` instance calls an internal method called `UpdateSelf`. Unfortunately, in ASP.NET 2.0 and ASP.NET 3.5 this method is not public or protected, let alone being defined as virtual, so the behavior of this method is a black box. What happens is that after the state of the `MembershipUser` instance is modified, the base class internally triggers a call to `GetUser()` on the user object's associated provider instance. If you look at an SQL trace on the `SqlMembershipProvider`, or if you trace method calls on a custom provider, this is why you always see an extra user retrieval running after most of the methods on `MembershipUser` are called.

With the `MembershipUser` instance returned from the `GetUser` call, the internal `UpdateSelf` method transfers the latest property values from the returned `MembershipUser` instance to the properties on the original `MembershipUser` instance. The idea here is that some of the public methods on `MembershipUser` cause changes to related properties (for example, calling `ResetPassword` implicitly changes the `LastPasswordChangedDate`). The theory was that it wouldn't make sense for a method call to change the state of the `MembershipUser` instance and then have the instance not reflect the changes. However, arguably there isn't anything wrong with a different approach that would have left the original `MembershipUser` instance intact despite the changes in the data store. Some developers will probably find it a little odd that the original `MembershipUser` instance suddenly changes on them.

Because some of the properties on a `MembershipUser` instance are public read-only properties, the behavior of this self-updating gets a little weird. The `UpdateSelf` method transfers updated values for read-only properties directly to the private variables of the `MembershipUser` base class. For properties that have setters, `UpdateSelf` transfers property data by calling the public `MembershipUser` setters instead. This means that if you have written a derived `MembershipUser` class, and overridden the public setters and the constructors, the `UpdateSelf` behavior may either bypass your custom logic or it may call your logic too many times.

For example, if a derived `MembershipUser` class overrides the constructor and performs some manipulations on `PasswordQuestion` prior to calling the base constructor, then the private variable holding the password question will reflect this work. If you then subsequently call `ChangePasswordQuestion AndAnswer` on the `MembershipUser` instance, the internal `UpdateSelf` method will cause the following to occur:

1. A new `MembershipUser` instance is retrieved from the call to `GetUser` (assume that you write a custom provider that returns a derived `MembershipUser` instance). As a result, this new instance will have its password question processed in your custom constructor.

2. UpdateSelf then takes the result of MembershipUser.PasswordQuestion and transfers its value directly to the private variable on the original MembershipUser instance that stores the question.

With this sequence you are probably OK because the custom processing in your constructor happened only once and then the result was directly stored in a private variable on the original instance. What happens, though, for a property with a public setter (for example, the Comment property)? Now the sequence of steps is:

1. A new MembershipUser instance is retrieved from the call to GetUser. The new instance does something to the Comment in your custom constructor.

2. UpdateSelf takes the result of MembershipUser.Comment and calls the public Comment setter on the original MembershipUser instance. If you have custom logic in your setter as well, then it will end up manipulating the Comment property a second time, which will potentially result in a bogus value.

To demonstrate this, start out with a custom MembershipUser type, as shown below:

C#

```csharp
using System.Web.Security;
...
public class CustomMembershipUser : MembershipUser
{
    public CustomMembershipUser() {}

    //Copy constructor
    public CustomMembershipUser(MembershipUser mu) :
        base(mu.ProviderName, mu.UserName, mu.ProviderUserKey, mu.Email,
            mu.PasswordQuestion, mu.Comment, mu.IsApproved, mu.IsLockedOut,
            mu.CreationDate, mu.LastLoginDate, mu.LastActivityDate,
            mu.LastPasswordChangedDate, mu.LastLockoutDate) { }

    public override string Comment
    {
        get
        {   return base.Comment; }
        set
        {
            base.Comment =
                value + " Whoops! Extra modification occurred in property setter";
        }
    }
}
```

VB.NET

```vbnet
Imports System.Web.Security

    ...


Public Class CustomMembershipUser
    Inherits MembershipUser
```

```
        Public Sub New()
        End Sub

        Public Sub New(ByVal providerName As String, _
                       ByVal name As String, ByVal providerUserKey As Object, _
                       ByVal email As String, ByVal passwordQuestion As String, _
                       ByVal comment As String, ByVal isApproved As Boolean, _
                       ByVal isLockedOut As Boolean, ByVal creationDate As DateTime, _
                       ByVal lastLoginDate As DateTime, _
                       ByVal lastActivityDate As DateTime, _
                       ByVal lastPasswordChangedDate As DateTime, _
                       ByVal lastLockoutDate As DateTime)
            MyBase.New(providerName, name, providerUserKey, email, _
                       passwordQuestion, comment, isApproved, _
                       isLockedOut, creationDate, lastLoginDate, _
                       lastActivityDate, lastPasswordChangedDate, lastLockoutDate)
        End Sub

        Public Overrides Property Comment() As String
            Get
                Return MyBase.Comment
            End Get
            Set(ByVal value As String)
                MyBase.Comment = value & _
                " Whoops! Extra modification occurred in property setter"
            End Set
        End Property
End Class
```

Try using this custom type to retrieve a MembershipUser and perform what should be a no-op update:

C#

```
…
MembershipUser mu = Membership.GetUser("testuser");

//Convert the MembershipUser into the custom user type
CustomMembershipUser cu = new CustomMembershipUser(mu);

Response.Write("Comment before update: " + cu.Comment + "<br/>");
Membership.UpdateUser(cu);
Response.Write("Comment after update: " + cu.Comment);
```

VB.NET

```
…
Dim mu As MembershipUser = Membership.GetUser("testuser")
mu.Comment = "This is the original comment"
Membership.UpdateUser(mu)

Dim cu As New CustomMembershipUser(mu)

Response.Write("Comment before update: " & cu.Comment & "<br/>")
Membership.UpdateUser(cu)

Response.Write("Comment after update: " & cu.Comment
```

When you run this code snippet in a page load event, the output is bit surprising:

```
Comment before update: This is the original comment
Comment after update: This is the original comment Whoops! Extra modification
occurred in property setter
```

Even though the code snippet appears to change none of the properties on the MembershipUser instance, after the update the Comment property has clearly been modified. This is due to the behavior of the internal UpdateSelf method on MembershipUser; in this case, UpdateSelf was triggered by code inside of the Membership class implementation of UpdateUser. (Membership.UpdateUser calls an internal method on MembershipUser which in turn calls UpdateSelf). You will see the same side effect from calling methods on MembershipUser as well. If you run into this problem, you can avoid the "stealth" update by calling UpdateUser on a provider directly. Doing so bypasses the refresh logic hidden inside of the Membership and MembershipUser classes.

It is likely, though, that derived versions of MembershipUser probably won't be changing the data that is returned inside of property setters. However, developers may author derived classes that implement custom dirty detection (that is, if the setters weren't called and an update is attempted, do nothing with the MembershipUser object) as well as throw exceptions from unsupported properties.

For the case of dirty detection, the only real workaround is to override the methods as well as the properties on MembershipUser. Then you can write code in the method overrides that does something like:

C#

```csharp
using System.Web.Security;

public class CustomMembershipUser : MembershipUser
{
    //Used by a custom provider to determine if the user object really
    //needs to be updated.
    internal bool isDirty = false;
    ...
    public override string Comment
    {
        set
        {
            base.Comment = value;
            isDirty = true;
        }
    }

    public override bool ChangePassword(string oldPassword, string newPassword)
    {
        //When this call returns, UpdateSelf will have triggered the object's
        //dirty flag by accident.
        bool retVal = base.ChangePassword(oldPassword, newPassword);

        //reset your private dirty tracking flags to false at this point
        isDirty = false;
    }
}
```

VB.NET

```vbnet
Imports System.Web.Security

Public Class CustomMembershipUser
  Inherits MembershipUser

  'Used by a custom provider to determine if the user object really
  'needs to be updated.
  Friend isDirty As Boolean = False

...

  Public Overrides WriteOnly Property Comment() As String
    Set(ByVal value As String)
          MyBase.Comment = value
          isDirty = True
    End Set
  End Property

  Public Overrides Function ChangePassword(ByVal oldPassword As String, _
                                    ByVal newPassword As String) As Boolean
      'When this call returns, UpdateSelf will have triggered the object's
      'dirty flag by accident.
      Dim retVal As Boolean = MyBase.ChangePassword(oldPassword, newPassword)
      'reset your private dirty tracking flags to false at this point
      isDirty = False
  End Function
End Class
```

On one hand, basically you need to explicitly manage your dirty detection logic and ensure that after you call the base implementation, your reset your internal dirty detection flags because they may have been spuriously tripped due to the way UpdateSelf works.

On the other hand, if you throw exceptions from some of your property getters and setters, you may be wondering if it is even possible to write a derived MembershipUser class. Theoretically, if the second the internal UpdateSelf method attempts to transfer property data back to the original MembershipUser instance, your custom class should blow up. In the finest programming tradition (and trust me; I mean this tongue in cheek), the solution in ASP.NET 2.0 and ASP.NET 3.5 is that the transfer logic inside of UpdateSelf is wrapped in a series of try-catch blocks. So, the guts of this method look something like:

C#

```csharp
try
{
    Comment = newUserFromGetUser.Comment;
}
catch (NotSupportedException) { }
```

VB.NET

```vbnet
Try
    Comment = newUserFromGetUser.Comment
Catch e1 As NotSupportedException
End Try
```

And here you thought jokes about Microsoft code relying on swallowing exceptions was a joke; however, `ildasm.exe` does not lie. Seriously though, the trick to making sure that a derived `MembershipUser` class does not fail because of unimplemented properties is to *always* throw a `NotSupportedException` (or a derived version of this exception) from any properties that you do not want to support. The internal `UpdateSelf` will always eat a `NotSupportedException` when it is transferring property data between `MembershipUser` instances. If you use a different exception type, though, you will quickly see that your derived `MembershipUser` type fails whenever its public set methods are called. Needless to say, making `UpdateSelf` protected virtual is on the list of enhancements for a future release!

The way in which updated property data is transferred back to the original `MembershipUser` instance is summarized in the following table:

Property Name	Transferred to Private Variable	Transferred Using Public Setter
Comment	No	Yes
CreationDate	Yes	No
Email	No	Yes
IsApproved	No	Yes
IsLockedOut	Yes	No
LastActivityDate	No	Yes
LastLockoutDate	Yes	No
LastLoginDate	No	Yes
LastPasswordChangedDate	Yes	No
PasswordQuestion	Yes	No
ProviderUserKey	Yes	No

Why Are Only Certain Properties Updatable?

Only a subset of the properties on a `MembershipUser` instance has public setters. The reasons for this differ depending on the specific property. The different reasons for each read-only property are described in the following list:

❑   `UserName`: In this release of the Membership feature, a username is considered part of the primary key for a `MembershipUser`. As a result, there is no built-in support for updating the username. There are no public APIs in any of the application services that allow you to make this change, though of course there is nothing stopping enterprising developers from tweaking things down in the data layer to make this work. From an API perspective, because username is not meant to be updated, this property is left as a read-only property.

❑   `ProviderUserKey`: Because this property is a data-store specific surrogate for `UserName`, the same feature restriction applies. The Membership feature doesn't expect the underlying primary key for a user to be updatable. Again, this may change in a future release.

- ❑ PasswordQuestion: This piece of user data is updatable, but you need to use the ChangePasswordQuestionAndAnswer method to effect a change. You cannot just change the property directly and then call Update on a provider.

- ❑ IsLockedOut: The value for this property is meant to reflect the side effect of previous login attempts or attempts to change a password using a question and answer challenge. As a result, it isn't intended to be directly updatable through any APIs. Note that you can unlock a user with the UnlockUser method on MembershipUser.

- ❑ LastLockoutDate: As with IsLockedOut, the value of this property is a side effect of an account being locked, or being explicitly unlocked. So, it is never intended to be directly updatable though the APIs.

- ❑ CreationDate: This date/time is determined as a side effect of calling CreateUser. After a user is created, it doesn't really make sense to go back and change this date.

- ❑ LastPasswordChangedDate: As with other read-only properties, the value is changed as a side effect of calling either ChangePassword or ResetPassword. From a security perspective, it wouldn't be a good idea to let arbitrary code change this type of data because then you wouldn't have any guarantee of when a user actually triggered a password change.

- ❑ IsOnline: This is actually a computed property as described earlier, so there is no need for a setter. You can indirectly influence this property by setting LastActivityDate.

- ❑ ProviderName: When a MembershipUser instance is created, it must be associated with a valid provider. After this association is established, though, the Membership feature expects the same provider to manage the user instance for the duration of its lifetime. If this property were settable, you could end up with some strange results if you changed the value in between calls to the other public methods on the MembershipUser class.

Among the properties that are public, Email, Comment, and IsApproved are pretty easy to understand. Email and Comment are just data fields, while IsApproved can be toggled between true and false, with a value of false causing ValidateUser to fail even if the correct username and password are supplied to the method.

LastActivityDate is public so that you can write other features that work with the Membership online tracking feature. For example, you could implement a custom feature that updates the user's LastActivityDate each time user-specific data is retrieved. The ASP.NET SQL providers actually do this for Profile and Web Parts Personalization. However the ASP.NET SQL providers all use a common schema, so the Profile and Personalization providers perform the update from inside of the database. The LastActivityDate property allows for similar behavior but at the level of an object API as opposed to a data layer.

The last settable property on MembershipUser is the LastLoginDate property. However, leaving LastLoginDate as settable may seem a bit odd. It means that someone can write code to arbitrarily set when a user logged in, which, of course, means audit trails for logins can become suspect. Some developers, though, want to integrate the existing Membership providers with their own authentication systems. For these scenarios, there is the concept of multiple logins, and thus the desire to log a user account into an external system while having the Membership feature reflect when this external login occurred.

If you want to prevent LastLoginDate from being updatable (currently only the SQL provider even supports getting and setting this value), you can write a derived MembershipProvider that returns a derived MembershipUser instance. The derived MembershipUser instance can just throw a NotSupportedException from the LastLoginDate setter.

DateTime Assumptions

There are quite a number of date-related properties on the Membership feature, especially for the `MembershipUser` class. For smaller websites the question of how date-time values are handled is probably moot. In single-server environments, or web farms running in a single data center, server local time would be sufficient. However, as the feature was being iterated on, a few things became pretty clear:

❑   The `ActiveDirectoryMembershipProvider` relies on AD/ADAM or ADLDS for storage. The Active Directory store keeps track of significant time-related data using UTC time, not server local time.

❑   If in the future the feature is ever extended to officially support database replication with the `SqlMembrshipProvider`, then problems with running in multiple time zones will become an issue.

For both of these reasons, the code within the providers as well as within the core Membership classes was changed to instead use UTC time internally. Unlike the forms authentication feature that unfortunately has the quirk of using local times as opposed to UTC times, the desire was to have the Membership feature always work in UTC time to avoid problems with multiple time-zone support as well as clock adjustments (that is, daylight savings time).

Although the Membership feature doesn't support database replication in ASP.NET 2.0 and ASP.NET 3.5 (it has never been tested), it is theoretically possible in future releases to have a network topology whereby different slices of Membership data are created in completely different time zones and then cross-replicated between different data centers. For this kind of scenario, having a common time measure is critical.

On a less theoretical note, it is likely that some websites will do things such as create new users right around the time server clocks are being adjusted. If information such as `CreationDate` were stored in machine local time, you would end up with some bizarre data records indicating that users were being created in the recent past or the soon-to-arrive future. Especially with security sensitive data this isn't a desirable outcome.

Some folks may also have server deployments that span time zones. For example, you may have multiple data centers with web servers running into two different time zones, with each set of web servers pointed back to a central data center running your database servers. In this kind of scenario, which time zone do you pick? If you don't use UTC time, you will always end up with weird date-time behavior because with this type of physical deployment some set of servers will always be in a different time zone than the time zone you selected for storing your data.

From a programming perspective, the .NET Frameworks traditionally returned machine local times from all public APIs. To handle this behavior while still handling UTC times internally, the Membership feature assumes that all date-time parameters passed in to public properties and methods are in local time. Furthermore, whenever date-time data is returned from public properties and methods, data is always converted back to machine local time. Internally though, the core Membership classes as well as the default providers manipulate and store date-time data in UTC time. If you look at the data stored by the `SqlMembershipProvider` in a database, you will see that all the date-time-related columns appears to be wrong (assuming, of course, that you don't actually live somewhere in the GMT time zone!). The reason is that by the time any Membership data is stored, the date-time-related variables have been converted to UTC time.

From the standpoint of someone using the Membership feature, this behavior should be mostly transparent to you. You can retrieve instances of MembershipUser objects, set date-related properties, or perform date-related queries all using the local time for your machine. The only potential for confusion occurs if you perform search queries using other features such as Profile that support date ranges for search parameters. If your query happens to span a time period when the clocks were reset, you will probably get slightly different results than if the Membership feature had stored data keyed off of a machine's local time.

Within the Membership feature, the way in which UTC times are enforced is:

❑   The various classes always call ToUniversalTime on any date-time parameters passed in to them.

❑   The MembershipUser class calls ToUniversalTime on all date-time parameters for its constructor as well as in the setters for any public properties. This means that you can set a machine-local date time for a property like LastActivityDate, and MembershipUser will still ensure that it is treated as a UTC time internally. Due to the way the .NET Framework System.DateTime class works, you can actually pass UTC date-time parameters if you want to the MembershipUser class (or any class for that matter). This works because the result of calling ToUniversalTime on a UTC System.DateTime is a no-op.

❑   For public getters, the MembershipUser class calls ToLocalTime on date-time data prior to returning it. As a result, all data retrieved from the Membership feature will always reflect machine-local times.

The one thing you should do for your servers, both web servers and whatever back-end servers store Membership data, is to regularly synchronize your server clocks with a common time source. Although this recommendation isn't made specifically because of any inherent problem with using UTC time, the implementation details for supporting UTC time highlight the need for synchronized clocks.

Especially for the SqlMembershipProvider, date-time values are usually created and compared on the web server, and then transmitted and stored on a database server. In any web farm with more than one server, this means that no single master server is responsible for generating date-time values. You could definitely end up with one web server logging a failed login attempt (and hence updating the date-time-related failure data) and a different server loading this information during the course of processing a second login attempt. Excessive amounts of clock skew across a web farm will lead to incorrect time calculations being made in this type of scenario. A few seconds of time skew isn't going to be noticeable, but if your servers are minutes apart, you will probably see intermittent problems with date-time-related functionality.

If you plan on writing custom providers for the Membership feature, you should keep the "UTC-ness" of the feature in mind. If at all possible, custom providers should follow the same behavior as the built-in providers, and store all date-time information internally as UTC date times.

The MembershipProvider Base Class

The central part of the Membership feature is its use of providers that derive from System.Web.Security .MembershipProvider. Out of the box, the Framework ships with two implementations of this class: SqlMembershipProvider and ActiveDirectoryMembershipProvider. Both of these providers are discussed in more detail in succeeding chapters. Because the Membership feature allows you to configure any type of provider, you can also write your own custom implementations of this class.

The base class definition that all providers must adhere to is shown below. The class definition falls into three major areas: abstract properties, abstract and protected methods, and a small number of event-related definitions.

C#

```csharp
public abstract class MembershipProvider : ProviderBase
{
    //Properties
    public abstract bool EnablePasswordRetrieval { get; }
    public abstract bool EnablePasswordReset { get; }
    public abstract bool RequiresQuestionAndAnswer { get; }
    public abstract string ApplicationName { get; set; }
    public abstract int MaxInvalidPasswordAttempts { get; }
    public abstract int PasswordAttemptWindow { get; }
    public abstract bool RequiresUniqueEmail { get; }
    public abstract MembershipPasswordFormat PasswordFormat { get; }
    public abstract int MinRequiredPasswordLength { get; }
    public abstract int MinRequiredNonAlphanumericCharacters { get; }
    public abstract string PasswordStrengthRegularExpression { get; }

    //Public Methods
    public abstract MembershipUser CreateUser( string username,
        string password, string email, string passwordQuestion,
        string passwordAnswer, bool   isApproved, object providerUserKey,
        out    MembershipCreateStatus status )

    public abstract bool ChangePasswordQuestionAndAnswer(string username,
        string password, string newPasswordQuestion, string newPasswordAnswer)

    public abstract string GetPassword(string username, string answer)
    public abstract bool ChangePassword(string username, string oldPassword,
        string newPassword)

    public abstract string ResetPassword(string username, string answer)
    public abstract void UpdateUser(MembershipUser user)
    public abstract bool ValidateUser(string username, string password)
    public abstract bool UnlockUser( string userName )
    public abstract MembershipUser GetUser( object providerUserKey,
        bool userIsOnline )

    public abstract MembershipUser GetUser(string username, bool userIsOnline)
    public abstract string GetUserNameByEmail(string email)
    public abstract bool DeleteUser(string username, bool deleteAllRelatedData)
    public abstract MembershipUserCollection GetAllUsers(int pageIndex,
        int pageSize, out int totalRecords)

    public abstract int GetNumberOfUsersOnline()
    public abstract MembershipUserCollection FindUsersByName(
        string usernameToMatch, int pageIndex, int pageSize,
        out int totalRecords)

    public abstract MembershipUserCollection FindUsersByEmail(string emailToMatch,
        int pageIndex, int pageSize, out int totalRecords)
```

```
//Protected helper methods
protected virtual byte[] EncryptPassword( byte[] password )
protected virtual byte[] DecryptPassword( byte[] encodedPassword )

//Events and event related methods
public event MembershipValidatePasswordEventHandler ValidatingPassword
protected virtual void OnValidatingPassword( ValidatePasswordEventArgs e )
}
```

VB.NET

```
Public MustInherit Class MembershipProvider
    Inherits ProviderBase
    ' Properties
    Public MustOverride Property ApplicationName() As String
    Public MustOverride ReadOnly Property EnablePasswordReset() As Boolean
    Public MustOverride ReadOnly Property EnablePasswordRetrieval() As Boolean
    Public MustOverride ReadOnly Property MaxInvalidPasswordAttempts() As Integer

    Public MustOverride ReadOnly Property MinRequiredNonAlphanumericCharacters() _
    As Integer

    Public MustOverride ReadOnly Property MinRequiredPasswordLength() As Integer
    Public MustOverride ReadOnly Property PasswordAttemptWindow() As Integer

    Public MustOverride ReadOnly Property PasswordFormat() _
    As MembershipPasswordFormat

    Public MustOverride ReadOnly Property PasswordStrengthRegularExpression() _
    As String
    Public MustOverride ReadOnly Property RequiresQuestionAndAnswer() As Boolean
    Public MustOverride ReadOnly Property RequiresUniqueEmail() As Boolean

    ' Public Methods
    Public MustOverride Function CreateUser(ByVal username As String, _
                                            ByVal password As String, _
                                            ByVal email As String, _
                                            ByVal passwordQuestion As String, _
                                            ByVal passwordAnswer As String, _
                                            ByVal isApproved As Boolean, _
                                            ByVal providerUserKey As Object, _
                                            <Out()> ByRef status As _
                                            MembershipCreateStatus) _
                                            As MembershipUser

    Public MustOverride Function ChangePasswordQuestionAndAnswer(_
                                            ByVal username As String, _
                                            ByVal password As String, _
                                            ByVal newPasswordQuestion As String, _
                                            ByVal newPasswordAnswer As String) _
                                            As Boolean

    Public MustOverride Function GetPassword(ByVal username As String, _
    ByVal answer As String) As String
```

```vbnet
        Public MustOverride Function ChangePassword(ByVal username As String, _
        ByVal oldPassword As String, ByVal newPassword As String) As Boolean

        Public MustOverride Function ResetPassword(ByVal username As String, _
        ByVal answer As String) As String

        Public MustOverride Sub UpdateUser(ByVal user As MembershipUser)

        Public MustOverride Function ValidateUser(ByVal username As String, _
        ByVal password As String) As Boolean

        Public MustOverride Function UnlockUser(ByVal userName As String) As Boolean

    Public MustOverride Function GetUser(ByVal providerUserKey As Object, _
                                ByVal userIsOnline As Boolean) _
                                As MembershipUser

    Public MustOverride Function GetUser(ByVal username As String, _
                                ByVal userIsOnline As Boolean) _
                                As MembershipUser

    Public MustOverride Function GetUserNameByEmail(ByVal email As String) _
    As String

    Public MustOverride Function DeleteUser(ByVal username As String, _
                                ByVal deleteAllRelatedData As Boolean) _
                                As Boolean

    Public MustOverride Function GetAllUsers(ByVal pageIndex As Integer, _
                                ByVal pageSize As Integer, _
                                <Out()> ByRef totalRecords As Integer) _
                                As MembershipUserCollection

    Public MustOverride Function GetNumberOfUsersOnline() As Integer

    Public MustOverride Function FindUsersByEmail(ByVal emailToMatch As String, _
                                ByVal pageIndex As Integer, _
                                ByVal pageSize As Integer, _
                                <Out()> ByRef totalRecords _
                                As Integer) _
                                As MembershipUserCollection

    Public MustOverride Function FindUsersByName(ByVal usernameToMatch As String, _
                                ByVal pageIndex As Integer, _
                                ByVal pageSize As Integer, _
                                <Out()> ByRef totalRecords As Integer) _
                                As MembershipUserCollection
    ' Protected Helper Methods
    Protected Overridable Function EncryptPassword(_
    ByVal password As Byte()) As Byte()

    Protected Overridable Function DecryptPassword(_
    ByVal encodedPassword As Byte()) As Byte()

        ' Events and event related methods
```

```
Protected Overridable Sub OnValidatingPassword(_
ByVal e As ValidatePasswordEventArgs)

Public Event ValidatingPassword As MembershipValidatePasswordEventHandler

End Class
```

If you are thinking about writing a custom provider, the extensive abstract class definition may seem a bit intimidating at first. An important point to keep in mind, though, is that not only is the Membership feature pluggable by way of providers; the breadth of functionality you choose to implement in a provider is also up to you. Although the SQL and AD based providers implement most of the functionality defined by the abstract class (the SQL provider implements 100% of it and the AD provider implements about 95% of it), it is a perfectly reasonable design decision to implement only the slice of provider functionality that you care about. For example, you may not care about exposing search functionality from your provider, in which case you could ignore many of the Get* and Find* methods.

The way to think about the available functionality exposed by a provider is to break it down into the different areas described in the next few sections. If there are broad pieces of functionality you don't care about, you can just stub out the requisite properties and methods for that functionality in your custom provider by throwing a NotSupportedException.

Basic Configuration

A portion of the MembershipProvider class signature deals directly with configuration information that is usually expected to be available from any custom provider.

All providers should at least implement the getter for the ApplicationName property. The concept of separating data by application name is so common to many of the provider-based features in ASP.NET 2.0 and ASP.NET 3.5 that the getter should always be implemented. If it turns out that you are mapping Membership to a data store that does not really have the concept of an "application" (for example, the AD provider doesn't support the concept of an application but it does implement the getter), you can have the setter throw a NotSupportedException. Internally, your custom provider can just ignore the application name that it loaded from configuration.

User Creation and User Updates

Most of the functionality on a MembershipProvider isn't of much use unless users are created in the first place. You have two approaches to this:

❑ You can write a full-featured provider that implements the create-, delete-, and update-related methods.

❑ You can stub out all the create-, delete-, and update-related methods if you have some other mechanism for populating the data store. For example, your provider may only expose the ability to validate a username-password pair. The actual user accounts may be created through some other mechanism. In this scenario, your custom provider could just choose not to implement the ability to create and update users.

The properties related to user creation and user updates mostly deal with the user's password.

❑   MinRequiredPasswordLength: On one hand, if a provider supports enforcing password strengths, it should return the minimum length of passwords allowed when using the provider. On the other hand, if a provider does not enforce any kind of password strength requirements, it should just return either zero or one from this property. If a provider doesn't care about password lengths, then it can return the number one as a reasonable default. The CreateUser Wizard and the ChangePassword controls both use this property when outputting error information. However, neither of the controls automatically generates any type of validators based on this property; they just use the property value for outputting default error information if an invalid password was entered into the controls.

❑   MinRequiredNonAlphanumericCharacters: A provider that enforces password strength rules can choose to also require a minimum number of nonalphanumberic characters in passwords. A custom provider that either does not enforce password strength or does not have the additional requirement around nonalphanumeric characters should just return zero from this property. The CreateUserWizard and the ChangePassword controls both use this property when outputting error information. However, neither of the controls automatically generates any type of validators based on this property; they just use the property value for outputting default error information if an invalid password was entered into the controls.

❑   PasswordStrengthRegularExpression: Because some developers have more complex password rules, they may use regular expressions instead of (or in addition to) the previous constraints. A provider that supports custom regular expressions should return the regular expression that was configured via this property. If a provider does not support enforcing password strength via a custom regular expression, it should just return an empty string from this property. You could argue that throwing a NotSupportedException would make sense, but returning a hard-coded empty string is just as effective and doesn't result in an unexpected exception when reading the property. Note that the CreateUserWizard and ChangePassword controls *don't* make use of this property. Both of these controls also support specifying a regular expression for password validation; however, the regular expression on these controls is intended for use in a client-side regular expression validator (that is, a regular expression that works in JavaScript) and as a result they do not use the value returned from this property.

❑   ValidatingPassword: This is a public event defined on the base MembershipProvider class. Because it is not defined as virtual, it's possible for developers to register custom password validation handlers even though a custom provider may not support extensible password validation and, thus, will never fire this event. For now, the best way to inform developers that a provider doesn't support extensible password validation is to document the limitation. There is a related protected virtual method that providers use (OnValidatingPassword) to fire the event.

❑   RequiresUniqueEmail: If you want to ensure that any user created with your custom membership provider has a unique email, return true from this property. If you do not care about email uniqueness return false from this property. The CreateUser control in the Login controls will add a validator that requires a valid email address in the event a provider returns true from this property.

The methods related to user creation and updates deal with both the MembershipUser object as well, changing just the user's password.

❑   CreateUser: If your provider supports creating users, you would implement this method. However, if you have some other mechanism for creating users you should just throw a

NotSupportedException from this method. If your provider requires unique email addresses (based on the requiresUniqueEmail configuration attribute), then its implementation should perform the necessary validations to enforce this. If your provider doesn't support explicitly defining the data-store-specific primary key with the providerUserKey parameter, it should throw a NotSupportedException in the event that a non-null value is supplied for this parameter. For other parameters, your provider should perform validations based on the password strength enforcement properties and password question and answer configuration properties. If a provider supports extensible password validation routines, it should raise the Validating Password event as well. This allows developers to provide custom password validation, with the most likely place to do this being global.asax. Because the CreateUser method returns a status parameter of type MembershipCreateStatus, you can set the status to one of the error codes (that is, something other than MembershipCreateStatus.Success) in the event that a validation check fails. Normally, the CreateUser method should not return an exception if a parameter validation fails because there is an extensive set of status codes that can be returned from this method. A NotSupportedException should only be thrown for cases where a parameter is supplied but the provider doesn't support the functionality that would make use of this parameter (that is, attempting to set the providerUserKey or supplying questions and answers when the provider can't store these values or make use of them). The CreateUserWizard internally calls this method on the provider configured for use with the control.

❑ DeleteUser: The companion to the CreateUser method. If a custom provider supports creating users, it likely also supports deleting users. Depending on how a custom provider is written, other features may depend on the users created with the provider. For example, the SqlMembership Provider uses a database schema that integrates with other features such as Role Manager. If this is the case for a custom provider, it should support the ability to perform a "clean" delete that can remove related data from other features prior to deleting the membership user data. As with CreateUser, if a provider doesn't support user deletion it should just throw a NotSupported Exception from this method.

❑ UpdateUser: After a user is created there is a subset of data on MembershipUser that is updatable. If a custom provider supports updating any user information (Email, Comment, IsApproved, LastLoginDate, and LastActivityDate), the provider should implement this method. A custom provider can choose to only allow a subset of these properties to be updatable. If email addresses can be updated, a custom provider should enforce the uniqueness of the new value based on the requiresUniqueEmail configuration attribute. The best way to enforce this is by creating a derived MembershipUser class that goes hand in hand with the custom provider. The custom MembershipUser class should throw NotSupportedExceptions from the property setters for properties that are not updatable. In this way, you prevent a developer from updating property data that you don't want to be changed via the provider. The custom provider should also ignore these properties and not use them when issuing a user update. Additionally, a custom provider that uses a derived MembershipUser type should ensure that the derived MembershipUser class is always passed as a parameter to the UpdateUser method. If some other type is used (for example, the base MembershipUser type), the provider should throw an ArgumentException to make it clear to developers that only the derived Membership User type is allowed. This is the general approach used by the ActiveDirectoryMembership Provider. This provider has a related MembershipUser-derived class that does not allow updates to LastLoginDate or LastActivityDate; it prevents updates to these properties by throwing a NotSupportedException from these properties on the ActiveDirectory MembershipUser class. However, the AD-based provider skips some performance optimizations in its update method internally if the wrong MembershipUser type is passed to it. I recommend throwing an `ArgumentException` instead for custom providers because it makes it clearer that there is a specific `MembershipUser`-derived type that must be used. Of course, if your provider doesn't support updating any user data, it should just throw a `NotSupportedException` instead.

❑ `ChangePassword`: If your provider supports creating users, you should support the ability for users to at least change their passwords via this method. Your provider should perform validations based on the password strength enforcement properties if your provider supports any type of strength enforcement. Furthermore, if a provider supports extensible password validation routines, it should raise the `ValidatingPassword` event as well. Because a user's old password is required to change the password, if a provider keeps track of bad passwords, it should include tracking logic in this method that keeps track of bad password attempts and locks out users as necessary. On one hand, users who have already been locked out should never be allowed to change their password. On the other hand, if you create users through some other mechanism, it is possible that you also have a separate process for allowing users to update their passwords, in which case you should just throw a `NotSupportedException`. The `ChangePassword` control in the Login controls calls this method on the provider associated with the control.

❑ `OnValidatingPassword`: This protected virtual method is defined on the base `Membership Provider` class and should be used by custom providers to raise the password validation event from the `CreateUser`, `ChangePassword`, and `ResetPassword` methods. If the event argument for this event is returned with an exception object, the provider should throw the returned exception rather than continuing. If instead the returned event argument just has the `Cancel` property set to `true`, a custom provider should throw a `ProviderException` stating that the password validation failed. If a custom provider doesn't allow for custom password validation logic to be registered by way of the `ValidatingPassword` event, there is no great way to communicate this to developers other than through documentation. Unfortunately, the internal property that holds the event delegates for this event is not accessible, so a custom provider has no way to check whether or not events have been registered for it.

Retrieving Data for a Single User

The provider signature supports a number of methods for retrieving single user objects and sets of user data. If a custom provider supports more than just the `ValidateUser` method, it should at least support the ability to fetch a single `MembershipUser` instance for a given user.

❑ `GetUser`: There are two `GetUser` overloads: one that retrieves users by name and one that retrieves users by way of a data-store-specific primary key. At a minimum, a custom provider that supports retrieving users should support fetching a `MembershipUser` by username. This is probably the most common approach for many developers because the username is available off of the `HttpContext` after a user logs in. If you don't want to support the concept of retrieving a user with a `ProviderUserKey`, you can throw a `NotSupportedException` from this overload. The `ChangePassword` and `PasswordRecovery` controls internally call the `GetUser` overload that accepts a username.

❑ `GetUserNameByEmail`: If your provider supports storing email addresses for users, it should support the ability to retrieve users by way of their email address. Of course, requiring unique email addresses is pretty much a requirement if you want this method to return any sensible data. Although a provider could allow storing users with duplicate email addresses, calling this method will result in ambiguous data because it can only return a single username. If there are duplicates, a custom provider can either return the first matching username, or it can throw some kind of exception. The general convention, though, is to return the first matching username if unique emails are not required and to throw a `ProviderException` if unique emails are required and more than one matching user record was found. If a provider does not need to support email-based retrieval, it should just throw a `NotSupportedException` instead.

Retrieving and Searching for Multiple Users

The ability to search for and retrieve multiple users is considered to be more of an administrative task than a normal runtime task. Administrative applications have the most need for the ability to search for users and return arbitrary sets of users. There are no provider properties on `MembershipProvider`-related to this functionality, though custom providers may have provider-specific configuration properties that deal with search functionality. For example, the `ActiveDirectoryMembershipProvider` has configuration properties that control how search related methods work. There are number of search-related methods, though, that provider implementers can choose to write.

❑   `GetAllUsers`: As the name implies, a provider should return all users from the underlying data store. This method is mostly useful for small numbers of users (the low hundreds at most), because for any large quantity of user records, retrieving every possible user is ungainly. The method on the provider class includes parameters to support paging. However, paging can sometimes be difficult to implement, especially for data stores that don't natively expose any concept of paged results. If your provider doesn't support paging, it can just ignore the `pageIndex` and `pageSize` parameters; there isn't really any good way to communicate the existence or lack of paging based on this method's parameter signature. The ASP.NET configuration tool that is available from inside of the Visual Studio environment makes use of this method. If your provider doesn't support this type of search functionality, throw a `NotSupportedException`.

❑   `FindUsersByName`: A filtered search method that can retrieve a set of users based on username. As with `GetAllUsers` some provider implementers will be able to support paging semantics, while other custom providers will need to ignore the paging-related parameters. Another aspect of this search method is support for wildcard characters in the `usernameToMatch` parameter: you will need to document the level of support a custom provider has for wildcard characters. The general expectation is that if the underlying data store (that is, SQL Server) supports wildcards in its native query language, the provider should allow the same set of wildcard characters in the `usernameToMatch` parameter. The ASP.NET configuration tool that is available from inside of the Visual Studio environment makes use of this method. If your provider doesn't support this type of search functionality, throw a `NotSupportedException`.

❑   `FindUsersByEmail`: This method has the same functionality and guidance as `FindUsersBy Name` with the one difference that it instead supports searching by email address.

Validating User Credentials

When you boil the Membership feature down to its basics, validating passwords is at its core. All other areas of functionality described in this section are pretty much optional; there are other ways that you can support functionality, like user creation or searching for users. Without the ability to validate user credentials, though, it would be sort of pointless to write a `MembershipProvider`. The basic support expected from all `MembershipProviders` is the ability to validate a username-password pair.

More advanced, and thus optional, functionality allows for tracking bad password attempts and bad password answer attempts. If certain configurable thresholds are met or exceeded, a provider should incorporate the ability to lock out user accounts and then subsequently unlock these accounts. If a provider does support tracking bad password and bad password answer attempts, it needs to keep track of this whenever `ValidateUser`, `ChangePassword`, `ChangePasswordQuestionAndAnswer`, `ResetPassword`, and `GetPassword` are called. Each of these methods involves a password or a password answer to work properly, although the password answer functionality in `ResetPassword` and `GetPassword` is also optional (see the next section on self-service password resets and retrieval). Furthermore, in each of these methods if the correct password or password answer is supplied, then a custom provider should reset its internal tracking counters (either password counters or password answer counters) to reflect this fact. In the next chapter, on `SqlMembershipProvider`, you will see how the SQL provider handles these types of counters in various `MembershipProvider` methods.

The properties related to validating user passwords are:

❑ `MaxInvalidPasswordAttempts`: For more secure providers that support tracking bad passwords (and also bad password answers if they support question-and-answer-based password resets or password retrieval), this setting indicates the maximum number of bad password attempts. If a provider supports tracking bad password answers, this configuration setting is also intended to be used as the maximum number of allowable bad password answers. Although the `MembershipProvider` could have specified two different properties for tracking bad passwords versus bad password answers, the decision was made to support the same upper limit for both pieces of data. There is always a debate over exactly what "maximum" means when tracking bad attempts; some folks would choose maximum to mean a threshold that can be reached but not exceeded. A reasonable case can be instead be made that this type of limit should instead be triggered only when it is exceeded. Realistically, either approach is valid; the ASP.NET providers consider the maximum number of attempts to have occurred when internal tracking counters exactly equal the value of this configuration setting. This means that if this property is set to five, then when the fifth bad password is supplied something happens; that is, the user account is locked out. Custom provider implementers may choose to be slightly different and instead carry out some action on the sixth attempt. The main thing is to communicate clearly to folks exactly how this property triggers account lockouts and other behavior. If a custom provider does not support any type of bad password or bad password answer tracking, it should return an appropriately large value instead (`Int32.MaxValue`, for example). Custom providers should avoid throwing an exception because developers may want to use administrative UI that lists all providers configured on a system along with their current configuration settings based on the `MembershipProvider` properties. Returning a very large value gets across the point that the provider does not enforce anything without causing the administrative UI to blow up with an unexpected exception.

❑ `PasswordAttemptWindow`: If a provider supports tracking bad passwords or bad password answer attempts, there usually needs to be some finite time window during which the provider actively keeps track of bad attempts. The value returned from this property indicates the length of time during which a provider would consider successive failed attempts to be additive; for example, the provider would increment internal tracking counters that are compared against `MaxInvalidPasswordAttempts`. The specifics of how a provider deals with the password attempt window over time are considered provider-specific. It is up to the provider implementer to document exactly how the `PasswordAttemptWindow` interacts with the value for `MaxInvalidPasswordAttempts`. If a provider does not support the concept of tracking bad attempts, it can instead return a dummy value such as zero from this property rather than throwing an exception. A return value of zero implies that the provider considers each new failed attempt as an isolated event unrelated to prior failed attempts.

There are only two methods for credential validation, with `ValidateUser` being the method that most developers expect to be implemented by all providers.

❑   `ValidateUser`: If there is one core method that "is" the Membership feature, this is it. Any custom provider will be expected to support this property. After a successful login, the user's `Last LoginDate` should be updated. Login controls such as the `Login` control and the `CreateUser Wizard` depend on this method. Providers that support tracking bad password attempts should increment tracking counters in this method and lock out user accounts as necessary. In general, if a user account is already locked out, `ValidateUser` should always return `false`. Similarly, if a custom provider supports the concept of approving a user prior to allowing the user to log on to a site, the provider should also return `false` if the user's `IsApproved` flag is set to `false`.

❑   `UnlockUser`: This is an optional method for providers that can lockout user accounts after an excessive number of bad passwords or bad password answers. If a custom provider supports this concept, then there needs to be a way to unlock user accounts. There are two general approaches to this. A provider can internally support the concept of auto-unlocking user accounts. Although auto-unlocking is not explicitly supported by the Membership feature, there is nothing to prevent a custom provider implementer from building this type of logic into any of the methods that deal with passwords and password answers (i.e. `ValidateUser`, `ChangePassword`, and so on). However, if a provider doesn't support auto-unlocking behavior, it should support explicitly unlocking a user account via the `UnlockUser` method. At a minimum an unlocked user account should have its `IsLockedOut` property set to `false`. Typically, internal tracking counters are reset as well, and the `LastLockoutDate` property for the user can be reset to a default value. If a provider doesn't cause users to be locked out, or if some other mechanism outside of Membership is used to unlock users, a custom provider should throw a `NotSupportedException` instead.

Supporting Self-Service Password Reset or Retrieval

Several properties provide information about the self-service password reset and password retrieval capabilities of Membership. The general idea behind this feature is that website users can retrieve their password, or have the system reset their password, if they forget the original password. Typically, for enhanced security the user needs to answer a special password question before the system retrieves or resets the password.

Although you may author a provider that supports only one of these options (that is, only password retrieval or only password resets), or none of these options, you should still implement the following properties so that server controls and administrative tools can determine the level of support that a custom provider has for password reset and retrieval:

❑   `EnablePasswordRetrieval`: Indicates whether the provider instance allows passwords to be retrieved in an unencrypted format. If you author a provider that supports password storage with reversible encryption, the value of this property may be retrieved from a provider configuration attribute just as it is with the `SqlMembershipProvider`. If you never plan to support this functionality just return `false`. The `PasswordRecovery` control in Login controls looks at the value of this property to determine what kind of UI to render.

❑ `EnablePasswordReset`: Indicates whether the provider allows a user's password to be reset to a randomly generated password value. As with the `SqlMembershipProvider`, you can derive this value from your provider's configuration. If you don't plan on ever supporting this functionality, you can instead always return `false` from this property. The `PasswordRecovery` control also looks at this property value to determine what kind of UI to render.

❑ `RequiresQuestionAndAnswer`: If your provider requires that a password question be successfully answered before performing either a password reset or retrieving a password, then you would return `true` from this property. As with the previous two properties this value can be driven from configuration as the `SqlMembershipProvider` does. Or if you don't support this kind of functionality just return `false`. The `CreateUser` control in the Login controls uses this property to determine whether it should prompt a new user for a password question and answer. The `PasswordRecovery` control in the Login controls also looks at this property value to determine whether or not it should challenge the user before resetting or retrieving a password.

❑ `PasswordFormat`: Indicates the way in which passwords will be stored in a backend system by the provider. Providers that are configurable, such as the `SqlMembershipProvider`, can derive this value from configuration. Other providers, such as the `ActiveDirectoryMembership Provider`, always return a hard-coded value because the underlying data store only supports a single storage format. None of the Login controls directly depends on this property. However, you may write Membership-related logic that only makes sense for certain password formats. For example, sending an email with the person's old password is never going to work unless the provider stores the password using reversible encryption as opposed to hashing.

The methods related to password resets and password retrieval are described in the following list. In some cases password reset and retrieval influences only part of the parameter signature of a method. In other cases, entire methods can be removed out if you don't plan on supporting either piece of functionality.

❑ `CreateUser`: You can always create a user even if you don't plan on implementing password resets and password retrieval. The `passwordQuestion` and `passwordAnswer` parameters to this method will be important to you if your provider returns `true` from `RequiresQuestion AndAnswer`. Developers will probably expect your `CreateUser` implementation to enforce the requirement that both parameters be supplied in the event you return `true` from `Requires QuestionAndAnswer`. Note that if you want to, you can choose not to support password resets or retrieval and yet still require a question and answer. Though not recommended, this would give your provider two extra properties for storing user-related data. From a security perspective, a custom provider should always store the password answer in a secure format. Because the password answer is essentially a surrogate password, providers should not store the password answer in cleartext.

❑ `ChangePasswordQuestionAndAnswer`: This method should be implemented if your provider returns `true` from `RequiresQuestionAndAnswer`. If you don't implement this method, then after a new user account is created your users will not have the ability to ever change their secret password question and answer. Because this method requires a user's password in order to complete successfully, providers that keep track of bad password attempts should increment their tracking counters in this method and lock out users as necessary. Providers also need to handle the case where a user is already locked out; locked-out users should not be allowed to change their password question and answer. If your provider does not use password questions and answers (either you do not support reset/retrieval or you do not want to impose the added security measure of a question-answer challenge), then you should throw a `NotSupported Exception` from this method.

❑ GetPassword: Implement this method if your provider is able to store passwords with reversible encryption and you want to give your users the ability to retrieve their old passwords. On one hand, if a custom provider requires a password answer prior to retrieving a password, and if the provider also keeps track of bad password answer attempts, it should increment tracking counters from inside of this method and lock out users as necessary. Providers need to also handle the case where a user is already locked out, in which case locked-out users should not be allowed to retrieve their password even if they have a valid answer. On the other hand, if a custom provider does not require an answer, then it can just ignore the answer parameter. If your provider's underlying data store does not support reversible encryption or if you do not want this type of functionality to be available, then throw a NotSupportedException instead. The PasswordRecovery control in the Login controls will use this method if it detects that the current provider supports password retrieval (that is, EnablePasswordRetrieval returns true). Note that if your provider does not require a valid password answer to a password question (that is, RequiresQuestionAndAnswer returns false), then your provider should ignore the answer parameter to this method.

❑ ResetPassword: If your provider allows users to reset their own passwords, then your provider should implement this method. If a provider supports extensible password validation routines, it should raise the ValidatingPassword event from this method as well. The PasswordRecovery control in the Login controls will use this method if your provider returns true from Enable PasswordReset. If a custom provider requires a password answer prior to resetting a password, and if the provider also keeps track of bad password answer attempts, it should increment tracking counters from inside of this method and lock out users as necessary. Providers also need to handle the case where a user is already locked out, in which case locked-out users should not be allowed to reset their password even if they have a valid answer. However, if a custom provider doesn't require an answer, it can just ignore the answer parameter. If a custom provider does not support password resets, your provider should return a NotSupportedException from this method. When resetting passwords, a custom provider can call the Membership .GeneratePassword static helper method. This method can be used to auto-generate a valid random password that meets minimum length and minimum nonalphanumeric character requirements. Note though that this helper method cannot guarantee a random password that matches a password-strength regular expression; attempting to programmatically reverse engineer a regular expression would have made this helper method way too complex, and it is doubtful that you could even write code to successfully accomplish this. It is up to the custom provider implementation whether or not it should even try to validate an auto-generated password against a specified regular expression. By way of comparison, neither the SQL nor AD-based ASP.NET providers attempt this.

Tracking Online Users

The Membership feature has the ability to keep track of users who are considered active on a website (that is, online) versus users who are in the system but have not necessarily been active within a configurable time period. The time period in which a user must be active, and thus considered online, is defined by the Membership.UserIsOnlineTimeWindow property. As discussed earlier, the internal implementation of MembershipUser.IsOnline uses this configuration property in conjunction with the user's LastActivityDate to determine whether a user is considered online.

For this functionality to work, though, a custom provider must update the LastActivityDate inside of various methods. The MembershipProvider also exposes a method that can be used to get the count of online users for a website.

❑ GetNumberOfUsersOnline: If a provider stores the LastActivityDate for its users, it should implement this method. The return value is a count of the number of users whose LastActivity Date is greater than or equal to the current date time less the UserIsOnlineTimeWindow. Note that an implementation of this method may result in a very expensive query or aggregation being performed. Although the ASP.NET SqlMemebershipProvider does not do anything to mitigate this issue, custom providers may want to implement some kind of internal caching logic so that calls to the GetNumberOfUsersOnline method do not trigger incessant table scans or other expensive operations in the underlying data store. If a provider does not support keeping track of when users are online, it can instead throw a NotSupportedException from this method.

❑ ValidateUser: Each time a user attempts to login, the LastActivityDate should be updated. There is no strict rule on whether this date should only be updated for successful logins, or for both successful and failed logins. The SqlMembershipProvider happens to update the date for both cases, but it is also reasonable to say a user is not truly online until after a successful login has occurred.

❑ GetUser: Both GetUser overloads have a parameter called userIsOnline. If the provider supports updating a user's LastActivityDate, and if this parameter is set to true, then each time a user object is retrieved it should first have its LastActivityDate updated. Providers that do not support counting online users can just ignore the userIsOnline parameter. It also would not be unreasonable for a custom provider to throw a NotSupportedException if userIsOnline is set to true and the provider does not support tracking online users.

❑ CreateUser: Custom providers can choose to set the LastActivityDate to the creation date (SqlMembershipProvider does this) or instead set LastActivityDate to a default value. It is up to you to determine if it makes more sense to say that a newly created user is immediately online or not. Some developers will probably prefer to not have CreateUser mark a Membership User as online if users are usually created in a batch process of if user accounts are created by someone other than a live user on a website.

❑ UpdateUser: A provider can support updating a user's LastActivityDate using the value on the MembershipUser object passed to this method.

In the SqlMembershipProvider there aren't any other Membership operations that result in updating a user's LastActivityDate. Other methods that update a user's password or password question and answer do not cause any changes to LastActivityDate when using the SQL provider. Again, though, this is a philosophical decision that can be argued either way. There would be nothing wrong with a custom provider when you feel that these types of operations should result in an update to LastActivityDate.

General Error-Handling Approaches

If you look closely at the MembershipProvider definition, you can see that there is one method with an out parameter (the status parameter on CreateUser), whereas all the other methods just handle input parameters. Furthermore, the default providers typically have different error behavior depending on whether a Boolean is used as a return value. Unfortunately, there wasn't enough time in the ASP.NET 2.0 development cycle to fine-tune error handling and exception behavior for the Membership feature, so the end result can be a bit confusing at times and less than elegant. It is important to mention that ASP.NET 3.5 does not introduce any changes to the error handling and exception behavior for the Membership feature and hence what applies to ASP.NET 2.0 in this field applies also to ASP.NET 3.5.

The general rules of thumb are listed here. Both the SQL- and AD-based providers follow these rules:

❑ For all methods, if the provider is asked to do something that it doesn't support, it should just throw a NotSupportedException. This can be the case when an entire method is simply not supported. This can also occur if a method is implemented, but another configuration setting on the provider indicates that the method should not succeed. For example, the default providers implement ResetPassword, but if EnablePasswordReset is set to false in configuration, then the providers throw a NotSupportedException. Another example is when a parameter to a method was supplied (for example, providerUserKey for CreateUser) but the provider cannot actually do anything with the parameter.

❑ If a method has an out parameter for communicating a result status, the method should usually return error conditions via that parameter.

❑ A well-written provider should perform a rigorous set of parameter validations that ensures method parameters have reasonable values. The ASP.NET providers throw an Argument Exception for parameter validations that fail for non-null values, and they throw an Argument NullException for parameter validations that fail because of unexpected null values.

❑ If the return type of a provider method is Boolean, and if the success of the method depends on a correct password being passed to the method, the method should simply return false for bad passwords. This means methods like ValidateUser, ChangePassword, and ChangePassword QuestionAndAnswer should simply return false if the provider determines that the user either supplied the wrong password or if the user was already locked out or not approved. The theory here is that especially for a method like ValidateUser, it makes more sense to provide a "thumbs-up/thumbs-down" result than to throw an exception for a bad password.

❑ For the other methods that return a Boolean value (DeleteUser and UnlockUser), the provider can return a value of false if the operation failed because the user record couldn't be found. As you will see shortly, in other methods a nonexistent user record instead causes an exception with the default ASP.NET providers. Although no Login controls depend on these two methods currently, it is possible that future Login controls might use these methods, in which case the controls would expect custom providers to follow the same behavior.

❑ A provider should throw the special MembershipPasswordException type when a bad password answer is supplied to either ResetPassword or GetPassword. This type allows developers and the Login controls to recognize that the specific problem is an incorrect password answer. Unfortunately, this behavior is a perfect example of the somewhat schizophrenic exception and error-handling behavior in the default providers; it would have been better to rationalize the behavior of bad passwords and bad password answers in a more consistent manner.

❑ If a provider performs business-logic-related checks in the provider or in the back-end data store, it can use the ProviderException class to return the error condition. The kinds of checks that can fail include not finding the specified user in the system (for example, you attempt to update a nonexistent user) or attempting to use a mal-formed regular expression for password validations. This was the approach used by the ASP.NET providers to eliminate the need to spam the System.Web.Security namespace with many custom exceptions. However, it is also a reasonable approach for building a rich exception hierarchy that is more expressive and return. If you intend for a custom provider to work with the various Login controls, though, your custom exceptions should derive from `ProviderException`. The Login controls will, in many cases, suppress exceptions in order to perform failure actions or to display failure text configured for a control. The Login controls can only do this, though, for exception types that they recognize, `ProviderExceptions` and `ArgumentExceptions` being two of the exception types that they handle.

❏ Last, the default ASP.NET providers usually don't handle unexpected exceptions that can arise from the underlying classes they call into. For example, the `SqlMembershipProvider` doesn't catch and remap SQL-Server-related exceptions. The `ActiveDirectoryMembershipProvider` for the most part also doesn't suppress or remap exceptions from the `System.Directory Services` namespace. The assumption is that data-layer exceptions are usually indicative that something has seriously gone wrong, and as a result these types of exceptions are not error conditions that the provider knows how to handle.

The "Primary Key" for Membership

I have alluded to the fact that the Membership feature considers a username to be part of the "primary key" for the Membership feature. Because the feature is provider-based, and all the ASP.NET 2.0 and ASP.NET 3.5 SQL providers support an "applicationName" attribute in configuration, the precise statement is that the Membership feature implicitly considers the combination of `applicationName` and username to be an immutable identifier for users. Although a more database-centric definition of a primary key could have been modeled in Membership and other related features, the intent was to keep the user identifier as simple and as generic as possible.

Because it is likely that just about any conceivable Membership store ever devised will support a string type, choosing username and application name seems pretty safe. This also means that it is possible for developers to write custom features that link to Membership data at an object level in a reliable manner. For example, if you had an inventory application running off in a corner somewhere that you needed to integrate with a website running Membership, it is pretty likely that you will at least be able to find a string-based username in the inventory system that has some mapping and relevance to your website. Using a database primary key/foreign key relationship probably will not work if your inventory system is running on some "interesting" relic that has been repeatedly upgraded over the decades, other systems that you need to integrate with are black boxes, and you can't just dive down and set up relationships at the data layer.

In other words, username and application name were chosen as the "primary key" because you can always pass these values around in a middle-tier object layer without requiring any kind of compatibility between features lower down in the data layer. In some cases, though, there may not be a concept of an application name for some data stores. The `ActiveDirectoryMembershipProvider`, for example, does not do anything with the `applicationName` attribute in configuration, whereas the `SqlMembershipProvider` does use the application name to create part of the primary key and actually stores the application name in the database.

However, even in the case of the AD-based provider you could argue that each separate instance of an AD provider defined in configuration logically correlates to an "application." So, if you wanted to use Web Parts Personalization (using the SQL provider) with the AD membership provider, you could still separate user data in the Web Parts Personalization data store based on which AD provider was actually used to authenticated a user. It would be up to you to set up the `applicationName` attribute for your Web Parts Personalization providers in a way that correlated to the different configured AD membership providers, but you could do this pretty easily.

Although having a common identifier for objects is useful, it does not perform well. If you know that you have features that are compatible at the data layer with Membership (for example, maybe you have all the tables for your feature and the Membership feature in the same database), it is probably easier and more natural to pass around database primary keys (for example, GUIDs, integers, and the like). There is an even bigger issue if you allow changes to usernames. Although the Membership API does not support this, and none of the other provider-based features support it, it is a common request by developers to have the ability to change usernames after a user has been created. Because all the ASP.NET features key off username, this can be a bit awkward; from a data integrity standpoint primary keys really are not supposed to be updated.

The way most developers deal with this design problem is to create a data-store-specific primary key value, and then to mark the username as some type of alternate key. The alternate key ensures uniqueness, while the primary key ensures that data relationships are not mucked up each time someone updates a username. Of course, you may already be thinking, what about that ProviderUserKey property we just saw a while back? That property (and it also shows up as a parameter in a few places in Membership) was the start of an abortive attempt to provide a more data-layer-centric approach to handling Membership data. However, further integration of this property into the Membership feature and other provider-based features was halted due to time constraints.

If you do not care about the portability of the username and application name, you can create and retrieve users based on the ProviderUserKey. The reason for the name of this property on MembershipUser is to make it clear that not all providers are necessarily databases. So, rather than calling the property PrimaryKey, the more generic name of ProviderUserKey was chosen.

The CreateUser method lets you pass in an explicit value for the database primary key, assuming that the underlying provider allows you to specify the primary key. The GetUser method has an overload that allows you to retrieve a user based on the data store's primary key value. Of course, this probably strikes you as a rather limited offering: What about updating a user based on the ProviderUserKey? Well, you can't do that. For that matter, other than creating a user and getting a single user instance back, there is no other support in the Membership feature, or any other feature, for manipulating data based on the data-store-specific primary key. There may (or may not) be work in a future release to bake the concept of a primary key more deeply into the Membership feature as well as the related Profile, Role Manager, and Web Parts Personalization features.

One very important thing to keep in mind, though, with data-store-specific keys is that after you start designing provider-based features with a hard dependency on a specific key format, you have potentially limited your interoperability with other features, including features that no one has dreamed up yet. Although the combination of username and application name can be a bit awkward at times, it does it make it possible for completely random features to integrate at the level of the various provider-based object APIs.

For example, although Role Manager is frequently referred to as a companion feature to Membership, the reality is that you do not need to use Membership to leverage Role Manager. You can use Role Manager on an intranet web server with Windows authentication. Because Role Manager keys off of username and application name, it is very easy to use the domain credentials of the user as the username value in Role Manager even though no data-layer relationship exists between Role Manager and an Active Directory environment. The application name in Role Manager can then be set based on the name of the website that is using the feature, or it can be set based on the AD domain that users authenticate against prior to using the application.

Supported Environments

Although the Membership feature is technically a part of ASP.NET 2.0 and ASP.NET 3.5 (the feature exists in the `System.Web.Security` namespace and is physically located in `System.Web.dll`), you can use the Membership feature outside of ASP.NET. This means that you can call any of the functionality in the Membership feature from console applications, NT service applications, fat client applications (that is, Windows Forms apps), and so on. Although you will need to reference the appropriate ASP.NET namespace and assembly, beyond this requirement nothing special is needed to get Membership working outside of ASP.NET.

The Membership feature always requires at least Low trust to work. For ASP.NET applications, this means that you must run in Low trust or higher. For a non-ASP.NET application, the `AspNetHosting Permission` must be granted to the calling code with a level of Low or higher.

As an example of using the feature outside of ASP.NET, you can write a basic console application that creates `MembershipUser` instances. This can come in handy if you need to prepopulate the database for the `SqlMembershipProvider`. When you create a non-ASP.NET application, it must reference `System .Web.dll`. Figure 11-1 shows the proper reference for a console application set up in Visual Studio 2005.

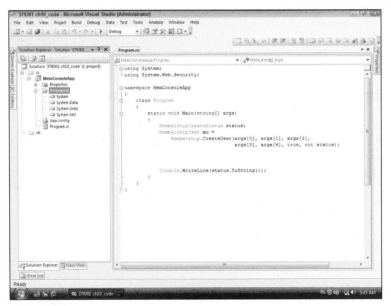

Figure 11-1

Because the Membership feature has default settings defined in `machine.config`, you do not necessarily need to configure the feature for your applications. However, the default `applicationName` as set in configuration is `/`. This value probably will not make much sense for complex applications, so you may need to change it for both your web and non-web applications. Additionally, the default Membership provider in `machine.config` points at a local SQL Server Express database, which is probably not useful for a lot of corporate applications.

In non-ASP.NET applications, you can add an `app.config` file to the project that contains the desired `<membership />` configuration section. One thing to note is that if you add `app.config` to a non-ASP.NET project, it is created without the namespace definition on the `<configuration />` element. This has the effect of disabling IntelliSense within the design environment. Don't worry, though, because the configuration syntax is the same regardless of whether you are working with an ASP.NET application or a non-ASP.NET application.

The `app.config` file for the sample console application is shown here with the type of the provider snipped for brevity. The connection string shown below also assumes that you have already set up the `aspnetdb` database in SQL Server using the `aspnet_regsql` tool:

```
<configuration>
   <connectionStrings>
     <add
      name="ConsoleDatabase"
      connectionString="server=.\SQL2005;Integrated Security=true;database=aspnet
db"
     />
   </connectionStrings>
```

Even though it may look a little strange, it is perfectly acceptable to have a `<system.web />` configuration section located inside of a configuration file for a non-ASP.NET application. From the Framework's point of view, `<system.web />` and its nested configuration sections are just another set of information to parse. There is no dependency on an ASP.NET application host for the Membership-related configuration classes.

The previous sample configuration clears the `<providers />` collections. It is usually a good idea to clear out provider collections if you don't need any of the inherited definitions. In the case of the sample console application, you need your own definition to set the `applicationName` attribute appropriately. As a result, there is no reason to incur the overhead of instantiating the default provider defined up in `machine.config`. Also notice that the configuration file resets the `defaultProvider` on the `<membership />` element to point at the `ConsoleMembershipProvider` definition.

At this point, you have done everything necessary from a configuration perspective to get the console application to work with the Membership feature. The only thing left to do is to write some code.

C#

```csharp
using System;
using System.Web.Security;

namespace MemConsoleApp
{
    class Program
    {
        static void Main(string[] args)
        {
            MembershipCreateStatus status;
            MembershipUser mu =
                Membership.CreateUser(args[0], args[1], args[2],
```

```
                                        args[3], args[4], true, out status);

                Console.WriteLine(status.ToString());
            }
        }
    }
```

VB.NET

```
Imports Microsoft.VisualBasic
Imports System
Imports System.Web.Security
Namespace MemConsoleApp
    Friend Class Program
        Shared Sub Main(ByVal args() As String)
            Dim status As MembershipCreateStatus
            Dim mu As MembershipUser = Membership.CreateUser(args(0), _
                                                args(1), _
                                                rgs(2), _
                                                args(3), _
                                                args(4), _
                                                True, _
                                                status)

            Console.WriteLine(status.ToString())
        End Sub
    End Class
End Namespace
```

The sample application uses the static Membership class to create a user. To reference the feature, it includes a namespace reference at the top of the file to System.Web.Security. It expects the command-line parameters to be the username, password, email address, password question, and password answers respectively. For brevity, the application doesn't include any error checking on the arguments. You can see how little code is necessary to take advantage of the Membership feature; it probably takes more time to set the assembly reference and tweak the configuration file that it does to write the actual code that creates users.

After compiling the application, you can invoke it from the command line, and the results of the user creation will be output to the console. A successful user creation looks like this:

```
MemConsoleApp.exe testuser pass!word test@nowhere.org Question Answer
Success
```

Because the console application uses the CreateUser overload that returns a status, if you attempt to create the same user a second time, you see the following error message.

```
MemConsoleApp.exe testuser pass!word test@nowhere.org Question Answer
DuplicateUserName
```

In this case, the error message is just the string version of the returned MembershipCreateStatus. Although the sample application only shows user creation, the full spectrum of the Membership feature is available for you to use outside of ASP.NET. You can consume the existing API as well as write custom providers for use in non-web environments. In future releases, Membership may also be extended further so that features such as Web Service-callable providers will be available right out of the box.

Using Custom Hash Algorithms

The `<membership />` configuration element includes the `hashAlgorithmType` configuration attribute. By default the Membership feature (or more specifically the `SqlMembershipProvider`) uses SHA1 when storing passwords. You can set this attribute to any string that the .NET Framework recognizes as a valid hashing algorithm, and the `SqlMembershipProvider` will use that algorithm instead. If you look at the documentation for the `System.Security,Cryptography.HashAlgorithm` class's `Create` method, there is a list of the default strings (that is, simple names) that the .NET Framework recognizes and supports for referring to hash algorithms. Any one of these strings can be used in the `hashAlgorithmType` attribute. You can retrieve the name of the hashing algorithm configured for the Membership feature by getting the value of the `Membership.HashAlgorithm` property.

Although the hash algorithm is a feature-level setting, it is really more of an opt-in approach for individual providers. The setting on the `<membership />` element would be useless if individual Membership providers didn't explicitly read the value from the `Membership.HashAlgorithm` property and then internally make use of the correct algorithm. Currently, the hashing functionality for the `SqlMembership Provider` calls an internal method on `MembershipProvider`. This internal method, in turn, creates the appropriate hash algorithm based on the `hashAlgorithmType` attribute and then hashes the password with a random salt value. In a future release, the internal method that does this may be made public. For now, though, this means custom provider implementers that support password hashing need to write code that follows the same approach:

1. Fetch the value of `Membership.HashAlgorithm`.

2. Call `HashAlgorithm.Create`, passing it the string from step 1.

3. With the resulting reference to the hash algorithm class, hash the password and optionally other information such as a random password salt if the provider supports this.

4. Store the hashed value in the back-end data store

Assuming that you can depend on providers to follow these steps, you have the ability to influence a provider's hashing processing by configuring different hash algorithms. Using any of the default hash algorithms in the Framework is very easy; you just set the `hashAlgorithmType` attribute to something else such as `SHA256`, `SHA512` and so on.

What happens, though, if you need to configure a hash algorithm that doesn't ship in the 2.0 or 3.5 Framework? In this case, you have the option of writing your own hash algorithm implementation and registering it with either the .NET 2.0 or 3.5 Framework. Although you can definitely create your own custom hashing algorithm that you instantiate and call directly from inside of a web page, because Membership depends on the loosely typed `HashAlgorithm.Create` method, you *must* register your hash algorithm with either the .NET 2.0 or 3.5 Framework for it to be used by the `SqlMembershipProvider` or any other providers that follow the same programming approach.

To see how this works, you can create a basic hash algorithm class like the one shown here:

C#

```
using System.Security.Cryptography;
using System.Text;

namespace CustomHashAlgorithm
```

```
    {
        public class DummyHashClass : HashAlgorithm
        {
            protected override void HashCore(byte[] array, int ibStart, int cbSize)
            {
                return; }

            protected override byte[] HashFinal()
            {
                return Encoding.UTF8.GetBytes("DUMMYHASHVALUE"); }

            public override void Initialize()
            {
                return;  }
        }
    }
```

VB.NET

```
Imports System.Security.Cryptography
Imports System.Text

Namespace CustomHashAlgorithm
    Public Class DummyHashClass
            Inherits HashAlgorithm
        Protected Overrides Sub HashCore(ByVal array() As Byte, _
                                    ByVal ibStart As Integer, _
                                    ByVal cbSize As Integer)

        Return
    End Sub

    End Class
End Namespace
```

Clearly, you would never use an "algorithm" like this in production, but for showing the hashAlgorithm Type attribute in configuration, it is good enough. Rather than actually hashing anything, the custom class always returns a hard-coded string. After you compile this class and deploy the assembly into the /bin folder of an ASP.NET application, the next step is to make the class visible to the cryptographic infrastructure in the .NET Framework.

You register custom cryptographic algorithms, both hashing and encryption algorithms, using the <crytpographySettings /> configuration element found within <mscorlib />.

```
<mscorlib>
  <cryptographySettings>
    <cryptoNameMapping>
      <cryptoClasses>
        <cryptoClass
        MyDummyHashClass="CustomHashAlgorithm.DummyHashClass, CustomHashAlgorithm"/>
      </cryptoClasses>

      <nameEntry name="TestAlgorithm" class="MyDummyHashClass"/>
```

```
        </cryptoNameMapping>
      </cryptographySettings>
  </mscorlib>
```

The way this configuration works is:

❑ The <cryptoClass /> element associates a name (in this case MyDummyHashClass) with a .NET Framework type. In this case, I am using a reference to just a class and an assembly. In production applications, your custom hash algorithm type would probably be in the GAC and, thus, you would instead use a strong-named reference here. Because the sample is not strong-named, the assembly CustomHashAlgorithm has to be deployed in an ASP.NET application's /bin directory for the type to be loaded.

❑ The <nameEntry /> element associates a friendly name with the custom hash algorithm class. In the sample configuration, this allows TestAlgorithm to be passed to HashAlgorithm.Create, which will then return a reference to the DummyHashClass type.

A very important note about this configuration: You must place the configuration in machine.config! If you try to place the configuration section inside of web.config, the cryptography infrastructure will never see your custom type because the <mscorlib /> cryptography settings are only valid when defined in machine.config. Although you can place them in other configuration files, they will never be processed. If you end up banging your head against a wall wondering why your custom hash class is never being used, it is probably because the configuration for it is not in the right place.

With the sample hash algorithm configured in machine.config, you can create a sample ASP.NET application that makes use of it. The following configuration element tells the Membership feature to use the custom type.

```
<membership hashAlgorithmType="TestAlgorithm" />
```

Now if you create a new user with the SqlMembershipProvider, the new user's password will be hashed using the custom hash algorithm. You can verify this by looking in the database—you will see that the password value is RFVNTVlIQVNIVkFMVUU=. This is just the base64-encoded representation of the byte[] returned by any hash algorithm. If you run the following code snippet to decode this string, the Membership feature successfully use the custom hash algorithm and end up with a password of DUMMYHASHVALUE.

C#

```
byte[] dbResult = Convert.FromBase64String("RFVNTVlIQVNIVkFMVUU=");
string dbString = Encoding.UTF8.GetString(dbResult);
Response.Write("The encoded password is " + dbString);
```

VB.NET

```
Dim dbResult() As Byte = Convert.FromBase64String("RFVNTVlIQVNIVkFMVUU=")
Dim dbString As String = Encoding.UTF8.GetString(dbResult)
Response.Write("The encoded password is " & dbString)
```

Because the registration of custom hash algorithms has to occur in machine.config, you will probably find custom hash algorithms (that is, non-Framework algorithms) primarily useful when they need to be used globally for many applications on a server. Although it is possible, it probably doesn't make much sense to use Membership in a way where custom hash algorithms are defined on a per-application basis (that is, dozens of applications on a machine with each application using a completely different custom hashing implementation). This kind of approach would result in dozens of custom algorithms needing to be registered up in `machine.config`.

Summary

For a lot of developers, the Membership feature will be equivalent to using the Login controls and the public static `Membership` class. If you never have to deal with multiple providers, or provider-specific functionality, everything you need to use can be found on the `Membership` class. However, more complex sites will probably need to code against the `MembershipProvider` class, especially if they need to handle multiple providers.

Because the Membership feature deals with various aspects of a user, the `MembershipUser` class is available for carrying out user-oriented functions such as password management and user updates. As with the `MembershipProvider` class, you can also choose to implement a custom `MembershipUser` class. The usual coding approach is for custom provider implementers to optionally supply a custom `Membership User` class as well.

For custom provider implementers, it can be helpful to group the functionality of a `Membership Provider` into different areas. Depending on how you plan to use a custom provider, you can choose to implement a very narrow set of functionality and eliminate the remainder of the provider implementation. For each of the functional areas, though, there are usually a few basic expectations that should be met for higher level applications and controls like the Login controls and the Web Administration Tool.

If you are thinking about integrating the Membership feature with custom providers for other ASP.NET application services, or with your own features, then understanding the definition of a "user" is very important. Keep in mind that across the ASP.NET application services, a user is identified by a combination of username and an application name defined in a provider's configuration. Although this combination of identifiers can be a bit cumbersome from a database-centric viewpoint, it does make it much easier to integrate different features written by completely different companies and development teams when there are no common assumptions on data types and primary keys.

Probably the biggest "stealth" feature of Membership, and other application services, is that the Membership feature works outside of ASP.NET. This makes it much easier to administer Membership data, and it also opens up a number of interesting possibilities for reusing authentication information across a spectrum of different client front ends.

SqlMembershipProvider

The Membership feature comes with two different providers by default: one that works with SQL Server and one that works with Active Directory. The subject of this chapter is the SQL-based provider. This provider is sort of the showcase provider for the Membership feature because it implements the full range of functionality exposed by the Membership API. It can be used by applications with only a handful of user accounts as well as very large sites with hundreds of thousands of user accounts. The provider can be used inside of ASP.NET applications as well as in non-ASP.NET applications. As with the parent Membership feature, SqlMembershipProvider can be used with Low trust and above, although when running it with Low trust, you need to explicitly add SqlClientPermission for the provider to work.

This chapter will cover the following aspects of SqlMembershipProvider in detail:

- ❑ The common database schema used by all SQL-based providers in ASP.NET.
- ❑ The database schema that supports SqlMembershipProvider.
- ❑ Caveats to keep in mind when using SQL Server Express instead of SQL Server.
- ❑ Security for the Membership database.
- ❑ How to change password formats.
- ❑ How to change the way that passwords are automatically generated.
- ❑ How to use custom encryption.
- ❑ How to enforce custom password strength rules.
- ❑ How account lockout works with the provider.
- ❑ How to extend the provider to implement auto-unlock behavior.
- ❑ How to support multiple portal-style applications with a single provider.
- ❑ How to manage application's users through IIS 7.0.

After covering these topics, you should have a good sense of how the provider works, as well as how you can build extended functionality on top of the SQL provider without needing to write a custom provider from scratch.

Understanding the Common Database Schema

All the default SQL-based providers in ASP.NET 2.0 and ASP.NET 3.5 share a common schema. The common tables and supporting stored procedures allow ASP.NET to share the same user data across the Membership, Role Manager, Profile, and Web Parts Personalization features. If you choose to use multiple features, and you take the extra step of pointing the various features at the same database, the end result is that all ASP.NET features will share a common set of user and application data. With this scenario, you can work with data through a feature's object API or directly against the database. At both levels of programming, you will be dealing with the same piece of user data.

This integration is not actually required to use any of the features. The integration support is nice to have if you choose to install all the feature schemas in a single database. However, it's possible to install each feature's database schema into a separate database, potentially on completely different servers. If you do this, all the features will still work. Because each one depends on a username and the application name from configuration as the identifying data for a user, each feature's database will have its own unique row of data identifying a user. For example, if you install three ASP.NET features into three different databases, over time the user "foo" will end up with three records: one in each feature database.

This approach leads to object level integration of user data; the only way features "know" they are dealing with the same user is from the username and application name data that is available from the various features of the APIs. At the database level, though, there are no foreign key relationships or common primary keys linking together the same user record across multiple databases or multiple servers.

As a developer or administrator, you don't ever need to install the common database schema directly. Instead, each time you choose to install at least one of the SQL-based ASP.NET features, the common schema elements are also created on your behalf. If you want to see where these common schema elements are defined, though, you can look in the file `InstallCommon.sql`, which exists in the framework's install directory.

Storing Application Name

You have seen references to the concept of an application name in a number of the previous chapters. The idea behind an application name is that providers (such as the SQL providers) that work with relational data can horizontally partition data in a table through the use of a partitioning key. That key is the application name. The ASP.NET SQL-based providers all use the `applicationName` configuration attribute internally when working with the database. For example, when `SqlMembershipProvider` attempts to a retrieve a user, foo, from the database, in reality it is looking for a user, foo, who belongs to application name "bar." In this way, it becomes possible to host multiple web applications with a single SQL Server database installation. The horizontal partitioning by application name ensures that each application works with its own slice of data.

The application names are stored in the common feature schema's table `aspnet_Applications`:

```
CREATE TABLE [dbo].aspnet_Applications (
    ApplicationName          nvarchar(256)          NOT NULL UNIQUE,
    LoweredApplicationName   nvarchar(256)          NOT NULL UNIQUE,
    ApplicationId            uniqueidentifier       PRIMARY KEY NONCLUSTERED
                                                    DEFAULT NEWID(),

    Description              nvarchar(256) )
```

As you can see, there isn't much stored for an application. In fact, the only portion of the row that is generated by a provider is the data for the `ApplicationName` column. Within the stored procedures for many of the SQL-based features, you will see code like the following:

```
EXEC dbo.aspnet_Applications_CreateApplication
                    @ApplicationName, @ApplicationId OUTPUT
```

Each time an SQL-based provider attempts to create a new row of data, it issues a command like this to ensure that a row is first created in the `aspnet_Applications` table. The application data that is registered corresponds to the value of the `applicationName` attribute set in the provider's configuration. This means that in ASP.NET 2.0 and ASP.NET 3.5, applications are auto-magically registered on behalf of providers. There is, unfortunately, no public API for accomplishing this.

Other stored procedures that retrieve or update data (as opposed to creating new rows of data) usually have a stored procedure parameter for application name that is used as a join key into the `aspnet_Applications` table.

```
SELECT  …
FROM    dbo.aspnet_Applications a, …
WHERE   LOWER(@ApplicationName) = a.LoweredApplicationName
AND     …
```

In these cases, the expectation is that the row in the `aspnet_Applications` table already exists. These types of stored procedures will not automatically cause creation of a row in the `aspnet_Applications` table because without a row in this table, there is no way any data for that application will exist in the feature's tables anyway.

The other columns in the table are either filled in by the application creation stored procedure (that is, `LoweredApplicationName` and `ApplicationId`) or are unused in ASP.NET 2.0 and ASP.NET 3.5 (the `Description` column will always be null). If a basic object model is built for developers to manipulate these common tables in a future release, then unused columns like `Description` will become accessible.

The Common Users Table

The central user table that is common to all feature schemas is `aspnet_Users`:

```
CREATE TABLE [dbo].aspnet_Users (
ApplicationId     uniqueidentifier     NOT NULL FOREIGN KEY REFERENCES
                                       [dbo].aspnet_Applications(ApplicationId),
UserId            uniqueidentifier     NOT NULL PRIMARY KEY NONCLUSTERED
                                       DEFAULT NEWID(),
```

```
UserName            nvarchar(256)      NOT NULL,
LoweredUserName     nvarchar(256)      NOT NULL,
MobileAlias         nvarchar(16)       DEFAULT NULL,
IsAnonymous         bit                NOT NULL DEFAULT 0,
LastActivityDate DATETIME             NOT NULL)
```

As you can see, this table has a foreign key relationship to the `aspnet_Applications` table. Because of this providers can partition their data based on application name. Every time an SQL-based provider retrieves data from the database, it always includes application name as part of its WHERE clause. The result is that the application's `ApplicationId` value is used as part of the filter when retrieving data from `aspnet_Users`.

The object APIs for the various ASP.NET features and of the stored procedures contain no functionality for querying tables like `aspnet_Users` without using an application name. In other words, no API allows you to query across all the data in the users table. All database operations are always constrained to just the slice of data relevant to a specific application name.

As with the application table, whenever various ASP.NET features need to create a row of data associated with a user, they first ensure that a record in the `aspnet_Users` table exists for that user.

```
EXEC @ReturnValue = dbo.aspnet_Users_CreateUser @ApplicationId, @UserName, 0,
                                              @CreateDate, @NewUserId OUTPUT
```

Here once a feature has the correct `ApplicationId` (perhaps just newly created from the application creation stored procedure mentioned in the last section), it usually checks to see if a user record exists for a given username. If no record exists, it creates one in the `aspnet_Users` table with a call to this stored procedure.

As with applications, this means in ASP.NET 2.0 and ASP.NET 3.5 that user records in the common `aspnet_Users` table are auto-magically created just before they are needed. There is no public API for creating generic user records in this table. Also note that a user record in the `aspnet_Users` table doesn't mean that the user is registered in the Membership feature. The `aspnet_Users` table's purpose is to map from an application name and a username to a GUID (that is, `uniqueidentifier`). This GUID is then used as a key to index into a feature's data tables.

Usually, a feature accomplishes this mapping with a piece of SQL similar to the following:

```
SELECT   @UserId = u.UserId
FROM     dbo.aspnet_Applications a, dbo.aspnet_Users u, ….
WHERE    LOWER(@ApplicationName) = a.LoweredApplicationName
AND      u.ApplicationId = a.ApplicationId
AND      LOWER(@UserName) = u.LoweredUserName
AND      ….
```

You can see how a feature first indexes into the `aspnet_Applications` table to get the GUID key for an application. The application's key is then used as a filter when looking in the `aspnet_Users` table for the data record corresponding to a specific username. Assuming that the user exists, the end result is the GUID key that represents a (username, application name) pair. For the SQL providers, there is code all over the place that translates from this somewhat cumbersome identifier, to the more compact and database-centric primary key identifier for a user.

If you make use of the ASP.NET provider-based features, and if you choose to install the entire feature schema in a single database, then the aspnet_Users table is very useful albeit in a mostly silent manner. With all the features pointed at the same database, each time one feature needs to create or reference a row of user data, it will end up pointing at the same row of data in aspnet_Users. For example, if you register a new user in the Membership feature, when that user personalizes a page with Web Parts Personalization, the personalization data will be linked to the same row in the aspnet_Users table assuming that the personalization provider is configured with the same application name as the membership provider.

This use of common user data is what enables the Membership.DeleteUser method to clean up data from other features. Although you could go feature by feature and issue delete commands to clean up user data, the DeleteUser method takes advantage of the fact that all the SQL-based features will key off of the same ApplicationId and the same UserId when running in the same database and all providers are configured with the same application name. As a result, if you call the DeleteUser method and pass it a value of true for the deleteAllRelatedData parameter, SqlMembershipProvider will call a stored procedure that iterates through all the other user-specific feature tables deleting data based on the common GUID identifier for a user.

Currently, only the Membership feature exposes the GUID UserId column by way of the provider UserKey parameter supported on CreateUser and GetUser. If you create a new user, you can optionally specify the GUID you want to store in the UserId column. You can retrieve a MembershipUser based on the UserId column with the GetUser overload that accepts a providerUserKey. However, other than these special methods in Membership, the linking of feature data to the same record in aspnet_Users and providing a global delete method, there is currently no other public functionality in ASP.NET that relies on the common users table. Furthermore, it is only the Membership feature that even provides a public API into the common users table. Future releases may expose the provider UserKey more broadly in other APIs, which would allow you to work with user data based on the UserId column as opposed to the somewhat awkward (username, application name) pair.

As with the aspnet_Applications table, the aspnet_Users table includes a number of other columns that are automatically filled in when a new user is created: LoweredApplicationName and ApplicationId. The LastActivityDate column is filled in with a UTC date time that is passed down from the provider running on the web server. (See Chapter 11 for a discussion on how datetime data is handled across the entire ASP.NET 2.0 and ASP.NET 3.5 SQL-based providers.) This date is intentionally stored in the aspnet_Users table rather than a feature-specific table. This allows the different ASP.NET features to update a common piece of date-time data whenever certain events occur within a feature. Features can then reference the LastActivityDate column to determine things like whether the user is online (Membership) or whether a user is considered stale and thus the associated data for that user can safely be purged from the database (Profile and Web Parts Personalization).

Currently, the LastActivityDate column is periodically updated in the following cases:

❑   Membership updates this column whenever a user logs in. The date is initially set when the user is created. It can also be optionally updated when retrieving a MembershipUser object.

❑   Role Manager will put the current UTC date time in this column if it needs to automatically create user records prior to assigning the users to roles. For example, this can occur if you use Role Manager in combination with Windows authentication.

❑   The Profile feature updates this column each time a user's profile data is retrieved or updated.

❑   The Web Parts Personalization data updates this column each time a user's personalization data for any page is retrieved or updated. It also updates this column each time a user's personalization data for any page is reset.

The general idea behind the updates to LastActivityDate is that for an ASP.NET site that makes use of a number of the SQL-based providers, an active user on a site will probably regularly cause one of the listed events to occur. Users do log in to sites, view pages with personalized web parts and use other pieces of functionality that retrieve information from their user profile.

As a result, it is likely that the LastActivityDate will be a rough indicator of the last time the user did anything significant. Of course, the activities that update this column aren't guaranteed to occur on any kind of regular interval. It would be possible for someone to log in to a site, and then never access a page with a web part on it. Or a very long period of time could pass between a user logging in and a user hitting a page that retrieves data from their user profile. As a result, any feature APIs that depend on this data work on the "good enough" concept—that is, the value in the LastActivityDate column is good enough as an indicator of user activity. Especially for APIs that are used for purging stale user data, you do not need accuracy down to the second to determine whether a user has been active on a website in the past three months. However, if you are looking for a very precise and deterministic indicator of user activity on a website you will need to create your own solution.

The IsAnonymous column is set based on whether the provider on the web server is issuing a command on behalf of an authenticated user or an anonymous user. For ASP.NET 2.0 and ASP.NET 3.5, you will only see a value of true in this column if you enable the Anonymous Identification feature and then store data with the Profile feature for anonymous users. The Membership, Role Manager, and Web Parts Personalization features all exclusively work with authenticated users in ASP.NET 2.0 and ASP.NET 3.5 and, hence, they always store a value of false in this column.

The MobileAlias column is an orphan in ASP.NET 2.0 and ASP.NET3.5. It was originally placed in the table early on in the development of ASP.NET 2.0 when mobile clients were being considered. However, as the mobile work in ASP.NET 2.0 was scaled back, there wasn't a driving need to expose this column via the providers. The original idea was to have an alternate identifier for mobile users who sometimes are identified by a shorter identifier than a username. For example, a mobile user might be identified by a just one or two characters and a few numbers (for example, JS1234) because it is easier for someone to tap in a few digits on a handset as opposed to laboriously typing in a text-based username. In a future release, this column may end up finding a use, though it is equally likely that it remains an orphan column in future releases. For now, I would recommend that curious developers avoid using the column for other uses.

Versioning Provider Schemas

Because feature requirements and thus database schemas change over time, the common database schema includes a version table aspnet_SchemaVersions and related stored procedures. Although the table is not exposed through any public APIs, the ASP.NET features register their schema versions when they are installed. At runtime, the SQL-based providers check the schema version in the database to ensure that the provider and the installed database schema are in sync. Although this table and the version checks may seem a bit pointless for ASP.NET 2.0 and ASP.NET 3.5, it is highly likely that the database schemas will change in future major releases.

```
CREATE TABLE [dbo].aspnet_SchemaVersions (
Feature                    nvarchar(128)  NOT NULL PRIMARY KEY CLUSTERED
                                          ( Feature, CompatibleSchemaVersion ),
CompatibleSchemaVersion    nvarchar(128)  NOT NULL,
IsCurrentVersion           bit            NOT NULL )
```

Each time a feature installs its database schema into the database, it writes the name of the feature into the `Feature` column. It also fills in the current version signature in the `CompatibleSchemaVersion` table. If the schema that is being installed is considered the most current version of the feature's schema, then the installation script also sets `IsCurrentVersion` to true. For ASP.NET 2.0 and ASP.NET 3.5 of course there is only one row in this table for each feature. Each feature currently sets the schema version to the string "1" and marks `IsCurrentVersion` as `true`.

The intended use of this table is that in future versions, service packs, and so on each new version of a feature schema installs a new row into this table. Furthermore, if a new version of a feature schema is not structured to support older providers, the older version rows in the database are deleted. For example, the current Membership feature inserts a row into the table with the values `Membership, 1` and `true`. If a major release of the Framework results in an entirely new Membership schema in the database, the Membership SQL installation scripts would probably insert a new set of data with the values `Membership, 2` and `true`.

However, if the new version of Membership does not support the older ASP.NET 2.0 or ASP.NET 3.5 `SqlMembershipProvider` implementation (meaning that the old stored procedures no longer existed), when the new Membership script runs, it would delete the old version 1 row from the database. When an ASP.NET 2.0 or ASP.NET 3.5 `SqlMembershipProvider` checks for a row in this table for the Membership feature with a version of "1" it will not find it. If this happens the provider throws a `Provider Exception` stating that the provider is pointed at an incompatible database. The version check and exception behaviors just described are coded into all the ASP.NET 2.0 and ASP.NET 3.5 providers. These checks come in handy for future releases where you may be running web servers with different versions of the framework all pointed at a single database.

Now this previous example is theoretical only; there are no plans to break ASP.NET 2.0 and ASP.NET 3.5 provider-based sites whenever new versions of the framework come out. In fact, the general idea is to have a database schema that versions well over time and that supports older and newer stored procedures and table layouts. In fact, one of the main reasons for the version table is to ensure that in the future if a *new* version of ASP.NET providers are pointed at an *old* database, then the new providers detect this and inform you of the problem. In an upgrade scenario, it is likely that after you upgrade a database, you will have two rows of data per feature in the schema version table:

```
Membership      1      false
Membership      2      true
Profile         1      false
Profile         2      true
Etc.
```

When a new provider runs, it expects to find a row of data indicating that the version "2" schema is installed. However, an older ASP.NET 2.0 or ASP.NET 3.5 provider would see that the database still supports version "1," and as a result it too would be able to run successfully. The fact that a newer database schema might "hollow out" the old stored procedures and map them to new stored procedures is something that would be entirely transparent to the providers. The `IsCurrentVersion` column just serves as a convenient indicator for you to determine the actual schema scripts that were last installed in the database. With the previous sample rows, this would mean although ASP.NET 2.0, ASP.NET 3.5, and newer providers are supported, the actual table schemas and stored procedures installed in the database are from the later version of the Framework.

A related piece of flexibility the version table gives ASP.NET is the ability to release out-of-band versions of the SQL providers for various external or experimental projects. The version table makes it much easier to play around with these types of releases in a way that ensures the various provider versions are actually pointed at compatible back ends. Because the version column in the database is just a string, it makes it easier to store more expressive version information for these types of releases than just a simple number.

You can see the version checks being performed by providers today if you sniff the network connection to SQL Server with a tool like SQL Profiler. Each provider will make a call to `aspnet_CheckSchema Version` to ensure that the provider is running against a database that supports the expected schema version. Because it would be expensive to make this check before each and every SQL call, the providers make this check just before the first SQL command is issued by the provider. Subsequent calls to the database over the lifetime of an app-domain simply reuse the original and now cached schema check result. This means that you could intentionally confuse a provider by using it once and then changing the database schema to an incompatible state. However, in production use making the schema check once during the provider's lifetime and then caching the result is sufficient.

Currently, all schema checks are implemented with private code, so the version functionality can be used by only ASP.NET providers. Although the version table is simple enough to use that you could hack in your own information, if you author your own SQL-based providers you should include your own custom mechanism for handling schema versioning over multiple releases.

Querying Common Tables with Views

There is technically one common public API available for use with the `aspnet_Applications` and `aspnet_Users` tables. As with the provider-specific features, the common table schema includes some SQL Server views for querying the underlying tables. Whenever the common database schema is installed, it includes two views: `vw_aspnet_Applications` and `vw_aspnet_Users`.

As the names suggest, the `vw_aspnet_Applications` view is simply a view that maps directly to all the columns in the `aspnet_Applications` table, whereas the `vw_aspnet_Users` table is a view that maps to all the columns in the `aspnet_Users` table. In both cases, developers are allowed to write *read-only* queries against these views because the development team plans to make sure that in future versions of the database schema the view definitions stay the same. Although nothing prevents you from writing inserts or updates against the views, the general guidance is that database level `SELECT` queries are supported against the views while any kind of data modification needs to go through a publicly supported provider API. As a result, if you are enterprising and you write inserts or updates to go against these views, do not be surprised if they break in a future release.

Linking Custom Features to User Records

Because all the ASP.NET features take advantage of the `aspnet_Users` and `aspnet_Applications` tables, you might be wondering if you can do so as well. For example, if you author a custom Profile provider that uses SQL Server, it would be reasonable to link your custom data with these tables. That way if someone used other ASP.NET SQL-based providers in conjunction with your custom Profile provider, everybody would be sharing a common set of data.

The "official" guidance is that this level of integration is technically not supported. Technically, the only way in which custom providers, or custom features, can be integrated with ASP.NET SQL-based providers is by way of the (username, application name) pair. However, because the existing SQL-based providers are so tightly integrated with these two tables, it isn't likely that the product team can easily change the primary keys for applications or users without causing some major data migration pain in future releases of the Framework.

With this in mind, it's reasonably safe for custom provider implementers and feature implementers to rely on the user and application tables. (Disclaimer: if something goes horribly awry in a future release, consider yourself warned!) Because `SqlMembershipProvider` explicitly supports the use of the GUID primary key via the `providerUserKey` parameter on various APIs, it isn't likely that this key will ever change. You have two general ways to take advantage of this:

❑ You could implement a custom database schema that has a `UserId` column of type `unique identifier`. For safety, though, you could always retrieve this key by calling `Membership .GetUser` and then storing the `ProviderUserKey` property in your database tables. However, you would not have any integration at the database level.

❑ You could create your tables with a foreign key dependency to `aspnet_Users`. Your stored procedures would work like the ASP.NET stored procedures. You would convert an application name parameter to an `ApplicationId` and then you would use `ApplicationId` and a username to get to a GUID `UserId`.

Of these two approaches, the second one makes the most sense. The only aspect of the second option that isn't officially supported is creating a foreign key on your tables that references `aspnet_Users .UserId`. You can perform the application name to `ApplicationId` resolution using the publicly supported `vw_aspnet_Applicatons` view. Similarly, you can then get the `UserId` by querying the `vw_aspnet_Users` view. So, the only risk you run is that a future version of ASP.NET creates a new users table and deprecates the old one, in which case all you would need to do is to update your foreign key references after a database upgrade.

Resolving an application name to an `ApplicationId` can be done with the following code:

```
create procedure getApplicationId
@pApplicationName nvarchar(256)
as
select ApplicationId
from   dbo.vw_aspnet_Applications
where  LoweredApplicationName = LOWER(@pApplicationName)
```

Fetching the `UserId` after you have the `ApplicationId` is just as easy:

```
create procedure getUserId
@pApplicationId uniqueidentifier,
@pUsername       nvarchar(256)
as
select  UserId
from    dbo.vw_aspnet_Users
where   LoweredUserName = LOWER(@pUsername)
and     ApplicationId   = @pApplicationId
```

And, of course, you can get to the `UserId` from a (username, application name) pair with just one query as well:

```
create procedure getUserId2
@pApplicationName nvarchar(256),
@pUsername        nvarchar(256)
as
select  UserId
from    dbo.vw_aspnet_Users u,
        dbo.vw_aspnet_Applications a
where   a.LoweredApplicationName = LOWER(@pApplicationName)
and     u.LoweredUserName = LOWER(@pUsername)
and     u.ApplicationId   = a.ApplicationId
```

All these pieces of T-SQL use views, so they don't depend on any unsupported functionality. If you author a custom provider that requires developers to use the existing `SqlMembershipProvider` to register users, then you don't need to worry about writing any other SQL. If you always create users with the Membership feature first, the necessary rows of data will already exist in the application and user tables. In essence, with this approach you are depending on ASP.NET to set things up ahead of time for you, and the only risk you are taking with your schema is a foreign key directly into an ASP.NET table.

However, what happens if you want to create your own custom Membership provider, but you still want your data to be integrated with other features such as Profile and Web Parts Personalization? Now you have the problem of getting a row of data into the user and application tables. If you wanted to, you could still require that `SqlMembershipProvider` be used even though someone really uses your custom provider for user management. You could register a user with `SqlMembershipProvider` simply to take advantage of the fact that by doing so you will get user and application rows set up properly.

That approach, though, is admittedly pretty clunky, and customers would wonder why the Membership user table holds all this extra data. The better approach would be to insert the common data into `aspnet_Users` and `aspnet_Applications`—but, of course, the catch-22 here is that ASP.NET 2.0 and ASP.NET 3.5 have no publicly supported way to do so. Assuming that you are fine with taking the added risk of using officially undocumented and unsupported stored procedures, you can solve this problem by using the stored procedures that already exist in the default ASP.NET schemas:

❑   `aspnet_Applications_CreateApplication`: Other ASP.NET features use this undocumented and unsupported feature to automatically create an application as needed. You pass it the string value for the application name, and it returns as an output parameter the GUID for the newly created application.

❑ aspnet_Users_CreateUser: This undocumented and unsupported stored procedure creates a row in the aspnet_Users table for a new user. You pass it the ApplicationId, username of the new user, and the settings for IsAnonymous and LastActivityDate. The procedure returns the GUID for the newly created user.

To at least mitigate the risk of these stored procedures changing or being renamed, you should limit the places where you call unsupported stored procedures. For example, if you wrote a stored procedure for a custom Membership implementation and you wanted to create a new user, you could write something like this:

```
create procedure MyCustomUserCreation
@pApplicationName nvarchar(256),
@pUsername        nvarchar(256),
@pUserId          uniqueidentifier OUTPUT
as

declare @applicationID uniqueidentifier
declare @retVal        int
declare @rightNow      datetime

set @rightNow = getutcdate()

--this ensures the row in the application data exists
--if the application already exists, the sproc just performs
--a select
exec dbo.aspnet_Applications_CreateApplication @pApplicationName,
                                               @applicationID OUTPUT


--if for some reason the user record was already registered
--just return it
select  @pUserId = UserId
from    dbo.vw_aspnet_Users u,
        dbo.vw_aspnet_Applications a
where   a.LoweredApplicationName = LOWER(@pApplicationName)
and     u.LoweredUserName        = LOWER(@pUsername)
and     u.ApplicationId          = a.ApplicationId

if (@pUserId is null)
begin
   exec @retVal = dbo.aspnet_Users_CreateUser @applicationID, @pUsername,
                                      0, @rightNow, @pUserId OUTPUT

End

if (@retVal = -1) --other error handling here
  return @retVal

--if you make it this far, create the rest of the user
--data in your custom tables

return 0
```

This stored procedure uses a mix of supported views and the unsupported stored procedures for creating applications and users. It starts by ensuring that a row in aspnet_Applications already exists by calling the aspnet_Applications_CreateApplication stored procedure. Internally, this stored procedure first attempts to return a row of application data if the application already exists. If the application does not exist, the stored procedure creates it for you. As a result, it is safe to repeatedly call this stored procedure with the same application name, because only the very first call results in an insert.

The user creation stored procedure then checks to see if the user record was already registered in the aspnet_Users table. If the user already exists, it just fetches the existing UserId by querying the view. However, if the user is not already in aspnet_Users, then the stored procedure calls the aspnet_Users_CreateUser stored procedure to insert a row into the aspnet_Users table. Assuming that no errors occur by this point, you would then write additional code to perform the necessary inserts into your custom data tables.

On one hand, wrapping this kind of logic inside of your own stored procedure ensures that if the ASP.NET procedures change in a future release, you have to edit only this one stored procedure. On the other hand, if you spam your code base with calls to the ASP.NET application creation and user creation stored procedures, you risk having to implement mass rework each time you upgrade the database with newer ASP.NET stored procedures. And, of course, in the extreme you could clone and rename the two ASP.NET stored procedures that are being used, though such an approach is likely to break if the underlying schemas for the aspnet_Users and aspnet_Applications tables change.

Why Are There Calls to the LOWER Function?

In a few of the previous samples there is code that looks like LOWER(@pUsername) and LOWER (@pApplicationName). You might be wondering, why not just perform joins directly against the UserName and ApplicationName columns in the views? If you install your database using a case-insensitive sort order, you do not need to muck around with the LOWER function. However, because ASP.NET can't control the collation orders of customer databases, many of the stored procedures in ASP.NET use columns whose sole purpose is to store the lowered representation of string data.

For example, the aspnet_Users table has a UserName column and a LoweredUserName column. If you install this schema in a database that is *case-sensitive*, you will see that the ASP.NET features still work in a *case-insensitive* manner. You could create a new user called "TEST" using SqlMembershipProvider, and you could still log in by typing in a username of "test". This means that ASP.NET stored procedures have to perform extra work during inserts, updates, and selects to ensure that string data is being queried in a case-insensitive manner regardless of the collation order for the underlying database.

Typically, at insert time (and updates in the case of data like email addresses), various stored procedures explicitly lower the data prior to inserting it into a Lowered* column. The original casing is preserved in a separate column. So, when you create a new user, the value TEST goes into the UserName column, but the lowercased representation of test goes into the LoweredUserName column. Whenever an ASP.NET feature performs a username-based query, it always lowercases the search parameter and then compares it against the LoweredUserName column. This is why some of the view samples earlier used the syntax LoweredUserName = LOWER(@pUserName). However, when you get a MembershipUser from the database, the Username property reflects the original casing used at creation time.

The reason that the ASP.NET stored procedures enforce the lowercasing is that, for the most part, the string data managed by the various features is intended to be used in a case-insensitive manner. Usernames and email addresses are typically not expected to be case-sensitive. When you log in to a

Windows desktop, for example, you can type your username in all capitals if you want, and the login still works. Similarly, you can email yourself using all capital letters, and the email will still reach you. In general, this behavior means that the following pieces of data are stored using two columns of data and are treated as case-insensitive for search and data modification purposes:

❑   Application name

❑   Username

❑   Email address

❑   Role names

❑   Virtual paths stored by Web Parts Personalization

If you are an experienced database developer all this probably raises a second question: Why the kludgy workaround? You may not realize it, but the database schemas for the provider-based features in ASP.NET are actually supported on SQL Server 7.0, 2000, and 2005.

Unfortunately, due to the wide range of supported SQL Server versions, there is not a single silver bullet for enforcing case-insensitivity. Only with SQL Server 2000 or later are you able to explicitly control collations on a column-by-column basis. Although the development team could have created a 2000/2005 table schema that was separate from the 7.0 schema, the workaround for handling lowercased data would still have been necessary for the 7.0 specific schema. Because supporting SQL Server 7.0 requires a workaround in all the stored procedures anyway, it did not make much sense to fork the database schemas and then have to support two subtly different sets of stored procedures and tables going forward.

The Membership Database Schema

The Membership database schema (contained in `InstallMembership.sql`) deals with storing Membership-specific data. Where overlaps exist with the common table schema (the username and application name), the data is stored using the common tables. As a result, only one additional table is added by Membership: the `aspnet_Membership` table. There is also a view called `vw_aspnet_MembershipUsers` that maps most, though not all, of the columns on this table. The vast majority of the Membership database schemas that are installed are for stored procedures used by `SqlMembershipProvider`.

The `aspnet_Membership` table is:

```
CREATE TABLE dbo.aspnet_Membership (
ApplicationId                              uniqueidentifier    NOT NULL
                    FOREIGN KEY REFERENCES dbo.aspnet_Applications(ApplicationId),
UserId                                     uniqueidentifier    NOT NULL
                    PRIMARY KEY NONCLUSTERED
                    FOREIGN KEY REFERENCES dbo.aspnet_Users(UserId),
Password                                   nvarchar(128)       NOT NULL,
PasswordFormat                             int                 NOT NULL DEFAULT 0,
PasswordSalt                               nvarchar(128)       NOT NULL,
MobilePIN                                  nvarchar(16),
Email                                      nvarchar(256),
LoweredEmail                               nvarchar(256),
PasswordQuestion                           nvarchar(256),
```

```
PasswordAnswer                            nvarchar(128),
IsApproved                                bit                NOT NULL,
IsLockedOut                               bit                NOT NULL,
CreateDate                                datetime           NOT NULL,
LastLoginDate                             datetime           NOT NULL,
LastPasswordChangedDate                   datetime           NOT NULL,
LastLockoutDate                           datetime           NOT NULL,
FailedPasswordAttemptCount                int                NOT NULL,
FailedPasswordAttemptWindowStart          datetime           NOT NULL,
FailedPasswordAnswerAttemptCount          int                NOT NULL,
FailedPasswordAnswerAttemptWindowStart    datetime           NOT NULL,
Comment                                   ntext )
```

Many columns in the table should be familiar to you because they map directly to properties on the MembershipUser class. A brief summary of each of the column values is listed here:

❑   ApplicationId: This column is included solely as a performance optimization for few stored procedures. Including the ApplicationId allows these procedures to perform a select directly against the aspnet_Membership table without first having to join through the aspnet_Applications table. From a data consistency standpoint though, the column isn't necessary, because UserId represents the combination of username and application name.

❑   UserId: The primary key for the table. You can think of a MembershipUser as being a "derivation" of the base user record stored in aspnet_Users. The UserId column is used by SqlMembershipProvider to join back to aspnet_Users to fetch the actual username as well as the LastActivityDate for a user.

❑   Password: Stores the password for the user in the format configured on SqlMemershipProvider. As a result, the value of this column can contain a cleartext password, an encrypted password, or a hashed representation of the password plus the salt value from the PasswordSalt column.

❑   PasswordFormat: This column is used internally by SqlMembershipProvider when decoding the value in the Password and PasswordAnswer columns. When you set the password format on a provider, that format is used to encode the password and password answer. The specific password format that was used is then stored by the provider in this column. If you subsequently change the password format for the provider, preexisting passwords and password answers are still usable. SqlMembershipProvider will continue to decode and encode preexisting passwords and answers using the format that was originally used when the record was created. The possible values for this column are: 0 = clear text, 1 = hashed, and 2 = encrypted.

❑   PasswordSalt: If you choose a hashed password format with SqlMembershipProvider, the provider will automatically generate a random 16-byte salt value and then hash passwords and password answers using a string that consists of the text and the random salt values. The result of the hashing operation is stored in the Password column. Because the salt value is always required to validate the password and password answer, it is stored in this column.

❑   MobilePIN: Another leftover from earlier plans for more extensive support for mobile users. The idea was that in conjunction with MobileAlias from aspnet_Users, you would be able to validate a mobile user's credentials using a custom PIN. Just as a traditional username could be too unwieldy for mobile users to type in, a traditional password could also be unwieldy. Instead, the idea was that you could validate a mobile user with just a PIN, much in the way you use ATM cards today and validate them using just a PIN code. None of this functionality was implemented in ASP.NET 2.0 or ASP.NET 3.5, but the column was left in the table in case a future release chooses to implement this.

❏ `Email`: The email address for a user. `SqlMembershipProvider` enforces uniqueness of this value based on the `requiresUniqueEmail` configuration setting.

❏ `LoweredEmail`: The result of calling `LOWER` on the email column. This ensures the provider can perform case-insensitive lookups based on email address, regardless of the collation order of the underlying database.

❏ `PasswordQuestion`: If a provider is configured to use password questions and answers (that is, `requiresPasswordQuestionAndAnswer` is set to true in configuration), this is the column where the question is stored. Note that the question is always stored in cleartext and that, furthermore, the expectation is that the entire question is stored in this column. Some developers may instead want to have a limited list of common password questions, in which case a domain lookup table of questions would be more useful. In this case, the functionality of `SqlMembershipProvider` would result in the same question text repeatedly showing up in this column for many users. If you want to use a domain table to limit the number of possible password questions, you could instead store the string value of the question's primary key in this column and write extra code to resolve this value against a lookup table.

❏ `PasswordAnswer`: The user's secret answer to a password question is stored in this column. For security reasons, `SqlMembershipProvider` actually stores an encoded representation of the password answer based on the password format that was applied to the user's password. This means that if the user's password was stored as a hash value, a hash of the secret answer is also stored as opposed to storing the answer in cleartext. If you configure the provider to use hashing or encryption, you will need to test the effective maximum length of password answer that be stored. For hashing and encryption, a base64-encoded representation is stored in this field. Stronger hash algorithms can result in a base64-encoded representation that is too large to store in this field because the column is an `nvarchar(128)`. Similarly, the encrypted version of a password answer may also be too large to store in this field after taking into account the overhead of encryption and base64 encoding.

❏ `IsApproved`: Stores the value of the `MembershipUser.IsApproved` property.

❏ `IsLockedOut`: This column is set to `true` whenever the provider detects that too many bad passwords or bad password answers have been supplied. The provider configuration attributes `maxInvalidPasswordAttempts` and `passwordAttemptWindow` control this behavior.

❏ `CreateDate`: The UTC date time when `SqlMembershipProvider` was used to create the user record in the table. There can be an edge case where a different type of authentication is used initially on a website with other ASP.NET provider-based features. At a later point, the website may be switched over to use Membership with `SqlMembershipProvider`. In this case, `SqlMembershipProvider` will only insert a user into the `aspnet_Membership` table because the user record already exists in `aspnet_Users`. For this reason, you may see that for newly created users the value of `CreateDate` in `aspnet_Membership` is different than the `LastActivityDate` column in `aspnet_Users`.

❏ `LastLoginDate`: `SqlMembershipProvider` stores the UTC date time of a successful login attempt in this column whenever `ValidateUser` is called. When a user is first created, the provider sets this column to the same value as the `CreateDate` column.

❏ `LastPasswordChangedDate`: The last UTC date time when the provider changed the password stored in the `Password` column. When a user is first created, the provider sets this column to the same value as the `CreateDate` column.

❏ `LastLockoutDate`: Used in conjunction with the `IsLockedOut` field. If the user is in a locked-out state, this column contains the UTC date time when the lockout occurred. For users that are not locked out, this field instead contains a default value of "01/01/1754."

❑ FailedPasswordAttemptCount: The provider keeps track of bad password attempts in this column. Even though determining account lockout for bad passwords and bad password answers uses the same configuration attributes (maxInvalidPasswordAttempts and passwordAttempt Window), the provider keeps track of bad password attempts separately from bad password answer attempts. Any time that an account is unlocked or any time the correct password is used for an account, this field is reset to zero.

❑ FailedPasswordAnswerAttemptCount: If the provider is configured to allow question-and-answer-based password retrieval or password resets (that is, requiresQuestionAndAnswer is set to true in configuration and either enablePasswordRetrieval or enablePasswordReset is set to true), then the provider keeps track of failed password answer attempts in this column. After a user account is unlocked, this counter is reset to zero. Any successful use of a password (that is, ValidateUser succeeded) or password answer (that is, GetPassword is called using a password answer) will also reset this column to zero.

❑ FailedPasswordAttemptWindowStart: When the provider keeps track of bad passwords, it needs to know the start of the time window in UTC time during which it should track bad attempts. It stores the start of this time window in this column. Any time an account is unlocked, or any time the correct password is used for an account, this field is reset to a default value of 01/01/1754.

❑ FailedPasswordAnswerAttemptWindowStart: When the provider keeps track of bad password it needs to know the start of the time window during which it should track bad attempts. It stores the start of this time window in UTC time in this column. Notice how the provider keeps track of bad password answer attempts separately from bad password attempts by storing the tracking information for each type of event in a different set of columns. Any time an account is unlocked, or any time the correct password or correct password answer is used for the account, this field is reset to a default value of 01/01/1754.

❑ Comment: A catch-all column that you can use to store miscellaneous data. Because this is an ntext column, you can actually store an immense amount of data in this field and then retrieve it from the MembershipUser.Comment property.

In addition to the single database table, the Membership feature also installs a single view: vw_aspnet_MembershipUsers. This view maps most of the columns from aspnet_Membership one for one. However, the Password and PasswordSalt columns aren't included in the view because the view is really intended for reporting purposes. From a security standpoint these columns were left out of the view because they are intended for internal use only by the provider and its stored procedures. The PasswordAnswer column probably should also have been left out of the view, but because the answer was actually stored in cleartext for most of the development cycle, it ended up being left in the view.

The view also joins in all the columns from the aspnet_Users table. This makes the vw_aspnet_ MembershipUsers view easier to use because most reporting queries written against this view will at the very least need the UserName column from the aspnet_Users table.

SQL Server-Specific Provider Configuration Options

Because SqlMembershipProvider connects to SQL Server, it uses two SQL Server-specific configuration attributes on the provider definition:

❑ connectionStringName: As you would expect, the provider needs to know what database and server to connect to. The value of this attribute must point at a named connection string defined up in the <connectionStrings /> section.

❑ commandTimeout: As you work with larger databases, you may find that the default ADO.NET SqlCommand timeout of 30 seconds is too short for certain operations. For SqlMembership Provider the Find* and Get* search methods can result in long-running queries especially with poor query parameters. You can change the command timeout that the provider uses with this configuration attribute. You can increase or decrease the amount of time that ADO.NET will wait for a SqlCommand to complete.

Working with SQL Server Express

Sometimes folks think that there is a separate set of providers for SQL Server 2005 Express different from the regular SKUs of SQL Server. SqlMembershipProvider as well as all the other SQL-based providers in ASP.NET 2.0 and ASP.NET 3.5 work equally well against the Express and non-Express versions of SQL Server 2005. However, there are some differences in how the database schema is installed when using SQL Server Express.

SQL Server Express (SSE) is the low-end SKU of SQL Server 2005. It normally installs on a machine as a named instance: SQLEXPRESS. As a result, you can install SSE on machines running SQL Server 2000 or other versions of SQL Server 2005 without interfering with these installations. There is also a special mode of operation supported by SSE called user instancing. The internal database code shared across all the ASP.NET SQL-based providers includes special logic in the event a provider runs against SSE that has user instancing enabled.

The idea behind user instancing is that the central SSE named instance (identified in a connection string as server=.\SQLEXPRESS) can be used to spawn additional instances of the SQL Server worker process. These spawned instances are referred to as user instances. They are referred to as "user" instances because the SQLEXPRESS named instance spawns these extra worker processes to run with the account credentials of a user—specifically, the Windows user credentials that opened an ADO.NET connection in the first place.

To make use of SSE user instancing, you use a special form of ADO.NET connection string. You can see an example of a user-instanced connection string by looking at the <connectionStrings /> section in machine.config:

```
<connectionStrings>
    <add name="LocalSqlServer"
        connectionString="data source=.\SQLEXPRESS;
                          Integrated Security=SSPI;
                          AttachDBFilename=|DataDirectory|aspnetdb.mdf;
                          User Instance=true"
        providerName="System.Data.SqlClient"/>
</connectionStrings>
```

The bolded portions of the connection string cause ADO.NET and SSE to handle the initial database connection in a different manner from when connecting to a regular version of SQL Server.

The data source portion of the connection string tells ADO.NET to initially open a connection against the named SSE instance. The User Instance=true portion of the connection string is a hint to ADO.NET and SSE that the connection should really be rerouted to a spawned worker process running with the account credentials currently active on the operating system thread at the time the ADO.NET connection was opened. The AttachDBFilename portion of the connection string tells SSE that once the spawned user instance is up and running, it should attach the SQL Server mdf data file at the specified location as a database in the spawned user instance.

ADO.NET actually preprocesses the `AttachDBFilename` syntax and substitutes in the full physical path information in place of `|DataDirectory|`. This syntax refers to an app-domain-level variable that host processes fill in. A client application such as a ClickOnce application will place one value inside of this app-domain variable. You can see what an ASP.NET host process uses with the following code:

```
Response.Write(System.AppDomain.CurrentDomain.GetData("DataDirectory"));
```

If you run this code in an IIS-based web, you will get back a path that looks something like:

```
C:\inetpub\wwwroot\379301_code\379301 ch12_code\cs\SSESample\App_Data
```

After ADO.NET substitutes the value of the `DataDirectory` app-domain variable in the connection string, it then passes the information down to SSE. So by the time SSE gets the connection string information, it is actually looking at a full physical file path to an `.mdf` file located somewhere within the directory structure of the web application.

SSE is able to attach a database in the user instance because within the user instance your code is running with System Administrator privileges. Because the user instance is spawned with some set of credentials, and that same set of credentials is sending commands over an ADO.NET connection, from the point of view of SSE those credentials have SA privileges. This makes sense because the credentials had the right to spawn a worker process in the first place, so the same credentials might as well have full control over any database operations within the user instance. Note that by default interactive users on a machine, as well as accounts like NETWORK SERVICE and ASPNET, have rights to connect to the default SSE named instance. As a result, this same set of accounts also has rights to request user instancing, thus elevating themselves to the System Administrators role within the scope of the spawned user instance.

There is still another set of rights that must be satisfied for SSE user instances to work: NTFS file ACLs. If you start out designing your application inside of Visual Studio, and if you create an `App_Data` directory, then Visual Studio will automatically grant Read and Write ACLs on this directory to ASPNET and NETWORK SERVICE. As a result, when SSE attempts to read or write data to or from the `.mdf` file, the calls succeed because the credentials for the user instance have write access to the file.

However, if you just copy a bunch files to a location on the filesystem and then map an application in IIS to this file location, attempts to use SSE user instancing will probably fail. By default, the ACLs on `inetpub\wwwroot` don't normally grant any Write access to the traditional web process accounts. As a result, if you rely on the automatic database creation process, you will instead end up with an error to the effect that SSE does not have write access to the database file. The simplest way to ensure that everything works properly is to create the web application inside of Visual Studio initially and let the design environment automatically place the correct ACLs on the `App_Data` directory for you.

When your website opens a connection with SSE user instancing requested:

1. An instance of `sqlservr.exe` is running initially as NETWORK SERVICE. This is the named SSE instance.

2. A new SSE user instance is spawned resulting in a second instance of `sqlservr.exe` running. This instance runs with user credentials based on the identity of the operating system thread that opened the connection.

3. If this is the first time that a user instance with the credentials from step 2 has ever been launched on the machine, SSE clones the master, msdb, and tempdb databases to support the user instance. If you look in the AppData directory on your hard drive, and then drill down to `users\user name\AppData\Local\Microsoft\Microsoft SQL Server Data\SQLEXPRESS`, you will see that these three databases have been created.

4. The special logic contained in ASP.NET's internal SQL provider code detects whether or not the `.mdf` file specified in the connection string even exists at the specified file path. If the `.mdf` file does not physically exist, then the providers incur about a 15 second delay while they run all the SQL installation files for the application services (that is, everything except session state gets installed) against the user instance. The end result of this work is that an `.mdf` file is created in the file location specified by the connection string. As the last part of this work, the provider infrastructure detaches the newly created `.mdf` file.

5. Within the new user instance, the database file specified by `AttachDBFilename` is attached to the instance and registered in the metadata tables in the user instance's master database. If you are accustomed to working with databases as a named database in other versions of SQL Server, this might seem a bit strange. However, using the attach syntax in the connection string causes the SSE user instance to attach the database on your behalf.

The connection string shown earlier exists in `machine.config` to allow developers that use Visual Studio to get up and running "auto-magically" with the application services. Rather than running `aspnet_regsql.exe` manually to install the database scripts into a specific database on a database server, you can write code against a feature like Membership, and the database will automatically be created for you.

From an ease-of-use perspective, this is actually pretty powerful and makes features like Membership so straightforward to use that developers potentially don't need to understand or muck around with databases. Of course, this rosy scenario actually has a few streaks on the window, as you will shortly see. The automatic database creation behavior was originally intended for client applications such as ClickOnce apps. In a client environment, a user instance makes a fair amount of sense because someone is actually running interactively on a machine with a well-established set of credentials.

Furthermore, while running in a client environment, there is likely to be sufficient processing power on the machine to handle the overhead of user instancing. Just running the named SSE instance plus a user instance with the ASP.NET database tables in them incurs up to about 45-75MB of memory overhead. That's a pretty hefty wallop, but nonetheless manageable on a single desktop machine. When the user instancing capability was used for the ASP.NET application services, the main scenario was to support development in Visual Studio (in essence, this is another client application scenario, albeit in this case the client application is a development environment).

However, the SSE story on a web server starts to break down because of a few constraints with user instancing. The most obvious one is that user instancing is tied to a specific user identity, which leads to the potential for multiple user instances floating around on a server. With around a 45MB overhead when the SQL providers auto-create the database, and around 25MB of overhead once the database exists, it would not take long for a shared web server to run out of memory space.

The next issue with user instancing deals specifically with the operating system thread identity that is used when making the initial ADO.NET connection. As mentioned earlier, this identity is critical because SSE needs to ensure that cloned databases like the master database exist for these user accounts. Additionally, SSE needs the security token of the client to create a new child process running the SQL Server executable. It turns out, though, that for SSE to actually know where to create and look for the cloned versions of master and other databases, a Windows user profile needs to be loaded into memory.

In the scenario with a client application, the dependency on the Windows user profile is a nonissue. The second you log on to a Windows machine with some credentials, your Windows user profile is loaded. Hence, any application that you choose to run, including Visual Studio, will be able to find data that is stored in the Windows user profile. What happens, though, for a noninteractive scenario like IIS 7.0 application pools? It turns out that when you run ASP.NET (any version of ASP.NET for that matter) on IIS 7.0, the Windows user profile *is never loaded* for the account identity used for the application pool when the application pool uses an account other than NETWORK SERVICE.

If you write an ASP.NET application that uses Membership with the default connection string, in some circumstances the application services database is automatically created for you. The reason this works is basically by accident. Because the default identity for IIS 7.0 application pools is NETWORK SERVICE, and NETWORK SERVICE is commonly used for other services on a Windows Server 2008 machine, the Windows user profile for NETWORK SERVICE gets loaded as a side effect of the operating system starting up. As a result, when you use SSE with the default connection string using the default IIS 6 application pool identity, the named SSE instance is able to query the Windows user profile for the location of the Local Settings folder for NETWORK SERVICE.

However, if you attempt to use application impersonation or to change the application pool identity to a different account, any code you write that uses the default SSE connection string will fail. For all other application pool identities, there is no Windows user profile available. As a result, if you attempt to use SSE user instances, you will instead end up with the following exception:

```
Failed to generate a user instance of SQL Server due to failure in retrieving the
user's local application data path. Please make sure the user has a local user
profile on the computer. The connection will be closed.
```

Other information is displayed along with this error, but if you see this error, you aren't ever going to get SSE user instancing to work (ignoring any crazy hacks that forcibly load a Windows user profile using an NT service or schedule batch job).

This behavior basically leaves you wondering when to use the default connection string and when to change it. If you perform most of your development using file-based, as opposed to IIS-based, websites on your own machine, then you can leave the SSE connection string as is. File-based webs use the Cassini web server instead of the IIS 7.0 process model. Cassini runs with your logged-in credentials, so SSE will always be able to find your Windows user profile. This security model meshes well with SSE's assumptions about user instancing.

However, if you are developing websites with IIS 7.0 (some of you probably run Windows Server 2008 for a development "desktop"), or if you are developing websites *that will be deployed* to IIS 7.0, then you definitely should consider changing the SSE style connection string. There are a few reasons for this suggestion:

❑   As noted earlier, unless your IIS 7.0 application pool runs as NETWORK SERVICE, the SSE style connections are not going to work anyway.

❑   There is a somewhat non-obvious problem with handshaking between an IIS 7.0 website and the development environment over who has control over the .mdf file (more on this in a bit).

❑   From a security perspective, you should *not* run with user instancing on any of your production machines if untrusted applications are deployed on them.

The last point may not be something that many of you run into. Most companies have SQL Server installations running on separate machines, in which case user instances would never come into the picture. (You can't connect to an SSE *user instance* from across the network; only local connections are accepted against user instances.) If you happen to be in an environment where SSE is installed locally on your web servers as a sort of low-cost database, you still should be aware of the security implications of user instancing.

Imagine a scenario where you have two different application pools on IIS 7.0 both running as NET-WORK SERVICE. If you put applications from two different untrusted clients into the two different application pools, you may think that you have enforced a reasonable degree of isolation between the two applications. The idea is that the two clients do not know or trust each other; perhaps for example this is an Internet facing shared hosting machine. Because their sites are in different application pools, the applications can't reach into each other's memory spaces and carry out malicious tasks. If you are running in something like Medium trust, the applications can't use file I/O to try to read each other's application files. So, you might think you are reasonably safe at this point.

However, if these applications use a connection string that specifies SSE user instances, you will come to grief. Because both application pools run as NETWORK SERVICE, SSE will spin up one, and only one, instance of sqlservr.exe running as NETWORK SERVICE. Both applications will connect to this single user instance, and both applications as a result will be running with System Administrator privileges within this single user instance. The end result is that two untrusted applications have access to each other's data. And, of course, attempting to switch the application pool identities to something else immediately breaks SSE user instancing!

There is a scenario, though, where SSE user instancing is reasonable for IIS 7.0 production machines. If you are running in a corporate environment (and this can be an intranet, an extranet, or the Internet) and all the applications on the machine are from trusted sources, SSE user instancing can probably be left in place. Because all the code authors are presumably from the same or trusted organizations, there probably aren't any concerns with snooping each other's data. Also, corporate developers running local SQL Server installations on their web servers probably are not storing confidential information in these databases. You may just be storing information such as Web Parts Personalization data; if the worst happens and someone walks away with everyone's preferred background color for a web part on page two of your application, it is not the end of the world.

A cautionary note for this scenario is still needed, though. Even if all the applications on a machine trust each other, I still would not store any security-sensitive data in an SSE user-instanced database. For example, I would still recommend storing Membership and Role Manager data at a minimum inside of a regular SQL Server database that can be protected. And ideally such a database would be running on a remote machine, not locally on the web server.

Note that although this section is discussing the user instance mode of SSE, you can install SSE on a machine just as you would normally install any other version of SQL Server. You can then have local and remote web servers connect to SSE using the more traditional database connection string syntax:

```
"server=remoteserver\SQLEXPRESS;database=aspnetdb;Integrated Security=true"
```

This connection string works the same way as connections to named instances of SQL Server 2000 work today. With this approach you need to manually enable remote network connections to SSE because, by default, even the named instance of SSE only allows local connections. Also, you can turn off user instancing on your machines that are running SSE at install time. (There is an advanced option for turning off support.) Alternatively, you can connect to the SSE named instance using credentials that have System Administrator privileges. Then using a command line tool like OSQL.exe or SQLCMD.exe, you can run the following SQL commands:

```
exec sp_configure 'show advanced option', '1'
go
reconfigure with override
go
exec sp_configure 'user instances enabled', 0
go
reconfigure with override
go
```

Unless you intend to support user instancing for development purposes or web servers where you trust all the users and you aren't storing sensitive data, you should turn off support for user instances. Especially in environments such as shared hosting servers that support multiple untrusted clients, you should always disable SSE user instancing.

Sharing Issues with SSE

If you work with an IIS-based web application inside of Visual Studio, you will probably run into cases with lock contention over the .mdf file containing the application services database. An .mdf file cannot be opened by more than one instance of sqlservr.exe at a time. If you are developing with file-based webs, you will not run into this issue because the Visual Studio environment and the Cassini web server run under the same credentials: the interactive user. Whenever either environment attempts to manipulate an .mdf both processes are routed to the same SSE user instance, and hence there is no file contention.

With an IIS-based web, you potentially have two different user accounts causing two different SSE user instances to be spawned. IIS will spawn a user instance running as NETWORK SERVICE, whereas the Visual Studio design environment will cause a user instance running as the interactive user to be spawned. You can run into a problem with this environment if you start debugging your application in IIS 7.0, thus causing the user instance running as NETWORK SERVICE to own the application services .mdf file.

Then if you go back into Visual Studio and try to run the Web Administration Tool (WAT), Visual Studio will start up a Cassini instance running as you. When you then surf around the WAT and access functionality that needs to access the .mdf, you may get an error message like the following:

```
Unable to open the physical file "C:\inetpub\wwwroot\379301_code\379301 ch12_code\
cs\SSESample\App_Data\aspnetdb.mdf".
Operating system error 32: "32(The process
cannot access the file because it is being used by another process.)".
An attempt to attach an auto-named database for file
C:\inetpub\wwwroot\379301_code\379301ch12_code\cs\SSESample\App_Data\aspnetdb.mdf
failed.
A database with the same name exists, or specified file cannot be opened,
or it is located on UNC share.
```

or

```
Cannot open user default database. Login failed. Login failed for user 'DOMAIN\
user'.
```

These errors can occur because the SSE user instance for IIS 7.0 is still up and running, and thus the SSE user instance for WAT in Cassini cannot get open the same .mdf file. Technically, this type of issue is not supposed to occur in many cases because within Visual Studio there are certain click paths that create an app_offline.htm file in the root of the IIS 7.0 website. Placing an app_offline.htm in the root of an application causes the application's add-domain to recycle and put the application in an offline mode that refuses any request targeting any resource within the application.

The idea behind Visual Studio placing a temporary app_offline.htm in the root of an IIS-based website is that when the app-domain recycles, all the ADO.NET connections to the SSE user instance drop. As a result, the SSE user instance should quickly detect that there are no active connections to the currently attached database, and therefore the SSE user instance should release any attached .mdf files. Unfortunately, the SSE auto-detach behavior and Visual Studio handshaking behavior have been flaky since day one, and therefore the extra work that Visual Studio does to force a detaching of the application services database sometimes does not work.

If you end up in this situation, the quickest way to force an app-domain restart in the IIS application is to touch the web.config. Put a space in the file, or make some trivial edit, and then save the updated web.config. ASP.NET will detect that web.config has changed, and it will cycle the app-domain, which in turn will trigger the auto-detach behavior in SSE. If you have problems going in the other direction (that is, the data designer in Visual Studio or the WAT has grabbed access to the .mdf file), you have two options. You can rectify the problem by finding the sqlservr.exe instance in Task Manager that is running with your logged-in identity and just kill the process. Or you can right-click on the application services database in the Visual Studio Solution Explorer and select Detach. When you then switch to your IIS 7.0 application, the SSE user instance running as NETWORK SERVICE will be able to grab access to the .mdf file again.

As you can see from this process of sharing the application services .mdf file between the design environment and IIS, this is yet another reason why using SSE for any of the ASP.NET application services is frequently more trouble than it is worth when developing against IIS 7.0. In general, I would only use SSE when developing file-based webs where the entire hand-shaking issue never arises.

Changing the SSE Connection String

So, what happens if you don't want to use SSE user instancing? Does this suddenly mean that you have to redefine every application provider just to switch over the connection string? Thankfully, the answer to this is no! All the ASP.NET providers, regardless of whether they are defined in machine .config or the root web.config, reference the connection string named LocalSqlServer. Because the <connectionStrings /> configuration section is a standard add-remove-clear collection, you can just redefine the LocalSqlServer connection string to point at a different server and database:

```
<connectionStrings>
    <remove name="LocalSqlServer"/>
    <add name="LocalSqlServer"
        connectionString="data source=.\SQLEXPRESS;
                    Integrated Security=SSPI;database=aspnetdb"/>
</connectionStrings>
```

This connection string redefines the common connection string shared by all SQL providers to point at the default local SSE named instance, but instead specifies connecting to a database called `aspnetdb`. This is the more traditional SQL Server connection string that you probably familiar with from SQL Server 2000. For other server locations, you can change the data source portion of the connection string to point at the correct server.

With the connection string shown previously, you can use the `aspnet_regsql` tool to install all the application services database schemas in a database called `aspnetdb` on the local SSE instance. The `aspnet_regsql.exe` tool is located in the Framework's installation directory:

```
aspnet_regsql  -S .\SQLEXPRESS -E -A all -d aspnetdb
```

For this to work with a remote SSE instance, you need to use the SQL Server Configuration Manager tool that comes with SSE and enable either the Named Pipes or TCP/IP protocol for the remote SSE instance. SSE by default disables these protocols to prevent connections made by remote servers.

After you have installed the application services databases, you still need to grant the appropriate login rights and permissions in the application services database. These steps aren't unique to SSE because you will have to do this for any variation of SQL Server other than user-instanced SSE installations. The subject of database security is the topic for the next section.

Database Security

After the database schema is installed using `aspnet_regsql`, your applications still won't be able to use the database. You need to grant the appropriate account login rights to the SQL Server. And then you need to grant the appropriate rights in the application services database. The first question that needs to be answered is, which account do the SQL-based providers use when connecting to SQL Server?

Internally, all the SQL providers, including `SqlMembershipProvider`, will suspend client imperson-ation if it is in effect. This means that the identity used by the providers for communicating with SQL Server when using integrated security will be one of the following:

❑   The process identity of the IIS 7.0 worker process. This is NETWORK SERVICE by default, but it can be different if you have changed the identity of the application pool.

❑   If you configured application impersonation for your application, then the provider connects using the explicit credentials specified in the `<identity />` configuration element.

If you have `<identity impersonate="true" />` and you are using Windows authentication, the providers always suspend client impersonation. From a security perspective, it is not a good approach to grant login and database access to all potential Windows accounts on your website. If your connec-tion string uses standard SQL security instead of integrated security, then the identity that connects to SQL Server is pretty easy to identify; it is simply the standard SQL user account that is specified in the connection string.

After you have identified the specific identity that will be used when connecting to SQL Server, you need to first grant login rights on the server to this identity. You can use the graphical management tools supplied with SQL Server 2000 and the nonexpress SKUs of SQL Server 2005 to do this. If you need to grant access to the NETWORK SERVICE account without a graphical tool, you can type in "NT AUTHORITY\NETWORK SERVICE" for the NETWORK SERVICE account of a local machine.

However, if you want to grant access to the NETWORK SERVICE account for a remote web server, you need to grant access to DOMAIN\MACHINENAME$. This special syntax references the machine account for a server in a domain. The MACHINENAME$ portion of this account actually references the NETWORK SERVICE account for a remote machine. If your website uses some other kind of domain credentials, you would just type DOMAIN\USERNAME instead.

If you want, you can also grant login rights using plain old TSQL to accomplish this:

```
exec sp_grantlogin N'bhaidar-PC\DEMOTEST$'
```

You use a standard SQL Server login account instead of a domain style name if your connection string uses standard SQL credentials. If you choose to use a locally installed SSE database, for some strange reason there is no graphical management tool for this type of operation that is available out of the box with the SSE installation. Instead, you need to use command-line tools like OSQL.exe or SQLCMD.exe to run this command. There is nothing quite like forward progress that throws you a decade back in time!

After login rights are granted on the SQL Server, you then need to grant permissions for that login account to access the application services database. Assuming that you want to grant login rights for a local NETWORK SERVICE account to a database called aspnetdb, the TSQL for this looks like:

```
use aspnetdb
go

exec sp_grantdbaccess 'NT AUTHORITY\NETWORK SERVICE'
go
```

You just use a different value for the username passed to sp_grantdbaccess, depending on whether you are granting login rights to a different domain account or to a standard SQL account. Of course, if you are using any of the graphical management tools, you can also use them to grant access to the database.

By this point, you have set things up in SQL Server so that the appropriate account can at least connect to SQL Server and reach the database. The last step is granting rights in the database to the account—this includes things like rights to query views and execute stored procedures. The ASP.NET schemas, though, are installed with a set of SQL Server roles that make this exercise substantially simpler.

Although you could make the application pool identity a dbo in the application services database, for example, this goes against the grain of granting least privilege. Furthermore, if you installed the ASP.NET schema in a preexisting database, you probably do not want the ASP.NET process identity (or whatever credentials are being used) to have such broad privileges.

The ASP.NET schema includes a set of roles for each set of application services with the following suffixes:

❑ **BasicAccess:** Database rights granted to this role are restricted to stored procedures that are needed for minimal feature functionality. The role does not have execute rights on stored procedures that deal with more advanced feature functionality.

❑ **ReportingAccess:** This role has rights to stored procedures that deal with read-only operations and search operations. The role also has rights to perform selects against the SQL Server views that were created for the feature.

❑ **FullAccess:** These roles have rights to execute all the stored procedures associated with the feature as well as having select rights on all of a feature's SQL views.

None of the feature-specific roles grant access directly to the SQL tables because the features deal with data by way of stored procedures and, optionally, views. As a result, there is no reason for a member of a feature's roles to manipulate the tables directly. This also means that in future releases the ASP.NET team has the freedom to change the underlying table schemas because all access to the data in these tables is by way of stored procedures or views.

Technically, the Health Monitoring feature (aka Web Events) is an exception to this rule because it does not provide any mechanism for querying data from the event table other than through direct SELECT statements. Other features like Membership, though, expect you to always go through the object API or for purposes of running reports, through the SQL Server views.

For the Membership feature, three roles are available to you:

- ❑ aspnet_Membership_BasicAccess: This role only allows you to call ValidateUser as well as GetUser and GetUserNameByEmail.

- ❑ aspnet_Membership_ReportingAccess: This role allows you to call GetUser, GetUserName ByEmail, GetAllUsers, GetNumberOfUsersOnline, FindUsersByName, and FindUsersBy Email. Members of this role can also issue select statements against the Membership views.

- ❑ aspnet_Membership_FullAccess: This role can call any of the methods defined on SqlMembershipProvider as well as query any of the Membership views.

Most of the time, you will just add the appropriate account to one of the FullAccess roles. The other, more restrictive roles are there for security-sensitive sites that may have separate web applications for creating users as opposed to logging users in to the website. You can add an account to a role through any of the SQL Server graphical tools, or you can use TSQL like the following:

```
exec sp_addrolemember 'aspnet_Membership_FullAccess',
                      'NT AUTHORITY\NETWORK SERVICE'
```

After this command runs, whenever a website running as NETWORK SERVICE has an SqlMembership Provider that attempts to call a Membership stored procedure in the database, the call will succeed because NETWORK SERVICE has login rights on the server and belongs to a database role that grants all the necessary privileges to execute stored procedures.

Database Schemas and the DBO User

Many of the previous topics assume that you have sufficient privileges to install the application services schemas on your database server. If you or a database administrator have rights to create databases (that is, you are in the db_creator server role), or have "dbo" rights in a preexisting database, then you can just run the aspnet_regsql tool without any worries.

However, there is a very important dependency that the current SQL-based providers have on the concept of the dbo user. If you look at any of the .sql installation scripts in the Framework's installation directory, you will see that all the tables and stored procedures are prepended with dbo:

```
CREATE TABLE dbo.aspnet_Membership
CREATE PROCEDURE dbo.aspnet_Membership_CreateUser
```

and so on.

Furthermore, the code inside of all the stored procedures explicitly references object names (that is, tables and stored procedures) using the explicit dbo username:

```
EXEC dbo.aspnet_Applications_CreateApplication …
SELECT  @NewUserId = UserId FROM dbo.aspnet_Users …
```

and so on.

If you disassemble any of the SQL providers with a tool like ildasm, you will also see that the providers themselves use the dbo owner name when calling stored procedures:

```
SqlCommand cmd = new SqlCommand("dbo.aspnet_Membership_GetUserByEmail",…);
```

If you install the database schemas as a member of the System Administrators role, or as a member of the Database Creators role, none of this will affect you because an SA or a database creator is treated as dbo within a newly created database. In this case, because you are dbo, you can of course create objects associated with the dbo username.

Problems arise, though, if you do not have dbo privileges in the database. For example, you can be running as someone other than dbo and still create tables in a database. Unfortunately, though, if you were to just issue a command like:

```
CREATE PROCEDURE aspnet_Membership_CreateUser
```

a table object called your_account_name.aspnet_Membership_CreateUser is created instead. If this were allowed to happen, a provider like SqlMembershipProvider would never work because the provider would always be looking for a stored procedure owned by dbo and would never see the user-owned stored procedure. The reason that all the providers explicitly look for a dbo-owned object is that at least on SQL Server 2000 (which is expected to be the main platform for running the application services databases for the first few years), there is a slight performance drain if you call stored procedures without including the owner name.

From experience, the ASP.NET team found that this slight performance drain was actually so severe with the SQL Server schema for session state back in ASP.NET 1.1 that they had to QFE the session state database scripts and Session State server code to always use owner-qualified stored procedure names. To prevent the same problem with contention over stored procedure compilation locks from occurring with the ASP.NET 2.0 or ASP.NET 3.5 database schema, the decision was made to owner-qualify all objects in the application services schemas.

Of course, that decision created the problem of which owner name to use. Because dbo is a common owner name that is always available in SQL Server databases, the decision was made to hard-code the dbo owner name into the schemas and the providers. After ASP.NET 2.0 Beta 1 shipped, problems arose with shared hosting companies that sell SQL Server databases for their customers.

Some of these hosters do not grant dbo privileges in the database purchased by the customer. If you attempt to run the older ASP.NET 2.0 Beta 1 versions of the database scripts the attempt fails. To work around this, the new requirement is that you must be one of the following to install the database schemas for the application services:

❑   You can be dbo in the database.

❑   You must be a member of both the db_ddladmin and db_securityadmin roles in the database.

If you belong to both the db_ddladmin and db_securityadmin roles in a database, then as long as a shared hoster or some other entity creates the database for you ahead of time, you can log in to the database and successfully run any of the SQL installation scripts. You need to be in the db_ddladmin role to issue commands like CREATE TABLE or CREATE PROCEDURE. Other than db_ddladmin, only dbo has this right by default. As strange as it may seem, a db_ddladmin member can create database objects owned by other user accounts. However, just because a db_ddladmin can create such objects does not mean a member of that role can use those objects.

As a result, you also need to belong to db_securityadmin because at the end of the SQL installation scripts there are commands that create SQL Server roles and then grant execute rights and select rights on the stored procedures and views to the various roles. If you aren't a member of the db_securityadmin role, the scripts won't be able to setup the SQL Server roles and associated permissions properly. Although some hosters or companies might still be reticent to grant db_ddladmin and db_securityadmin rights, this set of rights is appropriate for most scenarios where all you want to do is prevent handing out dbo rights to everyone.

A very important point to keep in mind from this discussion is that although you need to run with some kind of elevated privileges to *install* the database scripts, you don't need these privileges to use the database objects. For any SQL-based provider to successfully call the stored procedures, you only need to add the appropriate security accounts to one or more of the predefined SQL Server roles. You don't have to grant the security accounts on your web servers dbo privileges or either of the two special security roles just discussed. In this way, at runtime you can still restrict the rights granted to the web server accounts and thus maintain the principle of least privilege when using any of the SQL-based providers.

For future Framework releases, the ASP.NET team is considering tweaking the SQL-based providers to allow for configurable owner names. Implementing the feature would allow you to install the application services schema using any arbitrary user account. The account would only need rights to create tables, views and stored procedures, which is an even lower set of privileges than those available from db_ddladmin and db_securityadmin. Then the providers would have an extra configuration attribute for you to specify the correct owner name to be prepended by the providers to all stored procedure calls.

Changing Password Formats

When you configure SqlMembershipProvider, you have the option of storing passwords in cleartext, as hashed values, or as encrypted values. By default, the provider will use SHA1 hashing with a random 16-byte salt value. As mentioned in the Membership chapter, you can change the hashing algorithm by defining a different algorithm in the hashAlgorithmType configuration attribute on the <membership /> element. If you choose encrypted passwords, the provider by default uses whatever is configured for encryption on the <machineKey /> element. The default algorithm for <machineKey /> is AES, although you can change this to 3DES instead with the "decryption" attribute.

If you choose to use encrypted passwords with `SqlMembershipProvider`, then you *must* explicitly provide a value for the `decryptionKey` attribute on `<machineKey />`, because if you were allowed to encrypt with the `<machineKey />` default of `AutoGenerate,IsolateApps` your passwords could become undecryptable. For example, there would be no way to decrypt passwords across a web farm. Also, whenever the Framework is upgraded or installed on a machine, the auto-generated machine keys are regenerated. Overall, the danger of leading developers into a dead end with encryption was so great that the provider now requires you to explicitly supply the decryption key for `<machineKey />`.

Normally, you set the `passwordFormat` configuration attribute on the provider just once. However, some confusion can arise if you change the password format after you create Membership user accounts, thus storing passwords (and potentially password answers) in the database. When a user account is first created, and the password is encoded, the format used to encode the password and the password answer is stored in the database in the `PasswordFormat` column. After this occurs, the format that was used at user creation time is used for the lifetime of the record in the database. Even if you switch the password format configured on the provider, existing user records will continue to use the old password format.

You can see this if you use a basic test site and start out with cleartext passwords:

```
<membership defaultProvider="formatTest">
    <providers>
        <add
            name="formatTest"
            ...
            passwordFormat="Clear"
            ...
    </providers>
</membership>
```

You can create a new user and look in the database to confirm that the password is stored in cleartext. If you then modify the provider definition to instead use `passwordFormat='Hashed'` and then create a second user, this user's password is stored as a base64-encoded hash value along with the random salt.

However, you can still log in with the first user account despite the fact that the password format used for the first user differs from the current setting on the provider. Additionally, you can use a control like the `ChangePassword` control to change the password of the first user. After you change the first user's password, the new password is still being stored using cleartext.

There really isn't a great way to work around this behavior, though it admittedly isn't likely that this would ever happen in a production environment. However, you may run into this problem in a development environment if you start with a set of test accounts using one password format and then later during the development a final decision is made to use a different password format. In this case, you may not want to migrate existing accounts into production using the old password format, especially if everything started out using cleartext.

If you just need to convert existing accounts with cleartext passwords to use a more secure format, you can query the database directly to extract the original passwords (and if necessary the original password answers as well). Then you can delete all the existing users using cleartext passwords and regenerate the accounts using the cleartext passwords that you stored off to the side. Of course, even this approach will lead to a problem if you depend on the user's primary keys for other data—perhaps you linked some of your own custom tables to the `aspnet_Users` table and, thus, you don't want the keys for each of the users to change. In this case, you can just use the old GUID `UserId` value as the `providerUserKey` parameter to `CreateUser` when you recreate the new user accounts.

However, what happens if you want to roll existing users over from encrypted or hashed passwords to a different format? For this scenario, you are stuck; there is no way to force existing user accounts to use a new password format. The problem is that to regenerate a password you need to call the `ChangePassword` method on the provider. As part of this method, you have to supply the old password, so it isn't likely that you can automate this process because you don't know the original password. You will probably need the users who know their passwords to log into a site and change their password.

But even this doesn't solve the problem because as part of the logic inside of `ChangePassword`, the provider first fetches the existing password information, including the password format from the database. The provider internally validates the `oldPassword` parameter of this method using the password data and format retrieved from the database. Assuming that this validation succeeds, the provider encodes the `newPassword` parameter using the password format that is stored in the database. As a result, there isn't a way to get in between the validation of the `oldPassword` and the encoding of `newPassword` parameter to tell the provider to use a new password format.

For this reason, you should avoid situations that require changing the password format for a production system. If you try to change a production system from using hashed passwords to using encrypted passwords, you really don't have any option other than recreating user accounts on the fly when users log in. With hashed passwords, you can't automate the change, because there is no way to get back to the cleartext versions of the passwords.

If you try to change a production system from using encrypted passwords to using hashed passwords, you can potentially automate this because you at least know the decryption key. However, you will need to write code that converts from the base64-encoded representations of the password and password answers into a `byte[]`, at which point you have to write your own code to decrypt the passwords using the correct algorithm. This method comes with a potential privacy issue because your website customers probably don't expect to have their passwords decrypted for any reason other than logging in.

As you can see, neither of these scenarios is optimal, so make sure that the password format you plan to use is determined well before your website goes into production. After you have live users on your site, changing your mind about the password format can require you to delete and then regenerate existing user accounts.

Custom Password Generation

If you use the password reset feature of `SqlMembershipProvider`, then you will be depending on the default behavior the provider supplies for automatically generating passwords. The default behavior uses the `Membership.GeneratePassword` method to create a password that conforms to the configured password strength requirements. These are defined by the provider's `minRequiredPassword Length` and `minRequiredNonAlphanumericCharacters` configuration attributes. Note that even if you set the `minRequiredNonAlphanumericCharacters` attribute to zero, it is likely that the auto-generated password will still contain nonalphanumeric characters.

The internal implementation of `Membership.GeneratePassword` randomly selects password characters from a predefined set of nonalphanumeric characters as well as the standard set of uppercase and lowercase alphanumeric characters and numbers. As a result the `GeneratePassword` method only guarantees that there are *at least* as many nonalphanumeric characters as required by the `minRequiredNonAlphanumericCharacters`. The method does not guarantee creating exactly as many nonalphanumeric characters as specified in the configuration attribute; instead, it is likely that GeneratePassword will generate a few more nonalphanumeric characters than specified by minRequiredNonAlphanumericCharacters.

If you don't want this behavior, or if you have your own requirements and algorithm for creating random passwords, you can choose to override the public virtual GeneratePassword method defined on SqlMembershipProvider.

```
public virtual string GeneratePassword();
```

An override of this virtual method does not take any parameters and is expected to return a string containing the randomly generated password. You have access to the provider's configured password strength requirements via MinRequiredPasswordLength and MinRequiredNonAlphanumeric Characters that are defined up on MembershipProvider.

As an example of this, you can write a provider that derives from SqlMembershipProvider and that overrides just the GeneratePassword method. For simplicity, you can implement the derived provider in the App_Code directory of your website; although if you needed this functionality available across all your websites you would instead create a derived provider using a standalone class library.

The following sample code shows a custom password generator that handles the case where *zero* nonalphanumeric characters are required:

C#

```
using System;
using System.Web.Security;
using System.Security.Cryptography;

public class CustomPasswordGeneration : SqlMembershipProvider
{
    private static char[] randChars =
    "a0bcde1fghij2klmno3pqrst4uvwxy5zABCD6EFGHI7JKLMN8OPQRS9TUVWXYZ".ToCharArray();

    public override string GeneratePassword()
    {
        if (MinRequiredNonAlphanumericCharacters == 0)
        {
            RNGCryptoServiceProvider rcsp = new RNGCryptoServiceProvider();
            //Always generate at least 14 characters in the random password
            int desiredLength =
                MinRequiredPasswordLength < 14 ? 14 : MinRequiredPasswordLength;

            byte[] randBytes = new byte[desiredLength];
            char[] convertedResult = new char[desiredLength];

            //First get some random values
            rcsp.GetBytes(randBytes);
            //Then convert these values into characters
            for (int i = 0; i < desiredLength; i++)
            {
                int indexOffset = ((int)randBytes[i]) % randChars.Length;
```

```
                    convertedResult[i] = randChars[indexOffset];
            }

            return new String(convertedResult);

        }
        else
        {
            return base.GeneratePassword();
        }
    }
}
```

VB.NET

```
Imports Microsoft.VisualBasic
Imports System
Imports System.Web.Security
Imports System.Security.Cryptography
Public Class CustomPasswordGeneration
    Inherits SqlMembershipProvider

    Private Shared randChars() As Char = _
"a0bcde1fghij2klmno3pqrst4uvwxy5zABCD6EFGHI7JKLMN8OPQRS9TUVWXYZ".ToCharArray()

    Public Overrides Function GeneratePassword() As String
        If MinRequiredNonAlphanumericCharacters = 0 Then
            Dim rcsp As New RNGCryptoServiceProvider()
            'Always generate at least 14 characters in the random password
            Dim desiredLength As Integer

            desiredLength = _
            If(MinRequiredPasswordLength < 14, 14, MinRequiredPasswordLength)

            Dim randBytes(desiredLength - 1) As Byte
            Dim convertedResult(desiredLength - 1) As Char
            'First get some random values
            rcsp.GetBytes(randBytes)

            'Then convert these values into characters
            For i As Integer = 0 To desiredLength - 1
                Dim indexOffset As Integer = _
                (CInt(Fix(randBytes(i)))) Mod randChars.Length()

                convertedResult(i) = randChars(indexOffset)
            Next i
            Return New String(convertedResult)
        Else
            Return MyBase.GeneratePassword()
        End If
    End Function
End Class
```

The sample code overrides just the `GeneratePassword` method of `SqlMembershipProvider`. In the event that the custom provider is configured to not require nonalphanumeric characters, then the custom password generation logic runs. Otherwise, the override just delegates to the base class. You can of course extend this to handle cases that require a nonzero number of nonalphanumeric characters, and you want to specify the exact number of nonalphanumeric characters allowed.

The custom password generator follows the same approach as the default Membership providers by always generating at least a 14-character-long random password. In the unlikely event that the provider is configured to require even more characters, it will honor the longer length instead. The custom provider first gets the appropriate number of random byte values using `RNGCryptoServiceProvider`. This ensures that the values are truly random as opposed to having some hidden dependency on a known seed.

The byte values are then converted into characters by treating each random byte value as an integer and then performing a modulus operation on the integer. The resulting value is used as an index into the fixed character array `randChars` defined at the start of the class. The custom provider implementation allows only uppercase and lowercase representations of a-z as well as the numbers 0-9 in a randomly generated password. Using this approach you can easily change the characters allowed in a random password by editing the characters in the `randChars` variable. Because the modulus operation always runs based on the length of `randChars`, you can change the length of the array without worrying about updating constants elsewhere in the code.

After each random byte has been converted into a character, the array of characters is returned as a string. You can try this code out with the sample configuration shown here:

```
<add name="customPasswordGeneration"
    type="CustomPasswordGeneration"
    connectionStringName="LocalSqlServer"
    minRequiredNonalphanumericCharacters="0"
/>
```

Notice that the type string for the provider contains only the name of the class. This works because the ASP.NET `ProvidersHelper` class that you saw earlier in Chapter 10 has extra logic that can resolve types from special ASP.NET directories, including the `App_Code` directory. As a result, the assembly name and optional string name information is not required for this case.

If you run a sample page with code like the following:

C#

```
CustomPasswordGeneration cgprovider =
        (CustomPasswordGeneration)Membership.Providers["customPasswordGeneration"];

Response.Write(cgprovider.GeneratePassword());
```

VB.NET

```
        Dim cgprovider As CustomPasswordGeneration = _
CType(Membership.Providers("customPasswordGeneration"), CustomPasswordGeneration)

    Response.Write(cgprovider.GeneratePassword())
```

you will get random passwords output like the following strings:

```
E73iDeRIs68USd
Ws25gpbZU6P2wo
U5EcY4WxissPfY
```

and so on.

If you change the configuration for the custom provider to require one or more nonalphanumeric characters, the random password generation reverts to the default behavior implemented by `SqlMembershipProvider`.

Implementing Custom Encryption

In the previous chapter, you saw how to implement custom hash algorithms that work with `SqlMembershipProvider`. Unlike hash operations, encryption is not something that can be declaratively customized using the `<membership />` element. While hash operations are pretty straightforward from an API standpoint (a `byte[]` goes in, and a different `byte[]` comes out the other side), encryption operations are not as simple to make universally configurable.

If you choose encrypted passwords with Membership, by default `SqlMembershipProvider` will use the encryption routines buried within the internals of the `<machineKey />` configuration section. There had been consideration at one point of making the encryption capabilities in this configuration section more generic and more customizable. However, that work was never done because configuring encryption algorithms can involve quite a number of initialization parameters (initialization vectors, padding modes, algorithm specific configuration properties, and so on).

Therefore, if you want to use a custom encryption algorithm in conjunction with `SqlMembership Provider`, you will need to write some code. The base class `MembershipProvider` exposes the `EncryptPassword` and `DecryptPassword` methods as `protected virtual`. You can derive from `SqlMembershipProvider` and override these two methods because internally the SQL provider encrypts and decrypts data by calling these base class methods. The method signatures for encryption and decryption are very basic:

C#

```
protected virtual byte[] DecryptPassword( byte[] encodedPassword )
protected virtual byte[] EncryptPassword( byte[] password )
```

VB.NET

```
Protected Overridable Function DecryptPassword(ByVal encodedPassword As Byte()) _
As Byte()
Protected Overridable Function EncryptPassword(ByVal password As Byte()) As Byte()
```

Your custom encryption implementation needs to take a `byte[]` in C# or `Byte()` in VB.NET, either encrypt or decrypt it, and then return the output as a different `byte[]`in C# or `Byte()` in VB.NET. By the time decryption override is called, `MembershipProvider` has already converted the base64-

encoded representation of the password in the database back into a `byte[]` in C# or `Byte()` in VB.NET. Similarly, after your custom encryption routine runs, the provider will convert the resulting `byte[]` in C# or `Byte()` in VB.NET back into a bas64-encoded string for storage in the database.

Remember that `SqlMembershipProvider` stores passwords and password answers as an `nvarchar(128)`. Custom encryption routines that cause excessive bloat need to keep this mind. If you suspect that a custom encryption algorithm may increase the size of the password and password answer (taking into account the subsequent base64 encoding as well), you should have extra maximum length rules to prevent this problem. For passwords, you could make sure to hook the `ValidatingPassword` event or override password-related methods on the provider to enforce a maximum password length. For password answer maximum length enforcement, you always need to derive from `SqlMembershipProvider` because this is the only way to validate password answer lengths prior to their encoding.

`SqlMembershipProvider` gives some protection against excessively long encoded values because it always validates that the encoded (that is, base64 encoded) representation of passwords and password answers are less than or equal to 128 characters. If an encoded representation exceeds this length, the provider throws an exception to that effect. However, proactively checking the maximum lengths of the cleartext password and password answer representations makes it easier to communicate to users to limit the size of these strings. Having some kind of a client-side validation check on the browser for such lengths means that users will not be scratching their heads wondering why a perfectly valid password or password answer keeps failing.

As a simple example for implementing custom encryption, the following code shows a custom provider that has overridden the encryption and decryption methods to instead preserve the cleartext representations of the passwords and password answers:

C#

```csharp
using System;
using System.Web.Security;

//Just replays the password/answer
public class CustomEncryption : SqlMembershipProvider
{
    protected override byte[] EncryptPassword(byte[] password)
    { return password; }

    protected override byte[] DecryptPassword(byte[] encodedPassword)
    { return encodedPassword; }
}
```

VB.NET

```vbnet
Imports Microsoft.VisualBasic
Imports System
Imports System.Web.Security

'Just replays the password/answer
Public Class CustomEncryption
  Inherits SqlMembershipProvider
```

```
    Protected Overrides Function EncryptPassword(ByVal password() As Byte) As Byte()
         Return password
    End Function

Protected Overrides Function DecryptPassword(ByVal encodedPassword() As Byte)_
         As Byte()
         Return encodedPassword
    End Function
End Class
```

Obviously, you would never use this kind of code in production—but the sample does make it clear how simple it is from an implementation perspective to clip in your own custom encryption and decryption logic. Assuming that you are using a commercial implementation of an encryption algorithm, the byte[] parameters to the two methods are what you would use with the System.Security.Cryptography .CryptoStream's Read and Write methods.

To use this custom provider, configure a sample application with a reference to the provider, making sure that you explicitly set the passwordFormat attribute for the provider.

```
<add name="customEncryptionProvider"
     type="CustomEncryption"
     passwordFormat="Encrypted"
     connectionStringName="LocalSqlServer" />
```

Now if you create a user with the following lines of code:

C#

```
CustomEncryption cencprovider =
             (CustomEncryption)Membership.Providers["customEncryptionProvider"];

MembershipCreateStatus status;
cencprovider.CreateUser("customEncryption22", "this is the cleartext password",
                    "foo@nowhere.org", "question",
                    "this is the cleartext answer", true, null, out status);
```

VB.NET

```
Dim cencprovider As CustomEncryption = _
    CType(Membership.Providers("customEncryptionProvider"), CustomEncryption)

    Dim status As MembershipCreateStatus

    cencprovider.CreateUser("customEncryption2", _
            "this is the cleartext password", _
            "foo1@nowhere.org", "question", _
            "this is the cleartext answer", _
            True, Nothing, status)
```

The database contains the base64-encoded representations stored for the password and the password answer, which are really just 16-byte salt values plus the cleartext strings preserved by the custom encryption routine. It turns out that when SqlMembershipProvider encrypts passwords and password answers, it still prepends a 16-byte random salt value to the byte representation of these strings (that is, password --> unicode byte[16 byte salt, then the byte representation of the password or answer]). However, I would not recommend taking advantage of this because the existence of the salt value, even in encrypted passwords and password answers, is an internal implementation detail. The existence of this value as well as its location could change unexpectedly in future releases. For example, the password is stored as:

```
we0UiiaUuwqIdS1dS0M5nQAaABpAHMAIABpAHMAIAB0AGgAZQAgAGMAbABlAGEAcgB0AGUAeAB0ACAAcABh
AHMAcwB3
AG8AcgBkAA==
```

If you convert this to a string with the following code:

C#

```
string result = " base 64 string here";
byte[] bResult = Convert.FromBase64String(result);
Response.Write(Encoding.Unicode.GetString((Convert.FromBase64String(result))));
```

VB.NET

```
Dim result As String = "base 64 string here"
Dim bResult() As Byte = Convert.FromBase64String(result)
Response.Write(Encoding.Unicode.GetString((Convert.FromBase64String(result))))
```

the result consists of eight nonsense characters (for the 16-byte random salt value) plus the original password string of "this is the cleartext password". The size of the base64-encoded password representation demonstrates the bloating effect the encoding has on the password. In this case, the original password contained 30 characters; adding the random salt value results in a 38-character password. Each character consumes 2 bytes when converted in a byte array, which results in a byte[76]. However, the base64-encoded representation contains 104 characters for these 76 byte values, which is around 1.37 encoded characters for each byte value and roughly 2.7 base64 characters for each original character in the password.

If you use the default of AES encryption with SqlMembershipProvider, the same password results in 108 encoded characters—roughly the same overhead. This tells you that most of the string bloat comes from the conversion of the Unicode password string into a byte array as well as the overhead from the base64 encoding; the actual encryption algorithm adds only a small amount to the overall size. As a general rule of thumb when using encryption with SqlMembershipProvider, you should plan on three encoded characters being stored in the database for each character in the original password and password answer strings.

This gives you a safe upper limit of around 42 characters for both of these values when using encryption. For passwords, this is actually enormous because most human beings (geniuses and savants excluded!) can't remember a 42-character long password. For password answers, 42 characters should be sufficient when using encryption as long as the password questions are such that they result in reasonable answers. Questions like what is your favorite car or color or mother's maiden name? probably don't result in 40+-character-long answers. However, if you allow freeform password questions where the user supplies the question, the resulting answer could be excessively long. Remember, though, that even with password answers, the user has to remember the exact password answer to retrieve or reset a password. As a result, it is unlikely that a website user will create an excessively long answer, because just as with passwords, folks will have trouble remembering excessively long answers.

Enforcing Custom Password Strength Rules

By default, `SqlMembershipProvider` enforces password strength using a combination of the `minRequiredPasswordLength`, `minRequiredNonalphanumericCharacters`, and `passwordStrength RegularExpression` provider configuration attributes. The default provider configuration in `machine .config` causes the provider to require at least seven characters in the password with at least one of these being a nonalphanumeric character. There is no default password strength regular expression defined in `machine.config`.

If you choose to define a regular expression, the provider enforces all three password constraints: minimum length, minimum number of nonalphanumeric characters, and matching the password against the configured regular expression. If you want the regular expression to be the exclusive determinant of password strength, you can set the `minRequiredPasswordLength` attribute to one and the `minRequiredNonalphanumericCharacters` to zero. Although the provider still enforces password strength with these requirements, your regular expression will expect that passwords have at least one character in them—so effectively only your regular expression will really be enforcing any kind of substantive rules.

You can see that just with the provider configuration attributes you can actually enforce a pretty robust password. However, for security-conscious organizations password strength alone isn't sufficient. The classic problem of course is with users and customers "changing" their passwords by simply using an old password, or by creating a new password that revs one digit or character from the old password. If you have more extensive password strength requirements, you can enforce them in one of two ways:

❑ **Hook the ValidatingPassword event on the provider:** This approach doesn't require you to derive from the SQL provider and as a result doesn't require deployment of a custom provider along with the related configuration changes in `web.config`. However, you do need some way to hook up your custom event handler to the provider in every web application that requires custom enforcement.

❑ **Derive from SqlMembershipProvider and override those methods that deal with creating or changing passwords (CreateUser, ChangePassword and ResetPassword):** You have to ensure that your custom provider is deployed in such a way that each website can access it, and you also need to configure websites to use the custom provider. Because you would be overriding methods anyway, this approach also has the minor advantage of having easy access to other parameters passed to the overridden methods. With this approach, you won't have to worry about hooking up the `ValidatingPassword` event.

Realistically, either approach is perfectly acceptable. The event handler was added in the first place because much of the extensibility model in ASP.NET supports event mechanisms and method overrides. For example, when you author a page, you are usually hooking events on the page and its contained controls as opposed to overriding methods like `OnClick` or `OnLoad`. For developers who have simple password strength requirements for one or a small number of sites, using the `Validating Password` event is the easier approach.

Using the `ValidatingPassword` event is as simple as hooking the event on an instance of `SqlMembership Provider`. To hook the event for the default provider, you can subscribe to `Membership.Validating Password`. To hook the event on one of the nondefault provider instances, you need to first get a reference on the provider instance and then subscribe to `MembershipProvider.ValidatingPassword`. When the event is fired, it passes some information to its subscribers with an instance of `ValidatingPassword EventArgs`.

C#

```csharp
public sealed class ValidatePasswordEventArgs : EventArgs
{
    public ValidatePasswordEventArgs(
            string userName,
            string password,
            bool   isNewUser )

public string UserName { get; }
public string Password { get; }
public bool IsNewUser { get; }
public bool Cancel {get; set; }
public Exception FailureInformation {get; set;}
}
```

VB.NET

```vbnet
Public NotInheritable Class ValidatePasswordEventArgs
    Inherits EventArgs

    Public Sub New(ByVal userName As String, _
                ByVal password As String, _
                ByVal ByVal isNewUser As Boolean)

    Public Property Cancel As Boolean
    Public Property FailureInformation As Exception
    Public ReadOnly Property IsNewUser As Boolean
    Public ReadOnly Property Password As String
    Public ReadOnly Property UserName As String

End Class
```

An event handler knows the user that the password creation or change applies to from the UserName property. You know whether the password in the Password parameter is for a new password (that is, CreateUser was called) or a changed password (that is, ResetPassword or ChangePassword was called) by looking at the IsNewUser property. If the property is true, then the UserName and Password are for a new user; otherwise, the event represents information for an existing user who is changing or resetting a password. The event handler doesn't know the difference between a password change and a password reset.

After an event handler has inspected the password using whatever logic it wants to apply, it can indicate the success or failure of the check via the Cancel property. If the custom password strength validation fails, then the event handler *must* set this property to true. If you also want to return some kind of custom exception information, you can optionally new() up a custom exception type and set it on the FailureInformation property. Remember that SqlMembershipProvider always returns a status code of MembershipCreateStatus.InvalidPassword from CreateUser. As a result of this method's signature, the provider doesn't throw an exception when password strength validation fails; instead, it just returns a failure status code.

SqlMembershipProvider will throw an exception if a failure occurs in either ChangePassword or ResetPassword. It will throw the custom exception from FailureInformation if it is available. If an event handler only sets Cancel to true, the provider throws ArgumentException from ChangePassword or ProviderException from ResetPassword. Remember that if you want to play well with the

Login controls, the exception type that you set on `FailureInformation` should derive from one of these two exception types.

The reason for the different exception types thrown by `SqlMembershipProvider` is that in `Change Password`, the new password being validated is something your user entered, and hence `Argument Exception` is appropriate. In the case of `ResetPassword`, though, the new password is automatically generated with a call to `GeneratePassword`. Because the new password is not something supplied by user input, throwing `ArgumentException` seemed a bit odd. So instead, `ProviderException` is thrown because the provider's password generation code failed. Unless you use password regular expressions, you probably won't run into `ProviderException` being thrown from `ResetPassword`. Because you can't determine if you are being called from `ChangePassword` or `ResetPassword` from inside of the `ValidatingPassword` event, it is reasonable to throw either exception type.

Hooking the ValidatePassword Event

When you hook the `ValidatingPassword` event, `SqlMembershipProvider` will raise it from inside of `CreateUser`, `ChangePassword`, and `ResetPassword`. The simplest way to perform the event hookup is from inside `global.asax`, with the actual event existing in a class file in the `App_Code` directory.

A custom event handler needs to have the same signature as the event definition:

C#

```
public delegate void MembershipValidatePasswordEventHandler(
                Object sender,  ValidatePasswordEventArgs e );
```

VB.NET

```
Public Delegate Sub MembershipValidatePasswordEventHandler( _
    ByVal sender As Object, _
    ByVal e As ValidatePasswordEventArgs)
```

The following sample code shows a password strength event handler that enforces a maximum length of 20 characters for a password. If the length is exceeded, it sets an `ArgumentException` on the event argument:

C#

```
public class ValidatingPasswordEventHook
{
  public static void LimitMaxLength(Object s, ValidatePasswordEventArgs e)
  {
    if (e.Password.Length > 20)
    {
      e.Cancel = true;
      ArgumentException ae =
        new ArgumentException("The password length cannot exceed 20 characters.");
      e.FailureInformation = ae;
    }
  }
}
```

VB.NET

```
Imports Microsoft.VisualBasic
Imports System
Imports System.Web.Security
Public Class ValidatingPasswordEventHook
    Public Shared Sub LimitMaxLength(ByVal s As Object, _
                                     ByVal e As ValidatePasswordEventArgs)
        If e.Password.Length > 20 Then
            e.Cancel = True
            Dim ae As _
            New ArgumentException("The password length cannot exceed20 characters.")
            e.FailureInformation = ae
        End If
    End Sub
End Class
```

The event handler is written as a static method on the `ValidatingPasswordEventHook` class. Because the event may be called at any time within the life of an application, it makes sense to define the event handler using a static method so that it is always available and doesn't rely on some other class instance that was previously instantiated.

The sample event handler is hooked up inside of `global.asax` using the `Application_Start` event:

C#

```
void Application_Start(object sender, EventArgs e)
{
  SqlMembershipProvider smp =
      (SqlMembershipProvider)Membership.Providers["sqlPasswordStrength"];

  smp.ValidatingPassword +=
      new MembershipValidatePasswordEventHandler(
          ValidatingPasswordEventHook.LimitMaxLength);
}
```

VB.NET

```
Sub Application_Start(ByVal sender As Object, ByVal e As EventArgs)
    Dim smp As SqlMembershipProvider = _
    CType(Membership.Providers("sqlPasswordStrength"), SqlMembershipProvider)

    AddHandler smp.ValidatingPassword, _
    AddressOf ValidatingPasswordEventHook.LimitMaxLength
End Sub
```

In this case, the event hookup is made using a provider reference directly as opposed to hooking up to the default provider via the `Membership.ValidatingPassword` event property. Now if you attempt to create a new user with an excessively long password, you receive `InvalidStatus` as the output parameter. For existing users, if you attempt to change the password with an excessively long password, `ArgumentException` set inside of the event handler is thrown instead.

Implementing Password History

A more advanced use of password strength validation is enforcing the rule that previously used passwords not be reused for new passwords. Although SqlMembershipProvider doesn't expose this kind of functionality, you can write a derived provider that keeps track of old passwords and ensures that new passwords are not duplicates. The sample provider detailed in this section keeps track of password history when hashed passwords are used. Hashed passwords are used for this sample because it is a somewhat more difficult scenario to handle.

Neither SqlMembershipProvider nor the base MembershipProvider class exposes the password salts for hashed passwords. Without this password salt, you need to do some extra work to keep track of password history in a way that doesn't rely on any hacks or undocumented provider behavior. The remainder of this section walks you through an example that extends SqlMembershipProvider by incorporating password history tracking. The sample provider checks new passwords against the history whenever ChangePassword is called. It adds items to the password history when a user is first created with CreateUser, and whenever the password subsequently changes with ChangePassword or ResetPassword.

As a first step, the custom provider needs a schema for storing the password history:

```
create table dbo.PasswordHistory (
  UserId          uniqueidentifier    NOT NULL,
  Password        nvarchar(128)       NOT NULL,
  PasswordSalt    nvarchar(128)       NOT NULL,
  CreateDate      datetime            NOT NULL
)

alter table dbo.PasswordHistory add constraint PKPasswordHistory
PRIMARY KEY (UserId, CreateDate)

alter table dbo.PasswordHistory add constraint FK1PasswordHistory
FOREIGN KEY (UserId) references dbo.aspnet_Users(UserId)
```

The provider stores one row for each password that has been associated with a user. It indexes the history on a combination of the UserId as well as the UTC date time that the password was submitted to the Membership system. This allows each user to have multiple passwords, and thus multiple entries in the history. The table also has a foreign key pointing to the aspnet_Users table just to ensure that the user really exists and that if the user is eventually deleted then the password history rows have to be cleaned up as well. As noted earlier in the chapter, this foreign key relationship is not officially supported because it is directly referencing the aspnet_Users table. However, this is the only part of the custom provider that uses any Membership feature that is considered undocumented.

As you can probably infer from the column names, the intent of the table is to store an encoded password representation and the password salt that was used to encode the password. Because the custom provider that uses this table supports hashing, each time a new password history record is generated the custom provider needs to store the password in a secure manner. It does this by hashing the password with the same algorithm used to hash the user's login password. Just like SqlMembershipProvider, the custom provider will actually hash a combination of the user's password and a random salt value to make it much more difficult for someone to reverse engineer the hash value stored in the Password column. Because of this, the table also has a column where the random salt value is stored, though this salt value is *not* the same salt the provider uses for hashing the user's login password.

Whenever a password history row has to be inserted, the following stored procedure will be used:

```
create procedure dbo.InsertPasswordHistoryRow
@pUserName              nvarchar(256),
@pApplicationName       nvarchar(256),
@pPassword              nvarchar(128),
@pPasswordSalt          nvarchar(128)
as

declare @UserId uniqueidentifier
select @UserId = UserId
from    dbo.vw_aspnet_Applications a,
        dbo.vw_aspnet_Users              u
where   a.LoweredApplicationName  = LOWER(@pApplicationName)
and     a.ApplicationId           = u.ApplicationId
and     u.LoweredUserName         = LOWER(@pUserName)

if not exists (select 1 from dbo.vw_aspnet_MembershipUsers
                            where UserId = @UserId)
     return -1

begin transaction

 select 1
 from   vw_aspnet_MembershipUsers WITH (UPDLOCK)
 where UserId = @UserId
 if (@@Error <> 0)
  goto AnErrorOccurred

 insert into dbo.PasswordHistory
 values (@UserId,@pPassword,@pPasswordSalt,getutcdate())
 if (@@Error <> 0)
  goto AnErrorOccurred

 --trim away old password records that are no longer needed
 delete
 from   dbo.PasswordHistory
 where  UserId  = @UserId
 and    CreateDate not in
 (
     select TOP 10 CreateDate   --only 10 passwords are ever maintained in history
     from   dbo.PasswordHistory
     where  UserId  = @UserId
     order by CreateDate DESC
 )
 if (@@Error <> 0)
  goto AnErrorOccurred

commit transaction

return 0

AnErrorOccurred:
  rollback transaction
  return -1
```

The parameter signature for the stored procedure expects a username and an application name: the object-level primary key of any user in Membership. The stored procedure converts these two parameters into the GUID UserId by querying the application and user table views as shown earlier in the chapter. The procedure also makes a sanity check to ensure that the UserId actually exists in the Membership table by querying its associated view. Technically, this should never occur because the custom provider only calls this stored procedure after the base SqlMembershipProvider has created a user row in the aspnet_Membership table.

After the procedure knows that the UserId is valid, it starts a transaction and places a lock on the user's Membership record. This ensures that, on the off chance that multiple calls are made to the database to insert a history record for a single user, each call completes its work before another call is allowed to manipulate the PasswordHistory table. This serialization is needed because after the data from the procedure's password and password salt parameter are inserted, the procedure removes old history records. The procedure needs to complete both steps successfully or roll the work back.

It is at this point in the procedure that you would put in any logic appropriate for determining "old" passwords for your application. In the case of the sample provider, only the last 10 passwords for a user are retained. Passwords are sorted according to when the records were created, with the oldest records being candidates for deletion. When you get to the eleventh and subsequent passwords, the stored procedure automatically purges the older records. If you don't have some type of logic like this, over time the password history tracking will get slower and slower. After the old password purge is completed the transaction is committed. For the sake of brevity, more extensive error handling is not included inside of the transaction. Theoretically, something could go wrong after the insert or delete statement, which would warrant more extensive error handling than that shown in the previous sample.

The companion to the insert stored procedure is a procedure to retrieve the current password history for a user:

```
create procedure dbo.GetPasswordHistory
@pUserName              nvarchar(256),
@pApplicationName       nvarchar(256)
as

select [Password], PasswordSalt, CreateDate
from    dbo.PasswordHistory ph,
        dbo.vw_aspnet_Applications a,
        dbo.vw_aspnet_Users         u
where   a.LoweredApplicationName  = LOWER(@pApplicationName)
and     a.ApplicationId           = u.ApplicationId
and     u.LoweredUserName         = LOWER(@pUserName)
and     ph.UserId                 = u.UserId
order by CreateDate DESC
```

This procedure is pretty basic. It accepts the username and application name and uses these two values to get to the UserId. At this point, the procedure returns all the rows from the PasswordHistory table with the most recent passwords being retrieved first.

The next step in developing the custom provider is to rough out its class signature:

C#

```csharp
using System;
using System.Configuration;
using System.Configuration.Provider;
using System.Data;
using System.Data.SqlClient;
using System.Security.Cryptography;
using System.Text;
using System.Web.Configuration;
using System.Web.Security;

public class ProviderWithPasswordHistory : SqlMembershipProvider
{
  private string connectionString;

  //Overrides of public functionality
  public override void Initialize(string name,
      System.Collections.Specialized.NameValueCollection config)

  public override string ResetPassword(string username, string passwordAnswer)

  public override MembershipUser CreateUser(…)

   public override bool ChangePassword(string username,
       string oldPassword, string newPassword)

  //Private methods that provide most of the functionality
  private byte[] GetRandomSaltValue()

  private void InsertHistoryRow(string username, string password)

  private bool PasswordUsedBefore(string username, string password)
}
```

VB.NET

```vbnet
Imports Microsoft.VisualBasic
Imports System
Imports System.Configuration
Imports System.Configuration.Provider
Imports System.Data
Imports System.Data.SqlClient
Imports System.Security.Cryptography
Imports System.Text
Imports System.Web.Configuration
Imports System.Web.Security

Public Class ProviderWithPasswordHistory
   Inherits SqlMembershipProvider

  Private connectionString As String

   'Overrides of public functionality
```

```
    Public Overrides Sub Initialize( _
        ByVal name As String, _
        ByVal config As System.Collections.Specialized.NameValueCollection)
    End Sub
    Public Overrides Function ResetPassword( _
            ByVal username As String, _
            ByVal passwordAnswer As String) As String
    End Function
    Public Overrides Function CreateUser( _
        ByVal username As String, _
        ByVal password As String, _
        ByVal email As String, _
        ByVal passwordQuestion As String, _
        ByVal passwordAnswer As String, _
        ByVal isApproved As Boolean, _
        ByVal providerUserKey As Object, _
        <System.Runtime.InteropServices.Out()> ByRef status As MembershipCreateStatus) _
        As MembershipUser
    End Function

    Public Overrides Function ChangePassword(ByVal username As String, _
                                    ByVal oldPassword As String, _
                                    ByVal newPassword As String) As Boolean

        End Function

    'Private methods that provide most of the functionality
    Private Function GetRandomSaltValue() As Byte()
    End Function

    Private Sub InsertHistoryRow(ByVal username As String, ByVal password As String)
    End Sub

    Private Function PasswordUsedBefore(ByVal username As String, _
                                    ByVal password As String) As Boolean
        End Function

End Class
```

The custom provider will perform some extra initialization logic in its Initialize method. Then the actual enforcement of password histories occurs within ChangePassword and ResetPassword. Create User is overridden because the very first password in the password history is the one used by the user when initially created. The private methods support functionality that uses the data layer logic you just saw: the ability to store password history as well as a way to determine whether a password has ever been used before. The GetRandomSaltValue method is used to generate random salt prior to storing password history records.

Start out looking at the Initialize method:

C#

```
public override void Initialize(string name,
        System.Collections.Specialized.NameValueCollection config)
{
    //We need the connection string later
    //So grab it before the SQL provider removes it from the
```

```
        //configuration collection.
        string connectionStringName = config["connectionStringName"];

        base.Initialize(name, config);
        if (PasswordFormat != MembershipPasswordFormat.Hashed)
            throw new NotSupportedException(
                "You can only use this provider with hashed passwords.");

        connectionString =
WebConfigurationManager.ConnectionStrings[connectionStringName].ConnectionString;
}
```

VB.NET

```
    Public Overrides Sub Initialize(ByVal name As String, _
                ByVal config As System.Collections.Specialized.NameValueCollection)
        'We need the connection string later
        'So grab it before the SQL provider removes it from the
        'configuration collection.
        Dim connectionStringName As String = config("connectionStringName")
        MyBase.Initialize(name, config)
        If PasswordFormat <> MembershipPasswordFormat.Hashed Then
            Throw New NotSupportedException("You can only use " & _
                                            "this provider with hashed passwords.")
        End If
        connectionString = _
        WebConfigurationManager.ConnectionStrings _
        (connectionStringName).ConnectionString
    End Sub
```

The override uses the connection string name that was configured on the provider (that is, the provider's connectionStringName attribute) to get the connection string from the <connectionStrings /> section. The provider also performs a basic sanity check to ensure that the password format has been set to use hashed passwords. If you want you can follow the same approach shown for this sample provider and extend it to support password histories for encrypted passwords.

The first step in the lifecycle of a user is the initial creation of that user's data in the Membership tables. Because the custom provider tracks a user's password history, it needs to store the very first password that is created. It does this with the private InsertHistoryRow method. The first part of this private method sets up the necessary ADO.NET command for calling the insert stored procedure shown earlier:

C#

```
    private void InsertHistoryRow(string username, string password)
    {
        using (SqlConnection conn = new SqlConnection(connectionString))
        {
            //Setup the command
            string command = "dbo.InsertPasswordHistoryRow";
            SqlCommand cmd = new SqlCommand(command, conn);
            cmd.CommandType = System.Data.CommandType.StoredProcedure;

            //Setup the parameters
            SqlParameter[] arrParams = new SqlParameter[5];
            arrParams[0] = new SqlParameter("pUserName", SqlDbType.NVarChar, 256);
```

```
            arrParams[1] = new SqlParameter("pApplicationName",
                                            SqlDbType.NVarChar, 256);
            arrParams[2] = new SqlParameter("pPassword", SqlDbType.NVarChar, 128);
            arrParams[3] = new SqlParameter("pPasswordSalt", SqlDbType.NVarChar, 128);
            arrParams[4] = new SqlParameter("returnValue", SqlDbType.Int);
```

VB.NET

```
Private Sub InsertHistoryRow(ByVal username As String, ByVal password As String)
    Using conn As New SqlConnection(connectionString)
            'Setup the command
            Dim command As String = "dbo.InsertPasswordHistoryRow"
            Dim cmd As New SqlCommand(command, conn)
            cmd.CommandType = System.Data.CommandType.StoredProcedure

            'Setup the parameters
            Dim arrParams(4) As SqlParameter
            arrParams(0) = New SqlParameter("pUserName", SqlDbType.NVarChar, 256)
            arrParams(1) = New SqlParameter("pApplicationName", _
SqlDbType.NVarChar,256)
            arrParams(2) = New SqlParameter("pPassword", SqlDbType.NVarChar, 128)
            arrParams(3) = New SqlParameter("pPasswordSalt", SqlDbType.NVarChar, 128)
            arrParams(4) = New SqlParameter("returnValue", SqlDbType.Int)
```

So far, this is all pretty standard ADO.NET coding practices. The next block of code gets interesting, though, because it is where a password is hashed with a random salt prior to storing it in the database:

C#

```
            //Hash the password again for storage in the history table
            byte[] passwordSalt = this.GetRandomSaltValue();
            byte[] bytePassword = Encoding.Unicode.GetBytes(password);
            byte[] inputBuffer = new byte[bytePassword.Length + 16];

            Buffer.BlockCopy(bytePassword, 0, inputBuffer, 0, bytePassword.Length);
            Buffer.BlockCopy(passwordSalt, 0, inputBuffer, bytePassword.Length, 16);

            HashAlgorithm ha = HashAlgorithm.Create(Membership.HashAlgorithmType);
            byte[] bhashedPassword = ha.ComputeHash(inputBuffer);
            string hashedPassword = Convert.ToBase64String(bhashedPassword);
            string stringizedPasswordSalt = Convert.ToBase64String(passwordSalt);
```

VB.NET

```
            'Hash the password again for storage in the history table
            Dim passwordSalt() As Byte = Me.GetRandomSaltValue()
            Dim bytePassword() As Byte = Encoding.Unicode.GetBytes(password)
            Dim inputBuffer(bytePassword.Length + 16 - 1) As Byte

            Buffer.BlockCopy(bytePassword, 0, inputBuffer, 0, bytePassword.Length)
            Buffer.BlockCopy(passwordSalt, 0, inputBuffer, bytePassword.Length, 16)

            Dim ha As HashAlgorithm = _
        HashAlgorithm.Create(Membership.HashAlgorithmType)
            Dim bhashedPassword() As Byte = ha.ComputeHash(inputBuffer)
```

```
Dim hashedPassword As String = Convert.ToBase64String(bhashedPassword)

Dim stringizedPasswordSalt As String = _
Convert.ToBase64String(passwordSalt)
```

As a first step, the provider gets a random 16-byte salt value as a `byte[]` in C# or `Byte()` in VB.NET. Because this salt value needs to be combined with the user's password, the password is also converted to a `byte[]` in C# or `Byte()` in VB.NET. Then the salt value and the byte representation of the password are combined using the `Buffer` object into a single array of bytes that looks like: `byte[password as bytes, 16 byte salt value]` in C# or `Byte(password as bytes, 16 byte salt value)` in VB.NET. This approach ensures that the hashed password will be next to impossible to reverse engineer, but it does so without relying on the internal byte array format used by `SqlMembershipProvider` when it hashes passwords. This means more code in the custom provider, but it also means the provider's approach to securely storing passwords won't break if the internal implementation of `SqlMembershipProvider` changes in a future release.

With the combined values in the byte array, the provider uses the hash algorithm configured for Membership to convert the array into a hashed value. At this point, both the resultant hash and the random salt that were used are converted in a base64-encoded string for storage back in the database.

C#

```csharp
//Put the results into the command object
arrParams[0].Value = username;
arrParams[1].Value = this.ApplicationName;
arrParams[2].Value = hashedPassword;
arrParams[3].Value = stringizedPasswordSalt;  //need to remember the salt
arrParams[4].Direction = ParameterDirection.ReturnValue;

cmd.Parameters.AddRange(arrParams);

//Insert the row into the password history table
conn.Open();
cmd.ExecuteNonQuery();

int procResult = (int)arrParams[4].Value;
conn.Close();
if (procResult != 0)
    throw new ProviderException(
        "An error occurred while inserting the password history row.");
    }
}
```

VB.NET

```vbnet
'Put the results into the command object
arrParams(0).Value = username
arrParams(1).Value = Me.ApplicationName
arrParams(2).Value = hashedPassword
arrParams(3).Value = stringizedPasswordSalt
arrParams(4).Direction = ParameterDirection.ReturnValue

cmd.Parameters.AddRange(arrParams)
```

```
                    'Insert the row into the password history table
                    conn.Open()
                    cmd.ExecuteNonQuery()

                    Dim procResult As Integer = CInt(Fix(arrParams(4).Value))
                    conn.Close()
                    If procResult <> 0 Then
                        Throw New ProviderException("An error occurred while " & _
                            "inserting the password history row.")
                    End If
```

The remainder of the InsertHistoryRow method packages up all the data into SqlCommand object's parameters and then inserts them using the InsertPasswordHistoryRow stored procedure. Because the stored procedure returns a -1 value if it could not find the user in the vw_aspnet_MembershipUsers view or if an error occurred during the insert, the provider checks for this error condition and throws an exception if this occurs.

Because this method relies on generating a random 16-byte salt, take a quick look at the private helper method that creates the salts:

C#

```csharp
private byte[] GetRandomSaltValue()
{
    RNGCryptoServiceProvider rcsp = new RNGCryptoServiceProvider();
    byte[] bSalt = new byte[16];
    rcsp.GetBytes(bSalt);
    return bSalt;
}
```

VB.NET

```vbnet
Private Function GetRandomSaltValue() As Byte()
    Dim rcsp As New RNGCryptoServiceProvider()
    Dim bSalt(15) As Byte
    rcsp.GetBytes(bSalt)

    Return bSalt
End Function
```

This code should look familiar from the earlier topic on custom password generation. In this case, the random number generator is used to create a fixed-length array of random bytes that will be used as a salt for the provider's hashing. The use of a salt value makes it substantially more difficult for anyone to guess a password stored in the password history table using a dictionary-based attack.

The create user method looks like this:

C#

```csharp
public override MembershipUser CreateUser(
    string username, string password, string email, string passwordQuestion,
    string passwordAnswer, bool isApproved, object providerUserKey,
    out MembershipCreateStatus status)
{
```

```
    MembershipUser mu;
    mu = base.CreateUser(username, password, email,
                                        passwordQuestion, passwordAnswer,
                                        isApproved, providerUserKey,
                                        out status);
    if (status != MembershipCreateStatus.Success)
        return mu;

    //Only insert the password row if the user was created
    try {
        InsertHistoryRow(username, password);
        return mu;
    }
    catch(Exception ex)
    {
        //Attempt to cleanup after a creation failure
        base.DeleteUser(username,true);
        status = MembershipCreateStatus.ProviderError;
        return null;
    }
}
```

VB.NET

```
PPublic Overrides Function CreateUser(ByVal username As String, _
                ByVal password As String, _
                ByVal email As String, _
                ByVal passwordQuestion As String, _
                ByVal passwordAnswer As String, _
                ByVal isApproved As Boolean, _
                ByVal providerUserKey As Object, _
                <System.Runtime.InteropServices.Out()> _
                ByRef status As MembershipCreateStatus) _
                As MembershipUser
        Dim mu As MembershipUser

        mu = MyBase.CreateUser(username, password, email, _
                        passwordQuestion, passwordAnswer, _
                        isApproved, providerUserKey, status)

        If status <> MembershipCreateStatus.Success Then
            Return mu
        End If
        'Only insert the password row if the user was created
        Try
            InsertHistoryRow(username, password)
            Return mu
        Catch ex As Exception
            'Attempt to cleanup after a creation failure
            MyBase.DeleteUser(username, True)
            status = MembershipCreateStatus.ProviderError
            Return Nothing
        End Try
    End Function
```

The custom provider doesn't attempt to save the password unless the user is successfully created by `SqlMembershipProvider`. If the base provider is successful, then the password history is inserted with a call to the custom provider's `InsertHistoryRow` method. If the call is successful (which should always be the case unless something goes wrong with the database), then the `MembershipUser` instance returned from the base provider is returned to the caller. If something does go wrong, the custom provider attempts to compensate by deleting the newly created user. This is intended to prevent the case where the user is created in the database, but the password is not properly logged to the password history. In the error case, the custom provider returns a `ProviderError` status code to indicate to the caller that the `CreateUser` method did not succeed.

At this point, you can test the custom provider with a page that uses the `CreateUserWizard` control. Configure the wizard control to use an instance of the custom provider:

In config:

```
<add name="passwordHistoryProvider"
    type="ProviderWithPasswordHistory"
    connectionStringName="LocalSqlServer"
    applicationName="passwordHistory"/>
```

On the page:

```
<asp:CreateUserWizard ID="CreateUserWizard1" runat="server" …other attributes…
                    MembershipProvider="passwordHistoryProvider" />
```

Now you can use `CreateUserWizard` to create new users. For each newly created user, the initial password is logged to the `PasswordHistory` table:

```
UserId        {A71E13F5-DB58-4E10-BEB4-9825E5A263F2}
Password      tJUZ5K1A5JuWcrZoJjF1OMXGM+8=
PasswordSalt  B8sbL04yOYwGyYZHT7AADA==
CreateDate    2005-07-27 21:04:10.257
```

So far so good. A user is registered in the Membership tables and the initial password is stored in the history. The next step is to get the custom provider working with the `ChangePassword` method. Changing a password requires the provider to retrieve the history of all the user's passwords and then search through the history to see if any of the old passwords match the value of the new password passed to `ChangePassword`.

The private method `PasswordUsedBefore` returns a `bool` value indicating whether or not a given password has ever been used before by a user. The first part of the method just uses standard ADO.NET calls to retrieve the password history using the `GetPasswordHistory` stored procedure:

C#

```
private bool PasswordUsedBefore(string username, string password)
{
    using (SqlConnection conn = new SqlConnection(connectionString))
    {
        //Setup the command
        string command = "dbo.GetPasswordHistory";
        SqlCommand cmd = new SqlCommand(command, conn);
        cmd.CommandType = System.Data.CommandType.StoredProcedure;
```

```
//Setup the parameters
SqlParameter[] arrParams = new SqlParameter[2];
arrParams[0] = new SqlParameter("pUserName", SqlDbType.NVarChar, 256);
arrParams[1] = new SqlParameter("pApplicationName",
                                    SqlDbType.NVarChar, 256);
arrParams[0].Value = username;
arrParams[1].Value = this.ApplicationName;

cmd.Parameters.AddRange(arrParams);

//Fetch the password history from the database
DataSet dsOldPasswords = new DataSet();
SqlDataAdapter da = new SqlDataAdapter(cmd);
da.Fill(dsOldPasswords);
```

VB.NET

```
Private Function PasswordUsedBefore(ByVal username As String, _
                                    ByVal password As String) As Boolean

    Using conn As New SqlConnection(connectionString)
        'Setup the command
        Dim command As String = "dbo.GetPasswordHistory"
        Dim cmd As New SqlCommand(command, conn)
        cmd.CommandType = System.Data.CommandType.StoredProcedure

        'Setup the parameters
        Dim arrParams(1) As SqlParameter
        arrParams(0) = New SqlParameter("pUserName", SqlDbType.NVarChar, 256)
        arrParams(1) = New SqlParameter("pApplicationName", _
                                        SqlDbType.NVarChar, 256)
        arrParams(0).Value = username
        arrParams(1).Value = Me.ApplicationName

        cmd.Parameters.AddRange(arrParams)

        'Fetch the password history from the database
        Dim dsOldPasswords As New DataSet()
        Dim da As New SqlDataAdapter(cmd)
        da.Fill(dsOldPasswords)
```

The end result of this code is a DataSet and a DataTable containing one or more rows of old passwords for the user from the PasswordHistory table. The interesting part of the method involves comparing each row of old password data in the returned DataSet to the password parameter that was passed to the method.

C#

```
HashAlgorithm ha = HashAlgorithm.Create(Membership.HashAlgorithmType);
foreach (DataRow dr in dsOldPasswords.Tables[0].Rows)
{
    string oldEncodedPassword = (string)dr[0];
    string oldEncodedSalt = (string)dr[1];
    byte[] oldSalt = Convert.FromBase64String(oldEncodedSalt);
```

```
            byte[] bytePassword = Encoding.Unicode.GetBytes(password);
            byte[] inputBuffer = new byte[bytePassword.Length + 16];

            Buffer.BlockCopy(bytePassword, 0, inputBuffer, 0, bytePassword.Length);
            Buffer.BlockCopy(oldSalt, 0, inputBuffer, bytePassword.Length, 16);

            byte[] bhashedPassword = ha.ComputeHash(inputBuffer);
            string hashedPassword = Convert.ToBase64String(bhashedPassword);

            if (hashedPassword == oldEncodedPassword)
                return true;
        }
    }
    //No matching passwords were found if you make it this far
    return false;
}
```

VB.NET

```
        Dim ha As HashAlgorithm = _
        HashAlgorithm.Create(Membership.HashAlgorithmType)
        For Each dr As DataRow In dsOldPasswords.Tables(0).Rows
                Dim oldEncodedPassword As String = CStr(dr(0))
                Dim oldEncodedSalt As String = CStr(dr(1))
                Dim oldSalt() As Byte = Convert.FromBase64String(oldEncodedSalt)

                Dim bytePassword() As Byte = Encoding.Unicode.GetBytes(password)
                Dim inputBuffer(bytePassword.Length + 16 - 1) As Byte

                Buffer.BlockCopy(bytePassword, 0, _
                        inputBuffer, 0, _
                        bytePassword.Length)
                Buffer.BlockCopy(oldSalt, 0, inputBuffer, bytePassword.Length, 16)

                Buffer.BlockCopy(bytePassword, 0, _
                        inputBuffer, 0, _
                        bytePassword.Length)

                If hashedPassword = oldEncodedPassword Then
                        Return True
                End If
        Next dr
    End Using

    'No matching passwords were found if you make it this far
    Return False
End Function
```

Once again, an instance of `HashAlgorithm` matching `hashAlgorithmType` for the Membership feature is used. Each row of password data from the database has the password salt that was used to hash and encode the result that is stored in the corresponding `Password` column. Much like the original hashing done inside of `InsertHistoryRow`, the `PasswordUsedBefore` method converts the password parameter into a byte array and combines it with the byte array representation of the password salt retrieved from the database. This combination is then hashed using the hashing algorithm created a few lines earlier in the code.

To make it easier to compare the hashed value of the password parameter to the old password from the database, the result of hashing the password parameter with the old salt value is converted to a base64-encoded string. As a result, the comparison is as simple as comparing the string from the database (that is, the Password column) to the base64-encoded representation of the encoded password parameter. If the two strings match, the method knows that the password parameter has been used before for that user, and the method returns true. If the method loops through all the password history records in the database and never finds a match, the method returns false, indicating that the password parameter has never been used before.

One thing to note about the password history implementation is that each old password is encoded using a different random salt value. That is why, for each row of password history data retrieved from the database, the custom provider must rehash the password parameter for comparison. A second thing to note about the implementation of the PasswordUsedBefore method is that it does not include any protections against two different threads of execution both attempting to change the password for the same user. It is theoretically possible that on two different web servers (or two different threads on the same server) a change password operation could be occurring at the same time.

However, if this occurs one of two things happens. Both operations could be attempting to change the user's password to the same value, in which case one of the two password change operations would effectively end up as a no-op, but the same password would show up twice in the password history table. In the alternative outcome, one change password successfully completes before the other change password attempt, in which case the second password change attempt would fail because it would be using the wrong value for the oldPassword parameter. The net outcome, though, is that this scenario has a low likelihood of occurring, and even if it does occur it has little effect on the overall security and accuracy of the password history feature.

Now that you have seen how the custom provider can compare a new password against all the old passwords in the database, look at how it is used from the ChangePassword method:

C#

```
public override bool ChangePassword(string username, string oldPassword,
                                    string newPassword)
{
    if (PasswordUsedBefore(username, newPassword))
        return false;

    bool result = base.ChangePassword(username, oldPassword, newPassword);

    if (result == false)
        return result;

    //Only insert the password row if the password was changed
    try
    {
        InsertHistoryRow(username, newPassword);
        return true;
    }
    catch (Exception ex)
    {
```

```
            //Attempt to cleanup after a failure to log the new password
            base.ChangePassword(username, newPassword, oldPassword);
            return false;
        }
    }
}
```

VB.NET

```
Public Overrides Function ChangePassword(ByVal username As String, _
                                    ByVal oldPassword As String, _
                                    ByVal newPassword As String) As Boolean
    If PasswordUsedBefore(username, newPassword) Then
        Return False
    End If

    Dim result As Boolean = MyBase.ChangePassword(username, oldPassword, newPassword)

    If result = False Then
        Return result
    End If

    'Only insert the password row if the password was changed
    Try
        InsertHistoryRow(username, newPassword)
        Return True
    Catch ex As Exception
        'Attempt to cleanup after a failure to log the new password
        MyBase.ChangePassword(username, newPassword, oldPassword)
        Return False
    End Try
End Function
```

First, the ChangePassword override validates the newPassword parameter against the password history. If the newPassword parameter matches any of the old passwords, then the method immediately returns false. Remember that because ChangePassword returns a bool, the convention used by the Membership feature is to return a false value as opposed to throwing an exception.

If no old matching passwords were found, the provider calls into the base provider to perform the password change operation. If for some reason the base provider fails, a false is also returned. If the base provider succeeds, though, the custom provider needs to store the new password in the password history table with a call to InsertHistoryRow. Normally, this operation succeeds, and the caller receives a true return value indicating that the password was successfully changed.

If the password history was not successfully updated, the custom provider compensates for the failure by resetting the user's password to the original value. If you look at the call to the base provider in the catch block you can see that the two password parameters from the original method call are simply reversed to cause the user to revert to the original password. And, of course, in the failure case a false value is again returned to the caller.

You can try the password change functionality with a simple page using the ChangePassword Login control configured to use the custom provider.

```
<asp:ChangePassword ID="ChangePassword1" runat="server"
                MembershipProvider="passwordHistoryProvider" />
```

After logging in with an account created using the custom provider, you can navigate to the change password page and try different variations of new passwords. For each new unique password another new row shows up in the `PasswordHistory` table. However, for each new non-unique password the `ChangePassword` control displays an error message saying the new password is invalid. Although I will not show it here, you can easily write some code that integrates between the custom provider's behavior and the `ChangePassword` control that would allow error messages to be more precise whenever duplicate passwords are used.

The last piece of functionality that the custom provider implements is the `ResetPassword` method:

C#

```csharp
public override string ResetPassword(string username, string passwordAnswer)
{
    string newPassword = base.ResetPassword(username, passwordAnswer);

    //No recovery logic at this point
    InsertHistoryRow(username, newPassword);

    return newPassword;
}
```

VB.NET

```vbnet
Public Overrides Function ResetPassword(ByVal username As String, _
                        ByVal passwordAnswer As String) As String
    Dim newPassword As String = MyBase.ResetPassword(username, passwordAnswer)

    'No recovery logic at this point since once the reset has occurred
    'there is not a way to "undo" a call to ResetPassword
    InsertHistoryRow(username, newPassword)

    Return newPassword
End Function
```

The custom provider delegates to the base provider to reset the password. There's no need to compare the reset password against the password history because the default reset password logic generates a completely random new password. Unless you are worried about the one in a billion chance (or so) of repeating a random password, you can save yourself the performance hit of checking against the password history for this case. If the password reset succeeds, the override calls `InsertHistoryRow` to store the auto-generated password in the `PasswordHistory` table.

Unlike `CreateUser` and `ChangePassword`, the sample code does not attempt to recover from a problem at this point. A simple `try-catch` block can't compensate for errors in the case of resetting passwords. You could use the new ADO.NET 2.0 `TransactionScope` class, though, to wrap both the base provider SQL calls and the password history SQL code in a single transaction. This approach would also be a more elegant solution to the compensation logic shown earlier for the `CreateUser` and `ChangePassword` overloads.

Account Lockouts

Membership providers can choose to implement account lockouts as a protection against brute force guessing attacks against a user's password and password answer. `SqlMembershipProvider` implements protections against both attacks and will lock out accounts for both cases. Deciphering the provider configuration attributes for account lockouts and trying to understand exactly when accounts are locked in SQL can be a bit confusing when using the SQL provider.

`SqlMembershipProvider` keeps track of failed attempts at using a password by storing tracking information in the `FailedPasswordAttemptCount` and `FailedPasswordAttemptWindowStart` columns of the `aspnet_Memership` table. The provider tracks failed attempts at using a password answer separately in a different set of columns: `FailedPasswordAnswerAttemptCount` and `FailedPassword AnswerAttemptWindowStart`. When a user is first created, the counter columns are set to a default value of zero while the date-time columns are set to default values of `01/01/1754`.

Each time a provider method is called that accepts a password parameter, the provider internally validates that the password is correct. `ValidateUser` is the most common method where this occurs, but password validation also occurs for `ChangePassword` (validating the old password) as well as `Change PasswordQuestionAndAnswer`. The first time an incorrect password is supplied, two things occur:

❏   The `FailedPasswordAttemptCount` in the database is incremented by one.

❏   The `FailedPasswordAttemptWindowStart` column is set to the current UTC date time.

The next time a method that accepts a password parameter is called, the provider realizes that a bad password was supplied sometime in the past. Therefore, the provider configuration attributes `password AttemptWindow` and `maxInvalidPasswordAttempts` are used.

Assume that a method call is made that requires a password, and that on the second attempt a bad password again is used. The provider needs to determine whether or not this second bad attempt is a discrete event, or if it should be considered part of a continuing chain of correlated password attempts. To make this determination, the provider compares the value of [(current UTC date-time) − "password AttemptWindow"] against the `FailedPasswordAttemptWindowStart` value in the database. If the current bad password attempt has occurred within `passwordAttemptWindow` minutes from `Failed PasswordAttemptWindowStart`, then the provider considers the current bad attempt to be related to previous bad password attempts, and the provider increments `FailedPasswordAttemptCount`. The provider also updates `FailedPasswordAttemptWindowStart` to the current UTC date time.

For example, if the data indicates a bad password was supplied at 10:00 AM UTC, and the `password AttemptWindow` is set to 10 (that is, 10 minutes), a subsequent bad password attempt that occurs anywhere from 10:00AM UTC through 10:10 AM UTC is considered related to the original bad password attempt. As a result, the bad password attempt counter will be incremented by one, and the window start will be updated to the current date-time. This last operation is very important to note. You might think that a `passwordAttemptWindow` setting of 10 minutes means that all bad passwords within a fixed 10 minute period are counted. However, this is not how the SQL provider works.

Instead, the tracking window is always rolled forward whenever a bad password attempt occurs within `passwordAttemptWindow` minutes from the last bad password attempt. The reason for this behavior is that if the provider only tracked bad password attempts in a fixed window you could end up with the following sequence of events (assume a lockout on the fifth bad attempt and a 10-minute tracking window):

```
Bad password attempt #1 at 10:00 AM UTC
Bad password attempt #2 at 10:08 AM UTC
Bad password attempt #3 at 10:09 AM UTC
Bad password attempt #4 at 10:10 AM UTC
Bad password attempt #1 at 10:11 AM UTC   <-- what happens here?
Bad password attempt #2 at 10:12 AM UTC
Bad password attempt #3 at 10:13 AM UTC
Bad password attempt #4 at 10:14 AM UTC
```

If the provider started a fixed tracking window at 10:00 AM UTC in this example and started counting, it would eventually count four bad attempts by 10:10 AM UTC. But when the next bad password attempt occurs at 10:11 AM UTC, the provider would throw away all the old attempts because the first 10-minute tracking window had expired. You could now continue to rack up more bad password attempts starting at 10:11 AM UTC. In the example, you could have four more bad password attempts starting at 10:11 AM UTC with no ill effect. The problem with this behavior is that if you look backward in time, you see that from 10:08 AM UTC through 10:14 AM UTC there have been seven bad password attempts in a 10-minute period, and yet the provider did not trigger an account lockout.

Of course, this is only a theoretical example because SqlMembershipProvider instead rolls the start of the tracking time window forward with each bad attempt. If you step through the same sequence of events with the SQL provider, you instead have the following behavior:

```
                                                    FailedPasswordAttemptWindowStart
Bad password attempt #1 at 10:00 AM UTC                 10:00 AM UTC
Bad password attempt #2 at 10:08 AM UTC                 10:08 AM UTC
Bad password attempt #3 at 10:09 AM UTC                 10:09 AM UTC
Bad password attempt #4 at 10:10 AM UTC                 10:10 AM UTC
Bad password attempt #5 at 10:11 AM UTC   lockout!   10:11 AM UTC
Cannot login due to lockout at 10:11 AM UTC
Cannot login due to lockout at 10:11 AM UTC
Cannot login due to lockout at 10:11 AM UTC
etc…
```

In this case, with each bad password attempt the provider looks back in time to determine whether or not the current attempt is correlated to the last bad attempt as stored in the FailedPasswordAttempt WindowStart column. Because the first five attempts all occur less than 10 minutes apart, each attempt causes the bad password attempt counter to increment and the start of the tracking window is updated as well. As a result, when the fifth attempt occurs at 10:11 AM UTC, the provider increments the counter and realizes that the maxInvalidPasswordAttempts threshold has been hit. As a result the provider locks the account out at this point. Any subsequent password attempts never make it far enough to attempt validating the password because the provider sees that the account has already been locked out.

Note that SqlMembershipProvider interprets the maxInvalidPasswordAttempts configuration attribute as a trip wire. If the number of bad password attempts exactly matches the value of this configuration setting, the account is immediately locked out. So, technically, a setting of 5 really means a user is allowed only four bad passwords; the fifth incorrect password results in a lockout. If you happen to write a custom provider, you can certainly choose to interpret this configuration attribute differently (for example, a custom provider could choose to lock out the user only on the sixth attempt, in which case the attribute would be considered a threshold rather than a limit that triggers a lockout).

The previous discussion focused on bad password attempts; the exact same logic applies, though, to bad password answer attempts. Any methods that accept a password answer (ResetPassword and

GetPassword) cause the provider to keep track of bad answer attempts using the exact same logic and the exact same provider configuration attributes. The only difference is that the counter and window start information is stored in a separate set of columns than the tracking information for bad passwords.

This raises an interesting question: What happens if a user enters bad passwords and bad password answers for an account? Until the limit specified by maxInvalidPasswordAttempts is reached, the provider increments counters and updates the start windows using different columns in the database. For a time, this means that bad password attempts and bad password answer attempts are considered separate occurrences that have no effect on each other. Assume that the bad password and bad password answer counters both reach 4 (the default for maxInvalidPasswordAttempts in machine.config is 5).

The next bad attempt that occurs (either password or password answer) within the tracking time window will trigger an account lockout. So even though bad attempts for passwords and answers have been tracked independently up to this point, after one of the counters hits the tripwire defined by maxInvalidPasswordAttempts, the user is locked out. A locked-out user account is no longer allowed to validate passwords with the provider *and* a locked-out user account can no longer use the password-answer-related methods. An account lockout triggered by one type of bad information locks everything out. The provider doesn't lock out only password-related functionality, only answer-related functionality.

Of course, after a user account is locked out, you need some way to unlock the account. The SQL provider does not incorporate the concept of automatic account lockouts (more on this in the next section). However, the AD-based provider does support automatic unlocking because the Active Directory engine natively has this functionality. For the SQL provider, you need to explicitly call the UnlockUser method to unlock user accounts. When UnlockUser is called the following occurs:

1. The user account is unlocked: IsLockedOut is reset to false.

2. The password counter in the database is reset to zero, and the password window start column is reset to 01/01/1754.

3. The password answer counter in the database is reset to zero, and the password answer window start column is reset to 01/01/1754.

This behavior means that when you inspect a MembershipUser object, the LastLockoutDate property contains a useful value only when IsLockedOut is set to true. When a user account is not locked out, the LastLockoutDate property contains a bogus default value. Furthermore, the MembershipUser object does not indicate what caused the lockout (was it bad passwords or bad password answers?). It only indicates that a lockout has occurred. If you need to determine the specific reason for the lockout, you can query the vw_aspnet_MembershipUsers view because the view exposes the four columns that store the password- and password-answer-tracking information.

The tracking information is also reset during the normal course of calling provider methods with valid passwords and valid password answers. The automatic reset of the tracking information occurs in the following ways:

❑ When a valid password is used for ValidateUser, ChangePassword or ChangePassword QuestionAndAnswer both the password- and password-answer-tracking columns are reset to their defaults (that is, zero and 01/01/1754).

❑ When a valid password answer is used for ResetPassword or GetPassword *only*, the password answer tracking columns are reset to their defaults.

All tracking information is reset when a good password is supplied because the password is considered the main source of security for a user account. If a user supplies a correct password, that is considered proof that at a specific point in time the user knows the "master" credential for the account. As a result, the password answer counters are also reset because the password answer is considered a "secondary" credential for the account. However, if a correct password answer is supplied to a method, that is only considered good enough to reset the answer-related-tracking counters. Knowing the password answer is not considered sufficient proof that a user also knows the "master" credential for the account.

Implementing Automatic Unlocking

One potential issue that folks raise about `SqlMembershipProvider` is that the current lockout behavior can lead to a denial of service (DoS) attack. Theoretically, a malicious user could spam a login page with likely user accounts to force account lockouts for a large number of website users. After the user accounts are locked out, the users have no way to get back onto the website until an administrator intervenes and unlocks the accounts.

Although an auto-unlock feature for accounts is a partial deterrent to this type of DoS attack, you should be aware that after you have automatic unlocking, the DoS attack can now be turned into a long-running brute force password attack. Instead of cutting the attack off after a few attempts per user account, an auto-unlock feature allows an attacker to iterate through a few passwords, back off for the duration of the account lockout, and then iterate through some more passwords for each user account. If you don't monitor web logs (and potentially add custom auditing on top of the SQL provider) for this type of activity, you can literally end up with a brute force password attack running for weeks on end.

For example, if you have a 30-minute auto-unlock period after five bad passwords, and an attacker tries guessing passwords for 4 weeks, the attacker can run 240 bad passwords per account per day for a rough total of 6720 bad passwords per user account per month on a site. I would highly recommend that if you add automatic unlock behavior as shown in this section, you also implement additional security measures to mitigate a long-running password-guessing attack. Even if an attacker never successfully guesses a password because of password strength rules, a long-running password-guessing attack can also look like a denial of service attack because each user account that is being attacked ends up in a locked-out state for the vast majority of the time. Other than for a few seconds at the expiration of the auto-unlock period, accounts end up locked out again when the password-guessing attack sweeps through the same set of accounts on its next iteration. And, of course, a really savvy attacker will probably only guess (lockout limit –1) passwords at a time for a user, thus keeping a long-running password guessing attack below the radar if you are only looking at rates of account lockouts.

As a result, the best argument for implementing auto-unlocking is as a convenience for sites that are already partially protected against brute force attacks by other security measures. For example, if you run your site under SSL, then a brute force attack is less likely due to the increased likelihood that the spike in SSL processing overhead from an attack would be detected by the site's administrators. If your website is only accessible over VPNs or private frame relay networks, the likelihood of a random attacker getting in and wreaking havoc is lower. In these cases, automatic unlock behavior provides a better user experience and cuts down on password-related support calls.

A custom provider that implements auto-unlock behavior needs a place for users to configure the timeout beyond which the provider should automatically unlock the user account. For this example, you want the provider configuration to look like the following:

```
<add name="autounlocksample"
     type="AutoUnlockProvider"
     connectionStringName="LocalSqlServer"
     autoUnlockTimeout="30"
     applicationName="passwordHistory"/>
```

The custom attribute `autoUnlockTimeout` tells the provider how many minutes after a lockout a user account should be automatically unlocked. The provider stores this attribute inside of an override of the `Initialize` method:

C#

```csharp
using System;
using System.Configuration.Provider;
using System.Web.Security;

public class AutoUnlockProvider : SqlMembershipProvider
{
    private int autoUnlockTimeout = 60;  //Default to 60 minutes

    public override void Initialize(string name,
                   System.Collections.Specialized.NameValueCollection config)
    {
        string sunlockTimeOut = config["autoUnlockTimeout"];
        if (!String.IsNullOrEmpty(sunlockTimeOut))
            autoUnlockTimeout = Int32.Parse(sunlockTimeOut);
        config.Remove("autoUnlockTimeout");

        base.Initialize(name, config);
    }

    //other overrides
}
```

VB.NET

```vbnet
Imports Microsoft.VisualBasic
Imports System
Imports System.Configuration.Provider
Imports System.Web.Security

Public Class AutoUnlockProvider
  Inherits SqlMembershipProvider

  Private autoUnlockTimeout As Integer = 60 'Default to 60 minutes

  PPublic Overrides Sub Initialize(ByVal name As String, _
          ByVal config As System.Collections.Specialized.NameValueCollection)

      Dim sunlockTimeOut As String = config("autoUnlockTimeout")
      If (Not String.IsNullOrEmpty(sunlockTimeOut)) Then
          autoUnlockTimeout = Int32.Parse(sunlockTimeOut)
      End If
      config.Remove("autoUnlockTimeout")
      MyBase.Initialize(name, config)
```

```
        End Sub

        'other overrides

    End Class
```

Before calling the base class `Initialize` method, the custom provider looks for the `autoUnlockTimeout` attribute in configuration. If it finds the attribute, it stores its value and removes it from the configuration collection. If the attribute is not supplied in the provider's configuration, it defaults to a 60-minute-long timeout after which locked accounts can be automatically unlocked.

Because there are a number of different provider methods that should automatically unlock the user, the core functionality is implemented in a single private method:

C#

```csharp
private bool AutoUnlockUser(string username)
{
    MembershipUser mu = this.GetUser(username,false);
    if ((mu != null) &&
        (mu.IsLockedOut) &&
        (mu.LastLockoutDate.ToUniversalTime().AddMinutes(autoUnlockTimeout)
            < DateTime.UtcNow)
        )
    {
        bool retval = mu.UnlockUser();
        if (retval)
            return true;
        else
            return false; //something went wrong with the unlock
    }
    else
        return false; //not locked out in the first place
                      //or still in lockout period
}
```

VB.NET

```vbnet
Private Function AutoUnlockUser(ByVal username As String) As Boolean
    Dim mu As MembershipUser = Me.GetUser(username,False)
    If (mu IsNot Nothing) _
        AndAlso (mu.IsLockedOut) _
        AndAlso (mu.LastLockoutDate. _
            ToUniversalTime(). _
            AddMinutes(autoUnlockTimeout) < DateTime.UtcNow) Then
            Dim retval As Boolean = mu.UnlockUser()
            If retval Then
                Return True
            Else
                Return False 'something went wrong with the unlock
            End If
        Else
            Return False 'not locked out in the first place
```

```
                End If
                                        'or still locked out
    End Function
```

For any given username, this method loads the `MembershipUser` instance for that user. If the `MembershipUser` instance indicates that the user is locked out, the provider checks to see how much time has elapsed since that last lockout. If more than `autoUnlockTimeout` minutes have elapsed, the method calls `UnlockUser` to automatically unlock the account. The return value from the method indicates whether the user account was unlocked. Normally, calling this method for users still within the `autoUnlockTimeout` period returns `false`, whereas calling the method for users who are past the timeout period results in a `true` return value.

To demonstrate how this method works with methods that deal with passwords, the following code shows `ValidateUser` automatically unlocking users as necessary:

C#

```csharp
public override bool ValidateUser(string username, string password)
{
    bool retval = base.ValidateUser(username, password);

    //The account may be locked out at this point
    if (retval == false)
    {
        bool successfulUnlock = AutoUnlockUser(username);
        if (successfulUnlock)
            //re-attempt the login
            return base.ValidateUser(username, password);
        else
            return false;
    }
    else
        return retval;  //first login was successful
}
```

VB.NET

```vbnet
Public Overrides Function ValidateUser(ByVal username As String, _
                    ByVal password As String) As Boolean
    Dim retval As Boolean = MyBase.ValidateUser(username, password)

    'The account may be locked out at this point
    If retval = False Then
        Dim successfulUnlock As Boolean = AutoUnlockUser(username)
        If successfulUnlock Then
                're-attempt the login
                Return MyBase.ValidateUser(username, password)
        Else
                Return False
        End If
    Else
        Return retval 'first login was successful
    End If
End Function
```

First, the custom provider lets the base provider attempt to validate the user's credentials. If the base call succeeds, no further work is necessary. However, if the initial result is false, the method attempts to unlock the user. There may be other reasons why ValidateUser fails (for example, the user account specified by username may not even exist in the Membership database). If the unlock attempt succeeds, though, the custom provider again calls the base class's ValidateUser. This sequence of calls will usually result in the second attempt succeeding, assuming, of course, that that password parameter is valid. If the automatic unlock attempt did not succeed, then the custom provider returns false because there isn't any point in calling base.ValidateUser again for a user that is still locked out.

The same implementation pattern can be used with the password-related methods ChangePassword and ChangePasswordQuestionAndAnswer. The override for these methods looks the same as the ValidateUser override with the one difference being that the calls to the base class use the appropriate method. With the custom ValidateUser implementation, you can try logging in with an account and intentionally force a lockout. After autoUnlockTimeout minutes pass, the next call to ValidateUser will succeed if you supply the correct password. In fact, this functionality also works transparently with a control like the Login control. This is another example of how provider customization can be completely transparent to the user interface layer.

The other aspect of automatically unlocking users is in methods that deal with password answers. The override for ResetPassword is:

C#

```csharp
public override string ResetPassword(string username, string passwordAnswer)
{
    //A MembershipPasswordException could be due to a lockout
    try
    {
        return base.ResetPassword(username, passwordAnswer);
    }
    catch (MembershipPasswordException me) {}

    bool successfulUnlock = AutoUnlockUser(username);
    if (successfulUnlock)
        //re-attempt the password reset
        return base.ResetPassword(username, passwordAnswer);
    else
        throw new ProviderException(
            "The attempt to auto unlock the user failed during ResetPassword.");
}
```

VB.NET

```vbnet
Public Overrides Function ResetPassword(ByVal username As String, _
                    ByVal passwordAnswer As String) As String
    'A MembershipPasswordException could be due to a lockout
    Try
        Return MyBase.ResetPassword(username, passwordAnswer)
    Catch [me] As MembershipPasswordException
    End Try
    Dim successfulUnlock As Boolean = AutoUnlockUser(username)
    If successfulUnlock Then
```

```
                    're-attempt the password reset
                    Return MyBase.ResetPassword(username, passwordAnswer)
            Else
                Throw New ProviderException("The attempt to auto " & _
                        "unlock the user failed during ResetPassword.")
            End If
    End Function
```

In this case, the `ResetPassword` method will throw a `MembershipPasswordException` if the user is locked out. As a result, the first call to the base class is wrapped in a `try-catch` block that suppresses this exception. In the event that the user is locked out, the override calls `AutoUnlockUser` to attempt to unlock the user account. If the user account was successfully unlocked, the custom provider attempts to reset the password again by calling into the base class. However, if the automatic unlock attempt failed for some reason, it throws a `ProviderException` to alert callers to the fact that the reset attempt failed. You could also choose to rethrow the `MembershipPasswordException` if you put extra logic into `AutoUnlockUser` to determine exactly why the unlock attempt failed.

If you use a sample page that calls `ResetPassword`, you can intentionally supply five bad password answers to cause the user account to be locked out. As with `ValidateUser`, if you now wait `autoUnlockTimeout` minutes to pass, the next call to `ResetPassword` with a valid answer will succeed. Note, though, unlike the `Login` control, if you use the `PasswordRecovery` control with this custom provider the `Password Recovery` control is unable to load the `MembershipUser` object for a locked-out user. Therefore, you will need to customize the `PasswordRecovery` control to work with the automatic unlock logic in the custom provider. The `GetPassword` method in the custom provider implements the same logic shown for `Reset-Password`. The only difference, of course, is that the `GetPassword` method calls `base.GetPassword` in the appropriate places. Overall though, you can see how straightforward it is to add automatic unlock logic to `SqlMembershipProvider` with a little bit of code. The best part is that you can implement this functionality using publicly available APIs, so you don't have to worry about any future changes in the provider breaking your custom code.

Supporting Dynamic Applications

Normally, an instance of `SqlMembershipProvider` knows which application name to use by looking at the value of the `applicationName` configuration attribute. The default configuration in `machine .config` sets `applicationName` to /, so most developers will probably want to explicitly redefine membership providers in their applications to use a more suitable name. Many of the previous examples of extending `SqlMembershipProvider` showed configurations that used more appropriate values for `applicationName`.

The one constraint on the `applicationName` attribute, though, is that it is statically defined. After you set the value in configuration, the provider remembers that value for the rest of its lifetime. If you look at the `MembershipProvider` base class definition, though, you see that the `ApplicationName` property for the provider is abstract and that a setter is also defined. Concrete providers like `SqlMembershipPro-vider` can choose to implement the setter so that developers can change the application name at runtime.

This means that you can write code that switches between different application data living in the same Membership table with code like the following:

C#

```
p = (SqlMembershipProvider)Membership.Provider;   //assume default provider is SQL
p.ValidateUser("someuser","somepassword");

p.ApplicationName = "A_Different_Value_Than_Configuration";

p.ValidateUser("some other user", "password");
```

VB.NET

```
p = CType(Membership.Provider, SqlMembershipProvider) _
        'assume default provider is SQL

p.ValidateUser("someuser", "somepassword")

p.ApplicationName = "A_Different_Value_Than_Configuration"

p.ValidateUser("some other user", "password")
```

Supporting the setter for ApplicationName can actually be quite useful for single-threaded applications. For example, if you used an application like the console application shown in the previous chapter for creating users, you could easily pass the desired application name as a command-line argument and then set this value on the provider instance. In this way, the create user console application would have no hard-coded dependencies on the application name.

The flaw with this approach is that in any kind of multithreaded environment, such as ASP.NET, it is likely that multiple pages will be running simultaneously. If two pages both have code like that in the preceding example, which one wins? Remember that each configured provider is instantiated only once and that the same instance is used by all threads in an ASP.NET application. The answer to this question for SqlMembershipProvider is that it depends.

❑　At best, no corruption of the internal application name variable occurs, and the two pages run in just the correct sequence that each page works with the correct application name value.

❑　One page stomps on the application name value that was just set by the other page, and as a result one of the two pages ends up working with the wrong set of data.

❑　The worst-case scenario is that both pages attempt to update the provider's private application name variable, with unknown results. This outcome would probably occur intermittently on a multiprocessor machine where you not only have threads logically running in parallel, but you also physically have different threads running simultaneously on different processors. The "nice" thing about this outcome is that it would probably only occur intermittently under stress, so you would go nuts trying to reproduce the problem!

The ASP.NET development team had considered at one point adding some locking to the get and set properties in SqlMembershipProvider's ApplicationName property. However, the setter for this property was not really intended to support dynamically switching application names in a high-concurrency application like ASP.NET. Even if the locking semantics were added, you would end up with a "hot" lock. Developers who wrote web applications that constantly set and reset the application name would find that a fair amount of time was being spent entering and exiting a lock section around the application name variable.

Even if the team had added locking, it still would not prevent multiple pages running simultaneously from overwriting each other's application name. It is the old problem with the Singleton pattern: access to shared state not only has to be serialized, but any operations that depend on the shared state are also liable to cause errors if the intent was that the change to shared state was supposed to be private to the calling thread.

The solution to this problem in ASP.NET 2.0 was to make the `ApplicationName` property abstract, and, of course, this is being inherited by ASP.NET 3.5. Although `SqlMembershipProvider` doesn't take advantage of this fact, you can. If you have an application where each page request needs to run in the context of a specific application name, and you want `SqlMembershipProvider` to dynamically use the correct application name, then you need to write a custom provider that overrides the `Application Name` getter. You can leave the setter alone because internally `SqlMembershipProvider` never uses it. Common scenarios that require this type of dynamic functionality are portal applications where one ASP.NET app-domain may actually be serving up multiple virtual "applications." In this type of scenario, it would be incredibly unwieldy to have to register a separate provider instance for each application. In the case of self-registered "applications," you wouldn't even be able to use a configuration-driven approach.

You have two design choices for the `ApplicationName` override. You can make the provider directly aware of contextual information for the request that determines the correct value for application name. Or you can write some other code (for example, an `HttpModule`) that processes information from a request and then stores the resulting application name in a convenient location such as `HttpContext`. For this sample, I use the latter approach. From an architectural perspective, you probably don't want a custom provider to know all the details about how an application name is determined. Instead, you want the provider to look at a central location that holds the code that determines the correct value neatly factored out into a separate class.

An `HttpModule` is the logical place to centralize the logic for determining the correct application name:

C#

```
using System;
using System.Web;

public class PortalApplicationProcessor : IHttpModule
{
    public void Dispose()
    {  return;  }

    private void DetermineApplicationName(Object sender, EventArgs e)
    {
        HttpApplication app = (HttpApplication)sender;
        HttpContext context  = app.Context;

        string qAppName = app.Request.QueryString["appname"];
        if (!String.IsNullOrEmpty(qAppName))
            context.Items["ApplicationName"] = qAppName;
        else
            context.Items["ApplicationName"] = "NOTSET";
    }

    public void Init(HttpApplication app)
    {
```

```
        app.BeginRequest +=
            new EventHandler(this.DetermineApplicationName);
    }
}
```

VB.NET

```
Imports Microsoft.VisualBasic
Imports System
Imports System.Web

Public Class PortalApplicationProcessor
  Implements IHttpModule
  Public Sub Dispose() Implements IHttpModule.Dispose
        Return
  End Sub

  Private Sub DetermineApplicationName(ByVal sender As Object, _
                                    ByVal e As EventArgs)
      Dim app As HttpApplication = CType(sender, HttpApplication)
      Dim context As HttpContext = app.Context
      Dim qAppName As String = app.Request.QueryString("appname")
      If (Not String.IsNullOrEmpty(qAppName)) Then
          context.Items("ApplicationName") = qAppName
      Else
          context.Items("ApplicationName") = "NOTSET"
      End If
  End Sub

  Public Sub Init(ByVal app As HttpApplication) Implements IHttpModule.Init
        AddHandler app.BeginRequest, AddressOf DetermineApplicationName
  End Sub
End Class
```

This module hooks the `BeginRequest` event to ensure that the application name has been determined before anything significant, such as authentication, has occurred. The module looks on the query-string for a variable called `appname`. If it finds this query-string variable, it stores it in the `HttpContext`'s `Items` collection. If the query-string variable is not found, then a default value is stored in the context instead. The only link required between `HttpModule` and a custom provider is a common agreement on what to call the variable in `HttpContext`. In this example, the context variable is called `ApplicationName`. Although this sample uses a query-string variable, you could certainly determine the application name from a form variable, a custom HTTP header, and so on.

The next step is to write a custom provider that overrides the `ApplicationName` property getter:

C#

```
public class ApplicationProvider : SqlMembershipProvider
{
    public override string ApplicationName
    {
        get
        {
            string appNameFromContext =
                (string)HttpContext.Current.Items["ApplicationName"];
```

```
                        if (appNameFromContext != "NOTSET")
                            return appNameFromContext;
                    else
                            return base.ApplicationName;
                }
        }
}
```

VB.NET

```
Imports Microsoft.VisualBasic
Imports System
Imports System.Web
Imports System.Web.Security

Public Class ApplicationProvider
  Inherits SqlMembershipProvider
    Public Overrides Property ApplicationName() As String
        Get
            Dim appNameFromContext As String = _
        CStr(HttpContext.Current.Items("ApplicationName"))
            If appNameFromContext <> "NOTSET" Then
                Return appNameFromContext
            Else
                Return MyBase.ApplicationName
            End If
        End Get
        Set(ByVal value As String)
            Throw New NotSupportedException()
        End Set
    End Property
End Class
```

The code for the custom provider is trivial. The ApplicationName property first looks in the context to see if a nondefault value for the ApplicationName variable was set. If such a value is found, the provider returns it. Otherwise, the provider reverts to the application name value stored in the provider's configuration.

At this point, all coding necessary to support dynamic application names is complete. You can test the custom provider by configuring a test application to use the provider as well as the associated HttpModule.

```
<system.webServer>
        <modules>
<add name ="PortalProcessor" type="PortalApplicationProcessor"/>
</modules>
</system.webServer>

<membership defaultProvider="portalAware">
    <providers>
        <add name="portalAware" type="ApplicationProvider"
            connectionStringName="LocalSqlServer" />
    </providers>
</membership>
```

Now that the sample application knows about the custom `HttpModule`, you can start authoring pages that make use of Membership in a dynamic manner. For example, you can drop the `CreateUserWizard` control onto a page and then request it with different URLs:

```
http://localhost/ChangingApplicationName/CreateUser.aspx?appname=fooapp2
```

—or—

```
http://localhost/ChangingApplicationName/CreateUser.aspx?appname=barapp
```

After stepping through the wizard, new users are automatically created in the Membership database and associated with different application names based on the `appname` query-string variable. If you use other controls like the `Login` control with the query-string variable, you can log in using credentials from different application names.

This all works so transparently because internally `SqlMembershipProvider` *always* calls the public `ApplicationName` getter whenever the provider needs this value. In the stored procedures for `SqlMembershipProvider`, almost every single stored procedure needs an application name. When the `SqlMembershipProvider` is building its `SqlCommand` objects, it fills in the application name stored procedure parameter with the value returned from the `ApplicationName` getter. Because the custom provider overrides this getter, the fact that the application name value is changing on each request is transparent to `SqlMembershipProvider`.

This approach is also safe from a concurrency perspective because the custom provider is depending on the `HttpContext` for the application name value. Because the context is local to each ASP.NET request, there is no chance that simultaneous page requests will tromp on each other's application name. Even if two different page threads are simultaneously calling the `ApplicationName` getter, each thread will end up with a different value pulled from that thread's associated `HttpContext`.

Although this sample demonstrates how to dynamically set the application name for a web application, the same technique is applicable to Web Service calls using `.asmx` files. The `.asmx` requests also have an `HttpContext` associated with the request, so the one difference is where you pull the application name from. Assuming that your web requests are submitted via HTTP, you could use the query-string, or you could use custom SOAP headers for storing the application name value. About the only tricky thing with overriding `ApplicationName` occurs if you want to use Membership from a "lights-out" application like an NT service. In this type of scenario, the same architectural approach applies, but instead of an `HttpModule` you will need to write code that determines the application name from some other data (for example, the request data that is queued to the service thread) and then initializes a shared memory location (for example, thread local storage being the most likely candidate) prior to calling into a custom provider.

If you are working with a portal application that can change its application context on each request, keep a few security points in mind. Even though it is trivial to make providers pick up a different application name on each request, remember that other features like forms authentication still work at the level of an ASP.NET application. If you validate credentials with a custom Membership provider, make sure that the forms authentication ticket you issue to one portal is not accidentally honored by another portal running in the same ASP.NET application. Similarly, if you write a custom Role Manager provider that overrides `ApplicationName`, make sure that your different portal applications don't accidentally honor each other's role information. In other words, customizing the ASP.NET providers is only one part of the broader architectural problem of making ASP.NET applications "act" like hundreds or thousands of virtual applications.

One other architectural solution has been proposed for dealing with dynamically setting the application name: why not just add applicationName as a parameter to every method on the entire ASP.NET provider and feature classes? Certainly, this is a technically viable option. There are problems with this approach, though:

❑ Developers would have to explicitly manage the application name throughout their code, whereas today the value gets set once and you can forget about it.

❑ From a testing perspective, the test cost of having another parameter inside of every provider and feature method is rather expensive. Although for your own development it doesn't seem like much overhead, for the ASP.NET team there is a nonzero cost each time a new method is added or a method signature widens.

For both of these reasons, it is unlikely that future releases of ASP.NET will add an applicationName parameter back into the APIs. What is more likely is that the general approach outlined in this section will get baked into the provider APIs in some future release.

Managing an Application's Users Through IIS 7.0

As part of the IIS 7.0 and ASP.NET integration, administrators and developers now have the chance of managing an application's users through a new IIS 7.0 applet. Figure 12-1 shows the .NET Users applet in the ASP.NET category of the IIS 7.0 Manager tool.

Figure 12-1

To access the users' management section, simply double-click the .NET Users applet. Figure 12-2 shows the details of the .NET Users applet.

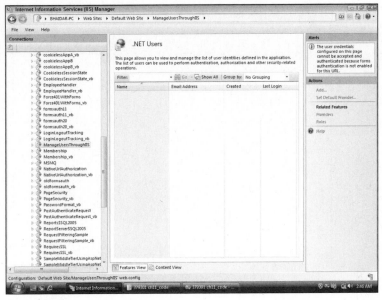

Figure 12-2

The main features the administrator or the developer can make use of are listed on the right Action pane. If you have any registered users in the database, they will show up in the middle grid with the following columns:

- Name
- Email Address
- Created
- Last Login

By default, the .NET Users applet communicates with the default Membership provider set in the application's `web.config`. If you do not specify any provider, the one set in the `machine.config`, `AspNetSqlMembershipProvider` will take effect.

To add a new user to the database, click on the Add link. Figure 12-3 shows the resulting dialog box.

To create a new user, you have to supply data for the following fields:

- User Name
- Email
- Password
- Confirm Password
- Question
- Answer

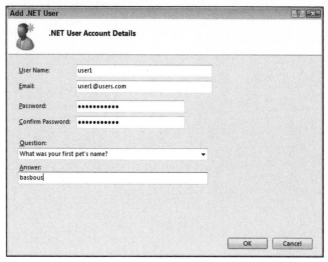

Figure 12-3

Once you are done, click the OK button. A new user has been created in the database and now will be listed in the middle grid, as mentioned above.

Now if you click on a user record listed in the middle grid, you get a new set of actions that you can perform on the user. You can reset the user's password, edit the username and email and, finally, remove the user from the database.

In addition, if you have registered more than one Membership provider in the application's `web.config` file, you can select which provider to be the default provider by clicking on the Set Default Provider option in the Action pane. A small pop-up Windows Forms is shown with a single combo box listing all the Membership providers added in the application's `web.config` file or the ones added directly into the `machine.config`.

You can also use the .NET Users applet to manage the Membership, Role, and Profile providers in an application. Figure 12-4 shows the Provider's applet in the IIS 7.0 Manager tool that can be reached once you click on the Providers menu in the Action pane.

Note that Figure 12-4 shows the Features combo box. This is used to choose which feature you want to manage its providers. Currently, there are three features: Users, Roles, and Profile.

The middle grid, in this case, lists all the registered providers for the application. You can add additional providers by clicking on the Add menu in the Action pane. Figure 12-5 shows the dialog box that allows you to add a new provider.

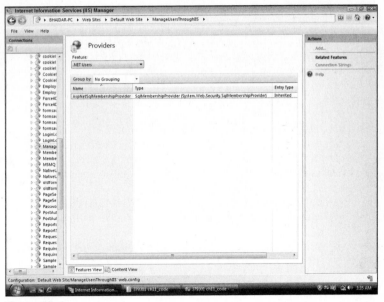

Figure 12-4

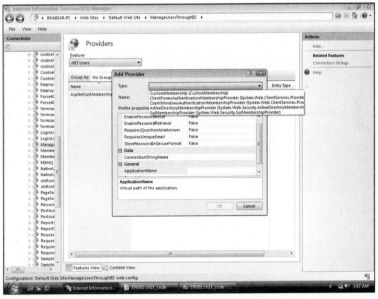

Figure 12-5

The two major fields to fill are the Type and Name fields. These two fields have been explained before and their importance was highlighted. In the Type field, you can either select a provider that ships with the .NET 2.0 or .NET 3.5 Frameworks or even select a custom provider that you have already defined in the App_Code ASP.NET folder or you have added a reference to it from a class library. Once the Type field is filled, you have to give a name for the newly added provider. Moreover, you can set values for all the properties defined on the base MembershipProvider, including RequiresUniqueEmail, Connection-StringName, and so on.

In addition, if you have specified a connection string name that has not yet been defined in the application's web.config file, you can easily add it by clicking on the Connection Strings menu in the Action pane. A new applet in IIS 7.0 opens, called the Connection Strings applet. Using this applet you can add as many connection strings as you may require and store them in the application's web.config file.

The middle grid now holds the details about the defined connection strings in the application's web.config file. To define a new connection string, simply click on the Add menu in the Action pane.

Figure 12-6 shows the dialog box that pops up to provide the details of the new connection strings.

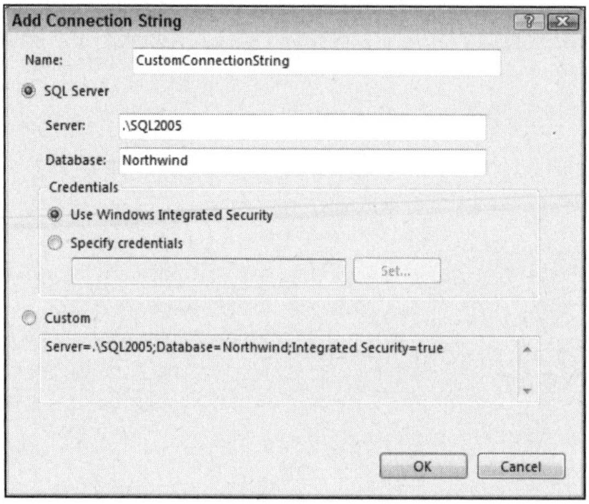

Figure 12-6

For a new connection string, you need to provide the name of the connection string, SQL Server address, database name, and credentials whether Windows Authentication or specify credentials. In addition, you have the choice of defining the connection manually by selecting the Custom option on the Form. Choosing this option allows you to write the connection string manually.

In chapter after chapter you are noticing the deep integration between IIS 7.0 and ASP.NET. This section highlighted a new integration feature—a set of UI tools that allow you to manage an application's users, providers, and connection strings.

Summary

The provider works in both ASP.NET and non-ASP.NET environments that are running at Low trust or higher. Remember, though, that the provider needs `SqlClientPermission` in partial trust environments and that this permission is not granted by default in Low trust. `SqlMembershipProvider` implements all the security functionality available in the Membership feature. This includes advanced security features such as question-and-answer-based password resets as well as account lockouts when bad passwords or bad password answers are used. The provider stores user-related data in a combination of tables: some common to all SQL-based providers, and some are specific to `SqlMembership-Provider`. Although there is nothing technically preventing you from using these tables directly, the expectation is that public APIs like the `MembershipProvider` class should be used for inserting and updating data. Only in the case where you need more extensive read-only access to Membership data should you query the database directly. ASP.NET ships with a number of SQL views that expose the data from the underlying tables for you to write `SELECT` queries against.

Although the default database engine used by `SqlMembershipProvider` is SQL Server 2005 Express, developers can easily change the `LocalSqlServer` connection string in `machine.config` to point the provider at any database server running SQL Server 7.0, 2000, or 2005. The only special logic that `SqlMembershipProvider` supports (and for that matter all the ASP.NET SQL-based providers) for SSE is the automatic generation of a database containing the schema for all the SQL-based features. Although this integration makes it very easy to develop using file-based webs in Visual Studio, you will probably be better off using the `aspnet_regsql` tool to manually install the schema when you develop against IIS 6-based webs.

`SqlMembershipProvider` can also be extended by developers who want to integrate additional functionality. Because the provider is unsealed, most of the public properties and methods can be overridden by you. In this chapter, you saw how you could take advantage of this functionality to make simple changes in custom password generation and custom password encryption. More extensive changes allow you to extend `SqlMembershipProvider` with new features such as password history tracking and automatic unlocking of unlocked accounts. Last, with a just a few lines of code you saw how you can override the `ApplicationName` property to make `SqlMembershipProvider` work with multiple "applications" in portal environments.

13

ActiveDirectoryMembership Provider

The `ActiveDirectoryMembershipProvider` supports almost the entire set of functionality defined by the Membership API. You can create and manage users with either Active Directory (AD) or the standalone directory product Active Directory Lightweight Directory Service (ADLDS), which resembles the ADAM on Windows Server 2003. Furthermore, you can use the provider in both ASP.NET and non-ASP.NET applications. Because the `ActiveDirectory MembershipProvider` closely mirrors the `SqlMembershipProvider` in terms of functionality, the interesting parts of `ActiveDirectoryMembershipProvider` are how the provider works with the directory server and how certain Membership operations are mapped to AD and ADLDS.

This chapter will cover the following aspects of `ActiveDirectoryMembershipProvider` in detail:

- ❑ How the provider works with different directory structures.
- ❑ Provider configuration settings.
- ❑ Notes on various pieces of provider functionality.
- ❑ The `ActiveDirectoryMembershipUser` class.
- ❑ Working with Active Directory.
- ❑ Configuring ADLDS to work with the provider.
- ❑ Using the provider in partial trust.

Supported Directory Architectures

Because the `ActiveDirectoryMembershipProvider` uses a directory store, you should understand the various domain architectures that it supports. The `ActiveDirectoryMembershipProvider` can work against either an Active Directory (AD) domain (Windows 2000, Windows Server 2003, and Windows Server 2008) or against what is called an application partition deployed in an Active Directory Lightweight Directory Service (ADLDS) on Windows Server 2008 or Active Directory Application Mode (ADAM) on Windows Server 2003. Of the two directory server types, AD is the one with more varied options and, thus, requires a little more preplanning on your part.

The most important thing to keep in mind when using the AD/ADLDS-based provider is that the provider treats AD and ADLDS as Lightweight Directory Access Protocol (LDAP) servers. In essence, the provider is talking to these "databases" using LDAP commands. The provider does not interact with AD as an NT LAN Manager (NTLM) or Kerberos authentication service. This means that the provider does not return any kind of authenticated domain principal, and the provider cannot be used to generate a login token. It simply makes LDAP calls and LDAP binds to a directory server, and it returns the results of those calls. This behavior is sometimes a point of confusion for folks who think that `ActiveDirectoryMembershipProvider` generates security tokens and sets the security context on a thread. Because the provider is implementing the `MembershipProvider` base class, and the Membership API has no concept of returning security tokens or switching security contexts, the provider has no support for such operations.

The provider always works in the context of a directory container. This means that the provider is always pointed at the root of some container, and all provider operations occur within that single container, or in most cases through the hierarchy of nested child containers. For ADLDS, this is not particularly surprising because ADLDS servers are basically standalone LDAP directories. Even though a single ADLDS server can host multiple application partitions (that is, these are sort of like mini-domains), the provider always needs to be pointed at a specific application partition when using ADLDS. Typically, for developers working with ADLDS, this is common practice; your application knows which application partition in ADLDS it should be using.

However, for AD you can have a forest with multiple domains, and for many customers the forest infrastructure is very large and complex. If you use the provider in an AD environment, each configured provider can only be pointed at a *single* domain or at a specific container within a *single* domain. The provider does not support the concept of multidomain operations; realistically, the concept of seamless support for multiple domains is baked more into the authentication aspect of Active Directory as opposed to the LDAP aspect of AD.

Even though AD has a global catalog (GC) that can be used for LDAP queries that need to work with data from many domains, for the most part the `ActiveDirectoryMembershipProvider` does not make use of GC functionality. (There are a handful of verification checks where the provider will query the GC, but this functionality is all internal to the provider.) The provider also does not chase referrals, so you can't set up user objects in one domain that are really referrals to objects in another domain and expect the provider to work. When using AD, you also cannot point the provider at a global catalog (that is, use `GC://` in the connection string). If this were allowed the provider's search and get methods would probably work, but all the data modification methods would fail because GC replicas are read-only.

If you want to use the provider in a multidomain AD environment, you need to configure multiple provider instances, one for each domain or domain-container that you need to work with. In your application, you can implement logic that determines which domain it should work with, and your code can then select the appropriate `ActiveDirectoryMembershipProvider` instance from the `Membership` `.Providers` collection. In this fashion, you can still effectively work in a multidomain environment with only a little extra code on your part.

Note, though, that this means the machine on which the providers are running needs network connectivity to each of the different domains. For an extranet environment that has only a handful of domains, this probably is not an issue. However, if you have a more complex scenario where you need to access remote domains from an extranet environment, chances are that a web server in your DMZ is not going to have network connectivity to reach back into the internal corporate network and then communicate with some random directory controller. If you are architecting an application that needs to have multiple provider instances communicating with many different domains, make sure that your network topology will support this before you go too far down the coding path!

I have been making a number of references to containers for both AD and ADLDS. The provider "knows" the context that it should be using based on the connection string configured for the provider. Just like the SQL providers, the `ActiveDirectoryMembershipProvider` uses a connection string, although in its case the connection string is an LDAP connection string. (You will see many examples of LDAP connection strings later in this chapter.) The connection string tells the provider which domain, directory server, or application partition it should work against, and the connection string also gives the provider enough information to know which container within the domain or directory server the provider should work with.

If you are working with ADLDS, you always work explicitly with a container because you need to configure an application partition within which your user data is stored. As a result, the connection string you have in configuration when using ADLDS *always* includes some container information in it. For AD this is not necessarily the case. In AD, you can point the provider at a domain, or a specific domain controller, without specifying a container. If you do this, the provider will default to using a combination of the default naming context for the domain and the "Users" container because this container is commonly available in AD domains. (User creation/deletion will occur in the Users container, whereas all other methods are rooted at the default naming context.) If you want to create your application's users within only the Users container, then you can define your connection strings without an explicit container in the AD case. Of course, you also have the same ability in AD as you do in ADLDS to create organizational units (OUs) and to specify these OUs as part of the connection string.

If your user data is spread across multiple containers, you have a few options for configuring the provider. If the user data exists in containers that are peers of one another, and all the containers have a common parent, you can point a single provider instance at the parent container. Except for user creation and user deletion, the provider always performs subtree searches starting with the container determined from the connection string. For example, if you call `GetUser` on the provider and the provider is pointed at a parent container, then the provider will be able to find the user object if it is located in the parent container, or if it is located in *any* of the containers nested within the parent, regardless of how deep the nesting may occur.

If your application needs to create and delete users, then you will need to configure a separate provider instance for each separate container in which creation and deletion occurs. The reason for the different behavior is that for user creation and deletion there is no such thing as a subtree operation. When you create a user object it must be created in a specific location, and as a result the provider limits user creation and deletion to the container specified (or implicitly determined) on the connection string. For applications that have a number of OUs, though, it can be awkward to have to always manipulate different provider instances for each OU when calling common methods like `GetUser` or `ValidateUser`. Therefore, except for `CreateUser` and `DeleteUser`, all the provider methods use subtree searches.

What happens if your application deals with multiple OUs sharing a common parent and you *do not* want the provider to perform broad search operations across all the OUs? If you intentionally want to limit all provider operations to a single OU, you can configure multiple provider instances and point each instance at a specific OU as opposed to a parent container. However, if you have a container structure that nests multiple OUs in a chain, and you want to limit the provider to only a single OU in the nesting chain, the reality is that any provider pointed at a nonleaf OU will still perform subtree searches down through all the remaining OUs. About the only thing you can do for this scenario is to restrict access on a per-OU basis using different user accounts and then configure the different provider instances with different sets of credentials.

Provider Configuration

If you configure the provider with the minimum number of required configuration attributes, most of its functionality will work against existing AD installations. About all you need to get up and running is a provider definition and a valid connection string:

```
<connectionStrings>
    <add name="adconnection" connectionString="LDAP://mydomain.dns.name"/>
</connectionStrings>

<membership defaultProvider=" someprovider ">
  <providers>
    <clear/>
    <add name="someprovider"
         type="System.Web.Security.ActiveDirectoryMembershipProvider, …"
         connectionStringName="adconnection" />
  </providers>
</membership>
```

It is pretty much guaranteed that for production applications, though, you will need to delve a little more deeply into the provider's configuration. The section "Working with Active Directory" walks you through a number of the common configuration tasks for setting up the provider.

For now, take a look at the various configuration settings that are available in the <add /> element of the provider. The available settings fall into the following general groups:

❑   Directory connection settings

❑   Schema mappings

❑   Search-specific settings

❑   Membership provider settings

Directory Connection Settings

As with SQL provider, you need to at least supply a connection string so that the provider knows where it should read and write data. However, unlike SQL Server connection strings, there is no such thing as specifying explicit connection credentials inside of the connection string. Also, connection security settings cannot be supplied inside of an LDAP connection string. As a result, the provider supports a number of additional configuration settings.

The connection string that you use for the provider is placed in the <connectionStrings /> section. The provider references the connection string via the connectionStringName attribute. The connection string that you create supports a number of different formats, depending on whether you are connecting to AD or ADLDS. For example, if you are running in a domain called foo.org and you have an AD domain controller called dcserver, the most prevalent forms of the connection string when connecting to AD look like:

❑   LDAP://foo.org

❑   LDAP://dcserver.foo.org

❑   LDAP://foo.org/OU=SomeOU,DC=foo, DC=org

❑   LDAP://dcserver.foo.org/OU=SomeOU,DC=foo,DC=org

However, if you are connecting to an ADLDS server, you always need to have an application partition defined. Assuming that you have an ADLDS server called adldsbox in the foo.org DNS namespace, you could use connection strings like:

❑   LDAP:// adldsbox.foo.org/O=myorg,DC=foo,DC=org

❑   LDAP:// adldsbox.foo.org/OU=SomeOU,O=myorg,DC=foo,DC=org

Unlike AD, ADLDS servers can be listening on nondefault LDAP ports. If you install ADLDS to listen on other ports, then the connection string can look like:

❑   LDAP://adldsbox.foo.org:50001/O=myorg,DC=foo,DC=org

❑   LDAP://adldsbox.foo.org:50001/OU=SomeOU,O=myorg,DC=foo,DC=org

If you do install ADLDS on a nondefault port, and you plan on using secure connectivity to the ADLDS server, you must make sure that SSL support has been configured properly on the ADLDS server and on each of the machines that needs to connect to the ADLDS server. If you do not change the default port settings for ADLDS, then SSL traffic by default occurs on port 636 (unsecured traffic occurs on port 389 by default). If your ADLDS server uses these default ports, then you do not need to specify a port number in the connection string.

Because both AD and ADLDS can replicate changes across servers, the type of connection strings that you use will have an effect on when the provider sees changes made on other machines. For example, if you use an AD connection string that points only at a domain, it is possible that across a web farm different web servers will end up connecting to different domain controllers. This can lead to odd behavior where changes made to a MembershipUser on one server do not show up immediately on other servers in your farm. Unfortunately, there is nothing the provider itself can do to mitigate the inherent latency of AD's multimaster behavior. However, you can at least use connection strings that explicitly specify a server; in this case, all provider instances pointed at the same server will see a consistent set of information.

One very important aspect of connecting to the directory server is connection security. From the sample connection strings, you saw that there is no indication of the secured state of the connection. You request security for the connection to the directory server via the connectionProtection provider configuration attribute. This attribute can be set to either None or Secure. By default, if you do not specify the attribute in your provider's configuration, the provider will default to Secure.

The reason that the attribute has only one of two settings is that attempting to expose the vagaries of negotiating secure connections with a directory server can quickly become very complicated. So rather than leaving it up to you to get things working, the provider simplifies the issue into a simple binary decision. Either you want connection security automatically established, or you do not. Of course, there is a bit more complexity than that occurring underneath the hood. There are a number of mix-and-match combinations you can use with `connectionProtection` and the credentials used by the provider when connecting to the directory, though only a subset of settings really make sense.

❑ **connectionProtection=None for AD:** This is not a combination you should ever use. In AD environments, any operations that set or change passwords must be done over secure connections, so with a setting of `None`, the provider will always fail when it attempts things like `ChangePassword` or `ResetPassword`. Also, you need to always use explicit connection credentials with this setting. Because AD has built-in support for automatically securing connections, there is not much reason for ever using `None` in an AD environment.

❑ **connectionProtection=None for ADLDS:** You may find yourself using this combination in a development environment where you do not have SSL certificates set up for your ADLDS server and client machines. As with AD, you will need to configure the connection credentials explicitly to use the `None` setting. Note that for ADLDS this means that you will be limited to using *only* ADLDS user principals for the explicit credentials; domain credentials cannot be explicitly specified for ADLDS when `connectionProtection` is set to `None`. Unlike AD, though, you can manually configure ADLDS to allow password changes and resets to occur over unsecured connections. The section on "Using ADLDS" later in the chapter shows you how to do this. Note, though, that I would not recommend using `None` in a production setting with ADLDS; it only makes sense as a convenience early on during a development cycle. Even for development scenarios, at some point you should get SSL set up so that you are coding in an environment that more closely matches your, deployment environment.

❑ **connectionProtection=Secure for AD:** This is the default when connecting to an AD server, and it is the setting that you should use for most cases when working with AD. Internally, the provider will first make a check to see if SSL is supported on the directory server. If it is, all LDAP traffic will flow over Active Directory's SSL port (that is, port 636). If SSL is not configured for AD, which is normally the case for at least intranet directory servers, then the provider will fall back and use signing and sealing for all LDAP traffic. If you have configured SSL in an extranet directory environment for example, then the provider will make use of SSL in preference to signing and sealing. Because the provider internally makes use of the Active Directory Services Interface (ADSI) API, it turns out that setting up SSL for AD environments gives the best performance when using the provider to connect securely to AD. Using SSL reduces the number of network connections that ADSI will open on behalf of the provider when making secure connections to AD.

❑ **connectionProtection=Secure for ADLDS:** This is the default when connecting to an ADLDS server. As noted earlier, this setting will not work unless you have explicitly set up SSL on your ADLDS server as well as on all machines that need to communicate with that server. The reason for this restriction is that unlike when connecting to AD, the provider *only* supports the use of SSL for securing network traffic with the ADLDS server. Even if the ADLDS instance is running on a server joined to a domain, the provider will not attempt to use signing and sealing.

When you set `connectionProtection` to `Secure`, you can find out the actual connection security that was chosen at runtime by querying the provider's `CurrentConnectionProtection` property. This property returns a value from the `System.Web.Security.ActiveDirectoryConnectionProtection` enumeration that will tell you if SSL or signing and sealing were chosen.

The last set of connection information that you can configure in the provider's <add /> element is explicit connection credentials. The configuration attributes connectionUsername and connection Password can be used to explicitly specify the username and password to use when connecting to the directory server. If you don't explicitly specify values for these settings the provider attempts to connect to the directory using either the process credentials from the IIS 7.0 worker process, or the application impersonation credentials if application impersonation is in effect. If you explicitly specify the username and password, make sure to use protected configuration (discussed in Chapter 5) so that the credentials are not stored in cleartext on your production servers.

The format of the username differs, depending on whether you are connecting to AD or ADLDS:

❑ **AD:** You can specify the username in any format that is supported by Windows. The two most common username formats are the NT4-style format of *DOMAIN\USERNAME* and the user principal name format of *username@domain.name*.

❑ **ADLDS:** If you are connecting to an ADLDS server with connectionProtection set to Secure, then you can explicitly specify either an ADLDS user principal or a domain user account. For a protection setting of None, though, only an ADLDS user principal can be specified. An ADLDS principal looks something like CN=Username,OU=AccountOU,O=MyOrganization, DC=bhaidar,DC=net. In the section on "Using ADLDS," there is a walkthrough of how to use an ADLDS user principal when connecting to an ADLDS server.

Directory Schema Mappings

By default, the provider attempts to map the properties of the MembershipUser class to an appropriate set of default attributes on the user class in AD and ADLDS. Some aspects of this mapping are configurable, whereas other aspects are not. The most important constraint is that ActiveDirectoryMembership Provider always binds to objects of type user.

The following properties on MembershipUser have fixed schema mappings to attributes in the directory:

❑ ProviderUserKey: This value maps to the objectSID attribute on the user object. As a result, you can get the user's security identifier (SID) from the ProviderUserKey property and you can also retrieve MembershipUser instances using the SID as a key.

❑ Comment: Maps to the comment attribute on the user class.

❑ CreationDate: Maps to the whenCreated attribute on the user class.

❑ LastPasswordChangedDate: Maps to the pwdLastSet attribute on the user class.

❑ IsApproved: Maps to the userAccountControl attribute when using AD. Maps to the mDS-UserAccountDisabled attribute when using ADLDS.

❑ IsLockedOut: Maps to msDS-User-Account-Control-Computed attribute when using AD on Windows Server 2003 or Windows Server 2008 or when using ADLDS. This property is computed from the lockoutTime attribute and the directory's account lockout duration setting when running against Windows 2000 AD (W2K's schema did not include the msDS-User-Account-Control-Computed attribute). If you have configured the provider to support question-and-answer-based password reset, then the provider will also look at the custom tracking information for bad password answers when determining whether a user is considered locked out.

❑ LastLockoutDate: Maps to the lockoutTime attribute on the user class. If question-and-answer-based password reset has been enabled, then the lockout date may also come from the custom attributes that track bad password answer attempts.

Other properties on MembershipUser are either not mapped by default or have default mappings to directory attributes that you can change.

❑ Username: By default, the provider maps this property to the userPrincipalName attribute in the directory. This mapping will work for you if each of your directory users is created with a user principal name. For older directories, though, you may be using the NT4-style SAM account names, in which case you will need to change the mapping for this property. You can change the mapping to the sAMAccountName attribute in this case. Note that if you try to use the provider with an already populated directory, and you are scratching your head wondering why you can't find any users or successfully validate any credentials, it is probably because your users have SAM account names, but you have not configured the provider to use the sAMAccountName attribute for MembershipUser.Username.

❑ Email: By default, the provider maps this property to the mail attribute. If you want, you can change this mapping to any single-valued attribute on the user class that is of type Unicode String.

❑ PasswordQuestion: This property is not mapped by default to anything in the directory. If you intend to use question-and-answer-based password resets with the provider, there are actually five different attributes that need to be mapped on the user class. The section on "Working with Active Directory" walks you through adding custom attributes to the AD schema and setting up password reset functionality.

Because Active Directory operates in a multimaster environment, some of the properties on Membership User cannot be reliably implemented based on directory attributes.

❑ LastActivityDate: This property has no mapping and is not supported by the provider. There is no concept in either AD or ADLDS of touching the user object every time something happens. Unlike the SQL providers where different features all update a LastActivityDate column in the database, attempting to engineer a similar approach for AD was not feasible. First, there would be no way for other features such as Profile to reach into a user object in a directory and update an arbitrary field (suddenly you would have System.DirectoryServices code sitting in the middle of the SQL provider code, which would be a bit strange to say the least). Another problem is that for this value to make any sense in a multimaster environment you would have to replicate the field to all the various domain controllers. Because it is not likely that most customers would want to add a custom attribute and then replicate it across their domain infrastructure each and every time the attribute was changed, the decision was made not to support the concept of a last activity date for the provider.

❑ LastLoginDate: Both AD and ADLDS store the last logon time for a user using the lastLogon and lastLogonTimestamp attributes, respectively. However, these attributes aren't replicated across domain controllers, and the property is not available from the global catalog. So, it is very likely that the provider would either get differing values for this property or stale property values in any domain that had at least two domain controllers. Rather than having the provider iterate through all domain controllers in a domain attempting to find the latest value, the decision was made to not implement this property.

If you want to change any of the configurable attribute mappings for the provider, you can do so by using the following configuration attributes in the provider's <add /> element:

❑   attributeMapUserName: You can use this provider configuration attribute to change which attribute on the user class the provider uses for identifying a user. You can set this to either userPrincipalName (the default) or to sAMAccountName.

❑   attributeMapEmail: If you don't want to store user's email addresses in the default mail attribute, you can tell the provider to use a different directory attribute instead. The only restriction is that the directory attribute must be of type Unicode String.

❑   attributeMapPasswordQuestion: This configuration attribute must be defined for the provider if you set enablePasswordReset to true. The configuration attribute must reference a directory attribute of type Unicode String.

❑   attributeMapPasswordAnswer: This configuration attribute must be defined for the provider if you set enablePasswordReset to true. The configuration attribute must reference a directory attribute of type Unicode String.

❑   attributeMapFailedPasswordAnswerCount: This configuration attribute must be defined for the provider if you set enablePasswordReset to true. The configuration attribute must reference a directory attribute of type Integer.

❑   attributeMapFailedPasswordAnswerTime: This configuration attribute must be defined for the provider if you set enablePasswordReset to true. The configuration attribute must reference a directory attribute of type Large Integer/Interval.

❑   attributeMapFailedPasswordAnswerLockoutTime: This configuration attribute must be defined for the provider if you set enablePasswordReset to true. The configuration attribute must reference a directory attribute of type Large Integer/Interval.

Later on in the "Working with Active Directory" section, I walk you through enabling question-and-answer-based password reset, including the necessary configuration steps for extending the schema in the directory.

Along with the directory schema mappings comes a set of default size restrictions on the length of various string properties. With the SQL provider, it is pretty easy to determine length restrictions by just looking in the database at the column definitions. For the AD provider, this is harder to accomplish unless you can look at the actual directory schema. The default length restrictions for various MembershipUser-related properties are shown in the following list. Note, though, that it is possible for you to edit the AD and ADLDS schemas to enforce even shorter size restrictions. If you have done this, the provider will honor the size restrictions defined in your directory's schema.

❑   Username: If you mapped username to sAMAccountName then your username cannot be longer than 20 characters. This is a hard-coded size restriction from NT4 days. If you mapped username to userPrincipalName, then a username cannot be longer than 64 characters.

❑   Password: As with the SQL provider, the plaintext password for a user cannot be longer than 128 characters.

❑   Comment: The provider only allows comments up to 1024 characters in length. This differs from the SQL provider, where you could basically store the entire English dictionary if you wanted in a user's Comment property.

❑ `Email`: A user's email property cannot be longer than 256 characters.

❑ `PasswordQuestion`: A user's password question cannot be longer than 256 characters.

❑ `PasswordAnswer`: A user's cleartext password answer cannot be longer than 128 characters. However, the end result of encrypting the password answer also cannot be longer than 128 characters. Because the `ActiveDirectoryMembershipProvider` always encrypts the password answer using the same encryption method described in Chapter 11 for `SqlMembership Provider`, this limits users to around a 42-character-long cleartext password answer.

Provider Settings for Search

There are a handful of other custom configuration attributes supported on the provider that deal specifically with how the provider interacts with AD and ADLDS.

❑ `enableSearchMethods`: By default, the provider sets this property to `false`. You can choose to set it to `true` to enable the following provider methods: `FindUsersByName`, `FindUsersBy Email`, and `GetAllUsers`. When you carry out LDAP search operations against AD and ADLDS the most efficient way to query large numbers of users is through the use of stateful search facilities. For example, if you perform directory searches using the `System.DirectoryServices` classes, you can perform paged searches to limit the amount of processing the directory server incurs during any one query operation. This type of search implies that your code hangs on to an object (the `DirectorySearcher`) over the course of moving through multiple pages of results. However, the `ActiveDirectoryMembershipProvider` is designed for use in stateless web applications. This means after each call to a provider search method, all the underlying `System.DirectoryServices` objects that were used during the search are released. As a result, the provider is not able to take advantage of the paged search facilities in AD and ADLDS. This means that if the search methods were allowed by default, it would be possible for a developer to accidentally point the provider at a large directory and then grind the directory servers to a halt by searching through sets of users. For this reason, the search methods on the provider can be enabled or disabled—with the default state being disabled.

❑ `clientSearchTimeout`: By default, the provider does not set this property. You can set this attribute to the number of seconds you want the provider to wait for a response from any LDAP query it sends to the server. This configuration attribute is used to set the `ClientTimeout` property on the `DirectorySearcher` instance that the provider uses internally. Note that this timeout applies to any LDAP search operation that the provider issues and, thus, also applies to methods like `UpdateUser` or `GetUser` that need to find a single user object as part of their normal processing.

❑ `serverSearchTimeout`: By default, the provider does not set this property. You can set this attribute to the number of seconds the directory server should spend performing a single search operation. The configuration attribute is used to set the `ServerPageTimeLimit` property on the `DirectorySearcher` instance that the provider uses internally. As with `clientSearch Timeout`, the value for this configuration attribute will affect any LDAP query that the provider issues and, thus, the configuration setting will affect methods like `UpdateUser` and `GetUser`.

As you can see, the area of searching users caused some degree of concern with the feature team. Searching for a specific user wasn't the problem because that type of operation yields one or no results and involves searching for a single user object in the directory. But performing broad searches has the potential to yield a large number of users, and the problem of mapping the provider's paging semantics on top of AD's paging semantics can exacerbate performance issues.

If you have ever used the `DirectorySearcher` class, you know that the class also supports a `PageSize` property that is normally used in conjunction with the timeout properties. However, there is no provider configuration attribute that exposes a page size. Instead, when you run a provider method like `FindUsersByName` the provider requests results from AD and ADLDS in fixed page sizes of 512 entries. Then the provider internally iterates through the results and determines whether any search results in a 512-entry page also lie within the set of rows that were requested by the calling code. Effectively, the provider has to map the page size and page index parameters on methods like `FindUsersByName` to the underlying set of pages that the provider is retrieving via the `DirectorySearcher` class.

Because of this behavior, the `clientSearchTimeout` and `serverSearchTimeout` attributes really only apply to each page of 512 search results retrieved by the provider. For example, if you specify a `server SearchTimeout` setting of 10 seconds in configuration, and the provider internally needs to retrieve 10 different pages of results from the directory server to complete a method call, the provider can take up to 100 seconds to retrieve all the data without exceeding the server's timeout.

The net result of this is that for a single method call to the provider, the provider internally may need to fetch multiple pages of results from the directory server in order to fulfill the request. For this reason, if you choose to enable the search methods on the provider, be sure that you do the following:

❏ Do not call `GetAllUsers`. This method is going to start with the first user in a directory container and keep on walking through all the other users. On a large directory, this will be an incredibly expensive method to call.

❏ For `FindUsersByName`, always specify at least a partial value for the `usernameToMatch` parameter. This will at least allow the directory server to narrow the set of results based on either the `userPrincipalName` or `sAMAccountName` attributes.

❏ For `FindUsersByEmail`, always specify at least a partial value for the `emailToMatch` parameter. This will allow the directory server to narrow the set of results returned based on the "mail" attribute.

MembershipProvider Settings

Because the `ActiveDirectoryMembershipProvider` inherits from `MembershipProvider`, it supports many of the same configuration settings as found on the `SqlMembershipProvider`. However, even though many of the settings are the same, in some cases the way the `ActiveDirectoryMembership Provider` uses the settings will differ.

❏ `applicationName`: Although you can configure this setting on the provider (and you can retrieve it from the `ApplicationName` property), it has no effect on the provider's functionality. The directory scope within which the provider operates is determined solely by the connection string. The provider supports configuring `applicationName` simply for visual consistency with the `SqlMembershipProvider`(that is, the configuration looks the same, but that's about it).

❏ `requiresUniqueEmail`: If this is set to `true`, then the provider's `CreateUser` and `UpdateUser` methods will perform a subtree search rooted at the location specified by the connection string and look for any other user objects with a matching value in their `mail` attribute. This means that the provider is guaranteeing local uniqueness of the email value; the provider does not guarantee that the email value is globally unique in the domain or the forest. Of course, if your connection string is pointed at an AD domain (that is, you have no container specified in your connection string), the provider will effectively be guaranteeing email uniqueness for that domain because the search will be rooted at the domain's default naming context.

❑ enablePasswordReset: The default setting is `false`. If you set this attribute to `true`, then you must also set `requiresQuestionAndAnswer` to `true`, and you must specify the five mapping attributes described earlier so the provider knows where to store bad password answer-tracking information.

❑ requiresQuestionAndAnswer: The default setting is `false`. You can actually set this attribute to `true` *without* setting `enablePasswordReset` to `true`. If `requiresQuestionAndAnswer` is set to `true`, then you must tell the provider the schema mappings in the directory for the password question and answer by using the `attributeMapPasswordQuestion` and `attribute MapPasswordAnswer` attributes. You might require questions and answers in order to start having users enter this information when their accounts are being created, and then at a later point turn on password resets. Alternatively, you could just use the `PasswordQuestion` property on the `MembershipUser` object to store some more information about the user (that is, use it as a second property like the `Comment` property).

❑ minRequiredPasswordLength: By default, this property is set to 7. The provider uses this setting to enforce a minimum password length prior to sending the password down to the directory server. Note that this property setting only *adds* a layer of password validation on top of the directory's existing password strength enforcement rules. Regardless of the setting you use for this configuration attribute, a user's password must always pass the password strength restrictions defined for the directory server.

❑ minRequiredNonalphanumericCharacters: Defaults to requiring one nonalphanumeric character. As with `minRequiredPasswordLength` this restriction is enforced in addition to whatever password strength restrictions are currently enforced by the directory server.

❑ passwordStrengthRegularExpression: There is no regular expression set by default. If you do set a regular expression for this attribute, the regex is enforced in addition to the password strength restrictions currently enforced by the directory server.

❑ maxInvalidPasswordAttempts: By default, this is set to 5. In the case of the `ActiveDirectory MembershipProvider`, the name of this configuration attribute is a little misleading. In reality, the provider always depends on the directory server for dealing with bad password attempts. Because AD and ADLDS already have extensive support for tracking bad password attempts and locking out users as a result of too many bad password attempts, this setting *only* affects bad password *answers*. If you have enabled question-and-answer-based password reset, then the provider will mark the account as locked out when the number of bad password answer attempts reaches the limit specified in this configuration attribute.

❑ passwordAttemptWindow: Defaults to 10 minutes. The value of this configuration attribute is used by the provider in conjunction with the `maxInvalidPasswordAttempts` and `password AnswerAttemptLockoutDuration` configuration attributes for tracking bad password *answer* attempts. Although the name of this attribute is a bit misleading, it has no effect on what happens when bad passwords are used. The provider always relies on AD and ADLDS to handle tracking bad passwords as well as locking users out when too many bad password attempts have occurred.

❑ passwordAnswerAttemptLockoutDuration: Because AD and ADLDS have the concept of automatically unlocking a user account after a configurable time period, the `ActiveDirectory MembershipProvider` supports the same capability when tracking bad password *answer* attempts. By default, this attribute is set to 30 minutes—which is the same default setting used by AD and ADLDS for auto-unlocking user accounts that had too many bad password attempts. After 30 minutes have passed, the provider will consider a user account unlocked in the case that the account was originally locked out because of too many bad password answer attempts.

Unique Aspects of Provider Functionality

In general, the `ActiveDirectoryMembershipProvider`'s implementation of `MembershipProvider` properties and methods matches the functionality described in earlier chapters for the Membership API and the `SqlMembershipProvider`. However, there are some differences in functionality that you should keep in mind so that you are not surprised when you start working with the provider.

Each of the provider's methods is listed here with a description of the directory-specific functionality that occurs in each method.

❑ `CreateUser`: You cannot create users with an explicit value for the `providerUserKey` parameter. If you attempt to create a new user with a non-null `providerUserKey`, the provider will throw an exception. If the creation was successful the provider returns an instance of `Active DirectoryMembershipUser`: this custom class is discussed further in the next section. If you create a user in AD, and the username is mapped to `userPrincipalName` (UPN), the provider will perform a GC lookup to confirm that the UPN is not already in use elsewhere in the forest. This means that if you use the provider in an extranet environment and you use UPNs for the username, your web servers will require network connectivity to a global catalog server to perform this check. Also if you use a UPN for the username the provider will automatically generate a random 20-character value for the `sAMAccountName` attribute (this will look something like `$A31000-2B7QQ9PMDFOG`). Even though the provider never uses this random value, it must generate a unique value because AD enforces uniqueness of SAM account names within a domain. On an ADLDS server, the provider does not do anything special for `sAMAccountName` because this attribute does not exist in the ADLDS schema. For both AD and ADLDS, the provider also automatically sets the `cn` attribute (that is, the common name for the user object) to the value passed in the `username` parameter. If `requiresUniqueMail` is set to `true` in the provider's configuration, then the provider also verifies that the email address is unique by performing a subtree search for other users with the same email address. The subtree search is rooted at the container specified by the connection string. Users are always created in the directory container determined by the connection string. The actual process of creating the user takes three to four steps: first, the user object is created, then the password is set on the object (effectively `IADsUser ::SetPassword` is called), and then the disabled status of the user object is set. In the case of ADLDS, the new user account is also added to the Readers security group for the application partition. If any phase of user creation after the first step fails, the provider will attempt to clean up after itself by deleting the partially created user object from the directory. This last step is the reason the identity used by the provider needs the ability to both create and delete user objects for the `CreateUser` method to work.

❑ `ChangePassword`: The provider relies on AD and ADLDS to keep track of bad passwords that may be passed to this method. If `enablePasswordReset` is set to `true`, the provider will also disallow password changes if the user account was already locked out because of bad password answers. If `enablePasswordReset` is set to true, the provider resets the password-answer-tracking fields each time a good password is used with this method. The password change is effectively being invoked with a call to `IADsUser::ChangePassword`.

❑ `ChangePasswordQuestionAndAnswer`: As with `ChangePassword` and `ValidateUser`, the provider lets AD and ADLDS handle tracking of bad passwords. If `enablePasswordReset` is set to true, the provider will also disallow changes to the question and answer if the user account was already locked out because of bad password answers. If `enablePasswordReset` is set to true, the provider resets the password-answer-tracking fields each time a good password is used with this method.

❑   DeleteUser: No directory-specific functionality. Deleting a user is just a straightforward removal of the user from the container determined by the connection string.

❑   FindUsersByEmail: If the provider configuration attribute enableSearchMethod is not set to true, this method will throw a NotSupportedException. You can use the LDAP wildcard character * to perform the equivalent of SQL LIKE queries with this method. See the earlier "Provider Settings for Search" section for details on how the provider performs broad searches against a directory. The MembershipUserCollection that is returned contains instances of the ActiveDirectoryMembershipUser class.

❑   FindUsersByName: If the provider configuration attribute enableSearchMethods is not set to true, this method will throw a NotSupportedException. You can use the LDAP wildcard character (*) to perform the equivalent of SQL LIKE queries with this method. See the earlier "Provider Settings for Search" for details on how the provider performs broad searches against a directory. The MembershipUserCollection that is returned contains instances of the ActiveDirectoryMembershipUser class.

❑   GeneratePassword: This method generates a random password using the same logic used by the SqlMembershipProvider. Internally, this method just calls Membership.GeneratePassword. The important thing to note here is that the provider's ResetPassword method relies on GeneratePassword. However, Membership.GeneratePassword has no awareness of the password complexity policy set for the domain or ADLDS server. As a result, it is possible that the password generated by this method will not pass the directory's password complexity rules. If you encounter this situation, you will need to derive from ActiveDirectoryMembership Provider and override this method with custom logic that generates conforming passwords.

❑   GetAllUsers: If the provider configuration attribute enableSearchMethods is not set to true, this method will throw a NotSupportedException. See the earlier "Provider Settings for Search" section for details on how the provider performs broad searches against a directory. The MembershipUserCollection that is returned contains instances of the ActiveDirectory MembershipUser class.

❑   GetNumberOfUsersOnline: This method always throws a NotSupportedException because the provider does not implement any logic for keeping track of the online state of a user.

❑   GetPassword: This method always throws a NotSupportedException. Even though theoretically you can configure your directory to use reversible encryption, this is not a recommended security practice for AD and ADLDS. The feature team decided not to support this functionality because they did not want to encourage the usage of reversible encryption.

❑   GetUser: Both overloads look for the user object using a subtree search rooted at the container determined from the connection string. In the case of the overload that accepts the provider UserKey parameter, you can supply an instance of System.Security.Principal.Security Identifier to the provider, and it will search for a user with a matching SID in its objectSID attribute. The user object that is returned is an instance of ActiveDirectoryMembershipUser. Both overloads ignore the userIsOnline parameter because the provider does not track the online status of users.

❑   GetUserNameByEmail: Performs a subtree search rooted at the container determined by the connection string for a user with a matching email address. If the requiresUniqueEmail configuration attribute is set to true, and more than one match is found, the provider throws a ProviderException. Otherwise, the provider returns the username from the first matching user object that is found.

❑ ResetPassword: If enablePasswordReset is set to false, the provider just throws a Not SupportedException. The provider disallows password resets for locked-out users, regardless of whether the user was locked out because of too many bad password attempts or too many bad password answer attempts. The provider will automatically keep track of bad password answer attempts using the custom attributes that you configure for the provider. If a valid password answer is supplied in the passwordAnswer parameter, the provider resets the bad-password-answer-tracking attributes in the directory to their default values (the counter and two date-time tracking fields are all set to zero). Assuming that a good password answer is supplied and the user is not locked out, the provider effectively calls IADsUser::SetPassword to reset the password to a randomly generated new password value. See the earlier notes on Generate Password for caveats about the randomly generated password and the directory's password complexity policy.

❑ UnlockUser: Resets the user to an unlocked state. For bad password attempts, this means that the user object's lockoutTime attribute is reset to zero. The bad-password-answer-tracking attributes (both the counter field and the two date-time fields) are also reset to zero. Note that unlike SqlMembershipProvider, after a user is locked out in AD the account will automatically become unlocked, assuming that the account lockout policy in AD and ADLDS has been configured to allow this. As noted earlier, if you are also using the question-and-answer-based password reset, the provider also supports automatically unlocking a user account after a configurable time assuming that the lockout occurred because of too many bad password answers.

❑ UpdateUser: You can pass either a MembershipUser instance or an ActiveDirectory MembershipUser instance to this method. If an ActiveDirectoryMembershipUser instance is provided, the provider will check to see which updatable properties have changed and will only write the subset of changed properties back to the directory. The provider supports updating only the Email, Comment, and IsApproved properties in the UpdateUser method.

❑ ValidateUser: Because the provider always operates within the scope of the container (or container hierarchy) determined by the connection string, the provider makes an extra check in this method. If a valid username-password pair is supplied, then the provider checks to see if the user actually exists within the scope determined from the provider's connection string. If the user does not exist within the directory scope, the method still returns false. For example, if user foo exists in OU=bar, but the provider is pointed at a peer container called OU=baz, then even if the foo account supplies the correct password, the method still will return false because the user account does not exist within OU=bar. The provider relies on the bad password lockout mechanism provided by AD and ADLDS for handling bad password attempts. If a correct password is supplied and enablePasswordReset is set to true, the provider will automatically reset the bad-password-answer-tracking attributes to zero. Because ValidateUser is probably the most heavily called method, you should keep in mind the performance overhead of enabling password resets on this method. If you do not use password resets, this method performs one directory search to verify the user is located within the provider's container scope, and one LDAP bind to actually verify the credentials. If password resets are enabled, then an additional LDAP call is always made to check the password-answer-tracking attributes. If these attributes need to be reset, a second call is made to reset the password-answer-tracking attributes.

The provider also implements the public properties defined by the MembershipProvider base class as well as a few extra directory-specific properties. The directory-specific properties and Membership Provider properties with special behavior are:

❑ ApplicationName: The getter just returns the value set in the provider's configuration. Like SqlMembershipProvider, if this value was not set in configuration it returns either the virtual path of the current web application or the name of the `.exe` (sans the `.exe` extension) that is currently running. Again, this behavior was done just to make the property somewhat consistent with the SQL provider's behavior. Internally, the provider never uses the `ApplicationName` property, and thus the trick of overriding the `ApplicationName` getter to handle dynamic portal-style applications will not work. The setter for this property throws a `NotSupportedException`.

❏ `CurrentConnectionProtection`: This returns the type of connection protection that the provider ultimately settled on. This property *doesn't* return the value of the `connectionProtection` attribute in configuration. Remember that when you set the `connectionProtection` attribute to `Secure` in configuration, the provider still needs to follow its internal heuristics to determine the precise type of connection security it will use. If you set `connectionProtection` to `None`, this property returns the enumeration value `ActiveDirectoryConnectionProtection.None`. If you set `connectionProtection` to `Secure`, then this property will return either `Active DirectoryConnectionProtection.Ssl` or `ActiveDirectoryConnectionProtection. SignAndSeal`, depending on which type of connection security the provider settled on.

❏ `EnablePasswordRetrieval`: Because the provider never supports password retrieval, this property always returns `false`.

❏ `EnableSearchMethods`: Returns the value of the `enableSearchMethods` provider configuration attribute. This allows you to write code that conditionally exposes search logic based on the provider's configuration.

❏ `PasswordAttemptLockoutDuration`: Returns the value of the `passwordAttemptLockout Duration` configuration attribute. If you enabled question-and-answer-based password resets for the provider, then this property indicates the number of minutes after which an account that was locked out because of too many bad password answers will be considered to have automatically unlocked.

❏ `PasswordFormat`: Regardless of whether the underlying directory server has enabled reversible encryption for passwords, this property always returns the value `MembershipPasswordFormat .Hashed`.

ActiveDirectoryMembershipUser

As part of the provider's implementation, it uses a custom derivation of `MembershipUser` called `ActiveDirectoryMembershipUser`. This custom user type serves the following purposes:

❏ It makes the `SecurityIdentifier` that is the `ProviderUserKey` property serializable. Because the Membership feature expects `MembershipUser` instances to be serializable, and the `Security Identifier` class itself is not serializable, the `ActiveDirectoryMembershipUser` has some special logic to translate the `ProviderUserKey` property into a serializable format.

❏ The `LastLoginDate` and `LastActivityDate` properties are overridden to throw `NotSupported Exceptions` from both their getters and setters. This ensures that developers will recognize that user objects returned from AD or ADLDS do not support these property values.

❏ The class implements a constructor that matches the wide constructor overload on the `MembershipUser` base class. The `ActiveDirectoryMemberhipUser` class makes a validation check inside of its constructor to ensure that if a non-null value is supplied

for the `providerUserKey` parameter that it is of type `System.Security.Principal`
`.SecurityIdentifier`.

❑   The custom class overrides the `Email`, `Comment`, and `IsApproved` properties. Inside of the setters the `ActiveDirectoryMembershipUser` class sets internal flags marking each property value as dirty. This is done as a performance optimization to cut down on the need to update properties on the directory server if their original values have not changed. The provider checks the dirty flag for each property inside of its `UpdateUser` implementation. If the `ActiveDirectory` `MembershipUser` instance indicates that a property has changed, then the provider adds it to the set of attributes that will be updated in the directory. Note that the user class considers a call to a property setter as sufficient indication that the property has changed. It does not attempt a value comparison to confirm that the value has really changed. Additionally, the provider does not compare the current value of any of the user properties to the corresponding values in the directory. The provider assumes that if the user class has marked a property as dirty, its value should be written back to the directory.

IsApproved and IsLockedOut

Both the `IsApproved` property and the `IsLockedOut` properties are computed by `ActiveDirectory` `MembershipProvider` when a user object is retrieved from the directory. For the `IsApproved` property, the provider will compute the value as `false` if the user object is marked as disabled in the directory (for example, if you view the user with the AD Users and Computers snap-in, the Account is Disabled check box is checked). If the user object is enabled in the directory, though, then the `IsApproved` property is computed as `true`. In other words, there is a one-to-one correspondence between the value of the `IsApproved` property and the enabled status of the user in AD and ADLDS.

However, this is not the case for the `IsLockedOut` property. If the user was locked because of too many bad password attempts, then both the `IsLockedOut` property and the locked-out status stored in the directory will match. However, if you have enabled question-and-answer-based password resets, it is possible that `IsLockedOut` will return `true` because the user had too many bad password answer attempts. In this case when you look at the user object in the directory (that is, you look at the `msDS-User-Account-Control` `-Computed` attribute in a Windows Server 2003 or Windows Server 2008 AD or an ADLDS directory), the account *won't* show as being locked out.

This also means that a user could attempt to log in to your website, and have the login fail, yet if that same user sits down at her desk, she will be able to successfully log on to her machine. If you have management tools or scripts that query for locked-out users, you will need to update them to also look at the failed password answer lockout time attribute that you have to add to the directory's `user` class when enabling password resets. If the difference between the current UTC time and the lockout time stored in the directory is less than or equal to the lockout duration specified in the provider's `password` `AnswerAttemptLockoutDuration` configuration attribute, then the user should be considered in a locked-out state.

Using the ProviderUserKey Property

The `ActiveDirectoryMembershipUser` class conveniently returns the user's SID in the `Provider` `UserKey` property. If you have other code that manipulates users via their SID, you can use this property, both by reading it for use elsewhere as well as for looking up an `ActiveDirectoryMembershipUser` instance by SID.

The following code outputs the string representation of a user's SID:

C#

```
using System.Security.Principal;
...
//code to retrieve a MembershipUser in the mu variable
...
SecurityIdentifier sid = (SecurityIdentifier)mu.ProviderUserKey;
Response.Write("The user's SID is: " + sid.ToString());
```

VB.NET

```
Imports System.Security.Principal
...
' code to retrieve a MembershipUSer in the mu variable
...
Dim sid As SecurityIdentifier = CType(mu.ProviderUserKey, SecurityIdentifier)
Response.Write("The user's SID is: " & sid.ToString() & "<br/>")
```

The output from this looks like:

```
The user's SID is: S-1-5-21-1582693030-3413920651-2689569351-1110
```

This format is the Security Descriptor Definition Language (SDDL) representation of the `objectSID` attribute on a user object in the directory. You can use the SDDL representation to create your own instance of a `SecurityIdentifier`.

C#

```
//Load a user instance using the SID
string sddlSID = sid.ToString();  //gets the SDDL form
SecurityIdentifier pkey = new SecurityIdentifier(sddlSID);

ActiveDirectoryMembershipUser admu =
    (ActiveDirectoryMembershipUser)Membership.Provider.GetUser(pkey, false);

Response.Write("The username is: " + admu.UserName + "<br/>");
Response.Write("The user's SID is: " +
    ((SecurityIdentifier)admu.ProviderUserKey).ToString());
```

VB.NET

```
'Load a user instance using the SID
Dim sddlSID As String = sid.ToString()
Dim pkey As New SecurityIdentifier(sddlSID)
Dim admu As ActiveDirectoryMembershipUser = _
    CType(Membership.Provider.GetUser(pkey, False), _
    ActiveDirectoryMembershipUser)
Response.Write("The username is: " & admu.UserName & "<br/>")
Response.Write("The user's SID is: " & _
    (CType(admu.ProviderUserKey,SecurityIdentifier)).ToString())
```

This code takes the `SecurityIdentifier` instance that was returned from the previous sample code and converts it into the string SDDL syntax. It then constructs a new instance of a `SecurityIdentifier` passing the SDDL representation to the constructor. The resultant `SecurityIdentifier` is then passed to `ActiveDirectoryMembershipProvider` as the key for looking up a user in the directory. When you run this code you see that with the SDDL version of the SID, you can successfully get back to the original user object:

```
The username is: demouser@bhaidar.net
The user's SID is: S-1-5-21-1582693030-3413920651-2689569351-1110
```

It is worth mentioning at this stage that the above code samples have been tested and executed on a machine with Windows Server 2008 installed and a domain called `bhaidar.net`.

Working with Active Directory

Out of the box, there is a reasonably high likelihood that you can get the provider to start working with an AD domain. Because the first hurdle you will face is the question of connectivity to the directory, getting the correct connection string is important. Luckily, if you know what your options are it is also pretty easy to set up. For starters, you can configure a sample application with the provider that attempts to retrieve a user object from the `Users` container that is found on all domains. Because `ActiveDirectoryMembershipProvider` is not configured in either `machine.config` or the root `web.config` files, you will need to explicitly configure it in `web.config`.

```
<membership defaultProvider="appprovider">
  <providers>
    <clear/>
    <add name="appprovider"
         type="System.Web.Security.ActiveDirectoryMembershipProvider, …"
         connectionStringName="DirectoryConnection" />
  </providers>
</membership>
```

Because none of the other provider-specific configuration options are used, the provider will connect to the directory using the underlying process credentials. This is an important point because it means that, by default, when running on IIS 7.0 the provider will connect to your directory as NETWORK SERVICE (that is, the machine account from the perspective of the directory server). For now, let's use a connection string that looks like:

```
<connectionStrings>
    <add
        name="DirectoryConnection"
        connectionString="LDAP://aspmvp.bhaidar.net"
    />
</connectionStrings>
```

This style of connection string tells the provider to explicitly connect to a specific directory server. Note, though, that there is no other information in the connection string, which means that the provider will automatically attempt to bind to the `Users` container. To see whether this configuration works, a simple test page writes out some of the properties of a user that already exists in the directory:

C#

```
MembershipUser mu = Membership.GetUser("demouser@bhaidar.net");
Response.Write("Email address is: " + mu.Email + "<br/>");
Response.Write("Creation date is: " + mu.CreationDate.ToString() + "<br/>");
```

VB.NET

```
Dim mu As MembershipUser = Membership.GetUser("demouser@bhaidar.net")
Response.Write("Email address is: " & mu.Email & "<br/>")
Response.Write("Creation date is: " & mu.CreationDate.ToString() & "<br/>")
```

When I ran this sample app against a directory server, the following information was returned:

```
Email address is: demouser@bhaidar.net
Creation date is: 4/27/2008 2:33:29 AM
```

This isn't exactly earth-shattering information, but if you think about it, with only some standard configuration entries and some boilerplate Membership code, you are now accessing a user object in a directory. No need for kung-fu coding with classes in the `System.DirectoryServices` namespace, let alone mucking around with the older ADSI programming APIs.

You can make things more interesting by first trying different variations of the connection string. One variation simply points the application at the domain, as opposed to a domain controller.

```
<add name="DirectoryConnection" connectionString="LDAP://bhaidar.net"/>
```

Notice how the connection string no longer points at a specific server. Now the provider is simply leveraging the default connectivity behavior supported by AD where you can just supply the DNS name associated with the domain, and the underlying network stack performs the magic of looking up special directory service entries in DNS to route the request to an actual domain controller.

Although this type of connection string is interesting to know about, and it can be useful in a development environment just to get things up and running, in an extranet environment you need to be careful with this type of connection string. Because you aren't guaranteed a connection to any specific directory controller, you can end up in cases where an operation against a user object occurs against one domain controller, and then at a later point in time the provider connects to a different controller that has not yet received the replicated changes. This behavior is not a bad thing; you just need to be aware of whether your application can tolerate this. The nice thing about a serverless connection string is that your application isn't tied to the uptime of any specific directory server. Instead, the provider will connect to whatever is available, and if a DC goes down then the provider will simply be routed to a different server.

Another connection string variation (and probably the most common one you will use) includes the container name.

```
<add
  name="DirectoryConnection"
  connectionString="LDAP://aspmvp.bhaidar.net/CN=Users,DC=bhaidar,DC=net"
/>
```

With this connection string, the provider will bind to the container specified after the server name. In this case, the connection string is binding to the Users container. If you have ever used ADSI or System .DirectoryServices, this should be a familiar syntax to you for binding to the Users container.

If you use the provider in an extranet environment where different user populations are segmented into different organizational units (that is, OUs), then you would use a connection string like the following:

```
<add
  name="DirectoryConnection"
  connectionString="LDAP://aspmvp.bhaidar.net/OU=UserPopulation_A,DC=bhaidar,DC=net"
/>
```

Now instead of referencing a built-in container, the connection string references an OU that was created in the domain. In this case, the OU is a peer of the Users container. However, you can just as easily bind to OUs that are nested any number of levels deep.

```
<add
  name="DirectoryConnection"
  connectionString="LDAP://aspmvp.bhaidar.net/OU=SomeNestedOU,OU=UserPopulation_A,DC
=bhaidar,DC=net"
/>
```

For nested containers, you just build up the second part of the connection string with the walk-up path from the nested OU to the top of the container hierarchy.

UPNs and SAM Account Names

In the previous examples, the provider was implicitly binding to the directory and looking for user objects based on the user principal name. In my test directory, I always created a UPN for each new user, so the provider can find user objects and bind to them. For older directory infrastructures, though, user principal names may not be in wide use, or they may not even be used at all. The provider supports binding to user objects using the sAMAccountName attribute instead. However, you need to explicitly configure this behavior. The configuration for the provider using a SAM account name looks like:

```
<add name="appprovider"
  type="System.Web.Security.ActiveDirectoryMembershipProvider, …"
  attributeMapUsername="sAMAccountName"
  connectionStringName="DirectoryConnection" />
```

With this configuration, the provider expects that any usernames passed to its methods will be *just the username* portion of the NT4-style DOMAIN\USERNAME format. For example, the following code retrieves the user object for bhaidar\demouser:

```
MembershipUser mu = Membership.GetUser("demouser");
```

Notice how the username parameter *doesn't* include the domain identifier. This is important because if you attempt to pass full NT4-style usernames to the provider, the calls will never return anything (that is, if you pass DOMAIN\USERNAME the provider is literally looking for a user object whose SAM account name is DOMAIN\USERNAME). Because the provider already knows the domain within which it is operating, it does not need the domain portion of the username. Remember that the provider is effectively acting like a database provider, except that the "database" is really an LDAP server. When the provider looks for objects using a SAM account name, it is performing an LDAP search where the sAMAccount Name attribute on the directory's user object equals a specific value. As a result, you only need to supply the username.

If you happen to set up ActiveDirectoryMembershipProvider, and you are unable to retrieve any existing users, keep in mind the attributeMapUsername attribute. It is likely that if the connection string works and you are getting back nulls from methods like GetUser, than your directory users have been configured only with SAM account names, not UPNs. Switching attributeMapUsername over to sAMAccountName is probably the most common configuration step that developers need to make to get the provider working with their directory.

However, if you have been creating user accounts in the directory using the ActiveDirectoryMembership Provider with its default setting of UPN-style usernames, you may run into a different problem. When you create users in the Active Directory Users and Computers MMC, the UI conveniently auto-selects a domain suffix for your UPN. In fact, the UI remembers previous UPN suffixes that have been used with the tool, and it displays a drop-down list where you can choose any one of them. However, if you create users directly with the provider, you may find yourself creating users with just a username and no suffix (for example, "demouser98" as opposed to "demouser98@bhaidar.net"). This kind of a UPN will sort of work with Active Directory, but you will find that if you also write code with System.DirectoryServices there are cases where a UPN without an @ will fail. As a result, you should always ensure that UPNs have an @ sign and some kind of domain suffix in them. For Internet-facing sites, it makes sense to create user accounts with some kind of domain suffix, with the user's email address being the most likely candidate.

This raises the question of whether you should eventually switch your user population over to UPNs. Although as far back as Windows 2000, the guidance was to create users with UPNs, the reality is that many folks still rely on the older NT4-style usernames, especially if their current domain infrastructure was the result of an NT4 domain upgrade. I certainly wouldn't recommend reworking your user population to use UPNs just because ActiveDirectoryMembershipProvider defaults to UPNs. (That's why the username mapping is configurable!) However, it does seem to be a recurring theme that UPNs are architecturally preferable. For e-commerce sites or extranet sites that rely on Active Directory, UPNs do make more sense because, typically, you don't want external users to be aware of AD domain names. Technically, external sites that do this are leaking a little bit of their security architecture to the public by requiring a domain name. Also UPNs frequently mirror a person's email address, so they can be a more natural username for your website users to grasp.

Container Nesting

You already saw a simple example where nested OUs were used in a connection string. However, container nesting raises some interesting issues when working with the provider. If you have different sets of users in different OUs, and you want some provider operations to span all these sets of users, how do you go about configuring the provider? Remember that data modification operations can occur only in the container specified by the connection string, whereas search-oriented operations are rooted at the container specified by the connection string.

Using the sample directory structure, so far there are users laid out as follows:

```
Cn=Users
    demouser
OU=UserPopulation_A
```

```
demouserpop
OU=SomeNestedOU
        demousernestedpop
```

If you use the following connection string:

```
<add name="DirectoryConnection" connectionString="LDAP://aspmvp.bhaidar.net"/>
```

then all search operations are rooted at what is called the default naming context for the domain. What this means is that all containers and OUs are considered children of the default naming context, so this type of connection string allows searches to be performed across all available containers. Because the provider performs its search operations using subtree searches, the following code searches across all containers, as well as down through the container hierarchy to its lowest nested level:

C#

```
MembershipUserCollection muc = Membership.GetAllUsers();
foreach (MembershipUser mu in muc)
    Response.Write("Username: " + mu.UserName + "<br />");
```

VB.NET

```
Dim muc As MembershipUserCollection = Membership.GetAllUsers()
For Each mu As MembershipUser In muc
    Response.Write("Username: " & mu.UserName & "<br />")
Next mu
```

The result from running this code is:

Username: demouser@bhaidar.net
Username: demousernestedpop@bhaidar.net
Username: demouserpop@bhaidar.net
Username: reader@bhaidar.net
Username: useradmin@bhaidar.net

The bolded identities are the three accounts used earlier in the chapter. The demouser account as well as all the other unbolded user accounts are located in the CN=Users container. The other two demouser* accounts are from OU=UserPopulation_A and OU=SomeNestedOU.

Similarly, if you perform get operations such as:

C#

```
MembershipUser mu = Membership.GetUser("demousernestedpop@bhaidar.net ");
```

VB.NET

```
Dim mu As MembershipUser = Membership.GetUser("demousernestedpop@bhaidar.net")
```

The code will return a valid user object because even though the user account is nested two OUs deep, the Get* methods on the provider start their search at the default naming context (because the connection string from earlier doesn't specify a container) and then work their way down. If you explicitly specify a container hierarchy in your connection string, then get and search methods will be rooted at the container you specify and then searches will work their way down through any remaining container hierarchy.

However, if you attempt to create a new user or delete an existing user, then these operations only occur in the container specified on the connection string. In the case of the sample connection string that doesn't explicitly specify a container, this means that user creation and deletion only occur in the CN=Users container. There are other provider methods that involve modifying information for a user, including UpdateUser, ChangePassword, and so on. Although these methods are technically data-modification operations, all these methods first bind to a specific user in the directory (a get operation) prior to making a change. As a result, updates to existing users also have the behavior of being rooted at a specific point in the directory, and then searching for the user object down through the nested containers.

With this behavior, it is possible to come up with some interesting provider configurations. For example, if your site supports multiple sets of users, you could allocate each set of users to a different OU. You could then configure a separate provider instance for each different OU (and hence each provider instance would have its own unique connection string). These different providers could be used exclusively for create and delete operations. For the rest of your site, you could then configure one more provider pointed at the default naming context or at a root OU, depending on how you structured your containers. This last provider would be used for things like calling ValidateUser or for fetching a MembershipUser object to display information on a page. In this way, you would get the flexibility to create and delete users in different OUs, while still having the convenience of searching, retrieving, and modifying users across the OUs with a single provider.

Securing Containers

So far, the sample code has been running with the credentials of the IIS 7.0 worker process. The reason that the samples have worked so far is that the NETWORK SERVICE account is implicitly considered part of the Authenticated Users group. If you look at the default security configuration in the directory, you will see that this group has rights to list objects in a container as well as having some read permissions on individual object. The concept of read permissions on objects though differs depending on the object in question.

In the case of the provider, the object types you care about are user objects. The default permissions that any authenticated user in a domain has on any other user object in the directory are read general information, read personal information, read web information, and read public information. General information, personal information, web information, and public information are just property sets that conveniently group together dozens of different directory attributes so that permissions can be granted to them without having to spam dozens or hundreds of ACLs on user objects. These default permissions are why the sample pages running as NETWORK SERVICE were able to find the user object in the first place and then read the various directory attributes in order to construct an instance of ActiveDirectoryMembershipUser.

If you attempt to use the sample configuration shown earlier to update an existing user object or create a new user object, you will get a System.UnauthorizedAccessException. The exception bubbles up from the underlying System.DirectoryServices API and is triggered because, for obvious reasons, authenticated domain users don't have the right to arbitrarily make data modifications to other objects or containers in the directory. This behavior is roughly equivalent to the exceptions you get when you haven't granted login rights to SQL Server or execute permissions to the Membership stored procedures and you attempt to use the `SqlMembershipProvider`.

One obvious solution would be to just add rights in the directory granting NETWORK SERVICE the required rights. However, in general this is not the correct approach. Each machine in a domain has a corresponding machine account in the directory. Because the account is comparatively well known, granting broad rights to it is not something you should do. Additionally, if you are running in a web farm, each individual server has a different machine account in the directory that locally is known as NETWORK SERVICE. So if you granted broad rights to the machine account, you would have to repeat this task for each and every server running in your web farm.

A better approach would be to at least assign your application's worker process a different domain identity and then grant this domain identity the necessary rights in the directory depending on what your code needs to do with the provider. With this approach, if you run multiple machines in a web farm, each web server can be configured with the same domain account for the worker process. For a lot of application scenarios, this is actually a reasonable approach. However, if you need to host multiple applications in a single worker process, with each application having a different set of privileges in the directory, or if you want to configure multiple providers in a single application with each provider having a different set of privileges, then you will need to use explicit provider credentials instead.

The `ActiveDirectoryMembershipProvider` exposes the `connectionUsername` and `connection Password` configuration attributes. With these attributes, you can explicitly set the domain credentials that the provider will use when connecting to the directory. Even though the default provider behavior is to revert to either the process credentials, or application impersonation credentials if application impersonation is being used, when explicit credentials are configured the provider always uses them in lieu of any other security identity.

The advantage of using explicit credentials in combination with application-specific OUs (as opposed to just using the `Users` container) is that you have the ability to specify granular permissions for different sets of application users. With the provider configuration attributes you then have the flexibility to fine-tune individual providers to allow only certain operations through specific providers. Let's see how this works by creating a new admin account to work with the `UserPopulation_A` container: `userpopaadmin`. You want this account to have the ability to create and delete user objects, as well as the ability to reset passwords and unlock users.

Remember that for a provider instance to be able to create users, it also needs the ability to delete users (in the event that the multistep user creation process failed) and to set passwords (because part of the process of creating the user is setting password). Note that the ability to set passwords for new accounts as well as reset existing passwords is shown as the Reset Password inside of the security dialog boxes shown in the MMC.

The Active Directory Users and Computers MMC has a Delegation of Control Wizard that steps you through delegating control over containers like the OUs used here. You can open up the MMC to display all the containers that are currently available in a directory. In the test directory I am running, right-clicking the UserPopulation_A container and selecting Delegate Control opens the first step of the wizard, as shown in Figure 13-1.

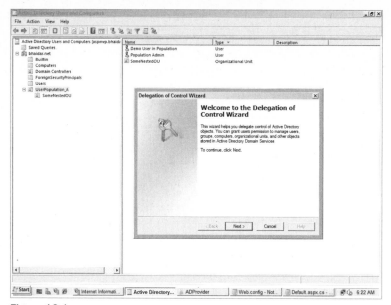

Figure 13-1

In the next wizard step, you can select one or more user/group accounts that will all be granted a specific set of rights over the OU. In Figure 13-2, you can see that I have selected the `userpopaadmin` account.

On the next step of the wizard, you can select multiple rights to grant to the accounts. Because you want the admin account to have the ability to create/delete users, reset passwords, and unlock users, the first three sets of tasks are selected in the wizard (see Figure 13-3).

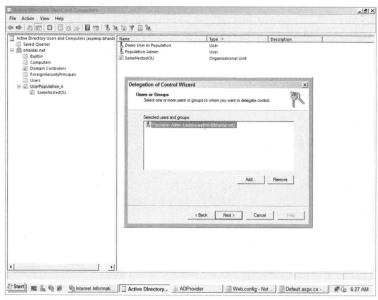

Figure 13-2

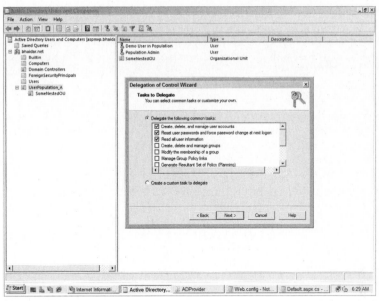

Figure 13-3

The final step of the wizard (not shown) just asks for confirmation of the selections. When you click the Finish button on the last wizard step, the security changes take effect. You can see the new set of security rights if you right-click the `UserPopulation_A` OU and then drill into the security settings for `userpopaadmin`. Figure 13-4 shows the two sets of rights highlighted in the Advanced Security Settings dialog box.

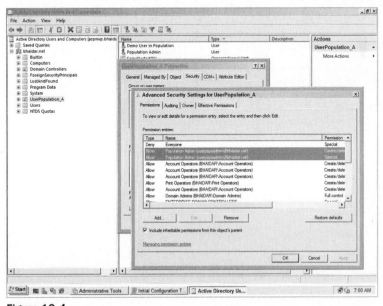

Figure 13-4

Notice that the account now has Full Control on any user objects in the container as well as the Create/Delete User Objects privilege on the container. The account needs to have two different sets of rights because the intent is for the `userpopaadmin` account to have a set of specific user object rights within the container as well as the ability to add and remove user objects in the container. Notice that the account *doesn't* have Full Control on the container itself. This allows other object types that are managed by other user accounts to be stored in the container.

If you highlight the Full Control row and click the Edit button, you will see the set of permissions that `userpopaadmin` now has on any user object located in the container. Specifically, it has Write All Properties permission as well as the Reset Password and Change Password permissions. These permissions will allow `userpopaadmin` the ability to set all of the properties on a newly created user object (including the password property) as well as the ability to reset the password when the `ResetPassword` method is called on the provider. These permissions also allow the account to be used when calling the `Update` method because this method updates a number of different properties on a user object in the directory.

With the security configuration for the admin user complete, you can make use of it to connect to the directory with a connection string which points directly at the OU:

```
<add
 name="DirectoryConnection"
 connectionString="LDAP://aspmvp.bhaidar.net/OU=UserPopulation_A,DC=bhaidar,DC=net"
/>
```

In this example, you configure two providers: one for admin operations and one for get/search operations:

```
<membership defaultProvider="readonlyprovider">
 <providers>
   <clear/>
   <add name="adminprovider"
        type="System.Web.Security.ActiveDirectoryMembershipProvider, …"
        enableSearchMethods="true"
        connectionUsername="userpopaadmin@bhaidar.net"
        connectionPassword="p@ssw0rd"
        connectionStringName="DirectoryConnection" />

   <add name="readonlyprovider"
        type="System.Web.Security.ActiveDirectoryMembershipProvider, …"
        enableSearchMethods="true"
        connectionStringName="DirectoryConnection" />
 </providers>
</membership>
```

The provider named `adminprovider` uses the explicit credentials with elevated privileges. The second provider instance named `readonlyprovider` depends on the default rights that the Authenticated Users group has to read various attributes on a user object. Note that in a production environment you should use protected configuration (discussed in Chapter 5) so that the explicit credentials are not stored as cleartext. You can now create users with the admin provider:

C#

```
MembershipCreateStatus status;
MembershipProvider mp = Membership.Providers["adminprovider"];

mp.CreateUser("demouser103@nowhere.org", "pass!word1", "demouser103@nowhere.org",
              null, null, true, null, out status);
Response.Write(status.ToString());
```

VB.NET

```
Dim status As MembershipCreateStatus
Dim mp As MembershipProvider = Membership.Providers("adminprovider")

mp.CreateUser("demouser103@nowhere.org", "pass!word1", _
    "demouser103@nowhere.org",Nothing, _
    Nothing, True, Nothing, status)
```

Read operations use the default provider running as NETWORK SERVICE, and thus the default provider can only search for users and read attributes on the `user` object. Note that you can take security lockdown a step further by removing the Authenticated Users ACL from the default ACL defined for the `user` class in the directory's schema. Doing so gets into the nitty-gritty of managing Active Directory default ACLs, which is a bit far afield from the topic of how to use `ActiveDirectoryMembership Provider`.

However, if you have changed the default ACL for the user object (you can see the default ACL using the Active Directory Schema editor, look at the Default Security tab on the Properties dialog box of the `user` class) by removing the Authenticated Users group, you can create a read-only user account using the same approach just shown for the administrative user. Just create a new read-only user account and, with the Delegation of Control Wizard, grant read permissions on all user objects in the container to the account. Because the wizard will end up granting read permissions on all attributes of user objects, you can right-click the container and use the Security tab to fine-tune the specific sets of user attributes that you really want the read-only account to have access to. The default set of permissions granted to the Authenticated Users account as described earlier is a good starting point.

Configuring Self-Service Password Reset

Self-service password resets are the one piece of provider functionality that is not "auto-magically" supported without a moderate amount of intervention on your part. Unlike `SqlMembershipProvider`, where this functionality is just a matter of setting the `enablePasswordReset` configuration attribute to `true`, `ActiveDirectoryMembershipProvider` requires schema changes prior to turning on the functionality. Furthermore, after the schema changes are made you need to configure the ACLs appropriately in the directory so that a provider has rights to read and update these properties.

You could use preexisting directory attributes to store password question-and-answer-related information. Although this saves you from having to modify the directory schema, from a long-term perspective it makes more sense to extend the schema with attributes to support the provider, rather than attempt to reuse existing directory attributes. This will prevent problems down the road if you overloaded a directory attribute for use with the provider, but then find out you actually need to "take back" the attribute for its original purposes.

The attributes that you need to add are those for the following pieces of information:

❑ **Password question:** A Unicode string attribute to store the user's password question.

❑ **Password answer:** A Unicode string attribute to store the user's password answer.

❑ **Failed password answer count:** An attribute of type `Integer` that is the counter for keeping track of the number of failed password answer attempts.

❑ **Failed password answer time:** An attribute of type `Large Integer/Interval` that will store the beginning of the time tracking window for failed password answer attempts.

❑ **Failed password answer lockout time:** An attribute of type `Large Integer/Interval` that stores the time the account was locked out because of too many failed password answer attempts.

You can use the Active Directory Schema snap-in to create five new attributes for storing these values. Before you do so, note that you have to have rights to edit the schema for your domain. This right is normally reserved for members of the Schema Admins group because of the sensitive nature of schema edits. Schema edits are a one-way affair; after you add an attribute, you can never actually delete it. Instead, you can only deactivate attributes. For this reason, enabling self-service password reset for the provider makes sense only for Internet facing websites that rely on Active Directory. Making irreversible schema edits to an extranet directory is less of an issue than making schema edits to your core corporate directories.

Whenever you create a new directory attribute you need to have a name for the attribute as well as an X.500 OID. The need for the OID is sort of weird, but it is a necessary part of creating any new classes or attributes in Active Directory. If you happen to have the Windows 2000 Resource Kit lying around, it has a handy command-line tool called `oidgen.exe` that will automatically generate a base OID for new attributes. I created five new attributes in my directory as follows:

Attribute Name (Both LDAP and Common)	OID
ampPasswordQuestion	1.2.840.113556.1.4.7000.233.28688.28684.8.311583.60825.551176.463623.1
ampPasswordAnswer	1.2.840.113556.1.4.7000.233.28688.28684.8.311583.60825.551176.463623.2
ampFailedPasswordAnswerCount	1.2.840.113556.1.4.7000.233.28688.28684.8.311583.60825.551176.463623.3
ampFailedPasswordAnswerTime	1.2.840.113556.1.4.7000.233.28688.28684.8.311583.60825.551176.463623.4
ampFailedPasswordAnswerLockoutTime	1.2.840.113556.1.4.7000.233.28688.28684.8.311583.60825.551176.463623.5

You can see what configuring the new password answer attribute looks like in Figure 13-5.

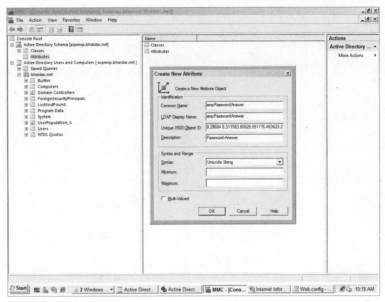

Figure 13-5

The configuration for the password question attribute looks exactly the same. Figure 13-6 shows how the password answer count attribute is configured as an `Integer` type.

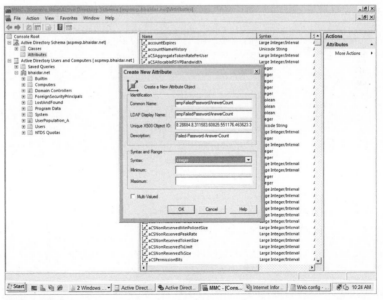

Figure 13-6

The configuration of the failed password answer time attribute is shown in Figure 13-7.

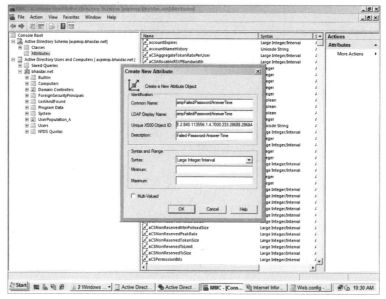

Figure 13-7

Configuring the failed password answer lockout time works the same way, just with a different attribute name and OID.

With the attribute configuration completed, you can add these attributes to the user class in the directory. You just right-click the user class in the MMC, select Properties and in the Attributes tab, add the five new attributes as optional attributes. After you have done this, the Attributes tab will look something like Figure 13-8.

Now that the user object has been modified to include extra attributes for storing password-reset-related information, you can configure a provider to make use of the new attributes. Using the administrative provider shown earlier, you can modify its configuration to allow for question-and-answer-based password resets.

```
<<add
  name="adminprovider"
  type="System.Web.Security.ActiveDirectoryMembershipProvider, System.Web,
  Version=2.0.0.0, Culture=neutral, PublicKeyToken=b03f5f7f11d50a3a"
  enableSearchMethods="true"
  connectionUsername="userpopaadmin@bhaidar.net"
  connectionPassword="p@ssw0rd"
  attributeMapPasswordQuestion="ampPasswordQuestion"
  attributeMapPasswordAnswer="ampPasswordAnswer"
  attributeMapFailedPasswordAnswerCount="ampFailedPasswordAnswerCount"
  attributeMapFailedPasswordAnswerTime="ampFailedPasswordAnswerTime"
  attributeMapFailedPasswordAnswerLockoutTime="ampFailedPasswordAnswerLockoutTime"
  enablePasswordReset="false"
```

```
    requiresQuestionAndAnswer="true"
    connectionStringName="DirectoryConnection"
/>
        enablePasswordReset="false"
        requiresQuestionAndAnswer="true"
        connectionStringName="DirectoryConnection"
/>
```

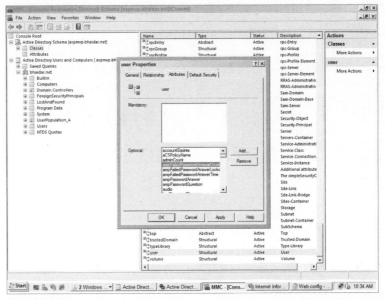

Figure 13-8

Because the provider now has to store a password answer, and you don't want the plaintext password answer to be easily viewable by arbitrary accounts (such as Authenticated Users), the provider always *encrypts* the password answer. Unless you derive from the provider and add your own custom encryption routines, this means that the provider encrypts the password answer using the encryption key specified in machine.config. Just like SqlMembershipProvider, though, ActiveDirectoryMembershipProvider requires you to explicitly set a decryption key. This requirement exists to prevent the problem that would occur if different machines have completely different auto-generated encryption keys. If this were allowed the password answer created on one web server would be useless on another server.

The hashing of the password answer is not supported, because there is no mechanism for having Active Directory hash anything other than a user's password. Rather than confuse things by adding a passwordFormat attribute on the provider that would be configurable for password answers and have no effect on the actual password, the feature team decided to support encryption of password answers only. In this way, there is no ambiguity around the protections for user passwords (AD hashes them) as opposed to the protections for password answers (they are always encrypted).

As a result of this requirement, the sample application now explicitly defines a decryption key as follows:

```
<machineKey
        decryptionKey="A225194E99BCCB0F6B92BC9D82F12C2907BD07CF069BC8B4"
        decryption="AES"  />
```

With the changes to the admin provider and the definition of a fixed decryption key, the sample application can now create users with question and answers. Because the Login controls work seamlessly with arbitrary membership providers, I just dropped a `CreateUserWizard` onto a form, configured it to use the admin provider, and started creating test accounts with questions and answers.

After creating a user with `CreateUserWizard`, you can dump the contents of the user object with a low-level tool like `ldp.exe` or the ADSI Edit MMC. Running `ldp.exe` and looking at the contents of the newly created user, you can see the following:

```
Dn:
    CN=demouser98,OU=UserPopulation_A,DC=bhaidar,DC=net
ampPasswordAnswer:
    DFHsKJYPjy8H8VWdAxifk07ystxUyICny/pzCRONJw45ZVY/pYNlm4XcLlRlW6Zw;
ampPasswordQuestion:
    what is my username?;
distinguishedName:
    CN=demouser98,OU=UserPopulation_A,DC=bhaidar,DC=net;
mail:
    demouser98@bhaidar.net;
name:
    demouser98;
objectCategory:
    CN=Person,CN=Schema,CN=Configuration,DC=bhaidar,DC=net;
objectSid:
    S-1-5-21-1582693030-3413920651-2689569351-1133;
sAMAccountName:
    $AOEH63-9E39GDNR1GC0;
userPrincipalName:
    demouser98;
whenCreated:
    4/27/2008 12:10:23 PM Pacific Daylight Time;
```

As you would expect after all of the configuration work, the password question was successfully stored, as was the encrypted version of the password answer.

If you keep using the `adminprovider` provider, you can create a test page where you attempt to reset the password using the `PasswordRecovery` control. If you intentionally supply the wrong answer a few times, you will see the tracking information stored in the other attributes of the user object.

```
ampFailedPasswordAnswerCount: 3;
ampFailedPasswordAnswerTime: 128537972320482544;
```

These attributes are showing that so far three failed password answer attempts have been made. The weird-looking password answer time is just the integer representation of the UTC date-time that is the start of the bad password answer tracking window. Because the default number of failed password answer attempts that can be made is five (the same setting as `SqlMembershipProvider`), after the fifth bad password attempt occurs, the tracking information for the user looks like this:

```
ampPasswordQuestion:
    what is my username?;
ampPasswordAnswer:
    DFHsKJYPjy8H8VWdAxifk07ystxUyICny/pzCRONJw45ZVY/pYNlm4XcLlRlW6Zw;
```

```
ampFailedPasswordAnswerCount:
    5;
ampFailedPasswordAnswerTime:
    128537973410049264;
ampFailedPasswordAnswerLockoutTime:
    128537973410049264;
```

Any attempt at this point to log in with the user's credentials, change his password, or reset his password will immediately fail because the provider sees that user is now locked out. As with the failed password answer time, the lockout time is stored as an integer representing the UTC time when the lockout occurred. Remember that one difference between this provider and the SQL provider is that if you wait 30 minutes (the default lockout timeout duration if one is configured for the domain), then the user account auto-unlocks despite the previous failed password answer attempts.

Of course, if you are impatient, you can use the Unlock method on the provider to forcibly unlock the user:

C#

```
MembershipProvider mp = Membership.Providers["adminprovider"];
mp.UnlockUser("demouser98@bhaidar.net");
```

VB.NET

```
Dim mp As MembershipProvider = Membership.Providers("adminprovider")
mp.UnlockUser("demouser98@bhaidar.net")
```

The result of unlocking the user with the admin provider looks like this:

```
ampPasswordQuestion:
    what is my username?;
ampPasswordAnswer:
    DFHsKJYPjy8H8VWdAxifk07ystxUyICny/pzCRONJw45ZVY/pYNlm4XcLlRlW6Zw;
ampFailedPasswordAnswerCount:
    0;
ampFailedPasswordAnswerTime:
    0;
ampFailedPasswordAnswerLockoutTime:
    0;
```

After an unlocking operation, the provider resets the count to zero and also stores a zero value in the two time-tracking fields. At this point, if you choose to reset the password, the new password will be sent to you. As a side note, if you want to get the PasswordRecoveryControl to work on a web server that has the default SMTP service installed, you will need a configuration entry like the following:

```
<system.net>
  <mailSettings>
    <smtp deliveryMethod="PickupDirectoryFromIis">
      <network host="localhost" port="25" defaultCredentials="true"/>
    </smtp>
  </mailSettings>
</system.net>
```

Without this entry, the `PasswordRecoveryControl` will fail when it attempts to email the password. In the case of my sample application, because I reset the email address of my test user account to match the domain address of my web server (that is, the `demouser98@bhaidar.net` account now has an email address of `demouser98@aspmvp.bhaidar.net` and my local SMTP server is running on a machine with the DNS address of `aspmvp.bhaidar.net`), the `PasswordRecoveryControl` sent the password reset email to my local mailroot directory, `C:\inetpub\mailroot\`. The text of the email looks like:

```
Please return to the site and log in using the following information.
User Name: demouser98@bhaidar.net
Password: NfRDSzlDsi*DVR
```

This entire process shows the power of the provider model used in conjunction with `ActiveDirectory MembershipProvider` and the various Login controls. Although the initial schema edits in the directory are a bit of a hassle, after those are completed you can see that with some edits to `web.config` to configure the Membership provider and the mail server, the self-service password reset process is pretty much automated. Attempting to hand-code a similar solution yourself, especially using Active Directory (or ADLDS for that matter) as the backing store, would be substantially more complex than the process you just walked through.

Note that I intentionally used the admin provider because that provider was running with security credentials in the directory necessary to allow it to reset the password of any user in the `UserPopulation_A` OU. Clearly, running with the other named provider (`readonlyprovider`) won't work for resetting passwords because the Authenticated Users group doesn't have the privileges necessary to reset arbitrary user passwords.

Within the `ActiveDirectoryMembershipProvider`, methods like `ValidateUser`, `ChangePassword`, `ChangePasswordQuestionAndAnswer` and `GetUser` will be able to read the new password answer tracking fields to determine whether the user is considered locked out. This holds true for the special administrative account that was created earlier, as well the NETWORK SERVICE account that is being used by the default provider. This behavior is okay because you want the failed-password-answer-tracking information to be readable by these methods.

There is a subtle requirement, though, for the `ValidateUser` and `ChangePassword` methods. Both of these methods will reset the password-answer-tracking information if the following conditions are met:

❑ The user supplies the correct password.

❑ The password-answer-tracking information contains nondefault values due to previously logged bad password answer attempts.

If both of these conditions are met, then the provider will reset the password answer tracking counters inside of `ValidateUser` and `ChangePassword`. For this reason, if you setup a nonadministrative account to handle user logins, make sure to grant this account write access to the three bad-password-answer-tracking attributes.

However, if you feel uncomfortable with running a nonadministrative provider under the default privileges of Authenticated Users, you can lock things further. For example, to prevent a nonadministrative provider from ever being able to read the encrypted password answer, you can go through the following steps to lock down access.

1. Create a read-only account that will be used by the nonadministrative provider to access the OU.

2.   Configure a nonadministrative provider instance to run with the read-only user account, just as was done for the administrative provider that we have been using.

3.   In the Active Directory Users and Computers MMC, configure the read-only account by denying specific granular user object property rights.

Figure 13-9 shows a special read-only user account being configured.

Notice how the ability to *read* and *write* the encrypted password answer field is being revoked from the `userpopareader` account. The password answer field needs to be readable only for accounts that fetch the answer from the directory for comparison with the answer typed in by a user. For `Active DirectoryMembershipProvider`, this only occurs when calling `ResetPassword`, so only the administrative account that was configured earlier needs read access on this attribute. Write access to the password answer attribute is only necessary for methods that the update this information. The only methods on `ActiveDirectoryMembershipProvider` where these updates occur are `CreateUser` (where the question and answer are initially created) and `ChangePasswordQuestionAndAnswer` (where the question and answer are updated). For this reason, it makes sense to have a separate provider instance (like the administrative provider used in the examples in this chapter) configured for creating users, updating questions and answers and carrying out password resets.

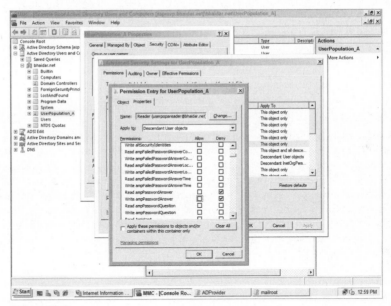

Figure 13-9

Using ADLDS

From the `ActiveDirectoryMembershipProvider`'s perspective, using ADLDS as a backing store is pretty much the same as using Active Directory as the backing store. ADLDS's schema supports the `user` class, and just as with Active Directory, you can extend the schema in ADLDS if you choose to enable self-service password resets. In terms of directory structure, you can use the same general approaches for both AD and ADLDS: using a single container for storing users, or separate user containers for different applications. The behavior around user creation/deletion as opposed to other operations works the same way in ADLDS as well (that is, creation and deletion always occur in the container pointed at by the connection string, whereas searches and operations that bind to a user start at the root of the specified container and then wend their way down through the container hierarchy looking for a match). If you are wondering, ADLDS encompasses the same functionality of the ADAM that was available for Windows Server 2003 and Windows XP.

The differences you will encounter when using ADLDS as a directory store with the provider are:

❑   You can choose to run ADLDS on a machine that is not joined to a domain. This will probably not be common for folks that run a lot of Windows Server machines, but it would be familiar to UNIX shops that just need to talk to an LDAP server and do not need the security mechanisms supported by an AD domain infrastructure.

❑   ADLDS can be installed multiple times on a single machine, with separate ADLDS installations running on different ports. Unlike AD, this means you can install ADLDS to listen on something other than port 389 (if using non-SSL connections) or port 636 (if using SSL connections).

❑   For an ADLDS server that is part of a domain, you can connect to the ADLDS instance using either a domain principal or an ADLDS principal. An ADLDS principal is simply a user account that only exists inside of the ADLDS instance and is unknown in the general AD directory.

❑   You need to manually set up ADLDS properly to store the data needed by the provider. With that said, you can go through the GUI installer for ADLDS and have it perform 95% of the setup work for you. If you do not get the GUI portion of the install correct, though, you have to use the dsmgmt.exe command-line tool that comes with ADLDS to manually create an application partition for use by your application.

❑   Quite honestly, security management of ADLDS is either much simpler or much more complicated depending on which approach you take to securing your application data. You can take the simple approach where you use the application identity of your worker process (or application impersonation identity if you choose) and make it an administrator in an ADLDS partition. This gives your web servers easy access to read and write data via ActiveDirectoryMembership Provider. On the other hand, you can follow the lockdown approaches described in the previous section on Active Directory where you grant specific rights to specific accounts (for example, admin accounts versus read-only accounts) and then use different provider instances for different operations. The snag with this approach is that the administrative tool for modifying ADLDS ACLs is quite simply abominable for anyone who is not directory savvy (and I definitely do not fall in the directory guru camp!). You have to use the command-line dsacls.exe tool that comes with ADLDS to manually ACL your application containers. This same process with Active Directory can be a little intimidating, but the MMC management tools for AD help you through the process. No such GUI tool support currently exists for ADLDS. With that said, if you feel comfortable manually ACL'ing containers in ADLDS, you can definitely use that approach to narrow the privileges granted to different accounts.

❑   Connectivity to the ADLDS instance is either in the clear or over an SSL connection. Active DirectoryMembershipProvider does not support any type of connection security other than SSL. Of course, you can always use lower-level security measures such as IPsec, but that level of network security functions at a lower level and is transparent to both the provider and the LDAP networking stack.

Because using ADLDS has a bit of a different flavor from using Active Directory, you will see some common steps described in this section so that you get an idea of how to get an application partition installed properly. After you see how to get to that point, you will look at connecting to the ADLDS store and carrying out basic provider operations against the directory store.

Installing ADLDS with an Application Partition

The first thing you need to accomplish is the installation of an ADLDS instance that the provider can connect to. Unlike Active Directory, where you already have a server running with the default Users container, with ADLDS you are starting from scratch. The first step is to add the Active Directory Lightweight Directory Services role on Windows Server 2008. Once the role is added, you will notice a new snap-in in the Administrative Tools named Active Directory Lightweight Directory Services Setup Wizard. This is the setup you will use to install the ADLDS on the machine. The installer walks you through a number of wizard steps for setting up an ADLDS instance. The first important step in the installation process is the naming the ADLDS instance. This is important when you work with ADLDS through a tool like the services control panel, but the service name itself has no impact when using the provider. Figure 13-10 shows the wizard step where you name the ADLDS instance.

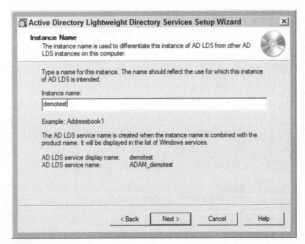

Figure 13-10

One of the next wizard steps lets you choose the port numbers for SSL and non-SSL communications. If this is the only ADLDS instance that will be running on the server, and the server is also not an AD domain controller (in which case AD already owns ports 389 and 636), you can just leave the default port selections as is.

Later on in the wizard, there is a step where you create an application partition. This is important because it determines the first part of the distinguished name that you will use in the connection string. Because ADLDS directories are their own little world, you can use any type of distinguished name that makes sense. However, if you plan to create organizational units within this application partition, you are limited to specific types of objects in the distinguished name that you choose. In Figure 13-11, you can see that I chose a distinguished name that ends in an organization because organizations in ADLDS can contain OUs.

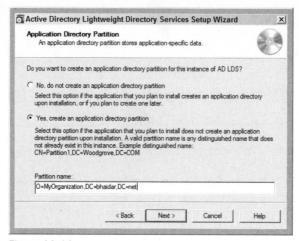

Figure 13-11

One of the steps in the wizard is to select the service account that ADLDS will use to perform operations. By default it uses the default Windows service account. For this installation, I will be satisfied with the default account, as shown in Figure 13-12.

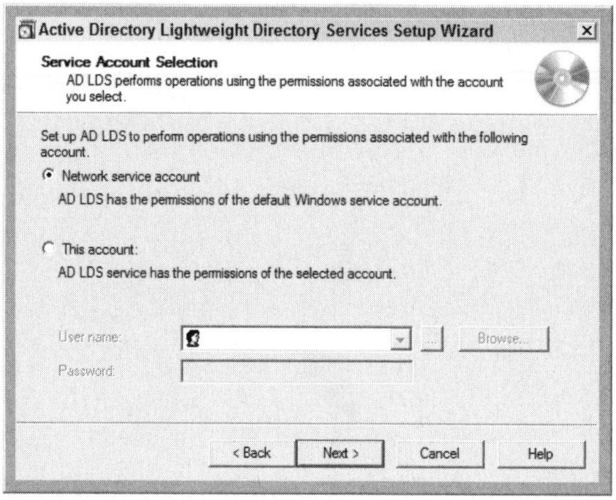

Figure 13-12

As you progress through the wizard, one of the next steps is choosing an administrative user for the application partition. This user account will by default be able to use command-line and GUI tools to configure ADLDS further. In Figure 13-13, I left the wizard with the default of the currently logged-on user.

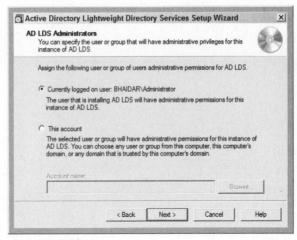

Figure 13-13

One of the last major steps in the wizard that you definitely want to take advantage of is the option to import an LDIF file. LDIF files are conceptually the same as running .sql files against SQL Server to install schema elements. In Figure 13-14, I selected the MS-User.ldf file to import because it contains the definition of the user class that is required by the provider. If you forget to choose anything in this step, then you have to import the LDIF file from the command line using a tool like ldifde.exe.

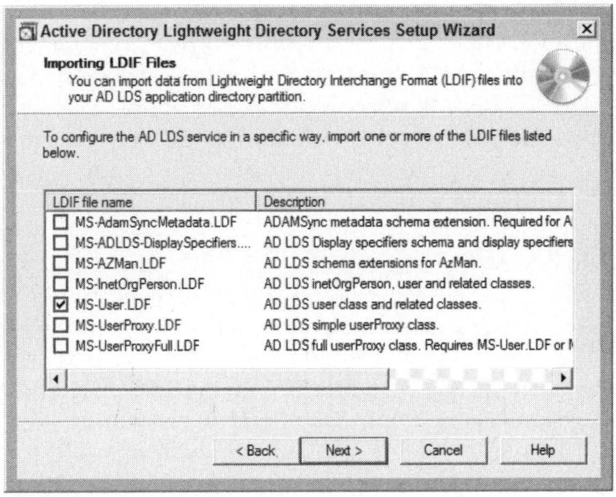

Figure 13-14

With these steps completed, you can finish the wizard, and after a brief pause you will have an ADLDS directory server running and available for use by the provider. To connect to the ADLDS instance and the application partition that you just created, you can use the adsiedit MMC tool, which is automatically installed with ADLDS on your machine. You will need to set up the connection settings by choosing Connect To from the ADLDS ADSI Edit node in the MMC. You can see how to set up the connection settings in Figure 13-15.

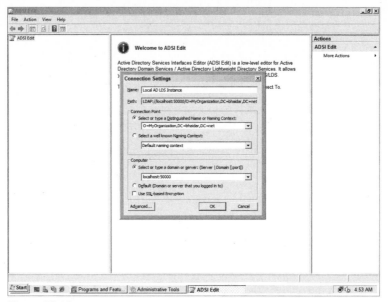

Figure 13-15

In this case, I have pointed the MMC at my local machine's ADLDS instance listening on port 50000. The connection settings also point at the application partition O=MyOrganization,DC=bhaidar,DC=net that was created with the ADLDS install wizard. Because you probably do not want user objects to be stored directly at the root of the application partition, you should create a container to store your application's user objects. In my case, I created an OU by right-clicking the partition node and choosing New ⇨ Object. In the dialog box that pops up after this selection, I chose an object of type organizationalUnit and then named it ApplicationUsers. Note that if you do not see the object type organizationalUnit in the selection list box, it is probably because your application partition used a container type that cannot be a parent of OU objects.

The last step at this point is to configure a domain account with administrative rights in the partition so that all of the methods on ActiveDirectoryMembershipProvider will work. Unlike AD where a familiar security UI is used, in ADLDS you have to go through a somewhat awkward configuration process. Using the adsiedit MMC tool, click the CN=Roles node. This displays all of the ADLDS groups (not Active Directory domain groups) that currently exist in the ADLDS application partition. In the right-hand side of the MMC, right-click the CN=Administrators entry and select Properties. This pulls up a list of all the attributes on the Administrators object. You need to scroll through this list and find the member attribute. Highlight that attribute and click the Edit button. This pulls up the clearly named Multi-valued Distinguished Name With Security Principal Editor dialog box. In this box, there are two buttons: Add Windows Account and Add DN.

This dialog box allows you to add either domain principals (such as domain users, as well as well-known accounts like the NETWORK SERVICE account) or ADLDS user principals into the Administrators group. For now, I just added the web server's NETWORK SERVICE account to the group. You can see what this all looks like in Figure 13-16.

If you do not plan on setting up SSL for your ADLDS instance, then you will need to add some other account aside from NETWORK SERVICE to the Administrators group. Remember that you can only connect to ADLDS with the `ActiveDirectoryMembershipProvider` in one of two ways: over SSL or in the clear. The provider is *not* able to connect to ADLDS over non-SSL connections using either the default process credentials or explicit domain account credentials. Instead, you *always* need an ADLDS user principal that can be used as the explicit username configured for the provider.

Because the demo code in the next section uses an ADLDS instance that is not configured to use SSL, you need to add some other security principal to the Administrators group. I created another OU in the application partition called `PartitionUserAccounts`, and I added a user to it called `Application UsersAdministrator`. The full distinguished name for this new account is:

```
CN=ApplicationUsersAdministrator,
OU=PartitionUserAccounts,
O=MyOrganization,
DC=bhaidar,
DC=net
```

You can add this account to the Administrators group using the same process described earlier, though you will want to click the Add DN (Distinguished Name) button for this case. Make sure that you have the distinguished name of the administrators account handy because you will not get any nice GUI for selecting ADLDS principals; instead, you have to type the full distinguished name. Figure 13-17 shows the end result of adding the ADLDS user principal to the Administrators group. Notice the highlighted account in the security principal dialog box.

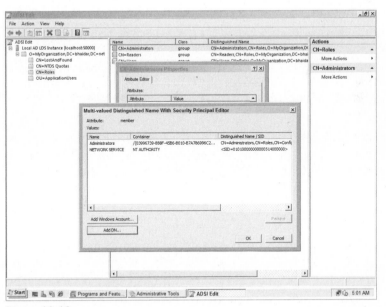

Figure 13-16

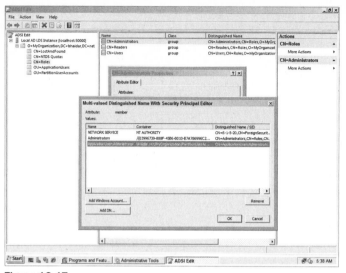

Figure 13-17

One thing to warn you about: even though you now have an ADLDS user principal, it is very likely that you still can't use it at this point. Unfortunately, the errors you will get back from the provider or from other tools like `ldp.exe` will not tell you the problem. There are two more things you need to do to get the ADLDS user principal working:

1 You need to explicitly set a password on it. You might have noticed that when you created the ADLDS user principal, at no point were you prompted for a password.

2 You need to enable the user account. By default newly created ADLDS user principals are created in a disabled state when running on Windows Server 2008 machines that have any type of password restrictions in effect. As a result, you need to enable the account after you set the password.

You can easily set the password for the ADLDS user principal by right-clicking the user object in the `adsiedit` tool and choosing Reset Password. After you have set the password for the account, right-click the user object again and choose Properties. Scroll down the list of properties until you find the property called `msDS-UserAccountDisabled`. Notice that it is currently set to `true`. Double-click it, and set the property to `false`. With these two steps the ADLDS user principal has a password and the account is now enabled so that you can actually use it for authentication purposes.

At this point you have an ADLDS instance, an application partition with an OU for storing users, and administrative security privileges on the application partition with an ADLDS user principal so that the `ActiveDirectoryMembershipProvider` can be configured with explicit connection credentials. So now you are at a point where you can hook up an ASP.NET application to the ADLDS instance and start making use of it.

Using the Application Partition

As with using Active Directory, the first step to getting `ActiveDirectoryMembershipProvider` to work is getting the connection string set up properly. Unlike connecting to Active Directory, for

ADLDS you must supply a container in the connection string. By now, this restriction should make sense because in ADLDS you saw that you always work in the context of an application partition, so at the very least you will be creating users starting in this partition. In this case, though, because there is also a user OU, you use a connection string that points at the OU:

```
<connectionStrings>
  <add
    name="adldsConnection"
    connectionString="LDAP://localhost:50000/OU=ApplicationUsers,O=MyOrganization,D
C=bhaidar,DC=net"
  />
</connectionStrings>
```

In this case, I explicitly specified a port number as well. Because the ADLDS instance on my machine is running on the default 389 port, the number is not really required. But if you installed ADLDS in a non-default port as in the case here, the syntax shown above is what you would use.

Because the sample application will be connecting over a non-SSL connection, the provider configuration needs to use an explicit set of credentials. In the configuration that follows, the provider is configured to use the ADLDS user principal that was just created.

```
<membership defaultProvider="adldsprovider">
    <providers>
      <clear/>
      <add
        name="adldsprovider"
        type="System.Web.Security.ActiveDirectoryMembershipProvider…"
        connectionProtection="None"
        connectionUsername="CN=ApplicationUsersAdministrator,OU=PartitionUserAccoun
ts,O=MyOrganization,DC=bhaidar,DC=net"
        connectionPassword="pass!word1"
        connectionStringName="adldsConnection"
      />
    </providers>
</membership>
```

As noted earlier, for a production environment you should use protected configuration so that the credentials are not visible in cleartext. Because the ADLDS instance does not support SSL, the connection Protection attribute is set to None. This causes the provider to skip looking for an SSL connection to the directory instance. For the explicit username, the full distinguished name of the user account is needed. This is one visible case where configuring the provider for ADLDS differs from AD. Unlike AD, ADLDS does not really have the concept of binding to a user object by way of a user principal name that is indexed in a global catalog. Instead, when you connect to ADLDS with an ADLDS user principal you need to supply the distinguished name so that ADLDS can actually find the user object in the directory.

Because the provider is configured to use a non-SSL connection, one last piece of ADLDS configuration is necessary. For security reasons, ADLDS does not allow passwords to be set or changed over non-SSL connections. You can change this behavior by using the dsmgmt.exe tool included with the ADLDS installation. The following output shows the command-line conversation with dsmgmt that re-enables the ability to set passwords over non-SSL connections:

```
C:\Windows\system32\dsmgmt.exe:
    ds behavior
```

```
AD DS/LDS behavior:
    connections
server connections:
    connect to server localhost:50000
Binding to localhost:
    50000 …
Connected to localhost:
    50000 using credentials of locally logged on user.
server connections:
    quit
AD DS/LDS behavior:
    allow passwd op on unsecured connection
    Successfully modified AD DS/LDS Behavior
    to reset password over unsecured network.
AD DS/LDS behavior:
    quit
C:\Windows\system32\dsmgmt.exe:
    quit
```

This type of configuration is acceptable for a development environment or a test-bed environment. However, I would not recommend doing this for a production environment unless you are securing the network traffic with some other mechanism such as IPsec. Although it requires more hoops to jump through (you need to obtain the SSL certificate and then follow the ADLDS help topics for installing the certificate on the ADLDS server and on all of the clients that will communicate with it), securing ADLDS traffic with SSL in your production environments is definitely the right thing to do.

By this point, I really promise that all of the mucking around with ADLDS configuration magic is done. To test things, you can drop a `CreateUserWizard` on a page and create a new user account. I created a new account called `testuser@bhaidar.net`. If you look in the `adsiedit tool` after running the test page (make sure to refresh the `ApplicationUsers` OU so that the tool will see the new user), you will see that a new user object with common name `CN=testuser@bhaidar.net` has been created in the OU. A few things to note about this user object:

❏ Although I typed in `testuser@bhaidar.net` for the username in the wizard, the provider automatically set the common name to `testuser@bhaidar.net` as well. If you look at the properties for the user object, both the "common name" (aka CN) and the `userPrincipalName` have been set to the same value. As a developer using the provider you do not ever deal with the common name, but other applications that are more LDAP-aware will depend on the CN as opposed to the `userPrincipalName` because in the world of LDAP you constantly reference objects using their distinguished name. The CN attribute is part of an object's distinguished name. So in the case of `testuser`, its distinguished name is now `CN=testuser@bhaidar.net, OU=ApplicationUsers,O=MyOrganization,DC=bhaidar,DC=net`.

❏ Unlike the `adsiedit` tool, the provider automatically set the `msDS-UserAccountDisabled` attribute to `false` for you. Of course, if you call `CreateUser` with the `isApproved` parameter set to `false`, then the `msDS-UserAccountDisabled` field will be set to `true` by the provider.

With the new user created, you can now try logging in using the Login control. Just type in the username `testuser@bhaidar.net`, and you will be logged in successfully. At this point, you can call any of the other methods on `ActiveDirectoryMembershipProvider`. Fetching the `MembershipUser` object and displaying its information works as expected. If you enable searching you can call the search related methods as well. If you extend the schema in ADLDS with the five attributes necessary for self-service password resets, you can use the `ResetPassword` method. Overall, you will see that after you get past the ADLDS-specific configuration work and unique aspects of connecting to ADLDS, Active DirectoryMembershipProvider works the same way against ADLDS as it does against AD. There is no difference in terms of supported provider functionality between the two directory stores.

Using the Provider in Partial Trust

All the examples shown so far for Active Directory and for ADLDS have been running in full trust. However, if you attempt to use the provider directly in a partial trust environment it will fail. Within the provider's Initialize method, an explicit check is made for Low trust. The provider itself is attributed with a link demand for System.DirectoryServices.DirectoryServicesPermission. Also, each of its public methods is attributed with a full demand for the same permission.

C#

```csharp
[DirectoryServicesPermission(SecurityAction.LinkDemand, Unrestricted=true)]
[DirectoryServicesPermission(SecurityAction.InheritanceDemand, Unrestricted=true)]
public class ActiveDirectoryMembershipProvider : MembershipProvider
{
…
[DirectoryServicesPermission(SecurityAction.Assert, Unrestricted=true)]
[DirectoryServicesPermission(SecurityAction.Demand, Unrestricted=true)]
[DirectoryServicesPermission(SecurityAction.InheritanceDemand, Unrestricted=true)]
  public override string ResetPassword(string username, string passwordAnswer)
…
}
```

VB.NET

```vbnet
    <DirectoryServicesPermission( _
        SecurityAction.LinkDemand, _
        Unrestricted:=True), _
    DirectoryServicesPermission( _
        SecurityAction.InheritanceDemand, _
        Unrestricted:=True)> _
        Public Class ActiveDirectoryMembershipProvider
        Inherits MembershipProvider
    …
    <DirectoryServicesPermission( _
        SecurityAction.InheritanceDemand, _
        Unrestricted:=True), _
    DirectoryServicesPermission( _
        SecurityAction.Assert, _
        Unrestricted:=True), _
    DirectoryServicesPermission( _
        SecurityAction.Demand,
        Unrestricted:=True)> _
    Public Overrides Function ResetPassword( _
        ByVal username As String, _
        ByVal passwordAnswer As String) As String
```

In the case of individual public methods, the provider actually asserts DirectoryServicesPermission at the same time it demands it. This cuts down on the overhead of walking the stack each time code in

`System.DirectoryServices` or `System.DirectoryServices.Protocols` makes a demand. Because the declarative demand will already have verified that all of its callers have the necessary privileges, there is no reason to rerun the stack walk when the provider makes calls into classes from these namespaces.

If you drop the trust level of an ASP.NET application down to High trust, any of the previous examples will immediately fail with an error like the following:

```
Request for the permission of type 'System.DirectoryServices.
DirectoryServicesPermission, System.DirectoryServices, Version=2.0.0.0,
Culture=neutral, PublicKeyToken=b03f5f7f11d50a3a' failed.
```

Thankfully, this error is at least clear enough to give you an idea of the problem, as well as a possible workaround. There are actually two approaches to getting the provider working again in partial trust:

❑ Add `DirectoryServicesPermission` to the appropriate ASP.NET trust policy file (or create a custom trust policy with the permission).

❑ Wrap all calls to the provider in a GAC'd assembly that asserts `DirectoryServicesPermission`.

The first approach is definitely the easiest to implement, but it is also less secure. Broadly granting `DirectoryServicesPermission` to a partially trusted application means that anyone can write code to start accessing your directory servers. In essence, it takes away the layer of protection on the web server and means that you are depending on whatever ACLs you set on your directory servers to protect against a malicious developer trolling through your data.

If you are running in the High trust bucket-though, this is effectively a trust bucket meant to be very much like Full trust, but without unmanaged code permissions. So, it isn't unreasonable for a High trust application to use the first approach. You can modify the High trust policy file with the following:

```
<SecurityClass
   Name="DirectoryServicesPermission"
   Description="System.DirectoryServices.DirectoryServicesPermission, … " />
   …

      <IPermission
          class="DirectoryServicesPermission"
          version="1"
          Unrestricted="true" />
```

By now, these types of changes should be pretty familiar. Register `DirectoryServicesPermission` with a `<SecurityClass />` entry in the `<SecurityClasses />` element. Then inside of the XML element defining the ASP.NET named permission set, add the `<IPermission />` element. With these two changes, your partial trust ASP.NET application will start working again when using `ActiveDirectoryMembershipProvider`.

Using a wrapper assembly involves a little more work, but it is actually pretty simple to accomplish. Create a new class library project in Visual Studio, making sure to reference the following assemblies:

❑ `System.Configuration`: Needed because the project will be creating a new provider.

❑ System.Web: Because the custom provider will be deriving from ActiveDirectory MembershipProvider

❑ System.DirectoryServices: This assembly contains the DirectoryServicesPermission.

You will need to generate a key file and enable strong naming for the project. Because the intent of the wrapper assembly is to assert DirectoryServicesPermission on behalf of partially trusted applications, you also need to add the APTCA attribute to AssemblyInfo.cs:

C#

```csharp
using System.Security;
...
[assembly: AllowPartiallyTrustedCallers()]
```

VB.NET

```vbnet
Imports System.Security
<Assembly: AllowPartiallyTrustedCallers()>
```

With these basic tasks completed, you can now "write" the wrapper provider. In reality, the wrapper provider is nothing more than a class definition where DirectoryServicesPermission can be asserted along with overrides for each of the methods you want available to partial trust applications.

C#

```csharp
using System;
using System.Configuration.Provider;
using System.Security.Permissions;
using System.Web.Security;
using System.DirectoryServices;

namespace ADProviderWrapper
{
    [DirectoryServicesPermission(SecurityAction.Assert, Unrestricted=true)]
    public class ADProviderWrapper : ActiveDirectoryMembershipProvider
    {
        //You must always override Initialize
        public override void Initialize(string name,
          System.Collections.Specialized.NameValueCollection config)
        {
            base.Initialize(name, config);
        }

        public override bool ChangePassword(string username,
          string oldPassword, string newPassword)
        {
            return base.ChangePassword(username, oldPassword, newPassword);
        }

        public override bool ChangePasswordQuestionAndAnswer(string username,
          string password, string newPasswordQuestion, string newPasswordAnswer)
        {
            return base.ChangePasswordQuestionAndAnswer(username, password,
                newPasswordQuestion, newPasswordAnswer);
```

```
        }

            //Additional overrides for methods you want available in partial trust
    }
}
```

VB.NET

```vb
Imports Microsoft.VisualBasic
Imports System
Imports System.Configuration.Provider
Imports System.Security.Permissions
Imports System.Web.Security
Imports System.DirectoryServices

Namespace ADProviderWrapper
  <DirectoryServicesPermission(SecurityAction.Assert, Unrestricted:=True)> _
  Public Class ADProviderWrapper
        Inherits ActiveDirectoryMembershipProvider
    Public Overrides Sub Initialize( _
      ByVal name As String, _
      ByVal config As System.Collections.Specialized.NameValueCollection)


    Public Overrides Function ChangePassword( _
      ByVal username As String, _
      ByVal oldPassword As String, _
      ByVal newPassword As String) As Boolean


    Public Overrides Function CreateUser( _
    ByVal username As String, _
    ByVal password As String, _
    ByVal email As String, _
    ByVal passwordQuestion As String, _
    ByVal passwordAnswer As String, _
    ByVal isApproved As Boolean, _
    ByVal providerUserKey As Object, _
    <System.Runtime.InteropServices.Out()> ByRef status As _
    MembershipCreateStatus) As MembershipUser


Return MyBase.CreateUser(username, password, _
 email, passwordQuestion, _
 passwordAnswer, isApproved, _
 providerUserKey, status)
End Function
  Public Overrides Function ChangePasswordQuestionAndAnswer( _
      ByVal username As String, _
      ByVal password As String, _
      ByVal newPasswordQuestion As String, _
      ByVal newPasswordAnswer As String) As Boolean

      Return MyBase.ChangePasswordQuestionAndAnswer( _
       username, password, _
```

```
                newPasswordQuestion, newPasswordAnswer)
     End Function
```

Code-wise, there isn't anything complex going on here. You start out referencing all of the related namespaces, derive from `ActiveDirectoryMembershipProvider` and then override the methods that you care about. The declarative assertion on the class means the common language runtime (CLR) will automatically assert this permission for any method that the class implements. The only method that you are required to override is the `Initialize` method. Because `Initialize` is always called when the Membership feature is instantiating providers based on configuration, you have to make sure the custom provider's implementation is called first in order to get the permission assertion onto the stack.

Other than the `Initialize` method, you can override whichever methods you care about exposing to partial trust applications. If your intent is to use all of the functionality of `ActiveDirectoryMembership Provider` from partial trust, then you would override all of the public methods on the provider. You might think that just adding the assertion for `DirectoryServicesPermission` would be sufficient and that you could avoid overriding any individual methods. Because the `ActiveDirectoryMembership Provider` has a class level link demand. though, any method that is not overridden means that the Framework will evaluate the link demand against the code that is directly calling it. Of course, for partial trust applications, this means that your partially trusted page code will be the immediate caller, and hence without an intervening override from the custom provider sitting on the call stack, the link demand will fail.

After you compile the custom provider and install it in the GAC, you can modify your partial trust application to use it:

```
<trust level="High" />

<compilation>
     <assemblies>
          <add
                 assembly="ADProviderWrapper, Version=1.0.0.0, Culture=neutral, Publi
cKeyToken=b95a0989e24f0920"
          />
     </assemblies>
</compilation>

<membership defaultProvider="gacdprovider">
     <providers>
     <clear/>
     <add
          name="gacdprovider"
          type="ADProviderWrapper.ADProviderWrapper,ADProviderWrapper,
               Version=1.0.0.0, Culture=neutral, PublicKeyToken=b95a0989e24f0920"
          enableSearchMethods="true"
          connectionStringName="directoryconnection"
     />
     </providers>
</membership>
```

The `<assemblies />` directive makes the ASP.NET application aware of the custom provider sitting in the GAC. The `<membership />` section adds the GAC'd provider and indicates that it should be used as the default provider for the Membership feature. At this point, you can run your partial trust application and make use of the functionality in `ActiveDirectoryMembershipProvider` without running into any security exceptions. From the point of view of the application developer, using the GAC'd provider is no different than using the base provider. The nice thing about using the GAC'd provider is that you have the ability to customize the subset of functionality on `ActiveDirectoryMembershipProvider` that you want to make available in your partial trust applications. For example, you could create a custom provider that only asserts permissions for read-oriented methods like `ValidateUser`, while choosing not to override more sensitive methods like `ChangePassword` or `ResetPassword`.

Summary

`ActiveDirectoryMembershipProvider` works with both AD and ADLDS directory stores. The provider implements all of the functionality of the Membership API with the following two exceptions: the provider does not keep track of users that are online, and the provider does not support password retrieval. You should probably invest some time planning for deploying and using the provider, especially in complex domain environments. When running against AD `ActiveDirectoryMembershipProvider` works in the scope of either a single domain, or a container within a domain. You can still leverage the provider in multidomain scenarios, but you will need to configure at least one provider instance per domain that you need to work with. Within the scope of a single domain, you can choose to point the provider at the root of the domain (that is, the default naming context), or at a specific container within the domain. In the case of ADLDS, though, you always have an application partition, so for ADLDS the provider will at least always be working in the context of the application partition (which itself is a container). As with AD, you can also configure containers in ADLDS and have the provider work within the context of these containers.

After you have settled on which domain and/or container you are working with, the next major decision is the type of username you plan to support. For ADLDS, the username in the Membership feature will always map to the `userPrincipalName` attribute in the directory. For Active Directory, you can choose to use either the `userPrincipalName` or the `sAMAccountName` attribute. Applications using older directories that were upgraded from NT4 will likely need to switch the provider to use `sAMAccountName`. The provider automatically maps other directory attributes to the various properties on a `MembershipUser` instance. A small subset of the `MembershipUser` properties can have these attribute mappings changed from their defaults. If you choose to enable password resets for the provider (not enabled by default), then you will need to edit the directory schema in order to store the question and answer as well as the bad password answer tracking information.

Although securing AD and ADLDS is an entire topic in and of itself, there are two main security decisions to keep in mind when using `ActiveDirectoryMembershipProvider`. By default, the provider attempts to establish a secure connection with AD or ADLDS. In the case of AD, this will normally "just work." For ADLDS, though, you need to explicitly configure SSL support on the ADLDS server and on the web servers for the provider to be able to securely connect to the directory. The other aspect of security to consider is locking down read and write access to user objects in the directory. If at all possible, you should plan on storing different user populations in different OUs in your directory, and you should also delegate control over those OUs to specific accounts. You can then configure different provider instances using different sets of explicit credentials that only have selected rights in a specific OU.

Although `ActiveDirectoryMembershipProvider` ships as part of ASP.NET, it has been tested and is supported for use in non-ASP.NET environments as well. For both ASP.NET and non-ASP.NET environments, though, the provider will only work in full trust by default. In partial trust ASP.NET environments, you do have the option of adding the `DirectoryServices` permission to a trust policy file. However, the more secure approach for any partial trust environment is to wrap access to the provider inside of a GAC'd assembly.

14

Role Manager

Role Manager is a feature that was added in ASP.NET 2.0 and fully supported in ASP.NET 3.5 that provides the basic functionality necessary to create an IPrincipal-based object associated with roles. The motivation for the Role Manager feature is to make it easy for developers to associate users with roles and then perform role checks both declaratively and in code. The Role Manager feature is sometimes referred to as a companion feature to Membership because Role Manager can be used to provide authorization for users that have been authenticated using Membership. However, Role Manager can also be used as a standalone feature that integrates with other authentication mechanisms, including Windows authentication.

As with the Membership feature, Role Manager can be used in non-ASP.NET environments such as the Windows Forms application and console applications, thus making it easier for developers to share a common set of authenticated users and role information across different client applications. This chapter will cover:

- ❑ The Role class
- ❑ The RolePrincipal class
- ❑ The RoleManager model
- ❑ RoleProvider
- ❑ WindowsTokenRoleProvider

The Roles Class

As with the Membership feature, the Role Manager feature has a static class that can be used as an easy way to access the functionality of the feature. The Roles class has methods and properties that cover the following areas:

❏ Public properties that primarily expose the Role Manager data from configuration.

❏ Public methods that act as façades on top of the default Role Manager provider.

❏ A single utility method that you can use for clearing the Role Manager cookie.

Because most ASP.NET provider-based features follow the same general design, I won't rehash how default providers work or the concept of façade methods mapping to the default provider. These areas work the same way in Role Manager as was described earlier in Chapter 11, which discussed Membership.

Regardless of where Role Manager is used, the feature always requires at least Low trust to work. This means that either an ASP.NET application must run in Low trust or higher to use the feature or, for a non-ASP.NET application, the AspNetHostingPermission must be granted to the calling code with a level of Low or higher.

The public properties on the Roles class for the most part just mirror the configuration settings from configuration. Some of the properties should be familiar to you because they work the exact same way on the static Membership class. Properties that are provider-specific or that involve unique behavior to the Role Manager features are described below.

❏ Provider: Returns a RoleProvider reference to the provider defined by the defaultProvider attribute on the <roleManager /> configuration element.

❏ Providers: Returns a RoleProviderCollection containing one reference to each provider defined within the <providers /> element contained within a <roleManager /> element.

❏ ApplicationName: Returns the value of the applicationName provider configuration attribute for the default provider.

❏ Enabled: Returns true if the Role Manager feature is enabled. The concept of being "enabled" though is based upon two different factors: the "enabled" attribute from the <roleManager /> configuration element and the current trust level. Unlike Membership, you can go into configuration and explicitly disable the Role Manager feature (effectively, the Membership feature is always "on"). In fact, the default configuration of the Role Manager feature is disabled; you won't see this in machine.config, but the hard-coded value for the "enabled" attribute in the RoleManagerSection class is false. Because machine.config does not redefine this attribute, Role Manager is turned off by default on all machines. Assuming that you explicitly enable the Role Manager feature by setting the "enabled" attribute to true, you still need to be running in Low trust or higher. If you are running in Minimal trust, Roles.Enabled will always return false, regardless of the setting in configuration. This is done because Role Manager (and for that matter Membership) is not intended for use in Minimal trust applications.

❏ CacheRolesInCookie: By default, this value is set to false. If it is set to true, the RoleManager Module attempts to improve the performance of the Role Manager feature by caching the roles for a user within a cookie and using the cookie during subsequent page hits. Cookie caching is covered in detail in the section on the RoleManagerModule.

❑   MaxCachedResults: The maximum number of roles that the RoleManagerModule will attempt to stuff into a cookie, assuming that CacheRolesInCookie is set to true. Because cookies are usually limited in size to around 4KB, you can use this setting to proactively hint the module so that it doesn't waste time attempting to pack enormous numbers of roles into a cookie.

There are seven more public properties on the Roles class, but I won't list them here because these additional properties all deal with the roles cookie. The corresponding configuration attributes are covered a little later in the section on role cache cookie settings. If you are familiar with the cookie options for forms authentication in ASP.NET 2.0 and ASP.NET 3.5, then the cookie settings available from the Roles class will make sense. For the most part, they control the same set of functionality (that is, cookie name, path, protection, and so on) as forms authentication. The one minor difference is that, unlike forms authentication, the Role Manager feature only supports the use of cookies for caching roles. There is no such thing as caching a user's roles in a cookieless value on the URL. The effective 4KB upper limit is already constraining for some Role Manager scenarios; attempting to cram cached roles into a path segment with an upper limit of 255 characters just wouldn't work.

Aside from the façade methods that provide easy-to-use method overloads for the default RoleProvider, there is one other method of interest on the Roles class: DeleteCookie. As the method name suggests, after you call this method the Roles class sends a clear cookie back to the browser that forces the Role Manager cookie in the browser to be deleted. Of course, if you never use cookie caching with Role Manager, you will never have a reason to call this method. However, if you create a logout page for your users, you should call Roles.DeleteCookie after clearing the authentication information as well:

C#

```
//Logout page logic
FormsAuthentication.SignOut();
Roles.DeleteCookie();

//Additional logic to prevent forms cookie re-use - see Chapter 6
```

VB.NET

```
'Logout page logic
FormsAuthentication.SignOut()
Roles.DeleteCookie()

'Additional logic to prevent forms cookie re-use - see Chapter 6
```

If you forget to call Roles.DeleteCookie from your logout page, it isn't the end of the world. The RoleManagerModule responsible for handling the cookie is smart enough to ignore and clear any role cookies sent by anonymous users. So if you have a role cookie lying around in the browser after a logout, the next time a user hits your site the RoleManagerModule will automatically call DeleteCookie.

One thing that developers sometimes look for when they start working with the Role Manager feature and the Roles class is some kind of role object. For ASP.NET 2.0 or ASP.NET 3.5, a role is just a string value; there is no rich object model for representing a role or manipulating a role. As a result, when you use the Roles class, you can see that most of the method parameters are just strings. You associate users (represented as a string username and an implicit application name) with role names. If ASP.NET ever creates a rich role object in a future release, it will probably require a substantial overhaul to the Role Manager feature because the current implementation is so tightly tied to the basic concept of a role as a string.

The façade methods include some extra logic for the case that the `Roles` class is called when the current user is represented by a `RolePrincipal`, and the method calls on the `Roles` class potentially affect that user. This allows the `Roles` class to take advantage of the caching behavior in the `RolePrincipal` class. For web applications, the current user is determined by looking at `HttpContext.Current.User`. Because the Role Manager feature is also supported for non-ASP.NET applications, the `Roles` class will look for the current user object in `Thread.CurrentPrincipal` for non-web applications.

This means that if you want the full functionality of the Role Manager feature to work consistently outside of ASP.NET, you should write some code that initializes `Thread.CurrentPrincipal` with a `RolePrincipal` for the current user of your application. As is described in the next section on `Role Principal`, you can create a `RolePrincipal` that wraps a `WindowsIdentity`. This means that you can have a fat-client application that requires a logged in Windows user but that fetches application-specific role information using the Role Manager feature.

The interaction between `Roles` and `RolePrincipal` is described here for each of the relevant façade methods:

❑ `IsUserInRole`: If the current user is a `RolePrincipal`, and the `username` parameter to this method matches the username (that is, `IIdentity.Name`) for the `RolePrincipal`, and the name of the provider associated with this `RolePrincipal` matches the name of the default Role Manager provider, the façade method instead calls `RolePrincipal.IsInRole`. The string comparison for username is a case-insensitive ordinal-based comparison. However, if the username or provider name of the `RolePrincipal` doesn't match the `username` parameter to the method or the name of the default provider, `Roles.IsUserInRole` calls the default `RoleProvider` instead. Note that for the parameterless `IsUserInRole` overload, the username is taken from `HttpContext.Current .User`. So if a `RolePrincipal` is attached to the context for this case, the parameterless `IsUser InRole` overload usually results in a call to `RolePrincipal.IsInRole` instead.

❑ `GetRolesForUser`: This method has the same behavior as `IsUserInRole`. If the current user is a `RolePrincipal`, and all of the other data matches, then the `Roles` class calls `RolePrincipal .GetRoles`. Otherwise, the `Roles` class calls the `GetRolesForUser` method on the default provider.

❑ `DeleteRole`: This method checks to see whether the current user is a `RolePrincipal` and if the `RolePrincipal` object uses the default provider. If both of these conditions are met, and if the `RolePrincipal` instance has cached role information within itself, the method checks to see whether the user represented by the principal belongs to the role that is being deleted. If this is the case, the method invalidates the `RolePrincipal` cache by calling `RolePrincipal.SetDirty`. Normally, you see this behavior only if you are in a management application and you change the role membership for the user that you are currently logged in as.

❑ `AddUserToRole`, `AddUsersToRoles`, `AddUserToRoles`, `AddUsersToRole`: All of these methods have logic similar to `DeleteRole`. If necessary, the current user represented by a `RolePrincipal` has its internal cache flushed if that user was added to a role using any of these methods. As with `DeleteRole`, you will probably only see this behavior when you are changing user-to-role assignments for yourself, and you are logged in to an administrative application as yourself.

❑ `RemoveUserFromRole`, `RemoveUsersFromRoles`, `RemoveUserFromRoles`, `RemoveUsers-FromRole`: These methods follow the same logic as described in the last two bullet points. In this case, the `RolePrincipal` cache is flushed if the current user has been removed from a role using any of these methods.

Just like the Membership feature, the Role Manager feature also has the concept of a primary key. The username and the application name from a provider's configuration are combined and used as the "primary key" when working with users and roles. See the section "The Primary Key for Membership" in Chapter 10 for a detailed discussion of how the username and application name are used to reference users. The only difference between Membership and Role Manager in this respect is that only the Membership feature went so far as to expose data-store-specific primary keys in its public APIs. The Role Manager feature doesn't do this—instead both the Roles class and the RoleProvider base class reference users with just a string username and roles with just a string role name. (The application name is implicitly used as well because it is obtained from a provider's configuration.)

The RolePrincipal Class

Because the Role Manager feature's main purpose is to supply an IPrincipal based object, it includes an implementation of this interface with the RolePrincipal class. The RolePrincipal is intended for use anywhere a Framework application (ASP.NET or non-ASP.NET) expects to find an IPrincipal for IsInRole calls. RolePrincipal also exposes some additional methods for retrieving all of a user's roles as well as for handling some of the work necessary when using cookie caching.

C#

```
public sealed class RolePrincipal : IPrincipal, ISerializable
{
    //Constructors
    public RolePrincipal(IIdentity identity, string encryptedTicket)
    public RolePrincipal(IIdentity identity)
    public RolePrincipal(string providerName, IIdentity identity)
    public RolePrincipal(string providerName, IIdentity identity,
                         string encryptedTicket)

    //Cookie caching related methods
    public string ToEncryptedTicket()

    //Role Manager and IPrincipal related functionality
    public string[] GetRoles()
    public bool IsInRole(string role)
    public void SetDirty()

    //Public properties not related to cookie caching
    public int Version { get; }
    public IIdentity Identity { get; }
    public string ProviderName { get }
    public bool IsRoleListCached { get; }

    //Public properties related to cookie caching
    public DateTime ExpireDate { get; }
    public DateTime IssueDate { get; }
    public bool Expired {get; }
    public String CookiePath { get; }
    public bool CachedListChanged { get; }
}
```

VB.NET

```
<Serializable(), AspNetHostingPermission( _
    SecurityAction.LinkDemand, _
    Level:=AspNetHostingPermissionLevel.Minimal)> _
Public NotInheritable Class RolePrincipal
    Implements IPrincipal, ISerializable

    'Constructors
    Public Sub New(ByVal identity As IIdentity)
    Public Sub New(ByVal identity As IIdentity, ByVal encryptedTicket As String)
    Public Sub New(ByVal providerName As String, ByVal identity As IIdentity)
    Public Sub New(ByVal providerName As String, _
    ByVal identity As IIdentity, _
    ByVal encryptedTicket As String)

    'Cookie caching related methods
    Public Function ToEncryptedTicket() As String

    'Role Manager and IPrincipal related functionality
    Public Function GetRoles() As String()
    Public Function IsInRole(ByVal role As String) As Boolean
    Public Sub SetDirty()

    'Public properties not related to cookie caching
    Public ReadOnly Property Identity As IIdentity
    Public ReadOnly Property IsRoleListCached As Boolean
    Public ReadOnly Property ProviderName As String
    Public ReadOnly Property Version As Integer

    'Public properties related to cookie caching
    Public ReadOnly Property ExpireDate As DateTime
    Public ReadOnly Property IssueDate As DateTime
    Public ReadOnly Property CookiePath As String
    Public ReadOnly Property Expired As Boolean
    Public ReadOnly Property CachedListChanged As Boolean

End Class
```

The first thing that may leap out at you is that RolePrincipal is *sealed*! This has important implications for more complex scenarios such as handling multiple RoleProviders in an application with cookie caching turned on. It also means that if you want to extend the principal to include custom functionality, you can't. Hopefully, in a future release the RolePrincipal class will be unsealed.

As you can see, although the RolePrincipal class implements the IPrincipal interface, it provides quite a bit more functionality beyond just a simple role check. Take a look at the portion of RolePrincipal that deals strictly with role information. There are two constructor overloads that can be used to create a RolePrincipal when you aren't using cookie caching. One constructor overload takes a single IIdentity parameter, while the second overload accepts both an IIdentity and the name of a provider.

The IIdentity reference is needed because any class that implements IPrincipal needs to be able to return the authenticated identity (that is, an IIdentity reference) associated with that principal. You can see from the constructor signature that the RolePrincipal is not hard-coded to any specific implementation of an `IIdentity`. That is why you can enable the Role Manager feature with any type of authentication mechanism available in ASP.NET. Forms authentication creates a `FormsIdentity`, Windows authentication results in a `WindowsIdentity`, and your own custom authentication mechanisms may use `GenericIdentity`. For all of these cases, the `RolePrincipal` is unaware of the underlying authentication implementation that generates an `IIdentity` reference.

One reason that you might use the less-than-obvious combination of Windows authentication and Role Manager is that you may not want to clutter your Active Directory with application-specific roles. It may be a somewhat laborious process to register application-specific groups in your directory if the directory is tightly managed by a central IT group. For this reason, storing application-specific roles off to the side using Role Manager can be very convenient. Also, if you develop "quick-hit" web applications that exist for only a few weeks or months, it's very easy to stuff application roles into a Role Manager database that can be deleted when the application has outlived its usefulness.

With that said (and before the Active Directory team comes after me!) with the introduction of Active Directory Lightweight Directory Services (aka ADLDS), application developers also have the option of storing user-to-group assignments in application-specific ADLDS instances. You can take this approach even further using the Authorization Manager (aka AzMan) feature of Windows Server 2003 and Windows Server 2008 by deploying an AzMan policy store in an application-specific ADLDS instance. These types of architectural decisions are beyond the scope of this book, but you should look into them especially for intranet web applications where you may be considering using Role Manager to get around operational or administrative hassles of a centrally managed Active Directory.

You now know that all of the ASP.NET-based features key their user records off of a combination of username and an application name usually found in a provider's configuration. In the case of the `Role Principal`, when you use the constructors the `RolePrincipal` "knows" how to look up user information from the default provider based on the following information:

❑   The username comes from `IIdentity.Name`.

❑   For the constructor with just a single `IIdentity` parameter, the application name is the one used by the default `RoleProvider` as defined in configuration.

❑   For the constructor that takes an additional `providerName` parameter, the application name is the one associated with `Roles.Providers[providerName]`.

In this way, the `RolePrincipal` can take an arbitrary string representation of a username, and it can associate the username with role data maintained by any of the configured providers.

Most of the methods on `RolePrincipal` that are not directly associated with cookie caching are pretty self-explanatory:

❑   `IsInRole`: Based on `IIdentity.Name` and the application name of the associated provider, the `RolePrincipal` indicates whether or not `IIdentity.Name` belongs to the specified role. If the `RolePrincipal` has not previously cached role information for the user, then the associated provider is called to get all of the user's roles. If this method is called for an `IIdentity` of an unauthenticated user (that is, `IIdentity.IsAuthenticated` returns `false`), then this method always returns `false`. This is because the Role Manager feature is only intended for use with authenticated users. Because many sites have public and secured pages, the Role Manager feature can silently run without error for unauthenticated users; it's just that methods like `IsInRole` will always return `false`.

- ❑ GetRoles: The RolePrincipal returns a string array containing all of the roles that IIdentity .Name belongs to. If the RolePrincipal has not previously cached role information for the user, then the associated provider is called to get all of the user's roles. As with IsInRole, this method has special behavior for unauthenticated users. For an unauthenticated user, this method always returns an empty string array (that is, string[0]).

- ❑ SetDirty: Tells the RolePrincipal object that it should invalidate any internally cached data. As a result, the next call to IsInRole or GetRoles will always result in a round trip to the associated provider.

The noncookie caching properties and their behavior are listed here:

- ❑ Identity: This property returns the IIdentity that was originally used when the RolePrincipal was constructed.

- ❑ ProviderName: The name of the provider associated with the RolePrincipal. This will return the name of the default provider (if you used the constructor that only accepts an IIdentity) or it will return the name of one of the providers configured for use with Role Manager. This property is a string parameter because the RolePrincipal is itself serializable. By storing the associated provider as a string name, RoleProviders don't themselves need to be serializable. Note that if your application does something funky like serializing a principal in one app-domain and deserializing it in another app-domain, you need to make sure that ProviderName is available in the Role Manager's provider collection for the app-domain where deserialization occurs.

- ❑ IsRoleListCached: This property returns true if RolePrincipal is currently caching the user's roles internally. This internal cache is discussed in the next few paragraphs.

- ❑ Version: Currently, this property will always return 1 for the 2.0 Framework. In future versions if the internal format or the public functionality of the RolePrincipal changes, the Version property will be changed as well.

Both the IsInRole and GetRoles methods rely on the RoleProvider associated with the Role Principal to carry out their work. It turns out that the internal implementation of IsInRole results in a call to RoleProvider.GetRolesForUser as opposed to RoleProvider.IsUserInRole. The reason for this behavior is that even if you have cookie caching turned off, the RolePrincipal still attempts to optimize performance of the IsInRole method.

Immediately after you new() up a RolePrincipal there is an empty internal dictionary that is ready and waiting to cache role information. The first call after object construction to either IsInRole or GetRoles causes the RolePrincipal to get a reference to its associated provider and retrieve a string array of the roles associated with the user. This array is then cached within the principal's internal role dictionary. Code can verify this is the case because after the role information is cached RolePrincipal.IsRoleListCached returns true. Now on subsequent calls to IsInRole, RolePrincipal recognizes that this dictionary contains data. So, instead of making a round trip to the provider again, the principal just looks for the requested role inside of the dictionary of cached role information. GetRoles has similar behavior, although in its case the method just returns the internal dictionary as an array because there is no need to search for a specific role.

Of course, at some point you may want to invalidate the cached role information. For example, after 15 minutes have passed, you may want to force the RolePrincipal to "forget" its current role information and refresh it from the provider. When you call the SetDirty method, it flips the value of Role Principal.IsRoleListCached to false. The next time either IsInRole or GetRoles is called,

`RolePrincipal` sees that the role information is now considered stale, and so it queries the provider again for all of the user's role data. This caching behavior has a few implications that you need to be aware of.

Because `GetRolesForUser` is called on the provider, users associated with large numbers of roles (that is, hundreds of roles) will find the `RolePrincipal` to be slow the first time either `IsInRole` or `GetRolesForUser` is called. In fact, for websites or other applications that need to support hundreds of roles per user, you should carefully assess the performance of retrieving all of a user's roles for these methods. To cut down on the number of round trips made to the back-end data store, you may find that you need to implement a custom `RoleProvider` that internally caches a user's role information.

The second issue is that the `IsInRole` method compares the `role` parameter against values in the internal dictionary with a case-insensitive comparison, using the casing rules for the invariant culture. If you happen to use a back end like SQL Server and you are running a case-insensitive sort order with the Latin collation order, the behavior of the `RolePrincipal` comparison won't matter to you. The standard Latin collation order is roughly equivalent to the Framework's invariant culture. But if you happen to use a non-Latin character set, you may run into issues where the casing rules in the database don't match the casing rules for `RolePrincipal`. Remember from Chapter 11, on `SqlMembershipProvider`, that all of the SQL based ASP.NET providers work in a case-insensitive manner. The `SqlRoleProvider` also works in a case-insensitive manner. However, even though the providers for Role Manager work in a case-insensitive manner, casing rules are still partially determined by the culture as well.

The casing rules for the invariant culture are not the same as the casing rules for Cryllic (as an example). As a result, you can end up in some edge scenarios where you create role names in your data store that are considered unique because the data store is using *culture-specific* casing rules. But when you attempt to use `RolePrincipal` it throws an exception because from a culture-invariant standpoint it thinks two role names are actually the same value. The array of strings returned from `RoleProvider` `.GetRolesForUser` could contain two strings that are considered the same value in the invariant culture. When the `RolePrincipal` attempts to add the strings to its internal dictionary (which is an instance of a `HybridDictionary`), the dictionary can throw an `ArgumentException` because it detects duplicate string values.

Another issue can arise where the result of `RolePrincipal.IsInRole` does not match the result from `RoleProvider.IsUserInRole`. The classic "Turkish I" problem is an example where a mismatch can occur for role comparisons. In the Turkish character set a capital "I" and a small "i" are actually associated with two completely different characters. Lowering "I" in Turkish will result in a completely different character than the English "i." This can cause a problem when `RolePrincipal.IsInRole` is called by URL authorization because if role names from the database differ only on characters like "I," then `RolePrincipal.IsInRole` may consider a user to belong to more roles than they really do. For example, from an invariant culture perspective a user may be considered to belong to both "ThIs role" and "This role." So if you had a URL authorization rule like `<add roles="ThIs role" />`, and the role in a database with the Turkish collation was "This role," the `RolePrincipal` object would return true from `IsInRole`. However, the same comparison made using `RoleProvider.IsUserInRole` against the database would treat these two roles as completely different and unique strings. A role check using the provider directly would succeed only for "This role." It would fail for the other role because in Turkish the capital "I" is from a different character pair.

Now granted that this discussion can be a bit mind-numbing, and when the ASP.NET team attempted to protect against this, the cure was worse than the problem. The main thing to remember is that if you use Role Manager with data stores that aren't running in the invariant culture (for example, the

Latin1_General collation is a close enough approximation in SQL Server), make sure that the role names you choose result in consistent string comparisons in your data store and on servers where you will be calling RolePrincipal.IsInRole.

At this point, take a look at a simple example of a console application that demonstrates how the internal caching behavior of RolePrincipal works. Just as Membership works in non-ASP.NET environments, Role Manager can be used outside of ASP.NET. The sample console application references System.Web.dll and includes configuration settings in its app.config file to enable the Role Manager feature:

```
<roleManager enabled="true"
             defaultProvider="roleprincipalcaching">
  <providers>
    <add name="roleprincipalcaching"
              etc… />
  </providers>
</roleManager>
```

The console application performs some initial setup for the example and then exercises the internal cache logic in RolePrincipal by calling GetRoles after the role assignments have been changed:

C#

```csharp
using System.Security;
using System.Web.Security;
…
static void Main(string[] args)
{
    //initial setup code - snipped for brevity…

    GenericIdentity gi = new GenericIdentity("testuser_rp");
    RolePrincipal rp = new RolePrincipal(gi);

    string[] currentRoles = rp.GetRoles();
    foreach (string r in currentRoles)
        Console.WriteLine(r);

    //Now change the user's role assignments
    Roles.AddUserToRole("testuser_rp", "role_2");
    Roles.RemoveUserFromRole("testuser_rp", "role_3");

    //The RolePrincipal's roles will not have changed at this point
    //Note that the sample code never sets Thread.CurrentPrincipal so
    //the RolePrincipal has not been invalidated at this point
    currentRoles = rp.GetRoles();
    foreach (string r in currentRoles)
        Console.WriteLine(r);

    //Force the RolePrincipal to flush its internal cache
    rp.SetDirty();

    //Now the RolePrincipal will reflect the changes
    currentRoles = rp.GetRoles();
```

```
        foreach (string r in currentRoles)
            Console.WriteLine(r);
}
```

VB.NET

```
Imports Microsoft.VisualBasic
Imports System.Security
Imports System.Web.Security

…

Shared Sub Main(ByVal args() As String)
    'initial setup code - snipped for brevity…

  Dim gi As New GenericIdentity("testuser_rp")
  Dim rp As New RolePrincipal(gi)

  Dim currentRoles() As String = rp.GetRoles()
  For Each r As String In currentRoles
        Console.WriteLine(r)
  Next r

  'Serialize the RolePrincipal
  Dim stringRP As String = rp.ToEncryptedTicket()
  Console.WriteLine("The length of the encrypted ticket is: " & stringRP.Length)

  'Now change the user's role assignments
  Roles.AddUserToRole("testuser_rp", "role_2")
  Roles.RemoveUserFromRole("testuser_rp", "role_3")

  'The RolePrincipal's roles will not have changed at this point
  currentRoles = rp.GetRoles()
  For Each r As String In currentRoles
        Console.WriteLine(r)
  Next r

  'Force the RolePrincipal to flush its internal cache
  rp.SetDirty()

  'Now the RolePrincipal will reflect the changes
  currentRoles = rp.GetRoles()
  For Each r As String In currentRoles
        Console.WriteLine(r)
  Next r

End Sub
```

A GenericIdentity is constructed with a username that has already been associated with three roles using the default provider. The first call to GetRoles causes this information to be loaded from the provider:

```
role_1
role_3
role_5
```

After dumping out this information, the test application changes the user's role assignments by adding the user to a new role, as well as removing the user from an existing role. However, because the first call to GetRoles caused the RolePrincipal to cache the role information internally, the next call to GetRoles still uses the cached information.

```
role_1
role_3
role_5
```

The RolePrincipal doesn't reflect the changes to the user's role assignments at this point. The test application then forces the RolePrincipal instance to flush the cached information with a call to SetDirty. Now when the test application calls GetRoles again, the principal goes back to the provider to reload the role data, and as a result the output reflects the changes that were made.

```
role_1
role_2
role_5
```

Keep this behavior in mind if you happen to be working with an administrative application where you change user-to-role assignments. If you Alt-Tab off to another browser window running as the user you just edited, and you are wondering why no changes are showing up, it is probably the caching behavior in RolePrincipal that is preventing your changes from taking effect.

Now that you have an understanding of how the internal cache within RolePrincipal works, you can explore how cookie caching is supported as an additional caching layer. The Role Manager feature has the ability to take the internal role cache within a RolePrincipal and store this information inside of a cookie. The RoleManagerModule is responsible for managing this process, but it is the RolePrincipal that supports the core functionality that makes this all work.

The method that makes this work is the ToEncryptedTicket method on the principal. This method serializes a RolePrincipal instance into a string. Internally, the method first runs RolePrincipal through the binary formatter. Because RolePrincipal implements ISerializable, some custom serialization logic runs at this point to handle the serialization of the principal's IIdentity. RolePrincipal *doesn't* serialize its associated IIdentity when serialization occurs as a result of a call to the ToEncrypted Ticket method. Note that if you just write some serialization code using the Framework's Binary Formatter directly, then the IIdentity reference will be serialized.

Because the intent of ToEncryptedTicket is to convert the RolePrincipal into a payload suitable for a cookie, it intentionally skips serializing the IIdentity reference. There is no need for it when reconstituting a RolePrincipal from a cookie because the constructor overloads that accept the stringized RolePrincipal also require an IIdentity reference. As a side note, RolePrincipal in the RTM version of the Framework uses binary serialization because theoretically this should make it easier in future versions to be able to run web farms with different versions of the Framework issuing different serialized versions of RolePrincipal. Both up-level and down-level versions of the Framework should be able to work with a serialized RolePrincipal without blowing up due to deserialization exceptions.

After ToEncryptedTicket gets back a byte array representation of the RolePrincipal, it converts the byte array into a string that can be safely stored in a cookie without triggering ASP.NET request validation. As part of this conversion, RolePrincipal secures the string using the settings from the cookieProtection attribute in the configuration element. By default, the string is encrypted using AES and signed with HMACSHA1. The algorithms used and the key values used are all determined from the section. If you want to change any of this information, you can change the configuration attributes on just as you would for controlling the encryption and signing information for forms authentication. Also, as with forms authentication, you can change the cookieProtection attribute on to None, All, Encryption, or Validation.

At this point, the work of ToEncryptedTicket is done; it doesn't actually validate if the resulting payload is too large for storage in a cookie. Furthermore, there isn't any functionality inside ToEncryptedTicket specific to ASP.NET. You can literally serialize RolePrincipal into a string, store the string somewhere (on a disk, in a database table, and so on), and then reconstitute the RolePrincipal from the string at a later point in time.

C#

```
//Serialize the RolePrincipal
string stringRP = rp.ToEncryptedTicket();

//Do some other work here...

//Reconstitute the RolePrincipal
RolePrincipal anotherRP = new RolePrincipal(gi, stringRP);
Console.WriteLine("User is in role_1: " + anotherRP.IsInRole("role_1"));
Console.WriteLine("User is in role_3: " + anotherRP.IsInRole("role_3"));
Console.WriteLine("User is in role_5: " + anotherRP.IsInRole("role_5"));
```

VB.NET

```
'Serialize the RolePrincipal
Dim stringRP As String = rp.ToEncryptedTicket()

'Do some other work here...

'Reconstitute the RolePrincipal
Dim anotherRP As New RolePrincipal(gi, stringRP)
Console.WriteLine("User is in role_1: " & anotherRP.IsInRole("role_1"))
Console.WriteLine("User is in role_3: " & anotherRP.IsInRole("role_3"))
Console.WriteLine("User is in role_5: " & anotherRP.IsInRole("role_5"))
```

The output from this sample code is:

```
User is in role_1: True
User is in role_3: True
User is in role_5: True
```

Using the sample console application from earlier, you can extend it by serializing the RolePrincipal prior to changing the user's role assignments (remember the user was removed from role 3 and added to role 2). If you add this code to the sample application, after creating a new RolePrincipal using the output from ToEncryptedTicket, the original role information is cached internally by the new RolePrincipal instance.

What is interesting, though, is if you take the new `RolePrincipal` and call `GetRoles` on it:

C#

```
currentRoles = anotherRP.GetRoles();
foreach (string r in currentRoles)
 Console.WriteLine(r);
```

VB.NET

```
currentRoles = anotherRP.GetRoles()
For Each r As String In currentRoles
        Console.WriteLine(r)
Next r
```

when you dump out the results you will see what might look like a discrepancy:

```
role_1
role_2
role_5
```

What happened here? For a second there it looked like the output of `ToEncrypedTicket` preserved the set of role assignments at the time serialization occurred. The previous code snippet with a series of `IsInRole` checks definitely confirms this behavior. The reason for this apparent schizophrenia of the `RolePrincipal` is that the principal handles the internal cache differently when a new `Role Principal` is initialized from the string output of `ToEncryptedTicket`.

After you call either of the two constructors that have an `encryptedTicket` parameter (the two constructor overloads are the companions to the two constructor overloads discussed earlier with the one difference being the extra string parameter for the encrypted ticket), `RolePrincipal` does a few special things with the extra string data:

1. The `encryptedTicket` parameter is decoded back into a byte array, and that array is then deserialized with the `BinaryFormatter`.

2. The `RolePrincipal` makes two sanity checks with the resulting data. It confirms that the username that was previously encoded into the `encryptedTicket` matches the username on the `IIdentity` that was passed to the constructor. Then `RolePrincipal` confirms that the provider name encoded in the `encryptedTicket` matches the name of the provider associated with the current `RolePrincipal` instance. Both of these comparisons are case-insensitive ordinal comparisons. If either of these checks fails, the ticket is discarded and the `RolePrincipal` instance functions as if it were constructed without the encrypted ticket.

3. If the expiration date contained in the deserialized ticket indicates that the information has expired, the ticket is discarded and the `RolePrincipal` instance functions as if it were constructed without the encrypted ticket.

4. `RolePrincipal` looks at `IssueDate` and `ExpireDate` that were extracted from the `encrypted Ticket`. If you have configured Role Manager to support sliding cookie expirations (that is, the `cookieSlidingExpiration` configuration attribute on the `<roleManager />` configuration element has been set to `true`), and if more than 50% of the encrypted ticket's lifetime has passed, the principal resets `IssueDate` to the current date-time and updates `ExpireDate` accordingly. As a side effect of this, the state of the principal is considered to have changed so the principal also marks itself for reserialization when `RoleManagerModule` runs at the end of a page request.

These validations ensure that the string-encoded version of the `RolePrincipal` is not spuriously used with a different user. It also ensures that whatever machine is responsible for decoding the encrypted string actually has a named `RoleProvider` matching the one defined within the `encryptedTicket` parameter. These checks imply a few things you need to do if you want cookie caching to work properly across multiple machines in a web farm.

First, you need to ensure that all of the providers are configured the same way across all of the machines. This means the same provider names need to be present for the encrypted string representation of a principal to work. It also implicitly means that providers with the same name in a web farm should be configured the same way. For example, the `RolePrincipal` is not going to validate that the application name for a provider called "foo" on one machine is actually the same application name as the provider "foo" that was associated with `RolePrincipal` when it was originally serialized on a different machine. If for some reason you use the same provider names across a web farm but with different application names, then it is likely you will end up with inconsistent role information depending on what machine servers up any given request.

The second assumption is that if a user is initially authenticated as foo when a `RolePrincipal` is serialized, then on another machine when a `RolePrincipal` is being deserialized the same user will be known as foo. Typically, for custom authentication schemes, or for forms authentication, the string value of the authenticated username is fixed after login. For example, the string used at login time against a site using forms authentication is encoded into the forms authentication cookie, and hence will remain the same for the duration of the login session.

Back to the original problem where the sample code appeared to lose the cached role information passed via `encryptedTicket`. Assuming that none of the validations just described failed, you have a `RolePrincipal` with its internal dictionary containing all of the roles from `encryptedTicket`. When this initialization occurs though, `RolePrincipal` "remembers" that it was initialized from an encrypted string, and *not* from a call to `RoleProvider.GetRolesForUser`. As long as your code just calls `IsIn Role`, `RolePrincipal` will continue to fulfill this request using the internal dictionary of roles.

However, after you call `GetRoles` as shown in the earlier code snippet, `RolePrincipal` decides that the role information from the encrypted string is not sufficiently authoritative to fulfill the request. So instead, the `RolePrincipal` flushes its internal cache and then calls `GetRolesForUser` on the provider. After `GetRolesForUser` is called, the `RolePrincipal` ends up with the latest role information for the user, which is why in the sample the dump of the user's roles after the call to `GetRolesForUser` was different from the results of the successive `IsInRole` checks. After `GetRolesForUser` has been called on the provider, the `RolePrincipal` remembers that this has occurred, and now all subsequent calls to either `IsInRole` or `GetRoles` will be served from the principal's internal cache.

Part of the reason for this discrepancy in behavior is that cookie caching is meant to be used only to speed up calls to `IPrincipal.IsInRole`. Hence, the reason for storing the `encryptedTicket` in a cookie is only to fulfill role checks. The general idea behind calling `GetRoles` is that the caller wants to have a reasonably up-to-date representation of that user's roles. Even though calling `GetRoles` more than once results in the use of cached data, in the normal use of a `RolePrincipal` on an ASP.NET page request, the page is running for only a few seconds. So, having `GetRoles` call the provider the first time ensures that for the duration of the page request your code has a very up-to-date array of the user's roles. The subsequent caching in this case is a minor optimization to ensure that if the page code continues to call `GetRoles` that the page doesn't end up thrashing the underlying data store. If your code actually requires different `GetRoles` calls to return different data, you can always manually force the principal to flush its internal cache through a call to `SetDirty`.

Aside from the extra constructor overloads and the `ToEncryptedTicket` method, there are a few properties on `RolePrincipal` that deal with cookie caching. These are briefly described in the following list:

❑   `CachedListChanged`: If the principal calls `GetRolesForUser` on its associated provider, if `SetDirty` is called, or if the `RolePrincipal` renewed the `IssueDate` and `ExpireDate` due to sliding expirations, the value of this property is set to `true`. However, if the principal is initialized from an encrypted ticket, the issue and expiration dates were not refreshed, and only `IsInRole` is called on the principal, this property returns `false`. This property is used by the `RoleManagerModule` to determine whether it needs to reissue the role cache cookie. If the state of the principle's internal cache initialized from an encrypted ticket has not changed and the date information also has not changed, then the `RoleManagerModule` can avoid the expensive overhead of reserializing the `RolePrincipal` and encrypting the results.

❑   `IssueDate`: Returns the machine local date-time the cached information in an `encrypted Ticket` was originally created. If the `RolePrincipal` was not initialized from an `encrypted Ticket`, this property always returns the current local date-time. Note that internally this data is stored as a UTC date-time, and the "UTCness" of this value is preserved when a `RolePrincipal` is serialized by `ToEncryptedTicket`.

❑   `ExpireDate`: Returns the machine local date-time that the cached information in an `encryptedTicket` is no longer considered valid. If the `RolePrincipal` was not initialized from an `encryptedTicket` (for example, the first time a `RolePrincipal` for a user is ever created), this value is set to the current local date-time plus the value of the `cookieTimeout` configuration attribute on the `<roleManager />` configuration element. As with `IssueDate`, internally this value is maintained as a UTC date-time.

❑   `Expired`: This property compares the private UTC value of `ExpireDate` against the current UTC date-time. If `ExpireDate` is less than the current UTC date-time, then the property returns `true`. This property is checked when the `RolePrincipal` is deserialized from an `encryptedTicket` to determine whether the encrypted information is stale. Note that you can end up in an edge case where the deserialization check succeeds, but then one millisecond later the encrypted information expires. In this case, for the duration of the lifetime of the `RolePrincipal`, the cached information from the `encryptedTicket` will still be used. This behavior is OK for a page request, because a page request is normally completed in a few seconds. However, if you are using the string ticket to initialize a `RolePrincipal` inside an application like a Winforms application, where a `RolePrincipal` instance may live for a very long time, then you should ensure that you have code in your application that periodically checks the `Expired` property on the principal and generates a new instance if the current `RolePrincipal` is expired.

❑   `CookiePath`: This property simply returns the value of `Roles.CookiePath`, which in turn comes from the `cookiePath` configuration attribute on the `<roleManager />` configuration element. At one point, the path information for a `RolePrincipal` was actually stored in the `encrypted-Ticket`. However, the path is no longer stored in the serialized string because you could end up bloating the size of the serialized string for applications that had lengthy URLs. Note that in a web farm environment all machines must be configured to use the same `cookiePath` for Role Manager. Otherwise, the role cache cookie issued by one web server may never be sent back to other servers in the farm.

In the next section, you will see how the `RoleManagerModule` works with the `RolePrincipal` to issue a cookie that contains the `encryptedTicket`. Keep in mind ahead of time that it's possible to create an `encryptedTicket` that is too large for the `RoleManagerModule` to store in a cookie. Because serializing a `RolePrincipal` and then encrypting and hashing the result is an expensive operation, you should test the size of the return value from the `ToEncryptedTicket` method for users with a large number of roles. If the resulting string is longer that 4096 characters, then the `RoleManagerModule` is never going to issue a roles cookie, and hence you should probably turn off cookie caching.

Because the `RolePrincipal` uses binary serialization, this adds a few hundred characters of overhead to the size of the role cache cookie. Roughly speaking, there is about an additional 350-character overhead due to using binary serialization as opposed to some type of custom serialization mechanism. This overhead is on top of the bloat caused by encoding the role information for storage in the cookie. For the earlier sample where the user belonged to just three roles, the `encryptedTicket` was 492 characters long, even though the length of the three role names was just 18 characters. Remember though that this cookie stores not only each role name, but also issue/expiry dates, a version number, the user's username, the provider name and a few pieces of internal tracking information. As a result, there is always some additional character overhead from storing all of this information. From testing the cookie caching feature with various numbers of roles, the ASP.NET team has been able to successfully store 300 roles (each role name was around seven characters long) in a role cache cookie with a cookie protection setting of "All."

The RoleManagerModule

The `RoleManagerModule` is an `HttpModule` that is responsible for two main tasks:

❑ Early during the request lifecycle, it places a `RolePrincipal` instance on `HttpContext.Current.User` if the Role Manager feature is enabled. This work occurs during the `PostAuthenticateRequest` event.

❑ At the end of a request, the module serializes the `RolePrincipal` into a cookie if cookie caching has been enabled for Role Manager. The module does this during the `EndRequest` event.

The `RoleManagerModule` also exposes an extensibility point with the `GetRoles` event. If you want, you can hook this event and add your own `IPrincipal` implementation to the context. This event is fired just before the module performs its regular processing during `PostAuthenticateRequest`.

PostAuthenticateRequest

The `RoleManagerModule` subscribes to the `PostAuthenticateRequest` pipeline event because it needs to set up a principal after an authenticated identity has been established but before any authorization occurs. In earlier versions of ASP.NET, doing this was a bit tricky because there were no `Post*` events. However, ASP.NET 2.0 introduced a set of `Post*` events for every major pipeline event, and this made it very easy for functionality like Role Manager to inject itself at precisely the right time during the authentication and authorization process in the HTTP pipeline.

If the Role Manager feature is not enabled, the module immediately exits. This is important because if you look at the default `HttpModule` configuration in the root `web.config`, you will see that the `RoleManagerModule` is always registered.

```
<httpModules>
  <add name="WindowsAuthentication"  …. />
  <add name="FormsAuthentication" … />
  <add name="RoleManager" type="System.Web.Security.RoleManagerModule" />
```

```
<!--- other modules --->
<add name="UrlAuthorization" … />
<add name="FileAuthorization" … />
<!--- other modules --->
</httpModules>
```

So, the module registration is basically a no-op in the case that the Role Manager feature is disabled. Assuming that the Role Manager feature is enabled though, the first thing the module does is fire the GetRoles event. The event argument for this event can be used by a custom event handler to communicate back to the module as to whether the event handler attached a user principal to the context. The framework's definition of the event argument is:

C#

```csharp
public sealed class RoleManagerEventArgs : EventArgs {
  //Constructor
  public RoleManagerEventArgs(HttpContext context)
  //Properties
  public  bool  RolesPopulated { get; set; }
  public  HttpContext Context { get; }
}
```

VB.NET

```vbnet
Public NotInheritable Class RoleManagerEventArgs
    Inherits EventArgs
    'Constructor
    Public Sub New(ByVal context As HttpContext)

    ' Properties
    Public ReadOnly Property Context As HttpContext
    Public Property RolesPopulated As Boolean

End Class
```

When an event handler needs to attach a user to the context, it can use the Context property from the event argument as a convenient way to reference it. Now if an event handler does attach a user to the context, it needs to indicate that this has occurred by setting the RolesPopulated property of the event argument to true. When the RoleManagerModule sees that RolesPopulated has been set to true, it will immediately exit from the PostAuthenticateRequest event. This is an important point because the normal behavior of the RoleManagerModule is to extract an IIdentity from whatever principal is on the context and then rewrap this IIdentity inside of a RolePrincipal. As a result, just setting a principal on the context from inside of the GetRoles event handler is not sufficient if your intent is to stop the RoleManagerModule from any further processing.

One question you may have is why would you hook the GetRoles event? Although you could certainly use the RolesPopulated event as a way to add your own custom principal to the HttpContext, the "correct" way to accomplish this is by writing code in global.asax that hooks AuthenticateRequest or PostAuthenticateRequest. Enabling the Role Manager feature just to hook the GetRoles event is complete overkill for this scenario. If the RolePrincipal class was not sealed, then GetRoles would have been a logical place to add a custom RolePrincipal-derived class to the context. But of course because RolePrincipal is sealed in ASP.NET 2.0 and ASP.NET 3.5, you can't do this either.

Probably the main use for the GetRoles event in ASP.NET 2.0 and ASP.NET 3.5 is for developers that configure multiple providers for use with the Role Manager feature. Unless you write extra code, the RoleManagerModule only works with the *default* provider. If you look at the Role Manager API, nowhere will you find a way to configure the RoleManagerModule to automatically choose a nondefault provider when it creates a RolePrincipal. The GetRoles event is the hook you need to be able to create a RolePrincipal that works with a nondefault RoleProvider. With some extra code, you can include extra logic that on a per-user basis selects the appropriate RoleProvider when new()'ing up a RolePrincipal. This technique is shown a bit later in the chapter.

Assuming that you don't hook the GetRoles event, the module performs the following:

❑   For anonymous users, any role cache cookie is ignored. In fact for anonymous users, if a role cache cookie is found, a clear cookie header is sent back to the browser to delete it. Remember that for anonymous users the RoleManagerModule just creates a RolePrincipal that always returns false from IsInRole and an empty array from GetRoles.

❑   For authenticated users if the request does not have a role cache cookie, the module creates a RolePrincipal that is based on the current IIdentity reference that can be extracted from HttpContext.User.Context. This means that for forms authentication a RolePrincipal that wraps a FormsIdentity is created. For sites using Windows authentication, a RolePrincipal that wraps a WindowsIdentity is created. The main idea here is that the current IIdentity of the authenticated user is preserved, while the outer IPrincipal based object is thrown away and replaced by a RolePrincipal. As part of this work, the RolePrincipal created is associated with the *default* Role Manager provider. As noted earlier, if you want to use a nondefault provider you must use the GetRoles event and write your own logic for creating a RolePrincipal.

❑   For authenticated requests that include a role cache cookie, the module creates a Role Principal based on the current IIdentity and the encoded role information stored in the role cache cookie. This means a RolePrincipal is initialized using the constructor overload that accepts an IIdentity and a string value for the serialized representation of the Role Principal's role information. This logic process is similar to that in the previous bullet point, with the one exception being that now the RolePrincipal has its internal role cache initialized based on the information from the role cache cookie. This also means that the default processing in the module associates the RolePrincipal with the Role Manager's default provider as well.

There are a few sanity checks that RoleManagerModule will follow when it finds a role cache cookie:

❑   If a role cache cookie is sent in the request, but cookie-based caching is not enabled (that is, the cacheRolesInCookie configuration attribute is set to false), then the cookie is ignored. In this case, the RolePrincipal is initialized with just the current IIdentity and the default provider.

❑   For anonymous users, the cookie is always ignored and cleared as mentioned earlier.

❑   If the cookieRequiresSSL attribute is set to true in configuration, and the current connection is not an SSL connection, the cookie is ignored and a clear cookie header is sent back to the browser. This check is intended to handle the case where a user agent does not honor the secure bit on the cookie, and the agent sends the cookie over an unsecured connection. In this case, the RoleManagerModule does not "trust" the cookie contents, and so it just drops the cookie and initializes the RolePrincipal using only the current IIdentity and the default RoleProvider.

So, one way or another `RoleManagerModule` eventually ends up with a `RolePrincipal` (potentially initialized from the cookie). As a last processing step during `PostAuthenticateRequest`, the module sets the `RolePrincipal` as the new value of `HttpContext.Current.User`, and it also sets the `Role Principal` on `Thread.CurrentPrincipal`.

Explicitly synchronizing `HttpContext` and `Thread` with the same principal is necessary because `DefaultAuthenticationModule`, discussed in Chapter 3, runs after the `AuthenticateRequest` pipeline processing is done. However, the `PostAuthenticateRequest` event runs *after* `Authenticate Request`, as well as *after* the hidden `DefaultAuthenticationModule`. If `RoleManagerModule` did not explicitly synchronize the principal across both `HttpContext` and the current `Thread`, then any authorization logic that used the `Thread.CurrentPrincipal` property would result in different results than authorization logic using `HttpContext.Current.User`. An example of this is declarative role authorizations; the `System.Security.Permissions.PrincipalPermission` attribute makes checks using `Thread.CurrentPrincipal`.

For example, if you had a method in a web page that should only be callable by members of the Administrators role, you could enforce this one of two ways. The imperative approach would be to write a line of code like the following:

C#

```
public void DoSomethingPrivileged()
{
    if (User.IsInRole("Adminstrators"))
        { //do some privileged work }
}
```

VB.NET

```
Public Sub DoSomethingPrivileged()
    If User.IsInRole("Adminstrators") Then
      'do some privileged work
    End If
```

However, because `RoleManagerModule` does the right thing and synchronizes values appropriately, you can use a declarative approach to security instead:

C#

```
[PrincipalPermission(SecurityAction.Demand, Role="Administrators")]
public void DoSomethingPrivileged()
{ //do something privileged here }
```

VB.NET

```
<PrincipalPermission(SecurityAction.Demand, Role:="Administrators")> _
Public Sub DoSomethingPrivileged()
      'do some privileged work
End Sub
```

Supporting declarative security with Role Manager also works in non-ASP.NET scenarios, though in non-ASP.NET hosts the `RoleManagerModule` never runs. If you want `RolePrincipal` to work in non-

ASP.NET applications with declarative security demands, you can write code during application initialization that sets the RolePrincipal onto the appropriate thread using Thread.CurrentPrincipal. With all of this said though, you will most likely use imperative (that is, write code) based authorization logic because it is substantially easier to write code that strings together complex rules involving OR logic (that is, if a user belongs to role_A or (role_B and role_C), then carry out some custom logic).

EndRequest

RoleManagerModule also runs during the EndRequest event of the pipeline. The only work the module performs during this event is to send the role cache cookie. If caching role information in a cookie is not enabled, then the module doesn't perform any work during EndRequest. Assuming that the role caching is enabled though, the module goes through the following steps to send a role cache cookie.

❏   If the current user is anonymous, the module never sends a role cache cookie. Instead, it just exits from EndRequest.

❏   If the cookieRequiresSSL attribute is set to true, the current user is authenticated, but the current connection is not secured with SSL, the module does not send a role cache cookie. In this way, RoleManagerModule is honoring the intent of the cookieRequiresSSL attribute; not only should browser agents not send the role cache cookie over unsecured connections, but the module itself should never be issuing the cookie in first place over non-SSL connections.

❏   If the user is authenticated, and there are no problems with the SSL state of the connection, then RoleManagerModule checks to see whether a role cache cookie needs to be issued. It does this by looking at the value of RolePrincipal.CachedListChanged. This property will always be set to true after a call to RolePrincipal.GetRoles (remember that for a "fresh" Role Principal the first call to IsInRole triggers a call to the GetRoles method). The property can also be set to true if the current RolePrincipal was previously initialized from a role cache cookie, and the principal determined that less than 50% of the cookie's TTL remains. In this case, the RolePrincipal internally refreshes the issue date and expiration date values for the RolePrincipal if the cookieSlidingExpiration configuration attribute is set to true. The principal then indicates that these changes have occurred by setting CachedListChanged to true. If sliding cookie expiration is not enabled though, this auto-refresh of the date information will never occur. The only things that change for the date-refresh case are the issuance and expiration dates; the internal role cache at this point has not changed. Regardless of what ultimately caused CachedListChanged to be set to true, the RoleManagerModule converts the current RolePrincipal into an encrypted ticket with a call to RolePrincipal.ToEncryptedTicket.

❏   If RolePrincipal.CachedListChanged is false, then the module exits because there is no need to update the role cache cookie.

❏   If the resulting string from ToEncryptedTicket is longer than 4096 characters, then the Role ManagerModule ignores the serialized value and does not send the cookie with the serialized role information. Instead, the module sends a clear cookie back to the browser. From testing both Internet Explorer and Mozilla, a role manager cookie with a value that is 4096 characters in length works with Role Manager. However, as you get above this limit, different versions of these browsers start exhibiting different behavior around accepting long cookies and sending such long cookies. For this reason, 4096 characters was chosen as a safe and reasonable upper limit for the maximum length of the value of the role cache cookie.

❑ If the result of serializing `RolePrincipal`'s role information is a null, then the module instead sends a clear cookie back to the browser. This normally will only occur if the current user belongs to more roles than specified in the `maxCachedResults` attribute. The reason that `RoleManager Module` sends a clear cookie in this case is to handle the scenario where a user once belonged to one or more roles and had a role cache cookie issued. Then at a later point in time the user belonged to a larger number of roles, and the cached role information expired and was subsequently refreshed from a provider. In this case, the role cache cookie needs to be reissued, but because there are now more roles than can be safely cached in the role cookie, a clear cookie is sent as the "new" role cache cookie.

❑ If the processing logic makes it past the previous security and length checks, then `RoleManager Module` creates a new `HttpCookie`, sets the various cookie properties based on the settings in the `<roleManager />` configuration element, and sends it back in the `Response`.

Role Cache Cookie Settings and Behavior

The previous discussions have alluded to a number of different configuration attributes on `<roleManager />` used to configure caching behavior with Role Manager. The following list summarizes the available settings and the effect they have on role cache cookies.

❑ `cacheRolesInCookie`: The default value in configuration is false. You need to explicitly configure `<roleManager cacheRolesInCookie="true" />` in your configuration to enable the cookie caching behavior of the `RoleManagerModule`.

❑ `createPersistentCookie`: By default, if role cache cookies are issued, they are sent as session-based cookies. This means no explicit expiration date is set on the cookie, and instead the cookie expires when the browser closes. Note though that even for persistent cookies, the validity of the information in the role cache cookie is determined by the issuance and expiration date values that are encoded within the serialized role information. The Role Manager feature never relies on the browser behavior as a determinant of the "freshness" of the role cache cookie. For performance reasons, you can set this configuration attribute to true, in which case an explicit expiration date is set on the cookie, which causes the cookie to be persisted to disk by most browsers. This gives you some capability for cross-browser-session persistence of cached role information. You should only enable persistent cookies though for sites where security is not terribly important. A persistent cookie is potentially available to be hijacked and moved to another machine. It also can result in stale role information being associated with a user even though an administrator has changed the user-to-role associations in the back-end data store.

❑ `cookieTimeout`: By default this is set to 30 minutes. This value really drives the expiration date for the cached role information that you get from calling `RolePrincipal.ToEncrypted Ticket`. If a `RolePrincipal` is initialized from an encrypted string, and if after deserialization the role information indicates that it has expired based on the current time and the expiration date that was determined from `cookieTimeout`, then `RolePrincipal` ignores the encrypted ticket and instead will fetch fresh role information from its associated provider. Because the most likely use of the ticket is as the value for the role cache cookie, the TTL for the serialized role information is configured with the `cookieTimeout` setting even though the setting really applies to the behavior of the `RolePrincipal` constructors that accept an encrypted ticket. If persistent cookies are used, then the timeout setting is also used to set the expiration date for the persistent role cache cookie sent to the browser.

❑ cookieRequiresSSL: By default, this attribute it set to `false`. If it set to `true` then any role cache cookies are issued with an additional setting indicating that the cookie should only be send back over SSL connections. This means compliant browser agents should not send the role cache cookie over non-SSL connections. The `RoleManagerModule` also enforces additional security measures by rejecting role cache cookies sent over non-SSL connections. The module will also not issue a role cache cookie over a non-SSL connection in the event that this attribute is set to `true`.

❑ cookieSlidingExpiration: Defaults to `true`, which means that whenever a `RolePrincipal` is initialized from an encrypted ticket, it checks the issuance and expiration date values that are also encoded in the ticket. If the data is still considered valid, but more than 50% of the TTL for the data has passed, then the `RolePrincipal` will update its `IssueDate` to the current UTC time and the `ExpiresDate` to the current UTC time plus the value from `cookieTimeout`. The next time that `RolePrincipal` is serialized back into an encrypted ticket, the new date information will also be serialized into the ticket. If sliding expirations are disabled though, `Role Principal` never updates it issuance and expiration dates, which means that after `cookie Timeout` minutes, the encrypted ticket sent in the role cache cookie will no longer be considered valid. Disabling sliding expirations is a good way to ensure that every `cookieTimeout` minutes the role information for users gets refreshed from a provider.

❑ cookieProtection: By default, the serialized representation of the role information returned by `ToEncryptedTicket` is digitally signed with an HMACSHA1 hash and the hash and principal's serialized data is then encrypted using AES. You can change the hash and encryption algorithms as well as the key material that is used by configuring the `<machineKey />` element. The `cookieProtection` attribute has the same options as the `protection` attribute on the `<forms />` configuration element, and the hashing/encryption behavior is the same as it is for forms authentication (remember the issue with synchronizing keys in a web farm!). Note that although this attribute is named `cookieProtection`, it really applies to the security of the serialized role information returned from `ToEncryptedTicket`. Because the most likely use of this information is in a cookie, the configuration setting is called `cookieProtection` as opposed to something else.

❑ maxCachedResults: The default value is 25. When `ToEncryptedTicket` is called, if the number of roles the user belongs to exceeds 25, then `ToEncryptedTicket` just returns a `null` value instead. If your users belong to a large number of roles or if the role names are very long, you will need to experiment and determine the best setting of `maxCachedResults` that results in serialized role representations being less than 4096 characters in length. Alternatively, your users may regularly belong to more than 25 roles, but the role names may be very short and thus the role information may still fit within the 4096 character limit; in this case, you will need to increase the value of `maxCachedResults`. Of course, if most users belong to so many roles that their serialized representation cannot fit within a cookie, then you might as well turn off cookie caching because it won't accomplish anything for you.

There are a few other cookie configuration options that aren't listed previously: `cookieName`, `cookie Path`, and `domain`. These attributes all work the same way as the similarly named attributes used by forms authentication.

One last note on the role cache cookie: as with forms authentication, `RoleManagerModule` *always* sets the `HttpOnly` property on the role cache cookie to `true`. This is not something that you can turn off or ever change. As a result, if you attempt to access the role cache cookie from a browser using JavaScript, even if the intent is to only replay the cookie on another request programmatically, you will not be able to access the role cache cookie. As with forms authentication, the intent of turning on HttpOnly is to minimize the likelihood of a cross-site scripting attack easily hijacking the role cache cookie. You can review the section on HttpOnly cookies back in Chapter 6 for more details on how HttpOnly cookies work.

Working with Multiple Providers during GetRoles

If you write complex applications that require the support of multiple Role Manager providers, then you will also need to write code that works with RoleManagerModule. As mentioned earlier, Role ManagerModule knows how to initialize a RolePrincipal on your behalf only if the user on the context should be associated with roles from the default RoleProvider. However, if your application allows logins against multiple back-end stores (perhaps you have multiple Membership providers configured as well), then chances are that users will need to be associated with roles from different back-end data stores as well. The extensibility hook you use to deal with this scenario is the GetRoles event raised by the RoleMangerModule.

Writing the code to handle this scenario properly though can be a bit tricky. The problem is that it is basically up to you to mirror RoleManagerModule's behavior in PostAuthenticateRequest. There are a number of security checks and other work that the module is doing, and you need to faithfully clone this behavior in a custom GetRoles event handler.

To demonstrate how you can use RoleManagerModule with multiple providers, set up a sample application that uses two RoleProviders:

```
<roleManager enabled="true" defaultProvider="roleStore_A"
             cacheRolesInCookie="true">
  <providers>
    <clear/>
      <add name="roleStore_A"
           applicationName="RoleStoreA"
           connectionStringName="LocalSqlServer"
           type="System.Web.Security.SqlRoleProvider, …"/>
      <add name="roleStore_B"
           applicationName="RoleStoreB"
           connectionStringName="LocalSqlServer"
           type="System.Web.Security.SqlRoleProvider, …"/>
  </providers>
</roleManager>

<authentication mode="Forms"/>
<authorization>
    <deny users="?"/>
</authorization>
```

This configuration defines two providers, roleStore_A and roleStore_B, by using two SqlRolePro-vider instances but with each provider using a different value for applicationName. The net result is that both providers work with the same database and same set of database tables, but they partition their data based on the application name. To set up some test data for this application, you can use the Web Administration Tool inside of Visual Studio to create a default user account. The following page then sets up some basic roles with each of the two role providers.

C#

```csharp
//Create a role with the "A" provider
RoleProvider rpA = Roles.Providers["roleStore_A"];
if (!rpA.RoleExists("Administrators in store A"))
    rpA.CreateRole("Administrators in store A");

//Add the test user account to a role in "A" provider's data store
if (!rpA.IsUserInRole("testuser", "Administrators in store A"))
    rpA.AddUsersToRoles(
        new string[] { "testuser" },
        new string[] { "Administrators in store A" });

//Create a role with the "B" provider
RoleProvider rpB = Roles.Providers["roleStore_B"];
if (!rpB.RoleExists("Administrators in store B"))
    rpB.CreateRole("Administrators in store B");

//Add the test user account to a role in "B" provider's data store
if (!rpB.IsUserInRole("testuser", "Administrators in store B"))
    rpB.AddUsersToRoles(
        new string[] { "testuser" },
        new string[] { "Administrators in store B" });
```

VB.NET

```vbnet
'Create a role with the "A" provider
    Dim rpA As RoleProvider = _
    Roles.Providers("roleStore_A")
If (Not rpA.RoleExists("Administrators in store A")) Then
    rpA.CreateRole("Administrators in store A")
End If

'Add the test user account to a role in "A" provider's data store
If (Not rpA.IsUserInRole("testuser", "Administrators in store A")) Then
        rpA.AddUsersToRoles(New String() {"testuser"}, _
                            New String() {"Administrators in store A"})
    End If

'Create a role with the "B" provider
Dim rpB As RoleProvider = Roles.Providers("roleStore_B")
If (Not rpB.RoleExists("Administrators in store B")) Then
    rpB.CreateRole("Administrators in store B")
End If

'Add the test user account to a role in "B" provider's data store
If (Not rpB.IsUserInRole("testuser", "Administrators in store B")) Then
        rpB.AddUsersToRoles(New String() {"testuser"}, _
                            New String() {"Administrators in store B"})
    End If
```

Now you have a test user account that belongs to two roles: one role managed by the first `SqlRole Provider` and one role managed by the second `SqlRoleProvider`. In production use, though, you would probably have different users associated with different authentication stores (for example, maybe different `SqlMembershipProvider` instances), and you would want to align these users with their corresponding `RoleProvider` instances. For this application, though, I am just using a single user account for demonstration purposes.

The sample application hooks up an event subscription for `GetRoles` in `global.asax`:

C#

```
void RoleManager_GetRoles(object sender, RoleManagerEventArgs re)
{
    HandlingMultipleRoleProviders.CreatePrincipal(re);
}
```

VB.NET

```
Sub RoleManager_GetRoles(ByVal sender As Object, ByVal re As RoleManagerEventArgs)
        HandlingMultipleRoleProviders.CreatePrincipal(re)
End Sub
```

This code takes advantage of ASP.NET's behavior for hooking up event handlers to events exposed on modules. Internally, the ASP.NET runtime interprets the method signature above to mean: find an event called `GetRoles` on the `HttpModule` called `RoleManager` or `RoleManagerModule` and subscribe the `RoleManager_GetRoles` method in `global.asax` to the `GetRoles` event exposed by the module. I have the event subscription forward the call to a static method on a class that will do the real work during this event.

C#

```
public class HandlingMultipleRoleProviders
{
    public static void CreatePrincipal(RoleManagerEventArgs re)
    {
      //logic goes here
    }
}
```

VB.NET

```
Public Class HandlingMultipleRoleProviders
   Public Shared Sub CreatePrincipal(ByVal re As RoleManagerEventArgs)
       'logic goes here
   End Sub
End Class
```

Because there are a number of different conditions the module needs to handle, the code inside of `CreatePrincipal` first determines whether it should just immediately return and defer processing to the `RoleManagerModule` instead.

C#

```
HttpContext c = re.Context;

//Logic to determine if the second provider is used
string flag = c.Request.QueryString["usenondefault"];
if (String.IsNullOrEmpty(flag) || flag != "true")
    return;

//Use default RoleManagerModule logic for anonymous users
if (!c.User.Identity.IsAuthenticated)
    return;
```

VB.NET

```
Dim c As HttpContext = re.Context

'Logic to determine if the second provider is used
Dim flag As String = c.Request.QueryString("usenondefault")
If String.IsNullOrEmpty(flag) OrElse flag <> "true" Then
        Return
End If

'Use default RoleManagerModule logic for anonymous users
If (Not c.User.Identity.IsAuthenticated) Then
        Return
End If
```

In the sample application, the code decides to use a nondefault provider if a query-string variable called "usenondefault" exists, and the variable is set to the string "true". In a production application, you would instead need a way to look at a logged-in user's username and determine the correct RoleProvider to select for that user. You could encode some extra information into the username (that is, set the username to "username + provider_name"). You could use another approach such as issuing a cookie at login time that indicates the appropriate RoleProvider to use for the logged in user. In the chapter on forms authentication, you also saw examples of using the UserData property from FormsIdentity.Ticket when running in cookied mode; you could use this approach as well to store information that allows you to figure out the correct RoleProvider for the user.

Regardless of the approach you choose, the main thing is that if a GetRoles event subscription determines that the *default* provider should be used, it can just exit and leave RoleManagerModule to do the processing for the request. The preceding sample code also checks to see if the user for the current request is authenticated; if the user is anonymous the method also immediately returns. Because Role Manager doesn't support the concept of associating roles to an anonymous user, there is no need for any custom processing.

At this point, there are two general scenarios the custom GetRoles event handler needs to deal with:

❑   Creating a RolePrincipal when cookie caching is in effect.

❑   Creating a RolePrincipal when cookie caching is not enabled.

If cookie caching is being used, the event handler mirrors the same security checks and behavior as the `RoleManagerModule`.

C#

```
if (Roles.CacheRolesInCookie)
{
    if ((!Roles.CookieRequireSSL || c.Request.IsSecureConnection))
    {
      //more custom logic here to create a RolePrincipal
    }
    else
    {
        if (c.Request.Cookies[Roles.CookieName] != null)
            Roles.DeleteCookie();
    }
}
```

VB.NET

```
If Roles.CacheRolesInCookie Then
    If ((Not Roles.CookieRequireSSL) OrElse c.Request.IsSecureConnection) Then
        'more custom logic here to create a RolePrincipal
    Else
        If c.Request.Cookies(Roles.CookieName) IsNot Nothing Then
            Roles.DeleteCookie()
        End If
    End If
End If
```

For an authenticated user, the custom event handler will carry out the necessary work to extract the encrypted role cache information from the cookie. However, if there is a mismatch between the cookie `RequireSSL` configuration attribute, and the current SSL state of the connection, then the custom event handler instead sets a clear cookie header. This behavior matches what `RoleManagerModule` does when it receives a role cache cookie in the clear, but the application configuration indicates that the role cache cookie should be issued and accepted only over SSL connections.

The logic for handling the encrypted role cache cookie is shown here:

C#

```
        try
        {
            HttpCookie cookie = c.Request.Cookies[Roles.CookieName];
            if (cookie != null)
            {
                string cookieValue = cookie.Value;
                if (cookieValue != null && cookieValue.Length > 4096)
                    Roles.DeleteCookie();
                else
                {
                    //ensure proper casing on some cookie properties
                    if (!String.IsNullOrEmpty(Roles.CookiePath) &&
```

```
                              Roles.CookiePath != "/")
                          cookie.Path = Roles.CookiePath;
                          cookie.Domain = Roles.Domain;


                      //create a new principal
                      c.User = new RolePrincipal("roleStore_B",
                                                  c.User.Identity,
                                                  cookieValue);
              }
          }
      }
      catch { /*ignore errors*/ }
```

VB.NET

```
Try
        Dim cookie As HttpCookie = c.Request.Cookies(Roles.CookieName)
        If cookie IsNot Nothing Then
            Dim cookieValue As String = cookie.Value
            If cookieValue IsNot Nothing AndAlso cookieValue.Length > 4096 Then
                Roles.DeleteCookie()
            Else
                'ensure proper casing
                If (Not String.IsNullOrEmpty(Roles.CookiePath)) _
        AndAlso Roles.CookiePath <> "/" Then
            cookie.Path = Roles.CookiePath
        End If

            cookie.Domain = Roles.Domain

            'create a new principal
        c.User = New RolePrincipal("roleStore_B", _
                            c.User.Identity, _
                            cookieValue)

    End If
      End If
      Catch ' ignore errors
End Try
```

The event handler gets a reference to the role cache cookie (Roles.CookieName makes it easy to get to the correct cookie). It then extracts the cookie's value because this is the encrypted representation of the user's role information. Just as with RoleManagerModule, the custom code makes a quick sanity check to ensure that it hasn't been sent an excessively long value. Because you know that RoleManagerModule will never issue a cookie during EndRequest where the value is longer than 4096 characters, you know that any inbound cookie with an excessively long value is bogus and, thus, should be ignored. If an excessively long cookie value is present, the custom code also sends back a clear cookie header to prevent the browser from continuing to send a bogus cookie.

The code just preceding the constructor call is boilerplate code from the ASP.NET RoleManagerModule. ASP.NET uses this code to ensure that if the casing of any of the cookie settings is wrong that the role cache cookie has these values reset with the correctly cased values. At one point, ASP.NET code would read these values back out of the request cookie, hence the logic for ensuring proper casing. Assuming that the cookie value's length is acceptable, the custom code creates a new RolePrincipal. Note that in the preceding custom code, it uses a constructor overload that accepts a provider name as the first parameter. This ensures that `RolePrincipal` internally will use the correct provider reference if it ever needs to call `GetRolesForUser` on the provider. For a production application the actual provider name would be selected (as opposed to being hard-coded) using some algorithm that tells you the correct `RoleProvider` to choose based on the username. The newly created `RolePrincipal` is also set on the `HttpContext`.

The custom code next has to handle the case where a `RolePrincipal` has not been created yet. For the custom code shown so far, this will occur either for authenticated users hitting the application for the first time (so no role cache cookie exists yet) or for authenticated users running over non-SSL connections where the role cache cookie was sent but the application's configuration only allows the role cache cookie to be processed when sent over an SSL connection.

C#

```
//Either no role cache cookie, or the cookie was invalid
if (!(c.User is RolePrincipal))
    c.User = new RolePrincipal("roleStore_B",c.User.Identity);
```

VB.NET

```
'Either no role cache cookie, or the cookie was invalid
If Not(TypeOf c.User Is RolePrincipal) Then
    c.User = New RolePrincipal("roleStore_B",c.User.Identity)
End If
```

This code ensures that if a `RolePrincipal` doesn't exist yet on the context, that one gets created. The constructor overload in this case also accepts a provider name, but no encrypted ticket is passed to the constructor. This means the first time the `RolePrincipal` is used, it will need to call `GetRoles ForUser` on the nondefault provider whose name was passed to the constructor.

The only tasks left at this point are to synchronize the principal on the context with the thread object, and telling `RoleManagerModule` that it should skip further processing in its `PostAuthenticate Request` handler.

C#

```
//Sync principal to Thread as well
Thread.CurrentPrincipal = c.User;

//Notify RoleManagerModule to skip its processing
re.RolesPopulated = true;
```

VB.NET

```
'Sync principal to Thread as well
Thread.CurrentPrincipal = c.User

'Notify RoleManagerModule to skip its processing
re.RolesPopulated = True
```

Remember that if you write your own code to handle the GetRoles event, you *must* set the Roles Populated property on the event argument to true. If you forget to do this, RoleManagerModule will still carry out its default processing and promptly overwrite any principal you created in a custom event handler.

Now that the sample application has the necessary custom logic to switch between the default provider and the nondefault RoleProvider, you can try out the custom behavior with a simple page. The test page allows you to flip between the two different providers by using two different URLs:

```
<form id="form1" runat="server">
<div>
 <a href="Default.aspx?usenondefault=true">Click to use second provider</a>
 <br />
 <a href="Default.aspx?usenondefault=false">Click to use default provider</a>
</div>
</form>
```

When the page runs, it lists the roles that the current user belongs to:

C#

```
protected void Page_Load(object sender, EventArgs e)
{
    foreach (string role in ((RolePrincipal)User).GetRoles())
        Response.Write("Belongs to: <b>" + role + "</b><br/>");
}
```

VB.NET

```
Protected Sub Page_Load(ByVal sender As Object, _
            ByVal e As EventArgs) Handles Me.Load()
    For Each role As String In (CType(User, RolePrincipal)).GetRoles()
        Response.Write("Belongs to: <b>" & role & "</b><br/>")
    Next role
End Sub
```

If you log in to the sample application initially, the test page lists:

Belongs to: **Administrators in store A**

If you then click the link that includes the query-string variable with a value of "true," the custom event handler creates a RolePrincipal that uses the second configured provider. As a result, the test page displays:

Belongs to: **Administrators in store B**

You can seamlessly flip back and forth between using a default provider (and hence the default Role ManagerModule logic) and the second nondefault provider by clicking on the two links. Aside from the simple logic in the custom event handler for determining which provider to use, the rest of the code shown in this section is exactly what you need to effectively use multiple Role Manager providers in an application.

Because the code manipulates both `Thread.CurrentPrincipal` and `HttpContext.Current.User`, the code must be running in Medium trust or higher. The policy files for Medium trust and above include the necessary permission to change the principal object. Alternatively, you can factor out the event handler code into a GAC'd assembly where you can create `SecurityPermission(SecurityPermission Flag.ControlPrincipal)` and then assert it. If you attempt to run the sample code in Low or Minimal trust, it will instead fail with a `SecurityException` because these trust levels do not allow user code to manipulate the principal on either context or the thread.

RoleProvider

As with the Membership feature, Role Manager depends heavily on providers. In fact, the major pieces of functionality within the Role Manager feature are effectively implemented in `RoleManagerModule`, `RolePrincipal` and concrete implementations of the `RoleProvider` base class. Because Role Manager does not have an object model for a role, the `RoleProvider` definition is pretty simple. Roles are just strings, and the users associated with those roles are also just strings. As a result, the `RoleProvider` base class is just an abstract class definition. Unlike `MembershipProvider`, `RoleProvider` does not have any helper methods or private methods implementing base portions of the Role Manager feature.

C#

```csharp
public abstract class RoleProvider : ProviderBase
{
    //Properties
    public abstract string ApplicationName { get; set; }

    //Authorization related methods
    public abstract bool IsUserInRole(string username, string roleName);

    //Methods that deal with fetching a user's role information
    public abstract string[] GetRolesForUser(string username);

    //Methods for creating, deleting and managing roles
    public abstract void CreateRole(string roleName);
    public abstract bool DeleteRole(string roleName, bool throwOnPopulatedRole);
    public abstract bool RoleExists(string roleName);
    public abstract void AddUsersToRoles(string[] usernames, string[] roleNames);
    public abstract void RemoveUsersFromRoles(string[] usernames,
                                              string[] roleNames);
    public abstract string[] GetUsersInRole(string roleName);
    public abstract string[] GetAllRoles();
    public abstract string[] FindUsersInRole(string roleName,
                                             string usernameToMatch);
}
```

VB.NET

```vbnet
Public MustInherit Class RoleProvider
    Inherits ProviderBase

    'Properties
```

```
Public MustOverride Property ApplicationName As String

'Authorization related methods
Public MustOverride Function IsUserInRole(ByVal username As String, _
                        ByVal roleName As String) _
                        As Boolean

'Methods that deal with fetching a user's role information
Public MustOverride Function GetRolesForUser(ByVal username As String) _
As String()

' Methods for creating, deleting and managing roles
Protected Sub New()
Public MustOverride Sub CreateRole(ByVal roleName As String)
Public MustOverride Function DeleteRole(ByVal roleName As String, _
                        ByVal throwOnPopulatedRole As Boolean) _
                        As Boolean
Public MustOverride Function RoleExists(ByVal roleName As String) As Boolean
Public MustOverride Sub AddUsersToRoles(ByVal usernames As String(), _
                        ByVal roleNames As String())
Public MustOverride Sub RemoveUsersFromRoles(ByVal usernames As String(), _
                        ByVal roleNames As String())
Public MustOverride Function GetUsersInRole(ByVal roleName As String) _
As String()
Public MustOverride Function GetAllRoles() As String()
Public MustOverride Function FindUsersInRole(ByVal roleName As String, _
                        ByVal usernameToMatch As String) _
                        As String()

End Class
```

Because the RoleProvider treats a role as a string, and some of the providers internally convert array parameters into comma-delimited strings, roles normally are not allowed to have a comma character. For example, if you attempt to create a role called "this,is,a,role", both the Roles class and most of the default providers will throw an ArgumentException. The reason for this restriction is that not all data stores can accept an array type. Methods like AddUsersToRoles that accept string arrays may have these arrays converted into a comma-delimited string of roles that is then passed down to a database for subsequent parsing and processing. To prevent confusion over whether a comma is a delimiter as opposed to part of a role name, the Roles class and all of the default role providers, except for Windows TokenRoleProvider, disallow the use of a comma when creating roles.

One thing to keep in mind if you are thinking about implementing a custom provider is the relative simplicity of the Role Manager feature. For custom providers implemented against relational data stores, it is a pretty trivial exercise to write a basic RoleProvider implementation. The core portion of RoleProvider is the GetRolesForUser method; if a custom provider does not implement this method, then the RolePrincipal class will not work properly. And of course without the RolePrincipal class there isn't much point to using Role Manager. The IsUserInRole method is a logical adjunct to GetRolesForUser. At one point, providers also needed to implement IsUserInRole for the RolePrincipal to work properly, but with some of the later changes to the way the role cache cookie works, it turns out that RolePrinicpal no longer calls IsUserInRole. However, given the nature of authorization checks, it is reasonable to expect a minimal RoleProvider implementation to also implement IsUserInRole (if your data store supports getting all roles for a user, then it implicitly supports role checks like IsUserInRole).

The remainder of the methods on the provider base class are optional from a runtime perspective. If you already create roles and associate users to roles using some other management tool or interface, then you can stub out the rest of the methods on a custom `RoleProvider` and just throw a `NotSupportedException` from them instead.

Note that the `RoleProvider` definition does not really expose the concept of nesting roles within roles. The administrative portion of `RoleProvider` does not have methods like `AddRoleToRole` or `Remove RoleFromRole`. If you have a custom data store that supports the nesting of roles, you can still expose most of this functionality from methods like `IsUserInRole`. There is nothing wrong with a custom provider that internally has the logic to recurse through a nested hierarchy of roles to perform authorization checks or to determine membership in a role. If necessary, a custom provider can add a few methods to its implementation to support the necessary administrative methods for nesting roles within roles.

The `AuthorizationStoreRoleProvider` discussed in Chapter 15 is an example of a `RoleProvider` that works against a data store that supports role nesting. Because the `AuthorizationStoreRole Provider` uses the Authorization Manager (aka AzMan) functionality that was first available as part of Windows Server 2003, when you call `IsUserInRole` on this provider it will properly handle group nesting. However, this provider does not expose any special methods to administer nested roles; instead, the expectation is that developers and administrators will use the MMC or management API available for AzMan policy stores.

Basic Configuration

Just like `MembershipProvider`, a `RoleProvider` can partition its data based on an application name from configuration.

❑   `ApplicationName`: Custom providers should at least implement the getter for this property. The concept of separating data by application name is so common to many of the provider-based features in ASP.NET 2.0 or ASP.NET 3.5, that the getter should always be implemented. If it turns out that you are mapping role data to a data store that doesn't really have the concept of an "application," you can have the setter throw a `NotSupportedException`. In this case, your custom provider can just ignore the application name that it loaded from configuration.

Authorization Methods

A basic provider implementation should always implement the following two methods:

❑   `GetRolesForUser`: As mentioned earlier, RolePrincipal always calls this method on a provider at least once prior to making an authorization check inside `RolePrincipal.IsInRole`. If the `username` parameter doesn't exist, the usual convention is to return an empty string array. Similarly, if the user exists in the data store but doesn't belong to any roles, a provider should return an empty string array as well.

❑   `IsUserInRole`: Developers may call this method directly on a provider as opposed to calling `IsInRole` on `RolePrincipal`. For users who belong to a large number of roles where `Get RolesForUser` may take an excessive amount of time to run, it will be faster (up to a point) to call `IsUserInRole` on a provider. There is a bit of a trade-off when developers need to balance the up-front cost of making a single round trip to the data store that returns a large result set when calling `GetRolesForUser`, versus calling the data store multiple times with `IsUseInRole`, in which case each individual query in the data store is much faster. For this reason, custom provider implementers should implement IsUserInRole and GetRolesForUser; furthermore, the implementation of IsUserInRole should ideally be faster than the implementation of Get-RolesForUser (technically, a custom provider could implement IsUserInRole in terms of GetRolesForUser, but then there is no performance gain for single authorization checks when calling IsUserInRole). If the user specified by the username parameter doesn't exist in the data store or if the role specified by the roleName parameter doesn't exist, a custom provider should return false. Developers normally would not expect an authorization check to throw an exception for these cases.

Managing Roles and Role Associations

The remaining methods on RoleProvider are primarily used by administrative tools like the Web Administration Tool (WAT) available inside of Visual Studio. If you already have other management tools for your custom role stores, you can stub out these methods and throw a NotSupportedException. If your intent, though, is for your provider to be useable from administrative tools like the WAT, then you should implement the following methods.

❑   CreateRole: Creates a new role in the data store. Providers should throw a Provider Exception if an attempt is made to create a role, and the role already exists.

❑   DeleteRole: Removes a role from the data store. If the parameter throwOnPopulatedRole is set to true, the provider should throw a ProviderException if an attempt is made to delete a role and the role still has users associated with it. If throwOnPopulatedRole is set to false, this is an indication that the caller is all right with deleting the role, and any remaining user-to-role associations. If an attempt is made to delete a role that doesn't exist in the data store, a custom provider should just return false from this method rather than throw an exception. If the role is found, and the deletion is successful, then a custom provider should return true.

❑   RoleExists: A provider returns true if the roleName exists in the data store; otherwise, a provider should return false.

❑   AddUsersToRoles: This method allows a developer to add one or more users to each of the roles specified in the roleNames parameter. A provider should check to see that each user specified in the usernames parameter exists and that each role specified in the roleNames parameter exists. If either of these checks fails, the provider should throw ProviderException. Also, if any user in the usernames parameter already belongs to one of the roles specified in the roleNames parameter, the provider should throw ProviderException. It is up to custom provider implementers to determine how the transactional semantics of adding multiple users to roles are handled. For example, the SqlRoleProvider performs all of the adds in a single transaction, or else it fails the entire chunk of work. However, not all authorization data stores will be able to use transactions.

❑   RemoveUsersFromRoles: This companion method to AddUsersToRoles enables a developer to remove each user specified in the usernames parameter from each role specified in the roleNames parameter. The validation checks noted earlier for AddUsersToRoles should also be implemented by custom providers for this method. Although in the case of removal, if an attempt is made to remove a user from a role and the user does not already belong to that role, a ProviderException should be thrown. (This is the reverse case of the validation that providers should implement in AddUsersToRoles.) It is also up to a custom provider implementer as to whether any transactional semantics are enforced. For example, the SqlRoleProvider will either successfully perform all requested removals, or it will roll the entire chunk of work back.

❏ GetUsersInRole: Returns a string array containing the names of all of the users that are currently members of the role specified by the roleName parameter. If the role is empty, the provider should just return an empty string. However, if a request if made to get the users for a nonexistent role then a ProviderException should be thrown.

❏ GetAllRoles: Returns a string array containing a list of all of the roles currently defined in the data store. If no roles currently exist, then a provider should return an empty string instead.

❏ FindUsersInRole: Returns a string array containing all of the users whose names match the search parameter specified by usernameToMatch that are members of the role specified by the roleName parameter. If no user matches are found, a custom provider should return an empty string array. However, if an attempt is made to search for users in a nonexistent role, a provider should throw a ProviderException. If the underlying data store supports wildcard characters for searches, a custom provider should allow these wildcard characters in the usernameToMatch parameter and pass the wildcard characters to the data store for further processing.

WindowsTokenRoleProvider

Although we will cover the SQL and AzMan providers in their Chapters 15 and 16, respectively, WindowsTokenRoleProvider has very limited functionality, so one section should suffice for explaining how it works. As the name suggests, the provider works with a Windows security token. Although the provider can theoretically run in any trust level (IsUserInRole will work in Minimal trust), it is intended for use at Low trust or above. Unlike other providers, WindowsTokenRoleProvider does not internally check the trust level during initialization. The reason for this is that if the runtime environment can get a Windows security token for a user, the provider will work. If the runtime environment cannot get a token, then the provider fails. So, explicitly checking trust levels at initialization time is not necessary for this provider.

The token the provider uses is the value from the Token property on a WindowsIdentity object. In an ASP.NET environment, the provider gets a WindowsIdentity from the User property on the HttpContext when using Windows authentication. In non-ASP.NET environments, the provider will get the token from Thread.CurrentPrincipal. For both runtime environments, these are the only two places the provider will look; there is no facility for passing an arbitrary token to the provider. In other words, WindowsTokenRoleProvider works only with the credentials of the currently executing user.

The provider supports only the following two methods defined on RoleProvider:

❏ IsUserInRole:There are two overloads for this method:the overload that is defined by the RoleProvider base class, as well as a special overload that accepts a System.Security .Principal.WindowsBuildInRole value. Both overloads carry out an access check against the current WindowsIdentity. There is also no trust level restriction on this method—it will work in any of the ASP.NET trust levels.

❏ GetRolesForUser: Note that inside of this method, the provider makes an explicit check for Low trust. Unlike IsUserInRole, if you new() up the provider and manually initialize it in Minimal trust, GetRolesForUser will still fail. Calling IsUserInRole, however, will succeed in Minimal trust because there is no explicit trust level check in that method.

The additional overload for `IsUserInRole` was added to the provider as a convenience. Internally, the additional overload just takes the current user's `WindowsIdentity`, wraps it in a `WindowsPrincipal`, and then calls the `IsInRole` overload on `WindowsPrincipal` that accepts a `WindowsBuiltInRole` parameter. These steps are necessary because when you use `WindowsTokenRoleProvider` with Role-Manager in ASP.NET, the principal object on the context is a `RolePrincipal` wrapping a `Windows Identity` (as opposed to a `WindowsPrincipal` wrapping a `WindowsIdentity` which is what happens when you use Windows authentication with an application and you have not enabled Role Manager).

There are two reasons why you might use `WindowsTokenRoleProvider` during development:

❑ You may need to start developing an application that will use Role Manager with a different provider, but you currently are only running Windows authentication in your development environment. Because Role Manager is provider-based, you can start writing code while using the `WindowsTokenRoleProvider` and then later point swap in the provider that will be used in production.

❑ Your application depends on fetching the group names for each authenticated user and then performing custom authorization checks and business logic against this set of group names. The `WindowsTokenRoleProvider`'s `GetRolesForUser` method already does this for you, so you can make use of the provider to easily retrieve a string array of a user's group membership. The Framework's `WindowsPrincipal` object doesn't provide this functionality.

If you use `WindowsTokenRoleProvider` on a site where the current user is considered anonymous (for example, a dummy `WindowsPrincipal` and `WindowsIdentity` were initially placed on the `HttpContext`), then `IsUserInRole` will always return `false` and `GetRolesForUser` will always return an empty string array. This behavior is consistent with the same values returned from Role-Principal for anonymous users. The extra `IsUserInRole` overload will also return `false` because the `WindowsIdentity` that ASP.NET sets on the context for anonymous users is just a dummy `Windows Identity` that doesn't belong to any built-in roles.

The internal logic of `WindowsTokenRoleProvider` compares the `username` parameter for `IsUser InRole` and `GetRolesForUser` to the string username of the current `WindowsIdentity`. This check is necessary because at the provider level there are no overloads that implicitly work with the current user. So, there is nothing preventing a developer from calling the provider's methods passing in arbitrary usernames in a domain. However, because the purpose of `WindowsTokenRoleProvider` is to work with the credentials of only the currently authenticated user, the provider makes a quick sanity check to ensure that the `username` parameter passed to it actually matches the username associated with the currently authenticated user. If a mismatch exists, `IsUserInRole` will always return `false`, and `GetRoles ForUser` always returns an empty string (that is, the same behavior as the anonymous user case).

Assuming that the current user is authenticated, and no mismatch occurs, the provider uses the security token of the user to carry out its work. For `IsUserInRole`, the provider converts the `roleName` parameter to a group security identifier (SID) and then checks the user's security token to see if that group SID exists. Depending on the value of the `roleName` parameter (that is, a Windows group name), translating from a string to a SID with a call to `LookupAccountName` may be an expensive operation. The `GetRolesForUser` method can be even more expensive because, internally, it must perform a SID-to-name translation on each of the group SIDs contained in the user's security token. This is a very important point to keep in mind because it means in complex domain environments a great deal of network traffic may be generated attempting to convert each user's group SID into a name. If some of the groups a user belongs to sit in remote domains, GetRolesForUser can be a very long call.

For this reason, you should experiment with using cookie caching in conjunction with WindowsToken RoleProvider because after the role information is retrieved with a call to GetRolesForUser, cookie caching can prevent you from having to resolve groups SIDs to names for the duration of a user's browser session. If it turns out that your users belong to so many groups that you can't fit them into a cookie, you could disable cookie caching but still increase the maxCachedResult limit so that you can call ToEncryptedTicket and get back a non-null value. Instead of storing the encrypted string in a cookie you can use an alternative data store like a database. Although the earlier code sample for RoleManager Module showed you how to use the GetRoles event to handle multiple providers, you could use the same approach to retrieve large encrypted tickets from a database and automatically reconstruct a RolePrincipal on each request during the GetRoles event.

When you call IsUserInRole, the value of the roleName you pass in must include the appropriate "domain" value of the role (that is, group) you are checking against. If the role is a well-known group (that is, a built in group or NT AUTHORITY-based group), then the roleName parameter may need to include NT AUTHORITY\\ or BUILTIN\\ before the group name. Note that the extra backslash is neces-sary for escaping this character in C#. If you leave out these specifiers, the IsUserInRole check will sometimes fail depending on the group you are checking. Always prepending either NT AUTHORITY\\ or BUILTIN\\ to the group name prevents any random problems. For domain groups, you always use the familiar syntax of "DOMAIN\\GROUPNAME". If you are calling IsUserInRole for a local machine group though, you can use either the syntax "MACHINENAME\\GROUPNAME" or just "GROUPNAME". Either syntax is interpreted as referencing a group in the local machine's SAM database.

As an example of this, the following code dumps the group membership for a user:

C#

```
WindowsTokenRoleProvider wp =
(WindowsTokenRoleProvider)Roles.Providers["AspNetWindowsTokenRoleProvider"];

    string[] roles = wp.GetRolesForUser(User.Identity.Name);
    foreach (string r in roles)
        Response.Write("You belong to: " + r + "<br/>");
```

VB.NET

```
Dim wp As WindowsTokenRoleProvider = CType( _
        System.Web.Security.Roles.Providers("AspNetWindowsTokenRoleProvider"), _
        WindowsTokenRoleProvider)

Dim roles() As String = wp.GetRolesForUser(User.Identity.Name)
For Each r As String In roles
    Response.Write("You belong to: " & r & "<br/>")
Next r
```

Aside from enabling Role Manager in configuration and disallowing anonymous access to the test site, this code is all that is needed to start using a WindowsTokenRoleProvider. The reason is that a pro-vider named AspNetWindowsTokenRoleProvider is defined by default in the machine.config file.

As a result every application, ASP.NET and non-ASP.NET, has access to this provider instance assuming that the Role Manager feature has been enabled. Running this code results in the following output when I am logged in:

```
You belong to: None
You belong to: Everyone
You belong to: TestLocalMachineGroup
You belong to: BUILTIN\Administrators
You belong to: BUILTIN\Users
You belong to: NT AUTHORITY\NETWORK
You belong to: NT AUTHORITY\Authenticated Users
You belong to: NT AUTHORITY\This Organization
You belong to: NT AUTHORITY\NTLM Authentication
```

You can see that on my test machine I belong to a variety of groups: one that is clearly a local machine group (the `TestLocalMachineGroup`), and a number of other default and built-in groups. One thing to note about this output is that when the provider's `GetRolesForUser` method returns the string names of groups located on the local machine, it *always* strips off the machine name. That is why the local machine group is shown as `TestLocalMachineGroup` instead of `MACHINE\TestLocalMachineGroup`.

Remember that the return value from `GetRolesForUser` can be cached internally by a `RolePrincipal` and that the internally cached set of roles in a `RolePrincipal` is used whenever you call `IsInRole` against the principal. From a completeness perspective, it would have been nice to store local machine groups that a user belongs to in both `MACHINENAME\\GROUPNAME` and `GROUPNAME` format. From a Windows API perspective both of these syntaxes are valid. However, if the provider did so, developers who depended on the count of roles returned from `RolePrincipal.GetRoles` would end up with twice the number of local machine groups because they would be stored twice.

As a compromise, the `WindowsTokenRoleProvider` strips the machine name off the local machine groups before returning the groups' names from `GetRolesForUser`. The local machine names are not left prepended to group names because if you need to deploy an application across different staging and production environments, and you are using Role Manager (and potentially URL authorization), you probably do not want to be incessantly changing the machine name string used in all of your authorization checks. So, it made more sense to strip off the machine name, thus making it easier to write applications that use local machine groups without needing to reconfigure group names each time the code is moved to a different machine.

You will not encounter this behavior if you make authorization checks by calling `IsUserInRole` directly on the provider; when calling the provider's `IsUserInRole` method directly you can use either syntax for local machine groups. However, if you depend on `RolePrincipal.IsInRole` for authorization checks you may run into this behavior and it may cause some unexpected problems. For example, using the `TestLocalMachineGroup` shown in the earlier results, the following URL authorization check when using Role Manager will fail:

```
<authorization>
    <allow roles="bhaidar-PC\TestLocalMachineGroup"/>
    <deny users="*"/>
</authorization>
```

This exact same check will succeed if you turn off Role Manager and just use Windows authentication instead. The `WindowsPrincipal` class never has to return roles as a string array, so when `Windows Principal.IsInRole` is called, internally, it can test local machine groups using alternative syntaxes. The reason that the preceding check fails when using Role Manager is that `RolePrincipal` internally caches the string array returned by `WindowsTokenRoleProvider.GetRolesForUser`. And this array has only a string entry of `TestLocalMachineGroup`, so the string comparison against `bhaidar-PC\ TestLocalMachineGroup` fails. The following configuration though will succeed:

```
<authorization>
    <allow roles="TestLocalMachineGroup"/>
    <deny users="*"/>
</authorization>
```

Now that the machine name is no longer part of the role name, the URL authorization check against `RolePrincipal` succeeds because there is a string match on just `TestLocalMachineGroup`. If you happen to be developing an application and authorization checks against local machine groups suddenly fail when you switch from using only Windows authentication to using Windows authentication and Role Manager with the `WindowsTokenRoleProvider`, the likely culprits are the group names in your `<authorization />` configuration element.

You can write some sample code that tries different ways of making role checks against the group names shown earlier that were returned from `GetRolesForUser`:

C#

```
Response.Write("This Organization: " +
    wp.IsUserInRole(User.Identity.Name, "This Organization"));
Response.Write("This Organization: " +
    wp.IsUserInRole(User.Identity.Name, "NT AUTHORITY\\This Organization"));
```

VB.NET

```
Response.Write("This Organization: " & _
                    wp.IsUserInRole( _
                    User.Identity.Name, _
                    "This Organization") & _
                    "<br/>")

RResponse.Write("This Organization: " & _
                    wp.IsUserInRole( _
                    User.Identity.Name, _
                    "NT AUTHORITY\This Organization") & _
                    "<br/>")
```

This code performs an authorization check against the `"This Organization"` default group. The first check does not include `"NT AUTHORITY\\"` in the `roleName` parameter, while the second role check does include it. This code results in the following output:

```
This Organization: False
This Organization: True
```

Now clearly the user account belongs to this group, but in the first case, without `"NT AUTHORITY\\"` prepended to the `roleName` parameter, the group name was interpreted as a local machine group and thus the check failed. If you use a different well-known group that has been around for a while, you get different behavior:

C#

```
Response.Write("Local administrators: " +
    wp.IsUserInRole(User.Identity.Name, "Administrators") + "<br/>");
Response.Write("Local administrators: " +
    wp.IsUserInRole(User.Identity.Name, "BUILTIN\\Administrators") + "<br/>");
```

VB.NET

```
Response.Write("Local administrators: " & _
                    wp.IsUserInRole( _
                    User.Identity.Name, _
                    "Administrators") & _
                    "<br/>")

Response.Write("Local administrators: " & _
                    wp.IsUserInRole( _
                    User.Identity.Name, _
                    "BUILTIN\Administrators") & _
                    "<br/>")
```

This code uses two different variations for checking to see if the current user belongs to the local Administrators group. As you can see in the following output, both coding styles result in the same results:

```
Local administrators: True
Local administrators: True
```

Because of the subtle differences in behavior when performing authorization checks with special group names, it is easier to always prepend either `"NT AUTHORITY\\"` or `"BUILTIN\\"`. It is important to note that if the above two lines of code were to be run on a machine running Windows Vista with the user logged in is a standard user and User Account Control (UAC) is turned on, the result would be a value of `False` for both lines. The discussion will not go into the details of UAC, but the standard user would be limited in privileges and hence not able to retrieve such information that requires elevation of privileges.

For local machine groups, it is always recommended to prepend the machine name to get exact results when calling `IsUserInRole`, as the following code snippet demonstrates:

C#

```
Response.Write("A local machine group: " +
    wp.IsUserInRole(User.Identity.Name, "TestLocalMachineGroup"));
Response.Write("A local machine group: " +
    wp.IsUserInRole(User.Identity.Name, "bhaidar-PC\\TestLocalMachineGroup"));
```

VB.NET

```
Response.Write("A local machine group: " & _
                    wp.IsUserInRole( _
                    User.Identity.Name, _
                    "TestLocalMachineGroup") & _
                    "<br/>")

Response.Write("A local machine group: " & _
                    wp.IsUserInRole( _
                    User.Identity.Name, _
                    "bhaidar-PC\TestLocalMachineGroup") & _
                    "<br/>")
```

The first line of code results in a value of False because the machine name was not prepended to the group under question. The second line of code succeeds due to the fact that the machine name was prepended to the group against which the code is doing the checking:

```
A local machine group: False
A local machine group: True
```

With either syntax for the roleName parameter, the provider interprets the roleName as a local machine group. For groups that you create in a domain, though, you must always prepend the group name with the domain name as the next sample demonstrates:

C#

```
Response.Write("The domain Users group: " +
    wp.IsUserInRole(User.Identity.Name, "AnyDomain\\Domain Users"));
Response.Write("The domain Users group: " +
    wp.IsUserInRole(User.Identity.Name, "Domain Users"));
```

VB.NET

```
Response.Write("The domain Users group: " & _
                    wp.IsUserInRole( _
                    User.Identity.Name, _
                    "bhaidar-PC\Domain Users") & _
                    "<br/>")


Response.Write("The domain Users group: " & _
                    wp.IsUserInRole( _
                    User.Identity.Name, _
                    "Domain Users") & _
                    "<br/>")
```

The first call will succeed because the provider can successfully resolve this to the default "Domain Users" group that is present in every domain. However, the second check fails because the provider is looking for a group called "Domain Users" on the local machine.

```
The domain Users group: True
The domain Users group: False
```

To summarize all of this, keep the following rules in mind when calling the provider's `IsUserInRole` method:

❑ Always prepend `"NT AUTHORITY\\"` or `"BUILTIN\\"` when working with these types of groups.

❑ Always prepend `"DOMAINNAME\\"` when working with nonlocal groups located somewhere in a domain.

❑ Always prepend `"MACHINENAME\\"` when working with local groups.

Summary

The Role Manager feature gives you an easy way to create roles, assign users to roles, and then carry out various authorization checks based on these associations. As with the Membership feature, the Role Manager feature can be used to make authorization checks in both ASP.NET and non-ASP.NET environments. The static `Roles` class is used for performing authorization checks if your application only has a single default provider, though for more complex sites you will probably end up getting references to specific `RoleProvider` instances directly instead. If your site uses multiple providers, you will probably also need to hook the `GetRoles` event on `RoleManagerModule` so that your `RolePrincipal` instances are associated with the proper provider.

`RoleManagerModule` is the "magic" that exposes the user-to-role associations stored by providers as a `RolePrincipal` instance available from `HttpContext.Current.User`. You have to explicitly enable the Role Manager feature (it is off by default in `machine.config`), but after you enable the feature, `RoleManagerModule` automatically handles looking at the current user, and constructing a `Role Principal` that represents the current user. `RolePrincipal` can be used for declarative authorization checks such as URL authorization as well as code-based authorization checks using `IPrincipal.IsInRole`. Because Role Manager has no hard-coded dependencies on a specific type of authenticated identity, the `RolePrincipal` can wrap authenticated identities obtained from Windows authentication, forms authentication, or any custom authentication mechanism you may author.

For performance reasons, `RolePrincipal` will fetch all of a user's roles the first time the roles are needed, and it will then cache that information internally for the duration of a page request. You can optionally enable caching this information in a cookie so that on subsequent page requests `RolePrincipal` will initialize its cached role information from the cookie as opposed to calling the provider. The `maxCached Results` configuration setting partially determines how many roles `RolePrincipal` is willing to stuff into a cookie. `RoleManagerModule` also enforces a maximum 4096 character limit on the size of a role cache cookie, so you will need to experiment with cookie caching in your applications to see if you can use it effectively.

One of the default providers supplied with the Framework is `WindowsTokenRoleProvider`. This provider is very basic because it only implements the `IsUserInRole` and `GetRolesForUser` methods, and these methods only work with the currently authenticated user. However, the `GetRolesForUser` method can be very handy for developers who want to get all of the roles that a domain user belongs to.

15

SqlRoleProvider

Role Manager ships with a number of different providers in the .NET 2.0 and 3.5 Frameworks: `WindowsTokenRoleProvider`, which was covered at the end of the previous chapter; `SqlRoleProvider`, which is the topic of this chapter; and `AuthorizationStoreRoleProvider`, which is discussed in the next chapter. `SqlRoleProvider` is already configured in `machine.config` as the default provider for the Role Manager feature. As with `SqlMembershipProvider`, `SqlRoleProvider` is the reference provider for the feature because it implements all of the functionality defined on the `RoleProvider` base class.

This chapter will cover the following areas of the `SqlRoleProvider`:

❑   The database schema used by the `SqlRoleProvider`.

❑   Database security and trust level requirements for the provider, including how to configure the provider for use in partially trusted non-ASP.NET environments.

❑   Using the `SqlRoleProvider` with Windows-authenticated websites.

❑   Extending the provider to support "run-with-limited-roles" scenarios.

❑   Leveraging role data for authorization checks in the data layer.

❑   Supporting multiple applications with a single provider.

❑   Managing an application's roles through IIS 7.0.

SqlRoleProvider Database Schema

The database schema contains tables, views, and stored procedures used by the provider. As with the Membership feature, `SqlRoleProvider`'s schema integrates with the common set of tables covered in Chapter 12. This allows you to use `SqlMembershipProvider` for authentication and then use `SqlRoleProvider` to associate one or more roles with the users already registered in the Membership feature. Keying off of the common tables also allows `SqlRoleProvider` to be used in conjunction with the other SQL-based providers (`SqlProfileProvider` and `SqlPersonalizationProvider`) supplied by ASP.NET. However, there is no requirement that `SqlRoleProvider` be used in conjunction with the Membership feature. The integration with the common provider schema is nice if you want to leverage it, but you can also use Role Manager and `SqlRoleProvider` as a standalone authorization feature. You will actually see how this works later on in the chapter, where using `SqlRoleProvider` with Windows authentication is described.

Because the concept of a role in Role Manager is very simple, and because Role Manager also does not support the concept of nested roles, the database tables for the `SqlRoleProvider` are also very simple. The first table in the database schema is the `aspnet_Roles` table shown in the following code:

```
CREATE TABLE dbo.aspnet_Roles (
        ApplicationId    uniqueidentifier   NOT NULL
                         FOREIGN KEY REFERENCES dbo.aspnet_Applications(ApplicationId),
        RoleId           uniqueidentifier   PRIMARY KEY
                         NONCLUSTERED DEFAULT NEWID(),
        RoleName         nvarchar(256)      NOT NULL,
        LoweredRoleName  nvarchar(256)      NOT NULL,
        Description      nvarchar(256)
)
```

Each of the table's rows is described here:

- ❑ `ApplicationId`: Because multiple provider instances can be configured to point at the same database, you can horizontally partition each application's role data using the `applicationName` configuration attribute supported in the provider's configuration. In the database schema, this attribute's value is translated to the GUID application ID that is stored in the common `aspnet_Applications` table. Whenever a `SqlRoleProvider` needs to look up role information, it always does so within the context of a specific application, and thus the provider always includes the `ApplicationId` column in the various stored procedures used by the provider.

- ❑ `RoleId`: The primary key for the table. Each role created using `SqlRoleProvider` is uniquely identified by its `RoleId`. Although the stored procedures perform most of their work using the `RoleId`, the public Role Manager API has no way to expose this value. As a result, the provider always starts its work with a role name.

- ❑ `RoleName`: For all practical purposes, this is the role "object" in the Role Manager feature. This is the value that you supply when creating new roles, and it is the value that you use when performing authorization checks with a `RolePrincipal`.

- ❑ `LoweredRoleName`: The case-insensitive representation of the `RoleName` column. Although you write code using the value stored in the `RoleName` column, internally the `SqlRoleProvider` enforces the uniqueness of role names by first lowering the role string and then attempting to store it in this column. The combination of this column, and the `ApplicationId` column, acts as an alternate primary key for the table. Also, whenever you call the `IsUserInRole` method on the provider, the provider looks at the value in this column as part of determining whether a specific user is associated with a role. In this way, the provider is able to enforce case-insensitive string comparisons on role names when performing role checks in the database. Note though that the culture setting (that is, collation order) of the underlying database still has an effect when the stored procedures are performing string comparisons. In the previous chapter, the potential mismatch between case-insensitive invariant-culture comparisons and case-insensitive culture-specific comparisons was discussed. You can always deploy the `SqlRoleProvider` schema in a database using the Latin1_General collation to roughly mirror the string comparison functionality used inside of `RolePrincipal`.

❑ `Description`: This is an orphan column because it is never used by the `SqlRoleProvider`. At one point, there were plans to make a full-fledged role object, but that work could not be fit into the ASP.NET 2.0 development schedule and nothing has been introduced in ASP.NET 3.5 on this issue. Because ASP.NET may introduce a role object sometime in the future, the column was left in the schema for future use. You should basically ignore the existence of the column, and you should not store anything in it.

The second table in the `SqlRoleProvider` database schema stores the mapping of users to roles:

```
CREATE TABLE dbo.aspnet_UsersInRoles (
    UserId    uniqueidentifier NOT NULL PRIMARY KEY(UserId, RoleId)
              FOREIGN KEY REFERENCES dbo.aspnet_Users (UserId),
    RoleId    uniqueidentifier NOT NULL
              FOREIGN KEY REFERENCES dbo.aspnet_Roles (RoleId)
)
```

The `aspnet_UsersInRoles` table is ultimately used by various stored procedures to determine which users belong to which roles. The table works in a self-explanatory way; however, a brief description of each rows is provided here.

❑ `UserId`: This is the user identifier from the common `aspnet_Users` table. For `SqlRoleProvider` to perform an authorization check, it must convert a string user name along with the application name specified on a provider, into a `UserId` value. Remember that the `aspnet_Users` table and `aspnet_Applications` tables together are used to accomplish this.

❑ `RoleId`: The role identifier from the `aspnet_Roles` table. During a database lookup, the string role name and the application name specified on a provider are converted into a `RoleId`. With the `UserId` and `RoleId` in hand, a stored procedure can perform a lookup in this table.

In addition to the database tables, two views are supplied with the schema: `vw_aspnet_Roles` and `vw_aspnet_UsersInRoles`. Both of these views map all of the columns in the corresponding tables. Later on in this chapter, you will see how you can use these views to perform authorization checks inside of your own stored procedures. Also note that, as with the Membership feature, the views are intended only for use with read-only queries. Although nothing technically prevents you from writing data through the views, the intent is that all data modifications flow through the provider API.

SQL Server-Specific Provider Configuration Options

Because the `SqlRoleProvider` connects to SQL Server, it supports two SQL Server-specific configuration attributes on the provider definition:

❑ `connectionStringName`: As you would expect, the provider needs to know what database and server to connect to. The value of this attribute must point at a named connection string defined up in the `<connectionStrings />` section.

❑ `commandTimeout`: As you work with larger databases, you may find that the default ADO.NET `SqlCommand` timeout of 30 seconds is too short for certain operations. For `SqlRoleProvider`, the `AddUsersToRoles` and `RemoveUsersFromRoles` methods are especially prone to timing out when working with large sets of role information (for example, the `aspnet_UsersInRoles` table contains 100K or more rows). If you run into timeout problems with either of these methods, you can boost the value of the `commandTimeout` configuration attribute to give the database server more time to complete its work. Alternatively, you can reduce the number of user-to-role associations being modified in a single method call and simply call these methods in a loop with only a chunk of user and role data being changed in a single iteration.

Transaction Behavior

Not all of the data modification work performed in the provider can be accomplished with single `INSERT` or `UPDATE` commands. The `SqlRoleProvider` methods `AddUsersToRoles` and `RemoveUsersFromRoles` both explicitly manage transactions within the provider's code. If you look inside of the stored procedures used by `SqlRoleProvider`, you will see that for operations like deleting or creating a role, all the work is encapsulated within a transaction managed within a stored procedure.

However, the `AddUsersToRoles` and `RemoveUsersFromRoles` methods can affect many rows of user-to-role associations. As a result of limitations in passing parameter data down to a stored procedure, there is not a great way to get all of the parameter data from these methods (an array of users and an array of roles) passed down to SQL Server. The most elegant approach would have been to use the XML capability in SQL Server 2000, but this approach would have required forking the code to support SQL Server 7.0. There are also edge cases where errors can occur in stored procedures without being able to properly clear up XML documents that have been parsed on the server.

So, the solution to the overall problem was to have `SqlRoleProvider` explicitly begin a transaction in the provider code. Then the provider passes chunks of user and role data down to SQL Server, potentially calling the underlying stored procedures multiple times. When all the parameter data has been chunked and passed to SQL Server, the provider issues an explicit `COMMIT TRANSACTION` to SQL Server. If anything fails along the way, all of the work is rolled back by the provider when it issues an explicit `ROLLBACK TRANSACTION`.

You should keep this transaction behavior in mind when calling `AddUsersToRoles` and `RemoveUsersFromRoles`. If you pass a large number of users and roles these two methods can take quite a while to run, and there is the possibility of a failure occurring along the way thus causing a rollback (just 100 users and 100 roles will result in 10K rows being inserted or deleted, so it does not take much to trigger large numbers of inserts or deletes). If you want to smooth out the load on your SQL Server while performing large numbers of adds or removes, you should call these methods iteratively, passing only a small number of roles and users on each iteration. In this way, you eliminate the possibility of SQL Server locking large portions of the `aspnet_UsersInRoles` table while it grinds through large data modifications.

The product team has successfully tested performing 100K and 250K inserts and deletes using these methods. However, the purpose of these tests was to exercise the `commandTimeout` provider configuration attribute. Issuing such a huge number of changes in a single transaction ends up locking most of the `aspnet_UsersInRoles` table. In a production application, this type of change could fail if the system was under load with other connections simultaneously attempting to get roles data from the same table. For this reason, limiting the number of associations being changed in any one method call to a small number makes sense for cases where the database needs to remain responsive to other applications using the same set of Role Manager data.

Provider Security

There are two levels of security enforced by `SqlRoleProvider`: trust-level checks and database-level security requirements. You influence the trust-level check by setting the appropriate trust level for your web application and optionally making other adjustments to the CAS policy on your machine. Database-level security requirements are managed through the use of SQL Server roles.

Trust-Level Requirements and Configuration

Inside of the provider's `Initialize` method, a check is made for Low trust. If the current application is running at Low trust or higher, then the provider will initialize itself. Otherwise, if the application is running in Minimal trust, the initialization process will fail. Outside of ASP.NET, local applications like console applications or Windows Forms application implicitly run in Full trust, so the trust level check in the `Initialize` method always succeeds.

For an ASP.NET application running in Low trust, the provider may still fail when you attempt to call any of its methods because the default Low trust policy file does not include `SqlClientPermission`. In this case, the `Initialize` method completes successfully because the Low trust-level check succeeds. But then when an individual method attempts to access SQL Server, the `System.Data.SqlClient` classes throw a security exception because the web application does not have `SqlClientPermission`. If you want to enable the provider for use in Low trust, you should do two things:

1. Create a custom trust policy file for the Low trust bucket, and add `SqlClientPermission` to the custom trust policy file.

2. Configure the database security for your application using one of the provider's SQL Server roles. Because, conceptually, Low trust applications are not supposed to be modifying sensitive data, the `aspnet_Roles_BasicAccess` role makes sense for use with the `SqlRoleProvider` in a Low trust environment.

Using Providers in Partially Trusted Non-ASP.NET Applications

If you happen to run partially trusted non-ASP.NET applications, you do not have the convenience of using the `<trust />` configuration element. For example, if you run an application off of a UNC share and you want that application to work with `SqlRoleProvider` (or for that matter, any other provider-based feature in ASP.NET, including the Membership and Profile features), you will initially end up with a rather obscure security exception.

For example, you can create a basic console application that triggers initialization of the feature and the `SqlRoleProvider` with the following code:

C#

```
using System;
using System.Web.Security;

namespace PartialTrustRoleManager
{
    class Program
```

```
    {
        static void Main(string[] args)
        {
            Console.WriteLine(Roles.Provider.ApplicationName);

            if (Roles.RoleExists("some random role name"))
                Console.WriteLine("The random role exists.");
            else
                Console.WriteLine("The random role does not exist");
        }
    }
}
```

VB.NET

```
Imports Microsoft.VisualBasic
Imports System
Imports System.Web.Security

Namespace PartialTrustRoleManager
  Friend Class Program
        Shared Sub Main(ByVal args() As String)
                Console.WriteLine(Roles.Provider.ApplicationName)

                If Roles.RoleExists("some random role name") Then
                        Console.WriteLine("The random role exists.")
                Else
                        Console.WriteLine("The random role does not exist")
                End If

                Console.Read()
        End Sub
  End Class
End Namespace
```

Because Role Manager is not enabled by default, the sample application also explicitly enables it in the application configuration file.

```
<configuration>
  <system.web>
    <roleManager enabled="true" />
  </system.web>
</configuration>
```

If you compile this on your local machine and run it, everything works. However, if you take the compiled executable and the configuration file, move them onto a remote UNC share, and then run the executable, you get the following exception.

```
Unhandled Exception: System.Security.SecurityException: Request for the permission
of type 'System.Web.AspNetHostingPermission, ...' failed.
<snipped for brevity>
    at PartialTrustRoleManager.Program.Main(String[] args)
```

```
The action that failed was:
LinkDemand
The type of the first permission that failed was:
System.Web.AspNetHostingPermission
The first permission that failed was:
<IPermission class="System.Web.AspNetHostingPermission, …"
             version="1"
             Level="Minimal"/>
```

Although the exception dump is a bit intimidating, parts of it should look familiar to you from Chapter 4 on trust levels. In this situation, the executable is on a UNC share; it runs with a permission set defined by both the .NET 2.0 and 3.5 Frameworks for applications running in LocalIntranet_Zone. You can see the zone membership and the permissions associated with it using the Microsoft .NET Framework 2.0 Configuration MMC, which is still being used in the .NET 3.5 Framework. The permission set associated with LocalIntranet_Zone is called LocalIntranet, and it includes only basic permissions like access to isolated storage, the use of default printers on the machine, and so forth.

The LocalIntranet permission set lacks AspNetHostingPermission. It also lacks SqlClientPermission, although the previous exception dump doesn't show this. The reason that the application immediately fails when run from a UNC share is that both the static Roles class and the SqlRoleProvider class are attributed with the following:

C#

```
[AspNetHostingPermission(SecurityAction.LinkDemand,
    Level=AspNetHostingPermissionLevel.Minimal)]
```

VB.NET

```
<AspNetHostingPermission( _
    SecurityAction.LinkDemand, _
    Level:=AspNetHostingPermissionLevel.Minimal)>
```

When the console application attempts to call into the Roles class, the declarative link demand immediately causes a SecurityException because UNC-based applications lack any kind of AspNetHostingPermission.

Because a fair amount of work was invested in making the Membership, Role Manager and Profile features ASP.NET-agnostic, it would be unfortunate if these features were limited to only fully trusted non-ASP.NET applications. Luckily, this is not the case, although, as you will see, it does require configuration work on your part to get things working. Because there is no convenient code access security (CAS) abstraction like trust levels outside of ASP.NET, you need to configure either the .NET 2.0 or 3.5 Framework's CAS system directly. The logical starting point is to add both AspNetHostingPermission and SqlClientPermission to the LocalIntranet permission set.

Because there is a convenient MMC tool that theoretically allows you to do this, you would probably think of using the tool first. Unfortunately, due to some bugs in the MMC you cannot add the System.Web.dll assembly as a policy assembly (that is, an assembly that can be used as a source of permission classes such as AspNetHostingPermission). So instead, you have to drop down to using the tool caspol.exe, which is located in the framework's installation directory.

There are a number of things you need to accomplish with caspol:

❏   Add the `AspNetHostingPermission` to a named permission set. You need to get it into a named permission set with the Level attribute set to at least "Low." Even though the link demand is for Minimal trust, the `Roles` class will trigger a demand for Low trust while loading the `SqlRoleProvider`.

❏   Add the `SqlClientPermission` to the named permission set because `SqlRoleProvider` will trigger a demand for this when it calls into ADO.NET.

❏   It is not immediately obvious, but because Role Manager and its providers internally depend on ASP.NET's `HttpRuntime` object, you also need to grant file I/O read and path discovery permissions to the installation directory for the framework. The `HttpRuntime` object depends on loading DLLs that exist in this directory, and without the correct `FileIOPermission` on the machine, it will fail to initialize.

One of the not-so-nice things about mucking with the Framework's CAS policy information directly is that the XML format for a named permission set is not easily discoverable. With a little enterprising hacking around, you can eventually stitch together the correct representation of a named permission set that is consumable by the `caspol.exe` tool. For the demo application, I simply looked for the named permission set called `LocalIntranet` inside of the file `security.config`, which is located in the CONFIG subdirectory underneath the framework's install directory. You can copy the `<PermissionSet />` element for `LocalIntranet` and all of its nested `<IPermission />` elements from this file and paste them into a separate file.

At this point, I admit that I could never get `caspol.exe` to properly recognize the class names used for the individual `<IPermission />` elements. Luckily, though, you can always use the fully qualified strong name in its place (the ASP.NET trust policy files use a short name that references `<SecurityClass />` elements at the top of the trust file). (The same approach seems to cause obscure errors in `caspol.exe` though.) The last step is to pop in the three additional `<IPermission />` elements for the three permissions that were discussed previously. The result is a file called `CustomSecurity.config` with the following XML definition (note that the strong names have been trimmed down for brevity):

```
<PermissionSet class="NamedPermissionSet"
               version="1"
               Name="LocalIntranet_MODIFIED"
               Description="Modified local intranet permissions">
   <IPermission
           class="System.Web.AspNetHostingPermission, System, …"
           version="1"
           Level="Low" />
   <IPermission
           class="System.Security.Permissions.FileIOPermission, mscorlib, …"
           version="1"
           Read="C:\Windows\Microsoft.NET\Framework\v2.0.50727\"
           PathDiscovery="C:\Windows\Microsoft.NET\Framework\v2.0.50727\" />
   <IPermission class="System.Security.Permissions.EnvironmentPermission, mscorlib…"
               version="1"
               Read="USERNAME"/>
   <IPermission class="System.Security.Permissions.FileDialogPermission, mscorlib…"
```

```
                         version="1"
                         Unrestricted="true"/>
        <IPermission class="System.Security.Permissions.IsolatedStorageFilePermission…"
                         version="1"
                         Allowed="AssemblyIsolationByUser"
                         UserQuota="9223372036854775807"
                         Expiry="9223372036854775807"
                         Permanent="True"/>
        <IPermission class="System.Security.Permissions.ReflectionPermission, mscorlib…"
                         version="1"
                         Flags="ReflectionEmit"/>
        <IPermission class="System.Security.Permissions.SecurityPermission, mscorlib…"
                         version="1"
                         Flags="Assertion, Execution, BindingRedirects"/>
        <IPermission class="System.Security.Permissions.UIPermission, mscorlib…"
                         version="1"
                         Unrestricted="true"/>
        <IPermission class="System.Net.DnsPermission, System…"
                         version="1"
                         Unrestricted="true"/>
        <IPermission class="System.Drawing.Printing.PrintingPermission, System.Drawing…"
                         version="1"
                         Level="DefaultPrinting"/>
        <IPermission
                class="System.Data.SqlClient.SqlClientPermission, System.Data…"
                version="1"
                Unrestricted="true" />
</PermissionSet>
```

The three bolded portions of the file indicate the new permissions that you need to add that are above and beyond the default set of permissions normally granted to applications running in the LocalIntranet zone. The FileIOPermission includes read and path discovery access for the framework install directory on the machine that will be running the application. You will need to tweak the physical file path to match the appropriate location on your machine.

With these changes made, you can now import the custom permission set (which is called LocalIntranet_Modified) using the following command line:

```
..\caspol.exe -m -ap CustomSecurity.config
```

In my case, I saved the preceding XML file into a file called CustomSecurity.config located in the CONFIG subdirectory of the framework install directory. Because the command line was running from the CONFIG subdirectory, the command uses ..\caspol.exe to reference the utility. The -m command line option tells caspol.exe that the named permission set in the file should be imported into the local machine's set of security informationas opposed to the enterprise- or user-specific security policies. The -ap switch tells caspol.exe that the file CustomSecurity.config contains a definition of a new named permission set.

After you run caspol.exe, you can open the Framework's MMC configuration tool. Expand the machine policy node so that you can see both configured security zones on the machine as well as the named permission sets that are available. You can see what this looks like in Figure 15-1.

Figure 15-1

Notice that underneath the Permission Sets node the new custom permission set appears. At this point, you can right-click the LocalIntranet_Zone node that is underneath the Code Groups node and select Properties. In the resulting dialog box, switch to the Permission Set tab and select LocalIntranet_MODIFIED from the drop-down list. You can see what this all looks like in Figure 15-2.

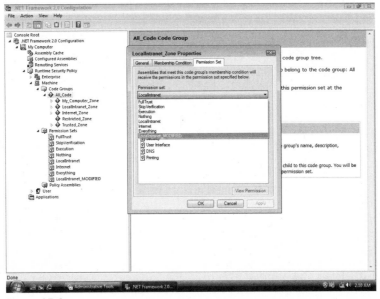

Figure 15-2

After you click the OK button, the Framework will consider all applications running in the `LocalIntranet` zone to be associated with the set of custom permissions listed in the XML file. Because applications running off of UNC shares are considered part of the local intranet zone, when you run the sample application for a second time from a remote UNC share all of the calls into Role Manager and the `SqlRoleProvider` succeed. Note that if you try this on your machine and the console application still fails, the definition for the Local Intranet zone in Internet Explorer may not include your remote machine. If you modify the Local Intranet zone definition in Internet Explorer to include a `file://your_remote_machine` URL, then the Framework will consider applications running remotely from that machine to be in the Local Intranet zone.

So, although this is a somewhat painful process, the end result is that you can absolutely use Role Manager inside of a partially trusted non-ASP.NET application. This means that you do not have to drop back to granting unmanaged code rights to your non-ASP.NET applications just because of the use of `AspNetHostingPermission` and other permissions like `SqlClientPermission`. After you create a custom named permission set and associate it with the local intranet zone, you will also be able to use the two other ASP.NET features that have been tweaked to work in non-ASP.NET environments: the Membership and the Profile features. Last, note that although this sample cloned the local intranet zone's permissions, you can be more creative with your customizations. For example, you could strip some of the extraneous permissions from the custom permission set (for example, maybe you do not need printer access or the ability to display file selection dialog boxes). You could also create custom code groups with more granular membership conditions than what is defined for the local intranet zone.

Database Security

Chapter 12 discussed the general database security requirements that are common to all of the SQL-based providers. Assuming that you have followed those steps, and you have a login created or mapped on your SQL Server machine, there are three database roles that you can use with `SqlRoleProvider`:

❑ **aspnet_Roles_BasicAccess:** This role only allows you to call the following methods on `SqlRoleProvider`: `IsUserInRole` and `GetRolesForUser`. These two methods represent the bare minimum needed to support the `RolePrincipal` object and authorization checks made directly against the provider.

❑ **aspnet_Roles_ReportingAccess:** This role allows you to call `IsUserInRole`, `GetRolesForUser`, `RoleExists`, `GetUsersInRole`, `FindUsersInRole`, and `GetAllRoles`. Members of this role can also issue select statements against the database views.

❑ **aspnet_Roles_FullAccess:** This role can call any of the methods defined on `SqlRoleProvider` as well as query any of the database views. In other words, a SQL Server login added to this role has the additionally ability to change the role data stored in the database.

As with the `SqlMembershipProvider`, the simplest way to use these roles is to add the appropriate SQL Server login account to the aspnet_Roles_FullAccess role. This gives you the full functionality of the feature without requiring you to run with DBO privileges in the database. The other two SQL Server roles allow for more granular allocation of security permissions. For example, you might run administrative tools in one web application (which would use aspnet_Roles_FullAccess), while only performing authorization checks in your production application (which would only need aspnet_Roles_BasicAccess).

Working with Windows Authentication

Although the most likely scenario that folks think of for `SqlRoleProvider` is to use it in applications with forms authentication, `SqlRoleProvider` and the Role Manager feature work perfectly fine in applications using Windows authentication. Typically, you would use NT groups or more advanced authorization stores such as Authorization Manager for many intranet production applications. However, it is not uncommon for developers to create intranet applications in which they do not want or need the overhead of setting up and maintaining group information in a directory store. This can be the case for specialized applications that have only a small number of users, and it can also be the case for "throw-away" intranet applications.

Although I would not advocate using `SqlRoleProvider` for long-lived internal applications or for complex line-of-business applications, knowing that you can use Role Manager for intranet applications adds another option to your toolbox for quickly building internal websites with reasonable authorization requirements. In the case of a web application using Windows authentication, `SqlRoleProvider` will automatically create a row in the common `aspnet_Users` table the very first time a Windows user is associated with a role. The important thing is to use the correct format for the username when adding users to roles or removing users from roles. The username that is available from `HttpContext.Current.User.Identity.Name` is the string that should be used when modifying a user's role associations. For example, the following code snippet shows how to add a domain user to two roles stored in a SQL database with the `SqlRoleProvider`:

C#

```
if (!Roles.IsUserInRole("bhaidar-PC\\bhaidar", "Application Role A"))
    Roles.AddUserToRole("bhaidar-PC\\bhaidar", "Application Role A");

if (!Roles.IsUserInRole("bhaidar-PC\\bhaidar", "Application Role C"))
    Roles.AddUserToRole("bhaidar-PC\\bhaidar", "Application Role C");
```

VB.NET

```
If (Not Roles.IsUserInRole("bhaidar-PC\bhaidar", "Application Role A")) Then
    Roles.AddUserToRole("bhaidar-PC\bhaidar", "Application Role A")
End If

If (Not Roles.IsUserInRole("bhaidar-PC\bhaidar", "Application Role C")) Then
    Roles.AddUserToRole("bhaidar-PC\bhaidar", "Application Role C")
End If
```

Note how the username is supplied using the familiar DOMAIN\USERNAME format. When you use Windows authentication in ASP.NET, the `WindowsIdentity` that is placed on the context will return the `Name` property using this format. If your web application is configured to use Windows authentication, when you enable the Role Manager feature, `RoleManagerModule` will automatically use the default provider to fetch the roles associated with the Windows authenticated user. The following configuration snippets show the required configuration to make this work:

```
<! connection string config and other config here >

<authentication mode="Windows"/>
<authorization>
    <deny users="?"/>
</authorization>
```

```
<roleManager enabled="true">
    <providers>
        <clear/>
        <add name="AspNetSqlRoleProvider"
            type="System.Web.Security.SqlRoleProvider, System.Web… "
            connectionStringName="LocalSqlServer"
            applicationName="WindowsAuthenticationDemo"/>
    </providers>
</roleManager>
```

Now, if you access a Windows authenticated web application as a user who has already been mapped to one or more roles, the `RolePrincipal` placed on the context will contain the expected role information.

C#

```
foreach (string s in ((RolePrincipal)User).GetRoles())
    Response.Write(User.Identity.Name + " belongs to <b>" + s + "</b><br />");
```

VB.NET

```
For Each s As String In (CType(User, RolePrincipal)).GetRoles()
    Response.Write(User.Identity.Name & " belongs to <b>" & s & "</b><br />")
Next s
```

Running this code sample while logged in as the sample user that was configured earlier results in the following output:

```
bhaidar-PC\bhaidar belongs to Application Role A
bhaidar-PC\bhaidar belongs to Application Role C
```

The only minor shortcoming that you will encounter getting this to work is that you will have to programmatically associate Windows users to roles. Although the Web Administration Tool inside of Visual Studio allows you to create and delete roles, you will not be able to leverage the tool for managing specific Windows users. Instead, you will need to use code like the sample shown earlier to add users to roles as well as removing users from roles.

One other concern you may have is keeping the format of the username stable over time. For the 2.0 and 3.5 versions of the Framework, the `WindowsIdentity` class will always return the value from the `Name` property using the DOMAIN\USERNAME format. Even if someone accesses your application with a different username format (for example, your application is configured to use Basic authentication in IIS and someone logs in using a UPN formatted username), `WindowsIdentity` always uses the older NT4-style username. As a result, you do not need to worry about accruing large amounts of user-to-role associations in a database only to find out that the username returned from `WindowsIdentity` suddenly changes on you.

For example, if you are running in a domain environment on Windows Server 2003 (that is, your domain controllers are Windows Server 2003 machines), you can run the following code sample:

C#

```
WindowsIdentity wi = new WindowsIdentity("bhaidar@bhaidar-PC ");
Response.Write(wi.Name);
```

VB.NET

```
Dim wi As New WindowsIdentity("bhaidar@bhaidar-PC")
Response.Write(wi.Name)
```

Even though the `WindowsIdentity` is constructed with a user principal name (UPN) format, the value returned by the `Name` property is still `bhaidar-PC\bhaidar`.

Running with a Limited Set of Roles

Typically, most of the users on a website are associated with a set of roles that make sense for their given purpose on the site. A limited number of website users, though, may have super privileges or the ability to act as an administrator on the site. Sometimes, it is desirable for this type of user to be able to limit the roles that he or she a part of while performing the normal daily routine on a site. For example, a business user may also have administrative privileges on a site. During the normal workday, though, he or she really does not need to have these privileges available and would rather perform most of the work as a normal user.

Because `RolePrincipal` depends on a provider for its role information, you can swap in a custom provider that supports the concept of a limited subset of roles being active at any given time for a specific user. As an example, you can create a derived version of `SqlRoleProvider` that is aware of role restrictions stored in the database. For convenience, I chose to store the set of role restrictions in the `Comments` property associated with a `MembershipUser`. You could certainly choose to store this type of role restriction in a different location, but because Membership is already available and has a convenient storage location for this type of information, the sample provider makes use of it. Because a `RolePrincipal` works exclusively with information returned from `GetRolesForUser`, the custom provider must override this method. Because a custom role provider should ideally also support at least `IsUserInRole`, the custom provider also provides the limited role functionality in an override of this method as well.

C#

```csharp
public class CustomRoleProvider : SqlRoleProvider
{
    public CustomRoleProvider() {}

    //overrides of GetRolesForUser and IsUserInRole
}
```

VB.NET

```vbnet
Public Class CustomRoleProvider
  Inherits SqlRoleProvider

  Public Sub New()
  End Sub

  ' overrides of GetRolesForUser and IsUserInRole

End Class
```

The custom provider works by looking at the set of restricted roles stored in `MembershipUser.Comment`. The string stored in this property is formatted as follows:

```
first restricted role;second restricted role; etc..
```

The custom provider converts this string into a string array by splitting the value on the semicolon character. For protection though, the custom provider always double-checks with `SqlRoleProvider` to ensure that the information stored in the `Comments` property is still considered a valid set of role associations by the provider. This prevents the problem where a set of restricted roles is stored in the `MembershipUser`, but later the user no longer belongs to some of those roles.

C#

```csharp
public override string[] GetRolesForUser(string username)
{
    MembershipUser mu = Membership.GetUser(username);

    //Anonymous user case
    if (mu == null)
        return new string[0];

    if (mu.Comment != null)
    {
        //Make sure user still belongs to the selected roles
        string[] currentRoleMembership = base.GetRolesForUser(username);
        string[] restrictedRoles = mu.Comment.Split(";".ToCharArray());

        List<string> confirmedRoles = new List<string>();
        foreach (string role in restrictedRoles)
        {
            if (Array.IndexOf(currentRoleMembership, role) != -1)
                confirmedRoles.Add(role);
        }

        return confirmedRoles.ToArray();
    }
    else
    {
        return base.GetRolesForUser(username);
    }
}
```

VB.NET

```vbnet
Public Overrides Function GetRolesForUser(ByVal username As String) As String()
        Dim mu As MembershipUser = Membership.GetUser(username)

        'Anonymous user case
        If mu Is Nothing Then
            Return New String() {}
        End If

        If mu.Comment IsNot Nothing Then
```

```
                             'Make sure user still belongs to the selected role
                             Dim currentRoleMembership() As String = _
                                     MyBase.GetRolesForUser(username)
                                     Dim restrictedRoles() As String = _
                                     mu.Comment.Split(";".ToCharArray())

                             Dim confirmedRoles As List(Of String) = New List(Of String)()
                             For Each role As String In restrictedRoles
                                     If Array.IndexOf(currentRoleMembership, role) <> -1 Then
                                             confirmedRoles.Add(role)
                                     End If
                             Next role

                             Return confirmedRoles.ToArray()
                     Else
                             Return MyBase.GetRolesForUser(username)
                     End If
             End Function
```

Just as with the `SqlRoleProvider`, the custom provider first checks to see if the user is anonymous. Assuming that you have never stored a `MembershipUser` object in the database for the username, the call to `GetUser` always returns `null` for anonymous users. If the user is authenticated, and if there is a set of restricted roles stored in the `Comment` property, then the custom provider parses the information from the property. Most of the work is just double-checking with the base provider that the set of roles the user currently belongs to still grants access to the roles listed in the `Comment` field. The end result of this processing is the subset of restricted roles that still apply to the user. Of course, if no restricted role information is stored in the `Comment` property, the custom provider defers to the base provider.

C#

```csharp
public override bool IsUserInRole(string username, string roleName)
{
    MembershipUser mu = Membership.GetUser(username);

    //Anonymous user case
    if (mu == null)
        return false;

    if (mu.Comment != null)
    {
        string[] restrictedRoles = mu.Comment.Split(";".ToCharArray());

        if ((Array.IndexOf(restrictedRoles, roleName) != -1)
            && (base.IsUserInRole(username, roleName))  )
            return true;
        else
            return false;
    }
    else
    {
        //No restriction is in effect
        return base.IsUserInRole(username, roleName);
    }
}
```

VB.NET

```
Public Overrides Function IsUserInRole( _
        ByVal username As String, _
        ByVal roleName As String) As Boolean
            Dim mu As MembershipUser = Membership.GetUser(username)
            'Anonymous user case
            If mu Is Nothing Then
                Return False
            End If
            If mu.Comment IsNot Nothing Then
                Dim restrictedRoles() As String = _
                mu.Comment.Split(";".ToCharArray())
                If (Array.IndexOf(restrictedRoles, roleName) <> -1) _
                AndAlso (MyBase.IsUserInRole(username, roleName)) Then
                    Return True
                Else
                    Return False
                End If
            Else
                'No restriction is in effect
                Return MyBase.IsUserInRole(username, roleName)
            End If
    End Function
End Function
```

The `IsUserInRole` override follows the same general pattern as `GetUserInRole`. The only difference is that in this case only a single role (the `roleName` parameter) is checked. As with `GetUserInRole` the `roleName` parameter must be found both in the restricted set of roles for the user, as well as in the set of roles currently associated with the user in the database.

Now that you have a customized version of the `SqlRoleProvider`, you can try it out in a sample application. The configuration for the sample application requires authorization for all pages. It also enables Role Manager and enables cookie caching as well. When you first try to access the test page in the sample application, you will be redirected to a login page. After you are logged in, and thus have a `RolePrincipal` attached to the context, the test page allows a user to restrict itself to a subset of the current role membership.

```
...
<asp:ListBox ID="lbxUserInRoles" runat="server" SelectionMode="Multiple" />
...
<asp:Button ID="btnRestrictRole" Runat="server" Text="Restrict Role"
        OnClick="btnRestrictRole_Click" />
...
<asp:Button ID="btnUndoRestriction" Runat="server" Text="Undo Role Restriction"
        OnClick="btnUndoRestriction_Click" />
...
<asp:Label ID="lblStatus" Runat="server" Text="" />
...
<asp:Literal ID="litIsInRoleTests" runat="server" />
...
```

A list box is displayed that contains the current set of roles associated with the user. Two buttons are available: one to restrict the user to the subset of roles that you can choose from the list box and a one that allows you to undo the role restrictions. Toward the bottom of the page is a literal control that contains the results of multiple calls to `RolePrincipal.IsInRole`.

Displaying the set of roles for the current user is accomplished by calling the `Roles` class. Remember that the parameterless version of `Roles.GetRolesForUser` actually results in a call to the `GetRoles` method on the `RolePrincipal` attached to the context. This means the list of information reflects the set of role information that `RolePrincipal` has fetched from the custom provider.

C#

```
lbxUserInRoles.DataSource = Roles.GetRolesForUser();
lbxUserInRoles.DataBind();
```

VB.NET

```
lbxUserInRoles.DataSource = Roles.GetRolesForUser()
lbxUserInRoles.DataBind()
```

To demonstrate the effect of the overridden `IsUserInRole` method, the page also dumps the result of making various authorization checks directly against the provider.

C#

```
StringBuilder sb = new StringBuilder();

if (Roles.Provider.IsUserInRole(User.Identity.Name,"Role A"))
    sb.Append("User is in Role A <br/>");

if (Roles.Provider.IsUserInRole(User.Identity.Name,"Role B"))
    sb.Append("User is in Role B <br/>");

if (Roles.Provider.IsUserInRole(User.Identity.Name,"Role C"))
    sb.Append("User is in Role C <br/>");

litIsInRoleTests.Text = sb.ToString();
```

VB.NET

```
            Dim sb As New StringBuilder()
            If Roles.Provider.IsUserInRole(User.Identity.Name, "Role A") Then
                sb.Append("User is in Role A <br/>")
            End If
            If Roles.Provider.IsUserInRole(User.Identity.Name, "Role B") Then
                sb.Append("User is in Role B <br/>")
            End If
            If Roles.Provider.IsUserInRole(User.Identity.Name, "Role C") Then
                sb.Append("User is in Role C <br/>")
            End If
            litIsInRoleTests.Text = sb.ToString()
```

Restricting a user to a subset of his or her available roles occurs when you click the role restriction button.

C#

```
protected void btnRestrictRole_Click(object sender, EventArgs e)
{
    string restriction = String.Empty;
```

```csharp
    foreach (ListItem li in lbxUserInRoles.Items)
    {
        if (li.Selected == true)
            restriction += li.Value + ";";
    }

    if (!String.IsNullOrEmpty(restriction))
        restriction = restriction.Substring(0, restriction.Length - 1);
    else
        restriction = null;

    MembershipUser mu = Membership.GetUser();
    mu.Comment = restriction;
    Membership.UpdateUser(mu);

    ((RolePrincipal)User).SetDirty();

    Response.Redirect("~/default.aspx");
}
```

VB.NET

```vbnet
Protected Sub btnRestrictRole_Click( _
ByVal sender As Object, _
ByVal e As EventArgs) Handles btnRestrictRole.Click
    Dim restriction As String = String.Empty
    For Each li As ListItem In lbxUserInRoles.Items
        If li.Selected = True Then
            restriction &= li.Value & ";"
        End If
    Next li

    If (Not String.IsNullOrEmpty(restriction)) Then
        restriction = restriction.Substring(0, restriction.Length - 1)
    Else
        restriction = Nothing
    End If

    Dim mu As MembershipUser = Membership.GetUser()
    mu.Comment = restriction
    Membership.UpdateUser(mu)

    CType(User, RolePrincipal).SetDirty()

    Response.Redirect("~/default.aspx")
End Sub
```

Because the list box allows for multiple selections, you can choose one or more roles from the set of roles currently associated with the user. The code bundles up the selected items into a semicolon delimited string and then stores this information in MembershipUser.Comment. Note that the page code then calls SetDirty on the current RolePrincipal. Because the restricted roles have been set, it is necessary to tell the RolePrincipal that it should ignore any currently cached information, and that instead it should refresh this information from the provider. The final redirect forces the page to be re-requested by the browser so that you can see the effect of restricting the roles.

You can undo the role restriction by clicking the second button:

C#

```
protected void btnUndoRestriction_Click(object sender, EventArgs e)
{
    MembershipUser mu = Membership.GetUser();
    mu.Comment = null;
    Membership.UpdateUser(mu);

    ((RolePrincipal)User).SetDirty();

    Response.Redirect("~/default.aspx");
}
```

VB.NET

```
    Protected Sub btnUndoRestriction_Click( _
ByVal sender As Object, _
ByVal e As EventArgs) Handles btnUndoRestriction.Click
        Dim mu As MembershipUser = Membership.GetUser()
        mu.Comment = Nothing
        Membership.UpdateUser(mu)

        CType(User, RolePrincipal).SetDirty()

        Response.Redirect("~/default.aspx")
    End Sub
```

The page code simply nulls the information in `MembershipUser.Comment`. Because the role information for the user has changed, this code also tells the `RolePrincipal` to invalidate its cached information. After the redirect occurs, you will see that the user has reverted to the original set of role assignments.

If you use the Web Administration Tool (WAT) from Visual Studio, you can configure a test user and set up some role associations. For example, I created an account called "testuser" that belonged to three different roles. After you log in, the information displayed on the page looks like:

```
Listbox contains:
   Role A
   Role B
   Role C

IsUserInRole checks:
   User is in Role A
   User is in Role B
   User is in Role C
```

So far so good: The user belongs to all of the roles that you would expect, and currently the custom provider is just delegating the method calls to the base `SqlRoleProvider`. If you choose a subset of roles (choose only Role A and Role C), when the page refreshes, it reflects the restricted set of roles that the user belongs to.

```
Listbox contains:
  Role A
  Role C

IsUserInRole checks:
  User is in Role A
  User is in Role C
```

Now the user can only accomplish tasks on the site allowed to Role A and Role C. Even though in the database the user is also associated with Role B, from the point of view of the website the user no longer belongs to that role. You can see how with just the added logic in the derived version of SqlRoleProvider, the rest of the authorization code in a site is oblivious to the fact that a set of restricted roles is being enforced. If you click the button to undo the role restrictions, you will see that you return to belonging to all of the original roles.

Although the sample just demonstrates the effect of role restrictions when calling RolePrincipal .GetRoles and Roles.GetRolesForUser, with the changes made in the custom provider any type of website authorization mechanism that depends on HttpContext.Current.User will be affected. For example, any URL authorization checks will be transparently made against the restricted set of roles because URL authorization calls IsInRole on the principal object attached to the context. Similarly, if you had a site that made calls to IPrincipal.IsInRole, these authorization checks would automatically work with the restricted role functionality of the custom provider.

Authorizing with Roles in the Data Layer

Because all of the user-to-role associations are stored in the database, and the SqlRoleProvider database schema includes SQL views that map to these tables, you can perform authorization checks in the database using this information. Depending on how your application is structured, you may find it to be more efficient to make a series of authorization checks in the database, as opposed to pulling information back up to the middle tier and then making a series of authorization checks using Role Manager. Older applications that have large amounts of their business logic still in stored procedures may need to keep their authorization logic in the database as well because it may be technically impossible to factor out the authorization checks to a middle tier.

As with the Membership feature, the first step you need to accomplish is the conversion of a (username, application name) pair to the GUID user identifier used in the database tables. You will want to store the result of converting an application name to a GUID identifier because you also need to convert a role name to its GUID identifier. Because role names are segmented by applications, just as usernames are partitioned by application, you will always be performing authorization checks in the context of a specific application name.

SQL Server 2000 conveniently supports user defined functions, so you can encapsulate all of this logic inside of a custom user-defined function.

```
create function IsUserInRole (
@pApplicationName nvarchar(256),
@pUsername        nvarchar(256),
```

```
@pRolename          nvarchar(256) )
returns bit
as
begin

    declare @retval bit

        if exists (
                    select  1
                            from    dbo.vw_aspnet_Users u,
                                    dbo.vw_aspnet_Applications a,
                                    dbo.vw_aspnet_Roles r,
                                    dbo.vw_aspnet_UsersInRoles uir
                            where   a.LoweredApplicationName = LOWER(@pApplicationName)
                            and     u.LoweredUserName = LOWER(@pUsername)
                            and     u.ApplicationId   = a.ApplicationId
                            and     r.ApplicationId   = a.ApplicationId
                            and     r.LoweredRoleName = LOWER(@pRolename)
                            and     r.RoleId          = uir.RoleId
                            and     u.UserId          = uir.UserId
                    )
            set @retval = 1
        else
            set @retval = 0

    return @retval
end
go
```

Much of the code in this function is the same as shown earlier in Chapter 12 in the `getUserId` stored procedures. The additional logic joins the `@pApplicationName` and `@pRolename` variables into the `vw_aspnet_Roles` view to convert from a string role name into the GUID identifier for the role. With the resulting role identifier, the select query looks in `vw_aspnet_UsersInRoles` for a row matching the GUID identifiers that correspond to the user and role name in the requested application. If a row is found, the function returns a bit value of 1 (that is, true); otherwise, it returns a bit value of 0 (that is, false).

With this function, it is trivial to perform authorization checks in the data layer. The following code snippet makes an authorization check based on the user and role data created for the earlier sample on restricting a user's roles:

```
declare @result bit
select  @result = dbo.IsUserInRole('LimitingRoles','testuser','Role B')

if @result = 1
  print 'User is in Role A'
```

Although performing authorization checks in the database is probably a rare occurrence given the types of application architectures in use today, it is still a handy tool to have available if you ever find that you need to authorize users from inside your stored procedures.

Supporting Dynamic Applications

The `RoleProvider` base class defines the abstract property `ApplicationName`. As a result, you can use the same approach for supporting multiple applications on-the-fly with `SqlRoleProvider` as was shown earlier for `SqlMembershipProvider`. After you have a way to set the application name dynamically on a per-request basis, you can write a custom version of `SqlRoleProvider` that reads the application name from a special location. Remember that in Chapter 12 an `HttpModule` was used that looked on the query-string for a variable called `appname`. Depending on the existence of that variable as well as its value, the module would store the appropriate application name in `HttpContext.Items["ApplicationName"]`. You can use the same module with a custom version of the `SqlRoleProvider`.

C#

```csharp
using System;
using System.Web;
using System.Web.Security;

public class CustomRoleProvider : SqlRoleProvider
{
    public override string ApplicationName
    {
        get
        {
            string appNameFromContext =
                (string)HttpContext.Current.Items["ApplicationName"];
            if (appNameFromContext != "NOTSET")
                return appNameFromContext;
            else
                return base.ApplicationName;
        }
    }
}
```

VB.NET

```vbnet
Imports Microsoft.VisualBasic
Imports System
Imports System.Web
Imports System.Web.Security

Public Class CustomRoleProvider
  Inherits SqlRoleProvider
    Public Overrides Property ApplicationName() As String
        Get
            Dim appNameFromContext As String = _
                CStr(HttpContext.Current.Items("ApplicationName"))
            If appNameFromContext <> "NOTSET" Then
                Return appNameFromContext
            Else
                Return MyBase.ApplicationName
            End If
        End Get
```

```
            Set(ByVal value As String)
                Throw New NotSupportedException()
            End Set
        End Property
    End Class
```

The code for handling the application name in the custom role provider is exactly the same as was used for writing a custom Membership provider. With this simple change, you can now create roles in different applications and work with user-to-role associations in different applications simply by changing the value of the appname query-string variable. This behavior is also completely transparent to the Role Manager API and the RolePrincipal object. As with Membership, though, if you write applications that depend on dynamically changing application name, you need to prevent accidentally associating authorization information for a user in one application with a similarly named user in a different application.

Managing an Application's Roles Through IIS 7.0

Chapter 12 demonstrates how to manage an application's users, providers, and connection strings using the new IIS 7.0 applets that are added to IIS as part of the deep integration between IIS 7.0 and ASP.NET.

I will continue to demonstrate the new features inside IIS 7.0 that make the developer's and administrator's life much easier by utilizing a set of UI applets away from all the error-pruning configuration file edits.

When you are inside the IIS 7.0 Manager tool, specifically looking inside the ASP.NET category, you will notice the .NET Roles applet. Figure 15-3 shows the applet when opened inside the IIS 7.0 Manager tool.

Figure 15-3

Inside the .NET Roles applet you can see a listing of all the roles that have been added to the application previously. Figure 15-4 shows the main view of the .NET Roles applet.

Figure 15-4

The available roles in the application are listed in the middle grid with the following two columns:

❑   Name

❑   Users

The Name column represents the name of the role, and the Users column indicates the number of users that are part of the role in the same row.

Similar to the other applets that were discussed in Chapter 12, you have a rich Action pane that contains a set of useful and handy options.

For example, you can add a new role into the application by simply clicking the Add menu. A tiny Windows form pops up that allows you to enter the name of the new role.

Moreover, you can set the role provider for the current application by clicking on the Set Default Provider menu. You also can disable the Role Management feature by clicking on the Disable menu on the Action pane.

If you click on any of the roles listed in the middle grid shown above, you get to see a new set of menu options inside the Action pane. Figure 15-5 shows the customized Action pane when a role is being selected inside the middle grid.

Figure 15-5

When you click on View Users, the .NET Users applet opens and lists all the users present in the current application that are part of the selected role. You can also rename the selected role and even remove it from the application's set of roles.

Summary

The SqlRoleProvider is a complete implementation of the RoleProvider base class with which you can quickly and easily set up user-to-role associations. The simplicity of the provider should not fool you though; the product team tested it regularly with 250,000 user-to-role associations and has stressed the provider with as many as 20 million user-to-role associations. So, even for large sites the provider is quite capable of scaling well with large numbers of users and roles. Note though that the provider does not support one often-asked-for feature: role nesting. In large part, this is because the Role Manager feature itself does not expose the concept of nesting roles within roles.

As with the Membership providers, you can use the SqlRoleProvider both inside of ASP.NET as well as in non-ASP.NET applications. Within ASP.NET the provider needs to run in Low trust or higher. The provider works equally well in partially trusted non-ASP.NET applications, although getting these types of applications to work properly with the provider does require a bit of rather arcane configuration work in the Framework's CAS system. With that said though, you can definitely get this scenario to work, and it is something that the ASP.NET team intentionally worked to enable in both the 2.0 and 3.5 .NET Frameworks.

Although the `SqlRoleProvider` is a rather simple provider to implement, you can still use it in a number of interesting ways. You can store authorization information in the database for Windows-authenticated users, which makes the provider ideal for applications where you don't need the extra time or hassle of getting NT groups setup for application authorization purposes. Because the `SqlRoleProvider` is unsealed, you can derive from it and add whatever custom authorization logic you want on top of it. In this chapter, you saw how you could use this approach to easily give power users and administrators the ability to restrict the set of roles that they act in while working on a site.

Because the provider's schema exists in SQL Server, and there are supported SQL views for querying this information, you can create your own custom data layer logic to perform authorization checks using the role data stored in the database. And just as with the Membership providers, you can write a simple derivation of `SqlRoleProvider` that can handle dynamically changing the application name on a per-request basis for portal-style applications.

16

AuthorizationStoreRoleProvider

AuthorizationStoreRoleProvider maps the functionality of the Role Manager feature onto the Authorization Manager (AzMan) authorization store that was first released as part of Windows Server 2003 and now is also part of Windows Server 2008 with several new enhancements. The provider supports most of the RoleProvider functionality as well as a handful of AzMan specific settings and behaviors. Although AzMan itself has the concept of more granular permission checks than just role checks, AuthorizationStoreRoleProvider only exposes the role-based functionality of AzMan.

In this chapter, will you will learn about the following aspects of the AuthorizationStore RoleProvider:

- ❑ How the provider interacts with AzMan.
- ❑ Role Manager functionality supported by the provider.
- ❑ Working with a file-based policy store.
- ❑ Working with an Active Directory AzMan policy store.
- ❑ Using the provider in partial trust.
- ❑ Using the ActiveDirectoryMembershipProvider and AuthorizationStoreRoleProvider together.

Provider Design

The AuthorizationStoreRoleProvider is a wrapper around a subset of the functionality available in Authorization Manager. The provider is supported for use in ASP.NET applications and non-ASP.NET applications. Although the provider depends on Authorization Manager, you can use it with Windows-authenticated and forms-authenticated websites. All of the samples in this chapter use forms authentication and `ActiveDirectoryMembershipProvider` in conjunction with `AuthorizationStoreRoleProvider`.

Authorization Manager is a feature that was first shipped as part of Windows Server 2003, and it supports role-based and "operation-based" security, and also ships with Windows Server 2008 with several new enhancements. There is also a runtime component that you can install that enables AzMan on Windows 2000 and Windows XP. AzMan supports role-based security because that has been the most prevalent type of security used by developers. It also introduced the concepts of tasks and operations that can be used to model more granular "things," which themselves can be authorized. For example, with AzMan, you could create an operation called `UpdateAccountData`, and then within your application you could ask AzMan if the current user has rights to `UpdateAccountData`. This is an elegant approach to the common authorization problem of separating authorization administration (adding users to roles, assigning users rights to operations) from the security model of "things" that can be authorized. The fact that you can model very granular operations makes AzMan a powerful authorization engine. Because `AuthorizationStoreRoleProvider` is an implementation of `RoleProvider`, the provider only exposes the subset of AzMan that deals specifically with associating users to roles and making checks to see if a user belongs to a role. The provider does not expose the AzMan functionality for making operation- and task-based access checks.

Throughout this chapter I will be focusing on AzMan running on top of Windows Server 2008. Whatever applies to AzMan on Windows Server 2008 applies to AzMan on Windows Server 2003, except the new improvements that have been added to AzMan on Windows Server 2008.

AzMan stores authorization information inside of a policy store. This policy store can be deployed in an Active Directory server, in ADLDS, or in a plain XML file. If you place the policy store in a directory, you can only use ADLDS or a Windows Server 2008 domain controller that has been upgraded to run at the Windows Server 2008 functional level. Note, though, that with the downloadable AzMan runtime you can still have web servers running Windows 2000 or Windows XP that make use of the policy store in a Windows Server 2008 domain controller. In addition, one of the major improvements on AzMan in Windows Server 2008 is the ability to store the authorization information in Microsoft SQL Server. Finally a new group that has been added to AzMan is the BizRule that allows you to add users to a role based on a script that you write and that runs at runtime to decide whether the user belongs to the group or not.

`AuthorizationStoreRoleProvider` works with AzMan through its COM primary interop assembly (PIA), so from the provider's standpoint the specific type of store is moot. Some partial trust issues arise when using different stores, but in Full trust the different types of policy store locations are just different connection string values to the provider. Back in the time of Windows Server 2003 SP1, AzMan did add support for nondomain principals stored in ADAM. This allows developers to use completely standalone ADAM instances and set up AzMan authorization information using ADAM principals. However, this AzMan functionality *is not* supported by `AuthorizationStoreRoleProvider`. Even though you can place the policy store in any one of the four locations supported by AzMan, in all cases the users and groups managed in the policy store must come from a domain.

The provider connects to the policy store specified in a connection string and then gets a reference to an AzMan application with a call to `IAzAuthorizationStore::OpenApplication`. Because AzMan also supports the concept of authorization scopes within an application, `AuthorizationStoreRoleProvider` has a configuration option that allows you to point the provider at a scope as well. In this case, the provider will internally ensure that any provider methods occur within the desired scope, as opposed to operating at the level of an AzMan application. Because AzMan itself can have multiple applications, as well as multiple scopes within an application, you can use the provider's `ApplicationName` and

ScopeName properties to point at any application or any scope within an AzMan application. In general, though, a single configured instance of AuthorizationStoreRoleProvider works with only a single AzMan application or a single scope in an AzMan application. If you need the provider to work with different AzMan applications or scopes, you should configure a separate provider instance for each AzMan application or scope you need to work with.

The other aspect of the provider's interaction with AzMan is how the provider gets a reference to a client context that represents a specific user. In AzMan, access checks for operations as well as the information needed for a role check all come from an application context represented as an IAzApplicationContext interface. Because the provider supports the IsUserInRole and GetRolesForUser methods, the provider has a number of different approaches to getting the appropriate client context for a given user:

❑   If an ASP.NET application is configured to use Windows authentication, and the username parameter to the provider exactly matches the username from HttpContext.Current.User.Name, then the provider initializes an AzMan client context using the token from the current principal's WindowsIdentity. This initialization approach is the fastest and most efficient way to get the correct client context because it doesn't incur extra round trips to a directory server. In the AzMan API, this means the provider makes a call to IAzApplication::InitializeClientContextFromToken. If you pass the value of HttpContext.Current.User.Identity.Name as the username parameter to IsUserInRole or GetRolesForUser, you will be able to have the provider initialize the client context from the Windows token.

❑   For non-ASP.NET applications, the provider follows the same process, but it looks at Thread.CurrentPrincipal. For non-ASP.NET applications, ensuring that the thread principal is set up with the correct WindowsPrincipal and WindowsIdentity is the most efficient approach for using the provider.

❑   If your application doesn't have a WindowsIdentity available (in ASP.NET this would probably mean you are using forms authentication), then the provider falls back and initializes the client context with a call to IAzApplication::InitializeClientContextFromName. This is the AzMan method that allows Authorization Manager to take just a plain string representation of a username (e.g. DOMAIN\USERNAME style or the user@domain.com UPN style) and look up the expansion of that user's group membership in Active Directory. Although this approach gives you the flexibility to use forms authentication in your web applications, it is slower than the token-based approach. Also note that for this approach to work the process identity or the application impersonation identity needs read privileges on the tokenGroupsGlobalAndUniversal attribute of any users that will be authorized in the application. By default, read access on this attribute is granted to members of the built-in domain group Pre-Windows 2000 Compatible Access. If this group has no members in your domain structure (for example, you may have locked down your domain by emptying the membership for this group), then the provider will return an access denied exception from the AzMan layer. You can fix this problem in a number of ways. The easiest approach is to add the appropriate accounts to a different built-in domain group called Windows Authorization Access Group. This group has read access to the tokenGroupsGlobalAndUniversal attribute for all users in the domain. You can also follow a more granular security approach by granting read access on the attribute at the OU level. This has the benefit of limiting the access granted to a process or application impersonation account to only the users in a specific directory container.

After the provider has the user's client context in hand, it can use it to get the role information needed by IsUserInRole and GetRolesForUser.

Internally, the provider will call the store's `UpdateCache` method to update its cached information after 60 or more minutes have passed. The duration between calls to `UpdateCache` is configurable, primarily so you can tune the provider to be more or less sensitive to changes in the underlying policy store. Because AzMan caches the authorization information it loads from the policy store, changes made to previously loaded authorization information are not reflected until the next time the provider asks AzMan to update its cached information.

In terms of unique AzMan functionality that does work with the provider, the following pieces of AzMan functionality will affect the results returned by the provider:

❑ AzMan supports nesting of Windows users and Windows groups in AzMan application groups, as well as nesting of AzMan application groups in other AzMan application groups. When you call the provider's `GetRolesForUser` or `IsUserInRole` methods, the results will reflect these nesting relationships. As noted in Chapter 13, this is a perfect example of being able to support nesting relationships for authorization checks even though the Role Manager feature doesn't explicitly support this kind of functionality.

❑ AzMan supports groups that have dynamic group membership; these are called LDAP query groups. The provider is oblivious to LDAP query groups. You can't create LDAP query groups via the provider. However, if you have preconfigured LDAP query groups in an AzMan policy store, the results returned from the provider will reflect a user's membership (or nonmembership) in the LDAP query groups.

Supported Functionality

`AuthorizationStoreRoleProvider` implements all of the methods defined on the base `RoleProvider` class with the exception of the `FindUsersInRole` method. The provider throws a `NotImplemented Exception` from this method, which is a bit of a deviation from the normal practice of throwing a `NotSupportedException` for such cases. Because the provider is basically a "shim" that maps `RoleProvider` method calls to their equivalent for AzMan, and AzMan has no concept of searching for users in a role, the `FindUsersInRole` method was not implemented.

If you have ever worked with the AzMan APIs directly, you are probably already getting an idea of how the provider makes use of AzMan. Internally, each supported `RoleProvider` method maps directly to a method call on an AzMan interface or object. The complete mapping is shown in the following list:

❑ `AddUsersToRoles`—`IAzRole::AddMemberName`

❑ `CreateRole`—Either `IAzApplication::CreateRole` or `IAzScope::CreateRole`

❑ `DeleteRole`—Either `IAzApplication::DeleteRole` or `IAzScope::DeleteRole`

❑ `FindUsersInRole`: Not implemented

❑ `GetAllRoles`: Iterates through the roles returned by either the `IAzApplization::Roles` property or the `IAzScope::Roles` property

❑ `GetRolesForUser`: `IAzClientContext::GetRoles`

❑ `GetUsersInRole`: `IAzRole::MembersName`

❑ `IsUserInRole`: Retrieves roles from `IAzClientContext::GetRoles` and then performs a string comparison between the requested role and the set of roles returned from the AzMan method. The comparison is case-insensitive and uses ordinal comparisons (that is, a case-insensitive byte-by-byte string comparison using the invariant culture).

❏ `RemoveUsersFromRoles:IAzRole::DeleteMemberName`

❏ `RoleExists:` Either `IAzApplication::OpenRole` or `IAzScope::OpenRole`

There aren't any implemented methods that have special or unexpected functionality. Beyond the internal mappings noted in the preceding list, the AzMan-specific aspects of the provider are in the area of a few properties and AzMan-specific handling of some configuration attributes.

The provider properties that directly affect how it works with AzMan are described in the following list:

❏ `ApplicationName:` `AuthorizationStoreRoleProvider` uses this attribute as the name of the AzMan application in the policy store that the provider instance should work with. An important difference from the SQL providers, though, is that the trick of overriding this property will not work. Internally, the provider *always* looks at a private variable that stores the application name; the provider doesn't call the getter on the public property. The assumption was that normally you would not have hundreds or thousands of AzMan applications in a policy store, so supporting the dynamic switching of application context on a per-request basis didn't really make sense. Note that this property also has a setter. After changing the application name via a call to the setter, the provider will reinitialize its reference to an AzMan application by calling `IAzAuthorizationStore::OpenApplication` again. This can be useful for limited administrative applications, but because the setter is not thread-safe you need to carefully manage calls to it. Otherwise two simultaneous requests attempting to set `ApplicationName` will interfere with each other. For this reason, you should configure different provider instances for different AzMan applications needed by your production applications.

❏ `ScopeName:` This is a custom provider property that allows you to get and set the AzMan scope used by the provider. Normally, you configure the AzMan scope in configuration and then the provider operates within the context of the scope for its entire lifetime. As with the `ApplicationName` property, `ScopeName` has a setter that you can use. After calling it, the provider will internally reinitialize its `IAzApplization` and `IAzScope` references. However, the setter for `ScopeName` is also not thread-safe, and so it is really only useful for administrative applications that implement some type of locking to ensure that competing threads don't tromp on each other's scope settings. The general guidance is that you should configure separate provider instances for each different AzMan application-scope combination needed by your application.

The AzMan-specific configuration properties supported by the provider are:

❏ `applicationName:` This attribute determines the AzMan application used by the provider. You must explicitly specify a value for this attribute if you want the provider to work. Although the provider will use ASP.NET's default logic for determining an application name if one is not specified, chances are you do not have an AzMan application with the same name as your web application's virtual directory (or executable name in the case of a non-ASP.NET application).

❏ `scopeName:` This attribute determines the AzMan scope in the AzMan application that will be used by the provider. If you specify the `scopeName` configuration attribute, be sure that the scope really does exist in the AzMan application pointed at by the `applicationName` attribute.

❏ `cacheRefreshInterval:` This attribute controls the interval in minutes between calls to update the cached representation of authorization information. If this attribute is not specified, the provider will call UpdateCache on the policy store every 60 minutes. You can lower the value on this setting if you have frequent changes occurring in your policy store, or you can increase it if your policy store does not change much. Note, though, that this setting affects only cached information derived from the AzMan policy store. For example, if you change the Windows groups that a user belongs to, adjusting this cache interval will not help because the AzMan cache has nothing to do with Windows group memberships that are cached in a user's security token.

Using a File-Based Policy Store

You can configure AzMan's authorization rules using an XML file as opposed to a directory or Microsoft SQL Server database (in this case, the XML file is the policy store. AzMan supports a file-specific connection string format for connecting to an XML file). AuthorizationStoreRoleProvider is configured with this connection string in the same way that you would configure a SQL-based provider with an ADO.NET-compliant connection string. You add the connectionStringName attribute to your provider definition and it references a connection string in the <connectionStrings /> section. For example, the following connection string uses a combination of the AzMan connection string syntax and a special syntax that is unique to AuthorizationStoreRoleProvider:

```
<add name="FileBasedPolicyStore"
     connectionString="msxml://~/App_Data/test.xml"/>
```

The bolded portion of the connection string uses the ASP.NET tilde shorthand. When the provider sees that the connection string starts with msxml it knows that it will be working with a file-based policy store. As a result, the provider makes an extra check for the tilde syntax. If it finds it, the provider gets the physical file path to the root of the web application and prepends it to the remainder of the connection string. In the preceding sample syntax, this means you could also use a connection string such as:

```
<add
    name="FileBasedPolicyStore"
    connectionString="msxml://C:\inetpub\wwwroot\379301_code\379301 ch_16_code\ ↵
        cs\UsingAzMan\App_Data\test.xml"
/>
```

For web applications, it makes sense to use the ~/App_Data shorthand because you can just deploy the web.config configuration file onto a web server without having to fix up the file path for the AzMan policy store. If you use the provider in a non-ASP.NET application, you can actually use the same tilde syntax. In this case the provider substitutes the file path to the current executable in place of the tilde character.

Using the provider with a file-based policy store is trivial after the authorization store has been set up and configured. In Figure 16-1 I have added the demouser98@bhaidar.net account to a role called Normal Users. There is also another role called Adminstrators defined in the application called UsingAzMan.

At this point, using the policy store is just an exercise in configuring Role Manager properly, and then calling the APIs. The abbreviated configuration for a test application is:

```
<connectionStrings>
    <!--special file based syntax supported only by the provider-->
    <add
```

```
            name="FileBasedPolicyStore"
            connectionString="msxml://~/App_Data/test.xml"
    />
</connectionStrings>
...
<roleManager enabled="true" defaultProvider="fileProvider">
    <providers>
    <clear />
    <add
        name="fileProvider"
        type="System.Web.Security.AuthorizationStoreRoleProvider,…"
        connectionStringName="FileBasedPolicyStore"
        applicationName="UsingAzMan"
    />
    </providers>
</roleManager>
```

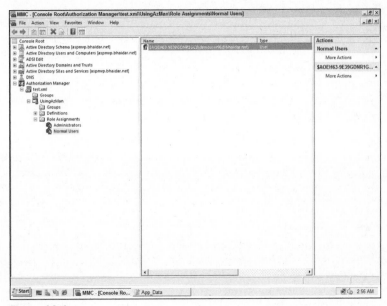

Figure 16-1

The provider definition points at a connection string using the tilde shorthand. The `applicationName` attribute on the provider definition corresponds to the AzMan application `UsingAzMan` that you can see in the policy store from Figure 16-1.

With the configuration steps completed, you can create roles and associate users to roles. If you want to, you can use the Web Administration Tool (WAT) to accomplish this. Because the WAT is oblivious to the type of provider being used, it will allow you to carry out role management against AzMan via the provider. Because I used the `ActiveDirectoryMembershipProvider` for my sample application, the WAT was able to find users and assign them to roles managed by the `AuthorizationStoreRoleProvider`. After you have set up some roles and user-to-role assignments, you can dump out the roles that the user belongs to.

C#

```
string[] roles = ((RolePrincipal)User).GetRoles();
foreach (string r in roles)
    Response.Write(User.Identity.Name + " is in role <b> " + r + "</b><br/>");
```

VB.NET

```
Dim roles() As String = (CType(User, RolePrincipal)).GetRoles()
For Each r As String In roles
    Response.Write(User.Identity.Name & " is in role <b> " & r & "</b><br/>")
Next r
```

This code snippet shows that the user account belongs to the Normal Users role:

```
demouser98@bhaidar.net is in role Normal Users
```

If you go back into the AzMan MMC and switch the account over to the Administrators role, you can see the change in role assignment take effect. First, though, you will need to cycle the web application (touch web.config or iisreset). This is because after browsing to the test page the first time, AzMan will have cached the results of the policy lookup. Changing a user's role membership in the MMC will not be reflected in the AzMan runtime until the next cache refresh interval (remember that the provider uses a 60 minute cache refresh interval by default). After you have cycled the web application, thus dumping the cached AzMan authorization information, refreshing the page in the browser will show the new role membership.

Note that from AzMan's point of view, the file is just an XML file, which has security implications for your web application. For web applications you should *always* place the XML file (or files if you are configuring multiple provider instances) inside of the App_Data directory. This prevents malicious users from downloading the policy store. If you were to place the XML file somewhere else in your directory structure, browser users that guessed the name of it would be able to download your entire authorization policy!

Of course, this raises the question of whether you should use file-based policy stores in production applications. Personally, I would lean away from doing so and limit use of the file-based policy store to development environments. Even though the policy store will be safe when it resides in App_Data, it still seems risky to have your authorization policy sitting on your web server's hard drive, available for anyone with local server access to browse. Some folks though like to use file-based policy stores in production because if the policy store is small ("small" is relative, but 1MB or smaller is a reasonable "guesstimate"), using an XML-based store is much faster than using the directory based store. Another argument, for using a file-based policy store is that in a web farm you now have the hassle of having to push updates to your authorization policy across multiple machines. Determining whether all of your servers have the same authorization rules can be a bit difficult. If you store the policy in a directory, you know that every web server pointed at the directory server is seeing the same consistent set of authorization information.

Because the policy store exists in a file, you can secure access to the store with NTFS file ACLs. Like other ASP.NET providers, AuthorizationStoreRoleProvider internally runs with either the process credentials or application impersonation credentials, assuming you have application impersonation enabled. If these credentials only have read access to the policy store, only the read-oriented methods on the provider will succeed. If the process or application impersonation credentials have write access to the file as well, then write-oriented methods (for example, CreateRole) will also work.

The default `App_Data` credentials set by Visual Studio grant both read and write access to the process account. As a result, for file-based policy stores, your web application will be able to modify the information in the store by default. To restrict policy stores to read-only on your web servers, you can simply revoke Write permission on the XML file from the process account or application impersonation account.

Using a Directory-Based Policy Store

From a programming and configuration standpoint, using a directory-based policy store is no different than using a file-based policy store, aside from the connection string. Instead of configuring the connection string with an `msxml` moniker, you use an `msldap` moniker with a valid LDAP path. Setting up an AzMan policy store basically involves choosing a location for the store in your directory. Instead of storing the policy store in a file, the policy store is located in a container somewhere in your directory structure. I created a policy store in the directory structure that you saw used earlier in Chapter 13 when you learned about working with `ActiveDirectoryMembershipProvider`. Figure 16-2 shows a policy store aptly named "Chapter16" that contains an application called UsingAzMan.

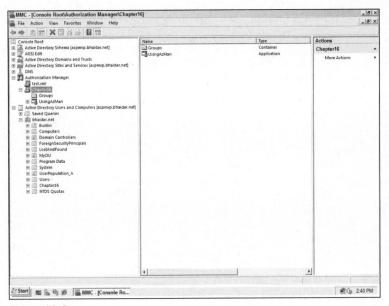

Figure 16-2

If you look at the containers underneath `bhaidar.net`, you will see that there is a container titled Chapter16 that is of type `msDS-AzAdminManager`. This container is the root of the AzMan policy store shown in Figure 16-2. Note that you will not see this container unless you enabled the advanced features view in the Active Directory MMC. Normally though, you work with the AzMan policy store via the AzMan MMC. Looking at the underlying container location is interesting in order to get an idea of how the abstract concept of a policy store maps to a physical container within a directory.

With the policy store and AzMan application created, you can connect to it with the following connection string:

```
<add
    name="DirectoryBasedPolicyStore"
    connectionString="msldap://aspmvp.bhaidar.net/CN=Chapter16,DC=bhaidar,DC=net"
/>
```

Unlike `ActiveDirectoryMembershipProvider`, where you could also use just a domain name, AzMan requires a server name and optional port name if you choose to supply this information. If you want, though, you can skip the servername and port name, in which case AzMan will use the default domain controller selected by the machine. The following connection string shows what this looks like:

```
<add
    name="DirectoryBasedPolicyStore"
    connectionString="msldap://CN=Chapter16,DC=bhaidar,DC=net"
/>
```

At this point, you might think you could take the sample code from the file-based policy example shown earlier and just use one of these two connection strings. If you do this, your code will connect to the policy store and then will promptly fail with an exception stating "Insufficient access rights to perform the operation." This is because the identity of your web application does not have any privileges to read or write information in the directory's policy store. Unlike the file-based policy store where NTFS ACLs control rights to the store, in a directory store you must explicitly setup the AzMan "roles" that grant access to applications and scopes.

I put "roles" in quotes because it can quickly become confusing dealing with AzMan "roles" used for connection access versus the real role information in the policy store. AzMan defines an Administrator role and a Reader role that control the kinds of operations a security account can perform in a policy store or application. As you would expect, a member of the Administrator role can do things like create applications, scopes, and roles. A member of the Reader role can only query information in the policy store; it cannot modify it.

Because I need to populate the store with some roles and set up a user-to-role mapping, I initially added the web server's machine account (which corresponds to NETWORK SERVICE) to the Administrator role for the AzMan application called "UsingAzMan." You can see what this looks like in Figure 16-3.

As you can see from the screenshot, the Administrators domain group and the Administrator domain user are members of this role by default. For a development environment where you are just loading test data, adding a server account to the Administrator role is acceptable. However, in a production environment, you clearly should not have your process accounts or application impersonation accounts in this role. At most you might have a machine off to the side running an administrative application, where the process or application impersonation credentials for that application are in the Administrator role.

Because the NETWORK SERVICE account was added to a management role associated with an AzMan application, you also need to add the machine account to the Delegated User role at the store level. You can see this in Figure 16-4.

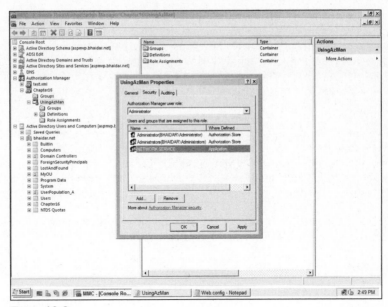

Figure 16-3

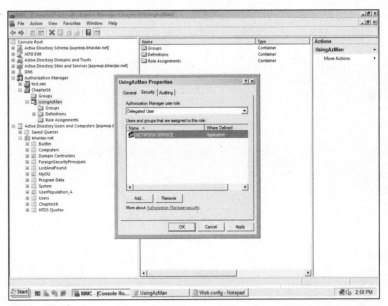

Figure 16-4

This extra step is necessary if you plan to delegate control over different applications, or different scopes within a single policy store. If you plan to store only a single web application's authorization information in a single policy store, then you can just grant rights at the store level (this would be a model of one business application mapping to one AzMan policy store). On the other hand, if you plan to store many different sets of authorization information within a single AzMan policy store, chances are that you do not want different web applications accidentally making use of each others' authorization rules.

In this case, you may allocate an AzMan application for each of your business applications, or you may allocate an AzMan scope for each business application. For these scenarios you need more granular access control down to the level of an AzMan application or an AzMan scope. As a result, you start out adding the appropriate accounts to the store level Delegated User group, and then add the appropriate accounts (that is, delegate control) to the Administrator or Reader role on a specific application or scope.

With this extra set of security configuration completed, you can now run the sample code from the file-based sample. The configuration looks almost exactly the same:

```
<connectionStrings>
        <add
                name="DirectoryBasedPolicyStore"
  connectionString="msldap://aspmvp.bhaidar.net/CN=Chapter15,DC=bhaidar,DC=net"/>

<connectionStrings>
   <add
        name="DirectoryBasedPolicyStore"
        connectionString="msldap://aspmvp.bhaidar.net/CN=Chapter16,DC=bhaidar,DC=net"
/>

<add
   name="FileBasedPolicyStore"
   connectionString="msxml://~/App_Data/test.xml"
/>
</connectionStrings>
...
<roleManager enabled="true" defaultProvider="directoryProvider">
    <providers>
    <clear />
    <add
       name="fileProvider"
       type="System.Web.Security.AuthorizationStoreRoleProvider, …"
       connectionStringName="FileBasedPolicyStore"
       applicationName="UsingAzMan"/>
    <add
       name="directoryProvider"
       type="System.Web.Security.AuthorizationStoreRoleProvider, …"
       connectionStringName="DirectoryBasedPolicyStore"
       applicationName="UsingAzMan"/>
    </providers>
</roleManager>
```

A second provider instance using a directory-based policy store was added to the <roleManager /> definition and was made the default provider for the feature. At this point, you can start creating roles and assigning users to roles. If you are running as an interactive user with privileges in the AzMan policy store, you can use the WAT to accomplish this. Alternatively, now that the process account is part of the application's Administrator role you can use the standard Role Manager APIs in .aspx pages to create roles and populate the roles with users.

Because most developers will probably work with prepopulated policy stores in their production environments, you can change the rights that have been delegated to the process account or application impersonation account. Although the account still needs to be in the Delegated User role at the store level (assuming that you want to work with many applications in a single policy store), you can instead add the account to the Reader role for the application. This will allow your application to read authorization information, but it will not be able to modify it in any way.

As noted earlier, the provider also supports working within the context of an AzMan scope. You can change the configuration for the provider to include a scope definition similar to the one that follows:

```
<add
    name="directoryProvider"
    type="System.Web.Security.AuthorizationStoreRoleProvider, …"
    connectionStringName="DirectoryBasedPolicyStore"
    applicationName="UsingAzMan"
    scopeName="Scope_A"
/>
```

Now, if you create new roles and assign users to roles, all of the operations will be occurring within the Scope_A scope nested within the UsingAzMan application. Figure 16-5 shows what this looks like:

Figure 16-5

The code to create the new roles and populate the roles consists of standard Role Manger API calls:

C#

```
if (Roles.RoleExists("Administrators in Scope A"))
    Roles.DeleteRole("Administrators in Scope A", false);

if (Roles.RoleExists("Normal Users in Scope A"))
    Roles.DeleteRole("Normal Users in Scope A", false);

Roles.CreateRole("Administrators in Scope A");
Roles.CreateRole("Normal Users in Scope A");

if (!Roles.IsUserInRole("Administrators in Scope A"))
    Roles.AddUserToRole(User.Identity.Name, "Administrators in Scope A");
```

VB.NET

```
If Roles.RoleExists("Administrators in Scope A") Then
    Roles.DeleteRole("Administrators in Scope A", False)
End If
If Roles.RoleExists("Normal Users in Scope A") Then
    Roles.DeleteRole("Normal Users in Scope A", False)
End If
Roles.CreateRole("Administrators in Scope A")
Roles.CreateRole("Normal Users in Scope A")

If (Not Roles.IsUserInRole("Administrators in Scope A")) Then
    Roles.AddUserToRole(User.Identity.Name, "Administrators in Scope A")
End If
```

As you can see, from a programming perspective nothing changes. You continue to write Role Manager code as you normally would, and the provider automatically takes care of working against the correct application scope.

Another unique aspect of using the AzMan policy store is the ability to nest group memberships. There are a variety of approaches to nesting:

❑ Add Windows users and Windows groups directly to a role you create in AzMan.

❑ Add Windows users and Windows groups to an AzMan application group. Then add the AzMan application group to a role you create in AzMan.

❑ Add Windows users and Windows groups to an AzMan application group. Then add the AzMan application group to a *different* AzMan application group. Add this second group to a role you create in AzMan.

So, you have quite a few different options that allow you to accomplish group nesting. Although AuthorizationStoreRoleProvider can add Windows users only directly to an AzMan role, the provider will properly handle the necessary group expansion computations when IsUserInRole or GetRolesForUser is called (more precisely, AzMan does this for you).

To see how this works, you can set up some test AzMan application groups. Set up an application group hierarchy like the following:

```
Application Group That Contains A
    |
    |
   ---> Application Group A
            |
            |
           ---> demouser98@bhaidar.net
```

You now have an example of a nesting relationship. The `demouser98@bhaidar.net` user account in Active Directory indirectly belongs to the top-level AzMan application group called Application Group That Contains A. You can add this application group to the Normal Users role that was created earlier, as shown in Figure 16-6.

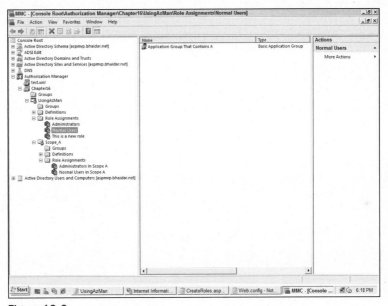

Figure 16-6

Now if you dump all the roles that `demouser98@bhaidar.net` belongs to with the following code:

C#

```csharp
string[] roles = ((RolePrincipal)User).GetRoles();
foreach (string r in roles)
    Response.Write(User.Identity.Name + " is in role <b> " + r + "</b><br/>");
```

VB.NET

```
Dim roles() As String = (CType(User, RolePrincipal)).GetRoles()
For Each r As String In roles
    Response.Write(User.Identity.Name & " is in role <b> " & r & "</b><br/>")
Next r
```

you will see the following output:

```
demouser98@bhaidar.net is in role Administrators
demouser98@bhaidar.net is in role Normal Users
```

Even though the user belongs to Normal Users by way of two intervening application groups, the provider is properly returning the full expansion of the user's role membership. If the underlying call to the provider's GetRolesForUser method did not properly expand all nested group relationships when computing a user's AzMan role memberships, the utility of the provider, and for that matter AzMan itself, would be rather hobbled. Keep this behavior in mind if you plan on using Authorization StoreRoleProvider. Even though you will not get the benefit of the AzMan access checks with this provider, the ability to use any type of group nesting in AzMan and still have role checks work properly gives you a powerful piece of role management that SqlRoleProvider lacks.

One other unique aspect of AzMan that you can leverage with the provider is LDAP query groups. The AzMan application groups you just saw are called basic groups in AzMan terminology. The companion group type in AzMan is an LDAP query group. As the name suggests, instead of statically defining the users and groups that belong to the AzMan application group, membership is determined on the fly based on an LDAP query. Depending upon what kind of user information you store in your directory, you can create some very rich user-to-LDAP query group assignments (for example, users that belong to the West coast region, users that have a specific area code, and so on).

Even though the concept of a MembershipUser in ASP.NET is very limited, this does not constrain the kinds of LDAP queries you can use in AzMan. This means that if you have some way of populating attributes for your user objects other than the Membership feature, you can create LDAP queries that make use of this information. For example, if you set the zip code (that is, the postalCode attribute) on a user object, you can then construct an LDAP query group that predicates its membership based on this value. A simple example of such a query definition is shown in Figure 16-7.

You can then add the LDAP query group to one of the AzMan roles that created earlier. Figure 16-8 shows adding the query group to the role called wrong.

I edited the user object for the demouser98@bhaidar.net user by setting its zip code to 11072. Now if you rerun the sample code that prints out a user's roles, you can see that the provider returns the third AzMan role as well.

```
demouser98@bhaidar.net is in role Administrators
demouser98@bhaidar.net is in role Normal Users
demouser98@bhaidar.net is in role This is a new role
```

Even though this kind of dynamic group functionality is not defined anywhere in the Role Manager feature, you can still take advantage of it via AuthorizationStoreRoleProvider. As long as you have set up user attributes and LDAP query groups through some other mechanism, you can take full advantage of the dynamic membership of LDAP query groups with the provider. With some planning around user attributes and LDAP queries, you can structure your AzMan authorization rules to automatically adjust to the changing information stored for your users.

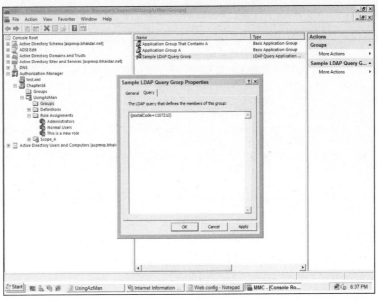

Figure 16-7

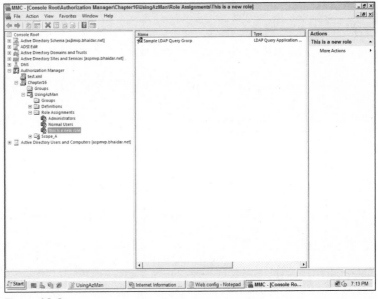

Figure 16-8

Using a Microsoft SQL Server Database-Based Policy Store

Windows Server 2008 enriches the AzMan Authorization Manager with a new feature: the ability to store the authorization information in a Microsoft SQL Server. The SQL Server can be a SQL Server 2000, SQL Server 2005, or SQL Server Express 2005. From a programming and configuration standpoint, using a Microsoft SQL Server database-based policy store is no different from using a file-based policy store or directory-based policy store, aside from the connection string. Instead of configuring the connection string with an `msxml` or `msldap` moniker, you can use an `mssql` moniker with a valid Microsoft SQL Server connection string. Setting up an AzMan policy store basically involves specifying a connection string that includes the database server, database name, and the Policy Store name at the very least. To create a new AzMan policy store based on a Microsoft SQL Server, right-click on the Authorization Manager node and select New Authorization Store. Figure 16-9 shows the GUI that pops up to help you in configuring the SQL Server based AzMan policy store.

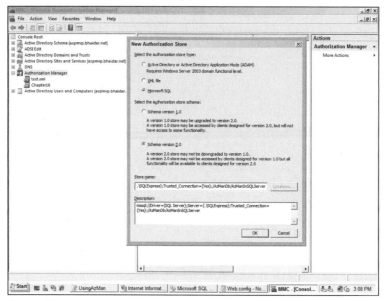

Figure 16-9

Notice in Figure 16-9 that a new authorization store type is now included as an option to select and use. Once you select the `Microsoft SQL` option, you need also to specify the schema version, and finally and most importantly the `Store Name`. If you are creating a Microsoft SQL policy store, the store name represents a URL beginning with the protocol prefix of `mssql`. I have pasted the same `Store Name` in the description area on the Form so that you can see the details of the how to specify a store name. The URL should first of all specify a valid connection string (in this case the authorization store is connecting to a SQL Server Express 2005 instance named ".\SQLExpress" where trusted connection is enabled), a database name that will hold all the tables required for the SQL Server authorization store to function properly, and finally the authorization store name to be listed as a subnode under the Authorization Manager root node.

If you are using Microsoft SQL Server Express Edition and the database name you specified is not pre-created, SQL Server automatically creates it once the authorization store is created. Figure 16-10 shows a table listing of all the tables that constitute the AzManDb database.

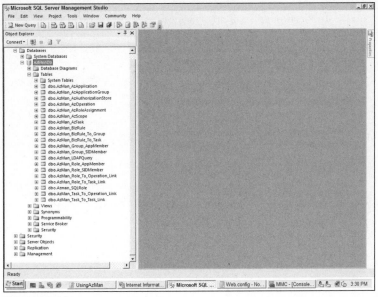

Figure 16-10

The database tables are mainly used to store all the related information about the authorization store and its authorization information. Any AzMan role, group, operations, tasks, and so on are stored in the different tables listed. I will not go into the details of every table since this is beyond the scope of this book, but the main idea is that any authorization information added to any authorization application in the current authorization store will be stored in these tables.

With the policy store and AzMan application created, you can connect to it with the following connection string:

```
<add
     name="SQLServerBasedPolicyStore"
     connectionString="mssql://Driver={SQL Server};Server={.\SQLExpress};Trusted_
Connection={Yes};/AzManDb/AzManInSQLServer"
/>
```

The preceding connection string represents the same store name that was used to create the authorization store. Now let us run the same application that we worked on in both the file-based policy store and the directory-based policy store examples shown above and see what happens. If you do so, your code will connect to the policy store and then will promptly fail with an exception stating "Access is Denied." This is because the identity of your web application does not have any privileges to access the database that is used to store the authorization information.

When an ASP.NET application is connecting to a database which client and application impersonation is disabled, the identity used to access the database is by default the identity that has been configured for the application pool that the current application is configured to, as discussed in Chapter 3. In this case, it is the NT AUTHORITY\NETWORK SERVICE account.

To be able to run the application without any exceptions, you need to add the web server's machine account (which corresponds to NT AUTHORITY\NETWORK SERVICE) to the Administrator role for the AzMan application called "UsingAzMan." You can see what this looks like in Figure 16-11.

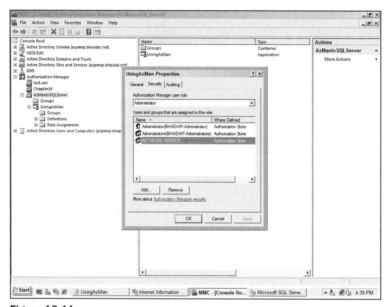

Figure 16-11

Explained in the preceding directory-based policy store section, you also need to add the NETWORK SERVICE account to the Delegated User role at the store level in case you plan to delegate control over different applications, or different scopes within a single policy store.

Now that the NETWORK SERVICE account is added, you will notice that a new user has been added to the list of users that are allowed to access the database. Figure 16-12 shows the list of users configured to access the AzMan database including the NETWORK SERVICE account.

Now try running the same application again and you will notice that the application runs fine whether you are listing the roles a user belongs to or creating new roles. I have already created a sample role called "Sample Microsoft SQL Server Role" and added to it the famous demouser98@bhaidar.net that is part of the AD defined earlier. When you run the Default.aspx page of the "UsingAzMan" application and log in with the aforementioned user, you will see a listing of all the roles that the current user belongs to.

```
demouser98@bhaidar.net is in role Sample Microsoft SQL Server Role
```

Figure 16-12

In this case, it is only a single role that I have previously added manually to the AzManInSQLServer authorization store.

Working in Partial Trust

Because the provider works with file-based AzMan policy stores, directory-based AzMan policy stores, and Microsoft SQL Server AzMan policy store, there are two different approaches to getting the provider in a partially trusted application. Regardless of the policy store location, the provider always requires `AspNetHostingPermission` with at least Low trust (see Chapter 15 on `SqlRoleProvider` to learn how you can grant this permission in a non-ASP.NET application) during the initialization process.

The provider always checks for `AspNetHostingPermission` with a setting of Medium for any write-oriented methods. Because Low trust is conceptually a read-only trust bucket, while Medium trust is the conceptual read-write trust bucket, `AuthorizationStoreRoleProvider` only allows the following methods to work when running in a web application at Medium trust or above:

❑ `CreateRole`

❑ `DeleteRole`

❑ `AddUsersToRoles`

❑ `RemoveUsersFromRoles`

You will see this behavior for ASP.NET applications. If you plan to use the provider outside of ASP.NET in a partial trust application, you effectively need to run at full trust, as is discussed a bit later in this section.

If the policy store is located in an XML file, *and* you are using the provider inside of an ASP.NET application, then the provider will also partially rely on the application's file I/O code access security (CAS) permissions for read-oriented methods. The idea here is that if you are using a file-based policy store, then the file I/O CAS permissions of the application are a good indicator of whether a partial trust web application has rights to use the provider. When the provider is initializing itself, it will check to see if the web application has read access to the XML file. This effectively means that in High trust you can point the provider at a policy file that is located anywhere on the file system. In Medium and Low trust though, due to the FileIOPermission(s) granted at these trust levels, the provider will only work with a policy file located somewhere within the application's directory structure. This kind of restriction makes sense because you probably do not want a Medium or Low trust application to read policy files located in other applications' directory structures. Assuming that your application passes these trust level checks, the provider internally asserts unrestricted security permissions so that it can call into the AzMan PIA without triggering any security exceptions.

To demonstrate how all of this works, you can take a sample application like the one shown earlier for the file-based policy store, and change the trust level setting. For example, if you drop the trust level down to Low and then attempt to create or delete roles, you will get an error stating "This API is not supported at this trust level." If you bump the trust level up to Medium, though, role creation and deletion will work again. However, if you reset the trust level to Low, you will still be able to use read-only methods like GetRolesForUser. Also, in both Medium and Low trust, if you change the connection string to point to a location outside of the web application's directory structure, you will get an exception like the following:

```
[HttpException (0x80004005): Access to path 'test.xml' was denied. The location
does not exist or is not accessible because of security settings.]
System.Web.HttpRuntime.CheckFilePermission(String path, Boolean writePermissions)
System.Web.Security.AuthorizationStoreRoleProvider.InitApp()
System.Web.Security.AuthorizationStoreRoleProvider.GetClientContext(String
userName)
System.Web.Security.AuthorizationStoreRoleProvider.GetRolesForUserCore(String
username)
System.Web.Security.AuthorizationStoreRoleProvider.GetRolesForUser(String username)
...
```

From the stack trace you can see that the provider is explicitly checking for FileIOPermission by way of an internal HttpRuntime helper method and that this check causes the failure.

If you use the provider in a partial trust web application and your policy store is located in a directory store, your code will simply not work regardless of the configuration steps you take. For example, if you run an application in High trust and attempt to use the provider, you will instead get error information like the following:

```
[SecurityException: Request for the permission of type 'System.Security.
Permissions.SecurityPermission...' failed.]
...
System.Activator.CreateInstance(Type type, Boolean nonPublic)
System.Activator.CreateInstance(Type type)
System.Web.Security.AuthorizationStoreRoleProvider.InitApp()
System.Web.Security.AuthorizationStoreRoleProvider.GetClientContext(String
userName)
```

```
System.Web.Security.AuthorizationStoreRoleProvider.GetRolesForUserCore(String
username)
System.Web.Security.AuthorizationStoreRoleProvider.GetRolesForUser(String username)
System.Web.Security.RolePrincipal.GetRoles() +248
...
```

In this case, when the provider attempts to open the policy store via the AzMan PIA, the call fails. Like many CAS-related errors, the error information is less than enlightening, and you can't tell what the problem is. Furthermore, the stack trace shows the provider calling `Activator.CreateInstance`, which probably seems a bit weird. Internally, the provider actually does not have any compile time dependency on the AzMan PIA. Instead, the provider dynamically loads AzMan types through reflection and then invokes methods on the resulting runtime callable wrappers through reflection as well. I intentionally chose High trust to demonstrate the error condition because High trust applications do have full reflection permissions. So, clearly it is not a lack of reflection permissions that is causing the security error.

The reason for the error is that the provider and the rest of the call stack require unmanaged code permissions to call into the COM PIA. There is no reasonable surrogate permission that can be used by the provider in return for asserting unmanaged code permission (as is done in the case of a file-based policy store) when connecting to a directory-based policy store. Neither `AspNetHostingPermission` nor `FileIOPermission` make sense to use as surrogate permissions. Theoretically, the development team could have used `DirectoryServicesPermission` that you saw in Chapter 13 on `ActiveDirectory MembershipProvider`, but doing so would be a bit awkward. Granting `DirectoryServices Permission` just to get `AuhtorizationStoreRoleProvider` working would also mean that any code in your web application could use the `System.DirectoryServices` class and start connecting to arbitrary directory stores. That level of access was considered excessive just for enabling a single provider.

Instead, if you want to use the provider in a partial trust web application with a directory-based policy store, you will need to wrap the calls to the provider's methods inside of a trusted GAC'd assembly. The wrapper assembly will need to assert a `SecurityPermission` for unmanaged code permissions prior to calling into the provider because internally the provider uses the AzMan PIA to talk to AzMan through COM interop. Because COM classes are considered unmanaged classes, a wrapper assembly must assert unmanaged code permissions. The same analysis also applies for the case when the AzMan authorization store is using the Microsoft SQL Server. Either you set the application to run in the full trust mode, or you use the aforementioned solution of wrapping the calls to the provider's methods inside of a trusted GAC'd assembly.

So far, I have discussed how to use the provider in partial trust web applications. For partial trust non-ASP.NET applications, you always need unmanaged code permissions. This holds true even for file-based policy stores. This means you need some kind of trusted code on the stack that calls into the provider. As a result-using a GAC'd wrapper assembly that asserts unmanaged code permissions is the correct approach for using the provider in partially trusted non-ASP.NET applications.

The reason that there is no special `FileIOPermission` behavior for partially trusted non-ASP.NET applications is the base requirement for unmanaged code permissions. After an application or a piece of code has that permission, checking the `FileIOPermission` is pointless. Unmanaged code permission means the application can just use Win32 or COM calls to directly manipulate the file system, so checking for `FileIOPermission` would not prove anything about the trust level for the application.

Using Membership and Role Manager Together

The previous samples have been exclusively using a username in a UPN format: demouser98@bhaidar.net. Even though the full configuration for the samples was not shown, they were using the ActiveDirectoryMembershipProvider configuration shown in Chapter 13. This allowed me to first log in with forms authentication against the directory, and then Authorization StoreRoleProvider initialized its client context with the same UPN. The nice thing about the UPN format is that using both the Membership and Role Manager providers together works.

Logging in with a UPN places that value in the forms authentication ticket. When it comes time for AuthorizationStoreRoleProvider to fetch role information for the user, it calls Initialize ClientContextFromName to set up the client context. This method accepts and parses usernames following the same rules defined in the Win32 API method LookupAccountName. UPNs provide unambiguous identification of a user account, which is why UPN style usernames work well with both providers.

Problems can arise, though, if your Membership provider is configured to use the sAMAccountName attribute. Because ActiveDirectoryMembershipProvider already knows the domain that it operates in, the provider does not allow the username parameter to include the DOMAIN portion. As a result, if you validate a forms authentication login with ActiveDirectoryMembershipProvider, the username that ends up in FormsAuthenticationTicket will lack the domain name. When Authorization StoreRoleProvider subsequently attempts to initialize a context from that username, it goes through a lengthier process trying to determine the correct user. The problem is that in even moderately complex domain environments you can have duplicate sAMAccountName(s) in different domains. For that matter, the same username can show up in a machine's local account SAM and in the domain. These cases can lead to ambiguity for AzMan and in the worst case can cause the wrong user account to be selected and used for authorization purposes.

The solution to the SAM account name problem is to layer support for NT4 style account names on top of ActiveDirectoryMembershipProvider. This allows users to log in with the older DOMAIN\ USERNAME syntax, which in turn means AuthorizationStoreRoleProvider will find the correct user when it looks for it in the directory. The inclusion of the DOMAIN portion of the username means that in multidomain environments you will be able to use forms authentication with both ActiveDirectoryMembershipProvider and AuthorizationStoreRoleProvider without having to worry about duplicate usernames in different domains confusing AzMan.

You can use the familiar approach of just deriving from ActiveDirectoryMembershipProvider to create a custom provider with the necessary functionality. The custom provider will add some basic validation logic that ensures the username parameter supplied to any method has the correct domain name. You set the domain name that the custom Membership provider expects in the applicationName configuration attribute. Because this attribute is not used by ActiveDirectoryMembershipProvider, it is a convenient place to store the expected DOMAIN prefix for a username.

C#

```
public class NTUsernameProvider : ActiveDirectoryMembershipProvider
{

    private string StripOffDomainValue(string username)
```

```csharp
    {
        string[] userParts = username.Split(new char[] {'\\'});
        if (userParts.Length == 1)
            throw new ArgumentException(
                "You must supply a domain name in the form DOMAIN\\USERNAME.");

        string domain = userParts[0];
        string user = userParts[1];

        if (String.Compare(domain,this.ApplicationName,
                        StringComparison.OrdinalIgnoreCase) != 0)
            throw new
            ArgumentException("The supplied username is in an incorrect format.");

        return user;
    }

    public override bool ValidateUser(string username, string password)
    {
        string user;
        try
        {
            user = StripOffDomainValue(username);
        }
        catch (ArgumentException ae)
        {
            return false;
        }

        return base.ValidateUser(user, password);
    }

    public override MembershipUser GetUser(string username, bool userIsOnline)
    {
        string user = StripOffDomainValue(username);
        return base.GetUser(user, userIsOnline);
    }

    //Override additional methods as needed.
}
```

VB.NET

```vbnet
Public Class NTUsernameProvider
  Inherits ActiveDirectoryMembershipProvider

  Private Function StripOffDomainValue(ByVal username As String) As String
        Dim userParts() As String = username.Split(New Char() {"\"c})
        If userParts.Length = 1 Then
                Throw New ArgumentException( _
                "You must supply a domain name in the form DOMAIN\USERNAME.")
        End If

        Dim domain As String = userParts(0)
```

```
            Dim user As String = userParts(1)

            If String.CompareOrdinal(domain,Me.ApplicationName) <> 0 Then
                    Throw New ArgumentException( _
                    "The supplied username is in an incorrect format.")
            End If

            Return user

    End Function

    Public Overrides Function ValidateUser(ByVal username As String, _
            ByVal password As String) As Boolean
        Dim user As String
        Try
                user = StripOffDomainValue(username)
        Catch ae As ArgumentException
                Return False
        End Try

        Return MyBase.ValidateUser(user, password)
    End Function

    Public Overrides Overloads Function GetUser(ByVal username As String, _
            ByVal userIsOnline As Boolean) As MembershipUser
        Dim user As String = StripOffDomainValue(username)
        Return MyBase.GetUser(user, userIsOnline)
    End Function

        'Override additional methods as needed.

End Class
```

The code to accomplish this is pretty simple. The private helper method StripOffDomainValue splits apart a username parameter into the domain name and the plain user name. It then verifies that the username did contain a domain identifier and that the domain portion of the username matches the domain name specified in the provider's applicationName configuration attribute. If these validation checks succeed, the helper method returns just the username portion of an NT4-style username.

The custom provider uses this helper method in its overrides of ActiveDirectoryMembershipProvider. Prior to calling in to the base class, the custom provider strips the domain portion of the username. This allows the underlying provider to function as it expects when usernames are mapped to the sAMAccount Name attribute. However, from an application perspective, a user is always known by a full NT4-style username. To use the custom provider, you change the Membership configuration to point at it:

```
<add
    name="appprovider"
    type="NTUsernameProvider"
    attributeMapUsername="sAMAccountName"
    connectionStringName="DirectoryConnection"
    applicationName="BHAIDAR"
/>
```

Notice how the `applicationName` attribute now contains the old NT4-style name of the domain. With the Membership feature configured to use the custom provider, you can now log in using NT4-style credentials like BHAIDAR\testuserpopa (this was an account created in Chapter 13). After logging in with these credentials, you can then retrieve the role information for this user with the usual Role Manager API calls. These calls will work because the username retrieved from `User.Identity.Name` will always be BHAIDAR\testuserpopa. Because this username includes the domain of the user, when `AuthorizationStoreRoleProvider` initializes a client context, AzMan has all of the information it needs to correctly identify the domain and the specific user in that domain that it should work with.

Summary

`AuthorizationStoreRoleProvider` maps most `RoleProvider` functionality (with the exception of the `FindUsersInRole` method) onto the Authorization Manager (AzMan) feature of Windows Server 2003 domains. The provider works with AzMan policy stores located in Active Directory, ADAM or ADLDS (in Windows Server 2008), Microsoft SQL Server (Microsoft SQL Server 2000 and above), or file-based policy stores. You can use the provider in both ASP.NET and non-ASP.NET applications. If you want to use the provider in partially trusted applications, though, there are a number of restrictions around using file-based, directory-based, and Microsoft SQL Server database-based policy stores.

Using a directory-based, database-based, or file-based AzMan policy store with the provider is straightforward. After the AzMan policy store has been created and populated, you need to grant access to the store. With the appropriate access rights (NTFS rights for the file-based policy store and AzMan-specific roles for directory-based and database-based policy stores), `AuthorizationStoreRoleProvider` can then connect to the AzMan policy store. The provider carries out its operations in the context of either a specific AzMan application or in the context of an AzMan scope.

Even though the `RoleProvider` class does not expose the concept of role nesting, if you have structured your AzMan policy store with any of its nesting features, the `GetRolesForUser` and `IsUserInRole` methods will correctly reflect the results of any these relationships. The advanced LDAP query group functionality also works with both of these methods. Remember that if you are working in a domain environment that uses SAM account names for its users and your application is using forms authentication with `ActiveDirectoryMembershipProvider`, you will need to write a simple wrapper around the Membership provider in order to accommodate NT4-style account names. When using SAM account names, `AuthorizationStoreRoleProvider` will only work reliably if the full NT4-style username is available from the `HttpContext`.

17

Membership and Role Management in ASP.NET AJAX 3.5

Membership and role management have been included since the days of ASP.NET 2.0. These features, among others, are based on the ASP.NET provider model discussed in Chapter 10. The ASP.NET membership feature enables you to manage users and validate their credentials against a data store of your choice. The ASP.NET role management feature provides an easy way to implement role management in a web application to authorize users and manage their roles. As mentioned several times throughout this book, the ASP.NET 3.5 runtime is based in its core on the ASP.NET 2.0 runtime and hence ASP.NET 3.5 inherits all the features included in the ASP.NET 2.0 and adds to them new features, modifications, and improvements, including ASP.NET AJAX.

ASP.NET AJAX that ships with the .NET Framework 3.5 contains web services that act as an interface to the ASP.NET application services. These services have to be enabled in your application and once enabled the authentication and role services will be accessible from the client-side (that is, the browser side where JavaScript code is running).

This chapter covers the topics of membership and role management and their integration with ASP.NET AJAX that ships as an integrated part of ASP.NET 3.5 and the .NET Framework 3.5. After reading this chapter, you will have a good knowledge of the following:

❑   How to enable membership management in a web application (Chapter 11 includes a detailed discussion on the ASP.NET membership feature).

❑   How to enable role management in a web application (Chapter 14 includes a detailed discussion on ASP.NET role feature).

❑   How to enable an existing ASP.NET application with ASP.NET AJAX 3.5.

❑   How to enable client-side authentication and role services in an ASP.NET application.

❑   Working in depth with the AJAX authentication service.

❑   Working in depth with the AJAX role service.

ASP.NET Membership and Role Services Overview

Chapters 10 through 16 discuss in detail the provider model, membership, and role services, and their different built-in provider implementations. This section recaps those features to make it easier to understand the material presented later in the chapter on the integration between ASP.NET AJAX 3.5 and ASP.NET membership and role services.

In ASP.NET 3.5 the same application services that were introduced in ASP.NET 2.0 are still available and have not changed at all. This means all your code written for ASP.NET 2.0 to access the membership and role services is still valid and runs perfectly under ASP.NET 3.5 once again due to the fact that ASP.NET 3.5 runtime is solely based on the ASP.NET 2.0 runtime with additional features and improvements.

ASP.NET Membership

The ASP.NET membership feature facilitates validating user credentials against a data source and helps in managing and creating user accounts that belong to the membership system of a web application. The membership feature is built on the provider model and hence it gives you the option to interact with any data source of choice by simply creating a concrete provider implementation for the data source.

By default, when you create a new ASP.NET website or application in Visual Studio 2005/2008, membership will be enabled automatically. Thus, you can benefit from the implicit definition of the membership feature inside the `machine.config` configuration file.

Membership is composed mainly of the `Membership`, `MembershipProvider`, and `MembershipUser` classes. These classes encapsulate the functionality of the membership feature and hide all the nasty coding details of connecting to the configured data source and converting the database user account record into a strongly typed user object. The `Membership` class consists of a list of static methods that act as an interface to most of the functions that can be called and executed against the data source storing all the user-related information. For instance, there is a method to create a new user account, a method to retrieve a user account record, a method to validate user credentials, and many more methods. The `MembershipUser` class represents a single user in the database and has some static methods mainly to manage the password of the user. The `MembershipProvider` class is the base class for the built-in provider implementations that have shipped with ASP.NET membership feature and can also be used for developing your own custom membership providers.

There are two built-in providers that ship with the ASP.NET membership feature: `SqlMembershipProvider` and `ActiveDirectoryMembershipProvider`. As you might have noticed from their names, the former is used to enable membership with the Microsoft SQL Server as a backend data store, and the latter is a read-only provider used to enable membership with the Windows Active Directory to manage the users stored in the active directory.

By default, when you create a new ASP.NET website or application, the application will have the `SqlMembershipProvider` configured automatically to run with the Microsoft SQL Server 2005 Express edition. You can keep the same provider configuration or change its properties according to your preferences. The following code snippet shows the complete membership provider configuration section that is located in the `machine.config` configuration file and you are free to change its properties inside the application's `web.config` configuration file according to what your application requires:

```
            <membership>
                <providers>
    <add
      name="AspNetSqlMembershipProvider"
      type="System.Web.Security.SqlMembershipProvider, System.Web,
      Version=2.0.0.0, Culture=neutral, PublicKeyToken=b03f5f7f11d50a3a"
      connectionStringName="LocalSqlServer"
  enablePasswordRetrieval="false"
  enablePasswordReset="true"
  requiresQuestionAndAnswer="true"
  applicationName="/"
  requiresUniqueEmail="false"
  passwordFormat="Hashed"
  maxInvalidPasswordAttempts="5"
  minRequiredPasswordLength="7"
  minRequiredNonalphanumericCharacters="1"
  passwordAttemptWindow="10"
  passwordStrengthRegularExpression=""/>
                </providers>
            </membership>
```

For more information on the preceding properties, refer to Chapters 11 and 12.

Now that the membership provider is configured, it is time to configure the web application to use an authentication type (in this case, the forms authentication). This can be easily done by configuring the `<authentication>` configuration section inside the application's `web.config` configuration file to use forms authentication as this example shows:

```
<authentication mode="Forms">
  <forms
    cookieless="UseCookies"
    defaultUrl="~/Default.aspx"
    loginUrl="~/Login.aspx"
    name="AUTHWEB"
    path="/"
    protection="All"
  />
  </authentication>
```

The application is now configured to use forms authentication and the membership provider is set correctly. Now you can create a login page that programmatically accesses the membership provider to authenticate a user. The following shows the code for the login page:

C#

```
string username = Server.HtmlEncode(this.txtUsername.Text);
string passowrd = Server.HtmlEncode(this.txtPassword.Text);

if (Membership.ValidateUser(username, password))
{
    FormsAuthentication.RedirectFromLoginPage(username, true);
}
```

VB.NET

```
Dim username As String = Server.HtmlEncode(Me.txtUsername.Text)
Dim passowrd As String = Server.HtmlEncode(Me.txtPassword.Text)

If Membership.ValidateUser(username, password) Then
    FormsAuthentication.RedirectFromLoginPage(username, True)
End If
```

The membership feature not only provides an API for programmatic access but a collection of web server security controls that you can use in your application and are bound internally to call methods on the configured membership provider. One example of those controls is the `Login` control. The `Login` control is used to provide the form that users use to enter their credentials for validation. It is internally bound to call the membership provider `ValidateUser()` method. There are other server controls that ship with the membership feature including the `CreateUserWizard`, `PasswordRecovery`, and so on. You use these controls without having to write any single line of code since those controls embed the required and necessary method calls on the configured membership provider.

In later sections, the ASP.NET membership feature integration with ASP.NET AJAX is discussed in detail explaining all the needed methods and web services required to allow the client-side code (JavaScript) to access the membership service on the server-side.

ASP.NET Role Management

ASP.NET provides a role management API to manage the application roles that you create to group the application's users. Using this API, you can create new roles, assign users to roles and check if a user belongs to a certain role. Role management is also based on the provider model and hence, gives you the chance to create your own custom role management provider to interact with any data source of your choice. You can refer back to Chapters 14-16 for a thorough explanation on the Role Manager and the two concrete provider implementations that ship with the ASP.NET role service.

Role management can be integrated with both forms and Windows authentication. However, it plays only a small role with Windows authentication. For example, you cannot use the role management API to create a new role or group when Windows authentication is configured for the application. The API can be used as a read-only API to check if a user belongs to a specific role defined in the application.

To use the role service in an application, you need to enable it by adding the `<roleManager>` configuration section group into the application's `web.config` configuration file, as follows:

```
<roleManager enabled="true" />
```

The `Roles`, `RoleProvider`, and `RolePrincipal` classes make up the core classes of the role management feature in ASP.NET 2.0 and 3.5. The `Roles` class contains a list of static methods that provide all of the functionality of the role management feature. For instance, there is a method to create new roles, a method to add users to a role, a method to get roles of a user, and many more useful methods. The `RoleProvider` class is the base class for the built-in role management providers and can be used as a base class for any custom role management provider that you wish to develop. At run time, ASP.NET checks if role management is enabled in the application. If so, the role management module gets a reference to the identity of the logged-in user, if any, accessed using `HttpContext.User` and then creates a new instance of the `RolePrinciple` class loaded with the roles of the currently logged in user and assigns it to the `User` property of the `HttpContext` instance object.

There are basically two built-in role management providers that ship with ASP.NET: `SqlRoleProvider` and `AuthorizationStoreRole`. The former is the default provider and is a read/write provider that handles the management of roles in a Microsoft SQL Server data store. The latter is a read-only provider that interacts with the Windows security built-in groups.

Now that the application is configured for role management, it is time to configure the authorization policy of the application. You can do so by adding an `<authorization>` configuration section into the application's `web.config` configuration file, as follows:

```
<authorization>
        <allow roles="Admin"/>
        <deny users="*"/>
</authorization>
```

The application is now configured to allow access only to users that belong to the Admin role and deny access to all other users. For more information on the ASP.NET role provider, see Chapter 14.

Creating a new role is easy:

C#

```
Roles.CreateRole("Admin");
```

VB.NET

```
Roles.CreateRole("Admin")
```

To check if a user belongs to the Admin role, you can do the following:

C#

```
// Get the RolePrincipal object
RolePrincipal rolePrincipal = (RolePrincipal)HttpContext.Current.User;

if (rolePrincipal.IsInRole("Admin"))
    Response.Write("User is in Admin Role!");
```

VB.NET

```
' Get the RolePrincipal object
Dim rolePrincipal As RolePrincipal = CType(HttpContext.Current.User, RolePrincipal)

If rolePrincipal.IsInRole("Admin") Then
        Response.Write("User is in Admin Role!")
End If
```

The above discussion aimed at refreshing your memory on the ASP.NET membership and role features that you have read about throughout this book. The next sections will start dealing with the integration between the membership and role management and ASP.NET AJAX. You will see how you can make use of these features by writing client-side code and hence, provide a more responsive web application, yet a secure one, based on features already existing in ASP.NET.

ASP.NET AJAX Application Services

The previous section served as an overview of the ASP.NET application services that were initially introduced with ASP.NET 2.0 and still constitute a solid block in ASP.NET 3.5. The ASP.NET application services are not only used by ASP.NET applications but also by several other clients like Windows and AJAX client applications. This chapter focuses mainly on discussing how an AJAX client application can make use of the ASP.NET application services from the client-side by writing client-side JavaScript code to access the different functionalities of these services.

An AJAX client application is an ASP.NET application enabled with AJAX features so that it gives its users a better user experience with higher response rate in processing requests. To create an ASP.NET AJAX application, simply create a new ASP.NET application, configure the application's web.config configuration file with ASP.NET AJAX 3.5 configuration sections and finally, add a reference to a Base Class Library (BCL) that encapsulates the AJAX functionality needed for the application to function properly.

The ASP.NET AJAX library allows .aspx pages to call web service methods from the client-side using JavaScript code. For security reasons, AJAX client applications exchange data with the server-side web services, including the ASP.NET application services, over HTTP using POST requests. This behavior can be overridden to use GET requests, but it is recommended to use POST requests as much as possible. The data being exchanged is usually packed with JavaScript and Object Notation (JSON) format, which is a lighter format to use than XML, especially when it comes to processing the response data on the client-side. In addition, AJAX client applications usually generate (on the server) client-side JavaScript proxy classes that are later sent into the browser. These proxy classes are mainly used by the AJAX applications on the client-side to communicate with the server and connect to web services, .aspx pages, and ASP.NET application services to handle client-side requests that require access to server-side resources. In the following sections, two of the major built-in client-side proxy classes are discussed in detail.

Enabling ASP.NET Applications with ASP.NET AJAX 3.5

The first step in enabling ASP.NET application services in an ASP.NET AJAX client application is to make sure the application itself is configured and enabled to run ASP.NET AJAX. If you are creating a new ASP.NET application or website in Microsoft Visual Studio 2008 with the .NET Framework 3.5 option selected, the application will be automatically enabled with ASP.NET AJAX since ASP.NET AJAX constitutes a major part of the ASP.NET 3.5. An AJAX-enabled application means all the necessary configuration sections in the application's web.config configuration file are added together with the needed libraries added as a reference into the solution.

However, if you are inheriting an ASP.NET application or website and you want to enable it with the ASP.NET AJAX 3.5, you have to configure the application's web.config configuration file with several configuration sections.

<configSections> Configuration Section Group

To start, you have to create the configuration section element for the SystemWebExtensionsSection Group class inside the <configSections /> configuration section group. This configuration section includes subsections whose properties are to be configured later on inside the application's web.config configuration file.

```
<configSections>
  <sectionGroup
   name="system.web.extensions"
   type="System.Web.Configuration.SystemWebExtensionsSectionGroup, System.Web.
Extensions, Version=3.5.0.0, Culture=neutral, PublicKeyToken=31BF3856AD364E35"
   >
    <sectionGroup
     name="scripting"
     type="System.Web.Configuration.ScriptingSectionGroup, System.Web.Extensions,
Version=3.5.0.0, Culture=neutral, PublicKeyToken=31BF3856AD364E35"
     >
      <section
       name="scriptResourceHandler"
       type="System.Web.Configuration.ScriptingScriptResourceHandlerSection,
System.Web.Extensions, Version=3.5.0.0, Culture=neutral, PublicKeyToken=31BF3856AD
364E35"
       requirePermission="false"
       allowDefinition="MachineToApplication"
      />
      <sectionGroup
       name="webServices"
       type="System.Web.Configuration.ScriptingWebServicesSectionGroup, System.
Web.Extensions, Version=3.5.0.0, Culture=neutral, PublicKeyToken=31BF3856AD364E35"
       >
        <section
         name="jsonSerialization"
         type="System.Web.Configuration.ScriptingJsonSerializationSection,
System.Web.Extensions, Version=3.5.0.0, Culture=neutral, PublicKeyToken=31BF3856AD
364E35"
         requirePermission="false"
         allowDefinition="Everywhere"
        />
        <section
         name="profileService"
         type="System.Web.Configuration.ScriptingProfileServiceSection, System.
Web.Extensions, Version=3.5.0.0, Culture=neutral, PublicKeyToken=31BF3856AD364E35"
         requirePermission="false"
         allowDefinition="MachineToApplication"
        />
        <section
         name="authenticationService"
         type="System.Web.Configuration.ScriptingAuthenticationServiceSection,
System.Web.Extensions, Version=3.5.0.0, Culture=neutral, PublicKeyToken=31BF3856AD
364E35"
         requirePermission="false"
         allowDefinition="MachineToApplication"
        />
```

```
            <section
             name="roleService"
             type="System.Web.Configuration.ScriptingRoleServiceSection, System.Web.
    Extensions, Version=3.5.0.0, Culture=neutral, PublicKeyToken=31BF3856AD364E35"
             requirePermission="false"
             allowDefinition="MachineToApplication"
            />
         </sectionGroup>
       </sectionGroup>
     </sectionGroup>
    </configSections>
```

The main configuration section group is the `<system.web.extensions />` that acts as a parent configuration section group for all the configurations needed by ASP.NET AJAX 3.5. You will notice later that this section will be used to configure the authentication and role services, in addition to many other AJAX-related configurations. For instance, every section of the ASP.NET AJAX 3.5 has its own configuration section: Sections to handle JSON serialization/deserialization, web services, and the rest of the features inside the framework.

<assemblies> Configuration Section Group

You need to register the `System.Web.Extensions` assembly that contains all the classes and JavaScript required by the ASP.NET AJAX 3.5 to function properly. To add the assembly, create a new entry for it inside the `<assemblies />` configuration section as follows:

```
    <assemblies>
      <add
       assembly="System.Web.Extensions, Version=3.5.0.0, Culture=neutral, PublicKeyTo
    ken=31BF3856AD364E35"
      />
    </assemblies>
```

The `System.Web.Extensions` assembly contains all the logic for the ASP.NET AJAX 3.5 from the different configuration sections, applications services, handlers, globalization, server controls, embedded JavaScript code, and the rest of the components that constitute the framework.

<controls> Configuration Section Group

The `<controls />` section usually maps tag prefixes for namespaces inside assemblies that contain server controls so that you can reference those controls without having to type the complete namespace name every time you want to add a server control onto an `.aspx` page.

```
    <asp:Button ID="btnAdd" runat="server" Text="Add" />
```

For instance, to declare an ASP.NET `Button` server control, you specify the tag prefix, which in this case, is the `asp` followed by a colon and the `Button` class name. ASP.NET AJAX 3.5 includes several server-side controls like the `ScriptManager`, `UpdatePanel`, etc. These controls are defined inside the `System.Web.UI` namespace that is located in `System.Web.Exensions` assembly and, therefore, you need to add a tag prefix mapping, so that you utilize these controls the same way you use the different ASP.NET server controls.

<httpHandlers> Configuration Section Group

ASP.NET AJAX 3.5 requires special HTTP Handlers to handle special HTTP requests for scripts and web service calls. Therefore, several handlers are to be added into the `<httpHandlers />` configuration section group so that the client script requests are handled and processed properly on the server-side by the ASP.NET AJAX engine.

```
<httpHandlers>
  <remove verb="*" path="*.asmx"/>
  <add
   verb="*"
   path="*.asmx"
   validate="false"
   type="System.Web.Script.Services.ScriptHandlerFactory, System.Web.Extensions,
Version=3.5.0.0, Culture=neutral, PublicKeyToken=31BF3856AD364E35"
  />
  <add
   verb="*"
   path="*_AppService.axd"
   validate="false" type="System.Web.Script.Services.ScriptHandlerFactory,
System.Web.Extensions, Version=3.5.0.0, Culture=neutral, PublicKeyToken=31BF3856AD
364E35"
  />
  <add
   verb="GET,HEAD"
   path="ScriptResource.axd"
   type="System.Web.Handlers.ScriptResourceHandler, System.Web.Extensions,
Version=3.5.0.0, Culture=neutral, PublicKeyToken=31BF3856AD364E35"
   validate="false"
  />
</httpHandlers>
```

The `System.Web.Script.Services.ScriptHandlerFactory` class is the main handler for HTTP requests that target web service calls. On the server-side it determines if the request is for a REST web service that is an AJAX web service call ending with an `.asmx/js` extension and calls a special handler to handle the REST request. If on the other hand, the call is for a normal web service, then it calls for the original handler for web services in ASP.NET. In addition, a new resource handler is also added known as the `System.Web.Handlers.ScriptResourceHandler` class. It provides an HTTP handler for processing requests for the script files that are embedded as resources in the assembly.

<httpModules> Configuration Section Group

ASP.NET AJAX 3.5 requires a special HTTP module to subscribe to the HTTP request pipeline to perform special handling for the requests targeting REST web service calls. To register HTTP modules, add the following element into the `<httpModules />` configuration section group.

```
<httpModules>
  <add
   name="ScriptModule"
   type="System.Web.Handlers.ScriptModule, System.Web.Extensions,
Version=3.5.0.0, Culture=neutral, PublicKeyToken=31BF3856AD364E35"
  />
</httpModules>
```

The new `HttpModule` is the `System.Web.Handlers.ScriptModule` class and it subscribes to several HTTP request pipeline events to give special consideration for the REST web service calls coming from AJAX clients' requests.

<system.web.extensions> Configuration Section Group

This configuration section group has already been defined as a section group in the `<configSections />` configuration section group above. This section is mainly used to configure the ASP.NET AJAX features and set some properties on these features. For instance, you can enable/disable the authentication service inside this configuration section.

```
<system.web.extensions>
    <scripting>
        <webServices>
            <!--
            <roleService enabled="true" />
        -->
              <!--
        <jsonSerialization maxJsonLength="500">
            <converters>
            </converters>
        </jsonSerialization>
        -->
              <!--
        <authenticationService
                enabled="true"
                requireSSL = "true|false"/>
        -->
              <!--
        <profileService
                enabled="true"
                readAccessProperties="propertyname1,propertyname2"
                writeAccessProperties="propertyname1,propertyname2" />
        -->
        </webServices>
              <!--
        <scriptResourceHandler enableCompression="true" nableCaching="true" />
        -->
    </scripting>
```

As you can see, the `<system.web.extensions />` configuration section group allows you to configure JSON serialization/deserialization, enable/disable authentication, profile, and role services and finally, configure the script resource handler.

<system.webServer> Configuration Section Group

This is the final configuration section you need to worry about before you make sure that ASP.NET AJAX 3.5 is configured into the existing ASP.NET application. This configuration section is essential if the application is configured to run with the default application pool inside IIS 7.0, (i.e., the integrated mode). As you know by now, all the `HttpModules` and `HttpHandlers` that were defined above in the application's `web.config` configuration file should be copied and added also to this section.

```
<system.webServer>
    <validation validateIntegratedModeConfiguration="false"/>
```

```
      <modules>
        <remove name="ScriptModule" />
        <add name="ScriptModule" preCondition="managedHandler" type="System.Web.
Handlers.ScriptModule, System.Web.Extensions, Version=3.5.0.0, Culture=neutral, Pub
licKeyToken=31BF3856AD364E35"/>
      </modules>
  <handlers>
    <remove name="WebServiceHandlerFactory-Integrated"/>
    <remove name="ScriptHandlerFactory" />
    <remove name="ScriptHandlerFactoryAppServices" />
    <remove name="ScriptResource" />
    <add
     name="ScriptHandlerFactory"
     verb="*"
     path="*.asmx"
     preCondition="integratedMode"
     type="System.Web.Script.Services.ScriptHandlerFactory, System.Web.Extensions,
Version=3.5.0.0, Culture=neutral, PublicKeyToken=31BF3856AD364E35"
     />
    <add
     name="ScriptHandlerFactoryAppServices"
     verb="*"
     path="*_AppService.axd"
     preCondition="integratedMode"
     type="System.Web.Script.Services.ScriptHandlerFactory, System.Web.Extensions,
Version=3.5.0.0, Culture=neutral, PublicKeyToken=31BF3856AD364E35"
     />
    <add
     name="ScriptResource"
     preCondition="integratedMode"
     verb="GET,HEAD"
     path="ScriptResource.axd"
     type="System.Web.Handlers.ScriptResourceHandler, System.Web.Extensions,
Version=3.5.0.0, Culture=neutral, PublicKeyToken=31BF3856AD364E35"
     />
  </handlers>
  </system.webServer>
```

There is nothing special here, except removing existing handlers and modules and adding them again so that the ASP.NET engine running in the integrated HTTP request pipeline can have access to those modules and handlers. One very important entry you should notice is the removal of the WebService HandlerFactory-Integrated HTTP handler. This handler, by default, only handles HTTP requests with an extension of .asmx. However, with ASP.NET AJAX 3.5 there is another web service extension that will be used most often and is represented by .asmx/js. Therefore, the ASP.NET handler for web services is to be removed and a new entry for the System.Web.Script.Services.ScriptHandler Factory is to be added. The aforementioned HTTP handler factory creates the correct handler for the web service request. If the request is for a REST web service, then it uses a new handler to handle REST requests and if the request is for a normal web service, it uses an ASP.NET handler to handle the web service call.

Now it is time to see how to enable the authentication and role services in an ASP.NET AJAX client application.

Enabling ASP.NET Application Services

Before you can make use of the ASP.NET application services in an AJAX client application, you need to enable the application services as you need. For instance, to enable an application with the authentication and role services you need to make sure the following configuration elements are present inside the `<system.web.extensions />` configuration section group:

```
<system.web.extensions>
  <scripting>
    <webServices>
      <roleService enabled="true" />
      <authenticationService enabled="true" requireSSL = "false"/>
    </webServices>
  </scripting>
</system.web.extensions>
```

It is important to include both the `<authenticationService />` and `<roleService />` element having the attribute `enabled` as `true`.

When an `.aspx` page, containing an instance of the `ScriptManager` control runs in the browser, all of the ASP.NET AJAX 3.5 scripts get loaded with the help of the `ScriptResource` script handler that was introduced in the previous section. Based on the `ScriptMode` property of the `ScriptManager` control, the JavaScript files that get loaded are the following:

❑ `MicrosoftAjax.js` in the case where `ScriptMode` property is assigned the value of Release or Inherit where the application is itself in the Release mode. When the `ScriptMode` property is assigned the value of Debug or Inherit where the application is itself in the Debug mode, then the `ScriptManager` control loads the `MicrosoftAjax.debug.js` JavaScript file name.

❑ `MicrosoftAjaxWebForms.js` in the case where `ScriptMode` property is assigned the value of Release or Inherit where the application is itself in the Release mode. When the `ScriptMode` property is assigned the value of Debug or Inherit where the application is itself in the Debug mode, then the `ScriptManager` control loads the `MicrosoftAjaxWebForms.debug.js` JavaScript file name.

The two preceding JavaScript files that constitute the ASP.NET AJAX 3.5 library contain all the client namespaces and classes that form the AJAX library. The definitions of the `AuthenticationService` and `RoleService` client classes are placed inside the `MicrosoftAjax.js` JavaScript file. For example, the `Sys.Services._AuthenticationService` client proxy class is defined as follows:

```
Sys.Services._AuthenticationService =
function Sys$Services$_AuthenticationService() {
Sys.Services._AuthenticationService.initializeBase(this);
}
Sys.Services._AuthenticationService.DefaultWebServicePath = '';
...

Sys.Services._AuthenticationService.prototype = {
_defaultLoginCompletedCallback: null,
_defaultLogoutCompletedCallback: null,
_path: '',
```

```
_timeout: 0,
_authenticated: false,

get_defaultLoginCompletedCallback:
Sys$Services$_AuthenticationService$get_defaultLoginCompletedCallback,

set_defaultLoginCompletedCallback:
Sys$Services$_AuthenticationService$set_defaultLoginCompletedCallback,

get_defaultLogoutCompletedCallback:
Sys$Services$_AuthenticationService$get_defaultLogoutCompletedCallback,

set_defaultLogoutCompletedCallback:
Sys$Services$_AuthenticationService$set_defaultLogoutCompletedCallback,

get_isLoggedIn: Sys$Services$_AuthenticationService$get_isLoggedIn,
get_path: Sys$Services$_AuthenticationService$get_path,
login: Sys$Services$_AuthenticationService$login,
logout: Sys$Services$_AuthenticationService$logout
}

Sys.Services._AuthenticationService.registerClass(
    'Sys.Services._AuthenticationService',
    Sys.Net.WebServiceProxy);
Sys.Services.AuthenticationService = new Sys.Services._AuthenticationService();
```

The preceding code is just an excerpt of the `Sys.Services._AuthenticationService` client-side proxy class generated by the AJAX library. The client class contains several functions and properties that are useful when dealing with authenticating a user. The above functions and properties are discussed in a later section.

One important line of code to notice is the following:

```
Sys.Services.AuthenticationService = new Sys.Services._AuthenticationService();
```

The `Sys.Services._AuthentictionService` registers itself with the ASP.NET AJAX 3.5 framework as a client proxy class called `Sys.Services._AuthenticationService` that has a base class called `Sys.Net.WebServiceProxy`. In other words, the authentication service is, after all, a web service client-side proxy class for the authentication service defined on the server-side. Once the client-side proxy class is registered with the framework, the code above creates a new instance of the `Sys.Services._AuthenticationService` client class and calls it `Sys.Services.AuthenticationService` without an underscore "_". This indicates that when you want to use the authentication service in your client-side code you can simply refer to the `Sys.Service.AuthenticationService` instance without having to create a new instance of the `Sys.Services._AuthenticationService` client proxy class.

The above discussion holds true for the `Sys.Services._RoleService` client proxy class. However, in order not to fill this chapter with repetitive discussions, this section discusses only the `Sys.Services.AuthenticationService` client-side proxy class and the same ideas apply for the `Sys.Services._RoleService` client-side proxy class.

AuthenticationServiceManager and RoleServiceManager Classes

The ScriptManager control has two public properties known as AuthenticationService and RoleService. The AuthenticationService property is of type AuthenticationServiceManager and the RoleService property is of type RoleServiceManager. The ScriptManager class subscribes to the PreRenderComplete event to register the custom scripts and services that are added to the ScriptManager control if any. At this stage, also the globalization scripts get loaded.

Internally the ScriptManager calls for the RegisterScripts() private method. It loops through all the script references added to the ScriptManager, resolves their paths and removes all duplicate script references. The final line of code inside the aforementioned method calls for another private method called RegisterUniqueScripts(). The list of unique script references is passed into this method as an input parameter The RegisterUniqueScripts() method loops through the unique custom scripts and adds them into the rendered HTML markup. In addition, this method calls another internal method called ConfigureApplicationServices() private method. This method is responsible for configuring the authentication, role, and profile services.

The ConfigureApplicationServices() method calls on the ConfigureProfileService(), ConfigureAuthenticationService(), and ConfigureRoleService() static methods that are part of the ProfileServiceManager, AuthenticationServiceManager, and RoleServiceManager classes, respectively. For the sake of this discussion the focus is on the AuthenticationService Manager.ConfigureAuthenticationService() method. The AuthenticationServiceManager has a single public property called Path that has, by default, a value of an empty string. The Configure AuthenticationService() method starts by checking if the AuthenticationService public property on the ScriptManager class has a custom value for the authentication service set by the developer. If there is a configured custom authentication service it determines its relative URL.

The method also loops through all the added instances of the ScriptManagerProxy class on the page if any. Without going into the internals, it makes sure of the following:

❑ If the developer did not set any custom authentication service URL and the *first* ScriptManager Proxy instance is using a custom authentication service URL, the relative URL of the authentication service will be the one that belongs to the first ScriptManagerProxy instance.

❑ Then for the rest of ScriptManagerProxy instances, if any one of them sets a custom URL for the authentication service and it happens that the URL is different from the one set by the first ScriptManagerProxy control instance, an exception is thrown.

Finally, the ConfigureAuthenticationService() method calls for the last method: the Generate InitializationScript() method. This method has three main tasks:

❑ If the authentication service is enabled, it injects into the HTML markup code the following JavaScript code:

```
Sys.Services._AuthenticationService.DefaultWebServicePath =
'Authentication_JSON_AppService.axd';
```

❑ The DefaultWebServicePath is already defined on the Sys.Services._Authentication Service client-side proxy class to an empty string. However, when an .aspx page is running that is enabled with ASP.NET AJAX 3.5, the value of the `DefaultWebServicePath` property is set to `Authentication_JSON_AppService.axd`.

❏ If a custom authentication service URL is set on the `ScriptManager` instance on the page, the following line of JavaScript code is injected into the HTML markup:

```
Sys.Services.AuthenticationService.set_path(
    '/website1/CustomAuthenticationService.asmx');
```

❏ Notice how the custom authentication service path is set on the `Sys.Services.Authentication Service` instance class. If the developer did not specify a custom authentication service URL, the default will be used to authenticate users on the client-side.

❏ Finally, if the authentication service is enabled or the custom authentication service URL is not empty and the current HTTP request is authenticated, the following line of JavaScript code is injected into the HTML markup:

```
Sys.Services.AuthenticationService._setAuthenticated(true);
```

❏ The above line of code internally set the value of a private field, `_authenticated`, on the `Sys.Services._AuthenticationService` client-side proxy class.

Later on, you will notice a function called `get_isLoggedIn()` on the `Sys.Services._Authentication Service` client-side proxy class. This function simply returns the value of the `_authenticated` private field to indicate whether the user is currently authenticated.

The above discussion once again applies to the `RoleServiceManager.ConfigureRoleService()` method with one difference: The method will inject into the HTML markup any roles assigned to the currently logged in user.

Now that you know the details of generating the `Sys.Services._AuthenticationService` client-side proxy class and what happens internally when the authentication or role services are enabled, it's time to go into the details of the authentication and role services client-side proxy and server-side classes.

Authentication Service

The authentication service feature that ships with the ASP.NET AJAX 3.5 allows users to enter their credentials and get validated and authenticated by the ASP.NET membership application service. At this time, the ASP.NET AJAX authentication service is only enabled to integrate with ASP.NET forms authentication; therefore, an application configured with any other type of authentication cannot make use of the AJAX authentication service.

The AJAX authentication service consists of two main classes, the server-side `System.Web.Application Services.AuthenticationService` class and the client-side `Sys.Services._Authentication Service` proxy class. The general architecture of the interaction between those two classes is that client-side proxy functions call asynchronously the methods defined on the server-side authentication service class. In the next section, both classes are explained in detail.

System.Web.ApplicationServices.AuthenticationService Class

The server-side `AuthenticationService` class is part of the `System.Web.ApplicationServices` namespace that is located inside the `System.Web.Extensions` assembly. The class contains the public methods listed in the following table:

Method Name	Description
Login	The `Login()` method takes as input the username, password, a custom string to include in the authentication process, and a Boolean specifying whether the cookie to be created is persistent or not. The method checks the input credentials against the configured ASP.NET membership service and issues a forms authentication ticket in the case of valid credentials.
Logout	The `Logout()` method clears the authentication ticket stored inside the authentication cookie (if any) in the browser.
ValidateUser	The `ValidateUser()` method takes as input the username, password serial, and a custom value that can be used in the authentication process. This method validates the user credentials against the ASP.NET membership service without issuing any authentication cookie. It simply returns a Boolean value of either `true` or `false` meaning that the user credentials are successfully validated or not.
IsLoggedIn	The `IsLoggedIn()` method takes no input parameter and returns a Boolean specifying whether the current user is authenticated or not.

In addition, the server-side authentication service class contains two public events shown in the following table that you can subscribe to perform some custom tasks:

Method Name	Description
Authenticating	The `Authenticating` event is fired just before the ASP.NET membership service is contacted to validate the user credentials that were sent from the client-side. You can subscribe to this event and perform some custom tasks like logging the users trying to login to the application.
CreatingCookie	The `CreatingCookie` event is fired just before generating and injecting an authentication cookie into the current HTTP response. This event is fired only when `Login` method, explained above, is called and not when the `ValidateUser` method is called, because the `ValidateUser` method just authenticates the user credentials and does not create any authentication cookie.

Sys.Services._AuthenticationService Client-Side Proxy Class

The server-side authentication service class alone is not enough for AJAX client applications to access the server-side membership services from the client-side using JavaScript code. Those applications need a client-side interface that allows them to perform asynchronous HTTP requests into the server to validate user credentials and, later on, logout users from an application. Therefore, there is a need for client-side proxy classes that can be used by the client-script developer to authenticate users by executing client-side JavaScript calls into the server-side membership service.

The AJAX library contains a definition of the client-side proxy `Sys.Services._Authentication Service` class that belongs to the `Sys.Services` namespace located in the `MicrosoftAjax.js` JavaScript file. The client class serves as a JavaScript class containing a set of functions that can be utilized to authenticate users. The following table lists the public functions defined on the `Sys.Services ._AuthenticationService` client-side proxy class:

Method Name	Description
login	The `login()` function takes three non-optional parameters mainly `username`, `password` and `isPersistent`. The function internally invokes the server-side `Login` method to authenticate a user. If the `isPersistent` input parameter is true then a persistent authentication cookie is created as a persistent cookie stored in the user browser, else a session-based cookie is created. There are optional input parameters that you can specify such as `customInfo`, `redirectUrl`, `loginCompletedCallback`, `failedCallback` and `userContext`. If the `redirectUrl` is specified and the user was successfully authenticated then they will be redirected to the specified URL in the `redirectUrl` parameter. If developers want to execute some custom code after the user has been successfully logged in, they can specify the `loginCompletedCallback` function to execute after the user has been successfully logged in. Moreover if the developers want to run some custom code when the user fails to successfully login, they can specify the `failed Callback` function.
logout	The `logout()` function can be called without providing any input parameter. The function internally invokes the `Logout` server-side method that clears out the authentication cookie that was generated upon a successful login of the user. The optional parameters include `redirectUrl`, `logout CompletedCallback`, `failedCallback` and `userContext`. If the user is to be redirected to a specific URL after they have been logged out from the application, the developer needs to specify a value for the `redirectUrl` input parameter. If developers wants to run some custom code after the user has successfully logged out, then they must specify a callback function for the `logoutCompletedCallback`. In addition, if the developers want to run some custom code for a non-successful logout operation, then they must specify a callback function for the `failedCallback`.
get_path	The `get_path()` function returns the path to the authentication service configured on the server-side. When the `Sys.Services._Authentication Service` class is constructed, the default authentication service path is set to an empty string. When the authentication service is enabled in an application by default the authentication service path is `~/Authentication _JSON_AppService.axd`.

Method Name	Description
get_isLoggedIn	The get_isLoggedIn() function returns a value of true or false based on whether the current user is authenticated or not.
set_defaultLogin CompletedCallback	The set_defaultLoginCompletedCallback() function is used to set the default callback function for the login function. When you set a default login callback function, this means that you can run the custom login callback function, when login is successful, without passing the name of that callback function to the login function. The authentication service will figure out on its own that the default login callback has to be fired. Unless you want to specify another login callback function instead of the default one, you need to explicitly pass the name of the login callback function, which at this time overrides the default one set previously, to the login function when called.
get_defaultLogin CompletedCallback	The get_defaultLoginCompletedCallback() function is used to retrieve a reference to the callback function configured as the login callback function.
set_defaultLogout CompletedCallback	The set_defaultLogoutCompletedCallback() function is used to set the default callback function for the logout() function. When you set a default logout callback function, this means that you can run the custom logout callback function, when logout is successful, without passing the name of that callback function to the logout() function. The authentication service will figure out on its own that the default logout callback has to be fired. Unless you want to specify another logout callback function, instead of the default one, then you need to explicitly pass the name of the logout callback function, which at this time overrides the default one set previously, to the logout() function when called.
get_defaultLogout CompletedCallback	The get_defaultLogoutCompletedCallback() function is used to retrieve a reference to the callback function configured as the logout callback function.

As previously mentioned, the ASP.NET AJAX creates a static instance of the Sys.Services._AuthenticationService client-side proxy class called Sys.Service.AuthenticationService excluding the underscore. You can always make use of the Sys.Services.AuthenticationService instance class instead of creating an instance of the Sys.Services._AuthenticationService client-side proxy class every time you need to contact the server-side membership service. Or another handy solution would be to simply create a global instance of the Sys.Services._AuthenticationService client-side proxy class and use it in case you are not happy with the static instance already created for you.

Now that you have a good knowledge of the server-side and client-side authentication service classes, it is time to go through some sample code to show you how to authenticate users by making use of the client-side proxy authentication service.

Login User

This section demonstrates how to use the AJAX authentication service to authenticate a user. The application we will be working with currently contains a single .aspx page that has two main ASP.NET panels. The HTML markup here shows the two mentioned panels:

```
        <asp:Panel ID="pnlLogin" runat="server">
<h3>Login First!!</h3><hr/>
<asp:Login
  ID="Login1"
  runat="server"
  BackColor="#F7F7DE"
  BorderColor="#CCCC99"
  BorderStyle="Solid"
  BorderWidth="1px"
  Font-Names="Verdana"
  Font-Size="10pt">

<TitleTextStyle
  BackColor="#6B696B"
  Font-Bold="True"
  ForeColor="#FFFFFF" />
</asp:Login>

</asp:Panel>

<asp:Panel ID="pnlPage" runat="server">
<h3>Normal Page!!</h3><hr/>
<p>If you can read this line, it means you are now authenticated!</p>
</asp:Panel>
```

The first panel contains an ASP.NET Login control that the user uses to enter his/her credentials. The other panel contains the normal content of the page, in this case simply a line of text. When the user is not authenticated, however, we want to show only the login panel so that they would enter their credentials to be authenticated using the AJAX authentication service. Once the user is authenticated asynchronously, the login panel is to be hidden and the main content panel is shown instead. All of this will be done from the client-side using the ASP.NET AJAX client library and authentication service.

To start, configure the application to use forms authentication and all anonymous users are prevented to access the application and are redirected to the default.aspx page that contains the login panel to allow them to enter their credentials and get authenticated.

```
<authentication mode="Forms">
    <forms loginUrl="Default.aspx" />
</authentication>

<authorization>
    <deny users="?"/>
</authorization>
```

Anonymous users are not allowed to access the application and are automatically redirected to the Default.aspx page. Remember that the AJAX authentication service up to this moment works only with ASP.NET forms authentication. For the sake of this example, the default ASP.NET membership service will be used and hence, no additional configuration is needed in the application's `web.config` configuration file.

After that, you should enable the authentication service as you learned from the section above that discussed enabling the authentication service in the application's `web.config` configuration file.

Once all the configuration settings are done, you need to add an instance of the `ScriptManager` control onto the `.aspx` page before trying to access any AJAX feature on the client-side.

```
<asp:ScriptManager ID="ScriptManager1" runat="server" />
```

The preceding `ScriptManager` instance will use the default authentication service. If instead you decided to use another authentication service, then you can specify it as follows:

```
        <asp:ScriptManager
  ID="ScriptManager1"
  runat="server"
  AuthenticationService-Path="~/MyAuthenticationService.asmx"
/>
```

Notice the above attribute in bold that is called `AuthenticationService-Path`. This represents the public property `Path` on the `AuthenticationServiceManager` class. Remember from previous sections that the `ScriptManager` class has a public property called `AuthenticationService` that is of type `AuthenticationServiceManager`. In a later section, you will use this property to define a custom authentication service.

What is left now is to add the JavaScript code that will handle authenticating users asynchronously using the AJAX authentication service. It is recommended to place all the JavaScript code for handling authentication in a single JavaScript file.

```
var username;
var password;
var ltFailureText;
var btnLogin;
var rememberMe;
var loginPanel;
var pagePanel;

// Subscribe to the Init function on
// the client-side Application object
Sys.Application.add_init(pageInit);

function pageInit()
{
    // Get panels on page
    loginPanel = $get("pnlLogin");
  pagePanel = $get("pnlPage");

    // If the user is authenticated
    // hide the login panel
```

```
        if (Sys.Services.AuthenticationService.get_isLoggedIn())
        {
            AuthenticatedState();
        }
        else
        {
            loginPanel.style.visiblity = "visible";
            pagePanel.style.visibility = "hidden";
        }
}
```

The preceding code starts by defining variable objects that represent the different elements on the HTML markup. For instance, the username, password, failure text label, remember me checkbox, login button, login panel, and normal page panel are defined.

The code then subscribes to the Init event that is fired by the Sys.Application global object. The Sys.Application object handles the client-side life-cycle of a request just as the server-side Page class handles the request's life-cycle on the server and fires several client-side events, among which are the Init, Load, and Unload events.

The pageInit() function handles the Init event of the Sys.Application object and it shows/hides the panels on the page according to the state of the user whether they are authenticated or not.

```
function pageLoad()
{
    // Get controls on page
    username = $get("Login1_UserName");
    password = $get("Login1_Password");
    ltFailureText = $get("Login1_FailureText");
    btnLogin = $get("Login1_LoginButton");
    rememberMe = $get("Login1_RememberMe");

    // Add handler for the Login button
    if (loginPanel != null)
        $addHandler($get("Login1_LoginButton"), "click", OnLogin);
}
```

The pageLoad() function is also controlled and fired by the Sys.Application object. Usually you should stick to this method to carry on most of the tasks required by an AJAX developer on the client-side. This function retrieves an instance to the previously defined global element variables and attaches an event handler for the Click event on the login button. In this case, when the user clicks on the login button, the client-side OnLogin() function is executed as you see here:

```
function OnLogin()
{
// Set the default LoginCompleted Callback function
Sys.Services.AuthenticationService.set_defaultLoginCompletedCallback(
    OnLoginCompleted);

    // Set the default Failed Callback function
    Sys.Services.AuthenticationService.set_defaultFailedCallback(OnFailed);
```

```
        // Login the user
        Sys.Services.AuthenticationService.login(
            username.value,                     //Username
            password.value,                     // Password
            rememberMe = "on" ? true : false,   // Create a persistent cookie or not
            null,                               // Custom Info
            null,                               // Redirect URL
            null,                               // Login Completed Callback
            null,                               // Failed Callback
            null);                              // User Context

        return false;
    }
```

The `OnLogin()` client-side function starts by setting the default `LoginCompleted` and `Failed` callback functions on the `Sys.Services.AuthenticationService` instance class. This way you do not need to specify those callbacks when you call the `Sys.Services.AuthenticationService.login()` function. The `LoginCompleted` callback is set to the `OnLoginCompleted()` function and the `Failed` callback is set to the `OnFailed()` function.

The `Sys.Services.AuthenticationService.login()` function is called passing to it the required parameters. As you know by now, the function would internally invoke the server-side `Login()` method on the server-side `System.Web.ApplicationServices.AuthenticationService` class. Finally, a `return false` is issued so that the page does not post back to the server.

```
    function OnLoginCompleted(validCredentials,
        userContext, methodName)
    {
        // If the user is authenticated
        // successfully
        if (validCredentials == true)
        {
            AuthenticatedState();
        }
        else
        {
            ltFailureText.innerHTML = "Invalid credentials. Could not login";
        }
    }
```

The `OnLoginCompleted()` function takes three input parameters:

❑   `validCredentials`: This parameter holds a value of `true` when the user is successfully authenticated, or a value of `false` when the user is not successfully authenticated.

❑   `userContext`: This parameter holds any value that is passed when the `Sys.Services.AuthenticationService.login()` function is called.

❑   `methodName`: This parameter contains a string that represents the name of the `login()` function as follows "`Sys.Services.AuthenticationService.login`".

The function above checks if the user has been successfully authenticated or not and shows/hides the panels on the page accordingly. The `AuthenticatedState()` helper client-side function shows/hides the panels on the page and this logic has been encapsulated in a function so that the same code can be used in several places in the same script file. If the user is not successfully authenticated, an error message is displayed to inform the user that the credentials entered were invalid.

```
function OnFailed(error,
    userContext, methodName)
{
    alert(error.get_message());
}
```

Finally, the `OnFailed()` function is called when the `Failed` callback is fired due to an error or exception that occurred during the process of authenticating the user. The function simply alerts the user with the exception generated.

Check If User Is Authenticated

To check from the client-side whether the current user is authenticated or not, simply issue a call to the `get_isLoggedIn()` function on the `Sys.Services.AuthenticationService` instance class, as follows:

```
if (Sys.Services.AuthenticationService.get_isLoggedIn())
{
    // user is authenticated
}
```

This is a very simple function call that you can embed in an if-statement to run on the client-side when the user is currently authenticated.

Logout User

To allow users to log out from the application, simply add the following `logout` button inside the normal page pane as follows:

```
<button id="btnLogout" name="btnLogout">Logout</button>
```

Next you need to attach a client-side handler for the logout `Click` event inside the JavaScript code, as follows:

```
// Add handler for the logout button
$addHandler($get("btnLogout"), "click", OnLogout);
```

The above means that when the logout button is clicked, the `OnLogout()` function is fired on the client-side.

```
function OnLogout()
{
    // Clear the authentication cookie and log out the user
    Sys.Services.AuthenticationService.logout(
        null,           // Redirect Url
        null,           // LogoutCompleted callback
        null,           // Failed callback
        null);          // User context

    return false;
}
```

The `OnLogout()` function wraps a call for the `Sys.Services.AuthenticationService.logout()` function passing null as a value for all the optional input parameters. That is all you need to do to enable the logout feature on the `.aspx` page.

Custom Authentication Service

Sometimes you might need to work with a different authentication service than the one configured by default with the ASP.NET AJAX authentication service. ASP.NET AJAX 3.5 gives you a straightforward and easy way of configuring a custom authentication service. All you need to do is develop a web service that includes at a minimum the `Login()` and `Logout()` methods. This is so that the client-side proxy `Sys.Services._AuthenticationService` class continues to function properly by calling these two main server-side methods and, of course, configures the `ScriptManager` control instance with the new custom authentication service URL.

To start, create a new web service that will serve as the custom authentication service and contains the following methods:

C#

```csharp
[System.Web.Script.Services.ScriptService]
public class CustomAuthenticationService : System.Web.Services.WebService {

    public CustomAuthenticationService () {

        //Uncomment the following line if using designed components
        //InitializeComponent();
    }

    [WebMethod]
    public bool Login(
        string userName,
        string password,
        bool createPersistentCookie)
    {
        bool isValid = Membership.ValidateUser(userName, password);
        if (isValid)
            FormsAuthentication.SetAuthCookie(userName, createPersistentCookie);

        return isValid;
    }

    [WebMethod]
    public void Logout()
    {
        FormsAuthentication.SignOut();
    }

    [WebMethod]
    public bool IsLoggedIn()
    {
        return HttpContext.Current.User.Identity.IsAuthenticated;
    }
}
```

VB.NET

```vb
<WebService(Namespace:="http://tempuri.org/"), _
WebServiceBinding(ConformsTo:=WsiProfiles.BasicProfile1_1), _
System.Web.Script.Services.ScriptService()> _

Public Class CustomAuthenticationService
    Inherits System.Web.Services.WebService
    Public Sub New()
        'Uncomment the following line if using designed components
        'InitializeComponent();
    End Sub
    <WebMethod()> _
    Public Function Login(ByVal userName As String, _
                          ByVal password As String, _
                          ByVal createPersistentCookie As Boolean) _
                          As Boolean
        Dim isValid As Boolean = Membership.ValidateUser(userName, password)
        If IsValid Then
            FormsAuthentication.SetAuthCookie( _
            userName, _
            createPersistentCookie)
        End If


        Return isValid
    End Function

    <WebMethod> _
    Public Sub Logout()
        FormsAuthentication.SignOut()
    End Sub

    <WebMethod> _
    Public Function IsLoggedIn() As Boolean
        Return HttpContext.Current.User.Identity.IsAuthenticated
    End Function
End Class
```

The above custom authentication web service is enough to make the AJAX authentication service function properly.

The first method included is the Login() method. This method should take the exact input parameter names; otherwise, the authentication service will generate exceptions. The input parameters are userName, password, and createPersistentCookie. You can choose the body of the method depending on the authentication you are using. In this example, the code simply validates the user credentials against the ASP.NET membership application service, creates the FormsAuthentication cookie accordingly, and finally returns a Boolean value representing a successful or failure login.

The other method is the Logout() method that takes no input parameters and simply clears the Forms Authentication cookie that was created previously when the user was authenticated for the first time.

The third method is the `IsLoggedIn()` method that returns a Boolean value representing the state of the current user, whether the user is authenticated or not.

Now that the custom authentication web service is finished, configure the `ScriptManager` control instance with the path to the newly created authentication service, as follows:

```
        <asp:ScriptManager
    ID="ScriptManager1"
    runat="server"
    AuthenticationService-Path="~/CustomAuthenticationService.asmx"
    />
```

That is all you need to do! Just run the application now and authenticate against the newly created custom authentication service.

It goes without saying that whatever applies to the `ScriptManager` control applies also to the `ScriptManagerProxy` class in all the features that we have been discussing so far and coming later in the next section.

Role Service

The role service feature that ships with the ASP.NET AJAX 3.5 allows a developer to retrieve a set of roles the currently logged-in user belongs to by issuing asynchronous client-side calls into the server. These calls would, in turn, query the server-side ASP.NET role service database to retrieve the user's information.

The AJAX role service consists of two main classes: the server-side `System.Web.ApplicationServices` `.RoleService` class and the client-side `Sys.Services._RoleService` proxy class. The general architecture of the interaction between those two classes is that client-side proxy functions asynchronously call the methods defined on the server-side role service class.

System.Web.ApplicationServices.RoleService Class

The server-side `RoleService` class is part of the `System.Web.ApplicationServices` namespace that is located inside the `System.Web.Extensions` assembly. The class contains the following public methods:

Method Name	Description
GetRolesForCurrentUser	The `GetRolesForCurrentUser()` method takes no input parameters and returns an array of strings representing the roles of the currently logged in user.
IsCurrentUserInRole	The `IsCurentUserInRole()` method takes a single input parameter that represents the role used to check whether the currently logged-in user belongs to it or not.

In addition, the server-side role service class contains a single public event that you can subscribe to set and use a `RoleProvider` concrete object of your choice:

Method Name	Description
SelectingProvider	The SelectingProvider event is fired just before a RoleProvider is selected inside the RoleService class to execute the preceding two methods. You can subscribe to this event and make use of the SelectingProviderEventArgs class to set its ProviderName public property so that the RoleService class internally uses the one set by you instead of the one already configured in the application's web.config configuration file.

Sys.Services._RoleService Client-Side Proxy Class

The server-side role service class alone is not enough for AJAX client applications to access the server-side role service from the client-side using JavaScript code. These applications need a client-side interface that allows them to perform asynchronous HTTP requests into the server to retrieve the currently logged in user's roles and to allow the client-side to check whether a user belongs to a specific role or not. Therefore, there is a need for client-side proxy classes that can be used by the client-script developer to work with the user's roles by executing client-side JavaScript calls into the server-side role service.

The AJAX library contains a definition of the client-side proxy Sys.Services._RoleService class that belongs to the Sys.Services namespace located in the MicrosoftAjax.js JavaScript file. The client class serves as a JavaScript class containing a set of functions that can be utilized to work with user's roles. The following table lists the public functions defined on the Sys.Services._RoleService client-side proxy class:

Method Name	Description
load	The load() function takes as input three optional input parameters: loadCompletedCallback, failedCallback and userContext. The loadCompletedCallback input parameter, if passed in, references a callback function that is executed when loading the currently logged in user roles into the client's memory. Also, the failedCallback input parameter, if passed in, references a callback function that is executed when the process of loading the currently logged in user fails. Finally, the userContext input parameter can be used to pass any custom data that can be retrieved later on when the loadCompletedCallback function is executing. Again it is important to mention that the callback functions are very helpful when you want to execute some custom code after the user's roles have been loaded into the client's memory or when an error occurs during the retrieval process.
get_Roles	The get_Roles() function takes no input parameters and returns an array of the roles names that the currently logged in user belongs to. It is important to know that you cannot call this function before calling the load() function that was explained above. The load() function is responsible for loading the user's roles into the client's memory and the get_Roles() function is based on the roles that were previously loaded by the load() function, if any.

Continued

Method Name	Description
isUserInRole	The isUserInRole() function takes an input parameter of type String. The input parameter represents the role name against which the method checks if the currently logged in user belongs. Once again, this function cannot be called without calling first the load() function, so that the currently logged in user gets his/her roles loaded into the client's memory.
get_path	The get_path() function returns the path to the role service configured on the server-side. When the Sys.Services._RoleService class is constructed, the default role service path is set to an empty string. When the role service is enabled in an application by default the role service path is ~/Role_JSON_AppService.axd.
set_default LoadCompleted Callback	The set_defaultLoadCompletedCallback() function is used to set the default callback function for the load() function explained above. When you set a default load callback function, this means that you can run the custom load callback function, when login is successful, without passing the name of that callback function to the load() function. The role service will figure out on its own that the default load callback has to be fired. Unless you want to specify another load callback function instead of the default one. Then you need to explicitly pass the name of the load callback function which overrides the default one set previously, to the load() function when called.
get_default LoadCompleted Callback	The get_defaultLoadCompletedCallback() function is used to retrieve a reference to the callback function configured as the default load callback function.

ASP.NET AJAX creates a static instance of the Sys.Services._RoleService client-side proxy class called Sys.Service.RoleService excluding the underscore. It represents a client-side singleton object that you can always reference without initiating a new instance of the Sys.Services._RoleService client-side proxy class. Or another handy solution would be to simply create a global instance of the Sys.Services._RoleService client-side proxy class and use it in case you are not happy with the singleton instance already created for you.

Now that you understand the server-side and client-side role service classes, it is time to go through sample codes to show you how to retrieve a currently logged in user's roles and to make sure the user belongs to a specific role.

Retrieving User Roles

This section demonstrates how to use the AJAX role service to retrieve the assigned roles to a logged in user that was previously authenticated using the AJAX authentication service. It is important to note that before being able to access the role service from the client-side, you need to enable the ASP.NET role service inside the application's web.config configuration file, as follows:

```
<roleManager enabled="true" />
```

The ASP.NET membership service is automatically enabled for you, so you need not enable it in your application (in contrast to the role service, which you have to enable explicitly).

Use the same .aspx page that was used in a previous section and include an additional button to show the roles attached to the user. The HTML markup below shows the added HTML button used to load the user's roles:

```
<button name="btnLoadRoles" id="btnLoadRoles">Load My Roles</button>
```

Now attach a handler for this button so that it executes a JavaScript function when clicked:

```
// Get the load-roles button
btnRoles = $get("btnLoadRoles");
$addHandler(btnRoles, "click", OnLoadRoles);
```

The HTML button is retrieved, first of all, as an object, and then a handler is set for that button to be executed when the Click event occurs.

```
function OnLoadRoles()
{
    // Load the user's roles first
    Sys.Services.RoleService.load(OnRolesLoaded);
}
```

When the user clicks on the Load Roles button, the above function gets fired. The function simply issues a call to the Sys.Services.RoleService.load() function specifying the loadCompletedCallback function. As previously mentioned, you cannot have access into the user's roles unless you first issue a call to the load() function. Then to retrieve the user's roles, you have to implement a loadCompleted Callback function where you will have safe access to the user's roles.

```
function OnRolesLoaded(roles)
{
    if (roles)
    {
        // format the roles in a string
        var strRoles = "You belong to the following roles:\r\n";
        for(var i=0; i<roles.length; i++)
            strRoles += "* " + roles[i] + "\r\n";

        alert(strRoles);
    }
}
```

This function starts by checking if there are roles returned for the currently logged in user and, accordingly, starts looping through all the role names joining them in a simple string to be displayed for the user, informing them of the set of roles they belong to.

It is only at this stage that you can safely access the Sys.Services.RoleService.get_roles() function to retrieve the user's roles. Before the OnRolesLoaded() function executes, calling the Sys.Services.RoleService.get_roles() function would return null and fail. The next section will show you how to check if a user belongs to a specific role.

Determining If User Belongs to a Specific Role

To find out whether the user belongs to a specific role, add two simple HTML buttons, as follows:

```
<button
  name="btnIsUserInRole"
  id="btnIsUserInRole"
  onclick="IsUserInRole('Guest'); return false;">
  Am I in 'Guest' Role?
</button>
   
<button
  name="btnIsUserInRole"
  id="Button1"
  onclick="IsUserInRole('Administrator'); return false;">
  Am I in 'Administrator' Role?
</button>
```

The first button checks whether the currently logged in user belongs to the Guest role. The second button checks if the currently logged in user belongs to the Administrator role. Each button calls a JavaScript function called `IsUserInRole()`, passing it the role name to check whether the user belongs.

The `IsUserInRole()` function is implemented as follows:

```
function IsUserInRole(roleName)
{
    // Check if the user belongs to a specific role
    var isUserInRole = Sys.Services.RoleService.isUserInRole(roleName);
    alert(isUserInRole);
}
```

The function takes as input a role name and issues an asynchronous call using the `Sys.Services` `.RoleService.isUserInRole()` client-side function that takes as input the role name that was originally passed into the parent function. The `isUserInRole()` function returns a Boolean value indicating whether the currently logged in user belongs to the role specified or not. Finally, the message alerts the user whether the user belongs to the role specified. Once again, this client-side function is used to handle the `Click` event of the above two HTML buttons.

Custom Role Service

Sometimes you might need to work with a different role service than the one configured by default with the ASP.NET AJAX role service. ASP.NET AJAX 3.5 gives you a straightforward and easy way of configuring a custom role service. You need to develop a web service that includes only the `GetRoles ForCurrentUser()` method, so that the client-side proxy `Sys.Services._RoleService` class continues to function properly by calling internally the server-side `GetRolesForCurrentUser()` method when a call is issued to the client-side `load()` function.

To start, create a new web service that serves as the custom role service and contains the following method:

C#

```csharp
[System.Web.Script.Services.ScriptService]
public class CustomRoleService : System.Web.Services.WebService {

    public CustomRoleService () {

        //Uncomment the following line if using designed components
        //InitializeComponent();
    }

    [WebMethod]
    public string[] GetRolesForCurrentUser()
    {
        return new string[] { "Guest", "Administrator" };
    }
}
```

VB.NET

```vbnet
<WebService(Namespace:="http://tempuri.org/"), _
WebServiceBinding(ConformsTo:=WsiProfiles.BasicProfile1_1), _
System.Web.Script.Services.ScriptService()> _
Public Class CustomRoleService
    Inherits System.Web.Services.WebService

  Public Sub New()

        'Uncomment the following line if using designed components
        'InitializeComponent();
  End Sub

  <WebMethod> _
  Public Function GetRolesForCurrentUser() As String()
        Return New String() { "Guest", "Administrator" }
  End Function
End Class
```

The implementation of the GetRolesForCurrentUser() method is simplistic and returns an array of role names as an array of strings. In a real-life scenario, you might contact a database server and retrieve the roles that the currently logged in user belongs to and return those roles as an array of strings containing the role names as entries.

The above custom role web service is enough to make the AJAX role service function properly.

Now that the custom role web service is finished, configure the ScriptManager control instance with the path to the newly created role service as follows:

```
<asp:ScriptManager
  ID="ScriptManager1"
  runat="server"
  RoleService-Path="~/CustomRoleService.asmx"
/>
```

That is all what you need to do! Just run the application and process the currently logged in user's roles using the newly created custom role service.

Summary

The application services introduced with ASP.NET played a very helpful role in providing developers with ready-made services that can they count on when developing small-scale web application. They can even customize and extend when working on medium- to large-scale web applications.

The application services introduced with ASP.NET played a very helpful role in providing developers with ready-made services that can be counted on when developing small-scale web application. These services can even be customized and extended to satisfy requirements for medium- to large-scale web applications.

Before using the authentication and role services, several steps have to be done beginning with enabling the ASP.NET application with the ASP.NET AJAX 3.5. Once an application is enabled with the ASP.NET AJAX, you need to enable the client-side authentication and role services by adding some configuration sections into the application's web.config configuration file.

The authentication services lets you authenticate users from the client-side JavaScript using the Sys .Services._AuthenticationService client-side proxy class that provides client-side functions that can be utilized by AJAX developers, which internally performs asynchronous calls against the server-side counterpart, the AuthenticationService class. The Sys.Services._AuthenticationService client-side proxy allows the developer to authenticate a user, check if the user is currently authenticated, logout a user by clearing their authentication cookie, and finally validate user credentials without creating any authentication cookie. The three major functions commonly used when developing the client-side part of the application are the login(), logout() and get_isLoggedIn() client-side functions.

The role service, on the other hand, allows the AJAX developer to retrieve information about the currently logged in user's roles. The ASP.NET AJAX 3.5 provides the Sys.Services._RoleService client-side proxy class that contains two main client-side functions used most of the time and represented by the load() and isUserInRole() functions. These functions are enough to gather information about the currently logged in user's roles. The counterpart class accompanying the client-side role service is the server-side RoleService class. The client-side functions on the Sys.Services._RoleService client-side proxy class functions internally issue asynchronous calls into the server-side class that takes care of querying the ASP.NET role service database to retrieve the currently logged in user's roles. One note before making use of the client-side role service is that you *must* enable the ASP.NET role service inside the application's web.config configuration file before you are able to access the role service from the client-side.

Finally, the ASP.NET AJAX authentication and role service do not limit you to use only the default authentication and role services. Developers are given the chance to develop their own authentication and role web services and configure the ScriptManager control instance on the .aspx page to use the custom authentication and role services, as needed.

18

Best Practices for Securing ASP.NET Web Applications

Having reached the last chapter of this book, you are now aware of all the features and modules provided by ASP.NET to help build secure web applications. All these features are out-of-the box features that ASP.NET provides to make the developer's life easy. However, a lot has to be done to secure an ASP.NET web application during its interaction with client users. In this chapter, you will be introduced to the best practices to secure an ASP.NET web application. The discussion is in the form of a list of best practices that you can follow and apply in your web application. Each recommended best practice is explained in detail with sample code, when possible.

In addition, the discussion introduces you to the vulnerabilities exposed by introducing AJAX techniques into your applications, for smooth and interactive user experiences, and the possible best practices in securing such applications.

In this chapter, will you will learn how to apply the following practices to secure your ASP.NET web application:

- ❑ How to trust your users.
- ❑ How to run applications with least privileges.
- ❑ How to validate user input properly.
- ❑ How to properly secure an `HttpCookie`.
- ❑ How to secure database access.
- ❑ How to handle SQL injection attacks.
- ❑ How to handle cross-site scripting attacks.

- ❏ How to handle cross-site request forgery attacks.

- ❏ How to handle application/page exceptions properly.

- ❏ How to guard against denial-of-service attacks.

- ❏ How to secure data transmission across the wire.

- ❏ How to handle information leakage introduced by AJAX-enabled web applications.

- ❏ How to protect against JSON hijacking.

- ❏ How to protect against amplified cross-site scripting.

Web Application Security Threats Overview

The focus throughout the previous chapters was how to best use and implement the different security features provided by ASP.NET 3.5, with its core based on .NET 2.0, and Internet Information Services 7.0. The major topics were as follows:

- ❏ How ASP.NET can have control on a request from its early entrance into IIS 7.0 new integrated mode

- ❏ How to best use the Code Access Security modes to give or deny permissions from an executing application

- ❏ How to protect sensitive sections of a `web.config` configuration file, how to use Forms and Windows Authentication modules to authenticate users accessing your application

- ❏ How to use URL authorization modules in ASP.NET and IIS to authorize users and make sure they can access resources that have permissions on them

- ❏ Many other important security features to implement and follow to build a more secure web application.

The discussion has always been on how to use the out-of-the box security features in ASP.NET and IIS 7.0 for a more secure and robust application. However, there are security threats and attacks that have no direct corresponding modules to use in ASP.NET to protect against them. It is the role of the developer to protect against the many threats using the ASP.NET 3.5 and .NET 3.5 Framework.

For instance, most of the important threats that an application might face is the improper input validation. Developers, who depend only on the client-side input validation through the use of ASP.NET validation controls, might face serious problems on the server due to the fact that not everything typed on the client-side arrives the same on the server-side. In addition, sometimes on some browsers, JavaScript is disabled by administrators and hence the ASP.NET validation controls will not even run! In other cases, the validation controls provided by ASP.NET might not help at all.

Consider the following example where you have a `Textbox` on a page that is labeled with "Name" that accepts input in the form of a string value representing the user's name and that the ASP.NET Request Validation is disabled. The user should type in their name in order to complete the registration form. The ASP.NET validation controls helps in controlling that the user has typed in a value, but it cannot help in the case where the user adds something like `<script>alert('You've been hacked!!');</script>` to the input. If at the server you did not provide any means of stripping out any character that you find illegal for the Name input Textbox, you will end up storing in your database an invalid name that will pop-up a JavaScript alert message every time you display the user's profile on the page. In the example you have seen, it is the responsibility of the application developer to make sure the input entered by the user on the client-side is valid and legal.

This example demonstrates a known threat which is the Cross Site Scripting (XSS) threat. There are many more such threats that can break down the normal execution of a web application. Microsoft categorizes the different threats an application might face and uses the acronym STIDE to represent these threat categories as follows:

- **Spoofing:** This is an attempt to gain access to an application by using stolen identities or credentials. What happens is that a user steals a locally-stored cookie and is lucky enough that the cookie contains the password in clear text. Or even worse is when a user is able to monitor the packets being interchanged between the client and the server and no SSL is configured and hence, in this case, the credentials exchanged might be easily retrieved and used to perform various attacks on the application. Of course, preventing this threat can be done by using strong and strict authentication; by not saving credentials in clear text inside cookies, and most importantly, by configuring SSL for communication at least in stages where credentials are being exchanged.

- **Tampering:** This is the process of modifying the data that is transmitted between network locations in an unauthorized way. It also follows from the preceding threat that a user might gain access to an application pretending they are someone else and start deleting or modifying resources on the web server in an unauthorized way, in this case, modifying data and resources in a hijacked way! Protecting against such a threat can be done by using data hashing and signing, digital signatures, and stronger authorization checking.

- **Information disclosure:** This is the exposure of private information and data that is not meant to be exposed for *unwanted* users. This type of security threat can take several forms. Hijacking a user's credentials and gaining access to an application is one form of this threat. The user will then be able to browse private data that they originally were not allowed to see and check. Spoofing data packets during their transmission from one place in the network to another is another form of information disclosure. In this case, the user will be able to view and modify data that they got control of in an illegal way. One more form of information disclosure is leaving sensitive sections inside the web.config configuration file in clear text. One such example is placing a database connection string in clear text without encrypting it. Leaving some sensitive comments inside the HTML markup might help attackers gain access to information that they should not have access to. Sometimes developers might be testing some sample code inside the markup page and then they decide to comment it out to try something else. The application goes into production and the comment lines show up when then page is requested and executing. Preventing such threats can be done through stronger authorization techniques, storing sensitive data in cookies, encrypting application variables, session variables, and other containers, and making use of SSL to protect the data that is being moved from one location on the network to another.

- **Denial of service:** This type of threat is caused by attackers bombarding your application with so many requests at the same time that it breaks your application and makes it unavailable for others. One way to protect against this threat is to develop a module that can monitor the number of requests coming from a single IP address in a certain amount of time and then accordingly deny requests from IPs that are requesting more than the usual requests. Also, IIS 7.0 helps in throttling an application by limiting the number of requests coming from a specific IP address.

❑ **Elevation of privilege:** It follows from the above threats that a user might be able to hijack the credentials of another user and gain access to resources and areas in an application to which they should not have access. Once an attacker enters the boundaries of an application with the identity and privileges of another more privileged user, the attacker can *elevate* the privileges already granted to their account. This gives the attacker access to more resources and secure areas that they could not access before.

In addition, there is a threat known as *repudiation*—the act of users (legal/illegal, authenticated and authorized) denying that they performed specific actions during their visit to an application. This can easily happen and users get away with their acts if an application does not implement proper auditing. In other words, logging auditing events in your application can help defend against such a threat.

Nowadays with the introduction of Web 2.0 and the demand for more responsive and interactive user experiences in applications, the trend is to move to utilizing more of the AJAX techniques in web applications. It is true that AJAX can improve the usability and interactivity of an application, but at the same time, it may open more areas for attackers to exploit an application if the AJAX-enabled application is not developed and designed with security in mind. The following points sum up the major threats that are caused with AJAX-enabled applications:

❑ **Increased Service Attack:** In a traditional web application an attacker might be able to hijack sensitive information to exploit an application, or if lucky enough to gain access to the web server itself and hence, gain physical access to the web application files and resources. However, with an AJAX-enabled web application that spans both the client and the server, AJAX continuously sends small web requests to the server, creating an increased service attack area that attackers can take advantage of.

❑ **Exposing functions:** An AJAX request usually gathers input from the elements located on the page and then sends calls to functions defined on the server side. All these calls are sent in clear text. Thus, the functions names, parameters, and data types are all exposed and any attackers listening to the network can gain access to all these methods. This gives them an opportunity to know more about the functions implemented on the server and hence, open an information leak that malicious attackers can use.

❑ **Amplification of Attacks:** Usually, an AJAX request is sent asynchronously in the background to the server. The server cannot tell the difference between a request done through AJAX (JavaScript) or upon the submission of a form. From the server-side point of view, the request is the same. This opens a very wide door to amplify all of the above threats and make them more harmful. The first effect you will notice is the amplification of the repudiation threat. AJAX will be sending more and more requests in the background allowing different kinds of attack and every user of the application will have the ability to deny their knowledge of such attacks. So many requests can now be sent from the client-side in the background that this opens the way to receive more response from the server; a response that might be full of scripts that are ready to be injected into the client-side and amplifying the XSS threat. Another threat that may be amplified is the denial of service attack. This kind of threat can be amplified easily without anyone noticing. Since the client requests performing the denial of service are JavaScript requests sent in the background, the user opening the page doesn't notice it.

Throughout this chapter, you will be introduced to several techniques you can follow in order to protect your application from malicious attacks and help in developing secure and robust applications.

Developers Beware

This section discusses a list of recommendations that you should follow to secure your ASP.NET web application against malicious attacks. Several books could be written on this topic, however, this section will cover as many recommendations as possible to give you an overview of some of the practices you can follow to protect your application.

Know Your Users

Knowing your users takes the form of both *authenticating* and *authorizing* users accessing the web application. Authenticating the user means making sure the user is a member of your user safe-list that can access the application. On the other hand, authorizing a user means knowing what rights and privileges the user has that allows them to access resources in the application.

Authenticate Users

ASP.NET 3.5 offers several options for authenticating users. As you have seen throughout the previous chapters in the book, you can make use of Forms Authentication and Windows Authentication as out-of-the-box authentication types offered by ASP.NET, or you can develop your own custom authentication mode. Forms authentication is mainly configured when the application is accessed online by users that do not necessarily correspond to users present in the Active Directory (AD) of a domain controller. It is best suited for web applications that store the users' credentials in databases or any other suitable and secure data store. On the other hand, Windows authentication best suits local intranets that allow only domain users to have access to the application. The details of using both types of authentication have been studied in detail previously, so you can refer to the corresponding chapters to read more on the different options available to use when configuring the types of authentication.

For read-only applications, anonymous authentication is enough to allow users to access the application. However, when private sections and resources exist in the application and need to be secured, it is a necessity to enable authentication.

Regardless of the authentication type you have configured for the application, your concern is with the identity of the user trying to access the application. In ASP.NET there are two main identities that you should look for: Application identity that is used to access the Windows resources (aspx pages, compiled assemblies, etc.) and the ASP.NET user identity that is used to identify the user to ASP.NET (the user logged in either in Forms or Windows authentication). An application can run without the ASP.NET user identity, which is the case when you offer your application as public, without securing any areas or resources within the application. However, ASP.NET cannot function without the presence of the application identity.

As covered in Chapter 3, when an ASP.NET page is running it is being executed inside a process or thread that is governed by a security context. This security identity or context is used to access all the physical resources on the Windows operating system, including databases if they are configured with integrated security through their connection strings. From the IIS 7.0 side, every application is running inside an application pool. When an application is created initially it is configured with a security identity that resembles a Windows account. By default, the identity configured with the default application pool in IIS 7.0 is the NT AUTHORITH\NETWORK SERVICE account that is present in Windows Server 2003 and Windows Server 2008. This account is already configured with the least privileges to access the necessary folders and files when an application is being executed. Therefore, by default, ASP.NET will have the NETWORK SERVICE account as the application identity when running your applications. This, however, is affected by a number of factors as mentioned in Chapter 3, including application and client impersonation in addition to any configured UNC credentials. The NETWORK SERVICE identity is already configured with the right ACLs to correctly run your applications without gaining any additional non-needed privileges that may be used to harm your application.

In case you want to configure another Windows account for the process identity, you should have a look at the ASP.NET Required Access Control Lists (http://msdn.microsoft.com/en-us/library/kwzs111e.aspx) article on MSDN that tells you exactly what ACLs you should assign for the custom user you want to configure as the process identity. For instance, the application's pool identity should have Read/Write access to the App_Data ASP.NET folder inside the application. The reason is that the App_Data folder usually contains all the data files and databases that are used by the application. Thus, ASP.NET needs to have read and write ACLs to be able to modify these resources. Granting your custom process identities additional privileges that are not used might reflect negatively on the safety of the application.

On the other hand, the ASP.NET user identity is determined by the authentication type that you have configured in the web.config application configuration file. Just as the ASP.NET application identity determines the rights of an executing ASP.NET application to access Windows resources, the ASP.NET user identity determines the ASP.NET resources and sections that users can access and view.

Authorize Users

In the preceding section, you were briefly introduced to authentication that takes places when an ASP.NET application is executing. Authentication and determining the ASP.NET user identity are not enough, however, to secure your application. In some cases, you allow one group of users to access a certain section of your application and another group to access other sections of your application. Authentication determines who can access the application, but authorization determines what every authenticated user can access on the application. ASP.NET 3.5 provides two main authorization modules that you may use in your applications: FileAuthorizationModule and URLAuthorizationModule. To get a detailed discussion on ASP.NET and IIS 7.0 authorization, it is recommended to refer back to Chapter 3.

The FileAuthorizationModule is mainly configured with intranet applications whose ASP.NET authentication is usually set to Windows authentication. On the other hand, the URLAuthorization Module is commonly configured with applications that make use of Forms authentication or any other custom form of authentication.

In addition, IIS 7.0 provides a new native authorization module that can be used by applications to authorize any content type in your application. The new URLAuthorizationModule is a native module that runs within the boundaries of IIS 7.0 and allows authorization rules the same as those used by ASP.NET URLAuthorizationModule rules.

The general rule is to make use of ASP.NET authentication and authorization features to limit access to your application when needed to protect the Windows and ASP.NET resources to the extent possible. Moreover, when a custom identity is to be used for the application pool running and executing your application, be sure to give the exact and necessary ACLs for that custom identity.

Run Applications with Minimum Privileges

As previously mentioned, the ASP.NET application identity is configured by default to be NET-WORK SERVICE identity and is affected by several previously mentioned factors. As you know, it is the ASP.NET application identity that is used to access any Windows resource while the ASP.NET is running and executing.

Usually administrators and developers create several application pools to categorize their applications and assign a different Windows identity for each of the applications pools that they have created. You should always make sure to give the custom Windows identity the least and most restrictive access control lists taking into consideration the required set of ACLs for the ASP.NET application to function properly. By configuring an application pool with an administrative identity you are exposing the application to a threat that might have harmful consequences on the safety of the application. In other words, make sure to always assign the custom Windows identity with the required set of permissions for your application to run properly, and not give attackers a chance to gain more privileges to do more harm to your application.

Validate User Input

As a general rule, never trust any input data that you receive from users browsing your application. Regardless of the source of the incoming data, always check for harmful and malicious information that might be sent from the client-side.

Consider the case when you have a registration form with several fields that require the user to fill in order for the user's registration to be processed and stored in the database. Figure 18-1 shows the simple registration form for users seeking access to profile themselves in your application.

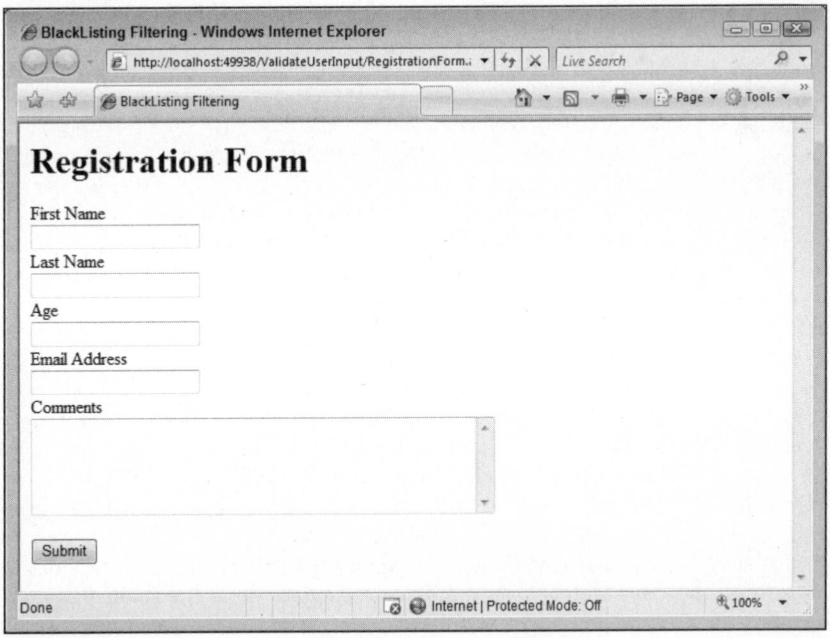

Figure 18-1

The registration form is very simple. The user has to provide input data for the first name, last name, age, email address, and optional comments. The form also includes a set of ASP.NET validation controls as follows:

- ❑ **RFVFirstName:** This required field validator makes sure that the user enters a value into the first name field, regardless if the data entered is valid or not.

- ❑ **RFVLastName:** This required field validator makes sure that the user enters a value into the last name field, regardless if the data entered is valid or not.

- ❑ **RFVAge:** This required field validator makes sure that the user enters a value into the age field, regardless if the data entered is valid or not.

- ❑ **RVAge:** This range validator makes sure that the user enters an age value that is between 18 and 65 only.

- ❑ **RFVEmail:** This required field validator makes sure that the user enters a value into the email address field, regardless if the data entered is valid or not.

- ❑ **REVEmail:** This regular expression validator makes sure that the user enters a valid email address into the email field.

As the first layer of defense against malicious user input, you can make use of the ASP.NET validation controls. There are a variety of validation controls including:

- ❑ Controls to force the user to enter some input the fields.

- ❑ Controls to compare fields to other fields on the page or some fixed text to compare against.

- ❑ Controls to validate the format of the entered text using regular expressions.

- ❑ Controls to validate the range of values that are acceptable for a field.

- ❑ A custom validator control that you can write to validate the field the way you want.

ASP.NET validation controls have the ability to run on both the client-side and the server-side. This is very helpful and harmful at the same time. It is important to run some validation on the client-side before sending the data to the server-side; however, validating on the client-side is not enough. One reason is that data might be scrambled before it reaches the server when coming from the client. For instance, assume that the client-side validators ran successfully and, while sending the request to the server, an attacker is there listening to the packets being sent from the client. The attacker is then able to change the content of the text, which was originally validated successfully, into some sort of harmful text. In this case, the client-side validation is not enough to make sure that the validate text on the client-side is truly safe.

Another problem that ASP.NET validator controls might face on the client-side is that some administrators in some organizations might have disabled JavaScript and hence, the validation controls will never run on the client-side. This gives you another incentive to not count on the client-side validation provided by the ASP.NET validation controls.

Now if we go back to the example mentioned above, using a set of ASP.NET validation controls helps in making sure the input fields will contain only validate data. Since it was mentioned above that the client-side validation is not enough, you should make sure the ASP.NET validation controls runs again on the server-side.

C#

```csharp
// Validate the page
Page.Validate();
if (Page.IsValid)
{
    // Process the input fields
}
```

VB.NET

```vbnet
' Validate the page
Page.Validate()
If Page.IsValid Then
    ' Process the input fields
End If
```

To make sure the validation controls are run again on the server-side when the page is being processed, and to make sure no errors exist on the page before processing the input fields, it is always recommended to call the `Page.Validate()` method which loops through all the validators placed on the page and calls their corresponding `Validate()` server method.

The validate method of every ASP.NET validation control executes its functionality by first setting the value of the `IsValid` public property on the validation controls to `true`. If the validation control is enabled, then the `EvaluateIsValid()` method is executed. This method usually contains the logic to execute for every validation control. The result of this method is set to the value of the `IsValid` public property. Finally, the method checks to see if the `IsValid` property is false, the `Page` instance is not null, and the validator control `SetFocusOnError` public property is set to true, it sets the focus to the validating control on the page.

After issuing a call to the `Page.Validate()` method, you should check if the page executing is valid with no errors. You call the page's public property, `IsValid`, to make sure none of the validation controls is invalid. The body of this property simply loops through all the validation controls and checks the `IsValid` property on every control. If only one of these controls has the value for this property as `false`, then the `Page.IsValid` property is set to `false` on the spot.

If the `Page.IsValid` property is `true`, then you are safe enough, according to the validation controls that you have placed on the page, to process the input fields' data and do whatever you want with them.

There are some cases where the ASP.NET validation controls do not help in validating the different scenarios. For such cases, you have the option of developing a custom validation control and provide functionality on both the client- and server-sides. Or you can live without such a custom validator and do some additional steps to make sure the specific validation is met.

Encoding and Filtering

Suppose you want the user to enter some HTML tags into the "Comments" field. However, you do not wish the user to enter harmful tags like a JavaScript `<script>` tag block. There are several steps you can take on the server-side code to protect your application against malicious user input. One of the options is to encode the contents of the "Comments" field. Encoding text that contains HTML tags means for instance the greater than ">" tag is converted to ">" representation. The same conversion applies to any other HTML tag. In ASP.NET you can HTML encode data by writing the following:

C#

```
string comments =
        System.Web.HttpUtility.HtmlEncode(this.txtComments.Text);
```

VB.NET

```
Dim comments As String = System.Web.HttpUtility.HtmlEncode(Me.txtComments.Text)
```

You make use of the `HttpUtility` class's method, `HtmlEncode()`, to encode all the incoming text that the user or some other third-party side has entered into the "Comments" field. HTML encoding means that all the HTML or JavaScript tags entered are now converted to string literals which have no effect when stored in the database or any other data store.

When it is time to display the comments on the page you should use the converse method, which is the `System.Web.HttpUtility.HtmlDecode()` method that will switch back all the string literals into their real form. Hence, all the ">" strings will be converted to ">" characters. For instance, suppose that the user entered some text in the "Comments" field surrounded by the "<b>" tag to make sure the text entered is bolded. If you do not decode the text before displaying it, the text will not be shown as bold text. It will be simply displayed as a string literal with no effect and cannot be interpreted by the browser as bold text. A new problem arises here! What if the original text contained tags other than safe and nice HTML tags? A malicious user might have entered some harmful or annoying JavaScript tags. For instance, the text might contain a JavaScript function to alert some annoying text to pop up every time the text is displayed on the page or even more harmful scripts.

From one side, you need to decode the text as explained above so that all the formatting HTML tags are interpreted well by the browser. But if you were not lucky enough and some JavaScript tags were originally embedded within the entered text, then you will always get a well formatted text displayed on the page with a little funny pop up message or some other form of harmful scripts! To get around this problem you have the option of filtering out any JavaScript tags, before doing any encoding, to make sure that it does not contain any harmful or annoying scripts. An example of a harmful script is one that is embedded on the page and is capable of stealing some locally stored cookies!

Filtering out characters before encoding involves removing some harmful characters that you deem harmful for your application. For instance, you decide to remove all JavaScript <script> tags from the input text and keep all other HTML tags to preserve the formatting set by the user and get rid of the harmful JavaScript scripts. Filtering out characters is also known as *sanitization*, where you remove the harmful characters and keep the good and clean text. Going back to our example above, I would consider any text entered into the "Comments" field valid unless it contained the JavaScript <script> block(s) and hence the sanitization of data includes filtering out these tags.

C#

```
// Validate the page
Page.Validate();
if (Page.IsValid)
{
```

```csharp
                    // Filter out what you think are harmful
                    string comments = SanitizeData(this.txtComments.Text);

                    // Process the input fields
                    comments = System.Web.HttpUtility.HtmlEncode(comments);
            }
    private string SanitizeData(string input)
    {
        Regex badChars =
            new Regex(@"(\n?<script[^>]*?>.*?</script[^>]*?>)|(\n?<script[^>]*?/>)");

        string goodChars = badChars.Replace(input, "");
        return goodChars;
    }
```

VB.NET

```vbnet
                    ' Validate the page
                    Page.Validate()
                    If Page.IsValid Then
                        ' Filter out what you think are harmful
                        comments = SanitizeData(comments)

                        ' Process the input fields
                        comments = Server.HtmlEncode(comments)

                    End If

    Private Function SanitizeData(ByVal input As String) As String
        Dim badChars As New _
        Regex("(\n?<script[^>]*?>.*?</script[^>]*?>)|(\n?<script[^>]*?/>)")
rs As String = badChars.Replace(input, "")
        Return goodChars
    End Function
```

The bold line above issues a call to a utility method that performs the sanitization of data by filtering out the JavaScript <script> tag block(s). These blocks are being replaced with an empty string. The SanitizeData() method makes use of a regular expression that simply locates the characters we think are harmful. Once any harmful sequence of characters is located, it is replaced with an empty string. Now if we encode the rest of the text and then decode it later when it is time to display it on the page, only the good HTML tags will be executed on the browser without any harmful scripts.

The above form of filtering is usually referred to as *blacklisting*. With blacklisting you search for all possible characters that *you* think are harmful for your application and filter them out. However, the blacklist you specify might not cover all available harmful characters out there. The above sample code showed only filtering out some of the characters that might be harmful for your application. If you want to filter out more harmful characters, or tags, you have to prepare a list of all the characters that you think are harmful and start replacing them with empty strings. However, with this technique there is a probability that you miss some of those characters and end up having harmful characters and scripts embedded in your data.

Another way of filtering user input data is known as *whitelisting*. Whitelisting is the preferred type of filtering and it is also called positive filtering. With whitelisting you accept only the data that you know is good for your application. To validate with whitelisting, you need to prepare a regular expression that you validate against. The expression should state the acceptable characters that an input field allows. This way, if there are any character sequences outside the regular expression, you will consider that the input text is exploited and reject it.

C#

```
// Validate the Email Address
if (
    !Regex.Match(
            this.txtEmail.Text,
            @"\w+([-+.]\w+)*@\w+([-.]\w+)*\.\w+([-.]\w+)*",
            RegexOptions.None).Success)
{
    // Invalid Email Address
}
```

VB.NET

```
' Validate the Email Address
If (Not Regex.Match( _
    Me.txtEmail.Text, _
    "\w+([-+.]\w+)*@\w+([-.]\w+)*\.\w+([-.]\w+)*", _
    RegexOptions.None).Success) Then
    ' Invalid Email Address
End If
```

The above sample code validates an email address against a regular expression. If the entered email address does not match the regular expression, then the entered email address is considered invalid. The difference between whitelisting and blacklisting is that blacklisting tries to strip out all the characters you consider harmful, while whitelisting compares the input data into a predefined good-format and rejects the entered text if there is no match with the good-format you have defined for your application. This is a better approach, since you are not worried whether you filtered out all the harmful characters or not. As long as the input text complies with a specific format and set of characters, the text is valid.

Now that the data is filtered out and you think it is now good and clean, the final step is to encode the text before processing it either for storage or anything else.

C#

```
// Process the input fields
comments = System.Web.HttpUtility.HtmlEncode(comments);
```

VB.NET

```
' Process the input fields
comments = Server.HtmlEncode(comments)
```

The above line of code simply HTML encodes the filtered data that might already contain some HTML tags that are allowed by the user to enter just to format the text. When it is time to display the comments on a page, you simply do the inverse by HTML decoding the already encoded text. This will make sure that the browser will be able to interpret all the HTML tags and apply them on the text displayed. However, the encoding/decoding process is a safe process since you are sure by now that all the text being processed is a safe text and contains no harmful or annoying scripts.

Request Validation

The above example has been tested with the `ValidateRequest` property on the `Page` class set to false. In Chapter 9 you were introduced to the Request Validation that has been added to ASP.NET since .NET 2.0. As you have read, this property, when enabled on the page, checks for any harmful scripts or characters in the forms variables, query strings, and cookie collections and, accordingly, it stops the execution of the page and prevents the page from being posted back to the server. It is very helpful and protects effectively against any harmful scripts that users try to submit to the server. In some cases you would like to allow users to enter some HTML tags like the example given above with the "Comments" field. If you want the above to work properly, you have to disable request validation on the page. This means, at the expense of allowing users to enter such HTML tags, you are exposing your page to harmful attacks by simply disabling that effective feature. So here you have a choice: either take the risk by disabling that protective functionality in ASP.NET to allow your users to enter the HTML tags they want, or come up with a solution that keeps the request validation enabled and allows user to enter the HTML tags they want.

The proposed solution was already mentioned in Chapter 9. What you need to do is apply the following steps:

1. Enable request validation in an ASP.NET page by setting the `ValidationRequest="true"` on the page directive.

2. Define a list of allowed HTML tags. For instance, <b>, <i>, and <pre> tags are the only allowed ones for the sake of explanation here. This way you have defined everything that is allowed.

3. Before the page submits back to the server, run a JavaScript function that replaces all instances of the allowed list of HTML tags with customized tags. For instance replace every <b> tag with a [b] tag. Apply the same replacements on the rest of the pre-defined list you have.

4. If the user enters any scripts or harmful tags other than those defined in the list you have, the ASP.NET request validation will prevent the user from submitting the page and present them with an error page. If on the other hand the user entered only the allowed tags, the page posts back to the server safely.

5. Before doing any processing or filtering on the entered text, you need to convert all the customized HTML tags back to the proper HTML format. In other words, you should convert all [b] tags back to <b> tags. Similar work should be done to all other HTML tags listed in the allowed set of tags.

6. You are now sure the text you received from the client contains only the allowed list of HTML tags with no harmful scripts or characters. HTML encoding in this case is enough without the need to filter out any additional harmful or annoying scripts.

The above steps are implemented in the `ValidaterUserInput` sample application that is part of the code that accompanies this chapter.

Verifying Data Input

You can always make use of the ASP.NET validation controls especially on the server side. There are many flavors of these controls. Most important is the regular expression validator with which you can specify a regular expression to force users to enter text into fields that are exactly what your application's business rules require. Whether you are counting on the validation controls or using usual `if` statements to validate your input data, you should always make sure to check for the type, format, length, and range of the values according to predefined rules as follows:

❏ Verify that the input entered can be successfully converted into the correct type you expect. In other words, if you are expecting an input of type Date in one of the fields, you should try to convert the input data into the specified type. If the conversion fails, then you should either throw an exception or stop processing and inform the user of the inconsistency:

C#

```
// Check to make sure the value entered
// in the Age field is an integer value
int ageValue = -1;
bool isAgeValid = Int32.TryParse(
    System.Web.HttpUtility.HtmlEncode(this.txtAge.Text),
    out ageValue);
if (!isAgeValid)
    throw new ArgumentException
    ("The value entered in the 'Age' field is invalid.");
```

VB.NET

```
' Check to make sure the value entered
' in the Age field is an integer value
Dim ageValue As Integer = -1

Dim isAgeValid As Boolean = _
Int32.TryParse( _
Server.HtmlEncode(Me.txtAge.Text), _
ageValue)

If (Not isAgeValid) Then
    Throw New ArgumentException("The value entered " & _
                    "in the 'Age' field is invalid.")
End If
```

❏ The code above tries to convert the value entered in the "Age" Textbox into an integer. If the conversion is successful then the output parameter, the second parameter of the Int32.TryParse() method, is set to true, else it is set to false. You can then check the value of the output parameter to see if the conversion was done successfully. If not, an exception is thrown to make sure the processing is stopped and the user is notified. You could, on the other hand, process this inconsistency in a friendlier way by checking all the other fields on the page and generate a single statement that lists all the inconsistencies that were found in the input data.

❏ You should validate the format of the text entered. For instance, if you want the user to enter their age in the form of two-digits you should construct a regular expression that accepts any age value entered in the form of two-digits and rejects anything else:

C#

```
// Validate the Age field
// to make sure it is composed of
// two digits
if (
    !Regex.Match(
```

```
                              this.txtAge.Text,
                              @"\d{2}",
                              RegexOptions.None).Success)
            {
                // Invalid Age value
            }
```

VB.NET

```
            ' Validate the Age field
            ' to make sure it is composed of
            ' two digits
            If (Not Regex.Match( _
                Me.txtAge.Text, _
                "\d{2}", _
                RegexOptions.None).Success) Then
                ' Invalid Age value
            End If
```

❑   The code above tries to match the value entered in the age field against an integer of two-digits. If the value entered passes the validation this means the format of the entered text is valid and can be processed safely.

❑   Once you are sure the input data is of the correct type and format, check the range of the entered values. For example, you might require that the user enters a value between 8 and 65 for the "Age" field from the above example:

C#

```
        if ((ageValue < 8) && (ageValue > 65))
            throw new ArgumentException("The value entered in " +
              "the 'Age' field should be between 8 and 65 only.");
```

VB.NET

```
            ' Make sure the Age value is within a valid
            ' range of values
        If (ageValue < 8) AndAlso (ageValue > 65) Then
            Throw New ArgumentException("The value entered in " & _
                "the 'Age' field should be between 8 and 65 only.")
        End If
```

❑   A simple `if` statement is used to make sure the value entered in the "Age" field falls within a valid range of values. An exception is thrown in case the value entered is invalid.

❑   Finally, you should check for the length of the entered input text. For instance, suppose there is an input field in which the user should enter a name. You have a requirement that the name field should not include more than 40 characters. This kind of validation can be grouped together with the format-checking mentioned above using a regular expression:

C#

```
        // Validate the Name input field to make
        // sure it is not greater than 40 characters
        // in length
        if (!Regex.IsMatch(this.txtName.Text, @"^[a-zA-Z\s]{1,40}$"))
```

```
                 {
                         // Invalid Name
                 }
```

VB.NET

```
                 ' Validate the Name input field to make
                 ' sure it is not greater than 40 characters
                 ' in length
                 If (Not Regex.IsMatch(Me.txtName.Text, "^[a-zA-Z\s]{1,40}$")) Then
                         ' Invalid Name
                 End If
```

❑ This example makes sure the value entered for the name field is no longer than 40 characters.

Validating user input does not only cover the Form's input fields, but also any kind of input that an application might receive including both cookies and query strings. When it comes to validating query strings, you should make sure the following apply:

❑ The number of query strings supplied for the page matches the number of query strings the page really requires—no more, no less!

❑ Make sure the query string keys the page expects are all included within the collection of query string keys posted by the end user.

❑ Validate the type of every value posted as a query string. For instance, if the page expects an integer value for a query string, make sure the value can be converted into an integer. If on the other hand the page expects a value for a query string to be a string, make sure the length of the value posted is within the range the page expects. You should validate all the data types the page might use and require.

Dino Esposito has an important article on validating query strings that you can reach at: (http://msdn .microsoft.com/en-us/magazine/cc163462.aspx). In this article, Dino shows you how to build a generic HTTP module to validate query strings.

You can see that whatever method you follow, either using ASP.NET validation controls or validating with if statements and regular expressions, the goal is to validate the user input and make sure it is valid according to the business rules your application employs.

Secure Cookies

Cookies are usually used to store small amounts of data locally on the client's machine. When the user visits the application again, it will retrieve the set of cookies previously issued and stored on the client's machine and use the data stored inside them.

A cookie is a knife with two edges! On one hand, cookies are useful to store some local data, like for instance the preferred background color that the user selects for all the pages in the application. This way when the user revisits the application again the preferred color will be retrieved from the locally stored cookie and applied on all the pages. On the other hand, since the cookies are stored locally on the machine, there is a possibility that an attacker who is able to gain access to them might exploit them and inject harmful scripts.

There are several steps you can take on the server-side to help protect and secure cookies. To start with, do not store any sensitive information inside cookies. For example, do not store a user's password inside a cookie and send that cookie to the client's machine. A more robust solution is to store only the location on the server where the user's information is stored. This way your application is aware of the location of the user's specific information without the need to store any sensitive data on the client's machine.

Another security precaution you can take is to set the expiration date for the cookie to a short period of time and try not to persist cookies locally for a long period of time:

C#

```
// Create a new cookie
HttpCookie cookie = new HttpCookie("MyKey", "MyValue");

// Set the expirtation on the cookie
cookie.Expires = DateTime.Now.AddHours(1.0);

// Add the cookie to the Response stream
Response.Cookies.Add(cookie);
```

VB.NET

```
' Create a new cookie
Dim cookie As New HttpCookie("MyKey", encryptedText)

' Set the expirtation on the cookie
cookie.Expires = DateTime.Now.AddHours(1.0)

' Add the cookie to the Response stream
Response.Cookies.Add(cookie)
```

In this example, you simply create a new HttpCookie instance and set its Expires public property to the value you want. Make sure to choose a small value for the expiration property so that an attacker, if any, has a smaller amount of time to break the locally-stored cookie.

ASP.NET provides you with two important properties on the HttpCookie class that you should make use of. The first is the Secure public property, which is set by default to the value false. When the property is set to true, the cookie will be transmitted only over HTTPS to the client's machine. It goes without saying that the page itself should be running over HTTPS. This property secures the transmission of the cookie from the server-side to the client's machine.

The second important property that was added to ASP.NET since the .NET 2.0 Framework is the HttpOnly public property. This property was discussed in Chapter 6. When this property is set to the value of true, no client-side code can ever read the contents of the cookie. The cookie can only be ready on the server-side. If you refer to Chapter 6, you will see a detailed explanation of this property with sample code. The following code snippet shows you how to enable both the Secure and HttpOnly public properties on an HttpCookie instance:

C#

```
// Create a new cookie
HttpCookie cookie = new HttpCookie("MyKey", "MyValue");
```

```
// Set the expirtation on the cookie
cookie.Expires = DateTime.Now.AddHours(1.0);

// Enable transmission of the cookie over HTTPS
cookie.Secure = true;

// Enable HttpOnly
cookie.HttpOnly = true;

// Add the cookie to the Response stream
Response.Cookies.Add(cookie);
```

VB.NET

```
' Create a new cookie
Dim cookie As New HttpCookie("MyKey", encryptedText)

' Set the expirtation on the cookie
cookie.Expires = DateTime.Now.AddHours(1.0)

' Enable transmission of the cookie over HTTPS
cookie.Secure = False

' Enable HttpOnly
cookie.HttpOnly = True

' Add the cookie to the Response stream
Response.Cookies.Add(cookie)
```

Finally, it is strongly recommended to encrypt the data before storing it inside an HttpCookie. This is very effective and protects your cookies from malicious attacks while being stored on the client's machine.

I have included a simple utility class in the application ValidateUserInput, which is part of the source code accompanying this chapter. It contains two methods to encrypt/decrypt text using the Rijndael algorithm, as shown here:

C#

```
// Encrypt the text
string encryptedText =
    RijndaelHelper.Encrypt("Data to Enrypt");

// Create a new cookie
HttpCookie cookie = new HttpCookie("MyKey", encryptedText);
```

VB.NET

```
' Encrypt the text
Dim encryptedText As String = RijndaelHelper.Encrypt("Data to Enrypt")

' Create a new cookie
Dim cookie As New HttpCookie("MyKey", encryptedText)
```

To encrypt the text before storing it in the cookie, simply call the `RijndaelHelper.Encrypt()` method to encrypt the text and after that initialize a new `HttpCookie` by setting its value to the encrypted text:

C#

```
// Read encrpted cookie
string cookieValue =
    RijndaelHelper.Decrypt(
        ((HttpCookie)Request.Cookies["MyKey"]).Value);
```

VB.NET

```
' Read encrpted cookie
Dim cookieValue As String = _
RijndaelHelper.Decrypt( _
        (CType(Request.Cookies("MyKey"),  _
                HttpCookie)).Value)
```

When it is time to process the encrypted data stored inside the cookie, call the `RijndaelHelper.Decrypt()` method passing it the cookie's value and the encrypted text in order to decrypt it and get it back into human-readable text.

Secure Database Access

When an application connects to the database store it usually uses a connection string. The connection string contains the location of the database, the database name, the username and password credentials required to access the database, the timeout used for the connection, and some other properties that are less important. For example:

```
<connectionStrings>
<add
 name="dbConnection"
 connectionString="server=.\SQL2005;database=aspnetdb;Integrated Security=SSPI;"
/>
<add
 name="anotherDbConnection"
 connectionString="Server=.\SQL2005;Database=Northwind;
Uid=myUsername;Pwd=myPassword;"
/>
</connectionStrings>
```

The code snippet above shows the definition of two connection strings inside the `web.config` configuration file in an application.

There are two ways of connecting to a database: either using Windows Authentication or using SQL Server authentication (this is the case when the application is depending on Microsoft SQL Server as a backend data store). The above code snippet gives an example for both techniques to connect to a database. The first represented by the `dbConnection` connection string makes use of Windows authentication by specifying `Integrated Security = SSPI` or it could have used `Trusted_Connection=Yes`. The second connection string represented by `anotherDbConnection` makes use of SQL Server authentication by specifying a SQL Server username and password directly inside the connection string.

Windows Authentication for Database Access

It is always recommended that you use Windows Authentication when connecting to the database server over the use of SQL-based authentication. With Windows Authentication the username and password credentials to access the database are not specifically embedded inside the `web.config` configuration file. So anyone who gains access to the configuration file will not be able to see any embedded credentials. Moreover, with Windows authentication you are relieved of the responsibility to manage the Windows user account and password, whether it is locked or unlocked, and other user management tasks. In addition you are not required to secure the network path between the application and the database server since there are no credentials being passed over the wire.

When an ASP.NET web application is configured with Windows authentication, there are two options the application can use to access the database server. If impersonation is enabled, then the ASP.NET web application will use the credentials that were negotiated with the user and in this case the Windows identity is used as the connection string credentials. On the other hand, if impersonation is disabled, then the ASP.NET application's process identity is used to connect to the database server. As you know, by default, the application's process identity is the `NT AUTHORITY\NETWORK SERVICE` and could be any other identity configured as the service account. If you decide on disabling impersonation, then make sure to create a SQL Server login and username for the NETWORK SERVICE account to have access on the database your application is connecting to and then you can configure the correct and required permissions you want on this account.

To begin, open the Microsoft SQL Server Management Studio and expand the Security node under the database instance you are working with. Now right-click on the Logins node and select New Login. Figure 18-2 shows the GUI that pops up to create the new login.

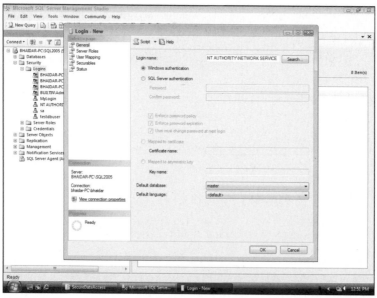

Figure 18-2

For the login name you have to click on the Search button and then type **NETWORK SERVICE**. Before creating the login make sure to select Windows Authentication since the NETWORK SERVICE account is a Windows account and it is managed by the Windows operating system.

Once the NETWORK SERVICE login is created, you still need to create the NETWORK SERVICE user that is specific to a database and configure the permissions on that username to decide what database objects it can access. Locate the specific database you want your application to connect to, expand the database node, after that expand the Security node, and finally right-click on the User node and select New User. Figure 18-3 shows the GUI that pops up to configure the new user to be created.

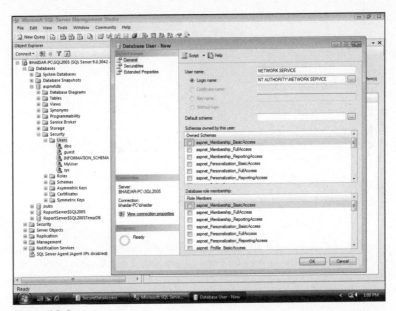

Figure 18-3

First, type or select the NETWORK SERVICE login name that you created in the previous step. Then, enter a username (in this case, "NETWORK SERVICE"). Then, select the database schema and roles that you find suitable for the application and hit OK to create the new configured NETWORK SERVICE user.

SQL Server Authentication

When it is not applicable to use Windows authentication, then you should be very careful when creating a new SQL Server login account. You can follow the steps shown here to create a new Microsoft SQL Server 2005 login user with the least permissions to access the database securely:

1. Expand the Security node on the database instance inside the Microsoft SQL Server Management Studio and right-click the Logins node and select New Login. Figure 18-4 shows the GUI that pops up to enter the information for the new SQL Server login.

   The important thing is to select the SQL Server Authentication option since this is a new login whose credentials are only present inside the Microsoft SQL Server.

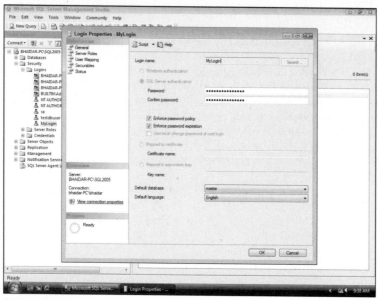

Figure 18-4

2.   Now that the login name is created, you still need to give it the right access permissions on the specific database you want to connect to. In other words you need to create a new Microsoft SQL Server user that maps to the already created Microsoft SQL Server login. To do so, expand the database tree you want to give access rights to, locate the Security node and expand it, and finally right-click on the Users node and select New User. Figure 18-5 shows the GUI that pops up to create a new SQL Server user.

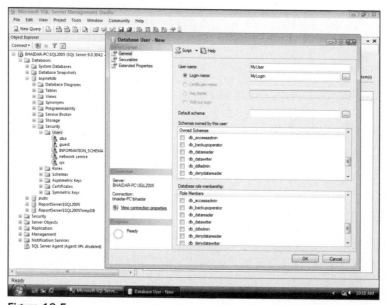

Figure 18-5

What you need to fill in mainly is the username and login name that you have already created. In addition, you need to specify the database schema and role that this new user will be part of. The database role you assign to the new user depends on your requirements. But always make sure to assign the least privileges to the user that is needed to access the database.

If you have decided to use SQL Server authentication that specifies the username and password credentials inside the `web.config` configuration file you should protect the connection strings' section by encrypting it and never leaving the credentials stored as clear text. It is true that in ASP.NET all HTTP requests to the `web.config` file are blocked, but if an attacker was able to get access into the web server by any chance, then they will be able to steal the configuration settings of the application, which might contain sensitive information. Since ASP.NET 2.0 you can encrypt several sections inside the `machine.config` and `web.config` configuration files. You should be aware that encrypting these sensitive sections is safe and recommended, but at runtime, ASP.NET pages has to decrypt these sections on its own to be able to access the settings in clear text. Thus, there is some overhead in decrypting these sections. That is why you should only encrypt configuration sections that only contain sensitive information, rather than encrypting all the configuration sections that ASP.NET allows you to encrypt.

Encrypt Your Data

You have two options when it comes to encrypting the connection strings' configuration section and other allowed sections: programmatically through code or using the `aspnet_regiis.exe` command-line tool. The .NET Framework 2.0, which ASP.NET 2.0 depends on in its core engine, has added support to encrypting several configuration sections based on the provider model, which allows you to develop your own providers to encrypt/decrypt the configuration sections. ASP.NET 3.5 ships with two main concrete provider implementations:

❑ **The Windows Data Protection API (DPAPI) Provider:** This provider is based on the built-in cryptography capabilities provided by Windows and is represented by the `DataProtection ConfigurationProvider` class. The provider can be configured to use either machine store or user store to keep the keys used by the provider for encryption/decryption stored safely.

❑ **RSA Protected Configuration Provider:** This is the default provider that uses RSA public key encryption to encrypt/decrypt the configuration sections and is represented by the `RSAProtected ConfigurationProivider` class. This provider requires that you create key containers to hold the public and private keys used for the encryption/decryption process.

This section shows you how you can encrypt/decrypt the connection strings' configuration section, but only the DPAPI provider is demonstrated. You can learn more on how to use the DPAPI provider from MSDN at `http://msdn.microsoft.com/en-us/library/ms998280.aspx`. In addition, if you require more reading on how to use the RSA provider to encrypt/decrypt configuration sections, you can check the article at `http://msdn.microsoft.com/en-us/library/ms998280.aspx`. The information in both articles applies both to ASP.NET 3.5 and ASP.NET 2.0.

With the DPAPI provider you have the choice of using either machine-level key storage or user-level key storage. The machine-level storage is best used when you have a dedicated server hosting a single application or you have multiple applications hosted on the same server and you want those applications to share the same sensitive encrypted data. On the other hand, the user-level key storage is best suited for scenarios where you run your application in a shared hosting environment and you want to make sure that the application's encrypted sensitive information are not accessible to other applications hosted on the same server. This, of course, requires that every application runs in the context of its own security identity.

As previously there are two options to encrypt/decrypt the connection strings' configuration section: programmatically through code or using the `aspnet_regiis.exe` command-line tool. The first example covers encrypting/decrypting the connection strings' configuration section using the `aspnet_regiis.exe` command-line tool, which can be found in `%WINDOWSDIR%\Microsoft.Net\Framework\version` directory.

The connection strings' configuration section to encrypt is as follows:

```
<connectionStrings>
<add
 name="aspnetdbConnectionString"
 connectionString="DataSource=.\SQL2005;Initial Catalog=aspnetdb;Integrated
Security=True"
 providerName="System.Data.SqlClient"
/>
</connectionStrings>
```

The above configuration section is stored as clear text inside the `web.config` configuration file. To encrypt the above section, type the following on the command prompt:

```
aspnet_regiis.exe
    -pef "connectionStrings"
    "C:\inetpub\wwwroot\379301_code\379301ch_18_code\cs\SecureDataAccess"
    -prov "DataProtectionconfigurationProvider"
```

The –pef switch is used to specify which configuration section you want to encrypt. You should then specify the physical path to the application to encrypt its configuration section. You could have specified the virtual path to the application, but then you would have used the –pe switch instead. Finally, you need to specify the provider you want to use to encrypt the configuration section by using the –prov switch.

After running the preceding command and opening the `web.config` configuration file, you will find the connection strings' configuration section encrypted as follows:

```
        <connectionStrings configProtectionProvider="DataProtectionConfigurationProvid
er">

        <EncryptedData>

            <CipherData>

<CipherValue>AQAAANCMnd8BFdERjHoAwE/Cl+sBAAAAdJbPl/G61UujsKYD/6KQEAQAAAACAAAAAAADZg
AAqAAAABAAAAA7zkWjDCLWelak33bIbX++A
AAAAASAAACgAAAAEAAAADZeRBFE7/O1BTpRrTJ4OUiwAQAA/o56qJKow745/
QfrQShyM1TNiL4Mz2nkhdWWc9EJO7i4L9uFR/TTljLdbvov4hGEdR7nqzk
ua9+g+hJpSmikQh7Q6J40c678sClIu15p0JbpxT9jrU13jPQT8oQmqA3pRlGoNtXQcUgfWds081T5YxYHUw
V5lbX2djUG3Aj3F+V/6uQvZUV8KMZS/zahD
IignByfjGYD4z4eUxIa+tTJW0vxDWhQPKpfiUH77fqvVFpcO2O8Nk+kkxGC4QBviNH+unriwTLAlDw7BGEZ
haqp1jA6N14HZkTg+hJNubaHWyb5yI2jZs9
xmdNngIdioHVEma82gCeh9zUwa5GwRh2c/MwLUbEGsiZEK1tGjYNLiTmWAYtul/Muj4Lb53AAq9n7+dSuId
tXcmCPSinprCKilyvaMIpteFHrBzMj0bk1O
NnDH4rXGxYu9Ync0I30zi5/g5TQCg7Ib7OagDaSHGVsLDqSmXzYjPo6/4o/miIWcR/
vXORoPlpx8J2r5G5LKuCyyWlOJbXJdGydntmnFuMzQ7iBtSxC5B5
NgGLn3MVKycsFMCRIzrgd+isWRxP8yLCpFAAAACUqhqidrDUelY2c/+xYYNA+JEpW</CipherValue>
```

```
        </CipherData>

    </EncryptedData>

</connectionStrings>
```

As a developer, you do not need to do any decryption when it comes time to access and use the connection string inside your code. ASP.NET will automatically decrypt the connection string and uses it to access the database.

You can also use the same command-line to decrypt the encrypted connection strings' configuration section as follows:

```
aspnet_regiis.exe -pdf "connectionStrings" "C:\inetpub\wwwroot\379301_code\379301
ch_18_code\cs\SecureDataAccess"
```

The -pdf switch is used to decrypt a configuration section when the physical path of the application is specified. When you specify the virtual path for the application you should use the -pd switch to decrypt the configuration section you previously encrypted.

The above example used the machine-level storage area to encrypt the connection strings' configuration, but you can also use a user-level storage store. The user-level storage procedure is not covered here, so you can check it out in the article mentioned few paragraphs earlier.

As previously mentioned, you can do the same encryption programmatically with few lines of code:

C#

```
// Open the web.config file
Configuration config =
    WebConfigurationManager.OpenWebConfiguration(Request.ApplicationPath);

// Get the connectionStrings configuration section
ConfigurationSection section = config.GetSection("connectionStrings");

// If the section is present and not already protected
// encrypt it
if (section != null && !section.SectionInformation.IsProtected)
{
 section.SectionInformation.ProtectSection("DataProtectionConfigurationProvider");
 // Save the changes
 config.Save();
}
```

VB.NET

```
        ' Open the web.config file
Dim config As Configuration = _
        WebConfigurationManager.OpenWebConfiguration(Request.ApplicationPath)

        ' Get the connectionStrings configuration section
        Dim section As ConfigurationSection = config.GetSection("connectionStrings")
```

```
' If the section is present and not already protected
' encrypt it
If section IsNot Nothing _
AndAlso (Not section.SectionInformation.IsProtected) Then
    section.SectionInformation. _
        ProtectSection("DataProtectionConfigurationProvider(")")

    ' Save the changes
    config.Save()
End If
```

The code above opens the application's web.config configuration file and retrieves the <connection Strings> configuration section. It checks if the section is not null and it is not already protected, if both conditions are true then the configuration section is encrypted using the ProtectSection() method that is part of the SectrionInformation public property on the ConfigurationSection class.

To decrypt the encrypted connection strings' configuration section above, you use similar code:

C#

```csharp
// Open the web.config file
Configuration config =
  WebConfigurationManager.OpenWebConfiguration(Request.ApplicationPath);


// Get the connectionStrings configuration section
ConfigurationSection section = config.GetSection(sectionName);

// If the section is present and already protected
// decrypt it
if (section != null && section.SectionInformation.IsProtected)
{
    section.SectionInformation.UnprotectSection();
    // Save the changes
    config.Save();
}
```

VB.NET

```vbnet
' Open the web.config file
Dim config As Configuration = _
WebConfigurationManager.OpenWebConfiguration(Request.ApplicationPath)

' Get the connectionStrings configuration section
Dim section As ConfigurationSection = config.GetSection(sectionName)
' If the section is present and already protected
' decrypt it
If section IsNot Nothing _
AndAlso section.SectionInformation.IsProtected Then

    section.SectionInformation.UnprotectSection()
    ' Save the changes
    config.Save()
End If
```

The preceding code starts by opening the application's `web.config` configuration file and retrieving the `connectionStrings` configuration section. The code then checks if the configuration section is not null and that is already protected or encrypted. If this is true, then the configuration section is decrypted back to clear text.

Finally, you can configure the communication between the ASP.NET application and the Microsoft SQL Server with a Socket Secure Layer (SSL). This provides an encrypted channel between the two parties and makes sure the connection string's credentials are passed as encrypted across the wire, which adds another layer of safety and security for the credentials and database access. To learn more on installing a certificate on a server that is running either Microsoft SQL Server 2000 or Microsoft SQL Server 2005 and how to enable SSL communication on a connection-string, see `http://support.microsoft.com/default.aspx?scid=kb;en-us;316898`

SQL Injection Attacks

SQL injection is one of the popular attacks that might severely harm your application and in particular the backend database store. SQL injection occurs when an attacker succeeds in injecting SQL commands into input fields and the application fails to correctly validate user input. It is mostly spread among applications or pages that construct dynamic SQL queries and simply concatenates the user input into the queries without having any (or poor) input validation.

This is a severe threat because an attacker is able with SQL injection to execute SQL commands on the database server using the application's login privileges. It gets worse when the application, by mistake, is using a database user account that has high privileges, for example, the privilege to delete a database. The common vulnerabilities that make SQL injection possible in your application are:

❑ Improper user input validation.

❑ Constructing dynamic SQL queries using simple string concatenation.

❑ Configuring an application with an over-privileged database login.

Assume that you have a database table called `Employees`, with `EmployeeID`, `EmployeeName`, and `EmployeeEmail` as columns. An `aspx` page displays a simple form with a single textbox that users can use to type in the Employee ID and accordingly check the details of the employee record. The code behind the form constructs the query dynamically by concatenating the input coming from the user input as follows:

```
SELECT
    EmployeeName AS [Name], EmployeeEmail AS Email
FROM
    Employees
WHERE
    EmployeeID = 1
```

An employee record is selected whose employee ID is "1". Now suppose the user entered some other type of input:

```
SELECT
    EmployeeName AS [Name], EmployeeEmail AS Email
FROM
    Employees
```

```
WHERE
    EmployeeID = '' OR ''=''
```

In other words, the user entered two single quotes, followed by a space, an OR, followed by a space, two single quotes, an equal symbol, and finally followed by two single quotes. The first two single quotes check for an Employee ID that is empty. However, the presence of the OR makes the WHERE clause evaluate the rest of the query after the OR. In this case, a single quote *equals* a single quote, so the above query selects all records in the Employees table and not just a single record. This is a simple example that shows how an attacker can exploit your database server and retrieve data that they are not entitled to access! A more serious example is the following:

```
SELECT
    EmployeeName AS [Name], EmployeeEmail AS Email
FROM
    Employees
WHERE
    EmployeeID = ''; DROP TABLE Employees
```

The user has entered two single quotes, a semicolon telling the Microsoft SQL Server that the first query ends and a new query is about to start, and finally a DROP statement to drop the Employees table. The above query executes smoothly and then deletes the Employees data table.

The above are just examples of SQL injection. The attacks can go even further and be more dangerous. There is an SQL Injection Cheat Sheet at http://ferruh.mavituna.com/sql-injection-cheatsheet-oku/ that you might be interested in looking at that provides detail to many SQL injections in ASP.NET, Microsoft SQL Server, and even other platforms and technologies. The next few sections show you how to protect an application from SQL injection.

Constrain User Input

An earlier section was dedicated to validating user input. The first step in protecting against SQL injection is to validate user input and make sure the input is safe and correct. As mentioned earlier, you need to validate the type, format, length, and range of the input data by using, for example ASP.NET validation controls like RegularExpressionValidator and the RangeValidator. In addition, you can use several techniques that were mentioned above, including the Regex class to validate against regular expressions on the server-side code.

C#

```
<%@ Page language="C#" %>
<form id="form1" runat="server">
    <asp:TextBox ID="txtEmployeeID" runat="server"/>
    <asp:RegularExpressionValidator ID="regexpEmployeeID" runat="server"
                                    ErrorMessage="Incorrect Employee ID"
                                    ControlToValidate=" txtEmployeeID "
                                    ValidationExpression="^\d{2}$" />
</form>
```

VB.NET

```
<%@ Page language="VB" %>
<form id="form1" runat="server">
    <asp:TextBox ID="txtEmployeeID" runat="server"/>
```

```
        <asp:RegularExpressionValidator ID="regexpEmployeeID" runat="server"
                                ErrorMessage="Incorrect Employee ID"
                                ControlToValidate=" txtEmployeeID "
                                ValidationExpression="^\d{2}$" />
</form>
```

The preceding HTML markup use the `RegularExpressionValidator` control to validate the `EmployeeID` textbox to make sure it only accepts integers with a maximum length of two. Hence, any attempt by the attacker to inject SQL commands will fail. Again, remember that you should not count on client-side validation only. Follow the detailed steps above to make sure the validator controls run again on the server-side.

If, on the other hand, you are using HTML input controls and not ASP.NET server controls, or you decided to validate with code, then you can use the `Regex` class to perform the validation as follows:

C#

```
if (Regex.IsMatch(this.txtEmployeeID, "^\d{2}$"))
    throw new FormatException("Invalid Employee ID");

// Data is safe!
```

VB.NET

```
If Regex.IsMatch(Me.txtEmployeeID, "^\d{2}$") Then
    Throw New FormatException("Invalid Employee ID")
End If

' Data is safe!
```

The above code throws an exception if the entered input for the `EmployeeID` textbox is anything other than two integers.

Use Parameters

When working with dynamic SQL queries and stored procedures, use parameters instead of directly concatenating the user input inside the queries or stored procedure's input parameters. Parameters convert the input data into literal values and prevent the input data from being executed in case it contains any SQL commands injected by the user.

Using stored procedures while accessing the database is strongly recommended and should be used side-by-side with parameters to prevent SQL injection:

C#

```
        DataSet employeeDataset = new DataSet();
        SqlDataAdapter myCommand = new SqlDataAdapter(
                "GetEmployeeByIDStoredProcedure", connection);
        myCommand.SelectCommand.CommandType = CommandType.StoredProcedure;
        myCommand.SelectCommand.Parameters.Add("@EmployeeID", SqlDbType.Int, 2);
        myCommand.SelectCommand.Parameters["@EmployeeID"].Value =
    this.txtEmployeeID.Text;
        myCommand.Fill(employeeDataset);
```

VB.NET

```
Dim employeeDataset As New DataSet()

Dim myCommand As New _
SqlDataAdapter("GetEmployeeByIDStoredProcedure", connection)

myCommand.SelectCommand.CommandType = CommandType.StoredProcedure
myCommand.SelectCommand.Parameters.Add("@EmployeeID", SqlDbType.Int, 2)

myCommand.SelectCommand.Parameters("@EmployeeID").Value =
Me.txtEmployeeID.Text()

myCommand.Fill(employeeDataset)
```

Assuming the stored procedure GetEmployeeByIDStoredProcedure is a stored procedure that accepts as input a parameter called EmployeeID, the code above creates a new instance of the SqlDataAdapter, then adds a SqlParameter instance into the collection of parameters on the SelectCommand of the adapter. The parameter added maps the value entered into the EmployeeID textbox to the stored procedure parameter as a literal string. Using the parameter also gives you the chance to specify and limit the type of the parameter to an integer having a length of two digits.

You can and should use parameters also when it comes to working with dynamic SQL queries. This again provides a shield against SQL injection:

C#

```
DataSet employeeDataset = new DataSet();

SqlDataAdapter myCommand =
    new SqlDataAdapter(
        "SELECT EmployeeID, EmployeeName,
        EmployeeEmail FORM Employees WHERE EmployeeID = @EmployeeID",
        connection);

myCommand.SelectCommand.Parameters.Add("@EmployeeID", SqlDbType.Int, 2);

myCommand.SelectCommand.Parameters["@EmployeeID"].Value =
    this.txtEmployeeID.Text;

myCommand.Fill(employeeDataset);
```

VB.NET

```
Dim employeeDataset As New DataSet()

Dim myCommand As New SqlDataAdapter( _
        "SELECT EmployeeID, EmployeeName,EmployeeEmail FORM " & _
                "Employees WHERE EmployeeID = @EmployeeID", _
        connection)

myCommand.SelectCommand.Parameters.Add("@EmployeeID", SqlDbType.Int, 2)

myCommand.SelectCommand.Parameters("@EmployeeID").Value = _
```

```
        Me.txtEmployeeID.Text()

        myCommand.Fill(employeeDataset)
```

The same code is used when dealing with dynamic queries with one difference, which is that the query is constructed dynamically without a call to a stored procedure. The input data needed by the query is added the same as above by adding a parameter into the collection of parameters of the `SelectCom-mand` of the `SqlDataAdapter` instance.

Additional Steps

There are times when you want to use dynamic SQL queries, yet you cannot use parameterized SQL queries. For such cases, you need to escape some characters that may be a serious threat on the SQL engine that processes the queries, for instance, the single quote. As you have seen, using a single quote can change the entire scope of the query and attackers can make use of a single quote to execute harmful commands on the database server. One way to get around this limitation is to escape a single quote with two single quotes. This way, even if the input text contained an injection using a single quote, replacing the single quote with two single quotes gets rid of the harmful effects:

C#

```
string safeEmployeeID = this.txtEmployeeID.Text.Replace("'", "''");
```

VB.NET

```
Dim safeEmployeeID As String = Me.txtEmployeeID.Text.Replace("'", "''")
```

As previously explained, it is always important to run your application with a least-privileged database login. For instance, say an attacker succeeds in their SQL injection and the SQL command injected is something like dropping a database table, or even the database itself. With a limited database account, such a query will not get executed and will be rejected by the SQL query engine. So, using a least-privileged user account to access a database is recommended.

Finally, it is important not to display any database server specific errors to the user. Usually, whenever your code wants to issue a call to the database server, you should place the calling code in a try/catch block. If any error occurs during the communication with or inside the database server, the catch block will catch the errors. In such cases your code should log the error first of all and maybe notify an administrator by email about the exception or error that has occurred. The application at that time should display to the user a friendly message informing them about an error that has occurred while processing their request. The user should not be able to see any details about the exception, nor any information about the database server.

Cross-Site Scripting

Cross-site scripting, also known as XSS or CSS, is a direct result of not having proper user input validation and failing to encode output to be displayed. The consequences of having improper input validation have been mentioned explicitly in detail. XSS is no different!

For instance, a user enters a public Forum, adds a post to a current or new thread that includes malicious script. The application, if there is improper user input validation and/or encoding for data embedded in the response, takes the input as is and stores it in the database. Now, any user who accesses the same page would have the malicious script executed silently when the application fails to encode the response. The browser is not able to distinguish between harmful and safe scripts. Whatever response the browser receives from the server is simply executed on the client-side. The malicious script could be an annoying one like displaying a pop-up message. Other malicious scripts might be more harmful and could steal stored authentication cookies and send them silently to the attacker.

An attacker usually looks for web applications that redisplay the text that was typed in the input fields via the query string, especially in the case of a search engine, or even a failed trial to validate credentials on a login page.

To protect against XSS, you should consider all input as malicious that requires input validation, encoding for all output, in case it contains HTML characters, regardless of the source for such data.

Validating input has been thoroughly discussed. Accordingly, the input data should be well-validated by checking that the correct type is received, the format of the input data is correct, and that the length and range of values are acceptable. ASP.NET validation controls like `RegularExpressionValidator` and `RangeValidator` play an important role in addition to the `Regex` class in the .NET framework that you can use to validate HTML input fields on the server-side. Programmatic checking for the type of input text can also be accomplished using the type-checking methods in the .NET framework like the `Int32.TryParse()` method.

As discussed previously, always encode whatever input text you receive from the client-side. The .NET framework provides the `System.Web.HttpUtility.HtmlEncode()` method to properly encode text before it is processed, whether for storage into the database or storage into files. Encoding text that includes HTML tags converts some of the tags into a different form. For instance, the space character is converted to ` ` and the "<" character gets converted to `&lt;`. In addition, if you need to embed URLs in the response on the server you can use the `System.Web.HttpUtility.UrlEncode()` method to properly encode the URL. Encoding not only covers the input fields, but also cookies, session variables, query strings, and database access methods. Any source of input data can be a source of harm to your applications.

When talking about encoding output to be displayed on the client-side, it is important to limit the ways in which data entered by end-users can be represented by the application on the server-side. Using a limited character set prevents malicious users from using canonicalization and multi-byte escape sequences to bypass the input validation routines on the server-side code. ASP.NET allows you to specify the character set in three different areas:

```
<meta http-equiv="Content Type" content="text/html; charset=ISO-8859-1" />
```

The first option is to use the HTML meta tag in the `<head>` section of an `.aspx` page. The above markup line sets the character set of the page to ISO Latin 1 (ISO-8859-1), which is the default character set for early versions of HTML and HTTP. In fact, the ISO Latin 1 is limited but it is recommended to use in your pages.

```
<%@ Page ResponseEncoding="ISO-8859-1" RequestEncoding="ISO-8859-1" %>
```

The second way to specify the character set is to set the `ResponseEncoding` and `RequestEncoding` properties on the `.aspx` page directive, as follows:

```
<configuration>
  <system.web>
```

```
        <globalization
            requestEncoding="iso-8859-1"
            responseEncoding="iso-8859-1"/>
    </system.web>
</configuration>
```

The third way is to make use of the `<globalization>` section in the `web.config` configuration file.

Protecting against harmful user input starts by enabling the `ValidateRequest` public property on the `Page` class. By default, request validation is enabled in any ASP.NET application. This property insures that no harmful scripts or HTML tags can ever be sent from the client-side to the server-side. However, as mentioned above, in some cases, there is a need to allow users to enter HTML formatting tags, for example, in a Rich Text Editor. As discussed earlier, you can do some character conversions on the client-side and convert back to the original text on the server-side! Enabling/disabling request validation takes two forms. The first is shown here:

C#

```
<%@ Page Language="C#" ValidateRequest="false" %>
```

VB.NET

```
<%@ Page Language="Vb" ValidateRequest="false" %>
```

You can configure this property on a page-level as the code snippet shows. The second form is as follows:

```
<system.web>
    <pages validateRequest="true" />
</system.web>
```

This way, you can configure validation at the application-level by configuring the `<pages>` configuration sections inside the `web.config` configuration file. Figure 18-6 shows the page that ASP.NET generates when request validation is enabled and a user enters some HTML tags or any other JavaScript scripts.

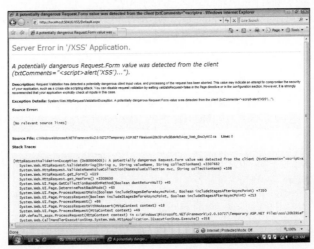

Figure 18-6

855

The ASP.NET and Application Consulting & Engineering (ACE) teams at Microsoft provided the Microsoft Anti-Cross Site Scripting Library V1.5 encoding library that is designed to help developers protect their web applications from cross-site scripting attacks. This library differs from other encoding libraries in that it uses the principle-of-inclusions technique. This technique is similar to the concept of whitelisting and it works by defining a set of allowable or valid set of characters and encoding anything outside this set:

C#

```csharp
namespace Microsoft.Application.Security
{
    public class AntiXss {

    public static string HtmlEncode(string s);
    public static string HtmlAttributeEncode(string s);
    public static string JavaScriptEncode(string s);
    public static string UrlEncode(string s);
    public static string VisualBasicScriptEncode(string s);
    public static string XmlEncode(string s);
    public static string XmlAttributeEncode(string s);
    }
}
```

VB.NET

```vbnet
Namespace Microsoft.Application.Security
    Public Class AntiXss
        Public Shared Function HtmlAttributeEncode(ByVal s As String) As String
        Public Shared Function HtmlEncode(ByVal s As String) As String
        Public Shared Function JavaScriptEncode(ByVal s As String) As String
        Public Shared Function UrlEncode(ByVal s As String) As String
        Public Shared Function VisualBasicScriptEncode(ByVal s As String) As String
        Public Shared Function XmlAttributeEncode(ByVal s As String) As String
        Public Shared Function XmlEncode(ByVal s As String) As String
    End Class
End Namespace
```

This code shows the set of methods that are available by the library that you can use to protect against the input you receive from end-users, and to properly send encoded data to the client-side.

The `HtmlEncode()` method is used to encode text that is to be displayed in the context of HTML. The container that will hold the encoded text can be any ASP.NET server control that can display text:

C#

```csharp
this.lblName.Text =
        Microsoft.Security.Application.AntiXss.HtmlEncode(
                            this.txtName.Text);
```

VB.NET

```vbnet
        Me.lblName.Text = _
        Microsoft.Security.Application.AntiXss.HtmlEncode( _
```

```
                              Me.txtComments.Text)
```

The `HtmlEncode()` method can also be used when displaying text directly inside HTML tags using `<%= %>` block:

```
<% = Microsoft.Security.Application.AntiXss.HtmlEncode(this.txtName.Text) %>
```

The `HtmlAttributeEncode()` method is used to encode attributes when embedding HTML elements into the page and specifying its attributes that might be used by attackers to send malicious and harmful scripts to the server:

C#

```
this.ltSeperator.Text =
    "<hr noshade size=" +
    Microsoft.Security.Application.AntiXss.HtmlAttributeEncode(
                    this.txtSizeInPixels.Text)+
    ">";
```

VB.NET

```
Me.ltSeperator.Text = _
        "<hr noshade size=" & _
        Microsoft.Security.Application.AntiXss.HtmlAttributeEncode( _
        Me.txtSizeInPixels.Text) & _
        ">"
```

This example shows how to safely encode HTML attributes when embedding dynamic HTML elements on the page.

The other methods available in the library are used in the same manner as the above sample methods. You can read more about the Anti-Cross Site Scripting library by reading the article on MSDN at: `http://msdn.microsoft.com/en-us/library/aa973813.aspx`.

Cross-Site Request Forgery

Cross-site request forgery, also known as *CSRF* or *see surf*, is an attack that exploits the trust between a web application and an authenticated and trusted user. What happens is that the attacker makes use of the trust between the user and the application and sends harmful HTTP requests through the trusted user to the application. In other words, the trusted user, on behalf of the attacker, sends an HTTP request to the server without knowing or noticing that they are sending a harmful request. The attacker in this case is able to make use of the victim, the user, to send harmful requests to the server.

Most of the attacks caused by CSRF are caused by embedding the HTML image tag on a page and setting its source to a page inside the application to perform or execute some code inside that page. Before giving an example on a CSRF attack, it is important to mention few concepts about how a browser interprets a response from the server.

When a browser receives a response from the server, it goes through the HTML and starts executing every line. If there is an HTML image tag embedded in the response, the browser issues a GET request to retrieve the content of the image from the server and then continues interpreting and executing the rest of the HTML content inside the original response.

For instance, when you want to embed an HTML image on a page you would add something like this:

```
<img src="http://localhost:50814/CSRF/image.gif" alt="" />
```

As mentioned above, most of the CSRF attacks are done through HTML images by setting the source of the image to something as in the following markup:

```
<form id="form1" runat="server">
<div>
    <img src="http://localhost:50814/CSRF/Default.aspx" alt="" /> <br />
    <asp:Button ID="btnSubmit" runat="server" Text="Submit" />
</div>
</form>
```

This markup is placed inside the CSRFPage.aspx page. As you can see, when you browse into this page, the browser will send a GET request to the server to retrieve the content of the image placed in the HTML and received from the server. The user (victim) using this page would not notice that they are doing something harmful. In the above code, the request is sent to just another page. But imagine if the request was for a page that executes some commands based on some query strings such as:

```
<form id="form1" runat="server">
<div>
    <img
 src="http://localhost:50814/CSRF/AccountManager.aspx?Acct=123289-212&Amount=1000"
 alt=""
/>
<br />" runat="server" Text="Submit" />
</div>
</form>
```

If the AccountManager.aspx page is used to transfer money to other accounts in the bank based on the query strings that include the account number to move the amount specified as a second query string, then this would be very harmful. The user issuing this request is authenticated and authorized from the application's point of view and the application would not differentiate between a request sent through accessing the page by typing the address on the browser or by an image requesting the page!

The way to "try" to get around the CSRF attack is to always use Request.Form["key"] in C# or Request.Form("key") in VB.NET instead of Request["key"] in C# or Request("key") in VB.NET when trying to access the Form fields. The Request["key"] or Request("key") searches for keys in both the GET and POST fields, whereas the Request.Form["key"] or Request("key") searches only among the POST fields (that is, fields inside the HTML form inside the current page). Even if the attacker changes the form's verb from POST to GET—thereby passing the form's field to the server as a query string—you will be on the safe side when accessing the form's fields with the Request.Form["key"] or Request.Form("key").

Here is a sample code to show one of the solutions you can come up with to prevent CSRF attacks:

C#

```csharp
    protected void Page_Load(object sender, EventArgs e)
    {
        if (!Page.IsPostBack)
        {
            ViewState["token"] = new Guid();
            this.csrfToken.Value = ViewState["token"].ToString();
        }
        else
        {
if (
    ((Request.Form["csrfToken"] != null) &&
      (ViewState["token"] !=null)) &&
    (Request.Form["csrfToken"].ToString().Equals(ViewState["token"].ToString()))
  )
{
    // Valid Page
    Response.Write("Safe Access");
}
else
{
    Response.Write("UnSafe Access");
}
        }
    }
```

VB.NET

```vbnet
    Protected Sub Page_Load(ByVal sender As Object, ByVal e As EventArgs) _
    Handles Me.Load()

        If (Not Page.IsPostBack) Then
            ViewState("token") = Guid.NewGuid()
            Me.csrfToken.Value = ViewState("token").ToString()
        Else
            If ((Request.Form("csrfToken") IsNot Nothing) _
                  AndAlso (ViewState("token") IsNot Nothing)) _
                AndAlso (Request.Form("csrfToken").ToString().Equals(_
                        ViewState("token").ToString())) Then

                ' Valid Page
                Response.Write("Safe Access")
                ' Update the key for the new response
                ViewState("token") = Guid.NewGuid()
                Me.csrfToken.Value = ViewState("token").ToString()
            Else
                Response.Write("UnSafe Access")
            End If
        End If
    End Sub
```

The first important technique to follow is not to place any functional code inside the Page_Load()
method and to make sure to distinguish between a normal page request and a postback request. Every

time an HTML image accesses the page (in the code shown above), the request will enter into the block that says this is not a postback request. Thus, nothing serious will be done or executed except creating a new GUID and setting the value of a hidden field on the page to this new GUID number as follows:

C#

```
if (!Page.IsPostBack)
{
    ViewState["token"] = new Guid();
    this.csrfToken.Value = ViewState["token"].ToString();
}
```

VB.NET

```
If (Not Page.IsPostBack) Then
    ViewState("token") = Guid.NewGuid()
    Me.csrfToken.Value = ViewState("token").ToString()
End If
```

This postback check always makes sure that embedding the page's URL into an HTML image will fail, since the request will always be a normal request. Even if the ASP.NET Button control, that is shown on CSRFPage.aspx, is clicked causing a postback request to the same page, when the browser renders the result, the HTML image contacts the server again asking for the specified URL in its source. And once again, it will not be handled as a postback to that URL, but as a normal request.

At this stage, making use of only the Request.Form["key"] or Request.Form("key") indexer, as shown in the following example, and checking for Page.IsPostBack are good methods for handling CSRF attacks:

C#

```
    else
    {
if (
((Request.Form["csrfToken"] != null) &&
    (ViewState["token"] != null)) &&
(Request.Form["csrfToken"].ToString().Equals(ViewState["token"].ToString()))
)
        {
            // Valid Page
            Response.Write("Safe Access");
        }
    }
```

VB.NET

```
    Else
If ((Request.Form("csrfToken") IsNot Nothing) _
        AndAlso (ViewState("token") IsNot Nothing)) _
        AndAlso (Request.Form("csrfToken").ToString().Equals( _
            ViewState("token").ToString())) Then
            ' Valid Page
```

```
                        Response.Write("Safe Access")
            End If
```

This code makes sure that the page handles any processing inside the block that says that this is a post-back request. Hence, you are sure now that the page was displayed by the browser and that the user clicked on one of the buttons on the page. A double check is done to make sure the token that was generated on the first request to the page is the same as the one stored inside the hidden field on the page. This insures that the page is being accessed properly.

The important thing to remember here is to always make sure to process any command only when the page posts back and not on the first access of the page. This prevents an attack that could be generated by specifying some query strings where the page simply grabs the query strings and performs the action. Also, checking for the token with the `Request.Form["csrfToken"]` or `Request.Form("csrfToken")` indexer makes sure you are dealing with the fields populated out of a POST request. Although sending silent POST requests might be possible with some sort of JavaScript and AJAX, following the whole process discussed above might help in resolving CSRF attacks.

Finally, the end-users should also protect themselves by not allowing any web application to create a persistent cookie when they log in to the application. When they are redirected to the login page they should make sure *not* to select the Remember Me checkbox. If this checkbox is selected, this means a persistent cookie has been created on the local machine. And this paves the way for CSRF attacks.

Handle Exceptions Properly

Exceptions and errors might happen anywhere in your application. Accessing a database, reading/writing to the file system, processing input data, sending emails, and many other actions all may cause problems at times. The first step in handling exceptions properly is to maintain a log of the problem that occurred and, of course, informing the user that the action they were performing caused an error or exception in the application. The important thing to keep in mind is to never send back to the client-side any details about the exception that occurred. Showing details, such as the line of code that caused the error(s), the database server name, or any other detail, could open your application up to potential attacks from malicious users.

In ASP.NET 3.5 there are several ways to handle exceptions in an application. These are divided into three categories as covered in the following sections.

<customErrors> Configuration Section

As you already know, the `<customErrors />` configuration section is used by an application to either display or hide details about the exceptions that occur inside it. The `mode` attribute of the `<customErrors />` configuration section determines how the application reacts to an exception. It can have one of the following values:

❑ **On:** With this option the application displays the default exception page that ASP.NET generates. Figure 18-7 shows the ASP.NET-generated error page that displays when the `mode` attribute is set to On.

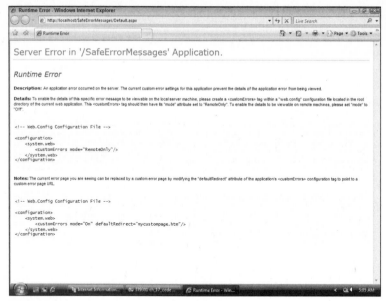

Figure 18-7

❑ The page, as you can see, tells you to set the value of the mode attribute to Off. Setting this attribute to a value of Off allows the end-user to check the details about the exception using an ASP.NET-generated error page. The value of On hides the details of the exception that occurred locally and remotely. To configure an application with this mode, add the following configuration section into the web.config configuration file:

```
<customErrors mode="On" />
```

❑ **Off:** This value causes the ASP.NET application to generate a detailed exception page to inform the only the local user about the exception that occurred in the application. In other words, with this setting, only local users, i.e., you the developers, are able to see the details about the exception that occurred. Figure 18-8 shows a detailed error page that was generated by ASP.NET due to an exception that occurred in the application.

❑ As you can see from Figure 18-8, many details about the exception and the code-behind the page are shown and displayed, in addition to the call stack trace. An attacker could make harmful use of such details to prepare a malicious attack on the application. That is why setting the value of the mode attribute to Off allows only local developers to view such vital details on the application and prevents remote users from viewing any of these details. To configure an application with this mode add the following configuration section into the web.config configuration file:

```
<customErrors mode="Off" />
```

❑ **RemoteOnly:** With this value set, the detailed explanation on the errors and exceptions is displayed only for local users (i.e., you the developers). Remote users that are not viewing the application on the same web server are not able to see the details of exceptions and errors. Only the ASP.NET default exception page is shown. To configure an application with this mode, add the following configuration section into the web.config configuration file:

```
<customErrors mode="RemoteOnly" />
```

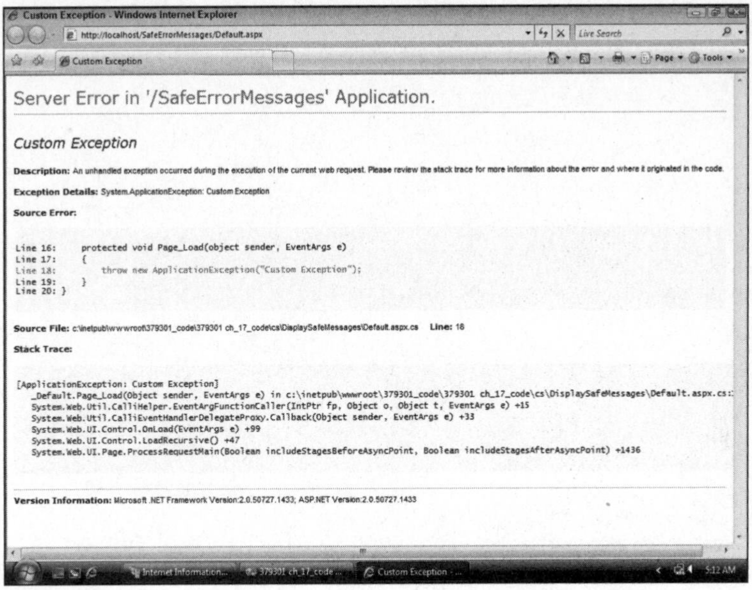

Figure 18-8

❑ In addition the `<customErrors />` configuration section has an optional attribute called defaultRedirect that allows you to specify a custom error page to be displayed to users instead of the default ASP.NET-generated page. To configure this attribute, add the following into the web.config configuration file:

```
<customErrors mode="RemoteOnly" defaultRedirect="GenericErrorPage.htm">
</customErrors>
```

❑ Furthermore, you can optionally specify error pages to display for specific error codes. For instance, you might want to show a customized error page when a resource inside the application is not found, which causes the 404 error code. To configure such pages, you need to use the `<error>` configuration section inside the `<customErrors>` configuration section as follows:

```
<customErrors mode="RemoteOnly" defaultRedirect="GenericErrorPage.htm">

    <error statusCode="404" redirect="FileNotFound.htm" /></customErrors>
```

❑ You can add as many custom error pages as you want for specific error codes.

Try/Catch Blocks

In addition to using the `<customErrors />` configuration section, you can make use of the Try/Catch block that is offered by both the C# and VB.NET programming languages. The try/catch block can be used effectively to handle exceptions in places that you think an exception might occur. This is different

863

from the previously explained way of handling exceptions, where the `<customErrors />` configuration section is used to handle errors globally for both handled and unhandled exceptions. The try/catch block is used to deal with handled exceptions.

For instance, any code written to access the database, file system, or any other source of data should be placed inside a try/catch block. This way, if any error was generated during the operation, you would be able to handle the exception and do whatever clean-up work is required. Here is an example of a try/catch block:

C#

```csharp
try
{
    FileStream fs = File.Open("path-to-file", FileMode.Open);
}
catch (ArgumentException argEcp)
{
    // Log the exception
}
catch (IOException ioExp)
{
    // Log the exception
}
catch (Exception ex)
{
    // Log the exception
}
```

VB.NET

```vbnet
Try
        Dim fs As FileStream = File.Open("path-to-file", FileMode.Open)
Catch argEcp As ArgumentException
        ' Log the exception
Catch ioExp As IOException
        ' Log the exception
Catch ex As Exception
        ' Log the exception
End Try
```

This code tries to open a file located on the file system. This operation is risky and might produce several exceptions that might result from a file not found or path not present on the current machine, in addition to other exceptions that might occur while reading the file. Several catch statements are added starting from the most specific exceptions that might occur down to the more general ones. This is the recommended way of handling such exceptions. In every catch statement you need, first of all, to log the exception. After that you might chose either to redirect the user to a custom error page located in your application or simply re-throw the exception. Re-throwing the exception assumes that you have already setup the `<customErrors>` configuration section, or you have implemented a global, programmatic way of dealing with handled and unhandled exceptions in the application.

Global Error Handling

ASP.NET offers another form of global error handling, side-by-side with the <customErrors /> configuration section. Global error handling can also be accomplished through code by using one of two major events. The first event is the Application_Error event that is fired on the HttpApplication instance whenever an error takes place within the application. As a developer, you can handle the implementation of the Application_Error event to deal with any exception. You can then log the exception, send an email to the administrator informing them about the exception, and use any other techniques for handling the exception.

You can implement the Application_Error event inside either the Global.asax file of the application or by creating a new HttpModule and subscribing to the global Error event:

C#

```csharp
void Application_Error(object sender, EventArgs e)
{
    // Get a reference to the source of the exception chain
    Exception exp = Server.GetLastError().GetBaseException();

    // Access all the details about the exception
    // and the page status when the error has occured
    string message = exp.Message;
    string source = exp.Source;
    string form = Request.Form.ToString();
    string queryString = Request.QueryString.ToString();
    string stackTrace = exp.StackTrace;

    // Optional: Add the exception details into the Event log

    // Optional: Send an email to the administrator with details
    // about the exception
}
```

VB.NET

```vbnet
Sub Application_Error(ByVal sender As Object, ByVal e As EventArgs)
    ' Get a reference to the source of the exception chain
    Dim exp As Exception = Server.GetLastError().GetBaseException()

    ' Access all the details about the exception
    ' and the page status when the error has occured
    Dim message As String = exp.Message
    Dim source As String = exp.Source
    Dim form As String = Request.Form.ToString()
    Dim queryString As String = Request.QueryString.ToString()
    Dim stackTrace As String = exp.StackTrace

    ' Optional: Add the exception details into the Event log

    ' Optional: Send an email to the administrator with details
    ' about the exception
End Sub
```

This implementation starts by collecting the exception that was raised in the application and then extracting the details of the exception. Then you can handle these details the way you want by either logging the exception into the Windows Event Log, send an email to the administrator, or any other way you may see it fit in this context.

This explains how to handle errors and exceptions on the application level. ASP.NET also allows you to handle exceptions and errors on the page-level. If you choose to handle exceptions on the page-level, then you need to implement the `Page_Error` event that is fired as part of the page life-cycle events. In this case, when an exception takes place, the ASP.NET runtime first checks to see if the page implements the `Page_Error` event. If this event is implemented, then the event handler for this error is executed. It also continues to check if the application global error event is also implemented and if so, executes it. You should implement one of those two events and not both of them. Either you place the `Page_Error` implementation in a base class that all pages inherit from, or you implement the `Application_Error` event inside the `Global.asax` file or inside a custom `HttpModule`. The same code is used for both cases, which makes it easier on you to decide on the way to handle global and page errors inside your application.

Guard Against Denial-of-Service Threats

In a denial-of-service (DOS) attack, an attacker floods the web server, hosting the web application, with a concentrated amount of requests causing the web server to reach its limit to serve any more requests. Thus, the web server will break down and will not be able to serve any legitimate user.

For instance, say the attacker is using DOS to attack a portal webpage that requires a lot of resources to be built on the server. And assume that the attacker is clearing out all the cookies that were generated by the portal page (so that less work is required on next visits from the same user). Then the sever will be using the same amount of resources in accessing the page, since requesting a portal page having all the generated cookies on the client-side deleted, means the page will redo the same tasks on every page request. Thus, the harm is doubled; because there is a limit that a web server can allow to accept requests and, of course, there is heavy work being done by the web application for the same page with multiple visits in a DOS attack.

It is very easy to simulate a DOS attack by executing the following piece of code:

C#

```
while (true)
{
    // WebClient used to send/receive
    // data from resources that are
    // identitifed by a URI
    System.Net.WebClient wb =
        new System.Net.WebClient();

    // Send request for DOS application
    wb.DownloadString("http://localhost:63626/DOS/Default.aspx");
}
```

VB.NET

```
Do
    ' WebClient used to send/receive
```

```
                            ' data from resources that are
                            ' identitifed by a URI
                            Dim wb As New System.Net.WebClient()

                            ' Send request for DOS application
                            wb.DownloadString("http://localhost:63626/DOS/Default.aspx")
                    Loop
```

This code sends an infinite number of requests for the http://www.asp.net/ website. If the web application being requested was not protected against DOS, at some point, the application will break down and will not be able to handle any further requests.

One of the solutions or precautions that you can take to help in mitigating DOS attacks is by building a solution based on the ASP.NET cache. What you need is a solution that keeps track of the number of hits in a certain amount of time based on the client IP address:

C#

```
public static class DOSHelper
{
    #region Constants
    /// <summary>
    /// Duration used to reset the
    /// number hits by a client IP
    /// thus allwoing normal processing for the web application
    /// </summary>
    private const double DURATION = 1;

    /// <summary>
    /// Number of allowed hits by a specific
    /// client IP during a Duration.
    /// </summary>
    private const int ALLOWED_HITS = 10;
    #endregion

    #region Methods
    public static bool IsDOS()
    {
        // Get the HttpContext
        HttpContext context = HttpContext.Current;

        // Prepare the key for the cache
        string key = context.Request.UserHostAddress;

        // Get number of hits from the cahe
        int numberOfHits = 0;
        if (context.Cache[key] == null)
            numberOfHits++;
        else
            numberOfHits = int.Parse(context.Cache[key].ToString());

        // If the limit is exceeded
        if (numberOfHits > ALLOWED_HITS)
            return true;
        else
```

```
                numberOfHits++;

        // First time visit, start tracking
        // the number of visits
        if (numberOfHits == 1)
        {
            context.Cache.Add(
                key,
                numberOfHits,
                null,
                DateTime.Now.AddMinutes(DURATION),
                System.Web.Caching.Cache.NoSlidingExpiration,
                System.Web.Caching.CacheItemPriority.Normal,
                null);
        }
        else
        {
            context.Cache[key] = numberOfHits.ToString();
        }

        return false;
    }
    #endregion
}
```

VB.NET

```
Public NotInheritable Class DOSHelper
  #Region "Constants"
  ''' <summary>
  ''' Duration used to reset the
  ''' number hits by a client IP
  ''' thus allwoing normal processing for the web application
  ''' </summary>
  Private Const DURATION As Double = 1

  ''' <summary>
  ''' Number of allowed hits by a specific
  ''' client IP during a Duration.
  ''' </summary>
  Private Const ALLOWED_HITS As Integer = 10
  #End Region

  #Region "Methods"
  Private Sub New()
  End Sub
  Public Shared Function IsDOS() As Boolean
        ' Get the HttpContext
        Dim context As HttpContext = HttpContext.Current

        ' Prepare the key for the cache
        Dim key As String = context.Request.UserHostAddress

        ' Get number of hits from the cahe
```

```vb
        Dim numberOfHits As Integer = 0
        If context.Cache(key) Is Nothing Then
                numberOfHits += 1
        Else
                numberOfHits = Integer.Parse(context.Cache(key).ToString())
        End If


        ' If the limit is exceeded
        If numberOfHits > ALLOWED_HITS Then
                Return True
        Else
                numberOfHits += 1
        End If


        ' First time visit, start tracking
        ' the number of visits
        If numberOfHits = 1 Then
        Context.Cache.Add(key, numberOfHits, Nothing, _
                        DateTime.Now.AddMinutes(DURATION), _
                        System.Web.Caching.Cache.NoSlidingExpiration, _
                        System.Web.Caching.CacheItemPriority.Normal, _
                        Nothing)
        Else
                context.Cache(key) = numberOfHits.ToString()
        End If


        Return False
    End Function
    #End Region
End Class
```

The DOSHelper class represents a utility class that contains a method to test against DOS attacks. The class defines DURATION as a constant variable to hold the number of minutes used to cache consecutive and repetitive requests from the same client IP. The other constant is the ALLOWED_HITS variable that holds the number of maximum requests a client IP can perform during a certain duration of time.

The only method included in the class is IsDOS().

C#

```csharp
    public static bool IsDOS()
    {
        // Get the HttpContext
        HttpContext context = HttpContext.Current;

        // Prepare the key for the cache
        string key = context.Request.UserHostAddress;

        // Get number of hits from the cahe
        int numberOfHits = 0;
        if (context.Cache[key] == null)
            numberOfHits++;
        else
```

```csharp
            numberOfHits = int.Parse(context.Cache[key].ToString());

    // If the limit is exceeded
    if (numberOfHits > ALLOWED_HITS)
        return true;
    else
        numberOfHits++;

    // First time visit, start tracking
    // the number of visits
    if (numberOfHits == 1)
    {
        context.Cache.Add(key, numberOfHits, null,
            DateTime.Now.AddMinutes(DURATION),
            System.Web.Caching.Cache.NoSlidingExpiration,
            System.Web.Caching.CacheItemPriority.Normal, null);
    }
    else
    {
        context.Cache[key] = numberOfHits.ToString();
    }

    return false;
}
```

VB.NET

```vbnet
Public Shared Function IsDOS() As Boolean
    ' Get the HttpContext
    Dim context As HttpContext = HttpContext.Current

    ' Prepare the key for the cache
    Dim key As String = context.Request.UserHostAddress

    ' Get number of hits from the cahe
    Dim numberOfHits As Integer = 0
    If context.Cache(key) Is Nothing Then
            numberOfHits += 1
    Else
            numberOfHits = Integer.Parse(context.Cache(key).ToString())
    End If

    ' If the limit is exceeded
    If numberOfHits > ALLOWED_HITS Then
            Return True
    Else
            numberOfHits += 1
    End If

    ' First time visit, start tracking
    ' the number of visits
    If numberOfHits = 1 Then
    Context.Cache.Add(key, numberOfHits, Nothing, _
```

```
                    DateTime.Now.AddMinutes(DURATION), _
                    System.Web.Caching.Cache.NoSlidingExpiration, _
                    System.Web.Caching.CacheItemPriority.Normal, _
                    Nothing)
        Else
                    context.Cache(key) = numberOfHits.ToString()
        End If

        Return False
    End Function
```

The method starts by retrieving an instance of the HttpContext of the current request. After that, the client IP address is stored in a local variable that is used later as the cache key to get the number of hits from a client IP address in a specific duration of time.

The cache is checked to see if there is an existing record for the current IP accessing the application. If not, this means that it is the first time the current IP is accessing the application. If there is a valid record in the cache then it is retrieved and hence, the user has already visited the same application during the DURATION time. A check is then performed to see if the number of hits is greater than the allowed number, if so, then a false value is returned meaning that the user has reached the maximum allowed number of visits in a specific amount of time. If not, the method continues to execute and checks if the number of hits is 1 and accordingly adds a new record into the cache, since this is the first time the current client IP is accessing the application. Notice that the DURATION variable is used as the absolute expiration of the cache record. Finally, if the number of hits is greater than 1 the IP address record inside the cache is updated.

To check for DOS attacks, add the following checks into your page:

C#

```
if (DOSHelper.IsDOS())
{
    Response.Clear();
    Response.End();
}
```

VB.NET

```
If DOSHelper.IsDOS() Then
    Response.Clear()
    Response.End()
End If
```

If the request is a DOS attack, clear the response and end it.

The idea here is that if the user exceeds the maximum allowed number of requests per a specific duration of time, this is considered a DOS attack. As long as the specific duration of time has not expired yet, and the user already exceeded the number of allowed requests, all requests performed by this specific user are considered DOS attacks. Once the cache is expired, the same user can start again sending normal requests to the application.

Secure Data Transmission

The transmission of data between the client and server is done many times using plain text. This threatens the data moved in and out to many threats across the network path. Attackers might be there sniffing the data packets sent from client to server or vice versa to extract sensitive information that might be used in a harmful and malicious way to attack the application.

For example, suppose you have a login page on your web application to authenticate users before accessing some parts of the application. In normal cases, the user will enter their credentials and submit the form to the server for authentication. The credentials are sent across the wire as plain text. Therefore, there is a possibility that the credentials may get stolen before they reach the server by attackers that are sniffing the network.

To help protect sensitive data being interchanged between the client and server, use Secure Sockets Layer (SSL). You can buy a legal certificate from many vendors online and install it on the server. Once installed you force some of your sensitive `.aspx` forms to be accessed securely by using the `https://` protocol when requesting any of them. Configuring sensitive pages within the application with SSL makes sure that the data transmission between the client and server is done securely, and all data is being encrypted properly so that no plain text is passed across the wire. This makes it nearly impossible for any attacker to have access to the data being transmitted.

AJAX-Enabled Application Threats

The introduction of Web 2.0 and the need for AJAX techniques to improve responsiveness and user experience have made the web application more vulnerable to attack. This section discusses some of the threats that an AJAX-enabled application might face from attacks. The focus is on the ASP.NET AJAX 3.5 when discussing the different threats that an AJAX-enabled Web application faces.

Information Leakage

As you know, ASP.NET AJAX allows the client-side JavaScript code to call web methods that are located in web services on the server-side. Hence, a JavaScript function on the browser can call asynchronously a web service, as if the server-side method is on the client-side. When you add a reference to a web service into the `ScriptManager` instance on the page, the ASP.NET AJAX engine creates a client-side proxy class similar to the server-side proxy class. And your JavaScript code now has a client-side class that acts as a proxy to the web service on the server-side.

The proxy class contains the methods that your client-side code can call from the browser using JavaScript. To view the client-side proxy, run the web service in a browser and append the `/js` extension to the web service URL. This URL is the URL of the client-side proxy class. It lists all the methods of the web service in the form of JavaScript functions that you can call asynchronously from the client-side. ASP.NET AJAX brought great flexibility to web applications, since more functionality is now exposed to the client-side code. Thus, the pressure is getting lighter on the server-side and fewer resources are needed to execute such calls, since there is no page life-cycle anymore to execute on the server, when a web method is called by the client-side code.

However, nothing comes without a cost! By exposing more functionality in your application to the client-side, you are potentially giving an attacker deep insight into your system's functionality. The attacker now can check a complete list of the server-side methods available together with information about the expected input parameters. This is really a problem. An attacker can now benefit from all the threats discussed from the beginning of this chapter and send their malicious attacks using other techniques than those that are available in a traditional web application.

The following JavaScript code represents the client-side proxy class for a web service called Web Service.asmx. The web service contains a single method called HelloWorld() and, as you can see, the HelloWorld() method has been added as a JavaScript function inside the client-side proxy class. JavaScript functions can now call the functions on the client-side proxy, which are internally submitted as asynchronous calls to the web server.

```
var WebService=function() {
WebService.initializeBase(this);
this._timeout = 0;
this._userContext = null;
this._succeeded = null;
this._failed = null;
}
WebService.prototype={
HelloWorld:function(
  succeededCallback,
  failedCallback,
  userContext) {

  return this._invoke(
      this._get_path(),
      'HelloWorld',
      false,
      {},
      succeededCallback,
      failedCallback,
      userContext);
  }
}
WebService.registerClass('WebService',Sys.Net.WebServiceProxy);
```

In an attempt to get around this threat, you should always separate the web methods to be called by AJAX from those that your application uses. In other words, place all the web methods that are to be called from the client-side code into a separate class and keep the web methods called by your .aspx pages separated in another class. This way, you can minimize the functionality that is exposed to the client-side and that is not needed by AJAX.

In addition, you should turn off Web Services Description Language (WSDL) for the web services that are to be called by AJAX. WSDL usually allows the developer to discover information about the available web services. When working with AJAX there is no need for the client-side code to know such information. The client-side code is required to call web methods that are located in internal web services only. This is by default the nature of the XmlHttpRequest class that allows calls only to local URLs and this is called *same origin policy*. Turning WSDL on can only help the attacker in discovering and revealing the web services available in your application. The following configuration shows you how to turn off WSDL by simply removing the element Documentation.

```
<configuration>
    <system.web>
```

```
            <webServices>
                <protocols>
                    <remove name="Documentation"/>
                </protocols>
            </webServices>
        </system.web>
    </configuration>
```

When working with AJAX, the developer now spends more time in writing JavaScript code. The developer tends to add many comments while developing. Adding comments to the server-side is not a problem at all and is recommended. However, when it comes to writing comments inside the HTML markup, you should be careful. You have two choices for adding comments inside the HTML markup: HTML comments or ASP.NET comments.

HTML comments are those comments that hide everything written inside them from showing and displaying on the page however anyone who views the source of the page can still see those comments.

```
    <!-- this is an HTML comment -->
```

Imagine that you are developing an .aspx page that connects to the database. For testing purposes you are connecting to a test database server to test the functionality of the page. You add the connection string as an HTML comment so that you do not forget it later on. Or you might put a username and password as an HTML comment so that you do not forget such credentials. You test the page and release it, but you forgot to remove the HTML comments. What you have done by mistake is give an attacker a present that they never dreamed of!

This is why, when it comes to adding comments into the HTML markup, it is always recommended to add ASP.NET comments.

```
    <%-- This is a comments --%>
```

An ASP.NET comment is never sent to the browser, hence protecting everything you place inside it.

When creating your own JavaScript files, any comment you place in the code is always sent down to the client-side. Therefore, you should be aware when writing your JavaScript files to include only necessary JavaScript comments, and not include any sensitive information, since there is no way around sending the JavaScript comments to the client-side.

Finally, to protect your application that is AJAX-enabled, try to minimize the logic written on the client-side. Let the client-side code be a UI code that asks the server for data, receives the response, and updates the UI. Keep all your logic stored on the server-side to protect it from allowing attackers to steal a look at it.

JSON Hijacking

Most of the popular AJAX libraries, including the ASP.NET AJAX library, use JavaScript and Object Notation (JSON) as the main format to interchange data between the client-side and server-side. It is recommended over XML because it is faster and easier to deal with. You can now say "AJAJ–enabled" web applications because of the fact that most of the AJAX libraries use JSON to transfer data instead of XML.

The JSON hijacking threat is one of the browser exploits that is performed by making use of the `<script src="" />` JavaScript tag inside the HTML markup of a web page to send HTTP GET requests to web services that do not originate from the same domain from which the current page is coming. Most of the major browsers only allow calls according to the same origin policy, and this applies on the `XmlHttpRequest` class. Attackers try to hijack transmitted data by sending these HTTP GET requests. Once they put their hands on the JSON payload, they can do anything they want with the data.

The ASP.NET team is aware of such attacks. That is why any web method that you add into a web service that is to be called from the client-side code is enabled only for HTTP POST requests. How does this help? Well, all HTTP requests that are fired from the `<script src="" />` JavaScript tag are done in the form of HTTP GET requests and hence, by allowing only HTTP POST client-side requests to call ASP.NET AJAX web service server-side methods, attackers will fail to hijack the JSON generated by these web services. You can enable the web methods to be called by HTTP GET requests by adding the following attribute:

C#

```csharp
using System;
using System.Collections;
using System.Linq;
using System.Web;
using System.Web.Services;
using System.Web.Services.Protocols;
using System.Xml.Linq;

[WebService(Namespace = "http://tempuri.org/")]
[WebServiceBinding(ConformsTo = WsiProfiles.BasicProfile1_1)]
[System.Web.Script.Services.ScriptService]
public class WebService : System.Web.Services.WebService {
    public WebService () { }

    [WebMethod]
    [System.Web.Script.Services.ScriptMethod(UseHttpGet=true)]
    public string HelloWorld() {
        return "Hello World";
    }
}
```

VB.NET

```vbnet
Imports Microsoft.VisualBasic
Imports System
Imports System.Collections
Imports System.Linq
Imports System.Web
Imports System.Web.Services
Imports System.Web.Services.Protocols
Imports System.Xml.Linq

<WebService(Namespace:="http://tempuri.org/"), _
WebServiceBinding(ConformsTo:=WsiProfiles.BasicProfile1_1), _
System.Web.Script.Services.ScriptService()> _

Public Class WebService
```

```
        Inherits System.Web.Services.WebService

  Public Class WebService
    Inherits System.Web.Services.WebService
    Public Sub New()
    End Sub

    <WebMethod, System.Web.Script.Services.ScriptMethod(UseHttpGet:=True)> _
    Public Function HelloWorld() As String
          Return "Hello World"
    End Function

  End Class
```

The bold statement in this example, above the `HelloWorld()` method, explicitly enables HTTP GET calls for this method. This is not recommended, but in case there is no way around it, you can see how it can be enabled.

Another protection against JSON hijacking that is provided by the ASP.NET engine is that ASP.NET requires that any request for an ASP.NET AJAX web method, whether it is an HTTP GET or POST, should always have the HTTP Content-Type header of the request set to the value of `application/json`. If this Content-Type is not set to `application/json`, then the ASP.NET AJAX engine will reject the request. This is a double-layer of protection that you will appreciate when you want to enable HTTP GET on a Web method. Even if the Web method is enabled for HTTP GET requests, an attacker will fail to call that method with the `<script src="" />` JavaScript tag, since there is no way for this tag to configure the value of the HTTP Content-Type header to be `application/json`.

Amplified Cross-Site Scripting

Cross-Site Scripting has been explained in detail in an earlier section. XSS happens when a malicious user is able to post some harmful scripts into the server and the server fails to validate the posted data and processes the harmful input text normally. AJAX-enabled applications amplify the effect of cross-site scripting by giving the attacker additional sets of tools to harm the server. In addition to all the JavaScript code that the attacker already has to attack the server with XSS, AJAX gives the attacker the ability to use the `XmlHttpRequest` class to perform asynchronous requests without having the application notice anything except a normal request submitted to the server.

For instance, suppose there is a page in a web application called `MyComments.aspx` that allows the user to enter some comments. The attacker can exploit such a page by sending their own type of comments:

```
<script language="javascript" type="text/javascript">
    // Instantiate the WebRequest object.
    var wRequest =  new Sys.Net.WebRequest();

    // Set the request Url.
    wRequest.set_url("MyProfile.aspx");

    // Set the request verb.
    wRequest.set_httpVerb("POST");

    var body = "Info=You've been Hacked!"
    wRequest.set_body(body);
```

```
            wRequest.get_headers()["Content-Length"] = body.length;

            // Execute the request.
            wRequest.invoke();
</script>
```

The attacker seems to be aware that there is already a page in the application called `MyProfile.aspx` that accepts as input a field called `Info` that is part of the form's variables. The attacker prepares a new HTTP POST request, poisons the `Info` field with some text of their own, and sends the request:

C#

```
        protected void btnSubmit_Click(object sender, EventArgs e)
        {
            Session["Comments"] = this.txtComments.Text;
Response.Write(
    "You have entered: " +
    "<br/>" +
    Session["Comments"].ToString());

        }
```

VB.NET

```
        Protected Sub btnSubmit_Click(ByVal sender As Object, _
                                      ByVal e As EventArgs) _
                                      Handles btnSubmit.Click
            Session("Comments") = Me.txtComments.Text
            Response.Write( _
                "You have entered: " & _
                "<br/>" & _
                Session("Comments").ToString())
        End Sub
```

The event handler for the button clicked inside `MyComments.aspx` stores the posted data without any input validation and writes back on the page whatever the user has entered from text. Once the input script is written on the page, the browser executes it and hence, the `MyProfile.aspx` page is now exploited with the attacker's text.

Now it is time for the `MyProfile.aspx` page to run and execute, since an HTTP POST was sent out from the attacker's harmful comments:

C#

```
        protected void Page_Load(object sender, EventArgs e)
        {
            if (HttpContext.Current.Request.Form["Info"] != null)
                Session["Info"] = HttpContext.Current.Request.Form["Info"].ToString();

            if (Session["Info"] != null)
                this.lblInfo.Text = Session["Info"].ToString();
        }
```

VB.NET

```
      Protected Sub Page_Load(ByVal sender As Object, _
                         ByVal e As EventArgs) _
                         Handles Me.Load()
        If HttpContext.Current.Request.Form("Info") IsNot Nothing Then
            Session("Info") = HttpContext.Current.Request.Form("Info").ToString()
        End If

        If Session("Info") IsNot Nothing Then
            Me.lblInfo.Text = Session("Info").ToString()
        End If
    End Sub
```

This code simply checks the Info field to see if it is null or not and accordingly stores the data inside a Session variable and displays the text on the page.

This example is very simplistic, but the main idea is to show you how an attacker can now amplify the effect of cross-site scripting by making use of the XmlHttpRequest class to send malicious attacks and harm existing pages inside the application.

Summary

The first step in protecting an ASP.NET web application starts by knowing and trusting the users accessing your application and to decide whether they can access the private sections of the application. Once the users are authenticated, the application should decide on what each user can access from resources in the application and hence, authorize those users.

Once the end-user starts using the application and submitting data into the application, it is very important to validate the user input and consider any input sent into the application as potentially bad and malicious. Every input should be well-validated. Thoroughly validating user input helps protect the application from many threats, including Cross-Site scripting, SQL injection, Cross-Site Request Forgery, and many other types of attacks. Validating user input primarily means validating the type, format, length and range of the input data.

User input not only targets form fields, but also covers cookies and query strings. These should also be validated as normal user input data. Moreover, cookies should be handled with special treatment, which includes encrypting the data that you store in a cookie, setting a small expiration date on the cookie, and finally, making use of the Secure and HttpOnly public properties to help better protect the application's cookies.

Finally, securing the communication between the web server and the different clients, and between the web server and the database server using SSL, can help in securing the transmission of data. This is true whether the data is interchanged between the web server and the browsers accessing the application, or when interchanging the data between the application on the server-side and the database server.

Index

W